The Cambridge
Australian English
Style Guide

Consultants

GRAHAM GRAYSTON
Canberra; formerly Australian Government Publishing Service
ALEC JONES
Department of English, University of Sydney
STEPHEN KNIGHT
Department of English, Media and Cultural Studies
De Montfort University
COLIN YALLOP
Dictionary Research Centre, Macquarie University

The Cambridge Australian English Style Guide

PAM PETERS

School of English and Linguistics
Macquarie University

CAMBRIDGE
UNIVERSITY PRESS

PUBLISHED BY THE PRESS SYNDICATE OF THE UNIVERSITY OF CAMBRIDGE
The Pitt Building, Trumpington Street, Cambridge CB2 1RP, United Kingdom

CAMBRIDGE UNIVERSITY PRESS
The Edinburgh Building, Cambridge CB2 2RU, United Kingdom
40 West 20th Street, New York, NY 10011–4211, USA
477 Williamstown Road, Port Melbourne, VIC 3207, Australia
Ruiz de Alarcón 13, 28014 Madrid, Spain
Dock House, The Waterfront, Cape Town 8001, South Africa

First published 1995
Paperback edition published 1996
Reprinted 2003

Printed in Australia by McPherson's Printing Group

Typeset in Times 10/12 pt

National Library of Australia Cataloguing in Publication data

Peters, Pam.
The Cambridge Australian English style guide.
Bibliography.
1. English language—Australia—Usage. 2. English language—
Australia—Style. 3. Australianisms. I. Title.
428.00994

Library of Congress Cataloguing in Publication data

Peters, Pam.
The Cambridge Australian English style guide / Pam Peters : consultants,
Graham Grayston . . . [et al.].
Includes bibliographical references.
1. English language—Australia—Style—Dictionaries. 2. English
language—Australia—Usage—Dictionaries. 3. Australianisms—
Dictionaries. I. Grayston, Graham. II. Title.
PE3601.P48 1994
427'.994 – dc20   94 – 4179

A catalogue record for this book is available from the British Library

ISBN 0 521 43401 7 hardback
ISBN 0 521 57634 2 paperback

Contents

Foreword   vii
Preface   ix
Overview of Contents and How to Access Them   xii

A to **Z** entries   1

Appendix I   International Phonetic Alphabet Symbols for
                    Australian English Sounds   831
Appendix II   Perpetual Calendar 1901–2001   832
Appendix III   Geological Eras   835
Appendix IV   International System of Units (SI Units)   836
Appendix V   Interconversion Tables for Metric and Imperial
                    Measures   838
Appendix VI   Selected Proofreading Marks   840
Appendix VII   Formats for Letters   842
Appendix VIII   Layout for Envelopes   844
Appendix IX   Time Line for the English Language and
                    Australian English   845
Appendix X   List of References   846

Foreword

In both Australia and the United States of America, efforts to codify the national language gathered strength about 200 years after the first European settlement. The publication of *Webster's Dictionary* in the USA and the *Macquarie Dictionary* here—both of them comprehensive accounts of the standard regional variety of English—was at that stage of national development; and they opened the field for a florescence of dictionaries and other works on usage and style.

In Australia the shadow of Fowler (*Modern English Usage*, OUP 1926, 1965) has fallen benignly over the late Stephen Murray-Smith, whose *Right Words* (Viking 1987, 1989) offered genial and personal guidance on contemporary usage. At the other end of the personality scale is the *Style Manual for Authors, Editors and Printers* (Australian Government Publishing Service, 4th edition 1988) which is now addressed not just to government writers, as formerly, but "to all those who have occasion to write for a general audience".

What then are the distinctive qualities of *The Cambridge Australian English Style Guide*? For me, as an interested outsider, there are several:

- Its author is not just an experienced writer, editor or publisher, expressing views that are the fruit of personal experience and judgement; she is a scholar well trained in the discipline of linguistics, who has done extensive research into the history of written English in its major varieties; she has excellent grounding and achievement in the languages that have contributed most to the history of English—Latin, Old Norse, French, German etc. So she writes with an authority that comes from a professional knowledge of language and languages.
- Her principles of style guidance are founded on descriptive accounts of actual language used in identifiable acts of written communication, in newspapers, magazines, books of fiction and nonfiction, all assembled in computerised databases here and elsewhere. Her guidance is not personal in origin, for the reader is first given the facts about a particular variant usage, then taken through the events that produced the variant, with grace, style and good humour in the telling; and in the end the reader may decide which of the possible variants is best for the work in hand.
- Australian English is not presented in a vacuum, but compared with and related to British, American and other varieties of English.
- The range of topics is exceptionally comprehensive, with ample cross-references to give easy access to some thousands of individual language questions and answers.

These things make it an altogether new type of style guide. Till now we have known only the Fowler type; from now on the benchmark will be the Peters type, here and (I suspect) internationally. So use it, enjoy it, and be proud of it!

Arthur Delbridge AO

Preface

If language stood still, there would be little need for new dictionaries or new guides to style and usage. But a living language needs to be accounted for at regular intervals as it responds to changing social, cultural and political circumstances.

Since World War II Australian English has emerged as a variety in its own right. Instead of simply taking its linguistic cues from Britain, it now absorbs language elements from North America as well and develops its own norms and standards. It embraces more alternatives than hitherto, and *The Cambridge Australian English Style Guide* aims to map this widened range of options in the 1990s— and to subject the older canons of English usage to fresh scrutiny in the light of modern linguistics.

The discipline of linguistics has added immensely to our understanding of the dynamics of language and of the patterning within it. It emphasises the need to look for evidence in assessing what is going on. *The Cambridge Australian English Style Guide* looks for primary and/or secondary sources of information on the current state of English wherever they are to be found, to ensure that the book represents the full spectrum of usage, not just the perspective of an individual author.

The compilation of large computerised databases of contemporary English provides us with new research tools for the study of usage. Statistics from the recently completed ACE corpus (Australian Corpus of English) can be directly compared with databases of American English (the Brown corpus) and British English (the LOB or Lancaster–Oslo/Bergen corpus), to highlight divergences between the three varieties of English. Each corpus has extracts from 500 different publications in a variety of prose genres, and thus a broad sampling of style and usage (see **English language databases** in the body of the book). Corpus evidence takes up where the citation records of historical dictionaries, such as the *Oxford English Dictionary*, *Webster's Dictionary*, *Australian National Dictionary* and the *Macquarie Dictionary of New Words*, leave off.

Secondary sources of information on English usage undoubtedly wield influence on current language practices, and their preferences and judgements are also discussed in examining the status of each variant. Some of the authorities referred to in writing this book are large, up-to-date dictionaries such as the *Macquarie Dictionary*, *Random House Dictionary*, and the *Collins Dictionary*; recent books on usage such as the Reader's Digest *Right Word at the Right Time* and Murray-Smith's *Right Words*; new grammars of English such as Halliday's *Introduction to Functional Grammar*, Huddleston's *Introduction to the Grammar of English*, and the *Comprehensive Grammar of English* by Quirk, Greenbaum, Leech and Svartvik. Because punctuation and the forms of words are affected by changing editorial practices, reference has also been made to the most recent accounts of editorial style, including the Australian Government *Style Manual* (4th ed.), *Copy-editing* (3rd ed.) by Butcher, *Hart's Rules* (39th ed.), and the Chicago *Manual of Style* (13th ed.). The full titles of these and all references mentioned in the book are to be found in Appendix X.

A third kind of information used in this book is that which comes direct from users of the language, by surveying their preferences and practices when faced with choices in usage and style. Elicitation tests conducted by researchers in Britain such as Mittins, and Collins in Australia, help to show how people deal with expressions whose status is ambivalent; and surveys of spelling preferences conducted in association with Style Council and other professional bodies yield information on how professional writers decide between alternatives.

With its broad range of sources, this book aims to provide a balanced and thoroughly informed account of Australian style and usage on the threshold of the twenty-first century. It steers a course between the extremes of prescription and description, invoking both linguistic principle and the usage evidence available when making recommendations. It sets itself apart from accounts of usage which enshrine conservative traditions without reference to language principle or practice, and it re-evaluates conventional notions of correctness case by case. Many traditional judgements on "correctness" reflect the prelinguistic conception of writing and literature as the only proper forms of language. A properly linguistic account of usage must take account of the various levels and different genres of language, written and spoken; and generic information from the ACE corpus and others is presented in association with the statistics of usage.

The interaction between colloquial and formal idiom provides rich stylistic resources for skilled writers to exploit. *The Cambridge Australian English Style Guide* draws attention to writing technique and to writing style in many of its entries. The book's title is deliberately ambiguous in this sense, because the book is concerned with both macro- and micro-aspects of style. Many entries begin with a small detail of word form or meaning or punctuation, but in the end this connects with broader issues of style, the tone in which the writer intends to communicate, or the stance which s/he wishes to adopt. Formal and conventional aspects of style are discussed, as in letter writing and reports, as well as more open-ended topics such as argumentation, figures of speech and the rhythm of prose.

Apart from serving the needs of those who write, the *Style Guide* pinpoints topics which are crucial to those who edit writing, whether for themselves or in a professional capacity. The use of wordprocessors means that more people than ever have to think about editorial matters and to decide on questions of style. The freedom to create one's own "house style" entails a need to know what the current options are, whether one is dominant, what principles underlie the selection of alternatives, and which would make for more consistent and easier implementation overall. Where there are options as with *traveller/traveler*, the less frequent word or word form may make good linguistic sense, and the fact that it is the "minor variant" does not invalidate its use here. The tendency to elevate one variant over others simply on the basis of tradition or strength of usage is stultifying, and to be resisted by anyone who cares about the life of the language. Yet editors do have to implement a single option in a given context, and editorial choices have been made for this book which are indicated between ruled lines at the end of certain entries. The choices made are not intended to disallow others however, and the book supplies material on which alternative decisions can be based.

The Cambridge Australian English Style Guide is designed to support the work of anyone who engages with written language in Australia. Professional communicators, advertising copywriters and computer programmers all have to decide on the forms of words by which to transmit information. Teachers of English to native and nonnative students have to consider what they will present as the norms of the language, to equip their students with the essentials as well as ensure that their knowledge is robust enough to cope with the vagaries of actual usage. (The inclusion of both traditional and modern grammar terminology will enable teachers to locate and describe elements of English.) And those members of the community who reflect on language at their leisure should find stimulation in exploring the finer points of Australian English.

The book owes much to several distinguished consultants: Graham Grayston, formerly of the Australian Government Publishing Service, Alec Jones of the University of Sydney, Stephen Knight of Simon de Montfort University and formerly the University of Melbourne, and Colin Yallop of Macquarie University. It has benefited by countless discussions with colleagues and friends in linguistics, lexicography and the study of the English language: John Bernard, David Blair, Sue Butler, Peter Collins, Tony Cousins, Peter Fries, Rhondda Fahey, Peter Peterson, Diane Speed and Sue Spinks, among many. The support of Cambridge University Press and Robin Derricourt is gratefully acknowledged. Above all *The Cambridge Australian English Style Guide* owes its inspiration to Arthur Delbridge, emeritus professor at Macquarie University, and its successful completion to John Peters, my computer adviser and constant companion.

Pam Peters

Overview of Contents
and How to Access Them

The alphabetical list in this book contains two kinds of entries: those which deal with general topics of language, editing and writing, and those dealing with particular words, word sets or parts of words. An overview of the general entries is provided on the opposite page. The particular entries, focusing on issues of usage, spelling and word form, are too numerous to be shown there, and simply take their places in the alphabetical list. But for many questions, either general or particular entries would lead you to the answer you're seeking, and the book offers multiple access paths via crossreferences.

Let's say you are interested in where to put the full stop in relation to a final bracket or parenthesis. Any of those terms (full stop, bracket, parenthesis) would take you to the relevant discussion under **brackets**. In addition the general entry on **punctuation** presents a list of all the entries dealing with individual punctuation marks, for both words and sentences.

Questions of grammar are accessible through traditional terms such as **noun** and **verb**, **clause** and **phrase**, and traditional labels such as **dangling participle** or **split infinitive** ... though the entries may lead you on to newer linguistic topics such as **information focus** and **modality**. Aspects of writing and argument (when is it OK to use **I**? what does it mean to **beg the question**?) are discussed under their particular headings, but can also be tracked down through more general ones such as **impersonal writing** and **argument**.

If your question is about current use of a word such as **hopefully**, or a pair such as **alternate** and **alternative**, or **gourmet** and **gourmand**, the discussion is to be found under those headwords. When it's a question of spelling, e.g. **convener** or **convenor**, the individual entry may answer it, and/or direct you on to another (**-er/-or**) where a whole set with the same variable part is dealt with. In the same way, the entry **-ise/-ize** discusses the alternative spellings of countless verbs like **recognise/recognize**, although there are too many to enter alphabetically. The key spelling entries are listed under **spelling** sections 2 and 3, in case you're unsure what heading to look under. Alternative plural forms can be located via the entry on **plurals**.

As in the text above, the use of boldface means that the word is entered as a headword, and it identifies all crossreferences at the end of entries. Within any entry, further instances of the headword(s) are often boldfaced to draw attention to strategic points about them. Words related to the headword(s) or derived from them are set in italics, as are all examples.

STYLE AND STRUCTURE OF WRITING

ARGUMENT & STRUCTURE OF DISCOURSE
Argument
Begging the question
Coherence and
  cohesion
Deduction
Fallacies
Introduction
Information focus
Paragraph
Topic sentence

RHETORICAL DEVICES
Analogy
Aphorism
Figures of speech
Irony
Metaphor
Oxymoron
Personification
Symbol
Understatement

SPECIAL STYLES
Commercialese
Impersonal writing
Jargon
Journalese
Plain English
Technologese

VARIETIES OF ENGLISH
Australian English
American English
British English
Canadian English
International English
Standard English

WRITING FORMS
Inverted pyramid
Letter formats
Narrative
Reports
Summary

AUSTRALIAN ISSUES
Aboriginal words
Dialect
Interstate differences

WORDS

FORMS OF WORDS
Affixes, prefixes, suffixes
Acronyms and initialisms
Compounds
Past tense forms
Plurals, English and foreign
Proper names
Zero forms

SPECIAL EXPRESSIONS
Cliché
Foreign phrases
Four-letter words
Geographic/scientific names
Intensifiers

WORD MEANINGS & SENSE RELATIONS
Antonyms
Euphemism
Folk etymology
Hyponyms
Synonyms

SPELLING
Alternative spellings: ae/e i/y -ise/-ize l/ll oe
  -or/-our -re/-er
Spelling rules: -c/-ck -ce/-ge -e -f/-v- i>y -o
  y>i, doubling of final consonant, i before e

USAGE DISTINCTIONS
Collocation
Near-but-not-identical words
Reciprocal words

EDITORIAL STYLE

EDITORIAL TECHNIQUE
Abbreviations
Bibliographies
Dating systems
Indexing
Lists
Prelims
Proofreading
Referencing
Titles

INCLUSIVE LANGUAGE
Aboriginal
Disabled
Half-caste
Nonsexist language
Racist language

PUNCTUATION
Apostrophe
Brackets
Colon
Comma
Dash
Full stop
Hyphen
Question mark
Quotation marks
Semicolon

TYPOGRAPHY
Accents
Capital letters
Dates
Headings
Indention
Italics
Numbers and
  number style

GRAMMAR

GRAMMATICAL ISSUES
Agreement
Dangling participles
Double negatives
First person
Modality
Nonfinite clauses
Restrictive relatives
Split infinitives
"Whom"

WORD CLASSES
Adjectives
Adverbs
Conjunctions
Determiners
Interjections
Nouns
Prepositions
Pronouns
Verbs

A

a or an Should you say *a hotel* or *an hotel, a hypothesis* or *an hypothesis, a heroic effort* or *an heroic effort, a heaven-sent opportunity* or *an heaven-sent opportunity?*

1 *The general rule* is that **a** is used before words beginning with a consonant, and **an** before those beginning with a vowel:

a doctor	*a secretary*	*a teacher*
an astronaut	*an engineer*	*an undertaker*

But note that the rule depends on sounds, not on the spelling. We say and write *a union* and *a once-in-a-lifetime experience* because the words following **a** actually begin with a consonant sound (the ''y'' sound and the ''w'' sound respectively). The same principle makes it *an hour, an honor,* and *an honest man*, because the first sound of the following word is a vowel. When writing abbreviations, the choice between **a** or **an** depends again on the pronunciation of the first letter. We would say *an HD*, or *an LBW* and *a UNESCO project*, and it dictates what is written.

I CAN FEEL	These advertisements force us to
A XXXX	think twice about how to say the
COMING ON ...	unpronounceable XXXX. The use
	of **A** (rather than **AN**) shows it
AUSTRALIANS WOULDN'T GIVE	should be read as ''four ex'' not
A XXXX	as ''exexexex''.
FOR ANYTHING ELSE	

---

2 *Words beginning with h* are usually treated according to the general rule above. Most people nowadays would say **a** rather than **an** in the four cases at the top of this entry, because the consonant sound *h* is used at the beginning of the next word.

But *h* has been an uncertain quantity over the centuries, a sound that comes and goes from people's pronunciation. Listeners notice this when they hear someone saying *'im* and *'er*, and call it ''dropping the h's''. It actually happened to most words beginning with *h* as they passed from Latin into French and Italian. The Latin word *hora* meaning ''hour'' became French *heure* (pronounced ''err'', with no *h* sound) and also the Italian *ora*, without an *h*

1

even in the spelling. In English there's an *h* in the spelling of *hour* but not in the pronunciation.

The tendency to drop the *h* affected many longer and more formal words in earlier times, including:

> *habitual hallucination herb heroic historical history*
> *hotel hypothesis hypothetical hysterical*

And for those who said *'eroic* or *'istorical*, it was natural to use **an** before them. So the tradition of saying *an heroic effort* and *an historical event* developed in times when the *h* was not pronounced. These days, since we all pronounce the *h* in those words, there is no reason to use **an**. Old traditions die hard, however, and you may still see and hear *an historical town* etc. occasionally.

3 *New words for old*. The alternation of **a** with **an** has actually altered the beginnings of some English words. Words such as *apron* and *auger* were originally *napron* and *nauger*. When they occurred as *a napron* and *a nauger* people misconstrued them as *an apron* and *an auger*, and so the *n* was deleted from the word itself. The word *orange* was created in the same way out of the Arabic word *naranj*.

For more about the grammar of **a** and **an**, see **articles**. For the presence/ absence of **a/an** in (1) journalistic introductions, see **journalism and journalese**; and (2) titles of books, periodicals, plays etc., see under **the**.

a- The **a-** prefixed to ordinary English adjectives and adverbs comes from two difference sources. In a few cases such as *afresh*, *akin* and *anew*, it represents the Old English preposition *of*, and so *anew* was once "of new". In many more cases it was the Old English preposition *on*, as in:

> *ablaze abroad afoot ahead apart aside asleep*

Thus *asleep* was literally "on sleep". In each set of examples the two words have long since merged into one, but the past still shows through in the fact that as adjectives they are only used predicatively, that is, in structures like *The fire was ablaze*, not "The ablaze fire ..." See further under **adjectives**.

a-/an- These are two forms of a negative prefix derived from Greek. In English it usually means "without" or "lacking". It appears as the first component in some of our more academic and technical words, such as:

> *achromatic*   *analgesic*
> *apathy, apathetic*   *anarchic, anarchy*
> *aphasia, aphasic*   *anhydrous*
> *atheist, atheism*   *anorexia*

As the list shows, the form **an-** occurs before vowels and *h*, and **a-** before all other consonants. In many cases the prefix combines with Greek stems which do not exist independently in English.

Amoral is an interesting exception, where **a-** combines with a Latin stem which is also an ordinary English word. The prefix **a-** then makes the vital difference between *amoral* "lacking in moral values" and *immoral* "contrary to moral values" (where *im-* is a negative).

For more about negative prefixes, see **de-**, **in-/im-**, **non-** and **un-**.

-a This suffix is really several suffixes. They come into English with loanwords from other languages, including Italian, Spanish, Latin and Greek, and may represent either singular or plural. In *gondola* (Italian), *siesta* (Spanish), *formula* (Latin) and *dogma* (Greek), the **-a** is a singular ending; whereas in *bacteria* (Latin) and *criteria* (Greek) it is a plural ending.

Loanwords ending in singular **-a** are not to be taken for granted because their plurals may or may not go according to a foreign pattern. Loanwords which come with a plural **-a** ending pose other grammatical questions. Let's deal with each group in turn.

1 *Words with the singular -a* mostly make their plurals in the usual English way, by adding an *s*. This is true for all the Italian and Spanish ones, and many of the Latin ones. So *gondola* becomes *gondolas*, *siesta* becomes *siestas*, and *aroma* becomes *aromas*. The numerous Latin names for plants, for example *acacia*, *angophora*, *grevillea* and *protea*, all take English plurals. However some Latin loanwords, particularly those in academic fields, have Latin plurals formed with *-ae* as well: *formulae* and *formulas*; *retinae* and *retinas* etc. The plurals with *-ae* prevail in writing intended for scientists and scholars, and the forms with *-s* in nonspecialised writing and conversation. The group with both Latin and English plurals includes:

abscissa alumna am(o)eba aorta *aura caesura cicada cornea echidna*
fibula *formula* hydra lacuna lamina larva mora nebula nova patella
penumbra *persona* piscina *placenta* pupa *retina* stoa tibia trachea ulna
urethra vagina vertebra

The words in italics are more likely overall to be found with English plurals, for various reasons. Those which serve as both the technical and the common term (e.g. *cicada*, *echidna*), and the more familiar medical words (*cornea*, *retina*) were voted English plurals by more than 90 percent of the professional writers surveyed in Melbourne and Sydney in 1992. For some other words (e.g. *trachea*) the occasions on which a plural might be needed are not very many, and the likelihood of an ad hoc English plural is all the greater.

Note that for *antenna* the two plurals are used in different fields (see **antenna**).

Greek loanwords with singular -a can also have two plural forms. They bring with them their Greek plural suffix *-ta*, though they soon acquire English plurals with *s* as well. The Greek *-ta* plurals survive in scholarly, religious or scientific writing, while in other contexts the English *s* plurals are dominant. Compare the *traumas of everyday life* with the *traumata* which are the concerns of medicine and psychology. Other loanwords which use both English and Greek plurals are:

dogma lemma magma miasma schema stigma

Note that for both *dogma* and *stigma*, the Greek plural is strongly associated with Catholic orthodoxy (see **stigma**).

2 *Words with the plural -a* from Latin are often collective in meaning, like *bacteria*, *data* and *media*. We do not need to pluralise them, nor do we often need their singular forms, though they do exist: *bacterium*, *datum* etc. (For more information see **-um**.) The grammatical status of words like *media* (whether they should be treated as singulars or plurals) is unclear, and can be hotly disputed.

Those who know Latin are inclined to insist on plural agreement in such cases, on the grounds that *data* and *media* (not to mention *candelabra*) ''are plural''. Yet the argument appeals to Latin rather than English grammar; and it is surely undermined by other cases, such as *agenda* and *stamina*, which are also Latin plurals but are always combined with singular verbs in English. For more about the question of singular/plural agreement, see **collective nouns** and **agreement**, as well as **candelabra**, **data** and **media**.

Greek loanwords with a plural **-a**, such as *automata*, *criteria*, *ganglia* and *phenomena*, are discussed at **-on**.

For the choice between **-a** and **-er** in spelling some Australian colloquialisms, see **-er/-a**.

à deux See under **au pair**.

a fortiori This elliptical phrase, borrowed from Latin, means roughly ''by way of something even stronger''. Far from being an oblique reference to fetching the whisky, it is used in debating and arguing to introduce a second point which the speaker or writer feels is more compelling than the first, and is intended to consolidate the argument.

à la With this French tag we sometimes create phrases on the spur of the moment: *à la Paul Hogan*, *à la Hollywood*, so as to describe a style or way of doing something by reference to a well-known name. Paraphrased, those phrases mean ''in the style of Paul Hogan'', and ''in the same way as Hollywood does it''. The roundaboutness of the paraphrases shows what useful shorthand **à la** is.

à la carte This is one of the many French expressions borrowed into English to cover gastronomic needs. Literally it means ''according to the card''. At a restaurant it gives you the freedom to choose what you will eat from a list of individually priced dishes—as well as the obligation to pay whatever the bill amounts to. The **à la carte** method contrasts with what has traditionally been known as **table d'hôte** (''the table of the host''), which implies that you will partake of whatever menu the host (or the restaurant) has decided on, for a set price. The phrase goes back to earlier centuries, when the only public dining place available for travelers was the host's/landlord's table. But the **table**

d'hôte menu is what most of us partake of when we travel as tourist class passengers on aircraft.

In restaurants more transparent phrases are used these days to show when the menu and its price are predetermined by the establishment itself—simply *fixed price menu*, or *prix fixe* (in France and francophone Canada). In Italy it's *menu turistico.* Many restaurants offer both fixed price and **à la carte** menus.

a posteriori Borrowed from Latin, this phrase means "by a later effect or instance". It refers to arguments which reason from the effect to the cause, or those which work from a specific instance back to a generalisation. **A posteriori** arguments are thus concerned with using empirical observation as the basis of reasoning, and with inductive argument. They contrast with **a priori** arguments, on which see next entry.

a priori This phrase, borrowed from Latin, means "from the prior (assumption)". It identifies an argument which reasons from cause to a presumed effect, or which works deductively from a general principle to the specific case. Because such reasoning relies on theory or presumption rather than empirical observation, an **a priori** argument is often judged negatively. It seems to make assertions before analysing the evidence. Compare **a posteriori**.

a quattr'occhi See under **au pair**.

abacus For the plural of this word, see under **-us**.

abattoir or abattoirs Abattoir is the older and more widely used form of this word worldwide, though **abattoirs** is certainly used (in reference to a single establishment) in Australia. Of the two, **abattoir** is the easier to use, because there's no doubt that the following verb is singular. If you use **abattoirs**, it poses the further problem as to whether the verb should be singular or plural (see further under **agreement**).

abbreviations These are standardised short forms of words or phrases. A few of them, like *AIDS* and *RSI*, are better known than the full phrase; and some abbreviated words like *bus* and *pram* stand in their own right (see further under **clipping**). **Abbreviations** are accepted as ways of representing the full word or phrase in many kinds of functional and informative writing. Some would say that they are unacceptable in formal writing, though we might debate which types of writing are "formal". **Abbreviations** would probably look strange in a novel or essay. Yet who can imagine a letter which does not carry **abbreviations** somewhere in referring to people and places. Business and technical reports can hardly do without them.

Provided they are not obscure to the reader, **abbreviations** communicate more with fewer letters. Writers have only to ensure that the abbreviations they use are either too well known to need any introduction, or that they are introduced and explained on their first appearance. Once the reader knows that in a particular document *CCC* equals the *Canberra Cat Club*, the short form can be used regularly.

1 *Punctuating* **abbreviations** raises questions of policy because of the differing conventions practised in Australia. They include:
a) using full stops with any shortened form:
   C.S.I.R.O. Mr. Rev. mgr. incl.
b) using full stops with abbreviations, but not *contractions* (see below):
   C.S.I.R.O. Mr Rev. mgr incl.
c) using full stops with abbreviations which have any lower case letters in them:
   CSIRO Mr. Rev. mgr. incl.
d) using full stops with abbreviations which consist entirely of lower case letters:
   CSIRO Mr Rev mgr. incl.
The options all have their advantages and disadvantages.

Option (a) is the easiest option to implement, and has been the standard practice in the USA. It's the one represented in the Chicago *Manual of Style* (1981), even though its editors admit the worldwide trend to use less punctuation, or no more punctuation than is really necessary. Many **abbreviations** are obviously such, and readers do not need full stops to remind them.

Option (b) turns on the distinction between **abbreviations** and *contractions*, which has developed in British editorial practice. (See further under **contractions**, section 1.) The distinction, also known in Australia, gives different punctuation to "true" abbreviations, that is, ones which cut words short (*Tas.* for Tasmania), and to contractions which telescope the word, keeping both the first and last letters (*Qld* for Queensland). Under this system the full stop only goes with **abbreviations**, and it shows where the word has been cut off. However it presents a conundrum with *pluralised abbreviations*. Should the plural of the abbreviation *fig.* be *figs*, *figs.* or *fig.s*? If we decide strictly by the abbreviation/contraction rule, as the Australian Government *Style Manual* (1988) does, it would be *figs* because with the plural *s* added the abbreviation becomes a contraction. To treat singular and plural shortened forms differently may seem unfortunate. Yet if we adopt either *figs.* and *fig.s* we create other anomalies, because the full stop no longer marks where the word has been cut. *Figs.* is nevertheless the practice for plural abbreviations in Butcher's *Copy-editing* (1992) and *Hart's Rules* (1989). (*Fig.s* does not seem to be recommended anywhere.)

Option (c) According to this option, full stops are dispensed with for **abbreviations** which consist of *full* capitals, but retained for those with just an initial capital, or consisting entirely of lower case. It accommodates the general trend towards leaving stops out of institutional abbreviations such as *ABC* and *ACTU*. So *NSW* is left unstopped, while *Tas.* and *Qld.* would have them. The treatment of abbreviated state names is thus still anomalous, and there are inconsistencies elsewhere where initialisms and capitalised abbreviations rub shoulders with each other, as in computer texts.

Option (d) simply draws a line between **abbreviations** which begin with a capital letter and those which do not. It leaves *NSW, Qld* and *Tas* all unstopped, while *a.m., a.s.a.p.* and *fig.* are all stopped. The distinction between *contractions* and **abbreviations** is dropped, making for consistency in both capitalised examples (*Qld, Tas*) and lower case ones (*fig., figs.*) whether singular or plural.

A fifth option, to use no stops at all in **abbreviations**, is not commonly practised though it would be easiest of all to implement. It would resolve the anomalies created by distinguishing contractions from abbreviations, and also break down the invisible barrier between abbreviations and symbols (see below). Removing stops from all abbreviations would (it's sometimes said) lead to confusion between lower case abbreviations and ordinary words. Yet there are very few abbreviations which could be mistaken for ordinary words. Those which are identical, such as *am, fig* and *no*, are normally accompanied by numbers: *10 am, fig 13, no 2*, and there is no doubt as to what they are.

2 *Policies and minimising anomalies.* Dictionaries, style guides, and publishers and their editors all have to determine a policy from among the options above. The Australian Government *Style Manual* (1988) uses a combination of options (b) and (c), preserving the abbreviations/contractions distinction, but recommending the removal of stops from **abbreviations** that consist entirely of capitals. Australia Post recommends the use of full caps and unstopped forms for the shortened forms of all states: *QLD, NSW, ACT, VIC, TAS, SA, WA, NT*, creating a self-consistent set with no distinction between abbreviations and contractions.

Professional writers surveyed in Melbourne and Sydney in 1992 voted very strongly for removing stops from fully capitalised abbreviations (97% in Melbourne, 93% in Sydney), and a majority in each case were against observing the distinction between abbreviations and contractions (60%, 52%). The vote on removing stops from abbreviations like *Rev* which combine upper and lower case was more mixed, endorsed by a majority (57%) in Sydney, but not in Melbourne (only 39%). In both places the majority were in favor of keeping stops in lower case abbreviations (72% Melbourne, 61% Sydney). The results suggest Melbourne writers generally incline to option (c) and Sydney writers to option (d), and that neither overall is inclined to perpetuate option (b). Individual writers and editors who are not committed to a given house style are free to choose whatever policy minimises anomalies for them.

The fourth option for punctuating abbreviations—using full stops only for abbreviations which consist entirely of lower case letters, and abandoning the distinction between contractions and abbreviations—has been adopted in this book.

Note that when an abbreviation with a stop is the last word in a sentence, no further stop is added according to the current convention of allowing the major stop to cover for any lesser ones. This poses a difficulty for readers who wish to know whether the abbreviation has its own full stop or not. Unless the matter is explained or exemplified nearby, it's best to remake the sentence so as to bring the abbreviation in from the end. (This was done in discussing *figs*, *figs.* and *fig.s* above.)

3 *Special categories of* **abbreviations**. Some groups of abbreviations are always written without stops, whatever the writer's policy on upper and lower case, contractions etc. They include:
a) the symbols for SI units: *kg*, *ml* etc. (See **SI units**.)
b) the compass points: *N*, *NE*, *SW* etc.
c) chemical **symbols**: *Na*, *Fe* etc.
d) **symbols** for currencies: *£*, *$* etc.
e) acronyms: *Anzac*, *laser* etc. (See further under **acronyms**.)
   For the use of stops with the initials of a person's name, see under **names**.
   (See also **Latin abbreviations**.)

ABC In Australia these letters usually stand for the *Australian Broadcasting Corporation*, as it has been named since 1983. It changed then from being the *Australian Broadcasting Commission* as it was for the first half-century of its existence. Founded in 1932, it was intended to be a national voice like the BBC; and since 1954 it has maintained a Standing Committee on Spoken English (SCOSE). The committee's prime role is to advise broadcasting personnel on the pronunciation of proper names, especially foreign ones. But it also gives attention to current usage issues, and has been concerned with instituting nonsexist language over the airwaves. The ABC's nickname *Aunty* is itself sexist, but a harder nut for SCOSE to crack. (See further under **auntie**.)
   Note also that **ABC** is used by sociologists and demographers to mean "Australian-born Chinese". (See further under **Chinaman**.)

-ability This ending marks the conversion of adjectives with *-able* into abstract nouns, as when *respectable* becomes *respectability*. Adjectives with *-ible* are converted by the same process, so *flexible* becomes *flexibility*. The ending is not a simple suffix but a composite of:
• the conversion of *-ble* to a stressed syllable *-bil* and
• the addition of the suffix *-ity*.

ablative This grammatical case operates in Latin and some other languages, but not English. It marks a noun as having the meaning "by, with, or from" attached to it. For some Latin nouns, the ablative ending is *-o*, and so *ipso facto* means "by that fact". (See further under **case**.)

-able/-ible Many good spellers have trouble knowing which of these endings should be used. Both sound the same, and which one should be used often seems arbitrary. Compare *indispensable* with *comprehensible*, *traversable* with *reversible*, and *enforceable* with *forcible*. Just a handful of these words can be spelled in more than one way, for example *collectable/collectible* and *deductable/deductible*. But most are fixed one way or the other, and only one spelling will do.

Overall there are more words with **-able**, because it combines with any English or French verb, and also comes with those from the Latin first conjugation. By contrast, **-ible** is restricted to those based on verbs from the other Latin conjugations. That's fine if you know Latin, but if you don't the table below will help you with the most important **-ible** words. It does not give both positive and negative (i.e. *possible* as well as *impossible*) but one or the other, because there's no difference in the way that their endings are spelled.

accessible adducible admissible audible combustible compatible compressible contemptible credible deducible digestible discernible divisible edible eligible expressible feasible flexible forcible gullible impressible incomprehensible incontrovertible incorrigible incorruptible indefensible indelible indestructible inexhaustible infallible intelligible invincible irascible irresistible legible negligible ostensible perceptible permissible persuasible plausible possible reducible reprehensible repressible responsible reversible sensible submersible suggestible suppressible susceptible tangible terrible transmissible visible

Note that if the word you wish to write is too new to be listed in a dictionary, you can confidently spell it with **-able** since all new formations go that way: *contactable*, *playable*, *ungetatable*. For the choice between *drivable* and *driveable*, *likable* and *likeable* etc., see further under **-eable**.

Aboriginal or **Aborigine** Which term to use when you refer to one of the original inhabitants of Australia has been a fraught question. Various Australian style guides try to give a lead, but are divided over which roles to assign to each word, and why. The Australian Government *Style Manual* (1988) recommends using **Aborigine** for the noun (singular and plural) and **Aboriginal** for the adjective. This is also the recommendation of the ABC in its usage guide *Watch your Language* (1992). It streamlines an older practice noted by Murray-Smith, in which **Aboriginal** was considered preferable to **Aborigine** for the singular noun, on the grounds that the latter was a **backformation** (see further under that heading). *Aborigines* was acceptable for the plural because it had precedents in Latin.

This nicety has inclined some, like Murray-Smith himself, to avoid **Aborigine** altogether and to use **Aboriginal** everywhere for simplicity's sake— for noun (singular and plural) as well as adjective. But this runs counter to both common written practice and Aboriginal preference. In the Australian ACE corpus **Aborigine(s)** heavily outnumbers **Aboriginal(s)** for the noun, by 11:3 in the singular and 133:18 in the plural. *Aborigines* themselves reject the designation **Aboriginal** because (according to the Aboriginal Research

Centre at Monash University) it perpetuates the phrase *aboriginal natives* which was used by the Australian government to deny them tribal identity and territory.

When referring to Aborigines it's preferable to use a range of Aboriginal names for their groups, depending on their region. Those in NSW and Victoria are **Koori(e)s** (see individual entry); while those in other states and regions are named as follows:

Murri	*south and central Queensland*
Bama	*northern Queensland*
Yolngu	*Northern Territory (northeastern Arnhem Land)*
Mulba	*Pilbara region, WA*
Yammagi	*Murchison River district and central WA*
Wongi	*around Kalgoorlie*
Nyunga(r)	*southwestern corner of WA*
or	
Nyoongah	
Nung(g)a	*South Australia* (See further under **Nyungar** and **Nungga**.)

According to the Aboriginal Research Centre at Monash University, two of those names can refer to Aboriginal people more broadly: *Koori(e)* is acceptable to Aborigines throughout southern and central Australia, and *Murri* is the one used for those in northern Australia. See also **Black**.

Whichever word you use, it should have a capital letter, as with any ethnic or tribal name (see **capitals**). Without a capital letter, **aborigine(s)** means the original inhabitants of any continent, not Australia in particular.

Aboriginal names The names of some Aboriginal groups can be spelled in more than one way, for example *Pintupi*, *Pintubi* or *Bindubi*. It happens most often with ones containing the letters **p** or **b**, **t** or **d**, and **k** or **g**. A little phonetics helps to explain why. The sounds ''p'' and ''b'' are hardly different when you say them (except for the way the vocal cords vibrate for ''b''), and the same is true for the other pairs. And though they are different sounds in English, most Aboriginal languages treat the members of each pair as one and the same. Whichever pronunciation you use—*Pintupi* or *Bindubi*—the word remains the same, and *Katoomba/Kedumba*, *Kakadu/Gagadu* etc. are really the same word.

Aboriginal words Most of the **Aboriginal words** in **Australian English** were borrowed during the first century of settlement. Typically they refer to flora and fauna and things in the Australian environment, although a few refer to aspects of Aboriginal culture. Almost all of them are nouns. The only one from the lists below which is also a verb is *boomerang*. It is also one of the few which has some currency outside Australia.

- flora:
  brigalow coolibah geebung jarrah kurrajong mallee mulga myall waratah

- fauna:
  barramundi boobook brolga brumby budgerigar currawong dingo galah gang-gang kangaroo koala kookaburra numbat potoroo quokka wobbegong wallaby wallaroo warrigal witchetty wombat wonga-wonga yabby
- environment:
  billabong gibber willy-willy
- Aboriginal culture:
  boomerang bunyip coolamon corroboree gin gunyah humpy lubra mia-mia nulla-nulla waddy woomera wurlie

The most significant loanwords ·from Aboriginal language in the twentieth century are **Koori** and other Aboriginal words for their own people. See under **Aboriginal** or **Aborigine**.

Because the Aborigines never wrote their languages, their words had no standard spelling; and they were later heard and recorded in different ways by different writers. As a result there are or have been alternative spellings for many Aboriginal loanwords, for example **budgerigar** and **Nyungar**. See under those headings.

abridgement or abridgment See -ment.

abscissa For the plural of this word, see under **-a**, section 1.

absolute As a grammatical term **absolute** refers to the ordinary uninflected form of an adjective, such as *hot, keen, tall*—as opposed to the inflected forms *hotter/hottest* etc., which embody the comparative and superlative degrees of comparison (see **adjectives**, section 2).

Yet many adjectives cannot be made comparative or superlative and have only an absolute form. Definitive adjectives such as *auxiliary, eternal, first, perpendicular, wooden*, all belong to this group. The group of *absolute adjectives* is in fact very much larger than usage commentators have recognised. For them it consisted only of words such as *extreme, perfect, unique*, whose very meaning expresses a superlative. From this they argued that the words could not be further compared. The argument assumed that there was no more to such words than their superlative meaning, whereas dictionaries recognise various senses for them, some of which are definitely comparable. See for example **unique**.

abstract nouns These words carry broad, generalised meanings that are not tied to the specific instance or a tangible, concrete item. In traditional grammar **abstract nouns** contrast with **concrete nouns** (see further under **nouns**). The essential **abstract noun** is the name for an intangible such as *honesty, justice* or *knowledge*, but modern grammarians recognise many other kinds of words which refer to abstractions or to imputed entities such as *energy, luck* and *research*. Many **abstract nouns** are constructs of the language itself, built up out of other, more specific words. Thus abstractions such as *flexibility, formality,* *prevention* and *severance* are generated out of descriptive adjectives such as *flexible*, *formal* and action verbs such as *prevent*, *sever*. Even ordinary and familiar words can become abstract in certain fields of writing. Think of *field* and *grain*. We usually imagine them in concrete terms, yet in expressions like "field of study" and "grain of truth", they become detached and abstract. Broad cover terms such as *article*, *creature* and *vehicle* are also abstract until instantiated in a particular object. A "vehicle" may thus take shape as a car, tram, bus, truck, bicycle or perhaps even a skateboard or wheelbarrow.

Abstract words are a useful means of building ideas. They help writers to extend their arguments and develop theories. They can encapsulate remarkable insights, and summarise diffuse material under manageable headings.

But they are easily overused by those who care little whether their meaning gets through, or who want to avoid an issue. They are the clichés of academic and bureaucratic documents, and the bane of the weary reader. Most books on good style alert writers to the need to replace abstract language whenever possible. Computer software is available which helps to identify some of the abstract language in a text: it picks up all the words which end in *-tion* and other identifiable endings. But the computer cannot identify the full range of abstract words. Writers and editors have to be alert themselves to the sound (and meaning) of their own words.

For more about this, see **gobbledygook** and **nominal**.

abstracts See under **summary**.

accents In speech an **accent** is a general style of pronunciation, one which strikes the listener as different, as in *a foreign accent*, *an Irish accent*. But the accents of writing (such as *circumflexes* and *umlauts*) relate to particular sounds. As small marks attached to particular letters of the alphabet, the **accents** show that their pronunciation is a little different from that of the ordinary unmarked letter.

English spelling does without accents, while other languages make systematic use of them for a variety of purposes. In Italian and Spanish, for example, accents can show where the stress falls in a polysyllabic word. Some Asian languages written in the Roman alphabet, such as Vietnamese, have accents to show the different tones or pitch that go with a particular word: rising, falling, level etc.

The most familiar kinds of accent are the ones which indicate a special pronunciation for the particular letter. Many European languages have accents of this kind, for vowels: the *acute*, *grave*, *circumflex* and *umlaut*; and for consonants: the *cedilla*, *háček* and *tilde*. (Further details about those kinds of accent will be found at their individual entries.) Less well-known kinds of accent are the small circle used over *ů* in Czech, and over *å* in Danish, Norwegian and Swedish, and the slash used with *ł* in Polish and with *ø* in Danish and Norwegian. The use of accents shows the need to extend the Roman alphabet for writing the sounds of diverse modern languages. (See further under **alphabets**.)

Foreign accents in English. **Accents** come into English with loanwords, and often remain part of their spelling until they are fully assimilated. Words like *gâteau* and *garçon* are still usually seen with their respective accents, whereas earlier borrowings such as *chateau* and *facade* have lost them. Their disappearance is helped by the fact that English typewriters and wordprocessors rarely have accents in their repertoire. In fact there's no reason for accents to be retained in words such as *role* or *debut* where the vowel letters themselves more or less match the pronunciation. **Accents** do persist in words where they serve to show, for example, that a final *e* is pronounced as a separate syllable, as in French loanwords like *lamé* and *exposé*. The accent is all that distinguishes those from common English words: *lame* and *expose*. Even so, the context usually helps us to know which word is meant, as in *an expose of corruption* versus *to expose corruption*, or in *a lame suit* versus *a lame duck*.

Note that the **accents** on well-known foreign names are rarely reproduced in English writing. So *Dvořak* is usually written without the háček, *Zürich* without the umlaut, and *Montréal* without its acute accent.

accessory or **accessary** Accessory is increasingly the all-purpose spelling. **Accessary** used to be (and sometimes still is) the one reserved for legal uses, when you're talking about a person as the *accessary to a crime* or an *accessary after the fact*. But **accessory** is now used in those expressions too; and it has never ceased to be the preferred spelling for the extras which go with any complex outfit, whether it is a set of clothes, a car or a computer.

acclaim Note that the associated noun is *acclamation*. See **-aim**.

accommodate This word, and the related noun *accommodation*, may well qualify as the most widely misspelled words of the late twentieth century. Yet "accomodate" was not uncommon in earlier centuries, as shown in *Oxford Dictionary* citations, and was indeed used by celebrated authors such as Defoe, Cowper and Jane Austen. The insistence on two *m*s thus seems to be a product of the last century or so, and it's unquestionably in line with the etymology of the word. (The root embodied in **accommodate** is the same as that in *commodity* and *commodious*.) But unless you know Latin and can make that connection, the reason for the two *m*s isn't obvious. One pair of doubled consonants (the *c*s) seems enough for some writers—as if a kind of *dissimilation* sets in. (See **dissimilate** or **dissimulate**.)

With the standard spelling still fixed on two *m*s, you may be able to get **accommodate** right when necessary by thinking of "commodious accommodation" … provided you're confident about the spelling of *commodious*. Otherwise you'll need to appeal to Jane Austen etc. as justification for using *accomodate*.

accusative This is a grammatical name for the case of the direct object of a verb. In *The judge addressed the jury*, *jury* is the direct object, and could be called **accusative**. The word is regularly used in analysing languages like German and Latin, because they have different forms for the direct and the indirect object (the latter is called the *dative*).

In English both direct and indirect objects have the same form. Compare:

The judge addressed the jury (where *jury* is direct object)

The judge gave the jury his advice (where *jury* is indirect object)

Because *jury* is the same in both roles, the term *objective case* is often used in English to cover both accusative and dative.

For more about grammatical case, see **cases** and **object**.

ACE This is an acronym for the *Australian Corpus of English*, a database of up-to-date written Australian English from which evidence on current usage has been drawn. For the composition of the corpus, see under **English language databases**.

-acious/-aceous There's a spurious likeness between these endings, although they need never be confused. The words ending in **-aceous** are uncommon unless you're a gardener or botanist. How recently did you see *herbaceous* or *rosaceous*, for example? *Farinaceous* comes closer to home in discussions of food or diet, yet all such words originate as scientific creations, referring to particular classes of plants.

By contrast, the words ending in **-acious** are unspecialised and used in many contexts. For example:

audacious capacious loquacious pugnacious vivacious voracious

Note that the *-aci* in these words is actually part of the stem or root of the word, to which *-ous* has been added. For more about words formed in this way, see the heading **-ious**.

acknowledgement or acknowledgment For the choice of spellings, see **-ment**.

For the location of *acknowledgements* at the front of a book, see **preface**.

acro- This Greek element, meaning either "top" or "end", brings both kinds of meaning into English in loanwords. In words like *acrophobia* and *acropolis* (including *The Acropolis* at Athens) it means a "high position". In others, like *acronym* and *acrostic*, it means the "tip" or "extremity" of the words involved. The *acrobat* is literally "one who walks on tiptoe".

acronyms An *acronym* is the word formed out of the initial letter or letters of a particular set of words. Thus an acronym, like an abbreviation, carries the meaning of a complex title or phrase:

ANZAC   *(Australia and New Zealand Army Corps)*

QANTAS   *(Queensland and Northern Territory Aerial Services)*

UNESCO   *(United Nations Educational Scientific and Cultural*
                Organization)

Acronyms, like many abbreviations, are written without full stops (see
abbreviations). Some also show their metamorphosis into words by reducing
their full caps to just the initial one. So *ANZAC* can also be written as *Anzac*,
and *UNESCO* as *Unesco*. When they become common words, acronyms are
written entirely in lower case. For example:

laser   *(light amplification by stimulated emission of radiation)*
radar   *(radio detection and ranging)*
scuba   *(self-contained underwater breathing apparatus)*
snag   *(sensitive new-age guy)*

Note that **acronyms** are not always nouns. The adjective *posh* is believed to
have begun as an acronym, standing for "port outward, starboard home"—
unquestionably the choicer sides of the ship, if you're a colonial journeying
between Britain and India. The adverb *aka* (as in *Garry McDonald aka Norman
Gunston*) is an acronym from "also known as".

The desire to create **acronyms** which are both pronounceable and meaningful
has exercised many an action group, such as:

ASH   *(Action on Smoking and Health)*
CARS   *(Committee on Alcohol and Road Safety)*
DOGS   *(Defence of Government Schools)*
LIFE   *(Lay Institute for Evangelism)*
SWAP   *(Students Work Abroad Program)*

Accidental **acronyms** sometimes work against the organisation they refer to, as
with the NSW Independent Commission Against Corruption *(ICAC)*. The
acronym unfortunately suggests that the commission's work isn't to be taken
seriously. Those involved in it read *ICAC* as an initialism.

Acronyms and **initialisms**. All the **acronyms** so far comprise strings of letters
which combine to form syllables, and can be pronounced as ordinary words. This
is not however possible with abbreviations like *ABC* or *GNP*, which have to be
pronounced letter by letter. Technically this makes them **initialisms** rather than
acronyms, although the term is not widely known (it is not yet registered in the
Oxford Dictionary, though the *Random House Dictionary* notes it originated
around 1900). Many people simply include **initialisms** under the general heading
of *acronym*; and as we've already seen, the same abbreviation can be both. Another
familiar example that can be read either way is *UFO*, which is pronounced as a
two-syllabled acronym by some, and a three-syllabled initialism by others.

active verbs The term *active* is applied by grammarians to a verb whose action
is performed by its own grammatical subject. A classical illustration is the
statement: *I came, I saw, I conquered.*

Active verbs contrast with **passive verbs**, where the subject is acted upon
by the verb's action. There are three passive verbs in: *He was hung, drawn and
quartered*, although only the first one is given in its full form.

In written documents, **active verbs** are vital because they express action directly as an event, rather than making it a passive process. They are the natural way to keep a narrative moving vigorously along, and many books on good style recommend their use in other kinds of writing to ensure vigorous prose.

For more about this, see **gobbledygook**, **passive verbs** and **impersonal writing**.

acute accents The meaning of this mark depends on the language being written. In some European languages it marks a special vowel quality, as in French where it's used for a tense *e* (one pronounced with the tongue higher than for other kinds of *e*). In Czech and Hungarian the acute accent can be associated with any of the five vowels. In Polish it goes with both the vowel *ó*, and the consonants *ć*, *ń*, *ś* and *ź*.

Other languages deploy the acute accent to mark prosodic aspects of words. In Spanish and Greek writing, **acute accents** are placed over vowels to show that the syllables they occur in are stressed. In Vietnamese writing, the acute accent represents a rising pitch for the syllable concerned.

Note that Hungarian uses double acute accents on *ő* and *ű*, which are distinct from an umlaut on those letters. (See further under **umlaut**.)

AD This abbreviates the Latin *anno domini*, meaning "in the year of the Lord". It represents a date calculated within the calendar devised centuries ago by the Christian church, which is still the standard for the western world. In the Christian calendar, all years are dated as being either before the presumed year of Christ's birth (**BC**), or after it (**AD**).

Historians and others have made a point of writing **AD** before a number: *AD 405*, and **BC** after a number: *55 BC*. The convention is not now rigidly observed, and *Webster's English Usage* (1989) shows that **AD** often appears after dates, as in *405 AD*. The Reader's Digest *Right Word at the Right Time* comments that it happens especially when such dates are frequent. Note also that **AD** often occurs following the word *century* at the end of a phrase, as in *the fifth century AD*. This is the order in which most people say it, but there were once objections to it too, on the grounds that the word *anno* ("year") in the **A** was awkward after "century". Yet **AD** is normally taken to mean "in the Christian era", and with that the objection disappears.

For the use of stops in **AD** see **abbreviations**.

For more about the writing of dates, see **dating systems**.

ad hoc In Latin this phrase means "to this" and by extension "for this matter". We use it in expressions like *ad hoc committee*, i.e. one set up for a specific and limited purpose, alongside the regular one. In this precise context **ad hoc** is neutral in meaning. But in wider use it has come to mean "impromptu", and more negatively "lacking in forethought or circumspection". Decisions made **ad hoc** often seem arbitrary.

These shifts in meaning show how thoroughly **ad hoc** has been assimilated into English, as does the abstract noun *adhockery* now derived from it. For the spelling of this word, see **-c/-ck-**.

ad hominem This phrase, borrowed from Latin, is part of the longer expression *argumentum ad hominem* (argument directed at the individual). It refers to diversionary tactics used in legal pleading and political rhetoric, either an appeal to the self-interest of the listener(s), or a personal attack on the opposition (the "mudslinging" of low-level parliamentary debate). Either way it diverts attention from the real issues, and jeopardises proper debate and discussion. It suggests that the speaker is unable or unwilling to answer the points raised by the other side. (See further under **argument**.)

Note that a nonsexist variant for **ad hominem** (literally "to the *man*") is **ad personam**.

ad infinitum This phrase obviously has something to do with the infinite, and in Latin it meant "to infinity". In medieval scholasticism it was used literally in theological and mathematical arguments; whereas in modern usage it's always a rhetorical exaggeration. We apply it to a process which seems to go drearily on and on.

ad lib In shortened form, this is the late Latin phrase *ad libitum*, meaning "at one's pleasure", or "as you please". Musicians have known it for centuries as a directive to do as they like with the musical score: modify the tempo, add a few grace notes, omit a few bars of repetition. Only in the twentieth century has the word been extended to other kinds of performance (particularly acting and public speaking), in which the speaker may extemporise beyond the script. Often it implies a complete absence of scripting. These more general uses of the phrase have turned it into a colloquial verb which is usually written with a hyphen: *ad-lib*. Note that when suffixes are added to it, the last consonant is doubled, as in *ad-libbed*.

ad personam See under **ad hominem**.

ad rem This Latin phrase means literally "to the matter". It is used to identify arguments which stick to the point at issue, and do not resort to diversionary tactics or argumentative tricks. (See further under **argument** and **fallacies**.)

adage See under **aphorism**.

adaptation or **adaption** These are both abstract nouns based on the verb *adapt*. **Adaptation** has the better pedigree, with an antecedent in late Latin, whereas **adaption** appears first in the eighteenth century, apparently formed on the analogy with *adoption*. **Adaption** has never been as popular as **adaptation**, perhaps because it can quite easily be mistaken for *adoption*. Fowler claimed that **adaption** was not in general use, yet it's acknowledged as an alternative to **adaptation** in current dictionaries such as *Collins* (1991) and *Macquarie* (1991).

adapter or adaptor Some -er/-or pairs complement each other, one being used for the person and the other for the instrument (as with *conveyer/conveyor*). The evidence of *Webster's English Usage* (1989) is that this is not so for **adapter/adaptor**, and that the two spellings are used interchangeably. The chief difference is that **adaptor** is much less frequent.

For some other kinds of complementation between *-er/-or* words, see under **-er/-or**.

addendum For the plural of this word, see under **-um**.

addition or additive Additives are of course **additions**, but **additions** are not necessarily **additives**. **Additive** has the much more restricted meaning of something added in a chemical process, as in photography, or in the processing of foods. But if you're extending your house or family, it will be an **addition**, not an **additive**.

addresses on letters The conventions for setting out addresses on letters and envelopes are shown in Appendixes VII and VIII.

Adelaidean or **Adelaidian** Although the *Australian National Dictionary* has more examples of the spelling **Adelaidean**, the examples are all from the nineteenth century, and the record suggests a trend towards **Adelaidian** as the preferred spelling this century. (The ending varies in some other words: see further under **-an**.) But with the occasional use of *Adelaider* and even *Adelaidonian*, there's clearly no standard word. The same holds for residents of other capital cities, however. (See further under **Australia**.)

adherence or adhesion Both these abstract words are related to the verb *adhere*, meaning "stick to". But they differ in that **adhesion** usually refers to the physical gluing of one thing to another, while **adherence** means a less tangible affiliation, such as the commitment to a religion, philosophy, code of behavior, or the groups of people who espouse them.

adieu In several European languages, speakers seem to invoke the divinity when taking leave of each other. **Adieu** (French) and *adios* (Spanish) both mean literally "to God", and the English *goodbye*, originally "God be with you", spells it out a little more. Such courtesies were originally the ones used by the person who was leaving, while those who remained behind said *farewell* (literally "go well") by way of a rejoinder. With changes to the meaning of the verb *fare*, this distinction has been lost and either party may now "farewell" the other. Only in *bon voyage* "(have a) good trip", borrowed from fifteenth century French, do we have a special phrase to address to the person going away. Other leave-taking courtesies such as *au revoir* have always been used by either party. See further under **arrivederci**.

The plural of **adieu** in English is usually *adieus*, though the French plural *adieux* is preferred by those who wish to emphasise its foreign origins. (See further under **-eau**.)

adjacent or **adjoining** While **adjoining** implies sharing a common wall (as in *adjoining rooms*), **adjacent** may or may not. *Adjacent angles* are certainly up against each other, but *adjacent houses* can simply be close to each other in the same street. Like many slightly formal words, **adjacent** is less specific than its more ordinary counterpart. So when a report says that certain companies have *adjacent offices* in the building, they may or may not be next door to each other.

adjectives Often thought of as "descriptive words", **adjectives** just as often work to define or to evaluate something:
  a sharp pin a *drawing* pin a *grotesque* pin
The same adjective may both describe and evaluate something, as in the first example. Writers can, of course, use more than one adjective in the same phrase, or several, in order to create a multifaceted image.

THE	**Adjectives** are the stock-in-
COLD	trade of advertisers, put to
HARD	work in this promotion for
PURE	the NSW Dairy Corporation.
PLAIN	Theoretically there's no
CLEAR	limit to the number of
SIMPLE	adjectives you can pile
REVEALING	up in front of a noun,
ILLUMINATING	but in general you risk
ENLIGHTENING	losing the reader with
UNADULTERATED	more than four or five
UNDILUTED	of them.
FACTS ABOUT	
NEW SOUTH	
WALES	
MILK	

Note that there is a conventional order in any string of **adjectives**: the evaluative ones come before the descriptive ones, which come before the definitive ones. You see it in:
  progressive state governments
  most popular living jazz artist
In the second example note also that the adjective modified by *most* comes first in the string, as do any comparable or gradable adjectives (see section 2 below). The nongradable definitive or categorial adjectives come next to the noun. A further point to note is that definitive adjectives are often nouns conscripted for adjectival service, like *state* and *jazz*. (On punctuating sets of adjectives like these, see **comma**.)

1 *Attributive and predicative* **adjectives**. When **adjectives** precede the nouns they qualify, as in the examples above, they are said to be *attributive*. But many also occur as an independent item after a verb, particularly if they are evaluative or descriptive. Compare for example *a sharp pin* with *The pin was sharp*. When used thus to complement the verb, they are said to be *predicative* (because they are part of the *predicate* of a clause; see **predicate**).

Some **adjectives** can *only* be used predicatively, such as:

aboard aground ajar alive asleep awry

We never say "the ajar door" only *The door was ajar*. Grammarians would debate whether *ajar* is an adjective or an adverb in that sentence. (See further under **copular verbs**.)

2 *Comparison of* **adjectives**. The adjective system allows us to compare one thing with another, or with a set of others. Comparisons are built into the basic adjective by means of the suffixes *-er* and *-est*, as in:

a *fine* house
a *finer* house
the *finest* house

These three different forms of the adjective are called the *absolute* (or *positive*), the *comparative* and the *superlative*, and they make the *degrees of comparison* in English. When adjectives consist of more than two syllables, the comparative and superlative are usually made up with *more* and *most*:

an *expensive* house
a *more* expensive house
a *most* expensive house

Adjectives with two syllables may go one way or the other, though some patterns can be seen. Those ending in *-le*, *-ow* and *-y* make comparisons with *-er* and *-est*. See for example:

humbler, humblest	*nobler, noblest*	*simpler, simplest*
hollower, hollowest	*narrower, narrowest*	*shallower, shallowest*
angrier, angriest	*earlier, earliest*	*merrier, merriest*

Two-syllabled **adjectives** with other endings usually take *more* and *most*:

more frequent   most frequent
more hopeful   most hopeful
more spacious   most spacious

The adjective *common* seems to permit both forms of comparison:

commoner/more common commonest/most common

Many **adjectives** do not permit comparative degrees at all. Definitive adjectives like the one in *drawing pin* cannot be compared in degrees. It either is or is not a drawing pin. Other adjectives which cannot be compared are those which refer to an absolute state, such as *first, double, last* and *dead*. Noncomparable adjectives like those are referred to as *absolute words*. (See further under **absolute**.)

3 *Compound **adjectives*** consist of two or more parts in their absolute/positive form. They are the staple of journalese, as in the *war-torn* Middle East or *power-hungry* executives, but are also used creatively by authors and poets for artistic purposes. For more about the structure of compound adjectives, see **compounds**, and **hyphens** section 2c.

Note finally that adjectival ideas can also be expressed as phrases or clauses. Thus *expensive* might be paraphrased as ''worth a fortune'' (a phrase), or ''that cost a lot of money'' (a clause). For more about the grammar of adjectival phrases and clauses, see **phrases** and **clauses** section 4.

adjoining or adjacent See **adjacent**.

adjuncts See under **adverbs**.

admission or **admittance** Both these words are abstract nouns related to the verb *admit* but they are not equally useful in all contexts. **Admission** is the one to use when it's a matter of what someone says or confesses to their own disadvantage, as in *by their own admission* or *an admission of guilt*. When it's a matter of entering or being allowed to enter, either word can be used, although **admission** is the more general word because it can be used of entering, or the right to enter, all kinds of public places. **Admittance** is often linked with entering something more exclusive, such as professional entry to the Bar. The official sign NO ADMITTANCE suggests the same kind of exclusiveness, even though it appears in ordinary places.

adopted or **adoptive** The relationship of the speaker/writer to the adoption is what differentiates these words. **Adopted** expresses the perspective of the one doing the adopting, while **adoptive** is the relationship as expressed by the one adopted. So **adopted** is the word used by parents when referring to the child they have taken in, and **adoptive** is the word used by the child to describe the parents he or she has acquired in this way.

adventurous or **adventuresome** See **venturous**.

adverbs Only recently have the many roles of **adverbs** begun to be recognised. The terms used to differentiate them below are mostly those of the *Comprehensive Grammar of English* (1985).

1 *Types of **adverbs***. Some **adverbs** do indeed modify verbs, as their name suggests. They specify more precisely the time or place of an action, or the manner in which it took place. For example:
   (time) *tonight tomorrow soon then*
   (place) *abroad downtown indoors upstairs*
   (manner) *well quickly energetically thoughtfully*
Such adverbs are **adjuncts** to the key verb in the clause.

But many **adverbs** modify adjectives and other adverbs, and for adverbs of degree, such as *almost, quite, very*, this is their most important or only role.

Such adverbs, called **subjuncts**, often have the effect of either softening or intensifying the word they modify, hence the two following groups:

(hedge words/downtoners) *fairly rather somewhat*

(intensifiers) *extremely most very*

Expletives like *bloody* are powerful intensifiers of other adjectives, as in: *a bloody good book*. (See further under **hedge words** and **intensifiers**.) Other subjunctive adverbs are words like *ever, only, too*, whose role is to spotlight others and clarify the focus of the sentence.

Other adverbs called **disjuncts** serve to modify a whole clause or sentence, as in:

Fortunately the letter got there.

Perhaps it will affect their decision.

Attitudinal and modal adverbs such as *fortunately, mercifully, maybe, perhaps* express the writer's perspective on and attitude to the whole statement or proposition. As such they have a subtle but significant interpersonal role to play in a writing style. (See further under **modality**.)

Finally there are **conjuncts** such as *however* and *therefore*, adverbs with a cohesive role to play between separate sentences. They indicate logical relationships such as contrast and causation. (See further under **conjunctions**.)

Note that the negative adverb *not* is treated separately from other adverbs in modern grammars such as the *Introduction to the Grammar of English* (1984) and the *Comprehensive Grammar of English* (1985). This is because of its affinity with negative words of other kinds, such as determiners and pronouns (*neither, no, none.*) *Not* has wide-ranging powers within sentences, to modify a word (verb, adjective or another adverb), a phrase, or a whole clause. See **not** and **negatives**.

2 *Adverbial structure and form*. In all the examples given above, it's clear that **adverbs** do not necessarily end in *-ly*. (See further under **-ly** and **zero adverbs**.) Many like *soon* and *well* consist of a single morpheme. There are also *compound adverbs*, for example *downtown* and *indoors*. (See further under **compounds**, and **hyphens** section 2b.) Many adverbs are phrases:

straight away   to the bottom   in no way   a little bit

without a care in the world

Adverbial ideas can be expressed through several kinds of clause. See **phrases** and **clauses** section 4c.

3 *Comparison of adverbs*. Like adjectives, many **adverbs** allow degrees of comparison. Those formed without *-ly*, e.g. *fast, hard, soon*, make their *comparative* and *superlative* forms with inflections in the same way as adjectives: *sooner/soonest* etc. Adverbs formed with *-ly* enlist the help of *more* and *most*:

more energetically most energetically

4 *Position of adverbs in sentences*. **Adverbs** can appear at almost any point in a sentence. Attitudinal and modal adverbs are especially mobile, yet even those which modify the verb can come at either end of the clause/sentence, or in the middle:

Yesterday burglars raided my flat.
Burglars yesterday raided my flat.
Burglars raided my flat yesterday.

Adjusting the position of the adverb often serves to alter the emphasis of a statement, and to control the focus. (See further under **information focus**.)

Note that a small group of **adverbs** (*hardly, never, scarcely*) require inversion of the normal word order when used at the beginning of a sentence. See for example:

Hardly had they arrived ...
Never would I have believed ...
Scarcely did they look at it ...

In each case the verb follows immediately after the adverb, rather than the subject. It's also worth noting that the verb has to be an auxiliary. Compare: *Scarcely did they look* with *They scarcely looked at it.*

adverse or **averse**   Both these words imply a negative orientation, but while **adverse** relates to abstract and external circumstances, **averse** gets inside the individual. **Adverse** often implies uncontrollable forces such as wind and weather, or collective public opinion, whereas **averse** highlights an idiosyncrasy:

With such adverse results from the election, he was not averse to a little whisky ...

Note that **averse** is normally followed by *to*, in spite of the pedantic argument raised in the past that it should be *averse from*. The argument was based on the fact that the *a-* in **averse** meant "away from" in Latin, and so *from* rather than *to* was needed, for the sake of consistency. We do in fact do this with the related verb *avert*:

They averted their eyes from his fierce gaze.

But for the adjective **averse**, the weight of usage is behind *to*.

advertisement or **advertizement**   The first spelling **advertisement** is given preference in dictionaries everywhere, including North America. The alternative spelling **advertizement** also gets dictionary recognition everywhere—perhaps on the assumption that *-ise* would naturally vary with *-ize*, especially in the American context (see further under **-ise/-ize**). Yet there is no sign of **advertizement** or even *advertize* in the Brown corpus of American English (1961), as against 74 instances of **advertisement/advertise**. The forms with *-ize* may have consolidated since then, or be more evident in signs and nonedited prose.

As far as Australia is concerned, there are no instances of **advertize(ment)** in the ACE corpus (1986). And with *-ise* spellings prevailing elsewhere, Australian English is likely to prefer **advertise(ment)** for some time to come.

adviser or **advisor** Both these spellings are in current use and recognised in standard dictionaries, including the *Macquarie Dictionary* (1991). The spelling **adviser** is consistent with the majority of agent words in modern English (see **-er/-or**), and it goes back to the seventeenth century, according to *Oxford Dictionary* citations. The spelling **advisor** is not recognised at all in the Oxford, even in the second edition (1989), though most other dictionaries acknowledge its existence. (It no doubt owes its currency to the analogy with *advisory*, and perhaps *supervisor*.)

Some British sources call **advisor** ''the American spelling'', yet both the *Random House* and *Webster's* dictionaries (1985/6) present it as the secondary alternative. It is the less frequent of the two in the American Brown corpus (6 instances as opposed to 18 of **adviser**). In the Australian ACE corpus, **advisor** has 3 instances to the 31 of **adviser**. Most Australian references on style recommend **adviser**, and preferences among Australian newspapers run about 4:1 in favor of **adviser**.

ae/e In words like *anaemic* and *aesthetic* the **ae** spellings present the classical Latin digraph **ae**, which was reduced to a ligature æ in medieval times. The ligature is still used in the second edition of the *Oxford Dictionary* and the *Shorter Oxford Dictionary*. But the digraph is reinstated in the smaller British dictionaries of Chambers, Collins and Oxford itself, either because of Fowler's support for it, or perhaps the lack of typographic options. In modern American English the ligature is replaced by just **e** (*anemic*, *esthetic* etc.), as happened sometimes in Britain in earlier centuries.

Australians have until recently gone along with the British practice, but the **e** spellings are on the increase. Most now use it in *medieval* and *encyclopedia*, and quite a number are extending the same treatment to *hemorrhage*, *leukemia*, *pediatrician* and other medical terms which have begun to be household words. The medical profession generally prefers to keep the **ae** spellings, judging by the responses of individual doctors surveyed through the *Australian Dr Weekly* in 1988. In other specialised fields, such as biology and classical studies, the **ae** spellings also seem to be preferred. But there is no doubt about the trend to **e** in common usage, a tendency which is already established in spellings such as *pedagogue*, *pederast* and also *pedophile*. Those contacted through a Macquarie Dictionary Society survey in 1986 were either already using **e**, or solidly in favor of its acceptance. Follow-up surveys conducted in 1991 through Style Council and professional writers' organisations in Melbourne and Sydney showed that a majority endorsed the use of **e** in:

leukemia orthopedic paleolithic pediatric pedophile septicemia toxemia
But the pattern of usage is still rather unsystematic: only a minority of those surveyed endorsed *anemia*.

The use of the **ae** digraph is sometimes defended on etymological grounds: that it helps readers to recognise the meanings of the classical words. Against this one might argue that the **ae** is hardly etymological when it is itself a Latin transcription of the Greek diphthong *ai*. (The Greek root in words like *an(a)emic*, *h(a)emorrhage*, *leuk(a)emia* and *septic(a)emia* is *haim-*, meaning "blood".) Having no Greek, most readers would recognise those words as wholes, not through one obscure syllable in them. The **ae** is inessential, and awkward as a vowel sequence which is not otherwise used in English words.

Some would say that the **ae** is more important at the beginning or end of a word: so they would keep it in words like *aesthetic* and *formulae*, but replace it with **e** in the middle of a word: *anemia*, *archeology*. This is a manageable compromise, not going all the way with the USA, yet moving with a trend which is already developing in Australia, and avoiding the idiosyncrasies of making individual decisions about such words.

The style just described—using **e** except when the digraph is first or last in the word—has been adopted in this book for all the more common words which may appear with the **ae** digraph. More specialised words which are noted as examples have the bracketed **(a)e**. The brackets are a double reminder that in specialist writing (in medicine, biology and elsewhere) such words are likely to be spelled out with **ae**, and that in linguistic terms it is unnecessary.

Final note, the **ae** at the beginning of words like *aerial* and *aerobics* is never reduced to *e*. In words like those it is part of the combining element *aer(o)-* "air", where *a* and *e* are separate syllables. See **aer(o)-**.

aeon or **eon** See ae/e.

aeq. See under **cum laude**.

aerie or **eyrie** See eyrie.

aer(o)- This is the Latin spelling of a Greek element meaning "air", which is built into words like *aerate*, *aerobics*, *aeronautical* and *aerosol*. The overall number of **aero-** words is not large, and the everyday words in the group are gradually being replaced by others:

    aerate(d) by *carbonate(d)*
    aerial by *antenna*
    aeroplane by *aircraft, airliner*
    aerosol (can) by *spray (can)*

Some **aero-** words have already gone. We no longer use *aerogramme* (air letter) or *aerodrome* (airport); and the use of *aerial* in Qantas (= Queensland and Northern Territory Aerial Services) sounds quite old-fashioned. Still **aer(o)-** seems to be surviving and remains productive with technical and scientific words, especially in relation to aviation and *aerospace* itself:

    aerobraking aerofoil aeromagnetic aeromechanic
    aeroneurosis aeropause aerostatic

As the examples show, it combines with both classical and English stems.

aesthetic or **esthetic** See under **ae/e**.

affect or **effect** For general purposes, the choice between these words is a matter of grammar: **affect** is a verb, and **effect** a noun. Compare:

The strike affected our beer supply.

We felt the effect of the strike on our beer supply.

These are by far the most common uses of those words. But because of their similarity, and the fact that **effect** appears about three times as often as **affect**, the spelling ''effect'' tends to be inadvertently given to the verb.

What complicates the picture is that in rather formal usage **effect** can itself be a verb meaning ''bring about'', as in:

To effect a change of policy, we must appoint a new director.

And in psychology **affect** can be a noun meaning ''the emotion a person attaches to a particular idea or set of them''. Yet these latter uses are relatively rare. The psychological use of **affect** makes no showing in the standard British and American corpus, and there is one instance of **effect** as a verb to every ten to fifteen as a noun. In the great majority of contexts, it's **effect** as a noun and **affect** as a verb which writers need.

affixes An **affix** is a meaningful element attached to either the beginning of a word (a *prefix*) or the end (a *suffix*). (See under **prefixes** and **suffixes**.)

afforestation See **reafforestation**.

afterward or **afterwards** See **-ward**.

-age Borrowed from French, this suffix came into English with words such as *courage* and *advantage*, and is now used to create all kinds of abstract nouns in English. Some examples are:

anchorage bondage breakage cartage dosage drainage frontage
leverage parentage percentage postage shrinkage storage sewerage
tonnage wastage wreckage

Some words ending in **-age** develop more specific meanings out of the abstractions they originally represented. They may refer to a specific amount of something, as do *dosage*, *percentage* and *tonnage*, or the payment associated with something: *cartage*, *corkage*, *postage*. Others express the result of a process, as do *breakage*, *shrinkage* and *wreckage*.

When new words are formed with this suffix, the final *-e* is dropped before the **-age**, as with most words ending in *-e*. See for example, *dosage*, *storage* and *wastage*. For more about this, see **-e**.

The most important exception is *acreage* where the *e* in the middle marks the fact that there are three syllables to the word.

Other words to note are **lin(e)age** and **mil(e)age**, which may be spelled either with or without the middle *e*. (See further under those headings.)

ageing or **aging** See aging.

ageism or **agism** See under aging.

agenda This loanword from Latin is strictly speaking a plural word, meaning "things to be done". But its singular *agendum* is hardly ever seen, and **agenda** itself is always construed as singular in a sentence, with a singular verb:
The agenda for the meeting is three pages long.
This singular use of **agenda** meaning "list of things to be discussed" is only about a century old, according to *Oxford Dictionary* citations. Yet the singular use of **agenda** was so quickly established that by 1907 an English plural **agendas** was on record. These days you may even hear it turned into a verb:
I'll agenda that for their next conference.
However, that extension of the word is not yet registered in dictionaries. (See further under **transfers**.)

agent words These are nouns like *teacher* and *calculator* which are very visibly based on verbs (*teach, calculate*), and represent someone or something as doing the verb's action. So *teacher* is the agent word for *teach*, and *calculator* for *calculate*. In linguistics they are also called *agentives*. **Agent words** have a very long history in English, going back to Anglo-Saxon times. Over the centuries they have been formed with *-er* (dancer), *-or* (investor), *-ant* (commandant) and *-ent* (superintendent). Only the first type is really productive in modern English.

aggravate For too long this word has been shackled by the idea that it shouldn't be allowed to mean "vex or annoy". The pedantic tradition says that **aggravate** should be used to mean "make worse", which is rather closer to the literal meaning of its Latin components. But the argument is about as sound as suggesting that the word *rivals* should only be used of people who share the same river, because that is how the word originated.
    The *Oxford Dictionary* has citations for **aggravate** meaning "vex or annoy" from 1611 on. They are typically associated with everyday rather than lofty prose, and in later nineteenth century writings John Stuart Mill claimed the usage was to be found in "almost all newspapers, and ... many books". Dickens and Thackeray are notable users of it in their novels. But the *Oxford Dictionary* labels it "fam." (= familiar), and others including Mill and Fowler actively censured the usage, the former calling it a "vulgarism of the nursery", and the latter "a feminine or childish colloquialism". Their condemnation seems to have led other usage commentators to do the same, and yet there are examples of its use in general twentieth century writing. Interestingly, the proscribed and the approved uses of **aggravate** seem to coexist, though recent citations in the *Webster's Dictionary* files show that the sense "annoy" is somewhat less common than "make worse". The editors of *Webster's English Usage* (1989) remind us that the citations are from edited prose, and that this issue is something of a fetish. (See further under **fetish**.) The narrow focus of the fetish

is nicely shown in their evidence that it does not seem to have affected *aggravating* and *aggravation* in the same way, where the meanings "annoying/annoyance" are more common than those corresponding to "make worse".

Aggravate has developed a new meaning in English, which is hardly unusual and not to be deprecated. It can scarcely be rejected on grounds of possible misunderstanding, because only a human subject or object of the verb can be annoyed, and other subjects or objects are made worse. There is every reason to accept it.

aging or **ageing** Both these spellings are current in Australia. **Ageing** has stronger support in terms of its overall representation in the Australian corpus (ACE), with 22 instances as opposed to 6 for **aging**. The data shows however that the two spellings are used equally within the verb phrase, whereas for adjective and noun uses of the word, **ageing** is definitely more common. Both the *Macquarie* and *Collins* dictionaries (1991) reflect these differences, giving priority to **ageing** for the adjective and noun, and making **aging** and **ageing** equal options for the verb.

The tendency to associate different spellings with different grammatical roles is to be seen elsewhere in Australian English (compare **burned** or **burnt**, **-ward** or **-wards**) where Australians draw on both British and American traditions. Modern American dictionaries prefer **aging** for the verb, and indicate its use also for the noun and adjective. The *Oxford Dictionary* (1989) does not give the verb forms, and **ageing** features as the spelling for the noun and adjective, especially in technical applications such as wine-making.

Yet **aging** conforms to one of the most fundamental rules of English spelling: that a final *e* is dropped before adding a suffix beginning with a vowel. (See **-e** section 1.) It is consistent with *raging*, *staging* and *changing*. Those who prefer **ageing** would say that *age* needs to keep its *e* because two letters are insufficient to maintain its identity. Their argument is somewhat undermined by the existence of words like *axing* and *icing*. **Ageing** is not a new word: it has been on record for well over a hundred years, according to the *Oxford Dictionary*, and it seems high time to be less tentative about the regular spelling of **aging** for all applications of the word.

The argument for *ageism* (rather than *agism*) is its newness—it was coined only in the 1960s. In the longer run, it too should come into line with **aging**, though dictionaries everywhere give preference to *ageism* for the moment.

agreement In grammar this refers to the matching of words within a sentence in terms of their number (singular or plural), and in terms of gender or person. A traditional name for the concept in English and other languages is *concord*.

1 *Verb-subject* **agreement**. In English a verb and its subject must be matched in terms of singular or plural (as seen in *the mouse moves* and *the mice move*). However this mostly affects the present tense (cf. *the mouse moved* and *the mice moved* with exactly the same verb) because English verbs do not normally change for singular/plural differences except in the present. The one exception is the verb *be*, which has the singular/plural difference (*was/were*) in its past tense.

English verbs and subjects also have to agree in terms of person (first, second or third), at least in the present tense. We say:

I *move* and
you *move* but
he, she or it *moves*

Most verbs are like this, in having the third person singular different from the other two. But once again, the verb *be* is exceptional in having different forms for all three persons:

I *am*
you *are*
he, she or it *is*

Matching pronouns with verbs is straightforward enough, until you come to cases like:

Neither she nor I ?am/?is/?are inclined to go or
One or both of us ?is/?are wrong.

None of the alternatives sits comfortably in those sentences. The best way out of the problem is to remake the sentence:

Both she and I are disinclined to go.
One of us is wrong, or both of us.

Verbs not only have to agree with the personal pronouns but other pronouns as well, including the demonstrative and indefinite pronouns. The demonstrative pronouns: *this/these* and *that/those* are straightforward, because *this* and *that* always take singular verbs and *these* and *those* always plural ones. Things are less clear with the indefinite pronouns, which include:

each everyone everybody
any anyone anybody anything
either neither
none no-one nobody nothing
someone somebody something

Those ending in *-one*, *-body* and *-thing* simply take a singular verb on all occasions. But with the others, a plural verb is a possibility. For example:

Any of the books he wrote is/are worth reading.
None of their suggestions appeal(s) to us.

A singular verb in such examples singles out one item, whereas the plural suggests that the writer has the whole set in mind. Other things being equal, the singular construction sounds more precise and perhaps more formal; but a plural verb is often used in such sentences and appears freely in writing.

For the choice between singular and plural agreement after phrases such as **half of**, **number of** and **total of**, see further under those headings.

2 *Agreement between pronouns.* Another question affecting indefinite pronouns is which personal pronoun to use in agreement with them:

> *Everyone likes to choose ?his/?her/?their own clothes.*

In strictest grammar, the pronoun should be either *his* or *her* in such cases. But the exclusiveness of opting for one gender or the other (and the clumsiness of saying "his or her") makes many people use *their*. Because it is gender-free, *their* helps to maintain the generality of the statement, and in many contexts this is preferable. *Their* is certainly being used in this way very often in speech, and increasingly in writing. A recent newspaper cartoon had the Prime Minister saying:

> *Everyone has to pay their tax!*

The use of *their* in singular agreement is recommended in many manuals on nonsexist writing. (See further under **they**.)

3 *Agreement for nouns ending in s.* Nouns that end in *s* seem to be plural, yet if they refer to a single object, we may wonder whether a singular or plural verb is required with them. There are definite tendencies for different groups of words.

a) *Plural agreement* is normal for many ordinary objects, for example:

> *The jeans look too large on me.*
> *These scissors are not sharp enough.*

Other examples of the two major groups are:

- clothes
  > *bloomers braces briefs knickers longjohns pyjamas pants*
  > *shorts slacks suspenders tights trousers*
- tools and instruments
  > *bellows binoculars forceps glasses pincers pliers scales shears*
  > *spectacles tongs tweezers*

Plural agreement is also usual with more abstract nouns ending in *s*, such as:

> *arrears congratulations contents credentials dregs dues funds goods*
> *grounds headquarters lodgings means odds outskirts pains premises*
> *proceeds regards remains savings surroundings thanks valuables*

But there are exceptions, as when *grounds* or *means* refers to a single and specific item, and a singular pronoun is quite possible: *on that grounds* and *by this means*. (See further under **ground** and **means**.) Singular verbs can sometimes be used with words like *headquarters* and other words which refer to a particular establishment (*abattoirs, barracks*) or operation (*cleaners, gasworks*). For example:

> *The printers is on the corner as you turn right.*

b) *Singular agreement* is usual for various groups of names:

- academic subjects
  > *Economics/linguistics/physics/statistics is your forte.*
- games and sports
  > *Athletics/dominoes/gymnastics/quoits is great spectator sport.*

- diseases

  Measles/mumps is rampaging through the school.

Note however that when words in any of these groups are used to refer to particular objects or instances (and are no longer names) they take plural verbs:

His economics are those of a shopkeeper.

The dominoes were all in the box.

4 *Agreement for collective nouns.* Words such as *committee* and *team* (which refer to groups or bodies of people) can combine with either singular or plural verbs. You could say:

The committee has decided to break for lunch or

The committee have decided to break for lunch.

It depends on whether you want to imply that they are of one mind (via the singular verb), or that it was a democratic decision (via the plural). The plural option is exercised less often in Australian and American English than in Britain—at least in print. They are nevertheless common in speech generally, and in sports reporting particularly in reference to a team: *Australia are all out for 152.* Other collective nouns which offer the option are:

assembly choir class clergy club crew crowd family group

government office orchestra pair parliament staff trio union

Note that a few collective nouns always take plural verbs, including *cattle*, *people*, *police* and *vermin*.

For the choice between singular and plural verbs with **data** and **media**, see under those headings.

agriculturist or **agriculturalist**   See under -ist.

aid or **aide**   The spelling **aide** comes from the French phrase *aide-de-camp*, meaning "assistant on the field (of battle)". It became part of English military usage, and was subsequently extended to the assistants of diplomatic representatives, and heads of government: *the governor's aide.* The same spelling is sometimes applied to those who assist in hospitals or schools: *nursing aide, teacher's aide.* However these are also spelled *nursing aid, teacher's aid*, as if some people would reserve the word **aide** for the more prestigious kinds of executive assistant. The spelling is always **aid** when it is a matter of the assistance being offered, e.g. *foreign aid.*

-aim   Verbs ending in **-aim**, such as *exclaim*, all have related nouns ending in *-amation*. The vital point to notice is that the *i* of the verb disappears before the *m* of the noun. Compare:

acclaim	with	*acclamation*
declaim		*declamation*
exclaim		*exclamation*
proclaim		*proclamation*
reclaim		*reclamation*

Both nouns and verbs originated in Latin with the *-am* spelling, but the verbs were respelled on the analogy of *claim* in the late sixteenth century. Pronunciation should help to remind you of the spelling difference. The **-aim** of the verb goes with its strong stress, whereas the *-am* of the noun is unstressed.

-ain The verbs ending in **-ain** are a curious lot when you compare them with their related nouns. See for example:

abstain	and	*abstinence*
detain		*detention*
explain		*explanation*
maintain		*maintenance*
ordain		*ordinance*
pertain		*pertinence*
retain		*retention*
sustain		*sustenance*

The verbs all go back to Latin ultimately, and to different conjugations, but they were streamlined to a single spelling in early modern English. The nouns meanwhile are a mixed bag with various suffixes. Those received through French end in *-nce*, while those from Latin end in *-tion*. The different vowels of the second syllable are mostly a link with their Latin originals. But the difference between *abstinence* and *sustenance* shows you just how erratic that linkage can be.

ain't This word created a furore when it first appeared in the lists of *Webster's Third International Dictionary* in 1961. It made the headlines of the *Chicago Tribune* in the sensational announcement: *"Saying ain't ain't wrong!"*

It had of course been used for centuries, probably well before the first *Oxford Dictionary* citation of 1778, though as an item from informal speech it was somehow not quite respectable. Perhaps the deeper problem is that **ain't** is a multi-purpose contraction, which may represent any of the following:

am not are not is not has not have not

Using **ain't** as a substitute for all those is no problem as far as communication goes, but it's more often seen as evidence of careless speech than the adaptability of usage.

Note that four out of the five expressions just listed have their own contracted forms:

aren't isn't hasn't haven't

But there's no exact equivalent for *am not*. The expression *amn't*, though consistent with the other four, is regarded as childish or provincial. The standard contraction is *I'm not* (which reduces the verb rather than the negative). In informal questions however, and in tag questions, the common contraction is *aren't I* (not *ain't I* or *amn't I*):

I'm supporting you, aren't I?

It looks a little strange written down, and the Harper-Heritage usage panel of the 1970s reacted strongly against it. But it's what everyone says and it fills a gap in the system.

aka See under **acronyms**. See also **nom de plume**.

-al This suffix has two major roles:
- to make nouns out of certain verbs
- to make adjectives out of nouns

1 *Nouns with -al* have an interesting feature in common. They are all based on verbs of two syllables with stress on the second. See for example:

acquittal appraisal approval arrival betrayal betrothal
committal denial dismissal disposal perusal proposal rebuttal
recital refusal removal reprisal retrieval reversal revival
survival upheaval withdrawal

Some of the earliest examples are from medieval legal English, and several of those just mentioned have strong legal connections. The type has spread into the language at large, though few new ones have been formed on the same pattern in recent times. *Deferral* and *referral* are apparently the only twentieth century examples.

2 *Adjectives* are made by adding **-al** to an ordinary noun, and new ones are continually being formed. A handful of examples are:

bridal critical cultural herbal magical musical national natural
parental seasonal sensational transitional

However a good many common adjectives ending in **-al** were borrowed ready-made from medieval Latin, and they may function in English either as adjectives or nouns or both. See for example:

animal annual capital casual final funeral liberal official oval
principal rival spiral total verbal

Some of these, e.g. *rival*, *total*, are even used as verbs. The question then arises as to whether we should double the final *l* before adding verb endings to them:

? rival(l)ed ? total(l)ing

The issues are discussed at **-l/-ll-**.

al dente A gastronomic phrase borrowed from Italian, it means literally "to the tooth". It describes a style of cooking in which foods such as vegetables are only lightly cooked, so as to preserve their natural flavor and texture—and so that there is something to sink your teeth into. The opposite is that style of cooking all too familiar to servicemen and boarding school students, in which vegetables are stewed so long that it wouldn't matter if you had no teeth at all.

al fresco This has nothing to do with frescos, though we certainly owe it to the Italians. Literally it means "in the fresh (or cool)", that is, in the fresh air or out of doors. When used as an adjective it is set solid: *an alfresco meal*, but as an adverb it may be either set solid or spaced.

algae This Latin word for the slimy growth in still water is strictly speaking a plural. Its singular is *alga* (see further under **-a** section 1). In Latin it meant "seaweed", though biologists have made it the family name for a much larger group of both salt and freshwater plants. In ordinary English **algae** serves as a collective noun, and as such it may take either singular or plural verbs and pronouns in agreement with it:

Blue-green algae are appearing on inland waterways everywhere.

Get rid of all that algae in the pool.

(See further under **agreement** section 4.)

alias See **nom de plume**.

all right or **alright** See **alright**.

allegory An allegory is a narrative or dramatic form which uses fictional people and events to portray aspects of real life. The play *Everyman*, Spenser's *Faerie Queene* and Langland's *Piers Plowman* are all examples of **allegory**. Taken separately, the people and events in them are *symbols* of other things, but collectively they form an allegory. Allegory was much favored in earlier historical times, partly because it offered artists an oblique way of presenting contentious matters, without running the risk of imprisonment or worse. Allegories often carry a strong moral or message, whether it is homiletic (as in *Pilgrim's Progress*) or satirical (as in the work of Byron).

alleluia or **hallelujah** See **hallelujah**.

alliteration This is the literary device of juxtaposing words containing the same initial sound, so as to weld them together as a group. Hopkins used it extensively in his lyric poetry:

kingdom of daylight's dauphin, dapple-dawn-drawn falcon ...

Tennyson used it to achieve sound symbolism or **onomatopoeia** as well, in:

The moan of doves in immemorial elms

And murmuring of innumerable bees ...

Not only the first sound of the word, but of successive syllables is used for onomatopoeic effect.

The same device can be used in prose, and by those with more commercial aims in mind. In advertisements, **alliteration** helps to highlight features of the product and package them together:

Machines That Make Money (a computer)

Your nose need never know (a deodorant)

A Philips Microwave will give late guests the Warm Welcome they don't deserve!

allusion or **illusion** See **delusion**.

allusive or **elusive** See **elusive**.

-ally See under **-ic/-ical**.

alma mater See under **alumni**.

alphabetical order Alphabetical systems aren't all alike, as you will see if you look closely at the order of items in a library catalogue, a computer-ordered list, and several dictionaries. The two major alternatives within alphabetical systems are *letter-by-letter* order, and *word-by-word* order. The differences show up in the sample lists below.

Letter by letter	Word by word
bitter	*bitter*
bitterbark	*bitter end*
bittercress	*bitter pill*
bitter end	*bitterbark*
bittern	*bittercress*
bitter-pea	*bittern*
bitter pill	*bitter-pea*
bitters	*bitters*

In the letter-by-letter order, all word spaces and hyphens are disregarded. The order often has unrelated words juxtaposed in the list. With the word-by-word system, you work only as far as the first word space, which brings spaced compounds in immediately after their base word, and compounds which are hyphenated or set solid follow after, sometimes jumbled in with unrelated words.

The *Macquarie Dictionary*, *Collins Dictionary* and major American dictionaries use the letter-by-letter system, while British dictionaries such as Oxford and Chambers use the word-by-word system broadly speaking. Yet most dictionaries modify these two basic ordering systems by putting suffixed forms of words under the base word itself. So in both systems, *bitterly* and *bitterness* are likely to appear in the entry for *bitter*, and ahead of other words in that list above. In computer-ordered lists with strict letter-by-letter alphabetisation, *bitterly* and *bitterness* would appear before and after *bittern* respectively.

The alphabetical system in indexes may be either letter-by-letter or word-by-word, with the first easier for the indexer and the second for the reader. Having said that, it makes little difference to the ordering of items in smaller-sized indexes. For the alphabetisation of names beginning with **Mac** or **Mc**, **St**, **Van** and **Von**, see under those headings.

alphabets The alphabet used for writing English and many other languages is derived from one developed by the Greeks more than 2000 years ago. The word **alphabet** itself confirms this, since it is made up of the Greek names of the first two letters: *alpha + beta*.

The alphabets in use today fall into three groups: (1) modern Greek; (2) Cyrillic (or Russian); (3) Roman. Note that other writing systems such as those used in the Middle East and India are sometimes called *alphabets*, though they developed independently of this group, and have their own sets of symbols.

1 The modern Greek alphabet with its 24 letters is most like the Greek original, and it preserves letters such as *lambda*, *pi* and *rho* which are extensively modified in the Roman alphabet. It is used, in Greece and elsewhere, for general communication in Greek, as well as within the Greek Orthodox Church.

2 The Cyrillic alphabet, associated with St Cyril and the Russian Orthodox Church, is used for the Russian language and several Slavic languages. It was also applied to certain non-Indo-European languages within the jurisdiction of the former Soviet Union, such as (Outer) Mongolian. Some of its letters are deceptively like those of the Roman alphabet, but with quite different sound values. For example, *B* in Cyrillic represents *V*, *N* is *H*, *R* is *P* and *S* is *C*. Ships bearing the initials *CCCP* were registered in the former USSR, which (in romanised transliteration of the Russian) is *Soyuz Sovetskikh Sotsialisticheskikh Respublik*.

3 The Roman alphabet is the written medium for all the languages of western Europe, and some in eastern Europe. It is also the standard medium for writing languages of all kinds in North and South America, in southern Africa, as well as some in Southeast Asia, in Australia and the Pacific. The original Roman alphabet was expanded in early modern times with the addition of the letters *j*, *v* and *w* (the first derived from *i*, and the second and third from *u*, which had been both consonant and vowel).

alright or **all right** Whether to write this as one or two words has been a curiously vexed question, and unfortunately something of a shibboleth (see further under **shibboleth**). Fowler condemned **alright** as a vulgarism, and almost all usage commentators disapprove of it, though without offering much justification, as *Webster's English Usage* (1989) notes. It comments that **alright** appears more often in draft manuscripts than in print because copy editors are trained to replace it with **all right**. In Australia teachers were for decades schooled to mark **alright** as wrong, and this is the judgement of all the newspaper style guides with an entry on it.

Yet the tendency to merge the two words into one (**alright**), is as natural as with *already* and *altogether*. It actually provides a means to distinguish **alright**, meaning ''OK'', from **all right**, meaning ''all correct''. In just the same way, we distinguish *already*, meaning ''by this time'', from *all ready*, meaning ''all prepared''.

The form **alright** was reported by the *Oxford Dictionary* as being on the increase before Fowler passed judgement on it in the 1920s, and the second edition of the *Oxford Dictionary* notes that it is a ''frequent spelling'' of **all right**. *Webster's Dictionary* (1986) says **alright** is ''in reputable use''. At this end of the twentieth century it is high time we used it without any second thoughts.

alter ego This phrase, borrowed from Latin, means ''the other I'', or ''my other self''. Those who know Latin are inclined to interpret it as referring to an alternative side of one's own character, though without the schizophrenic overtones of Jekyll and Hyde. For a while it was used by psychologists to refer to an altruistic dimension of individual personality. The form *alteregoism* is recorded in this sense.

A rather different use of the phrase is found in citations from the seventeenth century on, where it refers not to oneself, but to a close and dear friend—one whose attitudes and tastes are so similar that they might be our own. The phrase always has sympathetic overtones, with none of the offhandedness of "my other half", or the ominous implications of the "doppelgänger".

alternate or **alternative** These words are a shifty pair. Both embody the idea of "other", and in older usage both meant "the other one of a pair". So by referring to the *alternative plan* you would imply that there were only two to choose between, and *alternate years* meant in "every second year".

But **alternative** as an adjective now often relates to a set of more than two options, as recent dictionaries acknowledge. We find this meaning strongly associated with the noun **alternative** as well, as in *We have three alternatives.* The extended meaning for **alternate** is also well established in the USA according to both *Random House* and *Webster's* dictionaries. And though the *Oxford Dictionary* labels it *(US)*, its use in official English in postwar Britain is registered in a complaint of Gowers (1954). The *Collins Dictionary* (1991) records it with no restrictive label. Using **alternate** as a synonym for **alternative** is recognised in Australian English too, as in *alternate routes to Adelaide*, and is registered in the *Macquarie Dictionary* (1991).

Another more recent development for **alternative** is its use in idioms such as *alternative lifestyle* and *alternative theatre*, where it implies something which is different from the conventional mainstream culture. This meaning is also recognised in the major American and Australian dictionaries. **Alternate** too is being used in those contexts (e.g. *alternate lifestyle magazine*), though less often than **alternative**. *Webster's English Usage* (1989) acknowledges this "antiestablishment" use of **alternate** as something shared with **alternative** since the 1960s, but the major dictionaries do not yet note it. The tendency for **alternate** to take on the adjectival roles of **alternative** emerges in all this. As nouns, they are still keeping their distance, with **alternate** meaning "substitute delegate", and **alternative** as "option".

although or **though** See under **though**.

aluminium or **aluminum** Aluminium is the usual form of this word in Australia and Britain. **Aluminum** predates it, as one of the earliest forms of the word (along with *alumium*, and *alumina* for the ore from which it is extracted); and it has remained the standard spelling in the USA and Canada. British English was perhaps influenced by Sir Humphrey Davy's comment in 1812 that **aluminium** "has a more classical sound than **aluminum**", and/or by its consistency with names of other elements such as *potassium*, *chromium* and *zirconium*.

alumni and **alumnae** Both of these words connect graduates with the institution which gave them their degree: the choice between them is a matter of gender. If you know Latin, it's clear that the **alumni** are male graduates and **alumnae** are female, though often the male term is used to include the other, as in the Melbourne University Alumni Association. Note that both words are plural, and that for **alumni** the singular is *alumnus* while for **alumnae** it is *alumna*. (See further under **-us** and **-a**.)

Both *alumnus* and *alumna* are literally the "foster child" of the *alma mater* or "fostering mother", as the university was dubbed. This of course makes universities and colleges the ultimate extended family.

a.m., AM or **AM** This is the standard abbreviation for times that fall between midnight and midday. It stands for the Latin phrase *ante meridiem*, literally "before noon". Like other abbreviations, it is often punctuated with stops, in line with the practice of keeping them in abbreviations in lower case (see **abbreviations**). Without stops, it could perhaps be mistaken for the verb *am*, part of the verb *be*, although this is unlikely when it's usually accompanied by numbers, as in *10 am*. Among the 49 instances in the Australian ACE corpus 19 were **a.m.** and 30 were **am** (unstopped). The **a.m.** form was rare in the newspaper samples, but the two were evenly divided in other kinds of writing. The American convention of printing it in small caps, as *10 AM*, also makes the stops unnecessary.

What time is 12 a.m.? Most people translate **a.m.** as "in the morning", and so *12 a.m.* would mean *12 noon*. But *12 noon* is the better expression to use since, strictly speaking, **a.m.** is "*before* noon". The American practice is to use 12 M, where M again is Latin *meridies* "midday" for *12 noon*. Elsewhere the abbreviation M is not widely used.

Note also that with full capitals **AM** stands for "amplitude modulation". (See further under **FM**.)

ambi-/amphi- This prefix, meaning "on both sides", appears in a few Latin loanwords, such as *ambidextrous*, *ambiguous* and *ambivalent*. As those examples show, the prefix carries the sense of unsettled values, swinging like a pendulum from one side to the other.

Note that **amphi-** is the equivalent in Greek loanwords, such as *amphibian*, *amphora* and *amphitheatre*. In these words the prefix simply implies "both sides". The amphibian lives on both sides of the high-water mark; an amphora has handles on both sides; and the amphitheatre has its audience both in front and behind—in fact, all around.

ambiance or **ambience** Ambience has been the general-purpose form of this word, derived from *ambient*, meaning "surrounding", and applied to any kind of physical or atmospheric context. **Ambiance** enjoyed a more esoteric existence in the realms of artistic criticism, as a word for the setting or context of a piece of art or music. The spelling with *-ance* originates in French; and a

French nasal vowel is often heard with it in English, to emphasise its elite character.

Inevitably perhaps the words are falling together: it's difficult enough to keep *-ence* and *-ance* apart (see **-ance/-ence**). And real estate agents and property owners only stand to gain by speaking of the *attractive ambiance* that their premises afford, which encourages the coalescence of the two words.

ambiguity This word is often used in the general sense of "uncertainty of meaning" or "fogginess of expression". More literally it means "capacity for dual interpretation", which leaves the reader swinging between two possible meanings for the same string of words. **Ambiguity** in this second sense can occur in a single phrase, as for example in *progressive anarchy*. (Does it means "anarchy which leads to progress" or "anarchy which gets worse and worse"?) The shorthand language of classified advertisements can also generate ambiguity of this kind, as in:

WANTED: Second-hand windmill by farmer with water problems

The **ambiguity** here is no doubt unintentional, a chance result of the string of words, which creates an alternative meaning for the phrase *water problems*. The cure (for the ambiguity) lies in rearranging or rewording the string.

Yet **ambiguity** is also used creatively and deliberately. A classic study of it in English literature is Empson's *Seven types of ambiguity*; and modern advertisers and copywriters use it to stimulate and hold their readers. The tension between two competing meanings engages the mind, especially when both are applicable in the context. For example, in the headline:

Why public servants are revolting

and in the slogan of a used-car salesman:

We Give You a Good Deal

Ambiguity of this kind works rather like *double entendre*, except that neither of the meanings generated is risqué. (See **double entendre**.)

ameba or **amoeba** See under **oe** for the spelling, and **-a** section 1 for the plural form.

amend or **emend** See **emend**.

America The *Americas* take their name from Amerigo Vespucci, an Italian astronomer and navigator who sailed under the Spanish flag, and in 1497 explored the Atlantic coast of what we now know as South America (Brazil, Uruguay and Argentina). Ten years later, a German map-maker attached the name **America** to the coastline Vespucci had charted. Vespucci was the first to discover continental America, so it was christened in his honor, even though Columbus reached the Caribbean islands in 1492.

For most people, **America** means "the United States of America", not the whole of North America, let alone Central and South America. (See also **Latin America**.) The citizens of the United States usually refer to themselves as **Americans**, and "America the beautiful" does not seem to include Canada.

Canadians, in fact, prefer not to be thought of as Americans, so the feeling is mutual. Yet the accents of Canadians and those from the USA have enough in common to be called the "American accent" by many outsiders. (For the phrase *US citizen*, see further under **USA.**)

This book notes wherever possible whether the practice being described is specifically US usage, or common throughout English-speaking North America.

American English This variety of English now has the largest body of speakers in the world. It originated with pockets of English settlers on the Atlantic seaboard of North America: a small group from the West country who took land in Virginia in 1607, and the better known "Pilgrim Fathers", many of them from East Anglia, who settled in New England in 1620. Those English communities evolved into the "Thirteen Colonies", though it was a narrow coastal settlement by comparison with the vast areas to the north, west and south which were then under French and Spanish control. But within 200 years, the English-speaking immigrants had acquired a mandate for the whole continent, and English was its official language.

The American Declaration of Independence from Britain in 1776 meant much more than political separation. Pressure for linguistic independence was a concomitant, and its outstanding spokesman, Noah Webster, issued a series of publications proposing language reform from 1783 on. The movement also found expression in the phrase "the American language", first recorded in the US Congress in 1802. In his first dictionary, the *Compendious Dictionary of the English Language* (1806), Webster urged Americans to detach themselves from English literary models. The dictionary enshrined many of the spellings by which **American English** is now distinguished from British English, such as *color*, *fiber* and *defense*. (See further under **-or, -re** and **-ce/-se.**) Webster's later and much larger *American Dictionary of the English Language* (1828) included many Americanisms, words borrowed from Indian languages, e.g. *caribou*, *moccasin*, *tomahawk*, *wigwam*, and ones created in North America out of standard English elements, *land office*, *log house*, *congressional*, *scalp* (verb).

American English is distinctive also in its loans from other European languages represented on the continent. From Dutch come *boss*, *cookie* and *waffle*, from French *chowder* and *gopher*, and from Spanish *dago*, *plaza* and *tornado*. These various kinds of Americanisms are the unique contribution of the New World to English at large, documented in the *Dictionary of American English* (1944) and especially the *Dictionary of Americanisms* (1951). Other major twentieth century dictionaries are the *American Heritage* (1969, 1982), *Random House* (1966, 1985), and *Webster's* Second and Third International dictionaries (1934, 1961).

During the nineteenth and early twentieth century, **American English** developed independently of Britain, and this is reflected in the countless distinctively American expressions for material and technological innovations of that period. American use of *gas*, *kerosene*, *phonograph* and *tire* contrasts with the British *petrol, paraffin, gramophone* and *tyre*. **American English** remained untouched by spelling modifications which developed in British English during the nineteenth century, hence its preference for *check, curb, disk* and *racket*, where British English has *cheque, kerb, disc* and *racquet* for certain applications of those words. Other examples where **American English** preserves an older spelling are *aluminum, defense, distill* and *jewelry* (rather than *aluminium, defence, distil* and *jewellery*).

In the details of grammar and usage, **American English** shows considerable range from the liberal to the conservative. The liberal views of Webster on things such as the use of *whom* and *shall* v. *will* contrast with the strictures of school grammarians of the nineteenth century, the archetypal Miss Fidditch and Miss Thistlebottom. Usage books of the twentieth century show the same wide range of opinion, some allowing American usage to distance itself from accepted British usage (e.g. on whether *bad* can be an adverb), and others seeking to bring it back into line with British English.

American divergences from British English are shown in many entries in this book. **American English** is often quite regular in its writing practices, as in the use of **-or** rather than **-our** in *color* etc., and of single rather than double *l* in *traveler*. In some punctuation matters, the American practice is more streamlined, as for example in the preference for double quotation marks, and the rules for deploying other punctuation marks with them. (See further under **quotation marks**.)

amid(st) or **among(st)**   The choice between **amid** and **among** depends first and foremost on what kind of noun you're coupling it with. Try it on the following:

among the trees	*among the landscape*
amid the trees	*amid the landscape*
among the rafters	*among the ceiling*
amid the rafters	*amid the ceiling*

You probably found all those acceptable, except *among the landscape* and *among the ceiling*. At first sight then, it looks as if **among** only goes with plural nouns, whereas **amid** can go with either singular or plural. The difference goes deeper however, because it *is* possible to say *among the audience* and *among the herd*—where the nouns are collective and comprise a number of similar and separable entities. *Landscape* is not a collective but a mass noun, and so it emerges that **among** goes with collective or count nouns, but not mass nouns. (See further under **count nouns**.)

There are no grammatical restrictions on where you use **amid** or **amidst**, but they do have a slightly literary flavor to them. Neither is used anything like as much as **among**, which outnumbers them by a ratio of more than 10:1 in the Australian (ACE) corpus. The corpus also shows that **amid** is used rather more often than **amidst** (15:9).

Among is more common than **amongst** in Australian usage, by a ratio of 5:1, but the latter is much less close to obsolescence here than in American English where the ratio is 80:1. The distribution of **amongst** through the various genres of the Australian (ACE) corpus is quite uneven however. It hardly appears at all in newspapers, while in most other kinds of nonfiction the level of use is around the average. Above-average use of **amongst** is to be found in more rhetorical and literary styles, in religious writing as well as higher-brow fiction and humor.

Some style books argue that **amongst** is to be preferred before a word beginning with a vowel, because of its final consonants. Yet **among** also ends in a consonant sound, so the phonetic argument turns out to be specious. The differences between **among** and **amongst** are a matter of frequency and style rather than euphony.

Compare **while** or **whilst**.

amoeba or **ameba** See under **oe** for the spelling, and **-a** section 1 for the plural form.

amok or **amuck** The first spelling is closer to the original Malay word *amoq* meaning ''frenzied'', while the second reflects the common pronunciation of the word. The spelling **amuck** is perhaps also an attempt to make sense of the word in English terms, though the connection with ''muck'' sheds little light on it.

Both spellings are current in the Australian press, though **amuck** is the preferred form of the *Macquarie Dictionary* and the *Oxford Dictionary*. *Chambers* and *Collins* dictionaries meanwhile make **amok** the primary spelling, as do both *Webster's* and *Random House*.

among See **amid(st)** or **among(st)**, and **between** or **among**.

ampersand This word covers a variety of symbols and squiggles used to represent the word ''and''. In official names and company titles, it has a shape like the figure 8, as in *Herald & Weekly Times*. An alternative and older shape for it looks like the Greek epsilon: &, as in Beaumont & Fletcher. Both these forms have been available in printing, though only the first one is common on typewriters and wordprocessors. Another form of **ampersand** is the one many people use in handwriting, which is like a cursive plus-sign: +, as in *bread + butter*.

But the **ampersand** is not used for general purposes in printed text. Its use is restricted to company names and titles in display work, and it is sometimes used in references to the work of joint authors, in bibliographies or in parentheses:

Bernard, J. & Delbridge, A. *Language as a Sign System*

In the body of a text, the word ''and'' itself replaces ampersand.

The word **ampersand** is hybrid Latin, a telescoping of ''and per se and'' which can only be translated as '' & by itself makes 'and' ''. This phrase records the fact that for centuries **ampersand** stood at the end of the list of alphabetic symbols A–Z in school primers—as the final symbol which in itself represented a whole word. No doubt the list was chanted in many a nineteenth century classroom, and the word ''ampersand'' stands as a monument to rote learning.

amuck or **amok**   See amok.

an   For the choice between *an* and *a*, see **a** or **an**.

-an   This common suffix generates adjectives from proper names, both personal and geographical. See for example:
> *Elizabethan Gregorian Hungarian Lutheran Mexican Mohammedan*
> *Republican Roman San Franciscan Tibetan*

As these examples show, the suffix may be simply added to the end, or may replace a final *-e* or *-o* in such words. If the final letter is *-y* it changes to *i* before the suffix. (See further under **-e** and **-y>-i-**.)

In many cases, the suffix coincides with the final *-a* of a name, as in:
> *Alaskan Asian Australian Estonian Jamaican Indian Persian Romanian*
> *Russian Spartan Syrian Tasmanian Victorian*

Because the resulting ending is quite often *-ian* (as in *Asian, Hungarian*), the **-an** suffix has given birth to *-ian* as a suffix in its own right. It is common with proper names, as in:
> *Bostonian Brazilian Canadian Christian Darwinian*
> *Freudian Miltonian Wagnerian*

The *-ian* suffix also appears in some ordinary adjectives, such as *mammalian* and *reptilian*, and a good many nouns referring to roles and professions:
> *grammarian guardian musician optician physician politician*

Note that a number of similar-looking words like *comedian, historian, librarian* are really examples of final *y* becoming *i* before the suffix **-an**.

One other variant of this suffix is *-ean*, which belonged originally to a number of classical words:
> *Chaldean Epicurean European Herculean Mediterranean*
> *Promethean Procrustean*

It has given rise to few new words since the English Renaissance, apart from *Jacobean*. Note however that several words may be spelled either *-ean* or *-ian*: **Adelaidean/Adelaidian**, **Argentinean/Argentinian**, **Aristotelean/Aristotelian**, **Caesarean/Caesarian** and **Shakespearean/Shakespearian**. (See under those headings.)

-ana   See under **-iana**.

anacoluthon   This is a learned word for a very common feature of spoken language—the lack of grammatical continuity in a sentence. As we speak off the cuff or on the run, we frequently start a sentence, stop, and continue on another tack. For example:

"That problem of yours—Why didn't I—Hell! All we need is to tell the computer to call up … "

In grammatical terms those are all incomplete sentences. But because everyday talk relies a lot on predictable idioms and phrases, the listener gets enough to follow the speaker's drift, and to understand the point at which something important and really unpredictable comes out. So the anacoluthon doesn't hinder communication.

For the plural of **anacoluthon**, see under **-on**.

anaemic or **anemic** See under **ae/e**.

anaesthetic or **anesthetic** See under **ae/e**.

anagrams An *anagram* is a word puzzle in which the letters of one word can be rearranged to form another. For example:

instead	*sainted*
mastering	*emigrants*
parental	*paternal*

The letters may be arranged in any order, as the examples show. Compare **palindrome**, in which the same letters must be read in reverse order.

analogue or **analog** The spelling **analogue** is the primary one, everywhere in the world, when the word is used to refer to something which is analogous in function to something else. Thus you might describe the American Congress as the **analogue** of the British parliament, and it would be spelled that way even in the USA. In Australia the earliest (scientific) computers in Australia were called *analogue computers*, because they worked by using physical quantities as analogues of mathematical variables, in order to calculate and solve problems.

But the spelling **analog** was used in technical and technological contexts in the USA, and is enshrined in items such as *analog clock* and *analog watch*, not to mention the *analog computer*. Australia's commercial resources in computing came first from the USA, and so the spelling **analog** is well known here too in compounds such as those just mentioned—even though analog systems have given way to digital ones.

So the difference between the two spellings in Australia (broadly speaking) is that **analogue** is the noun, while **analog** works like an adjective. In this way **analog** is quite well established in Australia, certainly better than any of its spelling counterparts such as *catalog*. (See further under **-gue/-g**.)

analogy Analogy is a matter of the perceived likeness between things. Analogies work rather like metaphors in poetry, but are used in speaking and writing either to explain something, or to bring the audience to a particular point of view. An imaginative geography teacher might explain how a cyclone moves by analogy with the way spaghetti behaves when you twirl it up a fork. And the parliamentarian who is determined to lower the speed limit for heavy semitrailers might refer to them as juggernauts of the highways. As the second example shows, the **analogy** may embody a judgement (positive or negative), which gives it its persuasive force. The word *juggernaut* not only projects the semitrailer as a large, rolling object on the road, but as something primitive and harsh, which mows people down indiscriminately in its path.

A *false analogy* is one which suggests conclusions which are misleading or inappropriate to the topic. Take for example the suggestion that crosscultural communication is like a game between people who are playing badminton on one side of the net and tennis on the other. It makes an amusing analogy. But it misses the point that crosscultural communication is often not a game but a serious business, and the principles being exercised by either party are probably not reducible to a set of sporting rules.

analyse or **analyze** See under -yse/-yze.

analytic or **analytical** See under -ic/-ical.

-ance/-ence Because these suffixes sound exactly alike, and both make abstract nouns, it seems perverse that they are not interchangeable in most English words. Usually there's no option, and only one spelling will do. So how do you know which one to write? There are a few principles which will save you having to look them all up in the dictionary.

The previous letters or sounds in the word often serve as a clue. With any of the following, the spelling is **-ence**:
- *-cence* (with the first *c* pronouced ''s'')—innocence magnificence reticence
- *-gence* (with the *g* pronounced ''j'')—convergence diligence indulgence
- *-quence*—consequence eloquence sequence
- *-scence*—convalescence effervescence fluorescence

With any other letters before the ending, you may be able to discover the right spelling (**-ence** or **-ance**) by thinking of related words. So to get *preference* correct, think of *preferential*; and the same technique works for:

confidence deference difference essence influence penitence
providence prudence reverence sentence

For **-ance** words, a related word ending in *-ate* or *-ation* can help you to get some of them right. So *dominance* can be reliably spelled by thinking of *dominate* or *domination*. The same technique works for:

luxuriance radiance significance tolerance

and many others.

Two small groups require special attention, because of their sheer perversity:

assist*ance* resist*ance*

versus

exist*ence* insist*ence* persist*ence* subsist*ence*

By rights they should all have **-ence** because they go back to the same Latin stem. But the French were inclined to spell them all with **-ance**, and their legacy remains in *assistance* and *resistance*. Would that the classical respellers of the English Renaissance had done a more thorough job on this set (see further under

spelling)—or that it was permissible to spell them either way. As it is, there's
no guiding rule to cover them, and those without graphic memories may need
to invent their own mnemonic for them.

A very few words may be spelled with either **-ance** or **-ence**. They include
dependence/dependance and *independence/independance*. The spelling with
-ance is in each case more common in the USA (see further under **dependent**).
For **ambiance/ambience**, see under that heading.

Note that some words vacillate between *-ance* and *-ancy*, or *-ence* and *-ency*,
and with some it makes a difference of meaning (see **-nce/-ncy**).

For the choice between *-ence* and *-ense*, see **-ce/-se**.

-ancy/-ency These suffixes, like *-ance* and *-ence*, create many a spelling
problem. But there are ways of predicting which spelling to use, just as with
-ance and *-ence*. (See **-ance/-ence** for details.)

and The word **and** is the commonest conjunction, and among the top three
English words overall in terms of frequency. It serves to join together words,
phrases and whole sentences, in all kinds of communication. Because it simply
adds something to whatever went before, speakers can easily build ideas with
it on the run. A vital element in the breathless narratives of children, it also
helps impromptu speech-makers:

> *"And now let me tell you a little about the background to this proposal
> and the petition. And before I raise the question of …"*

As the example shows, **and** can just as readily appear at the start of a sentence
as in the middle, although this has raised the eyebrows of grammarians and
teachers for many years. "It's wrong to use **and** at the start of a sentence",
they say. Their judgement is based on a very literal interpretation of the role of
a conjunction—that it must conjoin things *within* a sentence, and that it cannot,
should not, must not link things across sentence boundaries. There is no
recognition of the fact that **and** can provide helpful cohesion and a semantic
link across sentences. (See **coherence** or **cohesion**.)

It would still be a pity to begin too many sentences with **and** (or *but*, or any
other word). It becomes monotonous and predictable. Unless of course there's
a special stylistic or rhetorical reason for repeating it …

> *he commanded the multitude to sit down on the grass, and took the five
> loaves, and the two fishes, and looking up to heaven, he blessed, and
> brake, and gave the loaves to his disciples, and the disciples to the
> multitude.*
> *And they did all eat, and were filled: and they took up the fragments that
> remained ten baskets full.*
> *And they that had eaten were about five thousand men, beside women and
> children …*

The *ands* which begin each sentence, and each phrase, help to stress the
enormous scope of the miracle.

and/or At its best, this compound conjunction is a succinct way of giving three alternatives for the price of two. Thus:

The child's mother and/or father should attend the meeting.

is equivalent to:

The child's mother, or father, or both of them should attend the meeting.

As long as it involves just two items, the meaning of **and/or** is clear, though the reader may have to pause over it to tease out the alternatives. When there are more than two items, the number of possible alternatives goes up and becomes unmanageable. Try:

The child's mother, father and/or guardian should attend the meeting ...

With three items, the meaning is inscrutable, and expressions of this kind are no doubt the ones which gave **and/or** its bad reputation for ambiguity. It is sometimes said to belong in the contexts of legal and business writing, yet the citations in *Webster's English Usage* (1989) show that it's widely used in informative writing for the general reader.

anemic or **anaemic** See under ae/e.

anesthetic or **anaesthetic** See under ae/e.

angle brackets See **brackets** section 1e.

anorexic or **anorectic** See under -ctic/-xic.

-ant/-ent These suffixes are alike in sound and meaning, and both are found in common adjectives and nouns. Yet for most words, convention has made one or other the only one acceptable. You can predict the standard spelling for some of them from the letters or sounds immediately before the ending.

For the following, it is always **-ent**:

- *-cent* (when *c* is pronounced ''s'')—magnificent
- *-gent* (when *g* is pronounced ''j'')—diligent indigent intelligent
- *-quent*—eloquent
- *-scent*—evanescent obsolescent

Note that the words that fit these patterns always have at least two syllables before the ending.

If the word you're pondering falls outside those four groups, you may be able to predict its spelling from other related words whose pronunciation makes the elusive vowel unmistakable. So the sound of *accidental* would put you right on *accident*, and *consonantal* helps with *consonant*.

A very small number of these words can appear with either **-ant** or **-ent**. They are typically ones which work as both adjectives and nouns, like **dependant/dependent** (see further under that heading). In such cases writers may (as the *Oxford Dictionary* suggests) reserve the **-ent** for the adjective, and use **-ant** for the noun. But this distinction does not sit comfortably with the fact that **-ant** is the ending of many adjectives, or that adjectives and nouns shift into each other's roles. Both spellings are current for **propellant/propellent** and **repellant/repellent** (see under those headings).

Note that with **ascendant**, **defendant** and **descendant**, the **-ant** spelling has become dominant: see under individual headings. There is of course a difference of meaning for **confidant/confident**. (See **confidant(e)**.)

antagonist and **protagonist** See protagonist.

Antarctic(a) Because it is a geographical term, this word typically appears with a capital letter (see **capital letters**). We may use either the **Antarctic** or **Antarctica** to refer to the region around the South Pole. But when used as an adjective, the word may be spelled either with or without a capital, depending on whether it refers directly to the South Pole, or is being used figuratively. This makes the difference in:

Mawson succumbed to the Antarctic climate and
My azaleas are slow to flower with this antarctic weather.

ante-/anti- These prefixes mean very different things. The Greek **anti-** (meaning "against, opposed to") is well established in words like:

anticlimax anticyclone anti-intellectual antisocial
not to mention
antidisestablishmentarianism

It is also regularly used to create new words, such as *anti-abortion, anti-ALP* and *anti-business*. As those examples show, newer words with **anti-** often carry a hyphen, whether or not the base word begins with a capital letter (see **hyphens**). As they become established the words lose their hyphens, except before *i* or a capital letter.

Ante- from Latin means "before", as in:

antecedent antedate antediluvian antenatal antepenultimate anteroom
It is never hyphenated. It is hardly ever used nowadays to form new words, but has yielded its place to *pre-* (see **pre-**).

One curious exception to all the above is the word *antipasto*, borrowed from Italian. Though it means the things you eat *before* the main meal, the Italians have fixed the spelling with **anti-** not **ante-**.

antechinus For the plural of this word, see **-us** section 1.

antenna This Latin **loanword** has two plurals: *antennae* and *antennas*, which belong to different fields of endeavor and are not interchangeable. *Antennas* is the plural used for the devices linked to our radio and television sets which receive the broadcast signal. *Antennae* is used in biology, in reference to the feelers of insects. As often, scientists preserve the original Latin plural of the word, while the English one is in more general use. (See further under **-a** section 1.)

anthrax For the plural of this word, see **-x** section 3.

anthropomorphism See under **personification**.

anti- See ante-/anti-.

anticlimax See under **climax**.

antipodes This remarkable word was coined by Plato, to mean "those with their feet placed opposite". It is a reminder that the Greeks of the fourth century BC understood not only that the world was round, but also that through gravity all the world's inhabitants trod the earth in the same way, whether in the northern or southern hemisphere. Those on one side of the world therefore had their feet opposite to those on the other. Or, as Shakespeare expressed it, they were "counterfooted".

The word has been used of both people and places on opposite sides of the globe, and so Mongolia and Argentina are antipodes, just as are Britain and Australia (or New Zealand). Strictly speaking, the word could be used by Australians in reference to Britain, although the whole course of history has meant that it is most often used by Britons in reference to Australia. And because when Britons spoke of going to "the **Antipodes**" they made it sound as if they were going to the end of the earth, the expression is not so warmly received in Australia. The expression "Down Under" seems friendlier and less pretentious, but it too represents the idea that there's something quaint about living in the southern hemisphere.

antivenin, antivenene or **antivenom** The spelling **antivenin** is given preference in the major American and British dictionaries, with **antivenene** offered as the lesser or earlier alternative. The *Oxford Dictionary* does so in spite of having more citations for **antivenene**, which has been the more familiar form for Australians. However Australian health authorities now endorse **antivenom**, a form of the word which is more transparent, and which might make for more reliable communication in a life-threatening situation. (Compare **flammable/inflammable**.) **Antivenom** has been offically adopted elsewhere in the world following a recommendation of the *Lancet* magazine in 1979, and is established in the World Health Organization's Committee on Venoms and Antivenoms.

antonyms These are pairs of words with opposite meanings, like *wet* and *dry*, or *dead* and *alive*. Many **antonyms** like *wet/dry* are words from opposite ends of a scale, and it is possible to imagine intermediate stages on the scale between them, like the ones expressed as "rather wet" and "almost dry". Linguists refer to these as *gradable antonyms*.

Antonyms like *dead/alive* are opposites too, but with no intermediate stages between them. If you say that an animal is "half-dead", you are really saying that it's still alive. In fact the use of one word entails negating its opposite: *alive* means "not dead", just as *dead* means "not alive". The two words complement each other in meaning, and linguists refer to them as *complementary antonyms*.

A third kind of antonym, such as *buy/sell*, *parent/child* and *before/after*, is not so much opposite as reciprocal in meaning. As those examples show, the words may refer to reciprocal actions, or relationships, or corresponding relationships in time or space. The term for such **antonyms** is *relational opposites*, or *converses*. Comparative expressions, such as *higher/lower* also fall into this class.

All pairs of **antonyms** have a common denominator between them:

wet/dry	*(level of moisture or saturation)*
dead/alive	*(life itself)*
buy/sell	*(exchange of goods for money)*

So any pair of antonyms is in fact concerned with the same thing—it's just that they take contrasting perspectives on it.

ANZAC or **Anzac**   See under **acronyms**.

aorta   For the plural of this word, see under **-a** section 1.

Aotearoa   See **New Zealand**.

apeing or **aping**   See under **-e** section 1.

apex   Dictionaries allow both *apexes* and *apices* for the plural of this word, in that order. For more about their use, see **-x** section 2.

aphorism, adage, axiom, maxim, proverb   All these words refer to statements of received wisdom, and brevity is the soul of all of them. Dictionaries often use the words as synonyms for each other, yet there are aspects of each to differentiate.

An **aphorism** is above all pithy and terse, as in *Least said, soonest mended*, whereas the wording of an **adage** has a centuries-old flavor to it: *He who pays the piper calls the tune*. A **proverb** expresses its practical wisdom in homely terms: *A stitch in time saves nine*. The **maxim** is also drawn from practical experience, but turned into a general principle and rule of conduct: *People who live in glass houses shouldn't throw stones*. The **axiom** is the most abstract of the set, a statement embodying a recognised truth which is felt to need no proof: *Crime does not pay*. Its wording is a little more flexible than that of the other four, and it could, for instance, be turned into the past tense.

All five types of saying express common wisdom, and they seem to evoke a widely held set of values which can be used to bring people on side. With their more or less fixed wording, many can be invoked without even being quoted in full. You only have to say "People who live in glass houses ..." to remind an audience of that maxim, and of how vulnerable they are. Many an argument has deflected a challenge or gathered strength in this way.

aping or **apeing**   See under **-e** section 1.

apoplectic or **apoplexic**   See under **-ctic/-xic**.

apostrophe This has two distinct meanings:
1 a punctuation mark, for which see **apostrophes** (next entry);
2 the rhetorical practice of "turning aside", (translating the Greek word as literally as one can).

The term **apostrophe** was first used of dramatic speeches in which an actor, turning aside from fellow actors on stage, directs his remarks towards the audience. It may be an appeal to someone present, or an invocation to an absent party. An example of the latter is found on the lips of Shakespeare's Antony in *Julius Caesar*:

"O Cicero, thou shouldst have been present at this hour ..."

In other literary works, poetry or prose, an **apostrophe** is any section in which the author diverts attention away from the main narrative with an invocation. In his novel *Lolita*, Nabokov does it with *Gentlemen of the jury ...*, and *Gentlewomen of the jury ...*

apostrophes As punctuation marks, **apostrophes** are used primarily:
- for marking the omission of a letter or letters from a word;
- for marking possession or attribution.

In spite of its Greek name, the *apostrophe* began to be used as a punctuation mark only in the seventeenth century. It was first and foremost a mark of omission, used to show, for example, when the vowel had been dropped from the suffixes of verbs, as in *think'st* or *dislik'd*. The use of **apostrophes** to mark possession grew out of this. In earlier centuries the genitive suffix for many nouns had been *-es*; and though it had long been contracted to plain *-s* without any obvious problems of communication, seventeenth century scholars wanted to mark the lost letter. Some even assumed (amid the shortage of information about older English) that a genitive expression like *the kings castle* was really a contraction of *the king his castle*—which gave them a still stronger motive for writing it with an apostrophe as *the king's castle*. They managed to ignore the fact that it was the same for *the queens ship*, although the pronoun *his* could never have been part of expressions like that.

The *apostrophe* became a mark of possession on *singular* nouns during the eighteenth century, and was extended to plural nouns in the nineteenth century. Its sense of possession was at one time so strong that it was thought improper to say *the table's legs*, because this seemed to attribute the power of possession to something inanimate. Scruples of this kind have long since gone by the board, and daily papers are full of phrases like *today's announcement* and *Japan's ambassador*, where the *apostrophe* marks association or affiliation rather than possession.

The role of the *apostrophe* has thus expanded over the course of time. From its use in contracted verbs, it became the way of marking omissions and contractions of other kinds in the verb phrase, as in *it's*, *I'll*, *we'd* and *John's not here*, as well as *hasn't* and *won't*. (See further under **contractions** section 2.)

1 *Standard uses of the apostrophe with nouns* are as follows:

a) *apostrophe s* for singular nouns, marking possession or attribution, as in *the spectator's car, the class's response*. It makes no difference for common nouns if they end in an *s* or not, whereas proper nouns ending in *s* may be given special treatment (see section 3 below).

b) *apostrophe s* for plural nouns not ending in *-s*, such as *the women's work, the mice's squeaking*.

c) an apostrophe alone for the possessive of plural nouns ending in *-s*, as in *the spectators' cheers*.

Note that the *apostrophe s* is normally added to the final word of a compound possessive expression, as in *mother-in-law's tongue* or *Laurel and Hardy's comedy*. But when a compound phrase identifies two independent possessors, the *apostrophe s* may be added to both, as in *his father's and mother's property*.

For the choice between the singular and plural apostrophe in *each others* and other ambiguous cases, see under **number**.

2 *The disappearing* **apostrophe**. **Apostrophes** are not now obligatory in a number of kinds of expressions. They include:

a) plural nouns in phrases which express affiliation, for example, *teachers college, visitors book* and *Veterans Affairs*. The Australian Government *Style Manual* (1988) recognises these plural words as "descriptive" ones, and the tendency to omit the apostrophe in such expressions is growing, particularly in institutional names. Note however that *a visitor's guide* would require an apostrophe because of the preceding *a*, whereas *Visitors guide to Darwin* need not have one. This distinction is recognised by the American Associated Press stylebook, and is widely practised in the USA though not yet mentioned in the Chicago *Manual of Style* (1981). The *Right Word at the Right Time* notes it is happening in Britain too.

b) plural expressions of time and space, such as *five weeks leave* (compare *a week's leave*), and *three kilometres distance* (cf. *a kilometre's distance*).

c) numbers and dates, such as *in his 60s, fly 747s,* and *in the 1980s*. However, the apostrophe is still used with single numbers, as in *All the* 2's *and* 3's *were missing*.

d) sets of letters, such as *PhDs* or *MPs*. Single letters in lower case still usually take apostrophes, as in *Do try to dot the i's and cross the t's*. (See further under **letters as words**.)

e) placenames involving possessive forms. The apostrophe is no longer used in cases like *St Albans* and *St Leonards*, or those like *Frenchs Forest, Kings Cross* and *Wheelers Hill*. This was originally proposed by the Geographical Names Board in 1966, and has been adopted by Australia Post in the post-code book. It also guides the spelling of placenames on road signs and railway stations.

f) company names such as *Georges, Woolworths* and *Diners Club*. Those which are registered trademarks are, of course, fixed either with or without an apostrophe.

3 *Apostrophes with names ending in -s.* What to do for the possessive form of proper names ending in *-s* has led to great diversity of opinion and a variety of practices. The earlier convention was to exempt all of them from the general rule, and simply to add the apostrophe, as in *James', Menzies'* etc. Since then the number of words exempted has been drastically reduced by other more specific conventions:

a) exempt only literary, classical and religious names ending in *s*:
   James's Menzies's Keats' Jesus' Xerxes' Euripides'
b) exempt names with two or more syllables:
   James's Menzies' Keats's Jesus' Xerxes' Euripides'
c) exempt names whose last syllable is pronounced "eez":
   James's Menzies' Keats's Jesus's Xerxes' Euripides'
d) exempt names whose possessive form is pronounced with the same number of syllables as the plain form. The application of this rule depends on individual pronunciation.

As the examples show, there are different outcomes depending on whichever of these "rules" is applied. The only way to achieve consistency is to do away with exemptions altogether, and to treat all names ending in *-s* to the full *apostrophe s*, like any other noun. This practice is easy to apply, and is recommended for general use by the Australian Government *Style Manual* (1988), and the Chicago *Manual of Style*. However both authorities allow a little of rule (a) for writing which focuses on literary, classical and religious subjects, where the older tradition of using the apostrophe alone is strongest.

For the choice between *it's* and *its*, see **its**.

The choice between using apostrophe *s* and nothing at all in statements like "They wouldn't hear of *Henry('s)* coming" is a matter of grammar. (See further under **-ing**.)

4 *The superfluous* **apostrophe**. The use of apostrophes in ordinary plural words in shop signs is certainly a phenomenon to behold from one end of Australia to the other. Alexander Buzo found it in northern Queensland in "Townsville: land of the wandering apostrophe"; and in the Deep South, a ginger group known as "Citizens Resisting Apostrophe Plague" was able to make its bicentennial award to a Melbourne store which featured the following sign:

CUSTOMER'S. HEALTH REGULATION'S DO NOT ALLOW CARTON'S OF EGG'S TO BE CUT IN HALF	**Apostrophes** like these are not grammatical devices but decorative flourishes—baroque accessories to the letters.

The "Apostrophe Man" keeps tabs on apostroflation in Sydney, with a constant supply of examples to report to the *Sydney Morning Herald*, both downmarket (*auto's*) and upmarket (*gateaux's*).

Although the superfluous *apostrophe* is so public, it is still very much associated with signwriting, and firmly resisted in edited and printed documents. It would indeed be a pity to extend the use of the apostrophe to ordinary plurals—as if it didn't have enough functions already. The eighteenth century developed the use of **apostrophes** in order to distinguish possessive singulars from the plurals of nouns, and it would be perverse for the twentieth or twenty-first century to obscure the distinction by using **apostrophes** in all of them. We could all rally to support the Association for the Abolition of the Aberrant Apostrophe. Some might even support the abolition of all apostrophes.

appall or **appal**   See under **single for double**.

apparatus   For the plural of this word, see under **-us** section 2.

appareled or **apparelled**   See under **-l/-ll-**.

appendix   Like many **loanwords** from Latin, **appendix** has two plurals: *appendixes* and *appendices* (see further **-x** section 2). *Appendices* is becoming less common, although it is still used when referring to the supplementary sections at the back of a book. *Appendixes* is also acceptable then. But in anatomical and medical contexts, when you're referring to the bodily appendage which can cause appendicitis, the only plural used is *appendixes*. The operation of excising the appendix used to be called an *appendicectomy*, but increasingly in Australia it is just *appendectomy*, the form which has been used for a long time in the USA.

appointer or **appointor**   See under **-er/-or**.

apposition   Phrases which are in **apposition** provide alternative descriptions of something already mentioned:
   Their teacher, Swami Svaratnaram, prescribed the routine.
   She was born in Claremont, a suburb of Perth.
   He ordered a martini, the drink which went with the company he used to keep.
Items in **apposition** may supply extra information about the subject, object, or any other noun phrase in the sentence. Because they stand in parallel to key elements in the clause, appositional items are grammatically integrated with it, unlike *parentheses* (see under **parenthesis**). Appositional phrases are framed by commas before and after, as shown above, while *parentheses* are usually set off with brackets.

In newspapers and other informative kinds of writing, the appositional phrase offers alternative names, descriptions, or relevant facts which readers may not know. For journalists, they are a convenient device for packaging information. But they also allow fiction writers (as in the third example above) to add extra dimensions to their characters amid the narrative of events.

apropos This telescopes the French phrase *à propos*, meaning "to the purpose". As a simple adverb or adjective, **apropos** means "right or opportune" in relation to whatever is going on: *The remark was apropos*. But when followed by *of* and another word or phrase, e.g. *apropos of the election*, it serves as a discourse marker to highlight a new topic of conversation (see **discourse markers**). The phrase draws attention to the change of subject.

Sometimes speakers change the topic of conversation more or less abruptly, with the phrase *apropos of nothing* ... Whether the new topic is really unrelated to what went before, and entirely unmotivated, is for the listener to judge. The phrase still implies that the speaker is very conscious of altering the topic of conversation.

See also **malapropism**.

aquarium For the plural of this word, see **-um**.

-ar This ending appears on a few nouns and many adjectives in English. The nouns are a mixed bag, representing:

- people:
  beggar burglar bursar friar liar pedlar scholar vicar
- objects and animals:
  agar altar briar budgerigar calendar caterpillar cellar cigar collar cougar dinar dollar exemplar fulmar grammar hangar molar nectar pillar poplar seminar sugar vinegar

In some cases, the **-ar** is a direct legacy of medieval Latin. *Bursar* is from *bursarius*, and *calendar* reflects *calendarium* (see further under **calendar** or **calender**). Others, e.g. *collar* and *pillar*, were written with *-er* in earlier English and later respelled with **-ar**, perhaps to show that they were not agent words and that the ending was not really a suffix (see further under **-er**).

The desire to differentiate homonyms probably helps to account for others like *altar* (as opposed to *alter*) and *hangar* (as opposed to *hanger*). The spelling of *liar*, "one who tells lies", differentiates it from the possible agent word *lier* "one who lies around". But the **-ar** spelling seems awkward for words like *beggar*, and *pedlar*, which also look like agent words and might be expected to have *-er* spellings. In American English, *pedlar* has indeed been replaced by *peddler*, whether it refers to someone peddling cocaine in New York, or pots and pans in the Alleghenies. In fact, neither *beggar* nor *pedlar* is an agent word. Their origins are rather obscure, but they appeared fully fledged in Middle English, and the verbs *beg* and *peddle* are backformations from them (see **backformation**). Here again the **-ar** spellings show that, historically speaking, they are not agent words.

Apart from that tricky set of nouns, **-ar** is normally found on adjectives borrowed from classical or medieval Latin. See for example:

angular cellular circular crepuscular familiar globular insular jocular linear lunar muscular particular perpendicular planar polar rectangular regular singular solar stellar titular triangular vehicular vulgar

For the choice between *peninsular* and *peninsula*, see **peninsula**.

Arab, Arabic or **Arabian** All three words ultimately relate to the inhabitants of Arabia, though each has its particular collocations. **Arab** is the form used for both people and horses, as in *desert Arabs* and *Arab stallions*, whereas **Arabic** is mostly used in reference to the language, scripts and symbols associated with Arab peoples. Curiously, what we know as *Arabic numerals* actually originated in India, and are known by the Arabs themselves as "Indian numerals". **Arabian** is used in more general references to the culture and geography of Arabia, as in *Arabian Nights*, and *Arabian deserts*. But of the three words, **Arab** is now the most frequent and widely used, no doubt because of the power and influence of Arabs outside Arabia itself.

arbor or **arbour** See under **-or/-our**.

arced or **arcked** See under **-c/-ck-**.

arch-/archa-/archae-/arche-/archi- These five forms represent just two prefixes, both inherited from Greek: (1) **arch-/archi-**, meaning "principal, chief" and (2) **arch(a)(e)-/archi-**, meaning "beginning".
Words embodying the first prefix are:
    archangel archbishop archduke archenemy architect
    archiepiscopal archipelago
Words embodying the second prefix are:
    archaic archaism arch(a)eology arch(a)eometry
    archiplasm architrave archetype
The different forms and pronunciations of the prefixes are the result of the way they were treated in Latin, Italian, French and English—not strictly in line with the Greek. The choice between *archaeology* and *archeology* etc. depends on whether you wish to apply the British convention of using *ae* instead of *e* in such words. (See under **ae/e**.)
    In fact, the two prefixes seem to have developed from the same source. The Greek word *arche* meant both "beginning" and "principality", just as the verb *archein* meant both "be first" and "govern or rule". So there's a common source for the idea of being first in time and being first in terms of a hierarchy. The two ideas come together in *archives*, documents which record the origins of things, and which were kept at the Greek *archeion* or headquarters of the local government.

-arch/-archy The suffix **-arch** means "chief" or "ruler", just like the prefix **arch-/archi-** (see previous entry). It is a familiar element in words like *matriarch, monarch* and *patriarch*. The related suffix **-archy**, meaning "rule or system of government", makes the corresponding abstract nouns:
    matriarchy monarchy patriarchy
as well as
    anarchy hierarchy oligarchy

archaeology or **archeology** See under **ae/e**.

archaisms These are words and expressions that reflect times past. They may refer to the material culture or social relations of past centuries, as do *liege lord* and *yeoman* from feudal times, or *emancipists* and *ticket-of-leave men* from Australia's nineteenth century history. They help to conjure up a sense of an earlier historical period. Measuring distances in *leagues* and giving prices in *guineas* have the same archaising effect.

Archaisms of another kind are the ordinary function words and expressions which have somehow gone out of fashion. Examples of this second kind of archaism are: *forsooth*, *methinks*, *howsoever* and *verily*. They have less power to set a particular historical period, and are more likely to draw attention back to the writer and the writer's style. They suggest a certain self-conscious use of language, which can either be effectively ironic, or annoyingly precious.

The boundary between archaic and old-fashioned language is somewhat fluid and subjectively determined. Whether you class words like *albeit*, *goodly*, *perchance* and *rejoice* as archaisms or just old-fashioned words depends on individual education and experience of language. Those who read older literature are more likely to feel that such words are part of the continuum of the English language, and only a little old-fashioned. Those whose reading is of the twentieth century will probably feel the words are archaic.

archeo- or **archaeo-** See under **arch-**.

archipelago For the plural of this word, see under **-o**.

aren't I See **ain't**.

Argentinean, Argentinian, Argentine or **Argentina** The first three words serve to connect something or someone with **Argentina**, officially known as the *Argentine Republic*, and also as the **Argentine**. There are alternative names for the inhabitants of **Argentina** as well: *Argentines* (in three syllables), or *Argentineans* or *Argentinians* (in five). Choosing between the five-syllabled options, you might as well toss a coin—or go by your preferred dictionary. *Webster's* (1986) and *Macquarie* (1991) give preference to **Argentinean** and *Collins* (1991) and the *Oxford Dictionary* to **Argentinian**. Both **Argentinian** and **Argentinean** serve as adjectives, as in *Argentinean beef*.

For other examples of **-ean/-ian**, see **-an**.

argument Many things pass for **argument** which do not merit the name. All too often those who would persuade actually shortcircuit the argumentative process, by attacking or appealing directly to the interests of the listener (*argumentum ad hominem*), or to the listener's hip-pocket nerve (in neo-Latin *ad crumenam*). The argument may be just a **non sequitur**, **ad hoc**, or **ex silentio**, and worse perhaps, goes on **ad infinitum**.

A proper argument addresses the issues (*argumentum ad rem*), and develops either inductively (**a posteriori**) or deductively (**a priori**).

We owe these Latin phrases to scholars in rhetoric and philosophy between the sixteenth and eighteenth centuries (see under the individual heading for more about each). A few other argumentative tactics and tricks go by English names, for example: *begging the question*, and posing *a leading question*. (See also under **analogy**, and **fallacies**.)

Note also the spelling of **argument**. Without the *e* of *argue*, it looks like an exception to the rule for words formed with **-ment** (see under that heading). In fact the word was borrowed ready-made from French, and its spelling harnessed to the Latin *argumentum*.

-arian A latter-day suffix, **-arian** has developed from several sources. Some of the words embodying it, like *librarian* and *veterinarian*, derive from medieval Latin words ending in *-arius*; while others like *egalitarian* are modeled on French antecedents. Many have simply been formed by analogy in English. Whether adjective or noun, they refer to attitudes of mind, and moral, religious or political beliefs. For example:

> *antiquarian authoritarian disciplinarian humanitarian libertarian*
> *millenarian parliamentarian proletarian sabbatarian sectarian*
> *totalitarian utilitarian vegetarian*

arise or **rise** See rise.

Aristotelian or **Aristotelean** All modern dictionaries give preference to **Aristotelian**, and for some it's the only spelling recognised. And though the *Oxford Dictionary* in the nineteenth century preferred the more classical-looking **Aristotelean**, it noted that **Aristotelian** was actually more common. For other words which vary between *-ian* and *-ean*, see under **-an**.

armfuls or **armsful** See under -ful.

armor or **armour** See under -or/-our.

-aroo This is one of the few distinctively Australian suffixes. It is derived from, or supported by, several Aboriginal words for flora and fauna (*kangaroo*, *wallaroo*, *willaroo*, *calgaroo*), and by placenames such as *Coorparoo* (QLD), *Gundaroo* (NSW), and *Liparoo* (VIC). It also appears in established common nouns such as *jackaroo* and *jillaroo*.

But in transients such as *jambaroo*, *jigamaroo* and *shivaroo*, noted by Sidney J. Baker in *The Australian Language* (1945), the **-aroo** suffix has become confounded with *-eroo*, a suffix popular in the USA in the 1940s. It coined ad hoc words such as *flopperoo* and *jokeroo*, which were spread around by military movements in World War II (see **-eroo**). The popularity of such words probably fostered the alternative spelling *jackeroo* for **jackaroo** (see further under that heading). Note the divergent spellings in placenames such as *Boolaroo* (NSW) and *Booleroo Centre* (SA).

Note also the spelling of *potoroo*, the only word with *-oroo*.

arouse or **rouse** See **rouse**.

arrivederci This Italian phrase allows English speakers to say goodbye with more syllables and nostalgia than any English word provides. In Italian it is *a rivederci*, meaning "till we see each other again", just like the French *au revoir*, German *auf Wiedersehen*, and Spanish *hasta la vista*. The tone of such phrases is courteous and somewhat formal, and they do not imply that the next meeting has already been arranged. In this they differ from parting phrases like *à bientôt* "till very soon" (French), and *hasta luego* "until then" (Spanish), which do carry such an implication. The English *see you later* has more in common with the latter pair, though it is definitely informal in style. Compare **adieu**.

ars gratia artis This sententious phrase borrowed from Latin means "art for the sake of art" or "art for art's sake". In its French form "l'art pour l'art", it was much touted by French romantics of the nineteenth century, and was used in support of the notion that art could be indifferent to moral and social values. The phrase is wonderfully enigmatic, and can be quoted either to invoke a lofty aestheticism, or to justify irresponsible artistic activity. It serves as the motto of MGM films, displayed at the start of each movie along with the roaring lion. Whether you read the motto as an artistic affirmation or an ironic comment will depend on whether it prefaces *Out of Africa* or *Tarzan the Apeman*.

artefact or **artifact** See **artifact**.

articles This is a grammatical term for two kinds of words: (1) the definite article (*the*) and (2) the indefinite article (*a/an*). Articles are the commonest words on the page and there's one in almost every English sentence. Their role and meaning is nevertheless elusive, and getting them right is often a problem for people learning English as a second language.

The prime function of **articles** is to signal that a noun is to follow, sooner or later. See for example:

the brown fox
the proverbial quick-moving brown fox
a fast car
a surprisingly fast classic sports car

Articles are almost always the first word of a noun phrase. The only exceptions are when a predeterminer or quantitative expression such as *all, both, some of* or *one of* occurs in the same phrase, e.g. *all the brown foxes*. In that case, the *article* comes second (see further under **determiners**).

The chief difference between definite and indefinite articles is in the specifications they put on the following noun. The indefinite article indicates that the noun is being mentioned for the first time in the discourse in which it occurs. See for example, how it works in:

On my way through Hong Kong, I bought a camera.

Compare the effect of the definite article:

When I showed the camera to customs men, they charged me 33% duty.

Using the word *the* often implies that you have referred to the thing already. In this case, *the camera* must be the one bought in Hong Kong. It isn't any camera, but one about which something has already been specified.

Note however that in writing we don't always work through those two stages. We may go straight for *the*, but add the specifications immediately after:

The camera which I bought in Hong Kong cost me 33% duty.

Still the use of *the* implies that the reader will find specifications for the noun in the immediate context.

The is one of the many language devices which make for cohesion in English. (See further under **the** and **coherence** and **cohesion**.)

For the choice between *a* and *an*, see **a** or **an**.

artifact or **artefact** All major dictionaries recognise both spellings, but while **artefact** is cited first by Australian and British authorities (*Macquarie* (1991) and *Collins* (1991)), American dictionaries prefer **artifact**. The *Oxford Dictionary* changed its position from giving **artifact** as the primary spelling in the nineteenth century, to preferring **artefact** in its second edition (1989). Yet its twentieth century citations seem to show that **artefact** prevails mostly in technical and scientific contexts, while **artifact** still appears in more general ones.

The word has few close relatives in English, the nearest being *artifice* and *artificial*. The analogy with those has no doubt helped to maintain **artifact**, whereas **artefact** has little but its closeness to the original Latin *arte facto* ("made by art") to support it.

-ary/-ery/-ory In Australian pronunciation, these three suffixes all sound alike. Whether the vowel is *a*, *e* or *o*, it is pronounced as an indeterminate vowel (or *schwa*) which gives no clue as to the spelling. (American pronunciation puts more stress on the first vowel of the suffix, and the sound is quite clearly one vowel or the other. Think of how Americans pronounce *dormitory* or *secretary*.)

Because Australian pronunciation offers no help with these words, we need other guidelines as to how to spell them correctly. Most of the time only one spelling will do, and we must appeal to grammar and meaning to sort them out. The first thing to check is whether the word is an adjective or a noun.

If it is an adjective, the ending is either **-ary** or **-ory**. Overall there are fewer ending in **-ory**. To discover which ones should be spelled **-ory**, it is worth looking at the previous letters in the word. If they are *-at*, *-ct* or *-s*, you are most likely to be dealing with cases of **-ory**. See for example:

compulsory cursory derogatory illusory introductory mandatory obligatory perfunctory satisfactory valedictory

The very many with **-ary** have other combinations of letters before the suffix:

complementary dietary disciplinary elementary hereditary plenary revolutionary rotary rudimentary sedimentary solitary

If the word is a noun, the ending could be **-ary**, **-ery** or **-ory**. Overall there are more ending in **-ery** than either of the other two, but you can be more certain of the spelling by being aware of how these words fall into certain groups. For example:

- **-ary**. These are typically either nouns referring to a person's role:
  actuary dignitary legionary mercenary secretary
  or else to something in which a collection of objects is to be found:
  aviary breviary dictionary dispensary granary library rosary summary
- **-ery**. These nouns may refer to general states or styles of behavior:
  buffoonery drudgery flattery mystery savagery slavery snobbery trickery
  or else to occupations, trades and the tools or goods associated with them:
  archery bakery brewery butchery confectionery drapery grocery hosiery joinery machinery millinery printery saddlery surgery tannery winery
- **-ory**. Nouns ending this way typically refer to a place in terms of the characteristic activity that takes place there:
  conservatory depository dormitory factory laboratory observatory repository

For the difference between **accessary/accessory**, **mandatory/mandatary** and **stationary/stationery**, see individual entries.

as Though a neat conjunction, **as** leads a double life (or rather triple), and is not to be relied on. Some of the time it is a simple comparative, for example in *as clear as mud*. But it also divides its time between being a synonym for "when", and for "because". Compare:

As I walked through the door the music began.
As no-one else knew the tune, I had to whistle it.

The sense intended by **as** may only be clear once you've digested the whole sentence. In some sentences **as** may remain ambiguous:

They stopped brawling as the police arrived.

Does **as** express time or reason there? It could be either. In conversation such ambiguity is harmless, and a poet or dramatist may deliberately use it to allow more than one interpretation of whatever is being described. But in argumentative and expository writing, it is usually important to make explicit the links between statements, and to show whether they are connected through time or reason, or something else.

For the distinction between **as** and **like**, see **like**.

ascendant or **ascendent** Most dictionaries have **ascendant** as the first spelling, whether the word is a noun or an adjective. In the nineteenth century the two spellings were given equal billing by the *Oxford Dictionary*, though even then citations ran heavily in favor of the *-ant* spelling. The phrase *in the ascendant*, borrowed from astrology, may have helped to popularise it.

Likewise *ascendancy* (and *ascendance*) seem to have prevailed over *ascendency* and *ascendence*, according to dictionaries and language databases. (See further under **-ant/-ent**.)

Asian or **Asiatic** These words are almost equally old, but they are not now equally usable. **Asiatic** has become much rarer than **Asian**, and is generally felt to have disparaging overtones, both in the USA and Britain. The reasons for this are obscure, though it may have something to do with the use of **Asiatic** as a racial designator in South Africa. Since the 1940s **Asian** has increasingly replaced **Asiatic**: what were once *Asiatic languages* are now commonly called *Asian languages*.

The fact that Australia is sometimes said to be part of Asia has not changed our normal understanding of **Asian**—as applying to the large continent north of Australia and all the adjacent islands. In theory it can refer to any land between the eastern Mediterranean and the western coast of the Pacific. But in everyday Australian usage, as in *Asian students*, it often equates with the countries of *Southeast Asia*, bordered by India in the west and Japan to the northeast.

aspect This is part of the grammatical meaning of some verbs, interleaved with the tense yet independent of it. It gives a perspective on the verb, indicating whether its action is complete or still going on. The difference is clear in:

The governor's party had arrived and

The governor's party was arriving.

Both verb phrases are in the past tense, but the first one is *perfect* in its aspect (i.e. the action is complete), whereas the second is *imperfect* or *continuous* in its aspect (i.e. the action is still going on).

In some languages this difference is shown entirely by the endings of the main verb, but in English it is a combination of the choice of auxiliary verb, and the particular participle. English uses the auxiliary *have* plus the past participle for the perfect aspect, and a part of the verb *be* plus the present participle for the imperfect. (See further under **auxiliary verbs** and **participles**.)

Note that some kinds of verb do not usually have continuous forms, especially verbs of perception, emotion and desire. Australians do not say "you are liking" or "I am not remembering", although this is done in some other varieties of English, notably Indian English.

assonance A half-rhyme in a string of words is known as **assonance**. It involves either words with the same vowel sound but different consonants following (*Feed the man meat*), or using different vowels between the same consonants (*Butter is better*). As in those advertising slogans, assonance helps to bind the key words together. The echoic link in the sounds reinforces the underlying grammatical structure.

assume or **presume** A good deal of ink has been spilled over the difference between these words, about their relative strength in expressing the idea of "take for granted", and whether facts or beliefs are involved. One of the most important differences is the simple fact that **assume** is much more common in Australian English than **presume** by about 6:1, using the evidence of the ACE corpus. **Assume** slips readily into everyday discussion, and draws less attention to itself and more to the particular point which the speaker wants to foreground. **Presume** seems to draw attention to itself and to the presumptive act on the part of the speaker.

assurance or **insurance** When is **insurance** not **insurance**? The answer used to be "When it's life **assurance**". But while this point is noted in a late nineteenth century volume of the *Oxford Dictionary*, it also observes that the distinction was not made originally (there are cases of *marine assurance*), and implies that the phrase *life insurance* is also to be found. In Australia, remnants of the old distinction are only to be found in the names of a few companies incorporated as *Life Assurance* bodies. But *life insurance* is the phrase now commonly used in company titles and policy documents, and secured by the *Commonwealth Life Insurance Amendment Act* of 1945.

assurer or **assuror** See under -er/-or.

asterisk The asterisk sign * has no standard role in punctuation, and so it is put to a variety of different purposes by writers and printers. They include:
1 as a mark of omission or ellipsis
2 as a typographical dividing line, to make a break in a narrative (a set of asterisks spaced across the whole page)
3 to indicate unknown characters (a *wildcard*) in computer programming (a search for *affect** would find instances of *affected*/*affecting*/*affects* as well as *affect*)
4 to mark levels of probability
5 to refer readers to footnotes
    The first of those uses is vigorously discouraged by both the Chicago *Manual of Style* and *Hart's Rules* (1989), and it is clearly unnecessary when we have the apostrophe to mark an omitted letter, and three dots for the ellipsis of whole words. There remains the question of what to do when quoting four-letter words without wanting (or being permitted) to spell them out. To use asterisks for the missing letters, as in "F*** you" seems to draw attention to the word, which may of course be what the writer intends. The row of asterisks embellishes the places of the missing letters so as to positively invite the reader to fill them in.
    The second and third uses are indicated above. The fourth use, endorsed in the Chicago *Manual of Style*, requires specialised knowledge of the levels of probability conventionally used in statistics. Three asterisks correspond to a probability of less than .001 that the phenomenon occurred by chance; two asterisks to a probability of less than .01, and a single asterisk to less than .05.
    The fifth use, as a footnoting device, is the most commonly encountered of all uses of the **asterisk**. One or more asterisks helps to lead readers to the occasional footnote at the bottom of a page, particularly in writing which also makes use of numbered endnotes. The asterisked footnote can be added by the editor, while the author creates the endnotes as part of the text. Some authors find a use for both, however.

Two other uses of asterisks are as follows:

- among linguists and historians of language, to mark conjectural or reconstructed forms of words;
- in tables of numbers, to draw the reader's attention to footnotes, as a substitute for superscript numbers which could possibly be confused with the numbers of the table itself. However square-bracketed numbers, not asterisks, are often used these days within tables of numbers.

astro- This Greek element meaning "star" is built into a number of words relating to the sciences of star-watching, both ancient and modern. Some of these words, like *astronomy* and *astrology*, come direct from Greek. Others, like *astronaut*, *astronavigation*, *astrophysics* and *astrosphere*, are modern formations. The *astrolabe* was a medieval navigating instrument. All these words have retained their scientific roles—apart from *astronomic(al)*, which doubles as a colloquial word for "skyhigh". (Like many paired adjectives of this kind, *astonomic* and *astronomical* differ little in meaning. See **-ic/-ical**.)

Also related to **astro-** are *asterisk* and *aster* (the flower), where the emphasis is on the visual shape of stars rather than their uses.

ate See under **eat**.

-ate A slightly curly question: how would you pronounce the following?
animate articulate designate duplicate graduate
moderate separate syndicate
All those words, and some others ending in **-ate**, are pronounced in two ways. The pronunciation depends on the words' grammatical role—whether they serve as adjectives, verbs or nouns.

Adjectives ending in **-ate** are pronounced with just one main stress which is early in the word, either on the first syllable (as in *animate*), or the second (as in *articulate*). They often have a past passive meaning: *designate* (in the *governor designate*) means "having been appointed", and *separate* "having been divided off". (Those who know Latin would recognise that they are clones of the past participle of first conjugation verbs.) These adjectives often provided the stem for the development of verbs in English, and from those verbs we have a fresh crop of participial adjectives alongside the older ones. See for example:
animate/animated designate/designated separate/separated
The meaning of the later ones is of course more closely related to the verb. A few **-ate** adjectives have no verb counterparts however:
affectionate considerate dispassionate proportionate

Verbs ending in **-ate** are the most common words of this kind. They are pronounced with two stresses, one early and one on the final syllable, so that it rhymes with "mate". Many such verbs date from the fifteenth century, as do all of the following:

> *abbreviate consecrate contaminate dedicate equate frustrate inoculate incorporate mitigate recreate terminate translate*

All those have Latin stems. The more remarkable development is when **-ate** is attached to non-Latin stems, as in:

> *assassinate hyphenate marinate orchestrate*

All those are based on French stems, and all originate in the sixteenth century. Since then **-ate** has remained a highly productive verb suffix, attaching itself to stems from any language. Occasionally there are duplicate verb forms in **-ate**, such as *commentate* (alongside *comment*) and *orientate* (alongside *orient*). To some, such **-ate** forms seem redundant, though they often develop their own specialised meaning. (See further under **comment** and **orient**.)

The nouns ending in -ate are few in number, and have a single early stress like the adjectives. There are two distinct kinds, one official and the other scientific. The older ones are official words referring either to an office or institution:

> *consulate directorate electorate syndicate*

or to the incumbent of a particular office or status:

> *curate graduate magistrate*

Many were borrowed from Latin, though some have been formed in English on non-Latin bases, e.g. *caliphate*, *shogunate*. The scientific words ending in **-ate** refer to chemical compounds which are salts of acids ending in *-ic*, including:

> *acetate lactate nitrate permanganate phosphate sulfate*

(Compare the scientist's use of the suffix **-ite**.)

-athon This freshly evolved suffix refers to an endurance test of some kind, taking its cue from the word *marathon*, the Olympic contest in long-distance running. That word was actually a placename, the site of the Greek victory over the Persian army in 490 BC. Yet its latter syllables have helped to generate many a suburban contest, like the *dance-a-thon* and the *skate a thon*, and the *rockathon* (for continuous rocking in the rocking chair) registered in the *Guinness Book of Records*. Even when punctuated with hyphens, the connection with *marathon* seems to be there. The *readathons* and *spellathons* of the primary school no doubt help to make schoolchildren feel like Olympic champions.

-ation Many an abstract noun in English ends this way. Some have been borrowed from Latin; many more have been formed in modern English from verbs ending in *-ate*. Almost all the verbs in the entry on **-ate** above have nouns ending in **-ation**.

The close relationship between *animation* and *animate*, *articulation* and *articulate* etc. makes it very easy for writers to vary and modify their style without having to hunt for synonyms. For example:

> *There was animation in their faces at the prospect of a meal.*
> *The prospect of a meal animated their faces.*

Verbs in *-ate* provide a ready cure for writing which is heavy with **-ation** words. They require some rewording of the sentence, but that is part of the cure.

Note that a small group of nouns ending in **-ation** are related to verbs ending in *-ify*, not *-ate*. See for example:

beautify/beautification   gratify/gratification
identify/identification   justify/justification

-ative This is the ending of a body of adjectives which form a tight network with nouns ending in *-ation*, and to a lesser extent the verbs ending in *-ate*. The following are some of many **-ative** adjectives with counterpart nouns in *-ation*:

administrative   affirmative   conservative   consultative
declarative   evocative   representative

Other adjectives of this kind relate to the noun in *-ation* and the verb in *-ate*:

creative   cooperative   generative   illustrative   participative

Note that some adjectives in **-ative** are used unchanged as nouns as well, e.g. *affirmative, alternative, cooperative*. (See further under **transfers**.)

-ator This is a very productive agentive suffix, associated with verbs ending in *-ate*. As the following examples show, it may refer to either instruments or people who are agents of the verb's action:

calculator   demonstrator   investigator   perpetrator   radiator

These **-ator** words form a large and open-ended group of agentive words which are spelled with *-or* rather than *-er*. The reason is that many **-ator** words come direct from Latin, where agentives of this kind were always *-or*. The Latin spelling has provided a firm model for any similar formations in modern English.

atrium For the plural of this word, see under *-um*.

attend or **tend** These verbs live separate lives most of the time, and coincide in just one area of meaning: "take care (of someone or something)".

He was attending to the fire.
He was tending (to) the fire.
A nurse attended to the injured at the scene of the accident.
A nurse tended (to) the injured at the scene of the accident.

Note that **attend** in this sense is always accompanied by *to*, whereas **tend** can do without it. However this use of **tend** is declining, and is now mostly restricted to dealing with fires and first aid. **Tend** could not replace **attend** (to) in other contexts, for example, in phrases like *attending to the customers*, or *attending to his business*.

Note the very different use of **tend** to "be inclined to", as in *the press tends to overreact*, which is well established. There, **tend** works as a kind of auxiliary verb or **catenative** (see further under that heading). **Tend** "be inclined" and **tend** "take care of" are in fact independent words: the origins of the first are to be found in the French verb *tendre* "stretch", while the second is actually a reduced form of *attend*.

attester or **attestor** See under *-er/-or*.

attorney-general The plural of this word is discussed under the heading **governor-general**.

attributive adjectives See **adjectives** section 1.

au naturel This French phrase meaning "in the natural (state/way)" was first used in gastronomy, to make a virtue of leaving food items uncooked, or else cooked plain without spices and garnishes. Ideally it allows you to taste the natural flavor of the food, just as *al dente* cooking gives you the natural texture (see **al dente**).

By the beginning of this century **au naturel** began to be used in its second sense "undressed"—or as the coy phrase has it "as nature intended". In 1905 it was just a matter of *ankles au naturel*, according to an *Oxford Dictionary* citation, but it now implies a state of undress which would appeal to a naturist (see **naturalist** or **naturist**).

au pair This phrase adopted from French means not so much "in a pair" as "on an equal footing". It is thus rather a euphemism for the financial arrangement whereby someone lives with a well-to-do family, acting as an all-purpose assistant in exchange for board and lodging, but with no standard wage.

Au pair is significantly different from **à deux**, another French phrase which does mean "in a twosome", but implies a private meeting or meal from which others are excluded. An Italian phrase which picks up the same idea of privacy and exclusiveness is **a quattr'occhi**, meaning "between four eyes".

au revoir See under **arrivederci**.

audi(o)- This Latin element meaning "hear(ing)" occurs in its full form in *audiology* and *audiovisual*, and blended into *audible, audience, audition* and *auditorium*

The same element is found in *audit* and *auditor*, reminding us of the historical practice of checking accounts in a public hearing: they were actually read aloud. Because this is now a private business, the sense of "hearing" is lost from both *audit* and *auditor*, except when they refer to a student who *audits* a series of lectures as a spectator rather than a participant in the course.

audiovisual media The need to refer to material other than print has raised new questions for bibliographers. Audiovisual materials require their own bibliographical practices, depending on whether they are films, videos, sound recordings of music, speeches or interviews, computer programs, maps, works of art, or museum objects.

Many such items are available only in limited editions, and in the case of works of art they are unique, so that the place where they are kept (i.e. the repository) is very important. An additional issue with sound recordings is the need to recognise the role of both the originator/composer of the work and the performer; or for interviews, both the subject (interviewee) and interviewer (the person with substantial responsibility). In citing all such kinds of material, the medium needs to be identified, in square brackets immediately after the title.

1 *Films, videotapes, television programs.* Most films and video recordings etc. are the product of collaboration, and so the title rather than any individual author is featured first:
    —*Crocodile Dundee* [motion picture] Directed by Peter Faiman. California. Rimfire Films. 1986. Distributed by CBS FOX.
    —*The Story of English* [video recording] Directed by Robert McCrum, William Cran and Robert MacNeill. London. BBC Enterprises. 1986.
After identifying the title and medium, the reference may mention the person with either artistic or administrative responsibility (the director and/or producer). If the item is not in the hands of a commercial distributor, the repository where it's kept should be mentioned.

2 *Recordings of music and the spoken word, including interviews.* Recordings of music usually feature the work of a composer or author, as well as that of a performer. But for citation purposes, the first gets priority:
    —Beethoven, L. van *Beethoven or bust* [sound recording] Realised by Don Dorsy on digital synthesiser in Anaheim, California. (1988) Compact Disc by Telarc International.
    —Mansfield, K. *The garden party* [sound recording] Read by Dame Peggy Ashcroft in Marlborough, Wiltshire. (1983) Cover to Cover Cassettes.
In citations of interviews, the name of the interviewee takes precedence, though that of the interviewer should also be given:
    —Suzuki, David. *Margaret Throsby in conversation with David Suzuki and Edward Goldsmith* [sound recording] Perth WA (1989) ABC Radio Tapes.
For sound recordings made from a general broadcast, titles may have to be supplied, as in that last example. Note also that it helps to indicate to the reader what kind of format the sound is recorded on: audiocassette, compact disc etc.

3 *Computer programs.* These are usually referenced first by title, although if there is a known author, his/her name is to be given first. A typical example is as follows:
    —*Grammatik* [computer software] San Francisco, California. Reference Software International. (1991)

4 *Maps.* References to individual sheet maps usually begin with a regional title, and include any series identifier, as well as the scale:
    —North Island New Zealand [map] New Zealand Department of Lands and Survey (1966) 1:1,637,000.

5 *Works of art, archival and museum objects.* Because these items are unique, the repository in which they are kept is a vital element. For works of art, the reference highlights the creator and its title:

—Senbergs, Jan *The Constitution and the States* [wall panels] (1980) High
Court of Australia, Canberra.

For archival objects and museum realia, a descriptive title must be found as the
focus of the reference:

—*Black-glazed bowl* [realia] fourth century BC. Item MU 328 Ancient
History Teaching Collection, Macquarie University.

As in the last example, a catalogue number leads the reader to the particular
object, if there's more than one of the kind in the repository.

auf Wiedersehen See **arrivederci**.

augur or **auger** Neither of these is a common word, which leaves some writers
in doubt as to which is which. **Augur** is a verb that mostly makes its appearance
in the phrase *augurs well*. It is related to the words *augury*, *inaugural* and
inaugurate. The second word, **auger**, is a tool or machine for boring holes. The
-er ending makes it like other workshop instruments, e.g. *screwdriver*, *spanner*
(though **auger** is not itself an agentive word). For more about the history of
auger, see **a or an**, section 3.

auntie or **aunty** Both spellings are current for the cognate female relative,
though **auntie** is the primary one in the major British and American dictionaries.
The *Macquarie Dictionary* (1991) gives preference to **aunty**, perhaps to keep it
apart from the numerous Australian colloquialisms ending in *-ie*, such as *cabbie*,
postie and *schoolie* (see further under **-ie/-y**). The spelling **aunty** puts it into
the group of kinship words which includes *daddy*, *granny*, and *mummy*, and
which are usually spelled with *-y*.

The use of **Aunty** in reference to the Australian Broadcasting Corporation is
relatively recent. It parallels the British use of **Auntie** (note the alternative
spelling) in reference to the BBC, which dates from 1962. The underlying
semantics of **Aunty** were critical rather than affectionate—implying, as Kenneth
Inglis puts it, that the nation's broadcaster was less manly and youthful than its
commercial rivals. However things were turned around by affirmative action
during the 1970s, notably with Graham Bond's *Aunty Jack Show* 1972–3, and
the ABC staff newsletter which titled itself *Aunty*, not to mention the Melbourne
support group who styled themselves *Aunty's nephews and nieces*.

aura For the plural of this word, see **-a**.

Australia and **Australians, Aussies** and **Oz** During the seventeenth and
eighteenth century, Australia was known as *New Holland*, a reminder of the fact
that the Dutch were the first Europeans to locate and visit the land. The name
Australia, derived from the Latin *terra Australis* "Southern Land" was used
by Cook, but owes its establishment to Governor Macquarie in the early
nineteenth century. **Australian** was first applied to Aboriginal people in 1814
by Matthew Flinders, but within ten years it also referred to others living on

the continent. The word is used in the original sense by linguists speaking of the *Australian languages*.

The clipped form **Aussie** originated in World War I as a term for "Australia", "an Australian", and as the general-purpose adjective. The spellings *Ossie* and *Ozzie* showed up very infrequently in the same period, according to the *Australian National Dictionary*. But the use of **Oz** took off in the 1970s, no doubt helped by the publicity surrounding the radical *Oz Magazine* (1963–73).

Australians are sometimes identified by names coined out of the states or cities where they live. State names are straightforward, except for residents of NSW, who have to choose between *New South Welshmen* and *New South Walers*, and for Tasmanians (see under **Tassie**). The metropolitan names are not fully standardised, see for example, **Adelaidean** or **Adelaidian**. For the rest we're most likely to use *Brisbanite*, *Canberran*, *Darwinian*, *Hobartian*, *Melburnian*, *Perthite* and *Sydney-sider*, though alternatives such as *Darwinite*, *Melbournian* are on record.

Australian English With the arrival of the First Fleet, **Australian English** began among settlers and convicts drawn mostly from southern and eastern England. Within a generation, the differentness of Australian speech was being commented on, for better for worse. Yet only in the twentieth century (and after two world wars) did Australian English attain its majority, and secure recognition of its place in the English-speaking world.

Distinctively Australian vocabulary developed in response to the new social and physical environment. The conditions of transportation, the development of new pastoral lands and the gold rushes all demanded their own terminology. Some of it came from standard English (e.g. *block*, *bush*, *squatter*, *emancipist*), and some (e.g. *barrack*, *billy*, *fossick*) from English dialects. Convict slang drawn from the British underworld provided other words such as *swag*. (See further under **flash language**.)

But new vocabulary was required for Australian flora and fauna, and the naming process went on throughout the nineteenth century. The names for Australian fauna were sometimes borrowed from Aboriginal languages, and sometimes compounded out of English elements, and the same animal or bird might be referred to either way. So the *dingo* was also the *native dog*, the *kookaburra* was the *laughing jackass* or *settler's clock*, and the *koala* the *native bear*. By the end of the nineteenth century, this variation had mostly been ironed out, leaving us with fewer rather than more Aboriginal names. Few people remember that *bettong* was the name for a small kangaroo, *tuan* for a flying squirrel, and *wobbegong* for the carpet shark. The names for Australian flora and fauna were the staple of a dictionary titled *Austral English*, which was published in 1898 by E. E. Morris. Morris's list of Australianisms was incorporated in both the *Oxford Dictionary* and *Webster's*.

A wide-ranging account of the informal and colloquial aspects of **Australian English** was first made by S. J. Baker in a volume first published in 1945, titled *The Australian Language* (echoing the H. L. Mencken's *The American Language* of 1919). Baker recorded the slang of many Australian subcultures: the racetrack, the pub, the two-up alley, and above all that of Australia's military forces in two world wars. Not all the words that he discussed were strictly speaking Australianisms, but they were and are part of the resources of **Australian English**. Like Mencken, he presented his findings in a series of essays with word lists embedded in them, not as a dictionary.

The first comprehensive dictionary of **Australian English**, the *Macquarie Dictionary*, appeared in 1981 with 80 000 headwords. It made it its business to include all standard Australian words and meanings, as well as *Australianisms* (expressions which originated here and are often still unique to this country): words for new cultural and social phenomena, for the unusual flora and fauna, and local slang and colloquialisms. Other "Australian" dictionaries have since appeared, with a quota of Australian words interpolated into a comprehensive dictionary of British English. The *Australian National Dictionary* published in 1988 concentrates on Australianisms alone. It gives a long historical perspective through citations on 10 000 headwords.

Australian English does not seem to have diverged in its grammar from that of standard English elsewhere. In casual conversation some Australian speakers (like English speakers elsewhere) make nonstandard selections of tense, such as *come* for *came*, *done* for *did*, and *kep* for *kept*; and *but* occurs as a sentence-final item (see **but**). However, none of this appears in print, except when an author quotes or aims to represent nonstandard speech. The morphology of **Australian English** words is based on the same resources as English everywhere, although Australians make fuller use than others of informal shortenings of words with *-o* (as in *milko*), and with *-ie* (as in *barbie*). The latter suffix is sometimes said to be childish, but in Australia its use is widespread among adults, and words formed with it are part of the informal style of popular daily newspapers.

The only distinctively Australian detail of morphology one might point to is in the handful of reduplicative words (e.g. *mia-mia*, *willy-willy*), which embody the exact reduplication used in various Aboriginal languages. In English generally the echoic type of reduplication (*ping-pong*, *walkie-talkie*) is much more common, and words with exact reduplication remain informal (see further under **reduplicatives**). Apart from general expressions such as *willy-willy*, exact reduplication is found in Australian placenames such as *Wagga Wagga* and *Woy Woy*.

The details of Australian written style (i.e. editorial style) are not strongly standardised, in that most publishing houses and newspapers print their own style guides for their writers and editors. The *Style Manual* produced by the Australian Government Publishing Service (and extensively revised for its fourth edition in 1988) sets the standard for federal government publications, and is referred to by other Australian institutions and corporations.

Yet beyond the genres of official publishing, different editorial practices may seem appropriate, and with both British and American publishing houses at work in Australia, the range of styles is probably increasing rather than decreasing. The institution of regular "Style Councils" since 1986 has helped to inform editors about variable and changing trends in style. (Contact the Dictionary Research Centre, Macquarie University, for information about them.) There is no language academy to refer to in Australia (any more than in Britain or USA), but the Style Council conferences do provide a consultative forum for discussing and assessing the options in written Australian English.

Australian Rules Australians developed their own style of football in the nineteenth century. Like rugby, **Australian Rules** began as a private school sport, the first game being played in 1858 between Melbourne Grammar School and Scotch College. It has remained most popular in Victoria and in Western Australia. Its official name since 1927 has been *Australian National Football*, though the earlier names *Australian Football* and especially **Australian Rules** are more widely used. Informally it's **Aussie Rules**.

Compare **rugby union**.

Australianisms See Australian English.

authoritarian or **authoritative** These words take rather different attitudes towards authority. In **authoritarian** there is resentment of high-handed leadership, whereas in **authoritative** the leadership provided is welcome and respected. **Authoritative** is much the older of the two, dating from the seventeenth century, whereas **authoritarian** dates only from the nineteenth century. Meditate if you will on the social and political practices of the Victorian era, which are immortalised in the latter.

auto- Borrowed from Greek, this prefix meaning "self" or "on its own" is familiar enough in words like:

autobiography autocracy autocrat autograph auto-immune
autism autistic automatic automation automaton automobile
autonomy autonomic autonomous

A less obvious example is *autopsy*, which is literally "inspection with one's own eyes". Its reference nowadays is so restricted to postmortems that one would hardly venture a joke about an "autopsy" of the food served in the company canteen—though in past centuries (up to the eighteenth), the word was not so specialised in its meaning.

Because of its use in *automobile*, the prefix **auto-** can also mean "associated with motor cars", and this is certainly its meaning in *auto-electrician*.

Note that in the phrase *auto-da-fé*, borrowed from Portuguese, *auto* means "act" (of faith). It was a euphemism for the execution of those tried by the Inquisition, and usually applied to the burning of "heretics".

auxiliary verbs These verbs combine with others to make up a verb phrase, and help to indicate **tense, aspect, voice, mood** and **modality**. (See under those headings for more about each.) Auxiliaries complement the *main* verb, typically bringing grammatical meaning to bear on its lexical meaning. There may be three or even four auxiliaries in a single phrase, as the following set shows:

was added
was being added   had been added
might have been added
might have been being added (at that time ...)

A verb which has no accompanying auxiliary is known as a *simple verb* (see further under **verbs**). The auxiliaries are often classed into two subgroups: *primary auxiliaries* and *modal auxiliaries.*

1 *The primary auxiliaries* are *have, be* and *do. Have* and *be* have the special characteristic of combining with participles, present and past, in order to express **aspect**, and the **passive** voice (see further under those headings). *Have* and *be* never combine with the "bare" infinitive, as do the *modal auxiliaries* and indeed the verb *do.* In the continuous flow of discourse, the auxiliaries *have* and *be* sometimes appear unaccompanied by participles, but this is when the relevant participle can be inferred from a previous sentence. So for example it is natural enough to say (or write):

I haven't met the new assistant yet. Have you?

The main verb participle *met* (and its object) are all understood with *have* in the question.

Note however that *have* and *be* can also occur on their own as simple main verbs, as in:

He hasn't any money and
They are in the office.

In those cases, each verb carries its own lexical meaning: *have* a possessive meaning, and *be* an existential meaning.

The auxiliary *do* has special roles in helping to formulate the interrogative (*Do I like spaghetti?*) and negative statements (*I don't like spaghetti*). All interrogative and negative statements are phrased with *do*, unless they already contain one of the other auxiliaries (primary or modal). *Do* has other roles as a substitute verb:

I enjoy spaghetti much less than they do.

Here *do* stands for the main (lexical) verb *enjoy* and its object in the second clause. Once again, *do* performs this function unless there is another auxiliary present. Compare the following with the previous example:

I wouldn't enjoy the spaghetti as they would.
I can't enjoy the spaghetti as they can.

Note that as a simple main verb, *do* means "work on (something)", as in *doing one's accounts* or *doing the milk run.*

2 *The modal auxiliaries* express modalities, shades of possibility, certainty and obligation, with a "bare" infinitive following. Two of them, *will* and *shall*, can also express tense (the future), although there may be a modal overtone of certainty or obligation there as well. See for example:

You will be in my power!

The winner shall receive a free trip to Hawaii.

The essential modals are:

can could may might shall should will would must

To these may be added a number of what the *Comprehensive Grammar of English* (1985) calls "marginal modals" and *semi-auxiliaries*. Many of these correspond to the modals in meaning but are often if not always followed by the *to-* infinitive:

ought to	(compare with *should*)
need (to)	
used to	(approximating to *would*)
dare (to)	(compare with *could*)
have to	(compare with *must*)
be able to	(compare with *can*)
be going to	(compare with *will*)
be likely to	
be obliged to	*must*
be supposed to	*should*
be willing to	*would*

See further under **modality** and individual headings. See also **catenatives**.

avenge or **revenge**   See **revenge**.

averse or **adverse**   See **adverse**.

await or **wait**   See **wait**.

awake or **awaken**   See under **wake**.

aweing or **awing**   See under **-e** section 1.

axe or **ax**   The spelling **ax** is earlier, and standard in North America. It is "better on every ground" according to the *Oxford Dictionary* (including etymology, phonology and analogy). Yet its citations show that the spelling **axe** gained support in Britain during the nineteenth century, and the second edition of the *Oxford Dictionary* (1989) confirms that **ax** is no longer used in Britain.

Australia has inherited the spelling with *e*, and the best argument in its favor is that it contrives to make the word consist of three letters. It thus conforms to the principle that whereas the function words of English (such as *we*, *to*, *as*) may have less than three letters, the content words never do (see further under **words**). Though we use the spelling **axe** for the noun, we drop the *e* when it becomes a verb: *axing*, thus treating the word like any other one ending in *e*. (See further under **-e** section 1.)

axiom See under **aphorism**.

axis For the plural of this word, see **-is**.

aye or **ay** These two spellings essentially represent two different pronunciations and two different meanings. **Ay**, pronounced to rhyme with "day", is an old-fashioned word for "ever". **Aye**, pronounced to rhyme with "eye", is a formal expression of affirmation in public meetings, and institutionalised in the Navy response: *Aye aye sir*. In the Australian parliament it means "one who votes in the affirmative", as in: *The ayes have it*.

The shorter spelling **ay** is occasionally used for the parliamentary vote, but it creates an unfortunate overlap with the other word, and also violates the principle that the content words of English should have a minimum of three letters. (For the distinction between content and function words, see under **words**.) All this makes **aye** much the better spelling for the affirmative word.

B

bacillus For the plural of this word, see under **-us** section 1.

back- This is a formative element in quite a few English compound words:
> *backbench background backhand backlash backlog backslider*
> *backstroke backwash backwater*

Back- serves to indicate location or direction, and like other adverbs and particles it is normally set solid with the word it's prefixed to. (See **hyphens** section 2b.)

As the examples above show, it normally combines with ordinary English stems, whereas *retro-*, its classical equivalent, combines with scholarly words from Latin and Greek (see further under **retro-**).

back matter See **endmatter**.

back of This collocation has wider currency in Australia than in Britain, in fixed expressions like *back of beyond, back of Bourke, back o' Cairns* and *back o' the sunset,* as well as in ones made up freely:
> *back of Mudgee back of Holland's property back of the silos*
> *back of the irrigation channel*

It means "beyond" rather than strictly "behind".

Note that the expression *in back of* meaning "behind" is still American rather than Australian English, and does *not* mean "in the back of". For Americans *in back of the shop* means "outside and behind the shop". In fact their use of *in back of* complements *in front of*, in exactly the way we use it. But because *in back of* may be misunderstood in Australia, we need to replace it with *behind* or *in the back of* as appropriate.

backformation New words are most often developed from smaller, simple words, as *rattler* is from *rattle* and *assassination* from *assassin.* Just occasionally words (especially verbs) are formed in the opposite way, distilled out of pre-existing words which are construed as complex ones (see further under **complex words**). So *burgle* is from *burglar, surveil* from *surveillance,* and *electrocute* from *electrocution.* Some other verbs derived in this way are:
> *donate edit enthuse laze liaise reminisce resurrect*
> *scavenge stoke swindle televise*

Most of the *backformations* just mentioned have become standard English, though some remain informal and colloquial, such as *buttle* (from *butler*) and *jell* (from *jelly*).

Backformations of any kind are unacceptable to some writers, almost as if their unusual origin makes them illegitimate words. Some backformations are indeed unnecessary, because they duplicate a much older verb. The verb *adaptate* (backformed from *adaptation*) is scarcely needed when we already have *adapt*, and strictly speaking *orientate* only duplicates the verb *orient*. But others like *commentate* (from *commentator*) are certainly earning their keep alongside *comment*, by covering different areas of meaning (see further under **comment**). It seems pedantic to deny the legitimacy of such formations merely on account of their origins.

Note that for some, the singular **Aborigine** was not to be used because it was a **backformation** from the plural *aborigines*, the only form of the word used in Latin (see further under **Aboriginal**). For examples of other words derived in a similar way, see **false plurals**.

backward or **backwards** See under -ward.

bacteria Should it be *This bacteria is dangerous* or *These bacteria are dangerous*? Plural agreement is still more usual, according to *Webster's English Usage* (1989). Yet singular agreement is sometimes found, suggesting that **bacteria** is gradually being reinterpreted as a collective noun in English. It is of course a Latin plural (see **-a**), whose singular is *bacterium*. However the latter makes only rare appearances outside specialist writing.

bad or **badly** Which of these goes with verbs such as *feel, look, need, smell, think, want*? For some people, either would do, but the frontiers have been shifting, especially in the USA, leaving a trail of uncertainty.

The grammatical fundamentals are that **bad** is first and foremost the adjective (*a bad shot*), and **badly** the adverb (*He played badly*). This division of labor was stressed in the eighteenth and nineteenth century, and continues in **British English**. But American English now sanctions the use of **bad** with all the verbs mentioned at the start of this entry, according to *Webster's English Usage* (1989). It functions there as a **zero adverb** (see further under that heading). Some argue that *feel badly* and *feel bad* have slightly different meanings, though others would say it is just a stylistic difference, one of greater and lesser formality.

In Australian English **bad** is acceptable with *feel, look* and *smell* (i.e. with **copular verbs**: see further under that heading). Meanwhile **badly** goes with *need, think* and *want*. Note that after *do*, **bad** is possible in a negative expression in casual speech:

I didn't do too bad, did I?

In more formal contexts, it would be **badly**.

bail or **bale** These two spellings overlie several different uses of these words.

The least problematical cases are the agricultural uses in *bale of wool* and *bail up a cow*. The spellings are uncontroversial and reflect etymology in each case: **bale** is from Old French *balle* meaning "package", and **bail** is older

English *baile* meaning "stick". In Australia **bail** is the bar by which farmers hold a cow's head through a wooden fence, in order to constrain its movements for milking. A figurative extension of this was found in the bushranger *bailing up* travelers for their valuables. As bushranging became a thing of the past, the expression *bail up* gained a further figurative extension to anyone who holds another person up in spite of the other's unwillingness.

The legal uses of **bail** derive from another Old French word, the verb *bailler* meaning "keep in custody". The expression *bail (someone) out* originates from this legal context, hence its spelling. The same spelling is right for the more general use of the expression, meaning "help someone out of difficulty".

Nautical use of *bail out* was traditionally spelled the same way, but by coincidence, since the phrase embodies the Old French word for a bucket *baille*. In the USA it is still spelled this way, but the *Oxford Dictionary* comments that the spelling *bale out* for this idiom was gaining ground in the nineteenth century, and it is the preferred spelling in the second edition of the *Oxford* (1989). *Bale out* is the first spelling in the *Macquarie Dictionary* (1991).

When it comes to airmen making a parachute jump from their aircraft, this is again *bail out* in American English. It is *bale out* in the second edition of the *Oxford Dictionary*, yet not because it's regarded as an extension of the nautical usage (an emergency measure in/from a vehicle). Instead, the dictionary relates it to the noun **bale**, and sees the manoeuvre as one where the parachutist exits from the aircraft like a bale through a trapdoor.

In all this we see two solutions to a dilemma. The American solution is to use **bail** for every meaning except the noun (**bale** of wool etc). The British solution is to give additional uses to the spelling **bale**, as the verb associated with taking emergency measures, and to differentiate it from legal (and agricultural) uses of the verb **bail**. But when both are figuratively extended they are harder to separate, and the reason for one spelling or the other becomes obscure. Why, for example, should one *bale out of a failing enterprise*, but *bail out a failing company*? They generate contrasting headlines:

BOND BALES OUT OF HONG KONG
The cash-strapped empire of Mr Alan Bond has released up to $364 million in funds by selling out its half-stake in Hong Kong's Bond Centre …

LANGE BAILS OUT BNZ
Wellington. The Lange Government was forced yesterday to bail out the Bank of New Zealand.

A grammarian would note that the first headline was intransitive and the second transitive, but is it worth the trouble? The American practice of using **bail** for both is the more straightforward one, and sounder in terms of etymology.

Note that there is no dilemma for cricketers the world over: the small pieces of wood which top the wicket are always **bails**. And the quite independent word

baleful is always spelled that way, because it's related to the Old Norse word *bal* meaning "fate".

balk or baulk The first spelling **balk** has much to recommend it. Apart from the analogy with common words such as *chalk*, *talk* and *walk*, it's more widely used than **baulk**, being standard in the USA and one of the alternatives used in Australia and Britain. **Balk** is also the earlier spelling, but the *Oxford Dictionary* noted increasing use of **baulk** in Britain in the later nineteenth century, especially in billiards.

Compare **caulk, calk** or **calque**, where several meanings are involved.

ballot Should the *t* be doubled when this word has verb suffixes added to it? See under **t**.

banquet On whether to double the *t* before verb suffixes are added, see under **t**.

barbaric, barbarous or **barbarian** All these serve to express the civilised person's distaste for savagery and condemnation of it. All three have been recorded in English since early modern times (the sixteenth century). There is little to differentiate them, except that **barbarian** is, these days, less often an adjective than a noun for someone with savage or uncivilised ways. The other two can only be adjectives. Note also that whereas **barbarous** always expresses condemnation, the judgement in **barbaric** varies with the phrase it appears in. In *barbaric cruelty* it's clearly negative, while in *barbaric hospitality* it connotes something which though primitive is impressive in its own way.

In origin all three words represent a much less harsh judgement about those who stand outside our society and culture. The root *barbar-* embedded in them was used by the Greeks to describe the speech of the neighboring nations, which they found unintelligible. Thus *barbarians* were originally people who spoke a different language; and the name given to the *Berbers* may have originated in this way also. In modern English the tables are turned in the idiom "It was all Greek to me".

barbarism Older commentators on usage, including Fowler, made use of **barbarism** to stigmatise the misuse of words. In principle it was used for a particular class of error (words malformed according to conventional usage or normal patterns of coining, e.g. *normalcy*); while other kinds of error in syntax were termed **solecisms** (see under that heading). Those who know the technical application of **barbarism** might find it less heavy-handed, but those who do not find it a powerful word, as Fowler himself noted. And those less scrupulous than Fowler about matters of usage have been known to deploy **barbarism** with all its primitive force to put down another's usage, when they found "unacceptable" and "wrong" too lightweight for the task. One suspects they resorted to it when there was plenty of popular support for the expression they wished to expunge from the language; and with the word **barbarism** they could invoke social sanctions against it, implying that no civilised person would utter it. (See further under **shibboleth**.)

barbecue or **barbeque** The first spelling is more common by a ratio of 10:1 in the Australian ACE corpus. It is also closer to the origins of the word in Haitian Creole *barbacoa*, which referred to a framework of sticks on which meat was smoked. It was borrowed into English in the seventeenth century, and was *barbacue* until the early nineteenth century. The rites of the backyard barbecue are now central in Australian cuisine, with the high priest of the beer and prawns tending the fires of the garden altar. But lest it become too solemn an affair, we also use the informal word **barbie**, one of the many Australian colloquialisms in *-ie* (see further under **-ie/-y**).

The second spelling **barbeque** seems at first sight to frenchify the word, although the French would pronounce such a word with just two syllables, to rhyme with "dalek". In fact the *-que* probably represents the third syllable of the various abbreviations for the word, as *bar-b-que*, *Bar-B-Q* and *BBQ*.

barrel On whether to double the *l* before adding verb suffixes, see **-l/-ll-**.

bases *What are the bases of power in this country?* The reader may well puzzle over whether this is the plural of **base** or **basis**. It could be either, and though pronunciation would make it one or the other, the difference is masked in the spelling. Often the context helps to make it one or the other, as in *American bases overseas*—but not always, as the example above shows, and clarification may be needed.

For more about the plurals of words like *basis*, see **-is**.

bassinet or **bassinette** See under **-ette**.

bathe or **bath** It is well known that ablutionary practices are culture-specific. Misunderstandings can arise from that alone, apart from the fact that the verbs **bath** and **bathe** connote different uses of water in different parts of the English-speaking world.

Australians use the verb **bath** to mean "take a bath" or "give a bath" (to a baby), while **bathe** normally refers to washing a wound. In Britain, **bathe** has the additional meaning of "take a swim" in the sea, but this is not common in Australia, even though Australians may wear *bathing costumes* when they venture into the surf. (Others less formal would call the garb their "swimmers", "bathers", "togs" or "cozzie".) In the USA meanwhile, *bathe* refers to swimming as well as taking a bath or shower for the purposes of hygiene; and there is no verb *bath* except in technical usage.

Note that when written down, *bathing* and *bathed* are ambiguous for readers familiar with both **bath** or **bathe**. Which verb do they relate to? Unless the context makes it clear, writers need to paraphrase them, by such means as *having a bath/bathe* and *had a bath/bathe*.

bathos In spite of its Greek name, the literary effect of **bathos** is not one of profundity. Instead it means either a slide from the sublime to the ridiculous, as in the idiom *making a mountain out of a molehill*; or triteness or banality of style. Either way the effect is not one of **pathos** (see further under that heading).

baulk or **balk** See balk.

bayonet Dictionaries all give preference to *bayoneted* and *bayoneting* over the spellings with two *t*s (*bayonetted, bayonetting*). The spellings with two *t*s can only be justified if the main stress falls on the third syllable (see **doubling of final consonant**). But with main stress on the first syllable, the spellings with one *t* are appropriate—and may as well be used if, as often, the pronunciation is unknowable or unimportant.

BC or **BCE** The letters **BC** (before Christ) remind us that our dating system has a religious foundation. Yet the fact that **BC** is an English phrase shows that it has only been used in the modern era (since the eighteenth century, in fact). Compare with the Latin abbreviation *AD* (short for *anno domini*), which has been used in Christian annals and records since the sixth century.

The inescapably Christian connotations of **BC** have led some to prefer **BCE** which is intended to represent "before the common era", and to avoid imposing a Christian framework on the world's history. Unfortunately **BCE** can also be read as "before the Christian era", and the problem remains. But for the antireligious it has the advantage of making the religious allusion rather more oblique. The corresponding term to replace *AD* is **CE**, meaning either "common era" or "Christian era".

Note that **BCE** and **CE** are both placed after the date itself: *50 BCE*, like *50 BC*. Compare with the position of **AD**, discussed under that heading.

All these abbreviations can be written without stops. The fact that they consist of capitals is one reason for this (see further under **abbreviations**). Another is the fact that they are almost always accompanied by numbers, which make plain their dating function.

For alternative ways of indicating dates, see **dating systems**.

be The verb **be** in its numerous forms is the most common in English. It has more distinct forms than any other verb, with three for the present: *am, are, is*; two for the past: *was, were*; and of course, two participles: *being, been* as well as the infinitive *be*.

The most essential role of **be** is as one of the *primary auxiliary verbs* of English, used to express continuous action (to grammarians, the imperfect aspect), and the passive voice, as in the following:

you are asking (continuous action/imperfect)

you are asked (passive)

Compare with *you ask* (no auxiliary, simple action, active voice). (See further under **auxiliary verbs, aspect** and **voice**.)

The verb **be** can also be used as a main verb on its own, in an existential sense:

I think therefore I am.

Or it can be used as a *copular verb*, linking the subject of the clause with its complement:

Their plan is a great leap forward.

(See further under **copular verbs**.)

The present forms of **be** are often contracted with their subject pronoun in the flow of conversation, as *I'm, you're, she's, we're, they're. Is* can form contractions with many kinds of nouns, both proper and common:

Jane's being taught the piano.

Stalin's dead.

Dinner's in the oven.

For the use of these forms in writing, see **contractions** section 2.

Note that **be** (and **were**) have residual roles as subjunctives in modern English. (See further under **subjunctive**.)

be- Being one of the oldest English prefixes, it's now hard to separate in verbs like *become, begin, behave* or *believe*. In some cases it turns intransitive verbs into transitive ones, as in *belie, bemoan* and *bewail*. In others it creates new verbs from nouns and adjectives: *becalm, befriend, bejewel, belittle* and *bewitch*.

Although it is not particularly productive in modern English, it still generates **nonce words** which are transparent enough to be understood on first encounter:

They stood ready for the rodeo, leather-jacketed and bespurred.

beau ideal This phrase is often interpreted in reverse. In French *le beau idéal* means "ideal (form of) beauty" or "the abstract idea of beauty" (because *idéal* is an adjective following the noun, as it normally does in French). Those who understand the French use it this way in aesthetic discussions in English.

But without an accent, *ideal* looks like an English word, and so the phrase is often taken to mean "beautiful ideal", and applied in many contexts to the ideal type or perfect model of something: *the beau ideal of the family.*

bedevil On whether to double the final *l* before adding verb suffixes, see **-l/-ll-**.

beg the question This phrase refers to a frustrating argumentative tactic, though it may be understood in more than one way. These days it's often used to mean "evade the question", as some dictionaries including *Collins* and *Webster's* recognise—even though that strains the meaning of the verb *beg*. Because of this, some users of the phrase reinterpret it to mean "raise the question", as in:

Some say that women should be paid to stay at home, which begs the question as to who is going to pay. We must consider the fiscal implications of such a proposal ...

The traditional use of the phrase is more abstract. In begging the question, a speaker or writer takes as a proven fact the very question which should be discussed. The issue is woven into another assertion which effectively submerges it. See for example:

We must reintroduce capital punishment to deter murderers.

The statement begs the question as to whether capital punishment really serves to discourage murder. It makes it sound as if we can take that for granted, and preempts discussion of it by focusing on the urgent need to resume capital punishment. The speaker is more interested in whipping up support for the cause than in allowing any discussion of the underlying assumptions.

The Latin name for this ancient rhetorical trick is *petitio principii*, literally "begging of the principle", hence the English phrase. For more about argumentative tactics, see **argument**.

behavior or **behaviour** See under -or/-our.

Beijing See under **China**.

belie This word implies that things are not as they seem:

Her coolness belied her real feelings about the problem.

With **belie** appearances give the lie to what is really going on inside or underneath, hence the fact that **belie** is sometimes confused with *underlie*. But while *underlie* refers to the actual structure of things physical or psychological, **belie** always implies a misrepresentation of them.

Note that because **belie** is derived from the verb *lie* "tell lies", its past tense is *belied* (not *belay*). For the past tense of *underlie*, see **underlay**.

benefit Should you double the *t* before adding verbal suffixes? See under **t**.

Benelux See under **Netherlands**.

benzine or **benzene** These two spellings are used to distinguish different chemical substances. **Benzine** is a mixture of hydrocarbons obtained in the distillation of petroleum. For Americans it is also a synonym for petrol. **Benzene** is a single species of hydrocarbon molecule, with various industrial applications. Confusion of the two spellings by nonchemists is hardly surprising, given that *-ine* and *-ene* are interchangeable in the names of other household chemicals (see further under **-ine**). In fact **benzene** was originally **benzine**.

beside or **besides** Do these mean the same thing? The answer is yes and no. As a preposition **beside** has the more immediate physical meaning "next to" and "in comparison with", while **besides** covers the more detached and figurative ones "in addition to" and "apart from". Compare:

The ticket machine was beside the bus driver.

There was no-one besides the driver in the bus.

But just occasionally **beside** is used in a figurative sense like the one shown in the second sentence, according to the *Macquarie Dictionary* (1991) and *Webster's English Usage* (1989). And as adverbs, **beside** and **besides** share the figurative role:

He enjoyed a big salary, a company car, and everything else beside(s).
When the sense is physical proximity, only **beside** can appear:
The president was on the platform and his wife stood beside.
Overall then, **beside** seems to be gaining on **besides**, at least in the roles of preposition and adverb. (The growing preference for adverbs without *s* can also be seen in the group ending in *-ward* (see **-ward**).

Yet **besides** is unchallenged as the conjunct meaning "moreover":
Besides, he felt they owed it to him.
In that role it cannot be replaced by **beside**.

bet The past form of this verb can be either *bet* or *betted* according to all major dictionaries, with odds-on chances of its being *bet* in the past participle:
Being a mathematician, he bet(ted) for years by a random number table.
He had bet all his savings on that horse.
See further under **zero past tense**.

bête noire Borrowed from French, this phrase allows us to refer discreetly to something or someone we can't stand. Literally it means "black beast". There is a touch of the sinister supernatural in it which puts it higher up the stylistic scale than *bugbear* (though it too has a supernatural element in *bug*—if you know the Welsh *bwg* meaning a "ghost").

Note that in the phrase **bête noire**, the *e* of *noire* is there to agree with *bête*, which happens to be a feminine noun in French. So the *e* should remain, even if your difficult person is masculine: **bête noire** applies to either gender. But the phrase is sometimes seen in English as *bête noir*, a spelling which is registered in *Webster's Dictionary* (1986) as an alternative.

better or **bettor** The spelling **bettor** for a person who lays bets undoubtedly helps to distinguish it from the adjective/adverb **better**. It would be indispensable if you had to write:
He was a better bettor than his partner.
Yet the juxtaposition of the two seems far-fetched: most of the time they move in different circles.

In fact the spelling **better** is used generally in Britain and Australia for the person who lays bets, and it had the backing of Fowler. It is more natural than **bettor** as the agent noun from the English verb *bet* (see further under **-er/-or**). In the USA however, **bettor** is the preferred form, as shown in the *Random House* and *Webster's* dictionaries. Australians who are concerned about the problem can avoid it altogether by using the word *punter*.

between or **among** These words share more common ground than they used to. **Between** was formerly reserved for situations where just two things or people were being related: *shared between husband and wife*, and **among** complemented it when there were three or more: *shared among the relatives.* This restriction on the use of **between** has certainly gone by the board, and Gowers declared it to be "superstition" in *Complete Plain Words* (1954). It is now quite common for **between** to be used in expressions referring to groups of more than two. But **among** is still reserved for situations where there are at least three parties involved. One could not say ''among husband and wife''.

between you and me (or I) Those of us who always use **between you and me** have it easy, because it's in line with what the traditional grammarians regard as correct use of pronouns. Yet **between you and I** is certainly used too, and for some people it is the usual formula to highlight a confidential point of conversation. The real issue is whether it should appear in writing.

The phrase **between you and I** has a long history of both use and censure. It has been used for centuries by literary authors, from Shakespeare on. Yet it fell foul of eighteenth century's zeal to ''correct'' the language, and to preserve the remaining case distinctions (nominative/accusative) among the English pronouns. It was argued that in **between you and ???**, both pronouns are objects of the preposition, and must therefore be accusative. This makes no difference for *you* but it demands *me* rather than *I* as the second pronoun. And of course, if it were *between me and my dog*, no-one would say or write otherwise. The use of *me* comes naturally then, because it is directly governed by *between*. The *I* probably gets into **between you and I** because it's further away from the governing word.

Other factors may help to foster the use of *I*, such as the fact that the phrase quite often comes immediately before the subject/nominative of a clause, as in:
   Between you and I, they won't be here much longer.
Some grammarians including the authors of the *Comprehensive Grammar of English* (1985) suggest it is a hypercorrection based on oversensitivity about using *me* (see further under **me**).

Research among young Australian adults by Collins in the 1970s showed that many thought that **between you and I** was standard and even formal English. This suggests it must at least be recognised as a colloquial variant of **between you and me**. But because **between you and I** seems to have become a shibboleth (see **shibboleth**), it's to be avoided in writing. In fact a confidential **between you and I** is unlikely to occur to anyone writing a formal document.

beveled or **bevelled** For the choice between these spellings, see **-l/-ll-**.

bi- This prefix comes from Latin with the meaning ''two'', though in a handful of English words it means ''twice''. Examples of the first meaning (''two'') are easily found in everyday and general words such as:
   bicentenary bicycle biennial bifocals bigamy
   binary binoculars bipartisan
as well as scientific words such as:
   bicarbonate biceps bicuspid biped bisexual bivalve
The second meaning (''twice'') is found only in *biannual*, and sometimes in *bimonthly* and *biweekly*. It arose only last century, and unfortunately makes for

chronic difficulty in interpreting those words. None of the other number prefixes one to ten has this duality of meaning (see **number prefixes**).

The distinction between *biennial* and *biannual* is easiest to remember if you're a gardener working with *biennial asters* which last for two years, or someone who attends *biennial exhibitions* which take place every two years. But without the support of such contexts, the reader may well be in doubt. Does a *biannual meeting* take place twice a year or every two years? Dictionaries which distinguish *biennial* "every two years" from *biannual* "twice a year", also note that *biannual* is sometimes used with the meaning of *biennial*. For a writer, there is always the risk of not being interpreted as you intend and it's safer to use a paraphrase to clarify the point. One can replace *biannual* with "twice a year", and *biennial* by "every two years".

Alternatively you could use the prefix *semi-*, and *semiannual* instead of *biannual*, as *Webster's English Usage* (1989) suggests. This works well enough for *semimonthly* and *semiweekly* also, because *semi-* combines with both classical and English words (see **semi-**). *Fortnightly* is also useful as a paraphrase for "every two weeks/twice a month", in something intended for Australian or British readers. To Americans, however, the term *fortnight* is unfamiliar.

Compare the prefix **di-**.

biannual or biennial See under **bi-**.

bias When **bias** becomes a verb, should its inflected forms be *biased* and *biasing*, or *biassed* and *biassing*? The spellings with one *s* are given preference in the major dictionaries in Australia, Britain and the USA, while those with double *s* are recognised variants. In Canada however, the *Gage Canadian Dictionary* prefers the spellings with double *s*.

The forms with double *s* were evidently quite common in the nineteenth century, but with both the *Oxford Dictionary* and Fowler arguing against them their currency was reduced. Still they survive as evidence to show people's uncertainty about how to spell the inflected forms of verbs ending in a single consonant. The rules are not entirely consistent, and they diverge in American and British English (see **doubling of final consonant**).

Note that the plural of the *noun* **bias** is not commented on in the dictionaries, which implies that it is the regular *biases*. It helps to reinforce the single *s* forms for the verb.

bibliographies *Bibliography* is the general name for the consolidated list of works referred to by the author. Note that in some academic disciplines, the *bibliography* includes any item read or consulted in writing the book; but others prefer to restrict the list to items which are actually cited in the text, which makes it a *List of references* or *Works consulted*.

The form of the *bibliography* varies with the chosen referencing system in matters such as the order of items, alphabetisation, and the forms of names. There are also many small points of style in punctuation and abbreviations which vary with the publishing house, the journal and its editor, and authors should always check for their particular preferences. What follows are token **bibliographies** for the main referencing systems: (A) short-title references, in the text and footnotes/endnotes; (B) author-date references (or "Harvard" system); (C) number system (with Vancouver style). For the forms of the references themselves, see **referencing**.

A) *Bibliography to go with short-title references*
—Bell, Philip B. and Staines, Phillip J. *Reasoning and argument in psychology.* Kensington, NSW University Press: 1979.
—Guy, Gregory and Vonwiller, Julia "The meaning of an intonation in Australian English". *Australian Journal of Linguistics* (7) 1984.
—Oasa, Hiroaki "Phonology of current Adelaide English". In *Australian English: the language of a new society,* edited by Peter Collins and David Blair. St Lucia, University of Queensland Press: 1989.

B) *Bibliography to go with author-date references*
—Bell, P. B. and Staines, P. J. (1979) *Reasoning and argument in psychology.* Kensington, NSW University Press.
—Guy, G. and Vonwiller, J. (1984) "The meaning of an intonation in Australian English". *Australian Journal of Linguistics* (7).
—Oasa, H. (1989) "Phonology of current Adelaide English". In *Australian English: the language of a new society,* edited by P. Collins and D. Blair. St Lucia, University of Queensland Press.

C) *Number system, with Vancouver style*
1 Guy G, Vonwiller, J. The meaning of an intonation in Australian English. Aust J of Linguistics 1984; 7.
2 Bell PB, Staines PJ. Reasoning and argument in psychology. Kensington: NSW University Press, 1979.
3 Oasa H. Phonology of current Adelaide English. In: Collins P, Blair D eds. Australian English: the language of a new society. St Lucia: University of Queensland Press, 1989.

Points to note
• The order of entries is alphabetical in (A) and (B). In (C) the order is dictated by the numbers, which run in accordance with the appearance of each item within the text.
• In all three systems the names of all authors are inverted. The practice of inverting only that of the first among joint authors is disappearing. Only the first practice is supported in the Australian Government *Style Manual* (1988).
• Initials are occasionally used in (A) for the full first names of authors, usually in (B), and always in (C). In (C) the initials are written without stops, and the word *and* is omitted between the names of joint authors.

- The date is placed immediately after the name(s) of the author(s) in (B), but not (A) or (C).
- The use of capitals in titles and subtitles varies, though the minimal capitalisation of librarians has much to recommend it. See further under **titles**.
- The titles of articles or chapters of books have in the past been set in inverted commas. This practice is declining in the social and natural sciences, and *Webster's Style Manual* (1985) notes it also in the humanities. The Chicago *Manual* (1981) presents it simply as an alternative style.
- Italics are normally used in (A) and (B) to set off the title of the book or the name of the journal.
- In Vancouver style the recurrent parts of the names of journals are abbreviated. The recognised abbreviations for medicine and biomedical research are detailed each year in the January issue of the *I:dex Medicus*. Abbreviations for other fields of research may be found in *Chemical Abstracts* and *World List of Scientific Periodicals*.
- In references to chapters or parts of a book, the book's title should appear before that of the editors, according to the Australian Government *Style Manual* as well as Chicago's *Manual of Style*. However the Vancouver system gives the name(s) of the editor(s) first.
- In the publication details, the place of publication often precedes the name of the publisher. This was not always so, but it's the practice of both the Australian Government and Chicago style manuals; and it makes good sense these days in the era of multinational publishing. If the place is subsumed in the actual name of the publisher, as for *Melbourne University Press*, there's no need to repeat it.
- The trend in punctuating bibliographical entries is to greater simplicity, and periods are preferred as the device *between* separate items, instead of the array of commas and parentheses used in the past. *Within* each component, commas and colons may be used, as shown above.

bicentennial or **bicentenary** When Australia celebrated its two-hundredth birthday, a curious division of labor was given to these words. **Bicentennial** had official backing in the *Australian Bicentennial Authority*, but the event itself was officially called the **Bicentenary**. Many people nevertheless referred to it as the **Bicentennial**, under the influence of the phrase *Bicentennial Authority* as well as the fact that the American **Bicentennial** had been on everyone's lips only a few years before. The ABC had the unenviable task of trying to promote **Bicentenary**, when **Bicentennial** seemed to come naturally, and you may wonder why it seemed important.

The explanation seems to lie in British reluctance to use **bicentennial** as a noun. It was certainly in use as an adjective, but Fowler had argued that **bicentenary** was preferable as the noun on grounds of analogy (see further under **centennial**). Yet the *Oxford Dictionary* suggests that **bicentennial** actually has the better etymology of the two, because it has the root for ''years''

(Latin *enn-*) built in. The fact that **bicentennial** was well used as a noun in **American English** may have gone against it for adherents of the Fowler tradition.

Classical adjectives like these often evolve into independent nouns in English (see under **-al** and **-ary**). It is indeed a moot point whether they are still adjectives in constructions like *bicentenary celebrations* and *Bicentennial Authority*. They can be nouns as much as "birthday" and "Electricity" would be if inserted into those same structures. There is no grammatical or other reason for Australians to perpetuate a **shibboleth** which artificially restricts the role of **bicentennial** to adjective.

biceps The plural of this word could be *biceps*, *bicepses* or even *bicipites* if you know your Latin. Most people choose between the first two, effectively using either the zero plural or the regular English *-es* plural. The use of just *biceps* as the plural is probably swelled by those who are unsure whether one or more rippling biceps is being referred to. With its final *s*, **biceps** looks already like a plural, and it probably diverts the uncertain user from adding a further plural ending to it. In any case, it's a perfectly acceptable form. Other muscles such as the *triceps* and *quadriceps* have the same alternative plurals.

Forceps is both similar and a little different. The plural could be *forceps*, *forcepses* or *forcipes*. (The Latin plural of **forceps** differs from that of **biceps** because it derives from the verb *capere* (*cip-*) "take" rather than the noun *caput* (*capitis*) "head".) With **forceps** there is a stronger incentive to settle on the zero plural, because of the analogy with *pliers*, *scissors* and other familiar tools with double blades or arms. On whether **forceps** takes a singular or plural verb, see **agreement**, section 3.

bid Two Old English verbs have coalesced into one in **bid**, one meaning "ask, demand" and the second "declare, command". By the fifteenth century the meanings and past forms of each were inextricably mixed, and the modern legacy is our uncertainty as to which past forms to attach to which meaning.

At auctions and in card games, both the past tense and the past participle are **bid**:

They said he bid $4 million for the house.
I've never bid three no trumps so often in one evening.

But when the verb comes up in reference to commands and greetings, the past tense is *bade*, and the past participle *bidden*, as in *She bade him a quick goodnight*. This use of the word now has a slightly old-fashioned flavor.

As a noun, the word shows up regularly in newspapers (see **headline words**).

biennial or **biannual** See under **bi-**.

bikie or **biker** A difference of lifestyle hangs around these two, though both may be devoted to their bikes. A **bikie** is associated with a motorbike gang, and with their often violent and lawless activities. A **biker** is any person who rides a motorbike, or even a bicycle.

-bility See -ability.

billet On whether to double the final -*t* when this word becomes a verb, see **t**.

billion Usage of this word in Australia has been changing during the last twenty years. No longer should it be taken to mean "a million million" (i.e. 10^{12}), but rather "a thousand million" (i.e. 10^9).

Although the latter meaning used to be regarded as peculiarly American, it is now current in many other parts of the world. In Britain, the Treasury and the London *Financial Times* have switched over, and the Australian Treasury and the Commonwealth and Reserve Banks have done the same.

All the major Australian newspapers take the stand that a **billion** is "a thousand million". However there are warnings in their style guides of the danger of misunderstanding, as long as there are readers who still assume the older meaning of the word. Both newspaper guides and the Australian Government *Style Manual* urge writers to spell out numerical values involving billions whenever they are critical. So however convenient it is to put $4 billion in the headline, or anywhere else, it is less ambiguous as $4000 000 000, or $4000 million. The word *million* is still the standard term, whereas both the (new) **billion** and the old term for it *milliard* have less than general currency. For mathematicians and scientists there's a definitive way around the problem by speaking in powers of ten.

Note that the dual value of **billion** also affects the value given to *trillion, quadrillion, quintillion* etc. Thus the American **trillion** is 10^{12}, and equal to the *older* British **billion**.

bimonthly See under **bi-**.

bindi-eye or **bindy** This prevalent suburban weed has a very old Australian name, borrowed from the Kamilaroy Aborigines in northern NSW. The original word was something like "bindayah", and the earliest recorded spelling in 1896 *bindeah* comes closer to it than any others since, including *bindiyi, bindei* and *bindii*, apart from the two standard ones given above. In those two we see English folk etymology at work, trying to interpret the Aboriginal syllables. (See further under **folk etymology**.)

bingeing or **binging** See under **-e** section 1d.

bivouac On how to spell this word when used as a verb, see **-c/-ck-**.

biweekly See under **bi-**.

black or **Black** This word has been used in reference to Aboriginal people from the time of the earliest settlements in 1788. Numerous compounds have been formed with it, witness:

    blackboy black fellow (or fella) black gin black man
    black police black people

These expressions were of course those of white Australians, and their overtones varied from the neutral to the negative. Since about 1970, the word **Black** (note the capital letter) has been vigorously taken up by Aborigines as a positive affirmation of their ethnic identity. This development paralleled the affirmation of Afro-Americans that "Black is beautiful", and their new practice of referring to themselves as "Blacks". (See further under **Aboriginal** or **Aborigine**.)

blackboy For the species of grasstree known as **blackboy**, see under **yakka**.

blanch or **blench** Both these verbs can be related to the French adjective *blanc* "white": **blanch** means "make something white" and **blench** "become white or pale". The first is usually transitive, as in a practical action:
First blanch the almonds in boiling water.
The second is intransitive, expressing a human response to a fearful situation:
He blenched at the sound of the approaching siren.
Yet **blanch** can also be used intransitively in such sentences, instead of **blench**. It seems in fact to be gaining ground, while **blench** is losing it. The *Oxford Dictionary* records the extinction of several meanings of **blench**, and it suffers from a homonymic clash with an identical Old English word meaning "recoil or shy away". In fearful situations a human being may (1) turn pale and/or (2) shy away, and **blench** could mean either or both. It can be important to know whether the protagonists stood their ground or not, and the indeterminacy of **blench** lets a narrative down at the critical moment. With **blanch** things are more straightforward: just a matter of turning pale.

blanket On how to spell this word when it's used as a verb, see **t**.

blends See **portmanteau words**.

blond or **blonde** How to spell this word is a curiously vexed issue. As often when there is a choice of spellings, people tend to assign different roles to them, and some dictionaries make **blond** the one to use in male references, and **blonde** the one for females. This of course is rather like what the French do with their genders, except that they apply it to grammatical gender as well as natural gender (see **gender**).

But Australian authors do not seem to work consistently with such a system, witness a recent travel article in a respected newspaper, which spoke first of "the blonde and jovial giants" (of Scandinavia), then "the blond and friendly giants", and topped it off with a headline to the effect that "Blonds Have More Sun". It seems unlikely that male/female differences were the point of the spelling differences.

That article apart, it is the grammatical differences which emerged in a wider survey of Australian newspapers. **Blonde** is more often used as the noun (usually the stereotyped female), whereas **blond** serves as the general adjective in *blond-haired*. These trends are nicely illustrated in a citation from *Webster's English Usage* (1989), taken from the *New York Times Book Review*. It concerned:

"The 'British Blondes' ... Thanks to them, blond hair ... became a mark of feminine beauty."

Yet the citations also show adjectival use of **blonde** varying with **blond** in references to the color of hair, wood and beer.

blue For the spelling of *blu(e)ish* and *blu(e)ing*, see under -e section 1g.

bogy, bogey or **bogie** These three spellings represent four different words for Australians, and may refer to: (1) a score in golf (nowadays one over par); (2) the wheel assembly under a railway wagon; (3) a bugbear; something you dread; (4) swim (noun or verb).

Each word has its primary spelling, yet in two cases there are alternatives. They make a nightmare set for any dictionary to catalogue. A table helps to show the differences and overlaps in Australian usage:

	bogy	bogey	bogie
1 golf		*	
2 wheel assembly			*
3 bugbear	*	+	
4 swim		*	+

(The primary spellings are asterisked, secondary ones given a plus sign.) Note that in Australia **bogy** is also an underlying possibility for the golfing word, because the plural is more often *bogies* than *bogeys*.

Clearly these spellings are fluid. None has a long history of being written down: the *Oxford Dictionary*'s record for words (2) and (3) begins in the early nineteenth century, while the others are from later in the century. Word (4) was borrowed from the Dharuk Aborigines by Australian settlers, and like other Aboriginal words it has been subject to variation, with slightly more support for **bogey** than **bogie** in the *Australian National Dictionary* citations.

Instability of spelling is scarcely a problem because all but **bogy** "bugbear" appear in quite distinct contexts of use. **Bogy** "bugbear" sets itself apart from the others as a construct of the individual mind (*my bogy*), while the others (*a bogey*, *the bogie*) are physical or objectively verifiable things. Even the golfer who says:

My bogy is to get a bogey on the last hole

is unlikely to be misunderstood. Perhaps the spellings will settle down to those asterisked above, but in the meantime writers can enjoy the taste of freedom with them.

For other words which allow the choice between -*ie* and -*y* and -*ey* and -*y* in spelling, see **-ie/-y** and **-ey**.

bon mot/mot juste These phrases, borrowed from French, are not about words which are good or just. **Bon mot** (literally "a good word") refers to a memorable witticism or clever remark. The plural is *bons mots*—if one aims to maintain the authentic French effect (but see **plurals** section 2). Le **mot juste**

(literally "the right word") is "the well-chosen word", one which suits the context perfectly.

bon vivant or **bon viveur** The French phrase **bon vivant** has the longer history in English (from the end of the seventeenth century), whereas **bon viveur** is a latter-day pseudo-French formation of the nineteenth century. **Bon vivant** is still much more widely used to refer to one who enjoys the pleasures of good living, but the presence of the other has prompted some demarcation disputes over meaning.

For some, the two phrases are synonymous. For others, the focus of **bon vivant** is especially on the epicurean delights of the table, whereas **bon viveur** implies the more urbane indulgences of the trendy man-about-town (and is sometimes coupled with "Don Juan"). The connotations of the phrases vary with people's attitudes to such codes of behavior, some finding them redolent with sophistication, others with reprehensible self-indulgence.

See also **gourmet** or **gourmand**.

bon voyage See under **adieu**.

bona fides and **bona fide** These are two forms of the same Latin phrase with different applications. The first one **bona fides** is used in English to mean "good faith or honest intention", and agrees with a singular verb as in:

The litigant's bona fides was queried by the judge.

Yet **bona fides** is sometimes found with a plural verb, suggesting that people think of it as plural:

The bona fides of the unlikely counterspy were yet to be ascertained.

This plural usage seems to anticipate a recent extension of the word, to mean "proof(s) of being genuine", which according to *Webster's English Usage* (1989) originated within intelligence operations, but is beginning to be used in other contexts:

With a brilliant recital, there is no questioning his bona fides as a musician.

Bona fide is the ablative of the phrase, meaning "in good faith" (see further under **ablative**). It serves as an adverb-cum-adjective in expressions like *bona fide offer* and *bona fide traveler*, where the nouns themselves have strong verb connections.

bonus For the plural of this word, see **-us** section 1.

bony or **boney** See under **-y/-ey**.

book titles For details about how to set out the titles of books, in bibliographies and elsewhere, see **titles**.

born or **borne** Though identical in pronunciation, the spelling of these words marks their different domains of meaning. **Born** is only used in expressions which refer to coming into the world, whether it is an actual birth ("born on

Christmas Day'') or a figurative one (''not born yesterday''). **Borne** serves as the all-purpose past participle of the verb *bear*, as in:

The oil slick was borne away by the tide.

Both **born** and **borne** are related to the verb *bear*, and there was no systematic difference in their spelling until the last quarter of the eighteenth century. Earlier editions of Samuel Johnson's dictionary (up to 1773) gave the past participle of *bear* as either ''bore or born''. But **borne** had been widely used in sixteenth and seventeenth century English, and it gradually replaced the other two as the general past participle, leaving **born** a restricted role.

Bosnia Herzegovina See under **Yugoslavia**.

bossa nova Not Italian for ''under new management'', but the name of a lively dance rather like a tango, with a jerky rhythm. The phrase is actually Brazilian slang for a new style or approach, and is not to be interpreted literally in terms of its Portuguese components, which mean ''new bump''.

botanic or **botanical** Both words are adjectives associated with *botany*, though **botanic** has had little general use since the eighteenth century. We're mostly aware of it because of its appearance in official names and titles such as ''Botanic Gardens'' and ''Royal Botanic Society''. Elsewhere **botanical** is the form normally used, as in *botanical specimens*.

For other pairs of words like this, see under **-ic/-ical**.

boulevard or **boulevarde** The French spell this word without a final *e*, as in *Boulevard St Germain*. Yet **Boulevarde** makes its appearance in Australia, particularly in Sydney. Suburban street directories show that when the word appears in its own right as a street name (*The Boulevarde*), it always carries a final *e* in Sydney, and almost never in Melbourne. In both cities, however, it is just **Boulevard** when it functions as the second element of the street name, as in *Yarra Boulevard*. Why the *e* should be added so regularly to Sydney street names is an intriguing question.

(See further under **-e** section 3.)

bow or **bows** Whether it's *in the bow* or *in the bows*, the action is at the front of the ship. For sailors, the plural **bows** is the usual expression because there is both a port and a starboard bow which meet at the stem in front. But landlubbers see only ''the pointed end'' of the ship, and are more inclined to use **bow**.

BP These letters, when preceded by an approximate date: *5000 BP*, stand for ''before the present'' (i.e. before AD 1950). The abbreviation refers to a chronological system based on radiocarbon dating, used increasingly by archeologists, historians and scientists. The system relies on measuring the radioisotopes of remains from a particular culture or era, and deducing their age from the relative decay of carbon atoms in them. The method is not particularly exact: one has to allow a plus or minus factor around any date proposed. But it does offer an approximate dating within undocumented periods of history and prehistory.

See further under **dating systems**.

bracket On whether to double the final consonant before adding verb suffixes, see **t**.

brackets The role of **brackets** is to separate a string of words or characters from those on either side. They come in five different shapes each with its own functions which are detailed below. The punctuation problems which arise with parentheses in particular are also discussed below, sections 2 and 3.

1 *Types of* **brackets**.
a) *Parentheses ()* (sometimes called *round brackets*) often enclose a parenthetical comment or *parenthesis* within a carrier sentence:
   Angkor (the ancient capital of the Khmer empire) is situated hundreds of miles upstream from Phnom Penh.
In such a sentence the parenthetical words are occasionally set off with commas or dashes (em rules). However some writers and editors use the three types of punctuation to represent degrees of separation: commas make the least separation between the parenthesis and the rest of the sentence, then parentheses, and then dashes making the biggest break. It seems unlikely however that all three levels can be usefully exploited in the same sentence.

Even for indicating two levels of parenthesis there is a variety of opinion and practice. Some recommend combining dashes with the parentheses, though the Chicago *Manual of Style* has dashes outside the brackets, whereas the *Right Word at the Right Time* recommends dashes inside. The Chicago *Manual* also allows a combination of square brackets and parentheses (with the square ones inside the others); but *Hart's Rules* warns specifically against it, because of the convention of using square brackets for editorial interpolations in a MS (see below). Instead it suggests simply using parentheses within parentheses, taking care to close each set in turn.
Other uses of parentheses are to:
   i) enclose optional additions to a word, when the author wants to allow for alternative interpretations or applications of a statement. For example:
      Students will take their additional subject(s) in their own time.
   ii) enclose numbers or enumerative letters in a list. If they are in continuous text it's usual to put brackets on either side: (i), (ii) etc., but when they stand at the margin in a list (as in this entry), the second bracket alone is enough.
   iii) enclose a whole sentence which forms a parenthesis within a paragraph.
   iv) provide a locus for author-date references (see **referencing**).

b) *Square brackets [ ]* are conventionally used in prose to indicate editorial additions to the text, whether they explain, correct, or just comment on it in the form of *[sic]*. Other examples are:

... went home [to Cairns] and was never heard of after.
... [cont. p.166]

In mathematics, square brackets are used in a hierarchy with parentheses and braces, but there is some divergence about the order of the first two. *Right Word at the Right Time* has it that the square brackets are to be dealt with before the round, whereas the Chicago and Australian Government style manuals put them in opposite order. All agree that the braces come last.

In linguistics, square brackets are used to enclose phonetic symbols.

c) *Braces { }* (sometimes called *curly brackets*) are used as a distinguishing bracket in mathematics, after round and square brackets. In linguistics they identify the morphemes of a language.

d) *Slash brackets / /* (also called *diagonal brackets*) serve to separate the numbers in a date, as in *11/11/88*. In Britain they were also used in sums of money, separating pounds from the smaller denominations (see further under **solidus**).

In linguistics, slash brackets mark phonetic symbols which have phonemic status for the language concerned. The phonemes of Australian English are listed in Appendix I, using the symbols of the International Phonetic Alphabet.

e) *Angle brackets ⟨ ⟩* have special uses in mathematics; and in linguistics to show the graphemes or units of orthography in a particular writing system, for instance ⟨gh⟩ in *ghost*. As printed they are sometimes identical with paired **chevrons** (see further under that heading).

2 *Use of other punctuation with parentheses.* Punctuation outside any pair of parentheses, and especially after the parenthesis, is determined by the structure of the host sentence. Compare the following sentences:

Their last act was passable (no unexpected mishaps), and so the show earned a modicum of applause.
The last act of the show was passable (no unexpected mishaps) and amusing.

Without its parenthesis, the second sentence would certainly not have had a comma, so there's no reason to add one with the parenthesis.

Within the **brackets** themselves there is minimal punctuation—only exclamation or question marks if required—unless the parenthesis stands as an independent sentence. Compare:

He said (no-one would have predicted it) that he would run for president.
He said that he would run for president. (No-one would have predicted it.)

Note in the first of those sentences, the absence of initial capital and full stop in the parenthesis, because it is embraced within another sentence. Only when the parenthesis contains a title, or some stock saying would capitals be introduced:

Tomorrow's lecture (Language and Social Life) has been cancelled.

Their grandmother's prudent advice (Waste not want not) had them saving every plastic bag that came into the house.

3 *The final period: is it inside or outside a parenthetical bracket?* When a sentence ends with a parenthesis, the point to check is whether the parenthesis forms part or all of the sentence. If it is the whole sentence, the full stop goes inside; if the parenthesis is only the last part of the sentence, the full stop goes outside. Compare:

He said he was guilty. (No-one believed him.)

He said that he was guilty (in spite of appearances).

Note that this rule for the placement of the final period is the same throughout the English-speaking world, whereas the ones relating to full stops and quotation marks are variable. (See **quotation marks** section 3c.)

Brahman or **Brahmin** Modern dictionaries all make **Brahman** the primary spelling, whether you're referring to a member of the highest caste among the Hindus where the word originated, or to a person of great culture and intellect, or to a breed of Indian cattle used in Australia for crossbreeding animals for warmer latitudes. The capital can be omitted from the word when used in the second or third sense. (On the removal of capitals from animal names, see **capital letters** section 2.)

    Brahmin is essentially the older spelling, which took precedence over **Brahman** in the nineteenth century according to the *Oxford Dictionary*. This probably helps to explain why it's the spelling used for the *Boston Brahmins* (members of the old established families of New England—highly cultivated and aloof), and elsewhere in American English for individuals of the same type. The concept is transported in rare references to the *Adelaide brahmin* (lower case). Yet **Brahman/brahman** elsewhere maintains its ground, and remains the primary spelling in Australia for other meanings.

breach, breech or **broach** The first two of these sound alike, whereas the first and third overlap in meaning. **Breech** is the least common of them, referring to the rear end of something, and mostly used in association with childbirth (*breech birth*) and with a style of guns (*breechloaders*).

    Breach comes from the same root as our word *break*, but it is more often used as a noun than a verb. Sometimes it refers to a physical break, as in a *breach in the dike* (or in the defences of the football team). More often it connotes a figurative rupture, in law or in personal relations: *a breach of the peace*, *a breach of promise*. When used as a verb, **breach** can mean "break", as in *breach the agreement*.

    The verb **breach** occasionally has something in common with **broach**, because the effect of breaching a dike is not unlike that of broaching a keg:

liquid pours through the hole. There is still a difference, in that *breaching* is normally the work of nature, and *broaching* a human act. The word **broach** comes from joinery and carpentry, where one uses a **broach** (a tapered spike) to enlarge a hole. The more figurative use of **broach** in *broaching a subject* is again a matter of opening something up, this time a reservoir of discussion.

Note also *brooch* "a piece of jewellery", pronounced exactly like **broach**. The two words come from the same French source and were spelled alike until about 1600.

breathalyser or **breathalyzer** How much more discreet the name is than its American counterpart: the *drunkometer*!

The Australian word is a blend of *breath* and *analyse*. The alternative spellings arise because of the variation between *-yse* and *-yze* in some verbs (see **-yse/-yze**). Evidence from the Australian ACE corpus gives more support to *-yse(r)*, though some newpaper style guides and the *Collins Dictionary* spell it with *-yzer* and an initial capital (**Breathalyzer**), as if it is believed to be a current trademark. (If it were, it would hardly be subject to the normal *s/z* variation of English spelling.)

breech, breach or **broach** See **breach**.

brethren or **brothers** Brethren was the ordinary plural of *brother* until the late sixteenth century, when it gave place to *brothers*. The King James Bible nevertheless keeps it all through, and it still survives in more conservative religious discourse. It is enshrined in the names of certain evangelical Protestant groups, such as the *Plymouth Brethren*, whereas Catholic orders use the regular plural as in *Christian Brothers*.

(See further under **plurals** section 1c.)

brilliance or **brilliancy** See under **-nce/-ncy**.

briquet or **briquette** See under **-ette**.

Britain and **British** Strictly speaking, **Britain** doesn't exist. It is either *Great Britain*, the island which embraces England, Wales and Scotland; or else the *United Kingdom*, a political entity comprising Great Britain and Northern Ireland (see **UK**); or the *British Isles*, including Great Britain, the whole of Ireland, and all the offshore islands.

The adjective **British** may be used in reference to many aspects of the culture of Great Britain, though there's no satisfactory general term for its inhabitants. *Briton* is faintly prehistoric, while *Britisher* is an Americanism which the British do not take kindly to. The recent abbreviation *Brit* is too informal for many contexts, and *Pom* may be offensive. In any case, the inhabitants of Wales and Scotland do not relish being grouped under the British label, so the best way out generally is to go for more specific terms such as *English*, *Welsh*, *Scottish*, as appropriate. The Irish also demand their own adjective (see further under **Irish**).

British English The expression **British English** is generally used to distinguish the standard form of English used in Great Britain from the varieties used in other parts of the world. In its pronunciation, standard **British English** is associated with the southern and eastern dialects (and with speakers from the middle and upper classes), but the grammar and vocabulary are also those of southern England.

Contemporary standard **British English** is not of course the variety that was transported to America from 1600 on, or to colonies in other parts of the world in the eighteenth and nineteenth centuries. (See under **American English**, **Australian English** etc., for the particular dialects which are believed to have contributed to those varieties.) This is just one reason for the many differences between British and other Englishes. Another is the fact that standard **British English** has itself evolved over the last four or five centuries. The characteristic features of written **British English** are often the products of linguistic movements of the eighteenth and nineteenth centuries, which were not felt so strongly elsewhere. Even in Britain the effects were uneven, and **British English** is in some ways more pluralistic than other varieties, for example in allowing both *-ize* and *-ise*, both *-able* and *-eable* etc.

The language and usage of Shakespeare, which was often invoked as the basis of **British English**, was itself very pluralistic. Examples can be found both to satisfy and subvert the principles enunciated by later language commentators of the eighteenth and nineteenth century. Their efforts to codify English grammar and usage fostered prescriptive attitudes which persist into our own time, in routine judgements of ''correctness'' pronounced in many quarters. This pressure to standardise English runs counter to the vast quantities of evidence in the *Oxford Dictionary* which document the sheer variety of English usage. (See further under **descriptive** or **prescriptive**.)

In *Fowler's Modern English Usage* (1926) both prescriptive and descriptive tendencies can be found. Yet Fowler is more often associated with the former, and his name invoked as the final arbiter in many a usage dilemma. Successive reprintings of his book have extended Fowler's influence through the twentieth century; and being widely distributed overseas the book still articulates his view of English for the world at large.

broach, breach or **breech** See breach.

brooch or **broach** See under breach.

brother-in-law See in-laws.

brothers or **brethren** See brethren.

brush See bush, brush or scrub.

bucketfuls or **bucketsful** See under -ful.

budgerigar This now seems to be established as the standard spelling, although *budgerygah* is preferred by some ornithologists, and *budgerygar*, *betcherrygah* and *betshiregah* had some currency in the nineteenth century. The name is a hybrid formation, probably based on the Aboriginal word *gijirrigaa*, borrowed from the Yuwaalaraay people near Lightning Ridge, but remodeled under the influence of the word *budgeree* "good" borrowed from the Dharuk Aborigines near Port Jackson. The early settlers also called the bird by descriptive English names such as "shell parrot" and "undulated grass parrakeet", but they have been eclipsed altogether by **budgerigar** in the twentieth century. The colloquial form *budgie* has been on record since 1935.

budget On how to spell this word when verb suffixes are added to it, see under **t**.

buffalo On the plural of this word, see **-o**.

buffet This string of letters represents two different words, both of which raise spelling queries when used as verbs. The older **buffet** has been a verb meaning "strike with repeated blows" since the thirteenth century. It keeps a single *t* when suffixes are added: *buffeted, buffcting.*

The other **buffet**, associated with a flat-topped piece of furniture on which food can be displayed (as for a *buffet lunch*), is an eighteenth century borrowing from French. It is still pronounced in the French fashion, so that it half rhymes with "cafe". Very occasionally it is used as a verb (in the same way as *banquet* is). It is then given the standard suffixes and written in exactly the same way as the older word (*buffeted, buffeting*), even though still pronounced as if the *t* were not there. See further under **t**.

bugbear See under **bogy** and **bête noire**.

bureau For the plural of this word, see **-eau**.

Burma Within the United Nations, the *Burmese* nation is represented as Myanmar, the name decreed in 1988–9 by the Law and Order Restoration Council of the military government. It was intended to replace the English colonial name **Burma**; however it is not acceptable within **Burma** to the National League for Democracy, who won the 1990 election by a huge majority but have not yet been allowed by the military to assume their place in government. The Australian government uses **Myanmar** in official correspondence to the *Burmese* regime, but not otherwise.

burned or **burnt** These alternative past forms of *burn* raise some questions. Are they interchangeable? Or is there some crucial distinction? In Australia and Britain, both forms are used, whereas in the USA it is almost all **burned**. As often when there are alternatives, people seek a reason for the difference. The suggestions among Australian newspaper guides include:

1 **burned** is continuous action; **burnt** is completed

2 **burned** is intransitive; **burnt** is transitive

3 **burned** relates to people; **burnt** to objects

4 **burned** goes with a final "d" in the pronunciation; **burnt** with a final "t".
The last suggestion is untestable—who is to be sure how the word would be
pronounced in a given context?

The other suggestions (1–3) do not appear to be implemented by Australian
authors at large. What does emerge from the Australian ACE corpus is that
burned is much more common than **burnt** (7:1) as the simple verb, but the
scores are reversed when it comes to appearing as the past participle (6:16).
Australians do not make the transitive/intransitive distinction for **burnt/burned**
which many do in Britain (according to *Webster's Dictionary of Usage* (1989)).
Amid the ACE data **burned** was used for 5 transitive participles, and **burnt** for
3 intransitive ones. With such mixed evidence it makes sense to standardise on
the regular form **burned** for all past forms of the verb—rather than assuming
that any systematic or meaningful distinction can be made with the two
spellings.

For the adjective the issues are a little different in that **burnt** is established
in expressions such as *burnt offering*, *burnt sienna* and *burnt toast*. The ACE
data showed a clear preference for **burnt** as the attributive adjective (i.e. within
noun phrases such as those), and it is evident in both British and American
English according to the *Contemporary Grammar of English* (1985). The
spelling **burnt** is associated with this grammatical role worldwide.

For other verbs with the same alternative past forms, see **-ed**.

burst This verb is exactly the same for past and present tense. For other
examples, see **zero past tense**.

bus Should it be *buses*, *bused* and *busing*, or *busses*, *bussed* and *bussing*? All
major dictionaries present these as alternatives for the noun as well as the verb,
and citations in the second edition of the *Oxford Dictionary* run 50/50 each way.
The dictionaries almost always give priority to the spellings with a single *s*,
though the *Macquarie Dictionary* (1991) suggests that for the verb, the forms
with *ss* are to be preferred (which brings them into line with the verb *gas*). (See
further under **gas**.)

The forms with double *s* are more regular generally for a single-syllabled
word of this kind. (See further under **doubling of final consonant**.) But the use
of the regular form is perhaps inhibited by the unusual origin of the word: **bus**
is a clipped form of the Latin word *omnibus*.

bush, brush or **scrub** These words have developed separate meanings in the
course of Australian history. **Bush** is the most general of them, referring to all
the uncultivated, natural tracts of land, in contrast with those cleared to make
way for agriculture or suburbia. This usage is not really unique to Australia, for
it was current earlier in South Africa and the USA. But it is embodied in the

Australian phrase *gone bush*, and shows how **bush** could be a cover term for anything from tropical rainforest to semi-arid **scrub**.

Scrub refers to the miscellany of low-growing trees and bushes typical of poorer soils and in drier parts of Australia. (The word **scrub** here is actually a variant of *shrub*.) **Brush** also referred originally to lower growing vegetation, except that it was the dense understorey of forest trees, rather than on the open plains. In the course of the nineteenth century, however, **brush** was increasingly used to refer to the whole forest coverage, and especially to the rainforests of eastern Australia.

bushy or **bushie** The first is a standard adjective. The second is a casual Australian noun for someone from the **bush**.

For other word pairs like this, see under **-ie/-y**.

bust This informal verb originated as a variant form of the verb *burst*. (It has no connection with the noun **bust**, referring to a person's head, shoulders and more.) But **bust** has now struck out independently from *burst* in both form and meaning. It has developed a regular past tense *busted* alongside the zero past tense *bust*. Its divergent sense makes it a synonym for *break/broke/broken*, as in *dam-busters*, *bust their way in* and *a busted ankle*. These usages are now widespread, according *Webster's English Usage* (1989), though not evidenced in the most formal kinds of writing. The use of the word in *gone bust* "gone bankrupt" is nevertheless standard English.

but The fact that **but** is a conjunction does not prevent it from being used at the beginning of a sentence—yet generations of students were taught to avoid it there. The lesson seems to have left a lingering guilt, without affecting the expression of the ordinary Australian. In conversation it's frequently heard at the beginning of an utterance, and in newspapers it serves as a sentence opener on 40% of its appearances.

But serves to alert the listener/reader to an imminent change of viewpoint or substance in whatever is being communicated. Signaling this to one's audience is vital, if they are to follow new developments in an argument. (See **discourse markers**.) Still it is a pity to use **but** or any other word or discourse marker too often. There are alternative devices to be had which express contrast. (See under **conjunctions**.)

Note that in spoken Australian English, **but** sometimes occurs at the end of a sentence:

I didn't want to go, but.

This usage is exactly like the more generally accepted one with *though*:

I didn't want to go, though.

In such cases **but** is a kind of adverb or adjunct, one which serves to soften the force of the whole statement. Other, more standard expressions which have the same effect are discussed under **hedge words**.

buzz words See **vogue words**.

by, **by-**, **bye-** and **bye**   The English particle **by** appears as a prefix meaning "near to" or "beside" in words like:

bypass byroad bystander byway

It appears with the less physical meaning "associated with" or "derivative from" in others such as:

byname byplay byproduct byword

The trend is to set these words solid, though dictionaries differ as to which particular words from the second set are still to be hyphenated. All give a hyphen to the most recent word of this type *by(-)line* ("the indication of authorship at the head of a newspaper article"); but those in the newspaper business are less inclined to do so. The fact that the word is increasingly used as a verb (*bylined*) is another factor that fosters the set-solid form.

When it comes to *by(e)law*, you may choose between **by** and **bye**. The spelling with **bye** hints at the word's history in the Old Norse word *byr* meaning "town"; while **by** implies a modern reinterpretation of the first syllable as the English prefix **by-**. (Most recent dictionaries prefer *bylaw* set solid.) The word *by(e)-election* is allowed the same options by some, though it really is based on the prefix **by-**, and there's no historical justification for **bye-**. The Australian ACE corpus showed a strong preference for *by(-)election*—with or without hyphen.

By/bye also appears in a few places as an independent noun. In various sports it is the round or part of a competition when a team temporarily stands out; and in cricket a bye or *leg bye* is a run gained on the side, i.e. not from contact between bat and ball. In *by the bye*, **bye** is again a noun meaning "something aside", though it's often written as *by the by*, as if it had something in common with *by and by* (which is correctly written with two *bys*).

Note also that the informal *bye-bye* is a telescoping of "(God) be with you", said twice over. (See further under **adieu**.)

The English prefix **by-** is not to be confused with the Latin *bi-*, though they are identical in pronunciation. (See further under **bi-**.)

C

c. or **ca.** See under **circa**.

-c/-ck- English spelling sometimes demands that we double the last letter of a word before adding *-ed*, *-ing* and other suffixes. Normally this means simply repeating the letter, as with *beg* > *begged* and *slam* > *slammed*. But when the last letter is **c**, we "double" it by adding in a *k*. See for example:

bivouac	*bivouacked*	*bivouacking*	*bivouacker*
frolic	*frolicked*	*frolicking*	*frolicker*
mimic	*mimicked*	*mimicking*	*mimicker*
panic	*panicked*	*panicking*	*panicker*
picnic	*picnicked*	*picnicking*	*picnicker*
traffic	*trafficked*	*trafficking*	*trafficker*

The same happens when *-y* is added, witness *panicky* and *colicky*.

This special treatment for a final **c** is necessary to ensure that it keeps its "k" sound before the suffix. (When followed by *e*, *i* or *y*, a *c* usually sounds as "s", as in *accent, pencil* and *fancy*.)

Adding the *k* into *panicked* etc. looks strange—partly because those forms are used much less often than the simple form *panic*. And because *k* is always there in the spelling of thousands of words such as *deck, derrick* and *rickshaw*, we're unused to a variable *k*. In fact the *k* has come and gone from some of the words in the list above. Spellings such as *frolick, mimick* and *panick* were used up to the eighteenth century, until it was felt that the *k* in them was superfluous, as with *logick* and *musick*. But the *k* reappears before the suffix in *panicked* and the rest, like a ghost from the past.

Note that some technical words ending in **c** do not add in a *k* before suffixes beginning with *e* or *i*. Engineers and scientists prefer *arced/arcing* to *arcked/arcking*. Technical words derived from *zinc* are written *zincic, zinciferous, zincify* and *zincite*. The less technical *zincky* follows the general rule, however.

ça va sans dire This phrase borrowed from French means "it goes without saying", i.e. it's something too obvious to mention. So at one level of interpretation, the phrase plays down the importance of whatever it refers to; at another, it seems to draw attention to it. This ambivalence can make it difficult for others to know how to respond, and speakers can use it thus to disarm the audience on an issue.

A similar French phrase *ça ne fait rien* is more straightforward with its meaning: "it doesn't matter" or "it's nothing". Used to play down an embarrassment or conversational accident, it means that you should not trouble yourself about what happened.

Different again is the French courtesy phrase **de rien**, which roughly equals "it's nothing", but is used as a rejoinder after thanks have been expressed for some favor or service rendered. It can be translated as "think nothing of it", or "don't mention it", though they are laborious in comparison. In American English, the nearest equivalent is *you're welcome*, and in British English it's *not at all*. Australians may use either of those.

cabanossi or **kabanossi** See under **k/c**.

cabbala, cabala, kabbala, kabala or **qabbalah** All these refer to an esoteric Jewish tradition, or more broadly, to any mystical doctrine. Choosing among the spellings is a matter of where you live in the world, and whether you want to stress the Hebrew origins of the word. The major British and Australian dictionaries give priority to the forms with two *b*s, while American dictionaries prefer those with one *b*. The spellings with one *b* are in line with antecedents in medieval French and Latin (and other related words such as *cabal*); those with two *b*s reflect the spelling of the Hebrew original—although getting closer to it requires other adjustments as in **qabbalah**. The spellings with *k* enjoyed some currency in the nineteenth century. But in the twentieth, those with *c* seem to have prevailed, as in derivatives such as *cab(b)alism*, *cab(b)alist* and *cab(b)alistic*.

For other examples of the same spelling variation, see under **k/c** and **single for double**.

cabby or **cabbie** See under **ie/y**.

cactus For the plural of this word, see **-us** section 1.

caddy or **caddie** When it's a matter of golf, **caddie** is the usual spelling. The word is believed to have come from Scottish English in the nineteenth century. Originally it was the French *cadet*, but you may hear the informal Scots *laddie* in it also. The *-ie* spelling coincides with Australian use of the same ending in informal words. See **-ie/-y**.

Caddy is the only spelling for a container of tea. The word is derived from Malay *kati*, which actually refers to a particular measure of weight, approximately 600 grams.

Caesarean, Caesarian, Cesarean or **Cesarian** With the added choice between capitalised and uncapitalised spellings, there are eight possible ways of writing this word. Is there a reasonable way of choosing among them?

Let's deal first with the question of whether to use a capital letter or not. It depends very much on whether you're referring to something associated with the Caesars, or to an obstetrical procedure. If your writing is concerned with the Caesars it must have a capital letter. But if it's a matter of obstetrics many writers use a lower case letter to begin the word.

As far as the choice between *-ae-* and just *-e-* goes, historians everywhere prefer to use the first. A Roman name such as *Caesar* (and any derivative such as **Caesarean**) keeps to its classical *ae* spelling—even in the USA, where an *ae* is usually reduced to *e* in common classical words (see further under **ae/e**). So **Cesarean**, **Cesarian** and their lower case equivalents are reserved for obstetrics.

With the choice between *-ean* and *-ian*, the lines are less clearly divided. In historical references, the *Oxford Dictionary* shows that both have been freely used in the past, although there's now a tendency for *-ian* to consolidate in that role. The major American dictionaries still show *-ean* and *-ian* as equal alternatives. The spelling with *-ean* is strongly preferred for obstetrics everywhere in the world.

All this means that historians have the choice of **Caesarian** or **Caesarean**, whereas doctors and nurses in Australia are most likely to use **caesarean**.

The use of **c(a)esarean** in reference to the obstetrical procedure is a small reminder of the classical legend that Julius Caesar was himself born by c(a)esarean section. The course of medical history makes this very unlikely. Only in the last century have surgical births become a regular procedure, and safe enough to ensure the survival of both mother and child. In earlier times surgical deliveries like this were indeed performed, but only to release an unborn child from a dying mother. Julius Caesar's mother bore two more children after him, so she can scarcely have had a c(a)esarean performed on her. The tradition probably arises from folk etymology—from the fact that the name *Caesar* seems to embody the Latin stem *caes-* meaning "cut", coupled with ignorance of the fact that the name *Caesar* was borne by several of Julius Caesar's ancestors.

caesura For the plural, see **-a** section 1.

caftan or **kaftan** See under **k/c**.

cagey or **cagy** See under **-y/-ey**.

caldron or **cauldron** See **cauldron**.

calendar or **calender** The spelling of the last syllable makes a difference. With **calendar** you have the word for a system by which time is calculated, whereas with **calender** you're referring to machinery used in manufacturing cloth or paper.

Calendar is the commoner of the two words by far. Its *-ar* ending is an integral part of the stem of its Latin forebear *calendarium* "account book". The Roman account book took its name from the fact that accounts were tallied on the first day of each month, known in Latin as the *calendae* (or *kalendae*). So time and money were reckoned together.

The other word **calender** refers to the machine whose rollers put a smooth finish on paper or cloth as it passes through. The word originates as a medieval spelling for the word "cylinder"—which helps to explain the *-er*.

caliber or **calibre** See under **-re/-er**.

calico For the plural of this word, see under **-o**.

caliph, calif, khalif or **kaliph** Modern dictionaries give preference to **caliph** as the most common spelling of this word for an Arab ruler. Arabic scholars prefer **khalif**, as being closer to the original form of the word. On the variation between **caliph** and **calif**, see **f/ph**, and for **caliph** v. **kaliph**, see **k/c.**

calix and **calyx** The *i* and *y* make a significant difference with these. The first **calix** is the ancient Latin word for the chalice used in the Catholic Church. It maintains its Latin plural *calices*. The second word **calyx** refers to the protective covering of a flower bud (and collectively to the sepals). At bottom it's a neoclassical use of the Greek *kalux* "shell". Its plural in scientific discourse is always *calyces*, but in general use it would be *calyxes*. See **-x** section 3.

calk or **caulk** See **caulk**.

callous or **callus** These complement each other as adjective and noun referring to a thickened patch of skin. (For other examples see under **-ous**.) **Callous** also has the figurative meaning "having a thick skin", i.e. hard-hearted and even brutal.

calque See under **caulk**.

Cambodia The name **Cambodia** has been reinstated for the Southeast Asian republic. It replaces **Kampuchea**, promoted during the Khmer revolution as the proper noncolonial name, and proclaimed in the official name *People's Republic of Kampuchea* in 1979. It has since become notorious, and **Cambodia** continues as the name registered at United Nations.

can or **may** There is no simple division of labor between these, and like any well-worked words they have shades of meaning which are sometimes hard to pin down. **Can** and **may** vacillate between:
> *be able to* (ability)
> *be allowed to* (permission)
> *be possible that* (possibility)

The meaning often depends on context, and the status of the speakers. So **can** could express either ability or permission in "I *can* come with you", depending on whether the speaker ("I") is allowed to exercise his or her discretion in such matters. In a similar way, circumstances would decide whether in "It *can* make things hard for you" **can** expresses ability or possibility.

The most frequent use of **may** nowadays is for the sense of possibility, as in "It may decide our future". Occasionally however, it embodies a sense of permission like **can**, because of the circumstances and the status of the speakers. The point of "They may leave by the first train" could be either permission (if the speaker enjoys lofty status), or else possibility (with neutral status).

When expressing permission, **may** seems more conspicuously polite than **can**. Compare the statements:

You may leave if you wish.

You can leave if you wish.

and the requests:

May I open the door?

Can I open the door?

Both in requests and statements, **may** is felt to represent a higher level of politeness and deference. Usage books have lent their weight to this notion, and in Australian speech it is underscored by the fact that **may** is used much less frequently than **can**. Collins's research (1988) puts the ratio at 1:15.

In written documents the meanings of **can** and **may** are less variable than in speech, partly because the writer's status is less directly involved in the interpretation of the words. **May** is most often used in connection with a possibility, and **can** for ability or possibility.

Compare **could** and **might**. (See further under **modality**.)

Canadian English Outside North America, Canadians are sometimes mistaken for Americans, but the Canadian variety of English is its own unique blend of British and American English. The foundations were laid by American Loyalists in the eighteenth century, who moved into Canada from the eastern seaboard of the USA, and were subsequently joined in the nineteenth century by new immigrants from Britain, especially Scotland. The **Canadian English** vocabulary includes loan words from Canadian Indians, such as *caribou*, *kayak*, *toboggan* and *totem*, which have become part of English worldwide. The same goes for certain French words such as *anglophone*, *francophone*, which were first assimilated into English in Canada through contact with French speakers in Quebec. When written or printed, **Canadian English** varies in the extent to which it reflects the practices of American or British English. In newspapers and magazines, American spellings such as *color*, *center* and *anemic* are typical, whereas Canadian book publishers tend to use the British alternatives (*colour*, *centre*, *anaemic* etc). Recent research also indicates some regional differences, that publishers based in Toronto were more likely to use British spelling, while those in the Prairies and further west use American spelling. The punctuation of **Canadian English** again shows both American and British tendencies, but American practices prevail in the preference for double quote marks in many book publishers, as well as the newspaper and magazine press. Notable exceptions are the University of Toronto Press, and Macmillan, who both prefer British style.

canceled or **cancelled** See under **-l/-ll-**.

candelabra This is a Latin plural, like *bacteria* and *data*. Its singular—for those who know Latin—is *candelabrum*. But common English usage nowadays allows either *candelabrum* or *candelabra* when you refer to a single branching candlestick. And in botanical names such as *candelabra tree* (*Euphorbia ingenuus*), **candelabra** also seems to be singular. In fact, unless you know Latin it's natural to treat **candelabra** as a singular, and then to create an English plural for it: *candelabras*. This new plural is recognised in all major dictionaries, Australian, British and American. So if it's important to say that there was more than one silver candelabra on the table, *candelabras* does it!

candidature or **candidacy** Both mean the status or standing of a candidate, and date from the mid-nineteenth century. Both words are current in Australia, though only **candidature** appears in the ACE corpus. The major American dictionaries label **candidature** as "chiefly Brit.", suggesting that they themselves are more accustomed to **candidacy**. Evidence from the Brown corpus bears this out, with 6 instances of **candidacy** and none of the other.

cannon or **canon** What's in a letter? In these words, it is the difference between war and peace.

The spelling **cannon** is reserved for a large gun, formerly mounted on a carriage, and for the shot fired by it. (It also refers to particular shots made in billiards and croquet.)

Canon is the spelling for two kinds of words, both originally associated with the Church.

1 A **canon** can be either a law or the body of laws associated with a church. From that use it has been extended to mean any law or standard referred to when judging something, or to a reference list of items which are deemed authentic (e.g. the *canon of Shakespeare plays*). The *canon of saints* comprises those officially recognised by the Catholic church.

2 A **canon** may be a member of a religious group living under *canon law*, or a clergyman attached to a cathedral.

Both aspects of **canon** go back to a Latin word meaning "rule or measuring line". Ultimately it was the Greek *kanon*, a derivative of *kan(n)e* meaning "a rod or reed". This, strangely enough, is also the ultimate source of **cannon**. The hollowness of the reed and its usefulness as a firing tube gave rise to **cannon**, whereas the straightness of the rod is the semantic basis of **canon**. Other derivatives of the same Greek word are *cane* and *cannelloni*.

canoe Should it be *canoeing* or *canoing*? See under **-e** section 1f.

cantaloupe or **cantaloup** The fruit known in most of Australia as "rock melon" is sold as **cantaloupe** in Victoria and Tasmania. Like other fruit and vegetable names, its spelling varies somewhat with the greengrocer, and those above are only two of the eight spellings registered in the *Oxford Dictionary*. The first spelling is given preference in major Australian and American dictionaries, though they all highlight the second as a frequent alternative. Among the other spellings noted in both *Oxford* and *Webster's* are *cantalope* and *cantelope*, reflecting a common pronunciation of the word which rhymes with "hope". They also create a folk etymology for the word, in a spurious link with *antelope* (see further under **folk etymology**).

Cantaloupe in fact enshrines the name of a quite different animal. The origins of the word are in *Cantalupo* "song of the wolf", the name of one of the Pope's former estates near Rome on which the fruit (brought from Armenia) was first developed. This confirms that the vowel of the middle syllable should be *a* rather than *e*, but leaves us with several alternatives for the last syllable.

Canton See under **China**.

canvas or **canvass** Dictionaries give the spelling **canvas** to the noun referring to a heavy fabric, and **canvass** to the verb meaning "solicit votes or voting support". However the spelling distinction is only about a century old, and the largest dictionaries (*Oxford*, *Random House* and *Webster's*) note that either spelling has been and is possible.

The noun **canvas** comes from *cannabis* "hemp", and so a single *s* is all that etymology can justify. The verb **canvass** apparently derives from the noun, though authorities disagree on how. Dr Johnson believed it originated in the practice of sifting flour through a piece of canvas, which is figuratively extended to the sifting through of ideas, one of the earliest recorded meanings. The *Oxford Dictionary* however relates the verb to the noun through a jolly practice alluded to by Shakespeare: that of tossing someone in a large canvas sheet, which could by extension suggest using the word for the public thrashing and airing of ideas. Yet neither explanation fully accounts for the sense of soliciting votes, which is also an important element of the verb's meaning.

Spelled as **canvass**, the verb presents no problems when suffixes are added: *canvassed, canvassing*. As **canvas** it raises the question as to whether to leave the *s* single as in *canvased, canvasing*. (See further under **doubling of final consonant**.) The plural of the noun **canvas** is simply *canvases*, on the analogy of *atlas(es)*.

capital or **capitol** In Australia we are fortunate to have spelling consistency in that Canberra is the nation's *capital*, and our federal parliament is on *Capital* Hill. The seat of federal government in the USA—and the name of the building which houses the US Congress—is the **Capitol** (with an upper case initial). It was the name of the temple of Jupiter in ancient Rome. The same name **capitol** (with lower case) is given to any of the state assemblies. The word **capital** is always lower case, and refers to the chief city in any state or country.

capital letters These are so named because they "head" the beginning of a sentence, or a word or expression of special significance. (*Capital* embodies the Latin word *caput* "head".) **Capital letters** are always larger than ordinary letters, and are often different in shape—angular rather than rounded, as is evident in the differences between *F* and *f*, *H* and *h*, and *M* and *m*. Printers refer to them as *upper case letters* because they were stored in the upper section of the tray containing the units of typeface, while the ordinary letters (*lower case letters*) were kept in the lower and larger section of the tray. (For the use of small capital letters, see **small caps**.)

Fewer initial capitals are now used in writing English than in earlier centuries. In the eighteenth century they were used not just for proper names, but also for any words of special note in a sentence, especially the noun or nouns under discussion. This practice survives to some extent in legal documents, which still use more capital letters than any other texts, partly perhaps to provide a focus for the reader in long legal sentences. Elsewhere the use of capitals has contracted to the items mentioned in the following sections 1a to 1f. The use of capitals in abbreviated references (section 3) is more variable, as also in the writing of book titles (see under **titles**). The gradual disappearance of capital letters from proper names which become generic words is discussed in section 2.

Note that British writers and editors are more inclined to use capital letters where Americans would dispense with them. This divergence may well owe something to the fact that the original *Oxford Dictionary* put a capital letter on every headword, whereas *Webster's Dictionary* has them all in lower case, and adds a note to say whether each is usually or often seen with a capital. Australian practices with capitals lie somewhere between those extremes.

1 *Capitals for proper names.*
a) Unique names and designations are always given initial capitals. In some cases, e.g. *Patience Strong*, the capitals serve to confirm that the common words do indeed form a personal name, but mostly the words could only be a personal name anyway. Capitals are used with names whether they are true given names, pseudonyms like *Afferbeck Lauder*, or nicknames such as *Old Silver*. Even the names of fictitious characters like *Edna Everage* are capitalised.

In English there's a tendency to give capital letters even to elements of foreign names which would not be capitalised in the language from which they come. So words like *da, de, della, le, la, van* and *von* quickly acquire capitals, as a glance at the telephone book would show. A Dutch personal name like *van der Meer* becomes *Van Der Meer*, and eventually *Vandermeer*. Celebrated names of this kind, such as *da Vinci, de Gaulle, della Robbia* and *van Gogh*, do resist this capitalisation more strongly. Yet they too acquire a capital letter when used at the beginning of a sentence. On the use of one or two capital letters in names such as *FitzGerald/Fitzgerald* and *McLeod/Macleod*, see under **Fitz-** and **Mac-**.

National and ethnic names are regularly capitalised, whether they refer to nations, races, tribes, and religious or linguistic groups. Hence:

Danish	*Japanese*	*Tongan*
Hausa	*Navaho*	*Tiwi*
Aztec	*Caucasian*	*Tartar*
Christian	*Hindu*	*Moslem*
Semitic	*Altaic*	*Ugric*

References to Australian *Aborigines* and *Aboriginal* people are always capitalised for this reason.

The names of organisations and institutions are to be capitalised, whenever they are set out in full. (For abbreviated references, see below section 3.) Most institutional names consist of a generic element e.g. *department* and another word or words which particularise it e.g. *education*; *immigration and ethnic affairs*. When cited in full, both generic and particularising words are capitalised, but not any small function words linking them (prepositions, articles, conjunctions). See for example:

Department of Immigration and Ethnic Affairs
Museum of Applied Arts and Sciences
Pioneer Concrete Services
Returned Services League of Australia
Printing and Allied Trades Union
Church of Jesus Christ of Latter Day Saints
Royal Society for the Prevention of Cruelty to Animals

The names of vehicles of transport are capitalised, whether they are brand names such as *Boeing 767* or *Ford Falcon*, or unique names such as the *Indian–Pacific* or HMAS *Melbourne*. Individual names such as the latter are normally italicised as well.

b) Official titles and offices are capitalised whenever they are used in reference to a particular holder, e.g.

the Lord Mayor of Brisbane, Sally-Ann Atkinson
the Premier of South Australia, Don Dunstan
the Prime Minister of Australia, John Curtin

But generic or plural references to such offices are left in lower case, as in the *prime ministers of Australia.*

Second and subsequent references to senior title- or office-holders are also capitalised in Australia, even if they are abbreviated. This tendency to capitalise all references to chief executives is not maintained in the USA, where it is often just *Richard Nixon, president of the United States.* In Australia the tendency disappears at lower levels in public organisations, and does not hold in business and industry. For general purposes it would be:

the chairman of Monsanto Chemicals
the managing director of Kodak Australia

However, in-house company publications and prospectuses may capitalise all references to their executives.

c) Geographical names and designations are capitalised whenever they appear in full. In some cases this helps to distinguish them from phrases consisting of identical common words e.g. *Snowy Mountains*, but in most cases the capitals simply help to highlight unique placenames for countries and cities e.g. *India*, *Delhi*, as well as local and street names e.g. *Adelaide Hills*, *Park Street*. They are also used for individual topographical names such as the *Darling River* and the *Atherton Tableland*. The names of special buildings and public structures are also capitalised whenever they are given in full form, as with the *Big Pineapple*, the *King Street Bridge*. Whenever two or more of such names are combined in a single expression, the generic part of the names is pluralised and kept in lower case:

the Murray and Murrumbidgee rivers
the Perth and Sydney town halls

(See further under **geographical names**.)

Compass directions are capitalised when abbreviated: *S, SW, SSW,* but lower-cased when written out in full: *south, southwest, southsouthwest*.

d) References to unique historical events and periods are capitalised if they are the standard designation, e.g. the *Eureka Stockade, World War II*. However ones which are paralleled in different places at different times need not be: *the gold rush, the industrial revolution*.

Special feast days, holidays and public events are given initial capitals:

Good Friday
Yom Kippur
Boxing Day
Melbourne Cup Day
the Adelaide Festival
the City-to-Surf

While the regular names of days and months are capitalised (*Saturday, September*), those for less well-known points in the calendar are left in lower case: *solstice, equinox*.

e) Scientific terms for animals and plants (in Latin) have a capital letter for the genus, but not for the species name:

Larus pacificus
Begonia semperflorens

Both parts of the expression are normally italicised. However the common English names for flora and fauna are not capitalised, even if they are ultimately derived from Latin (or Greek):

funnel-web spider megalomorph wombat diprotodon

(See further under **scientific names**.)

Astronomical names for the stars, planets, asteroids etc. are capitalised:

the Milky Way
the Southern Cross

However when the name consists of both a particular and a generic element (e.g. *the Crab nebula*), only the particular part bears a capital.

f) Commercial names, including trademarks, brandnames and proprietary references should be capitalised as long as their registration is current. Those which become household words do steadily lose the initial capital, witness *masonite, pyrex, thermos*. Yet the value of the trademark seems to be undermined by generic use of the word, and to protect it the current trademark owner will insist on it being capitalised on every appearance. Dictionaries usually indicate when a particular word originated as a trademark, though many a trademark has lapsed in the course of time. The Patents Office in each capital city keeps records on the status of trademarks, for those interested in consulting them. (See further under **trademarks**.)

In computer terminology, the names of computer languages and proprietary programs and systems are often in full caps:

FORTRAN LISP LOTUS 123 MSDOS SGML WORDSTAR UNIX

The names of newspapers, magazines and serials always bear capital letters: the *West Australian*, the *Women's Weekly*, *New Idea*, the *Bulletin*. The Australian Government *Style Manual* (1988) affirms that the definite article (*the*) is not to be capitalised (or italicised) in such references. Note however that *The Economist* and *The Times* in London still insist on such treatment for their respective names.

2 *When capitals disappear from proper names.* Since a *capital letter* marks the fact that a name is unique (or at least relatively so, in the case of "common" personal names such as *John, Thomas* etc.), we might expect them to disappear when the name becomes the byword for something. This has certainly happened to words such as *sandwich* and *wellington*, whose transitions into ordinary words took place long ago. It is also true in the case of most eponymic words (see further under **eponyms**), and most likely to happen when the name itself undergoes some further adjustment, as in *wellies* or *spoonerism*.

Capital letters disappear more slowly from geographical and national names which have become the byword for something. No doubt this is because the regular geographical/national use of the word (with a capital) is current, and some writers flinch at *french polish* (with lower case) because they are so accustomed to *French exports*. Dictionary makers are also reluctant to decapitalise such words because of the inconsistencies they seem to create in a column of compound expressions.

Yet Fowler and others have recommended lower-casing expressions like *french windows* and *venetian blinds*, because the geographical/cultural connection is tenuous and scarcely felt. We might all agree to delete the capital letter in phrases such as *dutch courage*, *french leave* and *chinese burn*, which owe more to Anglo-Saxon prejudice than anything else (see further under **throwaway terms**). Many people would remove the capital from the names of fruits and vegetables, such as *french beans*, *swiss chard*, because they are now grown all over the world. The same is true of animal breeds, e.g. *alsatian*, *siamese*, *friesian*, although official breeding organisations resist this. In books and daily papers however, the trend away from capitals is clear. The Australian Wine Board encourages the use of capitals for grape varieties (but not wine names), so that it should be *Chardonnay*, *Riesling* and *Shiraz*, but *champagne*, *moselle* and *sauterne*. Yet the uncertainty in the general public about this distinction, and the unfamiliarity of the placenames embodied in them, means that many people simply lower-case them all. Few people know the town names enshrined in the names of cheeses: *cheddar*, *edam* and *stilton*, and they are increasingly seen without a capital letter. Overall then the trend is for capitals to disappear, though the trend is retarded in certain contexts. It leaves us with room to choose.

3 *Capitals in abbreviated designations and titles.* After introducing a name or the title in full, most writers abbreviate it for subsequent appearances. It would be cumbersome otherwise. So the *Murray River* becomes *the river*, *Brigadier J. Sands* becomes *the brigadier*, and *the Art Gallery of NSW* becomes *the gallery*. The word retained is lower-cased, which helps to show that it is not the official name, and avoids drawing unnecessary attention to it once it is a "given" rather than "new" item in the stream of information.

Note however that some established abbreviations may be capitalised:
a) *the Reef* (for the Great Barrier Reef); *the Rock* (for Ayers Rock/Uluru).
b) Abbreviated names of organisations continue to bear capitals when they consist of the particular, rather than the generic part of the name, such as *a new look for Veterans Affairs, the budget for Health.*
c) Many organisational names are abbreviated as an initialism or acronym in full caps: *ABC, ACTU, BHP, CSIRO.*

Exceptions to these general principles are the tendency mentioned above in section 1b to capitalise even abbreviated references to the chief executive roles in Australia, e.g. *the Prime Minister, the Vice-Chancellor*; and the tendency to retain capitals in in-house publications, when referring to company or organisation personnel, e.g. *the Personnel Manager, the Directors.* Most publications, including daily papers, will capitalise the word *Government* when it is an abbreviated reference to the federal government, probably to distinguish it from references to state and local government.

For information about the use of capitals in the titles of books and other compositions, see **titles**.

The use of capitals for typographical effects is discussed under **headings** *layout and typography.*

capital punishment See under **corporal**.

capitol or **capital** See **capital**.

cappuccino According to dictionaries, this is the standard spelling for Italian-style coffee made with a topping of frothy steamed milk. The occasional spelling variants with only one *p* or one *c* are not however acknowledged. The reason for the two *p*s and two *c*s is not obvious unless you know that at the core of the word is the Italian word *cappuccio* meaning "hood". The hood gave a name to the *Capuchin* order of friars, and in that name we again note how one of the two *p*s has got lost. (See further under **single for double**.)

The connection with the Capuchins is more important than you might expect. The Capuchin (in Italian *cappuccino*) wore a chestnut-colored robe, and the color itself became known as *cappuccino*. So what could be more natural as the name for a type of coffee which was neither black nor white but brindle! This is the explanation of the *Grande Dizionario della Lingua Italiana* (1962).

In Australian English the plural of *cap(p)uc(c)ino* is normally *cappuccinos*, though in Carlton, Melbourne, and Leichhardt, Sydney it could well be *cappuccini*. (See further under **Italian plurals**.)

capsize This is the one word (of more than one syllable) which must always be spelled *-ize*, even by writers who prefer to use *-ise* in *organise, recognise* etc. (see further under **-ise/-ize**). This is because the second syllable is not something added to the root, but an integral part of it: it originated in the Spanish verb *cabezar* "sink by the head", as far as we can tell.

carat, karat or **caret** Both **carat** and **karat** are used in assessing the value of gold, though the first is much more common than the second. In **American English** the two spellings sometimes correspond with different measures, **carat** being a unit of weight (about 200 milligrams), and **karat** a measure of its purity. (Pure gold is 24 karats.) Yet **carat** often serves for both according to the major American dictionaries, and in Britain this is standard practice. The abbreviation for **carat** is *ct.* or *car.*, and for **karat** when used is *kt.*

Both **karat** and **carat** seem to have developed from the same source, though neither comes very close to the Arabic *qirat*; rather they reflect the mediating languages: Greek *keration* and Italian *carato*. Both meanings (weight, and purity) were current in sixteenth century English, and the fact that the second one is sometimes spelled *caract* suggests that it may have developed under the influence of the Middle English word *caracter*, which was later used to mean both "sign, symbol" and "worth, value".

Different altogether is the word **caret**, a technical word used by editors and printers for the omission mark λ. Borrowed from Latin in the seventeenth century, it means literally "(something) is lacking"—whatever is supplied. The use of the mark is explained with other proofreading marks in Appendix VI.

carburettor, carburetter or **carburetor** The spellings with two *t*s are usual in Australia. **Carburettor** is more common and found in many a car maintenance manual, but **carburetter** has its adherents, at least in Western Australia. The spellings with two *t*s are preferred in Britain, in keeping with the practice of doubling the last consonant before suffixes when the stress comes late in the word. (See further under **doubling of final consonant**.) With stress on the first syllable, **carburetor** is preferred in the USA.

Whatever the spelling, the word stands as a monument to a little known verb/noun *carburet*, coined at a time when chemical compounds were named with the addition of the French suffix *-uret*. The same compounds are nowadays christened with *-ide*.

carcass or **carcase** For many people these spellings are interchangeable, although for some, they carry slightly different meanings. The Department of Agriculture prefers the spelling **carcase** for an animal body prepared at the abattoir for human consumption (with head and entrails removed); and **carcass** is then used for the bodily remains of animal or human in other contexts. Nonspecialists in meat do not usually make this distinction, and may use either spelling. Some newspaper style guides prefer **carcase** (notably the *Age*, *Adelaide Advertiser*), where others are for **carcass**.

In fact **carcase** is closer to the original pronunciation of the word, which was spelled as *carcays* and *carkeis* in Middle English. Those spellings were replaced in the sixteenth century by the French *carcasse*, and **carcass** has been the one preferred in dictionaries since Dr Johnson. The *Oxford Dictionary* notes however that **carcass** and **carcase** were almost equally common in the late nineteenth century; and **carcase** is still in general use, perhaps because it seems to make sense of the second syllable (see further under **folk etymology**). Australian English may even have made something of the first syllable, deriving the colloquial verb *cark/kark* "die" from it (see under **kark**).

cardinal or **ordinal** See under **ordinary**.

cargo For the plural of this word, see **-o**.

cark or **kark** See kark.

caroled or **carolled** See under **-l/-ll-**.

carpe diem This Latin phrase means "seize the day", or less literally "make the most of the here and now". The phrase originated with the Roman poet Horace (*Odes* I xi 8), and was taken up by the English poets Donne and Marvell in the seventeenth century. It has enjoyed new life in our own century as the theme of a successful film *Dead Poets Society*.

case See **in case of, in case, in the case of**.

cases Nouns and pronouns turn up in various roles in clauses, and their particular function in a given sentence is known as their *case*.

In many languages, the *case* is associated with a particular ending or inflection. English nouns show it only for the genitive or possessive, as in: *cat's breakfast*; *today's program* etc., although several pronouns adjust their forms for the accusative as well as the genitive:

nominative:	I	he	she	we	they	who
accusative:	me	him	her	us	them	whom
genitive:	my	his	her	our	their	whose

In some languages such as German, there are separate *accusative* and *dative* forms for many nouns, and Latin had them for the *ablative* and *vocative* cases as well. (See further under **ablative**, **dative** and **vocative**.) Aboriginal languages use other cases which are hardly found in European languages at all, including the *instrumental*, the *locative*, the *ergative* (subject of a transitive verb), and the *privative* (expressing the lack of something).

In the absence of distinctive case endings, English nouns are sometimes assigned a case on the basis of their function in the clause. So a word (or phrase) that is the subject of the verb can be said to be in the *nominative (or subjective) case*, while the word or phrase which is the object of the verb is *accusative* (or *objective*) in its case. The so-called *dative case* is found only residually in English, when there's an indirect object expressed without a preceding preposition (see further under **dative** and **objects**).

Modern *case grammar* works by the functions of English words in clauses, but uses its own analysis and terminology. Thus the grammatical subject of an active verb is typically the *agent*, while the subjects of passive verbs are the *patient*.

castor or **caster** These spellings are sometimes interchangeable, sometimes not. If you're referring to (1) a particular type of fur hat, or (2) the oil used in making perfumes, the spelling is **castor** because of their historical association with the beaver (in Greek *kastor*). The *castor-oil plant* which provides a similar oil for medicinal purposes is also spelled *-or*.

Caster refers naturally enough to one who casts (as in a *caster of pearls before swine*), because it's the agent word from the English verb *cast*. It should also spell the name of any object which casts, such as the container which dispenses sugar, pepper or some other condiment, and any of the swiveling wheels attached underneath movable furniture. The spelling **caster** is indeed used for them in American English, but not necessarily in British or Australian English, where it shares the field with **castor**. The etymology has not been obvious enough to separate them from the other **castor** words, and the overlap between *-er* and *-or* generally is also a factor in the confusion. (See further under **-er**.)

Yet there's hope on the sugar front in Australia, where the fine grade of sugar is now labeled *caster sugar*, and this should influence the spelling of the sugar dispenser. (It would seem perverse to dispense *caster sugar* from a **castor**.)

cata-/cath- This Greek prefix means "down or down to the end", and so also "complete". It appears in a number of loanwords, such as:

> *cataclysm catalepsy catalogue catalyst catapult cataract catarrh
> catastrophe catheter cathode catholic*

The form **cath-** occurs before words that began in Greek with an *h*.

The word *catechise* involves the same prefix, and means literally "din into a person's ears" and so "instruct orally"—the original rote learning.

catalogue or **catalog** See under **-gue/-g**.

catalyse or **catalyze** See under **-yse**.

catapult This is the only spelling recognised for this word, and some dictionaries recognise only one pronunciation for it (which has the last syllable pronounced like the first one in *ultimate*).

However a little attention to what people say shows that there are several pronunciations for the last syllable, one of which makes it sound like the first syllable in *poultry*. Since this is a diphthong, it's not surprising that an alternative spelling *catapault* has been sighted several times over in a highly respected newspaper (Weiner, 1984) without being subedited out. The word is one to keep your eye on.

catchup, catsup or **ketchup** See under **ketchup**.

catenatives These verbs resemble and yet differ from auxiliaries. Common examples are:

He seems to think the same way.
We began planning the Christmas party.
They remembered leaving the keys under the mat.
You love to surprise your family.

Like auxiliaries, **catenatives** forge links with other nonfinite verbs, though with *to* infinitives or *-ing* forms, not ''bare'' infinitives. The **catenatives** also differ from auxiliaries in the meanings they express. Instead of paraphrasing the modals like other semi-auxiliaries (see under **auxiliaries**), they qualify the action of the following verb (as do *seem, begin*), or else set up a mental perspective on it (as do *remember, love*). Other examples like *seem* are:

appear cease chance continue fail finish get happen help keep manage stop tend

Others like *remember* are:

attempt consider detest endeavor expect forget hate hope intend like prefer regret resent risk strive try want

Note that some **catenatives** can take both *to* infinitives and *-ing* constructions, others only one of them.

Catenatives are relatively new in the classification of English verbs, and grammarians are still debating which belong to the class. The *Comprehensive Grammar of English* (1985) admits only the first group mentioned above, whereas the *Introduction to the Grammar of English* (1984) allows both. The latter questions whether a third group of verbs could also belong, ones which also link up with a nonfinite verb, but which require a noun phrase in between:

He advised her parents to come.

Other examples are:

ask entreat invite oblige remind request teach tell urge

These verbs typically express some kind of speech act.

cathode or **kathode** See under **k/c**.

Catholic or **catholic** What's in a capital letter? Written without a capital, **catholic** is an uncontroversial adjective meaning ''universal, all-embracing''. With a capital, it begins to be the focus of theological argument. Technically **Catholic** refers to the whole Christian church, the Church universal, irrespective of orthodoxies and denominations. However the word is also used by many

Australians to refer to the Catholic church based in Rome, and to distinguish it from the Orthodox churches (Greek and Russian). At this point **Catholic** equals *Roman Catholic*, but it may seem to preempt the more comprehensive sense of the word. In Great Britain a further issue arises in the need to distinguish between *Roman Catholic* and *Anglo-Catholic* (a "high" movement within the Church of England), and the term **Catholic** is often qualified one way or the other. This use of *Roman Catholic* is alive among Protestants in Australia too, although Australian Catholics very much prefer to be called just *Catholics*. The presence of both Irish and Italian Catholic traditions in Australia makes it a neutral term, and one which contrasts sufficiently with *Protestant*.

cauldron or **caldron** Whatever the brew, **cauldron** is the usual spelling in Australia and Britain. In the USA the field is divided, **caldron** being *Webster's* first preference, **cauldron** that of *Random House*. Both are respellings of the original loanword *caudron* from medieval French, designed to show its connection with the Latin *caldarium* "hot bath". The spelling **caldron** is the earlier of the two, dating from the Middle Ages, whereas **cauldron** is a Renaissance respelling. Dr Johnson's dictionary put its weight behind **caldron**.

caulk, calk or **calque** These three spellings represent several developments from the Latin verb *calcare* "tread".

1 To **caulk** (a boat or anything else) is to press a filler substance into the spaces between the pieces of wood, tile etc. of which it's made, in order to make it water- or air-tight. The spelling **caulk** is given preference for this over **calk** in all major dictionaries throughout the English-speaking world.

2 **Calk** is the primary spelling for the small projection on a horseshoe designed to prevent slipping. **Caulk** is registered as the secondary spelling for this meaning. In Australia **calk** is also used of an industrial process in which a design is transferred by pressure from one sheet to another. This usage is occasionally spelled in the French way as **calque**.

3 **Calque** is the regular spelling for a "loan translation", the linguistic analogue of that industrial process. A **calque** is an expression created in one language to parallel a particular word or phrase in another. It matches the original expression in structure, but slots into it words from the borrowing language. For an English example of a **calque**, think of *commonwealth* coined in the sixteenth century to represent the Latin "res publica". They are equivalent if we allow that adjectives and nouns are differently arranged in the two languages. (See further under **Commonwealth**.)

caveat emptor This Latin phrase borrowed into English in the sixteenth century means "let the buyer beware". In law it expresses the principle that the seller of goods is not responsible for the quality of the goods, unless the goods are under warranty. In more general use it urges buyers to subject purchases to close scrutiny.

caviar or **caviare** See under **-e** section 3.

c.c. or **cc** This abbreviation found at the foot of business and institutional letters stands for "carbon copy". It is followed by the name of one or more people, and it indicates to the addressee of the letter that an exact copy has been sent to those other people. Its purpose may be to save the addressee the effort of sending further copies to those people, or to warn him or her that they too have been informed about the contents of the letter. For more about commercial letter writing conventions, see under **commercialese**.

Note that **c.c.** also stands for "cubic centimetre(s)" in measurements of volume, although its place among SI units has been taken by cm^3. (See Appendix IV.)

CE This abbreviation coming after a date means "Common Era". (See further under **BC**.)

-ce/-cy See **-nce/-ncy**.

-ce/-ge Words ending in **-ce** or **-ge** need special attention when suffixes are added to them. Most words ending in *-e* drop it before adding any suffix beginning with a vowel. (Think of *move*, *moving* and *movable*; and see further under **-e**). But with **-ce** and **-ge** words it depends on which vowel the suffix begins with.

If it begins with *a* (as in *-able*, *-age*, *-al* or *-an*) or *o* (as in *-ose*, *-ous* or *-osity*), the word remains unchanged and keeps its *e*. See for instance:

replaceable manageable outrageous

In words like those, the *e* serves a vital purpose in preserving the *c* or *g* as a soft sound. Compare *replaceable* with *implacable*, and *outrageous* with *analogous*.

But if the suffix begins with *e* (as in *-ed* or *-er*), *i* (as in *-ing*, *-ism* or *ist*) or *y*, words ending in *-ce* or *-ge* can drop their *e*. Think of the following words based on *race*:

raced racer racing racism racist racy

The soft *c* is maintained in each of them through the vowel of the suffix.

Note the different spellings of *forcible* and *unenforceable*, *tangible* and *changeable*, which preserve soft sounds in the middle by different means. The words ending in *-ible* have come direct from Latin, while those with *-eable* have been formed in modern English. (See further under **-able/-ible**. See also **-eable**.)

-ce/-se In pairs such as *advice/advise* and *device/devise*, the *-ce* and *-se* have complementary roles with **-ce** marking the noun and **-se** the verb. The **-ce** is of course pronounced "s", and the **-se** "z". In Australia and Britain this spelling convention also affects *license* and *practice*, so that *license* and *practise* must be verbs, while *licence* and *practice* are nouns. But with those words there's no difference in the way verb and noun are pronounced, and we need a little grammar to get *-se* and *-ce* in the right place. In the USA one spelling predominates for each word: *license* and *practice* (whatever their grammatical role). In the American Brown database they vastly outnumber *licence* and *practise* (by 53:0 and 179:3 respectively), though the latter are recognised as minority variants in American dictionaries.

Regional differences also emerge in the British spelling of *defence, offence* and *pretence,* as opposed to American *defense, offense* and *pretense.* The American practice spares them the inconsistency of pairs such as *defence/defensive, offence/offensive* and *pretence/pretension,* an extra detail which those in the British tradition have to master. (Compare *defense/defensive* etc.) The spellings *defense, offense* and *pretense* are not only more straightforward, but just as old as the spellings with **-ce**.

The **-se** spellings have been used in this book for *defense, offense* and *pretense,* for the reasons just given.

-cede/-ceed Why should words like *exceed, proceed* and *succeed* be spelled one way, and *concede, intercede, precede, recede* and *secede* in another?

All these words go back to the Latin verb *cedere* "yield or move", but the second group are much more recent arrivals in English, mostly post-Renaissance, whereas the first set were actively used in the fourteenth and fifteenth centuries. Middle English scribes turned the Latin *ced-* into **-ceed** to bring those words into line with native English ones such as *feed* and *need,* which were pronounced the same way. The words ending in **-cede** came into English from written sources during the Renaissance, and keep their bookish flavor and their classical spelling as a result.

This helps to explain the difference between *proceed* and *precede,* as well as the further anomaly of *proceeding*(s) and *procedure.* The classical spelling of *procedure* confirms that it was borrowed later into English (in the seventeenth century). A further point to note is that the *-ced-* spelling goes with the foreign suffix *-ure,* whereas the **-ceed** goes with the native English *-ing.*

For the choice between *supersede* and *supercede,* see under that heading.

cedilla This is one of the less familiar foreign accents which comes into English with a handful of loanwords from French and Portuguese. Some examples are the French *façade* and *garçon,* and Portuguese *curaçao.*

In both languages the cedilla keeps a *c* soft (i.e. sounding like "s") before *a, o* and *u.* Before *e* and *i* it's not needed, because those vowels keep the *c* soft anyway. The cedilla comes and goes in the spelling of French verbs, depending on the following vowel:

> *nous annonçons* "we announce"   *vous annoncez* "you announce"
> *vous recevez* "you receive"   *ils reçoivent* "they receive"

In English the cedilla on loanwords is often left out because of its absence from many typewriters and wordprocessors. It is the only accent to be written beneath the letter it affects.

The name **cedilla** comes from the Spanish *zedilla*. It means "little *z*"—a rough way of describing its shape. It was first used in writing French words in the sixteenth century, as an alternative for *cz* in *faczade* or for *ce* in *receoivent*.

Celsius or **Centigrade** Celsius is the official name for the **Centigrade** scale of temperature used within the metric system. The scale was devised by the Swedish astronomer Anders Celsius (1701–44), using the freezing and boiling points of pure water as its reference points. They establish a scale from 0° to 100°. The **Celsius** scale dovetails with the Kelvin scale of temperature, which offers an "absolute zero" temperature of –273°, the theoretical temperature at which gas molecules have zero kinetic energy. **Celsius** temperatures were adopted in Australia along with other metric measures in the 1970s, to replace the Fahrenheit system. Older kitchen stoves, and cookery books, are of course calibrated in degrees Fahrenheit. In the USA, temperature is still generally measured on the Fahrenheit scale. (See further under **Fahrenheit** and **metrication**.)

The name **Celsius** is preferred to the metric name **Centigrade** as a way of highlighting the names of famous scientists, which is part of the naming policy of the Bureau International de Poids et Mesures.

Celtic or **Keltic** As used in Australia, the name **Celtic** often refers to the people of Wales, Scotland and Ireland, who emigrated across Europe more than 2000 years ago. Thus the term *Anglo-Celtic* used in Australia refers collectively to immigrants from all parts of the British Isles, as opposed to those who emigrated from continental Europe and elsewhere.

Yet in the pre-Christian era the original *Celts* left traces of their civilisation in various places across continental Europe, in Switzerland, Spain and in France. The people of present-day Brittany still speak a **Celtic** language: *Breton* which is closely related to Welsh. Together they make up the larger body of **Celtic** speakers (over one million), whereas the speakers of Scottish and Irish Gaelic total between one and two hundred thousand, according to estimates in the *Cambridge Encyclopedia of Language* (1987).

The spelling **Keltic** reflects the original Greek name for the Celts: *Keltoi*. It has been more used by scholars than writers at large, and serves to distinguish the ancient nomadic people from their twentieth century descendants.

cement or **concrete** These words are sometimes interchanged, as when a *concrete mixer* is referred to as a *cement mixer*. **Cement** is of course the bonding agent in **concrete**, although it is the steel reinforcing or crushed stones which give concrete its strength, not the cement. Using the word **cement** instead of **concrete** may be seen as an everyday instance of *meronymy*: referring to something by means of one of its constituents. (See further under **metonymy**.)

censor or **censure** As verbs these seem to overlap because both involve strong negative judgements. They differ in that **censor** implies official control of information which is deemed dangerous for the public, and results in the proscription or banning of such things as books, films or news items. It is a preventive measure, whereas **censure** means voicing public criticism of things already done, as when members of parliament are censured in a formal motion.

As nouns the two words go their separate ways, **censor** as an **agent word** "one who censors", and **censure** as the **abstract noun** for "strongly voiced criticism".

centennial or **centenary** Some Australians worry more than they need about which of these words to use. In the USA, Canada and New Zealand, they serve as both nouns and adjectives, and there are no restrictions on which you use when referring to a one hundredth year celebration. In British usage however there has been a reluctance to use **centennial** as a noun, which probably stems from a note in the *Oxford Dictionary* that **centenary** has the better pedigree for use as a noun, as well as Fowler's emphasis on the analogous forms of *bicentenary, tercentenary, quatercentenary* etc. and *sesquicentenary* (150 years). The argument has its force if one is looking from one centennial celebration to the next, but otherwise the enormous gap in time between the actual celebrations makes it relatively unimportant.

center or **centre** See under -re/-er.

centi- This prefix means "one hundredth", as in *centimetre, centisecond* and other words of measurement used within the metric system (see further under **metrication** and **number prefixes**). Yet **centi-** is derived from the Latin word *centum* meaning "one hundred", and this is its meaning in words like *centenary* and *century*, borrowed direct from Latin.

Note by way of curiosity that most *centipedes* do not actually have 100 feet or legs (50 pairs), but anywhere between 15 and 170 pairs. (Compare **millipede**: see under **milli-**.)

Centigrade or **Celsius** See under **Celsius**.

centuries In our Anglo-Saxon historical tradition, we always number **centuries** by thinking ahead to the boundary with the next one. So the *nineteenth century* includes any dates from 1801 to 1900; and the *twentieth century*, all those from 1901 to 2000. The tradition is based on the fact that the first century of the Christian era dates from AD 1 to AD 100, and could not be otherwise since there was no AD 0.

Whatever the justification, this system of reckoning seems rather perverse. For one thing, it runs counter to our ordinary numerical system, in which we think of decimal sets running from 0 to 9 in each "ten", or 00 to 99 in each "hundred". We might reasonably expect the present *century* to include dates from 1900 to 1999: at least they would all have the number 19.. in common.

But no, it's 1901 to 2000, and the third millennium will begin on 1 January 2001.

That will also be the first day of the *twenty-first century*, again somewhat perversely, since all but the last year in it will begin with *20..* (2010, 2020 etc.). Yet the convention of referring to the years of one century by the next one on is thoroughly established in English, and in other (north) European languages including French, Dutch and German. In both Italian and Spanish however, a reference to a century such as the *Quattrocento* or *el Siglo XIV* means "the *1400s*" (the famous century of Renaissance painters). In formal English *quattrocento* would be translated as "the fifteenth century", though expressions such as *the 1400s* recommend themselves as a more direct, if less formal equivalent.

There are a number of abbreviations for indicating particular centuries:

C15 15C 15th century XV century   XVth century

The first two are often used in note-taking, but they could be ambiguous in print unless the *C* is in a larger font than the numbers.

None of the abbreviations is actually recommended by the standard style manuals. The Chicago *Manual of Style* speaks for them all in saying that any century references should be spelled out in full, as *fifteenth century* etc. This advice is in keeping with their general reluctance to use abbreviations in discursive writing. But abbreviations of all kinds are appearing more and more in factual publications, and the abbreviations for **centuries** will no doubt do the same. (See further under **dates**.)

ceramic or **keramic**   See under **k/c**.

ceremonial or **ceremonious**   Both words relate to the noun *ceremony*, and **ceremonial** even substitutes for it occasionally: *the ceremonials associated with graduating*. But as an adjective **ceremonial** simply means "used in, or as of a ceremony", for example *a ceremonial sword*. **Ceremonious** meanwhile often suggests a certain satisfaction in ceremony for its own sake. It may imply pretentiousness and self-importance, especially in an unstructured situation: *a ceremonious nod from their neighbor*.

c'est à dire   In French it means "that is to say". The Latin abbreviation **i.e.** says the same in fewer letters, and its efficiency is important in documentary writing. In more discursive writing the bulkier French phrase may serve to underscore a reformulation of ideas which the author is about to offer.

c'est la vie   This phrase, borrowed quite recently from French, means "That's life". It gives elegant expression to an acceptance of the way things are or how they happen. The equivalent Italian phrase **che sarà sarà** "what will be will be" is much less used, though it was originally borrowed into English in the sixteenth century. It was popularised in the 1950s as the chorus line of a song.

ceteris paribus Borrowed from Latin, this phrase means "all other things being equal". It is used in argument to limit a conclusion or generalisation on which writers feel they may be challenged. It provides academic protection for their claim, since it is usually impossible to show whether all other things are equal or not.

cf. In English scholarly writing this stands for the Latin *confer* meaning "compare". In Latin it is a bald imperative, but in English it invites the reader to look elsewhere for a revealing comparison.

chacun à son goût Drinking habits and gout are not really uppermost in this phrase borrowed from French, which means "each one to his own taste". In French the word *chacun* is masculine, though the phrase is intended as a general observation: everyone has their own tastes. It is often used to preempt debate based on differences in taste, and it therefore functions in the same way as the older Latin maxim: **de gustibus** *non est disputandum* "concerning matters of taste there can be no argument". Both the French and Latin sayings can also be used more offhandedly, to say "There's no accounting for taste".

chairman This word has come under fire from feminist action groups, along with many other compounds involving the word *man*. (See further under **man**.) As with other issues raised in the sexist language debate, the problem is seen differently by different people, and so the solutions vary.

Some critics are primarily concerned that **chairman** seems to make women in that role invisible. The alternatives they suggest are *chairwoman* or *lady chairman*, which draw attention to the sex of the person concerned, as do terms of address such as *Madam Chairman* and *Madam Chair*.

Others feel that **chairman** fosters the general expectation that only a man could fulfil that role. They propose nonexclusive, gender-free alternatives, such as *chairperson* or *chair*. Yet neither of these seems very satisfactory. *Chair* combines awkwardly with any verb implying human action, as in:

The chair reported the minutes from the previous meeting.

And *chairperson* suffers from the known fact that it is usually used as a substitute for *chairwoman* (men do not usually resort to *chairperson*), so it too has acquired a gender coloring. The best way out of the impasse may be to use a completely independent term, such as *convener, coordinator, moderator* or *president*.

Note that some women who chair meetings are quite content to be called *chairmen*. They see **chairman** simply as a functional title, like that of *secretary* and *treasurer*, which indicates a person's official role in an organisation.

For further discussion of these issues, see under **nonsexist language**.

chaise longue This French expression meaning "long chair" is applied in English to that eminently relaxing piece of furniture which supports the legs in a resting position, and keeps the upper body at a sufficient angle to allow us to keep up a conversation.

Because of the comfort it offers, the **chaise longue** is sometimes referred to as a *chaise lounge*—with just a slight rearrangement of the letters of the second word. It is after all a chair in which you lounge about, and it shows folk etymology in action, trying to make sense of an obscure foreignism (see **folk etymology**). This alternative was recorded well over a century ago in Ogilvie's *Imperial Dictionary* (1855), and it's recognised in the *Macquarie Dictionary* (1991) as well as *Random House* and *Webster's*. If it is a *chaise lounge*, the French order of words still helps to distinguish it from the *lounge chair* which is less obviously designed for lounging in—and rather for the Australian *lounge room*.

American dictionaries present three possible plurals for the phrase: *chaise longues* and *chaise lounges*, which treat it like an ordinary English compound (see under **plurals**); and *chaises longues*, the all-French plural, but the least likely of the three in Australian English.

chalky or **chalkie** The endings distinguish the adjective **chalky** "covered with or consisting of chalk" from the noun **chalkie**, one whose professional tool is a piece of chalk, which may mean either a teacher or, before computerisation, a stock exchange assistant.

chamois, chammy or **shammy** Chamois is the French name for the European antelope from whose skin a soft leather was originally prepared. Similar leathers prepared from the skins of goats or sheep are also called **chamois**, and even **chammy** or **shammy**, reflecting the sound of the word in English. Several major dictionaries associate the spelling **shammy** with the soft polishing cloth made of imitation leather—*sham chamois*, as you might say—so that the spelling also provides a folk etymology.

channeled or **channelled** The choice between these spellings is discussed at **-l/-ll-**.

chaperone or **chaperon** These spellings are given equal billing in the *Macquarie Dictionary* (1991); and there are arguments for both. **Chaperon** is the normal French way of writing the word, and it's given preference in British and American dictionaries. However **chaperone** reflects the ordinary Australian pronunciation, and also the fact that a **chaperone** is usually female. For other examples of French words given a feminine *-e*, see under **-e** section 3.

chart or **charter** These verbs can be mistaken for each other, particularly when it comes to the past forms *charted* and *chartered*. As Australians pronounce them, they're indistinguishable (whereas in most American pronunciation, the *r* of the second syllable sets them apart; and in most British pronunciation the vowels of the second syllable are different).

The verb **chart** is a matter of cartography or mapping, either literally or figuratively. During the eighteenth century, the coasts of Australia were finally *charted*; in the twentieth century, areas of social and political behavior are what remain uncharted.

As a verb **charter** means "set up by charter", and so institutions may be *chartered* to fulfill public functions; and individuals such as *chartered accountants* or *chartered engineers* have obtained the right to engage in professional practice. The idea of being hired under a specialised contract underlies the *chartering* of a vehicle (a bus, ship, helicopter etc.), but the fact that it means contracting to cover a particular geographical distance brings it close to **chart**.

chassis In the plural this French loanword is usually left unchanged:
A pile of rusty automobile chassis lay at the foot of the cliff.
An English plural *chassises* is however recognised in *Webster's Dictionary*.

chateaus or **chateaux** For the choice of plurals, see **-eau**. In French the word has a circumflex but it is now rare in English.

chauvinism This word has always represented extreme attitudes: bigoted devotion to one's own nation, race or sex, and a corresponding contempt for those who do not belong to it. The word enshrines the name of Nicolas Chauvin, an old soldier of Napoleon I whose blind devotion to his leader was dramatised in popular plays of the 1820s and 30s. The chauvinists of the twentieth century are those who assume the superiority of their own country or race, and close their minds to the value of others. (See further under **racist language**.)

The phrase *male chauvinism*, dating only from 1970, is the attitude which assumes the superiority of men over women. (See further under **feminist**.)

che sarà sarà See under **c'est la vie**.

check or **cheque** The English-speaking world at large uses the first spelling for many applications of the word as a verb meaning "stop, restrain, verify, tick", and the corresponding nouns. Only when it comes to money is there a great divide, with Americans continuing to use **check** for a personal bank note, while **cheque** is preferred by Britons and Australians.

Cheque is very much a latter-day spelling, first appearing at the beginning of the eighteenth century. It was used by the Bank of England to refer to the counterfoil issued for a money order— literally a way of checking each one and preventing forgery. **Cheque** soon became the name for the money order itself in Britain. The system was adopted somewhat later in the USA, though the spelling has remained **check**.

In the same way British English of the eighteenth century adopted the spelling **chequer** for a pattern of squares, as in the game *chequers* and the *chequerboard*, as well as the figurative *chequered career*. It replaced the longer established *checker* which has continued in American English. American motoring writers are therefore spared the anomaly that confronts their British and Australian counterparts, of referring to a *chequered flag* which has black and white *checks* on it.

chef d'oeuvre Borrowed from seventeenth century French, this phrase means "masterpiece". More literally, it means "the culmination of the work". It can be used of an outstanding work in any artistic field: literature, music, opera, painting, sculpture, and even gastronomy. But when your hired cook produces *hors d'oeuvres* which are a **chef d'oeuvre**, that is a lucky coincidence. (See **hors d'oeuvre**, and **magnum opus**.)

chemist, pharmacist or **druggist** See under **pharmacist**.

cheque and **chequer** See under **check**.

cherubs or **cherubim** See under **-im**.

chevron This refers to a V-shaped bar. One or more chevrons are set horizontally on the sleeves of military and police uniforms to show the rank of the wearer.

In mathematics and statistics, a chevron-shaped mark turned horizontally has a specific meaning depending on its direction: $<$ before a number means "is less than", and $>$ means "is greater than". Computer programmers use the same sign to indicate:
- take input from, and
- direct output to.

In computer programming, chevrons are used in pairs like *angle brackets* to frame special codes and commands (see **brackets** section 1). Note however the angle brackets used in mathematics have a broader span, $\langle\ \rangle$ as opposed to $<\ >$, where full type resources are available.

chiasmus This word, borrowed from classical Greek, refers to an elegant figure of speech. It expresses a contrast or paradox in two parallel statements, the second of which reverses the order of items in the first:

Martyrs create faith; faith does not create martyrs.
Glory to God in the highest, and on earth peace towards men.

As the examples show, the second statement may play on the words and/or the structure of the first. Both are played on in the following newspaper headline, highlighting the opening up of the Berlin Wall in 1989:

TUMBLING WALL SENDS WALL STREET SOARING

The **chiasmus** has a pleasing symmetry in which the contrasting statements are balanced. It draws attention to word order, which we tend to take for granted in English prose because it is largely regularised. It provides elegant variation on the standard patterns of clause and phrase.

chilli, chili, chile or **chilly** The first three are alternative spellings for a pepper or a peppery vegetable discovered in the New World. In Britain and Australia the primary spelling is **chilli**, which is believed to render the original

Mexican Indian word most exactly. But in American English the spelling **chili** is given preference and often featured in the spicy Mexican dish *chili con carne*. The actual Spanish form of the word is **chile**, which also appears in *chile con carne* where Spanish is better known.

In Australian and American English, the fourth spelling above is a separate word meaning "rather cold", mostly used in relation to the ambient temperature. But in British English it's yet another possible spelling for the pepper, according to the *Oxford Dictionary* (1989).

China Since 1949 it has been important to distinguish two Chinas:

Chinese People's Republic = Mainland China (capital: Beijing)
Chinese Nationalist Republic = Taiwan (capital: Taipei)

The first has a population of approximately one billion, the second about twenty million.

In *Mainland China* the communist revolution has led to far-reaching linguistic reforms, including the development of a standard form of Chinese *Putonghua*, which involved the modifying and streamlining of more than 2000 traditional characters of the Chinese system. Like "Mandarin" it's based on the Beijing dialect, but serves as the native language of more than half the people. Other major dialects are clustered in the south of the country:

- *Wu* in Shanghai and on the Yangzi valley;
- *Yue* in Guangzhou and Guandong;
- *Min* in Taiwan and adjoining provinces on the mainland;
- *Hakka* used by small groups within the other southern dialect areas.

A phonetic alphabet *Pinyin* has been used to develop romanised scripts for minority language groups, and for children beginning their education. It also has public uses on street signs and the railway system. *Pinyin* was officially adopted in 1938, though it was far from the first attempt to romanise Chinese characters. Earlier systems include the *Wade-Giles*, developed by British scholars in the nineteenth century; *Gwoyeu Romatzyh*, designed by Chinese scholars in the 1920s; and *Latinxua* devised by Russians in the 1930s. *Pinyin's* roots are in the third, but it differs in the spelling of certain consonants. Some which strike westerners as unusual are the use of:

q for pre-palatal "ch"
x for pre-palatal "sh"
zh for retroflex "j"
c for alveolar "ts"

Amid these linguistic movements, many Chinese placenames have changed, at least in the forms now reaching the western world. Some of the most dramatic are the substitution of *Beijing* for "Peking", *Guangzhou* for "Canton", and *Tianjin* for "Tientsin". Others less revolutionary are *Xian* for "Sian", *Shandong* for "Shantung", *Chong Qing* for "Chungking" and *Nanjing* for "Nanking". The changes of consonants in those examples show which letters are typically affected, but it's a good idea to check Chinese names in a large up-to-date atlas.

Chinaman or **Chinese** In a number of books on usage, the word **Chinaman** is said to have derogatory overtones. If so they may originate in its being a slightly awkward formation by comparison with the more regular *Dutchman*, *Englishman*, *Frenchman* etc. (combinations of adjective plus noun, rather than noun plus noun). More likely it's a matter of colonial prejudice. In Australia nowadays it seems old-fashioned rather than derogatory, and that is probably sufficient reason for seeking an alternative. A neutral substitute can be found in using **Chinese** as a noun, though some people find it unsatisfactory for use in the singular: *a Chinese*. Possible paraphrases are *Chinese person* or *Chinese citizen*. (See further under **racist language**.)

Note that the abbreviation *ABC* for "Australian-born Chinese" is used by demographers, but it would seem curt in other contexts.

chiseled or **chiselled** For the choice between these, see under **-l/-ll-**.

chlorophyll or **chlorophyl** The first spelling is given preference in all English dictionaries, and it recommends itself on grounds of etymology. The word is a modern compound of the Greek *chloro-* "green" and *phyllon* "leaf". The alternative spelling **chlorophyl**, used occasionally in American English, connects inappropriately with another Greek word *phyle* "tribe". Yet the word's etymology is probably unknown to most people, and no-one reading **chlorophyl** would mistake its meaning. The extra *l* at the end may seem inessential, as with double consonants in a number of foreign borrowings. For other cases, see **single for double**.

chord or **cord** Is it vocal *chords* or vocal *cords*?

In technical writing *cords* is preferred; but the *vocal cords* are so often mentioned in connection with sounds and singing that writers are tempted to use *vocal chords*, and *Macquarie*, *Collins* and other major dictionaries register it as an alternative.

Both **chord** and **cord** derive from a Greek and then Latin word spelled *chorda*, which meant both "gut" and "string of a musical instrument". In the Middle Ages it was just **cord**, and this is still the spelling for plain ordinary string etc., and for anatomical uses of the word, as in *spinal cord* and *umbilical cord*. The *vocal cords* are however not cord-like in shape, and are more accurately described as "vocal folds".

The spelling **chord** in mathematics results from the "touching up" of **cord** during the English Renaissance, when many words with classical ancestors were respelled according to their ancient form. The musical **chord** was also respelled, as if it came from the same source. In fact its origins are quite independent. It is a clipped form of *accord* "a set of sounds which agree together". Of all the cases of **cord** mentioned so far, it least deserves to have an *h* in its spelling.

Christian name See **first name** or **forename**.

chrom(o)- and **chron(o)-** Chromo- is a Greek root meaning "color". In English it occurs as the first part of modern compounds such as *chromosome*, and as the second part in others such as *monochrome*. It also occurs by itself as *chrome*, the nontechnical equivalent of the element *chromium*.

Chrono-, also a Greek root, means "time". It is embodied in words such as *chronology* and *chronometer* as well as *diachronic* and *isochronous*.

In almost all cases, the prefixes and suffixes help to make the distinction between the two roots. Only in *chromic* and *chronic* does the difference depend entirely on their respective roots.

cicada For the plural of this word, see under **-a** section 1.

cider or **cyder,** and **cipher** or **cypher** See under **i/y**.

circa This prefix meaning "around" comes direct from Latin. Historians use it with dates that cannot be given exactly and should be interpreted with some latitude. For example:

Chaucer was born circa 1340.

When spelled out in full as in that example **circa** is often italicised. When abbreviated as *c.* or *ca.* it is now usually set in roman (see further under **Latin abbreviations**). On whether or not to put a stop on *ca.*, see **abbreviations** section 1.

In the antique business, the abbreviation helps to protect the vendor against too literal interpretation of the dating of items in the catalogue:

—*Chippendale chair* c.1760

circum- This prefix meaning "around" appears in a number of Latin loanwords in English:

circumambulate circumcision circumference circumnavigate
circumscribe circumspect circumstantial

It has generated few new words in modern English, perhaps because of its ponderousness, which the examples demonstrate.

circumflex This is an accent which has come into English with quite a few French loanwords, such as *château*, *entrecôte* and *fête*, as well as in phrases borrowed from French:

chacun à son goût   raison d'être   tête à tête

The absence of the **circumflex** from most English typewriters and wordprocessors means that it is quickly lost and forgotten once the loanword becomes assimilated. Those unacquainted with French are unlikely to know that there might ever have been a **circumflex** on words like:

baton chassis crepe depot hotel role

In French the **circumflex** often marks the disappearance of a letter (such as *s*) from the spelling of the word, as is clear when we compare *château* with *castle*, *fête* with *feast*, and *hôtel* with *hostel*. Circumflexes have also marked the loss of vowels from particular words, or the fact that the vowel was once long. But from its first appearance in sixteenth century French, the applications of the **circumflex** have been various and inconsistent. Unlike the acute and grave accent, it does not correspond to a particular pronunciation of the vowel it surmounts. The etymological information it provides is less important to English than French users of the word (though even in France there have been moves to do away with the **circumflex** in many words). All this means that there is little incentive to keep the circumflexes on French loanwords in English.

civil or **civic** Both these adjectives relate ultimately to the city and its citizens, but they differ in their range of meaning. **Civic** enters into expressions which are strongly associated with a city, such as *civic centre* and *civic pride*; whereas **civil** often relates to the citizens of the country at large, as in *civil service* and *civil war*.

    Civil is the older of the two, appearing first in Chaucer's day, and developing a wide range of meanings in the following centuries. The different kinds of antonyms it has developed are revealing:

    civil as opposed to *uncouth, rude*
    civil   "   *military*
    civil   "   *ecclesiastical*

Civic meanwhile dates from the sixteenth century, is still narrow in its range, and occurs much less often according to the evidence of language databases.

-ck/-cq These provide alternative spellings in pairs such as **racket/racquet, lackey/lacquey** and **lacker/lacquer**. (See further under those headings.)

clamor or **clamour** See under -or/-our.

classic or **classical** The relationship between these words is changing. Both imply that something is in a special *class*, and in their three centuries of use there has been a great deal of overlap between them, as with other *-ic/-ical* pairs (see further under **-ic/-ical**). Both words relate things to the *classics* of high culture, and especially to the civilisations of ancient Greece and Rome—hence the phrase *to study the classics.*

    But since the late nineteenth century, **classic** has been widening its frontiers and associating itself with all sorts of everyday things, not just matters of culture. The noun **classic** was applied to important horse races last century, and to motor races this century. That which is dubbed **classic** may be anything from a political ploy, to a dress of simple style, to the perfect shot in tennis. The criteria for using the word may or may not be obvious to others, and more and more its role is simply to express approval and to commend. The *Oxford Dictionary* noted this usage in the late nineteenth century, commenting that it is ''burlesque, humorous''. A century later it seems perfectly standard and straightforward.

    While **classic** has become a more popular and subjective word, **classical** maintains the higher ground. It is suffused with a sense of history and great artistic traditions: *classical music* is associated with a period of outstanding music in western Europe in the eighteenth and nineteenth centuries; and *classical ballet* embodies what for many is still the acme of balletic technique, developed last century.

Occasionally **classical** is used in the freer ways now enjoyed by **classic**. There is however another rival for that informal terrain: *classy*. Its links with the word *class* ("high class") are still quite strong, but it is acquiring overtones of "stylish", "superior" which bring it close to the attitudinal uses of **classic**. *Classy* is more direct and down-to-earth however, so it can probably coexist with **classic** for some time to come.

clauses The *clause* is the basic grammatical unit in any sentence. Whether they know it or not, people produce many more **clauses** than sentences whenever they communicate.

At its bare minimum, a *clause* consists of two elements:
- a subject (S) (whatever is being identified for comment), and
- a predicate (P) (whatever is stated about the subject)

For example:

The dollar is rising.
     S   P

A dreamy expression came over her face.
        S   P

The predicate always contains a finite verb (e.g. *is rising*, *came* in those examples), and there may be other elements such as objects, complements or adverbs. (See further under **predicate**.)

Clauses generally distinguish themselves from phrases by having both subject and predicate. Note however that modern grammarians also recognise *nonfinite clauses* (usually without a subject) in subordinate constructions. (See below, section 3 for *subordination*, and also **nonfinite clauses**.) The number of clauses, and the relationship between them in a sentence, is the basis of recognising several different types of sentence.

1 *Simple sentences* consist of a single clause, like the two examples above. They may however embody extra adverbs and dependent phrases:

After months of decline, the dollar is rising.
       (phr)   S   P

The dollar is finally rising, despite economic predictions.
  S   P (adv) P   (phr)

Simple sentences may have several phrases in them.

2 In *compound sentences* there are two or more **clauses** which are *coordinated*, i.e. they are linked in such a way as to have equal status as statements. Usually they are joined by conjunctions such as *and*, *but*, *or* or *nor*, though a semicolon or occasionally a comma can also serve to coordinate. For example:

a) *They came and they brought their dog.*
b) *They came; their dog came with them.*

c) *I came, I saw, I conquered.*

d) *She didn't answer or show any emotion.*

Note that when the same subject appears in two clauses coordinated by a conjunction, it may be omitted in the second clause. This is shown in sentence (d). In sentence (a) however the subject is repeated in the second clause to draw extra attention to it.

3 In *complex sentences* the **clauses** are linked so as to give one of them superior status. The superior one is known as the *main clause* (or *principal clause*), while the other is subordinated to it and is therefore called the *subordinate clause*. This differentiation of roles is achieved through the use of particular conjunctions, sometimes called "subordinating conjunctions" (see further under **conjunctions**). The following are complex sentences:

They pleaded insanity so that the charge would be dropped.
             main clause   subordinate clause
Because they pleaded insanity, the charge was dropped.
             sub. clause   main clause

Notice the different effect of the subordinate clause in those sentences. In the first it simply acts as a coda to the main clause; in the second it draws attention to both the main clause and itself, because of its prime position. (See further under **information focus**.)

4 *Types of subordinate clause.* In traditional grammar the three types distinguished are:

relative (or adjectival)

noun

adverbial

As their names suggest, they function as adjectives, nouns and adverbs respectively, in relation to the main clause.

a) *Relative clauses* attach further information to nouns or pronouns in the main clause:

The book which I had in my hand had been banned.

The book was written by someone who mocked traditional values.

As in those examples, relative clauses may serve either to define or to further describe the noun or pronoun which they modify. (See further under **relative clauses** section 4.

b) *Noun clauses* take the place of a noun or noun phrase in the main clause:

They explained what was going on.

What was going on took some explaining.

The noun clause works as either subject, object or complement of the main clause. In the first example it is the object: in the second, the subject.

c) *Adverbial clauses* attach further information to the verb of the main clause, detailing such things as how, when, where or why the action or event took place:

Her eyes lit up as they hadn't for days. (HOW)

Her eyes lit up when she heard the news. (WHEN)
She would succeed where others had failed. (WHERE)
She would succeed because the time was ripe. (WHY)
She would succeed although they weren't yet out of the woods.
(CONCESSION)
She would succeed if she could only raise the funds. (CONDITION)
*The enterprise would flourish so that no-one would dare question it
again.* (RESULT)
Note that modern English grammars such as the *Comprehensive Grammar
of English* (1985) distinguish *adverbial clauses* of similarity and comparison
(introduced by *as*, or *as if/though*) from *comparative clauses* proper. The
latter have a comparative or equative element in the main clause which is
connected by *than* or *as* with the subordinate clause, as in:
He liked the film better than I did.

cleave This word is really two words, both verbs, meaning:
1 stick (to), be attached (to), as in
A man shall cleave to his wife …
2 split, cut through, as in
They cleaved their way through the jungle.
Neither verb is actively used nowadays. The first is an archaism, and the second
quite old-fashioned. But the second has provided us with *cleavage*, the butcher's
cleaver, and a number of expressions such as *cloven-footed, cloven hoof, cleft
palate* and *cleft stick*. These fossils show the earlier confusion between the two
verbs as to their past forms. The form *cloven* belongs only to **cleave** (2), while
cleft was originally part of **cleave** (1), but eventually annexed by **cleave** (2).

cleft sentences A *cleft sentence* is one in which the normal sequence of
subject/verb/object is interrupted and even rearranged, so as to spotlight one of
them in particular. Compare:
Jane noticed the unusual signature.
with its cleft counterparts
It was Jane who noticed the unusual signature.
It was the unusual signature that Jane noticed.
The *it was* (or *it is*) of the cleft sentence draws special attention to whatever
follows, underscoring it as the topic of the sentence. (See further under **topic**.)
A similar rearranging of the basic sentence elements (known as the *pseudo-cleft
sentence*) helps to foreground the action of the verb, as in:
What Jane noticed was the signature.
Both cleft and pseudo-cleft sentences help to sharpen the information focus in
a sentence, and to signal a change of focus when necessary. (See further under
information focus.)

Cleft sentences sometimes raise questions of grammatical agreement:

1 Can the verb in the clause after *It is/was* be plural? Yes, and in fact it should be if its subject is plural:

It is her relatives who are insisting on it.

2 What happens with the pronouns?

In formal style it's conventional to use the subject (nominative) form of pronouns: *I, he, she, we, you, they*, and to make the verb agree with it:

It is I who am unsure.

It is s/he who is unsure.

It is we/you/they who are unsure.

However informal usage allows the object pronouns: *me, him, her, us, them*. The third person singular verb is then used for either first or second person singular:

It's me who is unsure.

It's you who's in need of help.

3 What other conjunctions apart from *who* can be used? The relative *that* is often used in cleft sentences, in references to people as well as objects. *That* is also preferred to *when* and *where* by some. They would correct:

It was on Sunday when I saw him to

It was on Sunday that I saw him.

The basis of this objection is not explained, and *when/where* are certainly used in the cleft constructions one hears. In speech, intonation makes their role clear, whereas in writing it may be ambiguous until you reach the end of the sentence. As often, our control of written language has to be tighter for reliable communication.

clench or **clinch** These words both suggest an intense grip. Hands or teeth are *clenched*, and a bargain may be *clinched*. The second one really derives from the first, with the vowel changing under the influence of the following *n*. In earlier centuries they shared some meanings, especially in carpentery (*clenching* or *clinching* nails) and in nautical usage. But **clench** has lost ground, collocating mostly with the hands, fists and teeth of an individual; and **clinch** has developed new meanings such as the hold used by boxers or wrestlers on each other, and even the embrace of people in noncombative encounters.

clichés These are tired, overworked turns of phrase like the one in the sign on a certain news editor's desk which read:

All clichés should be avoided like the plague.

The advice of Spike Milligan on the same subject did succeed in avoiding cliché itself:

Clichés are the handrails of an infirm mind.

Clichés are a particularly tempting resource if you have to write a lot in a short time. For journalists it's a way of life, and a crop of clichés can be harvested from the pages of most daily papers, predictable phrases which readers can skim over: "Urgent——held behind closed——". Fill in the blanks! The word *cliché* means "stereotype(d)" in French, where it once referred to the stereotype block cast from an engraving, from which multiple copies could be printed. Our **clichés** recast unique events in a standard mould. Resisting clichés takes mental energy, and for mass media communicators there is the depressing prospect that today's striking thought is tomorrow's platitude, and next week's cliché—as Bernard Levin (1986) put it.

Writers sometimes use **clichés** deliberately as a way of parodying a style, and the parody itself controls and limits their use. There's more danger of clichés getting out of hand when writers use them to make things effortless for the reader, a danger of losing the reader altogether. Information theory reminds us that readers need at least a modicum of stimulation from the unexpected, to keep them reading. When the content of a text is itself predictable, the language has to provide the stimulation.

Writing the word **cliché**. *Cliché* comes to us from French with an acute accent, showing that the final *e* is a separate syllable. Like many other accents, it's often left off in English, though without it *cliche* just could be a one-syllabled word like *creche, cache* etc. Those who know the word would never pronounce it with one syllable—hence the Tory jibe about the British prime minister whose speeches consisted of "clitch after clitch after clitch".

When *cliché* becomes a verb in English, its past participle or adjective can be written in several ways:

clichéd cliché'd clichéed cliche'd cliched

The first three depend on having an acute accent in your typing or printing facilities. If it's not available, the fourth helps the reader more than the fifth. For more about adding the past tense ending to foreign words, see under **-ed** section 2.

climax In Greek this meant "ladder", and in rhetoric it implied an ascending series of steps, each one more impressive than the one before. Nowadays we apply the word only to the last step in the series, the point which is the culmination of all that has gone before.

Developing a **climax** is the core of narrative art, whether the composition is as long as a novel or as brief as a fable. A build-up is achieved by many writers through the space they devote to setting the scene and developing characters. All such detail helps to involve the reader, to raise the level of tension gradually, and to build the **climax**.

In argumentative writing also, one needs to plan to develop the discussion step by step towards a **climax**, in order to convince the reader. Many writers make their strongest argument the last one in the series, to ensure the impact and prevent *anticlimax*—that sense of let-down—creeping in at the end.

Even when drafting sentences, it pays to work up to the most compelling item when you have a series to present. Compare

Next across the line were an Olympic athlete, a wheelchair victim pushed by his red-hot companion, an army recruit in battle gear, a footballer, and a runner in a dinner jacket.

with

> *Next across the line were a footballer, an Olympic athlete, a runner in a dinner jacket, an army recruit in battle gear, and a wheelchair victim pushed by his red-hot companion.*

Assuming that the order in which the competitors finished is unimportant, the second version is more effective because it exploits the escalating amount of detail in each item to engage the reader. The first version simply has one thing after another, like a jumbled catalogue in which you could easily get lost. In the second version the items have all been harnessed to create a mini-climax.

See further under **rhythm** (*rhythm and rhetoric of a series*) and **bathos**.

clinch or **clench** See **clench**.

clipping New words are sometimes formed from older ones by a process of cutting back or **clipping**. Either the beginning, the end, or both ends may be clipped, as with the following:

> *bus (from omnibus)*
> *exam* (from *exam*ination)
> *flu* (from *in*flu*enza*)

Of the three types, the ones which are clipped back to the first syllable(s), like *exam*, are the most common. Some other common examples are:

> *ad deb deli gym lab memo mike (microphone) pram*
> *pro taxi telly uni zoo*

Among those examples, *bus*, *pram*, *taxi* and *zoo* have become the standard word, replacing the original word or phrase. The others are still an informal counterpart to the standard word, to be avoided in more formal styles of writing. Many clippings belong to the in-house or in-group *jargon* of a particular institution or social group.

As if brief was not really beautiful, Australians often extend their clippings with the addition of informal suffixes such as *-ie* or *-o*. This is of course the source of numerous colloquialisms, such as:

> *bookie cozzie footie mozzie pokie*
> *arvo compo milko rego*

(See further under **-ie/-y** and **-o**.)

cliquey or **cliquy** See under **-y/-ey**.

cloven See under **cleave**.

co- This useful prefix implies joint activity in a particular role:

> *co-author co-editor co-pilot co-sponsor co-star*

This meaning is a relatively new one, developed from the meaning "together" which it has in older formations such as:

> *coaxial coeducation coequal coexist cohabit coincide*
> *co(-)operate co(-)ordinate*

These older words show how **co-** was originally used with words beginning with a vowel or *h*, and as a variant of the Latin prefix *con-* or *com-*. **Co-** is the only one of them which is productive in modern English, and since the seventeenth century it has increasingly been used with words beginning with any letter of the alphabet. A number of mathematical words show this development:

coplanar coset cosine cotangent covalence

Co- has even replaced the earlier *con-* in *coterminous*, and the seventeenth century raised *cotemporary* as a variant for *contemporary*. It seems to stress the historical sense of that word (living in the same period).

One of the perennial questions with **co-** is whether or not to use the hyphen with it. As the examples show, the **ad hoc** words in which it means "joint" are often given hyphens, but the hyphen is left out of the established ones, except those which are liable to be misread. The only ones over which there is any debate are ones where **co-** precedes an *o*, as in *co(-)occur*, *co(-)operate* and *co(-)ordinate*. In America they are set solid like the rest, while in Britain they are hyphened. In Australia, usage is divided, so the choice is open. If you do set them solid, there can be no problem misinterpreting them because there are no words remotely like them.

Note that in short or clipped words with **co-**, such as *co-ed*, *co-op* and *co-opt*, the hyphen is vital to ensure that their two syllables are obvious.

cocotte or coquette Both these French **loanwords** are about women and sexuality, but if the **coquette** makes men her victims, men have the advantage over the **cocotte**. **Cocotte** is colloquial French for prostitute, while *grande cocotte* is the expression for the upmarket type kept in luxury by her lover. Alternatively, the latter is a *poule de luxe* (roughly "a luxury bird"). The **coquette** differs in maintaining a flirtatious independence while exploiting the affections of her admirers. Both words are ultimately derived from *coc*, the Old French word for rooster.

codex For the plural of this word, see **-x** section 3.

cogito ergo sum This Latin phrase meaning "I think therefore I am" is surprisingly well known in the English-speaking world. They are the words of the French philosopher Descartes, uttered in 1637 but mediated through British philosophers of the nineteenth and twentieth century. The words seem to express the essence of existentialism, and the ultimate syllogism (see **syllogism**). Descartes himself insisted that the statement was simply a way of asserting the involvement of self in any act of thinking. He was concerned about the basis of knowledge, and how far intuition plays a part in it.

coherence or **cohesion, coherent** or **cohesive** There are broad differences between **coherence/cohesion** and **coherent/cohesive**, even though all four are related to the verb *cohere* ("stick together"). None of them retain the literal meaning of the verb itself, but the second word in each pair still carries a sense of bonding together, as in *the cohesion within the party* or *a* *cohesive defence force*. The first word in each pair has moved further away, and implies a consecutive and logical linkage from one thing to the next, as in *the coherence of his argument* or *a coherent plan*. This extended meaning is underscored in the negatives *incoherence* and *incoherent*. Note the lack of established negatives for **cohesion** and **cohesive**, another sign that they are more recent arrivals (dating from the late seventeenth and eighteenth century, whereas **coherence/coherent** are from the sixteenth century).

1 Coherence *in writing*. Communication of any kind needs to be both **coherent** and **cohesive**: to be integrated and logical in its development, as well as effectively bonded in its expression. The **coherence** comes from thinking about the sequence of ideas, whether you are writing or speaking. Even in fiction the world created has to be imaginatively consistent and provide plausible dramatic development. In nonfiction it's vital that the statements made are somehow related, as being matched or deliberately contrasted, or linked as general/ particular, problem/solution or cause/effect. Some underlying logic of development, e.g. deduction or induction, is needed, though it may not be spelled out as such. (See further under **deduction, induction** and **argument**.)

2 Cohesion in writing is the network of verbal connections on the surface of the text, which link one reference with another and mark the continuity of ideas. In fiction, the pronouns *he* and *she* help to keep tabs on the protagonists, as in the following extract from Cliff Hardy's *Heroin Annie*:

> *When she came out at twenty to six she was recognisable from her walk; she still moved well, but there was something not proud about the way she carried her head. Her hair had darkened to a honey colour and she wore it short. In a lumpy cardigan and old jeans she headed across the pavement to a battered Datsun standing at the kerb; no-one stood aside for her ...*

This detective "portrait of a lady" keeps its focus on Annie with the unobtrusive aid of *she* and *her* in successive sentences. **Cohesion** is also provided by the sequence of references to her appearance, and then the street phenomena, pavements, car, the crowd, as reminders of the dramatic context.

In nonfiction, the pronouns (especially *it, this* and *that*, and *the* as well) are again important in ensuring continuity of reference. Other **cohesive** aids in informative and argumentative writing are the conjunctions, which forge links between one statement and another, and make explicit the underlying relationship (of similarity, contrast, cause and effect, etc). (See further under **conjunctions**.) The links between clauses or phrases can also be made by **ellipsis** (see under that heading). Yet much of the **cohesion** still comes through the words that express the subject matter, and through synonyms and antonyms which maintain the same meaning. (See further under **synonyms, antonyms, hyponyms** and **synecdoche**.)

Most writers succeed in maintaining enough **cohesive** links in the texts they compose. But the conjunctions deserve extra thought, and it pays to check on any sequences of pronouns, in case ambiguity has crept in. See for example:

He waited until the boss had finished reading his letter ...

(Whose letter was it?)

Such problems are always more obvious when you come back to edit at a later stage.

Ironically, it's quite hard to write something which is totally lacking in **coherence** and **cohesion**. One author who tried was hailed as a great poet, in a notorious Australian literary hoax. This was "Ern Malley", the pseudonym adopted by James McAuley and Harold Stewart when they offered for publication a set of verses concocted out of bits and pieces from the books that happened to be on their desks at the time. "We opened books at random, choosing a word or phrase haphazardly. We made lists of these and wove them into nonsensical sentences ..." A sample of the result, from the poem "Egyptian register", begins:

The hand that burns resinous in the evening sky
Which is a lake of roses, perfumes, idylls
Breathed from the wastes of the Tartarean heart.
The skull gathers darkness, like an inept mountain
That broods on its aeons of self-injury.
The spine, barbed and venomous, pierces
The one unmodulated cumulus of cloud ...

Knowing the intention behind it, you are unlikely to look for **coherence** or meaningful connections in it. But Max Harris who published the poems in 1944 certainly did. It shows how ready we are to assume that printed text is **coherent** and **cohesive**, though it's as well to maintain a little skepticism. (See further under **gobbledygook**.)

coliseum or **colosseum** Any place of entertainment which calls itself a **coliseum** or **colosseum** invokes the famous **Colosseum** of Rome, the huge amphitheatre built by Vespasian in the first century AD. Its name expresses all that we know in the word *colossal*, and it was evidently the ultimate entertainment centre. Smaller amphitheatres and stadiums, built on the same model elsewhere in the Roman Empire, turned it into a generic word, and it comes to us through medieval Latin (and Italian) as **coliseum**. This form of the word is used by Byron in reference to Vespasian's original, when he declares (through Childe Harold):

While stands the Coliseum, Rome shall stand ...

Journalists in Melbourne who use **Coliseum** for the original in Rome are no doubt less influenced by the memory of Byron than the requirements of their style guides. It serves to distinguish any classical reference from the Victorian *Colosseum Hotel*, and other private enterprises which perpetuate the name.

collapsable or **collapsible** Either spelling is acceptable. (See under the heading **-able/-ible**.)

collectable or **collectible** These spellings are given equal status in the *Macquarie Dictionary* (1991), and each is perfectly acceptable. **Collectable** is the simple English formation and the one preferred in Britain, according to the *Oxford Dictionary*; whereas the latinate form **collectible** is given priority for American English in the *Webster's* and *Random House* dictionaries. *Webster's English Usage* (1989) notes further that there's no sign of a grammatical division of labor (noun v. adjective) correlating with spelling.

collective nouns A *collective noun* is a singular term which designates a group of people, animals or objects. Those referring to people connote some kind of organisation or structure:
> *audience class committee congregation crew council family*
> *government orchestra parliament squad staff team tribe*

Such words raise questions of grammatical agreement: each can represent either the collective body or its individual members, according to whether it is used with a singular or plural verb. Compare:
> *The crew is training as hard as it can.*
> *The crew are training as hard as they can.*

The first sentence gives you a picture of the team members all synchronising their strokes on the river, while the second has them doing time on individual exercise machines in the gym. The choice of verb and pronoun (singular or plural) accords with the writer's meaning, rather than being dictated by grammar. (See further under **agreement** section 4.)

Collective terms for animals usually work as the head of a phrase, e.g. *herd of elephants*. This is so with examples like:
> *flock mob pack school shoal swarm troupe*

Because they are not species-specific we must specify, at least for the first reference, what the *flock* or *mob* consists of. (*Flock* can be used with animals or birds, and there is more than one possibility for *mob*.) This is also true of collective terms for objects such as:
> *bunch cluster collection crop heap mass pile*

The possibilities for them are in fact much wider than for animal terms.

The convention of specifying the species lingers with some very traditional collective words which are applied to one species only, witness: *covey of partridges, gaggle (of geese), pride (of lions)* etc. These are the models for various facetious formations for specialised human groups, such as the *haggle of vendors* and the *decorum of deans* (or the *decanter of deans*). Among the many others created for amusement are:
> *a column of accountants*
> *a consternation of mothers*
> *a goggle of tourists*
> *a guess of diagnosticians*

a quaver of coloraturas
a recession of economists
a slumber of old guard

The danger of libel looms larger, the further you go with such phrases—which probably explains why their use is limited.

collocation and **collocations** This is the tendency of words to go with particular others in a sequence. There may be only one word which can go with a particular verb, as in *the mind boggles* or with *lips pursed*. Why this is so is not obvious, any more than the reason why we speak of *Scotch whisky* and *Scottish people*. Why should it be *melted butter* and *molten lead*? They are just some of the conventional **collocations** of English.

Collocations of another kind are to be found in phrasal verbs: *bear up*, *browned off*, *butt in*, *carry out* etc., where the same particle is always used. Knowing which particle it is makes life hard for the second language learner, and even native Australians can be bushed when slightly different **collocations** are used in speech and in writing. In standard written English, it's usual to have *wait for* (someone) while in speech you quite often hear it expressed as *wait on*. Thus some **collocations** vary according to context, and others according to the structure of the sentence. The choice of particle after *different* (*from/ than/ to*) often depends on what comes next. (See further under **different**.)

Collocations differ from *idioms* in that their meaning is not removed from the literal value of their components. Compare expressions such as *a red herring* and *shoot (oneself) in the foot* (true idioms) with any of the examples in the previous paragraph. (See further under **idiom**.)

Collocations differ from *clichés* in that they have an established place in the language, whereas *clichés* are hackneyed expressions which seem to need replacing. (See further under **clichés**.)

colloquialisms These are expressions used in casual conversation. They smack of easy-going exchanges between people, when not too fine a point is being put on the medium of communication:

If you'll get a wriggle on with the painting—we can have a barbie this arvo, and get the neighbors round to have a bite. We'll have a bash at doing the garden tomorrow ...

The most conspicuous **colloquialisms** in a casual conversation are words like *barbie* and *arvo*, where the word itself or the particular use of it is reserved for informal use. They appear in writing only in texts which are designed to conjure up the flavor of natural talk. Colloquial idioms like *get a wriggle on* and *have a bash at* also contribute to the flavor and are unlikely to appear in formal writing, even though the words within them can be used in noncolloquial ways.

Colloquial expressions are often allusive rather than specific. Examples such as *have a bite*, and *doing the garden* rely a lot for their meaning on the context and on the knowledge shared by the speakers. When conversing we take a lot for granted. We also tend to telescope the less essential parts of words and phrases, resulting in contractions such as *you'll* in the sample above.

In formal writing those are things to avoid because they undermine the serious effect you would want to have on the reader. The style should not appear casual, imprecise or to gloss over details. But in friendly communication, a sprinkling of **colloquialisms** helps to lighten the style, and show that you are human.

colloquium For the plural of this word, see under **-um**.

Colombia or **Columbia** See Columbia.

colon The **colon** is a handy punctuation mark for showing that examples or specific details are about to come. The examples may continue the line of the sentence, as in the following case:

> *Most of their books are technical: textbooks for students of economics and law, and manuals for computer users.*

Alternatively, the examples after the colon may be set out on the line(s) below, as in countless entries in this book.

The **colon** reassures readers that what follows will give them the specifics, and that they will be offered more than an empty generalisation. It allows the writer to detail something or give a set of examples without overloading the introductory part of the sentence. Note that what comes after the **colon** is not usually a sentence itself—a point on which colons differ significantly from semicolons (see under **semicolon**). The word following the **colon** is kept in lower case, unless it's a formal statement, slogan or motto. For example:

> *On the laboratory door was a new sign: Trespassers prosecuted.*

Colons are often used these days before presenting extended quotations. A long quotation from a printed source is nowadays introduced by just a colon, not a colon plus a dash (:—). Direct quotations from someone's speech are also prefaced by a **colon** nowadays, especially in newspapers and magazines, where once a comma was the standard punctuation. The use of commas with quotations is increasingly confined to literary fiction. (See **quotation marks** section 3.)

Other uses of colons:
- to separate the headings in memos from the specific details:
  > *MEMO TO:*   *Leslie Smith, Manager*
  > *FROM:*   *Robin Jones*
  > *SUBJECT:*   *Uniforms for staff*

  (In American correspondence the colon is also used after the salutation in ordinary letters, as in:
  > *Dear John:*
  > *Your last letter arrived after I'd left for Detroit ...*)
- to separate the main title from the subtitle of a book. (See further under **titles**.)
- to separate elements in literary and biblical citations:
  > *Romeo and Juliet* Act V:ii Revelation 12:20

- to separate elements in bibliographical references, such as the publisher from the place of publication, or the date of publication from the page numbers. (See **referencing** sections 2 and 3.)
- to indicate ratios in mathematics, as in *3:1*.

Note that in the USA the **colon** is also used in expressions of time, e.g. *5:30 pm*, whereas in Australia and Britain it is *5.30 pm*.

color or **colour** See under -or/-our.

colosseum or **coliseum** See coliseum.

Columbia or **Colombia** Both names honor Christopher Columbus, as does *Colón*. The different forms of his name result from its being differently written in Italian, Spanish and Latin. Columbus was of course an Italian by birth, and the Italian form of his name *Colombo* is preserved exactly as the name of the capital city of Sri Lanka. In South America his name is written into the mountainous state **Colombia** and the *Colombian Basin* to the north of it. When Columbus settled in Spain, he adopted the name Cristobal Colón, and *Colón* lives on as the name of cities in Argentina, Panama and Cuba.

Columbus, the form most familiar to us, is the Latin version of the great explorer's name. In North America it becomes **Columbia** in the several towns that bear the name, as well as the *District of Columbia, Columbia University* and the Canadian state of *British Columbia*.

So English-speaking countries use **Columbia** along with *Columbus*, whereas **Colombia** and *Colón* are used where Spanish or Portuguese culture has prevailed.

combated or **combatted** The spelling **combated** is preferred in all major dictionaries, Australian, American and British. The *Oxford Dictionary* shows that the spelling **combatted** was once more common, no doubt when the word's second syllable was stressed. (See further under **doubling of final consonant**.) The older spelling survives in the heraldic word *combattant*, whereas its modern military counterpart is *combatant*.

comic or **comical** The first of these adjectives is more closely linked with comedy, as in *comic opera* and a *comic character*. **Comical** is more loosely used of anything that generates laughter, as in a *comical expression*. But the boundaries between them are not too sharply drawn, as with other pairs of this kind. (See further under **-ic/-ical**.)

comma Commas are an underused punctuation mark, and the chief casualty of the trend towards open punctuation (see **punctuation**, section 1). They have a vital role to play in longer sentences, separating information into readable units, and guiding the reader as to the relationship between phrases and items in a series.

1 A *single comma* ensures correct reading of sentences which start with a longish introductory element:

a) *Before the close of the last Ice Age, Tasmania was joined to the mainland of Australia.*

b) *Before the last Ice Age ended ten thousands years ago, Tasmania was joined to the mainland.*

Whether the sentence begins with a phrase as in (a), or a clause as in (b), it benefits by having a **comma** to show where the introductory element ends and the main statement begins. The **comma** allows the reader to pause between the two parts, and to absorb each one properly. Introductory strings of words often express the ongoing theme of a paragraph, or they highlight a change or adjustment to the theme (see **information focus**).

When the introductory string is short (just two or three words), the separating **comma** may not be necessary—except to prevent misreading. The **comma** is essential in a case like the following:

Fourteen months after the rains came to other parts of the Kimberleys.

A **comma** following *after* will prevent the reader having to go over the sentence twice to get its structure. Commas can also make a difference to the reading of a sentence with a relative clause (see **relative clauses** section 4), and those with negatives in them (see **negatives** section 2).

2 *Pairs of commas* help in the middle of a sentence to set off any string of words which is either a parenthesis or in apposition to whatever went before.

The desert trees, casuarinas and acacias, were sprouting new green needles. (Apposition)

The dead canyons, all nature in them reduced to desiccation, came alive with the sound of rain slithering down the crevasses. (Parenthesis)

Note that a pair of dashes could have been used instead of commas with the parenthesis, in both formal and informal writing.

3 *Sets of commas* are a means of separating:

a) strings of predicative adjectives, as in: *It looks big, bold, enticing.*

b) items in a series, as in: *The billabongs at sunset drew flocks of galahs, gang-gangs, budgerigars and cockatoos of all kinds.*

A curious amount of heat has been generated over whether or not there should be a **comma** between the two last items in such a series (the so-called *serial comma* debate). Older editing practice tried to legislate on the matter, and insisted that there should always be a **comma** before the *and*. Yet *Webster's Standard American Style Manual* (1985) admits that the serial comma is as often absent as present in its citation files. The ongoing trend is to use the final serial comma only when it is needed to prevent ambiguity, as noted also in British English by the authors of *Right Word at the Right Time*, and recommended by the Australian Government *Style Manual*. In a sentence like the one shown above, there is no problem if the serial comma is absent. However it's a different matter with the following:

Drinking their fill at the billabong were rabbits, emus, flocks of galahs and wallabies.

The word *flock* does not collocate with *wallabies*, and a **comma** before *and*, to separate *flocks of galahs* from *wallabies* is desirable.

Note that once there are commas within individual items in a series, semicolons must be used to separate each item from the next:

Drinking their fill at the billabong were a tribe of rabbits, large and small; emus with rippling plumage; flocks of galahs, jostling each other for positions; and a tentative group of wallabies.

4 *The disappearing* **comma**
- with numbers (see **numbers** section 1)
- with dates. Depending on the order (day, month and year or month, day and year), the **comma** may or may not be necessary. (See under **dates**.)
- with addresses on envelopes. To ensure accurate reading by the electronic scanners, Australia Post and Australian Government Publishing Service now recommend the *omission* of commas (and all punctuation) from addresses on envelopes. (See further in Appendix VIII.)

For **inverted commas**, see **quotation marks**.

commands In English, **commands** are most directly expressed through what grammarians call *imperatives*. They are the short, sharp forms of verbs which are used on the parade ground, or in written instructions:

Switch on the automatic control to the oven. Turn the clock to whatever starting time you want. Set the temperature control ...

In recipes imperatives are regularly found at the start of sentences.

But other, less direct ways of expressing **commands** are also available in English, particularly if you want to soften the abruptness of the imperative—and to adopt the role of counsellor rather than commander in the document you're writing. The following are some of the possibilities, graded more or less from most to least direct:

Switch on the oven.
You must switch on the oven.
Make sure you switch on the oven.
The oven should be switched on.

In face-to-face situations we generally use something even less direct, such as *Could you switch on the oven*? It seems to allow more discretion to the other party, and disguises the instruction. In writing that might seem to be going too far, however. (See further under **imperative**.)

comme il faut Borrowed from French, this phrase means "as it should be". Adopted into English in the courtly eighteenth century, it refers to matters of etiquette and correct social behavior. It commends as proper conduct whatever it is attached to. The phrase allows more freedom of choice than certain other French phrases which refer to etiquette. **De règle** means "required by rule or convention''; and **de rigueur** (roughly ''in strictness'') suggests that the whole weight of social opinion is behind it, to make it an absolute necessity.

comment or **commentate** These verbs both have their place. **Commentate** conveys the sense of commenting as a means of earning your living, providing continuous commentary on events at which you're the official media representative. **Comment** usually implies making an ad hoc set of remarks, or just one of them.

Yet **commentate** is sometimes disparaged, as a clumsy and unnecessary extension of **comment** (which it isn't), or else because it's a backformation from *commentator*. (See further under **backformation**.) There is no need to avoid it on either count if it carries its distinctive meaning.

commercialese Letter writing has its conventions, and letters written in the name of business can be the most stylised of all. The routine nature of many business letters has fostered the growth of jargon and formulaic language, in phrases such as:

further to your letter of the 12 inst.
re your order of the 27 ult.
your communication to hand
please find enclosed
for your perusal
at your earliest convenience

Clichés such as those sound increasingly stilted, and business firms these days generally encourage their letter writers to avoid them: to use direct and natural language instead, and to communicate in friendly terms if possible. For the conventional layout of letters, see Appendix VII. (See also **letter writing**.)

commitment or **committal** Both words are of course from the verb *commit* and provide an abstract noun for it. Some dictionaries seem to say that they are interchangeable, yet they differ in their breadth and frequency of use. **Commitment** is much more common and widely used, for committing oneself to anything, be it a religion, or amateur sport, or ridding the bush of nonnative plants. The statement ''I have another commitment'' can mean almost any activity. **Committal** by contrast has been particularly associated with legal processes, the *committal hearing* and *committal proceedings*, which involve the examination of evidence before a full trial. **Committal** is also the word used in connection with the formal burial of a body. So there are ritual and legal overtones to **committal** which **commitment** is free of.

common or **mutual** Common has numerous meanings, but it contrasts with **mutual** in emphasising sharing rather than reciprocation in a relationship, as in *common origin* or *common interest*.

Mutual involves reciprocity. *Mutual satisfaction* implies the satisfaction which two people give to each other, and *mutual agreement* emphasises the fact that something is agreed to by both parties (assuming there is no tautology). Reciprocity is carried to excess in a *mutual admiration society*.

Mutual has also long been used to refer to a reciprocal relationship which is enjoyed by more than one other person, as in the title of Charles Dickens's *Our Mutual Friend*, published in 1865. Yet for some reason this usage was censured in the later nineteenth century, as the *Oxford Dictionary* notes. The dictionary also noted that **mutual** was the only possible word in expressions like Dickens's title. (When class distinctions were so important, who would take the risk of referring to "our common friend".) The linguistic propriety of using **mutual** has never bothered insurance companies, which offer thousands of "mutual insurance" policies, and many build the word *Mutual* into their company titles.

common gender See under **gender**.

common nouns These contrast with *proper nouns*. (See further under **nouns**.)

Commonwealth The phrase *Commonwealth of Australia* has been a political football for most of the one hundred years of its existence. It was voted in as the official title for Australia (by a majority of one) at the Federal Convention held in Sydney in 1891. Other former British colonies such as Canada and New Zealand adopted the title *Dominion*.

The word **commonwealth** was first used by English social reformers of the early sixteenth century, who wanted the state to be the ideal *republic* existing for the common good, and not advantaging the rich and powerful. (*Common* was to parallel *public*, and *weal*(th) then meant "welfare" rather than "affluence".) Several of the original American states, Kentucky, Massachusetts, Pennsylvania and Virginia, are *commonwealths* by charter, and the word expressed republican and antimonarchic ideals which were popular in nineteenth century America. It appealed to Australian federationists for the same reason.

But the republican associations of **commonwealth** were presumably not strongly felt by the British government when it renamed what had been the *British Empire* as the *British Commonwealth*. The recruitment of the word for that other purpose led both Menzies and Whitlam in the 60s to declare publicly their preference for "Australian Government" rather than *Commonwealth of Australia*. (The comments of other Australian historians are documented in *Right Words* (1989).) Whitlam went further, in reducing *Commonwealth of Australia* to *Australia* on banknotes, and removing the word **Commonwealth** from the Governor-General's title. The latter change was however revoked by Fraser in 1975. The interim state of affairs can also be seen in the fact that the Australian Government Publishing Service still uses the Commonwealth Government Printer. The CSIRO (Commonwealth Scientific and Industrial Research Organisation) has yet to join the trend, though in 1986 it modified the spelling of the word *organisation* (from *organization*) to bring it into line with Australian government style.

For the *Commonwealth of Independent States*, see **Russia**.

comparatives For comparative forms of adjectives, see under **adjectives**. See also **than**.

compare with or **compare to** Is there any difference between:

Compared with other products, it's inspired and
Compared to other products, it's inspired.

Some suggest there is a slight difference in meaning: that **compare with** is used when the comparison is part of a broad analysis, and **compare to** when it's a matter of specifically likening one thing to another. This distinction goes back to separate definitions in the major English dictionaries. But whether they are distinct for the common user seems doubtful, and *Webster's English Usage* (1989) cites instances in which the two meanings can scarcely be separated. *Webster's* evidence shows little correlation between the particles and the two meanings; if there is any tendency to use *to* with the meaning "liken", it's only when it works as an active verb. When passive or just a past participle, *to* and *with* are used indifferently.

Fowler believed that in one context **compare with** still reigned supreme, i.e. in intransitive statements such as:

The product compares very favorably with imported ones.

Yet the evidence collected by *Webster's* shows that even here, *with* shares the field with *to*.

Compare(d) to is thus an established option to **compare(d) with**, occurring in a ratio of about 1:3 in over one hundred instances in the Australian ACE corpus. **Compare with** was once underpinned by the Latinists' insistence that *with* was the only possible particle when the prefix in *compare* is the Latin *cum* "with". (Compare **averse**.) But with the decline in common knowledge of Latin, *compare(d)* works more and more on English analogies, and for words such as *liken* and *similar* the regular particle is *to*.

comparison of adjectives and adverbs For degrees of comparison, see **adjectives** section 2 and **adverbs** section 3.

compendium For the plural of this word, see under **-um**.

competence or **competency** Dictionaries often give these as alternatives, and in some contexts they are synonymous in their now dominant sense of "sufficient capability or skills". But English databases show that **competence** occurs a good deal more often than **competency** in general use, and dictionaries record newly developed specialist meanings for it in linguistics, biology and geology.

The two words have an extraordinary trail of meanings behind them. When first recorded in English they shared several meanings related to our verb *compete* ("contest"). These meanings have been totally eclipsed, and those we know are related to a different verb, *compete* meaning "come together" and figuratively "be convenient or fitting". That verb itself has disappeared, no doubt under pressure from the other one. But **competence/competency** with their sense of sufficiency or adequacy are fossils of the second verb, and legal extensions of this (meaning "fitness or adequacy in law") were the ones which dominated the record until the eighteenth century. Strictly speaking however, in Australian law it is *capacity* (not either **competence** or **competency**) which stands as the legal term.

One other development of **competency** (but not **competence**) has been for it to acquire a plural form *competencies*. It thus becomes a *count noun*, whereas **competence** remains a *mass noun* only. This grammatical differentiation is not uncommon for word pairs like these. (See further under **-nce/-ncy**, and **nouns**.)

complacent or **complaisant** Complacent has been making inroads into the domain of **complaisant** during the last two centuries. Both words derive from the Latin verb "please", though this is more evident in the spelling of **complaisant**, the French derivative. In English it has meant "eager to please" or "obliging" in a positive sense. **Complacent**, the regular Latin form, usually means "pleased with oneself and with the status quo". Its overtones are somewhat negative, suggesting undue satisfaction with one's self and a reluctance to improve things.

Complacent is occasionally used as a synonym for **complaisant**, and seems now to be infecting it with negative connotations. Examples quoted in *Right Word at the Right Time* show **complaisant** meaning not just "eager to please" but "overready to condone". This perhaps is the final stage in this verbal encounter.

Note also that the older *complacence* is giving way to the newer *complacency*. (See further under **-nce/-ncy**.)

complement or **compliment** These identical-sounding words represent earlier and later developments of the same Latin word *complementum* "something which completes". The spelling **complement** still corresponds to that kind of meaning, as in:

> *His creativity and her business sense are the perfect complement for*
> *each other.*

A similar meaning is the one used by grammarians when they speak of a **complement** to the verb. (Note that the term **complement** is reserved by some grammarians for the item following a copular verb (especially *be*), whereas others apply it to any item which completes the verb phrase: objects, adverbs, verb phrases or complements (as just defined). See further under **predicate**.)

The spelling **compliment** which we use to mean "a commendatory remark" comes to us through Italian and French. This extension of meaning can be explained in terms of etiquette, where a **compliment** is that which completes or rounds off an act of courtesy. Until the seventeenth century, the spelling **complement** represented this sense also. Since then **compliment** has helped to distinguish the two, though it adds yet another detail which the competent speller has to know.

complex sentences See **clauses** section 3.

complex words A *complex word* embodies more than one distinct component, but only one which can stand alone. See for example:
    *child*ren *denigrate*d *evolution*ary re*model* unpre*meditate*d *water*ing
The independent (or free-standing element) has been italicised in each case. In cases such as *hungri*est, *rac*ism and *traffick*ing, the italicised part should still be regarded as the free-standing element, since there's no doubt that *hungry*, *race* and *traffic* can stand alone. The alternative forms they take in those words are simply dictated by the following suffix and certain basic rules of English spelling. (See under **y>-i-**, **-e** and **-c/-ck-** for the three involved in those cases.)
    Complex words have either prefixes, suffixes or both attached to their free-standing element, which add extra dimensions of meaning. (See further under **prefixes** and **suffixes**, and under individual examples, such as **-ate**, **be-** etc.)
    Compare **complex words** with **compounds**.

compliment or **complement** See **complement**.

compline or **complin** The name for the last church service of the day has been growing with the centuries. Its regular French antecedent had neither *n* nor *e*, being *compli* "completed". However on English soil it began to be called *compelin*, and it was **complin** in the sixteenth century when Cranmer removed it as a separate service from the *English Prayer Book*. In scattered references over the next three centuries it appears as **compline**, and when the service was reinstated by the Anglican church in 1928, it was **compline**. In the current prayer book of the Anglican Church in Australia, and in Catholic liturgical books, the spelling is **compline**.
    The second edition of the *Oxford Dictionary* (unlike the first) gave priority to **compline**, and it is preferred in all modern dictionaries including the *New Westminster Dictionary of Liturgy and Worship* (1986). It's remarkable that **complin** is nevertheless still supported by the standard pronunciation of the word. The addition of the unhistorical *-e* may be an instance of **frenchification**, though the motive is less clear than in other cases. (See under that heading.)

compos mentis See **non compos mentis**.

composed (of) or **comprise** See **comprise**.

compound sentences See **clauses** section 2.

compound verbs This phrase is applied to several kinds of verbs which consist of more than one word:

1 Those which embrace one or more auxiliary verbs, such as:
    was going am being taken would have liked
   (See further under **auxiliary verbs**.)

2 Those which combine with particular particles to express a meaning, such as:
   compare with differ from give up protest against
   (See further under **phrasal verbs**.)

3 Those which are compound words, such as *downgrade* and *shortlist*. (See
   further under **compounds**).

compounds These are expressions which consist of two (or more) separable
parts, each of which can stand as a word in its own right. English has very
many of them, of which the following are only tokens:
• nouns *car park football machine gun take-over*
• adjectives *airborne home-made icy-cold keen-eyed*
• verbs *baby-sit blackball blue-pencil overturn*
• adverbs *downtown overseas upmarket worldwide*
Although four examples have been given in each group, there are infinitely more
noun compounds at large. Note that in each group, some have hyphens and
others do not, either because they are spaced or set solid. It is sometimes said
that compounds develop from being spaced as separate words, are then
hyphenated, then become set solid; and there are some examples to prove the
point among the shorter noun compounds. But compound adjectives and verbs
often go straight to the hyphened (or set solid) stage, which ensures that they
are read as a single grammatical unit. With noun compounds this is less crucial.
(See further under **hyphens**.)
    Whatever the setting, the two parts of a compound come together in terms
of meaning, and this special integration of meaning is what makes a compound.
A *car park* is unlike a *national park* in almost every way, in spite of the common
element *park*, because both are **compounds**.
    For the plurals of compounds, see **plurals** section 2.
    Compounds differ from *complex words* in that the latter have only one part
which can stand alone. Compare *football* with *footing*, *machine gun* with
machinery, *worldwide* with *worldly* and so on. (See further under **complex
words**.) For blended words such as *brunch*, *electrocute* and *telecast*, see
portmanteau words.

comprehensible or **comprehensive** These words are both related to the
verb *comprehend*, which in Latin (and earlier English) meant ''take a grip on'';
and still the sense of holding or including (many things) is the most common
one for **comprehensive** nowadays. A *comprehensive approach* (to a problem)
takes in almost every aspect of it, just as a *comprehensive school* is intended to
teach subjects right across the educational curriculum, not just the academic or
technical strand.
    But the verb *comprehend* has for centuries also meant ''have a *mental* grasp
of or understand''. (The *Oxford Dictionary* notes that this is actually the first
recorded meaning in fourteenth century English, though the more classical
meaning was in use then too.) The notion of understanding is the primary

meaning for **comprehensible** "able to be understood". Just occasionally **comprehensive** also shows this development of meaning as well, when used in the sense of "having understanding":

They were not fully comprehensive of the corruption within their ranks.

Though recorded from time to time over the last three centuries, this usage is not common nowadays, and mostly confined to formal style and deliberately lofty writing.

comprise or **composed of** Comprise is a verb over which many people pause, and several constructions are now acceptable with it. Traditionally it meant "include or contain", as in:

The book comprises three sections: background, argument and
applications.

It was thus equivalent to the passive of **compose**:

The book is composed of three sections: background, argument and
applications.

The two constructions offer a stylistic choice—more compact expression (with **comprise**) or something less dense (with **composed of**).

Those two constructions seem to be blended in two other uses of **comprise**:
* *The book is comprised of three sections* … (where *comprised* means "made up of") and
* *Three sections comprise the book* … (where *comprise* means "combine to make up")

This last construction is the mirror-image of the traditional use: it begins with the parts that make up the whole, rather than the whole which consists of certain parts. The meaning of **comprise** thus depends on whatever the writer makes its subject (the whole, or its parts), and readers take their cue from that. The second edition of the *Oxford Dictionary* (1989) now recognises all three uses of comprise, as does the *Random House Dictionary* (1987) and none of them can now be considered incorrect.

concensus or **consensus** See consensus.

concerto For the plural of this word, see under **Italian plurals**.

concomitance or **concomitancy** See under **-nce/-ncy**.

concord See under **agreement**.

concrete or **cement** See cement.

concrete nouns These contrast with **abstract nouns**. They refer to visible, tangible things such as *apple, bridge, ceiling, house, student, water*, as well as observable aspects of behavior such as *laughing, running, shouting, typing*, and natural phenomena which have some measurable correlate, such as *electricity, heat, humidity* and *wind*. They may be either **mass nouns** like *flesh* and *water*, or **count nouns** like *apple* and *student*. (See further under **nouns**.)

concurrence or **concurrency** See -nce/-ncy.

conditional In languages such as French and Italian, this is the term for a special form of the verb which shows that an event or action *may* take place, not that it *will*. The **conditional** is formed rather like the future tense, though the suffixes are a little different:

- French   je viendrais   (*conditional*)
                   je viendrai   (*future*)
- Italian   (io) verrei   (*conditional*)
                   (io) verrò   (*future*)

Translators usually use the English modal verb *would* to translate *conditionals* from French and Italian.

Conditionals express the writer's judgement that the fulfillment of the verb's action depends on something else. For example:
Je viendrais mais je n'ai pas d'auto.
(I would come but I don't have a car.)
Si j'avais un auto, je viendrais.
(If I had a car, I would come.)
As the last example shows, *conditional statements* are often expressed in English by means of a *conditional clause*, prefaced by *if*, *unless* or *provided that* and are a type of *adverbial clause*. (See further under **clauses** section 4c).

condominium This legal word is used in **American English** (and increasingly in Australia) to refer to a high-rise apartment which can be owned by strata title. For the plural, see under **-um**.

The abbreviation *condo* originated in the USA, though it too has had some currency in Australia since 1984, no doubt because it chimes in with other informal words ending in *-o*.

confidant(e) or **confident** These both relate to *confidence*, but while **confident** (adjective) means "having confidence in oneself", a **confidant** (noun) is one who receives the confidences of others. Originally (up to the eighteenth century) **confident** was the spelling for both.

Although **confidant(e)** looks like a French loanword, the French themselves use *confidente*. Their word referred to a conventional stage character who was privy to the secrets of the chief characters. The English spelling of **confidant(e)** with *a* is thought to have been a way of representing French pronunciation of the last syllable (with stress and a nasal vowel). No doubt it was also a way of differentiating it from **confident**, in times when people tried to maintain formal differences between words with different functions. The presence or absence of *e* on the end might be expected to indicate the gender of the person in whom one confided (with **confidante** for a woman, and **confidant** for the man). However *Webster's English Usage* (1989) finds this is not systematically observed in contemporary English.

conform to/conform with Of these two possibilities, Fowler commented that "idiom demands *conform to*", and it is certainly the more common. But *conform with* is also used occasionally, perhaps under the influence of the phrase *in conformity with* where *with* is the standard collocation. There is no particular resistance to *with*, so the choice is open. Compare **compare with/to**.

conjugations The verbs of a language fall into distinct classes or **conjugations** according to their patterns of inflection and characteristic vowels.

In Latin there were five major **conjugations**, the most distinctive of which was the first with *a* as its stem vowel. Its descendants in English are the many words ending in *-ate*, *-ator*, *-ation* and *-ative*. Most modern European languages have many more than five different classes of verbs, with numerous subgroups created by changes to word forms over the centuries. In English the original seven types of "strong" verbs are now a mixed bag of remnants, and the so-called "weak" conjugation has also spawned many small subgroups.

Remnants of the strong conjugations (those which alter their vowels to indicate the past tense and past participle, often adding *(e)n* to the latter) include:

sing	*sang*	*sung*	cf. *ring, swim*
ride	*rode*	*ridden*	*drive, write*
bear	*bore*	*borne*	*tear, wear*
break	*broke*	*broken*	*speak*
take	*took*	*taken*	*forsake*

The weak conjugation simply added *-(e)d* or *-t* for both the past forms, though some of these verbs now show vowel changes (and spelling changes) as well:

live	*lived*	*lived*	cf. *love, move*
keep	*kept*	*kept*	*creep, meet, sleep*
sell	*sold*	*sold*	*tell*
say	*said*	*said*	*pay*

Strong and weak elements are also mixed in verbs such as:

do	*did*	*done*
shear	*sheared*	*shorn*
show	*showed*	*shown*

(See further under **irregular verbs**.)

conjunctions and **conjuncts** Though both these serve to link words together, only **conjunctions** are widely known. They join words in the same phrase or clause:

> *bread and butter   white or black coffee*
> *The children were tired but happy.*

They also link together whole clauses, as in:

> *The milkbar sold bread rolls* but *there was no supply of bagels.*

When joining clauses, conjunctions serve either to *coordinate* them as equals, as in the examples above, or to *subordinate* one to the other. Different sets of conjunctions are used for each type.

1 The major *coordinating* **conjunctions** are:

and but or nor yet

In grammatical terms they link together main clauses (see further under **clauses**). They appear at the head of a clause, and allow the subject following them to be deleted if it's the same as the one just mentioned. See for example:

Marion came and *(she) demolished the cheese cake.*

Others saw her at it yet *(they) didn't intervene.*

Note that **conjunctions** like these can appear at the start of a sentence, and are then strictly speaking **conjuncts** (see **adverbs** section 1). They forge a cohesive link with the previous sentence while being grammatically unconnected.

Others saw her at it. Yet they didn't intervene.

(See the table in section 3 for more examples of **conjuncts**.) Grammarians and some teachers have in the past objected to the use of *but* or *and* at the start of a sentence—presumably because they recognised them only as conjunctions, not as conjuncts. (See further under **and** and **but**.)

2 The *subordinating* **conjunctions** include:

how when where whether why while since as before after once till until (al)though if because for whereas than

In general terms, these **conjunctions** link a main clause with a subordinate one that details some point in it. (See **clauses** sections 3 and 4.) For the status of **directly, however, like** and **plus** as conjunctions, see under those headings.

Compound subordinating conjunctions include:

as if   as though   as soon as   as far as   in case   in order that provided that   so that

3 *The logic of* **conjunctions** *and* **conjuncts**. Apart from their role in sentence grammar, **conjunctions** and **conjuncts** relate ideas to each other, helping to show the logic of the information offered. In fact they express a number of logical relationships—addition, contrast, causation or circumstance (especially time). These logical meanings are embodied in both coordinating and subordinating conjunctions, as well as conjuncts and their paraphrases, as shown in the following table:

- Addition
  - **conjunctions**:   *and or nor*
  - **conjuncts**:   *additionally also alternatively besides furthermore likewise moreover similarly*
  - phrases: *as well in addition in the same way*
- Contrast
  - **conjunctions**:   *although but yet though whereas*
  - **conjuncts**:   *however instead nevertheless otherwise rather*
  - phrases: *against this by contrast on the contrary*
- Causation
  - **conjunctions**:   *as because for since so (that)*

conjuncts:	*consequently hence then therefore thus*
phrases:	*as a result because of this for this reason*
	on this account to this end

- Circumstance

conjunctions:	*(al)though as since when*
conjuncts:	*granted meanwhile next now soon still then*
phrases:	*at this point despite this even so in that case*
	in the meantime that being so
	under the circumstances up till now

The table shows that the same word may signal more than one kind of logical meaning. Examples such as *since* and *then* may express either causal relations or temporal circumstance, depending on what statements they are coupled with. In argumentative writing it's important to avoid ambiguous connections between ideas, and to choose **conjunctions** and **conjuncts** that underscore the logic of the argument. Variety is also important. If *thus* appears three times on the same page, it can arouse suspicion that its use is decorative rather than logical.

conjuncts See under **conjunctions**.

conjurer or **conjuror** Both spellings are acceptable, though dictionaries give preference to **conjurer**, and certainly it appeared earlier in English, in the fourteenth century. **Conjuror** is first recorded in the fifteenth century, and seems to gain ground over **conjurer** in the late eighteenth and nineteenth century. The *-or* spelling links **conjuror** with *juror*, and with other "role words" derived direct from French, whereas **conjurer** makes it an English formation based on the verb *conjure*. (See further under **-er/-or**.)

conk or **konk** See under k/c.

connectible or **connectable** Both spellings are acceptable, and **connectable** can be justified on the grounds that the word is a native English formation of the eighteenth century, based on the verb *connect*. Yet the pressure to spell it **connectible**, on the analogy of other Latin-derived adjectives such as *perfectible* is quite strong, and **connectible** is the first spelling in the *Oxford* and the *Collins* dictionaries. However the complete absence of the word from other dictionaries would lead readers to expect it to be spelled in the regular English way (**connectable**), as with any undocumented word. (See further under **-able/-ible**.)

connector or **connecter** These spellings are juxtaposed as equals in many dictionaries, though *Collins* puts the latinate **connector** first, and *Macquarie* **connecter**, which is the regular English formation. Both spellings have been recorded since about 1800. Faraday used **connecter**, but **connector** dominates in technical use now, perhaps by analogy with *conductor* and other technical items in the same field. (See further under **-er/-or**.)

connexion or **connection** See under -ction/-xion.

connotation The **connotations** of words are the associations which they raise in the minds of people using them. Some of these associations would be the same for most users of a particular word, as *holiday* connotes pleasure and relaxation (not to mention beaches and lazing in the sun) for students and many working people. Yet the same word may hold special **connotations** for individuals and subgroups in the population. For women who are the working mothers of school-age children, the word *holiday* raises mixed feelings because it connotes a time when life is actually more complicated—the need to arrange care and entertainment for the children (and relax with them as far as possible), as well as continue one's normal working routine.

The example just given shows how a word's **connotations** may be different for speaker and listener, or writer and reader. The connotations may also change over the course of time, as with *enthusiasm* for example, which is positively valued nowadays, though in the seventeenth and eighteenth century it was a derogatory word. (It was then associated with extreme religious emotion.) The fact that **connotations** vary and change shows how unstable they are.

In contrast, the **denotations** of words (whatever they refer to or identify) are quite stable. So *holiday* denotes a period of days which makes a break in the normal schedules of work or study. Both students and working mothers would agree on that. Yet some words, especially slang words, have relatively little denotation and their chief force is in their **connotation**. The slang uses of *screw* as a noun denoting "prison warder" or a verb meaning "have sexual intercourse" are heavy with contempt. The **connotations** serve your purpose if your aim is to insult, but make them unusable for neutral communication.

Apart from their positive or negative values, words often have stylistic **connotations**. Compare *holiday* with *vacation*. *Holiday* is the ordinary, standard word in Australia, whereas *vacation* is American English, and smacks of the overseas trip. Its style is relatively formal, contrasting strongly with the informality of the abbreviated form *hols*. A stylistic value is thus also a part of the **connotations** of a word, and again something which can change, as, for example, when a colloquialism becomes part of the standard language.

consensus or **concensus** Dictionaries all agree that the word should be spelled **consensus**, because like *consent* it goes back to the Latin verb *consentire* "agree". Yet the spelling **concensus** persists. The *Oxford Dictionary* registers it as a variant of **consensus**, though without giving any details, and *Webster's English Usage* (1989) reports a number of sightings in the last two decades, even in edited material. The *Right Word at the Right Time* notes that the spelling **concensus** may result from confusion with *census* or *concentric*, and the idea of movement towards a central point is apt enough. **Concensus** is thus a **folk etymology** (see further under that heading). Like other latinisms which are obscure to many in the twentieth century, **consensus** may eventually be credited with an alternative spelling.

consist of or **consist in** In the twentieth century, **consist of** enjoys much more widespread use than **consist in**, outnumbering it by 25:2 in the Australian ACE corpus. Yet some writers make a point of using **consist in** when identifying the (usually abstract) principle which underlies something; and **consist of** when they were about to specify the several (usually physical) components of something. The distinction is exemplified in the following:

His argument consists in casting aspersions at all previous work in the field.

The kit consists of scissors, thread and sewing cards.

However the distinction emerged only last century, and is more often observed in formal style than in impromptu speech. In fact the verb *consist* seems to leave a trail of obsolete *collocations* behind it. Once upon a time it was *consist on* and *consist by.*

consistence or **consistency** See under -nce/-ncy.

consonance or **consonancy** See under -nce/-ncy.

consonants See under **vowels.**

consortium For the plural of this word, see under **-um.**

constitutionist or **constitutionalist** See under -ist.

contagious or **infectious** These both imply that something spreads from person to person, and provided it is not an identifiable disease, you could use either. Both have been used figuratively since the eighteenth century. At first they mostly coupled with words implying negative social phenomena, such as *folly* and *panic*, but the nineteenth century saw **contagious** associated with *vigor*, and **infectious** with *good humor*, as well as other positive collocations of this kind.

In medical usage however, it is important to distinguish them. **Contagious** there has the quite specific meaning of being spread from person to person by physical contact, while **infectious** simply means "communicable or capable of being spread by any means". So **infectious** is the broader term. An *Infectious Diseases* hospital is concerned with those which are spread by water, moist air, insects etc., not just human contact.

contemporary or **contemporaneous** As adjectives, both mean "occurring at the same point or period in time", and both collocate with *with*:

Shakespeare was contemporary with Queen Elizabeth I.

The use of cast iron in China was almost contemporaneous with that of forged iron in Europe.

It has been suggested that **contemporaneous** usually couples with inanimates (and **contemporary** with human beings), as those examples happen to show. But if there is any such tendency, it probably results as much from the fact that

contemporary is an everyday English word, while **contemporaneous** appears most often in academic and abstract discussions.

In the last century, **contemporary** (as adjective) has developed a new meaning "modern" or "of *our* times", which it does not share with **contemporaneous**. It appears in expressions such as "contemporary artists" and "contemporary theatre", probably as a substitute for *modern*, which by now seems a bit old hat. This new meaning of **contemporary** occasionally lends ambiguity to statements in which the older meaning could also apply:

Dickens shares with contemporary novelists his concern with social issues.
Without further information the reader cannot tell whether nineteenth or twentieth century novelists are being invoked for comparison. Are they Dickens's contemporaries, or those of the writer/reader? The use of **co-temporary** attempts to spotlight the first meaning. (See under **co-**.)

Contemporary, as shown in the previous sentence, can be used as a noun. Unlike the adjective, it is followed by *of*:

Shakespeare was a contemporary of Queen Elizabeth I.
Contemporaneous is not used as a noun. It does however have a role as adverb (*contemporaneously*), while there is no adverb for **contemporary**.

Note the five syllables in **contemporary**, though it's sometimes pronounced and written as if there were only four. To secure the spelling of the last two vowels, think of **contemporaneous** and especially the two syllables after *-temp*.

contemptible or **contemptuous** These adjectives are complementary in meaning. **Contemptuous** is the attitude of those who hold something (or someone) in contempt. Whatever they hold in contempt is **contemptible**—for them at least.

Behind both words is the lost verb *contemn*, which was used by Shakespeare and in the King James Bible. By the nineteenth century it survived only in literary usage, and only in writing could it be clearly distinguished from *condemn*. Both verbs are extremely negative in their judgement, which is reinforced in the case of *condemn* by its use in law and religion.

continual or **continuous** Dictionary definitions in Australia, America and Britain show that the line of demarcation between these is no longer so clear. Both are now used in the sense of "nonstop", the meaning which used to belong to **continuous**. However **continual** still usually keeps to itself the meaning of "occurring repeatedly or persistently".

Even this distinction is liable to disappear soon, under the influence of educational jargon. What is known as *continuous assessment* is not actually that in practice, but rather *continual assessment*—luckily for the students concerned. To be assessed repeatedly is bad enough, but to be assessed nonstop would be intolerable.

For the grammatical concept *continuous aspect*, see under **aspect**.

continuance, continuation or **continuity** Both Australian and American dictionaries allow that **continuance** and **continuation** may be substitutes for each other, though each has its own centre of gravity. **Continuance** maintains stronger links with the verb *continue*, implying an unbroken operation or provision (the *continuance of your salary*), or an uninterrupted stay in the same place (*the prisoners' continuance in substandard conditions*). But **continuation** often implies resumption after a break, whether in the dimensions of space or time;

> *We had to wait a week for the continuation of the discussion.*
> *The continuation of this article is to be found on p.19.*

The second example shows how **continuation** comes to mean the physical extension of something. Its capacity to take on more concrete meanings helps to make it much more frequent than **continuance** in present-day English.

The word **continuity** emphasises the lack of breaks or disjunctions in something, as for example *continuity of service*. The word has assumed particular importance in the audiovisual mass media, where continuity of communication is a point of professional pride. Job titles such as *continuity girl* and *continuity man* identify the person who checks that there are no abrupt changes or unexplained pauses in the output. The *continuity* itself is the comprehensive script (for a broadcast) or scenario (for a film), which details the words, music, sound effects (and camera work) which are going on simultaneously.

contra- This prefix originated in Latin as an adverb meaning "against or opposed to". It appears in Latin loanwords such as *contradiction* and *contravene*, and in a few modern English creations, such as:

> *contraception contradistinction contraindication*

The prefix is the same in modern Italian and Spanish, and from there we derive *contraband, contralto* and *contrapuntal*.

The so-called *Contras* in Nicaragua were right-wing guerillas who enjoyed some support from the US government in their struggle against the left-wing regime of President Ortega. In this case *contra* is a clipped form of the Spanish *contrarevolucionario* "counterrevolutionary". As that example shows, English often prefers to use the prefix *counter-* instead of *contra-*. (See further under **counter-**.)

contractions In writing and editing this term now has two meanings:

1 abbreviated forms of single words in which the middle is omitted, e.g. *Mr, Dr*; as opposed to those in which the end is omitted, e.g. *Prof., Rev.* This difference entails a special punctuation practice for some writers and editors, who use a full stop with the second type but not the first. (See further under **abbreviations**.) The distinction between **contractions** and abbreviations was articulated by Fowler (1926), though he did not use the word *contraction*, and it seems to have developed as part of the British editorial tradition after World

War II. The *Authors' and Printers' Dictionary* (1938) does not mention it; but it is acknowledged as common practice in *Copy-editing* (1975), and shown in copious examples in the *Oxford Dictionary for Writers and Editors* (1981). In North America such *contractions* are known as **suspensions**, though the practice of punctuating them differently is not widespread. The Chicago *Manual of Style* (1981) mentions them only in a passing footnote; and in Canada they are mostly associated with government documents.

2 telescoped phrases such as *don't*, *I'll*, *there's*, *we've*. In all such cases the apostrophe marks the place where a letter or letters have been omitted. Note that with *shan't* and *won't*, a single apostrophe is all that is used, even though they have shed letters in more than one place.

Contractions like these affect one of two elements in the verb phrase:
- the word *not*, when it follows any of the auxiliaries:
  isn't wasn't can't couldn't doesn't don't didn't hasn't haven't hadn't mustn't etc.
- the auxiliary itself, especially following a personal pronoun:

I'm	*you're*	*s/he's*	*we're*	*they're*	(*be*, present only)
I've	*you've*	*s/he's*	*we've*	*they've*	(*have*, present)
I'd	*you'd*	*s/he'd*	*we'd*	*they'd*	(*have*, past)
I'd	*you'd*	*s/he'd*	*we'd*	*they'd*	(*would*)
I'll	*you'll*	*s/he'll*	*we'll*	*they'll*	(*will*)

Note that the last set are sometimes said to be contractions of *shall*, though this is unlikely. (See further under **shall** section 2.)

As the list shows, the contractions from different auxiliaries are sometimes identical (see *I'd*, *s/he's*). Whether they stand for *I had* or *I would*, *s/he is* or *s/he has* must be decided with the help of neighboring words. The most vital clue is the form of the verb after them. So with *I'd keep*, *I'd* must be "I would"; with *I'd kept* it is "I had". (See further under **auxiliaries**.)

In conversation and informal writing, auxiliary verbs can be telescoped with almost any kind of word or phrase which serves as the subject: a personal pronoun, a demonstrative or interrogative, a noun or noun phrase, and so on:
That's going too far.
There's a lot more rain coming.
Who'd want a thing like that?
The word's getting around.
The king of Spain's on his way here.
In just one instance the pronoun itself is contracted: *let's*. There were of course others like that in older English: *'tis*, *'twas*, *'twere*, all of which are now archaisms.

Contractions like those mentioned above are very common in speech, and increasingly they appear in writing, for example in newspaper columns and in magazines, including serious ones such as *Choice*. In the past they were felt to be too colloquial, and editors of academic journals are still inclined to edit them

out. The writers of formal reports may feel that they undermine the authority
and dignity of their words. But the informality that contractions lend to a style
is these days often sought, in business and elsewhere, as something which helps
to ease communication.

Contractions have been used from time to time in this book, for reasons of style
and the rhythm of particular sentences.

---

contralto For the plural of this word, see **Italian plurals**.

convener or **convenor** The spelling **convener** is older and better supported
in the *Oxford Dictionary*'s citations, and it is the first preference in other British,
American and Australian dictionaries. The Australian Government *Style Manual*
uses **convener** when recommending the word as an alternative to *chairman*.
Still **convenor** enjoys considerable support in Australian institutions—as if the
latinate *-or* suffix gives it a formal status that the common *-er* of English cannot.
(See further under **-er/-or**.)

convergence or **convergency** See under **-nce/-ncy**.

conversance or **conversancy** See under **-nce/-ncy**.

conversationalist or **conversationist** Of these two, Australians seem to
prefer the longer form, and it's given priority in both the *Macquarie* and *Collins*
dictionaries. For the preference in other similar pairs, see under **-ist**.

conveyer or **conveyor** Conveyer is the older form, and the one for **ad hoc**
agentive uses such as *a conveyer of good news* (see further under **-er/-or**). But
conveyor has established itself in the fields of law and engineering, and is the
spelling normally used for any mechanical carrying device.

cooperate or **co-operate** See under **co-**.

coordination In grammar this term implies that two clauses (or phrases or
words) are joined so as to be equal in status. Compare **subordination**, which
makes one clause subordinate to the other. (See further under **clauses**.)
    For the question as to whether to hyphenate **co(-)ordination** (as well as
co(-)ordinate and *co(-)ordinator*), see under **co-**.

Coori or **Koori** See under **Koori**.

copular verbs This term refers to verbs which forge a link between the subject
and complement of a clause. The verb *be* is the most common *copula*, and the
only one which is without semantic content of its own. Others typically show
that the complement is a current, or else resulting state of affairs. Examples
include:

- current *appear feel keep look remain seem smell sound taste*
- resulting *become come fall get go grow prove run turn*

The complement of a *copular verb* may be either an adjective, adjectival phrase, noun phrase, or an adverb (adjunct) or adverbial phrase, according to the *Comprehensive Grammar of English* (1985). The following are examples of each:

The reception was (highly) successful.
The reception proved a great success.
The reception went brilliantly.

Alternative names for the *copular verb* are *copulative verb* or *linking verb*.

coquette or **cocotte** See cocotte.

cord or **chord** See chord.

cornea For the plural of this word, see under **-a**.

cornerways or **cornerwise** For the choice between these, see **-wise**.

corporal or **capital (punishment)** Neither form of punishment is as familiar as it used to be. **Corporal punishment** involves the striking of another person's body (usually with an instrument such as a stick or whip, according to a prescribed formula) to induce that person to mend his or her ways. **Capital punishment** means the legal execution of a person found guilty of certain major crimes.

   Corporal punishment has been outlawed in most government school systems since 1980, after lobbying by pressure groups of teachers and parents. It remains only in some non-state schools as a form of discipline. **Capital punishment** has not been carried out in Australia since 1967, and the last case (in Victoria) was accompanied by fierce public protests. The unfamiliarity of the practices, the fact that they are no longer public issues, and the similar shapes of the words *corporal* and *capital* all contribute to the fact that the two phrases are sometimes confused … And one hears a caller on talkback radio urging the reintroduction of *capital* punishment in schools.

corps, corpse or **corpus** These are, respectively, the French, English and Latin word for "body", though none of them nowadays refers to the living human form. The oldest of the three in English is **corpse**, going back to the fourteenth century. It was earlier spelled *corse* and *corps*, and until about 1700 could refer to bodies either living or dead. Only since the eighteenth century has it been confined to the dead body, and only in the nineteenth century did the final *e* become a regular part of the spelling. Some explain the *e* as a backformation from *corpses*, the English plural of *corps*; yet many English words were spelled both with and without a final *e* in the early modern era.

   Corps came from French in the eighteenth century with the silent *ps* of its French pronunciation. It survives in references to organised bodies of people, especially the *corps de ballet*, the *corps diplomatique*, and the military unit which consists of two or more divisions. In *esprit de corps* ("common spirit") it means the group of people who are part of the same enterprise.

Corpus is the Latin form which appears only as a specialised word, in law, medicine and scholarship. Its legal use in phrases such as **corpus delicti** and **habeas corpus** is discussed under those headings. In medical and anatomical usage it appears in reference to complex structures such as the *corpus callosum* in the human brain. For scholars, a **corpus** may be either a collection of works by selected groups of authors, or a database of language material, sometimes homogeneous, sometimes heterogeneous. (See further under **English language databases**.)

Note that **corpus** is usually pluralised in English as *corpora* (its Latin plural form)—at least when it appears in scholarly documents. However the native English plural is often said and occasionally written. (See **-us** section 3.)

corpus delicti This legal phrase, borrowed straight from Latin, means "the body of the crime". Lawyers use it in an abstract way to refer to the various elements which make up a criminal offence. It is however often misused as a reference to material objects associated with a crime, and even to the victim in a murder case. More lightheartedly, it's occasionally used to refer to a shapely female figure, as if the Latin *delicti* were somehow related to the English words *delicious* and *delight*.

Note that the phrase *(in) flagrante delicto* "as the crime was being committed" employs the same Latin word *delictum* "crime". It too is subject to some ambiguity, partly because of *flagrante*. (See further under **flagrant** or **fragrant**.)

correspond to or **correspond with** In earlier usage, a clear distinction was made: **correspond with** meant "exchange letters with", and **correspond to** meant "have a similar function or shape", when two items were being compared. Nowadays **correspond with** is also used in comparisons of function and shape, though according to *Webster's English Usage* (1989) it's still the less common of the two. This is borne out in the Australian ACE corpus, where non-epistolary instances of **correspond with** were in the minority by 4:7. Yet the fact that the construction using *with* is gaining ground makes interesting comparison with what is happening after *compare*, where *compare with* is gradually losing ground overall. (See **compare with/compare to**.)

correspondent or **co(-)respondent** A correspondent is a person who regularly writes letters or dispatches. **Co(-)respondent** is the legal term for the third party in a divorce suit. The hyphenated spelling used in Australian and British English helps to prevent confusion between the two words—although in Australia the **co-respondent** no longer has to be named after radical changes to divorce procedures since the *Family Law Act* of 1975. But when the **corespondent** is referred to in American English, the word is set solid, according to both *Webster's* and *Random House* dictionaries, in keeping with their normal practice for longer words formed with *co-*.

corrigenda and **corrigendum**   See under **-um**.

corroboree   The spelling of this word for a ritual Aboriginal gathering was very unstable until the twentieth century. Nearly twenty different forms of it are recorded, of which *corobory, corrobbaree, corrobori, corrobory* and *corrobara* are the more common. Morris's *Dictionary of Austral English* (1898) had it as *corrobbery* in which the likeness with *robbery* was unfortunate. The standard twentieth century spelling **corroboree** likens it (more positively) to *corroborate*, though there is no etymological justification. Note also the *-ee* suffix, like that of various exotic words. (See further under **-ee**.)

The Aboriginal word which the early settlers were trying to render was *garaabara* "dance", borrowed from the Dharuk Aborigines in 1790. For the variability between the *g* of that word and the *c* of English spelling, see **Aboriginal names**.

cortex   The plural of this word is discussed under **-x**.

cosh or **kosh**   See under **k/c**.

cosher or **kosher**   See **kosher**.

cost   The past tense of this verb depends on its meaning. In its common use, meaning "be priced at", the past is the same as the present:
They're a bargain. Yesterday they cost twenty dollars. Today they cost fifteen.
For other verbs which have no distinct form for the past tense, see **zero past tense**.

In business usage, when **cost** means "estimate the dollar costs of doing or producing (something)", its past tense has the regular *-ed* inflection:
They costed the new product rather conservatively.

cosy or **cozy**   The spelling **cosy** is standard in Australia and Britain, whereas **cozy** is usual in the USA. The American spelling accords with the general American preference for *z* rather than *s* in the final syllable of words (see under **-ise/-ize** and **-yse/-yze**).

A number of other spellings (*cosey, cosie, cozie*) have been recorded for this informal word, which first appeared in print in the eighteenth century. It entered the language from the north of Britain, and may be an Old Norse loanword related to the modern Norwegian verb *kosa* meaning "be comfortable". Note that the alternative spellings apply not only to the English adjective, but also to the noun which refers to the padded cover that keeps a teapot warm.

could or **might**   These two modal auxiliaries share some uses, as well as having areas of independence. Like other modals they can express the writer's

judgement about the likelihood of an event—that it was or is possible, or that
it may occur in the future:

They could have been there. They might have been there.
You could be right. You might be right.
It could rain tonight. It might rain tonight.

Both **could** and **might** are used in polite requests:

Could I have the keys please? Might I have the keys please?

In such expressions, **might** is more tentative and self-effacing than **could**, and
both are less direct than *can* or *may*. (See further under **can** or **may**.) **Might** is
the least common of the four in Australian English, according to Collins's
research (1988).

Could has other minor roles relating to its origins as the past tense of *can*.
Like *can*, it sometimes expresses the ability to do something:

When he was younger, he could sing like Caruso.

It may also indicate something previously permitted or allowed:

Until then, researchers could do surreptitious recordings.

A curious detail of **could** is the *l* in its spelling, which is never pronounced,
and only began to be part of its written form from 1525 on. The *l* was added
to bring it into line with other modals *should* and *would*, where there are *l*s for
good historical reasons. By a further irony, the *l* later disappeared from the
pronunciation of *should* and *would*, so that they now rhyme with *could*.

(See further under **modality** and **modal verbs**.)

could of or **could have** See **have** section 3.

councillor or **councilor,** and **counsellor** or **counselor** The first word
in each pair shows the standard British spelling, and the more common one in
Australia. The second is the distinctive US spelling, although the major
American dictionaries differ a little on them, with *Random House* preferring the
spellings with a single *l* in each case, while *Webster's* gives preference to
councillor in the first pair and **counselor** in the second. The *Random House*
preferences accord with the usual American use of single rather than double
consonants in such contexts. (See **-l/-ll-**.)

The two pairs go back to separate Latin words: *concilium* "assembly or
meeting", and *consilium* "consultation, plan or advice". The older meanings
are still more or less there in *council of war*, and *wise counsel*. But the two
words were often mistaken for each other in Middle English, especially with
the interchanging of *c* and *s* by Anglo-Norman scribes (as with *defense/defence*
and others). The idea of consultation passed from the second to the first word,
so that a *council* became not just a meeting, but a consultative and deliberative
body constituted to meet at certain intervals. And *counsel* gained a collective
sense, being used for "a *group* of legal advisers" from the fourteenth century
on.

Yet the old distinction between public meeting and private consultation seems
to persist in the work of **council(l)or** and **counsel(l)or**, and helps to distinguish

them. The **council(l)or** is a member of a publicly constituted body, whereas the **counsel(l)or** is usually consulted privately for his or her advice.

counseled or **counselled** For the choice between these, see under -l/-ll-.

count nouns Many nouns refer to things which can be counted, and so they can be pluralised, witness:

  answers books doctors fences offices telescopes

They contrast with **mass nouns**, which are almost always used in the singular because they refer to concepts, substances or qualities with no clear-cut boundaries. For example:

  butter cream education honesty information keenness
  knowledge mud respectability rice

As those examples show, *mass nouns* may be either concrete or abstract. (See further under **nouns**.)

  Some *mass nouns* can be used as **count nouns** under special circumstances. The word *butter* is usually a mass noun, but cooks and supermarket assistants may speak of "all the butters in the fridge", meaning the various types of butter—salted, unsalted and cultured. This "countable" use of a *mass noun* is the reason why some grammars (such as the *Introduction to the Grammar of English* (1984)) prefer to speak of *countable* and *uncountable nouns* in particular cases.

  Knowing which are normally **count nouns** and *mass nouns* in English is one of the more difficult points for second language learners. The nonnative speaker who produces "informations" is up against this problem, with a word which is always a *mass noun* in English.

counter- This prefix meaning "against" was borrowed from French. It came into English with **loanwords** such as *countermand* and *counterpoint*. In modern English words formed with it, it has developed other shades of meaning, suggesting opposition, retaliation or complementary action:

  counterattack counterbalance counterfactual counterintelligence
  counterinsurgency counterproductive counteroffensive countersign
  countersink counterweight

In the USA *counter-* substitutes for *anti-* in *counterclockwise*, but this is the only instance.

  Counter- is normally set solid with the word it prefixes, though some British writers would insert a hyphen before a following *r*, as in *counter-revolutionary*. The more important point to note is that *counter* should have space after it in compounds such as *counter lunch* and *counter service*—where it represents the word *counter* "bench or table at which goods are sold", not the prefix **counter-**.

coup de ... The French word *coup*, literally "stroke", appears in several phrases which have become naturalised in English. To translate it as "act" (rather than "stroke") gets closer to the meaning generally, but it develops a special character in each of the following phrases:

coup d'état	a sudden political move, one which overthrows an existing government
coup de foudre	a thunder bolt, or love at first sight
coup de grâce	a blow or shot which finishes off someone in the throes of death
coup d'oeil	a quick glance which takes in a whole scene at once
coup de théâtre	a dramatic act designed to draw attention to itself

Clearly it's what goes with *coup* that dictates its meaning. Note however that when *coup* is used alone in English, it always means *coup d'état*.

coupe or **coupé** In French the accent always serves to distinguish these two, but in English the accent (and the pronunciation) is capricious. **Coupe** without an accent is really the French for "cup", and it appears most often on menus in the names of desserts—*coupe de fruits* etc.—for a sweet, colorful concoction served in a glass dish.

Coupé, literally "cut back", refers to a road vehicle. Originally a type of carriage, it now means a luxury car which seats only two people, with a long, sloping back aerodynamically designed for speed. However the distinguishing accent is not often there when the word is printed in English texts, and this has fostered a pronunciation of the word with one syllable. It makes it identical with the word used on menus.

Even stranger, confusion between the two means that some Australians give two syllables to the *coupe* mentioned on menus. To those aware of the difference, a *coupé de fruits* suggests the ultimate cornucopia: a luxury sports car used to transport a harvest festival supply of glorious fruits to your table!

cousins Are they my second cousins, or my first cousins once removed? Strictly speaking, they cannot be both. To sort it out, the first question to ask is whether they share one set of the grandparents with you. If the answer is yes, then you're first cousins. If the closest common ancestors are your greatgrandparents, then you're second cousins.

Removed registers the fact that you're a generation apart in either the first or second cousin line of descendants. So the children of your first cousins are your *first cousins once removed*. And if life and time permit, those cousins' children's children are your *first cousins twice removed*.

Having said that, the term *second cousin* is sometimes loosely applied to a *first cousin once removed*. But those more conscious of genealogy make a clear distinction between them.

Note that the term *cousin(s)-german* is an old legal way of referring to first cousins.

cozy or **cosy** See cosy.

-cracy This Greek element meaning "rule (by)" is used in both ancient and modern formations to identify specific kinds of government. We find it in purely

Greek words such as *democracy, plutocracy* and *theocracy,* as well as contemporary hybrids such as *bureaucracy, mobocracy* and *squattocracy.*

While **-cracy** forms abstract nouns, its counterpart *-crat* makes the corresponding agent noun "one who participates in rule by", for both older and newer formations. Thus *democrat* stands beside *democracy, bureaucrat* beside *bureaucracy* etc.

credible or **creditable** These words sometimes overlap in modern usage, because of the newer, colloquial use of **credible**. Essentially *credible* means "believable", as in *a credible account of the accident.* From this it is increasingly extended to mean "convincing", and applied to anything from a politician's words, to the performance by an artist or sports figure:

> *In this last race before the Melbourne Cup, he's looking very credible.*
> *Lew performed very credibly in the last A-grade season.*

At this point it's no longer clear whether this is an extension of **credible**, or a mistake for **creditable** "deserving credit or respect"—just the slip of a syllable. **Creditable** is a less common and more formal word altogether, one which is more often written than said, and it seems an unlikely target in many spoken situations.

But with this extension of **credible** to mean "convincing, impressive" we have the remarkable possibility of it coming to mean much the same as **incredible** in its colloquial sense. The use of *incredible* to mean "amazing, impressive" is widespread, no doubt helped by a gee-whiz television program called *That's incredible*! Not often do a word and its opposite coincide.

credulity or **credibility** These words once complemented each other, **credulity** meaning a "willingness to believe" and **credibility** meaning "quality of being believable". But the negative tones of the adjective *credulous* "being *too* willing to believe" seem to impinge on **credulity**, and make us uncomfortable about saying that something *strains our/your credulity.* Increasingly the phrase we hear uttered is *strains our/your credibility,* and dictionaries now add the meaning "capacity to believe" to **credibility**. Meanwhile *credulousness* is available if we want to stress the fact of being too willing to believe something.

crematorium For the plural of this word, see **-um**.

crème de la crème To be the cream of society is not enough. You have to be **crème de la crème** "cream of the cream". The elitist symbolism of cream goes back at least four centuries in English, to when Mulcaster described "gentlemen" as "cream of the common (= community)". Yet having floated to the top (in those days before milk was homogenised) it could be difficult to maintain your distinctive position except by cultivating things French ... and **crème de la crème** makes its appearance in the nineteenth century, to satisfy that need. To enhance the phrase even further in English, some writers replace the proper grave accents with circumflexes: *crême de la crême*!

Note that the French themselves distinguish carefully between *crème* "cream" and *chrême* "oil used for anointing". Both words actually derive from the same medieval French word *chresme* "oil for anointing". But in standard French they have always had different accents, reflecting the belief that they had separate origins.

creole See under **pidgins**.

crevasse or **crevice** These words are in fact from the same source, the medieval French *crevace*, but centuries of separation have helped their spellings and meanings to diverge. **Crevice**, meaning "fissure or crack", came into English in the fourteenth century as a variant form of the original French word. **Crevasse** entered English only in the nineteenth, with different meanings on either side of the Atlantic. In the Deep South (probably on loan from Louisiana French), it's recorded from 1814 on to mean a "breach in the bank of a river". A little later than that, British alpine explorers brought back from Switzerland the same word as meaning "deep chasm in a glacier", and this meaning has spread to other parts of the English-speaking world.

cri de coeur This French phrase means " a cry from the heart", a plea which is spontaneous, intense and free of affectation. A cry **de profundis** (Latin for "out of the depths") is less personal but more desperate. The words come from the Vulgate version of the beginning of Psalm 130: "Out of the depths have I cried unto thee …"

crime passionnel This French phrase meaning "crime of passion" is not an official legal term, yet it highlights the different treatment given under French and English law to crimes (especially murder) prompted by sexual jealousy. The *Encyclopaedia Britannica* of 1910 explains it thus: "French juries almost invariably find extenuating circumstances" by which to acquit the murderer. It coincides with an English stereotype of the French: as people for whom the affairs of the heart are paramount. The principle for "crimes of passion" seems to be there in the French *Code Penal*, article 324, which allows husbands finding their wives **in flagrante delicto** to shoot them. Whatever the legal issues, English spelling of the phrase is often erratic. Instead of the French spelling (as above), it may appear as *crime passionel, crime passionelle* and *crime passionnelle*.

criterion and **criteria** Dictionaries all present these as the standard singular and plural forms for this Greek **loanword** (see further under **-on**). **Criterion** is in fact rather uncommon, and **criteria** turns up as a plural/collective/singular almost three times as often (20:7) in the Australian ACE database. It is not uncommonly heard as a singular in conversation, and research among young Australian adults by Collins in 1979 showed that more than 85% treated it as a singular. *Webster's English Usage* has citations for it from the 1940s, from a variety of sources including the advertising flyers of certain well-known educational publishers, mass-circulating magazines and academic journals. It notes also the use of the analogical plural *criterias* in speech, though not yet recorded in print.

Meanwhile dictionaries regularly offer *criterions* as an alternative plural for the word, though according to *Webster's* it has had little use apart from "a spate of popularity in the late 1940s and early 1950s". This coincides intriguingly with the first records of **criteria** as singular, hinting at a reversal of roles whose repercussions are still being worked out.

Croatia   See **Yugoslavia**.

crocheted and **crocheting**   The final *t* is never doubled before a verb suffix (see **t**). Compare **ricochet**.

crossways or **crosswise**   See under -**wise**.

crudité or **crudity**   The *crudités* (raw vegetables served with a dip at cocktail parties) are certainly not intended to be seen as evidence of **crudity**. They remind us that *crude* has come a long way in English from meaning "uncooked, raw, unprepared", which its counterpart in French (*cru*) still does. This meaning was overtaken in eighteenth century English by figurative senses such as "lacking in maturity and polish" and "lacking in good character and manners", and these are now dominant in *crude* and **crudity**. The only fossil of the earlier meaning of *crude* is in *crude oil*, but that will scarcely help you to appreciate the delights of the crudités put before you.

crueler or **crueller, cruelest** or **cruellest**   The inflected forms of the adjective *cruel* are **crueler** and **cruelest** if we go by the *Oxford Dictionary*'s citations since the eighteenth century (when it was no longer spelled *cruell* in the absolute form). No further light is shed on the question in the second edition of the *Oxford Dictionary* (1989), in spite of the famous use of the **cruellest** in T.S. Eliot's *Waste Land*, which begins:

    April is the cruellest month …

From a London publisher (Faber and Faber) it suggests the readiness of twentieth century British editors to use two *l*s in these words, though very few dictionaries give a lead on it. Perhaps it's assumed that because the word has two syllables, writers will prefer to use *more cruel/most cruel* for comparisons rather than the inflected forms (see further under **adjectives**). *Webster's Dictionary* is one of the few which presents the alternative inflected forms of the adjective, giving preference to **crueler** and **cruelest** with one *l* as we might expect. (See further under -**l/-ll-**.)

-**ctic/-xic**   These endings create variant forms for the adjectives associated with *anorexia* and *dyslexia*:

    anorectic/anorexic   dyslectic/dyslexic

The two are used interchangeably. In both cases, the form with -**ctic** is the older one, dating (in the case of *anorectic*) from the nineteenth century. The spellings with **-xic** have been current since the 1960s, and clearly forge a stronger link with the name of the disorder.

Note that the much older adjective *apoplectic* (relating to *apoplexia*) has no alternative in "apoplexic", though the oldfashioned-sounding *apoplectical* is recorded as a variant.

-ction/-xion These have been alternative spellings for a small group of nouns:

connection	or	*connexion*
deflection		*deflexion*
genuflection		*genuflexion*
inflection		*inflexion*
reflection		*reflexion*

Current usage everywhere nowadays prefers **-ction**, and **-xion** seems increasingly old-fashioned. The forms with **-xion** were borrowed straight from Latin, and reinforced by common knowledge of Latin. With declining knowledge of Latin, the words have been adapted under the influence of the related verb (*connect*, *deflect* etc). The only word like these which steadfastly remains as *-xion* is *complexion*—no doubt because of the lack of a related verb.

Note that the similar adjectives *reflective* and *reflexive* have developed quite separate realms of meaning, and are not interchangeable like *reflection/reflexion*. (See further under **reflective/reflexive**.)

cui bono This rather elusive Latin phrase asks the question "for whom (is/was) the benefit?" or, less literally "who gains (or gained) by it?". It was originally used by Cicero when defending his clients in court, as a way of querying the motivation for committing a crime. But since its first appearance in English in the seventeenth century, it has also been taken to mean "to what end". A number of *Oxford Dictionary* citations have it questioning whether something is of practical utility, and being used to express utilitarian values.

cuisine minceur See under **nouvelle cuisine**.

cul-de-sac Translated word for word, this unlikely French phrase means "bottom of the bag". But in English it expresses several things for which there are no ready alternatives. Essentially it covers structures and situations from which there is only one way out—the way one came in. In anatomy, a **cul-de-sac** is a bodily organ like the appendix which can indeed cause trouble because there is only one way in and out. In military manoeuvres, a **cul-de-sac** is the dangerous position of a force which finds itself checked in front and on both sides, so that the only way out is backwards. In suburban terrain however, the **cul-de-sac** means a quiet street with no through traffic. In the age of the motor car it's exactly the kind of street which town planners try to build into new subdivisions.

In French the plural is *culs-de-sac*, but the hyphens encourage writers to treat it as a compound, and to pluralise it as *cul-de-sacs*. (See further under **plurals** section 2.)

cum laude This phrase, borrowed from Latin, means "with praise". It is usually found in connection with American university and college degrees, to distinguish three levels of honors:

cum laude	with distinction
magna cum laude	with great distinction
summa cum laude ⎫	with the greatest distinction
maxima cum laude ⎭	

Those phrases all refer to degrees achieved competitively through the examination process. A degree given **honoris causa** is acquired without examination, and as a personal accolade.

Other Latin expressions used in connection with exam results are **aeq.**, an abbreviation for *aequalis* "equal"; and **proxime accessit** (or *prox. acc.*) "s/he came very close". The latter is some consolation to the person who was the runner up on a special award or prize.

cumquat or **kumquat** See under k/c.

cupfuls or **cupsful** See under -ful.

curb or **kerb** In Australian and British English the spelling **curb** serves for the verb "restrain", the noun "restraint", and various restraining devices; while **kerb** is for the concrete or stone step that divides the roadway from the footpath. In American English, all are spelled **curb**.

Surprisingly, those meanings all originated in the French word *courbe*, literally "curve". The idea of restraint comes from the **curb**, i.e. curved bit in a horse's harness. The **kerb** on the street evolved from the **curb** which was originally a curved frame or framework around wells and barrels, and then extended to frameworks of other shapes, including those around trapdoors and roof lines. The spelling for these extensions of the word varied from **curb** to *kirb* and **kerb**—hence the one which attached itself to the stone edge that marked the carriageway of improved London streets in the mid-nineteenth century. But like other late developments in British spelling, it has never caught on in American English.

curly brackets This is an alternative name for **braces**. (See **brackets** section 1c.)

currant or **current** Getting -ent and -ant in the right places is a problem with a number of English words (see under -ant/-ent), and with **current** and **currant** it affects the meaning. Most of the time writers want **current**, which has many more uses in English, as a noun for running water and electricity, as well as an adjective meaning "happening now". All those senses derive from the Old French word for "running" *corant*, though the word was respelled in English according to its Latin antecedent.

The spelling of **currant**, the small dried fruit which is the staple of Christmas cakes, has a bizarre history. *Currants* were originally named as "raisins of

Corinth'' (the Greek place with which they were associated), and some medieval recipes give their name in full, as *raisins de corauntz*. Many recipes then reduce the phrase to the last element *corauntz*, which reflected French pronunciation of the placename. The spelling *corauntz* had quite a vogue in fifteenth century England, but English cooks often interpreted it as a plural word, as we see from respellings of it as *corantes*, *currants* and even *currence*. (See under **false plurals** for other examples.) From these, singular forms were derived in the sixteenth and seventeenth century, including *coren*, *coran*, *curran*, *current* and *currant*.

The word **currant** is also applied to quite different plants of the family Ribes: the *redcurrant* and *blackcurrant*. They are shrubs, not vines, and their small berries are made into jams and jellies. The spelling catches people, witness the recipe on a supermarket product for *redcurrent* jelly—an electrifying dish!

currency This word acquired special significance in colonial Australia, becoming an **antonym** for **sterling** in two senses. **Currency** referred to the locally devised notes and coins (including the *holey dollar* and the *dump* struck from its centre), which served as a medium of exchange though they were continually devalued against **sterling**, the coins and notes brought from England. From this **sterling** came to refer to the British-born members of the Australian community, and so **currency** acquired the meaning of locally born white Australians. This usage is consolidated in the nineteenth century phrase *currency lads and lasses*.

curriculum The plural of this word is discussed under **-um**.

curriculum vitae This Latin phrase meaning ''the course of one's life'' should not be interpreted too literally in modern English. When a potential employer requests a **curriculum vitae** from applicants, what is needed is an outline of your working career so far, not a complete autobiography. In the USA, and often now in Australia, it's called a *resumé*. (See **resumé**.)

A **curriculum vitae** begins with a few personal facts, such as age, nationality, marital status, and highest level of education achieved; and then lists the positions you have held in chronological order, with notes on the responsibilities in each, in case the job titles are less than self-explanatory. The phrase is abbreviated as *CV* or *c.v.*

Note that, strictly speaking, the plural would be *curricula vitae* (for several versions of the CV for one person) or *curricula vitarum* (CVs for several people). But most people would pluralise it as *curriculum vitaes*, as for other foreign compounds in English. (See **plurals** section 2.)

curtsy or **curtsey** These spellings are offered as alternatives in most dictionaries, but the first is always the one preferred. Just as the practice of *curtsying* is disappearing (except on stage), its spelling has finally settled down. In the centuries when it was an important social gesture, the spelling was quite volatile, even for celebrated writers such as Jane Austen.

The word is a derivative of *courtesy*, and people's awareness of this is evident in earlier spellings such as *court'sy*, *curtesy* and *curt'sy*. However the spelling **curtsey** simply reflects the common variation between *-y* and *-ey* at the end of some traditional words. For other examples, see under **-ey/-y**.

Note that the two spellings allow two plurals: *curtsies* and *curtseys*.

CV See **curriculum vitae**.

cyclone, hurricane, tornado, typhoon or **willy-willy** Though all of these refer to a huge destructive whirlwind, each one has its association with particular parts of the world. The first and last are standard Australian terms, **cyclone** for the whirlwind which forms out of a barometric depression over water, and **willy-willy** for the dust and sand storms associated with northwestern Australia. The latter is an Aboriginal word from the Yinjibarndi people of the Fortescue River district, WA.

Cyclone is the term normally used of whirlwinds which affect the Australian coasts, from the Indian or south Pacific Ocean. It is a metereologist's word, borrowed straight from Greek. In the northwest Pacific and China Seas, **typhoon** is the usual term. Its etymology is much disputed, though it probably owes something to the Chinese *tai fung* "big wind", as well as the Greek monster god *Typhon* and the Greek word *typhon* "whirlwind". The Greek word is pervasive and seems to have found its way into Portuguese, as well as Arabic, Persian and Hindi; and it is clear that it could easily have been superimposed on the Chinese expression by Europeans who reached the west Pacific.

In and around the Atlantic, Spanish-derived words for whirlwind are the ones used. **Hurricane** is the standard term in the West Indies and the Caribbean coastline, and the Spanish word *huracán* mimics a West Indian one for it. Under American influence, **hurricane** has also spread to the northeastern Pacific and Hawaii. **Tornado** is a purely Spanish concoction out of their words for "thunder" *tronada* and "turn" *tornar*. It is most often associated with whirlwinds in Central America and West Africa. Dictionaries show that **tornado** serves both as a synonym for **hurricane**, and as a more specific word for the whirlwind that develops over land and cuts a much narrower path of destruction.

cyder or **cider, cypher** or **cipher** See under **i/y**.

czar or **tsar** This is hardly a common word in Australia, but both spellings are in use according to the ACE corpus, with **czar** outnumbering **tsar** by 4:2. The spelling **czar** is preferred in the USA, according to *Webster's* and *Random House*, while modern British dictionaries have **tsar**. A third, rare, spelling *tzar* is listed in some dictionaries. All three are attempts to transliterate a word from the Russian alphabet, whose symbols do not correspond exactly with those of the Roman alphabet. (See under **alphabets**.)

The spelling **czar** recommends itself to many because it's closer than **tsar** to the common pronunciation of the word (with a *z* as the first sound). It also seems to reflect the word's ultimate origin in *Caesar*. The argument for **tsar** rests on the fact that it's closer to the Russian spelling of the word; and even in the USA, scholars in Slavic studies prefer to use **tsar**. Yet in Britain the spelling **czar** is beginning to appear, partly because of the extended use of the word to mean "big chief or tycoon". This usage originated in the USA last century, and it has caught on in Britain since World War II. Its currency in Australia is shown in references to Rupert Murdoch as the "communications czar of the world".

These developments suggest that **czar** has the edge over **tsar** for general purposes. It also helps to decide the spelling of a number of derivative words:

czardom	rather than	*tsardom*
czarevna		*tsarevna* (in Russian, the daughter-in-law of the **czar**; in English, the daughter of a **czar**)
czarina		*tsarina* (term for the wife of a **czar** used in west European languages)
czarism		*tsarism*
czaritza		*tsaritsa* (Russian term for the wife of a **czar**; the empress)

Czechoslovakia This central European state was formed after World War I, a combination of Bohemia, Moravia and Slovakia. Strictly speaking, only the Bohemians are *Czechs*, but the term *Czech* was often extended to the Moravians and the Slovaks. However the Slovaks maintained their separate identity within **Czechoslovakia**, and negotiated a secession which took effect in January 1993, establishing two new states: the *Slovak Republic* with its capital in Bratislava, and the *Czeck Republic* (note the new spelling) whose capital is Prague.

D

da, dal and **dalla** On whether to capitalise these particles as parts of surnames (as in *Da Costa*, *Da Vinci*), see under **capital letters**. For indexing purposes they are best alphabetised by the particle itself. Compare **van** and **von**.

dais Thinking of "daisy" helps to secure the spelling of this word, and to underscore the pronunciation preferred by dictionaries everywhere.

The alternative pronunciation which has it rhyming with "bias" is acknowledged in American dictionaries, and it correlates with the occasional use of *dias* for the spelling, noted in *Webster's English Usage* (1989). Yet another, older pronunciation is recorded in some British dictionaries, making it one syllable rhyming with "pace", but its disappearance is noted in the second edition of the *Oxford Dictionary* (1989). The currency of the two-syllabled pronunciation is marked by occasional use of a dieresis in the spelling: **daïs**. (See further under **dieresis**.)

The meaning of **dais** has also shifted in the course of time. It is a derivative of the Latin *discus*, which is the rather surprising antecedent for a number of words for furniture: *desco* (in Italian) which becomes *desk* in English, and *Tisch* (the standard German word for "table".) In Middle English and up to 1600, *deis* was the term for a "high table" in a hall, and sometimes by association it referred to the platform the table stood on. The word then disappeared, to be revived by antiquarian writers after 1800, with the meaning "platform" alone.

Dame For the conventional form of names with this title, see under **Sir**.

dangling participles Depending on how and where they were educated, people may be highly sensitive or indifferent to **dangling participles** (also known as **unattached participles**, where dangling participle was too much of a stimulus to the imagination). Yet another name for the same peccadillo was *dangling modifier*. Whichever phrase is used, the problem is essentially about how to relate an independent introductory element to the grammar of the rest of a sentence.

Occasionally the *dangling participle* has strange consequences for the meaning of the sentence; more often it is unremarkable. See for example:

1 *Having said that, it would be a pity to do it too often.*

2 *Now damaged in the stern, the captain ordered the ship back to port.*

3 *Wondering irresolutely what to do, the clock struck twelve.*

Technically there are **dangling participles** in all three sentences: the opening phrase in each is unattached to the subject of the following clause. But only in the third sentence does it become a distraction, when the meaning is sabotaged by the grammar. Where the contents of the sentence are more abstract (as in the first), or where the opening phrase can be related to the object of the sentence (as in the second), the problem is hardly there.

Castigation of "dangling" constructions usually takes place with sentences taken out of context. In its proper context of discourse, the *dangling participle* of the first sentence would have a dual function: to draw preceding arguments together, and to alert readers to an imminent change in the argument. It works as an extended conjunctive phrase (see further under **conjunctions**.). The second sentence would sound natural enough in the context of narrative:

> *The bows of the vessel had been scarred by pack ice. Now damaged in the stern, the captain ordered the ship back to port ...*

The narrative keeps the ship in the spotlight—in the topic position in both sentences (see further under **topic**).

In their respective writing contexts the opening phrases of sentences 1 and 2 have a discourse function beyond the sentence itself. If we rewrite the sentences to eliminate the **dangling participles** we lose the topicalising effect they have. Any sentence in which the dangling modifier creates a bizarre distraction should of course be recast. But if it works in the context of discourse and draws no attention to itself, there's no reason to treat it like a cancer in need of excision.

*Established **dangling participles**.* Note finally that some kinds of dangling modifiers are actually the standard phrases of reports and documentary writing. Those who react on principle to dangling modifiers can be curiously unaware of how often they provide a sentence opening, for example:

> *Concerning the matter of ...*
> *Considering how ...*
> *Regarding your ...*
> *Seeing that ...*
> *Assuming that ...*
> *Judging by ...*
> *Provided that ...*
> *Given that ...*
> *Excepting that ...*

Phrases like these are a commonplace way of indicating the ongoing theme or topic of discussion. (See further under **information focus** and **discourse markers**.) Even the strictest grammarian is unlikely to insist that the substance of those carrier phrases must be attached to the nearest subject noun—any more than with stock phrases such as *barring accidents* or *failing that*. In fact, the most recent grammatical theory allows that there may be independent units within the English sentence.

danse macabre This phrase, borrowed from French, gives the English a way of referring to the traditional "dance of death" which so fascinated the medieval imagination—the dance in which a skeletal figure leads all kinds of people to their doom. Its power in medieval times derived from the ever-present threat of plague, but the motif showed itself as forceful as ever in the notorious "Grim Reaper" advertisement concerning the potential spread of AIDS in Australia.

Earlier forms of the phrase in English: *dance macabré, daunce of Machabree* show that it was once the dance associated with Maccabeus, the Jewish patriot who led a revolt again Graeco-Roman colonialism in the second century BC. Some suggest that there was a medieval miracle play about the slaughter associated with the revolt. The Dutch *Makkabeusdans* confirms that the tradition was known elsewhere in Europe. But the name *Maccabeus* was no longer recognisable as *Machabree* or *macabre*, and seems to have become confounded with Arabic words for gravedigger and graveyard or graves (pl): *maqabrey*, *maqbara* and *maqabir*. The confusion led to the dropping of the acute accent from the word *macabre*, and to the spelling *macaber* found occasionally in American English. (See further under **-re/-er**.)

The **danse macabre** expresses the threat of death in the form of frenzied energy, contrasting with the cold symbolism of the skull, the **memento mori** ("reminder of death") which was a subject for Renaissance painters. A third expression of mortality is the Latin phrase **dies irae** "day of wrath" (or Judgement Day), taken from the opening lines of the Requiem Mass.

dare (to) This verb often takes another verb in train, sometimes using *to* as a connecting rod between them, sometimes not:

They dared to speak their minds.
They dared not speak their minds.
They didn't dare to speak their minds.
He will curl up and die if you dare to do that.
Don't you dare do that!

Constructions with **dare** have been gradually changing. While the form with *to* is used freely in both positive and negative statements, the *to*-less form is mostly confined to negative statements (or ones with an implicit negative in them), and a few stock idioms: "I dare say", and "How dare you/he/she/they (+ verb) …!". The tide has clearly turned against the *to*-less form in Australian and American English, and it's increasingly rare in British English according to the *Comprehensive Grammar of English* (1985).

In constructions without *to* or *do/did*, **dare** works like an auxiliary, whereas with them it becomes a *catenative*. (See further under **auxiliary verbs** and **catenatives**.)

dashes The word *dash* is loosely applied to two types of horizontal line characters in printing: the *em rule* and the *en rule*. As those names suggest, the *em rule* is the length of an *m*, and the shorter *en rule* is the length of an *n*. An *en rule* is slightly longer than a hyphen, and where all three characters are available, each has its own roles:

em rule	to separate strings of words
en rule	to link words or numbers in pairs
hyphen	with compounds or complex words

However not all typewriters and wordprocessors have all three; and to compensate, a single hyphen is often used for both en rule and hyphen, and two hyphens (or a spaced hyphen) for em rule.

1 *The em rule* is used either in pairs, or singly. In pairs they mark off a parenthesis in the middle of a sentence:

> *The most important effect of British colonial development—apart from establishing the tea-drinking habit back home—was the spread of the English language throughout the world.*

Note that one pair of em rules is enough for any sentence. Within the main parenthesis, further parenthetical items should be marked off by means of brackets or commas. (See further under **brackets**.)

A single *em rule* may be used like a colon, particularly before a summarising comment which matches the first part of the sentence:

> *A loaf of bread, a jug of wine, and thou—it was the classic intimate meal.*

But the em rule is also used to indicate a break (or anacoluthon) in the grammatical structure of a sentence:

> *A loaf of bread, a jug of wine, and—What happened to you yesterday?*

This use of the *dash* (em rule) in unstructured writing has earned it a reputation as an informal punctuation mark. The other uses mentioned are quite standard, however.

The so-called *two-em rule* has several regular uses:

- to show when the text has been discontinued:

  > *A loaf of bread, a jug of wine, and——*

- to show the deliberate omission of (large) parts of a word, as for instance when representing ''four-letter words'' such as *f*——, *c*—— (see also under **asterisk**)

- to show where a whole word has been omitted

- to save repeating the name of an author when it occurs first in successive lines of a bibliography

Note that the Chicago *Manual of Style* recommends using a *three-em rule* for the last two purposes.

2 *The en rule* is used to connect two words or numbers which set up a span between them:

> *Sydney–Hobart yacht race   the Australia–China Foundation*
> *pp.306–9   1988–89*

Note that where both the en rule and hyphen are available, they can make a difference of meaning:

> *Lloyd–Jones (= a partnership between Lloyd and Jones)* and
> *Lloyd-Jones (= an individual with a double-barreled surname)*

But in headings and titles consisting of *full caps*, the en rule is used instead of the hyphen in words which are regularly hyphenated.

A spaced en rule is used when the words or numbers to be separated have internal spaces. See for example:

1 July 1991 – 30 June 1992

For the uses of **hyphens**, see under that heading.

data The fact that **data** is a plural in Latin (see under **-a**) has had a powerful influence on its use in English. Writers conscious of its Latinity have ensured that plural verbs or pronouns are used in agreement with it, as in the following:

These data are inconclusive; they do not entitle us to ...

Plural agreement is still insisted on by many in academic circles, where old scholastic traditions die hard. But in general usage we often hear **data** combined with singular verbs and pronouns, as if it is conceived of as a collective word:

This data is inconclusive; it does not entitle us to ....

In fact, the latter statement expresses something slightly different from the first one. It projects the data as a mass or block rather than a set of separable items. *Webster's English Usage* (1989) notes that both constructions are standard, and though the plural construction appears more often in print, this may have more to do with editorial intervention than authorial intention. The choice between singular or plural agreement is a matter of the writer's intended meaning, not a point on which the plural-using cognoscenti can pride themselves. The Australian Government *Style Manual* allows that singular agreement is acceptable in the context of data processing, and in any context where we deal with **data** as a batch, it seems natural. Singular and plural agreement appeared in the ratio 1:3 in the Australian ACE database, among 60 instances—nearly all of them in the categories of academic and bureaucratic writing.

dates Depending on where you are in the English-speaking world, dates may be written in several ways:

- day/month/year
  11 August 1988   11th August 1988   11th August, 1988
  11/8/88   11.8.88   11-8-88
- month/day/year
  August 11, 1988   August 11th 1988   August 11th, 1988
  8/11/88   8.11.88   8-11-88

The trend towards using the cardinal *11* rather than the ordinal *11th* is worldwide, and used in official correspondence everywhere. But the order of items has yet to be standardised. The first set above shows the order for dates in Australia and Britain, and it is the one recommended by the Chicago *Manual of Style* and used in American military documents. It is also usual in Britain. However, the second order is the one used very widely in the USA and in Canada, both with the month spelled out, and in the all-number style.

The potential for confusion among the all-number styles from each set is obvious, and something which those with overseas correspondents need to be careful about. Australian letters which give a date as 11/8/88 may very well be misinterpreted in North America, and the dates in letters *from* North America need to be read with caution here. The problem never arises, of course, if the month is given as a word, or else as a roman numeral (*11.viii.88*)—a convention used by some Europeans.

A third order for dates is *year/month/day*: *88/08/11* or *1988/08/11*. It avoids the problems of the other two all-number styles, and is the one recommended by the International Organization for Standardization, and endorsed in Australian Standard 1120–1978. It is already widely used in computing, by international companies based in Europe, and increasingly in the USA. As shown in our example, both month and day are indicated by two digits, with zero filling in the space beside the numbers 1–9. In computer usage the year is given its full four digits, and it may be set without spaces: *19880811*.

In data systems, a different convention has the day and month combined as a single, three-digit number between 001 and 365 (or 366 in a leap year). According to this system, the date *11 August 1988* would appear as *1988224* or *88224*. A space or hyphen can be inserted between the year and the day figure: *1988 224* or *1988-224*. The following table shows the range of numbers for each month:

January 1	*1*
February 1	*32*
March 1	*60 (61 in leap years)*
April 1	*91 (92)*
May 1	*121 (122)*
June 1	*152 (153)*
July 1	*182 (183)*
August 1	*213 (214)*
September 1	*244 (245)*
October 1	*274 (275)*
November 1	*305 (306)*
December 1	*335 (336)*

This method of dating is particularly useful for continuous accounting. It is described in Australian Standard 2297–1979.

Decades, years and spans of time. The standard writing style for these items has been changing. No apostrophe is used nowadays when referring to decades, either as *in the 1940s* or *in the 40s*. However in informal references to a particular year, such as *the class of '86*, the apostrophe may still appear.

When indicating spans of time, a dash (en rule) connects the two numbers, and it may be necessary to repeat more than one of the digits in the second number. A span between 47 BC and 42 BC would need to be given as 47–42 BC, not 47–2 BC, which might seem to be between 47 BC and 2 BC. Australian and American authorities (the Australian Government *Style Manual* and those of both *Chicago* and *Webster's*) recommend that with pairs of dates the last two digits should generally be given, even when only the last has changed: that it should be *1901–05*, *1955–58*, and so on. This contrasts with British style, as articulated for Oxford and Cambridge University presses in *Hart's Rules* (1989) and *Copy-editing* (1992), where writers are encouraged not to repeat more digits than it takes to show the change. They therefore recommend *1901–5*, *1955–8* and so on, but make an exception of numbers between 10 and 19, as in references to the *1914–18 War*. The exception seems to take account of the pronunciation of numbers in that decade: "fourteen", "eighteen" etc. The style authorities everywhere agree that when dates span the turn of a century, e.g. *1898–1901*, all four digits should be repeated (and that *1898–901* is unfortunate).

Note that while the dash (en rule) is used in expressing spans of time, the solidus or slash mark is often used to indicate a financial year or other statutory period (such as tenure of office) which does not coincide exactly with one calendar year: *1908/9*. In contrast *1908–9* would indicate a two-year span of time involving both years. This distinction between en rule and solidus then allows us to indicate spans between two financial years etc.: *1982/3–1988/9*.

For ways of referring to an individual century, see under **centuries**.

dating systems Several of the world's major religions have provided a calendar for dating historical events. The familiar Christian calendar dates things in relation to the putative year of Christ's birth, AD 1 (see further under **AD** and **BC**). The Islamic calendar is based on the year AD 622, when Muhammad fled from persecution in Mecca to Medina, where he began to develop a following. According to this system, events are dated with the prefix *AH* (= *anno Hegirae* "in the year of (Muhammad's) hegira or flight"). The Islamic years are however difficult to relate to Christian years because they work on a 355-day *lunar* cycle. Judaism meanwhile calculates historical time in years from the putative creation of the world. Under this system, the years are also sometimes prefixed *AH* (= *anno Hebraico* "in the Hebrew year"), which is clearly a trap for the unwary. Alternatively, dates using this reference point are prefixed *AM* (= *anno mundi* "in the year of the world").

Those seeking a dating system which is neutral as to religion have devised the term *Common Era*, and the abbreviations *CE* and *BCE* "(before) the Common Era". But contrary to intention, *CE* is quite often read as "Christian Era", a misunderstanding which is helped by the fact that the first year of the Common Era is AD 1. (See further under **BC**.)

Two other secular systems of dating have had their day. The Romans located historical events in relation to the founding of their city in 753 BC. They gave years with the suffix *AUC*, which to them meant *ab urbe condita* "from the city's founding", but is usually glossed nowadays as *anno urbis conditae* "in the year of the city's founding". In modern times the French Republican calendar was promulgated with the establishment of the Republic in September 1792, and used until the beginning of 1806. It created twelve months all of thirty days (and five intercalary days), and a new set of names for the months which express the flavor of the season:

Vendémiaire (= September/October: "the vintage") *Brumaire* ("mist")
Frimaire ("frost") *Nivôse* ("snow") *Pluviôse* ("rain") *Ventôse*

("wind") *Germinal* ("new shoots") *Floréal* ("flowers") *Prairial*
("grass") *Messidor* ("harvest") *Thermidor* ("heat") *Fructidor* ("fruit")
One aspect of the Roman calendar has been extremely long-lived. We owe to
Julius Caesar the system of allowing for a normal 365-day year, plus a 366-day
year once in every four. This so-called *Julian* (or "Old Style") Calendar
continued to be used in Europe up to the threshold of the modern era. By then
it was evident that the Julian equation for the solar cycle was a slight
overestimate and out by 11 minutes 10 seconds a year. The *Gregorian* ("New
Style") Calendar modified the old formula by reducing the number of leap
years. Instead of allowing that every turn of the century (1800, 1900, 2000,
2100, 2200, 2300 etc) was a leap year, only one in four was (2000, 2400 etc.).
The new system took its name from Pope Gregory XIII, and it has been observed
in most Catholic countries since 1582. However the state of religious politics
being what it was, England remained with the Julian Calendar until 1752, by
which time the British calendar was 12 days behind the rest of Europe. The
Gregorian Calendar was not adopted in Russia until 1918.

Finally, there is a dating system which uses neither sun, moon or climate as
its reference, but the known patterns of radiation in carbon atoms: *radiocarbon
dating*. It relies on the fact the radiocarbon (= carbon 14) in all living things
has a known level of radioactivity, which falls off at a predictable rate after the
organism has died. The half-life of carbon 14 is 5700 years, and it continues to
be just measurable up to 40 000 years. For obvious reasons the method is more
useful to archeologists than geologists generally, and has contributed much to
the study of the prehistoric environment and relatively recent climatic changes.
An Aboriginal footprint preserved in mud near Ceduna SA was dated as
5470 BP ± 190 years. (Dates achieved by radiocarbon dating carry the suffix
BP: see further under that heading.)

For **geological eras**, see under that heading. For a *perpetual calendar*, see
Appendix II.

dative   This is the grammatical name for the case of the indirect object. In some
languages such as German and Latin, there are distinct forms and suffixes for
nouns, pronouns, adjectives and articles in the **dative** case, to distinguish them
from the nominative and accusative. The pronoun *I/me* is as follows in German
and Latin:

German	*Latin*			
ich	ego	"I"	*nominative*	(= subject)
mich	me	"me"	*accusative*	(= direct object)
mir	mihi	"me"	**dative**	(= indirect object)

As the translation shows, the **dative** in English is identical with the accusative,
and it is only from the syntax of the sentence that its role as an indirect object
can be seen. (See further under **accusative**.) Further aspects of case-marking in
English and other languages are discussed under **cases**.

daughter-in-law   See in-laws.

de, del and **della** On the question as to whether to capitalise these particles in French, Dutch and Italian surnames (as in *De la Mare, De Haan* and *De Giorgio*), see under **capital letters**. For indexing purposes they are best alphabetised by the particle itself. Compare **van** and **von**.

de- The older meanings of this prefix differ from the new. It came into English and is embedded in familiar Latin loanwords such as *decline, depend* and *descend* where its meaning is "down or away", and in ones such as *delude, deplore* and *deride* where it means "put down" in a derogatory sense (*derogatory* itself is another example).

But its usual modern meaning is to reverse an action: either reducing or lowering it, as in *decentralise, de-escalate* and *devalue*; or removing something entirely, as in *defoliate, defrost* and *dethrone*. In *defuse* it may be one or the other, depending on whether the object is a situation or a bomb. This modern usage seems to have developed out of an earlier confusion with *dis-* (see **dis-**). In medieval French, words which had originally had **de-** and those with *dis-* were both written *des-*, because the *s* ceased to be pronounced and people were unsure which words it belonged in.

The earliest English examples of **de-** in its negative and privative sense were strictly technical: *decanonise* and *decardinalise* amid the religious turmoil of the seventeenth century, and *deacidify* and *de-aerate* out of empirical science in the eighteenth. Quite a few modern formations also began as technical jargon: *debrief, decontaminate* and *demilitarise*. But there are plenty of examples closer to home: *defrost, demist* and *deodorant. Debug* has gone further down the figurative path than *delouse*. As these examples show, new formations are as often based on nouns as verbs.

de facto This Latin phrase meaning "in fact" or "in reality" comes from the language of law where it forms a contrast with **de jure** "according to law" or "lawful". Even lawyers have had to recognise that things which have no legal standing are a force to reckon with, and the phrase **de facto** has had vigorous use both in law and in the turmoil of English religious and political history. But for many people it is the domestic use of **de facto** that comes first to mind, and it now appears on Australian tax forms, in references to the taxpayer's "spouse (married or *de facto*)". This usage is backed by the Family Law Reform Act 1980 and in NSW by the De Facto Relationships Act 1984–5. Thus the **de facto** now has legal status for such things as maintenance and division of property. In using the phrase as a noun for a domestic partner, Australians seem to be leading the English-speaking world. It is not yet recognised this way in British dictionaries, and among American dictionaries only *Random House* lists it (as Australian usage).

Yet even in Australia, there are many situations where **de facto** still does not solve the problem of how to introduce or refer to one's unmarried partner. It still carries some of the cold connotations of law, and while it may be possible to refer to someone else's **de facto**, few people would want to refer to their own (or a person associated with a member of their family) in that way.

Alternative English terms are still hard to find. To speak of one's "lover/ mistress" is too direct; "paramour" or "inamorato/a" too exotic; "significant other" rather intellectual; to use "fiancé(e)" invokes the very marital conventions that are being circumvented; and using "boyfriend" or "girlfriend" seems unsophisticated. Journalists create makeshift expressions such as "apartmate" and "live-in friend", but neither they nor the sex therapists with their talk of one's "spousal unit" seem to hit the mark. The term "partner" is perhaps the most widely acceptable, though subject to its own ambiguities. An advertisement featuring sophisticated conference accommodation for yuppie couples ran the intriguing line:

WHAT WILL YOU DO WHILE YOUR PARTNER IS MEETING HIS PARTNER?

The elusiveness of a standard term obliges people to invent their own, which is probably no bad thing, given the infinite variety of human relationships. (See further under **spouse equivalent**.)

de gustibus This is an abbreviated form of the Latin saying *De gustibus non est disputandum*. (See further under **chacun à son goût**.)

de jure See under **de facto**

de mortuis These words invoke the cautionary Latin statement: *de mortuis nil nisi bonum* "concerning the dead, nothing but good (should be said)", or "speak no ill of the dead". It represents an ancient taboo as well as a modern social convention, that the shortcomings of those who have died should not be aired: speak kindly or not at all. Though it comes to use in Latin, the saying is attributed to Chilo of Sparta, one of the legendary wise men of Greek tradition, from the sixth century BC. The sentiment is also expressed as **nil nisi bonum**.

de profundis See under **cri de coeur**.

de règle and **de rigueur** See under **comme il faut**.

de rien See under **ça va sans dire**.

de trop This French phrase means literally "too much" or "too many". In English it has long been applied to a person whose presence is superfluous, inappropriate or unwelcome in a given company. It parallels the idiom "playing gooseberry", expressing the idea more directly (if you know French), and more elegantly (if you do not).

déboutonné See **en déshabillé**.

debut Given the importance of *savoir faire* when making a debut, it is perverse that the word itself should create uncertainties. We all know that the *t* is not pronounced, but what to do when it becomes an English verb …? It must take the standard suffixes *-ed* and *-ing*, but how do they affect the pronunciation, and the spelling?

The normal practice is quite simple: simply write *debuted* and *debuting* (and continue to pronounce them as if there was no *t*). We do exactly the same with other French words ending in *-et* which have become verbs in English (see further under **-t**). But if the disjunction between spelling and sound bothers you, it is always possible to resort to paraphrase with *made/making a debut*.

deca-/deci- These prefixes both embody the Latin (and Greek) word for "ten". The prefix **deca-** expresses that meaning straightforwardly in words such as *decade, decagon* and *decahedron.* Spelled *deka-*, it is sometimes found with metric measures such as *dekalitre* and *dekametre*, though neither of these is an SI base unit (see further under **metrication**).

The prefix **deci-** means "one tenth", and it too used to be found with metric measures. But the potential for confusion between **deci-** and **deca-** has long been recognised, hence the attempts to replace **deca-** with *deka-*. In mathematical terms, the prefixes make all the difference between a cup of water (a *decilitre*) and enough for a bath (a *decalitre* or *dekalitre*). Even so, neither prefix is much used within the SI system because of the general preference for expressions which involve powers of 1000.

deceitful or **deceptive** Both words involve *deceiving*; but while **deceitful** suggests that it is part of a conscious intention by the perpetrator, **deceptive** just means that one can be misled by appearances. So *deceitful words* implies that the speaker is being deliberately dishonest, while a *deceptive account* only allows you to infer that those listening need to watch their own interests.

decessit sine prole This Latin phrase means "s/he departed (this life) without offspring". Used mostly in law and genealogy, it often appears abbreviated as **d.s.p.** It confirms the fact that the genealogy is complete, rather than a case where genealogists have been unable to trace all the progeny of the person being documented. The same idea is also expressed through **obiit sine prole** "died without offspring" (**o.s.p.**) and **sine prole** (**s.p.**).

decided or **decisive** These words only come into each other's ambit when *decided* is an adjective, as in *a decided advantage* (or *decisive advantage*?). In such contexts, **decided** means "definite", whereas **decisive** carries the sense of "that which clinches the issue". Thus *decisive* suggests finality, where *decided* is just an interim value.

decimate Does this mean reduce something by ⅒, by 9/10, or by some other fraction?

The meaning of **decimate** has been changing, so it is a word to handle with care. In its original Latin meaning it was mathematically precise: "reduce by one tenth", and it was used this way in English too. It served as a classical synonym for the English word *tithe*: "take one tenth of a person's goods, as a levy or tax''. On rare occasions, **decimate** has also been used by mean ''reduce *to* one tenth (i.e. by nine tenths). The *Oxford Dictionary* demonstrates this with an 1867 citation from the historian Freeman, who spells out his meaning with the aid of the fraction. Yet the fact that he does so suggests that there was a certain uncertainty about the word's meaning.

The *Oxford Dictionary* registers another use of the word, to mean ''devastate or drastically reduce'', though it dubs it ''rhetorical and loose''. We may read between the lines that there was some kind of shibboleth about it, fostered by more widespread knowledge of Latin. This is nowadays the commonest use of the word, and it's registered without comment in all modern dictionaries. The word appears in many contexts, to describe anything from the loss of financial capital, to severe cuts in educational resources. The meaning is less precise but more ominous.

The chief function now of **decimate** is emotive, to express the writer's disquiet about a reduction, not to specify its size. In fact, the word has had dark connotations since Roman times, when it referred to the punitive measure practised by the Roman army: the killing of one soldier in ten as a reprisal against units which mutinied or showed cowardice. The mathematical precision of that meaning has been lost, but the sinister implications are still there.

decisive or **decided** See decided.

declaim and **declamation** The spelling difference is discussed under **-aim**.

declarative Modern grammarians apply this term to sentences which embody a statement, as opposed to a question or command. In traditional grammar the verb of a *declarative sentence* was said to be **indicative** rather than **interrogative** or **imperative**. (See further under **mood**.)

declension *Declensions* are the different groups or classes to which the nouns of a language belong, according to the way they change for singular and plural, as well as the various grammatical cases such as nominative, accusative, genitive (see further under **cases**).

Classical Latin had elaborate noun *declensions*, with individual suffixes for many of the six standard cases, and often a characteristic vowel, such as *-a* (first **declension**), *-u* (second and fourth **declension**) and *-e* (third and fifth **declension**). The following are examples of nominative and accusative forms of each:

First **declension**:   *domina*   ''woman'' (nom.)   *dominam (acc.)*
Second **declension**:   *deus*   ''god''   *deum*
Third **declension**:   *miles*   ''soldier''   *militem*
Fourth **declension**:   *manus*   ''hand''   *manum*
Fifth **declension**:   *dies*   ''day''   *diem*

In the older Germanic languages such as Old English and Old Norse, there were numerous noun *declensions* within the two major groups, known as ''strong'' and "weak". And in modern German there are up to sixteen *declensions*, according to the paradigms in the *Langenscheidt Dictionary*.

Most Germanic languages either have or have had different *declensions* for their adjectives, also often referred to as "strong" and "weak".

décolletée See en déshabillé.

deductible or **deductable** In Australia both spellings are possible for this relatively new word, though only the first appears in the ACE corpus, and it dominates in finance and accounting. When first recorded in the nineteenth century, the spelling **deductible** was "rare" according to the *Oxford Dictionary*, and the regular English form **deductable** was the primary form. The latinate **deductible** has gained ground since then and according to the second edition of the *Oxford Dictionary*, it is now the more common spelling in Britain. In American English **deductible** is apparently the only spelling used—the only one listed in *Webster's* and the *Random House Dictionary*. (See further under **-able/-ible**.)

deduction This word is often loosely used to refer to any kind of argument. But in logic it denotes a particular kind of reasoning, a process in which a conclusion is drawn after certain premises have been established. Provided that the premises are true, they guarantee the validity of the conclusion. Deductive arguments contrast with inductive ones, in which the premises can only be said to *support* the conclusion (see **induction**).

One of the best known forms of **deduction** is the **syllogism**, in which a conclusion is drawn from a pair of premises. For example:

All mammals suckle their young. (major premise)

Platypuses are mammals. (minor premise)

Therefore the platypus suckles its young. (conclusion)

The validity of the conclusion depends on (1) the validity of both premises, and (2) the fact that the class of things introduced in the minor premise is included in the class mentioned in the major one. The class of things which links the major and minor premise is known as the *middle term*.

Similar deductive arguments are commonly used in establishing scientific theory and making predictions from it. They involve setting up and testing a hypothesis which is conditionally asserted within the major premise. The two well-recognised types of argument like this are the *modus ponens* and the *modus tollens*. The following illustrate the two types:

1 *Modus ponens.*

If there's an inverse relationship between IQ and the number of siblings in a family, then brighter children will come from smaller families.

Bright children typically come from smaller families.

Therefore there's an inverse relationship between IQ and the number of siblings in a family.

With the *modus ponens* argument we can assert the antecedent as the conclusion.

2 *Modus tollens*

> *If there's an inverse relationship between IQ and the number of siblings in*
> *a family, then brighter children will come from smaller families.*
> *Bright children don't all come from smaller families.*
> *Therefore there cannot be an inverse relationship between IQ and the*
> *number of siblings in a family.*

The *modus tollens* argument is the negative counterpart of *modus ponens*, and works by denying the consequent as the conclusion.

The two patterns of argument may be symbolically represented as follows:

1 Modus ponens	*2 Modus tollens*
If p then q	If p then q
p	not p
therefore q.	therefore not q.

(The letters *p* and *q* stand for indicative statements. See further under **indicative**.) The **modus tollens** provides the logical framework for testing the null hypothesis, used in statistics and much research in the behavioral and social sciences.

Deductive arguments are sometimes referred to as **a priori** arguments. (See further under that heading.)

defective or **deficient** Both these adjectives say that something is unsatisfactory, but they work in different domains. **Defective** is used of objects which have detectable flaws, or do not function properly because of missing or damaged parts. **Deficient** expresses a more abstract problem, where there is less than the full complement of a standard quality or attribute. Because of its abstractness, **deficient** is usually qualified in some way, such as "deficient in sensitivity".

The two words rarely rival each other in usage, because one word refers to concrete problems, and the other to abstract faults. Yet it has happened in the phrase *mentally defective/deficient*—and mental disorder may of course be seen in terms of impaired brain function or insufficient brain resources. Of the two phrases, *mentally deficient* is probably more common, though it too has been challenged by *mentally handicapped*, and most recently by *differently abled*.

defendant or **defendent** The first is now the regular spelling for the person answering a legal charge, whether the word is technically a noun or adjective. Compare:

> *The defendant showed no remorse.*
> *The judge gave a warning to the defendant lawyer.*

(See further under **dependent** or **dependant**.)

defense or **defence** See -ce/-se.

deficient or **defective** See defective.

definite or **definitive** The extra syllable in **definitive** makes it more like *definition*; and a **definitive** object has the archetypal qualities of its kind, and serves as a reference point for others. A *definitive performance of Shakespeare's Macbeth* is a classic interpretation.

To say something is **definitive** is to make much more ambitious claims for it than with **definite**. **Definite** simply implies that something is exact or has clear, firm limits, as in *a definite proposal*. In some contexts its meaning is further diluted, so that it is little more than an intensifier, as in *a definite step forward* or *They're definitely coming*. (See further under **intensifiers**.)

definite article See articles.

definitive or **definite** See definite.

deflection or **deflexion** See under **-ction/-xion**.

degrees of comparison See **adjectives** section 2.

deixis Borrowed from philosophy, this term is used in linguistics to refer to words whose meaning is tied to the situation in which they are uttered. Without knowing that situation we cannot decode their meaning. Some examples are:
* the pronouns *I*, *we* and *you*
* demonstratives such as *this* and *that*
* positional terms like *here* and *there*, *right* and *left*
  in front and *behind*
* time references such as *tomorrow* and *yesterday*
  next, *last* and *ago*
  now and *then*

Such items are called *deictics*. The adjective is *deictic*, and there's no sign yet of a rival "deixic" in dictionaries or grammars—though we might expect it in the longer run. (See further under **-ctic/-xic**.)

déjà vu This phrase, borrowed from French, means "already seen". In critiques of artistic or literary works it can be used almost literally to say that their substance is not new, and that they are trite and unoriginal.

But when used by psychologists and others, **déjà vu** is a peculiar mental phenomenon whereby a person feels he or she is seeing for the second time something which they can never have seen before. It seems to strike a chord in memory, and yet it can only be a quirk of the mind. The effect is uncanny, though not in the occult realms of "second sight". While the clairvoyant claims to have a view into the future, a **déjà vu** glimpse is always framed in the past.

dekalitre and **dekametre** See under **deca-/deci-**.

del and **della** On how to treat these elements of surnames, see under **de**.

delirium tremens Coined in the early nineteenth century, this medical phrase consists of Latin elements which mean "trembling delirium". The name describes the convulsive state of delirium brought on by prolonged and excessive consumption of alcohol—fits of trembling and sweating associated with terrifying optical illusions. The phrase can be abbreviated to **d.t.**, although it's often written and said in the plural **d.t.'s**, as if the word *tremens* were a plural noun. The abbreviation often appears in capitals: as **D.T.'s** or **DTs**.

delusion or **illusion** These words both refer to false perceptions, and though they seem interchangeable in some contexts, their implications are slightly different. **Delusion** suggests that the misapprehension is subjective and results from distorted thinking within the individual, or a disordered mind. *Delusions* are chronic or persistent, as for example with *delusions of grandeur*. An *illusion* is a temporary misapprehension produced by external objects or circumstances, as in an *optical illusion*. It can be dispelled relatively easily.

Note also the difference between **illusion** and **allusion**, the latter being a passing comment or fleeting reference to something. **Allusion** is the abstract noun from the verb *allude*. (There is no English verb associated with **illusion**.) (See also **elusive** or **allusive**.)

demagogue or **demagog** See under -gue/-g.

demeanor or **demeanour** See under -or/-our.

demi- This French prefix meaning "half" appears in a few borrowed words like *demi-sec* and *demitasse*, and in some hybrid English formations like *demigod* and *demirelief*. It appears as an independent word in the form *demy* (a now obsolete size of paper), with its spelling adjusted in accordance with the English rules for final letters of words. (The reverse process is described at **-y>-i-**.)

In musical terminology, **demi-** shares with *semi-* from Latin and *hemi-* from Greek the role of subdividing the length of musical notes. So a *hemidemisemiquaver* is one eighth the length of a quaver—a long word for a very brief sound.

Demi- seems to lend itself to ambiguity in *demivolt*—unless you happen to have some knowledge of electricity and/or dressage. In fact, it has no place in electrical measurement, but refers to the half turn (with forelegs raised) made by a trained horse.

demonstratives Words like *this/these* and *that/those* which draw the reader's or listener's attention to particular objects or persons are **demonstratives**. They function as both adjectives and pronouns:
This offer is worth accepting. (adjective)
This is worth accepting. (pronoun)
Those recruits did better than these.
(adjective)   (pronoun)
English also has *demonstrative adverbs (of time, place and manner)* including:
here/there   hence/thence   now/then   thus

In modern English the pairs of **demonstratives** (i.e. *this*/*that*, *these*/*those*) express the notion of being either closer to, or further from the writer/speaker. In older English, the words *yon* and *yonder* also worked as **demonstratives**, and expressed a third degree of distance, even more remote from the standpoint of the communicator. In some Aboriginal languages, the demonstrative system indicates not only relative distance but direction (i.e. "near to the south", "further away to the west" etc.).

(See also under **deixis**.)

denotation See under **connotation**.

denounce and **denunciation** For the spelling of these words, see under **pronounce**.

dependence or **dependency** Whether you spell these *-ence*/*-ency* or *-ance*/*-ancy*, there are matters of meaning to consider with them. Like some other *-nce*/*-ncy* pairs, the first is typically abstract in its use, so that it's usually modified (before or after) to make it more specific, as in *nicotine dependence* or *dependence on outside finance*. **Dependency** is more specific in itself, referring to a particular dependent unit, and probably best known in its use as a geo-political unit governed by another country: the *Falkland Island Dependencies*. However, **dependency** is also found in phrases such as *drug dependency*, suggesting that for some people it is quite interchangeable with **dependence**. (See further under **-nce/-ncy**.)

dependent or **dependant** Uncertainty over spelling this word goes back to the eighteenth century, when Dr Johnson offered both spellings for the noun and adjective, with the comment "Some words vary their final syllable". The *Oxford Dictionary* however commented that *-ant* was more common for the noun, and in this has firmed into the preferences of modern British dictionaries: **dependant** for the noun and **dependent** for the adjective. In Australia the authorities make the British distinction, and it is borne out in the ACE corpus with more than 60 instances of the adjective all as **dependent**, and 5 out of 6 instances of the noun as **dependant**. But in the USA **dependent** is used for both adjective and noun, and it was the only spelling in 42 instances of the word in the American Brown corpus. Both *Webster's* and *Random House* give it as the prime spelling, though they also allow **dependant** as an alternative.

Overall then, the spelling **dependent** seems to be dominant, helped by the fact that the adjective is much more frequent than the noun. The corpus evidence is however drawn from edited prose, and draft material in Australia is rather less consistent, with freer use of **dependant** for the adjective. It causes no misunderstanding, and could be accommodated as Johnsonian variation or American liberalism, according to taste. (Why not keep a little flexibility in the language, given the arbitrary rule of *-ent* or *-ant* in so many English words? See further under **-ant/-ent**.)

The variation noted with **dependent/dependant** also affects **dependence/ dependance** and **dependency/dependancy**, not to mention **independent/ independant** and **independence/independance**. The argument for flexibility applies equally to them. (See also the next entry.)

dependent clauses This is another name for *subordinate clauses*. (See further under **clauses** section 3.)

deposit On whether to double the *t* before adding verb suffixes, see **t**.

deprecate or **depreciate** From rather different origins, these similar-looking words have come to overlap in meaning in some contexts, especially when it comes to *self-deprecation* or *self-depreciation.*

In essence **depreciate** means "reduce in price or value". This is the meaning it still expresses in the domain of business and finance, as when "assets are depreciated by 10 per cent". But the word can take on the more figurative meaning of "represent as having little value, belittle", and it then comes close to the extended meaning of **deprecate**. **Deprecate** is essentially "argue against", but by extension means "disparage", as in *deprecating their efforts to form an alternative union.*

In this way *deprecatory comments* and *depreciatory comments* mean much the same, and compounds such as *self-deprecatory/self-deprecating* and *self-depreciatory* are indistinguishable. With the extra syllable, **depreciate** and its derivatives seem to be the losers in these close encounters. **Depreciate** nevertheless maintains its ground in the world of finance, which it never shares with **deprecate**.

derisive or **derisory** The distinction between these words seems to have developed during the twentieth century, and since the 1920s, to judge by citations in the second edition of the *Oxford Dictionary*, Both involve laughing something out of court, but while **derisory** attaches itself to the object of derision, e.g. *a derisory attempt at stage managing*, **derisive** expresses the attitude of those mocking: *derisive laughs from the audience*. In other words, **derisory** has become a synonym for "laughable", and **derisive** for "mocking".

dernier cri In spite of appearances, this French phrase (literally "the last cry") is closer in meaning to "the last word" than "the last gasp". Often translated as "the latest fashion", it is certainly not restricted to the world of *haute couture*, but can be applied to "the latest thing" in any field. In some English usage, it seems to carry a certain irony, as if the user was conscious of the literal meaning of the phrase. But in French it is an uncomplicated colloquial idiom which just means "the in-thing". Compare **bossa nova**.

derogatory or **derogative** Both forms are acceptable, though **derogatory** is the primary form of this adjective, and it has developed several distinct uses since it was first recorded in 1503. **Derogative** is in fact slightly older (dating from 1477), yet seems to have remained less common and without special applications. The dictionaries give it just a general definition, or crossreference it to **derogatory**.

desalination or **desalinisation** See under **salination**.

descendant or **descendent** The first spelling **descendant** has become standard for the "(one) originating from a particular ancestor"—whether it serves as a noun or adjective. The spelling **descendent** is confined to the realms of astronomy and heraldry. Compare **ascendant** and **dependent**.

descriptive or **prescriptive** Language changes all the time in small ways, offering us alternative words, idioms and spellings. Much of the time this passes unnoticed, but when people do notice a new usage around, they may react in one of two ways. They may simply remark on it without passing judgement (the **descriptive** approach). Or they may declare one particular form to be the right one to use (the **prescriptive** approach). Prescriptivists, whether they are experts or ordinary citizens, usually plump for the traditional form, whereas descriptivists recognise that language changes, and that there may be a choice of forms in certain contexts.

In the history of English, language commentators have swung from being typically descriptive in the sixteenth and seventeenth centuries, to prescriptivism in the eighteenth, nineteenth and earlier twentieth centuries. Under the influence of modern linguistics, a more **descriptive** approach has been fostered in the second half of this century. It goes hand in hand with better understanding of language change and better tools for describing it. A third factor is the generally more democratic climate of thinking, which allows that common usage and trends within it are really more powerful in language history than academic ideas about what is correct or "logical" in English. This principle was articulated in Roman times by the poet Horace in the comment "the arbiter, law and standard of speech lies in usage" (*Ars Poetica* lines 71–2); and Horace's words were known to and quoted by eighteenth century scholars. Yet the idea that common usage should influence judgements about language was hardly implemented in eighteenth century publications.

Twentieth century dictionaries and style manuals vary in their stance, though generally speaking, the smaller the volume the more likely it is to work prescriptively. You need space to offer the full descriptive detail on usage. Even larger volumes may resort to prescriptivism in the absence of linguistic evidence, a point which is not always obvious to the reader. It must also be said that some readers expect and perhaps prefer prescriptivism, because it seems to provide simple answers to language questions.

Style manuals have traditionally taken it as their raison d'être to pass judgement on usage, and to score things as correct and "acceptable" or the opposite. This book endeavors to provide **descriptive** information on usage wherever possible (where variant forms are used, and in what contexts)—

assuming that interested and intelligent watchers of the language would prefer to have the wherewithal to choose, rather than have choices made for them.

déshabillé See **en déshabillé**.

desideratum For the plural of this word, see under **-um**.

despatch or **dispatch** See **dispatch**.

determiners In modern grammars **determiners** are the words which occupy the first slot in the **noun phrase** (see further under that heading). They include:
   articles: *a an the*
   demonstrative adjectives: *this that these those*
   possessive adjectives: *my your his her its our their*
   quantitative adjectives: *few both some each every all no*
   all cardinal numbers: *one two three* etc.
Any of the above could go into the vacant slot in the following:
   ——*good book(s)*
Modern grammarians note that combinations of more than one *determiner* are to be found in English, as in *all those people* and *both my dogs*. The first *determiner* is then the **predeterminer**. Other words which can be *predeterminers* are *quite*, *such* and *what*, all of which can combine with the indefinite article: *quite an experience, what a business*. Note also the **postdeterminers**, usually numbers (either cardinal or ordinal), as in *the first two students/the two first students*; or else general quantifiers as in *a few books/the two next weeks*.

detract or **distract** See **distract**.

deus ex machina This Latin phrase meaning "god from the machine" captures an ancient Greek theatrical practice associated especially with Euripides. It involved hoisting up the divinities who appeared in the play to a position above the stage, from where they could observe and intervene in the affairs of ordinary mortals.

   Modern popular culture has a remarkable **deus ex machina** in *Superman* who descends miraculously to the aid of beleaguered people in innumerable comics, videos and movies. The expression is also applied in contemporary usage to any improbable event or device of plot which provides easy resolution of a difficult situation.

developing countries This term is now used instead of the less flattering "underdeveloped countries", to describe countries in which the majority of the population are engaged in agriculture rather than secondary industry, and where traditional customs and low rates of literacy prevail. The **developing countries** are typically in Asia, Africa, Latin America and the Pacific region, and they are often former colonies of European powers. Collectively they are sometimes referred to as the "Third World", a term coined when they were seen as independent of both the western and eastern blocs. (See further under **Third World**.) The developing countries still tend to have fewer resources and less economic and financial clout than the developed countries of Europe and North America. But they are at least equally represented at the United Nations, and at the Commonwealth Heads of Government meetings.

deviled or **devilled**   The choice between these is discussed under **-l/-ll-**.

devil's advocate   This phrase is a direct translation of the Latin *advocatus diaboli*, the official who was appointed by the Catholic Church to argue against a proposal for canonisation, and to draw attention to flaws in the case of the proposed saint. While sympathetic to the cause, he tries to prepare its advocate for any challenges that may be brought against it.

By extension it has come to mean a person who voices arguments against the position held by most others, and who seems to argue for argument's sake. It is most often used of those who produce negative arguments against what others propose, though it can also apply to those who recommend what most others reject.

devisor or **deviser**   See under **-or/-er**.

dexterous or **dextrous**   Both of these are acceptable, but **dexterous** is given as the first preference in all modern dictionaries. According to the *Oxford Dictionary*, **dexterous** was more common in nineteenth century prose, even though **dextrous** was "more regular". (For other cases in which *-er* becomes *-r*, see **-er>-r-**.) Note the survival of the "regular" spelling in *ambidextrous*, for which there is no alternative.

di   On whether to capitalise this particle in surnames (such as *Di Bartolo, Di Maggio*) see under **capitals**. For the purposes of indexing, the particle is best treated as the first part of the name. Compare **van** and **von**.

di-   This prefix meaning "two" appears in borrowed Greek words and neoclassical words such as:
> *dicotyledon digraph dihedral dilemma diode*
> *diphthong diptych di(s)syllable*

Most such words are in specialised fields of learning and scholarship, which **di-** to some extent shares with *bi-* (see under **bi-**). Although **di-** has generated far fewer words in the life sciences, it has been used much more extensively in chemistry, and has largely replaced *bi-* in the nomenclature of organic compounds. Only in the well-established names of acid salts, such as *bicarbonate* and *bisulfate*, has *bi-* retained its place.

dia-   A legacy of Greek, this prefix meaning "through, across" is a component of borrowed words such as:
> *diabetes diagonal diagram dialect diameter diagnosis*
> *diarrh(o)ea diathermy diatonic*

It becomes just *di-* when combined with a word beginning with a vowel, as in *dieresis, diorama* and *diuretic* etc.

Note that **dialogue** is essentially conversation across a group, not just between two people—because its prefix is **dia-** not *di-* "two". The misunderstanding about **dialogue** is probably fostered by the fact that it is often contrasted with *monologue*. The term *duologue* has been coined for a conversation between just two people, but it is little used. For the spelling question, whether to write *dialogue* or *dialog*, see **-gue/-g**.

diad and **diadic** See under **dyad**.

dialect Is there such a thing as **dialect** in Australia? Does it affect the way Australians write?

Most people are aware of dialect when they hear speech which sounds very different from their own, speech which they know belongs to a particular region. Most Australians would recognise the "Deep South" vowels of someone who comes from anywhere between Texas and Tennessee, and the "burr" of a Scots speaker of English. Yet *within* Australia, there are no systematic differences in pronunciation to help us identify speakers from say Perth or Melbourne. The broad Australian accent is clearly different from the cultivated one, but it's widely distributed over the whole continent, and in both metropolitan and country areas. (If anything, it identifies particular social groups in the community, although even this is variable, since many Australians adapt their accents in more and less formal circumstances.) People sometimes associate the particular pronunciation of a word such as *castle* rhyming with "hassle" with a particular region. But unless the difference extends to other similar words such as (in that case) *fast* and *plaster*, it hardly constitutes a dialect.

If **dialect** was only a matter of accent, it would scarcely impinge on writing. However a well-developed **dialect** also has its own distinctive features of vocabulary, idiom and even grammar. Once again we may be aware of the words and phrases which mark British or American regional dialects, but can point to few within Australia which are peculiar to one city or state. Apart from the words for delicatessen sausage (*devon, baloney*), for measures of beer (*schooner, pot*), for swimming costumes (*cozzie, bathers, togs*) and for a child's pram (*pusher, stroller*), they are thin on the ground. (See under **interstate differences**.) The differences would only matter if you were writing for Australians in several states, and were trying to use the same text for all. But otherwise Australian English, whether formal or informal, is quite homogeneous.

The only point at which **dialect** details may become an issue for Australians is when they write with an international audience in mind, and need to be aware of the points at which standard Australian English differs from standard British or American English. David Williamson's play *The Removalists* had to be titled "The Moving Men" when it was produced in New York. The need for adjustments like this is often indicated in larger dictionaries, where US alternatives are mentioned for particular words. When writing, there are also differences in idiom and collocation: for example, Australians say "write to me" where Americans say "write me". Many of the entries in this book highlight such differences.

Yet most of the language written in Australia is truly *standard English*, which can be understood anywhere in the English-speaking world and has no dialectal overtones. (See further under **international English** and **standard English**.)

dialectal or **dialectical** These adjectives are not interchangeable because they relate to different nouns. **Dialectal** relates to **dialect** (see previous entry), whereas **dialectical** relates to *dialectic(s)*, a form of philosophical argument in which the truth is sought through reconciling opposite positions. *Dialectic* originated with Socrates and Plato, but it was given new life by Kant and Hegel in the modern era, and subsequently adapted by Marx in the philosophy of *dialectical materialism*. A more recent extension of the noun *dialectic* makes it simply a way of referring to the tension between two opposing forces, such as church and state, without any philosophical implications. This usage is likely to irritate those with any knowledge of philosophy, and to intimidate those without it.

dialed or **dialled** The choice between these is discussed under **-l/-ll-**.

dialogue or **dialog** See under **-gue/-g**.

dialyse or **dialyze** See under **-yse/-yze**.

diarchy or **dyarchy** See **dyarchy**.

diarrhea or **diarrhoea** See under **oe**.

dicey or **dicy** See under **-y/-ey**.

dieresis Borrowed from Greek, this term has been applied to an accent used sporadically in written English. It consists of two dots placed above a vowel, and thus is rather like the German umlaut (see **umlaut**), though the latter consists of two strokes. The **dieresis** shows when two successive vowels are to be pronounced as separate syllables, and it is placed over the second one, as in *naïve*. These days it is used primarily in proper names such as *Aïda*, *Chloë* and *Noël*, though in earlier centuries it was also used to show the scansion of common nouns in editions of poetry. In British English it is spelled **diaeresis**. (See further under **ae/e**.)

dies irae See under **danse macabre**.

dietitian or **dietician** Both spellings are acceptable, though the first is more fully endorsed in Australia, by the *Macquarie Dictionary* and the major newspapers, and it alone appears in the ACE corpus. It is also the first preference of the major British and American dictionaries. With its two *t*'s **dietitian** has a clearer link with *dietetics*, and this may well have helped to secure its position against **dietician** in the twentieth century.

Dietician was endorsed by the *Oxford Dictionary* in the nineteenth century as the "proper" spelling, on the analogy of *physician* and *politician*. Yet uncertainty over the form of the noun was perhaps fostered by the variety of adjectives related to *diet*: *dietary*, *dietic*, *dietical*, *dietetic* and *dietetical*. The ones ending in *-ical* have dropped out of use, according to the *Oxford Dictionary*, and *dietic* does not seem to be current either. With them much of the support for the letter *c* as part of the stem has disappeared.

different from, different to, and **different than**   All three constructions have a long history of use, dating back to the sixteenth and seventeenth centuries. Yet much ink has been spilt over their relative correctness, with insufficient attention to their contexts of use. Consider what you would do in the following:

1a *Bob's approach was different ... Jo's.* (from/to/than)
 b *Bob had a different approach ... Jo.* (from/to/than)
2a *Bob's approach was different ... what we expected.*
 b *Bob had a different approach ... what we expected.*
3a *Bob's approach was different ... we expected.*
 b *Bob had a different approach ... we expected.*

Whatever you do in the first two pairs, there's a very strong chance that you will use *than* in the third pair. This is because sentences 3a and 3b require a conjunction, and *from* and *to* are essentially prepositions. Those who have learned to shun *than* after **different** may avoid it in 3a/b by rewriting them along the lines of 2a/b where either *from* or *to* can be used. Yet the use of **different than** in sentences like 3a/b is standard in American English, according to *Webster's English Usage* (1989), and Crystal (1984) argues that it's unremarkable in British English. Small wonder then if **different than** is now frequently heard in Australia. It was not however represented in the (written) material of the ACE corpus, but there were no sentences like 3a/b which would require it.

When choosing between *from* and *to* for constructions like 1a/b and 2a/b, Australians are more likely to write *from* (by about 6:1) according to the evidence of ACE. This is in keeping with British practice, where *from* is established and *to* tolerated. In the USA *to* gets little use, and *from* and *than* are widely used. Though the Harper-Heritage usage panel of the 70s registered strong objections to the use of *than*, *Webster's* evidence is that most Americans feel free to use it in all constructions with **different**.

The arguments which used to support **different from** no longer seem so powerful. The fact that **different** embodies the Latin prefix *dis-* "away from" does not require the use of *from* after it, any more than with *averse* (see **adverse** or **averse**). And there are natural English parallels for *to* in collocations such as *compared to* and *similar to*, and for *than* in comparatives such as *better than* or *worse than*. The verb *differ* also combines with other preposition/particles, for example *differ with*, and so provides only qualified support for **different from**.

Thus **different from** no longer reigns supreme but shares the field with both **different to** and **different than**. Writers who relish the resources of English would use all three collocations from time to time, according to the linguistic and stylistic context.

digraph or **diphthong** Only the first of these words really relates to writing. A **digraph** is a pair of letters which represents or corresponds to a single sound, such as both the *ch* and the *ie* of *chief*. As those examples show, *digraphs* have their component letters set apart, whereas those of a *ligature* are joined together to form a single character. In earlier phases of English printing, letter combinations such as *ct* and *ae* were **ligatures** (*ct* and *æ*), but in modern print they are normally set as *digraphs*. (See further under **ae/e** and **oe**.)

Diphthongs are sounds which contrast with pure vowels in that they have the quality of more than one vowel. Pure vowels are pronounced with the tongue held momentarily in one position, whereas *diphthongs* are moving vowels, pronounced by a tongue which is in transit from one position to another. This gives *diphthongs* their dual character, which is why the prefix *di-* "two" is embedded in their name. The Greek word *phthongos* "sound" is the second element, spelled with three of the *digraphs* of modern English. For a list of all the sounds of English (consonants and vowels) see Appendix I.

dike or **dyke** These spellings represent two different words:

1 a water channel and embankment
2 a lesbian.

For the first word, the spelling **dike** is preferred in the major British and American dictionaries, as well as the *Oxford Dictionary*, though **dyke** is a recognised alternative. **Dike** is better in terms of etymology as the word is a variant form of *ditch*. The *Macquarie Dictionary* (1991) gives the two spellings equal billing, at **dike** for the first word and at **dyke** for the second.

The origin of the second and much more recent word is not known, and dictionaries diverge over the preferred spelling. **Dyke** is the only spelling for it in *Random House*, whereas *Webster's* gives **dyke** followed by **dike**. Curiously, the second edition of the *Oxford Dictionary* puts **dyke** second, and has **dike** as the first spelling, even though its citations weight them the other way. The adjective *dykey/dikey* shows the same variation, and here again the Australian and American dictionaries give preference to *dykey* while the *Oxford Dictionary* prefers *dikey*. In general such words which vary between *i* and *y* tend towards *i* (see **i/y**); but in this case it may well be inhibited by the need to differentiate the second word from the first.

dilettante This Italian loanword of the eighteenth century is sufficiently assimilated in English to have an English plural: *dilettantes*. However the Italian plural *dilettanti* is still used by those who wish to emphasise its foreignness.

The existence of derivatives such as *dilettantish*, and *dilettantism* or *dilettanteism* suggests that it is high time to treat it as an ordinary English word.

diminutives A *diminutive* is an affix which implies smallness of size. It may be a suffix such as *-ette* or *-let*, or a prefix such as *micro-* and *mini-*. They are generally neutral in connotation, neither colloquial nor childish. Compare **hypocorisms**.

dingo This is among the first recorded Aboriginal words in Australian English, borrowed from the Dharuk Aborigines of Port Jackson. According to the *Australian National Dictionary* the plural of **dingo** is always *dingoes*, whether it refers to wild dogs, or their figurative human analogues. But the *Macquarie Dictionary* allows that its plural may be *-oes* or the regular *-os*. (See further under **-o**.) Other less familiar Aboriginal words ending in *-o* have plurals in *-os*, for example *euros* (for a species of wallaroo).

dinner Everywhere in the English-speaking world, this word can raise uncertainties about the sort of meal it refers to. While *lunch* is clearly a midday meal, and *supper* one in the evening, an invitation to *come to dinner at the weekend* can pose a most delicate dilemma until an exact time is mentioned.

There are two things at stake. Working Australians usually have their main meal in the evening, and so from Monday to Friday, and Saturday as well, **dinner** would be eaten with the setting sun, more or less. On Sunday however, **dinner** used to be the ample midday meal to which many returned from their morning church service. But with changing habits in both eating and church-going, the "Sunday roast" tradition is less common now than it used to be, and "Sunday dinner" is more and more an evening meal as on other days of the week.

Apart from the question of eating habits, the word **dinner** has had connotations which would be sought by some and avoided by others. It has always been the word for the formal meal arranged for special occasions, and one which might seem pretentious for those lower down the social ladder. Instead their natural word would be *tea*, which would still denote their main meal of the day—not just a pot of tea and scones. Within many Australian families, the regular evening meal is simply referred to as *tea*—not "high tea" as in Britain. In the USA and often in Britain, the term *supper* is used in much the same unpretentious way for the homely evening meal. In Australia *supper* only refers to a late evening snack. As far as *lunch* goes, the English-speaking world is in solid agreement that it refers to a midday meal, which may be light or quite substantial.

diphthong or **digraph** See **digraph**.

direct or **directly** Both these words may be used as adverbs, and in Australian English they may be used with any of the meanings attached to the adjective **direct**, in the dimensions of time and space. In contrast, British authorities insist that as an adverb, **direct** means "by the quickest route", while **directly** means "immediately". The two kinds of meaning are not always easy to separate, and the familiar instruction to Monopoly players:

Go directly to Gaol. Do not pass Go ...

seems to conflate the two meanings.

Apart from its role as an adverb, **directly** also works as a temporal conjunction:

They came directly they heard the news.

This last usage is recognised in all the major dictionaries, Australian, British and American. The original *Oxford Dictionary* dubbed it "colloquial", and some later British dictionaries and style manuals echo this judgement; yet Fowler commented that it was "defensible". And *Webster's English Usage* (1989) has enough citations from respected authors to show that it is unexceptionable, even in Britain.

direct object See under **object**.

direct speech The most dramatic way of reporting what someone said is **direct speech**, i.e. using not only their words, but their way of projecting them to the listener. Compare:

Speaking to the waiting journalists, Whitlam said: "Maintain your rage".
(direct speech)
Speaking to the waiting journalists, Whitlam said that they should maintain their rage. (indirect speech)

The quotation marks in the first version are a sign that the speech is being quoted verbatim. The imperative "maintain" is exactly the form of address that was used, and it re-creates the immediate effect of the words for the reader. In *indirect speech* this imperative is translated into the modal *should maintain*, and the third person pronoun *they* is used instead of the implied *you* (second person). (See further under **modality**, and **person**.) Both changes help to soften the impact of the statement and push it back into the past.

Between direct and indirect speech there are a number of other ways of quoting or reporting people's words. They include:

Whitlam told them to maintain their rage.
                    (narrative reporting of speech)
Whitlam said for them to maintain their rage.
                    (free indirect speech)
Whitlam urged maintaining their rage.
                    (narrative reporting of act)

These intermediate forms of reporting suggest several ways in which writers may modify the substance of the speech they're communicating, and subtly control the reader's response.

dis- This prefix, borrowed ultimately from Latin, often implies reversing the action of a verb. See for example:

disagree disarm disclaim disconnect discount discourage disengage
disentangle disinherit dislike dismount disobey disown distrust

As those words show, it is usually combined with words of French or Latin origin, and with few Old English roots.

When used with nouns and adjectives, it usually implies oppositeness and works as a straight negative:

disadvantage disapproval dishonest dishonor disorder dispassionate
displeasure disreputable dissimilar distaste disunity

Dis- replaced almost entirely the earlier French form of the prefix: *des-* in common loanwords of the Middle English period. (So *discharge* was *descharge* for Chaucer, and *disturb* was once *destourbe*.) The only modern word to have resisted this respelling is *descant*. The respelling of *dispatch* as *despatch* is a different process (see under **dispatch/despatch**).

Dis- overlaps with some other negative prefixes in English, notably (1) *mis-* and (2) *un-*. For the difference between:

1 **distrust** and **mistrust** see **mistrust**, and for **disinformation** and **misinformation**, see **mis-**;
2 **disinterested** and **uninterested**, and **dissatisfied** and **unsatisfied**, see under the first of each pair.

Note the distinction between **dis-** and *dys-* as prefixes, although *disfunctional* is sometimes seen for **dysfunctional**. (See further under that heading.)

disabled Used in reference to people, this word is now under scrutiny. Although it's institutionalised in *Disabled Parking* and elsewhere as a way of referring to individuals with a particular disability, it may seem to suggest total incapacity in the *disabled person*. The term *differently abled* is preferred by some because of its more positive implications, and the fact that it does not draw attention to the impaired bodily function, as do *blind, deaf, retarded, spastic* etc.

The lack of specificity in *differently abled* can be a liability however, for those who need to accommodate or provide for people with disabilities. Unless it's clear what the disability is, there could be problems on both sides.

disassemble or **dissemble** See **dissemble**.

disassociate or **dissociate** See **dissociate**.

disc or **disk** Though **disk** was the normal spelling of this word from the seventeenth century on, the *Oxford Dictionary* in the late nineteenth century noted an increasing tendency to use **disc**, and the second edition of the *Oxford Dictionary* comments that it is now the usual form in Britain. In Australia *disc* is used in most contexts except computing, where *floppy disk* and *hard disk* are the normal spellings, along with *diskette*. In the USA the picture is divided. Both *Random House* and *Webster's* give **disk** as the primary spelling for most contexts, including biology (*disk flower*), medicine (*intervertebrate disk*), agriculture (*disk harrow*), engineering (*disk wheel*), and of course computing. The remarkable exception in North America is the phonograph record industry, where *compact discs* (or *L-P discs*) are played over the airwaves by *disc jockeys*, who promote *discography* by day, and may wind up at a *disco(theque)* at night. The *videodisc* and the *optical disc* encapsulate the same spelling.

Either spelling could be justified by etymology. The word is a descendant of the Latin *discus* and Greek *diskos*, so it all depends on how far back you wish to go.

discernible This word was spelled *discernable* for the first three centuries of its existence. But the nineteenth century turned it into the more latinate **discernible**, and this is now the standard spelling. (See further under the heading **-able/-ible**.)

discourse markers In any longish stretch of discourse, whether spoken or written, the reader/receiver welcomes some passing indications as to its structure. Writers and speakers sometimes go so far as to enumerate every structural unit of their discourse: *first(ly)*, *second(ly)*, *third(ly)*; or they may simply mark the boundary between one unit and the next with the help of words such as *another* (point), a *further* (reason) etc. Such words mark both the beginning of the new unit and the end of the previous one. Contrastive conjunctions and conjuncts such as *but*, *yet* and *however* may also serve this function when used at the beginning of a sentence. (See further under **conjunctions**.) Like the Monty Python film, they imply: *And now for something (completely) different!*

More extended types of **discourse markers** are the ones which provide a carrier phrase for identifying the new unit or topic of discussion, such as:
apropos of …
as far as … goes
concerning the business/matter of …
(See further under **dangling participles**, and also **topic**.)

discreet or **discrete** These words both go back to the Latin *discretus* meaning "set apart". This meaning survives much more clearly in the scholastic word **discrete** ("separate, distinct, unrelated") than the common word **discreet** ("circumspect" or "careful in one's actions and words"). In spite of these considerable differences in meaning, the two spellings were not regularly used to distinguish them until the sixteenth century.

The nouns *discreteness* and *discreetness* correspond to the two adjectives in their contemporary meanings. Note that *discretion* is available as a synonym for *discreetness* only.

discriminating or **discriminatory** *Discrimination* has two different faces, one negative, one positive, which are picked up in the different adjectives related to it. *Discrimination against* a particular social group (whether based on gender, race or religion) is a negative phenomenon implying prejudice, and these negative values are embodied in **discriminatory**. The negative is neutralised in *nondiscriminatory*, a word applied to practices which are designed to avoid prejudicing or disadvantaging any social group.

But when *discrimination* is followed by some other word such as *in*, it implies good judgement, and has positive connotations. The adjective **discriminating** is also used to suggest good taste and positive values, whether it is applied in the choice of wines or cultural pursuits. Good judgement and taste are lacking in those who are *undiscriminating*, but the possibility of *discrimination* is still affirmed there. *Indiscriminate* implies the total absence of any principles of selection, and is used of wanton behavior and unmotivated actions, as in *indiscriminate shooting*.

disemboweled or **disembowelled**   The choice between these is discussed under **-l/-ll-**.

disfranchise or **disenfranchise**   Both these words have borne the meaning "deprive of a civil or electoral right" for centuries, though dictionaries all give their preference to **disfranchise**, the older one of the two. It dates from the fifteenth century, while **disenfranchise** made its first appearance in the seventeenth century. Being older, **disfranchise** has a wider range of meanings, and has been adding to them in the twentieth century, in parallel with new developments of the word *franchise* itself. Both noun and verb *franchise* can express "(the authority) to sell goods in a particular zone", and so **disfranchise** now comes to mean "lose one's franchise to sell". **Disenfranchise** lacks this commercial meaning, and associates itself with the loss of civil or electoral rights. Thus the two words seem to be acquiring some independence which would ensure the survival of both.

disfunctional or **dysfunctional**   See dysfunctional.

disheveled or **dishevelled**   For the choice between these, see under **-l/-ll-**.

disinformation or **misinformation**   See under **mis-**.

disingenuous   See under **ingenious** or **ingenuous**.

disinterested or **uninterested**   Is there a difference? Yes and no. Different kinds of meaning are certainly associated with these words, and twentieth century authorities on usage generally distinguish them as follows:
 disinterested = *"unbiased"*, *"having no vested interest"*
 uninterested = *"indifferent"*, *"feeling or showing no mental involvement"*
The Harper-Heritage usage panel stood 100% behind these distinctions in 1985.

But dictionaries all now recognise that **disinterested** is used in the sense of "indifferent". This usage goes back to the seventeenth century, and though the *Oxford Dictionary* declared it obsolete in the late nineteenth, it kept the files open, and there are up-to-date citations on it, and on *disinterest* (meaning "boredom") in the second edition. **Disinterested** can also carry the meaning "having lost interest", which arises easily enough out of its prefix. (See further under **dis-**.)

Webster's English Usage (1989) shows that while **disinterested** is still most often used to mean "unbiased" (in 70% of the instances in their files), it also takes in the meanings "indifferent" and "having lost interest", and is much more frequent overall than **uninterested**. Because **disinterested** carries several meanings, we must rely on the context to show which of them is intended. Given this, and all the surrounding controversy, it would be better to seek a synonym than use either **disinterested** or **uninterested**, if you aim to communicate clearly and directly. (Some possible alternatives are indicated above.)

disjuncts See under **adverbs**.

disk or **disc** See **disc**.

disoriented or **disorientated** The longer form seems to be preferred in Australia and Britain, the shorter one in the USA. The arguments for each are presented under **orient** or **orientate**.

dispassionate This word sets itself apart from both *impassive* and *impassioned*. See under **impassive**.

dispatch or **despatch** Both of these are acceptable spellings, although **dispatch** gets priority in all the major dictionaries, Australian, British and American. Of the two **dispatch** has the better pedigree. **Despatch** seems in fact to have been a typographic mistake from the headword entered in Dr Johnson's dictionary. (Johnson elsewhere in the dictionary used **dispatch**.) The mistake survived until corrected in an 1820 reprint of the dictionary, but by then it had established itself in usage. The fluctuation of other words between *dis-* and *des-* (see **dis-**) certainly helped to make it a plausible variant. However the word actually derives from the Italian *dispacciare*, and the frenchified spelling with *des-* is not justified by etymology.

dispersal or **dispersion** The first of these can be used in many contexts, and simply expresses the action of the verb *disperse*. It could appear in general nonfiction or fiction, in reference to the dispersing of a crowd or a mass of fog. **Dispersion** has technical overtones, because of its use in describing chemical, physical and statistical processes.

disposal or **disposition** Both these relate to the verb *dispose*, but **disposition** preserves the older and more formal of its meanings, in expressing the ideas of "arrangement", "control" and "temper or character". When it comes to *disposing of* something however, **disposal** has taken over, except in legal contexts. So in dealing with a deceased estate, the will may refer to the *disposition of property*, but in other contexts it is normally *disposal*, as in *waste disposal* and *army disposals store*. The idiom *at your disposal* "available for you to use as you see fit" also has *disposal* occupying a slot which was once filled by *disposition.*

dissatisfied or **unsatisfied** With their different prefixes, these mean slightly different things. **Dissatisfied** is usually applied to people, and it expresses a specific discontent with emotion attached to it. **Unsatisfied** is used in more detached and analytical ways, to suggest that a certain requirement has not been met. Compare:
> *The candidates were dissatisfied with their campaign manager.*
> *The party's need for leadership was unsatisfied.*

dissemble or **disassemble** These mean very different things. **Dissemble** is now a slightly old-fashioned synonym for "disguise", and one which may always have been on the outer fringe of English usage, to judge by the trail of obsolete meanings for it in the *Oxford Dictionary*. Borrowed from French, **dissemble** is not really analysable in modern English, and has been largely eclipsed by the more transparent **dissimulate**. (See next entry.)

   Disassemble is a straightforward combination of the prefix *dis-* and *assemble*, implying the taking apart of that which was joined together.

dissimilate or **dissimulate** What's in a letter? With these two it makes the difference between a latinate synonym for "disguise" (**dissimulate**), and the linguistic term **dissimilate**, meaning "make or become dissimilar". **Dissimilate** is used to describe the process by one or other of two identical sounds in a word becomes differentiated, e.g. with the medieval Latin word *peregrinus* "pilgrim" or "foreigner", "one who travels around". The word *pilgrim* is a direct descendant of *peregrinus* but with the first *r* dissimilated into *l*.

dissociate or **disassociate** Both these words mean "sever connections", and both have been used since the seventeenth century. The first is derived from Latin, while the second is a calque of the French *désassocier*. *Webster's English Usage* (1989) notes that **dissociate** is more common, and dictionaries reflect and/or promote this by giving it priority. Fowler gave **disassociate** the thumbs down by saying it was a "needless variant". Yet with its extra syllable **disassociate** spells out its meaning "put an end to an association", which gives it a raison d'être alongside **dissociate** in which the components are fused.

distill or **distil** Australians are caught between the American preference for **distill**, and the fact that the British still plump for **distil**.
   Distil was the spelling used by Dr Johnson, and yet he was distinctly erratic on such words (see **single for double**). The spelling **distill** is to be preferred because of its consistency with all other words derived from the same root, including *distillate, distillation* and *distillery*.

distinct or **distinctive** There's a subtle difference between these two. While **distinct** is a general-purpose word meaning "clear or definite", **distinctive**

means "having the special character or quality of …". Compare their use in the following sentences:

There was a distinct smell of marijuana in the room.
There was the distinctive smell of marijuana in the room.

As the examples show, the word **distinct** is often used simply as an emphatic, whereas **distinctive** invokes knowledge shared by both writer and reader on a particular matter.

distract or **detract** Both words suggest that the impact of something is undermined, but they identify different communicative problems. With **distract** the attention of the audience is sidetracked, whereas with **detract** we imply that there's some deficiency in the communication itself, which would devalue it for anyone.

The peacock in the dancer's arms distracted us from the dance itself.
The jerky movements of the bird detracted from the smooth choreography of the dance.

Note that **detract** is normally followed by *from*, whereas **distract** has a person or persons following it as the object. (See further under **transitive**.)

distracted, distrait or **distraught** These are all variants of the same Latin stem *distractus* meaning "drawn aside", but they designate a whole range of mental conditions. **Distrait** is the most recent of them, borrowed from French in the eighteenth century. It implies being mentally preoccupied and out of touch with whatever is going on, so that the *distrait* person hardly communicates with others around. **Distracted** was borrowed straight from Latin in the sixteenth century, and is used of people whose attention is temporarily diverted, or who suffer from too many demands on their attention. **Distraught**, implying severe emotional distress, is a curious anglicisation of the Latin word, dating back to the fourteenth century. The modern spelling is a result of its being thought of as a past form, like *caught* and *taught*.

distrust or **mistrust** Some style guides suggest that these words differ slightly in meaning (**mistrust** is more tentative), but dictionaries lend no support to it. If anything, the suggested difference probably reflects the fact that **distrust** is much more common nowadays, and this seems to make it less nuanced in meaning, as with some other pairs (see **assume** or **presume**). **Distrust** is actually the later word, a hybrid formation of Latin and English which had no currency until the sixteenth century. **Mistrust** is centuries older, and purely English.

ditransitive See under **transitive**.

ditto The **ditto** (") is a pair of marks which signify that the word(s) or number(s) immediately above should be read again in its place. The marks themselves may be vertical like an umlaut (¨), slanting ("), or curved like closing quotation marks (''), depending on the type resources available. The chief use of **ditto** marks is to avoid cumbersome repetition in successive lines of a list or catalogue.

Roster of Staff for Long Weekend

Saturday	24	January	am	Jones,	Smith,	Taylor
"	"	"	pm	"	"	"
Sunday	25	"	am	"	Walker,	Yeo
"	"	"	pm	"	"	"
Monday	26	"	am	Arnott,	Bowie,	Dodd
"	"	"	pm	"	"	"

Ditto marks were originally used in seventeenth century calendars to avoid repeating the names of months (the word **ditto** is old Italian for "aforesaid"). In older documents, the letters *do* also served as an abbreviation for it, instead of the pair of marks.

Djakarta or **Jakarta** and **Djogjakarta** or **Djokjakarta** See Jakarta.

do Like other auxiliary verbs, **do** has several functions in modern English. It regularly helps to phrase both negative and interrogative statements, and is occasionally used to express emphasis:

I don't like fresh air.
Do you like fresh air?
They do like fresh air.

Apart from those auxiliary roles, **do** also functions as a main verb in its own right. Broadly speaking it means "work on", as in *doing the dishes* and *doing the books*, but it takes on different shades of meaning according to whatever it's coupled with, and whatever context it occurs in. So *doing Germany* could mean completing an educational assignment on it, pursuing business connections in all quarters of the country, or touching down in Bonn and Berlin as one-night tourist stopovers.

docket On whether to double the *t* before adding verb suffixes to this word, see under **t**.

doggerel or **doggrel** The first spelling is now the usual one for this word for pseudo-poetry or bastardised verse, while the second is one of the various alternatives which show people's uncertainty about where the word comes from. A possible explanation is that it's derived from the Italian *doga* meaning "stick"—it being the kind of verse which hits you over the head with its subtlety. But English-speakers are inclined to find their own word *dog* in it, and a negative meaning like the one embedded in *dog Latin*.

dogma For the plural of this word, see under **-a** section 1.

doily, doiley, doyly or **doyley** The first of these spellings is nowadays the most common for the decorative linen or paper napkin used to grace a serving plate. The alternatives exist because the name embodies two variable features of English spelling, *i* varying with *y*, and *ey* with just *y* (see under **y/i** and **-y/-ey**). The word is the surname of a family of successful linen drapers in late seventeenth century England, who according to the *Spectator* magazine "raised a fortune by finding out materials for such stuffs as might at once be cheap and genteel". The aspirations to gentility emerge in yet another spelling of the word as *d'Oyley*, giving it a spurious French connection.

dolce vita This Italian phrase meaning "(the) sweet life" gives English-speakers a way of alluding to what they would describe as "the good life"—a lifestyle supported by a bottomless bank account, fast cars, country properties, and everything that indulges the senses. Fellini's film *La dolce vita* with all those ingredients helped to popularise the idea. A **dolce vita** lifestyle is for those who are free from regular working hours, so that there can be plenty of *dolce far niente* "sweet doing nothing", punctuated by moments of intensity.

-dom This Old English suffix still makes abstract nouns out of more specific ones, although those of the twentieth century have a certain ad hoc quality, and none of them have wide currency. The humorous *ockerdom* is Australia's most notable creation of this kind. In America such words have been created in media coverage to describe the people involved in particular industries, sports or entertainments, for example:

> *newspaperdom moviedom oildom theatredom turfdom*

But only *stardom* (actually dating from 1865) seems to be in common use. The US penchant for such words is believed to have been strengthened by the use of *rebeldom* in the American Civil War.

Apart from these mostly temporary formations, English makes use of the suffix in a few words which describe particular states and conditions, such as *boredom, freedom, martyrdom* and *serfdom*. It also serves to form words which refer to an extent of territory, including *Christendom, earldom, kingdom* and *princedom*. A recent formation of this kind is *officialdom*, where officials reign supreme.

domino For the plural of this word, see **-o**.

dopey or **dopy** The choice between these is discussed under **-y/-ey**.

dot dot dot This is an informal way of referring to ellipsis marks. (See further under **ellipsis**.)

double entendre This phrase borrowed from seventeenth century French is most often translated as "double meaning". The alternative meanings are not on the same plane however: one is straightforward and innocent, while the second is risqué. The second meaning is often occasioned by the context or conventional expectations, as in Mae West's legendary greeting to a male visitor:

> *Is that a gun you've got in your pocket, or are you just pleased to see me?*

In twentieth century French, the **double entendre** is referred to as *double entente* "double signification", and some English speakers use it instead of the older phrase.

double negatives All the following sentences contain double negatives, but is every one of them a no-no?

1 *He didn't say nothing.*
2 *He didn't speak, I don't think.*
3 *He wasn't incapable of speaking.*

Only one of them (the first) is the target of common criticism. The second would pass unnoticed as natural, considered speech; and the third is an accepted way of expressing a subtle observation. The third type of double negative often escapes attention because the second negative element is incorporated as a prefix into another word.

Sentences like the second and third are quite acceptable in writing, whereas the first type is strongly objected to. The negatives in it are of course conspicuous, but there's also an element of social discrimination since **double negatives** of that kind are used in many nonstandard dialects, but abhorred in standard English. Sociolinguists would note a certain amount of window-dressing in claiming that **double negatives** are illogical "because two negatives make a positive". The appeal to mathematics and logic is quite dubious when **double negatives** are standard in some languages such as Russian. No-one hearing such a sentence would doubt that it was meant to be an emphatic negative, with the second negative word reinforcing the first. (Shakespeare made use of **double negatives** to underscore a dramatic point.) But the construction is strongly associated with speech, and writers can seek other ways of accentuating the negative.

Negative constructions like those in the other sentences above are the opposite of emphatic. The sequence of negatives in the second underscores the tentativeness of the assertion, and gives the speaker subtle control over the force of the statement. Subtlety is also the effect achieved in the third through the use of a negative word plus a negative prefix (any from the group *in-*, *un-*, *non-*, *dis-* and *mis-*). The *double negative* again helps to avoid a bald assertion, and paves the way for a new perspective on the topic. Combinations of this kind are quite often used in argumentative writing, as are those which combine a negative with a verb involving a negative process, such as *challenge, deny, disclaim, dispute, doubt, miss, neglect, prevent, refuse* or *refute*. Other auxiliary negative elements are the adverbs *hardly* and *scarcely*, and the particles *unless* and *without*.

Writers who use two or more of the negative elements just mentioned are unlikely to be charged with producing substandard English. They may well create difficult English however, and sentences which require mental gymnastics of the reader:

*He would never dispute the claim that there were no persons in the
country unable to survive without a government pension.*

It is one of the precepts of the Plain English movement that such multiple
negatives are to be avoided, and the reasons are obvious. (See further under
Plain English.)

doubling of final consonant To double or not to double, that is the
question. It comes up with new verbs made out of nouns and adjectives: what
to do with the past forms of verbs derived from *banquet* and *sequin*, for example.
It is also the basis of some of the regular differences between British and
American spelling. Let's review the general rules before looking at the
variations.

In a two-part nutshell, the general rule is that you double the final consonant
if:

- the vowel before the consonant is a single one (as in *wetted*
  or *regretted*, not a digraph (compare *seated* and *repeated*); and
- the syllable before the suffix is stressed (as in *wetted* and
  regretted), not unstressed (compare *budgeted* and *marketed*).

The rule applies to any noun, verb or adjective ending in a single consonant,
when suffixes beginning with a vowel or *-y* are to be added. The following
examples show how the rule works with various suffixes and before words of
one and two syllables:

skim	*skimming*			*bosom*	*bosomy*
win	*winner*	*begin*	*beginner*	*sequin*	*sequined*
step	*stepped*			*gallop*	*galloped*
stir	*stirred*	*deter*	*deterred*	*butter*	*buttered*
knit	*knitting*	*admit*	*admitting*	*audit*	*auditing*

Further examples are discussed under **-p/-pp-**, **-s/-ss-** and **t**. Note that some
words, especially those ending in *-r*, vary their spelling because of changes in
stress before particular suffixes:

confer	*conferred*	*conference*
defer	*deferred*	*deferent*
prefer	*preferred*	*preferable*
refer	*referred*	*reference*

These changes are all in accordance with the rule above.

Exceptions, variations and anomalies. Certain kinds of words diverge from
the rules just mentioned, in all or some parts of the English-speaking world:

1 Words ending in *-x* (such as *tax* and *transfix*) are never doubled, even when
their last syllable is stressed

2 Words ending in *-c* (such as *panic*) are always "doubled" to *-ck*, to preserve
their "k" sound. (See further under **-c/-ck-**.)

3 Words in which the last syllable is identical with a one-syllabled word. For
example:

backlog eavesdrop fellowship format handicap kidnap leapfrog overlap program sandbag waterlog worship zigzag

In Australia and Britain, these words double the final consonant in spite of the lack of stress, to become *backlogged, handicapped, programmed* etc. In American English they may not: spellings such as *kidnaped, programed* and *worshiped* are certainly in use.

4 Words ending in *-l* are usually doubled in Australian and British English, whether or not the last syllable is stressed. In the USA the common practice is to apply the general rules given above, and to double only when there is stress on the final syllable. So most Americans write *reveled* with one *l* and *rebelled* with two, whereas Britons and most Australians write *revelled* like *rebelled*. These anomalies are discussed further under **-l/-ll-**.

doubtless or **undoubtedly** See **undoubtedly**.

down- This familiar particle combines like a prefix with both verbs and nouns, to indicate a descent, or the movement from a higher to lower position. It combines with verbs in *downcast, downfall, downpour* and *downturn*, and usually bears the stress in those words. When combined with nouns, in *downbeat, downhill, downstairs* and *downstream*, the stress is more variable, as if it is less fully integrated. Yet in each case, **down-** is set solid with the word to which it is attached.

downtoners See under **hedge words** and **adverbs**.

downward or **downwards** See under **-ward**.

doyly, doyley or **doiley** See **doily**.

draft or **draught** The borders between these two spellings are still being adjusted in Australian English. Both relate to the verb *draw* which has generated many descendants, ranging from words for pulling a load, or drawing water, air or money, to sketching, composing a document, dividing up one's livestock or choosing men for military service. The older spelling **draught** has few analogies in English except *laughter*, and the more phonetic **draft** gained ground on it in the late eighteenth and early nineteenth century. In American English **draft** is the standard spelling for all uses of the word, and even in Britain, it is now accepted in the contexts of banking, the composing of documents, and in references to selecting soldiers and livestock. Yet still the business of making technical drawings is distinguished with the spelling **draught**, and in *draughtsman/person*. **Draught** also persists in references to fluids, as in *draught beer*, a *cold draught under the door*, and the *draught of a ship*, as well as *draught horses*.

Australians generally deploy the spellings **draft** and **draught** in the same way as the British. In the ACE corpus most uses of **draught** were in reference to beer, apart from a sprinkling of references to the *draught horse*, and the spelling is perhaps entrenched there. However things are different when it comes to technical drawing, with **draft** recommended by some of the major newspapers for that use (as well as for the composing of documents). And the corresponding spellings *draftsperson* and *drafting officer/assistant* are codified in the Australian Standard Classification of Occupations (1990).

dramaturge or **dramaturgist** In the nineteenth century either form of this word referred to one who wrote dramas for the stage. But **dramaturge** is now applied to the specialist adviser to a theatre company, who devises the repertoire, and investigates and adapts the play scripts for performance. According to *Webster's Dictionary*, the role originated in European theatres, and *Random House* notes the alternative form *dramaturg*. Both **dramaturge** and *dramaturg* are used this way in Australia.

drank or **drunk** See under **drink**.

dreamed or **dreamt** For the choice between these, see under **-ed**.

drier or **dryer** The first spelling usually represents the comparative form of the adjective *dry*, while the second is the agent noun for referring to that which dries. However all dictionaries recognise **drier** as an alternative for the noun, and some in Britain and USA also allow **dryer** for the adjective. It is of course normal for the final *y* to change to *i* before the vowel of the suffix (see further under **-y>-i-**). In the eighteenth century this mutation was also found in *driness* and *drily*, though it is no longer seen in the first of those, and is disappearing from the second. The tendency not to change the final *y* asserts itself with the agent noun, and the *Oxford Dictionary* notes its use in the names of mechanical devices such as *clothes dryer* or *hair dryer*. It makes a useful contrast with **drier** for the adjective, as long as the latter remains unchanged.

drink, drank and **drunk** The parts of this irregular verb have been unstable for centuries, and they still seem to be shifting and changing places. Dictionaries present the three forms given above as standard, yet the larger ones indicate that there are alternative past forms with some currency. **Drunk** is a colloquial or dialectal form of the past tense; and **drank** is given as an occasional past participle. (According to a special note in the *Random House Dictionary*, **drank** is often used in this way by educated Americans.) The use of *drunken* (once a past participle) is now limited to being an attributive adjective, as in *a drunken rage*. It thus complements **drunk** as the predicative adjective, in: *They were drunk and disorderly*. (See further under **adjectives.**)

drivable or **driveable** See under **-eable**.

driveling or **drivelling** For the choice between these, see **-l/-ll-**.

druggist, pharmacist or **chemist** See under **pharmacist**.

drunk or **drunken** See under **drink**.

dryer or **drier** See drier.

d.s.p. See decessit sine prole.

d.t.'s or **DT's** See delirium tremens.

due to or **owing to** Due to has been under a cloud for three centuries, though the basis of objections to it has shifted. Early this century the problem, as articulated by Fowler, was that **due** should be seen as an adjective or participle and be attached to a relevant noun, not to a notion extracted from a whole clause/sentence. The first sentence below was therefore unacceptable, and should be rewritten as the second or third:

The dinner was postponed due to unforeseen circumstances.
The postponement of the dinner was due to unforeseen circumstances.
Owing to unforeseen circumstances, the dinner was postponed.

Similar objections had in fact been raised against **owing to** in the eighteenth century, which quietly faded away as it evolved into a compound preposition. **Due to** began to be used in the same way in the late nineteenth century (the first *Oxford Dictionary* citation is from 1897), and objections against it begin to appear early this century.

Yet Fowler himself noted that this prepositional use of **due to** was "as common as can be", and the *Oxford Dictionary* Supplement (1933) confirms its frequency in the USA. The tide of usage has swept it in, as Gowers admits in his 1965 edition of Fowler, when BBC announcers and even the Queen's own speech-writer have to be counted among its more conspicuous users. There is clearly no reason to perpetuate the shibboleth against **due to** in Australia, when the grammatical grounds for objecting to it are so dubious. *Webster's English Usage* (1989) affirms that it is "grammatically impeccable", and we may take our cue from the reputable writers who use it without qualms.

(See further under **shibboleths**, and **dangling participles**.)

dueling or **duelling** The choice between these is discussed under -l/-ll-.

dullness or **dulness** The first of these spellings is given priority in almost all modern dictionaries. The second exists as an example of the historical uncertainty as to what to do about a final *l*. (See further under **single for double**.)

duologue or **dialogue** See under dia-.

Dutch or **dutch** See under Holland.

dwarfs or **dwarves** The first form **dwarfs** is preferred by all dictionaries for the plural of *dwarf*, and it is sounder in historical terms. The *f* in its spelling is relatively recent, unlike others whose *f* turns into *v* for a plural which goes back to Old English. (See further under **-f>-v-**.) **Dwarves** seems to have arisen on the analogy of *wharf/wharves*, where the plural with *-ves* has some legitimacy. The number of words with *-ves* plurals is steadily declining, and there's no reason to count *dwarf* among them, on the strength of very sporadic uses of **dwarves**.

dwelt or **dwelled** Only the first of these enjoys much currency these days. The second is distinctly old-fashioned. For a discussion of other such pairs, see under **-ed**.

dyad, diad or **duad** The spelling **dyad** is preferred in all modern dictionaries. **Diad** is a current alternative in *Webster's* and the *Random House Dictionary*, though according to the second edition of the *Oxford Dictionary* it's obsolete. The rare third spelling **duad** also seems to be obsolete by the *Oxford's* dating, yet is glossed with no indication of obsolescence in the American dictionaries. New uses for **dyad** in sociology and theories of communication seem to account for its vitality in the USA, as well as the variation in spelling. The tendency to replace *y* with *i* is familiar enough in other nouns, and especially in American English (see **i/y**)—even if **dyad** represents the original Greek root more exactly.

dyarchy or **diarchy** Both are recognised spellings, yet dictionaries diverge over which should be given priority. *Webster's* stands alone in preferring **dyarchy**, while **diarchy** is preferred by *Random House, Macquarie, Collins* and the second edition of the *Oxford Dictionary*. The *Oxford's* preference is based strictly on etymology (*di + archy*), and it dubs **dyarchy** "erroneous", though its own citations support **dyarchy** rather than **diarchy** by 5:3. Perhaps users of the word feel it looks more consistently Greek as **dyarchy**.

The same divergence in spelling applies to adjectives based on the noun. While *Oxford* and *Random House* give priority to spellings with *i* in the stem: *diarchic, diarchical* and *diarch(i)al, Webster's* gives them as *dyarchic*, also *dyarchical* or *dyarchal*. Again the *Oxford's* citations offer rather more support for the spellings with *y*. For the choice between *-ic* and *-ical* endings, see **-ic/-ical**.

dyeing This word resists the standard spelling rule to drop *-e* before a suffix beginning with a vowel—with good reason, to distinguish itself from *dying*. The distinction is however only about a century old. For centuries, either word could be spelled either way, and those who preferred might spell both the same way, and rely on the context to communicate the difference. So Addison in the late seventeenth century spelled both *dye*, while Johnson made both *die*. (See further under **i/y**, **i>y**, and **-e**.)

dyke or **dike** See **dike**.

dys- This Greek prefix means "bad, faulty", and almost all the words it appears in are bad news. It may be that your breathing is labored (*dyspnoeia*), you're having trouble swallowing (*dysphagia*), your digestion is poor (*dyspepsia*), your bowels are in disarray (*dysentery*), and urinating is a problem (*dysuria*). Apart from its use in designating medical problems, **dys-** also serves to designate intellectual deficiencies (*dyslexia* and *dyscalculia*).

Note that **dys-** occasionally forms words which contrast with an opposite number formed with *eu-*, for example *dysphemism* as opposed to *euphemism* (see under **euphemism**). The recently coined *dystopia* works on that basis, as an antonym for *Utopia*—spuriously interpreted as "Eutopia". (The name *Utopia* created by Sir Thomas More for his perfect society actually comprises *ou* "not" and *topos* "place", i.e. "no place".)

dysfunctional or **disfunctional** The major American and British dictionaries recognise **disfunctional** as a variant of **dysfunctional**, and *disfunction* for *dysfunction*. The second edition of the *Oxford Dictionary* has several citations for them, and the substitution of the prefix *dis-* for *dys-*, or of *i* for *y* in the spelling (see **i/y**) is not so remarkable. The two prefixes both have negative meanings, and the occasional use of *dis-* for *dys-* suggests that the word is losing its academic flavor, and beginning to be assimilated among more general vocabulary.

E

-e The letter *e* is the most hardworked of all in written English, as every Scrabble player knows. Apart from representing its own sound (as in *let, send*), it often serves as a silent modifier of others (as in *mate, rage*). Sometimes (as in *some, true*) it is simply a relic of times when far more English words ended in *e*— times when there was many an "olde shoppe". In the course of history, final *e* has come and gone from many words; and in twentieth century English it still varies in the spelling of words. Its presence or absence is dictated by number of rules and conventions, including those following:

1 *The major rule affecting* ***e*** is dropping it before a suffix beginning with a vowel or *y*. This applies to an enormous number of words in English. It happens regularly with the parts of a verb: *hope* < *hoping, hoped*, and with adjectives: *simple* < *simpler, simplest*. It also applies whenever words with final *e* are extended into new words:

-able	note > notable
-age	dose > dosage
-al	arrive > arrival
-ation	conserve > conservation
-ator	demonstrate > demonstrator
-er	believe > believer
-ery	machine > machinery
-ify	false > falsify
-ise/-ize	pressure > pressurise
-ish	prude > prudish
-ism	elite > elitism
-ist	extreme > extremist
-ity	saline > salinity
-ous	virtue > virtuous
-ure	expose > exposure
-y	craze > crazy

The rule does not apply when the suffix begins with a consonant, for example:

-ful	hope, hopeful	cf. hoping
-ly	close, closely	closing
-ment	advertise, advertisement	advertising
-ness	humble, humbleness	humbling

Exceptions and variations to the major rule:

a) A handful of words such as *acknowledg(e)ment* and *judg(e)ment* are spelled either with or without the **e**, even though the following suffix begins with a consonant. (See under **judgement** and also **fledgling**.)

b) Words ending with *-ce* or *-ge* keep their final **e** before a suffix beginning with *a* (e.g. *embraceable*) and *o* (e.g. *courageous*). (See under **-ce/-ge**.)

c) Words ending with *-ee* such as *agree* and *decree* drop one **e** before *-ed*, but keep both before *-ing*. So *agreed* but *agreeing*.

d) Words ending in *-inge* such as *singe* may keep the **e** before *-ing*, and thus *singeing* is distinct from *singing*, *springeing* from *springing*, and *swingeing* from *swinging*. Some writers keep the **-e** in other rather uncommon verbs of this kind, e.g. *bingeing*, *hingeing*, *tingeing*, *twingeing* and *whingeing*, even though there are no parallel words without the **-e** to confuse them with. Note that well-established verbs such as *cringe*, *fringe*, *impinge* and *infringe* always drop their **e** in accordance with the major rule.

e) Words ending in *-ie*, such as *die*, *lie*, *tie* and *vie* change in two ways before *-ing*: they drop their **e** and change the *i* to *y* (see **i>y**). Note however that *tieing* is recognised in *Webster's Dictionary* (1986) as an alternative to *tying*; and for *stymie* there is both *stymying* and *stymieing* (see **stymie**). For *dying* v. *dyeing*, see under **dyeing**.

f) Words ending in *-oe* regularly keep their **e** before *-ing*: *canoeing*, *hoeing*, *shoeing* and *toeing*. Before *-ist*, it is the same for *canoeist*, but not for *oboist*.

g) Words ending in *-ue* often keep their **e** before a suffix beginning with *i* or *y*, particularly if they have only one syllable. So *clue* and *glue* retain it in *cluey* and *gluey* (to ensure that they are not read as words of one syllable like *buy*). This explains why *blue* appears with **e** in *bluey-green*, but not usually in *bluish*. As a technical term *blueing* is more likely to keep its **e** than in common idiom as a part of a verb: *bluing all his pay on the horses*. Established verbs normally drop their **e**, as do:

> *accrue argue construe continue ensue issue pursue*
> *queue rescue subdue sue value*

For the verb *cue* (in theatre and film usage), the regular *cuing* is the dictionaries' preferred spelling, but *Webster's* also recognises *cueing*. *Cueing* is also the spelling for technical uses of the word in audio systems, from multiple citations in the second edition of the *Oxford Dictionary* (1989).

h) Three-letter words which end in **e** may or may not keep it before suffixes: in *ageism* the **e** is always there, in *icing* never. Others such as *ag(e)ing*, *ap(e)ing*, *aw(e)ing* and *ey(e)ing* may appear either way. If the context is straightforward and helps to foster the intended meaning, there's no reason not to spell them according to the major rule. (See further under **aging**.)

Other spelling conventions of English with final e are:

2 A final **e** is sometimes added to a gender-free word ending in *-ant* or *-ist* to create an explicitly female form of it, for example:

　　　artiste clairvoyante confidante typiste

This is analogous to what happens in French grammar, though in French it is more often used for reasons of grammatical gender than natural gender (see further under **gender**). The use of explicitly female words is often beside the point, and to be discouraged if we care about nonsexist language (see further under **nonsexist language**). In cases like these, the gender-free equivalent is much better established anyway.

3 A final **e** is sometimes added to French loanwords used in English, even when they have none in French itself. So there are alternative spellings (with and without the **e**) for words such as *boulevard(e)*, *caviar(e)*, *chaperon(e)* and *complin(e)*. The spellings with **e** are really "more French than the French". This is one of several ways in which French loanwords are sometimes touched up in English. (See **frenchification**.)

4 A final **e** often distinguishes proper names from their common noun counterparts (in addition to the initial capital letter). Some examples are *Coote*, *Hawke*, *Lowe* and *Moore*. Not all bearers of such names use these spellings however, and writers should check whether they're corresponding with *Brown* or *Browne*, *Clark* or *Clarke*. (See further under **proper names**.)

5 A final **e** is used by chemists to distinguish the names of certain groups of chemical substances—though this technical distinction is not necessarily understood by those who use the spelling *glycerine* rather than *glycerin*. (See further under **-ine/-in**.)

-eable This ending is really a composite of the final *e* of a root word and the *-able* suffix. It is a matter of necessity for some words, and of choice for others. It is the necessary ending for words such as *changeable* and *traceable*, because *-eable* serves to preserve the "j" or "s" sound in them (see **-ce/-ge**). But for others such as *lik(e)able*, *liv(e)able*, *siz(e)able* and *us(e)able*, it's possible to use either **-eable** or just *-able*. Broadly speaking, the *Oxford Dictionary* tradition maintains the first spelling, while American English is squarely behind the second. Australians are divided in their preferences, and the *Macquarie Dictionary* (1991) gives them as equals, though with the plain *-able* spellings first. This is in line with the major rule over dropping final *e* (see **e**), and was indeed Fowler's recommendation for words suffixed with *-able*. The style guides for the *Sydney Morning Herald* and *News Limited* both settle the issue that way.

　　The major rule is applied by almost everyone when the root word has two or more syllables, such as *debatable*, *unshakable*, *reconcilable* and *(un)mistakable*. It is when the root word has only one syllable that writers diverge, some arguing that it needs its *e* before *-able* to prevent misconstruction. Yet established cases such as *curable*, *notable* and *provable* show that retaining the *e* in the middle need only be a temporary measure. Even new formations such as *drivable* are unlikely to be misread if motor vehicles are already part of the context. The words we read rarely have to stand alone for interpretation, as they do in dictionary lists.

each On the question whether **each** takes a singular or plural verb, see **agreement** section 1.

each other or **one another** Prescriptive style commentators have tried to insist that the first of these expressions was to be used between two people only, and the second when more than two were concerned. Yet Fowler spoke firmly against this distinction in 1926, saying it had "neither present utility nor a basis in historical usage"; and his judgement is confirmed in citations recorded in the *Oxford Dictionary* and *Webster's English Usage* (1989).

On the question of where to place the apostrophe in such expressions, see under **other's** or **others'**.

-ean See under **-an**.

earthen, earthy or **earthly** Only the first of these is still completely in touch with the ground. **Earthen** means "consisting or made out of earth or clay", as in *earthen floor*. **Earthy** usually highlights the natural properties of earth which can be recognised elsewhere, such as in an *earthy smell*, or its elemental characteristics, as in an "earthy sense of humor". Depending on context, **earthy** may carry positive or negative overtones. Even in the appreciation of wines, research has shown that it is ambiguous, implying a down-to-earth, robust wine to some tasters, and a mouldy bouquet to others.

Earthly takes its particular meaning from being the antonym of *heavenly*. When used in expressions such as *earthly pleasures*, it usually implies their limited or short-term nature, in comparison with the infinity of heaven. Note however that when it is negated as *unearthly*, it is no synonym for *heavenly*. Instead it denotes the weird and eerie elements of the supernatural, as in an *unearthly cry*. Different again is its meaning in expressions such as *not an earthly chance* and *no earthly reason*, where it simply acts as an intensifier. (See further under **intensifiers**.)

east, eastern or **easterly** When used with lower case, these words all relate straightforwardly to a point, area or direction which is 90° right of the north/south axis for a particular country or city. In the absence of any geographical reference points, it relates to the writer's or speaker's north/south axis.

The main thing to note is that when applied to winds, airstreams or currents, these words denote "*from* the east", whereas in other applications they mean "*to(wards)* or *in* the east". So an *easterly wind* will have its impact on the *eastern side* of a building, and wildflowers in the *eastern region* of a national park will have walkers heading **east** to see them.

When dressed with a capital letter, **East** often carries special historical or political overtones. In *Middle East* or *Far East*, it still represents the European colonial perspective. What was the *Far East* for Britons is the "Near North" for Australians, as Menzies observed in 1939. (Compare the expression *Southeast Asia*, which is free of any "user-perspective".) The difference between European cultures and those of colonial countries was the stimulus for Rudyard Kipling's comment last century that "East is East and West is West, and never the twain shall meet"... But the twentieth century recognises the need for mutual understanding, and the East-West Center was established at the University of Hawaii in 1960 for this very purpose.

After World War II and during the subsequent Cold War, **eastern** acquired a new political significance in the phrase *eastern bloc*, used in reference to the Soviet Union and its east European satellites. Its communist system and centralised economy contrasted with those of the capitalistic states of western Europe and North America, allied through NATO. Since 1991 however the old east-west division has dissolved with the breakup of the *eastern bloc*.

The implications of **Eastern** are different again in references to the *Eastern Orthodox Church*, where the word identifies the group of churches which developed in the **eastern** half of the Roman Empire, which were for centuries identified with Byzantium/Constantinople. They include the churches of Greece and Cyprus, Egypt and some cities in the Middle East, as well as Russia, Bulgaria, Czechoslovakia, Poland, Romania and Serbia. The group split off from the Catholic church (based on Rome) in AD 1054.

eastward or **eastwards** See under -ward.

eat The only point at issue with this verb is its past tense—how you say and spell it. Uncertainty about the pronunciation has made people less sure about the spelling. In twentieth century English the spelling has settled down so that it is now always *ate*, and many Australians and Americans pronounce it to rhyme with "late". However some Australians and many Britons pronounce it to rhyme with "let". The second pronunciation corresponds to the older past form **eat**, which was used until the nineteenth century for the past as well as the present tense. (Compare *read* for both present and past forms of another verb.) Nowadays *ate* has everything to recommend it, offering a distinct way of spelling the past tense, and a clear lead as to its pronunciation.

-eau Words which end in **-eau** (or *-ieu* or *-iau*) are borrowings from French where they are pluralised with *-x*, e.g. *tableau* > *tableaux*. However once they are at home in English they acquire English plurals as well, e.g. *tableaus*. Those which are totally assimilated may indeed shed their French plural, and so *bureaus* is now the only plural form current. But many others still have both French and English plurals, including:

bandeau bateau beau chapeau chateau flambeau
fricandeau gateau manteau morceau plateau portmanteau
reseau rouleau tableau tonneau trousseau

In English the *-x* plural is most likely to be used by writers who wish to emphasise the foreign origin of such words.

Like all those just mentioned, *adieu* in the plural may be spelled with either *-s* or *-x*, but the English plural *adieus* is the more frequent one now and entirely justifiable. (The word has been in English for centuries—since Chaucer—and its spelling was temporarily anglicised in the sixteenth and seventeenth centuries as *adew* and *adue*.) *Milieu* is also more commonly found with an English than a French plural, and *purlieu* has only the English one.

Note however that with *fabliau* the plural with *-x* is still preferred, no doubt because those who use it are aware of the French origin of that genre, and use the form *fabliaux* as a reminder of it.

echidna For the plural of this word, see **-a** section 1.

eco- The words formed with this Greek root have come a long way from its literal meaning "house". With *economics* we usually think of state or business finances rather than those of the home. And with *ecology*, coined only in the nineteenth century, we focus on the environment and systemic or symbiotic relationships within it. In the several new compounds formed with it, **eco-** certainly equals "environment":

ecocide ecofreak ecohazard eco-nut ecosphere ecospecies
ecosystem ecothriller ecotourist ecotype

The same item serves as an independent word in *Eco Rambo*, a movie which casts Sylvester Stallone in a new role as defender of the environment.

economic or **economical** As with many *-ic/-ical* pairs, there is common ground between these, as well as a demarcation difference, though the picture keeps changing. The "economical man" of nineteenth century political philosophy is the "economic man" of the twentieth century. Thus **economic** has generally displaced **economical** in references to matters of *economics* and the structure of the economy at large; and **economical** now relates to economy measures by which we avoid extravagance and wastage. So while treasurers and accountants concern themselves with **economic** strategies, those responsible for the household budget work on **economical** uses of the kitty. The two embody different perspectives on money, one theoretical, the other practical.

Note however that these distinctions are sometimes blurred, at least in colloquial usage, as is acknowledged in dictionaries all over the world. In any case the two different perspectives are not always easy to separate, for example in expressions like "an economic necessity". There is only one adverb for the two words *economically*, and we rely on the context to show which kind of meaning is intended. Only in the verb *economise* is the meaning unquestionably linked with the practical implementation of an economy measure. (See further under **-ic/-ical**.)

-ed The **-ed** suffix is used for the past (both past tense and past participle) of many an English verb:

bounded claimed departed liked organised wandered

Verbs like these are the *regular* verbs of English (see further under **irregular verbs**). In some cases the **-ed** makes a separate syllable (*bounded, departed*), in others it just adds an extra consonant sound, a "d" in *claimed*, and a "t" in *liked*.

The past forms of a number of verbs are actually spelled with *t*. For example:

> *bent built crept dealt dwelt felt kept left lent meant sent*
> *slept spent swept wept*

In some of those cases the *t* takes the place of a *d* in the stem of the word (*bent* < *bend*), in others it is a substitute for the **-ed** suffix (as in *dealt* < *deal*). The list was once longer: spellings such as *past* and *wrapt* are relics of some other cases.

1 *Verbs with both* **-ed** *and* **-t***.* Several verbs have alternative past forms, including:

> *burned/burnt dreamed/dreamt kneeled/knelt leaned/leant leaped/leapt*
> *learned/learnt smelled/smelt spelled/spelt spilled/spilt spoiled/spoilt*

The forms with **-ed** are dominant in American English, whereas in Australian and British English both forms are used. The use of the *-t* form may indeed have increased in Britain during the twentieth century, according to Gowers's 1965 edition of *Fowler's Modern English Usage*. In Australia the picture is mixed, with the **-ed** forms predominating for the simple past of *burn, dream, lean, learn* and *spill*, though not the rest, according to the ACE corpus. The *-t* forms are preferred for adjectival uses as in "spilt milk" and "learnt behavior", with the exception of "a learned man". Though some attach different meanings to the two forms (see under **burned**), they are not necessarily there for the reader. When **-ed** is clearly the more regular form, we might as well use it for the standard verb uses.

2 *The* **-ed** *after vowels.* When an **-ed** is added to a verb ending in *a e i o* or *u*, the result may look rather strange, especially with more than one vowel (as in *radioed* or *plateaued*), or the word is being newly used as a verb (as in *flambeed* or *mascaraed*). Fowler's answer to the problem was to use *'d* in such cases: *flambe'd, mascara'd, plateau'd, radio'd*, which accords well with the fact that the apostrophe has long been used to mark omission, and the fact that the **-(e)d** never makes a separate syllable on such words. (See further under **apostrophes**.) An alternative measure sometimes used in such cases is the hyphen: *mascara-ed, radio-ed*, though it has the disadvantage of seeming to create an extra syllable, and is little used, according to a survey reported in *English Today* in 1988.

Few words of this kind are entered as verbs in dictionaries (because they are essentially nouns being pressed into verbal service). When they are, the American dictionaries give them the regular spelling (as in *hennaed, umbrellaed* and *visaed*); whereas British dictionaries occasionally use the apostropheed (or apostrophe'd) spelling, as in *tiara'd*. Fowler's principle has a value when there are two or three different vowels preceding the suffix, as in *shanghai'd* and *plateau'd*, but seems unnecessary when there are two identical vowels before the suffix, as in *baaed* and *tattooed*. Words ending with double *e* (*agree, filigree, pedigree, referee, tee*) conform easily to the general rule by which a final *e* is dropped before a suffix (see under **-e**). In general the regular **-ed** spelling seems to work, and it does offer a clear principle for new or ad hoc uses of words as verbs.

Spellings with the regular **-ed** have been used in this book wherever there are choices like those discussed above.

---

edema or **oedema** See under **oe**.

edgeways or **edgewise** See under **-wise**.

educator, educationist or **educationalist** All these words seem to have aspirations beyond the familiar word *teacher*, and represent the desire to express the professionalism involved in pedagogy. **Educator** implies direct contact with students, whether it is as a lecturer, tutor, classroom teacher, or coach. The term **education(al)ist** implies someone specifically interested in the theory and methods of teaching. The shorter form is more common in both the USA and Britain, and it had Fowler's vote, although the longer one persists. (See further under **-ist**.) *Webster's English Usage* (1989) notes that **educationist** has unfavorable connotations in some of its recent citations, and that **educationalist** (provided it remains neutral) might serve instead. A more radical solution was proposed for Australians by Murray-Smith (1989): to use **educator** for all applications. Unfortunately it leaves us with no way of distinguishing the practitioner from the academic.

-ee This ending appears on English words for a number of reasons. Apart from a few simple ones like *knee* and *tree*, such words are often foreign loanwords in which **-ee** is the best way to represent the final syllable in English. So it stands instead of "i" in Hindi loanwords such as *dungaree, kedgeree* and *suttee*; and in *chimpanzee*, borrowed from a Bantu language. Yet its most common use in English is as counterpart to the French use of *e* for the past participle, a usage which was established in English law when legal matters were still discussed in hybrid French and English. Many of the words with the **-ee** suffix are ones which designate a legal or quasi-legal role, such as:

> *appellee assignee arrestee consignee deportee*
> *franchisee grantee internee lessee libelee licensee*
> *mortgagee parolee patentee payee trustee*

Yet as the last example shows, such words can become part of everyday language, as is unquestionably the case with:

absentee addressee amputee conferee devotee
divorcee employee escapee evacuee examinee interviewee
nominee referee returnee trainee

The legal or bureaucratic associations of many of those words have nevertheless given **-ee** a formal and organisational flavor; and this is no doubt part of the joke in ad hoc words such as *quizzee* and *holdupee*, formed with everyday verbs.

The words in those lists also show that **-ee** words do not necessarily form a pair with one ending in *-er/-or*. The cases which do, like *employee/employer* and *lessee/lessor*, are probably fewer than those like *addressee* or *devotee* which do not. The list also shows that **-ee** words are not necessarily passive, as is sometimes said. Examples such as *conferee* and *escapee* can only be active in meaning (see **active verbs**); and others such as *referee* and *retiree* have developed active meanings though they may have originated as passives.

All the examples so far have in common the fact that they designate *one* person. The word *committee* might therefore seem to be an alien form. Originally it too referred to a single person to whom some duty was assigned, but from the seventeenth century on, it became the word for a group of people with a collective brief.

Note that **-ee** is sometimes a respelling of the informal suffix *-ie*, especially in some words associated with children, such as *bootees* and *coatee*. (Brand names such as *Softees* are also formed with it.) (See further under **-ie/-y**.)

-eer First and foremost, this suffix serves to identify a person by whatever item they engage with in their work, as with *engineer, mountaineer* or *puppeteer*. A number of such words have been used in connection with military personnel, including *cannoneer, charioteer, musketeer* and *rocketeer*, and this seems to have paved the way for its use in civilian forms of contention, as in *auctioneer, electioneer* and *pamphleteer*. This in turn may have helped to attach a derogatory flavor to words with **-eer**, as with *profiteer, racketeer* and *(black) marketeer*. The negative implications of (black) *marketeer* were exploited in Britain by those who were reluctant to join the European Community.

Derogatory implications also infect the meanings of these words when they appear used as verbs, as in *profiteering* and *racketeering*. The coloring is there also in *commandeer* and *domineer*, though they are loanwords from Dutch.

Note that *pioneer* and *volunteer* are free of any derogatory or contentious associations, whether as nouns or verbs. In each case they were borrowed ready-made into English, and cannot be analysed in the same way as the English formations.

Compare **-ier**.

eerie or **eery** All major dictionaries prefer **eerie** for this Scottish dialect word, though **eery** is more regular as the spelling for an English adjective. (See further under **-y**.) The *Oxford Dictionary*'s record for **eery** stops in the eighteenth century, however, and **eerie** has clearly prevailed.

effect For the difference between **effect** and **affect**, see under **affect**.

effective, efficient or **efficacious** These words are all about getting things done and having the desired effect, but the first two have many more applications than the third. The third **efficacious** is now used principally to refer to medicines and remedies. It was once used more widely, in situations where we now use **effective**, but nowadays appears only in the most lofty style.

Effective has expanded its domain continually since the fifteenth century, when it was simply a scholar's word, and even since the seventeenth and eighteenth centuries, when it had particular uses in military and technical contexts. It can now be used in relation to almost anything that achieves the intended result, from *effective advertising* to *effective parenting*. It can be used of objects and instruments, as well as methods and strategies, and even of people who harness and mobilise others' efforts towards a particular goal: *an effective chairman*. In some contexts it carries the meaning of "being in force", as in *prices effective until December 31st*. It can also mean "in fact", particularly as an adverb: *It effectively rules them out.*

Efficient is most often applied to people who do not waste time or energy and other resources in fulfilling particular tasks, such as *an efficient waiter*. It can also be applied to engines and machinery which give relatively large amounts of power in relation to their consumption: *more fuel-efficient than the previous model*.

Note that the word *effectual* once served as an alternative to **effective** and **efficient**. Nowadays it hardly appears except in the negative: *ineffectual*, used to describe a person who fails to meet the demands of a task.

-efy/-ify See -ify/-efy.

e.g. This Latin abbreviation stands for *exempli gratia* meaning "by way of an example". In English it's regularly translated as "for example". Nowadays, like other Latin abbreviations, it is not usually italicised. As a lower case abbreviation, it is still usually accorded stops (see **abbreviations**), though increasingly it is printed without them. There were 51 instances of **e.g.** to 11 of **eg** in the Australian ACE corpus. A third alternative **eg** was represented by 5 instances, and is discussed further under **Latin abbreviations**.

The punctuation before and after **e.g.** has long been the subject of prescription. A comma used to be considered necessary *after* it, and still is, according to the Chicago *Manual of Style*. But most style guides now dispense with one after it, and emphasise only having one *before* it. Other punctuation marks, such as a dash, colon or opening parenthesis could equally well come before it, depending on the structure of the sentence.

The propriety of using **e.g.** in one's writing has also been subject to taboos and prescriptions. Generations of editors have translated it into "for example" whenever it appeared in running text, because it was deemed suitable only for footnotes (according to Fowler) or parentheses (Chicago *Manual*). Yet the

Chicago *Manual* also mentions that it may be used in "technical matter", and other style guides recognise its right to appear in various kinds of prose. The *Right Word at the Right Time* allows for **e.g.** in either "official or very informal writing"—one extreme or the other; and the Australian Government *Style Manual* recognises the need for the abbreviation in "general works", if there are many shortened forms. As far as Cambridge University Press is concerned, the decision is up to individual authors, and **e.g.** is used freely on the expository pages of *Copy-editing* (1992).

Compare **i.e.**

egoist or **egotist** These words have identical meaning for many people, both referring to individuals who are seen as preoccupied with themselves and their own interests. Dictionaries often suggest that they may be synonyms for each other, and yet for some users they embody slight differences due to their independent origins.

Egoist (and *egoism*) originated in eighteenth century philosophy, amid questions as to whether self-interest was the basis of morality. From this the **egoist** comes to be someone who finds more interest in himself or herself than anyone else. **Egotist** derives from *egotism*, a word used in eighteenth century stylistic discussions to refer to writing which makes excessive use of the first person (*I*). Nowadays the words *egotism* and *egotist* are not restricted to writing, and refer to self-important behavior of any kind, whether it is boasting about one's achievements, or building public monuments to oneself. Yet in this sense, *egotism* is simply the outward expression of *egoism*, and so the two words merge in describing the same kind of personality.

For the choice between *ego(t)istic* and *ego(t)istical*, see **-ic/-ical**.

ei or **ie** For the spelling rule which highlights this question, see **i before e**.

either The question of using singular or plural verbs with **either** is discussed under **agreement** section 1.

elder or **older** Elder (and *eldest*) were in use centuries before **older** (and *oldest*). But since the fifteenth century **older** and *oldest* have steadily gained the upper hand. Nowadays **elder** and *eldest* are hardly used except within the family, as in *his elder sister, their eldest son*. Even there, Australians can just as well say *his older sister, their oldest son*. In Britain the adjectives **elder** and *eldest* persist a little more strongly than in Australia or USA, occurring about twice as often in comparable English databases, but still much less often than **older/** *oldest*.

Examples such as *elder statesman*, and *elder partner* (used in Britain for the senior partner in a company), show how the meaning of **elder** has developed, so that it now seems to emphasise relative seniority and experience rather than age. That point is clear when we try to compare ages in a structure like: *X is elder/older than Y*. Only **older** can be used in this way nowadays, and it can be used to compare the relative ages of people in any social group from school students to pensioners, as well as objects and abstracts of any kind.

The changing meaning of **elder** is also evident from its use in reference to the senior members of a tribe *(Aboriginal elders)*, or the lay officers of certain Protestant churches. It also emerges in expressions such as *no respect for their elders*, where neither the experience of age, nor age itself, seem to be given their due.

electric, electrical and **electronic** The power of electricity is invoked in the first two words, and during the nineteenth century when the frontiers of electricity were being explored, both forms of the word appeared in its collocations. Expressions such as *electrical battery* and *electrical shock* seem a little surprising nowadays, because we now tend to use **electric** when referring to specific things which are either powered or produced by electricity, e.g. *electric light, electric radiator, electric current, electric shock.* **Electrical** is used in collocations which are generic: *electrical appliances, electrical equipment,* or which relate in a more general way to the nature of electricity: *electrical energy, electrical engineering.* (See further under **-ic/-ical**.)

Electronic embodies the discovery that electrons carry the charge in electric current, and involves the twentieth century science and technology of *electronics*. They are concerned with modulating and amplifying the electric charge, using semiconductor devices. Note also *electrolytic* which means "working by electrolysis", the process of using an **electric** current to break up a chemical compound.

electrify or **electrocute** There is an electric charge in both these verbs, but only with **electrocute** is it fatal. A person may be *electrocuted* by accident, or as a mode of execution (in the USA). **Electrify** is primarily used in connection with powering a system with electricity, as in *electrifying the railway to Canberra.* It can also be used figuratively to mean "excite" or "thrill", as in *His words electrified the audience.*

electrolyse or **electrolyze** See under **-yse/-yze**.

elegy or **eulogy** Either of these may be uttered in memory of someone who has died, but their overtones are different. An **elegy** is an artistic or literary composition which is mournful or contemplative in tone, and may express nostalgia for things past or persons lost. The **eulogy** is a ritual speech or statement which is consciously laudatory and affirmative of what the dead person achieved.

elementary or **elemental** These words did service for each other in the nineteenth century, but they are clearly distinguished nowadays, with **elementary** enjoying much wider use than **elemental**.

Elementary often refers to the elements or basics of any subject you could think of, from physics to piano-playing. *Elementary textbooks* are the ones designed to teach the basics to beginners. Because **elementary** connotes lack of knowledge and experience, it can also be used as a put-down, as in the proverbial "Elementary, my dear Watson" of Sherlock Holmes. However all *elementariness* is relative, and it's a relatively advanced mathematics student who can take *elementary nonhomogeneous linear differential equations* in his or her stride. And when physicists speak of *elementary particles*, or chemists of *elementary substances*, the discourse is likely to be technical and demanding.

Elemental relates to older notions about nature. When the physical world was believed to be formed out of the four elements of earth, air, fire and water, **elemental** was the relevant adjective. With the demise of such ideas, **elemental** lives on in figurative expressions such as *elemental fury*, implying the great forces of nature and human nature.

elfish or **elvish** See under -v-/-f-.

elision The disappearance of a vowel, consonant or whole syllable from the pronunciation of a word is known as **elision**. In writing it's represented by an apostrophe, as in *he's, won't* or *huntin', shootin' and fishin'*. The term **elision** was used by Fowler and others to refer to words or phrases which were contracted in this way (see further under **contractions**).

In certain poetic metres (especially those whose syllables are strictly counted), **elision** is the practice of blending the last syllable of one word into the first syllable of the next, particularly when both are vowels. It was and is a way of keeping the regular rhythm with otherwise awkward combinations of words.

For *elision of numbers* in spans, see under **dates**.

ellipsis Both grammarians and those concerned with punctuation make use of this term. In grammar it means the omission of a word or words which would complete or clarify the sentence. In punctuation practice, it refers to the mark, usually a set of three dots (...), which shows where something has been consciously omitted from a quotation. Let's deal with each meaning in turn.

1 *Ellipsis in the grammar of a sentence.* Many ordinary sentences omit a word or words which could be added in to spell out the meaning and clarify the sentence structure. All the sentences below show some sort of ellipsis. The ellipted elements are shown in square brackets.

a) *They took glasses from the bar and* [they took] *knives and forks from the tables.*

b) *They said* [that] *no-one was there.*

c) *The woman* [that/whom] *I spoke to yesterday was there.*

d) *Those results are better than* [those that] *our team could get.*

e) *They are enjoying it more than* [they did] *last year.*

f) *Herbert loves the dog more than* [he does] *his wife* [does].

g) *The politics of war are more straightforward than* [those of] *peace* [is].

Note that the last two sentences have alternative meanings, depending on which of two possible points of **ellipsis** is addressed. The ambiguity calls our attention to the **ellipsis**, though most of the time it passes unnoticed. Several kinds of **ellipsis**, such as of a second identical subject in a coordinated sentence, or of *that* and other conjunctions in subordinate clauses, are well known and recognised by modern grammarians (see further under **clauses** section 2 and **that**). The **ellipsis** of items in comparative statements with *than* is also very common, and it need not disturb communication. The concern of some grammarians about sentences like (d) and (e) above is focused on the function of **than** in them (is it a preposition or a conjunction?)—rather than whether the sentences fail to communicate. (See further under **than**.) Yet the last two sentences (f) and (g) do raise questions of meaning, showing the occasional problems caused by **ellipsis**.

Grammatical **ellipsis** is the hallmark of everyday conversation. In exchanges with others we continually omit elements of the sentence that would simply repeat what has gone before:

Are you coming to the barbecue?   Not until after the meeting.
I'll be gone by then.   Where to? ...

As the examples show, the **ellipses** help to connect an answer with the question, and a follow-up with a previous statement. **Ellipsis** is in fact part of the bonding or cohesion of such discourse (see further under **coherence** or **cohesion**). Apart from contributing to the efficiency of conversation, it is the medium through which we manipulate and expand utterances.

2 *Ellipsis in punctuation* usually means the set of dots which show where words have been omitted from a text. But because **ellipsis** refers in the first place to the omission itself, the term is sometimes applied to other punctuation marks whose function is the same, including asterisks, and dashes. (See further under **asterisk** and **dashes**.) To avoid ambiguity on this, some style books refer to *ellipsis points*, and reserve the right to discuss only the dots—as we shall.

Most style manuals recognise the practice of using *three* dots for an **ellipsis** occurring anywhere within a sentence or between sentences, and the Australian Government *Style Manual* endorses it without question. The practice is actively recommended as "sanity-saving" by the Canadian Freelance Editors Association. The alternative practice—of using three dots for an omission within sentences, and four dots (counting in the full stop) for an omission between sentences—creates many complexities. The spacing for the four dots is uneven, with the full stop set close to the final word, and the other three dots with equal space on either side of them. The difference is shown below:

He wanted no more of it. ...   But having said that ...

The use of four-dot ellipses is still the preferred practice of the Chicago and *Webster's* style manuals. Yet the difficulty of managing the spacing, and the lack of means to achieve it on many typewriters and wordprocessors leave many writers and editors with no choice but to use three dots for any **ellipsis**.

All the authorities agree that it's reasonable to begin with a capital letter after an **ellipsis** (whether or not there was a capital at that point in the original) if the resumed quotation constitutes a fresh sentence. It always helps the reader to have the start of a sentence marked, and only in legal and scholarly quotations is this consideration overruled by the need to keep every letter in the same case as the original. One other simplification of older ellipsis practice is dispensing with them at the start of a quotation. The opening quote marks themselves show that the words cited are an excerpt.

Note that a whole line of ellipsis points can be used to indicate the omission of a line or lines of verse from a poem, or where whole paragraphs have been omitted from a prose text.

else This word is usually classified as an adverb (or adjective) in dictionaries, yet its most important roles are as part of a compound pronoun or conjunction. Its legitimacy in those roles is only gradually being recognised. It is frequently used as part of an indefinite or interrogative pronoun, as in:

   anyone else   someone else   what else   who else

So well established are these phrases that **else** can take the possessive form quite easily:

   anyone else's umbrella   who else's car

This usage was once frowned on by those who insisted that **else** was an adverb and so could not be made possessive. The paraphrase they suggested was *whose car else*, which nowadays seems quite stilted and unacceptable.

Another common role of **else** is to join forces with *or* as the compound conjunction *or else*. At times it even stands alone as a conjunction, in:

   Take the car else you'll be late.

   You'd better come else they'll wonder what's going on.

This use of **else** as an independent conjunction occurs in commands and advisory statements, in the context of direct speech. Modern dictionaries do not however recognise it, and the *Oxford Dictionary* notes it as an *obsolete* "quasi conjunction", with a few citations from the fourteenth century. Yet its currency is acknowledged in the *Right Word at the Right Time*, at the same time as its use in writing is discouraged. Those who write formal documents are not likely to want to use **else** as a simple conjunction, seeing that it is associated with direct speech. But there's no reason to disallow it in other kinds of writing, where direct speech and advice have a natural place.

elusive or **allusive** These adjectives can easily be mistaken for each other in speech, being identical in most people's pronunciation, and in some contexts they are rather alike in meaning, as in: *an elusive charm*, and *an allusive comment*, for example. In both phrases the words imply that something is there and yet not there. But the different spellings confirm that they relate to different verbs (**elusive** to *elude*, and **allusive** to *allude*); so *an elusive charm* is one that eludes the beholder and cannot be pinned down: while *an allusive comment* just alludes to something, touching on it in passing, and not dwelling on it. **Allusive**

and *allude* are usually linked with things *said* (or not said), while **elusive** and *elude* relate to things (or people) that disappear or escape.

elvish or **elfish** See under -v-/-f-.

em-/en- See en-/em-.

em dash This is a name used for the *em rule*, especially in North America. See next entry.

em rule This is the traditional printers' name for the *full dash*. See **dashes** section 1.

embargo For the plural of this word, see -o.

emend or **amend** Neither of these verbs is in common use nowadays: both survive in specialist contexts. To **emend** is the work of scholars, as they edit individual words and expressions in older texts in order to produce a definitive version of the original. The fruits of this work are *emendations*. *Emending* is a matter of fine detail, whereas those who **amend** documents are either editors seeking to improve a draft manuscript by modifying its substance, or legislators modifying the provisions of legal codes and constitutions. Their work results in *amendments* and changes to the original text.

The plural form *amends* in *to make amends* is a fossil of the once much wider use of **amend**, in references to improving one's conduct and social behavior. Another fossil *They must amend their ways* is now usually expressed as *mend their ways*. As that example shows, *mend* has taken over most of the general functions of **amend** in modern English.

emergence or **emergency** There is a clear difference between these now, unlike many -nce/-ncy pairs (see further under that heading). Both are nouns derived from the verb *emerge*, with **emergence** serving as the abstract noun, and **emergency** as the highly specific one, meaning a situation which requires urgent action. In the seventeenth and eighteenth centuries the spellings were interchangeable, and only since the nineteenth century has **emergency** been the more common spelling for the urgent situation.

emigrant, émigré or **expatriate** All these refer to someone who has emigrated away from their native country, but each word has its own implications. **Emigrant** expresses the plain fact that someone has moved permanently away from their country of origin, and is neutral as to the reason for their move as well as their social background. **Émigré** carries more elitist overtones, as well as the implication that the emigration was necessitated by political circumstances. Historically the word **émigré** has been associated with those who fled from the French and Russian revolutions, though it might seem applicable to those who felt obliged to flee communist revolutions in Chile, Afghanistan and Vietnam. The higher social background of *émigrés* is clear when the word is contrasted with *refugees*, who may come from any social class.

The term **expatriate** may be applied to those whose emigration was either voluntary or involuntary, though it is often applied to individuals who choose for professional reasons to live in another country, as in:

London has its share of expatriate Australians.

This voluntary exile is sometimes seen as betraying a lack of patriotism, which no doubt explains why **expatriate** is sometimes misconstrued as *expatriot*. *Webster's English Usage* (1989) forecasts that it has some chance of becoming an acceptable variant spelling in the future, though it's not yet acknowledged in the major dictionaries.

For the distinction between **emigrant**, **immigrant** and **migrant**, see under **migrant**.

eminent or **imminent** While **eminent** is a term of commendation, meaning "outstanding", **imminent** means that something is on the point of happening. Typical uses are *an eminent scholar* and *their imminent defeat*. As the examples show, **imminent** is used of events, and **eminent** of people, generally speaking. The two are unlikely to come together in the same utterance—unless of course you're about to be visited by an eminent person, in which case it would be possible to speak of *an eminent, imminent visitor*!

Note that when **eminent** becomes an adverb it means "extremely or very", as in *eminently likely* or *eminently fair*.

emotive or **emotional** Though both of these recognise the role of emotion, they identify it in different places. **Emotive** implies that emotion is raised in the audience, and a phrase such as *emotive words* often suggests that the speaker's output is calculated to kindle the emotions of those listening. The word **emotional** simply implies that emotion was expressed by the speaker, or was characteristic of the speech itself. An *emotional speech* can of course have an *emotive effect* on the audience.

empaneled or **empanelled** See under **-l/-ll-**.

employee, employé or **employe** Employee is the standard form of this word nowadays, everywhere in the English-speaking world. Yet it seems to have established itself earlier in North America than Britain, and the *Oxford Dictionary* in the last decade of the nineteenth century dubbed it "rare except US". At that stage the *Oxford* gave much fuller coverage to the French form **employé**, and made a point of saying that **employée** was used for female workers. But in its 1933 Supplement, *Oxford* endorsed **employee** as the common English term, and the idea of a gender distinction seems to have disappeared along with the French accent. The *-ee* suffix is of course gender-free, as in many words. (See further under **-ee**.) The spelling **employe** is still recognised as an occasional alternative to **employee** in the major American and Australian dictionaries, but is not used in Britain.

emporium For the plural of this word, see under **-um**.

en-/em- These are variant forms of a prefix borrowed from Norman French in words such as *encircle, encourage* and *enrich*. The prefix has been put to fresh use in English, in forming new verbs out of nouns and adjectives:

> *enable embed embellish embitter emblazon encase encompass engulf enlarge enlist empower ennoble enrapture enslave ensnare enthrall entomb entrance entrench*

As those words show, the **em-** form is used before words beginning with *b* and *p*, and **en-** before all others.

en-/in- The prefix **en-** has long been interchanged with the **in-** prefix from Old English, and the identical one from Latin (see further under **in-/im-**). This vacillation has left us with optional spellings for a number of other words:

> *endorse/indorse enfold/infold engrain/ingrain enmesh/inmesh enshrine/inshrine enthrone/inthrone entrench/intrench entwine/intwine entwist/intwist enure/inure*

Note however that the different spellings entail different meanings for some users with **inquire/enquire** and **insure/ensure**. (See under those headings.)

In some cases the earlier spelling with **in-** has been totally replaced by **en-**, hence the strangeness of the following:

> *inclose incompass ingender ingross inlist inroll inthrall*

The reverse has happened in one or two such as *envigor* and *empassion*, where *in-/im-* have replaced the earlier *en-/em-*. (See also **incumbent**.)

-en These letters represent four different English suffixes:

- a plural ending on nouns, e.g. *children*. (See further under **plurals**.)
- a past participle ending, e.g. *taken*. (See **irregular verbs** section 7.)
- a means of forming adjectives out of nouns, e.g. *golden*; and
- a means of forming verbs out of adjectives, e.g. *sharpen*.

Only the fourth of these suffixes is still active and creating new words. The first two are fossilised, and the third is not much used except in poetic diction.

*Adjectives formed with **-en*** are derived from single-syllabled nouns:

> *ashen earthen leaden oaken silken wooden woollen*

The **-en** ending implies "made out of", and occasionally "looking as if it were made out of", as with *leaden skies* and *silken hair*. The pattern is so simple that we might wonder why its use is so limited nowadays. One reason is that it competes with the *-y* suffix, which has indeed generated alternative forms for many of the words above: *ashy, silky, woolly*. Another is that in everyday usage when referring to something actually made out of lead or silk, we would use just those words, as in *lead batteries* and *silk scarves*, and so *leaden, silken* etc. seem to be retiring to the leisured world of literature.

*Verbs formed with **-en*** are derived from single-syllabled adjectives (except for *quieten*). The regular pattern is seen in:

blacken darken deafen deepen lessen lighten madden moisten redden ripen sadden smarten stiffen thicken whiten widen

The verbs all imply a change of state, and as things may either *be made* blacker or *become* blacker, the verbs can be either transitive or intransitive. Words ending in *m*, *n*, *l*, *r* and any vowel are ineligible for phonetic reasons to become verbs this way, and so *blacken* is not matched by "greenen" or "bluen". Verbs of this kind could once be made out of nouns, as were *frighten*, *lengthen*, *strengthen* and *threaten*, but this is no longer possible.

en dash This is the name used especially in North America for the *en rule*. See further under **dashes**.

en déshabillé This French phrase, meaning literally "in (a state of being) undressed", is an elaborate way of noting that someone's dress is informal. The expression also appears in English simply as *déshabillé* or *deshabille*, or in the more anglicised form *in dishabille*. The degree of "undress" implied by such expressions is very much relative to the situation, sometimes a matter of careless dress, and sometimes its incompleteness. Just how incomplete is suggested by the fact that *dishabille* as a noun once referred to the garment we know as a *negligee*. Note again the French loanword.

Other delicate French loanwords used to describe modes of dress which defy convention are *décolletée*—wearing a dress with a low-cut neckline, and *déboutonné*, which means literally "unbuttoned". By extension it comes to mean "ready to exchange confidences".

en route This French phrase means literally "on the road or way", but it has acquired a number of meanings in English. It can mean "along the way", as in *We'll buy our food en route*; or "in transit", as in *Their neighbors were already en route for India*. Some also use it on its own (**En route**!) to mean "let's go". All have something to do with traveling, however, whereas the use of **en passant** (literally "in passing") is usually figurative. In examples such as *It indicates their existence only en passant*, the phrase is a synonym for "incidentally".

en rule This is the traditional printers' name for the *dash* which is intermediate in size between hyphen and the full dash. See **dashes** section 2.

enameled or **enamelled** For the choice between these, see under **-l/-ll-**.

encomium The plural of this word is discussed under **-um**.

encumbent See under **incumbent**.

encyclopedia or **encyclopaedia** See under **ae/e**.

endeavor or **endeavour** The choice between these is discussed under **-or/-our**.

endemic or **epidemic** Since **endemic** is an adjective and **epidemic** most often a noun, we might expect grammar to keep them apart. Yet because they look rather similar, and because both can refer to the presence of disease in a community, they are sometimes substituted for each other:

Cholera was an endemic/epidemic problem in that overcrowded city.

Their meanings are still rather different however. **Endemic** means "recurring or prevalent in a particular locality", while **epidemic** carries the sense of "(spreading like) a plague". Both words may represent aspects of the problem, but the writer needs to distinguish the two for discussion.

A third member of the set is *pandemic*, originally (in the seventeenth century) an adjective meaning "occurring everywhere", and contrasting with **endemic** which connects things with a particular locality. The nineteenth century saw the arrival of the noun *pandemic*, which owes something to **epidemic**, and is used to mean "a plague which affects the whole country".

The tendency of these words to converge need not surprise us, given their common Greek root *-demic*, related to *demos* "people". Literally **endemic** is "in the people"; **epidemic** is "upon or among the people" (see further under **epi-**); and *pandemic* is "all the people".

endmatter For the makers of books, this term covers the various items included at the back of a reference book, including the appendix(es), notes, glossary, bibliography and index(es). The typical order is as just listed. **Endmatter** is often printed in a slightly smaller typeface than the main text. In the USA the equivalent term is *back matter*.

endpapers These are the folded leaves glued inside the covers of a hardcover book which join the front cover to the first page and the last page to the back cover.

endways or **endwise** See under **-wise**.

-ene or **-ine** See **-ine**.

England See under **Britain** and **British**.

English or **Englishes** English is the world's most widespread language. Its history is one of almost continuous expansion—from being the language of a few thousand Anglo-Saxon immigrants to Britain in the fifth century AD, to being now the first or second language of at least seven hundred and fifty million people around the world. On all continents there are nation-states for which it is either the official language or one of them, including:

English as national language	**English** as auxiliary national language
Australia	*Brunei*
Bahamas	*Fiji*
Barbados	*Gambia*
Canada	*Ghana*
Falklands	*Kenya*
Guyana	*Liberia*
Ireland	*Nigeria*
Jamaica	*Papua New Guinea*
New Zealand	*Sierra Leone*
South Africa	*Singapore*
Trinidad and Tobago	*Uganda*
United Kingdom	*Zambia*
United States of America	*Zimbabwe*

In several others, **English** was until recently an auxiliary national language:

Bangladesh India Malaya Pakistan Philippines Sri Lanka Tanzania

The volume of international communication in **English** is enormous. Estimates (or guesstimates) have it that three quarters of the world's mail, cables and telexes, and 80% of the information on computers is in **English**. Its international reach has also been helped by the fact that it is the language of science and technology, and is the official medium of communication for ships and aircraft.

Facts like these are sometimes invoked to show that **English** is destined to become a universal medium of communication. But as you look more closely at the details of **English** in all those countries named above, you begin to be conscious of how various they are. Wherever it is used, **English** (like any living language) responds to its surroundings. Even in countries like Australia where it has always been the national language, **English** still tends to develop new regional characteristics, and to reflect the local culture, society and environment. (See further under **Australian English** and **dialects**.) In countries like Ghana and Singapore, where **English** is an auxiliary national language, it rubs shoulders with other languages, borrowing from them and adjusting itself in interaction with them. (See further under **pidgins**.) The phrase ''new **Englishes**'' represents nicely this panorama of new developments of **English**.

The development of multiple varieties of **English**, with their own styles of pronunciation, vocabulary and idiom, suggests that the concept of ''international English'' is not to be taken for granted (see **international English**). The natural tendency towards variation can be constrained in specialised contexts such as communication for ships and aircraft, and perhaps within the fields of science and technology. But as long as **English** responds to the infinitely variable needs of everyday communication in innumerable geographical and social contexts, it is bound to diversify. No single set of norms can be applied round the world, to decide what is ''correct'' or what forms to use. The analogy of Latin—which spread to all parts of the Roman empire and diversified into the various Romance languages—may well hold for English in the third millennium.

English language databases Statements about language or anything else are only as valid as the evidence that supports them. The evidence needs to be more than impressionistic and anecdotal if we are to evaluate linguistic diversity and change around us. To provide large bodies of evidence, a number of computerised databases of English have been built since 1960. The pioneering work in this field was done at Brown University, Rhode Island USA with the Brown corpus (database) of one million words of written American English, taken in a number of clearly defined categories. Its British counterpart is the LOB corpus (Lancaster–Oslo/Bergen), which used an equivalent range of samples, also from 1961. (In both Britain and the USA, larger multimillion word corpora have since been compiled, though they set less store by systematic sampling, and are not directly comparable with others.)

In Australia the ACE corpus (Australian Corpus of English) compiled at Macquarie University is exactly like Brown and LOB, with samples from a wide variety of local publications: newspapers, magazines, and books of fiction and nonfiction. The samples are all from 1986. Evidence from ACE has been offered wherever possible in the entries of this book.

enormity or **enormousness** Is there any difference between these, apart from their obvious difference in bulk? Both are used as abstract nouns for *enormous*, to express the notion of hugeness, vastness or immensity. However some people would reserve **enormousness** for that meaning, and insist that **enormity** carries a sense of strong moral outrage, connoting the heinousness of a deed or event. Compare:

The enormity of the crime made the people take the law into their own hands.
With the enormousness of the calculations, the computer crashed.

The distinction illustrated is rather difficult to maintain, especially when the adjective *enormous* can only mean "huge", (It once carried the additional meaning "heinous", but this is now obsolete.) Most modern dictionaries allow that **enormity** serves as a synonym for **enormousness**, as does the *Macquarie Dictionary* (1991). Dictionary usage notes in *Collins* and *Random House* dictionaries suggest that using **enormity** this way is still more acceptable in the USA than in Britain.

Yet the *Oxford Dictionary* record shows that **enormity** was in use well before **enormousness**, and has been used to mean "hugeness" since the eighteenth century. That usage was dubbed "obsolete" with the latest citation in 1848, though an intriguing note adds that "more recent examples might perhaps be found but the use is now regarded as incorrect". Even so the *Oxford Dictionary* has twice as many citations for **enormity** with that meaning as for **enormousness**. Common usage has never taken account of the shibboleth that somehow attached itself to the use of **enormity** for **enormousness**, and Fowler warned against trying to insist on any distinction between them. Those who need to communicate a sense of outrage should not put too much faith in **enormity**, and would be wise to seek an alternative.

enough This familiar adjective-cum-adverb is normally followed up by constructions with *to*. For example:

> *They have enough money to buy their own house.* (adjective)
> *They are rich enough to buy their own house.* (adverb)

An alternative construction for the adverb is also on the increase in Australia:

> *They're rich enough that they could buy their own house.*

This wording is less concise than the other, but it serves to draw extra attention to the subject *they* and their action, rather like a **cleft sentence**. (See further under that heading.)

enquiry or **inquiry** See **inquiry**.

enroll or **enrol** Both of these spellings appear in Australian documents, though the second **enrol** is given priority in the *Macquarie* and *Collins* dictionaries, and in several newspaper style guides. It is the traditional British preference, appearing in the present tense of the verb *I/you/he/she/we/they enrol(s)* as well as in the noun *enrolment*. Yet the word must still be spelled with two *l*s in the past tense (*enrolled*) because of the stress (see **doubling of final consonant**). The history of the spelling with one *l* is curious: see **single for double**.

 The spelling **enroll** is standard in American English for both present and past forms of the verb, as well as for the noun *enrollment*. This spelling has the advantage of making clear the origins of the word (*en* + *roll*), apart from stabilising the word's spelling for all its appearances. They are two good reasons for preferring **enroll**.

ensure or **insure** See **insure**.

enthrall or **enthral** The spelling **enthral** is the traditional British spelling, and it's given preference in *Collins* and *Macquarie* dictionaries. **Enthrall** is standard in American English. Given that the verb is made up of *en-* and *thrall*, the American spelling has everything to recommend it. (Compare **enroll**.) The alternative spellings *inthrall/inthral* are very old-fashioned nowadays. (See further under **en-/in-**.)

entrance or **entry** Both these nouns connect with the verb *enter*, and can mean "act of entering", "the place of entering" and "the right to enter". But corpus evidence shows that **entrance** is more often used of the place at which people enter premises, and **entry** of the fact or moment of entering. On entering the showgrounds you could then be charged either an *entrance fee* (because it is at the gate) or an *entry fee* (which secures your right to go in). The words are almost equally represented in the Australian ACE corpus (about thirty times each), but **entrance** is mostly a physical structure as in *main entrance* and *entrance foyer* while **entry** is often more metaphorical as in *entry into the war* and *student entry to Computing Science*. **Entry** has further developed to mean "something entered", such as a note in a diary or an account book, or an item in a competition.

Both nouns are loanwords from French, **entry** borrowed in the fourteenth century and **entrance** in the sixteenth. Quite distinct is the verb **entrance** with stress on the second syllable, formed in English out of *en-* and *trance*. (See further under **en-/em-**.)

eon or **aeon** The choice between these is discussed at **ae/e**.

-eous or **-ious** See **-ious**.

epi- This Greek prefix has several meanings, as seen in the various scholarly loanwords which brought it into English. Its most general meaning "on or upon" is represented in:

epaxial epicentre epicycle epidural epiglottis epithelium epizooic

Such words designate things which are physically situated on or above. In others, **epi-** refers to something which occurs or is added on afterwards:

epenthetic epigenesis epigram epilogue episode epitaph epithet epitome

When prefixed to a word beginning with a vowel, **epi-** becomes *ep-*, as in *epaxial*, *epenthetic* and *epode*; and this also happens before *h*, as in *ephemeral* ("happening on just one day").

The prefix **epi-** has mostly been productive in the specialised fields of science and scholarship. Yet **epithet** has acquired a new role in popular usage, meaning an abusive name or word which is flung at someone in anger or contempt (often a swear word). In scholarly use **epithet** is still a synonym for adjective, or a term for the nickname attached to a celebrated or notorious person, as in *Gregory the Great* or *Ivan the Terrible*.

epicene In the grammar of Greek and Latin, **epicene** was used of nouns which were strictly masculine (or feminine) by their grammatical class, but could refer to people and animals of either gender. Examples from Latin include *poeta*, a feminine noun which regularly referred to male poets, and *vulpes*, the feminine noun for "fox", which was used of both the vixen and the dog fox. (See further under **declension**.)

In English grammar the term has been transferred from grammatical to natural gender. It is applied to English words which could denote either male or female, such as *artist*, *cat*, *clerk*, *doctor*, *giraffe*, *student*, *teacher*, *they*, i.e. words which are **common** in gender. (See further under **gender**.)

epidemic or **endemic** See **endemic**.

epilogue or **epilog** See under **-gue/-g**.

epithet For use of this word, see under **epi-**.

eponyms Some people gain a curious immortality when their surnames become the byword (and eventually the common word) for a particular product or a practice with which they're associated. The *sandwich* originated this way (named after the Earl of Sandwich, 1718–92), and a *furphy* is the Australian eponym for a rumor or spurious information. It immortalises the name of

John Furphy, who manufactured the water and sanitation vehicles used by the Australian army in the field, which were the places where news, rumors and gossip were exchanged. *Bloomers* take their name from the American feminist Amelia Bloomer 1818–91. **Eponyms** sometimes perpetuate a nickname, as in the case of *grog*. "Old Grog" (referring to his grogram cloak) was the nickname of Admiral Edward Vernon (1684–1757), who reputedly added water to the sailors' rations of rum, and so lent his name to cheap varieties of liquor.

The items or behavior to which **eponyms** refer are not necessarily a credit to the family name, yet many are no worse than household words:

biro boycott braille brougham bunsen cardigan clerihew
derby doily guillotine leotard macintosh morse pullman quisling
shrapnel silhouette wellingtons

A more select group of **eponyms** are the ones specifically chosen by the community of scientists to refer to units of measurement, including:

ampere coulomb henry joule newton ohm pascal watt

The complete list is to be found in Appendix IV.

Note that **eponyms** do not need to be capitalised because they work as common nouns, and are no longer proper names. Their assimilation into the common vocabulary is even more complete in cases where they provide the basis for new complex words, as with:

bowdlerise chauvinism galvanise hansardise macadamise mesmerise
nicotine pasteurise sadism spoonerism

Eponymic names abound for Australian flora, sometimes celebrating national heroes, but also botanists and horticulturalists of many nationalities:

banksia bauera bauhinia boronia dampiera darwinia grevillea hakea
hardenbergia kennedya/kennedia kunzea leschenaultia patersonia
stackhousia swainsonia templetonia tristania wahlenbergia

These names are written with lower case when they're used as the common name for the plant. However when used as the name of the botanical genus, and accompanied by a species name, they are capitalised. (See further under **capitals** section 1e.)

equ-/equi- These are two forms of the Latin root *aequus* meaning "equal", which is found in *equal* itself and in other loanwords such as the following:

equable equanimity equation equator equilateral equilibrium
equinox equivalent equivocal

In modern English it has helped to create new scholarly words such as:

equiangular equidistant equimolecular equipoise equiprobable

The same Latin root is at the heart of *equit-*, a stem which comes to us in French loanwords such as *equity* and *equitable*, words which connote fair and equal treatment for all parties.

Note however that other similar-looking words such as *equestrian*, *equine* and *equitation* are extensions of a different Latin root: *equus* meaning "horse".

Its influence extends to *equip*, though the connection in that case is spurious. The word is of Germanic origin, but appears to have been remodeled in French in the belief that it was related to Latin *equus*.

equable or **equitable** What's in a syllable? A sizable difference in meaning hangs on that syllable, though these words are otherwise similar enough to be sometimes mistaken for each other. Both embody the Latin root *aequus* "equal, even" (see **equ-/equi-**), but **equable** preserves the meaning more directly, in its applications to people who have *an equable temperament* i.e. are even-tempered, and to regions with *an equable climate* i.e. one which is temperate. **Equitable** comes by a less direct path through French, and is associated with *equity*. It therefore means "even-handed", and implies the fair and just disposition of human affairs, as in *an equitable arrangement*. We trust that judges will deal *equitably* with the matters before them.

The two words are occasionally interchanged by mistake as in *equitable weather* which then carries the whimsical suggestion that "someone up there" might control the climate, and prevent it from raining indifferently "on the just and the unjust", as the King James Bible has it.

equaled or **equalled** For the choice between these, see **-l/-ll-**.

equilibrium The plural of this word is discussed under **-um**.

-er/-a These are alternative spellings for the last syllable of colloquialisms such as *feller/fella*, *gubber/gubba* and *yakker/yakka*. The **-a** is more common than **-er** in familiar forms of proper names such as *Bazza* for *Barry* and *Muzza* for *Murray*. (The additional change from "rr" to "zz" is known as *assibilation*.)

-er/-ers In colloquial English, an **-er** is sometimes substituted for the last syllable (or syllables) of a word, as in *feller* for *fellow* and *rugger* for *rugby*. The adaptation is taken a little further when *champagne* becomes *champers*, *pregnant* becomes *preggers*, and *chock-a-block* becomes *chockers*. Some Australian placenames get the same treatment, as when *Thredbo* is *Thredders* and *Macquarie* becomes *Makkers*. (See also **-er/-a**.)

-er/-or When you look over the various roles sustained by these two endings, it's remarkable that they overlap so little:

    -er functions   as an agent suffix for verbs, e.g. *hunter*
                                as an agent suffix with nouns, e.g. *farmer*
                                as a localising suffix with area and placenames,
                                    e.g. *New Yorker, Highlander*
                                as the comparative suffix for many adjectives,
                                    e.g. *older* (see under **adjectives**.)
                                as a colloquial replacement for a final syllable,
                                    e.g. *feller* (see under **-er/-a**.)
                                as a variant form of *-re* as in *centre/center*
                                    (see under **-re/-er**.)

> **-or** functions   as an agent suffix for verbs, e.g. *educator*
> as an ending on borrowed agent words, e.g. *doctor*, *ambassador*
> as a variant form of *-our*, as in *color/colour* (see **-or/-our.**)

The point at which **-er** and **-or** overlap most significantly is in forming agent words out of English verbs, and here even reliable spellers are sometimes in doubt. Should it be:

adapter or *adaptor*	*adviser* or *advisor*
*appointer or *appointor*	*assurer or *assuror*
*attester or *attestor*	*attracter* or *attractor*
attributer or *attributor*	**conjurer** or **conjuror**
*connecter or *connector*	*constructer* or *constructor*
convener or **convenor**	**conveyer** or **conveyor**
*deviser or *devisor*	*disrupter* or *disruptor*
*exciter or *excitor*	*executer or *executor*
*granter or *grantor*	*licenser or *licensor*
mortgager or **mortgagor**	*resister or *resistor*
settler or **settlor**	*warranter or *warrantor etc.*

The pairs in bold are discussed at their own entries in this book. Those asterisked are cases where the **-er** form is the one in general use, and the **-or** one is for specialists, usually in science, technology or law. The remainder are just a token of the ever-increasing group where there are both **-er** and **-or** agent words, and either can be used.

1 *Words with* **-er**. Overall there's no doubt that the **-er** group is growing at the expense of the **-or** group. This is because almost all agent words based on English verbs are formed that way. The **-er** suffix can identify people in terms of their work, their recreation or their behavior:

> *baker driver producer teacher dancer hiker runner surfer drinker smoker talker wrecker*

The suffix is also commonly used to designate machines and instruments by their function:

> *decanter dispenser divider propeller*

The **-er** ending is also the normal one for ad hoc formations, in phrases such as *a prolonger of meetings* or *an inviter of trouble*. Any agent words which are not listed in dictionaries you can safely spell with **-er**.

2 *Words with* **-or**. The most significant group of agent words with **-or** are Latin or neo-Latin in origin. Note especially those based on verbs ending in *-ate*, for example:

> *agitator calculator demonstrator elevator illustrator operator precipitator radiator spectator*

With other Latin verb groups, the endings are increasingly mixed. Older agentives such as *conductor, contributor, director, instructor* and *investor* retain the **-or**, while younger ones with latinate stems have **-er**, for example:

computer contester digester distracter molester presenter
promoter protester respecter

The older ones with **-or** can sometimes be identified by the fact that their standard meaning has moved some distance away from the formative verb, and seems to designate a role rather than a specific action, e.g. *conductor*. The new formations with **-er** express the ordinary meaning of the verb.

Note that the **-or** ending also goes with certain Latin loanwords such as *doctor, impostor* which clearly cannot have been formed from verbs in modern English. (There is no verb "doct" or "impost".) Other examples are:

divisor incisor interlocutor monitor precentor sponsor transistor victor

Also spelled with **-or** are a number of medieval loanwords from French, such as:

conqueror counsellor governor juror purveyor surveyor survivor

Their **-or** endings are actually a result of their being respelled in early modern English according to the Latin model. In short, you may expect **-or** spellings with older loanwords from either Latin or French, and with younger formations based on verbs ending in *-ate*.

3 *A case for spelling reform*? Because the **-er** ending is the dominant one for agent words in modern English, it would make excellent sense to allow writers to use it even with those which have traditionally been spelled **-or**, so as to remove the artificial distinction between *computer* and *calculator*, between *demonstrator* and *protester* etc. No vital meaning would be lost in such cases, and it would relieve writers of the unnecessary anxiety about the remaining **-or** spellings. If **-er** were used in all cases where there was a lively English verb, as in *calculater, demonstrater, instructer* and *invester*, the spelling would be more predictable for true agent words. We could still allow for continuing use of **-or** in words which cannot be interpreted as agentives, such as *author, doctor, sponsor, tailor* and *traitor*, in which the ending seems to be part of the identity of the word. (See **spelling** sections 1 and 4.)

-er>-r- When words are extended with extra suffixes, the less stressed syllables are often reduced in pronunciation, and occasionally this is registered in the spelling as well. It is built into pairs such as:

disaster	*disastrous*	*enter*	*entrance*
hinder	*hindrance*	*monster*	*monstrous*
tiger	*tigress*	*waiter*	*waitress*

For those who use the **-er** spelling in *fiber* etc., it can also be seen in

caliber	*calibrate*	*center*	*central*
fiber	*fibrous*	*luster*	*lustrous*
sepulcher	*sepulchral*	*theater*	*theatrical*

(See further under **-re/-er**.)

-eroo This was a popular suffix in America in the 1940s which created ad hoc words such as:
   bummeroo checkeroo flopperoo jokeroo kisseroo
The **-eroo** suffix generated a few recorded words in the South Pacific, including the New Zealand term *boozeroo*, and in Australia the name *Nackeroo*—the unit charged with the defense of northern Australia during World War II. Other Australian formations such as *jambaroo*, *jigamaroo* and *shivaroo* suggest by their spelling that their suffix was confused with the Australian **-aroo**. (See further under **-aroo**.)

erratum For the plural of this word, see under **-um**.

-ery This ending, modeled on the French *-erie* has been in use in English since the fourteenth century. It is the formative element in numerous abstract nouns, of which the following are only a token:
   imagery popery quackery rookery scenery vinery
For other formations see **-ary/-ery/-ory**.

escapee or **escaper** The first of these **escapee** is established throughout the English-speaking world as the term for someone who makes an escape from prison or internment. It appeared in the later nineteenth century, and one of its earliest applications was to refer to French convicts who escaped from New Caledonia to Australia, reported in the Melbourne *Argus* in 1881.
   The word **escaper** is actually older, if we count an isolated example in the King James Bible of 1611, or even the first one recorded after that in 1844. With its *-er* suffix, it seems a more regular formation than **escapee**—especially if one assumes that *-ee* is a passive suffix, which was Fowler's reason for preferring **escaper**. But not all *-ee* words are passive in meaning (see **-ee**), and the fact that *-ee* is often found on legal or bureaucratic words makes it apt for one who declines to remain a "guest" of the government. This may explain the popularity of **escapee**, which is endorsed in most Australian newspaper style guides. The Melbourne *Age* is alone in preferring **escaper**, perhaps following Fowler's lead.
   Note that the other agent words based on *escape* belong to different worlds altogether. For an *escapist* it's all in the mind, and for the *escapologist*, it is the dramatic art or sport of extricating yourself houdini-like from seemingly inescapable cages, chains or ropes.

-ese This suffix originated as a way of indicating geographical origin, as it still can. The earliest loanwords with it, dating from the fifteenth century, are *Milanese* and *Genoese*, and by its form the suffix itself must be Italian in origin, not French, as is sometimes said. Later examples of its use in English suggest that it came to be associated with exotic places, and their peoples, cultures and languages:
   Balinese Burmese Chinese Faroese Japanese Javanese Nepalese
   Portuguese Sudanese Vietnamese

The number of Asian places in that list is striking.

In the nineteenth century, the suffix **-ese** acquired another role in designating the distinctive speech style of an individual e.g. *Johnsonese*, or an occupational group e.g. *journalese, legalese, officialese*. Apart from established words such as those, **-ese** appears in ad hoc formations such as *brochurese* and *computerese*. Words formed in this way often have a pejorative flavor.

Note that the suffix *-speak* is now used in much the same way, to designate the speech styles of individuals (*Hawkespeak*) or occupational groups (*adspeak, eduspeak*). (See further under **-speak**.)

Eskimo This ethnic name may be pluralised either in the regular way with *-s*: *Eskimos*, or by means of the *zero plural*, i.e. as just **Eskimo**:
The Eskimos were trapping salmon for winter supplies.
The Eskimo were trapping salmon for winter supplies.
However the second (zero plural form) is actively discouraged these days, for reasons explained at **plurals** section 4. Those who use the French spelling *Esquimau* for these people should pluralise it as *Esquimaux*. (See further under **-eau**.)

But the name **Inuit** is now preferred to **Eskimo** and can be applied to **Eskimo** people right across North America from Greenland to Alaska. Within Canada it covers eight tribal groups: the Baffin Land, Caribou, Copper, Iglulik, Labrador, Netsilik, Ungava and Western Arctic. (Cf. *Koori* and others in Australia, discussed under **Aboriginal**.) **Inuit** is itself a plural form, the singular of which is *Inuk*.

esophagus or **oesophagus** For the choice between these, see **oe**.

especially or **specially** See **specially**.

espresso or **expresso** The strong black coffee made by Italians is *espresso*, literally "expressed or drawn out under pressure". The method relies on pressurised steam to extract the flavorsome liquid from the ground coffee beans. The spelling **expresso** anglicises the word and suggests a folk etymology, that it offers you a *fast* cup of coffee. This spelling is in widespread use, according to *Webster's English Usage* (1989) on menus and in edited prose.

Like most Italian loanwords it takes an English plural, and especially with the anglicised spelling: *expressos*. However in Lygon Street, Carlton in Melbourne and Parramatta Road, Leichhardt in Sydney, you may well hear the plural *espressi*, naturally enough. (See further under **Italian plurals**.)

esprit de corps See under **corps**.

Esq This abbreviation for *Esquire* has fallen out of general use, and the Australian Government *Style Manual* (1988) dubs it "archaic". It once appeared regularly on letterheads and envelopes, as a courtesy title for those who could not claim a title (*Sir, Dr, Professor* etc.) and were not in clerical orders, but were "gentlemen" by virtue of birth, position or education. This represented a large extension of earlier usage, whereby the title *Esquire* was only accorded to the higher gentry, those ranking next to knights. Nowadays the use of *Mr* before men's names has effectively taken the place of *Esq.* (See further under **forms of address**.)

Note that in American English, the abbreviation *Esq* is sometimes used after the surnames of professional persons, provided that no other title (such as *Dr*, *Mr*, *Ms*, *Hon*) prefaces the name. It is used especially for people associated with the law, such as attorneys, clerks of court, and justices of the peace, and after the surnames of woman lawyers, as well as their male counterparts.

-ess This suffix, borrowed from French, is loaded with gender, and its raison d'être in the past has been to draw specific attention to the female of the species (with animals, as in *lioness*), and to the female incumbents of particular roles and occupations (as in *hostess* and *waitress*).

The latter have come under fire as conspicuous examples of sexism in language, and ones which devalue women's participation in the work force. Many feel that words such as *actress, authoress, conductress, deaconess, directress, editress, manageress, mayoress, poetess, proprietress, sculptress, stewardess* and *waitress* tend to distract attention from the nature of the occupation itself: they make it somehow different from that of the *actor, author, conductor* etc., and seem to demean the work of the woman who does it. For many women the problem is easily solved by calling themselves *actors, authors, editors* etc., and this is the recommendation of the Australian Government *Style Manual* (1988) for most of the **-ess** words. Occasionally a synonym or paraphrase can be used, e.g. *flight attendant* for *stewardess*, but it's important that the alternative expression should (1) not be cumbersome, and (2) leave no doubt that the same occupation is being referred to. (See further under **inclusive language**.)

Other words of this kind do not really undermine women's rights to equal opportunity in the job market. Some are traditional titles: *countess, duchess, princess*; some designate specific female social roles, such as *heiress, hostess, mistress, patroness* which may need to be identified from time to time. Yet others are just literary fictions, like *enchantress, goddess* and *shepherdess*. Occasional or literary use of such words hardly poses any threat to the status of women at large; and where they relate to vanishing traditions, they will die a natural death. The **-ess** will simply become an archaic and irrelevant suffix.

essays The classic essays of the past were written by philosophers and gentlemen of leisure—from Montaigne and Bacon to Russell and T.S. Eliot— exploring ideas and views on a personally chosen subject. Today's university students who write essays are their heirs only in the sense that they use the essay as a format for discussion. Their essays are usually written on prescribed topics, and few would risk "flying a kite" in an assessable exercise. Having duly mastered the art of essay writing, students graduate to positions in which they never use that form of communication, and letters, reports and memorandums are the order of the day. The only professional equivalent to the traditional essay is perhaps the signed editorial column produced by celebrated journalists, who do indeed enjoy the essayist's licence to explore ideas and speak their minds.

esthetic or **aesthetic** See under **ae/e.**

estrogen or **oestrogen** See under **oe.**

et al. See under **etc.**

et seq. This Latin abbreviation stands for *et sequens* "and the following (page)". In the plural it takes the form *et seqq.* "and the following (pages)". It was once widely used in scholarly references, as in:
   Newton, Optics p.16 et seq. Newton, *Optics* p.16 et seqq.
While the first of those refers the reader to pages 16 and 17, the second is open-ended. It leaves it to the reader to decide how far to keep going from page 16 in search of relevant material. More specific references are preferred these days for each type, so that the first would be:
   Newton, Optics pp.16-17
and the second, say:
   Newton, Optics pp.16-21
Compare **loc. cit., op. cit.** and **passim**, which are also being replaced by more specific alternatives.

etc. This abbreviation is usually written with a stop, though this assumes an editorial policy of using stops for lower case abbreviations (see further at **abbreviations**). Making **etc.** a joint character with ampersand: *&c* is not recommended nowadays. It is printed in roman, not italics (see further under **italics**).
   Etc., standing for *et cetera* is the best known Latin abbreviation in English. (The complete list is shown at **Latin abbreviations.**) The Latin words in it are pronounced in full, unlike *e.g.* and *i.e.* which are simply said as initialisms. Further evidence of its assimilation is the fact that there's no standardised translation for it as there is for *e.g.* and *i.e.* Authors and editors translate **etc.** variously as "and so forth", "and so on", "and such like", "and the like" or "and others", and this too shows the gradual extension of its use. It also works as a fully fledged word *etcetera*, and it becomes a colloquial noun *etceteras* with the regular English plural ending.
   The original Latin phrase *et cetera* means "and the rest" or "and *the* others", implying a known set of items which might be used to complete the list preceding it. It relieves the writer of the need to list them, and calls on the reader to supply them. However **etc.** is quite often used more loosely to mean "and others", which presumes nothing of the reader, and just notes that the list is incomplete. Strictly speaking **etc.** refers to things, not people, because the *-a* makes it neuter in gender. For references to people, the Latin abbreviation

et al. (literally "and other persons") is available. (See further under **Latin abbreviations**, and **referencing**.)

1 *Punctuation with etc.* In spite of its thorough assimilation, the use of **etc.** has traditionally been discouraged (along with other abbreviations), and hedged about with rules. The use of commas with it has been the subject of editorial prescription: that there should be a comma before it if the preceding list consisted of at least two items (but not if there was only one); and that there must be a comma after it, except when it was the last word in a sentence. The Australian Government *Style Manual* takes a more liberal line on the comma preceding **etc.**, implying that it's usually unnecessary, and *Copy-editing* (1992) asks only for editorial consistency in either using or not using it. The policy of framing **etc.** with commas is still enjoined by the Chicago *Manual of Style*, yet *Webster's* style manual makes no mention of it.

2 *The use of etc. in various kinds of writing.* Like other abbreviations, **etc.** has been thought unsuitable for many kinds of writing. The Chicago *Manual* discourages its use in "running text", and would confine it to parenthetical references. The *Right Word at the Right Time* suggests that the problem of **etc.** is its inelegance or discourtesy to the reader, or that it lays the writer open to charges of being lazy or short of information. Yet all such problems are relative to the medium of writing, and to writers themselves. A writer who supplies a plethora of information is not likely to be thought ignorant because of an occasional **etc.** But as with any stylistic device used too often, it can easily become conspicuous and irritating. Alternatives are readily available, in the "translations" given at the start of this entry, and in phrases like *such as, for example* or *for instance*, to be used at the beginning of the list, instead of **etc.** at the end.

The use of **etc.** is certainly not confined to technical and business writing. The evidence of English databases in Britain and North America is that it appears in the majority of the genres sampled; and in the Australian ACE corpus it registered in all types of nonfiction, and in 5 out of 8 categories of fiction. There is no reason to avoid using it occasionally in a book like this.

ethnic This word has always been subject to ethnocentricity, i.e. the tendency to take your own culture as the reference point in judging any others. In early Christian usage it meant "heathen", while in the twentieth century many people use it to identify any other culture than their own. **Ethnic** thus often means "not of the mainstream", and acquires the connotations of "strange and exotic". It often implies a reluctance to differentiate between other cultures, and the tendency to lump them all together, a tendency which is not really helped by having a *Department of Immigration and Ethnic Affairs.* As a noun, **ethnic** is an offhanded word for "immigrant", and can all too easily acquire negative overtones, like *reffo, new chum* and *wog.* (See further under **racist language**.)

For all these reasons, **ethnic** is a troublesome word which lends itself to abuse, and there are few situations where it is really a neutral word for "multicultural". One of the few perhaps is *Ethnic Radio* which broadcasts in numerous languages *including* English. Would that there were more such usages! This problem is further discussed at **inclusive language**.

ethos In common usage this word refers to the characteristic attitudes and values of any group or institution, as in the *industrial ethos of the nineteenth century*. In rhetoric and art however it is a technical term for a way of appealing to the audience. (See further under **pathos**.)

-ette This suffix borrowed from French has three main uses in English, to mean:
1 "small" (as in *kitchenette, rosette*)
2 "female" (as in *suffragette, usherette*)
3 "substitute" (as in *leatherette, flannelette*).
    The first use of **-ette** has generated a few common terms, such as *couchette, dinette, diskette, flatette, sermonette* and *statuette*, where the suffix serves as necessary (and sometimes rueful) recognition that the size and scope of the object are diminished in comparison with any archetypes you may think of. The *supermarkette* in an Australian country town makes no false promises.
    The second meaning has had little use in English generally, although it had some vogue in America in the earlier half of the century, in formations like *freshette, (drum)-majorette* and *sailorette* for the members of certain (younger) female groups. *Undergraduette* had some vogue in Britain between the wars. But the pressure to do away with gender-specific suffixes goes against it now. (See **sexist language**.)
    In the names of fabrics such as *leatherette*, **-ette** serves to denote a product that is either a substitute for or an imitation of an old-established material. *Flannelette* and the British *winceyette* are further examples.
    *Loanwords with **-ette***. The use of the **-ette** ending is somewhat variable with *bassinet(te), briquet(te)* and *epaulet(te)*, as well as with musical terms like *minuet(te), quartet(te), quintet(te)*, and *sextet(te)*. It appears in full in cultural or consumer contexts where its French connotations are most valued (see further under **frenchification**). More functional loanwords which had earlier had **-ette** were trimmed back to *-et*, as happened with numerous French loanwords like *budget, bullet, facet, pocket, rivet, tablet* and *turret*. Other significant examples are **toilet** and **omelet** (see individual entries).

etymology This is the study of the origins and individual history of words— what languages they came from, and how their meaning and form have changed over the course of time. It confronts us with the mutability of language, although *etymological* knowledge has been used to try to prevent language change.
    Etymologies are sometimes used to identify an "original" form or meaning for a word, which is then held up as true for all time. This was the basis for a number of the strangest spellings of English, such as *debt, doubt* and *receipt*,

whose Latin ancestors (*debitum*, *dubitum* and *receptum*) are invoked in the letters *b*, *c* and *p*, added in during the fifteenth century. The *etymological* letters were and are superfluous in terms of our pronunciation of those words, which is based on French. Likewise, the fact that *aggravate* contains the Latin root *grav-* meaning "heavy, serious" moves some people to insist that the English word can only mean "make more serious", and ought not to mean "annoy".

Etymological arguments about language are ultimately arbitrary, choosing a fixed point in time (such as classical Latin) as the reference point for language questions. But usage stretches still further back in time. Many Latin words had Greek antecedents, and they can be traced back to Indo-European. (See further under **Indo-European**, and **spelling**.)

Apart from scholarly uses of **etymology**, there's no doubt that ordinary users of a language like to see a word's meaning reflected in its form or spelling. Words sometimes adjust their spelling in response to an *assumed etymology*. In cases like *bridegroom*, the *etymon* ("original word or form") now enshrined in the spelling is quite wrong. (See further under **folk etymology**.)

eu- This Greek prefix brings the notion of "good, fine, attractive or beautiful" to whatever roots it attaches itself to. See for example:

eugenics eulogy eupepsia euphemism euphony euphoria

The *euphonium* also owes its name to this prefix (it is simply a variant of *euphony*)—though people who live under the same roof as a beginner on the *euphonium* may feel that it is not well named.

The Australian *eucalyptus* tree (literally "fine-capped") is so named after the neat caps which cover the buds.

eulogy or **elegy** See **elegy**.

euphemisms Euphemisms are the fine-sounding words and phrases we use for things which are not so fine or beautiful. The word itself goes back to the Greeks and Greek civilisation, suggesting that they had found the need for inoffensive expressions to refer to what was unpalatable, unacceptable and unmentionable in their culture. A little later Cicero wrote about euphemisms in letters to his friends: *Epistolae ad Familiares* IX. Contemporary linguistic research suggests that it occurs in most languages, and even across languages, for bilingual speakers.

Any culture has its taboo subjects, and will find **euphemisms** for referring to them when reference is unavoidable. The basic bodily functions are a common focus of **euphemisms** in contemporary English, e.g. *urinate* for *piss*, and *copulate* or *have intercourse with* for *fuck*. Presumably most people feel some inhibitions or distaste about referring to them. These however are a relatively small group of **euphemisms** by comparison with those created by our social and political institutions—created as part of their public rhetoric, and as a means to avoid confronting people with uncomfortable and disturbing facts. The funeral industry does it with terms such as *casket* (for coffin), and *professional car* (for hearse), and has created the blended term *cremains*, to reduce people's awareness that they are dealing with *cremated remains*. The Australian government does it with the "higher education contribution scheme" or HECS, which attempts to put a positive coloring on an educational levy which strikes a negative chord in many people.

Apart from masking the awful truth, euphemisms also help to "dress things up", when people want to lend status to something—as when barbers call themselves "hair consultants", and when what used to be called "cooking" is referred to as *home science*. But euphemisms with pretensions can easily develop ironic overtones and begin to parody themselves. The burglar alarm expert who calls himself a *security executive* will soon need to find a new job title, if people are to take him seriously. One of the chronic problems with **euphemisms** is their built-in obsolescence. Hardly has a new one become established before its unmentionable past catches up with it. The turnover in terms for the public toilet: *WC, conveniences, rest rooms* etc., is well-known evidence, and we may wonder how long even the male and female icons for them can survive.

The search for replacement **euphemisms** can also be a source of comedy, and some seem deliberately aimed at comic effect. The phrases used to allude to a person's madness are legion, as *round the bend* becomes *round the twist*, *bats in the belfry* is Australianised as *kangaroos in the top paddock*, and being *not the full quid* becomes *a sausage short of a barbie*. The joke helps to cushion us from the real possibility of mental deterioration.

Euphemisms and writing. **Euphemisms** are a resource for tactful communication in many situations, and few people want to give unnecessary verbal offense. In written communication, when we cannot be sure how our words will be read, it seems safer to use the occasional *euphemism* in the approach to "touchy" subjects. Many **euphemisms** are drawn from more formal English (e.g. *dismissed* for *sacked*), and more formal vocabulary is part of the verbal repertoire of the professional writer.

This is not to say that writers should make a practice of seeking high-flown expressions. Those who do are indulging not in *euphemism* but *euphuism*, the artificially elevated and embellished prose of John Lyly's *Euphues* (an Elizabethan epistolary novel whose style was satirised by both Shakespeare and Walter Scott). The frontier between *euphemism* and public deception is also one to guard: George Orwell's *1984* reminds us that with the corruption of language we risk the corruption of thought.

Along with a sensitivity to **euphemisms**, writers should perhaps cultivate their sense of the opposite: *dysphemisms*—words and phrases which are likely to prove offensive to the reader. It helps to develop a scale from the most offensive, e.g. referring to someone as a *cunt*, up to the offhanded *bloke* which might only seem offensive in a formal context. Both *dysphemisms* and **euphemisms** are a resource for adjusting our expression to the needs of the situation. (See also **pejorative**.)

Europe For Australians, **Europe** includes both the British Isles and the continental mainland. It is the same for Americans—witness Henry James' novel *The Europeans*, about a British family who come to reside in New England. For many Britons, however, **Europe** is "the Continent"—that multilingual, multicultural land mass on the opposite side of the English Channel. Joining the EEC was for many Britons "going into Europe".

evasion or **evasiveness** In spite of obvious similarities, these words are different in their makeup and use. **Evasiveness** is the abstract noun derived from the adjective *evasive*, and normally used to describe verbal behavior which avoids confronting the issues that others would like to see addressed. **Evasion** is the verbal noun more closely linked with *evade* and used to refer to specific instances in which a duty or responsibility is shirked, e.g. *tax evasion*. Note that while *tax evasion* is a civil crime, *tax avoidance* (like *tax minimisation*) is strictly a legal crime.

even This word is often used to underscore and draw attention to neighboring words. In speech it can highlight a whole following phrase if the speaker's intonation carries it:
He didn't even sign a cheque today.
    (let alone sign a contract)
But the scope of **even** is more limited in writing because of the lack of intonation. Readers will not necessarily take it as affecting any more than the item immediately following. So the sentence just quoted would need to be slightly rearranged to make its point:
He didn't sign even a cheque today.
In that order, **even** draws full attention to *a cheque*, and thus makes it clear that nothing at all was signed.
    Compare **only** for a similar word whose position in writing is more critical than in speech.

-ever or **ever** This is both a suffix and an independent word. As a suffix **-ever** appears in *wh-* words:
however whatever whenever wherever whichever whoever
They have two different roles, as indefinites and as intensifiers.
    As *indefinites* the **-ever** words usually work as relative pronouns and conjunctions, as in:
Whoever thought of it deserves a medal.
The nurse will come whenever you call.
In casual speech they also function simply as indefinite pronouns or adverbs:
Bring your cup, mug, or whatever.
We'll find a spot in the park—wherever.
As *intensifiers* **-ever** words occur only at the beginning of sentences. (Compare the variable positions of the indefinites.) They underscore the focus of the question or exclamation that they preface.

Whichever did they mean?
However can you say that!
Fowler thought that in these cases **ever** should be written as a separate word,
as it sometimes is:
Which ever did they mean?
How ever can you say that!
But dictionaries all confirm that **-ever** is often set solid with the *wh-* word that
it intensifies. Note that when **ever** is used to intensify a superlative it must
remain separate, as in *their best result ever* or *their best ever result*.

every Because **every** is followed by a singular noun: *every dog, every week,*
there's little doubt that a singular verb is to be used in agreement with it.
Singular verbs are also used for *everybody, everyone* and *everything.* But when
it comes to pronoun agreement, there's a strong tendency now to use *they, them*
and *their* with **every** or any of its compounds. (See further under **agreement**.)

evoke or **invoke** There are subtle differences between these. When memories
or a reaction is *evoked* in someone, it happens as a byproduct of an activity,
not because that was the intended outcome:
His name evoked scenes from my student days.
The claim evoked a grunt of approval from the compere.
What is evoked is not directly solicited.
   With **invoke**, the subject of the verb is directly soliciting help and support
from outside parties, or else appealing to principles for confirmation of an
argument:
He invoked the help of the gods.
She invoked the principle of inertia to explain the problem.
In just one kind of context, there is potential for overlap—in speaking of contact
with departed spirits. Here your choice between **evoke** and **invoke** depends on
how much faith you have in the occult. **Invoke** implies some active response
from the dead spirits as conjured up in a seance, while **evoke** simply suggests
the conjuring up of their memory in the fellowship of their old friends.
   Note that *evocation* and *invocation* are distinguished in the same way as
evoke and **invoke**.

ex- This Latin prefix embodies two kinds of meaning in English:
   1 "out of, from"
   2 "former".
   The older meaning "out of, from" is blended into hundreds of classical
loanwords (nouns, verbs and adjectives), of which the following are only a
token:
excavate except excise exclaim exclusive exempt exorcise
explicit explosion export extend
In such cases, the prefix is always set solid.

Words with the newer meaning "former" (which originated in the eighteenth century) are normally hyphenated, as in:

ex-convict ex-husband ex-king ex-pilot ex-president
ex-serviceman ex-wife

Formations like this can be freely coined on the spur of the moment, as in:

ex-hairdresser ex-football coach ex-advertising man

-ex For the plural of words like *apex*, *index* or *vortex*, see under **-x**.

ex officio This Latin phrase means "by right of office". It connotes the duties and/or privileges of a particular office, especially when the incumbent automatically becomes a member of a committee to which others must be elected.

The privilege and authority of office are also vested in the Latin phrase *ex cathedra*, meaning "from the seat (of authority)"—either religious or judicial. From that authoritative seat, popes and judges wielded immense verbal power, and their pronouncements and judgements could not be challenged.

Neither **ex officio** nor *ex cathedra* needs a hyphen when it becomes a compound adjective, as in an *ex officio member* or an *ex cathedra statement*, since both are foreign phrases. (See **hyphens** section 2c iii.)

ex silentio Those who use an *argumentum e(x) silentio* "argument from silence" give themselves an enormous licence. They exploit the fact that an author or document is silent on the issue with which they are concerned, and use the *absence* of comment to bolster their own case. A silence or absence of comment can of course be interpreted in various ways—and in quite opposite ways, as the play *A Man for all Seasons* by Robert Bolt showed so well. The charges against Thomas More turned on arguing that his silence meant a *denial* of Henry VIII's claims, while the standard aphorism was that silence meant consent: *qui tacet consentire* "he who is silent (seems) to consent".

Arguments based on silence or the lack of contrary evidence are not really arguments at all, but rhetoric which works on the principle of "heads I win, tails you lose".

exalt or **exult** With only a letter between them, and some similar connotations, these can be mistaken for each other. Both belong to an elevated style, and elevation is built into the meaning of both. But while **exalt** usually means "raise in status", as in *exalted position*, **exult** ("rejoice, be jubilant") has the spirits running high. The distinction is complicated by the fact that **exalt** is occasionally used to mean "give high praise to", as in *exalted them to the skies*. Yet there's a crucial grammatical difference, in that **exalt** either takes an object or is made a passive verb, whereas **exult** never takes an object and is never passive.

When it comes to *exaltation* and *exultation*, there is little to choose between them. Both express high feelings. If we use *exaltation* for "elation", and *exultation* for "triumphant joy", there's still a lot of common ground between them.

excellence or **excellency** See under **-nce/-ncy**.

exception proves the rule The thrust of this axiom is widely misunderstood, no doubt because it depends on a rather old-fashioned use of the verb *prove*. The verb used to mean "test" (as it sometimes still does), and with this sense the axiom says that an exception will test or challenge the validity of the general rule. (Having identified an exception, we should indeed be reassessing the rule.)

However because *prove* is usually assumed to mean "confirm, corroborate", the statement seems to make the paradoxical claim that an exception *confirms* the rule. Alternatively, some interpret it simply as an analytic statement which validates itself through the word *exception*—something which is by definition outside a given rule. (See further under **induction**.)

exceptional or **exceptionable** The different values expressed in these words put a gulf between them. **Exceptionable** is always negatively charged, because it describes something people take exception to, as in:

Residents whose behavior is exceptionable will be evicted from the hostel.

Exceptional is an objective and definitive word, identifying something as an exception to the general rule, as in *exceptional case*. The *exceptional student* is outside the normal range, yet in Australian and British English the phrase is applied to those who are brilliant, whereas in American English it's used at either end of the scale, and *exceptional students* may be brilliant or in need of remedial schooling.

Note also that with a negative prefix (*unexceptionable, unexceptional*) the two words come close together in meaning. Both can mean "unremarkable" when applied to such things as programs or reports. Those which are *unexceptionable* will not raise objections, but they are as bland as those which are *unexceptional* and contain nothing out of the ordinary. Both words seem to damn with faint praise.

excitor or **exciter** See under **-er/-or**.

exclaim and **exclamation** For the spelling of these words, see **-aim**.

exclamation marks The exclamation mark has its most natural place in printed dialogue and reported speech, to show the dramatic or interactive force of a string of words. It occurs with greetings:

Good morning! G'day! Hi! How are you!

with interjections:

Hear, hear! Down with democracy!

with peremptory commands:

Don't do it! Get out of here!

and with expressions of surprise, ranging from enthusiastic and sympathetic to deprecating:

Absolutely superb! How lucky for you! What a shambles!

As the examples show, exclamation marks are often used with fragments of sentences that work as exclamations. They do also occur with fully formed exclamatory sentences:

Don't tell me!
You walked all the way!
Isn't that amazing!

As in the last example, exclamations may be phrased like questions, yet because no answer is being sought they take an *exclamation mark* rather than a question mark. Note also that the *exclamation mark* takes the place of a full stop at the end of a sentence.

The extended role of **exclamation marks**. Apart from marking utterances which are truly exclamations, **exclamation marks** are used by some writers to draw the reader's attention to a particular word, phrase or sentence which they find remarkable or ironic:

The divorce settlement divided the contents of the house equally, so now she can give dinner parties for three!

This use of **exclamation marks** has its place in interactive writing, for example in personal letters. But used this way in documentary writing, the effect is more dubious because of the diversity of readers' responses and attitudes. They may not share the writer's sense of irony, and so the reason for using an *exclamation mark* may be lost on them. Apart from the danger of inscrutability, **exclamation marks** lose their power to draw attention to anything if used too often. Even in informal writing they can be overdone, and those who write documentary prose must be very circumspect with them.

Exclamation marks and other punctuation.

1 An *exclamation mark* which belongs to a quoted statement goes inside the final quotation marks:

Their parting words were "It's on!"

2 The authorial *exclamation mark* which comments on a quoted statement goes outside the final **quotation marks**:

After all that drama they said: "It's not important"!
After all that drama they asked: "Who'd like a coffee?"!

3 An *exclamation mark* which belongs to a parenthesis goes inside the closing bracket (see **brackets** section 2).

4 The exclamation mark precedes points of ellipsis:

It's on! ... See you there.

5 The use of double (!!) or triple (!!!) **exclamation marks** generally looks naive or hysterical.

Note that the *exclamation mark* is known as the *exclamation point* in the USA but not in Canada.

exclamations The label *exclamation* has always been attached to a very mixed bag of utterances. Anything printed with an exclamation mark qualifies, ranging from:

Hell! Damn it! Brilliant!

to more fully fledged utterances such as:

The ideas you have!
What a way to go!
How brilliantly she plays!

Grammarians focus first and foremost on **exclamations** which begin with an interrogative word like *how* or *what* and contain the standard clause elements in the standard word order. (See further under **clauses**.) These are the only **exclamations** with a regular form, called *exclamative* in recent grammars such as the *Introduction to the Grammar of English* (1984) and the *Comprehensive Grammar of English* (1985), a term which matches up with *declarative*, *imperative* and *interrogative*. But grammarians also acknowledge that **exclamations** may be formed exactly like statements, commands or questions:

You tried it! Don't do it! Isn't it great!

These examples and the ones above show that the full range of **exclamations** cannot be identified by a particular grammatical form. They can be embodied in all types of sentences (declarative/exclamative/imperative/interrogative), or in fragments of sentences and phrases. (See further under **sentences**.) We know them by their function in discourse—their exclamatory force in dialogue, and the similar force invested in whatever bears exclamation marks in writing.

executor or **executer** See under **-er/-or**.

exhaustive or **exhausting** Though both link up with the verb *exhaust*, these words embody different views of human endeavor. **Exhaustive** has more intellectual connections, and represents the judgement that the endeavor was thorough and complete. An *exhaustive inquiry* is one which works through (exhausts) all possibilities. **Exhausting** is more physical, and is concerned with the using up of material resources and human energy. So an *exhausting day* is one which leaves you devoid of energy.

In some contexts it would be possible for either word to occur, and the writer's choice depends on which particular perspective is sought. An *exhaustive search* for lost bush walkers implies a full ground and air search with all available resources; whereas an *exhausting search* recognises that it was a grinding day for the rescue party. The first phrase is the detached comment of an administrator of emergency services, the second identifies with those who are actually doing the job.

existence or **existance** The first is still the only spelling recognised in dictionaries, though the second appears often enough for commentators to issue warnings about it, according to *Webster's English Usage* (1989). The word is one of an anomalous set. (See further under **-ance/-ence**.)

expatriate or **expatriot** See under **emigrant**.

expediency or **expedience** As with other *-ence/-ency* pairs, there's room for doubt as to which to use:

on grounds of expedience or *on grounds of expediency*

Expediency seems to have been the dominant form since the seventeenth century, but **expedience** persists and can be used with impunity, since it has no divergent meanings of its own. (See further under **-nce/-ncy**.)

expiry or **expiration** Either of these may be used in reference to the termination of a contract:

with the expiry of the present lease
with the expiration of the present lease

The chief difference between those phrases is one of tone. **Expiry** is a brisker word, suggesting tight planning and tidy systems—though this may have something to do with its brevity, and the fact that it's the word which confronts us every day, in the *expiry date* on credit cards, travel tickets and packaged foods. **Expiration** has the more detached qualities of a formal, latinate word. It seems to speak at a level above the gritty business of arranging contracts and observing their terms, and may indeed serve as something of a euphemism for **expiry** when the latter is an unwelcome fact. Apart from its legal use, **expiration** has some currency among biologists as a synonym for *exhalation*. Altogether, its usage is more academic and abstract than that of **expiry**.

explain and **explanation** For the spelling of these words, see **-ain**.

expose or **exposé** See under **accents**.

expresso or **espresso** See **espresso**.

extendible or **extendable** The first of these spellings is given first preference in most dictionaries, and it is the older spelling in English, dating from the fifteenth century. **Extendable** was first recorded in the seventeenth century, and is the more natural spelling, simply combining the verb *extend* with the English suffix *-able*. The word is one of the few which could be spelled either way. (See further under **-able/-ible**.)

external, exterior or **extraneous** Both **external** and **exterior** refer to what is physically on the outside, though with a slight difference of perspective. **External** is simply what can be seen from outside, as in *an external staircase*; whereas **exterior** suggests a judgement made from inside, as in *no exterior window*. **Extraneous** differs from both in implying that something neither belongs nor is intrinsic to the subject under discussion. *Extraneous suggestions* are not essential or relevant to the main plan, and *an extraneous substance* is foreign matter which has adhered or attached itself to a body, or become blended into a mixture.

extra-/extro- The Latin prefix **extra-**, meaning literally "outside or beyond", is a formative element in various English words, usually polysyllabic:

extra-atmospheric extracurricular extramarital extramural
extrasensory extraterrestrial

Such words are almost always scholarly ones.

The *extra* of common usage formations, such as *extra time* and *extra dry* is believed to be a clipped form of *extraordinary*, meaning "additional(ly) or special(ly)". (*Extraordinary* could be used as an adverb as well as adjective in earlier English.)

The form **extro-** appears instead of **extra-** in a few modern English words which were coined as opposites to those with *intro-*. Thus *extroduction* matched *introduction*, and *extroversion* matched *introversion*. This use of **extro-** seems to be falling into abeyance however. The *Oxford Dictionary* (1989) has almost as many citations for *extraversion* (and *extravert*) as for *extroversion* (and *extrovert*).

Compare **intra-/intro-**.

extraneous or **external** See external.

exult or **exalt** See exalt.

-ey This is both a regular and a variable ending for English words. It is regular in words such as *donkey*, *honey*, *jockey*, *journey*, and *monkey*; and the main point to note is that they form their plurals in the normal way by adding *s*, and unlike most nouns ending in *y*, whose plurals are with *-ies*. (See **-y>-i-**.)

But **-ey** is also a variable spelling for *-y* in a number of English words. In some cases both the older forms with **-ey** (*curtsey*, *doiley*, *fogey*) and the younger ones with *-y* (*curtsy*, *doily*, *fogy*) have survived, with no differentiation of meaning. In other cases the two spellings have developed different meanings, at least in some varieties of English. See for example the entries for **bog(e)y**, **stor(e)y** and **whisk(e)y**. The two different spellings mean that there are also two plural forms for each.

Note that spellings with **-ey** are transitional ones for a number of colloquial adjectives, such as *chanc(e)y*, *mous(e)y*, *phon(e)y* and *pric(e)y*. (See further under **-y/-ey**.)

For the choice between *Surrey* and *Surry*, see under **town names**.

eyeing or **eying** See under -e section 1h.

eyetie or **Itie** See Itie.

eyrie or **aerie** Or *eyry* or *aery*? If you have occasion to refer to eagles' nests, the choice of spellings is rich. The spelling **eyrie** is the primary spelling in Australia, and the dominant one now in Britain, according to the second edition of the *Oxford Dictionary*. However the original *Oxford* gave preference to **aerie**, and it's still preferred in American English, according to *Webster's* and *Random House* dictionaries. The *ae* spelling connects the word with its French origins, in *aire* "a threshing floor" or "high level stretch of ground". However words of that kind were variously spelled *ayre* and *eyre* in early modern English, and use of the second variant was reinforced by the English dialect word *eyre(n)* "eggs", which suggested a folk etymology for the word, as a place for eggs.

Compare **eerie** or **eery**.

F

f/ph The use of **f** or **ph** is fixed in most English words, reflecting their origins. The **ph** is used in words borrowed from Greek, such as:

> *phallic phenomenon philosophy phlegm phosphorus physics*

It also occurs in modern words formed with Greek elements, such as *-phil/ -philia*, *-phobia*, *phono-/-phony*, *-graph/-graphy* etc. Words from any other source (Latin, French, Italian or Anglo-Saxon) are spelled with **f**:

> *fashion federal fiasco flight foreign frame fuse*

As the examples show, words with the **ph** spelling are usually scholarly terms, while those with **f** are common usage.

For just a handful of words, the spelling may be either **ph** or **f**. In the case of *sulfur/sulphur*, it depends on whether the use is scientific or not (see **sulfur**). In other cases such as *calif/caliph* and *serif/seriph*, the **f** is closer to the original word (Arabic and Dutch respectively); yet people wrongly assume they are Greek and therefore should have **ph**. But for *fantasy/phantasy* and *griffin/ gryphon* there are enough parallels in modern English words to foster the spelling with **f**.

One other point at which we notice **f/ph** variation is in references to the *Filipino* people of the *Philippines*. The islands are named after Philip II of Spain, and the spelling remains in line with the Greek (and English) way of writing his name. However the name for the people comes to us via Spanish, where words with **ph** have all been respelled with **f**. See for example: *farmacia* "pharmacy", *filosofo* "philosopher" and *fotografia* "photographia". The same replacement of *ph* has occurred in Italian, and in a number of Scandinavian and Slavic languages. English has mostly preserved the **ph** in Greek loanwords, partly perhaps because it accommodates a number of other graphemes compounded with *h* (*ch, gh, sh* and *wh*).

-f>-v- A small group of very old English nouns ending in **f** make their plurals by replacing it with **v**, and adding *-es* for good measure. The group is shrinking, but its active members still include:

> *calf half leaf loaf self shelf thief wolf*

(*Elf, sheaf* and *wharf* may be added to that list, although dictionaries allow that they may also be pluralised simply by the addition of *s*.) Note also that a few words ending in **-fe** (*knife, life, wife*) also substitute **v** for **f**, before adding the plural *s*.

Beyond those, there are a number which have in the past replaced the **f** with **v** in the plural, but are now often (or usually) pluralised in the regular way, with no change except the addition of *s*:

    dwarfs (dwarves)   *scarfs (scarves)*
    roofs (rooves)   *turfs (turves)*

For *hoof*, the choice between *hoofs* and *hooves* is still in the balance, with dictionaries divided over them. The plurals of **staff** and **tipstaff** are discussed under their individual headings.

Many other nouns ending in *f, ff* or *fe* simply add *s* for the plural:
    beliefs carafes chefs chiefs cliffs cuffs giraffes griefs gulfs muffs
    proofs puffs reefs ruffs skiffs strifes surfs waifs
All are relatively recent, i.e. post-medieval additions to English.

For the choice between **f** and **v** in verbs and adjectives, see **-v-/-f-**.

Variation between **-f** and **-ve** in words such as **motif/motive, naif/naive** and **plaintiff/plaintive** are discussed under individual headings.

faceted For the spelling of this word when it becomes a verb, see **t**.

facility or **faculty** From a common origin in Latin, these two have developed quite distinct areas of meaning in modern English. **Facility** refers to the ease with which we perform any acquired skill, from opening wine bottles to speaking Spanish. A **faculty** is an innate power or capacity, attributed either to people in general, or to a particular individual. The *five faculties* by tradition are sight, hearing, taste, touch and smell. Younger people take all their faculties for granted; elderly people cannot, hence the phrase *in full possession of his/ her faculties*, usually said of an older person.

    Both **facility** and **faculty** are used of resources beyond those of the individual. *Facilities* has come to mean "physical and organisational resources", whether for arranging conferences or making coffee in your motel room. The term **faculty** is used collectively in Australia to mean a department or set of academic disciplines, such as *Arts, Science* or *Law*. In American English meanwhile **faculty** refers to the whole teaching staff of a university, college or school.

    Faculty is quite often used with a plural verb, as in:
    The faculty are likely to vote against it.
This usage has been increasing since the 1950s, according to the evidence of *Webster's English Usage* (1989) and is established among academics, even in North America. In Australia and Britain it's one of a set of collective words that can take a plural verb. (See further under **agreement** section 4.)

factious, factitious or **fractious** None of these is common enough to make its meaning well known. Both **factious** and **fractious** imply uncooperative behavior, and both once meant "tending to split up into petty divisions" (**factious** because it derives from *faction*, and **fractious** from *fraction*). Nowadays only **factious** carries that meaning, and **fractious** refers to the character of an individual who may be anything from unruly and violent to irritable, but at any rate difficult for others to handle:
    He was a fractious prisoner for the authorities.
    The baby was getting tired and fractious with waiting.

Factitious means "contrived or artificial". It may be applied to human behavior, as in *factitious charm*; or to things without the value they might appear to have, as in *factitious shares*. Distinguish **factitious** from the similar and much more common word *fictitious* (see under **fictional**).

faculty or **facility** See facility

Fahrenheit The Fahrenheit scale (°F) has given way in Australia to the centigrade or Celsius scale, in accordance with the Metric Conversion Act 1970. But it continues to be used in North America, despite official moves to "go metric". **Fahrenheit** temperatures are calibrated in relation to the lowest temperature that Gabriel Fahrenheit (1686–1736) could achieve by mixing ice, water and certain salts: 0°F. This sets the freezing point of pure water at 32°F, and its boiling point at 212°F. The so-called "comfort zone" for airconditioning is around 70-75°F.

To convert temperatures from Fahrenheit to Celsius, simply implement the formula below:

$$(°F - 32) \times \frac{5}{9} = °C$$

(See further under **Celsius** and **metrication**.)

Whether in degrees **Fahrenheit** or Celsius, we all continue to measure temperatures with the mercury thermometer invented centuries ago by Fahrenheit. It remains more reliable for many purposes than alcohol-based thermometers—except in the microwave oven.

faint or **feint** As verbs these are very different: **faint** is to lose consciousness, while **feint** is to pretend to punch or thrust forward, as a boxer does to draw his opponent's fire at the start of a bout.

As an adjective, **faint** is the only spelling possible for the common meaning "weak"; yet either **faint** or **feint** may be used in the technical sense of "lightly printed", used of the least conspicuous grade of lines on ruled paper. Printers prefer the spelling **feint**.

fair or **fairly** Both of these have a role as adverbs meaning "honestly" or "without resorting to underhand means", though **fair** is increasingly restricted to a few fixed collocations, such as *play fair* and *fight fair*. Others such as *bid fair*, *promise fair*, *speak fair* and *write fair* (where **fair** means "well") are becoming distinctly old-fashioned. Where it survives in ordinary conversation **fair** still has a role as an intensifier of other words, as in:

It hit me fair and square on the nose.

It fair gets me down.

(See further under **intensifiers**.)

In more formal discourse the adverb is **fairly**, and it still means "honestly" or "justly". See for example: *campaigned fairly, umpired fairly* and *divided it fairly*. Yet by far the commonest use of **fairly**, by more than 20:1 according to the ACE database of Australian English, is as a modifier of other verbs, adverbs or adjectives. Just occasionally it is an intensifier, as in *it fairly hisses through the broken window*. Most of the time it is a downtoner, as in *fairly quickly* and *fairly sure*. (See further under **hedge words**.)

fait accompli This French phrase means "accomplished fact". It is used of preemptive acts which bypass discussion and consultation.

falafel or **felafel** See **felafel**.

fallacies These are flawed arguments. Speakers and writers get away with them more often than they should, probably because they come in many guises. Some types of *fallacy* have traditional Latin names, others have English ones. The labels do help to distinguish them, so for those who would like to be able to detect **fallacies** in their own argument, or anyone else's, here is an inventory of the major types.

1 *Fallacies in the use of words and their representation of reality.*
a) false analogy (see under **analogy**).
b) reification: when an abstract word is used as if it referred to a concrete entity. It happens when a theory or principle is expressed as if it were a fact or element of the real world, as when a sociologist says "society forces us to ..."
c) faulty generalisation: when a sweeping generalisation is drawn from a small and not necessarily representative set of examples: "Our trains are always ten minutes late ..."
d) faulty classification: when the terms offered to cover a range of possibilities are insufficient to cover it. Tick-the-box questionnaires often oblige us to use very rough classifications—to show whether we do something *always/often/ irregularly/never*, but there's nowhere to register the fact that we do it rarely but regularly. In its crudest form, the faulty classification may be a *false dichotomy* and offer us only two alternatives: *true/false, yes/no, good/bad*. Other familiar forms of false dichotomy are the "black or white argument", and the idea that "whoever is not with us is against us".

2 *Logical fallacies*
a) faulty deduction: when the argument rests on affirming the consequent, or denying the antecedent. (See under **deduction** for their proper logical counterparts.)
b) using the *undistributed middle*. This is a flawed syllogism, where the *middle term* is not made universal through the use of *all*. If it only relates to some of the population in the major premise, no proper conclusion can be drawn. (See further under **deduction**.)
c) circular argument, sometimes called the *vicious circle*, is one which claims as its conclusion the very assumption on which it began. It happens in some essays and theses, when writers divide their material (say newspaper articles) into four categories, discuss each one in turn, and then declare "we may

conclude that there are four major types of news report''. Similarly flawed arguments are those which beg the question, also known by the Latin phrase *petitio principii*. (See further under **beg the question**.)

d) analytic-synthetic confusion, sometimes known as the ''no true Scotsman'' *fallacy*. Here an assertion is made which can be tested by empirical evidence, as with ''This publication can be obtained at all good bookshops''. If the statement is challenged by someone who was unable to get the book at what most people think of as a good bookshop, the defender shifts ground to the terms of the assertion itself, and claims that the bookshop visited could not be a good one. So what appears to be a synthetic statement is defended as an analytic one. (See further under **induction**.)

e) *non sequitur* arguments suffer from a logical gap between the premise and the conclusion. (See under **non sequitur**.)

f) *post hoc propter hoc* arguments make the mistake of assuming that what comes after is a result or effect of whatever went before. (See under **post hoc**.)

g) irrelevant conclusion, also known by the Latin phrase *ignoratio elenchi* ''ignoring of (the required) disproof''. Here the person arguing devotes great effort towards proving or disproving something which is beside the point at issue.

3 *Diversionary arguments* i.e. those which rely on diverting attention from the issues or sidestepping them:

a) forestalling disagreement, as when an argument is led by the statement: ''No intelligent person would think that …'', or ''The only proper response is …''

b) *argumentum ad hominem*. This is an argument which makes either a personal attack, or a special appeal to the other party in the debate. (See further under **ad hominem**.)

c) damning the origin: the technique of quashing an argument by discrediting its source or authority, and highlighting anything about them that can be made out to be reprehensible or ridiculous. It dodges the argument itself.

d) straw man argument. This works by attributing an exaggerated or extreme position to the other party, and attacking it as a way of undermining their credibility. It is often used in political debate.

For further discussion of types of argument, see **argument**.

false analogy See under **analogy**.

false plurals The assumption that words ending with *s* in English are plural is too familiar to need explaining. No surprise then if it has sometimes been misapplied to loanwords with a final *s* or *z*, and a special singular form been created for use in English. The fruit which we know as the *currant* got its name this way (see **currant**), as did the *pea*, the *cherry* and *sherry*. *Pea* was derived or backformed from *pease*, *cherry* from the medieval form of *cerise*, and *sherry* was *sherris*, an anglicised form of the Spanish name *Xerez*, the town where the liquor was made (now *Jerez*). (See further under **backformation**.)

falsehood, falseness or **falsity** The word **falsehood** differs from the other two in being applied to particular untruths or untrue statements: it often serves as a formal synonym for a lie. **Falseness** and **falsity** are used of general deceptiveness or lack of genuineness in someone's behavior: *the falseness of their excuses* or *the falsity of their position*. There is little to choose between **falseness** and **falsity**, except that the first is clearly the more common of the two in the twentieth century, to judge by the evidence of English databases.

farther or **further, farthest** or **furthest** See **further**.

fatal or **fateful** The emphasis in **fatal** is on death (whether actual or figurative), whereas in **fateful** it is on destiny. So **fatal** puts an end to something (*a fatal blow to their plans*) or to someone (*a fatal accident*). **Fateful** is more prospective, anticipating an inevitable future outcome for someone, and at the same time emphasising the perspective which hindsight gives on it:

> On that fateful morning my alarm clock went on strike, and I missed the plane which was to take me to sign the contract in Tokyo. There would be no further business for us in Japan ...

Fatal is the older word, borrowed from Latin in the fifteenth century. It could be associated with either death or destiny until the English formation **fateful** made its appearance in the eighteenth century. Both meanings are blended in the phrase "fatal shore" from the Ballad of Van Diemen's Land, 1825–30. Overall **fatal** remains much more common.

father-in-law See under **in-laws**.

fauna See under **flora**.

faute de mieux This apologetic phrase borrowed from French means "for lack of (something) better". It is said in rueful recognition that whatever has been done left much to be desired, lest anyone should think your judgement was defective. Things could be worse however, and once again a borrowed French phrase can say it all: **pis aller**. Literally (and in reverse order) it means "go worst", but it identifies the last resort—what one must be prepared for in the worst of all possible worlds. If nothing can be done, and you can only shrug your shoulders, the verbal equivalent is **tant pis** "too bad".

faux pas Translated literally, this French phrase means "false step", though it's always used figuratively of a breach of etiquette, or of a comment or move which disturbs the smoothness of proceedings. In the plural it remains unchanged:

> His faux pas were notorious in the club.

The comparable English idiom is "putting one's foot in it". Its colloquial overtones make it more suitable for informal contexts, while **faux pas** serves for formal ones.

favor or **favour** See under **-or/-our**.

fay or **fey** Both these smack of older notions of the supernatural: **fay** being an old-fashioned word for "fairy", and **fey** an adjective which originated as a synonym of "doomed". **Fey** connoted a weird state of excitement and heightened awareness in someone whose death was imminent; and so it has come to mean "under a spell", "lightheaded", and "given to elfish whimsy or eccentricity". In this way **fey** begins to overlap with the adjectival use of **fay**, particularly when used to describe certain kinds of imaginative writing. Shakespeare's *A Midsummer Night's Dream* could be called either *a fay tale* or *a fey tale*, in the developed sense of the word. And what of Gilbert and Sullivan's *Iolanthe*? Its unlikely fairies suggest that it's more *a fey tale*—but the choice is ultimately up to the critic.

Note that the word **fey** is apt to be misinterpreted as connoting "gay" in phrases such as *a slightly fey young man*—even though the speaker/writer is most probably referring to his mental rather than sexual orientation.

faze or **phase** See **phase**.

fecal or **faecal** See under **ae/e**.

federal or **Federal** For writers and editors, the question with this word is whether to capitalise or not to capitalise it. Authorities such as the Australian Government *Style Manual* and most newspaper style guides have it that it needs a capital letter only in official titles such as *Federal Constitution*, *Federal Government* and *Federal Parliament*. Two of the newspapers extend the treatment wherever there are comparable state and federal institutions to be distinguished, as with departments of health and education. But others (the majority) would use lower case in all nonofficial designations and descriptions, such as *federal department of health*, *federal-state relations* and the *federal executive of the Labor party*. In the context of Australian government, the word **federal** itself connotes all that's needed to make the point, and a capital letter is an inessential token of officialdom. We might note that in the USA, **federal** is not capitalised even in references to the *federal government*. (See **capitals** sections 1b and 3.)

Federation Like other events of general historical significance, this is given a capital letter (see **capitals** section 1d). The federation of the six former colonies of Australia into the six states of the Commonwealth of Australia on 1 January 1901 represented an important coming-of-age, after more than a decade of debate and two referendums. So **Federation** and the title *Father of Federation* (often given to Sir Henry Parkes) are usually capitalised.

Federation is also used (especially in Sydney) as an adjective to refer to a conventional style of domestic architecture, which was more or less contemporary with **Federation** and continued through to the end of World War I. The name preferred in Victoria is *Edwardian* architecture. In either state it was the architecture associated with what were then seen as *small* homes, i.e. ones with no servants' quarters, where the kitchen was integrated under the main roof. But since 1950, the comfortable proportions of such houses and their *art nouveau* motifs have acquired a certain cachet. They have a definite value for real estate agents, and this probably helps to maintain the capital letter on Federation, though with its sometimes dubious connections with Australian Federation it might otherwise shed it.

feint or **faint** See faint.

felafel, falafel or **filafil** The spellings of this Lebanese food agree on the middle syllable but not the others. Like other Arabic words, its vowels are not standardised in the writing system, and people render it by ear. The *Oxford Dictionary* (1989) made it **felafel**, as do the major Australian dictionaries. American dictionaries prefer **falafel**. But all allow at least three different spellings, with the letters *a*, *e* and *i* appearing variously in the first and third syllable.

feldspar or **felspar** The first of these spellings is recommended in the *Oxford Dictionary* and the major American dictionaries, and is the spelling preferred everywhere by geologists and chemists. It reflects the Swedish origins of the word, coined by D. Tilas in 1740 out of *feldt* "field" and *spar* "spat(h)", for a type of gypsum he identified in Finland. **Felspar** represents a mistaken etymology by which the first element is understood as the German *Fels* "rock". Though "corrupt", it's still the more common spelling according to the *Oxford Dictionary* (1989). The *Macquarie Dictionary* (1991) gives them equal status.

fellowship On whether to double the *p* when this word becomes a verb, see -p/-pp-.

female or **feminine** See feminist.

feminine gender See under gender.

feminist, feminine or **female** These words all pick up aspects of woman's identity, yet are remarkably different. **Female** is a straightforward word used to identify natural gender; and it contrasts with *male* in reference to both human and animal species. **Feminine** has long connoted the social and behavioral attributes of women which were felt to be archetypal of their sex, such as delicacy, prettiness, refinement of taste and feeling, and also weakness. The word also has a long history of use by grammarians, in reference to grammatical gender. In all these uses it contrasts with *masculine*.

While **female** and **feminine** have centuries of use behind them, **feminist** is very much a contemporary word, first recorded in 1894. It is applied to whoever or whatever advocates equal rights and opportunities for women. **Feminist** attitudes are diametrically opposed to *male chauvinist* ones. (See further under **chauvinism**.) Some women (and men) would regard the words **feminine** and **feminist** as mutually exclusive, but the assumption is not shared by all.

ferment or **foment** Only when used as verbs in the expression *fermenting trouble* or *fomenting trouble* do these two come close to each other. The expression is an ordinary collocation for **foment** meaning "foster", "instigate", but a figurative use for **ferment** because of its strong association with biological processes. So the chief difference between the two is in the physical imagery embodied in **ferment**.

Overall, **foment** seems likely to disappear. Its medical uses, as a verb meaning "warm" or "apply a warm poultice (or other substance) to", are outdated; and its only remaining use in *fomenting trouble* etc. is under pressure from **ferment** because the latter is the more familiar word. In Australian and standard British pronunciation, **foment** is often indistinguishable from **ferment** and can easily be mistaken for it. The additional fact that we can say *in a ferment* meaning "in a state of agitation", while there's no equivalent noun for **foment**, also strengthens the position of **ferment**.

ferret On how to spell this word when it becomes a verb, see under **t**.

fervent or **fervid** Both these adjectives derive from the Latin root *ferv-* meaning "glow(ing) hot", and both have developed figuratively, so that they're nowadays applied to intense relationships and attitudes. **Fervent** is the commoner of the two, used of strong commitments to ideals and causes as in *fervent prayer*, and to people as in *fervent admirer*. Though it connotes intensity, **fervent** does not bear the faintly pejorative aftertaste of **fervid**. In *fervid imagination* or *fervid preaching* there's a suggestion that things are overheated and excessive.

fervor or **fervour** See under **-or/-our**.

fetid or **foetid** The first of these spellings has by far the better claim, being in line with the Latin adjective *fetidus* which is the word's direct antecedent. In Latin it meant "stinking", as a derivative of the verb *fetere* "stink". Dictionaries all give **fetid** first preference. However variant spellings (both *foetid* and *faetid*) appear for it in the eighteenth century, in references to *foetid drugs*, among other things. This usage in prescientific medicine suggests a possible confusion with *fetus/foetus* (see further under **fetus**).

fetish This word is used by behavioral scientists (both psychologists and anthropologists) to refer to something apparently ordinary, to which some people give extraordinary attention and reverence. An outsider would call it "an obsession".

In certain circles, language discussion tends to be "fetishised". Particular usages and forms of expression may be subjected to intense attention, and revered or held up as models of correctness for the rest of the community to observe—such as not splitting infinitives or ending sentences with prepositions (see **infinitive** and **particles**). The observation of such things becomes the canon of "correctness" for all, irrespective of time and place. *Fetishes* of usage put an arbitrary stamp of "correct" on one expression rather than another, often out of conservatism and sometimes ignorance. Fortunately they are no longer the focus of English language education—yet they are still well enough known in the community to be a pernicious weapon in the hands of those who only want to pick holes in other people's expression. When writing we need to know about language *fetishes*, to decide when we can and should defy them. They are the subject of a number of entries in this book.

See also **shibboleth**.

fetus or **foetus** The first of these **fetus** has the better credentials. It is the standard spelling in American English, and the one recommended by the *Oxford Dictionary*. Yet **foetus** is very familiar in both Britain and Australia, and has centuries of tradition behind it. The spelling **foetus** seems to have originated through the misunderstanding that it derived from the Latin verb *foetare* "give birth" rather than the verb *fere* "conceive", of which it's the past participle. **Foetus** passed from medieval Latin into Middle English, and has maintained its place through to current debates in the British *Lancet* magazine. In the USA meanwhile the spelling **fetus** was preferred to the one with the *oe* digraph (see further at **oe**). Americans thus have the etymologically superior spelling **fetus**.

All this unfortunately complicates the matter in Australia. Those who might otherwise be amenable to the etymologically preferable spelling **fetus** (which comes with the *Oxford Dictionary*'s recommendation) are reluctant to accept what they see as an American spelling. For whatever reason, the doctors surveyed by *Australian Dr Weekly* (in 1988) were mostly disinclined to change from **foetus**, in spite of having the etymological evidence put before them. Doctors are not however the only users of the word, and both spellings appear in the Australian ACE corpus though the numbers are small: 2 of **fetus** and 3 of **foetus**. Writers at large are free to choose, and might prefer **fetus** either in terms of its own etymology, or because of the general principle of reducing *oe* digraphs to *e*—or for both reasons.

Note that the plural of **fetus** is *fetuses*, as for most other loanwords from the Latin fourth declension. (See further under **-us** section 2.)

few or **a few** Both mean a small number, yet there's an important difference. Compare:

They wrote few letters.

They wrote a few letters.

The first sentence implies that the number was lower than expected, whereas the second simply notes the small number without any evaluation. In fact it gives us no very precise idea as to how many were written: it's simply a casual alternative for "some".

Note that the quantity implied by **a few** is always relative to the population referred to. *A few apples* in the fridge might mean half a dozen, whereas *a few spectators* at the match might mean fifty. But one should never put too fine a point on it, because the very raison d'être for **a few** is that it means an indefinite number. It is on this point that **a few** contrasts with **several**. It too implies a small number, but one within the range from three or four to ten. **Several** differs also in that it's associated with written style and is free of the casual overtones of **a few**.

fewer or **less** The standard rule says that **fewer** goes with plural nouns, and **less** with singular or collective ones. So it should be *fewer books, fewer answers*, but *less publishing, less response*. Alternatively, we might put it that **fewer** goes with *count* or *countable nouns*, and **less** with *mass nouns*. (See further under **count nouns**.)

However, **less** is often found where the rule prescribes **fewer**, in speech as well as writing. See for example:

The costs must be less than twenty per cent.

Foreign oil companies had warned him less than forty-eight hours beforehand.

Express lane: fifteen items or less.

We now find ourselves with a lot less jobs and with different ones to offer.

A year ago he had worn less wrinkles and more clothes.

Even the strictest usage commentators now agree that **less** may well occur in expressions involving quantities of money, time, distance, weight etc. as in the first two sentences, especially before *than*. The very familiar third sentence is similar in its expression of a quantity, but is elliptical. The fourth and fifth examples from the Australian ACE corpus stretch the quantitative use somewhat further. In each, **less** is more conspicuous because it directly qualifies the count noun; yet a number or quantity of jobs is still implied in the fourth sentence, and a collective body of wrinkles in the fifth. This use of **less** (as a determiner) occurs much less often in print than the pronoun use illustrated in the first pair of sentences. Yet all five examples serve to show the current range of uses of **less** with things countable.

The second edition of the *Oxford Dictionary* notes that such use of **less** is frequent in spite of being "regarded as incorrect"; and *Webster's English Usage* (1989) has multiple citations of constructions like those above, gleaned from contemporary writing. Both *Webster's* and *Random House* dictionaries give "fewer" as one of the definitions of **less**, and *Random House* comments in a usage note that the replacement of **fewer** with **less** in such contexts is increasing in all varieties of English, and that only in formal written English is **fewer** more frequent than **less** in examples like the fourth and fifth. Their appearance in the ACE corpus confirms the trend in Australia.

The issue of using **fewer** rather than **less** is thus a stylistic matter rather than one of correct grammar. Using **fewer** makes for a more formal tone, **less** more informal. The *Comprehensive Grammar of English* (1985) recognises **less** as both pronoun and determiner, while noting the "prescriptive objections" to it. The objections seem to begin only in the late eighteenth century with Baker's *Reflections on the English Language* (1770), and to have consolidated in the nineteenth century. Before then **less** was used freely for "fewer", according to the *Oxford Dictionary* record.

fey or **fay**   See **fay**.

fiasco   For the plural of this word, see under **-o**.

fiber or **fibre**   See under **-re/-er**.

fibula   The plural of this is discussed under **-a** section 1.

fictional or **fictitious**   In **fictional**, the presence of the word *fiction* reminds us that the creative imagination is at work, as when we speak of the *fictional portrayal of Sir Joseph Banks* in a TV series about Captain Cook, or a *fictional conversation between Gough Whitlam and Sir John Kerr* in *The Dismissal*. Fictional creations like these stand in their own right, and are not to be assessed in terms of factuality.

A **fictitious** story cannot be respected as a work of art, but will be judged negatively against the known facts. People who use *fictitious excuses* to get out of a tight spot lose credibility with others, and those who give *fictitious evidence* in court may end up in jail. When the word **fictitious** is applied, it's clear that fact rather than fiction is being sought.

Distinguish **fictitious** from **factitious** (see under **factious**).

fidget   For the spelling of this word when it becomes a verb, see under **t**.

figures of speech   The phrase **figure of speech** is often nowadays used in a deprecating way to refer to a metaphor or hyperbole which is not to be taken literally: "It's only a figure of speech," people say, when a politician refers to Australia as "a banana republic". The taste or appetite for figures of speech has declined, and their range is not as well known as when rhetoric loomed large in the educational curriculum. Yet they remain powerful communicative devices when used occasionally.

Figures of speech include any unusual way of using words to refer to something, especially those which stimulate the imagination. Some work through establishing a likeness between two unlike things—either explicitly, in a **simile**: "My love is like a red, red rose"; or implicitly, through *metaphors* which develop sustained imagery or analogies (see **metaphor**). *Personification* (of abstract concepts) and *anthropomorphism* (of animals) are special kinds of metaphor (see under **personification**). *Metonymy* and *synecdoche* differ from metaphor in two ways: they are not usually sustained, and the verbal substitute is closely related to the item it replaces (see further under **metonymy** and **synecdoche**).

Any *figure of speech* may also gain its effect through exaggeration (*hyperbole*) or through understatement (*meiosis*). The latter term is often replaced by **litotes**, though *litotes* is more strictly a form of understatement in which you assert something by negative means, as in "He doesn't hate us". The intention is to impress by the moderation of the statement.

Some **figures of speech** work through the arrangements and patterns of words themselves. **Parallelism** involves the repetition of a particular phrase or clause structure with different words slotted in, as in "The bigger they are, the harder they fall". The *chiasmus* exploits the same words or related ones in a symmetrically opposed arrangement (see under **chiasmus**). The sound elements of words are exploited through figures of speech such as **alliteration**, **assonance** and **onomatopoeia** (see further under those headings).

Like any kind of ornament, **figures of speech** work best when integrated with the meaning and purpose of the discourse. The overuse of any kind of metaphor can easily result in a ludicrous mix, and an overdose of litotes or alliteration quickly becomes irritating. In scattered headlines or advertising slogans they may be indulged, but in continuous prose they must be used sparingly for optimum effect.

Filipino See under **f/ph**.

fill in or **fill out** In Britain people **fill in** application forms or personal file documents, whereas in the USA they **fill** (them) **out**. Australians have traditionally used the British collocation, but the American one is increasingly familiar. Users of each expression tend to find their own the more rational one to describe what you're doing when faced with the blank spaces on a form.

fillet For the spelling of this word when it becomes a verb, see under **t**.

fin de siècle This French phrase, meaning "end of the century", featured in the title of a novel by F. de Jouvenot and H. Micard (1888). It passed very quickly from being an adjective with the meaning "modern" and "avant garde", to meaning "decadent". The first meaning was there in the Melbourne *Punch* of 1891, in "this fin de siècle ballet". But by 1908 **fin de siècle** had become retrospective in meaning and associated with "fading glory". At this end of the twentieth century, its use is mostly historical.

As a compound adjective it is hyphenated by some writers and editors, although as a foreign phrase, and as one which is often italicised, there is no need. (See **hyphens** section 2c iii.)

final or **finale** Both of these serve as nouns referring to the last event in a series, though they are cultural worlds apart. **Final** is the term used in sporting competitions for the concluding match which decides the season's winners. The **finale** is the last movement of a musical composition, or the last item in a stage performance of some kind. Being a loanword from Italian it has three syllables, and the *e* is functional rather than decorative.

fingers and **thumbs** Our ability to write—*to put pen to paper*—is a remarkable fruit of both evolution and our sociocultural history. Both the opposed thumb (which we share with the other primates), and the use of a highly developed written code (which is ours alone), come together as we write. But English is still at sixes and sevens over how to refer to the digits of the hand. Some of the time we speak of having *five fingers*, and talking of *a middle finger* presupposes this too. The traditional marriage service spoke of placing a ring on the *fourth finger*. And nowadays musical scores all identify the fingers to be used by numbers 1 to 5 (the "Continental" system)—reversing an earlier system (the "English" system) by which the thumb was shown with an *x*, and the fingers as 1 to 4. The etymology of the word *finger* is also believed to be related to the number *five*.

Yet those who refer to the *first finger* usually mean "the index finger" rather than the *thumb*; and the question as to which *finger* bears the wedding ring is usually sidestepped by calling it the *ring finger*. In older tradition it was called "the medicinal finger", because of a superstition that potions should be stirred with it to test for their noxiousness. (The practice linked up with the notion that a nerve ran direct from that *finger* to the heart—which also explains the choice of *finger* for the wedding ring.) Contemporary medics and nurses avoid all possible ambiguity by referring to each *finger* by individual names: *thumb*, *index finger*, *middle finger*, *ring finger*, *little finger*.

finite verbs Every fully fledged clause has a *finite verb*. They are the forms of verbs which have a definite tense (either present or past) and mood (indicative or imperative). In the following sentences, all the verbs are finite:
You give a good performance. (present, indicative)
She gave a good performance. (past, indicative)
Give a good performance. (present, imperative)
Finite verbs can be either single words as in those sentences, or the first element of a compound verb phrase, as in the following:
She was giving a good deal.
She would have given a good deal.
She ought to give a good deal.
In compound verbs, the tense and mood are carried by the auxiliary verb(s); and the various parts of the main verb *giving*, *given*, (to) *give* are all *nonfinite*. On their own the nonfinite elements are insufficient to make clauses, and can only be the basis of a phrase:
Given encouragement …
Giving no thought for the others …
To give them a chance …
Note that the nonfinite *give* (often called the *infinitive*) is identical with some finite parts of the verb, as shown above in the imperative, and the present

indicative with *you*. (It would be the same for *I*, *we* and *they*.) In those cases, the finiteness is only evident in the fact that there is a subject directly governing the verb, expressed either as a pronoun or a noun phrase, or else left implicit in the imperative mood.

For many verbs, the past tense (finite) and the past nonfinite form (participle) are identical:

They supplied the goods quickly.

They have supplied the goods quickly.

Once again, the finiteness or nonfiniteness can only be seen by referring to the accompanying words. The subject *they* makes *supplied* finite in the first sentence, and the auxiliary *have* makes it nonfinite in the second.

An alternative name to the traditional one *finite verb* is *tensed verb*, used in the *Introduction to the Grammar of English* (1984). (See further under **phrases**, **nonfinite clauses**, **infinitives**, **participles** and **auxiliaries**.)

fiord or **fjord** Most British and Australian dictionaries give priority to **fiord**, which anglicises this Norwegian loanword, whereas the major American dictionaries prefer **fjord** as do the Norwegians themselves. The spelling **fiord** has the advantage of reflecting the normal pronunciation of the word, whereas **fjord** runs the risk of being misread with an extraneous ''j'' sound. (The names *Bjorn* and *Bjelke-Petersen* sometimes suffer in this way.)

first or **firstly** An old and peculiar tradition of style has it that when enumerating items, you should use **first** (not *firstly*), followed by *secondly*, *thirdly*, *fourthly* etc. The origins and basis of this are rather obscure. The absence of **firstly** from Dr Johnson's dictionary may have something to do with it, and perhaps an argument *ex silentio* was drawn from that, which became a fetish in the nineteenth century. By 1847 De Quincey calls **firstly** ''a ridiculous and most pedantic neologism''. But it was no neologism according to the *Oxford Dictionary*, being first recorded in 1530, and from time to time after that.

In any case, a contemporary of De Quincey comments that **firstly** was being used by a number of authors ''for the sake of its more accordant sound with *secondly*, *thirdly*''. Exactly the same policy is recommended by style books of the 1980s, such as the *Right Word at the Right Time*. There is also the obvious alternative of using *first*, *second*, *third* etc., and consistency of form can be achieved either way.

first cousin See under **cousins**.

First Fleet This phrase, referring to the group of ships which reached Botany Bay in 1788, has assumed increasing importance for Australians as time goes by. The fleet, consisting of eleven ships (two naval ships, including the flagship *Sirius*, and nine contracted commercial vessels) brought a total of about 1500 people, officers, sailors, civilians and convicts, as the human resources for the new Australian colony.

Descendants of those first arrivals now proudly refer to themselves as *First Fleeters*. In nineteenth century society, by contrast, people's convict origins were hushed up, and allusions to the "first fleet" and its population were not generally capitalised. The capital letters have become a regular feature of the phrase since World War II. Recognition has also been enhanced through the Fellowship of First Fleeters, which has published its own journal *First-Fleeters* since 1969.

first name or **forename** These are two of the several expressions by which we refer to someone's personal name, as opposed to their family name. Formerly it was the *Christian name* (or *baptismal name*), but the religious bias in that phrase is now recognised and avoided in multicultural communities. **First name** is the phrase most widely used in Australia or Britain, although it creates problems for those in whose culture the family name is given first, including Chinese, Japanese, Cambodians, Koreans and Vietnamese, among others. The same problem besets the term **forename**, even though it's intended to complement the word *surname*. Only the phrase *given name* avoids the various complications just mentioned, and is the least ambiguous in crosscultural use.

For more about the writing of people's names and titles, see under **forms of address** and **names**.

first person See under **person**.

First World War See under **World War**.

Fitz- Surnames with this prefix (the Anglo-Norman form of *fils* "son") are mostly written without a hyphen: *Fitzgerald, Fitzpatrick, Fitzroy, Fitzsimons*. However some families reserve the right to hyphenate their name, and in that case the following letter is usually capitalised: *Fitz-Gerald, Fitz-Simons*. (See **hyphens** section 1c.) In a handful of cases (judging by the metropolitan telephone directory) the same name has no hyphen, but still an internal capital letter: *FitzGerald, FitzSimons*. Although these are the minority, it's as well to check whenever you're writing to someone surnamed **Fitz-**. They are likely to be highly sensitive on this point. Compare **Mac** or **Mc**.

fjord or **fiord** See **fiord**.

fl. See **floruit**.

flack or **flak** See **flak**.

flagrant or **fragrant** Confusion between **flagrant** meaning "blatant" and **fragrant** meaning "sweet-smelling" goes back centuries. It is evident in medieval manuscripts, and some believe that it originated in popular Latin. The sounds "l" and "r" are easily substituted for each other (as happens in many Southeast Asian languages), and so we sometimes hear of "flagrant perfumes" (not ones that Christian Dior would be proud of) and "fragrant violation of the law" (? confounding the breath analyser by gargling with eau de cologne).

flagrante delicto See under **corpus delicti**.

flair or **flare** Flair is a recent (nineteenth century) loanword from French, meaning "a special skill or aptitude". **Flare** is centuries older, and probably a Germanic word though its origins are obscure. It has developed numerous meanings from the earliest known sense "spread out", and is used to describe shapes: "flared trousers"; sounds: "the flare of trumpets"; movements: "the aircraft flared"; and especially flames: "the tall flare of the refinery".

   Flair was an alternative spelling for **flare** until the nineteenth century, but since the arrival of the French loanword, each has kept its own regular spelling. Yet there are occasional confusions between them, as in: "He's a brilliant musician. A violinist with flare"! ... We may presume that he has "fire in the belly".

flak or **flack** The spelling **flak** is distinctly un-English, and serves to remind us that it is a German acronym which gained currency during World War II. It originally stood for **Fl**i*eger***a***bwehr***k***anone* "aircraft defence gun", and then referred to the anti-aircraft fire from such guns—shells that burst into a thousand jagged pieces. In the decades that followed, **flak** acquired its more familiar meaning of "damaging criticism", first recorded in 1968 according to the second edition of the *Oxford Dictionary*. It is occasionally spelled **flack**, another sign of its ongoing assimilation in English.

   But the spelling **flack** also belongs to a different word, used for a press agent or public relations officer. According to the *Random House Dictionary*, it made its first appearance just before World War II, and is believed to be an eponym harking back to Gene Flack, a Hollywood publicity agent.

flamingo For the plural of this word, see under **-o**.

flammable or **inflammable** Though these mean exactly the same: "liable to burst into flame", the first is preferred and to be encouraged wherever public safety is an issue. Apart from being slightly shorter, **flammable** is never subject to the faint ambiguity which dogs **inflammmable**—as to whether its *in-* is a negative or intensive prefix (see further under **in-/im-**). It is of course an intensive prefix, just as it is in the related word *inflame*. But with the risk of *in-* being read as a negative in **inflammable** (and failing to serve as a warning of fire), the spelling **flammable** is preferred by all those concerned with fire hazards. The US National Fire Protection Association adopted it in the 1920s, but in Australia it has only recently become standard on warning signs. **Inflammable** is still of course available for figurative use, as in *an inflammable mix of poverty and unemployment*.

flare or **flair** See **flair**.

flash language Australian English owes something to *flash*, the underworld jargon of thieves and those who lived "on the cross". It served as a private means of communication between convicts, as an expression of solidarity among them, and as a way of preventing outsiders from listening in. The authorities identified it with crime itself, and apparently tried to prevent it being used or recorded in official documents. Its presence is however acknowledged by Captain Watkin Tench in 1793, and there's a sprinkling of references to it in the decades that followed. Our best information about it comes from a glossary apparently compiled about 1812 for the benefit of Thomas Skottowe, commandant of the Newcastle prison, which was subsequently published in London as part of the memoirs of an ex-convict, James Hardy Vaux.

Vaux's *Vocabulary of the Flash Language*, published in London in 1819, offers definitions and notes on about 740 words and phrases. The vocabulary is not exclusively Australian, but common to convicts in other parts of the English-speaking world; and some of the items are ordinary colloquialisms. What is interesting among the lists is the number which were once thieves' jargon, and which have slipped with slightly changed meanings into informal Australian English. They include:

cadge	"beg" once an intransitive verb, now transitive
crack	"break open" now has multiple idiomatic uses
flash	"belonging to those *on the cross*" now "flamboyantly expensive"
frisk	"empty or search thoroughly" now "search (a person) for concealed weapons"
job	"a planned criminal action" now " a task" or "regular employment"
kid(dy)	"child thief" now "child"
lag	"sentence to transportation" now "arrest or imprison"
mob	"gang of thieves" now "herd, flock" or "angry crowd"
pal	"partner, accomplice" now "companion"
pig	"police runner" now "policeman"
pull up	"accost or arrest" now "stop (a horse)"
rig	"racket" once a noun, now a verb
square	"honest" now "conservative in one's habits"
swag	"booty, stolen goods" now "bundle of belongings"

The word *smiggins* from the same source meant a "soup or hash" made out of beef stock and barley—a lumpy mix which may indeed have helped to give *Smiggin Holes* in the Snowy Mountains its name. Skiers would find the name suggests both the shallow soup-bowl shape of the circular terrain, and the typically mushy snow that lies in it.

flaunt or **flout** The overtones of defiance are strong in both of these verbs, though their objects are different. **Flout** means "mock or treat with contempt", especially when it involves defying rules, conventions or the law. **Flaunt** means "display so as to draw public attention to", particularly something over which there might have been some discreetness or sense of shame. But the two often seem to overlap, since *flaunting* one's ill-gotten gains may also mean *flouting* the law, and *flaunting* oneself implies the *flouting* of social conventions—hence the common confusion between them.

flautist or **flutist** Since the nineteenth century, **flautist** has been the professional name for the flute player, at least in Britain and Australia. Those who play the flute in ABC symphony orchestras are *flautists*. Yet **flutist** has a much longer history dating back to sixteenth century English, and was challenged only in the later nineteenth century by the Italianate **flautist**. In the USA **flutist** has never been displaced as the standard term, and nonmusical people in Australia naturally find it a more accessible word.

fledgeling or **fledgling** Fledgeling is the more regular spelling in terms of the rules for a final *e* when a suffix with a consonant is added. (See further under **-e**.) This seems to be why the *Oxford Dictionary* puts it first. The other is made equal but second, on the strength of citations which as Fowler noted are all for **fledgling**. The strength of usage has certainly prevailed, and other dictionaries in Britain, Australia and America all give priority to **fledgling**.

Compare **judgement**.

flier or **flyer** There's little to choose between these, and all major dictionaries make them equal. The *Oxford Dictionary* (1989) names **flyer** first, on the strength of "recent quotations", which are indeed spread through the twentieth century and over many of the word's meanings. Other dictionaries give precedence to **flier**, and it's endorsed by most of the Australian newspaper guides. For some meanings **flier** may be preferred, as when the reference is to an aviator: *World War II flier*. The person who flies *in* a plane can then be contrasted as the **flyer**, as shown in the "frequent flyer" schemes offered by various airlines. For mechanical uses of the word, **flier** is the common spelling, and it's the one found for an express train: *the Newcastle flier*. In various idiomatic uses both spellings occur, as with *high flier/high flyer*. Yet when it comes to advertising leaflets, **flyer** is the more usual spelling.

Overall then **flyer** seems to be consolidating and setting itself apart from *crier*, *drier* etc., which as the *Oxford Dictionary* and Fowler noted were more regular in terms of the rule for turning final *-y* into *i* before a suffix (see **-y> -i-**). The rule makes greater demands on the reader for stems of three letters than for longer ones; and **flyer** is clearly easier for the reader than **flier**, if the word has to be understood with little support from the context.

Compare **drier** or **dryer**.

floor and **storey** Does a first floor room allow you to step out into the garden? It all depends on whether it's the American or British system for numbering the floors, both of which are used in Australia. In American usage, the level at which you enter is normally called the *first floor*. In the British system, the entry level is the *ground floor*, and above it is the *first floor*. Fortunately, in both traditions the first level of the building is the *first storey*, so there's no ambiguity there.

See **storey or story** for the variable spelling of that word, and its plural.

flora and **fauna** These two have been coupled together since 1745/6, when the botanist and naturalist Linnaeus published a *Flora* and *Fauna* of his native Sweden. In Roman mythology they were the names of divinities who led separate lives, Flora as the goddess of flowers, and Faunus as the god of agriculture and shepherds. In the twentieth century Flora has acquired a new realm in references to the micro-organisms that inhabit the internal canals and external organs of animals. In a sense this is a takeover, as it allows the term **flora** to subsume both fungi and bacteria (i.e. both plant and animal life).

Both words are used in modern English as collective words, referring to the whole gamut of plant (or animal) life in a particular location. In such references there's no need to seek a plural form, and writers may choose a singular or plural verb in agreement, depending on whether their discussion focuses on the whole range of species, or on individual varieties:

The flora of the western slopes is mainly dry sclerophyll.
The flora of the western slopes are mainly dry sclerophyll.

(See further under **agreement** and **collective nouns**.)

If there is an occasion to speak of the **flora** (or **fauna**) of more than one region in the same breath, a plural form is needed. Writers have the choice of either the regular English forms *floras/faunas* or Latin ones *florae/faunae*. (See further under **-a** for the use of each.)

floruit Borrowed by historians from Latin, this word means literally "s/he flourished". When followed by a date or a span of time, it indicates a significant point or period in someone's life, and it provides a historical benchmark for someone whose exact date of birth and death are not known. The date or time accompanying the **floruit** (abbreviated as **fl.**) may be drawn from circumstantial evidence, such as when the person was appointed to a particular position, or when s/he produced an outstanding literary or artistic work. For William of Ockham (or Occam) the year in which he was put on trial for heresy (1328) is the most precisely known date of his life; and since he managed to escape to Munich and lived in sanctuary for some years after, *fl.1328* serves to put a date on his career.

flounder or **founder** Hardly surprising that these get confused when you know that the first may indeed owe its existence to the second. **Founder** meaning "sink to the bottom (of the sea)" is commonly used of ships, or enterprises that come to grief. **Flounder** meaning "move clumsily" often seems to involve struggling close to the ground, as in the fisherman's story from the *Angler in Wales* (1834), in which "man and fish lay floundering together in the rapids" … and it no doubt got away.

The origins of **founder** are in medieval French, whereas those of **flounder**, first recorded in 1592, are not at all certain. Some scholars have suggested that it is a blend of *flounce* and *founder*: others that it is simply an embellishment of *founder* with *fl*, a sound unit which seems to carry a subliminal meaning of "heavy movement" (see further under **phonesthemes**). In popular etymology however, the verb **flounder** may also owe something to a well-known fish (also **flounder**) that inhabits the sea bottom. The fish itself derives its name from the Scandinavian languages.

The latter influence seems to be still at work in a memorial plaque set on the wall of a certain RSL club:

IN MEMORY OF FORMER MEMBERS OF THE SPORTS FISHING CLUB,
WHOSE BOAT FLOUNDERED ON THE PT CAMPBELL ROCKS,
MAY 16TH 1935.

---

flout or **flaunt** See flaunt.

fluorene or **fluorine** The endings make for very different chemicals. **Fluorine** is a nonmetallic element which occurs as a greenish-yellow gas. When impure it's fluorescent. **Fluorene** is a white crystalline hydrocarbon, used in the manufacture of resins and dyes.

flush and **hang** See under **indent**.

flutist or **flautist** See flautist.

flyer or **flier** See flier.

FM This abbreviation, meaning "frequency modulation", contrasts with **AM** "amplitude modulation", and they represent the two kinds of radio transmission now available. Being capitalised abbreviations, they need no stops. (See further under **abbreviations** section 1c.)

focus This word raises questions of spelling, both as a noun and as a verb. As a noun its plural is usually the English *focuses* rather than the Latin *foci* (see further under **-us**). As a verb with suffixes attached, it is written both as *focused/focusing* and *focussed/focussing*. The persistence of the second forms is remarkable, given that dictionaries are unanimous in giving their preferences to the first spelling. The spelling with only one *s* conforms to the general principle of not doubling the final consonant when the syllable it belongs to is unstressed (see under **doubling of final consonant**).

For ways of maintaining a clear focus in your writing, see **information focus**.

foetid or **fetid** See fetid.

foetus or **fetus** See fetus.

fogy or **fogey** The first spelling is preferred in all dictionaries, though the two are apparently more equal in British than in American English. The word's origins are obscure. It seems to have originated as a nickname for an invalid soldier, and was prefaced by "old" from its first recorded appearances in the late eighteenth century. Attempts to explain its etymology by reference to "foggy" seem a little far-fetched, and like various slang words, it comes from nowhere. The residual use of *-ey* in its spelling is discussed at **-ey**. Dictionaries usually spell its derivatives as *fogyish* and *fogyism*, though they too are subject to the variation between *-y* and *-ey*.

folk or **folks** These words diverge in both style and meaning. **Folks** has a warm informality to it, partly from its use to refer to one's own relatives (*the folks at home*), but also when addressing an audience, as in *Hi folks*. **Folk** is the neutral term for an identifiable community of people, e.g. *rural folk*, *literary folk*, and is usually modified by an adjective, as in those examples. The examples also show that it can be applied as a synonym for "people", and as a nonsexist substitute for "men".

folk etymology Popular interpretation of a word's structure and meaning can alter its spelling in the course of time. Loanwords are particularly susceptible to **folk etymology**, as English speakers seek to regularise them in terms of words they are familiar with. So the word *amok* (borrowed from Malay) is reinterpreted and respelled by some as *amuck*, as if it was a composite of the medieval English prefix *a-* (as in *abroad*, *awry*) and the word *muck*. Like most *folk etymologies*, it only fits where it touches and makes little sense of the word. Obsolete elements of English are also subject to **folk etymology**. Thus *bridegroom* suggests a spurious connection with horses, which comes from using *groom* instead of the unfamiliar *gome* as its second element. (*Gome* was an alternative word for "man" in early English.) *Folk etymologies* are by definition not true etymologies. (See further under **etymology**.)

foment or **ferment** See ferment.

font or **fount** Two different words lurk behind these spellings:
1 *fo(u)nt* meaning "fountain, source of water/inspiration"
2 *fo(u)nt* meaning "repository or repertoire of typefaces".

For the first and older word, derived from the Latin *fons* "fountain, spring", the different spellings correlate with different applications. **Font** is the spelling used in the Christian church, as in *baptismal font* (the vessel which contains the water used in baptisms and christenings.) The spelling **fount** survives in poetic diction as a synonym for *fountain*, and in more general use as a figurative word for "source", as in *fount of wisdom*.

The second word, when for a set of printing type, is modeled on the French *fonte* from *fondre* meaning "cast or found (a metal)". It was spelled *font*, *fond* and even *fund* in the seventeenth century, but then became confused with the first word **font/fount**. As often, the more radical spelling **font** crossed the Atlantic to become the standard term among printers in North America, while **fount** consolidated its position in Britain. Australian printers—in spite of the

British legacy—also use **font** (see Australian Government *Style Manual* (1988));
and it's the only form used for the choice of typefaces in computer programs.

foolscap This imperial paper size (13½ × 17 inches or 337 × 206 mm) was
long known by its distinctive watermark: that of a jester's cap with bells. Its
origins are rather obscure, and the traditions that link it with Caxton in the
fifteenth century and Sir John Spielman, the sixteenth century papermaker,
cannot be confirmed. The earliest hard evidence of the foolscap watermark is
in a seventeenth century copy of Rushworth's *Historical Collections*, kept in
the British Museum. The enigma of its origin made it a topic of speculation,
and partisan rumor had it that the fool's cap was substituted for the royal coat
of arms during the Rump Parliament (1648–53), on the paper used to record
the daily records of the House.

footnotes See **referencing**.

footy or **footie** See under **-ie/-y**.

for While this is one of the commonest prepositions, its role as a conjunction is
declining. Nowadays it yields to *because* and *since* to express reasons and
causes. It could have been replaced by either of them in the following sentence:
They missed the opening for it had been difficult to park the car.
Apart from its role as a subordinating conjunction, **for** was once more widely
used like a coordinator, alongside other conjunctions:
For when she called the maid, there was no answer ...
This usage now seems rather literary.

Note that some older grammar books class **for** as a full coordinating
conjunction, even though unlike others (*and, but* etc.) it does not allow deletion
of a repeated subject:
He came by bike and was late.
He came by bike but was late.
He came by bike for (he) was late.
(See further under **conjunctions**.)

forbade or **forbad** The first of these **forbade** is the preferred form for the past
tense of *forbid* in all modern dictionaries, and it's unquestionably more common
in contemporary English databases. This is all the more remarkable when one
notes the numerous other spellings used in the course of centuries. The *Oxford
Dictionary* gave preference to **forbad**, which had some merit in terms of its
correspondence with *forbid*, and with the pronunciation.

Note also the strong preference for *forbidden* as the past participle, in phrases
such as:
They had forbidden the students to leave.
The use of *forbid* in such contexts seems a little old-fashioned, if not archaic,
as *Webster's* suggests.
Compare **bid**.

forbear or **forebear** See under **fore-/for-**.

force de frappe This French phrase, borrowed only this century, is often translated as "(a) strike force". Though it can be applied almost literally to guerilla and commando units, the expression has gained world attention as a reference to nuclear capability, and especially the French insistence on their need for an independent nuclear strike force—the development of which impinges most closely on the Pacific region.

Yet even a nuclear **force de frappe** may be less powerful than the so-called *force majeure*, which in traditional legal French meant "a superior force". The concept itself was borrowed from Roman law, where it meant what we now call an "act of God". In modern contract law it covers any one of a set of natural or man-made forces (flood or hurricane as well as strikes, lockouts or a go-slow on the wharf), which may prevent the fulfillment of the contract. There, and in general usage, it implies a force over which the parties referred to have no control.

forceful or **forcible** Should it be *a forceful reminder*, or *a forcible reminder*?

Both these words involve force, but their implications are somewhat different. **Forcible** suggests that either sheer physical force or some other inescapable factor was felt or brought to bear on the situation, particularly when some other means might have been expected. The *forcible removal* of interjectors from a meeting implies that the strong arm of the law was exerted against them, and a *forcible reminder* is one which expresses itself through physical circumstances, not the spoken word itself.

Forceful just implies that noticeable energy is or was used in an action or activity, to maximise its impact. It can be physical energy, as in *a forceful blow*, but very often it is verbal and rhetorical, as in *a forceful argument* and *a forceful reminder*.

forceps For the plural of this word, see under **biceps**.

fore-/for- These two Old English prefixes have quite independent meanings, though they are sometimes mistaken for each other. Nowadays **fore-** "ahead, before" is much more familiar than **for-** "against, utterly". **Fore-** operates in numerous words expressing priority in time or position:

forearm forecast forefather forefront foreground
foreleg foreman forename foresee foreshadow forestall
foretaste foretell forethought forewarn

For- is fossilised in just a handful of words, including *forbid, forget, forgive* and *forsake*.

The difference between **fore-** and **for-** is most crucial in pairs such as:

forebear	"ancestor"	and	*forbear*	"hold back"
forego	"go before"		*forgo*	"do without"

Confusion within these pairs means that *forbear* is also used for "ancestor", and *forego* for "do without", and dictionaries recognise them as alternative spellings. Though it might seem preferable to keep the spellings apart, this doubling up is less problematic than one might expect. The two meanings of *forbear* are distinguished by their grammar, one being a noun, the other a verb. And *forgo* can be spelled *forego* with little chance of misunderstanding, since *forego* "go before" is very rare as an active verb, and mostly survives in expressions like *foregone conclusion.*

Note also the difference between *foreword*, a name for the introductory statement printed at the front of a book, and *forward* meaning "in an onward direction". For the distinction drawn between *foreword* and *preface*, see **preface.**

foreign names Foreign placenames are discussed under **geographical names**; foreign personal names in **capitals** section 1; and foreign titles under **forms of address.**

forename or **first name** See **first name.**

forestallment or **forestalment** The first spelling **forestallment** is definitely preferable, now that *forestall* is everywhere the standard spelling for the verb. Yet **forestalment** is still given as the primary spelling for the noun in British and Australian dictionaries, endorsed by the *Oxford Dictionary* in spite of its fewer citations. It represents a disused spelling of the verb *forestal* (see further under **single for double**).

Compare **installment.**

foreword or **forward** For the distinction between these, see under **fore-/for-.**

For the difference between a *foreword* and a *preface*, see under **preface.**

forgo or **forego** See under **fore-/for-.**

formal words A formal choice of words elevates the style of our discourse, as when the sign says *PROCEED WITH CAUTION* rather than *DRIVE CAREFULLY*, or when a public service administrator is said to *oversight* a matter, rather than "keep an eye on it". Formal language sets itself above both standard and colloquial English. It lends dignity, weight and authority to a message, and is used by individuals and institutions for that reason.

Formal words tend to put verbal distance between the people communicating, which may or may not be appropriate to the situation. With serious subjects such as religion or law, most people allow that formal language is somehow right, and would feel that a preacher or judge who relied heavily on colloquialisms was behaving unprofessionally. But those who use formal language in ordinary situations are likely to be seen as pretentious and unsympathetic to their audience. This is often an issue in business or institutional letter writing, where the writer must strike a balance between the need to communicate with dignity and seriousness, and the need to speak as pleasantly and directly as possible to the reader. Fortunately English has ample resources to provide for many styles and levels of communication.

(See further under **colloquialisms** and **standard English**.)

former and **latter** These words allow writers to refer back systematically to the first and then the second member of a previously mentioned pair of items or persons:

Hawke survived longer as prime minister than either of his immediate predecessors, Fraser and Whitlam. (The former served for seven years, the latter for only three.) Hawke was at the helm for more than a decade.

As the example shows, **former** refers to the first of the pair, **latter** to the second, and they neatly pinpoint the two people mentioned. Some cautions are in order, however:

1 Like pronouns, **former** and **latter** depend on words that have gone before for their specifics. Those antecedents should not be too far away or readers will have to search for them.

2 Because they identify the members of a pair, **former** and **latter** cannot be used in reference to a larger set of items. Instead, *first, second, third respectively* (etc.) should be used. (See further under **respectfully** or **respectively**.)

3 Some authorities argue that **latter** should not be used to refer back to a single preceding item, and that the ordinary pronouns such as *it* and *that* are available for that purpose. But **latter** draws much more attention to itself than *it* etc., and so is a useful device in longer sentences and denser discussion. Provided its antecedent is clear (as with any pronoun), there's no reason to proscribe this usage.

forms of address In spite of the trend towards informality, forms of address are still important in letter writing. Choices have always to be made for the envelope, and within the letter itself (in and above the salutation) for business and institutional correspondence. (See Appendix VII for the standard formats for letters.)

For both the envelope and the internal address above the salutation, it's a matter of using the correct title or honorific. The salutation itself involves some further considerations, according to whether we know the addressee or not. Let's deal with each in turn.

1 For envelopes, and the internal address of a business letter, it's a matter of selecting a title appropriate to the addressee's qualifications, gender, and in some cases, marital status and nationality. In the English-speaking world, the choice is from among the following:

• *Dr* for medical practitioners (except surgeons), and holders of university doctorates, *PhD, DSc, DLitt* etc.

- *Professor* for university professors
- *The Honorable Mr Justice* for judges
- *Captain/Major/Lieutenant* etc. for members of the armed forces
- *Reverend* for ministers of most branches of the Christian church, including the Protestant, Catholic and Orthodox. (For the combination of *Reverend* with other names, see **names** section 2.)
- *Rabbi* for Jewish priests
- *Senator* for members of the federal upper house
- *Sir* for holders of knighthoods
- *Dame* for women who have been made Dame of the Order of Australia, Dame of the British Empire, or admitted to certain other orders of chivalry (see **Order of Australia**)
- *Lady* for the wives of those knighted
- *Mr* for men not included in any of the above groups
- *Mrs* for married women not included in any of the above groups
- *Ms* for women who prefer a title which does not express marital status
- *Miss* an older title for unmarried women, and for young girls
- *Master* an older title for young boys, little used nowadays

For the use of *Messrs* see **plurals** section 3; for **Esq**, see under that heading.

Note that the convention of addressing a married woman by her husband's name or initials (as Mrs J(ohn) Evans) is disappearing, except in the most formal documents. (This once applied to a widow as well as a married woman, and served to distinguish both from a divorcee who used her own forename and initial. The convention is no longer observed.) On envelopes however, married women are still usually addressed jointly with their husbands, as in *Mr and Mrs J(ohn) Evans*. The use of *Mr J. and Mrs P. Evans* on envelopes is not yet widespread.

When addressing Europeans, the terms corresponding to *Mr* and *Mrs/Ms* are:

(French)	*Monsieur*	*Madame*
(Dutch)	*Meneer/Mijnheer*	*Mevrouw*
(German)	*Herr*	*Frau*
(Italian)	*Signor*	*Signora*
(Spanish)	*Señor*	*Señora*

When addressing Asians, they are:

(Burmese)	*U*	*Daw*
(India—Hindi)	*Shri*	*Shrimati*
—Sikh)	*Sardar*	*Sardarni*
(Laos)	*Thao*	*Nang*
(Malaysia)	*Encik*	*Puan*
(Thailand)	*Nai*	*Nang*

Note that for Chinese, Filipino, Indonesian and Sri Lankan people, the titles of *Mr*, *Mrs*, *Ms* and *Miss* should be used.

For more details, see *Naming Systems of Ethnic Groups* (1990).

2 The salutation in a business or institutional letter is no longer a predictable *Dear Sir*. Nowadays the salutation is expected to establish an appropriate relationship with the reader, and usually reflects their degree of acquaintance. If the correspondents are at all acquainted, it's likely that first names will be used in the salutation: *Dear John, Dear Helen*. If however the correspondents are not already acquainted, or if the recipient of the letter is unknown, there are a number of options.

- If only the recipient's name is known, it's usual to use *Dear Mr Brown* or *Dear M(r)s Brown*, depending on gender. (The choice between *Mrs* and *Ms* in this situation is delicate. Not all women like to be addressed as *Ms*; and yet with *Mrs* you would be implying that the surname following was her married name. See further under **Miss, Mrs** or **Ms**.) If the preferred title is not known, *Dear Patricia Brown* is increasingly used as a semiformal salutation.

- If only surname and an initial are known, and the gender of the recipient is unknown, the alternatives are to use *Dear P. Brown*, or *Dear Mr/Mrs/Ms Brown*.

- If only the gender of the recipient is known, it's still possible to use *Dear Sir* or *Dear Madam*, though they set up a rather formal tone for the letter.

- If neither gender nor name of the recipient are known, the options are to use *Dear Sir/Madam*, or else some relevant job or role title, such as *Dear Manager, Dear Teacher, Dear Customer*.

- If the letter is written to a company rather than a particular individual within it, there are two possibilities: (1) to use *Dear Jeffries Pty Ltd* as the salutation, or (2) just the company name without a preliminary "Dear". The second is often appropriate.

For further details, see under **first name**, **letter writing** and **names**, and also letter formats in Appendix VII.

formula For the plural of this word, see under **-a** section 1.

fornix For the plural of this word see **-x** section 3.

forum For the plural, see under **-um**.

forward The distinction between **forward** and **foreword** is discussed under **fore-/for-**.
For the choice between **forward** and **forwards** see under **-ward**.

founder or **flounder** See flounder.

fount or **font** See font.

four, fourteen and **forty** The inconsistency in the spelling of these words is a headache for many writers. The spelling of **four** naturally helps to distinguish it from its homonyms *for* and *fore*. To have it also in **fourteen** but not in **forty** seems perverse, especially when records show that it was spelled "fourty" in earlier times, and was only displaced by **forty** in the eighteenth century. The British *fortnight* (= two weeks) shows the same spelling adjustment, since it's a telescoping of "fourteen nights".

four-letter words This is a cover term for the group of swear words which refer to intimate bodily parts and functions, especially *fuck*, *shit* and *cunt*. For some people, *piss*, *frig*, *arse* and *turd* might be added to the group, though for others the uses of those words are more diverse (not necessarily associated with swearing and offensive language), and so they do not belong to the core group. Having four letters is not essential to being a "four-letter word", in spite of all the examples so far, and so *prick* could be included because it does represent a body part and is regularly used in offensive references to other people. Those seem to be the defining characteristics of the group, and serve to distinguish them from other general-purpose swear words, such as *bloody* and *bugger*.

Because four-letter words are taboo in many contexts, in printed texts they have traditionally been replaced by a set of asterisks, or hinted at by use of their first letter only, followed by a line or three spaces. Other strategies involve using a substitute word which begins with the same sound, such as *sugar* or *shoot* for *shit* (sometimes called *euphemistic dysphemisms*.) (See further under **euphemisms**, **swear words** and **taboo words**.)

fractious or **factious** See **factious**.

fragrant or **flagrant** See **flagrant**.

franchise For the spelling see **-ise/-ize**; for the form and meaning, see **disfranchise**.

frangipani or **frangipane** The first spelling **frangipani** applies to a small tree whose strongly scented flowers perfume the suburban gardens of Sydney and Brisbane. The plant is believed to take its name from the sixteenth century Marquis of Frangipani of Rome, who created a famous perfume for gloves. The word is sometimes spelled *frangipanni* or **frangipane**.

Frangipane is also the word for a pastry tart filled with cream, almonds and sugar. The *Larousse Gastronomique* (1984) associates it with the first word, and the fact that the Marquis's perfume was based on bitter almonds. But other etymologists connect the gastronomic word with *franchipane*, an old term for "coagulated milk", or more literally "French bread".

-freak See under **-head**.

-free This works like an adjectival suffix, to highlight the absence of something undesirable in a commodity or medium:

> *duty-free goods   gender-free language   lead-free petrol   nuclear-free zone*
> *rent-free accommodation   trouble-free run*

The regular hyphen in these words suggests that **-free** is not yet a fully established suffix. Yet that status cannot be far off, given that it forms new words so easily. Already it can be seen as complementing *-less*, the suffix long used in words which emphasise the absence of something desirable, such as *graceless, hopeless, shapeless*. (See further under **-less**.)

frenchification French culture has always been held in special respect by the English, and innumerable French words and phrases have been borrowed over the centuries. Apart from expressing things for which there was no suitable English word, French expressions often seemed to have a certain something about them, a ''je ne sais quoi'' which recommended them to the user.

Because the Frenchness of such borrowings is part of their value, unusual features of their spelling and pronunciation may be consciously maintained long after they might naturally have been assimilated to conform with ordinary English words. So *ballet*, as part of high culture, has kept its French pronunciation, whereas *bullet*, borrowed in the same century, has become fully anglicised. The desire to keep French loanwords looking French accounts for the preservation and even extension of their accents. So *crèche* and *crème* are often given circumflexes in English, where in French they have grave accents. Other words acquire accents in English which they never have in French: *châlet, compôte, côterie* and *toupée* (a refashioning of French *toupet*).

This habit of making loanwords more French than the French is also seen in the English addition of an *-e* to *boulevarde, caviare, chaperone* and others, and in the reversing of earlier anglicised spellings. So the frenchified *cheque* and *chequer* were superimposed on the earlier *check* and *checker*, and *omelet* was remade as *omelette*. Borrowings from classical sources (Greek and Latin) were also remade according to French models, as in the case of *program* (respelled as *programme*), *inquire* (as *enquire*), and *honor, labor* etc. confirmed as *honour, labour* etc. But the preference for French spellings has always been stronger in Britain than in the USA, and Australians are divided over them.

frescoes or **frescos** See under **-o**.

fresher or **freshman** In Australia the term **fresher** refers to a university student in his or her first year, just as **freshman** does in North America. However **fresher** is not institutionalised in the same way, and is mostly used by non-first-year students as a way of identifying those who are a target for orientation or initiation. In North America the term **freshman** is used by students and administrators alike, as part of a set used to identify students in each of the four years of the standard college program:

freshman	first year
sophomore	second year
junior	third year
senior	fourth year

In Australia the only term with which **fresher** is occasionally contrasted is *freshette* ''a female first-year student''. But **fresher** is also widely used for both male and female novices at university.

fridge or **frig** When you want to reduce *refrigerator* to a word of one syllable, **fridge** is a good deal more reliable than **frig**, though dictionaries will offer you both. **Fridge** not only registers the "j" sound unambiguously, but also avoids the risk of a double entendre (see **four-letter words**). Why not *frige*, you might ask. It isn't a recognised alternative, perhaps because it suggests a long vowel before the "j" sound, as in *oblige*. The manufacturer who chose *frij* for the name of his portable icebag was up against the same problem, but his distinctive spelling looks distinctly un-English.

frizz or **friz** Dictionaries all prefer the spelling **frizz** when referring to the making of a tightly curled hairstyle, while recognising **friz** as a secondary alternative. The rare homonym **frizz** meaning "fry", listed in the *Oxford* and *Webster's* dictionaries, only has the one spelling.

frolic For the spelling of this word when it's used as a verb, see **-c/-ck-**.

front matter See prelims.

fueled or **fuelled** See under **-l/-ll-**.

-ful This suffix has two functions: to create adjectives, and a special group of nouns.
It forms adjectives primarily out of abstract nouns:
beautiful blissful careful delightful doubtful fearful
graceful hopeful pitiful plentiful powerful sinful successful
thoughtful wonderful wrongful
Yet the stem in some of those words could also be construed as a verb, and in fact a few **-ful** words could only be based on verbs, e.g. *forgetful*, *thankful* and *wakeful*.
The special group of nouns created with **-ful** are expressions for measures of volume:
armful bucketful cupful handful mouthful plateful spoonful
These words function as compound nouns, and so their plurals are:
armfuls (of hay) *cupfuls* (of water) *spoonfuls* (of sugar)
According to an older tradition, their plurals should be *armsful*, *cupsful* etc., because their internal grammar was noun + adjective and the noun should bear the plural marker. But they have long been fully integrated compounds, and "good modern usage" (according to the *Oxford Dictionary*) sanctions *armfuls*, *cupfuls* etc.

fulcrum The plural of this word is discussed under **-um**.

fulfill or **fulfil** The first of these spellings is standard in the USA, the second in Britain. In Australia both are used, with 4 instances of **fulfill** and 9 of **fulfil** in the ACE corpus, and the *Macquarie Dictionary* (1991) gives them equal status. **Fulfill** is easier and more consistent, given the sense connection with *fill* in the second syllable, and the fact that double *l* is always used in *fulfilled* and *fulfilling*. The same considerations apply in choosing between *fulfillment* and *fulfilment.* The variation between the two spellings is a legacy of the more general problem of final *l*. (See further under **single for double**.)

full stop The most frequent of all punctuation marks is the **full stop**, its usual name in Australia and Britain. Among British editors and printers it's termed the *full point* (see *Hart's Rules* and *Copy-editing*): while in the USA and Canada it goes by the name **period**.

During the last three centuries, the **full stop** has acquired three major areas of activity:
- in marking the end of a sentence
- in marking abbreviated words
- in punctuating numbers and dates

We will deal with each in turn.

1 *The **full stop** in sentences. Full stops* are used at the end of most types of sentences, whether they are grammatically complete or fragments. The **full stop** gives way to an exclamation mark when the utterance it marks is intended by the writer to have exclamatory value (see **exclamations**). The **full stop** gives way to a question mark if the sentence is a *direct* question:

Why don't you take it?

But in indirect questions, and questions which function as requests or invitations to do something, a simple **full stop** is still used.

They asked why I didn't take it.
They asked why didn't I take it.
Do you mind taking it.

On where to place the final **full stop** of a quoted or parenthetical sentence, see **quotation marks** section 3c, and **brackets** section 3.

Note that *full stops* do not appear in headlines, captions or headings, although some editors use *full stops* with headings that run over on to a second line. *Full stops* are not used in the stub or column headings in tables, nor in vertical lists. (See further under **tables** and **lists**.)

2 *The **full stop*** in words. In the past *full stops* have been the means of marking abbreviated words or sets of them, in both upper and lower case. Current trends are towards removing them from upper case abbreviations, and increasingly when giving people's initials (see **names** section 3). The use of *full stops* with lower case abbreviations is an area of great variability (see **abbreviations** section 1).

Note that *full stops* are never used for *SI units* (see **abbreviations** section 3).

3 *The **full stop*** with numbers and dates. *Full stops* serve as a separating device among figures:

a) in lists. Successive numbers or enumerating letters are often accompanied by full stops:

1. 2. 3. or *1a. 2a. 3a.* or *1.a. 2.a. 3.a.*

Brackets *1) 2) 3)* are an alternative device, and can be usefully combined with full stops, especially when there are several subdivisional systems of numbering: *1.a.(i)*, *1.a.(ii).* (For the use of single or paired brackets, see **brackets** section 1.) Note that while brackets are effective with lower case roman numbers, they are best avoided with roman capitals because of possible misreading. Full stops are preferable there: *1.(a) I.*

b) in dates and times of day:
   26.4.89   7.30 pm

c) in sums of money
   $24.20 $1.32

d) as the decimal point:
   0.08 %   3.1417

(See further under **numbers** and **number style**.)

   Note that a raised **full stop** (rather than the normal low **full stop**) may be used for items covered under (b), (c) and (d).

fullness or **fulness**   All modern dictionaries give first preference to **fullness**. It was backed by the *Oxford Dictionary* on grounds of analogy, in spite of the observed frequency of **fulness** in the nineteenth century. That principled stand has helped to resolve one of the several points on which English has vacillated between single and double *l*. (See further under **single for double**.)

-fuls   See under **-ful**.

fungus or **fungous**   The first of these is a noun, the second an adjective. Compare: *Fungus was growing everywhere* with *a fungous growth*. **Fungus**, borrowed straight from Latin, still keeps its Latin plural *fungi* in botanical discourse, though *funguses* is common in nontechnical usage. (See **-us** section 1.)

   For other *-us/-ous* pairs, see **-ous**.

furor or **furore**   The older form of this word is **furor**, which is the standard spelling in the USA. It was replaced in nineteenth century Britain by the Italian **furore**, and a three-syllabled pronunciation developed with it. Australian English, according to the *Macquarie Dictionary*, seems to have a compromise by using the British spelling and the (two-syllabled) American pronunciation—though the spelling **furor** is also used.

further or **farther,** and **furthest** or **farthest**   The existence of these two has tempted people to differentiate between them—hence the tradition that **farther** related to distance in space or time, and **further** to figurative extensions of it. However the *Oxford Dictionary* commented that nineteenth century usage on this point was often arbitrary; and both are now freely used in referring to "spatial, temporal or metaphorical distance", according to *Webster's English Usage* (1989). Dictionaries generally give both words as meaning "additional(ly)", although on that point *Webster's* shows that **further** is squeezing the other one out. The authorities everywhere agree that only **further** can be used as a conjunct equivalent to "moreover", and as a verb.

   Any distinctions between **further** and **farther** are of more interest in the USA and Britain, where both are still in use. According to the evidence of

English databases, **further** outnumbers **farther** in the ratio of 7:1 in American English, compared with 17:1 in British English. But in Australian English **farther** is quite rare: in the ACE corpus it occurred twice against 299 instances of **further**. The low frequency of **farther** gives it formal and literary connotations, as noted in some dictionaries.

The presence of *far* in **farther** has no doubt helped the idea that it relates to sheer distance, as well as providing a folk etymology for the word, as the comparative of *far*. In fact **farther** is simply a pronunciation variant of **further**, dating from the fifteenth century, along with others which respelled it with an *e, i, o* or *y*. **Further** itself seems to be a comparative form of the word *forth*.

Note that the superlative forms **furthest** and **farthest** are used much less often than **further** and **farther**, but still the same relationship holds between them in Australian English. **Furthest** comes out ahead of **farthest** (3:1) in the Australian ACE corpus.

fused participle For the choice between:
>   *They heard him singing* and *They heard his singing*
see under **gerund**.

future tense English, like other Germanic languages, has no special suffix to add to its verbs to make the future tense. Instead it uses auxiliary verbs, or the present tense along with some other indicator of futurity. The best known auxiliaries are: *will*, as in *you will receive* and *shall* as in *I shall retire*. (For the traditional differences between those two, see **shall**.)

Other auxiliaries used to indicate futurity are:
>   *be going to   be to   be about to   be on the point of*
The first of these (*I am going to*) is the most straightforward with no particular implications that limit its use. The second (*I am to*) suggests that the projected event is the result of an arrangement made by other parties, and not something to decide for oneself. The last two (*I am about to*/*I am on the point of*) show that the projected event is imminent, and not just at some undetermined time in the future. The sense of imminence and immediacy is stronger with *on the point of* than with *about to*.

In certain circumstances, the plain present tense can be used to express futurity. An accompanying adverb (or adverbial phrase) which expresses future time is sufficient in a simple statement, and used very often in conversation:
>   *They come tomorrow.*
>   *My course finishes in two weeks time.*
In complex sentences (see **clauses** section 3), a plain present tense can be used to express future in the subordinate clause, provided that the main clause has one of the future auxiliaries:
>   *I'm going to wear a wig if you do.*
>   *Next year we'll celebrate when the yachts arrive.*

-fy See -ify.

G

gabardine or **gaberdine** Both spellings go back to the sixteenth century, when they were alternatives for a loose-fitting overgarment, sometimes called a "smock", sometimes a "cloak". But **gabardine** in particular is associated with the closely woven twill fabric, as documented in all the *Oxford Dictionary*'s citations for the word since the beginning of the twentieth century. American dictionaries reflect the distinction, preferring **gabardine** for the modern fabric, and **gaberdine** for the historical garment—while acknowledging that the spellings may be interchanged. The *Macquarie Dictionary* (1991) makes the spellings equal for both meanings. But with the *Oxford*'s citations running so strongly in favor of **gabardine** for the only current meaning, it seems likely to displace the other spelling.

The word itself is a curiosity. It has no relatives in English to provide analogies, and to pin the spelling down. Its French antecedents *gauvardine* and *galvardine* lend support to **gabardine**, and also show how scholars link it with the old German word *wallevart* "pilgrimage". They suggest that the cloak of **gabardine** was the uniform of pilgrims on their travels. The spelling of the word has been as mobile as those who wore it.

gaff and **gaffe** These spellings represent several different words—two of which are derived ultimately from a Celtic word for "boathook", which appeared in medieval French and English as **gaffe**. It became **gaff** in modern English, but has kept much of the original meaning when it refers to the hooked pole used by fishermen for landing large fish. In another nautical use it refers to the spar on the upper edge of a fore-and-aft sail, as in a *gaff-rigged boat.*

In French meanwhile, **gaffe** continued to refer to a boathook, and it is from nautical accidents (French sailors getting hooked on their own gaffs) that the meaning of **gaffe** as "social blunder" is believed to derive. The idiom *make/ made a gaffe* came into English early this century, embodied in the French spelling.

Independent of all this is the slang word **gaff** found in *blow the gaff*, recorded from 1812 on. Its origins are obscure, although **gaff** in this context seems to reflect the meanings "cheat" or "trick" of a homonym in underworld language (see **flash language**). Yet an earlier form of the phrase: *blow the gab* shows its association with the *gift of the gab*, and with glib or specious talk. Some dictionaries suggest a link between *blow the gaff* and **gaffe** "social blunder", but this is anachronistic by the *Oxford Dictionary*'s record.

Note that the word *gaffer* for the chief electrician on a movie or TV set owes nothing to either **gaff** or **gaffe**. A contracted form of *godfather*, it earlier developed meanings of its own, including "old man" and "foreman".

Gagadu or **Kakadu** See under **Aboriginal names**.

gage or **gauge** See **gauge**.

galah This has been the standard spelling for Australia's rose-breasted cockatoo since the beginning of the twentieth century. Before then it had several spellings (*galar, galaa, gulah, gillar*) like other Aboriginal loanwords (see under **Aboriginal words**). It probably comes from the Yuwaalaraay language, used by Aborigines in northwestern NSW.

Galah is one of the few Aboriginal words to have acquired a figurative meaning in English. The first record of the word to mean "fool" is from 1938, more than seventy years after the ornithological use was documented. The extension is not fully explained, but the simile *mad as a gumtree full of galahs* suggests it has something to do with what happens when galahs get together.

Gallup or **gallop** As the *Gallup poll* becomes a household word, and the memory of its founder recedes—he was Dr George Gallup, of the American Institute of Public Opinion—it's likely that **Gallup** will lose its capital and become *gallup*, like many another eponymous word (see further under **eponyms**). The possibility of *gallup* being confused with **gallop** is then real enough, and even a folk etymology which explains the "gallop poll" as giving a runaway victory to one party or the other.

Note that the verb **gallop** simply becomes *galloped/galloping* or *galloper* when suffixes are added, in line with the broad rules of English spelling. (See further under **doubling of final consonant**.)

gamboled or **gambolled** See under **l/-ll-**.

gamey or **gamy** See under **-y/-ey**.

ganglion The plural of this word is discussed under **-on**.

gaol or **jail** For the choice between these spellings, see **jail**.

gaoler, jailer or **jailor** See **jailer**.

garrote, garrotte or **garotte** This word for an old Spanish method of execution has acquired a new use in referring to a mugging tactic whereby the victim is half strangled. The spelling **garrote** is given first preference in American dictionaries, while **garrotte** is preferred in Australian and British ones. The third spelling is also recognised, showing how unstable the word is. Of the three **garrote** is closest to the original Spanish verb *garrotear*. But like other loanwords with double consonants, it presents difficulties for English users (see further under **single for double**).

gas The verb forms of this word are quite regular in their spelling, as *gassed/ gassing*, with the final consonant doubled as in most monosyllabic words of this kind. (See **doubling of final consonant**.)

The noun plural is somewhat variable: usually *gases* but occasionally *gasses*, according to the largest American dictionaries, as well as *Collins*. The disinclination to use the regular *gasses* is perhaps a reflection of the unusual origins of **gas**, as a Dutch transliteration of the Greek word *chaos*.

gasoline or **gasolene** See under **-ine** final note.

gateaus or **gateaux** See under **-eau**.

gauge or **gage** These spellings have been used to differentiate two different words: **gauge** for "measure" or "measuring instrument", and **gage** for the noun or verb "pledge". But the first spelling gives many writers trouble because it is eccentric in terms of English letter–sound correspondence, and is in fact the only one of its kind. The spelling **gage** is a much more natural way to represent the sound of the word, whichever sense is intended, and was in fact used for both words in past centuries.

The distinction between **gauge** ("measure/r") and **gage** ("pledge") is nevertheless upheld in Australian, British and American dictionaries, though they do acknowledge the use of **gage** for **gauge**. The *Random House Dictionary* notes that **gage** is particularly used as the spelling for "measure/r" in technical contexts, and its firm foothold there may help to establish it more generally. Nowadays there's little need to preserve the two spellings, with the uses of **gage** ("pledge") shrinking and those of **gauge/gage** increasing with every new measuring device. The acceptance of **gage** for all such uses would rid English of one more of its anomalies.

Gaulish or **Gaullist** There are ancient and modern links with France in these words. The first relates to the original Celtic inhabitants of France, to their culture and language, whereas the second relates very specifically to the post-World War II policies of General de Gaulle. Both **Gaulish** and **Gaullist** are subsumed by *Gallic*, which can be applied to either the ancient or the modern culture of France.

gay Because the standard use of this word has changed dramatically since World War II, it needs careful handling. The older meaning of **gay** "lighthearted" is still there in the adverb *gaily* and the abstract noun *gaiety*, but the adjective **gay** now usually means "homosexual". In that sense it can be applied to both men and women, and so if one speaks of either *a gay young man* or *a gay young woman*, it is potentially a comment on their sexual orientation, whether or not so intended. When *gay* itself is used as a noun, it regularly means "a homosexual male", as in:

The gays and lesbians gathered for the mardi gras parade.

The abstract noun *gayness* also connotes homosexuality, though it was earlier just a synonym for *gaiety*.

This new meaning for **gay** seems in fact to have been around before World War II in American prison and underworld slang, as a reference in Ersine's 1935 *Underworld and Prison Slang* shows us. And British evidence from the nineteenth century shows that **gay** (as an adjective) had a slang role meaning "licentious or living by prostitution". To say that a woman was "living a gay life" was to imply that she was "no better than she ought to be".

Gay is not the only English word to develop alternative meanings in the course of time. If we intend to target the older sense ("lighthearted"), either that word or one of its near-synonyms in *elated, cheerful, merry, lighthearted* or *in high spirits* is more reliable, and avoids any possible double entendre.

gelatine or **gelatin** For general purposes, the first of these is the preferred spelling in Australia and Britain, the second in the USA. Note however that chemists make a deliberate distinction between *-ine* and *-in* in the naming of chemicals. (See further under **-ine/-in**.)

gender Style guides are still inclined to insist that **gender** is a grammatical term, as if it is not to be used in discussing the sexual/social roles of men and women. Dictionaries often reinforce this view, by labeling the use of **gender** to mean "sex" as colloquial, jocular or "loose".

Yet much very serious writing about male/female roles makes free use of the term **gender**. Some prefer it to using *sex*, with its inherent double entendre, while others use both terms, drawing distinctions between them. For some, *sex* is associated with individual differences, and **gender** with group ones; *sex* with biological differences and **gender** with social ones. Yet others use them to distinguish between physical/sexual identity and socially or culturally constructed identity. **Gender** appears both on its own, and built into compounds such as:

gender-bias gender-marked gender-neutral gender-specific

There can be little doubt that the word has established its place in this field of discourse.

1 *Grammatical **gender**.* In codifying languages grammarians have traditionally used the notion of "gender" in classifying nouns into groups. Where there are two types, the categories are labeled "masculine" and "feminine"; and "masculine", "feminine" and "neuter" (= neither masculine nor feminine) where there are three. But the classification has little to do with male or female. Words for inanimate things may be classed as "masculine" or "feminine", and what is masculine in one language may be feminine in the next: a cloud is masculine in French (*le nuage*) and feminine in German (*die Wolke*). "Masculine", "feminine" and "neuter" are just convenient labels for classes of nouns which take different forms of the definite article and of adjectives. In modern English there are no such classes of nouns. All nouns take the same definite article *the*, and the same forms of adjectives.

2 *Natural* **gender**. In English grammar we become conscious of gender in the third person singular pronouns, with *he, she, him, her, his* and *hers*. But here it's a matter of *natural (not grammatical) gender*, since the pronouns are applied according to the sex of the person being referred to. So *she* is used after a reference to "mother", and *he* after one to "father". In a language with full-blown *grammatical gender*, the pronoun for "she" would also be used after any "feminine" noun, and the one for "he" after "masculine" nouns.

Because the English pronouns are so firmly associated with *natural gender*, the traditional use of masculine forms to express generic human identity is now felt to be unfortunate and ambiguous, if not sexist. (See further under **he** and/or **she**.) Ideally English would have a *common gender* singular pronoun, one which could refer to either a male or female without identifying their sex. The pronoun *it* has only limited uses in references to animals and perhaps babies in scientific or impersonal contexts. This explains why *they*, the *common gender* plural pronoun, is increasingly being use in singular references (see **they**).

The quest for expressions which are common in gender or gender-free has also put the spotlight on the so-called *epicene* words of English, e.g. *athlete, patient, writer*. (See further under **epicene**.)

generalisations See under **induction**.

genitive This is the grammarians' name for what in English is often called the "possessive". It refers to the form of nouns which indicates a possessive or associative relationship with the following word. In modern English the genitive is shown by the presence of an apostrophe and a following *s*, if the noun is an ordinary singular one:

> *the child's bike   a lawyer's answer   the horse's mouth*
> *Thursday's program   Japan's building industry*

As those examples show, the English genitive covers a wide range of relationships, including possession, attribution and association, as well as location in time and space. The genitive often provides a neat expression for a more wordy paraphrase. Compare the following with the genitive phrases above:

> *the bike belonging to the child*
> *the answer of a lawyer*
> *the program for Thursday*
> *the building industry in Japan*

Note however that a genitive phrase with a verbal noun, such as *John's appointment* is potentially ambiguous; it could refer to the person whom John appointed, or to the fact that John himself was appointed. The first meaning with active use of the verb is sometimes called the *subjective genitive*, and the second where the verb is passive, the *objective genitive*. The same expression could also mean "an appointment made for John (at the dentist etc.)". The context should clarify which of the three meanings is meant.

With plural nouns, the genitive is usually shown by the apostrophe alone, as in *the grammarians' term*. For more about the use of apostrophes with plural nouns, proper names, and words ending in *s*, see under **apostrophes**.

Note that although the English pronouns have special genitive forms, none of them take apostrophes:

my   your   his   her   its   our   their

Of those, *its* is the one to note particularly. (See **its** or **it's**.)

genius Like many words ending in *-us*, this is a Latin loanword which raises questions about its plural forms in English (see **-us** section 1). The English plural *geniuses* is used with the more common meaning of the word: "an unusually gifted and brilliant person". The plural *genii* is only used in reference to mythical spirits, as in *the genii of the forest*.

genre As its French pronunciation suggests, this is a relative newcomer to English. It is in fact a latter-day borrowing of the word which once gave us *gender*; and as *gender* once did, **genre** essentially means "type". In English it has almost always been associated with types of artistic creation—with works of literature and art in the late eighteenth century, and music as well as film and photography in the twentieth century. In the visual arts, *genre painting* has acquired the specific meaning of "art which depicts scenes of everyday life".

In reference to writing, the term **genre** is variously used. At the highest level, it identifies the archetypal forms of composition, such as poetry, drama and novel. But it's also used to broadly identify the purpose of a work, i.e. as comedy or tragedy, and its substance: fiction or nonfiction. Within any of those categories, **genre** can identify subgroups, such as biography, essays, letters and journalism within nonfiction; and within, say, journalism the subgroups of news articles, editorials and reviews. At these lower levels, individual *genres* still differ in form, purpose and style.

genteelism The term **genteelism** is applied by Fowler and others to expressions which are careful substitutes for common everyday words. So *obtain* is a genteelism for *get*, and *purchase* for *buy*. Genteelisms are typically longer words of French or Latin origin, and associated with more formal styles of communication. They are gentle euphemisms—not intended to disguise, but to lend a touch of class to a plain reference.

No-one would challenge a genteelism which is used in deference to the feelings of others. But when they become the staple of bureaucratic and institutional prose, it's time to rise in ungenteel revolution and campaign against them. (See further under **gobbledygook** and **Plain English**.)

genuflexion or **genuflection** See under -ction/-xion.

genus The plural of this may be *genuses* or *genera*. (See under **-us** section 3.)

geographic or **geographical** As with other *-ic/-ical* pairs, the longer form **geographical** enjoys more widespread use than the alternative **geographic**. The latter is only familiar because of its use in magazine titles, such as *National Geographic* and *Australian Geographic*. (See further under **-ic/-ical**.)

geographical names. Writing geographical names raises four kinds of issues:
- how to capitalise them
- how to abbreviate them
- whether to use anglicised or local forms of foreign placenames
- how to check placenames with variable elements

For the use of apostrophes in placenames, see under **apostrophes**.

1 *Capitalising* **geographical names**. Capital letters are used on all the nouns and adjectives that make up a proper geographical name:

> *Darling River Gulf of Carpentaria Mount Bogong Simpson Desert*
> *Cradle Mountain Torres Strait Lake Eyre the Great Dividing Range*
> *Whitsunday Island Cape York Peninsula*

Geographical names like these usually consist of a specific word or words, and a generic word. So *Darling* is specific and *River* generic. The order of the components is mostly fixed by convention. In North America *River* is usually the second element (*Colorado River, Hudson River*) whereas in Britain and Europe it's often the first (*River Thames, River Rhine*). With this dual tradition, it's not surprising that rivers in other parts of the world may be named either way in English writing: either the *Ganges River* or the *River Ganges*. So whether *River* comes first or second, it can be part of the official name, and therefore needs a capital letter.

But when the geographical reference is clearly a descriptive phrase, not an official name, the generic element is left without a capital:

> *the Canberra lake   the South Australian desert*

Note also that the generic component has no capital letter when it appears as an abbreviated, second reference, or when it is pluralised in a phrase which puts two or more geographical names together: *Murray and Murrumbidgee rivers*. (See further under **capital letters** sections 1c and 3.)

2 *Abbreviating* **geographical names**. There are standard abbreviations for the generic parts of geographical names, to be used when space is at a premium (for instance on maps), but not normally in running text:

C for	*cape*	*Pen* for	*peninsula*
G	*gulf*	*Pt*	*point*
I or *Is*	*island*	*R*	*river*
L	*lake*	*Ra*	*range*
Mt	*mount(ain)*	*Str*	*strait*

Note that none of these abbreviations need take a full stop, since all involve capital letters (see **abbreviations** section 1).

There are also standard abbreviations for whole geographical names, such as:
HK   NZ   UK   USA
Within particular continents, abbreviations are available for individual states or countries—for use in lists and tabular material, or for car registration plates and distribution of mail. Those approved by Australia Post are:
ACT NSW NT QLD SA TAS VIC WA
Americans now have two-letter abbreviations for all 51 states (see Chicago *Manual of Style* (1981)). Once again, full stops are not used in them. In Europe such abbreviations are mostly a single letter, as in *F* for France, *D* for Germany etc.
For the abbreviation of compass points, see **capital letters** section 1c.

3 *Foreign placenames—in anglicised or local forms?* This is a vexed question in a postcolonial world, when foreign names are no longer preserved in their imperial form. Even in Europe, English-speakers are sometimes surprised to find that "Münich" is *München*, and that "Athens" is *Athinai* to those who live there—and beyond Europe the discrepancies are even more marked, with "Cairo" expressed as *Al Qahirah* and "Canton" as *Guangzhou*. It is a reminder that **geographical names** are a product of our culture, and not always in touch with developments in other parts of the world.

Political developments sometimes force us to accept changes in placenames, as when "St Petersburg" became *Leningrad* under the Russian communist regime, and when "Northern and Southern Rhodesia" marked their independence with the names *Zambia* and *Zimbabwe*. In other cases there's a diplomatic imperative to accept a different form of an old name. *Beijing* and *Sri Lanka* are simply local forms of the names we had as "Peking" and "Ceylon", but we need to update with them, to avoid seeming to be still in the colonial era.

The updating of our geographical nomenclature is helped by the ABC's Standing Committee on Spoken English. It not only checks the pronunciations of foreign names that occur in the news, but also the forms of those names. The lead it provides in this area helps to alert us to changes, and to familiarise us with them. When using the new names in writing, we may need to remind our readers of the older form in parentheses, alongside the new one, at least on first mention. The change of the "Gilbert Islands" into the *Kiribati* is not self-explanatory. But recognising such changes in foreign placenames should seem no stranger than accepting the fact that *Tasmania* is no longer "Van Diemen's Land".

4 *Placenames with variable elements.* The variable spellings of personal names e.g. *Phillip/Philip*, *Macleod/McLeod* are another detail to reckon with in placenames. The question of whether it should be *Stuart* or *Stewart* can only be resolved by referring to the Master Names File, prepared by the Commonwealth Department of Administrative Services and updated every January. The divergent spellings of Australian towns and suburbs are listed under **town names**.

geological eras The origins of our planet go back well over 4000 million years, with the evolution of plant and animal life from about 2500 million years ago. The history of human evolution occupies only a tiny fraction of the last one million years.

For the standard names used in geology and paleontology for the major phases of earth's evolution, see Appendix III.

geometric or **geometrical** The shorter form **geometric** has fewer uses nowadays, though it is enshrined in some fixed collocations such as *geometric spider* and the *Geometric Age* (of Greek culture). But English "Geometric" architecture has become **geometrical**, and in maths and science, as well as in ordinary usage, **geometrical** prevails.

german or **germane** These words refer to relationships, **german** to those of kin, as in *cousin german*, and **germane** to more abstract logical relationships, as in:

His answer was not germane to the question.

In older usage **germane** could be used in *cousin germane* as well, but this is now archaic. For more about *cousin german*, see under **cousins**.

Note that a link between *german(e)* and *German(y)* is unlikely. Most scholars believe that the name *Germany* is Celtic in origin, whereas *german(e)* derives from a Latin adjective meaning "having common roots".

Germany After World War II Germany was divided into two:

Federal Republic of Germany (BRD) = West Germany
(Bundesrepublik Deutschlands)
German Democratic Republic (DDR) = East Germany
(Deutsche Demokratische Republik)

The first was a member of NATO and the EEC, while the second was a member of the Warsaw Pact and Comecon. This division of Germany put Berlin into East Germany. It too was divided into a Western and an Eastern sector, and to mark the boundary between them, the Berlin Wall was erected in 1961. The breaching of the Berlin Wall in November 1989 marked the beginning of a new era, and strong pressures for reunification. The two halves were officially reunited in 1990, as the FRG (Federal Republic of Germany).

gerunds and **gerundives** Both these are terms borrowed from Latin grammar. In Latin the **gerund** was a verbal noun, and the **gerundive** an adjectival future passive participle which carried a sense of obligation or necessity. Our word *agenda* was a Latin **gerundive**, meaning literally "(things which) should be done".

English grammar has nothing quite like the Latin **gerundive**. Words formed with *-able* from verbs (such as *likable*) are as near as we come: they are passive, but do not carry the sense of obligation. We do however have equivalents to **gerunds** in the verbal nouns which end in *-ing*, as in:

Singing is my recreation.

Gerunds in English lead double lives, in that they can behave like nouns or verbs (or both). As nouns, they can be qualified by adjectives, articles etc., and/ or followed by dependent phrases.

My singing alarmed the dogs next door.
The singing of grand opera caused the trouble.

English **gerunds** also have the capacity of verbs to take subjects or objects, adverbs and adverbial phrases:

Singing grand opera was the problem, or rather, the dogs reacting to it.

Does the gerund require a possessive? The last example: *the dogs reacting to it* exemplifies a construction which has long been a bone of contention in English. Some insist that it should be made possessive: *the dogs' reacting to it*; and Fowler argued long and hard that without the possessive marker the construction (which he called the "fused participle") was "grammatically indefensible". As with many such issues, it goes back to the eighteenth century, when the form with the possessive was attacked and defended, most notably by Webster (of *Webster's Dictionary*), who claimed that it alone was "the genuine English idiom". Others then and now would argue that both constructions (with and without the possessive marker) have their place, because their meaning or emphasis is slightly different. Compare:

The dogs reacted to me singing.
The dogs reacted to my singing.

The first sentence focuses on the fact that I sang, whereas the second seems to imply that it was the way I sang which caused a reaction. Yet that difference intersects with matters of style. The choice of *my* makes the sentence rather formal, while the use of *me* is acceptable in all kinds of writing these days. Still there's a grammatical point to note: that *my* or other possessive pronouns are necessary when the **gerund** is the subject of the sentence, as in *My singing alarmed the dogs.* The use of *me* there sounds ungrammatical. But when the **gerund** is the object either construction can be used.

The *Comprehensive Grammar of English* (1985) and others provide us with quite satisfactory analysis of either construction; and *Webster's English Usage* (1989) shows the construction without the possessive has been used by speakers and writers for centuries. The issue turns out to be another of those linguistic fetishes which has generated more heat than light.

get, got and **gotten** Get is a common and useful verb, especially in informal spoken English. It is an easy synonym for many others, such as *obtain*, *receive*, *fetch*, *buy*, *take*, *arrive* and *become*. Apart from these meanings, it has a number of roles as an auxiliary, both in its present form **get**, and its past **got**. Let's deal with each in turn.

1 Get often works as a substitute for the verb *be* in passive constructions:

I'm getting married in the morning.

Compare *I shall be married in the morning*, which is much more formal in style.

Get is also used as a causative verb in:

You're getting your car cleaned for the occasion.

I'm getting him to do it.

Once again, the alternatives are somewhat formal:

You will have your car cleaned for the occasion.

I have prevailed on him to do it.

As the examples show, **get** is often used in interactive situations, and is suitable for interactive prose as well as written dialogue. The alternatives are less flexible in style and meaning, and best suited to impersonal and documentary writing.

2 Got also has auxiliary roles, both as the past of **get** in its passive and causative roles, and in its own right in structures like *has/have got to*, where it serves as an informal substitute for *must* or *ought to* (see further under **auxiliaries**). The *got to* construction is so familiar in speech that the words seem to coalesce, and are sometimes written as *gotta*. But that blended form is used only in casual dialogue: in other genres of writing the construction is always expressed in its full form.

3 Got serves as the past tense of **get** in all parts of the English-speaking world. It is also the one and only past participle for many in Australia, as well as for Britons at large. But for Americans and some Australians, there are two past participles: **got** and **gotten**, with separate roles. **Got** is the only one used when obligation or possession are being expressed, as in

You've got to come.

I've got a weekender in the mountains.

He hasn't got a chance.

But when it's a matter of becoming, achieving or acquiring, **gotten** is the form commonly used:

He had gotten angry.

They had gotten good results by combining the data.

She had gotten a new car since we last saw her.

Webster's English Usage (1989) notes a few exceptions, but those do represent the dominant patterns.

By all the evidence above, **get/got** is a versatile verb, and with its numerous roles it is the staple of daily communication. English databases of printed material show that it occurs much more often in fiction than in nonfiction, though there are ample examples in all 17 genres of the Australian ACE corpus. It is scarcest in the categories of religious, bureaucratic and academic writing— no doubt the genres which can least tolerate informality of style. This stylistic point is the one to make to novice writers about **get/got**: that it is a verb to avoid in writing which aims to be formal, not that it should be rooted out everywhere like a noxious weed.

gh This notorious pair of letters represents a bizarre range of sounds in English. At the start of a word, they simply stand for "g", as in *ghost* and *ghastly*. At the end of a word they never represent "g", and often no consonant at all. The **gh** has no sound in any of the following:

> *inveigh neigh sleigh weigh*
> *high sigh thigh*
> *bough plough sough*
> *dough furlough though*
> *through borough thorough*

In three other groups of words, **gh** represents "f":

> *laugh*
> *enough rough tough*
> *cough trough*

Given such bewildering possibilities, it's surprising how few words ending with **gh** have alternative spellings. *Plow* has indeed replaced *plough* in American English, though not in British or Australian English; and though *draft* has taken over from *draught* in the USA, it has some distance to go elsewhere (see further under **draft**). *Thru* is still considered rather informal (see **through**); and *donut* is only just recognised as a variant of *doughnut*.

ghetto The plural of this Italian loanword was once *ghetti*, but now the choice is between *ghettos* and *ghettoes*. *Ghettos* is the spelling given priority in Australian dictionaries, and is all that's needed. Yet *ghettoes* persists to show that the word has been in English a long time (since the seventeenth century). (See further under **-o**.)

gibber This string of letters gives Australians two words for the price of one. The first is the noun (or verb) meaning "rapid, unintelligible talk" and pronounced with a "j" sound, which it shares with the rest of the English-speaking world. It is believed to be an "echoic" word, i.e. one which originated as onomatopoeia. (See further under **onomatopoeia**.) Compare **barbaric**.

The second word, a noun meaning "stone" and pronounced with a "g" sound, is an Aboriginal loanword from the Dharuk language once used around Port Jackson. It can refer either to individual stones and boulders, or to a substantial outcrop of rock, as the familiar compounds show:

> *gibber plain* ("arid, flat land littered with large weathered stones")
> *gibber gunyah* ("a rock shelter or shallow cave")

gibe, gybe or **jibe** These spellings are shared by three different words:

1 taunt (noun or verb)
2 sudden shift in the setting of a fore-and-aft sail from one side to the other (verb or noun)
3 accord (verb), as in:
> *It didn't jibe with what I knew of him.*

The different spellings were used interchangeably in earlier centuries, but in a division of labor established by the *Oxford Dictionary*, **gibe** is associated with the meaning "taunt" and **gybe** with the nautical term—at least in Britain. This distinction is maintained by some Australians. The spelling **jibe** is applied to the third word "accord", only recently recognised in dictionaries outside North America, though *Oxford Dictionary* (1989) offers citations for it going back into the nineteenth century.

Yet in Australia, Britain and North America, **jibe** also serves as an alternative for the word "taunt", and is preferred by Americans and others for the nautical term. It is thus the most freely used of the three spellings, and if it does service for all three words, the contexts will always clarify the meaning. The nautical term has its own context of use, and the other two words (as verbs) are differentiated by the fact that in the sense "accord" **jibe** is normally followed by "with".

Note also the word *jive* meaning "make sense", as in *It doesn't jive, man.*

gilgai This Aboriginal word, borrowed from the Kamilaroi and Wiradhuri people, refers to the uneven surface of clay pan country, with alternating hollows, rims and mounds, caused by expansion and contraction of clay soil. Occasionally it's spelled as *gilgie*, but it then overlaps with the Aboriginal word for a yabby. (See further under **jilgie** or **gilgie**.)

gin Alternatives to this word for an Aboriginal woman are discussed under **lubra**.

gipsy or **gypsy** Dictionaries support both spellings more or less equally, though differing on which has priority. The *Macquarie Dictionary* (1991) presents the pair at **gipsy**, whereas *Collins* does it at **Gypsy** (with a capital letter marking it as an ethnic name). The major American dictionaries also go one each way. The *Oxford Dictionary* gave **gipsy** priority, and speculated that it had become the common spelling because it avoided a spelling with two *y*'s (see further under **dissimilation**). Fowler however voted for **gypsy** to preserve the connection with *Egypt*, and his voice seems to be reflected in database evidence, with **gypsy** substantially outnumbering **gipsy** in the British LOB corpus (4:2), as well as the Australian ACE corpus (14:1) and Brown (5:0).

The idea that *gipsies* came from Egypt is a popular myth, even though their name is indeed a clipped form of *Egyptian*. In fact they emigrated into Europe from northern India. Using the spelling **gipsy** helps to quash that spurious connection with Egypt, and is in line with the general trend to prefer *i* to *y* spellings where there are alternatives. (See further under **i>y**.)

girl See under **nonsexist language**.

gladiolus This word has too many syllables for a household word, as Fowler noted, and one thing in favor of its Latin plural *gladioli* is that it makes the word no longer. The English plural *gladioluses* obviously does, and it's still the less common of the two plural forms, according to *Webster's English Usage* (1989). Other words with both Latin and English plurals are discussed at **-us**.

Yet the need to anglicise this classical word has been felt all along. In earlier centuries it was sometimes *gladiole*; and in our own time it sometimes appears as *gladiola*. The latter is an artificial creation, based on interpreting **gladiolus** as a plural "gladiolas". (For other words formed this way, see under **false plurals**.) *Gladiola* is now recognised in all the major dictionaries round the world, though *Webster's English Usage* notes that it appears only in mass circulation magazines.

Australians long ago found a serviceable form for the word and its plural in *gladdies*. The first recorded instance is in Morris's *The Township* (1947)— though Barry Humphries no doubt deserves the credit for making it known overseas. Yet neither it, nor the clipped form *glads* would pass in formal contexts.

glamor or **glamour**   See under **-or/-our**.

glycerine or **glycerin**   For general purposes, **glycerine** is the standard spelling in Britain and Australia, and **glycerin** in the USA. Neither spelling is however used by professional chemists, who prefer *glycerol*.

For a discussion of other pairs like this, see under **-ine/-in**.

go   This very common verb in English has as its prime function to express motion away from the speaker (cf. *come*), or to express continuous activity. Examples of each are:

Go away.   They've gone to the races.

and

The clock is still going.   If all goes well ...

One part of the verb **go** (*going*) also serves with *to* as an informal auxiliary to express future intention.

We're going to paint the town red.

(See further under **future**.) So well established is this usage, that it can combine with **go** itself as the main verb:

They're going to go to the races.

Another sign that *going to* has made it as an auxiliary is the fact that it's sometimes written as a single word: *gonna*. This assimilated form is however only used in writing casual dialogue.

The past forms of **go** are curious, and often a trap for the unwary learner. Children have first to learn that they must say *I went*, not "I goed", and then that it is *I have gone*, not "I have went". The use of *went* as the past tense for **go** seems to have become standard in the fifteenth century. *Went* was annexed from the verb *wend*, which then had to revive an earlier regular past *wended* for its own purposes.

gobbledygook or **gobbledegook**   Both are established spellings, though dictionaries differ over which to put first. The *Oxford* and *Webster's* dictionaries give preference to **gobbledygook**, while *Collins* and *Random House* dictionaries go for the second. Each allows the other as alternative however, and the *Macquarie Dictionary* (1991) presents them as equals.

By either spelling it's a nonsense word for wordy nonsense. It associates with pompous officials and professionals who seem less interested in communicating than in overwhelming their readers with long words. Whether they aim to impress or to cover their tracks, what they offer the reader is verbal fog:

The departmental reaction to the municipal government submission on recreational facilities was instrumental in discouraging philanthropic contributions towards them.

Decoded, this means (more or less):

The department was unhelpful about the council's proposal for a park, and people who might have given money have been put off by it.

You can just see it happening!

Choice magazine instituted a "gobbledegook award" in 1986, to highlight the problem in Australia, as well as the importance of the Plain English campaign. (See further under **Plain English**.)

goiter or **goitre** See under **-re/-er**.

Gondwanaland This is the name of the hypothetical supercontinent to which the continents of the southern hemisphere once belonged (Australia, Antarctica and parts of South America and Africa) as well as Arabia and peninsular India. According to the Wegener theory of continental drift, **Gondwanaland** was a single unit from Cambrian times (more than 500 million years ago) until its breakup somewhere between the start of the Permian period and the end of the Cretaceous, probably between 200 and 100 million years ago. (See Appendix III.) The breakup resulted in the formation of three new oceans: the Indian, South Atlantic and Antarctic oceans, and a substantially reduced Pacific Ocean. The evidence for this theory comes from parallel forms of animal and plant life in those now separate continents.

Gondwanaland owes its name to the Gondwana district in southern India, and was coined in the 1880s.

good and **well** Good is strictly speaking an adjective, and **well** an adverb. Yet there are idioms in which **good** seems to serve as an adverb too, such as:

It sounds good. It looks good. It seems good. You're looking good.

It also occurs in the colloquial Australian response *I'm good*, used in reply to the question "How are you?". To use *I'm well* in that context would seem rather formal, and would also emphasise one's state of health—rather than general state of well-being which is usually taken to be the point of the question.

Grammarians might indeed debate how to analyse any of the above clauses: are they instances of subject/verb/adverb or subject/verb/complement, in which an adjective could well appear? (See further under **predicate**.) The question turns on the nature of the verb in those utterances, and the role of copulars, now recognised in the major grammars (see under **copular verbs**).

good day or **g'day** Good day is the opposite of **g'day** on almost any scale you can think of. There is formality in **good day** where **g'day** is casual and familiar; and while **good day** is strictly for daytime use, **g'day** can be used at any time, day or night. **Good day** can be uttered either to begin or end a conversation, but these days it's mostly used as the final word and to show one's determination to close the conversation. **G'day** serves as a greeting and to open a conversation, but not to close it.

The standard polite greetings used currently are **good morning**, **good afternoon** and **good evening**, selected according to the time of day. The boundary between *good morning* and *good afternoon* is set at noon for those who work close to the clock (such as radio announcers), but is otherwise more loosely related to the before-lunch and after-lunch segments of the day. The boundary between *afternoon* and *evening* is even more fluid, and is set either by the end of the working day, or the evening meal. Note that all three may serve to open or close a conversation, but when used at the end, their overtones are rather detached and businesslike, and this makes them unsuitable for most social situations. **Good night** is only used to take one's leave at the end of the evening.

goodbye or **goodby** In Australia, Britain and the USA, **goodbye** is the standard spelling for the word by which we take our leave. Only in USA is **goodby** a possible alternative. Both spellings can be hyphenated but there's no need for it. For more about the formulas we use on leaving, see under **adieu**.

goodwill or **good will** All writers use **goodwill** when the word is an adjective, as in *goodwill mission*, and modern dictionaries all propose this form for the noun too, as in *the goodwill between author and publisher*. In older British usage **good will** (spaced) was used for some or all meanings of the noun. In one tradition, **good will** was for "benevolence" and **goodwill** for "the body of customer support built up by a business". But the meaning is usually clear in context, and if not, it's unfortunate to assume that the word's setting will differentiate it for the reader, when the settings of compound nouns are so variable. (See **hyphens** section 2d.)

gossiped or **gossipped** See under **-p/-pp-**.

got, got to and **gotten** See under **get**.

gourmet or **gourmand** The distinction between these is less sharply drawn in Australian usage than in Britain, where **gourmet** is a term of approval applied to the connoisseur of fine food, and **gourmand** carries a negative judgement against someone who seems to overindulge in food. In Australia the voluminous eating habits of the **gourmand** are not necessarily viewed with disfavor, even if they're seen as contrasting with the discriminating palate of the **gourmet**. A contrast in terms of quantity and quality rather than good and bad styles of eating is sometimes seen, though the two senses may be difficult to disentangle, as in the following newspaper article:

It takes a dedicated gourmand to keep up with the latest northside restaurants ...

The accompanying headline "Great Nosh on the Northside" kept the point ambiguous. The example shows a further new development, that the two words may be acquiring different grammatical roles. **Gourmand** is there used as a noun, whereas all examples of **gourmet** in the Australian ACE corpus were as adjectives: *gourmet foods*, *gourmet restaurants* among others. But this potential new line of demarcation has yet to be registered in dictionaries, and in the meantime writers who wish to target the older distinction will need to use alternative verbal means such as "epicure" and "glutton".

government In Australian English this word may take either a singular or plural verb in agreement, depending on whether the writer is concerned with it as a single institution or with the individuals it comprises:

The government is on the point of issuing an ultimatum.
The government are unable to agree on industrial policy.

The different patterns of agreement suggest two different ways in which a government may operate—the autocratic and the democratic mode—though we should not make too much political capital out of a point on which writers are forced by English grammar to make a choice. In American English the singular option is the one most often used.

Note that pronouns following **government** would also vary (either *it/its* or *they/them/their*) according to whether singular or plural verbs were being used. (See further under **agreement**.)

For the question of when to capitalise **government**, see under **capital letters**.

governor-general The plural of this has traditionally been *governors-general*, because the second part of the word is strictly speaking an adjective. However many people would interpret it as a noun, hence the naturalness of *governor-generals*, which enjoys widespread use in Australia, and is recognised in major Australian and American dictionaries.

In the similar cases of
• *major general*, the plural is always *major generals*
whereas for
• *attorney-general*, the dictionaries recognise both *attorneys-general* and *attorney-generals*, in that order.
(See further under **plurals** section 2.)

goyim This Hebrew word refers collectively to those who are not Jews. It is a plural: its singular counterpart is *goy* "a gentile". For others like it, see **-im**.

graceful or **gracious** A different kind of *grace* is acknowledged in these two words. In **graceful** it is an aesthetic grace of form, movement or verbal expression, as in *graceful proportions*, *a graceful leap* and *a graceful* *compliment*. In **gracious** it is the grace of sympathetic and respectful human interaction, as in:

The offer was graciously declined.

A *graceful compliment* could therefore be *graciously received*, without any sense of tautology.

Note that **gracious** is also combined in a handful of fixed collocations, notably *your gracious majesty*, but also as a traditional courtesy for those at somewhat lower levels in society, *your gracious self*. These conventionalised uses seem to hang around the relatively recent phrase *gracious living* (recorded first in the 1930s), and the use of **gracious** rather than **graceful** gives it a certain irony. It has social pretensions, though it can only connote a lifestyle which has a certain aesthetic charm.

graffiti This indispensable loanword from Italian is strictly speaking a plural, though it couples with either singular or plural verbs in English:

All this graffiti is a measure of protest.

There were graffiti scrawled from floor to ceiling.

When linked with a singular verb as in the first example, **graffiti** takes on a collective sense and works like a mass noun. With a plural verb it remains a count noun, as it is in Italian (see further under **count nouns**). The Italian singular form *graffito* is sometimes used in English, to refer to an individual scribble or message in a mass of **graffiti**.

grammar The deeper secrets of any language lie in its grammar, in the underlying rules and conventions by which words combine with each other. This is especially true of English, where word relationships are only occasionally marked in the forms of the words themselves. Many words can work as nouns, verbs or adjectives without showing it in their outward form:

in the clear (noun)

clear the table (verb)

on a clear day (adjective)

The grammar of the word, as well as its particular meaning, only emerges in the phrase or clause in which it is used.

In some other languages, such as German, French, Italian and Latin, the grammar is much more on the surface of words, hence all the different forms we have to learn for them. Grammarians would note that for those languages, the *morphology* of words (i.e. their form and their inflections) is vital to understanding the grammar; whereas in English it is the *syntax* (i.e. the order in which words are combined) which is more important.

In one sense, every native speaker of a language knows its grammar, learning it intuitively as part of the language acquisition process. Still accusations of "bad grammar" may be flung at native speakers who use nonstandard morphology, as in:

I kep it in the house.

Youse had better all be quiet.

Variant forms like *kep* and *youse* often have a long history of spoken use, but are not accepted as part of the standard written language. "Bad grammar" is also sometimes invoked to censure alternative collocations, such as *different than* (by those who were brought up on *different from*). An unwillingness to recognise variation in the grammar of English has resulted in a number of fetishes and shibboleths which are still used to identify "correct" and "incorrect" grammar. English grammar is nevertheless somewhat flexible from one context to another, and has certainly changed in its details over the course of time. In principle it embraces more than the current conventions of written language.

(See further under **clause**, **phrase**, **sentence**, **parts of speech** and **syntax**.)

gramophone or **phonograph** See phonograph.

grand prix How do you make its plural?

When the original *Grand Prix de Paris* was set up for three-year-olds at Longchamps racecourse in 1863, it was the one and only. But by 1908 there was a "grand prix" for motor racing, and after that, for the best product at an exhibition … etc., etc. To refer to more than one **grand prix**, the French use *grands prix*, and this is also used in English writing. However other English-style plurals are also seen, such as *grand prixs* and *grand prixes*, neither of which is very satisfactory since *prixs* is unpronounceable, and *prixes* adds a foreign syllable to what is still very much a French word. Those reluctant to use the French plural *grands prix* could resort to "big prizes", which is an exact calque of the French.

granter or **grantor** See under -er/-or.

grapheme A **grapheme** is a unit of a writing system. In English it can be a single letter, like any of those in *c-a-t* in "cat"; but we also recognise *graphemes* consisting of more than one letter, such as the *th* in "catharsis", and the *tch* in "catch". In languages such as French, the repertoire of *graphemes* is extended by means of accents. Thus *e*, *é*, *è* and *ê* are different *graphemes*. Note that *graphemes* are identified by means of chevrons, e.g. <*t*>, <*th*>, <*tch*>.

grave accent This accent has a number of uses depending on which language it's deployed in. In Italian it marks a stressed final vowel, while in Vietnamese it shows a falling tone. In French it has several functions:

● to mark an open variety of *e*, as in *père*
● to show when a final syllable is stressed as in *déjà*
● to distinguish between homonyms, such as *a* and *à* or *la* and *là*

The **grave accent** tends to disappear quickly from French loanwords in English, because it's less important than the acute accent in identifying a word's pronunciation. (See further under **acute accent**.)

The **grave accent** is occasionally used in printing English poetry, to show when a syllable is to be pronounced separately, e.g. *time's wingèd chariot*. It helps readers to recognise meters which depend on a strict pattern of syllables.

graveled or **gravelled**   See under **-l/-ll-**.

gray or **grey**   The use of these spellings is quite strongly regionalised, with **gray** as the standard form in the USA, and **grey** used in Australia and Britain. The choice of spelling for the *Oxford Dictionary* was apparently in the balance in the 1890s, and the chief editor Dr Murray conducted an inquiry to decide the issue. Though *The Times* was for **gray**, other printers and a majority of those he asked voted for **grey**. They settled the issue for him, in spite of the preference given to **gray** by previous lexicographers, including Dr Johnson. This older preference is presumably what underlies the American use of **gray**.

Great Britain   See under **Britain** and the **British**.

Greek or **Grecian**   Both as adjectives and as nouns, these have different meanings. **Grecian**, dating from the English Renaissance, relates to the ancient culture of Greece, its art and literature. A **Grecian** is a scholar of *Grecian antiquities*. **Greek** is actually the older word, dating from the fourteenth century and capable of referring to any aspect of Greece, ancient or modern. A **Greek** is any person of Greek nationality, from Aristotle to Onassis.

Whether ancient or modern, the language of Greece is always called **Greek**. *Classical Greek* was the language of Athens: "Attic Greek". In the twentieth century two varieties of the language have jostled for recognition as the standard: *katharevusa* (the "high" variety, with spellings that link it with the classical language) and *demotike* (the popular variety, written much more as it is spoken). *Katharevusa* was promoted for a while after the Colonels' coup in 1967, but its role has since diminished with the use of *demotike* in education, and for most communicative purposes.

Greek plurals   Some Greek loanwords into English have brought with them their Greek plurals, e.g. *criterion* whose regular plural is *criteria*, and *schema*, which has both a Greek plural *schemata* and an English one *schemas*. A third group of Greek loanwords with Greek plurals is little known except to scholars: *topos* plural *topoi*, though this pattern of plurals is fossilised in *hoi polloi* "the many", where both article and adjective show the Greek plural ending.

For words like *criterion*, see further under **-on**; for those like *schema*, see under **-a** section 1.

grey or **gray**   See gray.

griffin, griffon or **gryphon**   The first of these spellings (**griffin**) is standard for both a mythical and a real animal:

1 the mythical beast with the head and wings of an eagle, and the body of a lion—which was believed by the ancient Greeks to keep guard over the gold of the Scythians
2 a type of vulture, at home in southern Europe.

The first item became a feature of the family crests of many noble families in Europe, and a symbol of valor and magnanimity. This dignified role probably helped to generate the alternative spelling **gryphon** (reflecting its Latin antecedent "gryps"), which was used in heraldry and other contexts where the link with tradition was important.

The spelling **griffon** is used in modern English to refer to a breed of wire-haired terrier developed in Belgium in the 1880s. The word is ultimately the French word for "griffin", though its use may well be ironic. The dog is rather small and its head is more like that of a monkey than an eagle. Another sign of irony is the fact that the French also call it the *chien anglais* "English dog".

grill or **grille**   The **grille** is one of a number of French loanwords which lost its *e* as it was assimilated in the seventeenth century, and reappeared with it in the nineteenth century. By then it was felt necessary to differentiate the use of the word as "a decorative grating or set of bars over a window or opening" from its use in referring to a style of cooking over a set of metal bars, first recorded in 1766. The two meanings were distinguished this way in French (by means of *grille* and *gril*), and their differentiation in English is another sign of **frenchification** (see further under that heading). The distinction is maintained in both American and British English, with **grill** used for the kitchen or barbecue, and **grille** in discussions of architecture and automobiles.

grisly or **grizzly**   The first of these is used of anything which arouses horror in the beholder, as in *the grisly relics of the concentration camp*. **Grizzly** means "greyish or grey-haired", so that an elderly person or animal may merit the adjective.

The *grizzly bear* may owe its name to both words. In a real sense it is a **grisly** bear, formidable in size (sometimes 2.5 m), as is implied in its Latin name *Ursus horribilis*. However we could explain the name simply by reference to the bear's color—its fur being anywhere from creamy brown to near-black, but often tipped with white.

In Australian and British English, the word **grizzly** (or *grizzling*) is sometimes applied to a whining child, as Murray-Smith (1988) noted. Its derivation is quite different, from the colloquial verb *grizzle* "whine".

groin or **groyne**   These spellings are usually for two different words. The first is anatomical, used to refer to the groove where thighs join the abdomen, a usage which goes back to about 1400. The architectural use of **groin** to mean "a curve or edge where two vaults intersect", dating from the eighteenth century, seems to be a figurative extension of the use in anatomy.

A **groyne** is a breakwater designed to reduce the sideways movement of sand on a beach, first mentioned in the sixteenth century. It seems to be quite independent of the first word, though it too is occasionally spelled **groin**.

grotto For the plural of this word, see under -**o**.

ground or **grounds** The word **ground** has numerous physical and figurative meanings: "earth", "soil", "foundation", "position", "area of discussion" etc. It becomes **grounds** in three particular kinds of reference:

1 to the land surrounding a building: *the school grounds*
2 to the sediment or ground-up material associated with a beverage: *coffee grounds*
3 to the basis of an argument, or the reason or motive for an action: *grounds for divorce.*

In all three cases **grounds** regularly takes a plural verb, although singular agreement is just possible for the third meaning.

Note that some would argue that it's better to speak of the **ground** of an argument or decision when there is clearly only one. According to this principle, one should say:

The ground of my decision is this: I need the money.

rather than:

The grounds of my decision are this: I need the money.

But since **grounds** can just as easily be used to mean "basis" as "particular reason", its use in the second sentence seems quite idiomatic. The plural form **grounds** is now as well established as the singular, according to the *Right Word at the Right Time*, and this usage is registered in all the major dictionaries.

groveled or **grovelled** See under -**l/-ll**-.

groyne or **groin** See groin.

grueling or **gruelling** See under -**l/-ll**-.

gryphon, griffon or **griffin** See under griffin.

Guangzhou See under China.

guarantee or **guaranty** The older word **guaranty**, dating from the end of the sixteenth century, seems to have been steadily overtaken by **guarantee** which came onto the scene about a century later. Fowler noted that **guarantee** could be used for all senses of **guaranty** except the rather abstract verbal noun meaning "the act of giving security", and even that is now possible, according to the *Oxford Dictionary* (1989). Some dictionaries have suggested a legal distinction between the **guarantee** who receives an assurance, and the **guaranty** (= *guarantor*) who provides it. But the distinction is confounded by the difficulty of deciding which party merits the label "guarantee" (see further under -**ee**)—and the fact that **guarantee** is much more common generally, with

its everyday and figurative uses as well as legal ones. With its strength it lays
claim to all the meanings which were ever those of **guaranty**.

Compare **warranty**.

gubba, gubber or **gub** In its various longer and shorter forms, this is the
Aborigines' general and none-too-complimentary name for a white person. It
was first recorded after World War II according to the *Australian National
Dictionary*, though its use may go back much further. Its origins are unclear:
once regarded as an Aboriginal word, it's now thought to be a pidginised form
of *government man*. (See *Australian Aboriginal Words* 1990.)

-gue/-g Among the various words we owe to the Greeks is the following set:
> *analog(ue)   catalog(ue)   demagog(ue)   dialog(ue)   epilog(ue)*
> *monolog(ue)   pedagog(ue)   prolog(ue)   synagog(ue)*

In Australian and British English, spellings with **-gue** are the standard, with the
exception of *analog/analogue* for which both spellings are current, though for
different meanings. (See **analog**.)

The shorter spellings *dialog, prolog* etc. are sometimes said to be the
American spellings. Yet according to *Webster's* and *Random House* they are
usually alternatives rather than the primary spelling for Americans. The one case
in which the **-g** spelling is actually preferred in the USA is *catalog*. It is
sufficiently established for its verb forms to be spelled *cataloged* and *cataloging*,
in spite of the general rule about *-ge* (see further under **-ce/-ge**). Both *Random
House* and *Webster's* dictionaries give *catalogued* and *cataloguing* as their
second preferences. The strength of *catalog* may owe something to the mail
order system—or else to librarians.

The spellings with **-gue** are in fact French forms of the Greek words, mostly
borrowed into English during the sixteenth and seventeenth century. This helps
to explain why the **-gue** spellings are still established in American English,
whereas the frenchified spellings of the nineteenth century have not taken root
(see **frenchification**). And though **-g** spellings are accepted alternatives there,
the shift from **-gue** to **-g** has been less rapid than Noah Webster might have
wished, when he tried to usher in ''tung'' for *tongue* in his dictionary of 1806.

Note that alternative spellings with **-g** are only found for words which:
- end in *-ogue* (not *fatigue, intrigue* or *harangue, meringue*)
- have at least two syllables (not *brogue, rogue* or *vogue*)

guerilla or **guerrilla** Though American and British dictionaries give
preference to the second spelling, the first is probably commoner in Australia.
Certainly five out of seven major newspapers recommend it, and it's made the
first among equals in the *Macquarie Dictionary* (1991). And among the citations
in the *Oxford Dictionary*, **guerilla** outnumbers **guerrilla** by 5:1, suggesting that
ordinary users of the word do not connect it with the Spanish *guerra* ''war''
from which it was derived as a diminutive. This etymology no doubt influenced
the dictionary editors in their preference for **guerrilla**; and closer acquaintance

with Spanish may strengthen its use in the USA. Yet the persistent English spelling could also reflect the normal French way of writing the word (as **guerilla**). It also presents a case where a single consonant tends to replace a double one in an isolated loanword. (See **single for double**.)

guesstimate or **guestimate** This colloquial blend of *guess* and *estimate* reminds that many an "estimate" may be a figure plucked out of the air, rather than a carefully calculated forecast. Dictionaries all give preference to **guesstimate**, for which the *Oxford Dictionary* (1989) has twice as many citations as for **guestimate** (4:2). The double *s* no doubt helps to prevent misreading of the first syllable.

gunyah This Aboriginal word for a shelter was among the first to be registered by English settlers in New South Wales in the 1790s. The word came from the Dharuk language spoken around Port Jackson, and referred to the temporary shelter made by Aborigines from sheets of bark and/or branches. Its meaning was extended in the middle of the nineteenth century to refer to the goldminer's shack or stockman's hut, but it seems nowadays to have contracted to the Aboriginal sense.

During the nineteenth century its spelling varied greatly, over forms such as *guneah*, *gunneah*, *gunnie*, *gunyer* and *gunya*. By the end of World War I it had settled down as **gunyah**.

gybe, gibe or **jibe** See gibe.

gymnasium The plural of this word is discussed under **-um**.

gynecology or **gynaecology** See under **ae/e**.

gypsy or **gipsy** See gipsy.

H

habeas corpus This somewhat obscure Latin formula, requiring that "you shall produce the person (in court)", is the beginning of several writs in English law. It represents an important civil liberty, obliging anyone who holds a prisoner in custody to bring him or her to court, and state the reasons for their detention. The court then examines the law under which the person is held and decides whether imprisonment is justified or not. The process is designed to prevent people being imprisoned by the state without trial. On occasions it is also used to prevent a citizen holding another person captive, and to ensure that custody arrangements for the child of divorced parents are properly observed.

Another Latin phrase which obliges people to appear in court is the **sub poena** "under penalty". Once again it's the opening phrase of a writ, one which summons the defendant of a case (and those nominated as witnesses) to appear before the judge. As a noun and verb *subpoena* is set solid, and can also be spelled *subpena* in the USA (see further under **oe**). As a verb, its past form is normally *subpoenaed*, though a case could be made for *subpoena'd* (see further under **-ed**).

háček This accent, like an inverted circumflex, is used in a few east European languages, including Czech and Croatian. In English it's sometimes referred to as the "wedge". The **háček** is used to extend the number of consonant symbols (or *graphemes*): e.g. *č* has the sound "tch", while a plain *c* sounds as "s". In Czech where it's used most extensively, the **háček** creates alternative forms for *c*, *n*, *r*, *s* and *z*, upper and lower case, and also for the vowel *e*. The **háček** appears in English writing only in connection with foreign personal names, such as Beneš, Dubček and Dvořák.

hachure or **hatching** Both these refer to lines of shading. Parallel lines of **hachure** were used on nineteenth century maps to show the gradient of a slope, with thick ones for a steep slope and fine ones where it was gentle. (Modern maps use contour lines with the actual heights stated.) **Hatching** refers to the parallel or crossed lines used to show light and shade on drawings, engravings and diagrams. A much older word, it was earlier applied to inlay work in the fifteenth century, and to engraving in the sixteenth century. Yet both **hachure** and the anglicised **hatching** derive from the French verb *hacher* "chop up". Other related words are *hash* and *hatchet*.

haem- This prefix is discussed under **hem-/haem-**.

hail or **hale** See hale.

hairbrained or **harebrained** See harebrained.

haitch How do you pronounce the name of the letter *H*? Australians divide on this, between saying "aitch" and "haitch". The latter is frowned upon by those who are used to "aitch", and only *aitch* gets a place in the headword list of dictionaries. **Haitch** nevertheless has a certain logic to it, since the letter names of most consonants embody their own sound, often beginning with it ("bee", "cee", "dee" etc.); and the "dropping" of *h* draws criticism in other places. Yet instead of being seen as a case of hypercarefulness, "haitch" is more often than not censured. Some people associate it with Irish Catholic schools in Australia, and with working class education, so that the judgement against "haitch" is social rather than linguistic.

hale or **hail** Nearly a score of different words have clustered under these two spellings. **Hale** and **hail** have no less than nine separate entries each in the *Oxford Dictionary*, as nouns and verbs, not to mention others as adjective/ adverb. Not all the words are current and some have always been dialect words, but there are enough in general use to give us pause.

Of the two, **hail** still has more uses, as:
• "icy precipitation"
• "greeting" as well as "greet or accost verbally"
• "come from", as in:
  He hails from Amsterdam.

The surviving uses of **hale** include:
• "haul, pull or drag", as in:
  They haled him into court.
• "healthy" as in the phrase *hale and hearty*. It too was sometimes spelled **hail**, until the seventeenth century. (This older spelling is enshrined in the Christmas *wassail*, a drinking toast, literally *wes* + *hail* "(may you) be healthy".)
  The familiar megaphone with built-in amplifier is a *loudhailer*—a device which accosts people noisily.

half- This is the first element in numerous compound nouns and adjectives. In Australian English they are typically hyphenated, though there are variations to note in each group.

In adjectives, **half-** regularly appears with a hyphen, as in:
  half-baked half-cocked half-hearted half-size half-timbered
The chief exception is *halfway*, which commonly works as adverb as well as adjective, and is therefore set solid. (See further under **hyphens**.)

In compound nouns, **half** is usually hyphenated, witness:
  half-boot half-day half-deck half-hour half-life half-light
  half-mast half-moon half-nelson half-pint half-sister half-time
  half-title half-truth half-volley

Just a few words have **half** set solid, notably *halfback, halftone* and *halfwit*. Note also that in American English some of the *half-* compounds are spaced, for example:

half boot   half deck   half pint   half sister   half title

The disinclination to use hyphens is a feature of American style (see further under **hyphens**), although American dictionaries do not always agree on individual words. It is a particularly fluid area of spelling.

As in the examples above, **half** normally combines with Anglo-Saxon words, or with thoroughly assimilated French ones. Its counterpart in more formal, latinate words is **semi-** (see further under that heading).

half-caste   One of the most delicate questions of usage is how to refer to people of mixed race—a matter of embarrassment, and worse, of condemnation. The formal word for it *miscegenation* may have fueled the problem, since its first element is easily misconstrued as *mis-* "bad, faulty" (see **mis-**), instead of *misce-* "mixed", which is neutral in meaning. Less formal words have been coined on all continents to deal with and skirt around the problem, some of them euphemistic, some offhanded.

The settlers brought to Australia an array of words used in other parts of the British Empire: *colored* (from South Africa); *half-caste* (from India); and *half-blood, half-breed, half-white* and *mixed blood* (from the USA). Other terms such as *ladino, mestizo* and *mulatto* (from Spanish colonial territories) were also known here. In Australia, there were local variants: *bronze wing, halfie* and *muleteer*—none of them more sympathetic than the imported terms. At least they did not develop the fractional mathematics of *quadroon* and *octoroon*.

Most of the disadvantages of those terms are avoided by the term *part-Aboriginal* (and such like). It does not pretend to precise mathematics, nor does it invoke agricultural analogies of breeding, and its tone is neither patronising nor offhanded. It is suitably neutral for situations when complex ethnic origins and culture need to be acknowledged. As when avoiding racist language, it's the straight ethnic or geographical term (cf. *Eurasian*) which seems best to preserve the dignity of the individual. (See further under **racist language**.)

half-title   The short title of a book when printed on the page before the main title page is its **half-title**. An alternative name among the makers of books has been *bastard title*. (See further under **prelims**.) The name **half-title** is applied also to the titles of individual sections of a book when they appear on a separate page.

half of   This phrase leaves some writers in doubt as to whether the following verb should be singular or plural. What decides the issue is the noun following *half*. If it's plural, the verb is plural; if singular, the verb is singular. See for example:

Half of the responses are for it.

Half of his response was unintelligible.

(See further under **agreement**.)

Note that the word *of* can often be omitted in such phrases.

hallelujah or **alleluia** This Hebrew word of praise is literally *hallelu* "praise (ye)" *Jah* "Jehovah". Apart from **hallelujah** and **alleluia** it is spelled in a variety of other ways, including *alleluya, alleluja, halleluya(h)* and *halleluia*, as often happens with loanwords which cannot be decoded by English users. In Latin the word was **alleluia**, as it was in the earliest English tradition, and it appeared thus in Wyclif's translation of the Bible (1394), notably in Revelation chapter 19. But in Coverdale's translation of 1535 **hallelujah** appeared in a heading to the Psalms of Praise. The legacy of both appears in the Authorised Version of 1611.

During the next 250 years **hallelujah** seems to dominate, replacing **alleluia** in the Revised Standard Bible's translation of Revelation. Yet it was increasingly associated with dissenting groups of Protestants such as the Salvation Army, witness the term *hallelujah lass*. The exclamation **Hallelujah** associated with gospel church services contrasts with the formal use of **Alleluia** for the section of the mass immediately after the gradual. The Catholic tradition retains the spelling **alleluia** in the New Jerusalem Bible (1985), and it's also enshrined in the Anglican Book of Common Prayer, the English Hymnal and the New English Bible (1961). The preference for **alleluia** among established churches thus seems to complement the use of **hallelujah** within the gospel churches. But both are well represented on the pages of the ecumenical *Australian Hymnbook* (1977).

halos or **haloes** See **-o** for the choice of plurals.

handfuls or **handsful** See under **-ful**.

hangar or **hanger** See under **-ar**,

hanged or **hung** The past form of the verb *hang* presents some questions, though overall **hanged** has given way to **hung**. All the major dictionaries give priority to **hung**, though some note that **hanged** is still reserved for death by hanging (either as capital punishment or suicide). This distinction is not always observed, however, and for many people **hung** is the all-purpose past, used as much to speak of someone having *hung himself from the rafters* as of having *hung the clothes on the line*. The *Right Word at the Right Time* suggests rather cryptically that using **hung** is associated with American English and/or rough justice; and **hung** is usually the form to appear in *hung in effigy*, as *Webster's Dictionary of English Usage* (1989) notes. But *Webster's* citations from round the world show that "educated speakers and writers" have used **hung** for both capital punishment and suicide for many years.

So at this end of the twentieth century **hung** has mostly replaced the earlier past form **hanged**. It seems to have been coined in northern dialects of Britain on the analogy of *sing/sang/sung* etc., and spread to all parts of the country during the sixteenth century. The earlier **hanged** survived in conservative media, such as the Authorised Version of the Bible (where it serves for all meanings of *hang*), and in legal English, hence its use in references to execution. The phasing out of capital punishment in Australia deprives it of its official stronghold (see under **corporal** or **capital punishment**), though it enjoys a faint afterlife in informal idiom: *I'll be hanged if ….*

hanging indention See indents.

hanging participles See under **dangling participles**.

Hansard This is the unofficial name for the daily records of parliamentary proceedings, published by the government in Britain and in Commonwealth countries such as Australia, Canada, New Zealand, and Fiji. Their counterpart in the USA is the *Congressional Records*.

The name **Hansard** is a reminder of the long association of the Hansard family with this publication, originally a private enterprise. Some trace the association back to the eighteenth century and to Luke Hansard, who published the journals of the House of Commons from 1774. Others give the credit to T.C. Hansard, who was the printer, and subsequently publisher of the unofficial series of parliamentary debates from 1803 on. Younger members of the family kept it going as an independent publishing enterprise until 1855, but from then until 1890 it depended on government subsidies. During the 1890s and early 1900s Hansard records were produced by various commercial publishers; but it did not prove a viable business and in 1909 became the responsibility of His Majesty's Stationery Office. In Australia, **Hansard** has always been published by the Australian Government.

During the nineteenth century, **Hansard** records were not verbatim records of what was said. Instead, the debates and proceedings were summarised and reported in the third person. Only during this century have they been written in the first person, and efforts made to create a "substantially" verbatim record, with only needless repetition omitted and obvious mistakes corrected. The idea that it is a verbatim record underlies British use of the verb *hansardise*, to mean either "confront a member of parliament with what he is reported to have said", or "remind (anyone) of their previously recorded opinion on an issue".

hapax legomena See under **nonce words**.

harakiri or **harikari** This Japanese loanword for a ritual form of suicide by disembowelment (literally "cut belly") stays closest to the original with the spelling **harakiri**. Yet all dictionaries allow **harikari** as an alternative, a spelling which turns it into a reduplicating word like *walkie-talkie*. (See further under **reduplicatives**.)

harbor or **harbour** See under **-or/-our**.

hard or **hardly** Hard can be either an adjective or an adverb:

It was a hard hit. (adjective)
The champion hit hard. (adverb)
Either way it implies putting effort into the task.

Hardly works only as an adverb, and nowadays means "scarcely, almost not", as in:
They could hardly see through the smoke.
Grammars and usage manuals sometimes refer to it as a negative adverb, although it differs from *not* in being a relative rather than an absolute negative. *Not* and **hardly** contradict each other in very colloquial expressions such as "He can't hardly walk", though not as a case of double negative, as is sometimes said. (See further under **double negatives**.)

Because **hardly** expresses a relative degree or state, it is quite often followed by the comparative conjunction *than*:
Hardly had they gone than we wished them back again.
The use of *than* after **hardly** is quite often censured by twentieth century commentators on usage, taking their cue from Fowler who amplified a query about it in the *Oxford Dictionary*. The critics argue that a time conjunction (*when*) is the proper connecter after **hardly**, even though it would sit awkwardly in the sentence above. Alternatively, they suggest that the comparative element should be explicit, and that *hardly* should be replaced by "no sooner":
No sooner had they gone than we wished them back again.
Doubts about the construction *hardly ... than* may well have arisen in the nineteenth century because both words were developing new roles: *hardly* as a special kind of negative, and *than* as a conjunction when there was no explicit comparison (see further under **than**). The construction may have sounded unidiomatic earlier on. But Fowler himself acknowledged that it was quite common, and by now it is thoroughly established in ordinary usage. It need raise no eyebrows if it appears in writing.

Note that the construction *scarcely ... than* has been subject to the same censure as *hardly ... than*, with the same suggested alternatives: *no sooner* (for *scarcely*) or *when* (for *than*). But there's no reason to use alternatives if they sit awkwardly or alter the meaning. *Scarcely ... than* has been in use almost as long as *hardly ... than*.

harebrained or **hairbrained** Dictionaries make **harebrained** their preferred spelling, and some justify it with the help of the traditional simile "mad as a March hare". But they also recognise **hairbrained**, which suggests an alternative interpretation of the word in which *hair* means "very small", as it does in *hairline* and *hairspring*. Both spellings have centuries of use behind them, and of the 7 *Oxford Dictionary* citations, 4 are with *harebrained* and 3 with *hairbrained*.

Harvard system of referencing This is an alternative name for the *author-date* system of referencing (see **referencing** section 3).

hash In spite of its many functions, this familiar sign # has yet to be entered in most dictionaries. Computer programmers call it **hash** or the *hash sign* because of its configuration (see under **hachure**), and the name is catching on among editors though for them it is the "space sign". The Chicago *Manual of Style* refers to it as the "space mark". Its place among the standard proofreaders' marks is shown in Appendix VI. Note that while Australian and American editors use # for "space", it has been officially replaced in British editing practice by the sign Ɣ, following British Standard 5261, 1976.

In other contexts the **hash** serves as the "number sign", handy in mathematical table and computer codes because it can never be confused with the actual quantities in them. As a "number sign" or "unit sign" it's also used in North America and elsewhere to signal an individual flat or unit within the block at a particular address. For example:

Mr G. Michaels
#3 25 Captain St
Sun Valley NT 7999

The *hash mark* familiar to American soldiers is different from all the above. It refers to any of the diagonal stripes on the left sleeve of one's uniform, each one representing three years of service.

hatching or **hachure** See hachure.

haute or **haut** These are two forms of the French word for "high", closely related to the English word *haughty*. They come into English in a number of phrases, usually associated with the things of high society, such as:

haute couture	*haute cuisine*	*haute époque*
(high fashion)	(fine food)	(elegant furniture)

High society is not too far from the *haute bourgeoisie* (strictly speaking the upper-middle or professional class), or the contexts for *haute politique* (the art of high intrigue), which can refer to negotiations conducted by people of high standing, as well as extraordinary wheeling and dealing by those of any class.

In all of the foregoing phrases, **haute** is spelled with an *e* because it accompanies a French feminine noun and must agree with it. When it accompanies a masculine noun, as in *haut monde* "high society", it's just **haut**.

have This is the second most important verb in English, after *be*, and like *be* it is both an auxiliary and a full main verb.

1 *As an auxiliary* the prime function of **have** is to express the perfect tense, as in:

I have waited she has been waiting they had waited
(See further under **aspect**.)

Another auxiliary or semi-auxiliary function is to express obligation, as in:
They have to come with us.
They've got to come with us.
The latter is the more informal of the two constructions. See **get** section 2.

Have also serves as a causative verb and to express management of an action
or event:

We're having our house painted.
He'll have them start next week.

2 *When standing as a main verb* **have** regularly carries the sense of possession
or attribution, as in:

I have a book about it.
They have the right idea.

When we turn such sentences into negatives and/or questions, there are several
alternatives:

a) *I don't have a book about it.*   *Don't I have a book ...?*
b) *I haven't got a book about it.*   *Haven't I got a book ...?*
c) *I haven't a book about it.*   *Haven't I a book about ...?*

Construction (a) is typical for Americans. Australians use either (a) or (b)
with increasing use of (a), perhaps because of sensitivity about overuse of
got (see **get** final note). In British English (b) and (c) have been the informal
and formal options respectively. But *Comprehensive Grammar of English*
(1985) notes that (c) is now less common in Britain, and that (a) has gained
ground there.

Final notes concerning **have**. In speech it is often reduced to *'ve*, as in:

I've an idea they've arrived before they should've.

As the example shows, it can happen whether *have* is a main verb or an
auxiliary, or combining with other auxiliaries. In the third case, it isn't always
recognised as **have** and so is sometimes mistakenly written as *of*: hence the
naive writer's *should of, could of, would of* and even *had of.*

Note that in *had have*, **have** itself is redundant. It hardly occurs except in
impossible conditions:

If they had've realised how hopeless it was ... or
If they'd have realised how hopeless it was ...

But *have/'ve* is not necessary, and the sentence reads better without it:

If they had realised how hopeless it was ...

In fact **have** is often redundant when repeated in successive verb phrases:

I would have liked to have seen Darwin before the cyclone.

That sentence loses little when rephrased with only one **have**:

I would have liked to see Darwin before the cyclone.

he and/or **she** The third person singular pronouns *he* and *she* are one of the
few points in English grammar that make us gender-conscious. We are forced
to choose between them whenever we refer to a single human being, and the
choice (whether it is **he** or **she**) seems to exclude half the population. Try filling
the blank in the following sentence:

Every teacher must ensure that ... can do first aid.

Whether you put **he** or **she**, you seem to imply that teachers are all of the same
gender. The same problem affects *his/her* and *him*.

On arrival at the hotel, the tourist was expected to hand ... passport to the manager.

Here again, the choice of *his* or *her* begins to create a gender-specific identikit of the tourist.

In earlier centuries and before the general concern about sexism in language, it was assumed and accepted that *he/his/him* could be both masculine and common in gender (see **gender**). Common gender uses of the pronoun are still to be found in aphorisms and Bible quotations:

He who hesitates is lost.

He that shall humble himself shall be exalted.

Such statements make generic use of **he** to refer to every human being, and would be seriously compromised if they applied only to the male half of the human race. Some would argue that the use of *he/his* is also generic in:

The applicant must demonstrate his ability to work independently, and how he would develop the unit if appointed to the position.

However for many people, this use of *he/his* suggests that women are ineligible for the job. In ordinary usage *he/his/him* seems to be losing its capacity to be common and generic.

*Alternatives to using **he** include:*

1 *he or she: how he or she would develop the unit.* This spells out the fact that both sexes are in the mind of the person communicating, and that no discrimination is intended. Once or twice in a text it is alright, but it becomes cumbersome if used repeatedly.

2 a) *he/she: how he/she would develop the unit.* Both sexes are recognised as in section 1. The slash puts the alternatives more neatly, though it's rather impersonal. For some writers the lack of oral counterparts is a concern.

  b) *s/he.* This again is a neat way of showing that both sexes are included, though something else is needed for *him/her.*

3 *he* alternating with *she* throughout the text. This is suggested by some as a way of being absolutely even-handed, but it is extremely disconcerting to the reader. It gives the impression that two different identities are being referred to, when only one is intended.

4 *it.* You can use *it* to refer to a baby—though the child's parents are unlikely to. The pronoun cannot be used very far up the age range.

5 *they.* This works very well if you turn the whole sentence into the plural:

Applicants must demonstrate how they would develop the unit.

Nowadays *they* is used increasingly after a singular word. To some this is still a grammatical error; but to many it is not unreasonable, at least after an indefinite word:

Anyone who applies must demonstrate how they would develop the unit.

But using *they* after a more specific word is still contentious, and sounds awkward or ungrammatical:
The applicant must demonstrate how they would develop the unit.
(See further under **they**.)

6 *you*. In some situations, *you* can be substituted. It creates a style which addresses the reader much more directly:
When you apply you must demonstrate how you would develop the unit.

7 Avoid pronouns altogether and rely on abstract nouns:
The applicant must demonstrate an ability to work independently, and present plans for future development of the unit.
This style is very impersonal and detached. (See further under **abstract words** and **person**.)

8 Repeat the words which identify people in terms of their roles, provided this is not too clumsy. The word *applicant* could hardly be repeated in our illustrative sentence, but in successive sentences this is effective:
The applicant must demonstrate an ability to work independently. The applicant's plans for developing the unit should also be submitted.
With so many alternatives available within English, there's really no need to invent a new common gender pronoun to replace **he** and **she**. Some however feel that it is the only way to cut loose from the sexist traditions embedded in English, and have proposed items such as *Co, E, hesh, tey, ther* and *thon* ("the one"). This is only a handful of the scores of alternatives invented since about 1850 and discussed in *Grammar and Gender* (1986). Unfortunately most of them require some explanation, and concerted effort to implement them.

The most instantly accessible of such proposals is *s/he*, and it has been used from time to time in this book.

---

head The grammatical uses of this word are shown under **phrases**.

-head The original use of this suffix in reference to abstracts is still evident in old-fashioned words such as *godhead* and *maidenhead*. In the twentieth century, and especially since the 1960s it has developed a new use in characterising groups of people either by their behavior or their appearance: *skinhead, talking head, waxhead*, or by the object to which they devote their energies: *beerhead, petrolhead, revhead, winehead*. The latter are plainer and less flattering terms than those invented with the Greek element *-phile*. Compare *winehead* and *oenophile*, and see further under **phil-** or **-phile**.

Even so the words formed with **-head** seem less derogatory than those combined with *freak*, such as *ecofreak, juice freak, Jesus freak, speed freak*.

There the commitment to a cause or a drug has become obsessive. Compare **-mania**.

heading, headline or **header** These words all refer to a cue provided for the reader at the start of an item, though they belong to different kinds of documents. *Headings* are associated with nonfiction publications (e.g. textbooks and government reports), where they cue the reader as to the subject about to be discussed. Typically phrases, they are set apart by typographic means at the top of a chapter or section. (The setting of headings and subheadings, is the subject of the next entry.)

Headlines are the telescoped sentences used at the head of newspaper articles, designed to grab the reader's attention. Some aspects of their wording are distinctive: see **headline language**.

In computer software the term **header** refers to a wordprocessing facility which places certain items at the top of every page of a document, such as page numbers and *running heads*, i.e. abbreviated chapter or section titles.

headings and **subheadings** In many kinds of nonfiction, **headings** are a boon to readers, indicating the structure of information in the solid text below, and helping them over the potential problem of not being able to "see the wood for trees".

For the writer too, deciding on **headings** and **subheadings** is an important step in getting on top of the material, and being able to present it in manageable blocks. Choosing **headings** also obliges you to think about the order of the blocks—which may come easily if there's a conventional set such as primary/secondary/tertiary (education/industry etc.) But in more open fields writers have to invent their own series of **headings**, making sure that individually they are suitable for everything under them. The **headings** then correlate with the major structural divisions of the piece of writing. For example (for an essay on the flute):

A Uses of the flute
B The European concert flute
C Music composed for the flute

Within each structural block **subheadings** must be found to label smaller units of discussion, and link up with the major headings. Sometimes the main heading may need rewording, to enlarge its scope or to make it more specific:

A HISTORICAL USES OF THE FLUTE
　　1. Herdsman's pipes in the Mediterranean, and in South America
　　2. As an aid to courtship in mythology and literature
　　3. As a professional musician's instrument in ancient Egypt and in medieval Europe

Layout and typography of headings. In a table of contents, **headings** and **subheadings** would be set out as just shown, with subheadings indented from the main headings. Subsubheadings would be further indented. To enumerate them, a combination of letters and numbers (as above), or just numbers may be used. (See **numbers** and **number style** section 5.)

Both in the table of contents, and on the ordinary page, **headings** are distinguished from **subheadings** etc. by means of different fonts. So main headings may be in bold, and others in normal type, or the main heading in caps, and the others using only an initial cap. Printers, desktop publishers and others able to vary the type size can use that to distinguish the headings, e.g. 12 point for headings and the regular 10 point for subheadings. Small caps and italics, if available, serve as further typographic variables to show lower headings. Letter spacing is also a resource for differentiating the levels of heading. Compare *U S E S* with *USES*.

For those with less flexible typographical resources, the placement of **headings** and **subheadings** on the printed page can be used to distinguish one from another. Main headings may be centred, while subheadings are flush with the left margin. Additional line space below main headings also helps to make the difference.

Note that many publishers set flush left the first line of text after a heading or subheading. But others simply indent it like any other paragraph.

headline language Newspaper headlines have to say everything in a few words: preferably no more than eight, and ideally less than that. The statements they make are usually elliptical, and some grammatical items such as articles, conjunctions, the verb *be* and verbs of saying, are usually left out. Each is illustrated in turn below:

BOND TELLS OF MEETING WITH SPY
BULGARIAN LEADERS QUIT, PLEDGE REFORM
COOK MANUSCRIPT STOLEN
OFFICIAL: MANDELA CLOSE TO FREEDOM

As those examples show, verbs are a feature of many headlines, helping to highlight what is happening—whether they appear as finite verbs (*quit, pledge*), participles with the verb *be* omitted (*stolen*), or verbal nouns (*meeting*). Certain short verbs/verbal nouns are regulars in headlines, including:

aid axe ban bar bid call clash crash curb cut find flee leak
pact probe push quit rise seek slam slash wed win

Words like these suggest decisive action, though they often refer to processes which are a matter of discussion long before they become action. But then, the news is as often about what people say as what they do. Newspapers have to make the best of it.

headword In a dictionary, the **headword** is the one which begins each entry, and is then analysed and defined within it. For certain grammarians **headword** is another term for the *head* of a phrase. (See further under **phrases**.)

heavenward or **heavenwards** See under **-ward**.

Hebrew See under **Israel**.

hedge words One quick way to soften the impact of a statement is to insert a *hedge word*. There are four subtypes, according to the *Comprehensive Grammar of English* (1985), which presents them under the general heading of *downtoners*:

- approximators e.g. *almost, nearly*
- compromisers e.g. *quite, rather*
- diminishers (a) e.g. *partly, somewhat* (these modify the force of the following expression), (b) e.g. *only, merely* (these confine the reader's attention to a single item)
- minimisers e.g. *barely, hardly*

The examples so far are all from standard English, though there are numerous comparable expressions in colloquial English: *practically* (approximator); *kind of* (compromiser); *just* (diminisher); *a bit* (minimiser), in negative statements such as *He didn't like it a bit.* Note that in positive statements, *a bit* is a diminisher: *I was a bit hasty.* Those examples also show the different positions in which some *downtoners* may appear. Others however have a fixed position, e.g. *enough* which always follows the word it modifies. Compare:

> *It was rather good.*
> *It was good enough.*

Hedge words help to curb the assertiveness of a claim, and to prevent a style from sounding too arrogant. They put limits on statements which could not be defended in their absolute form. Yet like any stylistic device they offer diminishing returns and become conspicuous (and ineffective) if overused. Even if you "juggle" several of them in the same piece of writing, they eventually draw attention to themselves because they create repetitive phrase patterns. At that point, writers need to seek other ways of expressing a claim: to paraphrase "rather good results" with *promising results*, and "felt somewhat upset" with *was distressed.* Another resource for modifying the force of a statement (and one which again helps to vary phrase patterns) is the group of modal verbs including *can, could, may, might, should, would* etc. They too must be used sparingly, however. (See further under **modality**.)

Compare **intensifiers**.

helix The plural of this word is discussed under **-x**.

hello and **hooroo** Both words belong primarily to spoken English, and their spellings have not yet been standardised. **Hello** is also spelled *hallo* and *hullo*, on account of "the obscurity of the first syllable" as the *Oxford Dictionary* puts it. Australian and American dictionaries make **hello** the first spelling, and it's the most frequent in the Australian ACE database, followed by *hullo* and then *hallo* (in the ratio of 14:8:2). **Hello** is the one used in ordinary contexts such as the following advertisement for a seminar on conversation skills:

> *What Do You Say After You Say Hello?*

British dictionaries give their preference to *hallo*, even though the LOB database showed that **hello** had become the most common spelling in Britain. It emerged as a standard greeting in the nineteenth century, though its origins are rather obscure. The *Oxford Dictionary* sees it as a variant of *halloa* and *halloo*, hence its preference for *hallo*.

Meanwhile **hooroo**, alias *ooroo*, *hurroo* and *hooray* is an Australianism, in use for about a hundred years to mean "goodbye". The last of those spellings shows a variant pronunciation, and also an overlap with *hurray* (also spelled *hooray*), the shout of satisfaction and jubilation. In fact *hurrah* (which is *hurray* in more formal dress) is suggested by the *Australian National Dictionary* as the source of *hooray/hooroo*, though without any comment on the difference in meaning. Perhaps the offhanded *hooroo/hooray* is an Australian parody of the rather formal and ritual expression *hurrah/hurray/hooray*. Yet both words are known in Australia, and if *hooray* does service for both, we know from the context whether it's meant to express triumph and satisfaction or the intention to leave.

Compare **adieu**.

hem-/haem- This element of ancient Greek, meaning "blood", has been put to use in modern scientific words, especially in medicine and physiology. Some familiar examples are:

> *h(a)emoglobin h(a)emophilia h(a)emorrhage h(a)emorrhoid*

It appears as *-(a)em-* when it's not the first syllable of a word. See for example:

> *an(a)emia hypoglyc(a)emia leuk(a)emia septic(a)emia tox(a)emia*

The preference for *haemoglobin* and *anaemia* etc. is in line with traditional British spelling, whereas American English has long since moved to *hem-/-em-*. In Australia, the spelling of such words is far from uniform, and varies according to whether the word is in common use or specialised. Several major newspapers use *hem-/-em-* in *hemorrhage*, *leukemia* and other members of those sets, whereas doctors still prefer *haem-/-aem-*, according to a 1988 survey in *Australian Dr Weekly*. Yet American medical practice loses nothing of substance in preferring *hem-/-em-*, and some unnecessary clutter is shed from the spelling. (See further under **ae/e**.) The spelling/sound regularity is also improved for some words: spellings such as *hypoglycaemia* and *septicaemia* are unfortunate given the general convention that a *c* followed by *a* is a hard "k" sound. (See further under **-ce/-ge**.)

Some **h(a)em-** words are specialised terms in geology and chemistry, including *h(a)ematite* and *h(a)emat(e)in*. Once again their standard spelling in North America is *hem-*, and they are recognised in that form in Australia. The connection with "blood" in such words is remote, and it deflates the argument that **haem-** is a more meaningful spelling.

Note that words with **h(a)em-** leave some writers in doubt as to whether the letter immediately following that element should be *a* or *o* when it is an unstressed syllable. In most of them it is *o*: *h(a)emoglobin, h(a)emophilia* etc. The chief exceptions are those like *h(a)ematite* and *h(a)ematology*, where the basic element is *h(a)emat-*, not **h(a)em-**.

hemi- See under **demi-**.

hence In abstract argument **hence**, i.e. "from this point", is still a useful word for introducing a conclusion, an alternative to *therefore*, *thus* etc. (See further under **conjunctions**.) However its other uses in the realms of space ("from this place, from here") and time ("from this time, from now") are very much contracted. As an adverb of time it's mostly confined to fixed phrases such as: *two weeks hence, six months hence*. When used in references to place, e.g. *go (from) hence to Singapore*, it now sounds quite old-fashioned.

The sense of place was once fundamental to **hence**, and it contrasted with *hither* and *here*, as in the following:

Get thee hence!   (from this place)
Come hither!   (to this place)
I am here!   (in this place)

In spite of those neat distinctions, the system seems to have broken down for *hence/hither/here*—just as it has for *thence/thither/there* and *whence/whither/where*. In each case the third is the only one to survive in common English, and the others seem formal, old-fashioned or archaic. Yet there are signs that the status of **hence**, *thence* and *whence* was always a little uncertain. To write *from hence* is strictly redundant (because "from" is part of the meaning of **hence** itself), yet there are records of it from the fourteenth century on. The Authorised Version of the Bible has numerous instances of *from thence/whence* (including the famous line of the Psalm 121: "I will lift up mine eyes unto the hills from whence cometh my help"). Thus even centuries ago *hence/thence/whence* were simply formal variants for *here/there/where*.

hendiadys See under **hysteron proteron**.

hepta- See under **number prefixes**.

heritage or **inheritance** In law, these can both refer to the estate or property which passes to one's legal heirs. But in common usage they diverge. **Inheritance** still has the sense of tangible inherited assets and family property attached to it, while the meaning of **heritage** is wider and more abstract. It often refers to the accumulated culture and traditions which belong to a society or nation, and which are the birthright of all its citizens:

The architecture of modern Japan is part of a continuous heritage of elegant design.
Younger Germans are less conscious of the heritage of guilt which their parents bore from World War II.

In twentieth century usage, **heritage** has been further extended to the natural resources of a nation, ones which must be carefully preserved for posterity and for humanity as a whole. It can thus be applied to Queensland rainforests and wild rivers in Tasmania for which a *World Heritage* listing has been sought.

heroin or **heroine** See under -**ine**, and **morphine**.

hesitance, hesitancy and **hesitation** These three have all done duty for each other since the seventeenth century, so there's little to choose between them in terms of meaning. All have been used to express a specific instance or act of *hesitating* as well as the corresponding state or quality. In terms of frequency, **hesitancy** has overtaken **hesitance**, but neither appears with anything like the frequency of **hesitation** in the twentieth century. In the Australian ACE database there are seven instances of **hesitation** to one of **hesitancy**, and none at all of **hesitance**. Presumably **hesitation** gains by being closer in form to the verb *hesitate* than either of the others.

hetero- This Greek prefix, meaning "different, other", is probably best known in the word *heterosexual*. It's also found in a number of scientific and scholarly words, such as:
> *heterogamous heterogeneous heteromorphic heterorganic*
In such words it often contrasts with a similar word formed with *homo-* "same", hence pairs such as *heterorganic/homorganic*. (See further under **homo-**.) In just one pair, it forms a contrast with a different prefix: *heterodox/orthodox*. (See further under **ortho-**.)

hex- See under **number prefixes**.

hi- and high- Hi- is a quasi-prefix of the latter twentieth century. It stands for **high-** in all the words it appears in, and for some it's the more common form:
> *hifalutin hi-fi hi-hat hijack hi-tech*
Both *hi-fi* and *hi-tech* are favored for their simplicity, especially in business: *hi-fi set, hi-tech design methods*. To spell them out in full as *high fidelity* and *high technology* would be cumbersome, though the first (*hi-fi*) is better established than the second (*hi-tech*). *Hi-hat* is a spelling associated with the drummer's equipment, where it is the pair of cymbals operated by a foot pedal.

The origins of both **hifalutin** and **hijack** are obscure, and the alternative spellings *highfalutin* and *highjack* show folk etymology at work, trying to inject meaning into the first syllable. The major dictionaries all prefer **hijack**, and the *Oxford Dictionary* has only a couple of citations for *highjack* in the 1920s and 1930s. But with **hi(gh)falutin** their preferences go the other way—probably because "uppity" pretensions seem to be part of the word's meaning. (The word's spelling is unstable in other ways too, witness the variant endings in *highfaluting* and *highfaluten*.)

High- is clearly an element in numerous new compound adjectives listed in the second edition of the *Oxford Dictionary*:
> *high-brow high-grade high-headed high-powered*
> *high-rise high-speed high-tone high-up*
It will be of interest to see how many words are gradually respelled with **hi-**— a small step in the direction of reforming one of the notorious words with **gh**. (See further under that heading.)

hiatus For the plural of this word, see under **-us**.

hiccup or **hiccough** Dictionaries usually give **hiccough** as a variant of **hiccup**, though there's no support for it in either the word's origin or pronunciation. **Hiccough** is an old folk etymology (first recorded in 1626) which tries to interpret the second syllable. The *Oxford Dictionary* argues firmly against its use, whereas *Webster's English Usage* (1989) is inclined to back it as having been "in reputable use" for centuries.

The major British and American dictionaries give preference to the regular *hiccuped* over *hiccupped* as the past tense, and the *Macquarie Dictionary* does the same by the absence of commentary on it. Yet both the *Right Word at the Right Time* and *Right Words* (1987) claim that it should be *hiccupped*. For the issues underlying each spelling, see **doubling of final consonant**.

hifalutin or **highfalutin** See under **hi-**.

high- or **hi-** See **hi-**.

hijack or **highjack** See under **hi-**.

Hindi and **Hindu** A **Hindu** is a person who either speaks a **Hindi** language, or adheres to the Brahmanistic religion of India. **Hindi** refers to any of the languages of northern India, as well as the official language which represents them. *Hindustani* is a form of **Hindi** with elements of Persian, Arabic and Turkish mixed in, used in northern India as a lingua franca for trade and intercultural communication. It was the form of **Hindi** best known to the British in colonial India. *Urdu* the official language of Pakistan, is also a form of **Hindi**, but written in Arabic rather than Indian script.

Alternative but now archaic spellings for **Hindu** and *Hindustani* are *Hindoo* and *Hindoostani*.

Note that **Hindi**, **Hindu** and *Hindustani* all preserve the original Persian word for India: "Hind".

hinging or **hingeing** For the choice between these, see under **-e** section 1d.

hippopotamus Dictionaries all give preference to *hippopotamuses* rather than *hippopotami* as the plural of this word. It has the support of scholars as well as those who simply prefer to anglicise the plurals of well-assimilated loanwords. Why? Scholars argue that because the origins of **hippopotamus** are Greek (*hippopotamos*, plural *hippotamoi*), it should not be pluralised as if it were a Latin noun ending in *-us* (see **-us** section 1).

hippy or **hippie** See under **-ie/-y**.

hire The oldest recorded use of **hire** is to mean "employ for wages, recruit", and it has always been used in this sense in American English. In British English however, this use fell into abeyance, and is only now being revived under North American influence. The meaning is registered without comment in the *Macquarie Dictionary* (1991).

Other uses of **hire** continue the world over. The word is applied to making a payment for the temporary loan of objects such as boats, caravans, halls and dinner jackets. The fact that such loans are short term helps it to contrast with **rent**, the verb used for securing a fixed-period tenancy of business or private accommodation by means of regular payments. The word **lease** is usually applied to longer term arrangements for business premises or land, and usually implies a formal contract. So **hire**, **rent** and **lease** can be distinguished in terms of the kind of property involved, length of the loan period, and style of payment.

The distinctions between the words are nevertheless increasingly blurred. **Rent** has moved into the former domain of **hire** so that we can speak of *renting a truck* or *renting party gear*. And **lease** can now be used of shorter term tenancies.

historic or **historical** The distinction between these two is sharper than for many -*ic*/-*ical* pairs. **Historic** is more self-consciously associated with the making of history, so that *a historic event* is one which people feel is particularly significant in the life and culture of the nation. **Historical** is more neutral, acknowledging that something belongs to the past, or to the study of the past, or else that it really happened and is not fictitious.

For the question as to whether to write *an* before **historic** and **historical**, see **a** or **an**.

Note that *histrionic* is unrelated to *history*. It is derived from *histrio* "actor", hence its connotations of "melodramatic, artificial" and the implied contrast with "sincere".

hoard or **horde** These words are easily mistaken for each other with their identical sound and similarity in meaning: both can refer to a large mass. Yet while a **hoard** is a collection of inanimate objects stored away, as in a *hoard of old records*, the word **horde** refers to a large body of people or animals, as in a *horde of tourists*, or of *insects*. **Horde** often implies some discomfort or threat associated with that group, although in colloquial usage it just means "a large number", as in:
Hordes of passionfruit on that vine!
This rather figurative use is the point at which the line between **horde** and **hoard** becomes harder to draw. But perhaps we can still contrast that use of *hordes* with *hoards of passionfruit in the fridge*. The second conjures up the image of the golden food store: the first, that of nature running wild.

hodgepodge or **hotchpotch** See under **hotchpot**.

hoi polloi See under **Greek plurals**.

holistic or **wholistic** Holistic is closely related to the English word *whole* in meaning, but takes its spelling directly from the Greek element *hol(o)*- "whole, entire". It was in fact coined by General Jan Smuts in the 1920s as a philosophical term, and now appears in other academic fields as a synonym for "global". The underlying link with *whole* has naturally helped to generate the spelling **wholistic**, which is recognised in the major Australian and American dictionaries. The *Oxford Dictionary* (1989) offers multiple citations of **wholistic** in British English, as well as of *wholism*; and it treats them as "alterations" of **holistic** and *holism*, with no hint of censure.

Holland The home of the Dutch people has been called **Holland** in English-speaking countries since the seventeenth century. But for the Dutch themselves, **Holland** is the name of two out of their twelve provinces (North and South Holland). The official international name for the country is the *Netherlands*, a word which also serves for the adjective, as in *the Netherlands ambassador to the UN*. (See under **Netherlands** for the history of that name.) The adjective **Dutch** was coined by English-speakers out of *Deutsch* (the German word for "German")—a reminder that the language and people of the **Netherlands** are Germanic in origin.

The English have taken unfair advantage of the word **Dutch/dutch**, in none-too-flattering concepts such as *dutch bargain*, *dutch courage* and *dutch treat*. Since those expressions owe more to English prejudice than any demonstrable customs of the Dutch, there's no reason to use a capital letter in them, though old habits die hard. *Webster's Dictionary* (1986) notes that the capital is more likely to be used for the first two expressions than for the third.

See **capital letters** section 2, and **throwaway terms**.

home in on or **hone in on** The phrase **home in on** is used of pilots finding their direction beacons, or missiles heading for their target. Yet the relatively uncommon verb **hone** "sharpen" is sometimes used by mistake in that phrase. **Hone** can be used either literally (of sharpening a blade), or figuratively as in *honing his argument* i.e. making it more pointed. The sense of pointing in a particular direction is presumably why it seems to overlap with **home**, and comes to replace it in **home in on**. *Webster's English Usage* (1989) notes that **hone in on** seems to be on the increase, though not yet recognised in dictionaries.

home unit is the standard term for a strata-titled flat or dwelling in NSW, but usage in other states is variable. Victorians have in the past made use of **OYO** (or "own your own"), though **home unit** now has some currency. The term **condominium**, borrowed from law, is beginning to be used in Australia for this system of home ownership, as in the USA.

homely, homey or **homy** Homey and **homy** are two forms of a recent (nineteenth century) adjective which connotes all the familiar and comfortable aspects of home life. The spelling **homey** is given first preference in a number of dictionaries, although the *Oxford Dictionary* prefers **homy** as more regular in terms of the rules for final *-e* (see **-y/-ey**).

Originally (in the fourteenth century) **homely** meant "homelike", but it has long since become a value-laden word, for better for worse. So it has positive values in an example such as *homely way of entertaining*, where a lack of pretentiousness and artifice are appreciated. But the word is unflattering in *a homely girl*, implying that she is plain and unattractive.

homeopath, homoeopath, homeopathist or **homoeopathist** The Australian Federation of Homoeopaths plumps for the second spelling with the oe digraph. Yet not all those who practise *hom(o)eopathy* take their cue from that, and the first spelling gained overwhelming support (81%) in a 1988 poll of newspaper readers conducted by the *Macquarie Dictionary*. Like other words with *oe*, the case for reducing the spelling to *e* is mounting. See **oe**.

When it comes to choosing between four- and five-syllabled forms of the word, the latter (in **homoeopathist** and **homeopathist**) gets priority in the major British and Australian dictionaries, and in *Random House. Webster's* however prefers the shorter **homeopath**, and this form is effectively endorsed by the Australian Federation.

homeward or **homewards** See under -ward.

hommos or **hummus** See **hummus**.

homo- This Greek prefix meaning ''same'' is used extensively in scholarly and scientific vocabulary as in:

   homocyclic homodont homogamy homologue homophonic homopolar homotaxis homotransplant

A few examples of its use in common words are: *homogenise, homonym* and *homosexual*.

In one or two words, **homo-** is interchangeable with a look-alike Greek prefix: *hom(o)eo-* or *homoio-*, meaning ''similar''. So *homotransplant* varies with *hom(o)iotransplant*, and *homothermous* with *hom(o)iothermic*. But *hom(o)eo-* is the only one found in more common items such as *hom(o)eopath* and *homeostatic*. For the tendency to reduce *oe* to *e*, see **oe**.

Homo sapiens This neo-Latin phrase identifies the fully evolved human being, with intellectual powers not shared by animal species. Literally it means ''rational human'', though the words appear in reverse order as is usual in scientific nomenclature. **Homo sapiens** contrasts with earlier human species such as *Homo erectus* ''upright man'' (not stooping like a gorilla), and *Homo habilis* ''skilful man'' (able to make tools), now postulated as a stage in human evolution.

Further variants of **Homo sapiens** are ad hoc creations by philosophers of humanity: *homo loquens* ''speaking man'' (one who has the power of speech): and *homo ludens* ''playful man'' (the irrepressible joker).

Note that *homo* in colloquial usage is an abbreviation for *homosexual*, and not related to the Latin *homo* in the phrases above. (See further under **homo-**).

homoeopath, homeopath or **hom(o)eopathist** See **homeopath**.

homogeneous or **homogenous** These two seem to be merging into one, except for biologists. In biology **homogenous** still means "of similar structure and origin", and **homogeneous** "made up of the same kind of elements". But in common use **homogenous** is a synonym for **homogeneous**, as shown in all major dictionaries—Australian, British and American. The shift has perhaps been helped by the spelling (and pronunciation) of the verb *homogenise*, which has the meaning of "make homogeneous".

homonyms Words that are alike in form are **homonyms**. They may be alike in sound (*homophones*), such as *bail* and *bale*; *gibe*, *gybe* and *jibe*. Or they may be identical in their written form (*homographs*), such as *bear* "carry" and *bear* "large furry animal", or *minute* (one sixtieth of an hour) and *minute* "very small". As the latter examples show, *homographs* may or may not be identical in sound. The point is that although their spelling is identical, they are independent words by virtue of their separate etymology. Compare **polysemy**.

English is well endowed with **homonyms**, partly because of its many one-syllabled words: *I*, *eye* and *aye*. But there are also plenty of examples with two or more syllables, such as *cellar/seller*, *gorilla/guerilla*, *principal/principle* and *holy/holey/wholly*. Further **homonyms** are created when ordinary suffixes are added to words, as in *allowed/aloud* and *presents/presence*.

The quantity of **homonyms** in English is sometimes seen as a problem. Scholars in earlier centuries actually encouraged the use of distinctive spellings for *homophones*, as visual reminders of their different meanings. To their efforts we owe *flour/flower*, *draft/draught*, *check/cheque*, *curb/kerb* and many others. This tradition has been more energetically maintained by the British than the Americans, with Australians still observing many of the distinctions made in Britain. The different spellings are a two-edged sword: they help the reader, but they impose a heavier burden on the writer to know which goes with which meaning. When surrounding words help to settle the meaning, it seems rather unnecessary to insist on differentiated spellings. American writers who use fewer of them have no obvious difficulties in communicating.

homous or **humus** See humus.

hone in on See home in on.

honi soit qui mal y pense This ancient French exclamation, literally "shamed be (anyone) who thinks evil of it", is first recorded in English in the medieval poem *Sir Gawain and the Green Knight*. It may be a proverb, though in later tradition it was associated with an act of gallantry by Edward III, founder of the Order of the Garter. As legend had it, he was dancing with the countess of Salisbury when her garter slipped to the floor. He picked it up, and to save her embarrassment put it on his own leg, saying "honi soit qui mal y pense". Thus interpreted, the statement is intended to call the bluff of those who would entertain scandalous thoughts—which may well be the mock reason for making *Honi soit* the masthead of the students' newspaper at Sydney University.

honor or **honour** See under **-or/-our**.

honorable or **honorary** Different facets of the word *honor* are embodied in **honorable** and **honorary**. **Honorable** serves to express the idealistic side of *honor*, as in *honorable motives* where it applauds high-mindedness in the individual. There is also a conventional use of **Hono(u)rable** for all members of the Australian House of Representatives, as in *the Hono(u)rable the Member for Monaro.*

    Honorary also has its official uses, with two kinds of implication. An *honorary secretary* is one who works for an organisation without receiving any remuneration, and perhaps gains some honor and recognition from it. The *honorary president* meanwhile may well be appointed as a figurehead with no obligation to help run the organisation—as when the Prime Minister's wife is made honorary president of a charity, and presumably brings some honor and distinction to it. An *honorary degree* has something in common with both uses of **honorary**. It is usually awarded to a distinguished person who does not have to submit to the normal examination procedures; but it also gives recognition to his or her achievements in a particular field. In Latin it is simply said to be *honoris causa* "for reason(s) of honor". (See further under **cum laude**.)

honorarium For the plural of this word, see **-um**.

honorifics These are conventional words or phrases used to show respect to the holders of particular ranks or offices. Calling the ambassador "your Excellency", the bishop "His Grace", the judge "your Hono(u)r", the queen "your Majesty" and the pope "His Holiness" are all examples. Some dictionaries also apply the term *honorific* to items such as *Sir, Reverend* and *Professor*, which might more strictly be called *titles*. See under **forms of address** section 1.

honoris causa See under **cum laude**.

-hood This very old English suffix makes abstract nouns out of concrete ones, to create words which identify a state of being, such as *childhood, manhood* or *womanhood*. Yet others refer to groups of people with particular status and identity: *brotherhood, knighthood* and *priesthood*. The most recent formations in these groups are *nationhood* and *sisterhood*.

hoofed or **hooved** See under **-v-/-f-**.

hoofs or **hooves** See under **-f>-v-**.

hooroo or **hello** See **hello**.

hopefully This word has acquired a new use in the twentieth century (and especially since the 1960s according to *Webster's English Usage* (1989)), but it draws a remarkable amount of criticism:
    Hopefully the letter will arrive tomorrow.

Objections to this usage are based on the assumption that *hopefully* is and can only be an adverbial adjunct of manner—and so the sentence above would imply that the letter itself was feeling hopeful.

Yet no-one would seriously doubt that the word **hopefully** in such contexts expresses the hopes of the person communicating. It is an attitudinal adverb (or disjunct) which contributes interpersonal meaning to the statement. (See further under **adverbs**.) It takes its place beside numerous others, including:

> *confidentially frankly happily honestly incredibly luckily mercifully naturally sadly surprisingly thankfully unfortunately*

So why the objection to **hopefully**? Perhaps it is because use of the word developed so suddenly in the early 60s, and because the popular press put a critical spotlight on it. The usage seems to have originated in North America; and Britons and Australians too have been known to object automatically to American usage. Perhaps its frequent appearances as the first word of a sentence make it conspicuous and clichéd. It can of course appear elsewhere in a sentence: in the example above it could come anywhere except between "the" and "letter". Adverbs and especially disjuncts are very mobile elements in a sentence, and by moving **hopefully** out of the first position we may mitigate the reaction to it.

The *Right Word at the Right Time* is able to show that the word is now used as a disjunct by "much-admired and careful writers of English", and hopefully this will lay the foundation for its acceptance. *Webster's English Usage* believes that the high tide of objections to it in the USA was about 1975. To continue making a fetish of it seems perverse.

horde or **hoard** See hoard.

horrible, horrid, horrendous, horrific or **horrifying** All these are related to the word *horror*. Yet "desperate fear" is not always the motive for using them, especially when they are adverbs. In phrases such as *horribly awkward* and *horrendously expensive* they serve only as intensifiers of the following word. As adjectives too, their meaning is beginning to be diluted, as when people talk of a *horrible performance of Beethoven* or having *a horrid day*. In such expressions **horrible** and **horrid** connote a generally negative judgement, and could be paraphrased as "deplorable" and "disagreeable". In colloquial usage there's a persistent tendency for strong words to be overused and to lose their force. It has already happened to *awful* and *terrific*, and the word *formidable* has been diluted in a similar way in French. Fear and terror seem sooner or later to desert the very adjectives which embody it. But if you need a strong word, the last two in the list above, **horrific** and **horrifying**, still connote real horror.

hors d'oeuvre In English it's natural to pluralise this French expression for the appetising items served before a meal as *hors d'oeuvres*. Some writers feel it should be left unchanged (as it would be in French) because it's an elliptical phrase, meaning roughly "outside the meal". But in English it works as a compound noun, and we might as well give it an ordinary plural. (See under **plurals** section 2.)

horticulturist or **horticulturalist** See under -ist.

hotchpot, hotchpotch or **hodgepodge** These three show easily a word can transform itself over the centuries. **Hotchpot** originated in English law in the thirteenth century, as the term for the conglomeration of property which is divided equally between the children of parents who die without making a will. By the fifteenth century, as **hotchpotch** or **hodgepodge**, it had acquired a use in cookery as a term for a stew of meat and vegetables. Another century and both spellings are also used to refer to any mishmash or miscellany of items.

Nowadays, **hotchpotch** prevails in Australia and Britain as the usual spelling for "mishmash" and "stew", and as an occasional alternative to **hotchpot** for the term in law. **Hodgepodge** gets little use. In the USA all three terms are deployed: **hodgepodge** for "mishmash", **hotchpotch** "stew", and **hotchpot** is the usual spelling for the legal concept.

hoummos or **hummus** See **hummus**.

however Versatile and mobile, this word has several roles as adverb and conjunction.

1 As a conjunctive adverb **however** serves to emphasise a point of contrast in an explanation or argument:
> *We were keen to keep going; they however had had enough.*

However usually follows the item which makes the contrast, and its position in the sentence varies according to the intended scope of the contrast. In the sentence above it creates a sharp contrast between *they* and *we*. Broader contrasts can be achieved with **however** in other positions,
> *We were keen to keep going. However they had had enough.*

(contrast between the whole of the first sentence and the next)
> *We were keen to keep going. They had had enough however.*

(contrast between the two predicates *keen to keep going/had enough*)
By its mobility as well as its own bulk, **however** helps to mark contrast. Its three syllables make it a weighty substitute for *but*, and some computer style checkers flag it as "wordy". But used occasionally its effect is powerful.

2 Indefinite uses of **however** as adverb and conjunction are quite distinct:
> *However hard they walked, they would not get back before dark.*
> *However they went, it would take half a day.*

The position of indefinite **however** is fixed. As a subjunctive adverb in the first sentence above it must precede the word it qualifies; and as conjunction in the second it must appear as the first word of the clause. Note that as indefinite conjunction **however** heads a subordinate clause, whereas contrastive **however** works in a main clause. This grammatical difference is unmistakable as one reads on in the sentence, and prevents confusion between them. There is no basis for insisting that contrastive **however** should not appear at the beginning of a sentence, as some usage books have suggested. In fact the great majority of instances of contrastive **however** in the Australian ACE corpus were as the first word of a sentence.

For a discussion of indefinite **however** and **how ever** (spaced), see **-ever**.

3 *Punctuation with **however***. Older books on style often say that **however** should be hedged about with commas (or else a comma and full stop/semicolon). Accordingly our sentences from above would read:

> *They, however, had had enough.*
> *They had had enough, however.*

These days amid the general trend to reduce punctuation marks, there's a tendency to leave the comma(s) out.

Yet punctuation can have important consequences for the grammar of **however**. Compare:

> *We were keen to keep going. However, they had had enough.*
> *We were keen to keep going; however they had had enough.*
> *We were keen to keep going, however they had had enough.*

The third sentence with its preceding comma makes **however** a contrastive conjunction, whereas in the others the punctuation confirms its role as adverb. The shift to conjunction is disallowed in prescriptive grammar, but it has long been seen in informal writing, and there are four instances in quite different categories of the ACE corpus. (The three instances of **however** with a preceding semicolon were confined to the category of learned prose. The very many instances of **however** with a preceding full stop were spread over almost all categories.) Although this further conjunctive role for **however** is not yet fully recognised in the major American and British dictionaries, both *Macquarie* and *Collins* (1991) register it, the latter with the label "sentence connector". Meanwhile those concerned about the status of **however** as a contrastive conjunction can satisfy the strictest grammarians by using a semicolon in front of it (or a full stop) as shown in the last set of examples above.

human or **humane**   As adjectives these both appeal to the better characteristics of mankind. There are loftier principles in **humane**, and a *humane approach to the prisoners* connotes compassion and concern in situations where others might react harshly and unsympathetically. The reactions implied in **human** are much more down-to-earth and typical:

> *It was only human to find them disagreeable.*

In their negative forms (*inhuman* and *inhumane*), the two words differ again. *Inhumane* is somewhat formal and detached, pinpointing the lack of compassion, whereas *inhuman* is charged with a sense of outrage, implying the complete absence of any sympathetic traits, to the point of being monstrous:

> *Caging them up on the ship's open deck was inhuman.*

humanity, humanism or **humanitarianism** The last and longest of these abstract nouns is the most straightforward. **Humanitarianism** simply means the philosophy of serving and helping people. **Humanism** is the kind of scholarship which concentrates on the tradition of arts and literature in our culture, and the human values they express. The word is also used to refer to a nontheistic approach to life and our place in the universe, and so the word has negative connotations in fundamentalist theology.

Humanity is first and foremost the abstract noun for the adjective *human* (see **human** or **humane**), and also the collective word for ''people at large'' or ''mankind''. It can be a useful synonym for ''mankind'' for those who find that word sexist. The plural form *humanities* refers to the scholarly disciplines which are concerned with arts and literature (cf. **humanism**). The word then contrasts with *sciences* and *social sciences.*

hummus, hommos or **hoummos** For that tasty Arabic food made from ground chick peas and sesame oil, there are at least three spellings in English. American dictionaries give the first and second, while the *Oxford Dictionary* (1989) gives the first and third. Additional spellings are sometimes seen in Australia on menus and product labels, such as *homous, houmos, houmus* and other combinations of the vowels. The spelling *humus* is avoided by those who know that it coincides rather unfortunately with another English word—although it is the actual Turkish spelling. Dictionaries often trace the word to the Arabic **hummus**, hence their preference for that spelling in English. But as with other Arabic loanwords, its spelling is unstable.

Compare **felafel, kebab, tabbouleh, yoghurt**.

humor or **humour** See under -or/-our.

humus or **humous** The difference between these is discussed under -ous.

hurricane, tornado or **cyclone** See under **cyclone**.

hyaena or **hyena** See **hyena**.

hydr-/hydro- Either of these is the Greek element meaning ''water'', familiar in words such as:
hydrant hydrate hydraulic hydrofoil hydrogen hydroelectric
hydrophobia hydroponic hydrotherapy
But in the names of some chemical compounds, **hydro-** is a short form for ''hydrogen''. See for example, *hydrocarbon* and *hydrofluoric acid*.

Note that while a *hydrometer* measures the specific gravity of liquids, a *hygrometer* measures the humidity of the atmosphere. The latter embodies the Greek element *hygro-* ''moisture''.

hydra The plural of this word is discussed at -a section 1.

hydrolyse or **hydrolyze** See under -yse/-yze.

hyena or **hyaena** The classical spelling **hyaena** was introduced in the sixteenth century, to replace medieval forms such as *hiene*. But it has never been very popular, and the spellings *hyene/hyena* suggest that the earlier form with just *e* persisted and was preferred. Modern dictionaries all give **hyena** first preference.

hype See under **hyperbole/hyperbola**.

hyper- This Greek prefix means "over, excessive(ly)", as in:

hyperactive hyperbole hypercritical hyperglyc(a)emia hyperreactive hypersensitive hypertensive hyperthermia hyperventilation

Although **hyper-** is the Greek counterpart of Latin *super-*, the two cannot normally be interchanged because **hyper-** has negative connotations, and *super-* often positive ones (see **super-**). And in some pairs of words **hyper-** sets itself higher than *super-*, as in *hypermarket* (clearly one up on the *supermarket*), and *hypersonic* which is five times faster than *supersonic*.

A number of **hyper-** words have been coined to contrast with words beginning with *hypo-*. See for example *hyperthermia/hypothermia*, and further under **hypo-**. See also **hypercritical** or **hypocritical**.

Note that in chemistry, the prefix **hyper-** was formerly used in the naming of compounds as *per-* is nowadays, to show that a given element was at its maximum valence (or a relatively high one). (See further under **per-**.)

Hyper has also established itself as an independent word meaning "overstimulated", "obsessive" or "hyperactive". Once again there's a negative coloring in each of them.

hyperbole or **hyperbola** Both these words are modern uses of the Greek *hyperbole*, and originate in the image of throwing a ball high over something. **Hyperbola** is a mathematical term for an off-centre vertical section cut down through a cone to its base. **Hyperbole** is the term given in rhetoric to exaggeration used as a figure of speech. What is said should not be taken literally, but has an emotive or intensifying effect as in the following from a popular song:

The future's so bright I've gotta wear shades!

(See further under **figures of speech**.)

Note that the colloquial word *hype* "publicity designed to create excitement" is thought by some to be related to *hyperbole*. Others derive it from *hypodermic* and the drug culture.

hypercorrection People's anxiety about getting their usage right may actually help to produce questionable expressions which *over*correct normal usage. For example, the use of "haitch" (rather than "aitch") for the name of the letter *h* suggests a generalised worry about dropping *h*s, resulting in a tendency to "correct" words which do not need it.

hypercritical or **hypocritical** The first of these is easily explained in terms of *hyper-* "excessively" and *critical*:

> *The reviews were hypercritical of his technique.*

Hypercritical is a relatively recent word (only four centuries old), whereas **hypocritical** goes back to Greek theatre. It owes its meaning to *hypocrite*, a word which in Greek referred to the mime who accompanied the delivery of an actor with gestures. It then came to mean anyone speaking under a particular guise. (See further under **hyper-** and **hypo-**.)

hypernym This is an alternative name for the superordinate term in hyponymy. See under **hyponyms**.

hyphens The single most variable element in the writing of words is the *hyphen*, hence the large amount of discussion it generates. **Hyphens** serve both to link and to separate the components of words; and while they are established in the spelling of certain words, they come and go from many others. The use or non-use of **hyphens** varies somewhat in different Englishes round the world. In Britain under the influence of the Oxford dictionaries, **hyphens** seem to be used quite often, and certainly more often than in the USA, where according to *Webster's* dictionaries the same words may be set solid, or spaced (if compounds). Australians in their use of **hyphens** are somewhere between Britons and Americans.

There are few fixed conventions over **hyphens**. Authorities can agree on the underlying principles, such as:

- restrict the use of **hyphens** as far as possible;
- the better established the formation, the less need is there for a *hyphen* to link its components;
- **hyphens** should be used to separate letter sequences which distract the reader from construing the word correctly.

But how to apply those principles to words such as *co(-)operate* and *co(-)ordinate* is still a matter of debate. To resolve the issue, writers are sometimes encouraged to adopt the practices of one dictionary—although dictionaries themselves have mixed policies. Their use/non-use of **hyphens** with particular words may reflect either typical usage (in so far as they are able to research it), or else editorial policy and their desire to achieve consistency within their own headword list. A further problem is that dictionary lists do not include all possible compounds ("transparent" ones are omitted); nor do they always show what happens to compounds when they are used in new grammatical roles. Many noun compounds which are normally spaced, e.g. *cold shoulder* or *first night*, acquire **hyphens** when they become verbs (*they cold-shouldered him*) or adjectives (*first-night nerves*).

As in those examples, the grammar of words is quite often what helps to decide whether they should be *hyphenated* or not. This is why it's used below in presenting the general practices for *hyphenating* compounds. But when dealing with complex words, the issue of ease of reading is usually the most important one. Note that in the following sections we are concerned with the so-called "hard" hyphens (ones which would be used whenever the word appears), and not "soft" hyphens (ones used to show when a word has been divided at the end of a line, because of insufficient space). Questions about soft hyphens and where to divide words are discussed at **wordbreaks**.

1 *Complex words.* Complex words with prefixes are not normally *hyphenated*, but set solid. See for example:

amoral biennial counterrevolutionary debrief dissociate

In some cases however, as with *co-* and *ex-*, it depends on whether the word is an older or newer type of formation. (See further under **co-**, **ex-** etc.)

Other exceptions to that general principle are:

a) using a *hyphen* when the prefix ends in the same vowel as the first letter of the root word, as in:

anti-intellectual cf. *antireligious*
de-emphasise   *deactivate*

As these examples show, there's no apparent difficulty when a *different* vowel follows the prefix, at least in longer and established words. However with formations such as *de-ice* and *re-ink*, a hyphen seems desirable to prevent misreading.

b) introducing a *hyphen* in formations which would otherwise be identical with another word. So the hyphen in *re-cover* helps to distinguish it from *recover*, just as one in *re-mark* differentiates it from *remark* etc.

c) using a *hyphen* when the rest of the word involves a change in typography, such as capital letters, numbers, italics or quotation marks, as in:

anti-FBT post-1954 pre-perestroika un-"macho"

Complex words with suffixes are almost always set solid, witness:

advertisement chauvinism rationalise resourceful

However a hyphen is sometimes used in words where the root ends in a vowel and the following a suffix begins with a vowel, particularly in formations which are new or not commonly seen in print. So *more-ish* is preferred by some to *moreish* (which violates the general principle of dropping *-e* before suffixes beginning with a vowel. See **-e**.). Some writers also prefer a hyphen before *-ed* and *-ing* in ad hoc verbs such as *quota-ed* and *to-ing and fro-ing*. Alternatives to using the hyphen there are discussed at **-ed**.

2 *Compounds.* The use of **hyphens** with compounds at large seems rather unpredictable. Yet within certain grammatical groups, especially verbs, adverbs and adjectives, there are regular principles. Noun compounds (see below, d) are the most varied group of all.

a) *Compound verbs* are either hyphenated or set solid, depending on their components. Those consisting of a noun + verb, such as *baby-sit, gift-wrap, red-pencil* and *short-list* are typically hyphenated. Those consisting of an adverb + verb, such as *bypass, outlast, underrate* and *upstage* are set solid.

b) *Compound adverbs* are usually set solid, witness examples such as the following:

    barefoot downstairs overboard underground upstream

c) *Compound adjectives* are typically hyphenated, but see the exceptions (both set solid and spaced) below. The typical pattern is seen in established cases such as:

    tone-deaf red-hot all-embracing home-baked

    nuclear-free icy-cold labor-saving open-ended

Hyphens are also used in ad hoc compound adjectives, such as *open-door policy* and *red-carpet treatment*, to ensure they're construed as intended by the writer. They are also used regularly in compounds which contain numbers written as full words, for example *four-part*, *two-stage*, as well as in fractions used in adjectival roles: *two-thirds majority*. See however exception (iii) below, when numbers are written as Arabic numerals.

Exceptions to the hyphenated pattern are:

i) a few very well-established adjective compounds which are set solid. They usually consist of a simple adverb + verb, such as *everlasting*, *forthcoming*, *underdone* and *widespread*.

ii) compounds with an *inflected* adverb or adjective as their first element, which are normally spaced. So there's no hyphen in expressions such as the following:

    badly displayed goods   fully fledged scheme

    lower scoring students   best known example

The same applies to adjectives involving *more* and *most*, or *less* and *least*. **Hyphens** are only used if there is some danger of ambiguity: *More expert staff are needed to handle the problem* could be read differently from *More-expert staff*. In such a case it's probably better to reword the whole sentence, rather than let its meaning hang on whether the hyphen is there or not.

iii) compound adjectives which embrace items with a change of typography, including Arabic numbers, capitals, italics and quotation marks. For example:

    Year 12 students

    the US Airforce base

    their *haute cuisine* menu

    his "do or die" attitude

Note that some style manuals (including the Chicago *Style Manual*) recommend that **hyphens** should be dropped from any foreign phrase used as a compound adjective, whether or not it is italicised. So there would be no hyphens in expressions such as *a de facto marriage* or *an in camera hearing*. The foreign phrases in those examples are read as units, and their components do not need to be linked with a hyphen.

iv) compound adjectives which are institutionalised concepts, such as:

    equal opportunity employer

    city council elections

> *high school teachers*
> *twelfth century manuscript*

d) *Compound nouns* can be written with **hyphens**, spaced, or set solid, depending somewhat on what they consist of (see below). Yet quite a number of them have different settings according to different dictionaries. Noun compounds, more than any of the other kinds, are subject to the well-known principle that they begin life spaced, become hyphenated, and are finally set solid. See for example: *dark room, dark-room, darkroom*. However authorities often differ over how well advanced the integration of the two components may be, with British ones often prolonging the use of the hyphen, and American ones preferring to join up the components, or keep them spaced.

Of all the major types, noun compounds are least likely to need a *hyphen* (or solid setting) to ensure that their components are read together. The great majority of them have the qualifying component first and the qualified component second, so they can be read like any ordinary sequence of adjective and noun. Many may as well be left spaced, and dictionaries the world over show that this is the normal practice with some types particularly, such as:

those consisting of two polysyllabic words, e.g. *geography teacher, unemployment benefit*;

those whose first component has more than one syllable, e.g. *buffer state, concert pitch, customs house*;

those with strong stress on both components, e.g. *damp squib, green ban, tree fern*.

Apart from those considerations, the internal grammar of the compound can often suggest how it's likely to be set:

i) those consisting of a simple adjective + noun, such as *black market, red tape*. These are usually spaced. The exceptions are elliptical expressions such as *bigwig* or *redneck*, which combine to qualify an (understood) base component.

ii) those consisting of adverb + verb, or verb + adverb, such as *downpour* or *runoff*. These are usually set solid, except when a distracting sequence of letters is set up between the two components and requires the separating hyphen. See for example: *go-ahead, shake-out*. **Hyphens** are also employed, this time as a connecting device, when there are inflections on the verbal first element, as in:

> *goings-on hanger-on passer-by summing-up*

iii) those consisting of verb + noun or noun + verb, such as *rattlesnake* or *snakebite*. When the verb component comes first and is inflected, the parts are usually left spaced, as in *flying saucer, helping hand* and *revolving door*. When the inflected verb is the second component, the compound is usually set solid:

> *mindreader wordprocessor glassblowing sightseeing*

iv) those consisting of noun + noun. These can very often be left spaced—
except when the second component is a common and general word which
depends on the preceding qualifying word for its specificity. See for
example:

alderman anchorman chairman policeman
birthplace commonplace marketplace
bulkhead figurehead letterhead
jellyfish lumpfish oarfish tigerfish
earthwork roadwork wickerwork

The only noun compounds which *always* have **hyphens** are structured
differently from all of the above. They are:

those with a specifying phrase following the headword, e.g. *editor-in-chief,
mother-in-law, theatre-in-the-round;*

those in which the two components are very much equal terms, e.g. *city-
state, owner-operator, secretary-stenographer;*

those with rhyming or reduplicative components, e.g.
culture-vulture, hanky-panky, sin-bin.

As types, none of them is very common.

hypo- This Greek prefix means "under" or "lower in location or degree". It
appears in scholarly words, and a few which have become generally familiar,
such as:

*hypodermic hypoglyc(a)emia hyponym hypotaxis hypothermia hypothesis
hypoventilation*

In the names of chemical compounds, it indicates a low valency of the particular
element it qualifies, as in *sodium hypochloride*, the active element in household
bleach.

The familiar word *hypochondriac* embodies the idea that those showing a
gloomy preoccupation with their health are suffering from a problem associated
with the *hypochondria*, the medieval name for the abdomen: the soft part of the
body beneath the ribs.

For *hypocritical*, see under **hypercritical**.

hypocorisms A *hypocorism* is an affectionate name for a person, an animal
or a familiar object, such as *Libby* for *Elizabeth*; *pussy* for a cat; *potty* for a
chamber pot. **Hypocorisms** are often associated with talking to children,
although the familiarity and closeness they express is like that of "familiarity
markers" used colloquially among adults—in naming objects and events such
as *telly* and *tranny*, *quickie* and *sickie*. (See further under **-ie/-y**.)

Compare **diminutives**.

hypocrisy To spell this word correctly, think of *hypo-* "under", and "crisis".
For more about the word's meaning, see under **hypercritical**.

hypoglycemia or **hypoglycaemia** For the choice between these, see under
hem-/haem-.

hyponyms This is the linguist's word for specific terms (such as *carrot, onion* and *lettuce*) which are embraced and interrelated through a single cover term *vegetables*. *Vegetables* is the superordinate term, which serves to identify the class to which the set of **hyponyms** belongs. The classes themselves may be further subdivided, e.g. *vegetables* breaks into *root vegetables* and *green vegetables*, to add an extra level of hyponymy:

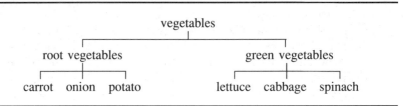

Root vegetables could itself be subdivided into *roots* (carrot), *bulbs* (onion), *tubers* (potato), to develop more **hyponyms** under each of those superordinates (also called *hypernyms*).

The relationship between **hyponyms** and their nearer or more remote superordinates is important in structuring our thinking and writing. It allows us to move up and down the "ladder of abstraction" in argumentative writing. (See further under **abstract words**.) **Hyponyms** also contribute to cohesion in writing. (See under **coherence** or **cohesion**.)

hypotaxis is an alternative name in grammar for *subordination*. In traditional grammar **hypotaxis** referred to the hierarchical relationship of a subordinate clause to the main clause (see **clause** section 3). Modern grammarians have extended its use. The *Introduction to Functional Grammar* (1985) has it embrace other constructions which paraphrase subordinate clauses, such as nonfinite clauses and expressions of indirect reported speech. In the *Comprehensive Grammar of English* (1985) it's used of the internal structure of phrases.

hysteron proteron This phrase, borrowed from Greek, means "the latter sooner", but is differently used in rhetoric and argument. In argument it refers to an inverted form of logic, in which a proposition can only be proved with the help of the proposition itself. In our terms it "begs the question". See also **fallacies** section 2.

As a rhetorical figure of speech, **hysteron proteron** reverses the expected order of events, as in "They died, they starved in their cave". A somewhat similar displacement is involved in *hendiadys*, which involves altering the normal construction of a phrase such as "with curious eyes", so that it reads as "with eyes and curiosity".

I

I When can **I** be used in writing?

It depends on the type of writing. Personal letters, diaries and autobiography are the natural medium for it, when talking about our attitudes and opinions ("I think", "I know" "I feel" etc.); and **I** occurs naturally in scripted dialogue and many types of fiction. But when we write as part of our profession or in the name of an institution, it's conventional to avoid **I** even when expressing individual opinions and attitudes. Thus a reviewer is less likely to say:

I was delighted by the freshness of the performance ... than

The performance was delightfully fresh ...

The personal opinion is thus expressed indirectly, through an attitudinal adverb which is blended into the description. It gives the illusion that anyone viewing the performance would see it that way, and implies a weight of opinion behind the comment. By avoiding the use of **I**, the writer masks the fact that it is a subjective reaction, and the comment sounds more authoritative and professional.

The desire to sound authoritative and/or professional has no doubt fostered the convention that **I** should be suppressed in scientific, academic and bureaucratic writing. It was not always so however. In their classic writings, scientists such as Newton used **I** quite freely, and the suppression of **I** only became a regular feature of science writing from the late nineteenth century on.

However since the 1960s the US Council of Biology Editors has actively encouraged the use of **I** instead of contorted impersonal expressions in the passive (see under **passive**). In Britain a study of science and engineering writing by Kirkman (1980) found a sprinkling of the pronoun **I** in many of the papers published in academic journals—even though the scientists studied still reacted negatively to frequent use of **I**, saying that it sounded either amateurish or arrogant.

Elsewhere there's a stronger drive towards using **I**. Some American editors of academic manuscripts will make a point of converting every passive verb ("it was found") to a first person active verb ("*I* found"). And in some Australian government departments, ministerial letters bearing the chief's signature are very firmly written in the first person. This may be motivated as much by the desire to project the image of a strong executive head as to avoid an impersonal bureaucratic style.

So the reasons for using **I** in writing, or suppressing it, are complex and vary with the context of writing. Writers who avoid it may be adhering to older convention, or trying to divert attention from the lack of evidence for their opinion. Saying "This is not acceptable" sounds much more powerful than "I cannot accept this", whether or not there's anything to support it. Let the reader beware!

Grammatical notes on I. Because **I** is the subjective or nominative form of the pronoun, it is not the one to use when it is the grammatical object—especially after verbs or prepositions. Instead *me* is the form to use. Few people would mistake this when the pronoun comes immediately after the verb/preposition, as in:

> *The nurse wants me over there. She was beckoning to me on the way in ...*

But when another pronoun comes in front, it's less obvious that *me* should still be used, i.e.:

> *The nurse wants you and me over there. She was beckoning to you and me ...*

So speakers are sometimes tempted to say:

> *The nurse wants you and I over there. She was beckoning to you and I ...*

In informal communication this could pass unnoticed, but it would raise eyebrows in formal writing.

See also **between you and me**.

i before e The well-known rule of English spelling "*i* before *e* except after *c*" needs some qualifying to make it fully reliable. What about *science, conscience* and *conscientious*, for example? Not to mention *their*, *height* and *weight*— among others which do not obey the "rule".

Both kinds of exceptions can be accounted for if we add one more line to the rule:

- *i* before *e* except after *c* when it sounds like "ee". In this fuller form, the rule doesn't claim to cover any of the exceptional words above, because none of them has the *ie/ei* sounding like "ee". And the rule is still a useful guide for spelling words like *ceiling, deceit* and *receipt* (*ei* after *c*), and for *achieve, belief, grief, niece, piece, relieve* and *siege* (*ie* because there's no preceding *c*). The only common exceptions to the rule in its fuller form are *seize*, and *either/neither* (for those who pronounce them with "ee" rather than "eye"), plus a few chemical words such as *caffeine* and *protein*.

  Note that we could use the variability over the pronunciation of *either* and *neither* to tighten up the rule even further:

- *i* before *e* except after *c* when it *always* sounds like "ee". Put that way, the only remaining exceptions are *seize* and words like *caffeine/protein*.

i/y In a handful of English words, the spelling can be either **i** or **y**:

> *cider/cyder cipher/cypher dike/dyke*
> *gipsy/gypsy pigmy/pygmy siphon/syphon*

In North America the common spelling is with **i**, and the same treatment is extended to *silvan* (*sylvan*); and also to the noun *tire* (for a car or bicycle). The spelling *sirup* is also recognised as a variant of *syrup*, though the latter still gets priority in American dictionaries. (See further under **tire** and **syrup**.)

In Australia and Britain things are very mixed, with **i** typically used in *cider*, *cipher* and *siphon*; but variable spelling (often **y**) for the other three: see **dike**, **gipsy** and **pigmy**. In each case it would make sense to standardise on **i**.

Other words which raise questions on this point of spelling are **myna** and **stymie**, as well as classical and neoclassical words such as **dyad, dyarchy, dysfunctional** and **tiro**. See under those headings, and also **calix** and **calyx**.

Alternation between **i** and **y** once affected a very much larger number of English words. In the first century and a half of printing (from 1475 on), words like *city* might be spelled *cyty*, and *ship* could be *shyp(pe)*; and **i** was routinely replaced with **y** because the letter **i** in earlier printing fonts was so flimsy. Since then, **i** has steadily recovered its ground, and the alternation between **i** and **y** persists only in the words mentioned above, and as a regular change before certain suffixes. (See further under **i>y** and **-y>-i-**.)

Note that the equivalence of **i** and **y** is still exploited in surnames like *Smyth* and *Whyte*, though the spelling is fixed for the individuals who bear them. Anyone who writes to them or about them must take care.

i>y The letter **i** is regularly changed to **y** in a small group of English words: *die*, *lie*, *tie* and *vie*, as well as complex words based on them, e.g. *belie*, *underlie*, *untie*. The change happens when *-ing* is added to the stem, so *die* becomes *dying*, *lie* becomes *lying* etc. The reason for the change is clear enough: it avoids awkward-looking forms like *diing*, *liing* which would result from going by the regular rule of removing final *e* before *-ing* (see **-e**). Only in recently arrived verbs such as *skiing* and *taxiing* is the double *i* permitted.

For the reverse process, see **-y>-i-**.

-ian See under **-an**.

-iana This suffix is the delight of scholars and antiquarians. It gives them a way of referring collectively to all the information and material resources on a particular subject, as in *Shakespeariana* or *Australiana*. As those examples show, it's attached to proper names of people, places or institutions. The pattern is well established and can be used to create ad hoc words, such as *Macquariana*.

Originally **-iana** referred to the recorded output of an author, as is evident from a seventeenth century publication titled:

> *Baconiana: certain genuine remains of Sir Francis Bacon, arguments civil and moral ...*

Nowadays the suffix is usually understood to mean publications *about* a particular author or culture, and is extended to cover archival material and even antique objects.

ibex For the plural of this word, see under **-x**.

ibid. This referencing device is an abbreviated form of the Latin *ibidem* meaning "in the same place". Used in follow-up references to a particular book, chapter or page, it directs readers to the same source or place as was mentioned in the preceding reference. It substitutes for the author's name, the title of the book or article, and as much of what follows as would be identical. For example:

> 1 Hardy, C. *"A family line" Australian Journal of Genealogy* 3 (1952), p.85
>
> 2 ibid. p.92

The reference with **ibid.** must come immediately after the full one: if not the follow-up reference must repeat the author's name or an abbreviated title. (See further under **referencing**.) **Ibid.** could once appear in the main body of text, but its use has steadily declined and is nowadays confined to footnotes and endnotes.

-ibility or **-ability**   See -ability.

-ible   See under -able/-ible.

-ic/-ical   Quite a number of English adjectives appear in two forms, for example:

analytic/analytical	*arithmetic/arithmetical*
astronomic/astronomical	*egotistic/egotistical*
fanatic/fanatical	*ironic/ironical*
magic/magical	*monarchic/monarchical*
mystic/mystical	*obstetric/obstetrical*
parasitic/parasitical	*philosophic/philosophical*
poetic/poetical	*problematic/problematical*
psychic/psychical	*rhythmic/rhythmical*

Is there any reason for preferring one over the other?

The short answer is *no*: many pairs do not differ significantly in meaning. But there are shades of difference in some, such as **comic(al)**, **electric(al)** and **lyric(al)**, discussed under their respective headings. Typically the **-ic** spelling corresponds more closely to the core meaning of the stem, while the meaning of the **-ical** spelling is rather generalised. In yet others such as **economic(al)**, **historic(al)** and **politic(al)**, the meanings diverge considerably (see individual headwords).

In past centuries (from the fifteenth to the seventeenth) there were many more such pairs derived from classical sources:

> *grammatic(al) identic(al) organic(al) tragic(al)*

Time has selected one or the other for us though not consistently **-ic** or **-ical**. The form with **-ical** has been the survivor when there was a comparable noun in *-ic(s)*. This explains why we now use:

> *logical musical physical rhetorical tactical*

all of which had counterpart adjectives ending in **-ic** in earlier centuries.

Adverbs for **-ic/-ical** *adjectives.* The parity of adjectives in **-ic** and **-ical** helps to explain why the adverbs for both types end in *-ically*. So, for example, the

adverbs for *organic* and *tragic* are *organically* and *tragically*. Even though the
-ical forms of the adjectives have long since disappeared, their ghosts appear in
the adverbs. The effect is there even for adjectives which never had a counterpart
ending in **-ical**. So *barbaric, basic, civic, drastic* and others become
barbarically, basically etc., and it is as if *-ally* is the adverbial ending for them.
This has become the general rule for all adjectives ending in **-ic**—except *public*,
whose adverb is still normally *publicly*. In centuries past there were others like
it: *franticly* and *heroicly* appear in the classics of English literature. But they
too now form adverbs with *-ally* (*frantically, heroically*). *Webster's Dictionary*
recognises *publically* as a secondary spelling, and we may speculate as to
whether it will one day become dominant, bringing the one exception back under
the rule.

-ic/-ics Nouns ending in **-ic** or **-ics** are very often the names of scholarly subjects:
> *acoustics arithmetic classics economics ethics linguistics logic*
> *mathematics music optics physics rhetoric semantics statistics technics*
As the examples show, there are more words of that kind ending in **-ics** than
-ic. Yet whichever it is, it takes a singular form of the verb:
> *Logic has something in common with mathematics.*
> *Mathematics has something in common with logic.*
Note that this only applies when the word with **-ics** refers to a structured course
or broad area of study. If its field of reference is narrowed down, a plural verb
is normally used:
> *The mathematics of gambling are based on probability theory.*
In such cases, the word ending in **-ics** is qualified either by a preceding pronoun,
or by a following phrase (as in the last example).

icon or **ikon** The first spelling **icon** is given preference in all modern
dictionaries, and the citations in the *Oxford Dictionary* show that it has always
been so. The spelling **ikon** brings the English word closer to the original Greek
word, though the very rare *eikon* is closer still, being an exact transliteration of
the Greek. But with derivatives such as *iconoclastic, iconography* and *iconology*,
there's no doubt that **icon** is the one to prefer. (See also **k/c**.)

identical with or **identical to** These days either *with* or *to* may be used
after **identical**. Traditionally it was *with*, which is still preferred among older
people. But the use of **identical to** is so common as to be unremarkable, and it
outnumbers **identical with** by 2:1 in the Australian ACE corpus.
For comparison see **compare with** or **compare to**.

identify with Although this expression has been used reflexively for two
hundred years, it seems to have been the focus of critical attention. Fowler felt
the need to defend its use in constructions such as:
> *She identified herself with the women's movement on campus.*

In Fowler's view the expression was acceptable so long as the affiliation was more than casual. Nowadays we have no such reservations about it, nor about omitting the reflexive pronoun:

She identified with the women's movement on campus.

This elliptical usage has increased steadily since World War II according to *Webster's English Usage* (1989), and is registered in modern dictionaries. And though it was declared obsolete in the original *Oxford Dictionary*, the construction is recognised and reinstated in the second edition (1989).

idiom This word has been used in two ways in English, to refer to:

1 the collective usage of a particular group, as in the *idiom of drovers*
2 a particular fixed phrase of ordinary usage, for example *a red herring*.

The second use of **idiom** is by far the more common nowadays. An **idiom** in this sense is a fixed unit whose elements cannot be varied. Neither *a red fish*, or *a herring red in color*, can capture the meaning of the **idiom** *a red herring*. The meaning resides in the whole expression, and cannot be built up or extracted from its parts.

The word **idiom** is extended by some to cover the conventional collocations of English, such as *hit by* (a car) versus *hit with* (a hammer). This meaning of **idiom** is involved when we say that "hit with a car" is *unidiomatic English*.

idiosyncrasy or **idiosyncracy** The second spelling seems more likely, and yet the first is the standard everywhere in the English-speaking world. The element *-crasy* is the Greek word for "mixture", and taken literally **idiosyncrasy** means "one's own-together-mixing", i.e. that special blend of things which makes up a unique constitution. Yet *-crasy* appears in no other English word, and not so surprisingly people are inclined to write **idiosyncracy**, with the ending they know from *autocracy, democracy* etc. (see further under **-cracy**). So prevalent is **idiosyncracy** that it is registered as an alternative in the major American dictionaries. In the *Oxford Dictionary* it's acknowledged but called "erroneous". Ironically the several citations for it are from literary and linguistic writing.

i.e. This common abbreviation stands for the Latin phrase *id est* "that is", used when offering further explanation or a paraphrase of a previous statement. For example:

He will come as soon as the meeting ends, i.e. at 4 p.m.

Note that **i.e.** is not used to introduce examples, which is the function of *e.g.* (see **e.g.**).

The standard punctuation for **i.e.** is to put stops after each letter (see further under **Latin abbreviations**); and the majority of the 40 instances in the Australian ACE corpus (67%) were punctuated this way. But 23% had no stops at all (*ie*), and 10% just one stop (*ie.*).

Traditionally **i.e.** has been framed by punctuation marks: preceded by a comma (or else a dash, colon, or an opening bracket), and followed by a comma.

All but three of the instances in ACE were preceded by punctuation of some sort. But there were commas *after* **i.e.** in only a minority of instances (17%)— in keeping with the general trend to reduce punctuation.

The writing contexts in which **i.e.** is acceptable are now much wider. Once confined to footnotes, the Chicago *Manual of Style* notes its appearance in the main text, at least in parentheses. The *Right Word at the Right Time* allows it in official documents, and the Australian Government *Style Manual* notes its usefulness in scientific and technical writing as well as "general works" which contain numerous shortened forms. In the ACE corpus it turns up in seven categories of nonfiction and two of fiction. The appearance of **i.e.** in an ever-increasing range of writing shows that it cannot be deemed inappropriate for formal writing.

-ie/-y These two spellings alternate in the suffix of some familiar Australian colloquialisms:

> *cabbie/cabby footie/footy hippie/hippy junkie/junky kiddie/kiddy*
> *tellie/telly wharfie/wharfy etc.*

Either spelling may be used. It makes no difference to the word's denotation, though **-ie** spelling seems more in keeping with their informal flavor and informal constitution. Often they are clipped versions of longer expressions as *footie* is for *football match*, and sometimes ad hoc in other aspects of their spelling, as *bikkie* is for *biscuit*.

Many words of this kind have only been recorded with **-ie** (the *bookie* and the *groupie*, the *rookie* and the *townie*); and they may as well keep that spelling rather than adding to the burden already borne by the suffix *-y* (see further under **-y**). In some cases it's essential to use **-ie** rather than **-y**, so as to distinguish the colloquial noun from a regular adjective ending in *-y*. See for example:

blowie	"blowfly"	*blowy*
bushie	"one from the bush"	*bushy*
chalkie	"teacher/stock exchange assistant"	*chalky*
chewie	"chewing gum"	*chewy*
mushie	"mushroom"	*mushy*
pokie	"poker machine"	*poky*
soapie	"soap opera"	*soapy*

The only subgroup of these colloquialisms in which **-y** is the usual spelling are those which refer to family relationships, such as:

> *daddy granny hubby mummy nanny*

Some writers make *aunty* a member of the set (see **auntie** or **aunty**). Words like those show the original hypocoristic (i.e. childish) use of the suffix. But in Australia the **-ie/-y** suffix has been put to use far beyond the familiar things of home and the neighborhood, to the naming of common trades and recreations. The suffix is now a "familiarity marker" in British English also, according to the *Comprehensive Grammar of English* (1985), but there are fewer signs of this development in American English. To visitors' ears the suffix may still sound childish, but extensive use has altered its connotations in Australia.

Personal names with -ie or -y. Sometimes there's a choice between *-ie* and *-y* in the spelling of popular names and abbreviations such as *Chrissie/Chrissy* and *Johnnie/Johnny.* But when *Kellie/Kelly, Kerrie/Kerry* or others are given names, the bearer will be very conscious whether it is spelled their way or not. Some performers' names are fixed on this point, e.g. *Johnny Farnham,* and they again are ones to get right.

-ienne This feminine suffix borrowed from French is found in only a few regular English words, such as *comedienne, equestrienne* and *tragedienne.* All such words were coined in the mid-nineteenth century, to provide conspicuously female counterparts to words ending in *-ian* (*comedian* etc.). They have never been very popular, and their extinction is probably assured amid the general drive towards nonsexist language. (See further under **inclusive language.**)

-ier This suffix appears on two kinds of English words:
1 a few agent words borrowed from French, e.g. *halberdier, bombardier.* This ending becomes *-eer* in later English formations. (See *-***eer.**)
2 a few English agent words, such as *clothier, furrier.* This ending was also spelled *-yer,* hence *lawyer, sawyer.*

-ies For the plurals of Latin loanwords such as *series* and *species,* see under **Latin plurals.**

if The ambiguities latent in this word are easily resolved by intonation in speech, but need careful handling in writing. **If** is often used as a substitute for *whether,* with the implicit meaning of "whether or not". This may be what was intended in:
>   *You'll let us know if you're coming ...*
The person who uttered that remark might have expected people to communicate their answer whether or not they were coming—yet it's not really clear. The sentence written down suggests another possible meaning: that the people addressed are expected to reply "if and only if" they intend to come. To avoid misunderstanding (especially over the lack of communication when it was expected), the sentence would be better expressed as:
>   *Would you let us know whether or not you're coming ...*
This leaves no room for misunderstanding, though the casualness of the original is lost.

   If can also be a source of ambiguity when combined in a phrase with *not:*
>   *There was a short if not hasty consultation with the coach.*
In such a string of words, the *if not* phrase could mean either "short although not hasty", or "short as well as hasty". In other words, *if not* could be either contrastive or additive (see further under **conjunctions**)—which makes a big difference in meaning. Writers no doubt use *if not* sometimes to opt out of

making a judgement and keep things ambiguous. But if the writer's judgement or meaning are important, *if not* is best avoided.

If and the subjunctive. In conditional clauses, **if** serves to express things which might be: some are real possibilities, others purely hypothetical. The two kinds of possibility can be distinguished by the choice of verb:

If she were more forgiving, they might have reached agreement.
If he was back from Adelaide he'd lend a hand.

In the first sentence, **if** is coupled with the past subjunctive *were* to express an impossible condition (see further under **subjunctives**). In the second the ordinary indicative form of the verb (*was*) is used to express a condition which is a real possibility. This distinction is not always clear-cut however; and the indicative tends to replace the subjunctive in less formal styles, as noted in the *Comprehensive Grammar of English* (1985). Even the fixed phrase *if I were you* gets casually rephrased as *if I was you*. The absence of past subjunctive forms for any verbs other than *be* is another reason why the distinction is breaking down. The use of *were* after *if I/he/she/it* is now a matter of formality of style rather than grammar.

-ify/-efy These verb endings are identical in sound and meaning, yet are attached by convention to different verbs. The less common ending by far is **-efy**, which makes its appearance in only four words: *liquefy, putrefy, rarefy* and *stupefy*. But **-ify** is the ending for many, of which the following are just a handful:

amplify beautify clarify classify exemplify fortify glorify gratify
identify justify petrify purify quantify simplify vilify

The reason why words have either **-efy** or **-ify** is a matter of their individual history. In twentieth century English it seems quite arbitrary, and so the minority group with **-efy** are sometimes spelled with **-ify**. It happens especially with *liquify* (no doubt because of *liquid*), and dictionaries recognise it as an alternative spelling. Large dictionaries also recognise the alternatives for two or three of the others. *Webster's* has *putrify* and *rarify*, and the *Oxford Dictionary* registers *stupify* as well, though it claims that the **-ify** spellings became obsolescent in the latter half of the nineteenth century. (The entries do not appear to have been updated for the second edition.) Yet the related adjectives *putrid* and *stupid* still nudge writers towards *putrify* and *stupify*, not to mention all the other verbs formed regularly with **-ify**.

Note that **-ify** is always the one used in nonce formations, such as:

They've potplantified the office.

The **-ify** is also the one used where we might have expected *-yfy*, e.g. in *countrify, gentrify* (not *countryfy, gentryfy*). The change from *y* to *i* is in fact regular before a suffix beginning with a consonant (see **-y>-i-**), and it also helps to dissimilate the two *y*s. (See further under **dissimilate**.)

ignoratio elenchi See under **fallacies** section 2g.

ikon or **icon** See **icon**.

illegal, illegitimate or **illicit** All these adjectives imply that things are not done according to law, but their connotations and uses are somewhat different. **Illegal** is the most neutral and widely used of them, and can be applied to any kind of crime from *illegal parking* to the *illegal slaughter of elephants*. **Illegitimate** is best known in the cold phrase *illegitimate child* i.e. one born outside the laws of marriage. Apart from this **illegitimate** is also used in academic discussion, to describe an argument, conclusion or inference which is unsound by the laws of logic. **Illicit** is applied to activities which are not permitted by law, e.g. *illicit gambling*, an *illicit love affair* or keeping an *illicit still*. Among those who are privy to such things, they are a well-kept secret, and so **illicit** has more than a whiff of enjoying forbidden fruits.

illiterate Essentially this adjective means "unable to read or write". Even in societies with compulsory schooling, there's a small percentage of the population with no command of the written word, and so **illiterate** has some application in that sense.

Yet because reading and writing are taken for granted by the majority, the threshold of "literacy" is often implicitly raised beyond the basic command of letters. Thus *literate* comes to mean "well acquainted with book learning", and **illiterate** "showing little acquaintaince with books" or "ill-educated". Only in this second sense can a student's writing be described as "illiterate". Those who use the word this way no doubt count themselves among the *literati*. (See **littérateurs** or **literati**.)

illusion or **delusion** See **delusion**.

im- See under **in-/im-**.

-im This is the plural suffix for certain loanwords from Hebrew, including the Biblical *seraph(im)* and the post-World War II *kibbutz(im)*. Another is *goyim*, a plural or collective word meaning "those non-Jewish" (its singular is *goy*).

Note that *cherub* has both Hebrew and English plurals, associated with quite different worlds. The *cherubim* who appeared so often to Ezekiel were divine messengers, while the childlike angels who appear in baroque decoration with trumpets aloft are *cherubs*.

image and **imagery** At this end of the twentieth century, **image** is established in its quasi-collective sense of the "total impression given by a person, institution, company or product etc.". This sense, though first recorded in 1908, did not gain much currency until the late 1950s. After that it enjoyed such a vogue as to raise anxiety in style manuals, such as the *Right Word at the Right Time*, about its overuse. Yet we need hardly be surprised at people's concern with their image in societies and cultures that are pervaded by the mass media. Use of the word simply reflects its importance for any person or product whose success depends on mobilising public opinion.

The **image** generated by publicity, and the **image** which a writer creates are somewhat different. The first kind of image is rather abstract, like the sophistication and glamor which is supposed to accompany drinking that glass of wine, held up by a manicured hand. The poet's image is much more tangible, when he says "Drink to me only with thine eyes", and conjures up the very act of drinking and toasting. Another difference is that the image of the advertised product is already a composite of ideas, whereas the images raised by a poem or piece of writing usually serve to develop its **imagery** sequentially. Yet both the *publicity image*, and the *writer's imagery* put a particular coloring or set of values on whatever they present, so as to influence people's thinking.

See also **analogy** and **metaphor**.

imaginary or **imaginative** These words express different attitudes to imagination and the products of our imagination. Phrases such as an *imaginative approach* and an *imaginative solution* show that **imaginative** is often a positive quality, and that the imagination is seen as a constructive and creative resource.

The word **imaginary** affirms that something has been imagined and is fictitious, such as an *imaginary conversation* or an *imaginary illness*. The adjective has negative connotations if what is imagined is used to deceive or to manipulate others, but otherwise it's neutral. So David Malouf's novel *An Imaginary Life* is a perfectly acceptable fiction. The book is also highly **imaginative**, but the author leaves it to readers and critics to apply that word to it.

immigrant For the choice between **immigrant** and **migrant**, see **migrant**.

imminent or **eminent** See eminent.

immoral or **amoral** See under a-/an-.

impassive or **impassioned** These words are almost opposite in meaning, since **impassive** means "showing no emotion", and **impassioned** means "expressing intense emotion". An *impassioned plea* by a speaker implies strong emotional input to the message, and the last thing such a speaker wants to see is *impassive expressions* on the faces of his audience.

Note that *dispassionate* differs from both *impassive* and *impassioned*. It connotes lack of personal bias or feeling, and is applied when fairness is important, as in a *dispassionate account of the conflict*.

imperative This is the grammarian's term for the special form of English verbs which expresses a direct command. For example:

Go back.
*Quick **march**.*
***Turn** off the lights before leaving.*

As the examples show, the imperative has no special suffix, and the subject is not expressed.

Negative imperatives are expressed with the aid of *do not*, or *don't*, as in:

> *Do not walk on the grass.*
> *Don't look now but ...*

Note that the abrupt effect of the imperative is softened by combining it with *please* or just *do*.

> *Please sit down. Please put it on.*   (polite and detached)
> *Do sit down. Do put it on.*   (collaborative and friendly)

For other ways of expressing commands and instructions, see under **commands**.

For the distinction between **imperative** and **imperious**, see under **imperial, imperious** or **imperative**.

imperfect For grammarians this is another name for the continuous aspect of the verb. See under **aspect**.

imperial, imperious or **imperative** With the decline of empires and emperors, there's less for **imperial** to do. It remains as a monument to former empires in *Imperial College* London, and to former emperors in the *Imperial Palace* to be visited by tourists in China and Japan. This is not to say that **imperialism** itself is dead, but rather that it's not now linked with recognised empires.

In Australia, the use of *Imperial* with a capital *I* has always been in connection with the British Empire, as it was in *AIF* (the abbreviation for the *Australian Imperial Force*) which served in both World Wars. With the commutation of the British Empire into the (British) Commonwealth, most *Imperial* institutions have disappeared, or been renamed. The most generally known Imperial institution to survive is the *imperial system of weights and measures*, on which see the next entry.

Neither **imperious** nor **imperative** have any connection with empires. Yet **imperious** implies the will to make others do your bidding, as in:

> *The imperious voice of the matron resounded ahead of her as she swept down the corridor.*

Imperious is usually applied to aspects of people's behavior, whereas **imperative** is mostly used of circumstances which force us to do something:

> *It's imperative that they decide before the next election.*

For the grammatical use of **imperative**, see under that heading.

imperial weights and **measures** The imperial system of weights and measures was formerly used in Australia, and continues to be used in Britain and elsewhere. In Australia it was officially replaced by the metric system in 1970. Younger people absorb the metric system as part of their schooling, even if older people still calibrate things in imperial measures, estimating distances in miles, and human weight in pounds and stones. The most common terms in the imperial system include:

> for length: *inch foot yard chain furlong mile*
> for mass: *ounce pound stone hundredweight ton*
> for volume: *fluid ounce pint quart gallon*

Some of those terms linger in common idiom:
a six footer
wouldn't budge an inch
miles from anywhere
drinking whisky by the gallon

Imperial measures persist in a number of specialised fields the world over. A tennis net is set at 3 *feet* or 1 *yard* (= 0.914 metres) above the ground, and a cricket pitch is still a *chain* or 22 *yards* in length (= 20.12 m). Printers calculate the dimensions of a piece of printed text in picas, which measure just on one sixth of an *inch*; and the screws used by engineers and carpenters are normally calibrated in terms of so many turns to the *inch*, and by British Standard Whitworth norms, rather than the ISO-metric system. The altitudes at which a jet flies are given in *feet* (e.g. 37 000 feet), and nautical usage maintains its own standard units for depth (*fathom*), speed (*knot*) and sea distance (*nautical mile*).

The metric system of units is discussed under **metrication**, and a full table for converting imperial measures to their metric equivalents can be found in Appendix V.

imperiled or **imperilled** See under -l/-ll.

imperious or **imperative** See imperial, imperious or imperative.

impersonal writing Writing can seem *impersonal* for different reasons. It may hide the character and attitudes of the writer, so that the information seems detached from both sender and receiver of the message, and shows no human perspective on it:
The Council will replace the twice-weekly garbage collection with a once-a-week system, as from March 1st.
Impersonal writing like that is often produced in the name of an institution, when the writer becomes an official voice, addressing a vast, mixed audience whose reactions are not known.

Writing can also seem *impersonal* when it avoids referring to human participation in the action it describes, as in:
It was decided that the meeting should be adjourned.
This is of course typical of the way in which the minutes of meetings are recorded. It can be frustrating if you want to know who prevailed in the debate. But the impersonal *it was decided* embodies the democratic principle that the majority decides the issue, whether or not there were dissenting votes from influential individuals. In science writing it's also conventional for experimenters to report their work impersonally, on the assumption that what was done (rather than who did it) is what other scientists need to know:
A small piece of sodium was added to a beaker of water.

This use of the passive (*was added*) instead of the active "I, the experimenter, added a small piece ..." is now being questioned by some scientists, however. (See under **I**.)

For the moment, the impersonal style serves a number of conventional purposes, bureaucratic and scientific. But in other contexts—where communication needs to be lively, human and sensitive to the individual—the impersonal style with its official and academic overtones is to be avoided.

imply or **infer** The distinction which is commonly drawn between these makes the two words reciprocal: a writer or statement may **imply** something, which readers may or may not **infer**. But usage commentators note the persistent habit of using **infer** rather than **imply** in sentences like the following:

I heard the doctor infer that she would never walk again. (assuming that the doctor was talking about a patient)

Such use of **infer**, making it synonymous with **imply**, is recognised in all modern dictionaries although they attach warning labels to it, dubbing it "colloquial" or "loose usage". The Harper-Heritage panel almost all rejected it, and the *Oxford Dictionary* (1989) notes that it is "widely considered to be incorrect". However *Webster's English Usage* (1989) shows that the stigma has developed in the course of this century, and that **infer** was used quite freely in this way earlier on.

The use of **infer** for **imply** may well be a hypercorrection actually generated by the fine reciprocal line that has been drawn between them. (A similar problem besets other reciprocal pairs such as *substitute/replace* and *comprise/compose*.) **Imply** is much more common than **infer** according to the evidence of English databases everywhere, and their distribution patterns are very different. In the Australian ACE corpus **infer** is found in only five samples, all either bureaucratic, legal or academic prose: whereas **imply** is found in all kinds of nonfiction, in nearly 40 different samples. In view of the relative rarity of **infer**, its use where the rule requires **imply** suggests writers/speakers who are overzealous about correctness, reaching beyond the word that comes easily.

Another complicating factor noted by *Webster's English Usage* is the logical use of **infer** with a nonpersonal subject, meaning "indicate" or "have or lead to as a conclusion"—a use which originated with Thomas More in 1530. For example:

The configuration of ankle bones in the x-rays inferred that she would never walk again.

This use of **infer** is acknowledged in all modern dictionaries.

It stands between the reciprocal uses of **imply** and **infer** distinguished above, and overlaps with the use of **imply** with a personal subject.

The shift from nonpersonal use of **infer** "indicate" to personal use as "imply" is no great move, as the two examples show. In conversation and debate many people do not distinguish between those constructions; and in context it's usually quite clear whether **infer** is intended to mean making an active suggestion (= **imply**), or a deduction made from something else. As often, the distinction is more important in writing, and writers may be reassured by the general facts of usage outlined above: that the word they need most of the time is **imply**. Like other shibboleths of language, the issue needs to be defused. (See further under **shibboleth**.)

impractical or **impracticable** See under **practical** or **practicable**.

in-/im- These two share the burden of representing two meanings in English:
1 "not" as in *inaccurate, indefinite, informal, imbalance, immortal, imperfect*
2 "in" as in *include, income, inroad, imbibe, immigrant, imprint*

As the examples show, the negative and intensive uses are indistinguishable. Only by analysing the composition of words can we tell which prefix is there. In both groups, the **im-** form is used regularly before *b*, *m* and *p*, and the **in-** form before any other sounds. Doubt as to which prefix is there lies at the heart of the problem with *inflammable*. (See further under **flammable**.)

Note that in- (= "in") varies in some words with en-. (See **en-/in-**.)

in-/un- Should it be:

inadvisable	or	*unadvisable*
incurable		*uncurable*
inescapable		*unescapable*
inharmonious		*unharmonious*
insanitary		*unsanitary*

For these, and various other negative adjectives, either prefix is acceptable, and there's no difference in meaning.

But for many, the prefix is fixed by a mixture of history and convention. The **in-** prefix is from Latin and generally goes with Latin formations, while **un-** is Old English and goes with English formations, even when the same root is involved. So we have:

incomplete	vs.	*uncompleted*
indiscriminate		*undiscriminating*
inedible		*uneatable*

Other points to note from those examples are that the English *un-* is often prefixed to words ending in *-ed*, *-ing* or *-able*, whereas the Latin **in-** heads words ending in *-te* and *-ible*, as well as *-ent*, *-(i)al*, *-ive* and *-ous*. For the choice between *impractical* and *unpractical*, see under **practical** or **practicable**.

Note finally the special group of Latin adjectives which do not use **in-**, but rather **un-**, *dis-* or *non*:
unindustrious unimaginative unintelligent unintentional
disincentive disinfectant disingenuous disintegrate
nonimperialist nonindigenous noninfectious nonintoxicating

For some of the *dis-* words, it's arguable that the prefix *dis-* is needed to express reversal rather than straight negation (see further under **dis-**). Yet in all those examples the stem itself begins with *in-*, and to add on the negative prefix **in-**

would be distracting, witness "inintelligent", "iningenuous", "ininfectious". The use of **un-**, *dis-* and *non* helps to dissimilate the prefix from the stem. (See further under **dissimilate** or **dissimulate**.)

-in/-ine See -ine/-in.

in back of See back of.

in camera This Latin phrase was adopted in the nineteenth century, to refer to legal proceedings conducted as a closed hearing. Literally the phrase means "in (the judge's) chamber", i.e. not in an open court. It is also applied to meetings of committees which are conducted in secret.

in case of, in case, and **in the case of** Between Australian and American English use of **in case of** there's a subtle difference. Australians use it in two ways:

> *In case of fire do not use the lifts.*
> *Bring an umbrella in case of rain.*

In the first sentence **in case of** means "in the event of", whereas in the second it means "on the offchance of". The first, rather official use at the start of a sentence sets up an inescapable condition; whereas the second is more casual, indicating a circumstance to prepare for, which may or may not happen. In Australian English the conditional meaning is associated with the topic position (i.e. being the first component in the sentence: see further under **topic**). But in American English it can appear later on, witness the following from a California newspaper:

> *The children would be sent home from school in case of disaster.*

To Australian ears, the sentence is ambiguous. Presumably it's concerned with emptying schools *if* there is a disaster, yet it seems to say that children may go home on the offchance that there may be one.

The conjunction **in case** is used with the more casual meaning in Australian English, whereas in American English it can have the stricter conditional meaning:

> *The machine should be turned off in case the red light comes on.*

The sentence hardly makes sense by the Australian meaning: it sounds as if you should never turn the machine on. By the American meaning however it has some purpose.

The phrase **in the case of** is often censured in style manuals as something wordy and overused. Looked at in isolation, it may seem extravagant in the following sentence:

> *In the case of that abusive letter, I would ignore it.*

Yet the opening phrase may well serve as a topicalising device, and as a way of spotlighting an item in a series of sentences that would otherwise submerge it. (See further under **topic** and **information focus**.)

in flagrante delicto See under **corpus delicti**.

in medias res This Latin phrase meaning "into the midst of things" refers to the narrative technique of plunging the reader straight into the heat of the action—and not working towards it through conventional introductions and setting of the scene. The phrase was coined by Horace (*Ars Poetica* 1.148). Twentieth century fiction quite often uses the technique, and it's increasingly common in movie-making.

in situ This Latin phrase means "on site", or less literally "in its original place". It has been used since the nineteenth century of such things as on-the-spot examinations of an object, as opposed to examining it after moving it to a laboratory. But it's also used more casually, to mean "in the usual place", as in:
> *He's still in situ at the Department of Education.*

in toto Borrowed from Latin, this phrase means "in total", and so "altogether, completely". Coupled with a negative it expresses reservations, as in:
> *She would not support the proposal in toto.*

Apart from negative adverbs, **in toto** is used with verbs of negative implications, such as *deny*, *disagree* or *reject*. Because it so often expresses a demurral, the phrase is sometimes thought to mean "on the whole"—though that translation shortcircuits its intrinsic meaning.

inapt or **inept** See inept.

inclusive language This is language which raises no sexist or racist stereotypes. It avoids terms like *businessman* and *businesswoman* in favor of ones like *executive* or *manager* which are gender-free. It shuns words with pejorative implications for members of other races and nationalities, such as *wog* and *Itie*. The use of such words creates instant disadvantage for the people referred to. The need to create equal opportunity is at the heart of **inclusive language**, to ensure that language itself neither raises nor maintains social barriers.

   Ways of avoiding sexist language are discussed at **nonsexist language**; and problems and solutions of racist terms under **ethnic**, **half-caste** and **racist language**. See also **disabled**.

incognito For the use of this word, see under **nom de plume**.

incredible or **incredulous** In standard English, only a person can be **incredulous** (i.e. "unable to believe something"), whereas facts and events are **incredible** (i.e. "unable to be believed"). Hence the television series about bizarre happenings, titled "That's incredible!"

   But we also have to reckon with a colloquial use of **incredible**, which often goes with an exclamation mark:
> *You're incredible!*
> *She's an incredible person.*

In expressions like those, **incredible** means roughly "amazing or extraordinary", but its connotations of intense surprise outweigh any particular denotation. As in those examples, it's often applied to people. The sense of amazement is also there in colloquial use of the adverb *incredibly*:

> *They were incredibly strong.*
> *I felt incredibly tired.*

Used this way, the word has little denotation, and becomes no more than a rather bulky intensifier. (See further under **intensifiers**.)

See also **credible** or **creditable**, and **credulity** or **credibility**.

incubus For the plural of this word, see under **-us** section 1.

incumbent or **encumbent** Only the first of these appears as a headword in modern dictionaries, though the second was used in earlier centuries, and is alive and well in Australia, according to Phillip Howard's cheerfully titled *Dictionary of Diseased English* (1977). He does not however declare his sources, and the *Oxford Dictionary* does not support his claims.

If **encumbent** shows up in Australia or anywhere else, it would be natural enough for two reasons. Firstly, the prefixes *in-* and *en-* have alternated for centuries in English words (see **en-/in-**); and secondly, *en-* is the usual prefix in the much more common (and deceptively similar) words *encumber* and *encumbrance*. In fact **incumbent** and *encumber* have quite separate histories, with **incumbent** formed out of the Latin verb meaning "lean upon", and *encumber* derived from French and meaning roughly "obstruct". Yet as the *incumbent* of an office, you may be *encumbered* with particular duties, and this overlap of meaning no doubt encourages the identification of the two words.

indefinite article See under **articles**, and **a** or **an**.

indention, indentation or **indenture** These all originate from the notion of making a notch or toothshaped mark in a document. However only the first two are interchangeable. Both **indention** and **indentation** refer to the practice of indenting: leaving a space at the beginning of a line of print, **indention** being the more widely used term. It is endorsed in the *Style Manual* of the Australian Government Publishing Service, as well as those by *Chicago* and *Webster's*. In Britain, *Copy-editing* (1992) also uses **indention**, whereas *Hart's Rules* is for **indentation**. (For more about indenting practices, see under **indents**.)

The term **indenture** was originally applied to legal contracts contained in documents with identical notches cut into the edge. The uniqueness of the notches was intended to prevent false copies of the document being drawn up. Nowadays **indenture** is still a contract or agreement (especially between an employer and an apprentice), but the documents are no longer notched.

indents The small space set at the beginning of a line of type is an *indent*. A single *indent* marks a new paragraph, and a vertical series of **indents** serves to set off a list of items from the main text. **Indents** are used in almost all print media, fiction and nonfiction; and in newspapers and magazines, whether the text runs across the whole width of the page, or is two or more columns.

The standard *indent* for paragraphs is 1 or 2 ems, varying with the length of the line. For line lengths over 26 picas, the longer *indent* is needed.

Regular indenting may be suspended in certain circumstances:

1 In textbooks and reference works, the line immediately following a heading or subheading is not usually indented, but set flush with the left margin. Most publishers do this at the beginning of a chapter as well. Yet the decision is partly a matter of looks, and needs to be coordinated with the size and placement of the headings: are they centred, flush with the left margin, or indented? Daily newspapers indent the first line under both headlines and subheadlines.

2 The first line of a block quotation is not usually indented, provided it's clearly set off from the main body of the text, either by italics, or change of type size, or by block indenting.

3 In fully blocked letter format. (See under **letter writing**, and Appendix VII.)

Hanging indention is the reverse of regular indention: the first line is flush with the left margin, and the second and subsequent lines in the same unit are all indented 1 em, as a block. (Note that while *hanging indention* is the standard term in Australian and British style manuals, it's *flush-and-hang* in American editorial practice.) The technique is often used in lists and indexes, as in the two examples in the entry for **indexing** under section 2. The same technique is sometimes used for setting out a series of points in the main body of the text. (The turnover lines are also indented.)

> *1. ʌʌʌʌʌʌʌʌʌʌʌʌ*
>   *xxxxxxx*
> *2. yyyyyyyyyyy*
>   *yyyyyyyyyyy*
>   *yy*

In statistical tables, *hanging indents* are used in the stub for turnover lines of subheadings. (See further under **tables**.)

Note that for footnotes, the standard practice is to use regular indention. The number itself is usually indented at the start of each note, and the turnover lines go back to the left margin:

>   *1. xxxxxxxxxxx*
> *xxxx*
>   *2. yyyyyyyyyyy*
> *yyyyyyyyyyyyyyyyy*
> *yyyyyyyyyy*

indenture or **indention** See under **indention**.

independent or **independant, independence** or **independance**
See under **dependent**.

index The plural of this Latin loanword can be either *indexes* or *indices*, though the context usually decides which. In statistical and technical writing, in mathematics, economics and the sciences, it's usually *indices*, as in:
> *Add the indices of all the numbers in the equation ...*
> *The latest indices of business turnover show ...*
In other contexts, especially when dealing with books and bibliography, the plural is *indexes*:
> *The book has two indexes, one of proper names, and one for ordinary*
> *words used and cited.*
For the two plurals see **-x** section 2.
For information on indexing books, see next entry.

indexing An *index* is an asset for almost any nonfiction book whose material is not already presented in alphabetical order. It helps both committed readers and browsers to access the book's fine detail, and is always a useful complement to the table of contents or chapter headings. Both by convention and convenience it's the last section of the book—since it cannot be started until the rest of the book has been paginated. It is usually set in slightly smaller type than the main text (2 points smaller), and usually in double columns, unless the book is in large format, in which case the index may be in three or four columns on a page. *Indexes* tend to be longer and more detailed in academic and technical books, and may indeed be specialised for particular aspects of the book. Hence the varieties of *index* such as: *Index of Names and Places* and *Subject Index* etc. as well as the *General Index*. When there's more than one index, the most comprehensive one goes last.

The labor of making the *index* may fall to the author of a book, or be done by the publisher or a professional indexer. *Indexing software* is increasingly available for personal computers, which can be used by anyone. But creating the *index* raises a number of questions.

1 What items should be entered in the *index*? The aim is to cover all the key concepts and terms used, as well as any specific references which readers might look for. The indexer needs to anticipate the nontechnical terms which browsers might use as their first port of call in the *index*. Established synonyms for concepts (and synonymous phrases), and alternative official and personal names will need to be entered. Crossreferencing within the entries should allow the reader to move from the specific to the general and vice versa. At the same time, the *index* should enable the reader to get information about a topic in one place, as far as possible.

2 How should the entries be set? There are two established ways of presenting entries in an *index*:
a) broken off;
b) run on (= *run in* in American editorial practice).

The methods differ in the way they treat subentries. The broken-off method has each subentry on a separate line, indented 1 em and with turnovers indented 2 ems. The run-on method blocks all subentries together, indented 1 em, with individual subitems separated by a semicolon:

broken off
brackets 102-6
   curly brackets 105
   round brackets (parentheses) 102-4
   slash brackets 104
   square brackets (in mathematics) 106, (in linguistics) 105
run on
brackets 102-6; curly brackets 105; round brackets (parentheses) 102-4;
     slash brackets 104; square brackets (in mathematics) 106, (in
     linguistics) 105

On the matter of page spans, see **numbers** and **number style** section 1. As the examples show, the run-on method takes less space, requires fewer word breaks, and is easy to set. It is however less easy for the reader to consult. The broken-off method always takes more space, especially if used for subentries as well as sub-subentries. (The text contracts to the right-hand side of the column.) In some *indexes* the two methods are combined, with broken-off setting used for subentries, while sub-subentries within them are run on.

3 Should the indexed words be in letter-by-letter or word-by-word alphabetical order? (These alternatives are presented at **alphabetical order**.) The letter-by-letter is more straightforward for the indexer or computer to produce. However the reader will locate entries more easily if word-by-word order is used, especially when there are many closely related words.

Indian This adjective has served to refer to peoples in many parts of the globe. It was originally applied to the inhabitants of the Indian subcontinent, as it still is. (See further under **Hindi** and **Hindu**.) During the European colonial era, it was also applied to the natives of the East Indies, to indigenous peoples in the Philippines, and to the Aborigines of Australia and New Zealand.

While **Indian** was extending its scope in English, it was being used in Spanish to refer to the indigenous peoples of both the Old World (India) and the New, in the American continent and in the *West Indies*. (Tradition has it that they owe their name to Columbus's mistaken idea when he first reached them that he had reached the *East Indies*.) In English too, **Indian** became applied to the indigenous people of North and South America, usually with some qualifying word as in *Plains Indians*, *Amazonian Indians*, *Mexican Indians*. The term *Red Indians* reflects the same tendency, though it smacks of frontier fiction, and is not used in American English.

International English has just a few stock phrases in which the adjective **Indian** (pure and simple) refers to North American Indians. They include *Indian corn* i.e. maize, *Indian file* (walk in single file as did American Indians on the move), and *Indian summer*. This phrase is recorded at regular intervals in nineteenth century America as a way of referring to a period of sunny and often hazy stable weather at the end of autumn. It is explained through the fact that such weather was typical of the inland areas then inhabited by American Indians, which differed from the changeable cool climate of the coasts settled by Europeans.

indicative This traditional grammar term is applied to verb forms which express factuality and contrast with those that express the hypothetical (termed *subjunctive*). The terms **indicative** and *subjunctive* are a legacy of Latin grammar, but there's little for them to do in English grammar because of the decline of subjunctive forms. (See further under **if**, **mood** and **subjunctive**.)

indict or **indite** In their ultimate origin and pronunciation, these are the same, but they have diverged in their spheres of activity. The verb **indict** is used in law to mean "bring a formal charge against (someone)". Both it and the related noun *indictment* are also used more widely, to mean "condemn/ation", as in:
His report was a damning indictment of the health service.
While **indict** and *indictment* are current terms, **indite** meaning "to compose or write a literary work" is very old-fashioned. The *Oxford Dictionary*'s latest citations for it are from Disraeli in the middle of last century, and we may wonder whether even then it was a conscious archaism on his part.
The spelling **indict** is an anomaly. The *c* was introduced around 1600 as a way of distinguishing the legal word from the other one, and as a visual link with its Latin forebear *indictare*. (Previously it had also been spelled *indite* or *endite*, see **en-/in-**.) But the additional letter has never registered in our pronunciation, as with various other respellings of the English Renaissance. Given the obsolescence of **indite**, the need to use the spelling **indict** disappears. We might as well accept the verdict of history, and allow **indict** to revert to **indite**. In doing so we'd remove one more trap for the unwary from the English language.

indirect object See under **object**.

indirect question See under **questions** section 4.

indirect speech The differences between *direct* and **indirect speech**, and other ways of reporting what someone has said are discussed under **direct speech**.

indiscriminate See under **discriminate**.

indite or **indict** See **indict**.

Indo-European This term links almost all the languages of Europe with those of Iran and North India into a single family. It represents one of the great linguistic discoveries of the colonial era: that English and Scots and French and

Greek, not to mention Russian and Iranian and Hindi, are all derivatives of the same original language, spoken perhaps 5000 years ago, somewhere on the frontiers of eastern Europe and western Asia. Within the Indo-European family the languages of individual branches are naturally more closely related, as are English and German in the Germanic branch, or Polish and Russian in the Slavic. However the genetic relationship with even the more remote branches, such as Celtic and Indo-Iranian, can be seen when you line up their basic vocabulary. The numbers used to count in each language provide the most striking evidence of common origin. See for example:

English	one	two	three
Dutch	een	twee	drie
Italian	uno	due	tre
Welsh	un	dau	tri
Russian	odin	dva	tri
Greek	heis	duo	treis
Hindi	ek	do	tin

Indo-European languages have spread by colonial expansion to all other continents—North and South America, Africa, Australia, New Zealand and the Pacific islands.

Indonesia The name means "Indian islands" and is a reminder of the vagueness of European geography in the early centuries of colonialism. **Indonesia** was just part of the East Indies, a region stretching from India to Japan.

The present population of **Indonesia**, now well over 150 million, is scattered over more than 13 000 islands, the largest of which are Borneo (in *Indonesian*, Kalimantan), Celebes (Sulawesi), Irian Jaya, Java, Sumatra, and the Moluccas. The wealth of **Indonesia** attracted the attention of the Portuguese in the sixteenth century, and then that of the English and Dutch East India companies. **Indonesia** was controlled by the Dutch from the seventeenth century until independence in 1949. However the Portuguese continued to govern East Timor until 1976.

See also **Jakarta**.

indorse or **endorse** See under **en-/in-**.

indubitably or **undoubtedly** See **undoubtedly**.

induction This is the process of reasoning whereby we draw a general proposition or generalisation from a series of instances or examples. The *inductive* process underlies much everyday communication, and is easily seen in newspaper headlines such as:

RENTS ON THE RISE IN PERTH

A generalisation like that is presumably based on evidence gathered by the reporter, and to see what it was we would read on. As in that case, the generalisation is often stated *before* the examples on which it is based. The soundness of the generalisation depends on whether it's based on plenty of examples, and on how representative they are. If the headline above was based on a few prices quoted by two real estate agents in two suburbs of Perth, it's potentially misleading and a *rash generalisation*.

Inductive generalisations both rash and reasonable are made all the time as people exchange ideas and information. Not often are they "perfect" inductions, i.e. ones based on *all* instances or entities which lend themselves to it. And even a perfect **induction** can only be said to *support* a general proposition, not to *prove* it in the philosophical sense of guaranteeing its truth.

Modern science owes a great deal to *inductive reasoning*, and it is the foundation of scientific method. Scientific laws are *induced* from recurrent instances of natural behavior, or tested and confirmed by them. In fact **induction** is the only logical way to validate many a statement. If someone says: *Melaleucas grow well on river banks*, the only way to verify the statement is by seeking out a significant number of instances in which this is so. Statements like that, whose validity must be tested *inductively* are called *synthetic statements*; whereas statements which are self-validating (i.e. true by virtue of the way they are formulated) are *analytic statements*. An example of the latter is "No maiden aunt is an only child". (See also **tautology**.)

Compare **deduction**.

industrious or **industrial** These adjectives involve two different uses of the word *industry*. Its older denotations of persistent and energetic application to a task are embodied in **industrious** meaning "hard-working", and this usage has persisted in English for five centuries. But **industrial** as in *industrial revolution* implies a connection with *industry* in its modern sense of a manufacturing concern or branch of business. The distance between **industrious** and **industrial** is clear in the ironic fact that *industrial action* means anything but industrious behavior on the part of the workers concerned.

-ine/-in This suffix appears on both adjectives and nouns in English, with variable pronunciation and some variation in its spelling. As an adjective ending it's used to mean "made of", as in *crystalline*, or "associated with", as in *tangerine*. The examples show two of the possible pronunciations for this suffix in English, to rhyme with "wine" or "ween". As a noun ending **-ine** has a minor role marking the feminine form of some masculine names, as in *Josephine* and *Pauline*, and in the common noun *heroine*. The latter shows a third pronunciation, rhyming with "win".

The most important role for **-ine** in twentieth century English is in marking the names of chemical substances, though in common usage both their spelling and pronunciation can vary. For the following the spelling may be either that of **-in** or **-ine**:

gelatin(e) glycerin(e) lanolin(e) saccharin(e)

The **-in** is strongly preferred in American English, whereas British English prefers **-ine**, and Australian usage as often is between the two. Product labels typically have *gelatine* and *glycerine*, but *lanolin* and *saccharin*, the latter helped by the currency of pronunciations rhyming with "win". (Another pointer in this direction is the Australian spelling and pronunciation of *mandarin* (the small, sweet citrus fruit), definitely preferred to *mandarine*.)

The spelling of chemical substances is less variable for professional chemists. The use of **-ine** and **-in** was systematically distinguished by A.W. von Hofmann, professor of chemistry in London and Berlin, whose classification was embodied in Watts' *Dictionary of Chemistry* (1866) and subsequently adopted by the Chemical Society. Hofmann reserved the **-ine** spelling for alkaloids and organic bases, such as:

caffeine cocaine morphine quinine strychnine

He assigned **-in** to neutral substances (including glucosides, glycerides and proteids):

albumin gasolin gelatin glycerin globulin

But Hofmann's system stands less clearly than it might (especially for the nonchemist), because **-ine** and **-in** have other uses in chemistry as well. A number of chemical elements (the so-called "halogens") are spelled **-ine**:

bromine chlorine fluorine iodine

Meanwhile, **-in** is the ending of a number of enzymes and hormones:

adrenalin insulin pepsin rennin

in addition to some well-known drugs and pharmaceutical products, such as:

aspirin heroin penicillin streptomycin

Chemists themselves have inside knowledge and access to chemical formulae which would resolve any ambiguity in using such words. And perhaps ignorance is bliss for ordinary users, who can simply decide between **-ine** and **-in** on the basis of habit and pronunciation.

Finally note that in some household chemical names **-ine** varies with *-ene*, and so both *gasoline* and *gasolene*, *kerosine* and *kerosene* are listed in dictionaries. Australian and American dictionaries prefer *gasoline* for the first and *kerosene* for the second. British dictionaries have a curious preference for *gasolene*, and vary over the other word. Their vacillation over *kerosene/kerosine* is effectively explained in the *Oxford Dictionary* (1989), with numerous citations showing the common preference for *kerosene*, but official backing given to *kerosine* by technical bodies in Britain and America (by the British Institute of Petroleum, the American Society for Testing Materials, the American Standards Association). For those two words, the choice of **-ine** or *-ene* makes no chemical difference— whereas with **benzine/benzene** and **fluorine/fluorene** there is a difference. (See further under those headings.)

inept or **inapt** The focus in these adjectives is different, though both imply that something is "not suited or unsuitable" for the purpose in hand. This is more directly expressed in **inapt**, in usages such as an *inapt use of resources*. The word was formed relatively recently in English (only two centuries ago), and has retained the literal meaning of its components. It is largely confined to formal styles of communication.

The much more common **inept** originated in Latin from the same elements, and had already developed the meaning "ineffectual" when it came into English. This is probably the dominant sense in English nowadays, though in particular contexts it can also mean "incompetent" (*inept management*) or "fatuous" (*inept remarks*). The word has a negative value judgement built in, whereas **inapt** is more dispassionate.

infectious For the difference between this word and *contagious*, see under **contagious** or **infectious**.

infer or **imply** See **imply**.

inferable, inferrable or **inferrible** Dictionaries give priority to the first spelling, though they also recognise the second and third. **Inferable** is in keeping with *inference*, whereas **inferrable** coincides with *inferred* and *inferring*, and observes the common rule of doubling the final consonant of a stressed syllable before adding a suffix. (See **doubling of final consonant**.) **Inferrible** uses the latinate suffix, but it sits strangely in an English formation. (See further at **-able/-ible**.)

Note that the same three options are recognised with *transferable/ transferrable/transferrible*, but not for *preferable*.

infinitives The basic nonfinite forms of verbs, such as *(to) ask, (to) go* or *(to) decide* are called **infinitives**. They combine with auxiliaries and other catenatives to form compound verbs and verb phrases:

I will *ask*	I wanted *to ask*
you may *go*	you meant *to go*
they couldn't *decide*	they tried *to decide*

Alongside simple infinitives such as those italicised, perfect infinitives can be formed with *have*, and passive infinitives with *be*:

I wouldn't *have gone*	I'd like *to have gone* (perfect)
you *will be asked*	you have *to be asked* (passive)

As the examples show, infinitives are not necessarily expressed with *to* in front, and historically *to* is not part of the English infinitive. Yet the idea that it was indissolubly attached underlies all the anxiety about **split infinitives**. (See under that heading.)

Infinitives also combine with certain adjectives in English:

eager to please   easy to undo   ready to go   sure to fly

They also combine with certain kinds of nouns, especially abstract nouns which embody verbal ideas:

decision to leave   desire to come   invitation to abscond

Other common combinations are with indefinite or general nouns:

moment to catch someone to love something to remember
time to reflect way to go

Yet another role of the infinitive is to serve instead of a verbal noun as subject or complement of a clause:

To err is human.

All they wanted was to rest.

Beyond all these uses, **infinitives** can be used to formulate a purpose in a nonfinite clause:

We walked fast to beat the rain.

The teachers brought bags to collect the bottles.

In more formal styles, the *to* is sometimes expanded into *in order to* or *so as to*, but most of the time the infinitive with *to* says it all. (See further under **nonfinite clauses.**)

inflammable or **inflammatory** These both have to do with lighting fires, but the fire lit by something **inflammmatory** is purely figurative, as by *inflammatory speech*, whereas what's generated by an *inflammable liquid* is dangerously physical. The possible ambiguity with **inflammable** has prompted official moves to replace it in public notices. (See **flammable.**)

inflections are the suffixes which add particular grammatical meanings to words of a particular class (nouns, verbs etc). Languages such as French, German and Italian have numerous **inflections** for individual classes and subclasses of words. English has relatively few. The most familiar ones are:

- for nouns
  's   possessive/genitive
  -(e)s   plural (see further under **plurals**)
- for verbs)
  -(e)s   3rd person singular, present tense
  -ing   continuous/imperfect aspect
  -ed   past tense and perfect aspect
                                    (see further under **irregular verbs**)
- for adjectives
  -er   comparative
  -est   superlative

Note that *inflectional suffixes* such as those do not change the class of the word to which they are attached, nor do they effectively form new words. Suffixes which do are termed *derivational* (see under **suffixes**).

For the choice of spelling between *inflection* and *inflexion*, see under **-ction**.

infold or **enfold** See under **en-/in-**.

informal style We typically use an informal style when talking impromptu with others. It consists of relaxed, easy-going language and ordinary colloquialisms rather than scholarly or academic words. We say *put up with* rather than "tolerate" or "endure", *buy* rather than "purchase", and *cut* or *trim* rather than "abbreviate". We use concrete examples and images rather than abstractions: *tool* rather than "implement", and *date* or *job* rather than "appointment" or "engagement". Abbreviated forms of words, such as *uni* for "university" and *rego* for "registration check" are natural elements of an

informal style, as are contracted forms of phrases, such as: *I'm*, *they're* or *mightn't* . The **informal style** also allows free and frequent ellipsis of the standard grammatical elements of a clause, so that sentences may be no more than:

Don't know.   A great idea.   To show the flag.

Because *informal language* is associated with conversation, its overtones are friendly and easy-going or perhaps offhanded. A hundred years ago, **informal style** would hardly have appeared in writing, except perhaps in the dialogue of novels, and *informal language* would have been almost synonymous with *incorrect language*. Nowadays informal features of style are seen as useful resources if used in moderation, especially for writers who want to avoid putting unnecessary distance between themselves and their readers. A few informal touches can help to ensure this, without undermining the purpose of the document or letter. One would of course avoid referring to grave or seriously contentious matters in an informal way. As always, it's a matter of deciding on the appropriate level of formality/informality for the item concerned.

(See further under **formal words**.)

information focus One of the arts of writing is to keep the reader with you. Amid the flow of words, readers can be distracted or diverted onto marginal things and miss the intended point or emphasis. Not all words in any text are important. But those which embody its themes need to stand out against those which are simply the ordinary medium.

There are several ways of spotlighting a word or words in an English sentence. It can be done by means of a focusing device, such as *only*, *even*, *also*, *too* and *as well*:

They wished only to identify the problem. (not to deal with it)
They had even brought the phone directory with them. (How well prepared can you be!)

Less marked versions of the second sentence would be:

They had also brought the phone directory.
They had brought the phone directory too.
They had brought the phone directory as well.

As the examples show, the focusing words sometimes go before and sometimes after the ones in the spotlight. *Too* and *as well* usually follow it, whereas the others usually precede. (For more about the position of **only**, see under that heading.) A bifocal spotlight can be achieved when *also* and *only* combine in the correlatives *not only ... but also*, drawing attention to two things of equal importance in parallel structures.

There are less dramatic but more pervasive ways of using English sentence order to provide a particular focus. The reading of any sentence is affected and framed by whatever it begins with, and the effect is cumulative. In a detective narrative, many a sentence will begin by referring to the hero:

Bond opened the door slowly. He stepped into the room ...

The repeated mention of the hero naturally makes him the focus of attention for the reader.

In nonfiction the writer can shift ground by drawing attention at the start of a sentence to the new focus:

From now on we will concentrate on present rather than past events.

Thus skilled writers of both fiction and nonfiction use their sentence openings to establish and to change the focus. (See further under **topic** and **dangling participles**.) Both phrases and subordinate clauses at the start of a sentence may help to refocus the reader's attention. See for example:

If any further action is required, we will call a meeting.

Though grammatically subordinate, the clause becomes prominent in that prime position in the sentence. (For more about subordinate clauses, see **clauses** sections 3 and 4.)

informer or **informant** Being similar in meaning and form, these words are sometimes substituted for each other. But because the standard connotations of **informer** are unpleasant, it's an unfortunate choice of words where the context is meant to be neutral.

Informer has been used for centuries (since the early sixteenth century) to refer to someone who gives information to legal authorities against another person. The more recent word **informant** was also used this way for about a hundred years until the later nineteenth century. But its common use nowadays is to refer to someone who gives information in response to an inquiry, whether solicited in a casual encounter (e.g. *Which way to the railway station?*), or in the name of social and linguistic research. **Informant** is definitely the one to use if you wish to avoid depreciating the help you've received.

-ing This familiar suffix is found on English verbs, adjectives and nouns. For all verbs, regular and irregular, it serves to form the present participle, and appears in many a compound verb:

it was wandering   they had been singing

These **-ing** forms have long been seconded from the verb to work as adjectives:

a wandering albatross   the laughing jackass

In *three kookaburras laughing for all they were worth*, the **-ing** word may be seen as adjectival (introducing an adjectival phrase) or participial (introducing a nonfinite clause), depending on your grammar. (See further under **phrases** and **nonfinite clauses**.)

Exactly the same suffix forms a verbal noun in English:

Their laughing heralded the dawn.

The fact that the verbal noun and adjective/participle are identical has caused a remarkable amount of anxiety in the last 200 years, over constructions in which it could be interpreted as either:

At dawn I heard the kookaburras laughing. (participle)

At dawn I heard the kookaburras' laughing. (noun)

For more about this controversy, see under **gerunds**.

Verbal nouns have been readily formed in English with **-ing** since the thirteenth century—before suffixes borrowed from French and Latin such as *-al, -ance, -ation, -ence* and *-ment* were put to the purpose. The long history of **-ing** words has allowed many of them to develop distinctive meanings, shifting away from the verbs on which they are based to materials used in the process, or the object of the process:

bedding clothing drawing dwelling icing mooring roofing
scaffolding seasoning stuffing

This transition into full nouns is most obvious when the **-ing** becomes plural, as in:

diggings earnings findings innings lodgings makings
savings shavings surroundings takings

Note that **-ing** is set solid except when attached to a short word ending in *-o*. In cases like *to-ing and fro-ing*, the hyphen helps to ensure that they are read as two syllables.

ingenuous or **ingenious** These similar-looking adjectives have distinctly different meanings. **Ingenious** means "inventive, clever", while **ingenuous** implies simplicity and a lack of guile or circumspection, so that it can mean "naive" as in *ingenuous acceptance of the contract*, or "candid" as in *an ingenuous smile*. **Ingenious** is far more common, occurring between 7 and 15 times in standard Australian, British and American corpora, while **ingenuous** appears once only or not at all.

The opposite of **ingenuous** is *disingenuous*, whose connotations are usually negative. A *disingenuous apology* is felt to be false or feigned, and a *disingenuous proposal* is one which should not be taken at face value and is seen as devious. A *disingenuous proposal* might however be seen as **ingenious**, by those who thought that the end was more important than the means.

Note that the noun *ingenuity* goes with **ingenious** in terms of meaning, in spite of its original link with **ingenuous**. *Ingenuity* has in fact meant "inventiveness" since the seventeenth century. A new abstract noun had to be found for **ingenuous**, and *ingenuousness* "naivety" has been in use since the eighteenth century.

inheritance or **heritage** See **heritage** or **inheritance**.

inhuman or **inhumane** See under **human** or **humane**.

initialed or **initialled** The choice between these is discussed under **-l/-ll-**.

initialisms For the distinction between acronyms and initialisms, see **acronyms**, last section.

initials For the question of using full stops when abbreviating a person's given names, see **names** section 3.

in-laws Dealing with **in-laws** takes some care. The plurals of *brother-in-law*, *father-in-law*, *mother-in-law* and *sister-in-law* are still formed according to French convention:

    brothers-in-law   *fathers-in-law*
    mothers-in-law   *sisters-in-law*

However the possessive forms are fully English:

    brother-in-law's   *father-in-law's* etc.

A well-known potplant *mother-in-law's tongue* is a useful reminder.

inmesh or **enmesh** See under **en-/in-**.

innuendo The plural of this word is discussed under **-o**.

inoculate This word was originally a technical term in horticulture, meaning to "engraft a bud into another plant". But it has long been used in medicine, to refer to the practice of immunising people against a disease, using a dead or weakened virus. In the earlier eighteenth century, **inoculate** simply implied scratching the patient's skin to implant the protective virus, the technique which Edward Jenner perfected in 1796. The virus used by Jenner was derived from infected cows and called a *vaccine* (*vacca* being Latin for "cow")—hence the term *vaccination*.

The nineteenth century saw extensive development of these medical practices, and both **inoculate** and *vaccinate* came to be applied to any process of immunisation whereby a protective form of a virus is implanted in a patient, whether by scratching the skin, injecting it under pressure, or consuming it orally.

Note the different spellings of *inoculate* and *innocuous* "harmless". Though inoculations ensure that future attacks of the disease will be innocuous, the two words have quite separate origins. **Inoculate** embodies the prefix *in-* "in" and the Latin *oculus* meaning "eye" or "bud"; while *innocuous* means "not noxious or noxious", and so involves the negative prefix **in-**. (See further under **in-/im-**.)

inquiry or **enquiry, inquire** or **enquire** The English-speaking world and Australia itself are rather divided over the use of these spellings. Some writers use both, giving them different applications: others simply use **inquiry** (and **inquire**) at all times. The distinction maintained by some is that **inquiry/inquire** refer to formal and organised investigations, whereas **enquiry/enquire** are used of single or ad hoc queries.

The distribution of these words in Australia is curious. Though *ENQUIRIES* is common on public signs, **inquiry** prevails in print. The Australian ACE database shows instances of **inquiry** outnumbering those of **enquiry** by more than 10:1. Many are references to an official or committee **inquiry**, thus going by the distinction mentioned above—except that at least one "committee of **enquiry**" is referred to, and both words are applied to intellectual investigations. Instances of **inquiry** are spread over a wide variety of prose including newspapers and magazines, whereas **enquiry** hardly appeared outside bureaucratic and academic prose. This suggests a stylistic difference: that **enquiry** has rather formal overtones in Australia, whereas the two are much more evenly matched in the comparable database of British English (LOB). But the ACE evidence shows Australians making very similar use of the verbs **inquire** and **enquire** (4 instances of the one to 5 of the other), and neither favoring **enquire** as in British English, nor **inquire** as in American English.

This worldwide variation in usage probably reflects the fact that English language authorities themselves have been divided over the issue. Fowler recommended using **inquiry** and **enquiry** for the different meanings mentioned above, while the *Oxford Dictionary* put its weight behind **inquiry/inquire**, and treats **enquiry/enquire** simply as variant spellings. The Oxford recommendations are most fully realised in American usage; and most major Australian newspapers indicate their preference for **inquire/inquiry**, whatever the application. They are the spellings to choose where regularity is needed.

Neither **inquiry** nor **enquiry** represents the original form of this word in English. It was borrowed from French as *enquery/enquere*, and was then gradually respelled under Latin influence in the fourteenth and fifteenth centuries. **Enquiry** represents a halfway stage, while in **inquiry** the latinisation of the root is complete. Uncertainty about its spelling has no doubt been perpetuated by the general vacillation over *en-* and *in-*. (See further under **en-/in-**.)

inshrine or **enshrine** See under **en-/in-**.

insistence or **insistency** See under **-nce/-ncy**.

inst. See under **ult.**

installment or **instalment** If you have the next repayment on your layby hanging over you, it seems beside the point to ask whether it's spelled with one *l* or two. In American English **installment** is preferred, whereas the traditional preference of Australian and British dictionaries is for **instalment**, for both a repayment in an *instal(l)ment plan*, and the ritual installing of a bishop in his see.

In fact **installment** has much more to recommend it in terms of consistency. The principle of using two *l*s is paralleled in *installation*, which all dictionaries recommend; and two *l*s are also the standard spelling everywhere for the verb *install*. (British dictionaries sometimes recognise *instal* as a rare variant for the latter, but it's never the first preference.) All this suggests that we make life easier for everyone by using **installment**.

Compare **forestallment**.

instantly or **instantaneously** Both these imply action without delay, but there's a touch of drama about **instantaneously** which is missing from its everyday counterpart **instantly**. While **instantly** is at home in both speech and writing, **instantaneously** is too bulky for casual conversation and much less common even in writing. But **instantaneously** carries the special sense of "happening only a split second afterwards", and so emphasises the close timing of two events:

The pilot touched down and the passengers cheered instantaneously.

Instantly often means just "straightaway", as in:

I'd go instantly if I had the afternoon free.

It has already ceased to mean "urgently", and unremarkable things such as *instant coffee* and *instant replay* may also have helped to dilute its force.

instill or **instil** While American dictionaries prefer **instill**, Australian and British authorities still plump for **instil**. Yet the *Oxford Dictionary*'s citations show that it is a latter-day spelling, first appearing in the nineteenth century, with the hardening up of "rules" over final *l*. (See further under **single for double**.) Dr Johnson used **instill**, which accords better with *instillation* and the word's Latin stem. When choosing between *instillment* and *instilment* writers take their cue from the spelling of the verb.

instinctive or **instinctual** Both words are related to *instinct*, but their connotations are a little different. **Instinctive** is the older and much more common word, used since the seventeenth century to mean "prompted by instinct". It's often used of actions and feelings which are intuitive, as in *an instinctive liking for her*, where the instinct involved would be hard to identify. With the meaning of **instinctive** extended in this way, another adjective was needed by psychologists to mean simply "relating to human instincts"—hence the coining of **instinctual** in the 1920s. It remains the more academic and formal of the two words.

institute or **institution** There's some overlap between these, because both can refer to specialised organisations and bodies of people, as well as to an established law or custom. **Institution** has a number of other roles. It can refer to a familiar practice, as in:

Friday wine-tastings are an institution in their office.

It also provides the abstract noun for the verb *institute*, as in:

The institution of regular on-site meetings kept them better in touch with construction problems.

Thirdly, **institution** is the generic word for organisations of all kinds, whether they're set up to provide social services, such as health, welfare, education or prisons, or to incorporate a particular trade or professional group.

In the *official titles* of trade and professional groups, the word **institute** prevails now in Australia, continuing a trend noted by Fowler. From the early *Mechanics Institutes* to the present *Institute of Actuaries* or of *Chartered Accountants*, the word **institute** is more common. Among organisations for professional engineers, we do find the *Institution of Engineers*, of *Chemical Engineers*, and of *Radio and Electronic Engineers*, as well as the *Institutes of*:

Automotive and Mechanical Engineers   Electrical Engineers
Electrical Inspectors   Engineering and Mining Surveyors
Hospital Engineers   Industrial Engineers   Marine Engineers

The first set with **Institution** are older, and offshoots of British foundations, while the second and much larger group with **Institute** are relatively recent.

Note also that for the titles of educational institutions, **Institute** is the word used. Again we might invoke the *Mechanics Institute* or "School of Arts" as they used to be in Australian country towns, as well as the *RMIT* (Royal Melbourne Institute of Technology), the former *NSWIT* and *QIT*, and other *institutes of higher learning*. Specialised research institutions are also called *Institutes*, witness those of *Counselling, Drug Technology, Navigation* and *Psychoanalysis*, to name a few.

instructive or **instructional** We learn something from it, whether the medium referred to is **instructive** or **instructional**. But things **instructional**, such as *instructional materials*, are expressly designed to provide instruction; while those which prove instructive, such as an *instructive interview*, are ones which teach us something incidentally. We learn through our own insights from an *instructive experience*, whereas a formal process of education is implied in **instructional**.

instrumental case In some languages there's a way of marking words which express the instrument of an action. Modern English no longer has a special suffix for this, and instead we use a phrase beginning with *with*:

They cut the window bars with a file.

In Old English the **instrumental case** was identical with the dative case for nouns, but there were special instrumental forms for some of the pronouns, notably the demonstratives and the interrogative. In Latin the instrumental was identical with the ablative case of nouns. In Aboriginal languages it can be distinctive, or identical with the ergative or locative. (See further under **cases**.)

insurance or **assurance** See assurance.

insure or **ensure** In Australian and British English these words have different meanings. To **ensure** is simply to make sure of something, while **insure** is the business of arranging financial guarantees against loss, theft or damage to your property, or against loss of life and limb. (Cf. **assurance** or **insurance**.) But in American English **insure** covers both meanings, and **ensure** is simply a variant spelling for it.

The use of the two spellings to distinguish the two meanings in Australia and Britain is only about a century old. For other cases of variation between *en-* and *in-*, see **en-/in-**.

insurgence or **insurgency** See under -nce/-ncy.

integral, integrate and **integration** To get the spelling right for any of these, think *integrity*. Its pronunciation helps to ensure you don't write the first part of the others as *inter-*. The prefix *inter-* has no part in any of them. Rather they are all related to *integer* "a whole, or whole number".

intense or **intensive** These have rather different implications: **intensive** implies sustained and constant attention over a given period, while the word **intense** targets the keenness of that attention at a particular moment. A more important difference is that **intensive** is often associated with organised and institutional activity, as in *intensive search* and *an intensive course*; whereas *intense* is used to characterise individual behavior and attitudes, as in *intense gaze* and *intense concentration*.

In *intensive care* we would of course hope to find that the patient is keenly watched by the nurse. But from the hospital's point of view it's a matter of ensuring the constancy of nursing attention, instead of periodic visits by the nurse, as in other wards.

intensifiers An *intensifier* is a word or phrase which reinforces the impact of others. Some work by underscoring the writer's/speaker's conviction:
actually certainly definitely really surely
These are dubbed *emphasisers* in the *Comprehensive Grammar of English* (1985). They add to the **interpersonal** aspects of the text (see under that heading). Other **intensifiers** work in the referential domain and lend strength to descriptive verbs, adverbs or adjectives, either as *boosters* (e.g. *greatly, highly*), or as *maximisers* (*altogether, completely, extremely, utterly*).

Apart from the standard repertoire of **intensifiers**, there are colloquial equivalents ranging from *awfully, incredibly* and *terrifically*, to *bloody, damn(ed)* and other swear words—suitable only for very informal styles of writing. In everyday speech, **intensifiers** serve to emphasise and pinpoint words, as well as to give the speaker a few more microseconds of time in which to develop an utterance. Both functions are reflected in the Kylie Mole speech pattern of talking about things being "roolly great".

Grammatically speaking, **intensifiers** are subjuncts (see further under **adverb**).

intensive or **intense** See intense.

inter- This prefix meaning "between, among" is built into hundreds of ordinary words borrowed from Latin, of which the following are only a token:
intercept interfere interjection interlude intermediate
interpolate interrupt interval
It also forms new words in English, many of which are hybrid Latin-English:
interact interchange interface interleave interlock intermarriage
interplay intertwine interview
New, purely Latin formations with **inter-** tend to be longish, academic and institutional words:
intercontinental interdenominational interdependent intergalactic
interinstitutional interpenetrate intertribal

In a few cases **inter-** contrasts with *intra-*, as in *international/intranational, interstate/intrastate.* (See further under **intra-/intro-.**)

inter alia This handy phrase, borrowed from Latin, means "among other things". It indicates that the set of items mentioned is not exhaustive:
> *The figures showed inter alia how audience ratings were going up.*

Inter alia also serves to highlight an item as the most important of a possible set. Notice the more casual effect of using *etc.* instead:
> *The figures showed how audience ratings were going up etc.*

There the same point about audience ratings is being made, but the use of *etc.* makes it just one thing indicated by the figure, not something particularly important.

Because **inter alia** is a neuter plural in Latin, it strictly speaking applies to things rather than people. Parallel forms for referring to people are *inter alios* (again plural, for all-male or mixed groups) and *inter alias* (for an all-female group). None of these phrases is abbreviated, unlike other Latin tags such as *e.g.* or *etc.* Whether to italicise them is a matter of choice. (See further under **Latin abbreviations** and **italics.**)

interdependence or **interdependency** Both these originate in the earlier nineteenth century, but **interdependence** is the more common and more generally useful of them. Fowler preferred it without giving his reasons, as if the meanings of the two words were indistinguishable. Yet *Oxford Dictionary* citations up to about 1900 show that **interdependence** was the more abstract of the two (as often), and **interdependency** was a countable noun, capable of taking a plural. The twentieth century seems to find more uses for the abstract **interdependence**, by the evidence of English corpora in Australia, Britain and the USA. (See further under **-nce/-ncy.**)

interjections Grammars and usage books often give short shrift to **interjections** because they have no place in formal written English. Seen as "natural ejaculation[s] expressive of some feeling or emotion" (to use the *Oxford Dictionary*'s terms), or as the tangential comments hurled by an unsympathetic listener at a speaker, they do not seem to contribute significantly to the fabric of discourse. They were however recognised by the earliest Greek grammarians as a special class of words, purely emotive in meaning, which could stand as independent sentences.

This ancient definition is echoed in many modern grammars and dictionaries, and the only examples offered are words such as *Wow! Ouch! Great! Hell!* Yet some modern grammars recognise other words in contemporary English which function as one-word sentences, and communicate an attitude or social orientation. The *Comprehensive Grammar of English* (1985) lists them as "formulae", and includes:
- reaction signals: *Yes, No, Right, Okay* and *Thanks*
- expletives: *damn, Jeez, shit*

- greetings and farewells: *Hello, Hi, Cheers, Goodbye*

All these, and even pause-fillers such as *Ah* and *Well*, can be included in an enlarged category of **interjections**.

In English **interjections** of more than one word also need to be recognised. Natural candidates are two-word greetings such as *Good evening*, as well as standardised expressions of emotion like *Hear, hear!*, *Good lord!* and *Stone the crows!* The latter have no referential content, and are therefore more like interjections than exclamations such as *What a day!*—though both are fragmentary sentences (see **sentences** section 2).

Beyond the grammar of **interjections**, their role in interactive discourse is now beginning to be recognised. So whether it's the collaborative *Of course* offered by one person to support another, or the skeptical *Tell us another!* designed to undermine a parliamentary speaker, **interjections** are an important element of communication. Even Hansard reporters try these days to capture them for the record.

international or **intranational** See under **inter-**.

international English The idea of "international English" has a lot of appeal to publishers and others who seek to market English language products to the world at large. It appeals also to teachers and learners of English as a second language, who are often concerned that their English should be neutral, without an Australian, American or British coloring. Any regional variety of English has a set of political, social and cultural connotations attached to it, even the so-called "standard" forms (see **standard English**). The regional associations can be quite distracting, witness the effect of translating an affirmative remark by the saintly Buddha as "Sure"! As that example shows, regional character can come through the printed word, though of course it's usually much more muted there than in living speech. As soon as we start to converse, we reveal what part of the world is home.

So the idea of a completely neutral form of English is something of a dream. Our best hopes of achieving it are in writing and the written medium. And if we take limited excerpts from English language newspapers printed in Canberra, New York, Singapore and London, they may not be distinguishable in their idiom—provided they do not refer to local institutions, and avoid any informal touches of style. **International English** exists only on the formal side of standard language, or in carefully controlled mediums such as "seaspeak" and the language of air-traffic control. (See further under **English** or **Englishes**.)

International Phonetic Alphabet The **International Phonetic Alphabet** (IPA) is the only one in the world whose symbols have a single, unvarying relationship with particular sounds. This is because they are defined in articulatory terms, i.e. by the speech organs used in producing them. The IPA symbols are indispensable whether we are attempting to describe sounds in a foreign language, or to pinpoint pronunciations of English words. A chart of the symbols used for Australian English can be found in Appendix I.

The symbols of the IPA are mostly drawn from the ordinary Roman alphabet, with permutated forms of them used to extend the inventory. A handful of others come from the Greek and Anglo-Saxon alphabets. Perhaps the most remarkable symbol of all is "schwa" represented by an upside-down, back-to-front *e*, which stands for the indeterminate vowel so often heard in English, and so variously written. (See further under **schwa**.)

International System of Units The "International System of Units" is Australia's way of referring to the *Système International d'Unités*, and the official French title explains why we often refer to the units themselves as *SI units*. *SI units* have been the basis of the Australian metric system of measurements since 1970, and replaced the earlier imperial system. (See further under **imperial weights and measures, metrication** and Appendix IV.)

interpersonal Writers do not always think of themselves as setting up a relationship with their readers. They may not know who their readers are likely to be, and tend to forget about them when the subject itself becomes all-consuming. If the writing is technical or philosophical this may not matter, though the style may still seem rather "dry". But for writing which is intended as individual or private communication, it's much more of an issue. A shortage· of **interpersonal** elements then seems not only dry but insensitive to the reader. It could undermine the very purpose of communicating. Many elements of English are in some way **interpersonal**, so writers do not have to look too far for ones which will contribute effectively but unobtrusively.

The **interpersonal** aspects of language or writing are all those elements which establish a particular relationship with the reader—as opposed to those which express information, or help to structure the text (the *referential* and *textual* aspects, respectively). The **interpersonal** effect is very strong and direct in the first and second person pronouns (*I*, *we*, *you*), and in grammatical structures such as questions, commands and exclamations. Both contribute to a sentence such as:

You really won't believe how brilliant the acting is!

The **interpersonal** effect in that sentence also comes from the use of the contraction *won't* (as from any word or structure which smacks of conversation); and from the word *brilliant*, which invites the reader to share a value judgement. Attitudinal adverbs and intensifiers such as *really* call for a reaction from the reader. Other words which have an **interpersonal** effect are those which mediate degrees of obligation, permission and possibility (modal auxiliaries such as *must*, *should* and *can*, as well as the adverbs which paraphrase them, such as *necessarily*, *perhaps*). Words which express the writer's judgement on the likelihood of something are again ones which call gently upon the reader.

He's likely to arrive on Friday.

The word *likely* highlights the fact that the statement is an estimate, one which the reader may either accept or re-evaluate. (See further under **modality**.)

Note that some words and expressions combine an **interpersonal** effect with their referential meaning. This is true of many evaluative words, though it varies with their use. The word *brilliant* has both when used in reference to someone's acting, but the **interpersonal** effect is hardly there when it refers to the light of the sun.

interpretive or **interpretative** Which of these gets priority varies from dictionary to dictionary, and either can be justified. According to the evidence of *Webster's English Usage* (1989), **interpretive** has been increasing its currency in the last few decades, and it certainly relates more directly to the verb *interpret*. In the past however, **interpretative** seems to have been the more common of the two—to judge by the *Oxford Dictionary*'s 12 citations over four centuries for **interpretative**, as opposed to 2 for **interpretive** in three centuries. Fowler argued from Latin word-forming principles that **interpretative** was more legitimate, though he elsewhere argued against unnecessary syllables. The *Macquarie Dictionary* (1991) gives both, though only **interpretative** is given as a headword (**interpretive** being listed as a run-on). Both *Collins* and *Random House* dictionaries prefer **interpretive**.

interrobang This yet-to-be-established mark of punctuation could be handy when we need to use both question mark and exclamation mark simultaneously. Shaped like a combination of the two: ‽ the **interrobang** allows us to query and to express incredulity in the same stroke:

   You want the report tomorrow‽

The complex of emotions you may feel at such a moment cannot be adequately expressed through the conventional sequence of *?!* or *!?*, and the **interrobang** would be a valuable addition to our repertoire of punctuation. According to the *Random House Dictionary* it originated in the 1960s as printers' slang, and its potential is discussed in Webster's *Style Manual* and in the *Right Word at the Right Time* (under *question mark*). Its future no doubt depends on its becoming a standard punctuation item in wordprocessing packages. Alternative spellings for it are *interrabang* and *interabang*.

interrogative This is the traditional grammarians' name for the form of verbs that expresses a direct question:

   Are they coming to the barbecue?
   When will he decide?
   Do you like red wine?

In **interrogative** constructions the normal subject-verb order is inverted, and the subject *they/he/you* follows the first (auxiliary) part of the verb. Compare the order in *they are coming, he will decide* etc. The third of those sentences shows how a simple verb *like* actually acquires an auxiliary (*do*) in the

interrogative. In Shakespearean English it was done by simply inverting subject and verb:

Like you red wine?

But in twentieth century English *do* is always brought in to form the **interrogative** if there is no auxiliary already.

Note that in modern grammars (*Introduction to the Grammar of English, Comprehensive Grammar of English*), the term **interrogative** is applied to the particular "sentence function" or "clause type" that expresses a question, rather than the distinctive verb form. (See further under **mood** and **questions**.) The **interrogative** verb can and does express other speech functions, such as the imperative. In American English the sentence *Why don't you open the window?* is a polite way of getting someone to do something.

interrogative words   With these words we signal the start and the focus of a question, as in "Who are you?" or "What's the time?" **Interrogative words** include both *pronouns*:

who   what   which   whose   whom

and *adverbs*:

when   where   why   how

Both can be used in either direct or indirect questions:

Who's there?   He asked who was there.

What do you want?   They inquired what I wanted.

Modern grammars such as the *Introduction to the Grammar of English* and the *Comprehensive Grammar of English* use the collective name *wh-words* for both groups.

Note that *wh-words* also work as conjunctions in other kinds of clauses. Interrogative pronouns can be relative pronouns in relative and noun clauses:

The man who came to dinner went away satisfied.

I asked them who had been invited.

And interrogative adverbs are used to introduce adverbial clauses:

They went where no human being had ventured before.

See **clauses** section 4.

interstate differences   There are relatively few words which vary from state to state in Australia. But those that do involve everyday things and are often associated with what we drink or eat or wear. They affect domestic life— whether we send our small children to *preschool* or *kindergarten*, and what we call the place we live in (see for example **home unit** and **Federation**).

Among beer-drinkers it's well known that the various sizes of beer glass change their names from state to state. Those from Western Australia would be disappointed with the size of a *pot* in the eastern states, while those from South Australia would be pleasantly surprised at the size of a *schooner* elsewhere, as the table shows:

7 oz (200ml)	8oz (225ml)	10oz (285ml)	15oz (425ml)	20oz (575ml)
QLD	glass	pot		
NSW seven		middy	schooner	pint
VIC glass		pot	schooner	
TAS	eight	ten/pot		
SA butcher		schooner	pint	
WA glass		middy	schooner	pot

The distribution of the various terms is no simple matter, with a different set used in each state. There is no overlap at all between South Australia and Western Australia, separated by deserts.

Research by Bryant (1989) confirms that regional variation is more than a matter of differences from state to state. Some words are shared by two or more states, but not all of them. Victoria, South Australia and Tasmania share terms such as *laundry trough* (for ''laundry tub''), while NSW and Queensland share *stroller*, *lobster* and *devon*, which are known by other names elsewhere. In any case the boundaries of different usages do not coincide with state borders. Some which defy them are *port* for ''suitcase'', which is used in northern NSW as well as Queensland; *nature strip* for ''footpath'', found in southern NSW (including ACT) and in Victoria; and *spider* ''ice cream soda'', used by Victorians and those in southeastern South Australia. Connections such as these can sometimes be explained in terms of older patterns of settlement, or in terms of current commercial contacts. At any rate, they show that interstate and metropolitan differences are not the only ones to reckon with in charting regional variation in Australia.

inthrone or **enthrone** See under **in-/en-**.

intra-/intro- This prefix meaning ''inside'' appears in a number of words coined for scientific or institutional usage. The form **intra-** is the more recent one, first recorded in the nineteenth century, in words such as:

> *intracranial intramuscular intramural*
> *intrastate intra-uterine intravenous*

A number of **intra-** words are obviously intended as counterparts to those prefixed with *extra-*, witness *intramural/extramural* for instance.

Formations with **intro-** are loanwords from Latin, which mostly date from the seventeenth century on, apart from *introduction* which was borrowed in the fourteenth. Unlike those prefixed with **intra-**, their second components are not usually independent words in English, and they maintain a classical flavor:

> *introgression introjection intromission introspection*
> *introvert/introversion introvolution*

Most are specialist words, except for those popularised through psychology such as *introspection* and *introvert/introversion*.

intra vires See under **ultra vires**.

intransitive This is the grammatical name for a verb which does not take an object. (See further under **transitive** and **intransitive**.)

intrench or **entrench**. See under **en-/in-**.

introductions First impressions are as important in writing as they are in spoken encounters. The first few sentences should combine to convince readers they are in competent hands, and that the writer is in control of the medium.

In nonfiction, the *introduction* needs to identify amd frame the topic to be discussed, with some indication as to the stages in which it will be treated, or the ultimate destination of the argument. The longer the document, the more some sort of map and signposts are needed. A long report may offer its concluding recommendations at the start, and then proceed to show how they were arrived at. The so-called *executive summary* in business documents serves this purpose (see under **reports**).

In fiction the introductory chapters serve to set the scene, create a particular tone, and secure the reader's engagement in the imaginative world.

Yet engaging the reader's imagination is not unimportant in nonfictional writing. The most effective **introductions** try to project some lively details of the subject, linking it with the real world and avoiding too many generalisations and clichéed observations.

For the relationship between the *introduction*, *foreword* and *preface* of a book, see **preface**.

intwine or **entwine** See under **en-/in-**.

intwist or **entwist** See under **en-/in-**.

Inuit See under **Eskimo**.

inure or **enure** The first spelling **inure** is given priority in American dictionaries as well as British ones, whether the meaning is "become accustomed", or "accrue". **Enure** is a recognised alternative, but less commonly seen in the USA than Britain, by the citations of *Webster's English Usage* (1989).

invaluable or **valuable** See **valuable** and **invaluable**.

inversion Any departure from the normal word order used in a clause (subject–verb–object/complement) can be called **inversion**. Inverting the subject and verb is a regular feature of certain English constructions, such as:
- direct questions:
  Have you finished?
  Are they on their way?
- after an adverb which highlights the timing or location of an event at the start of a sentence:
  Here comes the bus.
  Now is the time to run for it.

Down came the rain.
There stood a surprised passenger.
No sooner had she reached the bus-stop when she found she'd lost her wallet.
Never had she been so embarrassed.
Under no circumstances could she return home.

As the last three examples show, **inversion** with negative adverbs (or adverbial phrases) always requires an auxiliary verb immediately after. Exactly the same construction occurs after *hardly* and *scarcely*. Note that pronouns are normally inverted after auxiliaries (*Hardly had they come ...*), but not after a simple verb: we don't say "Here come they".

* stock phrases identifying the speaker in dialogue:
  "I'd like you to take the shot from my other side", says he.
  "Here we go again", said the cameraman.
* clauses which express an impossible condition may use **inversion** of the subject and verb instead of a conjunction:
  Had I known, I'd have been there. (= If I had known ...)
  Were I an expert on computers, I'd have solved the problem.

All the *inversions* so far, involving subject and verb, can appear in standard written or narrative prose. The **inversion** of object and verb is not often found in writing, but it's common enough in conversation:

Avocados they adore. Artichokes they hate.

Inversions of this kind give special prominence to the object as the **topic** of the clause (see further under that heading). The use of object–verb **inversion** by poets seems to serve the same purpose, although one suspects that more often it's motivated by the demands of rhyme and meter.

Brothers and sisters have I none ...

inverted commas This term is still used as an alternative to *quotation marks* in Britain. But the major style references in Britain (*Copy-editing* (1992) and *Hart's Rules* (1983)) use *quotation marks*, as do the *Chicago* and *Webster's* style manuals, and that of the Australian Government Publishing Service. (See further under **quotation marks**.)

inverted pyramid See under **journalism** and **journalese**.

invocation or **evocation** See under **evoke** or **invoke**.

invoke or **evoke** See **evoke** or **invoke**.

inward or **inwards** See under **-ward** or **-wards**.

-ion This is by far the most common suffix for nouns in English, in spite of its foreign origins. Most of the words embodying it are loanwords from French or Latin, yet many of them are ordinary enough:
ambition action decision instruction motion tension

Broadly speaking **-ion** forms abstract nouns, though many of them like *action* and *motion* express the product of the related verb (*act*, *move*), and so have at least some physical and material properties. New words of this kind are continually being formed from verbs ending in *-ate*. (See further under **-ation**.)

Words with **-ion** are often treated collectively as abstract nouns. Some computer style checkers work on the assumption that they always contribute to a woolly style, and draw attention to all of them. In cases like *declassification* or *transmogrification*, the point is taken, but with ones like *action* and *motion* there's no need to seek a simpler synonym.

-ious Three large groups of English adjectives end in **-ious**:
1 those like *furious*, *glorious* and *industrious*, which have related nouns ending in *-y* (*fury/glory/industry*)
2 those like *cautious*, *oblivious* and *religious*, which have related nouns ending in *-ion* (*caution* etc.)
3 those like *audacious*, *capacious* and *loquacious*, which have related nouns ending in *-ity* (*audacity* etc.)

Adjectives with **-ious** begin to be recorded in the English Renaissance, though whether they're really English formations is unclear, since many have counterparts in Latin and French. A handful of bizarre later ones like *bumptious*, *rumbustious* and *scrumptious* are unquestionably English inventions—words in which the more pretentious latinate **-ious** is juxtaposed to down-to-earth English syllables.

Words with -eous not -ious. The ending **-ious** sounds identical to *-eous*, but the endings are not interchangeable. The words with *-eous* (*bounteous*, *contemporaneous*, *herbaceous*) are far fewer, and usually distinctive by virtue of their length or specialised character. The oldest group like *bounteous* were French borrowings or based on French or Anglo-Norman models. (Compare Middle English *bounte* with modern *bounty*.) Examples include:
   beauteous courteous duteous gorgeous hideous
   piteous plenteous righteous
All have a rhetorical or literary flavor, except perhaps *courteous*.

Most of the other *-eous* words are based on Latin and associated with scholarship and science. Those like *contemporaneous* include:
   erroneous extraneous instantaneous miscellaneous
   momentaneous spontaneous
There are Latin models also for *aqueous*, *igneous*, *ligneous*, *vitreous*, and for the large number of biological names like *herbaceous*. (See further under **-acious/-aceous**.)

Three special cases with *-eous* are *advantageous*, *courageous* and *outrageous*, all spelled that way because of the need to preserve a soft "g" in them. (See further under **-ce/-ge**.)

Confusion between **-ious** *and* -uous. On occasions **-ious** is used by mistake for -uous, so that one hears and sees "presumptious" and "unctious", instead of *presumptuous* and *unctuous*. This problem happens because of the related nouns in -*ion* (*presumption, unction*) from which **-ious** adjectives could be generated (compare *cautious/caution* above.)

All such adjectives belong to the larger group ending in **-ous** (see further under that heading).

ipse dixit This Latin phrase meaning "he himself said it" was originally used in Greek by the acolytes of Pythagoras to refer to the utterances of the master. It has taken on a special meaning in English since the eighteenth century, encapsulating the idea of the self-appointed authority on language. Such authorities seemed to meet the needs of the age, and they created arbitrary linguistic rules and used them to condemn the language of earlier authors. The "ipse dixit" grammarians were not inclined to look at the facts of usage, even in their own times. Some of their pronouncements (such as those concerning the uses of *shall* and *will*) have been transmitted through the English language curriculums of the nineteenth and twentieth century to become the linguistic fetishes of contemporary English. (See further under **fetish**.)

ipso facto Used in argument, this Latin tag means "by that very fact". It draws attention to a point which the speaker/writer claims has a necessary consequence:
The defendant had a shotgun on the backseat of his car and was ipso facto planning for a fight.
There's no necessary connection between that piece of evidence and the interpretation put on it. Yet the use of **ipso facto** with its legal connotations serves to highlight the point which follows.

Iraq or **Irak** Dictionaries all give first preference to **Iraq** and *Iraqi*. But while some recognise only those forms, *Webster's, Random House* and the *Oxford Dictionary* (1989) also register the anglicised forms *Irak* and *Iraki*. The name has been in use in English for only a relatively short time—since 1921, when Mesopotamia became the kingdom and then the republic of Iraq—and it's not yet fully assimilated to English patterns of spelling. The use of *q* without a following *u* is un-English, as is the appearance of *q* as the final letter of a word.
For other words in which *q* and *k* vary, see **qu/k**.

Irish The division of the "Emerald Isle" into Northern Ireland (= "Ulster") and the Republic of Ireland (Eire) in 1921 has complicated the use of the adjective **Irish**. Only in geographical references and jokes can it refer to the whole island. When referring to the people and their language(s) it needs qualifying. Yet "Northern Irishman" is not an established term, and "Ulsterman" is not entirely accurate, since only 6 of the original 9 provinces of Ulster belong to Northern Ireland. (The other 3 are now part of Eire.)

To scholars, the original Celtic language of Ireland is "Irish", but in ordinary usage it's known as *Gaelic*, a reminder of its close similarity to the Celtic language of Scotland. The English of Ireland comes in three varieties:

1 *Hiberno-English*, the local variety spoken by the Catholic population of Ireland (including Northern Ireland)

2 *Anglo-Irish*, used by some Protestants in Eire

3 *Ulster Scots*, the English of the Protestants of Northern Ireland which owes rather more to Scottish English.

The three varieties get bundled together under the term *Irish English*, but its lack of regional and cultural sensitivity is evident.

irony This much-used concept originated on the Greek stage, in the duality of meaning created by the character whose words had a simple, immediate meaning as well as another, discrepant meaning for the audience who saw them in the context of the whole play and of the common culture.

From there the notion of **irony** has been extended to the similar effect achieved in modern forms of literature—when there's a discrepancy between the immediate meaning of a writer's words, and the shades of meaning they take on in a broader context. The effect may be gentle as in Jane Austen's works, or biting, as in those of Jonathan Swift. Either way the effect is cerebral, and depends on the comprehensiveness of the reader's response. In this respect **irony** differs from *sarcasm*, which uses taunting words to launch a direct and explicit attack on another person.

Irony is also to be seen in real-life situations and events which turn out contrary to what one might expect. It might for example seem ironic to appoint an emotionally unstable person to counsel others with emotional problems.

For the choice between *ironic* and *ironical*, see **-ic/-ical**.

irregardless Not a useful word—it negates itself from both ends, with a negative prefix and suffix, and what's left in the middle by way of meaning is unclear. It seems to be a blend of *irrespective* and *regardless*, either of which is to be preferred.

irregular verbs An important minority of English verbs are irregular in the way in which they form their past tense and past participle. Regular verbs simply add *-ed* for both the past forms, whether they go back to Anglo-Saxon, or are later acquisitions from French and Latin: *want(ed)*, *depart(ed)*, *precipitat(ed)*. Our **irregular verbs** are remnants of several groups that existed in Anglo-Saxon, as well as once regular verbs which have developed their own idiosyncrasies over the centuries.

The common **irregular verbs** are grouped below according to the number of changes that their stems undergo to form the past tense and past participle. Note that the classification is based on their spelling, not their sound; and so the doubling of a consonant, the loss of a final *e* or the alteration of a vowel from double to a single letter would qualify as a change. All those in bold are discussed further under individual headings.

1 *Those which use the same form for past and present*:
burst cast cut hit hurt let put read set shed shut slit split
spread thrust

The verb **cost** can also be included here for one of its uses. (See also below section 9.)

2a) *Those which keep the stem vowel as written and replace **d** with **t***:
bend build lend rend send spend

Two special cases are **have** and *make*, where *d* replaces other stem consonants.

b) *Those which simply add **t***, such as deal *and* mean. This also applies, for British and some Australian writers, to a number of other verbs including:
burn dream lean leap learn spoil

Other Australians and Americans at large would keep such verbs regular. (See further under **-ed**.)

3 *Those which have a single vowel change for both past forms*:
bleed breed feed meet speed ($ee>e$)
bind fight find grind wind ($i>ou$)
cling dig fling sling slink spin stick sting **string**
swing **wring** ($i>u$)

Special cases are *win* ($i>o$), *shoot* ($oo>o$), *sit* ($i>a$), *hold* ($o>e$), **hang** ($a>u$), all one-off examples of the same kind. Note also *come* and *run*, which form past tenses by changing the vowel to *a*, but revert for the past participle.

4a) *Those which change the stem vowel and follow it with **t***:
creep feel keep kneel sleep sweep weep ($ee>e$)

b) *Those which reduce a double consonant to single and add **t***:
dwell smell spell spill

As with the 2b verbs, these are kept regular by Americans and some Australians. (See under **-ed**.)

c) *Those which change the stem vowel and follow it with **d***:
sell tell ($e>o$)

A similar one-off example is **do** which becomes *did*.

5 *Those which change the stem vowel and one or more of the consonants, as well as adding **t***:
bring>brought buy>bought catch>caught leave>left seek>sought
teach>taught think>thought

Special cases which change vowels and consonants (but do not add *t*) are *stand>stood* and **strike**>*struck*.

6 *Those with two different stem vowels for the past tense and the past participle*:
    begin **drink** *ring* **shrink** *sing* **sink** *spring* *stink* **swim** (i>a>u)

Some of these are in the process of change. (See below section 9.)

7a) *Those with a different stem vowel for the past tense, and the present tense vowel for the past participle, with (e)n added on*:
    awake *forsake* **shake** *take* *wake* (a>oo/o>a)
    blow grow know throw (o>e>o)

Others of the same kind are *give, forgive* (*gave>given*.) One-off examples are **eat** (*ate>eaten*), *fall* (*fell>fallen*), *draw* (*drew>drawn*) and *see* (*saw>seen*). *Beat* with its past participle *beaten* may be included here, though with zero change for the simple past it is anomalous and has something in common with group 1 above.

  b) *Those which use a different stem vowel for the past (both past tense and past participle), and add (e)n to the latter*:
    break freeze speak steal weave (ea>o)
    bear swear tear wear (ea>o)

Note that for *bear* the past participle is **borne**. Others which belong here are **get** and *forget* (e>o), though the use of *gotten* with *get* is not found in all varieties of English. The verbs *awake, bite* and *hide* are further members of the set.

  c) *Those with two different stem vowels for the past tense and the past participle, plus -en added on*:
    drive ride rise **stride** *write* (i>o>i>)

Special cases are *fly* (*flew>flown*) and **lie** (*lay>lain*).

8 *Those which borrow forms from other verbs to make their past tense (sometimes called* **suppletive verbs***)*. The outstanding cases of this are **go** (*went*) and **be** (*was/were* and *been*). The verb *be* has more distinct parts than any other English verb. (See further at **be**.)

9 *Unstable* **irregular verbs**. Changes are still going on with some irregular verbs. For example, some of those with two different forms for the past tense and past participle work increasingly with just one. Thus *drink* (*drank/drunk*) is now often *drink/drunk*, as are *shrink* and *stink*. Already quite common in speech, these patterns will no doubt become unremarkable in writing, sooner or later.

    Other ongoing changes are with verbs which are reverting to the regular pattern for the past, as with:

light	*(lit)*	*now often*	*lighted*
shear	*(shore)*		*sheared*

shine	(shone)	shined
shoe	(shod)	shoed
speed	(sped)	speeded
strive	(strove)	strived

The same is true for the past of verbs such as **bet**, **bid**, **knit**, **quit**, **rid**, **shit**, **spit** and **wet**, which are more and more often formed with -*ed*. In some of them, the regular past form has a slightly different meaning from the irregular one (see under the individual headings).

Note finally that the number of verbs which are reverting to the regular pattern is much larger than that going the other way. There are two isolated cases in **hang** and **show**.

irrelevance or **irrelevancy** All dictionaries give priority to **irrelevance**. It actually appears later in the nineteenth century than **irrelevancy** (by more than forty years), yet seems to have overtaken it in terms of popularity. (See further under **-nce/-ncy**.)

-is Words ending in **-is** are mostly Latin or Greek loanwords, and they continue to behave like foreigners in the way they make their plurals, by substituting -*es* for **-is**. It happens whether they are ordinary words like:

analysis basis crisis diagnosis emphasis oasis

Or ones which are mostly at home in fields of science and scholarship:

amanuensis antithesis axis ceratosis ellipsis
genesis hypothesis metamorphosis neurosis parenthesis psychosis
synopsis thesis thrombosis

Note that the plurals of *axis* and *basis* (*axes/bases*) are identical in their written form with the plurals of *axe* and *base*. The context will clarify whether *axes* is the plural of *axe* or *axis*; but with *bases* it's less clear-cut since both *base* and *basis* are abstract enough to fit the same context. (See further under **bases**.)

The special cases of **chassis** and **metropolis** are discussed at their respective entries.

-isation/-ization These alternative spellings go hand in hand with the -*ise/-ize* option. Your preference for -*ise* entails **-isation** (*civilise–civilisation*), just as -*ize* entails **-ization**. The choice for one such pair is also your choice across the board. Attempts to link the choice of -*is/-iz* with the etymology and history of individual words have been abandoned as unworkable. (See **-ise/-ize** below.)

-ise/-ize In Australian English, as in British English, it's possible to use either **-ise** or **-ize** in the many verbs with that ending, whether they're as old as *baptise/baptize* or as new as *energise/energize*. In American English, the standard spelling is with **-ize**.

In Australian English spellings with **-ise** regularly outnumber those with **-ize**, according to the evidence of the ACE corpus. The margin of difference is often large: for *organise* it is 85:21; for *recognise* it is 102:34. The **-ise** has had the official backing of the Australian Government *Style Manual* since the 1970s, and it is standard in federal government departments, as well as the daily press. Its use in state government departments is less regular. A survey of education departments in 1987 showed that while **-ise** was consistently used in Victoria and South Australia, both it and **-ize** were in use in New South Wales and Queensland, in different sections of the department.

In the commercial sphere the two spellings for the suffix can be strangely juxtaposed, as in the chemist's sign opposite.	*For Hire* NEBULISERS VAPORIZERS CRUTCHES

The continuing use of **-ize** in Australia can be seen as reflecting one of several overseas forces: the fact that it is standard in the USA; or that in Britain it's preferred by both Oxford and Cambridge University presses; or that scientists the world over endorse it. (In Australia the CSIRO nevertheless decided in 1986 to change the spelling of its name from *Organization* to *Organisation*, to conform with the Australian government standard. And the Australian branch of Oxford University Press switched to **-ise** in 1991, with the publication of the *Australian Writers' and Editors' Guide*.)

Other factors which sometimes influence people's choice of **-ize** are linguistic:

1 that it seems to represent the "z" sound of the word more closely. (Note however that words like *raise* and *rise* are accepted with *s* for the same sound.)

2 that **-ize** was thought to be better etymologically (it corresponds to *-izein* in Greek, *-izare* in late Latin). Scholars have in the past tried particularly to give **-ize** to words which go back to Greek or Latin, and thus classical loanwords were to be distinguished from similar ones borrowed from French with **-ise**. However it often proved impossible to know whether the source was French or classical. This impasse prompted the present-day resolution of the problem—to choose either **-ize** or **-ise** systematically. Fowler opted for **-ize**, on the grounds of sound, the fact that **-ize** represented the ultimate origins of the suffix, and perhaps also the fact that his publisher was Oxford University Press. He noted however that "most British printers" opted for **-ise**, and could show that it was the easier option.

*Good reasons for choosing **-ise*** are in fact offered by Fowler. If we apply the **-ise** spelling to all susceptible words of two or more syllables, we are left with a single exception: **capsize** (see under that heading). But if you choose **-ize** the list of exceptions which need the alternative spelling is as least as long as the following:

advertise advise apprise chastise circumcise comprise
compromise despise devise exercise excise franchise improvise
incise revise supervise surmise surprise televise

Apart from those, which are all verbs, the problem arises with other words which are acquiring verb roles, such as *enterprise* and *merchandise*. Etymology dictates that **-ise** should be used in such words, and the policy of using **-ise** everywhere makes them part of the general pattern. With an **-ize** policy they are yet more special cases.

The argument of fewer exceptions is certainly used in Australia to support the official endorsement of **-ise** spellings. It loses a little of its force in the USA, where dictionaries already allow some of the words in Fowler's list to be spelled with **-ize** (e.g. *advertize, apprize, comprize*)—etymology notwithstanding. The same overruling of etymology is to be seen in American acceptance of *-yze* instead of *-yse* in *analyse* etc. (See further under **-yse/-yze**.) If and when all such words can be spelled with *z*, the argument for **-ise** will evaporate.

In a real sense, Fowler's exceptions "prove the rule". If you believe there's still good reason to spell *advertise* and the others with **-ise**, your better option is to go for **-ise** and **-isation** everywhere.

-ish This Old English suffix has been used for a thousand years and more to create ethnic adjectives out of proper names. Modern examples are:
British Danish English Finnish Flemish Irish
Jewish Polish Swedish Turkish
A similar and equally old use of the suffix is to create adjectives which connote the qualities of the noun they're based on:
bookish boyish childish churlish feverish fiendish foolish
freakish girlish owlish popish priggish prudish selfish
sheepish standoffish stylish waspish
Some of those have negative implications, and writers who are concerned about them in, say, *childish* often replace it with *childlike*, which is neutral (see further under **-like**). Often there is a tentativeness about **-ish**, which has made it productive in informal language. We readily invent suggestive color adjectives like *greenish, whitish, brownish*, and words which hint at but avoid asserting a quality: *biggish, oldish, thinnish*. In indicating time, we may use **-ish** words to avoid sounding too strict about the matter:
I'll be home latish.
Let's have dinner about eightish.
This use of **-ish** after "about" seems redundant, but it's often heard, and its informality and tentativeness are important in some situations.

-ism This suffix has come to us through early Christianity in Greek words such as *baptism*. But it's used very freely in modern English to form nouns which embody a particular philosophy or set of principles, or an individual preoccupation or way of life:
absenteeism catholicism chauvinism colonialism communism

cynicism egotism environmentalism existentialism fanaticism
favoritism federalism feminism hedonism idealism imperialism
jingoism minimalism realism romanticism

The strong feelings embodied in some of those have helped to develop a special use of **-ism** in referring to newly identified forms of prejudice:

ageism classism heightism racism sexism speciesism weightism

The suffix attaches itself easily to both adjectives and nouns, proper as well as common: *Calvinism, Darwinism, Platonism.*

Words based on **-ism** are not uncommon in medicine, to describe particular conditions such as *astigmatism, mongolism, rheumatism.*

A further role of **-ism** is to refer to the features of a given speech style, especially a distinctive word or idiom:

archaism colloquialism genteelism malapropism neologism
provincialism solecism truism vulgarism witticism

Here again the suffix can be used with proper names:

Americanism Gallicism Scotticism

even on an ad hoc basis: *a Paul Hoganism.*

Apart from attaching itself to almost anything, **-ism** also enjoys an independent existence of its own, as in:

Postwar affluence has fostered hundreds of isms among younger people.

Israel This name links both ancient and modern Jewish tradition. Since 1948 it has been the name of the Jewish state in the eastern Mediterranean, established after the horrors of World War II. The land was of course occupied by Jews in biblical times, though the area was then known as *Palestine*, and while **Israel** was the northern section, *Judah* was the southern. The word *Israelite* also goes back to biblical times, whereas *Israelitish* is a medieval word. Neither is in common use nowadays except in historical references, and instead the word *Israeli* serves to identify both the citizen of **Israel** and its culture.

The creation of the modern state of **Israel** was the culmination of half a century's work by *Zionists*. The *Zionist* movement was both mystical and practical; and with its emphasis on *Jewish* ethnicity and *Hebrew* culture, it united *Jews* scattered across Europe. Within contemporary **Israel**, *Zionists* continue to develop the common language and culture, though their emphasis on *Jewish* nationalism is felt by some to displace the essential *Jewish* religion.

The words *Jew* and *Jewish* seem to have outlived the pejorative associations which hung around them for centuries. They now serve to mark the religious identity of *Israelis* and others round the world, and therefore correspond to *Christian, Buddhist* etc.

The word *Hebrew* is used to name the official language of modern **Israel**. Again it's a link between past and present, being the name of the ancient Semitic language of the scriptures, as well as its updated and expanded counterpart. *Yiddish* is used more informally among Jewish emigrants from eastern Europe.

It is a dialect of German, with elements from Slavonic languages and Hebrew added in.

-ist This suffix is ultimately Greek, but it enjoys a lot of use in modern English, to mean "someone who specialises in". The word *specialist* itself is a familiar example, and words with **-ist** appear in almost any trade, profession or recreation. Many of the words are Latin and French loanwords, but others are simple English formations:

> *flautist harpist organist pianist soloist violinist*
> *artist cartoonist columnist diarist humorist archeologist*
> *botanist chemist dentist economist*

Apart from its use to designate fields of expertise, **-ist** also serves to create words which refer to particular attitudes or habits of mind:

> *anarchist conservationist defeatist escapist humanist materialist*
> *nationalist perfectionist theorist*

Proper nouns as well as common names can provide the base, witness *Marxist* and *Peronist* as further examples.

As with *-ism*, **-ist** attaches itself to both nouns and adjectives, and this sometimes results in double coinings. For example:

agriculturist	*agriculturalist*
constitutionist	*constitutionalist*
conversationist	*conversationalist*
educationist	*educationalist*
horticulturist	*horticulturalist*

Fowler noted that in British English the longer forms seemed to be preferred for all, for no very good reason (they're more cumbersome, and in some ways less effective in pinpointing their meaning). American English differs (according to *Random House* and the *Webster's* dictionaries) in preferring the longer forms for *constitutionalist* and *conversationalist*, but not the rest. The *Macquarie Dictionary* gives preference to *horticulturist* over the longer form, but otherwise endorses the long forms.

Note that the *naturalist* and the *naturist* are distinctly different in their pursuits. (See **naturalist**.)

-istic/-istical Adjectives ending in **-istic** sometimes have alternatives with an extra syllable: for example *logistic/logistical*. The choice between them is often arbitrary, and may as well be made on the basis of its effect on the rhythm of the phrase it appears in. The **-istical** form is however always the one on which the associated adverb is based. (See further under **-ic/-ical**.)

it This word can be a regular pronoun, or a "dummy" component in certain kinds of English sentences.

As the neuter pronoun, it's a meaningful element in a sequence such as:
> *They would drive to Canberra on Thursday. It was a perfect suggestion ...*

It picks up the nub of the sentence before, and makes it the subject of the next one, creating cohesion between them. (See further under **coherence** or **cohesion**.)

But elsewhere **it** is neither a pronoun nor cohesive. In statements like: *It was raining* or *It's hard to decide*, **it** serves as the grammatical subject without referring to anything in particular. Modern grammarians emphasise its emptiness, calling it a "dummy" subject (*Introduction to the Grammar of English*) or "prop **it**" (*Comprehensive Grammar of English*), because **it** simply fills an empty slot in the clause. Another dummy use of **it** is in the impersonal style used in reports and formal records, where it helps to formulate passive statements to avoid referring to the people involved:

It was agreed that the matter be postponed for the next meeting.

Yet another use of **it** for purely structural purposes is in cleft sentences:

It was only last Christmas that we decided to go.

In sentences like that **it** puts the spotlight on a significant phrase before everything else in the sentence. (See further under **cleft sentences**.)

All those uses of **it** explain why it often appears at the start of a sentence, and why **it** needs watching, whether or not you have a computer style checker to remind you.

Italian plurals Italian loanwords are better assimilated than most and pose few problems for English users. In ordinary usage they all take English plurals in *s*—witness *maestro(s)*, *opera(s)*, *studio(s)* or *regatta(s)*—and their Italian plural endings in *i* and *e* are never seen. Even in specialised fields such as art and architecture, Italian technical terms such as *fresco*, *loggia*, *pergola* and *portico* are given English plurals. In literature and music the same is true for loanwords ending in *a*, such as *aria*, *cadenza*, *cantata* and *stanza*. But in concert program notes, **Italian plurals** are sometimes put on musical loanwords ending in *-o*: *concerti*, *contralti*, *libretti*, *soprani*, *virtuosi* etc., by those who wish to kindle a sense of foreignness with their words. For musicians and many a music lover however, the Italianness of the words is irrelevant to their pleasure, and like the general public, they pluralise all such words with *s*.

(See further under **-a** section 1, and **-o**.)

italics Nowadays the sloping forms of *italic* type serve only to contrast with the ordinary upright forms of *roman*—though *italic* fonts were once the regular medium for printing. Modern wordprocessors usually offer them as a supplement to the main font, though their availability on the printer is the key to whether they can be part of your repertoire. (In handwriting, and on typewriters and wordprocessors where italics are not available, underlining is the equivalent practice.)

As the alternative typeface **italics** help to make a word or string of words stand out from the carrier sentence. Like any contrastive device, they work best when used sparingly, and are not very effective for whole sentences. Their use also raises certain questions and anomalies, which are dealt with in the final section of this entry.

*Uses of **italics**:*

1 With English words
a) to emphasise a particular word in its context:
   What I've just asked you was not intended as a *rhetorical* question.
b) to draw attention to an unusual word or one being used in an unusual way, such as an archaism, malapropism or neologism.
c) to highlight technical terms or words which are themselves the focus of discussion. Technical terms are usually italicised for first appearance only, whereas those under discussion would be italicised regularly.

2 With foreign words. **Italics** are often used to highlight borrowed words and phrases which are not yet fully assimilated into English. However judging the extent of their assimilation is a vexed question, and one on which it's difficult to be consistent. Dictionaries themselves wrestle with the problem, and their conclusions are sometimes inscrutable. Why should *a fortiori* and *carte blanche* have **italics** in the *Oxford Dictionary for Writers and Editors*, but not *a posteriori* and *carte-de-visite*? Instead of providing a canon of words to be italicised, other authorities leave it to individual writers and editors to decide, depending on the likely reader's familiarity with such foreignisms. "When in doubt, don't" is the most general piece of advice on italicising from the Chicago *Manual of Style*. To this we might add the comment of *Foreign Words in English* (1966): if the loanword needs its full quota of accents and diacritics, it probably needs **italics** too: witness *pièce de résistance* and *vis-à-vis*. Once the accents disappear, as in *debris* and *debut* (formerly *débris* and *début*), they might as well be printed in roman. Any reduction in the number of accents, as from two to one in *resumé*, is also grounds for not using **italics**.

3 With Latin abbreviations. These are no longer set in **italics**, though special exceptions are made by some editors (see under **Latin abbreviations**).

4 With individual letters. **Italics** are one way of setting off single letters against accompanying words, e.g. "minding your *p*s and *q*s". (For other ways, see under **letters as words**.)

5 With the titles of compositions. By general agreement you italicise the titles of books, periodicals and newspapers, of plays, films, works of art (including sculpture), and opera and music:

An Imaginary Life	*Crocodile Dundee*
The One Day of the Year	*Blue Poles*
Adelaide Advertiser	*Sun Music*
Australian Women's Weekly	*Voss*

An important exception is the Bible and its various books, and other sacred texts such as the Koran, which are always in roman.

The use of **italics** for TV and radio programs is not agreed upon. In Britain they are recommended by *Copy-editing* (1992), though both the Australian Government Publishing Service and Chicago *Style Manual* suggest roman + quote marks. Yet actual practice in Australia (as evidenced in newspaper reviews and entertainment guides) is to use **italics** for any program titles. Canadian editors are encouraged to use **italics** for the title of a series, and roman + quote marks for individual programs/episodes—a distinction which has traditionally been made between the title of a book and the titles of individual essays or poems within it. But it's more difficult to make in relation to radio and TV programs. The Chicago *Manual* notes that if you're making repeated references to the items in a collection, it's clearer then to use **italics** for all.

6 With official names:
a) the titles of legislative acts have in the past been set in **italics** or roman according to the jurisdiction; but the Australian Government *Style Manual* (1988) recommends that they should be italicised everywhere in Australia. This is providing they're quoted in their full form (complete with date); when referred to by their short title they should appear in roman. Note that in both Britain and the USA the full titles are themselves given in roman, according to *Copy-editing* (1992) and the Chicago *Manual of Style.*
b) the official names of court cases are italicised, as in *Kramer v. Kramer.* In the past, editors were enjoined to put the *v.* separating the names in roman, as *Copy-editing* (1992) still does. But the Australian Government Publishing Service and Chicago style manuals allow either **italics** or roman provided it's consistently one or the other.
c) the names of ships, trains and other special vehicles are italicised:
   HMAS *Vendetta   Indian Pacific   Challenger*
   Note that the prefix HMAS is not italicised.
d) the Latin names of plants and animals, both genus and species (as well as subspecies and variety), are italicised, as in:
   Tristania conferta   Ornithorhynchus anatinus
Note that when the generic name is also the common name, as for example with "banksia" and "melaleuca" and many Australian plants, it's printed in roman.

7 With performing directions. In the texts of plays or scripts of films, stage directions are printed in **italics** to separate them from the dialogue. In musical scores, **italics** are likewise used for references to the dynamics of performing, to separate them from the words of the score.

Questions and anomalies with **italics**. Italicised words raise the question as to what to do when they need to be made plural or possessive. Should the apostrophe *s* or plural ending be in **italics** or roman? The traditional answer for the possessive ending has been roman, and this is still the verdict of the major style guides. But they diverge over plural endings, where the Australian Government *Style Manual* recommends switching to roman, and *Copy-editing*

(1992) staying in **italics**. The Chicago *Manual of Style* notes that continuing the **italics** is preferable whenever the plural ending is something other than a simple English *s*, as for instance with the plural of *lingua franca* > *lingue franche*. In that way, a foreign plural is better integrated with the rest of the word.

Any punctuation mark immediately following an italicised word is usually in **italics** too, for the congruity of line. This is of course less important for a full stop than for a semicolon or question/exclamation mark. Note however that accompanying brackets, whether square or rounded, are still in roman.

Finally, how can items normally italicised be identified within italicised titles or headings? **Italics** within **italics** are somehow needed. Lacking that, editors and writers can resort to quotation marks, go back to roman, or simply leave the item undistinguished amid its *italic* carrier. *Copy-editing* (1992) notes the rather self-conscious effect of giving quotation marks to foreign words in titles or headings, and that it's best to leave them in **italics** just like the rest. But quotation marks are usually given to titles within titles. Latin biological names are normally turned into roman.

-ite Though ultimately from Greek, **-ite** is a lively suffix—whether you think of *socialite* or *dynamite*. It serves both in common and scientific usage to make nouns which refer to someone with a particular affiliation, and to form the names of certain minerals and chemical substances.

In common usage **-ite** normally attaches itself to proper names. Cases such as *socialite* and *suburbanite* are the exception. Much more often it picks up a place name, as in *Brooklynite*, *Canaanite* or *Muscovite*; or that of a notable person, as in *Ibsenite*, *Thatcherite* or *Trotskyite*; or that or a party or movement, as in *Laborite* and *pre-Raphaelite*. The suffix sometimes seems derogatory, though not all the examples given would show this. At any rate, the **-ite** word tends to be used by those opposed to the person or party named, while supporters and adherents are unlikely to apply it to themselves. *Darwinite* is probably less neutral than *Darwinist* or *Darwinian*. (See further under **-an** and **-ist**.)

In scientific usage, **-ite** again has more than one function. In geology it serves as a regular suffix for naming minerals, such as *anthracite*, *dolomite* and *malachite*; and for the names of various fossils: *ammonite*, *lignite* and *trilobite*. In chemistry it's used for naming both explosives such as *dynamite* and *melinite*, as well as the salts of certain acids (those whose names end in *-ous*), for example *nitrite* and *sulfite*. The fictional name *kryptonite* (the only substance that can reduce Superman to a trembling heap) seems to carry the aura of several of these scientific uses.

Itie, eyetie or **eytie** None of these makes good contact with the intended reference: an Italian. The first spelling has trouble representing the sound of the second syllable; the second and third spellings mask the fact that it is a proper name.

Yet we need feel no regrets if the word misses its target. Its overtones are derogatory, and it's most often heard in utterances that express ethnic discrimination. Better by far to replace it with the neutral word *Italian*, with its straightforward geographical and historical associations.

(See further under **inclusive language** and **racist language**.)

-itis This is essentially a medical suffix, creating nouns which mean "inflammation of ...", as in:

appendicitis bronchitis gastroenteritis mastitis tonsillitis

It also enjoys some popular use in coining words which refer to pseudo-diseases, such as *Mondayitis*.

its or **it's** Separated only by an apostrophe, there are few pairs in English which cause as much trouble as this. The problem is mostly that **it's** is written instead of **its**—which is to say that **its** is most probably the one you need, other things being equal.

Its without the apostrophe is a possessive pronoun or adjective, pure and simple. Like other pronouns: *his*, *her(s)*, *our(s)* etc, it has no apostrophe. What confuses the issue is the fact that nouns *do* have apostrophes when they are possessive, as in *the dog's breakfast* or *a baker's dozen*. Inexperienced writers therefore think that **it's** is the possessive they need, especially if they have been rapped over the knuckles for leaving apostrophes out.

It's is a contraction of *it is*, (usually *is*, but occasionally *has*). The apostrophe is a mark of omission, not possession. (See further under **apostrophes**.) Note that because it consists of a pronoun plus a verb, the contraction is often used to introduce statements:

It's true. It's blue. It's Australian.

Because **its** (without apostrophe) is a possessive pronoun/adjective (or *determiner*), it introduces a noun phrase:

its truth its blueness its Australianness

(See further under **determiners**.)

The problem of **its/it's** is an artifact of the last two centuries of English. Earlier on, the contracted form of *it is* was *'tis*, and because it didn't coincide with the pronoun, both **its** and **it's** were used interchangeably for the pronoun. The *Oxford Dictionary* shows that some writers continued to use **it's** for the pronoun until around 1800. But by then *'tis* had given way to **it's** as the normal contraction for *it is* (having been previously described as "vulgar", i.e. the nonliterary one). And as this new contraction made its appearance in writing, it became necessary to distinguish the pronoun from it, hence the insistence on **its** with no apostrophe.

-ity This is the ending of many an abstract noun which embodies the quality of a related adjective. As *ethnic* is contained in *ethnicity*, so *circular* is in *circularity*, and *readable* in *readability*. Many other nouns ending in **-ity** are not really English formations but words borrowed direct from French (e.g. *falsity*) or modeled on Latin (e.g. *sincerity*); and in some cases (e.g. *atrocity*, *hilarity*) the abstract noun was current in English quite a while before the related adjective. But their large numbers have helped to foster English formations of the same kind.

The most productive types in modern English are those like *readability*, based on adjectives ending in *-able* (*accountability*, *respectability*), or *-ible* (*compatibility*, *feasibility*). (See further under **-ability**.) Such words are surprisingly popular, in spite of all their syllables. History shows that in some cases they have replaced slightly shorter nouns ending in *-ness*. So the earlier *unaccountableness* has given place to *unaccountability*, *unavailableness* to *unavailability* and so on.

-ive Thousands of English adjectives bear this suffix. It originated in Latin, but is an element of both Latin and French borrowings, and has been thoroughly assimilated. The following are only a token of the innumerable familiar words with it:

> *active attractive collective competitive convulsive creative decisive*
> *exclusive impressive impulsive persuasive permissive repulsive*
> *retrospective speculative submissive subversive*

Some **-ive** adjectives have also established themselves as nouns, witness:

> *collective imperative native representative*

Adjectives in **-ive** are often members of tightly knit sets of words, with adjective/verb/noun members:

active	*act*	*action*
collective	*collect*	*collection*
decisive	*decide*	*decision*
persuasive	*persuade*	*persuasion*
repulsive	*repel*	*repulsion*
submissive	*submit*	*submission*

The same kind of network is evident with words ending in **-ative/-ate/-ation**. (See under those headings.)

-ization/-isation The choice between these depends on the same issues as are discussed under **-ise/-ize**.

-ize/-ise See **-ise/-ize**.

J

jackaroo or **jackeroo** This word is unsettled, and the *Macquarie Dictionary* (1991) gives equal status to the two spellings. The *Australian National Dictionary*'s citations run 3:1 in favor of **jackeroo**, and yet **jackaroo** is endorsed in five out of the six Australian newspaper guides. **Jackaroo** is the spelling used for the job title in the Australian Standard Classification of Occupations (1990), and it appears in the street as the name of a four-wheel drive vehicle. In a 1992 spelling survey of over one thousand Australians, a large majority (70%) were in favor of **jackaroo**.

The spelling with **-aroo** is more Australian, being the suffix that occurs in words for Australian fauna and flora, and a sprinkling of local placenames. (See further under **-aroo**.) Words with *-eroo* were however in vogue in the 1940s, in the USA and in the Pacific (see **-eroo**), and they probably boosted the frequency of **jackeroo**.

The origins of **jackaroo** remain obscure. Two Aboriginal words have been suggested as its source—*tchaceroo*, an old name for the talkative crow-shrike, or *dhugai-iu*, a loanword from the Moreton Bay area for "wandering white man"—though neither is endorsed in *Australian Aboriginal Words* (1990). Overseas origins have also been proposed: that the word is based on the Spanish *vaquero* "cowboy", thought to be the source for the American "buckaroo" as well. Yet **jackaroo** is first recorded in Australia in 1845, too early to have come across the Pacific with Americans prospecting for gold, which makes the Spanish–American etymology unlikely. Other explanations of **jackaroo** have it based on English personal names: *Jacky Rue*, *Jacky Raw* or *Jack Carew*, though all of them sound ad hoc.

After all those speculations, we are left with the popular explanation, that the word is simply a hybrid, a blend of *Jack* and *kangaroo*. This makes the **jackaroo** the Australian equivalent of a centaur—and a small contribution to mythology.

jacketed The *t* remains single when this word becomes a verb. See under **t**.

jail or **gaol** No English spelling is more perverse than **gaol**. With its peculiar sequence of vowels, it has been misspelled as *goal* for centuries, according to the *Oxford Dictionary*. The word **gaol** was borrowed from Norman French in the thirteenth century, and that spelling has been protected in English statutes and the legal code. The tradition behind **gaol** is thus much longer than that of **jail**, borrowed from Central French and used in English only since the seventeenth century.

But **jail** is the much more rational spelling, analogous with *bail, fail, hail* and others. It is the standard spelling in North America, and the Australian Government Publishing Service *Style Manual* (1978) made it an acceptable alternative to **gaol**. Almost all Australian newspapers (except the *West Australian*) take advantage of the licence to use **jail**. In fact, **jail** is preferred in British dictionaries including the *Oxford Dictionary*, although it has never had official backing in the penal system in Britain.

jailer, jailor or **gaoler** The choice between these depends first and foremost on whether you prefer *jail* or *gaol*. After that you choose between the English *-er* suffix and the Latin/French *-or*. (See further under **-er/-or**.) The major dictionaries around the world all give preference to **jailer**.

Jakarta or **Djakarta** The simpler spelling with just *J* is the usual one nowadays for the capital of Indonesia. The name has been successively modified since colonial days, when under Dutch rule it was *Batavia*. With the departure of the Dutch in 1949, it became **Djakarta**; it was then officially modified to **Jakarta** in the early seventies.

The second city of Indonesia has also seen adjustments to its name: once *Djokjakarta* or *Djogjakarta*, it was then written variously as *Jokjakarta*, *Jogjakarta* and *Jokyakarta*. The preferred spelling nowadays is *Yogyakarta*.

Jap or **Japanese** The use of **Jap** for *Japanese* has rarely been an innocent case of shortening. The word had derogatory implications from the beginning of the twentieth century, according to *Webster's English Usage* (1989), and these intensified during World War II. The full form **Japanese** is neutral and free of racist connotations. (See further under **racist language**.)

jargon This is the technical language of a special group. It smacks of inside knowledge, and implies membership of the inside group. You have to be a sailor to know what a *broad reach* is, or a wine connoisseur to comment on *oxidisation* in the wine. Those able to use the **jargon** with confidence enjoy a sense of solidarity with others who do the same. **Jargon** is thus inclusive in its effect for some—and very exclusive for others. Its power to exclude is what gives **jargon** its negative connotations. The word is quite often used to express the resentment felt by those who cannot "talk the lingo" and feel disadvantaged by it:

I couldn't get a word in. They talked economic jargon all through dinner.

Those who use **jargon** can be unaware of how specialised it is or how dependent they are on it. The jargon habit becomes ingrained in writing if you write only for a restricted audience or within a particular institution. (See further under **officialese**.)

Note that **jargon** has something in common with slang, though it differs in being standardised. So while the pressure in industrial pipes is measured in *kilopascals* (according to the jargon), it's a matter of so many "kippers" in the slang of those operating the plant. **Jargon** takes itself seriously, whereas slang can be playful or at least offhanded.

jaw's harp, jaws harp or **jew's harp** These are all names for a small folk instrument which originated in southern Asia (in India, Borneo and New Guinea) as well as Europe. It is has little in common with a harp, and consists of a single strip of vibrating metal, set in a frame which is held between the teeth, and plucked with a fingertip. The mouth itself acts as resonator, and as modifier of the pitch. Thus the plain names **jaw's harp** or **jaws harp** highlight the method of playing, as for other instruments, e.g. *viola da gamba* ("viol for the leg"). *Grove's Dictionary of Music* (1880) speculated that **jaw's harp** was the original name, and that **jew's harp** was a corruption of it. Yet things seem to be the other way round.

The instrument was in fact known as a **jew's harp** or *jew's tromp*, from the sixteenth century on, centuries before the first reference to the **jaw's harp** in *Grove's Dictionary*. The Jewish element is built into the English name for the instrument as well as one of the German ones (*Judenharfe*). Yet the instrument has no special connection with the Jews; nor is it necessarily a poor man's means of making music. Some of the *jew's harps* exhibited in museums are exquisitely worked in silver. Presumably **jew's harp** originated as a "throwaway name" (along the same lines as *dutch treat* and *french leave*), in times when people were less concerned about racist language. (See further under **throwaway terms**.)

je ne sais quoi This French phrase means literally "I do not know what", but in English it refers to a special, indefinable quality:
> *Their house has a je ne sais quoi about it.*
The phrase puts on airs. Yet it may have its place when you're writing of a quality which can't quite be pinned down.

jelly or **jello** In Australia **jelly** is a gelatinous, transparent, brightly colored dessert. In the USA the same food is called **jello**, a name derived from the trademark *Jell-O*. Americans need the additional term because **jelly** itself is used for the very thin, transparent type of jam. At the opposite end of the scale are *conserves*, jams which are almost solid fruit. They apply the term *jam* to concoctions somewhere between the extremes of **jelly** and *conserves*.

jerry can or **jerrican** The spaced form is usual in Australia, whereas **jerrican** is preferred by British dictionaries. The *Random House Dictionary* shares the Australian preference, and *Webster's* the British. Other variants are *jerrycan*, *jerry-can* and *jerican*. The form **jerry can** makes no bones about the fact that this useful steel container for petrol was modeled on a German prototype, and that we owe the invention to "Jerry" (a collective term for the Germans, used in British English since World War I). The spellings **jerrican** and *jerican* make its origin less obvious.

Jew and **Jewish** See under **Israel**.

jewellery or **jewelry** The standard spelling in Australia is **jewellery**, used by almost all the retail jewel stores listed in the metropolitan phone directories. In the USA the standard spelling is **jewelry**. Both spellings occur in Britain, according to Fowler and other authorities, though **jewellery** is the usual one. In fact **jewelry** is the older spelling, dating from the fourteenth century, whereas **jewellery** is first recorded in the eighteenth.

Style books are generally less concerned about the spelling of the word than its pronunciation, which they insist should be ''jewel'' + ''ry'', not ''jul'' + ''ery''. Yet the latter is common enough, and arguably accords better with the spelling **jewellery**. The pronunciation ''jewel'' + ''ry'' may indeed help to strengthen the use of **jewelry**.

Note also that the vendor of jewels is a *jeweller* in Australia and Britain, and a *jeweler* in the USA. (See further under **doubling of last consonant**.)

jew's harp, jaw's harp or **jaws harp** See jaw's harp.

jibe or **gybe** See under **gibe, gybe** or **jibe**.

jihad or **jehad** Whatever dictionary you consult, the first spelling for this word for a Muslim holy war is **jihad**. It is the primary spelling in the *Oxford Dictionary*, no doubt because it transliterates the Arabic original exactly. Yet the Oxford citations show that many English users of the word have preferred **jehad**, and the pronunciation of the first syllable (as ''ee'' not ''eye'') may still influence them that way. At any rate, **jehad** continues to be offered as an alternative.

jilgie or **gilgie** These are alternative spellings for a West Australian word for the yabby, borrowed from the Nyungar Aborigines in the southwest corner of Australia. The spelling **jilgie** is less well supported than **gilgie** by citations (2:5) in the *Australian National Dictionary*. But **jilgie** helps to distinguish this word from another Aboriginal loanword *gilgai*, which also has **gilgie** as a variant. (See further under **gilgai**.)

jillaroo or **jilleroo** This word for the female counterpart to the *jackaroo* was coined in the context of World War II, when landgirls were needed as farm labor to replace the men who had enlisted. **Jillaroo** seems to be the more common spelling, if we are to judge from the *Australian National Dictionary*'s citations which run 6:4 in its favor; and it's the preferred spelling of the *Macquarie Dictionary* (1991). (See also **-aroo**.)

The sexist implications of **jillaroo** are not commented on in the review of occupational titles in chapter 8 of the Australian Government *Style Manual*; and it stands (with that spelling) in the 1990 Australian Standard Classification of Occupations. But if girls are to be encouraged to take up farming apprenticeships, **jillaroo** may need replacing with ''farming assistant'' or some such. (See further under **nonsexist language**.)

jiujitsu or **jujitsu** See jujitsu.

job titles The ultimate Australian authority for the way we refer to occupational roles are the various statutes of labor, together with the standard list of names published by the Australian Bureau of Statistics as the *Australian Standard Classification of Occupations*. Job titles are part of the jargon of the workplace (though often complemented by unofficial slang titles, such as "sumpy" alongside *engine maintenance engineer* in the RAAF, and "sadie" alongside *cleaning operative* in business premises). Within the public service, the established classifications are often rather broad and cover a wide range in seniority, so that the jobs performed by bearers of the title *assistant, clerk, officer* etc. are very diverse. This fact, plus the thrust to replace sexist job titles with ones which are gender-free, tends to foster job titles which are less and less specific. (See further under **nonsexist language**.)

Where people are free to choose their own job titles (in private industry, and among the self-employed) their best aim would be to make them specific and distinctive. But for some it's tempting to use a euphemism or try to dignify the job with a formal name—and who are we to object if the makeup artist prefers to style herself a "cosmetologist", and those who install burglar alarms as "security executives"? If such terms seem inflationary they will sooner or later succumb to devaluation, like any other overpriced currency.

Jogjakarta or **Jokjakarta** See under **Jakarta** or **Djakarta**.

Jonathan or **Jonathon** The first spelling is traditional for this Hebrew name, borne by **Jonathan** the friend of the biblical King David (I Samuel 18), and many others since him. **Jonathon** is a recent variant, used by popular singers and others. The second spelling is no doubt influenced by the new suffix *-athon*, which is a formative element in a number of recent English words (see **-athon**). With lower case, **jonathan** and **jonathon** are also alternative spellings for a red-skinned type of apple sold through much of the year. The origins of the name, first recorded in the 1870s, are unclear although most dictionaries associate it with *Jonathan Hasbrouk*, an American jurist who died in 1846. Yet because this variety of apple originated in America, its name could well have been reinforced by nineteenth century use of **Jonathan** to mean "an American".

journalism and **journalese** Journalists are mass producers of words against deadlines. Small wonder then that what they write sometimes/often sounds pedestrian and predictable. Small miracle if they succeed in stimulating readers with the freshness and insightfulness of their writing. The best **journalism** is interesting and original in its expression, making readers more aware of the resources of the common language. It is achieved most often in the personal editorial columns of newspapers, by journalists who enjoy the privilege of a guaranteed number of words in which to develop their thoughts. (Cf. the **inverted pyramid** below.)

Bad **journalism** is hack writing with a witch-like power to turn anything into stereotyped dross, partly because it depends so heavily on **clichés** (see further under **clichés**). Predictable as the style is, it almost "writes itself". Even the awkward three- and four-letter words which are the staple of headlines (such as *ban*, *bid*, *leak*, *wed* etc.) seem curiously natural in it. This is **journalese** at its worst. (See further under **headline language**.)

Other hallmarks of **journalese** are the lumpish sentences with overweight beginnings:

St Edmund's Catholic Church Youth Orchestra organiser Jane Filomel ...

Keen amateur sports fisherman and RSL Vice President Jeff Bringamin ...

The vital information is all there at the start, but so condensed (shorn of articles such as *the*, *a* and connecting words) that it can generate its own ambiguities. However capacious the noun phrase is, there are limits on what it can effectively put across (see further under **adjectives** and **noun phrase**).

The **inverted pyramid** (or *triangle*) undoubtedly puts pressure on journalists to present everything "up front". This is the traditional structure for a news article in which the first sentence must encapsulate the essence of the whole event. This summary sentence is followed by background information and details which are increasingly marginal in importance.

Readers are often conscious that they get less and less, the further they go in an article. What the inverted pyramid offers is increasingly slender information.

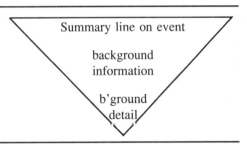

The **inverted pyramid** is certainly not intended to frustrate the thorough reader. Rather it is to ensure that if the journalist's report is cut short by the subeditor through lack of space on the page, only the less essential details will be omitted.

judgement or **judgment**   Either of these two spellings can be justified: they appear in almost equal numbers (24:25) in the Australian ACE corpus, and the *Macquarie Dictionary* (1991) gives them equal status. **Judgement** is the more regular spelling, according to the rule of leaving an *-e* on a verb before *-ment* is added (cf. *advertisement*, and others presented at **-ment**). The *Oxford Dictionary* preferred **judgement**, arguing explicitly against "the unscholarly habit of omitting the *-e*". It did however allow the use of **judgment** in legal contexts. Yet whatever its idiosyncrasies, **judgment** has been in general use since the sixteenth century, and was the spelling enshrined in the Authorised Version of the Bible (1611). This early use helps to explain why it is the standard spelling in American English. Even in Britain, dictionaries other than the Oxford give first preference to **judgment**.

While authorities can be found for either spelling, the tide of usage in Australia is with **judgement**, which was endorsed by a majority of 74% in a 1992 spelling survey of over 1000 people.

The spelling **judgement** has been preferred in this book, for reasons of usage as well as orthographical regularity as outlined above. Comparable spellings are recommended for **abridgement**, **acknowledgement** and **lodgement**.

---

judicious or **judicial** Though both link up ultimately with the work of judges, these words have distinct meanings. **Judicial** connects with the official role of the judge in phrases like *judicial hearing* and *judicial procedure*; it implies something done by a judge, or associated with the courts. It is strictly neutral in its implications, whereas **judicious** is discreetly positive in its overtones. It connotes sound judgement in any field of activity, from a *judicious comment* by a teacher, to a *judicious withdrawal* by an army commander. In principle, a **judicial** judgement is also **judicious**, but if the law is (sometimes) an ass, this cannot be taken for granted.

jujitsu Dictionaries prefer **jujitsu** as the spelling of the word for the ancient Japanese art of self defence, though it's still a little unsettled. Other recognised alternatives are *jiujitsu*, *jiujutsu* and *jujutsu*, the last being closest to the form of the Japanese word itself. As with the Japanese word *harakiri*, a tendency to dissimilate the syllables seems to be at work. (See further under **dissimilate**.)

junction or **juncture** These words have common origins in the Latin verb "join", but only **junction** is widely used in this sense. **Juncture** is mostly confined to the rather formal phrase *at this juncture*, meaning "at this critical moment" (or more loosely "as things come together like this"). **Junction** is much more common and familiar from being used to refer to the place at which roads, railway lines or wires come together. The uses of **junction** start up in the late eighteenth century (two centuries after **juncture**) and gather steam with the industrial revolution.

junketing The spelling of this word is discussed at **t**.

junkie or **junky** See under **-ie/-y**.

jurist or **juror** Both these have to take the law seriously, but for the **jurist** it is a profession, while for the **juror** it is simply an occasional commitment. The **jurist** is an academic expert on law, a scholar and/or writer in the field. The **juror** is an ordinary citizen, one of the group selected from the community at large to hear the proceedings of a trial, and to cast final judgement on it.

juristic or **juristical** See under -istic/-istical.

just and **justly** As an adjective, **just** means "fair, impartial or right". The related adverb is **justly**, as in:
She dealt justly with their complaints.
However **just** has other uses as an adverb in its own right. It carries several meanings, including "exactly", "by a near thing", "very recently", "only" and "really"; and only the context shows which of them is intended:
It's just what they wanted.
The food just lasted long enough.
They've just arrived.
It's just an ordinary day.
The idea was just brilliant.
In the first three sentences, **just** has an important interpersonal role expressing immediacy (see **interpersonal**). In the last two, **just** could be seen as a **hedge word** and an **intensifier** respectively (see under those headings). Some might argue that it's redundant in such sentences, though it does contribute to their rhythm and emphasis. The examples also show that **just** works as a discourse marker, spotlighting the word or phrase following (see **information focus**).

*Using **just** with verbs* raises a small point of style. British usage avoids putting **just** with the simple past form of verbs whenever it means "recently". Britons prefer the compound form with *has/have*. So for them it's important to write:
It has just come through not
It just came through.
Yet the latter idiom (without the auxiliary *has/have*) is well established in North America and Australia. Even in Britain the simple past verb can be used with **just** in any of several other senses. See for example the use of **just** = "only" in:
Not so outstanding this year—he just won two out of the seven prizes.
This concession (and the fact that the meanings of **just** are so intricately bound up with their context) suggests that we make trouble for ourselves if we try to restrict the use of **just** with a simple past verb.

K

k/c Many loanwords beginning with a "k" sound may be spelled with either *k* or *c*. The **k** is usually a sign of their foreign origin, which tends to be replaced by **c** as they become more assimilated into English. Among the following, only those in italics are more likely to have *k* spellings nowadays:

> *kabbala kabanossi kadi kaftan kaliph kalsomine kalpak* karat kark kathode kation kephalin keramic *keratin ketchup* kola konk kosh *kosher krimmer kris* krummhorn kumquat *kyanite kymograph*

Note that in some of those words, other letters also vary in spelling. (See under **cabbala, caliph, carat, ketchup** and **kosher.**)

The tendency to replace **k** with **c** can be seen also in the middle of a word: **ikon/icon, okker/ocker, okta/octa, skeptic/sceptic**; and at the end: **disk/disc, mollusk/mollusc.** All are discussed at individual entries. On *yakka, yacka* and *yacca*, see **yakka.**

Note also that **k** sometimes varies with *q(u)* in the spelling of a word. See **qu/k.**

kabob or **kebab** See under **kebab.**

Kakadu or **Gagadu** See under **Aboriginal names.**

Kampuchea See **Cambodia.**

kangaroo This archetypal symbol of Australia was the first Aboriginal loanword to be recorded. It appears in the journals of both Captain Cook and Joseph Banks, gathered during their landfall at Endeavour River in northern Queensland in 1770. They noted that *kanguru* was the local name for the large hopping animal they encountered there for the first time. But the name was unknown a few years later (1788) to Aborigines 1500 miles south around Port Jackson, even though they were familiar with similar names such as *wallaroo* and *potoroo*). Scholars now believe that the name originally given to Cook may have designated a very specific kind of kangaroo, and that the Europeans made it the general term for all. The spelling varied at first, from *kanguru* and *kangooroo*, to *kanguroo* and **kangaroo.** The latter became the regular spelling from the 1790s.

Note that the plural is normally *kangaroos*, though sportsmen are inclined to leave it as plain *kangaroo*:

> *They shot a dozen kangaroo …*

karat or **carat** See **carat.**

kark or **cark** Both spellings are used for this very informal word meaning "die". The *Australian National Dictionary* has slightly more citations for **kark** and makes it the primary spelling, though it derives it rather metaphysically from **cark**, the cry of the bird associated with carrion. *Collins Dictionary* spells it as **cark**, and explains it simply in terms of the onomatopoeia of **cark** as the cawing of the crow. The *Macquarie Dictionary* also lists it as **cark**, but with the suggestion that its etymology is associated with the word *carcase*. Whichever etymology you prefer, it adds weight to the spelling **cark**.

karri or **kauri** The timber from these quite different trees should never be confused. The **karri** is a tall eucalyptus, whose name is a loanword from the Nyungar people around Norseman in Western Australia. It produces hardwood, heavy and reddish in color. The **kauri** is a type of pine found both in Queensland and in New Zealand, whose name is borrowed from a Maori language. **Kauri** timber is light in color and easily worked.

Katoomba or **Kedumba** See under **Aboriginal names.**

kebab Modern dictionaries prefer **kebab** to *kabob, kebob* or *kabab*. They thus prefer the Turkish form of the word (**kebab**) to the original Arabic *kabab*, meaning "roast meat", which was first introduced into English in the seventeenth century. The Turkish spelling is the most common, whether the dish referred to is *shishkebabs* (small pieces of meat roasted on individual skewers), or *doner kebab* (slices of meat cut from a large cylinder of it, cooked on a vertical spit).

kelim or **kilim** See kilim.

Keltic or **Celtic** See Celtic.

Kelvin See under Celsius.

kenneled or **kennelled** For the choice of spellings when *kennel* becomes a verb, see under **-l/-ll-**.

keramic or **ceramic** See under k/c.

kerb or **curb** See curb.

kerosene or **kerosine** See under -ine.

ketchup, catsup or **catchup** In Australian and British dictionaries, **ketchup** is the first spelling for the well-known sauce, and **catsup** is made the secondary alternative. Both forms go back to Cantonese and to alternative pronunciations for the word for "tomato juice". The third spelling **catchup** shows folk etymology at work, attempting to make sense of an inscrutable foreign word, but with English elements which are scarcely relevant. (See further under **folk etymology**.)

In American English there's a great divide in usage between those who, like the *Random House Dictionary*, prefer **ketchup**, and those who line up with *Webster's* and **catsup**. *Webster's English Usage* (1989) notes however that people's preferences just might be linked to the spelling on the label of their favorite brand of sauce (Heinz or Del Monte)—rather than their dictionary.

key or **quay** See **quay**.

kibbutz When written down, this Hebrew loanword is usually pluralised in the regular Hebrew way as *kibbutzim* (see further under **-im**). In conversation it often acquires an English plural form "kibbutzes", and we need not be surprised to see it in print in due course.

kiddie or **kiddy** See under **-ie/-y**.

kidnapped or **kidnaped** The choice between these is discussed under **-p/-pp-**.

kilim or **kelim** Both spellings are used for this word for a rug woven without pile, originally from the Middle East. In Turkish and Persian it is a **kilim**, and that is the spelling endorsed in English dictionaries everywhere. Yet **kelim** is not uncommon in Australian advertising; and the citations for **kelim** actually outnumber those for *kilim* in the *Oxford Dictionary* (5:3), although it too gives **kilim** as the primary spelling. The decision was evidently based on etymology, and perhaps the feeling that a third spelling *khilim* (with two citations) provided extra support for **kilim**.

kilo This Greek prefix meaning "1000" is one of the key elements of the metric system. (See **metrication** and Appendix IV.) Note however that in the computer word *kilobyte*, **kilo** equals 1024. This is because computer systems are essentially binary (not decimal), and 1024 is 2 to the power of 10.

kind and **kindly** Both these words can be adjectives, with only a little difference in meaning between them. Both imply sympathy in the person to whom they are applied, but while **kindly** refers to a generally benign disposition, **kind** can be related to specific action. Compare:
The matron was a kindly person.
They were kind enough to drive me home.
As an adverb, **kindly** expresses the meaning of **kind**, and so *They kindly drove me home* paraphrases the second example exactly.

The adjective **kindly** has no accepted adverb because of the awkwardness of a formation like "kindlily". Instead we say "in a kindly way".

Note that the word **kindly** also works as synonym for "please", in polite requests and commands:
Kindly take your seats.
Would you kindly take your feet off the chair.
Here its function is definitely **interpersonal**. (See further under that heading.)

kind of In phrases like *kind of/sort of/type of*, singular and plural ideas come together: both a particular class of objects, and various examples we know. In formal English either the singular or plural is consistently maintained through the sentence:

> *This kind of film is one to avoid.*
> *These kinds of films are ones to avoid.*

(Of course, those sentences differ a little in meaning, because the second makes a more sweeping statement than the first. Yet the preference for one or the other is often a matter of personal and intellectual style.)

Rather less formal are the various constructions in which singular and plural are blended, all of which occur in impromptu speech and can also appear in informal writing:

> *This kind of films is not what they should be making.*
> *These kinds of film are the best yet.*
> *These kind of films are being made for television.*

Both the first and second sentences in that set are tolerable and justifiable in particular contexts, as long as the following verb is made to agree (*kind + is, kinds + are*). The third is a slightly uncomfortable hybrid, though it's heard on the lips of Shakespearean characters and in twentieth century conversation. It does however suggest imprecise thinking which needs to be sharpened up in writing. Are you really talking about one type of film or several?

One other indefinite use of **kind of** and *sort of* which is frequent in conversation is as a hedging device:

> *She works as a sort of au pair girl.*
> *He was kind of ready to leave by then.*

Usages like these are definitely informal and unsuitable for documentary writing. (See under **hedge words** for alternatives.)

kinesthetic or **kinaesthetic, kinesthesia** or **kinaesthesia** See under **ae/e**.

kn/n The **kn-** spelling is essential in various English words to prevent the convergence of homonyms. See for example:

> *(k)nave (k)new (k)night (k)nit (k)nob (k)not (k)now*

Compare **knickknack** or **nicknack**.

kneeled or **knelt** See under **-ed/-t**.

knickknack or **nicknack** The excess of consonants in the first spelling is enough to make anyone prefer **nicknack**, and it is the accepted alternative. Fortunately the *n* spelling is not already bespoken for another word. (See further under **kn/n**.)

knifed or **knived** See under **-v-/-f-**.

knit or **knitted** Both these serve as past forms of the verb **knit**, but the uses of **knit** are far fewer. It survives mostly in collocations such as *closely/loosely/*

tightly knit. The regular **knitted** is always used for *knitting* with yarn or something like it, as well as for many figurative uses. For example:

> *The broken bones knitted quickly.*
>
> *Tragedy knitted the two families together.*

In examples like those, British English might still use **knit**, whereas in Australian and American English it's most likely to be **knitted**, according to the *Macquarie* and *Random House* dictionaries.

KO See under **OK**.

koala Australia's **koala** has suffered many indignities. Its name is the result of early confusion, probably a misreading of *koolah*, which was believed to be the Aboriginal form of the word. According to *Aboriginal Words in English* (1990) even this was mistaken, the original word being more like *gula* or *gulawang*. But the form **koala** was created in the Philosophical Transactions of the Royal Society of London in 1808, and has proved tenacious. The *Oxford Dictionary* tried to get back to basics by putting the spelling *koolah* before **koala**, but to no avail, and in its second edition (1989) the Oxford recognises **koala** as "the usual spelling".

The phrase *koala bear* is also a misnomer, according to zoologists, because the **koala** is unrelated to the bears of the northern hemisphere. The use of that phrase probably reflects the image of the koala as a cuddly creature, which like the teddy bear takes its place in the toy menagerie.

konk or **conk** See under **k/c**.

kookaburra The Australian bird with the all-too-human laugh still rejoices in two names. The first settlers called it the *laughing jackass*, but since the 1830s it has also been known by its Aboriginal name **kookaburra**, borrowed as *gugubarra* from the Wiradhuri people of central NSW. Europeans who knew that name spelled it variously as *gogoberra* and *kukuburra*.

The settlers roused by the bird at dawn also knew it as the *colonist's clock*. But to the Aborigines the **kookaburra** was much more than an alarm clock. In Aboriginal mythology the bird's laugh was the signal to the sky people to light the fire that illuminates and warms the earth each day—and woe betide anyone who mocked it in its solemn duty.

Koori or **Koorie** This is the name by which Aborigines in New South Wales and Victoria prefer to be known. (In other parts of Australia, different names are preferred: see **Aboriginal** or **Aborigine**.) First recorded in 1834, it comes from Aboriginal languages of central and northern NSW where it's simply the word for "man" *guri*. Since the 1970s **Koori(e)** has acquired greater political significance, as a name to which many Aborigines respond, and one which is their own, not imposed by Europeans.

The spelling **Koori** is used generally in NSW, in the masthead of the *Koori Mail* edited in Lismore, and in the title of James Miller's book (1985) set on the NSW coast. The Koori Centre at the University of Sydney embodies it. **Koorie** is used officially in Victoria and by the Aboriginal Research Centre at Monash University; and it is equally represented in citations in the *Australian National Dictionary*. Other spellings recorded are *Coorie* and *Kuri*.

Koran, Quran or **Qoran**   In English the most familiar spelling for the Muslim holy book is **Koran**, replacing the earlier **Qoran**. Amid current efforts to confirm the Arabic origins of the word, **Quran**, and more correctly *Qur'an* are also seen.

kosh or **cosh**   See under **k/c**.

kosher or **cosher**   The Yiddish word **Kosher** meaning "in accordance with proper Jewish practices" has become a colloquial word for "genuine", usually written without a capital letter. In the past it has also been **cosher**, but this seems to have been eclipsed by **kosher** in the *Oxford Dictionary's* twentieth century citations. **Kosher** is also the preferred spelling in the major American dictionaries, with *kasher* (the Hebrew form of the word) given as an alternative.

kowtow or **kotow**   Kowtow is the first preference of all modern dictionaries, though **kotow** (and also *kootoo*) were used in the nineteenth century. Its obsequious meaning comes from the fact that in Chinese it meant "knock (the) head".

Kriol   is a name for an Australian Aboriginal creole spoken in the Kimberleys and the Roper River area. (See further under **pidgins** and **creoles**.)

kumquat or **cumquat**   See **k/c**.

L

-l/-ll The choice between one and two *l*s in uninflected verbs such as **distil(l)**, **enrol(l)**, **enthral(l)**, **fulfil(l)** and **instil(l)** is discussed under individual headings. (See also **forestallment**, **installment** and **single for double** for further cases.)

-l/-ll- Deeply embedded in English there are rules about doubling the final consonant of a word before you add a suffix beginning with a vowel. (See **doubling of final consonant**.) The rules are applied with reasonable consistency to most consonants, but *l* is singled out for special treatment in British (and Australian) English. If you use spellings such as *traveller, modelling, totalled*, note that they run counter to the more general rule of not doubling when the second (or last) syllable of the verb is unstressed. In American English the more regular *traveler, modeling, totaled* are standard.

The use of double *l* seems all the more erratic if you compare its use before verb suffixes as above, yet not in *equalise, finalise* etc.; before adjective suffixes, as in *cruellest, marvellous, woollen*, but *devilish* is an exception; and sometimes before noun suffixes, as in *medallist*, but never *specialist* or *federalism*. In American English all such words are spelled with a single *l*, and there are no inconsistencies or special cases. The spellings with single *l* are beginning to be used in Australia too, though dictionaries do not give them first preference, and many people dismiss them as "American spellings"—unaware that they embody some of the most widely accepted principles of English spelling.

Those who exempt words ending in *l* from the general rule make a rod for their own backs with any new words of this kind. New verbs are continually being formed from nouns and adjectives ending in *l*, and they test the consistency of our spelling. Should it be:

credential(l)ed enamel(l)ed initial(l)ed trial(l)ed

The spelling that seems "right" in *travelled* may not necessarily seem so right in less familiar words. This same issue arises with all of the following and their derivatives, e.g. *bedevil, empanel, disembowel*:

apparel barrel bevel bowel cancel carol cavil channel chisel counsel cudgel devil dial dishevel dowel drivel duel equal fuel funnel gambol gravel grovel gruel jewel kennel label laurel level libel marshal marvel medal metal model panel parcel pencil peril petal pistol pummel quarrel ravel revel rival shovel shrivel signal snivel spiral squirrel stencil swivel symbol tassel tinsel total towel trammel trowel tunnel weasel yodel

---

The broadest rule of English spelling leaves all such words with a single *l*. This is the policy adopted in this book.

La Trobe or **Latrobe** Charles Joseph La Trobe was lieutenant governor of Victoria 1851–4, and is remembered in a number of geographical and institutional names. In geographical names (the town of Latrobe in northern Tasmania, and the Latrobe River and Valley in Victoria), as well as the streets in Melbourne and its suburbs, the two parts of the name run together, and it has an initial capital only. However institutions such as *La Trobe University* and the *La Trobe Library* in Melbourne keep the name as two words, each with its own capital letter as La Trobe himself did.
   (See further under **capital letters** section 1a.)

labeled or **labelled** Whether to double the *l* is discussed under **-l/-ll-**.

labor or **labour** The choice between these is discussed at **-or/-our**.

Labor The Australian Labor Party has spelled its name thus (without a *u*) since early this century. The *Australian National Dictionary* records *Labor Caucus* in 1911, and the full title *Australian Labor Party* in 1918. The spelling contrasts with the use of *Labour* by its counterparts in both Britain and New Zealand.

lackey or **lacquey** Dictionaries all make **lackey** the primary spelling, and it was indeed the first to be recorded in sixteenth century English. The spelling **lacquey** connects it with its French antecedent *laquais* "footsoldier". The two spellings flourished in the seventeenth and eighteenth centuries, but **lackey** seems to have become dominant during the nineteenth, for both noun and verb. Perhaps the French spelling seemed out of keeping with the servile implications of the word in English. (See further under **frenchification**.)

lacquer or **lacker** The French spelling **lacquer** is given preference in all dictionaries. **Lacker** seems dated, though it's closer to the word's origins in the now obsolete French word *lacre* "sealing wax". But the word was mistakenly associated with the French *lacque* "lake", and the spelling **lacquer** has been used increasingly, from the late seventeenth century on.

lacuna The plural of this word is discussed under **-a** section 1.

laden or **loaded** In a few contexts either of these words would do, though they differ in their connotations. Compare the difference in:
   The table was laden with fine food.
   The table was loaded with fine food.
In both cases there is a wonderful excess, but the word **laden** makes its appeal more aesthetic. **Loaded** has strong physical connections with the noun *load*, and

with it you can almost see the table straining under the weight of goodies piled on it.

Laden is the last remnant of the old verb *lade*, which only appears otherwise in the fossilised phrase *bill of lading*. It is increasingly a literary word, as is clear when we compare *laden with cares*, and *loaded with responsibilities*. **Loaded** is common and usable in many kinds of context, whether it's a matter of carrying a load of ammunition, money, responsibilities, or in the colloquial sense "under the influence".

lady or **woman**   From humble origins in Anglo-Saxon, **lady** has climbed the social ladder to be a title of honor and courtesy. The word originated in the kitchen as literally "one who kneads the loaf"; but a thousand years later it was "my lady" to whom tea and scones were served in the drawing room. In the twentieth century *lady* still has genteel connotations:

   She received the unexpected guest like a lady.

This usage is no doubt helped by the fact that the word is still used as a courtesy title: witness *Lady Casey, Lady Fairfax* et al. In Australia **Lady** has been used in referring to the wife of someone who has received a knighthood; in Britain it can also be a hereditary title. Both in Australia and elsewhere, **lady** is also used (without a capital letter) as a courteous way of referring to women of no special class or connection, in public situations where they are the focus of attention:

   Give your seat to the lady.
   Would you ladies like to join in?
   Come in, young lady.

This courteous form of reference or address acquires a heavy irony in exclamations such as:

   Look where you're going, lady!

The courtesy is rather too conspicuous in job titles like *cleaning lady* and *tea lady*—euphemisms for the person who performs some of the menial tasks in homes and offices. Both those titles are now felt to be patronising, and the Australian Government *Style Manual* (1988) recommends using terms such as *cleaner* and *tea attendant* instead. The word *lady* is also unwelcome these days in designations such as *lady dentist, lady doctor*. Identifying the gender in such phrases is gratuitous, when *dentist, doctor* etc. is all that's needed for professional purposes.

Woman is the term most widely used to refer to a female human being. In the past it was the proletarian counterpart to **lady**, but its overtones are preferred by many in an egalitarian age. With younger females it's well established: less so with the older generation. In men's usage especially, the term *woman* is usefully nonspecific when referring to someone's female companion, as in:

   James and Sue came to the party, as well as Luke and his woman.

By using **woman**, the speaker avoids having to name her or imputing any particular relationship to the couple. Sporting competitions which were once "ladies singles" or "ladies open golf tournament" are now often referred to as *women's* events. For feminists **woman** is the preferred term whenever it's felt necessary to refer to gender, as in:

woman lawyer   women writers   women in publishing

However, the basic principle of inclusive language is that gender specification should to be avoided whenever possible. (See further under **nonsexist language**.)

laid or **lain** These belong to different verbs: *lay* and *lie* respectively. The overlapping parts of those verbs are a source of much confusion. (See under **lie** or **lay**.)

lairy, leary or **leery** See leery.

laissez faire This phrase, borrowed from French, means literally "let (them) do (whatever)". It stands for the longer phrase *laissez faire et laissez passer*, which was the maxim of the French free-trade economists of the eighteenth century. Nowadays it's used to refer to any noninterventionist policy of a government or an individual. When used as an adjective, as in *a laissez faire approach to gardening*, it does not need a hyphen because it's a foreign phrase. (See **hyphens** section 3c.)

Note that in modern French the same phrase is *laisser faire*.

lamé Is it safe to leave off the accent in *silver lamé*? See under **accents**.

lamina The plural of this word is discussed under **-a** section 1.

landslide or **landslip** The first of these **landslide** originated in mid-nineteenth century America to refer to a devastating movement of earth. In Britain the equivalent geological term was **landslip**. But **landslide** had also developed a figurative sense in American usage—that of an overwhelming election victory, and that was its meaning when it first appeared in British sources in 1896. The geological meaning was recorded not long after in Britain, and it soon eclipsed **landslip** there. In Australia **landslide** can refer to either earth or election results, and **landslip** has no currency.

languid or **languorous** Both these suggest a lack of energetic activity. But while **languid** usually implies that it is unfortunate, **languorous** can imply that there's something rather appealing about the slow pace. Compare the following:

There was a languid smile on the patient's face.

At low tide the languorous movement of the wave hardly rippled the surface of the pool.

Note that while the *u* in *languid* confirms the "g" sound preceding it, in *languorous* and *languor* it is really superfluous. The word was spelled *langor* for centuries in Middle English, and the *u* was inserted only in the seventeenth century, to make it match its Latin forebear.

lanolin or **lanoline** Both spellings are to be found in Australia. But while **lanolin** is the one featured on product labels, **lanoline** is the one more likely to show up in the fine print when the substance is listed as one of the ingredients in a pharmaceutical product. It reminds us of the chemist's distinctive use of *-ine* and *-in* (see **-ine/-in**), which breaks down where common household substances are concerned.

larva The plural of this word is discussed at **-a** section 1.

larynx For the plural of this word, see **-x** section 3.

lasso The plural of this word is discussed at **-o**.

last or **lastly** When enumerating a series of points, the old convention had it that you should begin with *first*, not *firstly* and end with **last**, not **lastly**. In between, however, you would use *secondly*, *thirdly*, *fourthly* etc. The rationale for this is obscure, and though it was certainly being challenged last century, it is still around this century. Fowler thought of it as "harmless pedantry". (See further under **first** or **firstly**.)

last or **latest** These words are often synonyms in informal language, yet they can also contrast in meaning. When they do contrast, **last** means "final, the one after which there can never be any more"; while **latest** just means "the most recent". The two meanings are enshrined in *your last chance* and *the latest fashion*.

Strictly speaking then, someone's *latest book* is not necessarily their *last book*. Yet the distinction is often blurred in comments such as:

I like this book better than his last one.

Out of context that sentence is ambiguous. Does it mean:

I like this latest book better than his previous one or

I prefer this earlier book to his final publication.

No doubt your knowledge of the author referred to and his various books would help to clarify the comment. But in writing it's still best to aim for a higher level of precision than in conversation, and to watch the relativities in **latest** and **last**.

Note however that **last** often equals **latest** in idioms of time:

Last Thursday they signed the contract.

During the last month we have taken on two new editors.

In official letter writing it's routinely used this way:

As I said in my last letter …

But in such cases both idiom and context clarify the meaning, and there's no reason to modify them.

late The quasi-legal phrase *the late* is a discreet reminder to readers that the person referred to has recently died, in case they are unaware of it. Just how long we should continue to use it after someone's death is a matter of individual judgement. Quotations in *Webster's English Usage* (1989) suggest anything from 10 to 50 years. It does seem a little superfluous to use it of those whose deaths are well known, though in cases like *the late president Kennedy* it probably serves as a mark of respect.

Note that **late** is sometimes used to mean that a person's term of office has ended, as in *the late premier Joh Bjelke-Petersen*. Such an expression could be misinterpreted as an allusion to someone's death rather than retirement from office. The point intended can be made more reliably with the prefix *ex-*, as in *ex-premier J. B.-P.*

lateish or **latish** See latish.

latex For the plural of this word see **-x** section 2.

Latin abbreviations Scholarly writing has transferred a number of **Latin abbreviations** into common usage, and others have gained currency through the conventions of letter writing. Some of them, like **e.g.**, **i.e.** and **etc.** are very well known; others like **ibid.** and **op. cit.** are more restricted, and are gradually being replaced (see under individual headings). Many still serve as useful shorthand, as the translations in the list below can show:

c. or ca.	*circa* "about, approximately" (with dates)
cf.	*confer* "compare"
c.v.	*curriculum vitae* "profile of (one's) life"
e.g.	*exempli gratia* "by way of an example"
et al.	*et alii* "and others"
etc.	*et cetera* "and so forth"
et seq(q).	*et sequen(te)s* "and the following (page/s)"
fl.	*floruit* "s/he flourished"
ibid.	*ibidem* "in the same place"
i.e.	*id est* "that is"
inf.	*infra* "below"
inst.	*instante* "in the present (month)"
loc. cit.	*loco citato* "in the place cited"
NB	*nota bene* "take good note"
op. cit.	*opere citato* "in the work cited"
pro tem.	*pro tempore* "for the time being"
prox.	*proximo* "in the next (month)"
PS	*post scriptum* "(something) written afterwards"
QED	*quod erat demonstrandum* "(that was the very point) which had to be demonstrated"
q.v.	*quod vide* "have a look at that"
RIP	*requiescat in pace* "may s/he rest in peace"
sup.	*supra* "above"
ult.	*ultimo* "in the last (month)"
v.	*vide* "see"
v. or vs.	*versus* "against"
viz.	*videlicet* "namely"

Latin abbreviations are given stops according to whatever editing principle you use for English abbreviations (see further under **abbreviations**). In the list above, stops are reserved for lower case abbreviations, or rather the shortened words within them (e.g. *al.* but not *et*). When both words in the abbreviation are shortened it's still usual to give each of them a stop, although the practice of working with just a final stop, as in *eg.* and *ie.*, is on the increase.

In older publications, **Latin abbreviations** were italicised like other foreign loanwords. But the tendency nowadays is to put them in roman. This is certainly recommended by the Australian Government *Style Manual*, as in the *Australian Writers' and Editors' Guide* and in the Chicago *Manual of Style*. However *Copy-editing* (1992) distinguishes between common and less common Latin abbreviations, and uses roman only for the most common ones such as *e.g.*, *i.e.*, *etc.* and *viz.* The question of whether to italicise *v.* when referring to legal cases is discussed under **italics**.

For the question as to where it's appropriate to use **Latin abbreviations** like **e.g.**, **etc.** and **i.e.**, as well as what punctuation to use with them, see under the individual entries.

Latin America This phrase is a reminder of how much of the "New World" is not English-speaking. It includes all the countries of North and South America in which Spanish or Portuguese is the official language. Almost all the independent states of South America come under that heading, except Guyana and Surinam, and the whole of Central America including Mexico.

Latin plurals English has borrowed words from Latin for over 1500 years. The older loanwords, like *cheese* and *oil*, have long since been assimilated and acquired English plurals. But younger loanwords (those borrowed from the Renaissance on) tend to keep their Latin plurals, at least as alternatives to regular English ones.

The Latin plurals in English are of five major kinds, for words ending in:

-a	(e.g. *formula*)
-is	(e.g. *axis*)
-us	(e.g. *corpus*, *fungus*, *hiatus*)
-um	(e.g. *atrium*)
-x	(e.g. *appendix*)

For details regarding each type, see the entries for each of those endings.

One other group to note are words like *series* and *species*, which have zero plurals in Latin. They too are maintained in English, so that the words remain the same whether singular or plural:

the latest series to be proposed

three new series since 1980

(See further under **zero plurals**.)

latish or **lateish** Dictionaries all prefer the first spelling, which has been on record since the seventeenth century. What is more, it's perfectly regular (see further under **-e** section 1).

Latrobe or **La Trobe** See La Trobe.

latter For the use of this word, both alone and in tandem with *former*, see **former** and **latter**.

laudable or **laudatory** If the verb *laud* "praise" were still in common usage, these adjectives would never be confused. As it is, *laud* is now closely tied to religious usage (apart from the quasi-religious idiom "lauded to the skies"), and is not familiar enough to many people to help decode the adjectives.

    Laudable is the passive adjective "able to be praised" or "worthy of praise", as in *a laudable undertaking*. The word is something of a two-edged sword however, since it expresses respect for the aims of an enterprise while not assuming that it will succeed. **Laudatory** means "full of praise", and so is applied to words, speech, or documents which commend someone's work: *a laudatory reference on the candidate's achievements*.

laudanum See under **morphine**.

laudatory or **laudable** See laudable.

lawful or **legal** See under **legal, legalistic** or **lawful**.

lay This is the present of one verb and the past of another. (See **lie** or **lay**.)

lay-by In Australian usage of the twentieth century, this compound is used to refer to buying an article on time payment. It can be a verb meaning "reserve something by putting a deposit on it", and it also functions as a noun referring to the article which is being bought in this way.

    In British English, **lay-by** is used quite differently, to refer to the area beside a highway where vehicles may pull off and park, out of the stream of traffic. (This is an extension of its earlier use in waterways and railways.) **Lay-by** thus corresponds to what Australians call the "rest area" beside a highway. People picnic there and, according to one *Oxford Dictionary* citation, may stop there for a *lay-by high tea*.

-le Several groups of English words end this way:

1 a largish group of two-syllabled verbs (or verb-related words) which express a quick, light movement or sound. The following are just a token:
    bustle drizzle fizzle giggle gurgle nibble rustle scramble
    scuttle shuffle sizzle trickle twinkle whistle
The source of such words is something of a mystery. In odd cases like *dazzle* we seem to have a diminutive form of *daze*, yet the roots of most of the list above are obscure and unparalleled elsewhere. The consonants in them often seem to suggest the process they refer to, as if some kind of sound symbolism is at work. (See further under **phonesthemes**.) Some have a playful character, witness *bamboozle* and *boondoggle* (rare examples with three-syllables), and *boggle, bungle* and *puzzle*.

2 two small groups of nouns. In some **-le** was once a diminutive, as shown by *speckle* and *nozzle*. But in others it was used to mark the physical object associated with a particular verb:

prickle spindle spittle treadle

3 a handful of abstract words all inherited from Anglo-Norman. They include *participle, principle* and *syllable*. (See further under **principal** or **principle**.)

Note also the **-le** has replaced *-el* in certain loanwords, or else provided alternative spellings. (See **mantle** or **mantel**.)

lead or **led** Written down, the letters **lead** could be a noun meaning a heavy metal, or a verb meaning "conduct"—though the grammar of surrounding words usually leaves no doubt as to which is intended. What more often causes trouble is the fact that the past form of the verb **lead** is **led**, which sounds exactly the same as the noun. Confusion of sound and spelling has many a writer inadvertently putting **lead** where **led** was intended. It is a point to watch.

leaders In older punctuation, **leaders** were the series of dots used singly or in groups to guide the eye across the page. They were used in the stub of a table, to draw readers to the right line within the columns, and to indicate empty cells in the table. These days an em rule is generally used to mark an empty cell.

Compare **ellipsis**.

leading question A **leading question** is one which foists its own answer on the person responding:

So you knew there were drugs in the refrigerator?

Thus a damaging piece of information is thrust into the discussion in the guise of a question. The question itself seeks a yes/no answer, and people being questioned like this can all-too-easily compromise themselves, whichever way they respond. The most notorious use of *leading questions* is in courts of law, although the defence lawyer is entitled to object to "leading" the witness or defendant in this way.

The phrase **leading question** is also used more loosely to refer to any embarrassing or pointed question. So a government minister being asked about a confidential decision may resist by saying "That's a leading question". Yet it wasn't, strictly speaking, unless the reporter's question embodied the very information it purported to seek.

leafed or **leaved** The choice between these is discussed under **-v-/-f-**.

leaned or **leant** **Leaned** is to be preferred. It is the more regular form; and it avoids one of the possible problems with **leant**—being confused with *lent*, the past tense of *lend*. (See **-ed**.)

leaped or **leapt** See under **-ed**.

learned or **learnt** See under **-ed**.

leary, leery or **lairy** See leery.

lease, rent or **hire** See hire.

leastways or **leastwise** See under -wise or -ways.

leery, leary and **lairy** Underlying these three spellings there are just two words, both of them slang. To American slang we owe **leery** meaning "distrustful", and to British Cockney slang **lairy** meaning "flashy (in dress)". **Leary** is an alternative spelling for either word.

Left A capital *L* makes this the broad term for those whose political persuasion runs counter to the conservative establishment, either by being more radical or more socialistic. This usage derives ultimately from the arrangement of seats in the French National Assembly, where the nobles sat on the president's right, and the members of the third estate (representatives of the common people) on the left. But the term **Left** has long since ceased to be simply a term for the Opposition, and has come to identify the more socialistic party in two-party politics. With the Australian Labor Party in government, the **Left** is in fact on the right of the parliament, and the political "Right" on the left.

Being described as the **Left** offers none of the linguistic advantages enjoyed by the **Right**. The word *right* itself suggests that those of Rightish persuasion are the "right and proper" party to govern; and it makes the party which opposes them somehow wrong. The **Left** must achieve what they can in spite of their name.

legal, legalistic, legitimate or **lawful** All four adjectives take the law as their starting point, but their connotations are rather different. **Lawful** is now rather formal and old-fashioned, being caught up in fixed phrases such as *lawful wife* or *lawful business*. It is often a reminder of traditional rights inscribed in the common law of the land. **Legal** is much more widely used to refer to any provision written into law (e.g. *legal access*), where a frontier between what's **legal** and *illegal* is being defined. Other general uses of **legal** are its association with the administration and profession of law, as in *a legal conference, a legal issue*.

Legalistic has a negative coloring. It implies an overemphasis on the letter of the law, and narrow interpretation of it. We use the word in any context where rules and regulations are being interpreted too literally, with too little attention to their broader purpose or how people are affected by them.

Legitimate has as many uses outside the law as within it. It can relate things to principles of logic and reasoning, as in *a legitimate answer/argument/ conclusion*; and its legal uses mostly relate to birthright, as in *legitimate child/ heir*. For the use of **legitimate** as a verb, see **legitimate, legitimise** or **legitimatise**.

legislation or **legislature** Both nouns relate to law-making. The **legislature** is the body which drafts and approves the laws of a country or state. In Australia the Parliament and the Senate together form the federal **legislature**, while the lower and upper houses in each state do the same. **Legislation** is a collective name for any act of law set up by one of the *legislatures*.

legitimate, legitimise or **legitimatise** Dictionaries do not distinguish these verbs in terms of meaning, though their crossreferencing makes **legitimate** the key to them all. **Legitimate** is indeed the oldest of the three, dating from the sixteenth century. But Fowler noted that it was being challenged by the other two in the 1920s, and *Webster's English Usage* (1989) notes the strength of **legitimise** since then. According to its evidence **legitimise** has been about as common as **legitimate** since the 1970s; and in the Australian ACE corpus only **legitimise** appears as a verb. All instances of **legitimate** in the corpus were as an adjective, and there were none of **legitimatise**.

leitmotif or **leitmotiv** See under **motif** or **motive**.

lemma The plural of this word is discussed under **-a** section 1.

lend or **loan** These are sometimes interchangeable, sometimes not. Only **lend** carries the figurative senses of adding or giving, as in *lend strength to the cause* or *lend color to an otherwise routine event*. But for other senses, as when property or money pass temporarily from one owner to another, either word could be used:
> *I'm happy to lend him my car* or
> *I'm happy to loan him my car*.

In Australian and American English the verb **loan** is readily used as an alternative to **lend** in such applications—but not so much in contemporary British English. A usage note in the *Collins Dictionary* suggests that it belongs to banking and the world of finance. However it's clear that **loan** was well used as a verb in earlier stages of English, and this use was presumably transported to the colonies, while it declined back home in Britain where usage commentators preferred to make **lend** the verb and **loan** the noun.

Outside Britain the division of labor is much less clear-cut: **loan** can be either verb or noun, and **lend** (apart from its verb role) serves as a noun in informal Australian English, for example:
> *Can you give me a lend of your notes?*

The construction could hardly appear in writing, though we might wonder why not when it's perfectly acceptable to say and write:
> *Can you give me a look at your notes?*

Modern English allows many conversions of verbs into nouns (see **transfers**), yet there's still a stylistic question mark about **lend** as a noun. It seems arbitrary when both **loan** and **lend** derive from the same Old English word for "loan", which was both a noun and a verb. **Lend** is a mutant of the older verb, formed in a southern dialect of Middle English, with a change of vowel and an extra consonant added on.

lengthways or **lengthwise** See under -wise or -ways.

lenience or **leniency** Fowler thought that there was a distinction opening up between these, with **lenience** referring to a lenient action, and **leniency** to a lenient disposition. Modern dictionaries do not support this, and simply crossreference one to the other as equivalents. In Australian and American dictionaries, **leniency** gets the guernsey, while British dictionaries give it to **lenience**.

For the differences between other pairs like this, see **-nce/-ncy**.

lesbian In all English-speaking countries this is the standard term for a homosexual woman, though only in Australia is it *lezzo* for short. Other colloquial abbreviations are *lezzy/lezzie* and *lez(z)*. The word **lesbian** was until quite recently (about 1970) written with a capital letter. This is because it originated as a geographical adjective, meaning "of or from the Greek island of Lesbos"; and the capital letter remained, even for the homosexual meaning, decades after it was first recorded in 1890. But why Lesbos? In the sixth century BC it was the home of the famous Greek poet Sappho, who surrounded herself with a circle of women who were said to have engaged in homosexual practices.

less or **lesser** The difference between these has exercised many a language watcher. Yet **less** is much more often the word needed, occurring about 25 times more often than **lesser** in the ACE, LOB and Brown databases of English. So what are the uses of **lesser**?

Lesser is almost exclusively an adjective, meaning "smaller in status, significance or importance". This is its meaning in *a lesser god* and *the lesser demands of the weekend*, as well as *Lesser men would have rushed for the exit*. As the examples show, it goes with **count nouns** (see further under that heading).

Less regularly goes with mass nouns as in *less demand for premium beef*, and in such contexts it commonly means "smaller in amount", as in that example. However **less** is also widely used to mean "fewer in number" (standing instead of *fewer*), as in *We want less taxes*; and in contexts like that it qualifies count nouns. For the objections raised to this usage, see under **fewer** or **less**.

As an adverb, **less** is very much the more common of the two. It modifies adjectives, adverbs and verbs. See for example: *less ambitious, advanced less rapidly* and *worried less than before*. **Lesser** hardly appears as an adverb except in compound adjectives: *the lesser known town of Okayama*. Note that it is not strictly necessary to hyphenate such adjectives because the *-er* ending (like *-ly*) ensures correct reading of the compound. (See further under **hyphens** section 2c iii.)

-less This suffix, meaning "without or lacking", is the formative element in many an adjective. It is enshrined in clichéd phrases like *a bottomless pit* and *a hopeless case*, and in paired adjectives like *cheerless/cheerful* and *graceless/*

graceful which pinpoint the absence or presence of something. Note however that some such "pairs" no longer pair up exactly in meaning.

faithless (not keeping faith)   *faithful* (loyal)
pitiless (showing no pity)   *pitiful* (demanding sympathy)
shameless (having no scruples)   *shameful* (very regrettable)
soulless (inhuman)   *soulful* (with deep feeling)

Not all **-less** adjectives have counterparts in *-ful*. Ones like *fatherless, headless, toothless* and *wireless* (originally an adjective) show how **-less** highlights an abnormal state of affairs, and we do not need a *-ful* adjective to describe the normal state of having a father, a head, or teeth. Note also that a very small number of **-less** adjectives are based on verbs, e.g. *ceaseless, tireless*, and they too have no counterparts ending in *-ful*.

let us or **let's** The difference between these is largely a question of formality, as often with contractions. Compare the ceremonious *Let us pray*, and the informal *Let's pray for rain*. The uncontracted **let us** is useful to writers of formal documents when they want to draw the reader into the discussion while maintaining an authoritative tone:

Let us now turn to the issue of accountability.

Compare the effect of:

Let's now turn to …

which minimises the distance between writer and reader.

Let us and **let's** both invite readers to join the writer in the activity proposed, i.e. they involve *you* and *us*. This sets them apart from similar constructions exemplified in *Do let us pay …*, where *let* stands as an independent verb meaning "allow", and *us* does not mean "you" as well. The *us* in such a construction cannot be contracted without changing the meaning. (Compare *Do let's pay …*)

Note that the pronouns used after *let* are always object pronouns. In **Let us** this is obvious, but not so much in *Let George and us decide*. (Some speakers and writers are tempted to use *Let George and we decide*, thus changing the construction in midstream.)

In its negative form this idiom becomes *Let us not (go into), Let's not (go into)* or *Don't let's (go into)*. Once again they represent degrees of formality. The first has a slightly rhetorical flavor, which might be suitable for a formal document. The second is broadly useful for writing and conversation. The third is definitely chatty.

letter writing The questions asked about **letter writing** often focus on format and the formalities. Those things need attention, but are really secondary to the question as to what the writer says and does through a letter. In other words, what sort of relationship is being set up through it?

Letters are one of the few writing mediums in which you normally communicate with a single individual, either an acquaintance, or someone with a particular role. What you write in personal letters is a way of maintaining your particular relationship.

Similarly when writing a letter in the name of an institution to an unknown person, ideally you're also establishing a basis for good relations with them. Institutional letters need to be positive in their tone as far as possible, and to offer a constructive exchange of information or points of view. Avoid correspondence clichés and stereotyped phrasing (see further under **commercialese**). Correspondence which sounds like a form letter (or something drafted by a machine) is liable to alienate the reader.

Letter formats matter most for institutional letters. For personal letters, you do as you please, guided only by the level of formality in the relationship. But with institutional letters there are format decisions to make, such as whether to use semiblocked or blocked presentation, and open or closed punctuation. Both these types are illustrated in Appendix VII. The blocked presentation with open punctuation requires fewest keystrokes and is therefore the most cost-effective. Starting everything at the left-hand margin is easy to explain to a new recruit. Yet questions about the look and readability of the letter also arise, especially in longer letters. Letter writers can and should adapt the standard blocked format in the interests of clear and attractive communication.

The conventions for beginning a letter are also set out in Appendix VII. The salutation itself varies according to whether or not you know the recipient's name. (See **forms of address** section 2.) The closing for most institutional letters these days is "Yours sincerely". It is used in any situation where the addressee can be named in the salutation, and even when that person can only be addressed through their role ("Dear Manager" etc). "Yours faithfully" is used only when the sender particularly wants to maintain a formal distance from the person addressed, and to emphasise that the correspondence is a matter of duty.

letters as words How to set isolated letters in print raises some questions, because they're very slight, especially in lower case. Italics are recognised as the most effective device by the Australian Government *Style Manual* and that of Chicago, though both acknowledge the occasional use of roman. Usually the roman is supplemented by something else: *Copy-editing* (1992) notes the practice of using roman with inverted commas round the letter, and certainly "g" is more distinctive than just g. Whenever the letter is made plural, an apostrophe inserted before the *s* serves instead of inverted commas, and this too makes the roman acceptable, as in *dotting the* i's *and crossing the* t's. Yet even the apostrophe is unnecessary if italics are used and the plural *s* itself is in roman, as in:

Dotting your is *and crossing your* ts ...

Upper case letters take care of themselves as in:

She had a curious record of three As and two Ds.

Other conventions with single letters:

- the letters used for enumerating a series may be either italics (*a*) (*b*) (*c*) or roman (a) (b) (c);

- when indicating musical notes, a roman capital is used: *middle* C, the *key of* D *minor*. Note that the convention of using capital letters for major keys and lower case for minor keys is still recognised for American texts by the Chicago *Manual of Style* (1981), but discouraged in Britain by *Hart's Rules* (1983) and *Copy-editing* (1992).
- letters used to represent hypothetical parties in a discussion or points in a description are capitalised, as in:

  If A sues B for breach of contract, ...
  Let C be a point midway on the hypotenuse ...
- letters used to designate shapes are capitalised, as in:

  a V-shaped valley an I-beam a J-curve

For the printing of initials in personal names, and the punctuation associated with them, see under **names**.

leukemia or **leukaemia** See under **ae/e**.

leveled or **levelled** The choice between these is discussed at **-l/-ll-**.

liable The meaning of this word varies according to the preposition following it: *for* or *to*. *Liable for* is a legal and quasi-legal phrase meaning "financially responsible for". *Liable to* is everyday English meaning "given to", as in *liable to fainting fits*; and also "likely to", as in *liable to go brittle*. Note that its use overlaps with *likely to*, but that *liable to* normally refers to a negative event as a general possibility, whereas *likely to* predicts either good or bad events on the strength of a specific past event. Compare for example:

That horse is likely to win tomorrow's race.
In the pack that horse is liable to bolt.

libeled or **libelled** The choice between these is discussed under **-l/-ll-**.

liberality, liberalism or **Liberalism** These three nouns all express different aspects of the adjective *liberal*: its material, intellectual and political manifestations. At bottom the word embodies the Latin root for "free", so that it can imply being free and generous with your goods (**liberality**), or being open-minded in your thinking and seeking to avoid imposing your own values and principles on others (**liberalism**).

   The latter meaning is theoretically the one enshrined in political **Liberalism**—a laissez faire approach to governing the country. The capital *L* is always used when the word refers to a political party, in Australia or elsewhere.

libertine or **libertarian** Both words have to do with freedom. But while *libertines* vote it all in their own direction and allow themselves every sexual licence, a **libertarian** argues for the rights of others to express themselves as they choose. In theological contexts a **libertarian** is one who maintains the doctrine of free will.

libretto For the plural of this word, see **Italian plurals**.

licence or **license** In Australian and British English, the choice between these is a matter of grammar: whether it's a noun or a verb. (See under **-ce/-se**.) In American English, **license** is preferred for both.

licenser or **licensor** For the choice between these, see under **-er/-or**.

licorice or **liquorice** The spelling of this dark form of confectionery is still rather unsettled, even in the twentieth century. The *Oxford Dictionary* lists eighteen different spellings for it since the fourteenth century, none of which is exactly **licorice** or **liquorice**. Common pronunciation still has the final sound as "sh", and this shows in most of the Oxford's spellings. Yet in modern dictionaries, **licorice** and **liquorice** are given preference, with American dictionaries giving preference to the first, and British ones to the second. The *Macquarie Dictionary* (1991) puts the two spellings on a par in Australia, and a glance at confectioners' labels suggests that **licorice** is gaining ground.

The spelling **liquorice** embodies a folk etymology, and a spurious connection with *liquor*. The word was originally Greek *glycyrrhiza* meaning "sweet root", which became *liquiritia* in medieval Latin and **licorice** in Old French.

lie or **lay** The reason why people confuse these verbs is clear enough when you set their principal parts side by side:

lie (1)	"tell lies"	lied (past tense)	lied (past participle)
lie (2)	"be in a horizontal position"	**lay**	lain
lay	"put, place, set down"	**laid**	laid

The different meanings of **lie** (1) and **lie** (2) keep them apart. But **lie** (2) and **lay** overlap in meaning and form (the past tense of one being identical with the present of the other).

The essential difference between **lie** (2) and **lay** is that **lay** takes an object, i.e. you always "lay *something*". See for example:

It lays eggs.

They lay the groundwork for the future.

In grammatical terms it's a transitive verb, whereas **lie** (2) is intransitive (see further under **transitive**). Without that point they are not easy to separate. Compare:

They lay the groundwork for the future. (= **lay**, transitive, present tense)

They lay on the ground while the bullets whistled overhead. (= **lie**, intransitive, past tense)

An awareness of the differences in tense as well as the transitive/intransitive distinction helps to distinguish the two uses of **lay**.

But the common colloquial trend is to use **lay** (and *laid*) instead of **lie** (and *lay/lain*) It happens in the present tense with the casual:

If you lay down for a while …

instead of

If you lie down for a while …

In the past tense, it's:
They laid on the ground ...
instead of
They lay on the ground ...
And for the past participle:
I had just laid down when the phone rang.
is more likely than
I had just lain down when the phone rang.
In fact *lain* has been falling into disuse since the eighteenth century. The grammarian Campbell corrects *laid* to *lain* in the 1770s, attributing the mistake to French influence. Whatever the cause, *lain* seems to be disappearing. In the Australian ACE database it occurs only 3 times in a million words, less than in equivalent British data where it occurred 6 times, and on its way to extinction, as in the American data where it made no showing at all.

All these replacements are used in common talk in all English-speaking countries, though in the written medium (certainly in edited writing) the standard forms **lie**/*lay (lain)* are still expected. We may speculate on when the pressure of usage will allow their replacements (**lay**/*laid*) to prevail in writing; but for the moment they remain markers of informal speech. In the longer run they spell the doom of **lie** (2).

ligatures A *ligature* is a written or printed character which embodies more than one letter. They come from two sources. In the earliest printing fonts, a small weak letter was often cast with a taller one to ensure that it stood in place during the printing process. Ligatures of *c* and *t* (ct) or *s* and *t* (st) were still quite common in the eighteenth century. The other source of ligatures was the special vowels of Latin in which *a* and *e* or *o* and *e* were joined as a single character, although Fowler argued against them (see further under **ae/e**). In modern typesetting, two or three letter ligatures are occasionally used, as for *ff, fi, fl, ffi* and *ffl*.

Compare **digraph**.

lighted or **lit** For the past tense of the verb *light*, **lighted** varies with **lit** in Britain and the USA; whereas Australians are still mostly inclined to use **lit**, according to the evidence of ACE and comparable databases. Only when the word serves as an adjective is it equally likely to be **lighted**: compare
a lighted cigarette
a lit match
The tendency to prefer **lighted** does however show up in Australians' usage with compound verbs, where *floodlighted, highlighted* and *spotlighted* are the common past tenses for their respective verbs.

lightning or **lightening** The word **lightning** has been associated with the enormously bright discharge of electricity in the sky since the fourteenth century. It originated from the verb *lighten* ("light up"), and was still occasionally

spelled with an *e* until the eighteenth century. Nowadays it's still sometimes pronounced as if the *e* were there; but the absence of *e* in **lightning** helps to differentiate it from words freshly derived from the verb(s) *lighten*, as in:
> *Fireworks lightening the sky were seen miles away ...* and
> *Some way of lightening their load must be found.*

likable or **likeable** See under -eable.

like or **as** Like is arguably the most versatile four-letter word in the English language. It serves as a verb, noun, adjective, adverb, preposition and conjunction. It even works as an interjection or pause-filler for some hesitant speakers: *I wanted, like, to come as soon as I could.* (Note however that the verb **like** and its noun (as in *likes and dislikes*) are an independent root from the adjective and the rest.) Yet the very versatility of **like** may have helped to foster doubts about where it belongs, and fueled criticisms of its use as a conjunction.

1 *The use of **like** as a conjunction* develops quite naturally out of its role as a preposition. Compare:
> *He behaves like a child with a new toy.* (preposition)
> *He behaves like a child does with a new toy.* (conjunction)

The parallel roles of preposition and conjunction are familiar enough with other words such as *before*, *since*, and *than*, so the objection to **like** doing the same is curious. The objections are relatively recent, dating only from the nineteenth century. Shakespeare did not shrink from using **like** as a conjunction, nor did other writers up to and including Darwin. The *Oxford Dictionary* notes in the late nineteenth century that it appears in "many recent writers of standing", in spite of being "generally condemned as vulgar or slovenly". The grammarian Jespersen listed examples from well published twentieth century writers such as Wells, Shaw and Maugham.

Modern British dictionaries often note that the use of **like** as a conjunction is colloquial, and this is confirmed by the data in the LOB corpus of British English, where the instances are mostly in fictional narrative. It is much more widely used in American English, appearing in all categories of fiction and nonfiction in the Brown corpus; and it's entered with no restrictive label in the major American dictionaries. The current pattern of use in Australian English is more like the American than the British. **Like** appears as conjunction in several categories of nonfiction (though not those for academic or bureaucratic readers), and in all categories of fiction in the ACE corpus.

Apart from the overall regional differences in the use of **like**, some senses are more widely used than others. As a conjunction it may mean: (a) "as if", (b) "(just) as", (c) "such as". Examples of each from the ACE corpus are:
> a) *It looks like he's done it this time.*
> b) *They don't pay your taxi fare home, like they do in the public service.*
> c) *It was a pram with large wheels like you used to see in English movies.*

In the Australian data, the first two senses are roughly equal in frequency with 23:17 instances, whereas in American English the first was way out in front, almost twice as frequent. In the British data meanwhile, it's the second and third senses which dominate. Britons make less use than Australians or Americans of of collocations such as *look like, feel like, sound like, seem like* and various others, all of which foster the use of conjunctive **like**.

The acceptability of **like** thus turns on several things, including the variety of English, the genre of writing and the particular meaning and collocation being used. It suggests that the routine advice to replace conjunctive **like** with **as** is an oversimplification. If we substitute **as** for **like** in:

They don't make bread like they used to
(They don't make bread as they used to)

both style and meaning seem to be affected: the revised statement is more formal, and seems to be about a method rather than a type of bread. (It seems to substitute sense (b) for sense (c).) **As** may sometimes be a useful replacement, but there's no virtue in using it to replace every instance of **like** as a conjunction.

2 *Like as a preposition.* There are no grammatical questions with using **like** as a preposition, but some care is needed to ensure its effectiveness in comparisons. For best effect the items being compared with it must be carefully paralleled, and so in the following examples the first sentence works better than the second:

Like Jane Austen, he creates characters from real life.
Like Jane Austen, his characters are created from real life.

While the first sentence compares author with author, the second is untidy and elliptical in the comparison it makes.

In writing, **like** is often more ambiguous than it would be in speech. The pause or lack of it before the final phrase would fix the meaning of a sentence like: *He would never reply like Raymond.* But in written form it could mean one of two things, either:

Like Raymond, he would never reply or
He would never reply in the way Raymond did.

Either of those paraphrases would clarify the meaning for the reader, and be preferable to the original.

Note finally that *unlike* is even more problematical than **like** for the reader when linked with a negative statement:

Unlike his predecessor, Rick didn't want a company car.

A sentence like that is an obstacle course for the reader. (See further under **double negatives.**)

-like For a thousand years and more, this English prefix has been used to create adjectives which express similarity with something or someone named. For example:

businesslike childlike craterlike godlike ladylike
lifelike statesmanlike warlike

Established words like those are normally set solid, whereas ad hoc formations with **-like** are usually hyphenated:

a rock-like resistance

a home of mansion-like proportions

Note that some words ending in **-like** have counterparts ending in *-ly*, witness *godlike/godly, statesmanlike/statesmanly*. In such pairs the one with **-like** is more literal and neutral in its meaning, while the one with *-ly* is more figurative and commendatory. Compare **-ish**.

likeable or **likable** See under **-eable**.

likewise As an adverb this can mean either "similarly" or "also". The two uses are illustrated in:

Go and do likewise.

Jane left then and John likewise.

The second usage makes **likewise** an additive word, and from this it gets used now and then as a conjunction between nouns and noun phrases. See for example:

The buses were on strike, likewise the ferries.

Purists object to this conjunctive use of **likewise**, just as they do to other newly emerging conjunctions. For them, the problem is cured by adding *and*:

The buses were on strike, and likewise the ferries.

But the use of **likewise** as a fully fledged additive conjunction is not uncommon in informal writing. It has yet to be recognised in dictionaries, however, even with the label "colloquial". Compare **plus**.

linage or **lineage** Both spellings are used for the (two-syllabled) printer's word meaning "number of lines printed on a page", but **linage** is greatly to be preferred. It is the more regular spelling (see **-e** section 1); and it avoids a clash with the quite independent word **lineage** with three syllables, meaning "ancestry or descent".

liney or liny See under **-y/-ey**.

lingua franca This Italian phrase refers to a hybrid and usually restricted language (with small vocabulary and syntactic resources), which is used for communication between people who do not understand each other's native language. The expression means "Frankish tongue", though the original "lingua franca" embodied elements of Italian, French, Spanish, Greek, Arabic and Turkish, and was used for trade purposes in the ports of the eastern Mediterranean. The word has since been applied to trading languages, and pidgins all over the world. (See further under **pidgins** and **creoles**.)

The word is also used simply to refer to any language which serves as a common medium for communication, as in:

Latin was the lingua franca of European scholars until the seventeenth century.

Those with a knowledge of Italian may pluralise **lingua franca** as *lingue franche*, but its normal plural in English is *lingua francas*.

linguist This word was first used in English (in 1550) to mean "someone who speaks a number of languages", and for many people this is still the only meaning. Almost anyone with a facility for languages can be a **linguist** in this sense. The other meaning of **linguist** is very strongly associated with *linguistics* (= the systematic study of language), and *linguists* of this kind are usually professionals or specialists in the field. The word **linguist** was used occasionally this way in earlier centuries, but the usage has only become common with the growth of the subject in the twentieth century.

linking verbs See **copular verbs**.

liquefy or **liquify** See **-ify/-efy**.

liqueur or **liquor** The first word **liqueur** is much more specialised. It refers to the sweet, flavored spirit often drunk at the end of a meal: *coffee and liqueurs*, as your host or the menu may offer. The second word **liquor** is the general word for spirits and for alcoholic drink, as in: *He can't hold his liquor*. In technical uses in industrial and pharmaceutical chemistry it normally refers to special solutions, although in brewing it's simply water.

    Liquor is centuries old in English. It was *licour* for Chaucer, but was respelled as **liquor** in the sixteenth century to show its Latin ancestry. **Liqueur** is the French form of the same Latin word, borrowed into English in the eighteenth century.

liquidate or **liquidise** The verb **liquidate** has only a figurative connection with *liquid*. In political contexts, it has sinister overtones as a euphemism for "execute" or "wipe out":

    Dissidents were all liquidated or driven into exile.

This usage is believed to have come from the equivalent Russian word "likvidirovat'". The first English use of the word in this sense dates from the 1920s, after the turbulent years of revolution. The financial uses of **liquidate** are much older, dating from the sixteenth century. They relate to *liquidity* rather than *liquid*, whether the procedure referred to is to "settle or pay (a debt)", "convert into cash" or "reduce (accounts) to order by deducing the amount owed or due".

    The more recent **liquidise**, coined in the nineteenth century, has a direct connection with *liquid* and means "turn into liquid form". It's often associated with food preparation, as in:

    Liquidise the carrots and add them to the soup.

Within such contexts it replaces *liquefy*, which is more often used to refer to scientific and industrial processes.

liquify or **liquefy** For the choice of spellings, see under **-ify/-efy**.

liquor or **liqueur** See liqueur.

liquorice or **licorice** See licorice.

lists Setting out a list always calls for some decisions. First of all, should it be set out horizontally or vertically? The two systems entail different punctuation practices, and details of layout are an issue with *vertical lists* but not *horizontal ones*. In both, but especially in vertical lists, it's important that the items listed are parallel in their wording, and that a consistent style is maintained all through.

1 *Horizontal lists* are best suited for items that consist of one or two words. Those in the list following vary somewhat, and are close to the limits of what can be comfortably presented along the line:

> There are seven major newspapers in Australia: the Adelaide Advertiser, the Age, the Australian, the Brisbane Courier-Mail, the Canberra Times, the Sydney Morning Herald and the West Australian.

(For questions about the serial comma, see under **comma**.) When the list is preceded by abbreviations such as *e.g., i.e., viz.* or the words that paraphrase them, the colon used above is replaced by a comma. But there's no punctuation at all when the list is the object or complement of the preceding verb, as in:

> Australia's seven major newspapers are the Adelaide Advertiser, the Age, the Australian …

Note that the commas used to separate the items in those lists could be replaced by semicolons. Semicolons are however most vital when you need two grades of punctuation in a list, as in the following:

> Australia's major newspapers are as follows: in NSW, the Sydney Morning Herald; in Queensland, the Brisbane Courier-Mail; in Victoria, the Age; in South Australia, the Adelaide Advertiser …

(See further under **semicolon**.)

2 *Vertical lists* can be used for both shorter and longer items, and are generally necessary for the latter. They are more often used in documentary writing than, say, in essays; and so the decision to turn a set of items into a vertical list depends somewhat on the genre. Our list of newspapers could very well be presented that way.

> There are seven major newspapers in Australia:
> Adelaide Advertiser
> Age
> Australian
> Brisbane Courier-Mail
> Canberra Times
> Sydney Morning Herald
> West Australian

Note the introductory colon preceding the list, and the absence of punctuation in the list itself. However a semicolon is often placed after each item (and a full stop after the last one) when the items listed have internal punctuation or are substantial parts of sentences:

Australia's major metropolitan newspapers are as follows:

in NSW, Sydney Morning Herald;

in Queensland, Brisbane Courier-Mail;

in South Australia, Adelaide Advertiser;

in Victoria, the Age;

in Western Australia, the West Australian.

Bullets or asterisks are increasingly used to mark a set of items in a vertical list, without further punctuation.

Numbers and/or letters give more specific enumeration to a vertical list, as in the example below. They may be used alternately to distinguish the headings, subheadings etc. See for example:

Australia's metropolitan newspapers are as follows:

1. Victoria

   a) Age

   b) Herald-Sun

2. New South Wales

   a) Sydney Morning Herald

   b) Telegraph-Mirror

Note that a closing bracket is all that's needed with the enumerators in a vertical list, whereas they must be enclosed in a pair of brackets in a horizontal list. See **brackets** section 1a. The details of styling a more extended vertical list are discussed under **numbers** and **number style**. For information about the indenting of items and runover lines, see *hanging indention* under **indents**.

Note finally that the items in any *vertical list* should be worded in parallel, as in the asterisked list above where each item begins with "in" and the name of a state. The list is then much easier to read. It's worthwhile working with the wording of nonconforming items (to express them all as verbs, or nouns preceded by "the"), so that they form a matching set. Consistency of wording in a *vertical list* is as important as consistency in the enumeration or punctuation.

lit or **lighted** See **lighted**.

literally Like any overworked word, **literally** has lost much of its force and credibility. Strictly speaking, it means "according to the letter", i.e. word for word or exactly as the utterance has it. Its use in the first sentence following is effective; in the second it's ridiculous:

The Metropolitan Sewerage Board needs literally to clean up its act.

They were literally green with envy.

In the second case, **literally** is only a general intensifier, used to bolster up an inadequate metaphor. It means little more than "really".

In impromptu conversation there's little we can do to reverse the trend to overuse and dilute the meaning of **literally**. Its essential meaning can perhaps only be captured by writers who choose their words with care, and invite the reader to savor the aptness of a metaphor or figure of speech with them.

litotes See under **figures of speech**.

litre or **liter** For the choice between these spellings, see **-re/-er**. For the use of the **litre** in Australia's metric system, see under *volume* in Appendix V.

littérateurs or **literati** These loanwords make people much more than literate. Both make them "men and women of letters", as the English phrase goes. But while **literati**, borrowed from Latin, indicates that they are of a scholarly or literary bent, the French **littérateurs** implies that they are writers of literary or critical works. The word *littérateur* is masculine in French, its feminine counterpart being *littératrice*. But *littérateur* usually serves for both genders in English, what with the decline in general knowledge of French, and the preference for nonsexist terms. The use of *litterateur* without an accent is another sign of its assimilation in English.

livable or **liveable** See under -eable.

loaded or **laden** See laden.

loafed or **loaved** See under -v-/-f-.

loan or **lend** See lend.

loanwords English has borrowed words from other languages throughout its recorded history. In earlier centuries the words came from Latin and other European languages; and since the beginning of the colonial era, they are from languages on all continents of the earth. **Loanwords** often bring with them unusual spellings, such as the *kh* of *sheik(h)*, or the accent of French *garçon*. These "foreign" features are slowly modified (*kh* becomes *k*, and French accents disappear), as the words become assimilated in English. In the same way, the foreign plural which comes with a borrowed noun (e.g. *kibbutzim*) is gradually replaced by an English plural with *s* (*kibbutzes*). These processes of assimilation are quite natural, and there's no reason to preserve the foreign features of **loanwords** in English—or to continue to set them in italics once they are visibly anglicised. (See further under **italics**.)

loath or **loth** All dictionaries prefer the first spelling for the adjective meaning "reluctant", even though it's more easily confused with the verb *loathe*. Note also that **loath** is the first element in *loathsome* "horrible", though its pronunciation links it with "loathe".

loc. cit. In scholarly referencing this abbreviation stands for the Latin phrase *loco citato* "in the place just cited". It saves the writer having to repeat the exact page or the title of the work, once they have been identified in a preceding footnote. See for example:

    1. G. Blainey *The Tyranny of Distance* p.56

2. C.M. Clark *A History of Australia* p.216
3. R. Hughes *The Fatal Shore* p.17
4. Blainey, loc. cit.

Footnote 4 thus refers to exactly the same page as footnote 1, and further details can be recovered there.

The use of scholarly Latin abbreviations is declining, and instead writers use the author's surname and/or a short title (depending on whether the author's name is given in the running text), and only repeat the page number. Compare **op. cit**.

locum tenens This handy Latin phrase means literally "place holder". In English it's applied to the person who keeps up the business or practice of a professional, such as a doctor, pharmacist or lawyer, while s/he goes away for a short period. Borrowed in the seventeenth century, it has been thoroughly anglicised: often abbreviated to *locum*, and pluralised as *locums*, rather than according to Latin principles as *locum tenentes*.

locus For the plural of this word, see **-us** section 1.

lodgement or **lodgment** See under **judgement** or **judgment**.

logistic or **logistical** See under **-istic/-istical**.

logogram, logotype and **logo** A **logogram** or *logograph* is a symbol for a word or phrase, as & is for "and" and % for "per cent". A **logotype** is a single piece of type with several uncombined characters on it. Compare **ligature**.

Note that *logo* is an abbreviation of **logotype** rather than **logogram**, according to most dictionaries.

-logy See under **-ology**.

longways or **longwise** See under **-wise** or **-ways**.

loose, loosen or **lose** The word **loose** is most familiar as an adjective meaning "slack or not tight" and "free or not tied up". Examples of its use are to be found in *a loose end*, and *Let the dogs loose*. The latter idiom has effectively taken the place of the verb **loose**, meaning "set free", which was in use in older English, but rare nowadays. The verb **loosen** ("make less tight") is by contrast very much in use, as in *He loosened his grip on the rope*.

Note that for centuries *unloose* and *unloosen* have doubled for the verbs **loose** and **loosen**. Their negative prefixes do not reverse the meaning of the root (see further under **un-**). *Unloose* is however increasingly rare, while *unloosen* seems to do service as both "make less tight" and "untie".

Note also that the verb **lose** meaning "suffer a loss" or "fail to keep" is a quite independent word—though often written "loose" by mistake. While **lose** comes from Old English, **loose** is a Scandinavian loanword.

loth or **loath** See **loath**.

loud or **loudly** Dictionaries these days all allow that **loud** can be either an adjective or an adverb, in certain contexts. So apart from qualifying a noun as in *a loud voice*, it can modify a verb as in:

Don't shout so loud!

They turned the radio up loud.

In the second case at least, **loud** seems to be the only possible word, and in the first it serves to make the imperative rather curt. Compare the more polite *Don't shout so loudly.*

Loud is also established as an adverb in idioms such as *read/say it out loud*, where it's used instead of *aloud*. There are several examples in the ACE corpus, and *Webster's English Usage* confirms its legitimacy with a number of citations.

The examples suggest that **loud** increasingly refers to the sheer impact of sound in a situation, while **loudly** is more detached and literary, and often implies a judgement that voices are being used in a rather blatant way:

They complained loudly about their poor accommodation.

lounge A **lounge** is both a piece of furniture you sit upon, and a room for sitting in. The first usage (**lounge** = "couch, divan, settee") is worldwide. But Australia seems to make more use than others of the second meaning, because **lounge** is short for the *lounge room* in a private house as well as the *lounge bar* of a public hotel. In both those cases the lounge is a cut above the general activities rooms for eating and drinking—one notch up in formality on the family room or the public bar. In both the room seems to be characterised by its furniture: armchairs, or at least more comfortable chairs designed for lingering and talking in.

Alternative names for the *lounge room* in Australia are *living room* or *sitting room*. The word *drawing room* is rather old-fashioned.

louvre or **louver** See -er/-re.

low and **lowly** These work as independent words, and do not correspond as adjective and adverb of the same word. **Low** is first of all an adjective or adverb meaning "not far off the ground", as in *a low wall* and *The plane flew low over the city*. More metaphorically, as in *a pretty low thing to do* or *They would lie low for a while*, **low** serves again as both adjective and adverb.

Lowly is normally an adjective meaning "humble", as in *of lowly origins*. Just occasionally it's pressed into service as an adverb, as in:

He began lowly in this organisation.

Yet there's a certain ambiguity about it—which is easily avoided by a phrase:

He began at a low level in this organisation.

Low Countries This phrase is still sometimes used by English-speakers as a collective reference to Holland, Belgium and Luxemburg. (See further under **Netherlands**.)

lower case Lower case letters are the ordinary, small letters of type, the opposite of capital letters (also known as *upper case*). In scholarly tradition they are known as *minuscules* and contrast with the *majuscules*. But in general usage, it's the printer's terms: **lower case** and *upper case* which have prevailed. Those terms are a reminder of the way the elements of type were stored in boxes in two large sets, with the capital letters in the higher rows—and at more of a stretch of the printer's arm, because he needed them less often. The small letters were in the more accessible lower rows, being needed all the time.

For the choice between using capital and lower case letters to begin certain kinds of words, see **capital letters**.

lubra Both **lubra** and **gin** are Aboriginal words for "woman". **Lubra** seems to have originated in southeastern Tasmania, as far as the *Australian National Dictionary* can say, and to have extended from there into Victoria. Its use during the nineteenth century was relatively neutral, given the context of colonial thinking, but it has developed derogatory overtones during this century. The word **gin** originated with the Dharuk Aborigines around Port Jackson, and became the general term north of the Murray for an Aboriginal woman, according to Morris's *Dictionary of Austral English* (1892). But in the outback **gin** too has since become a derogatory word, and both terms are to be avoided. For white Australians, *Aboriginal woman* is the proper, neutral way of referring to them, although Aboriginal women seem comfortable with the phrase *Black women* when referring to themselves. (See further under **black** or **Black**.)

lunch or **luncheon** Lunch is the standard word for a midday meal. *Luncheon* now sounds old-fashioned or extremely formal, as if the Prince of Wales has been invited. Note that *dinner* is also used occasionally in Australia for a midday meal. (See **dinner**.)

lustre or **luster** See under **-re/-er**.

lusty or **lustful** The first of these is an innocent word meaning "hearty, or full of energy and enthusiasm":
They joined in the hymns, singing with lusty voices.
This use of **lusty** is a relic of when *lust* itself was an innocent word in English, meaning simply "delight".

The second word **lustful** picks up the current meaning of *lust*. Quite literally it means "full of lust, lecherous", as in:
Punk-rock guitarists played with lustful gestures to the crowd.
The obvious danger of **lusty** being mistaken for the other word has reduced its use, though the adverb *lustily* is more freely used.

luxuriant or **luxurious** In spite of their similarity, these are used very differently. **Luxuriant** refers to abundant natural growth, either in the environment: *a luxuriant canopy of creepers in the rainforest*, or on the human head: *After six weeks he sported a luxuriant beard.*

Luxurious always relates to the man-made environment, and has strong links with the noun *luxury*. See for instance:

With their winnings they rented a luxurious hotel suite.

-ly This ending serves both adjectives and adverbs in English. It is better known as an adverb suffix, as in *coolly*, *excitingly*, *quietly* and *smoothly*, where it has clearly been added to a simple adjective (*cool* etc.). Adverbs with **-ly** often show some of the standard spelling adjustments of English, such as losing the final *-e* of the adjective in cases such as *simply* < *simple*. For the change from *y* to *i* in cases such as *merrily*, see under **-y>-i-**. Note also that adjectives ending in *-ic* usually add *-ally*, as with *organically* < *organic*. (See further under **-ic/-ical**.)

In earlier centuries **-ly** was also often used to form adjectives from nouns, as with *friendly*, *leisurely*, *lovely* and *scholarly*. Sometimes an existing adjective formed the base, as in *deadly*, *elderly*, *kindly* and *sickly*. Such words are well established, and can be compared by just adding *-er* or *-est*, e.g. *friendlier/ friendliest*, at least when they begin with no more than two syllables. (See further under **adjectives**.) Note that adjectives ending in **-ly** do not usually convert to adverbs by adding another **-ly**. The awkwardness of formations such as *friendlily* is obvious, and so it's normally replaced by a paraphrase: *in a friendly way*.

A distinctive group of adjectives with **-ly** are those designating points of the compass, such as *easterly*, *northerly* etc., and those referring to intervals of time, including:

daily hourly monthly nightly quarterly weekly yearly

These serve as adverbs as well as adjectives.

For questions about adverbs which may or may not have an **-ly** ending (such as *Go slow/slowly*), see **zero adverbs**.

lyric or **lyrical** The shorter adjective is closer in meaning to the origins of both words—the Greek *lyre*, and the song-like verse associated with it. So **lyric** usually collocates with things literary or musical, as in *lyric poetry* or a *lyric soprano*. **Lyrical** usually implies the graceful expression of emotion associated with lyric verse, as in:

She gave a lyrical account of the experience.

For a discussion of similar pairs of words, see **-ic/-ical**.

-lyse/-lyze See under **-yse/-yze**.

M

Mac or **Mc** How do you write the name of a well-known hamburger restaurant chain?

McDonald's MacDonald's Macdonald's

The first spelling is the one used by the company, although the second or third spellings are also used by many people with the same surname—as a glance at the metropolitan phone book will confirm. Apart from those three spellings, there are two other ways of writing Celtic surnames of this kind: *Mcdonald* (which is rare by comparison with the other three above); and *M'Donald*, used in the nineteenth century, and still to be seen in the names of Walter Scott's characters, and sometimes in references to *M'Naghten rules* (a legal plea which seeks to defend someone on the basis of diminished responsibility).

Ultimately, the decision about how to spell these surnames rests with the individual. Individual choices can put both **Mc** and **Mac** in the same sign, as in *McCulloughs of Macquarie*. Yet there are some general trends towards one or the other spelling, in that Irish surnames seem to stay with **Mc**, as in *McConnochie, McElroy* and *McEvoy*; while Scottish names more often convert to **Mac** (with or without a following capital). It means that Scottish names are around in two or three forms: *McDonald/MacDonald/Macdonald*. Other things being equal, the commoner the name, the more chance of it having the **Mac** forms. And **mac** is the spelling found in common words derived from **Mc** surnames, such as *macadamia (nut)*, with no capital letters. (See further under **capitals** and also **eponyms**.) In *mackintosh* ''raincoat'' the spelling adjustments have gone one stage further, with the insertion of the *k* to conform with standard *c/ck* rules. Compare the alternative forms of the original surname: *McIntosh/MacIntosh/Macintosh*.

1 *Geographical names in Australia* are written with both **Mac** and **Mc**, witness the *MacDonnell Ranges* and the *McPherson Range*, and in the suburbs of Canberra both *Macgregor* and *McKellar*. The spelling in such names is often dictated by the person being commemorated, and Governor *Macquarie*'s name has its exact echo in a number of places. *Macarthur* was less fortunate in this: the Victorian town has it right, but in northern Australia his name is respelled in the *McArthur River* and *Port McArthur*. Note that the names of larger country towns such as *Mackay* and *Maclean* are spelled out with **Mac**.

2 *Indexing names with **Mac** and **Mc**. Whichever way personal or geographical names are written, in an index all are alphabetised together as if they were* **Mac***, with their individual spellings being retained:*

Maas Y
Mabey L.
McAdam H.
MacAndrew S.
Macarthur A.
McArthur J.
MacArthur W.
Mace R.
Macfarlane M.
McFarlane P.

Three other points to note are that:

- names with **Mac/Mc** may be included at their natural place in an alphabetical list (after *Mab*) as in the list above, or else as a block at the start of the *M*s. The latter practice is best for short lists, where the beginning of *M* is easily seen from where **Mac** would be.
- names such as *Mace* which do not have the **Mac** prefix are alphabetised together with the *Mac*s in terms of their fourth letter;
- when you have several cases of the same surname with **Mc** and **Mac**, the order depends not on whether there's a second capital, but rather on the *initial letter* of the first given name. If the initials are identical in successive names, Telecom decides the order by the first letter of the person's suburb of residence.

macabre or **macaber**   See under **danse macabre**.

macaroni or **maccaroni**   The spelling **macaroni** is the usual one in English today, though the original Italian spelling **maccaroni** was used for centuries and is still recognised as an alternative in some dictionaries. The Italians themselves now use *maccheroni*, but this has made no headway in English.

macro-   This Greek prefix means "large or large-scale". It has been in service in English only since the 1880s, but the *Oxford Dictionary* (1989) has columns of new technical terms coined with it. Such words are often the opposites of ones formed with *micro-*, as with:

macrobiotic	*microbiotic*
macrocosm	*microcosm*
macroeconomics	*microeconomics*
macroscopic	*microscopic*
macrostructure	*microstructure*

Note that **macro-** usually combines with classical roots to form scholarly words. Its arena differs thus from that of *mega-*, another newish Greek prefix meaning "large", which combines with simple English roots as well. (See further under **mega-**.)

madam or **madame** Both these represent the French expression *ma dame*, literally "my lady", though as *Madame* it's the common French word for "Mrs". In English **Madame** and **madam** have quite different functions.

Madam can be used freely as a polite way of addressing a woman whose name and status are unknown. In restaurants of the more expensive kind, the waiter may ask: "Would madam like to see the menu?" In an upmarket department store, the sales assistant may suggest: "Madam might like to try a larger size". **Madam** also appears in the salutation of letters addressed to unknown female recipients. (See further under **forms of address**.) There's no established plural for it, because it singles out the individual woman.

Note that when **madam** is used as a common noun it may mean either:
- a bossy woman: *She's quite a young madam to deal with*;
- a woman in charge of a brothel: *She had no other prospects than to graduate from tart to madam.*

In both these uses, the plural form is *madams*.

The word **Madame** is usually used in English to preface the name of a celebrated artist, e.g. *Madame Melba, Madame Von Praagh*; or else as a courtesy title for the wife of a foreign dignitary, especially from Europe, as in:

> *The Governor received a visit from the Dutch ambassador Jan Peeters and Madame Peeters.*

(For equivalent courtesy titles for non-European women, see **forms of address**.) The English plural for **Madame** is like the French: *Mesdames*.

Note also the contraction *ma'am*, which is quite common in the USA and (differently pronounced) in the stately homes of England, but little used in Australia except on the occasion of visits by the Queen or other female members of the royal family.

magma For the plural, see **-a** section 1.

magnum opus This Latin phrase, meaning "great work", is applied in English to the major literary or artistic composition by a particular person. However it often seems to imply that the work is more remarkable for its size than anything else. (The French phrase *chef d'oeuvre* is not equivocal in this way.) In earlier centuries the phrase **magnum opus** appeared as *opus magnum*, and both word order and meaning were then more closely aligned with Latin.

maharaja or **maharajah** Australian and British dictionaries give preference to the first spelling, while American ones endorse the second. As often with loanwords, the *Oxford Dictionary* seems to prefer **maharaja** for reasons of etymology, and there's no doubt that it matches the Sanskrit *maha raja* "great king" exactly. Yet the *Oxford* citations also show that the spelling **maharajah** has been in regular use since the word was first recorded in English in 1698.

The wife of a **maharaja(h)** is a *maharani*, sometimes spelled *maharanee*— like other Hindi words ending in that sound. (See under **-ee**.) But once again, *maharani* is closer to the word's origins as *maha rani* "great queen".

Mahomet See under **Muhammad**.

main clause A **main clause** (or principal clause) is not grammatically dependent on any other in the sentence, and may indeed stand alone. A single **main clause** with one or more dependent (or *subordinate*) clauses forms a *complex* sentence. Two or more **main clauses** in the same sentence create a *compound* sentence. (See further under **clauses**.)

main verb In compound verbs, the **main verb** combines with one or more auxiliary verbs, to form a finite verb phrase. (See under **auxiliary verbs** and **finite verbs**.)

maintain and **maintenance** See under **-ain**.

majority When used to mean "larger number of people", **majority** can take either a singular or plural verb in agreement:
The majority of the party is/are behind it.
The silent majority is/are still a force to reckon with.
Constructions with the plural are more common in Australia and Britain than in American English (see further under **collective words**).

Apart from the question of agreement, a curious restriction on the use of this word seems to have evolved during the twentieth century. Compare the following:
The majority of the recruits were sent to the sports ground.
The majority of the field was under water.
Both types of sentence were acceptable in the nineteenth century, and dictionaries all define **majority** as "the greater number *or part*". But according to Fowler and other British books on usage, the second sentence is unacceptable. The reason is not a matter of whether the noun following is singular rather than plural: instead they say that **majority** must be used with something which is "numerical" (Fowler); and that it cannot be used with "a single item" (*Right Word at the Right Time*). Grammarians would comment that the first construction has **majority** coupled with a count noun, and the second with a mass noun (or one used noncountably). (See further under **count nouns**.) *Webster's English Usage* (1989) suggests that the use of **majority** with noncount nouns may be more common in speech, but that there is no substantial objection to such constructions. And from the citations in the *Oxford Dictionary*, it's clear that there was no objection to them in the nineteenth century, nor is there further comment on the matter in the second edition.

The construction with **majority** may of course seem a little heavy. *Most* would be sufficient in either of the sentences above. But that is a matter of style not correct usage, and there is no danger of misunderstanding.

majuscule See **lower case**.

mal- and **male-** Both these prefixes contribute negative meanings to English words. In the cases of *malediction, malefactor, malodor* and *maltreat* it means "bad" or "evil": with *maladministration, malformed, malfunction, malnutrition* and *malpractice* it means "corrupt" or "defective". Always it bodes ill.

Male- is the original Latin form of the prefix, and so examples like *malediction* and *malefactor* are really Latin compounds. **Mal-** is the French form of the same prefix, and English has borrowed a few words with it, and created more during the last four centuries. In the seventeenth century the French prefix was sometimes overwritten with the Latin, so **mal-** was written as **male-** in *mal(e)government* and *mal(e)practice*. But in modern English the French form of the prefix prevails in such words, and is the only one used to form new ones.

malapropisms A *malapropism* is the faulty use of a word which shows that the writer/speaker has confused it with another similar one. See for example:

The book I eluded to a little while ago ...

The ship floundered on the reef ...

The distinction between *elude* and *allude*, *flounder* and *founder*, and many others are detailed in this book. In serious prose they're an unfortunate distraction. But their incongruity has its funny side, and comedy writers from Shakespeare on have exploited their effect for amusement. Some of the most memorable examples were uttered by Sheridan's character *Mrs Malaprop* in *The Rivals*:

[What's the matter?] Why murder's the matter! ... He can tell you all the perpendiculars.

Mrs Malaprop's name has become the byword for this kind of word play, though her name itself derives from the French phrase *mal à propos* "not to the point".

Malaya, Malaysia and **Malay** **Malaya** is a geographical term referring to the southern end of the Malay peninsula which now forms part of the Federation of Malaysia. **Malaysia** is the name for the political unit formed in 1963 out of the mainland **Malay** states as well as those in North Borneo (Sabah and Sarawak) and Singapore. (Singapore left the federation in 1965.)

Note that the term **Malay** is strictly speaking an ethnic term for the indigenous people of **Malaya** and the *Malay Archipelago*, and parts of Indonesia. The population of **Malaysia** itself is only about half **Malay.** The other major community blocks are the Chinese (35%) and the Indian (10%).

malevolent, malicious, malignant or **malign** These words point to an area of meaning which is well supplied with adjectives. All imply a negative disposition or orientation to others, and dictionaries quite often give them as synonyms for each other. There are however some differences, in that **malicious** and **malevolent** are always associated with people and their behavior (*malicious intent*, a *malevolent smile*), whereas **malignant** and the adjective **malign** are often applied to forces and circumstances.

Further differences are that **malevolent** implies general ill-will towards another, while **malicious** suggests that the feeling is channeled into spiteful words or actions.

Malignant is most often used of relentlessly destructive forces, as in the medical phrase *malignant tumor*. **Malign** has also been used this way in the past (*malign syphilis*), but nowadays it most often serves as a verb meaning "speak unfavorably of", shown in *He maligned all the people he worked with*. The influence of the adjective **malign** is still to be found in its opposite *benign*, which serves as the antonym to *malignant* in *benign tumor* etc.

malignance or **malignancy** See under -nce/-ncy.

man For over a thousand years, this word has carried two meanings:
1 person, human being
2 adult male
The first meaning embraces the second, except where the context dictates otherwise. As often in language, the ambiguity of any particular word is resolved by others in the context. All this was taken for granted until recently, when feminist concerns were raised as to whether **man** was really being taken in its first, generic sense as often as was assumed. The debate drew attention to some of our oldest compounds, such as *mankind* and *manslaughter*. Were they interpreted in broad human terms or as "men only" references? Would it be a surprise to hear that a *man-eating* shark has taken a woman who was diving in the coral reef; or that a woman has fallen down a *man-hole*?

Doubts about individual **man-** compounds are reinforced by the large set where **-man** is the second element, as in *businessman, policeman, salesman*. Such words are thought likely to endorse and perpetuate sexist ideas about social and occupational roles, and to make being a businessman an exclusively male preserve. Of course those who use such words may not be male chauvinists: sexism may very well be in the eye of the beholder. Some women indeed prefer to be called *chairman*, because it's the usual way to refer to the role they are taking on. Yet many people feel we should avoid any expressions which raise such questions, and look for synonyms and paraphrases.

For individual job titles there are usually alternatives which focus on the job and bypass the gender of the person doing it. So for example:

businessman	can be replaced by	*executive, entrepreneur*
cameraman		*camera operator*
cattleman		*cattle breeder*
chairman		*convener, coordinator*
draftsman		*drafter*
fireman		*firefighter*
first-aid man		*first-aid attendant*
foreman		*supervisor, leading hand*
insurance man		*insurance agent*
juryman		*juror*
linesman		*linesworker*
mailman/postman		*mail deliverer*
newsman		*reporter, journalist*

policeman	*police officer*
railwayman	*railway worker*
repairman/serviceman	*repairer*
salesman	*shop assistant*
serviceman	*member of armed forces*
spokesman	*representative (of)*
sportsman	*athlete, player, competitor*
storeman	*stores officer*
weatherman	*weather officer*
workman	*worker*

In some of those cases, there is an exact female counterpart to the male term, as with *businessman/businesswoman*, and the latter could be used when it seems important to identify the gender of the person concerned. Yet *businesswoman* is no less sexist than *businessman*, and the better and broader principle of nonsexist language is to seek terms which cover both genders wherever possible (see **inclusive language**). Some would advocate the use of words ending in *-person* (e.g. *chairperson*) to cover both, but that policy too is has its problems (see under **-person**). Note also the need to avoid *man* in some nationality words such as *Englishman*. You could use either *English person* (if the reference has to be singular), or *the English* (for the plural/collective).

When **man** is the first element of the compound, satisfactory alternatives and paraphrases are not so easy to find. The following substitutes seem rather cumbersome and less precise:

manhours	*working hours*
mankind	*the human race, humanity*
man-made	*artificial, manufactured*
manpower	*the work force*

We might also ask whether the original word really works to the disadvantage of women. Do such generalised concepts prejudice women's chances of getting a particular job? The same may be argued in connection with certain conventional phrases containing **man**. Do they need to be paraphrased away?

every man for himself	as	*everyone for themselves*
man in the street		*average person*
man on the land		*farmer, grazier*
no man's land		*neutral territory; dangerous or unproductive place*
to a man		*to the last person*

Idiomatic expressions lose their vital connotations in a paraphrase.

Note finally that the hunt to eradicate **man** from the language is sometimes taken to strange extremes by those who find sexist problems in words such as *manicure, manipulate, manoeuvre, manual, manufacture* and *manuscript*. The first element in all those words is the Latin root *man(u)* "hand". The words have nothing to do with **man**.

manakin See mannequin.

mandarin or **mandarine** See under -ine.

mandatory, mandatary or **mandative** The first spelling **mandatory** is the common adjective meaning "obligatory", as in *a mandatory condition of employment*. **Mandatary** is a noun used to refer to a person or nation that holds a mandate over another. Australia was once the **mandatary** for Nauru and the northeastern section of New Guinea, which were among the various territories *mandated* by the League of Nations after World War I. Note that the spelling **mandatory** has also been used for this application of the word.

Mandative is mostly used by grammarians, to refer to the type of verb used after a persuasive word (verb, noun or adjective) which expresses the obligation in it. For example:

I insisted that he *explain* things in full.

Their demand that it *be sent* by the next post was unrealistic.

It is vital that she *join* us.

The verbs in italics are **mandative**. (See **subjunctive** section 2.)

manège or **ménage** See ménage.

maneuver or **manoeuvre** See manoeuvre.

mango For the plural of this word, see -o.

-mania This Greek root means "madness", but in English its meaning is more often "obsession" or "compulsion", as in

kleptomania   megalomania   pyromania

Words like those imply a deluded or perverse mentality rather than one which is disordered. Perfectly sane people can suffer from *regalomania* ("an obsession with rules and regulations").

The meaning of **-mania** can be quite positive, as with *bibliomania*, where it simply refers to a passion for something. This is also shown in other recent formations with English roots, such as:

balletomania   discomania   videomania

Older words with **-mania** generate nouns ending in *-maniac* for referring to the person with the obsession or compulsion, as in *kleptomaniac* or *pyromaniac*. But for the newer, less pejorative words with **-mania** there are various counterparts:

balletomania >   balletomane
bibliomania >   bibliophil(e)
discomania >   discophil(e)

(See under **phil-** or **-phile**.)

manifesto For the plural of this word, see -o.

manikin See mannequin.

manila or **manilla** The first spelling **manila** is the natural one for all the fibre products originally associated with **Manila** (see next entry). They include *manila paper* (envelopes, folders) and *manila rope*. The capital letter is unnecessary, since the items have long since lost their geographical connection with Manila. But it survives at least as an alternative in most dictionaries.

The spelling **manilla** is the secondary alternative in modern dictionaries, and it was preferred by the *Oxford Dictionary* in the nineteenth century, being then more frequent than **manila**. Its popularity may however owe something to confusion with other Spanish loanwords (*manilla* for a bracelet and one-time unit of African currency; or *manille*, the second highest card in games such as ombre and quadrille). Whether to use single or double consonants in foreign loanwords is in any case an endemic problem in English spelling. (See **single for double**.)

Manila or **Manilla** The first spelling gives the capital of the Philippines. The second is the name of a small town in the New England region of NSW, and an even smaller one in western Queensland.

mannequin, mannikin, manikin or **manakin** All these derive from the Dutch *manneken* "a little man", but their spellings put them in different worlds. The frenchified spelling **mannequin** is the one associated with fashion and the displaying of clothes to public gaze. It may refer either to a shopwindow dummy or a live model who parades up and down the carpeted catwalk.

A **manikin** is a small model of the human figure, as used by an artist, or in the context of teaching anatomy and surgery. Very occasionally it's used to refer to a small human (or quasi-human) figure: a pigmy or a dwarf. Alternative spellings are **mannikin** and **manakin**. Note however that **manakin** is also the name of a small brightly colored bird of Central and South America.

manoeuvre or **maneuver** The spelling **manoeuvre** seems to have an excess of vowels, but it's the standard spelling for this French loanword in Australia and Britain. (The spelling seems less awkward if you keep *hors d'oeuvre* in mind when writing it.)

The spelling **maneuver** is standard in the USA, making it a good deal easier for Americans to put on paper. However the use of *e* for *oe* will not recommend itself to those who associate this spelling adjustment with words of Greek origin (such as *am(o)eba*). (See further under **oe**.) For the use of *-er* instead of *-re* at the end of the word, see **-re/-er**.

Note that when **manoeuvre** becomes a verb, the forms with suffixes are *manoeuvred* and *manoeuvring*. As an adjective it is *manoeuvrable*. For **maneuver**, the corresponding forms are *maneuvered*, *maneuvering* and *maneuverable*.

mantle or **mantel** The first of these is a word for an old-fashioned garment, a loose, sleeveless cloak. By extension it also applies to any covering, such as the mantle on a portable gas lamp, or a blanket of snow over the earth. The metaphorical **mantle** which passes from one person to another is a symbol of authority—recalling the biblical story of how Elijah's mantle was passed down to Elisha.

A **mantel** is a shelf over a fireplace, often spelled out as a *mantelpiece* (or *mantelshelf*). However the spellings **mantle** and *mantlepiece* are also sometimes used with this meaning.

Look back into their history and you find that both words derive from the Latin *mantellum* "cloak". The word was used in Old and Middle English with various spellings and meanings, and only in the seventeenth century did **mantle** become the regular spelling for the garment or covering, and **mantel** for the structure around a fireplace.

marijuana or **marihuana** Dictionaries everywhere give first preference to **marijuana**, and it's the more common spelling in the *Oxford Dictionary* citations. Yet **marihuana** is regularly put up as an alternative, and some Australian newspapers ·(*Brisbane Courier-Mail*, the *West Australian*) give it preference. For most people, the spelling **marihuana** represents the word's pronunciation more satisfactorily than **marijuana** (you have to be familiar with Spanish pronunciation to make sense of the *ju*).

Yet **marijuana** is closer to the etymology of this curious word, as far as it's known. Originally an American Indian word, the Spaniards could only interpret it as *Maria Juana* "Mary Jane", and this folk etymology is still written into **marijuana**. (See further under **folk etymology**.)

marquess or **marquis** This might be a question if you ever visit the principality of Hutt River north of Geraldton in WA, or meet one of its leading citizens on the Queensland Gold Coast. They opt for **marquess**, in keeping with those who bear the title in Britain. Fowler's research earlier this century confirmed that **marquess** had replaced **marquis**, as foreshadowed by the *Oxford Dictionary* in the nineteenth century. It noted the preference for **marquess** in newspapers and that **marquis** was increasingly a literary spelling. But in the USA the spelling **marquis** is still the primary one—fossilised, presumably, because such aristocratic titles are foreign there, and perhaps because of the celebrated/infamous *Marquis de Sade*.

Note that the wife of a **marquess** is referred to in England (and Australia) as a *marchioness*, whereas in France she is a *marquise*.

marshal, marshall and **Marshall** Should it have one *l* or two?

As a proper name, **Marshall** almost always has two *l*s—witness geographical and historical names such as the *Marshall Islands* and the *Marshall Plan*, as well as the countless *Marshall*s in the metropolitan phone directory. There are columns of surnames with two *l*s, and only a handful with one *l*.

As a common word (noun or verb), or as part of a title, **marshal** is normally given only one *l*. See for example:

The sky marshal *is a new breed of plain-clothes police, designed to prevent hijacking of aircraft.*
The commander gave the signal to marshal the troops.
Field-Marshal Sir William Slim became governor-general of Australia in 1953.

After centuries when either spelling was acceptable, the spelling with one *l* seems to have become dominant in the nineteenth century according to *Oxford Dictionary* citations, and it is the only one now recognised in British dictionaries. Yet American dictionaries still register both spellings, and *Webster's English Usage* has citations for both as the noun and the verb. The use of **marshall** in the USA is fostered by American use of two *l*s in verbs such as *distill, enroll* and *fulfill,* where Britons use spellings with just one *l.* (See further under **-l/-ll-.**)

martin or **marten**   The first spelling refers to a small insectivorous bird, such as the *fairy martin* or the *tree martin.* The name is believed to come from the personal name *Martin.*

   The second spelling **marten** is for a small carnivorous animal like a weasel. It is native to North America and hunted for its fur, often referred to as "sable". The word **marten** seems to be an adaption of the French *martre.*

marvelous or **marvellous**   The choice between these, and between *marveled/ marvelled* and *marveling/marvelling* is discussed under **-l/-ll-.**

masculine gender   See under **gender.**

mass nouns   See under **count nouns.**

masterful or **masterly**   There is a subtle difference between showing who is master and showing that you are a master at something. Fowler believed that **masterful** expresses the first meaning (that you're in command of a situation), and that **masterly** is to be deployed when great skill has been demonstrated. Compare:
   He silenced the protests with a masterful gesture.
   His performance of the Mozart concerto was masterly.
Though Fowler's distinction is echoed in various usage books, modern dictionaries show that there is no simple dichotomy between the two words. Rather they show that **masterful** can be used in both senses, whereas **masterly** is only used in the sense of "showing great skill".

   The wider range of **masterful** is reinforced by the fact that it's the only one of the pair which can serve as an adverb (*masterfully*). Adjectives ending in *-ly* like *masterly* cannot satisfactorily add another *-ly* to become adverbs, and so *masterfully* has to do service for both words. In *He performed it masterfully* we assume the adverb means "in a masterly way".

   Note that both *mastery* and the verb *master* are sometimes the focus of feminist critiques of language, but *masterful* and *masterly* seem to have escaped attention in the Australian Government *Style Manual* (1988). Perhaps their meanings seem more removed from any possible charge of sexism.

matrix The plural of this word may be either Latin *matrices* or English *matrixes*, though modern dictionaries all present them in that order. The *Oxford Dictionary* originally gave preference to *matrixes* over *matrices*, but in its second edition the order has been reversed on the strength of numerous citations for *matrices*, derived from mathematics as well as various new technologies including photography, computing and broadcasting. The major American and Australian dictionaries also give preference to *matrices* for the plural. *Matrixes* is probably more often said than written, but it may be helped in the future by uses of the new verb *matrix*, and its inflected forms *matrixed* and *matrixing*.

maunder or **meander** Similar looks and uses have brought these together, though their origins are quite distinct. **Meander** is associated first and foremost with the winding course of a river, and was the Greek name for a Turkish river which flows into the western Mediterranean. (The river is now known as the *Menderes*.)
  Maunder means essentially "talk in a rambling way", as in:
  He maundered through his introductory speech.
It probably comes from a medieval French verb *mendier* "beg". Yet both words can be used figuratively to mean "wander aimlessly", so you could say either:
  The tourists meandered through the market stalls or
  The tourists maundered through the market stalls.
There are still slightly different implications. While the first sentence connotes leisurely movement, the second has overtones of confusion.

mausoleum For the plural of this word, see **-um**.

maxi- This new prefix of the 1960s is derived from Latin *maximus* "greatest or largest". In English it usually means "large-sized", as in:
  maxibudget   maxisingle   maxiskirt   maxi-taxi   maxiyacht
Although they are hybrid Latin/English formations, new words with **maxi-** quickly lose their hyphens. In some examples the **maxi-** word is obviously coined to match a similar word with *mini-*. So *maxi-taxi*, first recorded in 1961, seems to parallel *minicab* (1960), and *maxiskirt* (1966) appeared just a year after *miniskirt*. *Mini-* is also a relatively new prefix (see under **mini-**).

maxim See under **aphorism**.

maxima cum laude See under **cum laude**.

maximum The plural of this word is discussed under **-um**.

may or **might** For the uses of these verbs, see under the headings **can** or **may** and **could** or **might**.

May Day or **mayday** With its capital letters and a space between the words, **May Day** (1st May) is celebrated in the northern hemisphere as the first day of spring. But the traditional games and dancing and celebration of nature have given way, in the twentieth century, to parades celebrating the international labor movement.

Without capitals or space, **mayday** is the international distress call used by ships and aircraft to radio for help. The rhyming syllables represent the French cri de coeur *m'aider* (or *m'aidez*) "help me". The English spelling is a neat example of **folk etymology** (see under that heading)—but it ensures that we get the pronunciation right when in dire straits.

maybe or **may be** The space makes all the difference. **May be** with space between the words is a compound verb, as in *It may be vital*, where *may* is the auxiliary verb (see further under **auxiliary verbs**).

Maybe is an adverb meaning "perhaps". It has a slightly informal character for some people, perhaps because of its frequent appearances in conversation and "thinking aloud":
Maybe they'll arrive tomorrow.
Still it appears often enough in written English, and there are 106 instances of **maybe** to 335 of **perhaps** in the Australian ACE corpus—a ratio of approximately 1:3. The affinity between **maybe** and less formal writing may be seen in the fact that more than half the instances (60) are found in the fiction samples which make up only a quarter of the corpus. Yet there are instances in all nonfiction categories of writing as well, including government and academic prose.

me The pronoun **me** comes very close to us all, though grammarians and other language commentators of the past have made us rather self-conscious about it. People sometimes replace it with *myself*, as if to avoid putting the spotlight directly on themselves:
This was a gift to myself from my wife.
There is no need to do this. In fact we draw *less* attention to ourselves by using the ordinary **me**:
This was a gift to me from my wife.
Anxieties about **me** probably stem from two constructions which are censured by the grammarian, though they are quite common in informal dialogue. One is the use of **me** instead of *my* as a possessive adjective (especially by young people), as in:
I rode round there on me bike.
Written down, this **me** seems ungrammatical (a first person pronoun where an adjective should be used). In fact it looks worse than it usually sounds. As pronounced it's often more like *my* with a shortened vowel or a **schwa** (see further under that heading). When scripting informal dialogue there may be good reason to write **me** or *m'* instead of *my*, though it would seem out of place or substandard in most other kinds of writing.

Another vexed use of **me** is after *and* when two subjects are coordinated:

Jim and me left before the rest.

Here **me** substitutes for *I*: in standard written grammar it would be *Jim and I left before the rest.* But in casual conversation some speakers maintain the object pronoun whether its role is actually subject or object. It would of course be perfectly acceptable in:

They farewelled Jim and me before the rest.

(There it's part of the object of the verb. See **cases**.) But when the grammatical reasons for using *I* and **me** are not understood, the choice seems arbitrary. Hence also the substitution of *I* for **me** in *for you and I* and *like you and I.* (See further under **between you and me.**)

Whatever the vagaries of **me** in casual speech, its use in writing is still complementary to *I* as object and subject pronoun respectively, and it's not about to be eclipsed. In noncoordinated constructions the use of **me** is stable, and the *I/me* distinction is matched by *we/us, he/him, she/her* and *they/them* (though absent from *you* and *it*). For the moment then, there are more English pronouns with the subject/object distinction than without it.

mea culpa This Latin phrase meaning "by my fault" comes from the confession at the beginning of the mass. But it has long been used in secular English to mean simply "I am to blame" whenever we feel the need to admit responsibility for a problem—whether it's the mismatched cutlery on the table or the mistaken information which has made everyone late for dinner. Its Latin dress still makes it a rather earnest admission, however, and neither it nor *peccavi* "I have sinned" can be used very lightheartedly.

meagre or **meager** See **-re/-er.**

meander or **maunder** See **maunder.**

meaningful Overworked words lose their cutting edge, and the meaning of **meaningful** is threatened in this way. Even worse, *meaningful* tends to devalue the words it's combined with. In clichés such as *meaningful dialogue, meaningful discussion,* and *meaningful negotiation,* we begin to wonder what *meaningless* dialogue/discussion/negotiation might be. (Can anything be discussed or negotiated without some meaning being exchanged?) And does **meaningful** mean much in *meaningful experience* or *meaningful relationship*? In many cases it's redundant, or simply a substitute for "important", "worthwhile", or other words which embody a value judgement. They are better words to use, if **meaningful** is intended that way. If **meaningful** is a synonym for "significant", then the actual significance of the *meaningful experience* should be explained.

If we take the load off **meaningful** by these various means, it has a better chance of retaining its essential denotation "full of meaning" in expressions such as *meaningful look, meaningful smile* and *meaningful pause*—and of being a meaningful component of English.

means   This word looks plural, yet it can combine with either a singular or plural verb, depending on the meaning.

When it means "resources or income", it's always plural:

Their means were never large enough for her dreams.

When it means "method of doing something", it can be either singular or plural, according to whether the writer means one or several methods:

His ultimate means of gaining public attention was to fake disappearance.

We've tried all the means that are available to ordinary citizens.

As the last example shows, the use of words such as *all, many, several* (or any plural number) confirms the need for a plural verb; and the use of *a, any, each* and *every* would show where a singular verb is needed.

measles   Should it be *Measles is rampant at the school* or *Measles are rampant...*? See **agreement** section 4b.

media   In English this has long been used as the plural of the Latin *medium* "a vehicle or channel of communication", especially in reference to the various forms of visual art, such as fresco, mosaic, relief, oil-painting, charcoal, gouache. In the twentieth century the same term is used collectively in the phrase *mass media*, to refer to the various channels of mass communication, such as radio, TV and newspapers. *The media*, first recorded in the 1950s, is now a byword for the mass media at large.

Because of this collective usage, **media** is sometimes coupled with a singular verb and/or pronoun:

A politician is no sooner elected than the media begins to get its teeth into him.

The same sentence could equally well be:

A politician is no sooner elected than the media begin to get their teeth into him.

For some people the second version is the only "correct" one, because they insist that **media** is plural. No-one could deny that it's a plural word in Latin, but its collective use in modern English makes it more like *team* and *committee*, which can take singular or plural verbs and pronouns, depending on the meaning intended. (See further under **collective nouns**.) An *Oxford Dictionary* citation from 1966 notes the use of **media** as a singular noun "spreading into upper cultural strata"; and the fact that the dictionary still calls it "erroneous" is a remarkable example of a linguistic fetish. Many Latin loanwords undergo new grammatical and sense developments in the context of English. (Compare *stamina*, discussed under **stamen**.)

Webster's English Usage (1989) notes two further developments of the word: **media** as a count noun (for example in *a new recording media*), and the use of *medias* as its plural.

For the different uses of plural *media* and *mediums*, see under **-um**.

medieval or **mediaeval**   See under ae/e.

mediocre This word is spelled the same way everywhere in the English-speaking world. Even in North America the *-re* is standard spelling, never replaced with *-er* (see **-re/-er**)—no doubt to avoid having *-cer* for the last syllable, which might suggest a soft *c* sound. (In similar words such as *ochre/ ocher* and *sepulchre/sepulcher*, the *h* keeps the *c* hard.)

Some people take the word **mediocre** "middling" very literally, to mean "at the middle point of a scale", and argue that it cannot be qualified by words such as "rather" or "very": it either is or is not "in the middle". But for most people **mediocre** is more general in its meaning, appraising things as "ordinary and unremarkable". Taken that way there's no problem at all in qualifying the word with adverbs of degree. Compare **unique**.

medium The plural of this word is discussed under **-um**.

meet (up)(with) For centuries the verb **meet** has worked simply and effectively, with no extra particles:
We met the director in her office.
They meet at the bar after work.
In grammatical terms the first sentence is transitive, the second intransitive (see further under **transitive**); but each is self-sufficient.

The very simplicity of this seems to make English-speakers want to add to it, and many are inclined to use **meet with** as the transitive form, and **meet up** as the intransitive:
We met with the director ...
They meet up at the bar ...
There are some subtle differences in meaning perhaps, a certain formality about **meet with** and a sense of the importance of the encounter; while **meet up** seems to connote a more ordinary get-together. These differences in connotation may justify their use on occasions, though **meet** itself would often be sufficient.

Some usage commentators, especially British ones, present a different argument for avoiding **meet with** in the sense of "come into the presence of". They find it unfortunate that it coincides with **meet with** in the sense "incur or experience", as in:
I hope it meets with your approval.
She met with huge resistance.
Yet dictionaries allow both kinds of meaning for **meet with**, and the distinction is clear from whether the object of **meet with** is animate (as with "director") or abstract (as with "approval" and "resistance"). The second is more common than the first (by a ratio of 11:5), at least in the printed material of the Australian ACE corpus.

As if this were not enough, **meet** is quite often accompanied by *up* as well as *with* when it means no more than *meet* in its simple, transitive sense of "encounter or come together with". See for example:
At the conference they met up with their former colleagues.

This usage seems to have originated in the USA last century, and is current in Australia. (It appears twice in the ACE corpus.) Although the use of two particles after a simple verb may seem excessive, we take it for granted in quite a few other verb phrases, such as *come up with* and *walk out on* (see further under **phrasal verbs**). Their flavor is slightly informal, but they are established idioms.

mega- Derived from Greek, this prefix means "huge". In physical measurements, such as those calibrated in *megahertz, megatons* and *megawatts*, **mega-** means exactly "one million or 10^6". It takes its place among the standard metric prefixes, represented by the symbol *M* (see Appendix IV). In the computer term *megabyte* **mega-** equals 2^{20}.

But in other scientific and scholarly words, **mega-** means just "impressively large", as in:

    megalith   megaphone   megaspore   megastructure

Note that *megapod* meaning "having large feet" can be applied generally in zoological description; whereas *macropod*, literally again "having large feet", is strictly the term for the kangaroo family of animals. (For other uses of **macro-** see under that heading.)

Megalo- is an older form of **mega-**, which combines only with Greek words, as in *megalomania, megalopolis* and *megalosaur*. The older *megalocephalic* is being replaced by *megacephalic*.

In the past, the words coined with **mega-** were scholarly ones. A few of them have however taken root in everyday English, and provided the stimulus for more informal uses of **mega-** since World War II. Recent formations such as *megabucks, megadeath, megastar* and *megastore* are familiar journalistic terms, in which its meaning varies from "vast in numbers" to "awesomely large or great". Australia has been dubbed *Meganesia*; and in casual conversation you'll hear **mega** used instead of "very" as an intensifier: *It's megatrendy.* It even occurs on its own as an exclamation: "*Mega!*" as a substitute for "Great!"

meiosis See under **figures of speech**.

Melanesia See under **Polynesia**.

melodious or **melodic** For musicologists and others, **melodic** is the one to use when you're talking technically about the structure of music, and distinguishing its **melodic** component from the rhythm and harmony. But for other general purposes, **melodic** and **melodious** are synonyms. Both can be applied to a tune or pattern of sound which appeals to the ear. Effectively **melodic** has more applications than **melodious**, and this may explain why it's the commoner of the two, according to the evidence of English databases. Apart from its use as banter in "I heard your melodious voice …", **melodious** has a somewhat literary flavor these days, which also helps to account for its decreasing use.

melted or **molten** In modern English we conventionally speak of *melted butter* and *melted ice*, but *molten lead* and *molten lava*. The twin adjectives are reminders of the fact that there were once (in Old English) two verbs relating to the process of becoming liquid. Their parts were merged in Middle English, and **molten** was used as an alternative past participle for the verb *melt*, as in *molten tallow*. **Melted** first appeared in the sixteenth century, as the regular past participle (see **irregular verbs**). As it became established **molten** lost its connection with the verb and was confined to the adjective role, especially to phrases in which it combined with metals or other substances that are liquefied only by great heat.

Nineteenth century authors could write figuratively of "molten passions", but the hyperbole in that is probably too much for twentieth century taste. We do however make figurative use of *melted*, as in "At those words he melted …", to express a much gentler human emotion.

memento This word has been used in English for a token of remembrance since the eighteenth century. Just occasionally it appears written as **momento**, a variant which has only recently been registered in dictionaries (*Oxford Dictionary* (1989) and *Webster's Third International* (1986)), although the first evidence of **momento** is from the middle of last century, according to *Webster's English Usage* (1989). Reluctance to recognise the variant spelling is no doubt because it obscures the etymology of the word, the Latin root *mem-* "remember" in the first syllable. The respelling suggests folk etymology at work on the word, reinterpreting it to emphasise the *special moment*, rather than as a means of *remembering or commemorating* something.

For the plural of **memento**, see **-o**.

memento mori See under **danse macabre**.

memorandum and **memo** Both these refer to a genre of inter-office communication in government and industry, one which is more public and less personal than letters. Both forms of the word are current, and the longer one has more formal overtones, especially in any quasi-legal document which is a *Memorandum of Agreement* or *Memorandum of Association*. Its plural may be *memoranda* or *memorandums*. (See further under **-um**.)

In government offices **memorandum** is the standard form, yet **memo** is well established in its own right, and the two appear in equal numbers in the Australian ACE corpus. The *Oxford Dictionary* has recorded the use of **memo** as a noun for over a century, and *Webster's English Usage* (1989) even has evidence of its being used as a verb. Its plural is *memos*, as is usual for abbreviated words ending in *-o* (see under **-o**.)

ménage or **manège** These French loanwords refer respectively to the management of one's house and the management of one's horse, so they are not to be confused. Without their accents, they are easily mistaken for each other. One way to remember the difference is that **ménage** is like *menial*, and involves the humdrum business of running a household; whereas **manège** which embodies the Latin root *manus* "hand" has to do with *handling* a horse.

Ménage also refers to the structure of a household, and the people who comprise it. So the *ménage à trois* (literally "household with three") is a discreet way of referring to a nonstandard household of three persons—a husband, wife and a third who is the lover of one of them.

mendacity or **mendicity** These two are dangerously alike. **Mendacity** refers to the falseness of something, or a particular falsehood. A *mendacious report* embodies false and deceptive statements. But those accused of **mendicity** have the consolation of knowing that they are poor but honest about their condition. **Mendicity** is a formal word for begging, and a way of life for a *mendicant* ("beggar").

-ment This suffix, borrowed from French and Latin, forms many an English word. It makes nouns out of verbs, especially those which are French in origin. Here is a sample of them from the letter *A*:

> *accomplishment advertisement agreement alignment amusement*
> *announcement arrangement assessment*

Only a handful of **-ment** words are formed with English verbs, including *catchment, puzzlement* and *settlement,* and a special subgroup prefixed with *em-* or *en-*: *embitterment, embodiment, encampment, enlightenment* and *enlistment.*

Most words ending in **-ment** can express the action of the verb they embody, as well as the product which results from the action:

> *the development of the program   a new housing development*
> *an investment in their future   devaluing our investments*

The spelling of words with **-ment** usually means leaving the verb intact, as in all the examples so far. Verbs ending in *-e* retain it, in keeping with the general rule before suffixes beginning with a consonant (see under **-e.**) Note however that when the verb ends in *-dge,* two spellings are possible, as with *abridg(e)ment, acknowledg(e)ment, judg(e)ment* and *lodg(e)ment.* (See further under **judgement** or **judgment.**) For the spelling of **argument** see under that heading.

Note also that **-ment** words based on certain verbs ending in *l* may have one or two *l*s before the suffix, as with *enrol(l)ment* and *fulfil(l)ment.* In Australia and Britain such words often have only one *l,* because that is the spelling of the simple verb (*enrol, fulfil*), whereas in North America the two *l*s of the simple verb are taken into the **-ment** word. However the spellings *forestalment* and *instalment* reflect outdated spellings of the verb. (See further under **forestallment** and **installment.**)

merino For the plural of this, see **-o.**

meronymy See under **metonymy.**

meta- Derived from Greek, this prefix essentially meant "with, beyond or after" (in space or time), and often involved a change of place or condition. The idea of change is the one in *metamorphosis* (as well as *metaphor* and *metathesis*); and the meaning "after" is the original one in *metaphysics*, though in modern English it has been reinterpreted there as "beyond, transcending".

All those kinds of meaning are to be found in modern formations with **meta-**. In anatomical words such as *metacarpus, metatarsus* and *metathorax,* **meta-** means "beyond" in a simple physical sense. *Metabolism* and *metachromatism* build on the idea of change. And the most widely used sense of all, "transcending", is exemplified in new words such as *metalanguage, metapsychology* and *metempirics.*

metal or **mettle** These two spellings have evolved from one and the same word, to distinguish its concrete meaning from the more abstract one. The spelling **metal** remains close to the form and meaning of the original Latin and Greek word *metallum/metallon.* The word's more abstract and figurative meaning "spirit, strength of character" began to appear in the late sixteenth century, and by the beginning of the eighteenth had acquired its distinctive spelling (**mettle**), conforming with an English spelling pattern.

metaphor *Metaphors* are a life-force of language. They lend vitality to routine commentary on anything, as when a golfing shot is said to be "rocketing its way to the ninth green". The *metaphorical* word "rocketing" brings lively imagery to bear on a familiar subject, stimulating the reader's imagination.

Metaphors help to extend the frontiers of language all the time. Figurative uses of words often begin as *metaphorical extensions*, and end up as permanent additions to the word's range of meaning. The notion of seeking one's "roots" and discovering unknown "branches" of one's family are thoroughly established, and to understand them we do not need to invoke the "tree" metaphor on which they're based.

When *metaphors* like those become ordinary elements of the language, they are sometimes referred to as *dead metaphors.* Yet even dead metaphors have a phoenix-like capacity to revive, as when President Gerald Ford declared that solar energy is something that cannot come in overnight! The imagery in familiar metaphors is latent rather than dead. A *mixed metaphor* is achieved by using two (or more) divergent metaphors in quick succession. Between them they create a dramatically inconsistent picture, as when someone is said to "have his head so deep in the sand he doesn't know which side of the fence he's on"—to quote a former premier of Queensland, who knew how to use the *mixed metaphor* (or "mixaphor") to divert and disarm those interviewing him.

Metaphors, like most stimuli, need to be indulged in moderation—not too many at once, and none exploited too hard. An *extended metaphor* can work well provided it's not used relentlessly. The effectiveness of the **metaphor** in this passage begins to flag after the third or fourth attempt to extend it:

> *The boss entered them for all kinds of new competitive activities. They*
> *were spurred into presenting themselves at the starting gate for every*
> *government grant (whether it was the right race or not), and feeling*
> *thoroughly flogged, they yearned for greener pastures …*

Like the hard-worked public servants of that example, a **metaphor** can be
overextended. It then becomes too obvious, and runs the risk of parodying itself.

Metaphors and *similes*. Metaphors work best allusively, likening one thing to
another by passing implication. Their contribution is much less direct and
explicit than that of *similes*. Compare:

> *The ball rockets its way to the ninth green.*
> *The ball flies like a rocket to the ninth green.*

In a *simile*, the comparison is spelled out in a phrase beginning with *like* or *as*,
and the image it raises is set alongside the statement, not integrated with it as
in a **metaphor**. But *similes* do allow for more complex comparisons which
cannot be set up in a single word. See for example:

> *Talking with him is like wrestling with an octopus—he weighs in with one*
> *heavyweight topic after another.*

Similes, like *metaphors*, sometimes become regular idioms of the language:

> *mad as a gumtree full of galahs*
> *as happy as a bastard on Father's Day*

Examples like those lend color and (in the second case) irony to everyday talk.
Note finally the difference between a **metaphor** and a *metonym*. In a
metaphor, both the object referred to (e.g. "ball") and the metaphorical word
("rocket") are expressed; whereas a *metonym* actually replaces the object of
reference. (See further under **metonymy**.)

meteor, meteoroid or **meteorite** These words are sometimes
interchanged, yet they refer to different phases in the life of a celestial object.
It begins as a **meteoroid**, an inert mass of mineral traveling in space far from
the earth's orbit. When drawn into the earth's orbit and through earth's
atmosphere, it becomes white-hot and is seen as a fiery streak through the
heavens. In this form it's called a **meteor** or "shooting star". Small *meteors*
burn up to nothingness in the skies, but larger ones shoot through to the earth's
surface, sometimes creating a great cavity in it. The cold and once again inert
mass which remains is the **meteorite**.

meter or **metre** See metre.

metonymy This is a figure of speech in which you name something by
something with which it is regularly associated. So *the bar* comes to stand for
the legal profession, because of the railing in a courtroom which divides the
public space from the area which is exclusively for legal personnel. *The press*
stands for journalists and reporters whose writing is made public by the
newspaper press. A *metonym* thus often stands for an institution of some kind.
They can also be used in reference to familiar practices. In phrases such as *on*

the bottle, the word *bottle* is a *metonym* for heavy consumption of alcohol, and *the kitchen sink* can be one for female domestic duties.

Metonymy (which works by associated objects) should be distinguished from *meronymy*, the figure of speech which names *a part* of something as a way of referring to the whole. Thus the "roof over our heads" is a *meronym* for "house". In traditional rhetoric this was called **synecdoche**. (See further under that heading.)

metre or **meter** In Australian English these words mean several different things, unlike other **-re/-er** pairs (see under that heading).

A **metre** is first and foremost a measure of length, the standard SI unit for it, and the one from which the metric system itself takes its name (see Appendix IV). But **metre** is also the word/spelling for a particular rhythmic pattern in poetry. Both words come from the Greek *metron* "a measure".

The word **meter** "measuring instrument" is a native English word, based on the verb *mete* "distribute or give out", which once meant "measure". Our spelling thus serves to remind us of the different origins of the *gas meter* and the *poetic metre*. Yet whether we need such a reminder—and whether there's any real danger of confusing them—is doubtful. In American English the spelling **meter** is used for both (as well as for the SI unit).

-metre or **-meter** Is a *micrometre* the same as a *micrometer*?

Not at all. The spelling **-metre** is attached to words that are units of length within the metric system, like *millimetre, centimetre* and *kilometre* (see Appendix V). A *micrometre* is one millionth of a metre, but the special instrument that measures minute lengths such as that is a *micrometer*.

Note that words ending in **-meter** are of two kinds:

1 measuring instruments, such as:

   altimeter barometer odometer speedometer thermometer

2 poetic metres, such as:

   hexameter pentameter tetrameter

The use of *hexa**meter*** etc. alongside *(poetic)* **metre** is an unfortunate inconsistency of British (and Australian) English. In American English **meter** is used throughout. (See previous entry.)

metres square or **square metres** See under **square metres**.

metric or **metrical** Since Australia's metrication in 1970, the word **metric** is usually associated with the SI units of our *metric system*; whereas **metrical** is used as the adjective associated with poetic metres. In the past **metric** could also be used for the latter. So as with some other *-ic/-ical* pairs, the two adjectives are developing distinct areas of meaning. (See **-ic/-ical**.)

metrication and the **metric system in Australia** Australia went metric with the *Metric Conversion Act (1970)*, and dispensed with the old imperial system of weights and measures. The metric system originated in France, and after the international metric convention of 1870–5 it was officially adopted by many other nations in Europe and South America. *Metric measurements* were once standardised by reference to physical objects kept in Paris, such as the platinum–iridium bar from which the *metre* was calibrated. But measurements of length are now standardised by reference to wavelengths of light, and the standards themselves are checked regularly by laboratories in many parts of the world.

English-speaking countries have generally been rather slow to implement the **metric system**. In the USA the **metric system** was legalised by act of Congress in 1866, but attempts to make it the official system in the 1890s were resisted, especially by the manufacturing industries. Only now, with the adoption of the **metric system** by the US Army and Marine Corps and by NASA for their weapons and equipment, is there some pressure for a general change; and the US Metric Board, set up in 1975, has responsibility for developing a national conversion program. In Canada, the SI system was accepted in 1971, and is supported in government documents and in technical and scientific work. Canadian children are taught the **metric system** in school, though it's still unfamiliar to older adults. In Britain, the changeover began officially in 1965, yet the most noteworthy adjustment so far has been decimalisation of the currency. Britons do admittedly buy their wine by the litre, but their beer and milk are still sold in pints.

In Australia the changeover to the **metric system** in the 1970s was well managed, and few would turn the clock back, even if they still mentally calibrate distances in miles, and people's height in feet and inches. A few of the old imperial units survive in Australia as our official units in special fields (see **imperial weights and measures**). In schools however the **metric system** is the only one now taught, and the rising generation will ensure that Australia stays metric.

1 The **metric system** is essentially the one based on the seven key units of the Système International des Poids et Mesures (international system of weights and measures). They are:

metre	for	*length*
kilogram		*mass*
second		*time*
ampere		*electric current*
kelvin		*thermodynamic temperature*
candela		*luminous intensity*
mole		*amount of substance*

From these SI base units, others—either decimal fractions or multiples of them—are named, such as the *millimetre* and *kilometre*.

Apart from those, there are:

a) two *supplementary units*, namely the *radian* (a unit of plane angle) and the *steradian* (a unit of solid angle); and

b) the so-called *derived units*: ones whose values are a product of certain base units. The standard unit of area is the metre squared, while that of density is based on kilograms per metre cubed. Derived units with special names (such as the *joule* which calibrates energy, and the *watt* which calibrates power) are also calculated from a formula involving the base units: in the latter case 1 kilogram metre squared per second cubed.

The (non-SI) units employed within our metric system are also defined in terms of metric units. Thus the *litre*, our measure of liquid volume, is defined as $10^{-3}m^3$; and the definition of *bar*, used in measuring pressure, is 10^5 pascals. Other familiar non-SI units are the *hectare, tonne, day, hour, minute*, and the *degree Celsius*.

All the units mentioned so far are in general use in Australia. A few others have become officially "declared units" for limited uses only. Examples are the *knot* and the *(nautical) mile*, for marine and aerial navigation as well as meteorology; the *tex* (a measure of linear density), used in measurements of yarns, fibres and cords; and the *kilogram per hectolitre*, used in measurements of grains and seeds.

2 *Writing* **metric units**. Both base and derived units in the **metric system** have official symbols, many of which are written with a capital letter because they are proper names. This applies to units such as the *ampere* (*A*), the *joule* (*J*) and the *watt* (*W*), as well as to our scales of temperature: *Kelvin* (*K*) and *Celsius* (*C*). By convention the symbol for litre is *L* (also a capital, to make it more conspicuous than an ordinary lower case *l* would be). Other metric items written with upper case are the symbols for prefixes which express multiples of any base unit, including *mega-* (*M*), *giga-* (*G*), *tera-* (*T*), *peta-* (*P*) and *exa-* (*E*). The symbols are all listed in Appendix IV.

Note that metric symbols are never pluralised, whether they are upper or lower case. See for example:

The generator's output is 600 MW (= megawatts).

The city-to-surf run is 14 km (= kilometres).

But when metric units appear as full words, they're almost always lower case (e.g. *watt, metre*), the only exception being *Celsius*. As full words they should be pluralised like ordinary English nouns with an *s* (e.g. *watts, metres*), except in the cases of *hertz, lux* and *siemens* which have zero plurals. (See further under **zero plurals**.)

Other points to note are:

a) either full words, or symbols (not a mixture of them) should be used in any expression: either *kilometres per hour* or *km/h*, but not *km/hour* etc. The symbols lend themselves to use in tables and diagrams, and the full words are most likely in discursive text.

b) only one unit should be used in expressing quantities, i.e. not both metres and kilometres. The writer chooses the unit so as to ensure as far as possible that the numerical values are between 0.1 and 1000. So working in metres makes best sense if you're comparing distances such as *75.2 m* and *106.5 m*. (In kilometres they would be *0.0752 km* and *0.106 km* respectively.)

c) between the figure and the abbreviated unit of measurement a space is needed.

metronymic See under **patronymic**.

metropolis Though Greek in origin, this word was mediated through late Latin to modern Europe. Yet its plural has always been *metropolises* since it was recorded in English in the sixteenth century.

miall or **myall** See **myall**.

miasma The plural of this word is discussed under **-a** section 1.

micro- Derived from Greek, this prefix means essentially "very small, minute", as in *microcosm, micro-organism, microprint* and *microprocessor*. In twentieth century scholarship, science and technology, it has developed a number of new meanings as well.

One is "small in scale or focus", as in:

microclimate   microeconomics   microstructure

Another is associated with physical measurements, where **micro-** has the precise meaning of "one millionth" of a given unit, as in:

micrometre   micro-ohm   microsecond   microvolt

As such it's one of the standard prefixes in the metric system.

Note that *microwaves* are not a precisely defined element of this kind. They have traditionally been explained within a range of wavelengths, and the range itself has been shifting down the scale in dictionary definitions over the last two or three decades, from something "less than 10 meters and especially less than one meter" *Webster's New World Dictionary* (1966); to between 100 cm and 1 cm *Webster's International* (1985); to between 30 cm and 1 mm in the *Oxford Dictionary* (1989). Whatever the niceties of their length, microwaves are familiar in the kitchen nowadays, and the abbreviation **micro-** begins to embody the meaning "microwave", as in *micro-oven* (*not* a very small oven).

Other new meanings have developed out of the use of **micro-** to mean "amplifying what's very small", as in *microphone* and *microscope*. From the latter the prefix has come to mean "associated with the microscope", as in *microbiology, microphotography* and *microsurgery*. The *microdot, microfiche* and *microfilm* all depend on magnifying processes to yield the information stored on them; and through this **micro-** has come to refer generally to the vehicles on or in which vast amounts of data are stored, such as the *microchip* and the *microcomputer*. The last word is sometimes abbreviated to **micro**, and in informal usage at least, it stands in its own right as a word for "personal computer".

Micronesia See under **Polynesia**.

might or **could** See under **could**.

migrant or **immigrant** In Australia **migrant** is the standard term for someone who has migrated from another country to make a permanent home here. The word is enshrined in institutions such as the *Adult Migrant Education Service* (AMES).

In other parts of the world **migrant** connotes temporary rather than permanent residence in another country. It is applied to itinerant workers in *migrant labor*, and in references to *migrant workers in the Middle East*. An alternative term **immigrant** is therefore used for the permanent resident.

Australia does not play host to a mobile work force of the kind known elsewhere, and so there's no confusion if we refer to newly arrived permanent residents as **migrants**. But anyone who writes about them for readers in other parts of the English-speaking world would do well to use **immigrant** rather than **migrant**, to ensure being properly understood.

mileage or **milage** The first of these spellings is given preference in all modern dictionaries. The second is however a recognised alternative, and certainly the one we might expect by all the general spelling rules which apply to roots ending in *-e* (see further under **-age**). Perhaps **milage** will gradually gain ground in countries where the mile continues to be an official unit of distance, and the word is in regular use. But there's less chance in Australia since we switched to metric measurements, and the mile has only a residual role as a measure of distance. (See under **metrication**.)

Mileage itself has acquired a number of uses in motoring, where it stands broadly for the word "distance" or "performance over a distance". Yet as soon as we get specific about the distance involved, it's given in kilometres, as in:
What's the mileage to Adelaide? About 300 kilometres.
The word "kilometrage" has yet to be established, and in the meantime **mileage** lives out an active retirement. It still figures in casual idiom:
He gets a lot of mileage out of that story.

militate or **mitigate** Confusion between these two is a persistent malapropism of twentieth century English, with **mitigate** being used where it should be **militate**. **Militate** means "be a force", or "work", usually *against* something. The word is related to *military*, and once meant literally "serve as a soldier, go to war". Its current more metaphorical sense is shown in:
The fact that they are city people militates against their surviving on that desert island.
Instead of this, you may see (or hear):
"The fact that they are city people mitigates against their surviving ..."
It is an unfortunate misuse of **mitigate** which means "make less harsh". The word can be used in either a physical or figurative sense, as in:
The sun mitigated the effect of the cold wind.
The magistrate may mitigate the penalty for first offenders.

In some contexts **mitigate** means almost the opposite of **militate**—to soften rather than intensify an effect. Yet they get confused, probably because of uncertainty about the meaning of **mitigate**, which has no relatives among modern English words. (Perhaps *litigate* contributes to the confusion.) At any rate, misuse of **mitigate** is rather obvious because of the use of *against* following it, or just occasionally *for* or *in favor of*. **Mitigate** needs no particle after it, being a transitive verb. (See further under **transitive** and **intransitive**.)

millennium, millenarian or **millenary** The first word means essentially "a thousand years". But in Christian tradition the **millennium** was often used to connote the thousand year reign of Christ on earth, anticipated at the end of the Bible (Revelation 20:1–7). From this it has acquired the more general denotation of a future "golden age", in which every human ideal is realised. The latter meaning is at the heart of **millenarian**, both adjective and noun, which may be used, respectively, to describe anything relating to the **millennium**, and a believer in it. The word **millenary** can substitute for **millennium** as well as **millenarian**.

Note the single *n* in **millenarian** and **millenary**, both of which are based on the classical Latin adjective *millenarius*. **Millennium** with two *n*s is a neo-Latin formation dating from the seventeenth century, and formed from *mille* "a thousand" and *-ennium* meaning "a period of years" (cf. *biennium, triennium*). The spelling discrepancy has helped to foster *millenium*, which occurred in more than 25% of the instances of the word in the British *Guardian* newspaper in 1990. It is one of the best attested spelling variants in the files of both *Oxford* and *Webster's* dictionaries; and it appears in the headword list of several dictionaries, including two by Longman in 1978 and 1981, according to Kjellmer's research (1986). Other dictionaries do not yet recognise *millenium* as an alternative, though we might well ask why not? Etymology is of course with **millennium**, but it need not be regarded as the sole arbiter of correctness when the strength of analogy is with *millenium*. (Compare **memento**, **minuscule**.)

The plural of **millen(n)ium** can be either *millen(n)ia* or *millen(n)iums*. (See further under **-um**.)

milli- This prefix is derived from Latin *mille* "a thousand". In the metric system however it means "a thousandth part", as in *milligram, millimetre* and *millisecond*, and this very precise meaning is the one most widely known and used.

A different and rather less precise meaning is the one attached to **milli-** in biological words such as *millipede* and *millipore*, which refer to creatures with supposedly a thousand feet and a thousand pores. Alternative spellings *millepede* and *millepore* help to connect the words with *mille* "a thousand", rather than **milli-** "a thousandth part". There seems little point however, when the figure of a thousand is so wide of the mark: a *millepede* has up to 400 feet (200 pairs of legs) but nowhere near one thousand. The spelling *millipede* is probably helped by *centipede*, and is given preference over *millepede* in modern dictionaries, apart from the *Oxford Dictionary*, which prefers *millepede*.

milliard In Britain and elsewhere this term has been used to refer to "a thousand million", by those who wished to avoid using the term *billion* for this purpose. (They wanted to keep *billion* for "a million million".) However **milliard** has never had much currency, and the Australian Government *Style Manual* (1988) recommends firmly against it. The so-called "American" billion is now firmly established in Australia and even in Britain (see under **billion**), and the raison d'être for **milliard** is disappearing.

mimic For the spelling of this word when used as a verb, see **-c/-ck-**.

miner or **mina** See **myna**.

mini- This is very much a twentieth century prefix, believed to be an abbreviation of *miniature* (on which see below). Its earliest uses in USA in the 30s were in the naming of new and more movable or portable instruments, such as the *minipiano* and the *minicam(era)*. They were followed by the *minicar* (1945) and the *miniprinter* (1950). It was during the 60s however that the prefix "took off", and since then it's been used to name new vehicles (*minibus, minivan*), garments (*minicoat, miniskirt*) and sports (*minigolf*), as well as less tangible items such as the *minibudget* and the *miniseries*. New formations sometimes carry a hyphen which is quickly shed as the word becomes established.

Note the spelling of **miniature**. The *ia* suggests two syllables in the middle, but they are always pronounced as one. As often the spelling connects the word with its Latin antecedent *miniare* "paint red", which is connected to *minium* "red lead". The tiny decorations and illustrations in medieval manuscripts were often done with red ink, and from this we have derived the prime meaning for *miniature* nowadays, i.e. "very small scale (reproductions)".

Note also the spelling of **minuscule** "very small, diminutive". The normal pronunciation diverts us from the need for the first *u*—again a reminder of the word's origins and the Latin diminutive ending *-usculus* that's built into it. The lack of general knowledge of Latin combines with common pronunciation to produce the spelling *miniscule*, for which there are seven citations recorded since 1898 in the *Oxford Dictionary*. It still dubs that spelling "erroneous", whereas the major American dictionaries (*Webster's, Random House*) have it as an acceptable alternative. *Webster's English Usage* (1989) notes increasing use of it since the 1940s, in parallel with the growing use of *mini-* as a prefix. In the Australian ACE corpus *miniscule* is the only spelling to appear; and an independent search of Australian newspapers in 1990 showed the instances of *miniscule* outnumbering *minuscule* by a ratio of 4:1.

minimal or **minimum** Most of the time, these words simply complement each other: **minimal** is the adjective and **minimum** the noun, and it's a matter of grammar which you use to express "the least possible". Yet like many a noun,

minimum can be pressed into service as an adjective, and then it takes the place of **minimal**. Compare:

They got here in minimal time.

They got here in minimum time.

In such contexts, the two words are at most stylistic variants, with **minimal** having a slightly more literary flavor than **minimum**. Note however that **minimal** sometimes seems to have an evaluative cutting edge to it, which **minimum** as an adjective does not. Compare:

They gave minimum time to their patients.

They gave minimal time to their patients.

The first sentence seems to say that the amount of time given to patients was only as large as was absolutely necessary, whereas the second can also imply that this was negligible and reprehensible.

miniscule For the use of this spelling as a variant for **minuscule**, see under **mini-**.

minority This word is a slippery one, as when someone says:

The motion was lost by a minority of three.

Does this mean that out of say 25 people, only 3 voted for it? Or that the number of people voting for the motion was 3 less than the number who voted against it, so that the vote ran 11:14 against?

According to the second interpretation **minority** means "the shortfall between the votes for and against". In the first, **minority** just identifies the smaller set of voters, in contrast with the *majority*. This is certainly the meaning in:

A minority of members wanted more frequent meetings.

In phrases like this one, **minority** means "less than half", and so in a group of 25 could be any number from 12 down. The inherent vagueness in this use of **minority** makes some people qualify it, as in "a small minority" or "a large minority". Yet expressions like those are problematic in other ways: the first seems tautologous and the second contradictory.

Problems like these with **minority** (and *majority*) mean that it's best to paraphrase them whenever precision counts. For example:

The motion was lost by a vote of 11 to 14.

    (instead of "a minority of three")

Only about a third/quarter/fifth (etc.) of the members wanted ...

    (instead of "a small minority")

Just under half the members wanted more meetings ...

    (instead of "a large minority")

Note that the use of **minority** with noncomposite items, as in "a minority of her time" is sometimes challenged, echoing a reaction to the same kind of construction with *majority*. For a discussion of this, see under **majority**.

minus This mathematical word has been steadily acquiring more general uses, as a preposition, adjective and noun, but their status is not entirely clear. Some of these new uses are labeled as "colloquial" or "informal", while others are presented without comment.

Several dictionaries including *Webster's*, *Heritage* and *Chambers* attach the "informal" label to prepositional use of *minus*, as in:

He reappeared minus his tie.

The word undoubtedly draws attention to itself, in a way that "without" would not. Yet is it a matter of (in)formality, or that it's much less common as a preposition than "without"? The *Macquarie Dictionary* (1991) presents this prepositional use without any restrictive label, though it does label as "colloquial" the use of **minus** as an adjective meaning "lacking or absent", as in:

The profits were minus.

Other dictionaries apparently have no qualms about **minus** as an adjective when it means "negative", although it's unclear whether "negative" is understood mathematically or more generally as "lacking or absent".

Nonmathematical uses of **minus** as a noun are unproblematical. By now it's established as a general-purpose word, often coupled with *plus* as in:

The college had pluses and minuses for me.

Dictionaries express this meaning variously as "deficiency", "deficit" and "disadvantage", but without any restrictive labels.

minuscule For the variable spelling of this word, see under **mini-**. For the uses of **minuscule letters**, see **lower case**.

mis- This prefix, meaning "bad or badly", occurs in many an English verb and verbal noun, witness:

> *misadventure misalliance miscarry misconduct misdeed*
> *misdeliver misfit misgivings mishit mislay mislead mismanage*
> *mismatch misnomer misprint misrepresent misspell mistake*
> *mistrial misunderstand*

Mis- is actually a coalescence of prefixes from two different sources:

1 *mis-* which goes back to Old English, and is found in other Germanic languages (in modern German *miss-*)

2 *mes-* an early French prefix derived from Latin *minus* "less".

Both imply that a process has gone wrong, and the use of the older English *mis-* was reinforced by the arrival of French loanwords with *mes-* from the fourteenth century on. For a while the two prefixes were interchanged in a number of words, but by the seventeenth century **mis-** was the standard spelling for all. For Shakespeare and his contemporaries it was a very popular formative for new words.

Note that when words formed with **mis-** match those formed with *dis-* (as with *miscount/discount, misplace/displace*), they often contrast in meaning. The older *misinformation*, dating from the sixteenth century, contrasts with the twentieth century *disinformation*: incorrect information is supplied by accident in the first case, whereas in the second it's a deliberate strategy, as in counterespionage. Yet in the case of *mistrust/distrust* the meanings are quite similar (see **distrust**).

Compare **dis-**.

miscellanea This is a Latin plural (see **-a** section 2), literally "miscellaneous articles", and like *data* and *media* it raises questions of agreement in English. It normally refers to a literary collection and is not unnaturally given a singular pronoun and verb:

This miscellanea is a great advance on the other one ...

However the cognoscenti would construe the same sentence in the plural:

These miscellanea are a great advance on the others.

The first may seem awkward: the second pretentious. The word *miscellany* provides an escape route from both. It means the same and is unquestionably singular.

Note also the spelling of *miscellaneous*. The ending is *-eous* rather than *-ious* because of its connection with **miscellanea**. Other adjectives ending in *-eous* are discussed at **-ious**.

misinformation or **disinformation** See mis-.

Miss, Mrs or **Ms** Both **Miss** and **Mrs** are abbreviations of *Mistress*, which was once the general title for a woman. **Mrs** is the earlier abbreviation, which in the seventeenth and eighteenth century could be applied to any adult woman, irrespective of whether she was married or not. Only in the nineteenth century were **Mrs** and **Miss** used to identify different kinds of marital status. Dissatisfaction with the conspicuous **Miss/Mrs** distinction—as well as the spinsterly associations of **Miss** in some people's minds—has fostered the adoption of **Ms** by many women and institutions. Its present connotations of "liberated woman" and "career woman" will no doubt fade as older women make use of it. It certainly makes a neat counterpart to *Mr*. (See further under **forms of address**.)

A curiously academic objection is sometimes raised against **Ms**: that it can be mistaken for *MS* or *ms* (abbreviations for "manuscript"). The pedantic answer would be that the letters of those abbreviations normally match each other in either upper or lower case, whereas the female title has only an initial capital. The pragmatic answer is that **Ms** is almost always followed by a personal name (except as the title of a well-known magazine), and this serves to distinguish it from abbreviated references to a manuscript.

The plurals of **Mrs** and **Ms** are discussed under **plurals** section 3.

misspelled or **misspelt** See under -ed.

mistakable or **mistakeable** See under -eable.

mistrust or **distrust** See distrust.

mitigate or **militate** See militate.

mitre or **miter** See -re/-er.

mixed metaphors See under metaphor.

moccasin or **mocassin** The first spelling is the only one recognised in most dictionaries. The second is however recorded in *Webster's* and the *Oxford Dictionary* as an alternative, and quite a few of the *Oxford* citations show it, whether they refer to the shoe, or to the plant or animal which also embody the name. The spelling with one *c* seems to come closer to the original Indian word (its most obvious relatives are *mokussin*, in the Narragansett language, and *mohkisson* in Massachusetts). But like many a foreign word without relatives in English, its pattern of consonants gets varied. (See further under **single for double**.)

modality and **modal verbs** What is modality? It depends who you ask. Grammarians differ in their definitions of it, though most would agree that it's the factor which differentiates the two following sentences:
  The books are coming tomorrow.
  The books should come tomorrow.
In both sentences there are auxiliary verbs (*are/should*). But while the auxiliary in the first expresses purely grammatical things such as the verb's tense and aspect, the one in the second expresses something of the speaker's attitude to the fact being stated, her involvement in it and the degree of confidence she expects others to have in it. These extra dimensions of linguistic communication are what is now generally called **modality**, and **modal verbs** are a large subgroup of auxiliary verbs which express it. (For the connection between **modality** and **mood**, see under **mood**.)

Most **modal verbs** express more than one kind of modality, depending on the sentence they occur in and the broader context of communication: whether information is being exchanged, or whether people are formulating actions in words, such as making offers or issuing commands. The table on the next page shows the uses of the commonest *modals*. (There are periphrastic equivalents for some of them, e.g. *can/be able to*: see **auxiliaries**.)

The table represents uses of *modals* in main clauses: others can be found in subordinate clauses. The sequence of tenses in a sentence may dictate a slightly different choice (see under **sequence of tenses**). Compare: *I will come* with *I said I would come*.

Note that the choice of *modal verb* often varies according to whether the first, second or third person is involved. *Must* expresses inclination or obligation with the first person (as in *I must go soon*), and possibility, deduction, obligation or frequency with the third (as in *He must come* or *The sun must rise*). The relationship between those communicating can also affect the type or range of **modality** implicit in the expression. (See further under **can** or **may**.)

	can	could	may	might	must	shall	should	will	would
possibility									
weak	*	*	*	*			-		
moderate					-				+
strong						*		*	
deduction									
weak		*	+	*					
strong					*				
obligation									
weak							*		
moderate						+		+	
strong					*				
inclination									
weak			-						+
moderate						+		+	
strong					-				
permission	+	-	-	-					
ability	*	+							
frequency					-				-

The symbols * *major use*, + *secondary use*, - *occasional use* are estimates only of their relative frequency.

Modal verbs are fluid rather than fixed in meaning, and most have changed and extended their meanings over the centuries. Yet in their form they are more rigid than any other kind of verb. One form serves for all persons e.g. I/you/he *must*, and there is no regular adjustment for tense even though there were once present/past contrasts among them (as with *shall/should*, *will/would*). They have no infinitive forms.

In writing as well as speaking, the various shades of **modality** are enormously important. Speakers express and control relationships with each other through them; and writers use *modals* as way of fine-tuning the factuality and the force of the statements they make. *Modals* are often used to modify claims which could be challenged or prove difficult to substantiate, as in:

The number of applicants may go down with the recession.

Inexperienced writers sometimes rely too much on **modal verbs** to cover themselves. Yet whether they use the same *modal* repeatedly, or "juggle" the whole set of *modals* that express possibility, it becomes conspicuous—because the *modal* is always the first item in the verb phrase. If you need to be tentative and want to avoid "sticking your neck out", the stylistic strategy needs also to include *modal adverbs* expressing degrees of certainty (*likely, perhaps, possibly, probably* etc.) as well as *downtoners*. (See further under **hedge words**.)

Rewording the tentative statement is better still, so that the terms in which it's expressed are themselves appropriate and do not need to be toned down.

modeled or **modelled, modeling** or **modelling** The choice between these is discussed at **-l/-ll-**.

modifiers This term is used in two ways in English grammar:

1   to refer to whatever qualifies the head of a noun phrase, either as premodifier or postmodifier (see under **noun phrases**)
2   to refer to words or phrases that soften the impact of others, such as *rather*, *somewhat* or *a bit*. Some grammarians call them *downtoners*, though in this book we refer to them as **hedge words** (see under that heading). Compare **intensifiers**, words or phrases which reinforce or emphasise the force of others.

modus This Latin word meaning "way" is caught up in a number of phrases used in English. Two familiar examples are *modus operandi* "way of working or proceeding", and *modus vivendi* "way of life or living". Both also have specific meanings in law. A *modus operandi* is the characteristic way in which a criminal works; and *modus vivendi* is used of an interim working arrangement which precedes a legal settlement.

In logic the phrases *modus ponens* and *modus tollens* refer to two different kinds of reasoning. (See under **deduction**.)

Mohammed See Muhammad.

mold or **mould** See mould.

mollusc or **mollusk** Both spellings are recognised everywhere, but **mollusc** is the primary spelling in Australian and British English, and **mollusk** in American English. The spelling **mollusc** is matched by that of related adjectives such as *molluscan* and *molluscoid*, and is thus the more consistent one to deploy.

molt or **moult** See moult.

molten or **melted** See melted.

momento See under **memento**.

momentous or **momentary** These adjectives express very different meanings of the word *moment*. **Momentary** expresses the idea of a very short span of time, as in "a momentary lapse of dignity". **Momentous** picks up the idea of importance expressed in "an event of great moment", and is usually found in phrases such as "momentous event" or "a momentous occasion".

The adverb *momentarily* has several meanings, including:

• "for a brief span of time" *The car stopped momentarily*
• "with every moment" *Their excitement increased momentarily*
• "occurring at any moment" *This aircraft will be taking off momentarily*

The potential for ambiguity is obvious with such a pile-up of senses, and where precision counts some alternative is needed. The word *momently* is no help, having all three of those meanings in American English, and at least the first two in Australia according to the *Macquarie Dictionary*.

monarchal, monarchical, monarchic or **monarchial** Even republicans may need to distinguish between these adjectives, and to know that while **monarchal** means "relating to a/the monarch", **monarchical** and **monarchic** can express a connection with either monarch and/or the monarchy. Like many other *-ic/-ical* pairs, there's little to choose between them (see under **-ic/-ical**). **Monarchical** gets preferential treatment in most dictionaries however and is probably more common. **Monarchial** is a leftover variant of **monarchal**, which Fowler declared superfluous.

money, moneys or **monies** In ordinary usage **money** is a mass noun with a collective sense, and there's no need to pluralise it:

All the money they earned was pooled.

But in law and accounting, **money** is a countable noun which can be pluralised to express the idea of individual sums of money. (See further under **count nouns**.) For example:

The moneys derived from rents can be offset by the expenses of managing the flats.

The spelling **moneys** is given preference over **monies** in all dictionaries, and is in keeping with the usual *y/i* conventions (see **-y>-i-**). When **money** becomes a verb, the preferred spelling again is *moneyed*, not *monied*.

mongoose Should you ever encounter not one but two of these small ferret-like animals, native to India, the plural to use is *mongooses*. (Neither the animal nor the word has any connection with *goose*, so "mongeese" is unthinkable.) The word was borrowed from the Marathi language in western India; but the Marathi spelling *mangus* has been anglicised to clarify the pronunciation.

mono- This Greek prefix meaning "one or single" derived from loanwords such as *monochrome, monologue, monopoly* and *monotony*. New words formed with it are usually technical, though the items named may be familiar enough:

monofil monocle monohull monorail monoski monotype

Most other words formed with **mono-** are scholarly, like *monogamy, monograph, monolingual* and *monosyllabic*, or definitely scientific names for chemicals: *monoxide, monosodium* or for broad groups of animals and plants: *monotremes, monocotyledons*.

In strict scientific nomenclature the prefix **mono-** "one" is the counterpart of *di-* "two":

monocotyledon	*dicotyledon*
monoxide	*dioxide*

But elsewhere **mono-** complements *bi-*:

monocular	*binoculars*
monogamy	*bigamy*
monolingual	*bilingual*

Note that **mono-** can now combine with any kind of root, not just Greek ones. It therefore competes with the prefix **uni-** "one" (see further under that heading.)

monogram or **monograph** The first is a classical loanword of the seventeenth century meaning "single letter". It refers to the single figure made up of interwoven letters—usually a person's initials. *Monograms* may be printed as personal identification on stationery, or stitched on to garments.

Monograph is a nineteenth century formation from the same Greek roots as the other word, though it means a single piece of writing. It refers to a treatise on one particular subject or branch of it, which is published as a single volume. In both those respects the **monograph** contrasts with scholarly journals.

monologue or **soliloquy** Both these are a sustained utterance by a single speaker. But while a **soliloquy** is declaimed without anyone to respond (even if there's an audience to witness it), a **monologue** is uttered in the context of a larger dialogue. It does of course imply that the rules of turn-taking in conversation have been temporarily suspended.

For the choice between **monologue** and *monolog*, see **-gue/-g**.

monotransitive See under **transitive**.

mood In the grammars of Latin and Greek, **mood** referred to the different forms of the verb used according to whether a fact or hypothesis was being expressed. In traditional English grammar, the notion of **mood** was used to distinguish the indicative, subjunctive and imperative forms of verbs:

indicative	(making factual statements: *They are there*)
imperative	(issuing commands: *Be there*)
subjunctive	(expressing wishes or hypothetical statements:
	If only they were there …
	Were they there we would all feel easier.)

A few grammarians also include the *infinitive* among the moods of English (the infinitive verb is more or less distinct in form from the others, as in *to be or not to be*). And some would include the *interrogative* (where the verb phrase is inverted and therefore different: *Are they there?*).

Nowadays the usefulness of the notion of **mood** for English is seriously questioned. Except with *be*, the different forms of verbs do not correspond in a regular way with the expressive function of the clause/sentence. In fact the latter seems much more important in English grammar, and the set of *sentence functions* now usually recognised (in the *Introduction to the Grammar of English* and the *Comprehensive Grammar*) are:

declarative imperative interrogative exclamative

The meanings expressed through changing verb forms in classical languages are typically expressed through auxiliaries and modal verbs in English. Thus *modality* and *sentence functions* are more useful concepts for describing English grammar than **mood**.

(See further under **auxiliary verbs**, and **modality**.)

mora For the plural of this word, see **-a** section 1.

moratorium The plurals of this word are discussed at **-um**.

morphemes See under **morphology**.

morphine, morphia, laudanum, heroin or **opium** The soothing effects of the *opium poppy* have been known for thousands of years. It was prescribed by Greek and Roman physicians, and remained the most effective pain-reliever until the development of **morphine** in the early nineteenth century. **Laudanum** was an earlier medicinal preparation from opium, which owes its name to the Swiss physician Paracelsus (1493–1541). It was prepared as an alcohol solution and taken orally. **Morphine** is a chemical extract of **opium**, a crystalline alkaloid which is its most important narcotic; and **morphia** was an alternative name for it in the first century of its use. Both words had some currency, and the problems of morphine addiction could be called either *morphinomania* or *morphiomania*. However **morphine** seems to have had the edge, judging by the large number of derivatives from it, and it's the dominant form in the twentieth century.

Apart from their medicinal uses, **opium** and its relatives have long been misused as "pick-me-ups", and opium addiction is one of the recurring motifs of modern history both in the East and the West. **Opium, laudanum** and **morphine** were all available without doctor's prescription in nineteenth century Europe and America, and only in the twentieth century have governments legislated against it. But the illegal trade goes on. In its simple form, **opium** is still eaten or smoked in various parts of Asia. Its newest and most powerful form **heroin** ("the drug that makes you feel like a hero") was developed in pharmaceutical laboratories in the West, and is taken by intravenous injection. It has made "syringe" a notorious word. **Heroin** is the stimulus of crime and focus of internecine struggles between rival black marketeers. Whether declaring it illegal contributes to the problem, or keeps some rein on it, is an unsolved question.

morphology and **morphemes** The **morphology** of words is their form or structure, and the meaningful units of which they consist. The word *meaningful* has three such units or **morphemes**:

  mean + -ing + -ful

Morphemes may be roughly divided into the *free* and the *bound*, the first being independent units, able to stand without any attachments; whereas the second must be attached to a *free morpheme*. In the case of *meaningful*, *mean* is a free morpheme, and the other two are bound.

In English the various prefixes and suffixes are all bound **morphemes**, and they usually fit the definition just given. Apparent exceptions such as the prefix *ex-* and the suffix *-able* seem to be capable of standing alone, though it can be argued that they have somewhat different meanings when standing as words and as affixes, and so they are actually different **morphemes**.

More debatable is the question as to just how free some of the "free" morphemes are, when the basic stem to which suffixes are attached cannot itself stand alone. See for example in the word *driving* how the bound morpheme is *-ing*, which means *driv-* is the "free" one, even though it never stands alone in exactly that form. One way out of this dilemma is to regard *driv-* as a variant (or *visual allomorph*) of *drive*, which is unquestionably free.

mortgagor or **mortgager,** and **mortgagee** In legal contexts, **mortgagor** is the standard spelling and dictionaries all give it preference. **Mortgager** has however been in ordinary use since the seventeenth century, and is a much sounder spelling in terms of English spelling patterns (see under **-ce/-ge**). The *-or* ending is no doubt supported by the fact that it's first and foremost a legal word. (See further under **-er/-or**.)

When arranging the finance for a new home, some buyers are surprised to find that they are the **mortgagor** and the bank or building society is the **mortgagee**. The surprise probably has something to do with idea that the suffix *-ee* connotes someone who is on the receiving end of an action (as with *employee/employer*). In fact not all *-ee* words are passive expressions (see further under **-ee**).

How the word *mortgage* came to mean what it does is not at all clear, even when one knows that the first syllable is the Latin/French word for "dead" and the second means "pledge". The *Oxford Dictionary* offers its best help in a quotation from a seventeenth century lawyer, who explains that the property involved in a *mortgage* is a pledge which is "dead" to the provider of the mortgage if the owner repays the loan on time, and "dead" to the owner if he cannot. The **mortgagor** executes the "dead pledge" one way or the other.

mortise or **mortice** The first spelling has been in continuous use since this word came into English in the fifteenth century. **Mortise** is given preference in British as well as American dictionaries, and gets Fowler's backing. The *Macquarie Dictionary* (1991) gives equal weight to **mortice**, a spelling which first appears in the eighteenth century, and which is preferred in dictionaries of architecture and building. The spelling is perhaps influenced by other building terms such as *cornice* and *lattice*. Compare **vice** or **vise**.

Moslem See under **Muslim**.

mosquito For the plural of this word, see under **-o**.

most or **mostly** These two are not interchangeable, in spite of their similarity and the fact that both are adverbs. **Most** has two rather routine roles:
- in superlative constructions for the majority of adjectives with two or more syllables, such as *most vibrant* or *most beautiful*. (See **adjectives** section 2.)
- as an intensifier, where it substitutes for "very".

The latter use is the one exemplified in:
The doctor was most concerned that I should have a day off.

Compare with

The doctor was mostly concerned that I should have a day off.

As that second sentence shows, **mostly** has different meanings, including "chiefly, largely" and "for the most part".

Note that the use of **most** as a shortened form of "almost", as in *most everything* or *most everyone*, is gaining ground in Australia, but still has American overtones.

-most This Old English suffix means "in the extreme", but is only found in adjectives of location:

foremost hindmost innermost outermost topmost uppermost

and of direction:

easternmost northernmost southernmost westernmost

The suffix actually consists of two superlative elements from Old English: *-ma* and *-est*, the combination of which was later reinterpreted as **-most**. A comparative element has since been added in to some words, witness *innermost*, which has almost replaced the earlier *inmost*. *Utmost* with its counterpart in *uttermost* is another example of this phenomenon.

mot juste See under **bon mot**.

mother-in-law See in-laws.

motif or **motive** Either of these can be used if it refers to a dominant theme in literature or art, but only the second means the "goal or incentive which prompts a person's action".

The word derives from the Latin verb "move", and neither its spelling nor meaning are inclined to stay in place. It was borrowed into fourteenth century English from French as **motif**, meaning something like "that which creates a moving impression on the mind". In less than a century it was being respelled **motive** according to its Latin ancestor, and acquiring new meanings such as "argument" and "whatever spurs someone into action".

In French meanwhile it remained **motif**, and acquired the further meaning of "dominant artistic theme", which came into nineteenth century English as a fresh loanword. Quite soon however, it too could be spelled **motive**, though this remains the secondary spelling.

Note also the various ways of writing the related loanword *Leitmotiv* "leading theme", borrowed from German. While *Leitmotiv* is the regular German form, *Leitmotive* and *Leitmotif* also occurred in nineteenth century English, with an increasing tendency to drop the initial capital. The frenchified *leitmotif* is found in the majority of the *Oxford Dictionary*'s twentieth century citations, and is the preferred spelling in the *Random House Dictionary*. But *Webster's* and the *Macquarie Dictionary* (1991) give preference to the more Germanic *leitmotiv*.

Note that **motif** and *leitmotif* are both made plural simply by the addition of *s*. Not having an Anglo-Saxon history behind them, their final letter makes no change from *f* to *v* as with *leaf* etc. (See further under **-f/-v-**.)

motto For the plural of this word, see under **-o**.

mould or **mold** The first spelling **mould** is the standard one in Australia and Britain for all uses of this word, to mean "shape", "fungus" etc. It dates only from the sixteenth century, whereas **mold**, the standard spelling in the USA, goes back to Old English.
    The spelling of all derivatives of **mo(u)ld**, including *mo(u)ldboard*, *mo(u)lder* and *mo(u)ldy*, also depends on whether you are working within the imperial tradition (with *u*) or the American tradition (without *u*).

moult or **molt** Both are respellings of the medieval word *mout*. American English uses the sixteenth century **molt**, and British and Australian English use **moult**, first recorded in the seventeenth century. The word is believed to be related to the Latin root *mut-* "change", but etymology is overruled in both modern spellings.

mouse The plural of this is *mice* only if you're referring to rodents. For a certain computer accessory used to direct the cursor on screen, the plural is *mouses*.
    Note also that *mous(e)y* has been with us long enough to work without an *e*. (See **-y/-ey**.)

moustache, mustache *or* **mustachio** The first spelling is the standard one in Australia and Britain, and in the USA, according to *Webster's*. *Random House* however gives preference to the second. Both spellings reflect the French form of the word, whereas the third is a curious blend of the Italian *mustaccio* and the Spanish *mostacho*. It appears occasionally as an alternative to the other two, but is best known in the verbal adjective *mustachioed*.

mouthful The plural form of this word is discussed under **-ful**.

movable or **moveable** For general purposes, either spelling is available, and the *Macquarie Dictionary* (1991) gives equal status to the two. All dictionaries give priority to **movable**, and it is the more regular of the two (see **-eable**). But the spelling **moveable** is to be preferred in the context of law.

mowed or **mown** Both these serve as past participles for the verb *mow*. The *Macquarie Dictionary* (1991) gives preference to the older **mown**, while *Collins* and other dictionaries in Britain and the USA prefer **mowed**. **Mown** is a reminder that the verb was once "strong" or irregular, though it began to acquire regular parts (**mowed** for past tense and past participle) in the sixteenth century. The verb is still in transition. (See further under **irregular verbs**.)

Mr This has been used as a courtesy title for decades (cf. **Esq**). It lends dignity to the names of ordinary citizens, and in press reporting it is still conventional to preface the names of both famous and unknown people with **Mr** (or *Mrs/Ms*, as appropriate), unless they have some other title—or a claim to fame in the worlds of sport, entertainment or the arts. Adding **Mr** (and removing the first name) does little for the identity of Greg Norman (Mr Norman), Barry Humphries (Mr Humphries) or John Olsen (Mr Olsen). Historical figures are also exempted, as are children (for whom it would seem inappropriate). Those charged with criminal offences are a further category of exception, not felt to deserve any courtesy title: they are simply referred to by their surname.

For the use of **Mr** as a form of address in letter writing, see further under **forms of address**.

Mrs and **Miss** See Miss.

MS, ms and **Ms** The abbreviation for "manuscript" can be set either in full caps (**MS**) or all lower case (**ms**), though dictionaries give priority to the first. They give stops to both **MS.** and **ms.**, though this should depend on your policy for punctuating abbreviations—all, none, or only those in lower case. (See **abbreviations** section 1.) The plural forms are **MSS** and **mss**, with or without stops.

While **MS** and **ms** are the forms listed in standard dictionaries, **Ms** is also occasionally seen (for "manuscript"). Whether it represents an accident of typesetting or a decision of the editor is a further question. Set that way, the abbreviation for manuscript is identical with the modern title for a woman, though the likelihood of their being confused seems remote. (See further under **Miss, Mrs** or **Ms**.)

mucus or **mucous** The distinction is discussed under **-ous/-us**.

Muhammad, Mohammed or **Mahomet** These are the three most widely used spellings for the name of the founder of Islam, though there are others on record which vary the vowels, the use of double or single *m*, and the choice of *d* or *t* at the end. The variability of the vowels results from the fact that traditional Arabic script registered only the consonants of a word: and the vowels vary with the different forms of spoken modern Arabic which supplied them.

The earliest European spelling was **Mahomet**, used from the sixteenth century and still known through nineteenth century English literature. The form **Mohammed** gained currency in the seventeenth and eighteenth century, and is the primary spelling in most modern dictionaries. However **Muhammad** is felt to best represent the Classical Arabic form of the name, and it's the spelling given priority in *Random House*, *Webster's* and the second edition of the *Oxford Dictionary* (1989). It is better established in the USA than in Britain, according to corpus evidence, and the only one of the three to appear in the ACE corpus. However **Mohammed** is still used in the names of historical personages, such as *Mohammed II, Sultan of Turkey 1451–81*.

mulatto For the plural of this Spanish loanword, see under **-o**.

For a discussion of alternatives, see under **half-caste**.

multi- This prefix meaning "many" is derived from Latin loanwords such as *multifarious, multiply* and *multitude.* Since the nineteenth century it has helped to create various technical words, including:
> *multicellular multilaminate multimeter multipartite*

as well as ones which are part of our common vocabulary:
> *multicolored multicultural multifaceted multigrade*
> *multilateral multilingual multinational multimillionaire*
> *multiplex multipurpose multiracial multistorey*

A further development of the prefix can be seen in compound adjectives, such as *multi-handicapped* and *multi-tasking (abilities),* where **multi-** is an abbreviation of either *multiple* or the adverb *multiply.* The hyphen is a useful indicator of this extended meaning. Note that some dictionaries and writers are inclined to use hyphens in other words from the list above, though there seems little need for hyphenation.

multicultural See under **ethnic.**

mumps Though it looks like a plural word, it takes a singular verb. See under **agreement** section 3b.

Murri See under **Aboriginal.**

Muslim or **Moslem** The first spelling is the one preferred by English-speaking followers of Islam, and is the only correct one for the so-called *Black Muslims,* that is the "Nation of Islam" in USA. It is the form recommended by scholars as the best transliteration of the Classical Arabic. The *Macquarie Dictionary* (1991) and others published during the last decade recommend **Muslim,** whereas older dictionaries give **Moslem** as the primary spelling, and it has considerable currency still in journalism and popular usage. It remains the preferred spelling in the second edition of *Oxford Dictionary* (1989).

must See under **auxiliary verbs** and **modality.**

mustache or **moustache** See **moustache.**

mutatis mutandis Equivalent English for this compact Latin phrase is "changing those things which need to be changed". In effect it means that when a rule or principle from one case is being applied to another, the appropriate adjustments have been made.

mutual See **common** or **mutual.**

myall or **miall** These represent two words borrowed from the Aborigines, meaning:
> 1 a type of wattle tree whose fine-grained wood is used for carving **Myall** in this sense comes from the Kamilaroi people in northwestern NSW.

2 an Aborigine who lives in a traditional tribal way, not within European civilisation; or (as an adjective) "wild or uncivilised". It was borrowed from the Dharuk people of Port Jackson.

Both words could be spelled **miall** (or *myal, mial*) in the nineteenth century. The *Myall Lakes* involve the first sense of the word, according to *Placenames of Australia* (1973).

Myanmar See **Burma**.

myna, mynah, mina, minah or **miner** These five spellings have all been used to refer to two different kinds of bird, with much confusion of the two:

1 the native honey-eater, genus *Manorina*, whose members (*bell miner*, *yellow miner*, *noisy miner*) have in common a yellow bill and yellow legs. With black patches close to the eyes, they look rather like the archetypal coalminer, and this may have helped to give them the name **miner**.

2 the immigrant Indian starling *Acridotheras tristis*, a bird with brown body, yellow bill and yellow legs. Its Hindi name is *maina* "starling", usually spelled **myna** by Australian ornithologists (*Field Guide to Australian Birds* 1974, *Reader's Digest Australian Birds* 1976–7), though the *Australian National Dictionary* notes increasing general use of **mynah**. It also records earlier use of **mina** and **minah**. (No doubt the final *h* is the Indian touch, found also in *maharajah* and *verandah*.)

Their similar appearance has no doubt fueled the confusion over the names of the two birds: and the *Reader's Digest Australian Birds* notes **mynah** as an alternative to **miner** for the native bird, while also using the spelling as an occasional variant for **myna**, the immigrant bird. Both ornithology and general communication would be helped by using **miner** alone for the native bird, and reserving **myna(h)** for the immigrant.

myself This word is sometimes used as a rather self-conscious replacement for *me* or even *I*. The effect is not the one intended. (See under **me**.)

For emphatic use of **myself** to underscore a personal reference, see **self**.

mythical or **mythological** Both these adjectives derive from *myth*, but their implications are a little different. **Mythological** implies a connection with the body of myths, or study of them, as in "mythological elements in ancient history". **Mythical** can mean either "dealt with in a myth", or by extension "existing only in myth, i.e. fictional". In a sentence such as the following, either word would do:

Prometheus was a mythical/mythological king of Greece.

However only **mythical** could be used in:

He has a mythical Swiss bank account to cushion the takeover.

N

naive, naïve or **naïf** The second and third spellings (with diereses) are the masculine and feminine forms of this French loanword, though they make no gender distinction in English. Instead **naïve**, or rather naive (without a dieresis) is the spelling used in reference to men or women. Its use is fostered by the difficulty of producing a dieresis on many typewriters and wordprocessors, and it is given preference in the *Macquarie* and *Random House* dictionaries, though not in *Webster's* or the *Oxford Dictionary*. *Webster's English Usage* (1989) points to an increasing tendency to use **naïf** for the noun, a tendency which is confirmed by the second edition of the *Oxford Dictionary* (1989).

naivety or **naïveté** These two spellings represent the opposite ends of a scale from least to most French. At the points in between there are several combinations of the variable items, including forms with or without the dieresis, and with *é*, *e* or *y* as the last syllable.

As with *naive* (see above), the dieresis is generally disappearing, and the fully anglicised form **naivety** is recommended by the *Macquarie Dictionary* (1991). Fowler noted that it was already in use in the eighteenth century, but slow to catch on in Britain. The *Oxford*, *Webster's* and *Random House* dictionaries all have separate entries one after the other for the French and English spellings, perhaps to avoid having too large a cluster of variant spellings at one entry. The in-between forms (*naivety, naivete, naiveté*) have little to recommend them, and it seems sensible to use the fully anglicised form **naivety**—unless one's looking for the French effect, and can muster the necessary accents on the keyboard for **naïveté**.

named after or **for** In Australia and Britain one is **named after** someone. In American English the collocation is **named for**.

names What's in a name? The writing of *institutional names* is discussed under **capitals** (sections 1 and 3), and *geographical names* are examined under their own heading. This entry concentrates on *personal names*, which raise a number of points of style. Getting them right is often a matter of courtesy as well as diplomacy, for no-one is so aware of the mistreatment of a name as its owner. There are several aspects to consider.

1 *Order.* In western culture a person's given name comes first and so is their "first name". Asian names are very often ordered the other way, with the family name first and the given name(s) after it. For specific nationalities, see further under **first name** or **forename**. Note however that Asians when overseas sometimes invert the customary order of their names to comply with western practice. This will not be obvious with, say, a Japanese name unless you can pick Japanese given names. Note also that Spanish and Latin American names normally comprise three units: a given name, the family name (patronymic), and mother's family name. For men and unmarried children the names appear in that order, though after being introduced they drop the third and use the first two. Spanish women after marrying are known by four names: their given and family names, followed by *de* and their husband's two surnames. However once introduced they would be called by their husband's family name, like Australian married women. For more details see *Naming Systems of Ethnic Groups* (1990).

2 *Titles.* Most names are preceded by some sort of title. Those for a number of different nationalities are listed under **forms of address**. The Australian ones are familiar enough, but there are still some questions about how they combine with the rest of the name. The general principle is that the title is used in full if it's followed by the surname alone, as in:

  General Monash   Professor Waterhouse   Senator Button

The title may be abbreviated if followed by initials or a given name:

  Gen John Monash   Prof E.R. Waterhouse   Sen John Button

The title *Reverend* has been subject to special conventions of its own. According to the highest Anglican tradition, it must always be followed by initials or a given name, never just *Reverend Martin*. The convention is affirmed in the Australian Government *Style Manual* (1988), and it says that the sequences *Reverend Mr Martin* and *Reverend Dr Martin* are also to be avoided. The ABC style guide *Watch your language* (1992) agrees on the first point but not the second, and allows that titles such as *Dr* and *Mr* may well be used when the clergyman's name and initials are unknown. If we seek a third opinion from the *Right Word at the Right Time*, it agrees generally with the ABC guide, while noting that even the plain *Reverend Martin* would be acceptable in lower Protestant churches, and especially in the USA. In the USA itself we find the Chicago *Manual of Style* affirming the high church conventions, while *Webster's English Usage* comments that there is great variation—such that it becomes a matter of etiquette within individual churches rather than a common principle of style. Whatever conventions there may have been, there is no single "correct" way now.

  For the question of using stops in *Rev*, *Gen* and other abbreviated titles, see **abbreviations** section 1.

3 *Initials.* The practice of using initials to represent given names has been more common in Europe than in the USA or Australia. Various celebrated names, especially authors, are never given in any other form: *C.S. Lewis*, *G.B. Shaw*, *P.G. Wodehouse*. And in bibliographies and elsewhere nowadays, the use of initials only is well established. The Australian Government *Style Manual* (1988) recommends it, except where giving the full name makes for better recognition; and titles may also be entered for that reason. When initials appear in isolated references, they are normally still punctuated with stops; but stops are now used less often in lists printed in newspapers and journals and in official correspondence, and they're absent from the telephone directory. They are omitted in Vancouver-style bibliographies (see **bibliographies** section C). Unpunctuated initials still usually keep a space between each letter—though not in Vancouver style, or in naming public figures such as *JFK* and *FDR*. Note also that there should be no stop in *Harry S Truman*, because the *S* is simply a letter, not an abbreviated name. His parents wanted to represent a name belonging to each of his grandfathers (Solomon and Shippe).

For the convention of addressing a married woman by her husband's initials, see under **forms of address** section 2.

4 *Surnames*. Getting the surname right may require checking with *Who's Who*, a *Dictionary of Biography*, or the telephone directory. There are permutations and variants of most English surnames (e.g. *Mathews/Matthews, Philips/Phillips, White/Whyte*), apart from the rather fluid spelling of foreign names on the way to being anglicised. Following the initial capital there may be internal capitals in surnames beginning with **Fitz-** and **Mac** or **Mc** (see under those headings). Capitals are also an issue with the particles *da, de, van, von* etc., which begin numerous Italian, French, Dutch, German and other European names. (See **capitals** section 1.) Note also the use of space, and hyphens, in compound surnames such as *La Trobe* and *Lloyd-Jones*.

5 *Roman numerals*. Enumerators such as *III, IV, V* and the designation *Jnr* have been used in American families to differentiate older and younger bearers of the same name, as with *Joseph Kennedy Jnr, Joseph Kennedy III*. The original convention was for these designators to be updated once the first bearer of the name had died, so that *JK III* then became *JK Jnr* etc. But the convention has stopped with some celebrated figures such as *Adlai Stevenson III*, whose numeral was never updated. This monarchical use of Roman numerals is now widespread, according to the Chicago *Manual of Style*.

Nanking or **Nanjing** See under **China**.

narcissus The plural of this flower is often *narcissuses*, in spite of the number of "s"s. The English plural is given priority in the *Macquarie* and *Collins* dictionaries, as well as *Random House* and *Webster's*. But being a Latin loanword, its plural can also be *narcissi* (see further under **-us** section 1), and this is the preferred plural in the *Oxford Dictionary*.

narrative An ancient form of art and entertainment, **narrative** comes naturally to most of us when we have something to tell. The habit of recounting things in the order in which they happened, i.e. in chronological order, is what many people resort to in impromptu discussion, when they have to explain such things as how a meeting turned out, or what caused the accident. Making the order of a **narrative** match the order of happening is the simplest way for the speaker to relate the story, and for the listener to digest it—as long as there's time for the whole of it.

In documentary writing, **narrative** is definitely less satisfactory. Readers usually want to know more than what happened—to get a perspective on it, and some insights out of it. The writer's point of view comes through more clearly if only significant events are told, and this selection may be structured argumentatively rather than chronologically. (See further under **persuasion**.)

naturalist or **naturist** There's a dramatic difference between these two. The first is a student of nature and its flora and fauna, while the second is one who advocates or practises nudism.

naught or **nought** Both these mean "nothing", but in Australia and Britain they appear in quite different contexts. **Naught** mostly survives in phrases such as *come to naught*, *set at naught*, *all for naught*, which have a rather old-fashioned ring to them, especially the second and third. The word **nought** however still has some working life, as a reference to the number *0* in mathematics and elsewhere when numbers are being quoted (though *zero* is twenty times more frequent than **nought** in the Australian ACE corpus). The game of *noughts and crosses* also preserves the word.

Note that in American English, **naught** and **nought** are used interchangeably as variant spellings, and *noughts and crosses* is "tick-tack-toe".

The two words have converged from independent origins. **Naught** is a compound of *na* "no" + *wiht* "thing", and **nought** of *ne* "not" + *owiht* "anything". Yet each amounts to *nothing*, and nothingness seems indeed to be the imminent fate of both.

nauseous or **nauseated** According to older dictionaries, **nauseous** means "causing or engendering nausea", and **nauseated** "affected with nausea". However comments such as "I feel nauseous" (using the first word in the second sense) are often heard in Australia, and the usage is noted in the *Macquarie Dictionary* (1991), and in recent style manuals such as the *Right Word at the Right Time*. It is now the dominant sense, according to the evidence available to *Webster's English Usage* (1989), and has developed strongly in the USA since the 1940s—which may explain why there's no reference to it in Fowler.

Yet the original *Oxford Dictionary* has some intriguing seventeenth century citations of **nauseous**, used to mean "inclined to nausea" but labeled *obsolete*. We may wonder whether that label diverted researchers from updating the entry for the second edition. Is the current use of **nauseous** really a survival, or a revival?

NB These letters represent the Latin imperative *nota bene* "note well". Since its first appearance in seventeenth century scholarly writing, it has become one of our most familiar abbreviations. Its tone is almost confidential, and definitely

less formal than the word *Note* itself. It normally appears in capitals as the first item in a sentence, with the next word also capitalised:
  NB The keys are under the doormat.
Like other fully capitalised abbreviations, it appears these days without full stops. (See **abbreviations** section 1.)

-nce/-ncy Words which are identical but for these endings often seem to offer us a choice. Should it be *complacence* or *complacency, compliance* or *compliancy*? Some of the others pairs like this are:

brilliance/brilliancy	*competence/competency*
concomitance/concomitancy	*concurrence/concurrency*
consistence/consistency	*consonance/consonancy*
convergence/convergency	*conversance/conversancy*
insistence/insistency	*insurgence/insurgency*
lenience/leniency	*malignance/malignancy*
permanence/permanency	*persistence/persistency*
recalcitrance/recalcitrancy	*relevance/relevancy*

With *ascendance/ascendancy/ascendence/ascendency* there are four choices. (See further under **ascendant**.)

Many of these words embody abstractions which are on the margins of common usage, mostly invoked in formal and theoretical writing. One may have an old-fashioned ring to it, as with *brilliancy* and *consistence*, while the other *brilliance/consistency* is the standard word. As those examples show, it's impossible to predict which of the pair is likely to be the "ordinary" member.

The lack of clear distinction between the two endings is at least partly due to the fact that the abstract/concrete relationship between them is changing. Historically it was **-nce** which was the more concrete of the two, because it was the verbal noun, and the verb element can be seen and felt in some like *compliance* and *convergence* However many **-nce** words were formed in French from verbs which have not come into English. They therefore seem quite as abstract as those ending in **-ncy**, which represent Latin abstract nouns ending in *-ntia*, and express the state or quality of a related adjective.

In contemporary English, the **-ncy** word is often more specific than the **-nce** one. This shows up in the contrast between *emergence* and *emergency*, or between *dependence* and *dependency* (meaning "*dependent territory*"), and between *excellence* and (your) *excellency*. Other **-ncy** words with quite specific meanings are *constituency* and *vacancy*. When both **-nce** and **-ncy** words are current, it's the **-ncy** one which can become plural, as with *competence/ competencies, irrelevance/irrelevancies* and *insurgence/insurgencies*. To grammarians it's a sign that the **-ncy** word is a countable noun, while the **-nce** one is a mass noun. (See further under **count nouns**.) All this shows that the older distinction between the two groups is breaking down and being replaced by a fresh paradigm. We are caught between the two paradigms with the less common pairs.

ne plus ultra This Latin phrase means literally "no more beyond". It refers to the furthest point of achievement in anything, the acme of perfection. In ancient tradition it had a geographical meaning: "the furthest limits (of navigation)", which was the message inscribed on the Pillars of Hercules in the Straits of Gibraltar to discourage seamen from venturing beyond the safety of the Mediterranean. There's a play on both meanings in the *Plus ultra* on the Spanish royal coat of arms. This was Charles V's modification of the original phrase, amid the triumph of the discovery of America.

nebula For the plural of this word, see **-a** section 1.

necessities or **necessaries** Are they synonyms? Fowler believed so, and his point seems to be confirmed by dictionaries: among various definitions they do allow that both can mean "something necessary or indispensable". The first (**necessities**) is the more common of the two, judging by its greater frequency in contemporary English databases everywhere. It is also the one established in phrases such as the *necessities of life*. The **necessaries** seems less natural, perhaps because it's uncomfortable as an adjective which has been converted into a noun and then pluralised.

née This French word means literally "born", but in English it's always used to preface a woman's maiden name, as in *Thea Gregson nee Astley*. As in that case, the **née** usually follows the woman's married name. This use of **née** and the juxtaposition of the two surnames helps those who could only identify her by one of them. It is as close as Anglo-Saxons come to using two surnames, and then only for women. (Cf. the Spanish naming conventions discussed under **names** section 1.)

Note that **nee** often appears in English without its accent, but with proper names on either side it can hardly fail to be recognised.

need This verb works in three different ways in contemporary English: as a main verb, a quasi-modal auxiliary, and a catenative:

She needs a holiday.

She needn't take it now.

She doesn't need to take it before Christmas.

In the first sentence *needs* is a simple main verb, with an *s* ending for the third person singular present tense, and with its own object. In the second sentence **need** is a modal auxiliary with no *s* ending, and with a bare (*to*-less) infinitive to extend its meaning. Note also that the negative *n't* is attached directly to it—another feature of auxiliaries. The third sentence is a kind of compromise between the first two. It takes an infinitive with *to*, and the negative is formed in the normal way for main verbs, i.e. with the help of the verb *do* and the negative attached to it.

The use of **need** as a modal is probably not as common as it used to be, and research by Collins (1988) shows that it's less common in Australia and the USA than in Britain. Even there it's mostly confined to negative statements like the one above, or ones with negative implications embedded in words such as *hardly, only, scarcely.*

negatives In English, **negatives** may be expressed in several ways
- through whole words

not never	(adverbs)
no	(adjective)
none	(pronoun)
nobody no-one nothing	(nouns)

- through phrases embodying those words, such as
  not at all
  under no circumstances
  by no means
- through prefixes such as **a-, dis-, in-, non-** and **un-**, and the suffix **-less** (see under each of those headings)

Negative values are also implied in a number of other words, including *unless* (conjunction), *without* (preposition), *few, little* (adjectives/pronouns), and *barely, hardly, only, rarely, scarcely* and *seldom* (all adverbs).

Note that when a negative or quasi-negative adverb is the first word in a sentence or clause, the next item must be an auxiliary, followed by the subject:

Never would she believe that it was over.

Hardly had they arrived when the telephone rang.

Seldom did he speak of his former life.

This *negative inversion* also applies to adverbial phrases. (See further under **inversion**.)

1 *Communicating with* **negatives**. A single negative causes few problems. But when two or more are combined in the same sentence or clause it can make difficulties for the reader. This is the real problem with the so-called "double negative", though not the kind which has been the traditional target of criticism. (See further under **double negatives**.)

When formulating questions, even *single negatives* can complicate things unnecessarily and make it hard for anyone to know how to reply:

Were you not driving in excess of 140 kph?

Are you an unlicensed driver?

If you wanted to say (in answer to either question) that your behavior was perfectly legal, you would have to use two or three negatives:

No, I was not ...

No, I am not unlicensed ...

Removing the negative element from the original question helps to guarantee a more reliable answer.

2 *The scope of* **negatives**. A negative word has considerable reach both within its own clause and beyond it. When attached to a verb which expresses a mental process, it immediately affects the clause depending on it. In fact it's more idiomatic to say: *I don't think he speaks well* than *I think he doesn't speak well.*

Note also the way in which a negative can dominate a whole sentence and forge a cohesive link with the next sentence:

> *We didn't laugh because she fell into the water. The whole ceremony was so ridiculous that we were bursting at the seams …*

The scope of such a negative could however be limited by a strategically placed comma. With it, the meaning of the sentence changes dramatically:

> *We didn't laugh, because she fell into the water. She might have been crushed against the wharf …*

The extent of the negative is also the basis of choosing between *nor* and *or* later in a sentence. (See under **nor**.)

negligible or **negligent** Both these adjectives have a lot to do with putting things out of one's mind. **Negligible** is the one to apply to things which are so small that they can be discounted: *a negligible amount of makeup on her face.* **Negligent** is applied to the conduct of people who do not attend to things in the usual or proper way. The word embodies more or less criticism, depending on whether the word expresses legal sanctions or not. In *negligent driving* its censure is much heavier than in a *negligent attitude to the garden.* In general usage **negligent** sometimes seems to connote something as light as nonchalance—as if some forms of *negligence* are **negligible**. So if carelessness and failure to attend to things are really the issue, you may need to use *neglectful* rather then **negligent**.

Note that the word *negligee* (the slightest form of dress known to man or woman) embodies the same stem as **negligible** and **negligent**.

neighbor or **neighbour** See -or/-our.

neither This word plays several parts in English:
1 pronoun, as in *Neither of the two is perfect.*
2 determiner, as in *Neither player could serve reliably.*
3 conjunct, as in *They couldn't see straight. Neither could I.*
4 conjunction, as in *They didn't apologise, neither did they offer any explanation.*

As a determiner, conjunct, and conjunction, **neither** raises few problems. The only point to note when it's a conjunct or conjunction is that the verb comes immediately after it, displacing the subject of the clause. This is *negative inversion* (see under **inversion**.)

As a pronoun **neither** is often the focus of grammatical comment. When translated as ''not either'' it sounds like a singular pronoun and seems to require a singular verb—as it has in (1) above. Traditionally this has been regarded as correct. Yet when the phrase after **neither** ends in a plural noun, a plural verb is quite often used:

> *Neither of the films are what you'd call exciting.*

The plural verb is not surprising, seeing that **neither** can very well mean "not this one, nor that one" in such a context, and the sentence effectively reports on two things at once. The plural verb gives you a comprehensive statement while a singular verb in the same sentence seems to restrict its meaning. The frequent use of plural verbs with **neither** suggests it needs to be recognised as potentially either a singular or plural pronoun.

Neither with nor. The same questions of agreement come up when **neither** is paired up with *nor* as a correlative conjunction. Again the traditional view was that the following verb should be singular, and yet research shows that the use of a plural verb is common. Compare the effect of:

Neither director nor producer has much experience.
Neither director nor producer have much experience.

The singular verb seems to particularise while the plural one generalises. The use of a plural verb there is as natural as it would be in a positive statement:

Both director and producer have plenty of experience.

The plural verb is sometimes used as the way out of another dilemma with **neither**/*nor* constructions: what to do when the items paired are different grammatical persons, as in:

Neither John nor I ... ready to leave.

Some would argue that the verb should agree with the nearest person (in this case *I*), and so it should be *am*. Others would feel that here again the plural *are* seems quite natural. (Or could it be *is*?) There is no simple answer with that construction, and if you're not happy with any of them, it's best to recast the sentence using **neither** in a different way:

John isn't ready to leave, neither am I.

Note also that with any verb other than *be*, this problem fades away.

In formal writing, **neither** always combines with *nor* (and not *or*) in coordinated subjects like the ones in the sentences above. But in more informal usage, "neither John or I" is common enough. The use of *or* implies that the whole phrase is included in the scope of the first negative **neither**, and there's no need to reinforce it with *nor*. It also shows the general decline in the use of *nor*. (See further under **nor**.)

Note finally that the use of **neither** with more than two alternatives once raised eyebrows—because it was assumed that **neither** meant "not either one (of two)". Yet the use of **neither** with three alternatives is proverbial in *neither fish nor flesh nor fowl*. And there are examples of it from well-known modern writers in the *Right Word at the Right Time* and *Webster's English Usage*, showing that it is quite normal.

nem. con. This abbreviates the Latin phrase *nemine contradicente*, which means "with no-one speaking against (it)". When noted in the minutes of a meeting, it emphasises that all the votes registered were in favor of the motion. It does not preclude the possibility of abstentions, however, so that **nem. con.** does not necessarily mean a unanimous vote.

neo- Derived from Greek, this prefix means "new". It appeared first in the mid-nineteenth century, and gained popularity in both scholarly and general use.

In chemistry it has been used to name newly discovered forms of chemicals, such as *neodymium, neomycin* and *neoprene*; while in geology (and archeology) it marks the latter end of one of the classical periods, as in *Neocene, Neolithic* and *Neozoic*. In medicine **neo-** means "new or fresh" in *neonatal* and *neoplasm*.

In the humanities and in general usage, **neo-** helps to name new or recently revived practices and philosophies, especially those identified with a particular leader, thinker, group or style:

Neo-Darwinian Neo-Fascist Neo-Gothic Neo-Lamarckism Neo-Nazi

It can be attached in the same way to any proper name to create a nonce word, as in *neo-Thatcherism*, or to ordinary words, as in *neoclassical* and *neocolonial*. Its recent use to form *neophilia* "passion for things new" and *neophobia* "fear of things new" seems nicely ironic.

The setting of words with **neo-** is quite variable. Nonce words and those where the proper name is still crucial often capitalise **Neo** as well as the name, with a hyphen between them, as shown in all of those above. But established ones slowly advance from the hyphenated setting to a more integrated state, as with *Neo-Platonism* to *Neoplatonism* to *neoplatonism*. Dictionaries differ in their treatment of words in that group, though they usually concur about those formed with common word elements, which are integrated except when they contain a difficult sequence of vowels, as with *neo-impressionism*. Those in specialised fields such as chemistry and medicine are always fully integrated in lower case, while those in geology and archeology have a single capital.

-ness This Old English suffix forms abstract nouns out of adjectives, witness:

darkness freshness goodness kindness feebleness politeness tenderness usefulness

It takes verbal adjectives, either present or past participles in its stride:

contentedness drunkenness willingness

as well as compound adjectives:

kindheartedness levelheadedness longwindedness shortsightedness straightforwardness

and hyphenated compound adjectives:

matter-of-factness up-to-dateness

Note that adjectives with a final *y* normally change it to *i* before **-ness**, as with *prettiness, readiness* and *weariness*. The best known exception is *busyness* (from *busy*), where the *y* must remain so as to distinguish the word from *business*.

Because abstract nouns are so readily formed with **-ness**, there are numerous doublets with abstracts borrowed or made according to French or Latin patterns, ending in *-cy, -ion* and *-ty*:

abstractness/abstraction	*accurateness/accuracy*
considerateness/consideration	*crudeness/crudity*
enormousness/enormity	*falseness/falsity*

notoriousness/notoriety   *preciseness/precision*
sensitiveness/sensitivity   *tenseness/tension*
turgidness/turgidity   *vacuousness/vacuity*

The words formed with **-ness** always have a strong link with the adjective, whereas the other member of the pair has usually developed additional meanings. It means that there's room for both, though there may also be some confusion between them. (See further under **enormity** and **ingenuous**.)

net or **nett**   Dictionaries all give priority to **net** in uses such as *net weight, net income* and *net worth*, though the earlier spelling **nett** remains a recognised alternative. Both are in use in Australian English, but the instances of **net** ("remaining after all deductions") outnumbered **nett** by 23:7 in the ACE corpus.

Netherlands   This is the official name for what English-speaking people have long known as *Holland*. **Netherlands** means literally "low(-lying) lands", and much of the land was and is below sea level, continually threatened by flood tides until a protective wall of dikes was completed in the 1970s.

In earlier usage, the word **Netherlands** referred not only to Holland, but also to Belgium and Luxemburg. The British translated it as *Low Countries*, and have used that phrase since the sixteenth century to group the three countries together. But Belgium claimed its independence in 1830, and Luxemburg did the same in 1890, so the name **Netherlands** was left as the official name for Holland alone. (See further under **Holland**.)

In 1948 a fresh term *Benelux* was coined to refer to the three countries as a customs union, and this name is the one now used for the three as a unit within the European Community.

nett or **net**   See **net**.

neuralgia, neuritis or **neurosis**   All three are based on the Greek root *neur-* meaning "nerve" and connote problems with nerves. **Neuralgia** means literally "nerve pain", while **neuritis** is "inflammation of the nerve". However the two are usually distinguished in terms of the type of pain associated with each, **neuralgia** with sudden sharp pain along the course of the nerve, and **neuritis** with a more generalised and continuous pain. **Neurosis** involves emotional and psychological disturbance, often manifested in anxiety and obsessive behavior.

neuter   means literally "neither". For grammarians it means that a noun is neither masculine nor feminine, but a member of a third, catch-all class. In Latin **neuter** words were nonhuman and usually inanimate, but in German they are sometimes human, as with *Fräulein* "miss", *Mädchen* "girl" and other diminutives. (See further under **gender**.)

New Guinea   See **Papua New Guinea**.

New South Wales-person The name of Australia's premier state is somewhat cumbersome, and offers no easy way of referring to one of its residents. The *Australian National Dictionary* records *New South Waler*, *New South Welsher* and *New South Welshman*, but only the last is current, and its citations are mostly from cricket. We often make do with "someone from New South Wales", though perhaps it's time to offer a prize for something apt and better.

New Zealand The largest islands in the South Pacific were christened **New Zealand** by Captain Cook. There are now moves to replace that name with *Aotearoa*, a Maori word for the North Island meaning "land of the long white cloud". The new name has support in official government correspondence and in the media, but has yet to become well known outside New Zealand.

New Zealand English The vocabularies of New Zealand and Australian English have much in common, especially among colloquialisms. They share such words as:

> *barney bludger bluey compo crook digger drongo dunny fibro*
> *grog kero lolly possie razoo sheila sickie skite wowser*

Yet New Zealanders also have distinctive terms which are unfamiliar in Australia, such as *bach* "small weekender", *cadet* "jackaroo", *section* "block (of land)" and *tramping* "bushwalking". What New Zealand farmers call *aerial topdressing*, Australians call *cropdusting*. The largest distinctive element in their vocabulary is of course what they borrow from Maori languages—words which refer especially to native flora and fauna. They include words for local trees and shrubs, such as the *akeake* and the *kauri*, birds such as the *kakapo* and the *kakariki*, and the dangerous *katipo* (redback spider). Words associated with Maori culture, such as *haka*, *mana* and *poi* are known to some extent outside New Zealand. A small group of Australian Aboriginal words are used in New Zealand, including *willy-willy*, *yakka*, and *mai mai* (= *mia-mia*) used for a duckshooter's hide.

newspapers and **news reporting** No generalisation about **newspapers** could capture the wide range of writing in them. Their prose styles range from the clichéd to the creative and from sensation-seeking to cosy intimacy. They can be commonplace and pedestrian, or interesting and intelligent. The sheer variety of columns in any newspaper guarantees different styles. Along with the work-a-day reporting you get the argumentative thrust of editorials and the stimulating idiosyncrasies of the personal columns.

Those who criticise newspaper writing are usually working with generalisations which apply to a subgroup of tabloids. Yet one or two of our higher brow newspapers (the *West Australian* and the *Financial Review*) are tabloid-like in shape, and their reporting is like that of the "quality" broadsheet papers such as the *Age*, the *Australian*, the *Canberra Times* and the *Sydney*

Morning Herald. Not all broadsheet papers maintain a high standard of journalism, which again shows that one cannot generalise.

For particular aspects of **news reporting**, see under **clichés, essays, headline language** and **journalism**.

next or **this** The word **next** sometimes raises doubts when it's used to refer to dates in the future, as in *next Friday* or *next weekend*. In principle it means "nearest in time". But many people draw a distinction between **next** and **this**, using **this** to mean "during the current week" and **next** "in the week which has yet to begin". So on *Thursday* the "next weekend" would be the one in ten days time, and "this weekend" would be the one only two days away. Like the distinction between **this** and *that*, **this** is closer to the speaker/writer's standpoint, and *next* is further away. But it's always a point to check when making arrangements for "next weekend". By checking the actual dates of the weekend (3rd/4th or 10th/11th etc.), you'll discover whether the other person is mentally making use of both **next** and **this**, or just the first one.

nexus For the plural, see **-us** section 2.

nice The battle to defend the precise meaning of this word was lost some time ago, perhaps in Jane Austen's time when one of her characters in *Northanger Abbey* exclaims that *nice* "is a very nice word indeed! It does for everything". Barry Humphries made the same point when christening one of his shows "A Nice Night's Entertainment". Those who try to make **nice** mean "fine, discriminating" in phrases such as a *nice comment* or a *nice distinction* are likely to be misinterpreted by the majority of their audience. A paraphrase of some kind (perhaps using *discriminating*) is the most reliable way to ensure the point is communicated. Trying to defend that particular meaning of **nice** seems a little misguided anyway, given that the word has a long history of changing its meaning. Its original in Latin *nescius* meant "not knowing, unaware".

nil desperandum This Latin phrase rolls off the tongue with the advice "never despair". It was borrowed by seventeenth century Englishmen from Horace's *Odes* (I vii line 2), and has been uttered in much less literary contexts to encourage others to "keep their pecker up".

nil nisi bonum See **de mortuis**.

no This small word has considerable power as an absolute negative. It has several grammatical roles:
- determiner, as in *no bird sings*
- adverb, as in *no mean effort*
- interjection, as in *No, that's impossible*
- noun, as in *They would never take no for an answer*

Note that **no** has no quotation marks in that last sentence, nor would it in sentences where the **no** is part of an indirectly reported utterance:

She said no, she couldn't join them.

(For the scale from direct to indirect speech, see **direct speech**.)

Note also that when **no** is a noun meaning a "vote cast against a motion", its plural is *noes*.

no one See under **nobody**.

noblesse oblige This French phrase means literally "(one's) nobility obliges (one)" i.e. there are obligations and duties incumbent on those of noble rank. When first used in nineteenth century English, it was with the implication that the aristocracy should conduct themselves honorably and give generously. In the twentieth century it's used more widely, and said of other kinds of status and privilege that have duties attached to them.

nobody, no-one and **none** The first two words take singular verbs in agreement with them:

Nobody/no-one has arrived yet.

This is only natural, given the singular elements *-body* and *-one*. **None** works differently, with either singular or plural depending on the phrase that follows it. Compare:

None of the mixture is left.

None of the ingredients are expensive.

Pundits of the past would argue against the latter, yet the *Oxford Dictionary* notes that **none** as the plural of **no one** is commonly found with a plural verb. Fowler too comments that it is a mistake to suppose that it "must at all costs be followed by singular verbs".

The setting of **no-one** has been much debated. The *Oxford Dictionary* had it as two words, though Fowler in 1926 argued for the hyphenated version. Gowers reversed Fowler's recommendation in 1965, with the paradoxical comments that **no-one** "now represents the standard practice", yet **no one** "has more backing ... and is recommended". Presumably he was very conscious of Oxford University Press practice in this regard. Modern dictionaries and other publishers give **no-one** first preference, and the occasional use of *noone* (set solid) reminds us that the integration of the word could go still further.

nom de plume or **nom de guerre** These French phrases both refer to assumed names. The first is a "pen name", a phrase coined in English in the nineteenth century for the name assumed by an author to hide his or her identity. The second phrase is the one used by the French themselves, meaning literally "war name", and applicable to pseudonyms adopted for any strategic purpose, not just for getting one's books published.

Other kinds of pseudonyms identified in English are:

* *alias*—an assumed name, sometimes associated with criminal activities;
* *incognito*—a name assumed by a celebrity in order to avoid public attention;
* *aka* (also *known as*)—an alternative name to the one used in performing:
  Barry Humphries aka Edna Everage.

Note that *sobriquet* "nickname" can also be used to refer to an assumed name.

nominal In grammar **nominal** means "relating to the noun", and so *nominal phrase* is an alternative name for a **noun phrase** (see further under that heading.) A *nominal style* is one which relies heavily on nouns, especially abstract ones, and invests relatively little meaning in its verbs. They are typically *copular verbs* (especially parts of the verb *be*), which string the noun phrases together, but do not lend any dynamic to the message. (See further under **verbs**.)

The following sentence illustrates the *nominal style*:

Recent expansion of the company's offices in all capital cities requires the installation of new communication systems ...

The high proportion of nouns to verbs is obvious, and the only verb *requires* is itself rather abstract in its connotations. Compare a *verbal style* version of the same sentence:

The company has recently expanded its offices in all capital cities, which means that we must install new communication systems ...

The verbal style relies less on nouns generally, and replaces some of the abstract nouns with equivalent verbs. It is usually less impersonal and makes livelier reading.

To turn verbs (such as *expand, install*) into abstract nouns (*expansion, installation*) is to *nominalise* them. *Nominalisations* are one of the hallmarks of theoretical and official writing, and never reader-friendly if used continuously. Yet for the writer it's all too easy to acquire the **nominal** habit, and rely on one abstract noun after another linked with the verb *be*, to carry the message. Using a variety of verbs demands more versatility, and sharper thinking. It forces the writer to identify a suitable subject for each verb as well as its tense, aspect and modality.

Of course *nominalisations* have their place in documentary writing. But those who write either academic or institutional prose need to avoid becoming addicted to *nominalisations* and the *nominal style*. As always, it's important to control and vary one's style, and to make good use of both **nominal** *and* verbal styles.

nominative This is the grammatical name for the case of the subject of a clause. It was important in the grammar of ancient languages such as Greek and Latin, as well as Old Norse and Old English, where nouns acting as subjects had a distinctive form. In modern languages such as German, and in Aboriginal languages, the term **nominative** is used for the same reason. But in modern English there's no difference in the form of nouns according to whether they're the subject or the object of the clause—no external marking to show the **nominative** as opposed to the accusative case. Most of the English pronouns do however have different forms for subject and object, and the term **nominative** is used in *Introduction to the Grammar of English* to refer to *I, he, she* etc. However the *Comprehensive Grammar of English* prefers the term "subjective" (and "objective"), stressing the particular function of the word, rather than the different form. (See further under **cases**.)

non- Since the nineteenth century **non-** has become the most freely used negative prefix in English. Originally and for centuries it was used in law, in formations like *non-parole*, but it's now firmly embedded in everyday English. It is pressed into service in nonce words, apart from being the formative element in many established words. Dictionaries list only a quota of them.

The following list from the start of the alphabet will suffice to show that **non-** is most often used to form adjectives, though nouns can also be derived from them:

> *nonactive nonarrival nonbeliever nonclassifiable noncriminal*
> *non-English-speaking nonexistent nonfiction*

Many **non-** words come into being to show recognition of a problem, and raise hopes of a solution:

> *nondutiable nonnuclear nonsexist nontoxic*

Advertisers also find them useful for highlighting the virtues of their product. Witness *nonskid tyres, nonslip soles* and *nonstop entertainment.*

1 *Should **non-** words be hyphenated?* Dictionaries agree on one point: that **non-** words formed with a proper name e.g. *non-European* must have a hyphen, in keeping with a general rule of editing (see **hyphen** section 1c). But for the rest of the **non-** words, the dictionary may give hyphens to all or none of them: the *Oxford Dictionary* does the first, while *Random House* and *Webster's* do the second. The difference is in keeping with their general policy on hyphens. The *Macquarie Dictionary* (1991) is somewhere in between, removing hyphens from many **non-** words, but keeping them in those which might otherwise be inscrutable. That is the real issue, although dictionaries cannot answer it for all contexts, and it's up to writers to decide.

2 Non- *and other negative prefixes.* Words prefixed with **non-** are particularly useful for drawing attention to the word they're coupled with, and expressing its exact opposite. No doubt this is why new **non-** words are sometimes created alongside older negative words, whose meanings have diverged from being a strict opposite of the base word. There is therefore a use for both *nonappearance* and *disappearance*, for *nonedible* and *inedible*, for *nonproductive* and *unproductive*. The difference is perhaps clearest when we compare *non-Australian* or *non-American* with *un-Australian* or *un-American*. The words with **non-** simply denote the fact that something/someone does not originate in Australia or the USA. The words with *un-* have a range of emotional connotations, suggesting alien values, loyalties and cultural practices from which "true" Australians/Americans would distance themselves. (History has shown how dangerous the latter words can be, with the persecution of supposedly *un-American* activities by McCarthyist forces in the USA in the 1950s.) Words with **non-** are normally more neutral and specific—more literal in meaning—than their counterparts with any of the other negative prefixes.

non compos mentis This Latin phrase means "not of sound mind". Cicero used it in one of his famous court cases (*In Pisonem* xx 48), though its use in medieval law probably accounts for its currency in modern English. In legal and formal English it still means "mentally incapable"; but when shortened to *non compos* in colloquial usage it can simply mean "vague, distrait", or even "in an alcoholic stupor".

non sequitur In Latin this means "it doesn't follow". Used in analysing argument, it means there's a break in logic from the previous sentence or proposition. It may occur in the output of a single speaker/writer, especially one who is keen to express a conviction without too many preliminaries. For example:

> *Research shows that children who have been taught English grammar do not write better than those who have not. Lesson time would be better spent on other things such as social studies ...*

The second statement shortcircuits the first, not pausing to see what its implications might be. (Is grammar of value only as a means to writing? What things should be taught by direct and indirect methods?) Instead it introduces a new assertion. In the rush of argument the missing link(s) can unfortunately— or deliberately—be overlooked.

The same problem can easily occur in dialogue, as people debate ideas on the run. The term **non sequitur** can then be applied to a false or inappropriate inference drawn by one person from what the other has just said.

nonce words A *nonce word* is one coined on the spur of the moment. It works in its context but may never be used again. Thea Astley's use of "dactylled" roofs in North Queensland (presumably a reference to the particular pattern of corrugation in them) is an example. Strictly speaking a **nonce word** is only uttered once, though ones which appear in print have some chance of gaining currency—and ceasing to be **nonce words**. The English term **nonce word** corresponds to what classical scholars called a *hapax legomenon*, a Greek phrase meaning "something said only once" (*hapax* for short). They used it to refer to words or a phrase for which there is only one citation in a given author, or literature.

none See under **nobody**.

nonfinite clauses This term has been used by modern English grammarians for the various structures which express the same kind of information as a subordinate clause, but do not have all its regular components. Compare:

> He asked if he could come to the meeting.
> He asked *to come to the meeting.*

The second sentence is similar in meaning, with the point of the *if-* clause expressed through a nonfinite clause (italicised), with a nonfinite form of the verb (in this case, the infinitive). Other types of **nonfinite clause** centre on participles, past or present:

Leaving early we miss out on the details.

The new recruits, *bored by the formalities*, had stopped listening.

Note that **nonfinite clauses** do not usually have their own subject, but borrow it from the adjacent main clause. The rather uncommon cases in which they do express their subject are those where the subject of the **nonfinite clause** differs from that of the main clause, as in infinitive clauses with *for*:

His intention was *for you to be there*.

And also in certain past participle clauses:

That settled they became good friends.

Nonfinite clauses work as alternatives to all kinds of subordinate clauses, noun, adjectival/relative and adverbial. Stylistically they make for compactness of expression.

nonfinite verbs is a term used in modern English grammar to cover parts of the verb such as the participles and the infinitive, which do not by themselves constitute a finite verb. (See further under **verbs**.)

nonplussed or **nonplused** All dictionaries give priority to the spelling with two *s*s, and it's quite regular for the pronunciation which stresses the second syllable. (See further under **doubling of final consonant**.) The alternative pronunciation which stresses the first syllable is recognised in the major American dictionaries, along with the corresponding spelling with one *s*.

nonrestrictive This word usually comes up in the discussion of *nonrestrictive relative clauses*. (See under **relative clauses** section 4.)

nonsexist language The feminist movement has undoubtedly succeeded in making people more aware of how sexism can be built into language. Most people now think twice before talking about *manning* the switchboard or *mastering* the computer, and reflect on the implications of saying that someone is *bitching* about their colleagues or that the boss is *an old woman*. Expressions like those, which could suggest that it takes men to do the job properly, and that negative human behavior is associated with women, are unsympathetic to half the human race. The male users of such expressions may have nothing against women, yet the terms in which they project their ideas suggest stereotypes which either make women invisible, or at worst seem to trivialise and denigrate them. The use of sexist language by men or women helps to preserve its negative stereotypes, and social values which disadvantage women generally—just as cigarette smoking creates an atmosphere which endangers even nonsmokers.

Having identified the problem, feminist thinkers have also worked to provide replacements for sexist or potentially sexist elements of language. Their targets include:

1 generic use of the pronoun *he* when the reference is to both men and women (see under **he** and/or **she**)

2 uses of *man* in compounds and idioms (see under **man**)

3 reliance on female suffixes, especially *-ess* (see **-ess**).

They also urge the use of nonsexist job titles, ones which emphasise the job itself rather than the gender of the incumbent. A further area of action is in the adoption of *nonsexist conventions* in letter writing, in the standard salutations and modes of address. (See **forms of address** section 2.)

Many publishers and public institutions have endorsed codes of **nonsexist language**, and have manuals or style guides setting out their preferred alternatives, including those mentioned above. (See also **-person** and **spouse equivalent**.)

non-U See under **U** and **non-U**.

no-one See under **nobody**.

nor or **or** The choice between these is a matter of style and emphasis rather than fixed rules. Compare:

> *The museum will not be open on Sundays or public holidays.*
> *The museum will not be open on Sundays nor on public holidays.*

The first sentence can be read simply as a single statement. The second is definitely divided by the **nor**, which stresses the force of the negative on the latter part of the sentence. To some readers it may seem like "overkill", because the negation in *not* carries over to "Sundays" and "public holidays". To others it makes a more elegant sentence with its parallel phrases. It's a question of taste—and the context in which it is to appear … Does that call for functional simplicity, or something more artful?

Fowler attempted to formulate rules as to when **nor** was required, and concluded that it was firstly a question of whether the negative was expressed in *not* (rather than *nothing, nobody, none*); and then whether any second verb was prefaced by an auxiliary or not. According to his "rules", **nor** and **or** would be used as follows:

> *They could not have seen the play or read the review.*
> (the *not* goes with the first auxiliary, and is understood together with it before the second verb)
> *They could not have seen the play nor have read the review.*
> (the effect of the *not* is limited by the second auxiliary, so the negative must be restated with **nor**)
> *There was nothing to applaud in the play nor to commend in the review.*
> (the negative in *nothing* is confined to its own clause, so **nor** is needed to restate the negative for the second clause)

However even in the second and third sentences, you may feel that **or** would do, and that **nor** is just a stylistic device to draw attention to what follows. In fact the negative carries over into any clause or phrase with which it is coordinated, and has considerable "scope". (See further under **negatives**.)

For the use of **nor** after *neither*, see under **neither**.

normalcy or **normality** Both these make their first appearance in the mid-nineteenth century, though **normality** seems to have quickly become more common and to have developed more applications. In terms of word structure it's more regular, there being many similar nouns ending in *-ity* made out of adjectives ending in *l*, whereas there are none like **normalcy**. (The nearest analogue is *colonelcy* based on a *noun* ending in *l*.) On both counts then **normalcy** is an unusual word, and perhaps that was why President Harding used it in a famous speech of 1920. Unfortunately his use of it drew censorious comment from across the Atlantic, which still echoes in the *Chambers* dictionary note that it is an "ill-formed word". But the *Oxford Dictionary* has citations both before and after Harding, from both British and American authors. *Webster's* and *Random House* dictionaries enter it without any usage comment.

north, northern and **northerly** For Australians, both **north** and **northern** refer to a location nearer the Equator—whether it is the north side of Sydney Harbor, the northern beaches, or north(ern) Queensland. Before it existed as a state in its own right, Queensland was sometimes referred to as the "northern squatting district of New South Wales". The northern face of a house is its sunniest aspect, just as the south-facing side is for Britons or North Americans. **Northerly** can also be used to express the idea of "facing north or directed towards the north". Note however that when **northerly** is combined with *wind* (or breeze, gale, airstream etc.), it means "from the north".

When capitalised, the **North** in Australia can to refer to the broad band of thinly populated country in northern West Australia, Northern Territory and Queensland—the relatively untouched deserts and scrub plains and tropical forests which are the antithesis of urban Australia. Apart from its wilderness associations, the term *North* or rather *Deep North* (modeled on the American *Deep South*) has occasionally been used with social connotations, especially by the *Bulletin* in the 1970s and 80s, to refer to the more conservative aspects of Queensland culture.

Further afield, the phrase "Near North" has occasionally been used by Australians to refer to the *Far East* (see under **east**). In broader political and geographical terms **North** can refer to continental North America, as opposed to the Caribbean nations, hence the *North-South Center* in Miami.

nostrums In spite of its Latin origins, the plural of this word is always **nostrums**. It has long smacked of home remedies and quack medicines, and the eighteenth century compound *nostrum-monger* suggests that even then **nostrums** were associated more with the traveling salesman than with reputable pharmacy. With scant connections with science, and no antecedent noun in Latin (there it was an adjective), the word has no plural in *-a* (*nostra*). (See further under **-um**.)

nosy or **nosey** See **-y/-ey**.

not Although this is a simple negative word, it can bring ambiguity to the sentence which carries it. Its position in a sentence affects its meaning, and needs to be checked. In the following statement the position of **not** leaves the meaning in doubt: *All men are certainly not equal.* Does this mean that "all men are unequal", or that "not all men are equal"? In other words it's unclear which part of the sentence is covered by the negative—or what its scope is. (See further under **negatives.**)

When **not** or its abbreviation *n't* is used in a question, there may be no negation in it at all. *Didn't you write to them last week?* effectively asks the same question as *Did you write to them last week?* In such questions the **not/ n't** works simply as a kind of question tag, a telescoped version of *You did write to them last week, didn't you?* Tag questions are discussed further in the entry on **questions.**

not only ... but also These compound conjunctions must be used in tandem with each other. The first anticipates the second, and the second latches on to the first. The other important point is to make sure the words or clauses linked by them are in parallel—that they match up in the order of their constituents and should have some in common. The following three sentences all have problems in these respects:

- *They not only made $600 from the garage sale, but also neighbors came and introduced themselves.* (no common elements)
- *They made not only $600 from the garage sale, but also cleared the accumulated junk.* (*not only* comes after its verb)
  Try *They not only made ...* to match *but also* before the verb *cleared.* The two verbs then work in parallel.
- *They not only made $600 from the garage sale, but also were making friends in the neighborhood.* (Here there's a common verb, but the verb forms are not exactly matched, one being simple, the other a compound verb.)
  A simple solution would be: *They made not only $600 ... but also some new friends in the neighborhood.*

In this final version the two objects work in parallel; and *not only ... but also* have their full stylistic effect.

not un-/in- Because they are double negatives, constructions such as the following bear thinking about:

> *not unprecedented not unwelcome not indifferent not impossible*

Examples like those are so well established as to be almost clichés, and so they're less demanding of the reader than those which are freshly coined. The reader has to work harder with ones such as *not unoriginal* or *not incompetent,* to decide where the emphasis lies in them. Instead of negating the other word, **not** modulates its force; and so *not unoriginal* means "having some originality" rather than "most original". Occasional expressions like this can contribute to the subtlety of an analysis, though as already indicated, they present some obstacles for the reader, and look mannered if used too often. (See further under **double negatives**.)

nothing By itself this is a singular word, and when followed directly by a verb it's natural that it too should be singular:

Nothing is closer to my heart than that.

But when **nothing** is separated from its verb, and especially when it is followed by a phrase ending in a plural noun, a plural verb is common enough:

Nothing except a few minor criticisms were offered.

As with *none*, the number of the nearest noun tends to decide whether the verb is singular or plural. (See further under **nobody**.)

nought or **naught** See **naught**.

noun clauses A *noun clause* works as either the subject, object or complement of a main clause:

What they wanted was a lift to the station. (subject)

A lift to the station was *what they wanted*. (complement)

They hoped *that we could fit them in*. (object)

The first and second types are often used to foreground part of a simple statement: compare *They wanted a lift to the station*. (See further under **cleft sentences**.) However the third type is by far the most common, where the noun clause is found after a verb which expresses a mental activity, such as thinking, feeling, knowing or saying.

Noun clauses which detail a mental activity may be introduced by one of the *wh-words* (what, who, which etc.) or by *that*, or by nothing at all. For example:

He knows *what they're after*.

I believe *that he's our man*.

They were convinced *the group would come*.

The suppression of *that* is common in informal writing, and reflects a very common habit of speech. Just occasionally it leads to ambiguity in writing, because of the absence of intonation to show where the noun clause begins. See further under **zero conjunction**.

noun phrases These are the expanding suitcases of English grammar. In their most basic form they consist of a single word, such as a pronoun or proper name, but more often they consist of an ordinary noun as head with other modifying words on either side of it. The following **noun phrase** shows how the basic head can be embellished:

that very fine old Greek lady *from an outer suburb of Melbourne*
(premodifiers)   head   (postmodifiers)

As the example shows, the **noun phrase** is premodified by determiners and adjectives (one or more). General enumerators like *all* or *some* come before the determiners: *all those very fine* ..., while cardinal numbers come between the determiner and the adjectives: *those two very fine old Greek* ... When there are two or more adjectives, their order is from least to most specific, so that the most definitive one (*Greek*) is closest to the head, and any evaluative ones (*fine*) are further away. Adverbs (such as *very*) come in front of the adjective which they modify. The example also shows how postmodification is usually a matter of one prepositional phrase after another. Just occasionally an adjective comes immediately after the head, as in ... *old Greek lady resident in an outer suburb* ... The postmodification may also involve a relative clause: ... *old lady who was from an outer suburb* ..., but it often consists of prepositional phrases.

Noun phrases are all too easily extended with another and yet another phrase, and this is an unfortunate feature of some of the least readable prose styles. Sentences like the following need to have their long **noun phrases** recast as clauses:

The three newly appointed members of the interim committee for forward planning of the municipality have declared their support for our campaign against the building of freeways through bushland reserves.

See further under **nominal**.

nouns The words that express the tangible and visible things of our experience, such as *sand*, *cliffs* and *sea*, are all **nouns**, as are those expressing intangibles such as *love*, *humor* and *idealism*. The first type have traditionally been called *concrete nouns* and the second *abstract*, though there's no hard and fast boundary between the two. They represent opposite ends of a scale from very generalised concepts to highly specific things. Even among concrete and specific words, we have ones which are more general than others: witness the nouns *cat*, *siamese* and *seal-point*. (See further under **abstract nouns**.)

The distinction between *common* and *proper nouns* is also a matter of distinguishing between general and very particular words. *Proper nouns* or names are so particular and specific that they refer to single individuals. They purport to be unique names, even if there are a number of *John Hardy*s in any metropolis. (See further under **proper names**.)

Common nouns can be distinguished grammatically in terms of whether they refer to countable things, as do *cliffs* and *cats*, or to noncountable and unbounded things such as *sand*, *silver* and *idealism*. The first group are *count nouns* which regularly have plural forms, whereas the second, often known as *mass nouns*, are only pluralised under special circumstances. (See further under **count nouns**.)

Different again are the nouns which refer to groups or bodies of people or animals, such as *team*, *orchestra* and *mob*, sometimes called *collective nouns*, or "nouns of multitude" by Fowler. Once again they need to be identified for grammatical reasons, and for the questions of agreement which they raise. (See further under **agreement** and **collective nouns**.)

nouveau riche This French phrase, meaning "new rich", was borrowed into Victorian England, when it seemed important to know who belonged to the hereditary aristocracy, and who happened to be just as rich but to lack the pedigree. Those who regarded themselves as having "class" applied the phrase to individuals who (in spite of their wealth) did not. Yet while **nouveau riche** implies an aristocratic disquiet that wealth and nobility might not be indissolubly linked, it is not explicitly derogatory like *parvenu* "upstart". Compare also **yuppie**.

Note that the plural of **nouveau riche** (when you want to refer to more than one person of that kind) is *nouveaux riches.*

nouvelle cuisine This is the "new (style of) cooking" emanating from France, which emphasises the artistic appearance of food on the plate, and relies less for its appeal on richness and quantity. The chef no longer stakes his reputation on generous use of brandy and cream. In fact **nouvelle cuisine** aligns itself with concerns for one's diet, and is often a synonym for *cuisine minceur* "slim/thin (style of) cooking". It is certainly designed to satisfy the gourmet rather than the gourmand, in the traditional senses of those words (see **gourmet** or **gourmand**). Both **nouvelle cuisine** and *cuisine minceur* qualify as *haute cuisine*. (See further under **haute**.)

nova The plural of this word is discussed under **-a**.

nucleus For the plural, see **-us**.

null hypothesis The **null hypothesis** is a tool of statistical reasoning. It formulates the negative counterpart to the *experimental hypothesis* which proposes that there is a significant correlation between two nominated variables in given populations. The **null hypothesis** states that there's no significant correlation between them, and that any suspected or apparent connection is a matter of chance (or else due to skewed sampling or some other flaw in the experiment). If however the statistics show only a very small probability that the connection is due to chance, the **null hypothesis** may be rejected, and the *experimental* (or *alternative*) *hypothesis* affirmed.

For more about deductive reasoning, see **deduction**.

number To a grammarian, **number** is the concept lying above and beyond singular and plural—the idea that language may refer to one thing or to more than one, and that this distinction is shown in the form of words. In English it's most obvious with nouns, almost all of which add an extra suffix or change in some way for the plural (see further under **plurals**). Apart from being expressed in nouns, **number** also affects the English pronoun system, in the distinction between *I* and *we*, etc., and in the present tense of most verbs (not the modals). The present singular form for the third person, e.g. *goes* contrasts with the plural *go*, and in this case the singular adds the suffix. (See further under **-s**.)

Apart from its effect on the forms of words, **number** is of some importance in English syntax. Within the same clause, verbs must agree in number with whatever noun or pronoun is their subject, and pronouns should agree with the number of their antecedent. (See further under **agreement** sections 1 and 2.)

Number *problems.* The expression of number through the apostrophe is another small point on which writers sometimes have to pause. A choice between singular (apostrophe before the possessive *s*) and plural (apostrophe after the *s*) has to be made in cases like the following:

The students all read each others *essays.*

Married women sometimes use their husbands *initials.*

The witch(e)s hats are removed each evening.

In the first sentence, the presence of *each* seems to demand the singular *other's* while *all* and *essays* suggests the plural form (see further under **other's** or **others'**). In the second *their* suggests plural, yet it seems best to use the singular *husband's* to avoid suggestions of polygamy.

In the third sentence there are three options to consider. The plurality of the object *hats* encourages the use of *witches'*, and yet only a single, archetypal witch is involved. With *witch's* we seem to have a generic phrase (cf. *tailor's chalk*), except that it goes awkwardly with the plural *hats*. Neater than either would be to omit the apostrophe altogether: *witches hats*, on the analogy of *visitors guide* etc. (See further under **apostrophes**.)

number of Should the verb after **number of** be singular or plural? The decision rests on whether *the* or *a* precedes number:

The number of visitors is more than we expected. (singular)

A number of visitors are expected tomorrow. (plural)

The difference in grammatical terms is that **number** is the head of the subject phrase in the first sentence, but part of a premodifying enumerator in the second. (See further under **noun phrases**.)

number prefixes English makes use of a full set of number prefixes derived from Latin, and a less complete one from Greek:

Latin		Greek
uni-	"one"	*mono-*
bi-	"two"	*di-*
tri-	"three"	
quadr-	"four"	*tetra-*
quin-	"five"	*penta-*
sex-	"six"	*hexa-*
sept-	"seven"	*hepta-*
oct-	"eight"	*okta-*
nona-	"nine"	
deca-	"ten"	*deka-*
cent-	"hundred"	
milli-	"thousand"	*kilo-*
	"million"	*mega-*

The metric system borrows from both sets: see the list given in Appendix IV.

numbers and **number style** How to write and print numbers is partly a question of what field you're working in. In mathematics, statistics, science or something technical or commercial, there's every reason to present numbers as Arabic numerals. They are by far the most direct and efficient way to communicate quantities. In other kinds of writing (especially literary or humanistic) the occasional number will more than likely be written in words, within the various constraints mentioned below.

But in any kind of writing, the following are almost always given in figures:

- sums of money: *$30.65*
- weights and measures: *16 kilometres*
- percentages: *17 percent*
- dates: *22 October 1990* (see further under *dates*)
- times of day: *5.30 am*, *17.00 hours* (The convention of writing *five o'clock* has largely given way to *5 o'clock*.)

Other points of **number style**:

1 *Numbers as figures.* Strings of figures are hard to read, and the maximum number of digits set solid is four. However this only happens in the case of a whole number, as in *The mountain is 2379 m above sea level.* Otherwise numbers are grouped in threes on either side of the decimal point:

> *15 069.01*
> *1 506 901*
> > *1.506 901*

These days space alone is used to separate the groups, as recommended by the Australian Government *Style Manual* (1988). According to an older convention, commas were used to separate the groups in front of the decimal point, and the numbers after it were set solid:

> *15,069.01*
> *1,506,901*
> > *1.506901*

Note that in continental Europe, the comma is used as the decimal point (as "decimal comma"), so 1,506 901 would correspond to the last number in the set above. There was some attempt to introduce the decimal comma into Australia in the 70s, but it failed to catch on. For many people it was all too easy to confuse the decimal comma with the older use of the comma in writing numbers. The net effect was that commas disappeared from numbers generally, hence the present reliance on space.

In *spans of numbers* there's generally no need to repeat digits which hold for the second number. So *pp.280-5* will do when you mean between pages 280 and 285. Note however that when the span involves numbers between 10 and 19 in each hundred, the Australian Government *Style Manual* recommends repeating the last two digits: *pp.12-18*, *pp.212-18*. This convention is commonly applied in writing *spans of dates* (see under **dates**). References to decades, e.g. *1980s* are also discussed there.

2 *Numbers as words*. In texts where numbers occur only occasionally, they're usually spelled out as words. There are still some provisos however, and most editors have a threshold above which they would write numbers as figures. For some the threshold is 100, so that they would write *one hundred* in words, but *101, 112, 224* etc. in figures. For others, the threshold is much lower than that, often set at 20 or even 10, but using words for round numbers such as *twenty, fifty, a hundred*. Any threshold creates difficulties when the writer cites numbers both above and below the threshold in the same sentence. It looks inconsistent to write:

There were 19 letters on Thursday, and only eight on Friday. (assuming your threshold is 10)

In this situation, consistency calls for treating both words in the same way (as either words, or numbers). If comparing the two numbers is important, the figures speak louder than the words:

There were 19 letters on Thursday, and only 8 on Friday.

Style guides all recommend against using a figure at the start of a sentence— which might be a reason for preferring words in another version of that sentence:

Nineteen letters came on Thursday, and only eight on Friday.

The sentence could of course be reworded to avoid having a number as the first item.

The choice between figures and words gives a writer alternatives when there are ones from different sets to express in the same sentence:

The two-day course had 5 participants on the first day, and 12 on the second.

3 *Punctuating* **numbers**. Hyphens are regularly used in the numbers from *twenty-one* to *ninety-nine*, as well as in fractions used as adjectives, as in *three-quarter time*. (See **hyphens** section 2c.) In fractions used as compound nouns (e.g. *three quarters of our time was up*) the hyphen is not essential, and variant practices are noted and discussed in *Webster's Style Manual* (1985). The Australian Government *Style Manual* (1988) declares that hyphens are used in fractions whatever their role, but *Copy-editing* (1992) leaves the matter open. Note also that when numbers are written as plural words, they take the same kind of plural suffix as other words with the same final letter: *ones, twos, fours, sixes, twenties*.

4 *Roman numerals* are given in upper case as part of a title: *George VI* or family name: *Adlai Stevenson III* (see further under **names** section 5). But when they refer to such things as the introductory pages of a book, or the subsection of a play, they appear in lower case: *Romeo and Juliet* Act iii Scene 2. Note that the volume numbers of journals are usually expressed in Arabic numbers nowadays, though it was once the convention to give them in Roman numerals.

5 *Enumerating lists of headings and subheadings*. Roman numerals are still widely used in alternation with Arabic ones, and/or with alphabetic letters to enumerate the sections of a document. By using all three, together with strategic use of full stops and single as well as double brackets, a large number of different levels of heading can be identified. For example:

Level A	*I*	*II*	*III*	*IV*
Level B	*A.*	*B.*	*C.*	*D.*
Level C	*1.*	*2.*	*3.*	*4.*
Level D	*a)*	*b)*	*c)*	*d)*
Level E	*i)*	*ii)*	*iii)*	*iv)*
Level F	*(1)*	*(2)*	*(3)*	*(4)*
Level G	*(a)*	*(b)*	*(c)*	*(d)*

and so on.

If only two or three levels of heading are needed, any subset of those enumerators would do. Many reports simply use *1,2,3* etc. for main headings, and *1.1,1.2,1.3* etc. for the subheadings.

6 *Indenting enumerators.* Each level of enumeration is indented on the previous one, the amount of indention depending on how many levels have to be catered for. When there are many levels, the standard 1 em is as much as can be allowed, but with only two or three levels, a 2 em indent is manageable and effective:

> *1.*
>> *1.1*
>>> *1.11*
>>> *1.12*
> *2.*
>> *2.1*
>>> *2.11*
>> *2.2*
>>> *2.21*
>>> *2.22*

Note however that Roman numerals are normally aligned on the following bracket or full stop, as in:

> *i)*
> *ii)*
> *iii)*
> *iv)*

(See further under **indents**.)

For the use of different typefaces and settings for each level, see under **headings** and **subheadings**.

Nungga or **Nunga** This name, used by Aborigines in the south of SA, is believed to represent *Nhangka*, a language used by people living between Streaky Bay and Fowlers Bay, SA. According to the Aboriginal Research Centre at Monash University, the preferred spelling is **Nungga**, though *Australian Aboriginal Words* (1990) has it as **Nunga**.

Nyungar, Nyunga or **Nyoongah** These three words refer to the Aborigines of southwestern WA. **Nyungar** is the name of the language once spoken by more than a dozen groups in the Perth–Albany region, a name coined out of their word for "Aboriginal person". While **Nyungar** is the spelling regularly used in scholarly publications, the similar **Nyunga** is the form used in documents from the Aboriginal Research Centre at Monash University, and it also recognises the more phonetic **Nyoongah**. This last spelling is given priority in *Australian Aboriginal Words* (1990) and in the *Australian National Dictionary*—on the strength of two recent citations, though there are some for **Nyunga**, *Noongar* and *N-yoongar* as well. Other spellings in the entry seem to relate to the *Nungga*, an independent word for the Aborigines of South Australia. (See previous entry.)

See further under **Aboriginal**.

O

O or **Oh** These exclamations have different overtones and are used in very different styles. **O** pure and simple is associated with the high style of literature and religion, as in *O wild west wind, thou breath of autumn's being …* or *O God, our help in ages past.* As in those examples, it's often used in a rhetorical apostrophe to the supreme being, and supernatural or abstract forces. (See further under **apostrophe**.) The same spelling is the one used in hymnbooks, whether the saints above or below are being invoked. It always appears with a capital letter.

The spelling **Oh** is the ordinary, everyday exclamation which expresses various emotions from surprise and delight to disappointment and regret, depending on the context. It also serves as a pause filler in spontaneous outbursts:

I'd be there like a shot, but oh … who would look after everything here?

Other uses of **Oh** are to be found in the worried expression *Oh dear!* as well as in addressing other people: *Oh Meg, would you put the kettle on.* As the examples show, **Oh** doesn't necessarily have a capital letter, nor is it always followed by a comma or full stop.

-o- This is the combining vowel in various compound names, such as *Anglo-Saxon, Franco-Prussian* and *Graeco-Roman.* It works like a hyphen between them—though a hyphen is also needed because the second element begins with a capital letter. (See **hyphens** section 1c.) When **-o-** serves to combine two common words into a compound, no hyphen is used, as in *gasometer.*

-o Most words ending in **-o** in English are borrowings made more or less recently from Italian and Spanish, such as *fiasco, piano, merino, mulatto.* A handful come from Latin (*veto*), Greek (*echo*), and from non-European sources (*calico, dingo*). Those which originated in English are either:

1 transfers such as the noun *do* (see further under **transfers**)
2 clippings such as *pro* (for *professional*)
3 (especially in Australian English) informal and ad hoc words such as *compo, milko, rego,* where a longer word or phrase has been cut back and sealed with the suffix **-o**.

The plurals of such words vary. Older loanwords and English formations took *-es*, whereas recent borrowings simply add *-s*.

The group of words ending in **o** which must take *-es* is steadily declining. The list is longer in Britain (for those who adhere to *Hart's Rules* (1983)) than

for Australians or Americans. Those which Australians are likely still to give
-*es* to are, according to the *Macquarie Dictionary* (1991):

> *cargo domino echo embargo go* (n.) *hero no* (n.)
> *potato tomato torpedo veto*

Apart from that group there are many words whose plural may be spelled either
-*es* or -*s* in Australia. They include:

> *buffalo dingo fiasco flamingo fresco ghetto grotto*
> *halo innuendo mango memento mosquito motto peccadillo*
> *portico stucco tornado volcano*

Many of these are reverting to plain -*s* plurals, creating a trend which is likely
to affect even the core group, sooner or later.

Many other words with **o** are standing firm with plain -*s* plurals. The factors
which seem to go with the -*s* plural are:

- being an abbreviation for a longer word, e.g. *auto, arvo*
- being relatively uncommon, e.g. *salvo* "discharge of fire"
- having several syllables, e.g. *archipelago, manifesto*
- being conspicuously foreign, e.g. *sombrero, stiletto*
- having another vowel before the final **o**, e.g. *cameo, radio*

Several of those factors combine to ensure that the newer fruits to reach
Australian shores, e.g. *avocado, babaco, tamarillo* do not take -*es* plurals as
potato and *tomato* do. But pity the immigrant greengrocer who has to make up
signs for Australian customers!

Note finally that a very small handful of Italian musical terms ending in -**o**
are sometimes found with Italian plurals in English, e.g. *concerti grossi*. (See
further under **Italian plurals**.)

In view of the large number of words ending in -**o** which can or regularly do
take a simple -*s* plural, it makes sense to standardise on it, and that policy has
been implemented in this book.

---

oasis For the plural, see -**is**.

obiit sine prole See under **decessit sine prole**.

obiter dictum and **obiter dicta** These Latin phrases both mean "said by
the way, or as an aside". The difference is simply that the first (with *dictum*)
is singular "something said", and the second with *dicta* is its plural counterpart
"things said". The phrases originate in law, where they refer to incidental
remarks uttered by the judge which are not part of the judgement, and therefore
not binding. Such remarks contrast with the *ratio decidendi* "reason for the
determination", i.e. the principle(s) on which the case is decided.

object An essential yet elusive concept in English grammar is the **object**. It is a key element of clause structure, though not all clauses have them (see **predicate** and **transitive**). Some clauses effectively have two *objects* of different kinds, one *direct* and the other *indirect*. It takes several definitions to show the range of things a *direct object* can be, let alone the indirect kind.

1 *Direct **objects*** can be the thing affected or produced by the action of the verb:
She hit her thumb *with a hammer.*
He baked a pizza *for lunch.*
The **object** can also express the arena or extent of the action:
The maid will tidy the house.
The students walk 5 km *to school.*
The *direct object* is sometimes a person affected by the action, as in:
They put their mother *into hospital.*
In spite of their variety, those objects have one thing in common: they would all be the item identified if you took the verb and asked *what/who?* immediately after.
He baked *what?* A pizza.
The maid will tidy *what?* The house
They put *who in hospital?* Their mother.
In each case the direct object answers the question what/who?

2 *Indirect **objects*** only appear when there's already a *direct object* in the clause. They are associated particularly with a group of verbs that express the idea of transmitting something, or making something change hands; and the indirect object is the person or thing that receives whatever is being transmitted.
She sent the bride *a telegram.*
He gave the door *a kick.*
I wrote them all *a letter.*
As the examples show, the *indirect object* precedes the *direct object*. If the two were in reverse order, the *indirect object* would have to be expressed through a prepositional phrase:
She sent a telegram to the bride.
Grammarians then debate whether that final phrase is still an *indirect object* or whether it should be regarded as a prepositional phrase, on a par with:
She sent a telegram to the reception.
Recent grammars such as the *Introduction to the Grammar of English* and the *Comprehensive Grammar of English* take the latter view, whereas traditional grammars took the former.

In traditional grammar the case of the *direct object* is referred to as the *accusative*, and that of the indirect object (without any preposition) as the *dative*. They are identical in form however, whether they're nouns or pronouns.

Final notes:
• both noun phrases and noun clauses can function as objects of the verb

- in statements the **object** normally follows the verb, as in the examples above. In conversation however the order is occasionally altered, to put the **object** in front of both subject and verb. It serves to focus attention on it, as in:

  Rumballs they liked better than anything.

  (See further under **information focus**.)
- in questions, the **object** is also put up front:

  Which film did you prefer?

  What will they do now?

objective case This is the name given by English grammarians to the case of words which function as either direct or indirect objects (see previous entry). In other languages the two are distinguished as the *accusative* and *dative* cases, because there are changes in the form of words corresponding to each. (See further under **accusative** and **cases**.)

objet d'art Translated literally from French, this means "object of art". Though it serves as a general heading for things of artistic value, it's very often applied to the smaller objects kept by private collectors as decorative pieces. The term then contrasts with *objet de vertu*, which is used of pieces valued for their antiquity or their craftsmanship. The latter phrase can only be translated as "object of virtue", though it is pseudo-French, coined in English as a counterpart to **objet d'art**. Both expressions make their plurals in the French fashion, as *objets d'art, objets de vertu*.

obliged or **obligated** Either of these might be used in a given context, though their implications are a little different. **Obligated** is firmly associated with *obligation*, and implies a quite specific kind of indebtedness or duty, as in:

  I'm obligated to him for supporting my application.

In the past **obliged** was used in much the same way, but nowadays it's used in acknowledging more general kinds of indebtedness, as in:

  I'm much obliged to you.

Obliged is often used with a following infinitive, as in:

  I'm obliged to leave as soon as the meal ends.

As that example shows, *be obliged* has much in common with the so-called "periphrastic modals" (see under **auxiliaries**). It is equivalent to *have to* and *must* in expressing obligation.

oblique line or **stroke** The oblique stroke goes by other names, depending on the context. Its technical name in writing and editing is the **solidus** (see further under that heading).

oblivious In Latin and earlier English, this word meant "forgetful", and so was only used when the person concerned had indeed forgotten something s/he had previously known: *oblivious of his earlier vow*. More recently its meaning has developed to the point where it is a synonym for "unaware": *oblivious to everything going on around*. This meaning was for a long time censured, and

30% of the Harper-Heritage usage panel still found it unacceptable in the 1970s. However *Oxford Dictionary* (1989) says that it can "no longer be regarded as erroneous", and simply notes that the newer meaning is often though not always associated with the use of *to* after it. The major Australian dictionaries register it without comment.

observance or **observation** These abstract nouns relate to slightly different aspects of the verb *observe*. Its older (fourteenth century) meaning "attend to, carry out, keep (a practice)" is the one enshrined in **observance**. The word is often coupled with references to a ritual or tradition, as in *observance of Sunday*. But by the sixteenth century, *observe* could also mean "regard with attention", and this is the meaning embodied in **observation**:
   Close observation of the fish showed they preferred to feed at night.
Thus the two words represent quite different cultures: **observance** expresses the medieval reverence for tradition, whereas **observation** is the key to modern empirical science.

obstetric or **obstetrical** See -ic/-ical.

obverse or **reverse** These refer to the two sides of a coin. The **obverse** is the primary face, with the principal design on it, i.e. the one which identifies the nation or person in whose name it is minted. For Australian coins, this is the side with the Queen's head on it, and the one known as "heads" when tossing a coin. The **reverse** is the other face whose design varies with each denomination. It of course is "tails".

occupant or **occupier** These can be synonyms, and dictionaries give "one who occupies" among their definitions for both. Yet there are differences to note: **occupant** often connotes short-term occupancy, as of a bus seat or a phone box, whereas **occupier** refers to the longer term resident or tenant of particular premises. The distinction is clear in British English where both terms are regularly used; less so in Australian and American English where only **occupant** has much currency, according to the evidence of English databases.

ochre or **ocher** See under -re/-er.

ocker or **okker** The first spelling is the more common by far, judging by the numbers of citations in *Australian National Dictionary* and Wilkes's *Dictionary of Australian Colloquialisms*. The origins of the word are unclear, though most dictionaries treat **ocker** as a variant of the name *Oscar*. **Ocker** was first recorded in 1916, but its popularity was greatly increased by Ron Frazer in the 1960s with the **ocker** character he played in a satirical TV program (the *Mavis Bramston Show*). In the 1970s the word began to spawn derivatives: *ockerdom*, *ockerism* (1974), *ockerisation* (1975) and *ockerise* (1978), again a sign that it is established. **Ocker** and its derivatives have sometimes been printed with a capital letter, but the trend is to use lower case.

octa or **okta** See okta.

octaroon or **octoroon** See octoroon.

octopus What should its plural be? By its Latin appearance people have been inclined to make the plural *octopi*, as with other loanwords ending in *-us*. (See *-us* section 1.) Those with superior knowledge would say the plural should be *octopodes*, because the word was actually coined out of Greek elements as *oktopous*. This is the plural given preference in the *Oxford Dictionary*, though neither *Oxford* nor *Webster's English Usage* (1989) has any citations for it. What the *Webster's* files show is that both *octopi* and the regular English plural *octopuses* have been in use (in scholarly as well as general writing), but that the English plural is prevailing at this end of the twentieth century.

octoroon or **octaroon** The first spelling is given preference in all dictionaries, and the second is acknowledged only in some. The spelling with *octo-* keeps it in line with Latin number prefixes, as seems fitting when it's modeled on *quadroon*. The spelling with *octa-* would seem to link it with the Greek, as some commentators argue. Yet it may also be a simple spelling substitution, one which happens with other words involving the same prefix, witness alternatives such as *octosyllabic/octasyllabic* registered in the *Random House Dictionary*.

For a discussion of terms associated with mixed race, see under **half-caste**.

oculist For the distinctions between this and other words for related professions, see **optician**.

OD For the past tense of this initialised form of the verb "overdose", dictionaries all prefer *OD'd*, with the regular *ODed* as the alternative. For the participle, the regular *"ODing"* is not registered anywhere, and is clearly liable to be misread. Instead the dictionaries mostly prefer *OD'ing*, though *Random House* and the *Macquarie Dictionary* give *OD-ing* as an option. The apostrophe provides a consistent solution to the difficulties in both inflected forms—for the moment. (See further under **-ed** and compare **OK**.)

odor or **odour** See under **-or/-our**.

oe The **oe** digraph is one of the eccentricities of modern English. It is built into the spelling of a few common words, such as *shoe*, *toe* and *canoe*; and into the plurals of others ending in *-o*, such as *echoes* and *heroes*. In short, everyday words like those, it's a regular part of the spelling. But in longer and less common ones such as *innuendoes* and *mementoes*, the plurals are increasingly spelled without the *e*, and reverting to just *-(o)s*. (See further under **-o**.)

Another set of words in which **oe** is being slowly reduced to one letter (this time to *e*) includes ones such as *am(o)eba*, *diarrh(o)ea*, *hom(o)eopath*, *(o)edema* and *(o)estrogen*, all Greek loanwords put to scientific purposes in English. The classical **oe** digraph became a ligature in earlier English, as it still is in the

Oxford English Dictionary. But Fowler argued for its being printed as a digraph, and British English has standardised it (see further under **ae/e**). In American English the **oe** is normally replaced by *e*. Australians normally spell **oe** words like the British, although a spelling survey conducted by the *Macquarie Dictionary* in 1986 showed that many writers were ready to reduce **oe** to *e*, just as they were to replace *ae* with *e*. A questionnaire on individual words issued in 1988 showed a keen desire to adjust words such as *diarrh(o)ea* and *hom(o)eopath*, with 80% of the respondents preferring them with the *e* form. Changes to those two would suggest changes to others formed in the same way:

  dysmennorrh(o)ea gonorrh(o)ea logorrh(o)ea
and
  hom(o)eostatic hom(o)eothermic hom(o)eotransplant
In both sets the **oe** digraph creates a tricky string of vowels, which have no etymological significance for most users. However Australian doctors surveyed in 1988 through the *Australian Dr Weekly* were reluctant to move to *e* spellings—even in *foetus*, following a widely publicised discussion of the fact that it was an illegitimate spelling (see **foetus**). Tradition dies hard. Yet no-one would turn the clock back on words like *economic, ecumenical* and *ecology*, all of which were originally spelled *oe* in English. As those words show, the **oe** digraph in common words is likely to become just *e*.

Note that **oe** should not become *e* where the two letters belong to different syllables, as in words like *coefficient, gastroenteritis, poem* or *whoever*, nor to loanwords from modern German, such as *roentgen*, where the *oe* represents an umlauted vowel (see **umlaut**). On the choice between *manoeuvre* and *maneuver*, see **manoeuvre**.

oedema or **edema**, **oesophagus** or **esophagus**, **oestrogen** or **estrogen** See under **oe**.

of and **off** Of is a preposition used to join nouns and noun phrases together, as in *cup of tea* and *no hope of winning*. It occasionally appears also after adjectives, such as *aware of*, and after verbs such as *think of*.

In that position after a main verb, **of** can sound exactly like the auxiliary *have* which comes before main verbs. This is presumably why inexpert writers sometimes produce *could of* (for *could have*), *may of (may have), might of (might have), should of (should have)*, and *would of (would have)*. Even *had of* is sometimes produced, though there's rarely any need for *had have*. (See further under **have**.)

Note also the potential confusion between **of** and **off**, after certain verbs. After *give*, the more likely one is *give off* "emit", because *give of* is quite rare, except in the idiom *give of one's best*. After *write*, **of** yields the simple meaning "(write) about", whereas *write off* means "cancel or dismiss". In each case the mistaken use of **off** could have distinctly negative implications.

Informal uses of **of** *and* **off**:

- In impromptu speech, both are sometimes used in quick succession, as in *Take your feet off of the seat*. In such cases the **of** is redundant, and should be edited out of written text.
- **of** can appear in adverbial phrases of time, as in *Of a Friday they go to the trots*. They represent a very casual style, whose standard counterpart is *On Fridays ...*
- **off** is increasingly found instead of *from* when describing how things are transmitted or passed from one person to another. Compare
    I got it off my uncle.
    I got it from my uncle.
    The first version still has a colloquial flavor to it.

offense or **offence**   See under **-ce/-se**.

official or **officious**   As adjectives, both invoke the word *office*, but their implications are quite different. **Official** implies the proper execution of duties, as in *official appearance*, or the proper expression of an office, as in *official position*. **Officious** suggests intrusive exercise of authority, as in:
    An officious clerk wanted to double-check my passport.
Thus **officious** has negative implications, while **official** is neutral.

officialese   This is an institutional written style that everyone objects to. Officialese frustrates the reader with long words and interminable sentences, while seeming to emphasise the importance and authority of the institution it represents. Dissatisfaction with **officialese** helps to explain the appeal of *Plain English*, and why various government departments and private companies are endeavoring to restyle their publications to ensure better communication.
    Officialese is above all an impersonal style, the voice of an institution rather than an individual. It is fostered in bureaucracies where teams of people work in succession on the same letter or document. Yet when that same style comes from the pen of a single person writing to another, it can only seem pompous and insensitive. The components of **officialese**, and ways of eliminating them are discussed at **Plain English**. (See also **gobbledygook**.)

officious or **official**   See **official**.

Oh or **O**   See **O**.

-oid   This suffix is derived from the Greek word *eidos* meaning "shape or form". It creates an adjective or noun which implies resemblance to a known body shape, as in:
    alkaloid anthropoid arachnoid asteroid cricoid rhomboid
Most of the words formed with it are technical ones. The majority are based on Greek roots, though a few Latin/English examples have appeared in the twentieth century including *celluloid* and *humanoid*.

OK and **KO** These raise several issues of style, as each appears increasingly in print. Neither needs to have stops, given the trend away from them in abbreviations consisting solely of capitals (see **abbreviations** section 1). When used as a verb, **OK** (as *okayed*) is more likely than **KO** to be spelled out, though *kayoed* has been recorded. The alternatives are *OK'd* and *KO'd*. (See **-ed**.)

The origin of **KO** (as an abbreviation for "knock out") is well known, and after 70 years it still has the flavor of the boxing ring about it. The origins of **OK** are much more obscure and continually disputed. It was first recorded in Boston in 1839, and remained an Americanism until the 1920s. Some have sought its etymology in an American Indian language, others in European immigrant languages including French, Finnish, Scots English and especially German. The most persistent explanation is that it's an Americanised form of *Alles Korrekt*—though it would take a Dutch pronunciation of the first vowel to suggest spelling it with *O* rather than *A*. A Dutch connection also emerges in the explanation of A.W. Read (reported in the *Oxford Dictionary*) that **OK** represents *Old Kinderhook*, the nickname of Martin van Buren (US president 1837–41), who grew up in the Dutch community of Kinderhook, New York.

okker or **ocker** See **ocker**.

okta or **octa** Dating only from 1950, this word meaning a one-eighth sector of the sky is used in meteorology and aircraft control. The spelling **okta** is the standard one in the dictionaries which list it (*Macquarie*, *Collins*, *Oxford*), modeling it on the Greek number eight (see **number prefixes**). The variant **octa** makes it more Latin-looking, though it could be no more than a case of replacing the *k* in a foreign word with *c* (see **k/c**).

older or **elder** For the choice between these, as well as between *oldest* and *eldest*, see under **elder**.

olla podrida See under **potpourri**.

-ology This ending is strictly speaking a combination of the Greek combining *-o-* (like that in compounds such as *Anglo-Saxon*) and *-logy*, a element meaning originally "statement, discourse about something", from which it came to mean the "study or science of a subject". Yet so many of our sciences are named with words ending in **-ology** that it seems to be a single unit. In fact it occurs as a word in its own right, in the title of the publication on *Ologies and Isms: a thematic dictionary*.

Some of the various areas of science and scholarship which go by an **-ology** word are:

> *biology campanology cosmology criminology entomology etymology*
> *geology histology ornithology parasitology philology psychology*
> *sociology theology zoology*

(Note that those in which we have *-alogy* (such as *genealogy* and *mineralogy*) are cases where the *-al* belongs to the first root.)

The **-ology** ending is also used in the names of pseudosciences and recreations, such as:

graphology iridology numerology phrenology speleology

It contributes to the humor of hybrid formations such as *fruitologist* and *garbologist*.

Olympian or **Olympic** The adjective **Olympian** refers first and foremost to Mount Olympus in northern Greece, which was the mythological home of the Greek gods. **Olympic** is associated with the plain of Olympia in the Peloponnese, west of Athens, where the original *Olympic games* were held in ancient times. Nowadays it's the standard adjective for the modern international athletic contest which perpetuates the tradition. Yet as a noun **Olympian** can refer to either one of the mythological inhabitants of Mount Olympus, or someone who has competed at the Olympic games. Those who participate in the *Olympics*, and especially those who ''bring home gold'', do indeed seem to attain the status of demigods via the media.

The associated word *Olympiad* also has both ancient and modern meanings. It originally referred to the four-year interval between the **Olympic** contests; now it usually refers to the period during which the games themselves are held, as in the *XVII Olympiad*.

omelet or **omelette** The first spelling is the older one, and to be preferred, according to the *Oxford Dictionary* and the major American dictionaries. **Omelet** has been in use since the seventeenth century; while **omelette** gained currency in nineteenth century Britain, and dominates the twentieth century citations of the *Oxford*. The *Oxford* now gives the two spellings equal status with **omelet** first, while the *Macquarie* and *Collins* dictionaries make them equal but with **omelette** first. (See further under **-ette**.)

omission mark The various marks of omission are discussed under **asterisk**, **dashes**, **ellipsis** (section 2), and **carat, karat** and **caret**.

-on The **-on** ending is the mark of a number of Greek loanwords, including:

anacoluthon asyndeton criterion etymon oxymoron phenomenon

The main point to note with them is that their plurals are formed in the Greek way with *-a*. Most of the examples above are confined to the study of language and rhetoric, and handling them is a matter for the specialist. But *criteria* and *phenomena* occur in many kinds of contexts, and do need attention because they are not always recognised as plurals or as being in need of plural agreement with verbs and pronouns. (See further under **criterion** and **phenomenon**.)

Other Greek-derived words ending in **-on** usually take *-s* plurals in English. This is true of neoclassical scientific and scholarly words such as *automaton*, *cyclotron, electron, lexicon, neutron, photon, proton* and *skeleton*. Only *ganglion* is more likely to appear with an *-a* plural.

Many English words ending in **-on** have no Greek connections, or are so fully assimilated that the **-on** works as part of the stem. The following are just a token of these, which always have *-s* plurals:

canon cauldron chevron crayon deacon demon melon pylon tenon

Note the small set of twentieth century formations such as *nylon, orlon* and *teflon*, in which **-on** is a suffix meaning "synthetic material". The suffix originated in *rayon*, the first artificial fibre, whose name is simply French for "ray". The name was originally coined because of the sheen on the fabric made with it.

one This word has several roles in English, some of which are uncomplicated. Its use is straightforward when it's the first number in a counting system (*one, two, three*), and when it appears as a substitute word for nouns and noun phrases, as in:

I'd like a train ticket. This lady needs one too.

The children were at school, but one of them had gone on an excursion.

The most critical style question with **one** arises when it is used as a substitute for a personal pronoun, as in:

What can one say to that?

Just which personal pronoun it replaces is not entirely clear. In a given context it could be *I* or *you* or both of us. Yet it's really detached from both, not as ego-centred as *I*, nor as direct in its address as *you*. Sometimes called the *indefinite pronoun*, its very indeterminacy makes it ideal in certain situations.

Because **one** has no regular place in the pronoun system, we're in a quandary as to which pronoun should agree with it. There are several possibilities:

One just has to do one's best.

One just has to do his best.

One just has to do her best.

One just has to do their best.

The first version is the one endorsed in formal British usage, though it tends to sound pompous and even a little old-fashioned to Australians. The second version has been its common equivalent in American usage—for generic and/ or sexist purposes. Yet both the second and third versions seem to draw attention to gender, and only particular contexts can decide whether each is apt or not. With all those difficulties, the fourth version appeals to many, even though it has been subject to grammatical criticism because it follows the singular **one** with the plural *their*. That kind of agreement is however increasingly common after other indefinite pronouns such as *anyone* and *someone*, and avoids gender complications. (See **agreement** section 2.)

Whichever pronoun you choose, it should be used consistently: i.e. *one/one's/ oneself* or *one/their/themselves* etc. It is also important to avoid switching from *one* to *you* or *we*, when the going gets hard. With these various difficulties there are plenty of reasons for not using **one** as a personal pronoun.

one of Should it be:

I am one of those who likes things to stay as they are or
I am one of those who like things to stay as they are.

A perennial question of agreement is raised by the phrase **one of ...** whenever it is the subject of a following relative clause. Is the verb (or any pronoun) following to be singular or plural? Usage commentators in both Britain and the USA have been inclined to say it should be plural; and the Harper-Heritage usage panel voted heavily in its favor (78%). Yet *Webster's English Usage* (1989) has ample evidence for the singular construction. Writers using the singular are apparently responding to the word *one*, whereas those using the plural are responding to the cue provided by *those*.

Other similar constructions in which either pattern of agreement could be chosen are illustrated in the following:

He wrote an article about one of the pilots who was/were on strike.
It's one of the things that come/s as no surprise when you're past middle age.

For most people it depends on whether you're thinking of a single or general case. Grammarians would note that the problem turns on whether or not you take **one** as the head of the phrase. Compare **number of**.

only This puts a spotlight on its neighbors in a sentence. It usually focuses on the one following, and the point of the sentence changes according to where it's placed:

Only the Secretary received the letter.
  (nobody else got one)
The Secretary only received the letter.
  (did not reply to it)
The Secretary received only the letter.
  (not the cheque)

In conversation the placement of **only** is less critical, because intonation can extend the ''spotlight'' over several words to the one which matters. (With extended intonation we could communicate the meaning of the third sentence with the word order in the second.) But in writing **only** needs to be adjacent to the crucial word or phrase to ensure its full effectiveness. (See further under **information focus**.)

Note also that **only** has a minor role as a conjunction expressing contrast, in sentences like:

He'll certainly come, only don't wait for him to start the meeting.

For some this usage smacks too much of conversation to be suitable for formal writing. It was rejected by 85% of the Harper-Heritage usage panel. Yet its written record began in the fourteenth century, according to the *Oxford Dictionary*, and *Webster's English Usage* (1989) has enough recent citations to deem it standard. Those who find it too informal may replace it with *but* or *except that* as appropriate.

onomatopoeia This unlikely word refers to a figure of speech as well as a way in which words are formed. In both kinds of **onomatopoeia**, the word or words seem to express the sound of the very thing they refer to or represent. Individual words such as *croak*, *hiss*, *miaou*, *neigh*, *quack*, *rustle*, *splash* probably owe their origins to **onomatopoeia**, the ad hoc creation of a word on the stimulus of sound. This correlates with the fact that they have no relatives among English words or even in other languages, where the same sounds are represented by different words. Yet within English not only words, but individual sounds are sometimes felt to have equivalents in terms of meaning. (See further under **phonesthemes**.)

Onomatopoeia can also be generated as a figure of speech from sets of ordinary words which are strategically put together. Again the words seem to hint at sounds associated with whatever is being described. Poets of all ages have enriched their work with **onomatopoeia**, as did Gerard Manley Hopkins in the opening lines of *God's Grandeur*:

> *The world is charged with the grandeur of God*
> *It will flame out, like shining from shook foil.*
> *It gathers to a greatness, like the ooze of oil*
> *Crushed.*

The words provide "sound" support for the two images: the sound of static charge breaking out from foil when it's shaken, and the viscous spread of a heavy liquid. Apart from the *onomatopoeic* effect of the words, Hopkins also made use of alliteration and simile in those lines. (See further under **alliteration** and **metaphor**.)

Advertisers too find uses for **onomatopoeia**, as did the makers of Rice Bubbles with their "snap, crackle, pop" slogan. The same effect has been sought in other languages when the product is marketed in non-English-speaking countries. So in Sweden it's "piff, paff, puff"; in parts of Germany "knisper, knasper, knusper"; and in South Africa "klap, knotter, kraak". It demonstrates again that the sound effects of words are relative to a particular language, not universal.

onto or **on to** Some commentators claim that there's no place for **onto**. Others allow there is a place for both forms, and that they have distinct roles, as in:

> *He went on to become a consultant engineer.*
> *He jumped onto the wagon.*

With verbs of motion **onto** is more satisfactory than **on to**, which seems to divide the movement into two aspects. Combining the two words is as natural as with *into*.

Note also the idiomatic use of **onto**/**on to** with the verbs *be* and *get*, as in:

> *Next thing the police will be onto him.*
> *I'll get onto the agent tomorrow.*

Once again they seem good candidates for the spelling **onto**, though dictionaries vary. *Collins* recommends it, while the *Oxford Dictionary* uses the spaced version.

onward or onwards See under -ward.

op. cit. This Latin abbreviation is only used in footnotes and endnotes, as a follow-up to a previous reference. It means "in the work (already) cited". It saves the writer having to repeat the full title of the word referred to, provided it had been cited in full in an earlier footnote:
1. See G. Blainey *The Tyranny of Distance*, p.31.
5. Blainey op. cit. p.35.
As the footnote numbers show, the reference with **op. cit.** need not follow immediately after the full reference.

However the use of **op. cit.** is on the decline (and being actively discouraged by some publishers such as the Chicago University Press). Its place is being taken by follow-up references with a short title instead:
1. See G. Blainey *The Tyranny of Distance*, p.31.
5. Blainey *Tyranny*, p.35.
Note that if the author's name appears in the running text before the repeated reference, just the book title and the page number would be enough. And if no other work by Blainey is being referred to, just his name and the page number are sufficient.

Compare **loc. cit.** and see further under **Latin abbreviations**.

opacity or **opaqueness** These are effectively synonyms according to modern dictionary definitions. Both work as the abstract noun for *opaque*, and even its more figurative meanings "obscure" or "unintelligent" can be vested in either (cf. other nouns in **-ness**). **Opaqueness** is therefore just as possible as **opacity** when it comes to describing either murky prose or a mind that lacks lucidity. Fowler thought the figurative meanings were particularly linked with **opacity**, but this specialisation does not seem to operate now. The chief difference between the two is stylistic, that **opacity** is more formal in character, and probably less common.

opera Since its origins in the seventeenth century, **opera** has developed in scope and variety. There are large differences in scope between the one-hour music dramas of Scarlatti and the *grand operas* of Verdi. In the latter, the whole libretto is set to music, and its serious and heroic subject matter contrasts with that of *opera buffa* (or French *opéra bouffe*)—names for comic opera in which the musical climaxes are embedded in recitative. French *opéra comique* combines plain spoken dialogue with the musical highlights, but is not necessarily comic in its substance, witness examples such as *Carmen*. In English the term *operetta* is used for (1) short operas of any variety, and (2) light operas whose subjects contrast with *grand opera*. Light opera in the second sense has much in common with musical comedy. Both deal with humorous or sentimental subjects, and one can hardly distinguish them except that the term *musical comedy* is usually applied to those which were composed more recently in the USA, and are familiar through film as well as stage versions.

operator or **operative** Both can mean "worker in an industry", according to dictionary definitions. Yet in industry they are carefully distinguished, the **operator** having the specific skills for a specialised kind of machine, as in *computer operator*, *switchboard operator*; and **operative** used for someone whose skills are more generalised and range over a process, as in *cleaning operative*, *waste disposal operative*. The word **operative** never in fact appears among the occupational titles listed in the Australian Standard Classification of Occupations (1990), perhaps because of the general push to have any distinctive skills recognised under the title **operator**.

Both words have additional meanings outside the regular work force. **Operator** can be used to refer to the owners or managers of a particular industrial plant or mine, or to those who deal in shares on a large scale. In colloquial use it's also applied to those who manipulate others. **Operative** is used in the USA to refer to a detective or secret agent.

opium See under **morphine, morphia, laudanum, opium** or **heroin**.

opossum See under **possum**.

opportunity to, opportunity for or **opportunity of** Several different constructions are possible after **opportunity**:

1 *It gave them the opportunity to talk*
2 *It gave them the opportunity for talking*
3 *It gave them the opportunity for full discussions*
4 *It gave them the opportunity of talking*
5 *It gave them the opportunity of long-needed talks*

The first construction is the most common by far in the Australian ACE corpus (52 instances), and in other varieties of English, judging by the material in *Webster's English Usage* (1989) and citations in the *Oxford Dictionary*. In the Australian database the frequency of the third construction is a quarter of the first (14 instances), and the second and fourth types only 3 and 4 instances. *Webster's* notes the popularity of the fourth construction in its British examples, and the fact that it was popular up to 30 years ago in the USA, but the first construction presumably paraphrases it in Australia. The fifth construction is represented by only one example in the ACE corpus. Differences in frequency tend to make slight differences in formality (the less frequent seeming to be more formal), but all five constructions are perfectly acceptable.

opposite of or **to** The choice of word after **opposite** depends on whether it serves as a noun or an adjective. As a noun it's more often followed by *of*, as in *the opposite of what I expected*, though *to* is increasingly common. As an adjective, **opposite** is mostly followed by *to* but occasionally by *from*:

The entrance is opposite to where the bus-stop was.
Their house was on the opposite side from the shops.

The use of *to* after **opposite** is sometimes redundant, as in:

Their house was opposite (to) the sports ground.

In such cases **opposite** stands as a preposition in its own right.

optician, optometrist, ophthalmologist or **oculist** In Australia the **optician** is the person who supplies you with spectacles or lenses, while the **optometrist** is the person who tests your eyes and measures your vision. The **optometrist** may have tertiary training, but is not a qualified doctor and so cannot work with drugs or surgical procedures. Both **ophthalmologist** and **oculist** are words for trained doctors who specialise in eyes, with the former used increasingly because of conflicting use of the latter by those who were not medically trained. In the USA the term **oculist** is used by optometrists, in Britain two kinds of **optician** are distinguished: *dispensing opticians* (who make glasses etc.) and *ophthalmic opticians* (who test eyes and prescribe lenses).

Note the cluster of consonants in the spelling of **ophthalmologist**, based directly on the Greek word for eye *ophthalamos*. The first *h* is easily overlooked (*opthal ...*), no doubt under the influence of **optician** and **optometrist**.

optimum or **optimal** The noun **optimum** is often used as an adjective, as in:
The optimum conditions for ballooning are at dawn.
The adjective **optimal** could equally have been used:
The optimal conditions for ballooning are at dawn.
Yet **optimal** is still quite uncommon. The *Oxford Dictionary* (1989) no longer labels it as "rare" and belonging to biology, but it retains a formal flavor, and **optimum** is widely used instead.

optometrist, ophthalmologist, oculist or **optician** See under **optician**.

opus The plural of this Latin loanword is *opera*. (See under **-us** section 3.) For *opus magnum* see **magnum opus**.

Note that *Opus Dei* literally "work of God" is the title of a politico-religious organisation associated with the Catholic church, which originated in Spain this century. In that context *Opus* always bears a capital and is never pluralised.

or Though often used as a simple conjunction, **or** also appears in tandem with *either*, and with *neither*:
You could go on either Tuesday or Friday.
Neither Tuesday or Friday is perfect for me.
The choice between *nor* and *or* with *neither* is discussed under **nor**.

As an ordinary conjunction **or** raises several questions of agreement:
• singular v. plural verb
• which part of the verb to use with a mix of pronouns
• what gender to use in the following pronoun

1 When **or** links two things or people together, many style guides say it should be followed by a singular verb as in:
Perhaps John or David thinks the same.
The advice makes sense when the alternatives are mutually exclusive. But it needs to be modified when the alternatives are effectively added up (when **or**

is a synonym for *and*), and also when the alternatives are a mixture of singular and plural items. See for example:

> *Just the sound of paper rustling or chairs scraping were enough to disturb her concentration.*

The fact that the plural item is nearer the verb makes it natural to work with plural agreement, though it is almost as likely if the sentence read:

> *Just the sound of chairs scraping or paper rustling were ...*

2 The nearest item affects the choice of verb when different persons of the pronoun are joined by **or**:

> *He or I do this everyday.*
> *Are you or he responsible for this?*
> *They believe either you or I am responsible.*

In the first two examples the verb agrees with the nearest pronoun and also works as a plural agreeing with the pair. But the third example is awkward because the verb can only agree with the nearest item. It could be avoided by using a plural verb, or by unpacking and rewording the sentence, as:

> *They believe you are responsible, or that I am.*

3 Which gender to use in the following pronoun is a further issue when **or** connects male and female items. The rule of going by the gender of the nearer item would endorse the following:

> *Every boy or girl must cover her books with plastic.*

The statement seems unfortunate, as does the following—unless you have a very strong faith in generic *his*:

> *Every boy or girl must cover his books with plastic.*

Using the gender-free *their* seems the best way out of a difficult situation:

> *Every boy or girl must cover their books with plastic.*

Those who still find that sentence grammatically anomalous would need to reword it.

Punctuation with **or**. This is simply a matter of whether to put a comma before **or** when it introduces the last of a series of alternatives. The issue is exactly the same as for *and* in the same position. See the discussion of the *serial comma* under **comma**.

-or/-our These are alternative spellings for a sizable group of abstract nouns, such as *colo(u)r, favo(u)r, hono(u)r* and *humo(u)r*. Both spellings are current in Australia, though the ratios between them in the ACE corpus vary considerably. The instances of *labor* (excluding references to the Labor Party) outnumber *labour* by 129:95, whereas *behaviour* outnumbers *behavior* by 99:10. The ratios for the rest lie in between. Spellings with **-or** are more often used by newspapers and magazines than book publishers, and are house style for papers with big circulations in Adelaide, Brisbane, Melbourne and Sydney.

The variation between **-or** and **-our** goes back to uncertainties of the seventeenth and eighteenth century as to how such words should be spelled.

Scholars wanted to use **-or** for words received from Latin, and **-our** for the French loanwords. But in many cases it was unclear which language was the source, and the choice of ending became arbitrary. The dictionaries of the eighteenth century show a continuing trend towards **-or** for all of them, and this process was allowed to run its full course in the USA. But in Britain it was halted by the publication of Dr Johnson's dictionary in 1755, and more importantly, the fact that his dictionary was reprinted with the spellings virtually unchanged for many decades years after his death. Johnson had a mixture of spellings for words in this group (compare *anterior* with *posteriour*), and a study of spellings in his correspondence showed that they occasionally diverge from those in his dictionary. Yet the words he spelled with **-our** are by and large the very ones which British spelling preserves today.

Official Australian usage has followed the British tradition, though **-or** spellings could be found in scattered sources in the nineteenth century, including regional newspapers and some legal codes. The spelling *Labor* was adopted by the Australian Labor Party early this century (see under **Labor**). The Victorian Education Department began to encourage the use of **-or** spellings after an Imperial Conference on the matter in 1910, and reaffirmed the policy in the 1930s and the 1970s, though with **-our** as an acceptable alternative. Other state education departments have yet to follow their lead.

Yet the reasons for preferring **-or**, especially for teaching purposes, are clear when we compare the **-or/-our** words with their most common derivatives. For example:

glamo(u)r	*glamorous*	*glamorise*
hono(u)r	*honorary*	*honorific*
humo(u)r	*humorous*	*humorist*
labo(u)r	*laborious*	*laboratory*
odo(u)r	*odorous*	*deodorant*
vigo(u)r	*vigorous*	*invigorate*

Those who use **-or** have only to transfer that spelling to the derivative words, whereas those using **-our** are involved in further modifications. The occasional appearance of *glamourous* is a sign of the problem **-our** users have in remembering to adjust the ending of the base word.

For all the above reasons, **-or** seems preferable in:
> *arbor armor behavior clamor color demeanor endeavor*
> *favor fervor flavor glamor harbor honor humor labor*
> *neighbor odor parlor rancor rigor rumor savior savor*
> *splendor succor tumor valor vapor vigor*

and in all derivatives such as *colorful, favorite, honorable* etc. They have therefore been used throughout this book.

On the choice between *-or* and *-er* in agentive words such as *protester*, see **-er/-or**.

oratio This Latin word meaning "speech" is the key to the phrases *oratio recta* "direct (or quoted) speech" and *oratio obliqua* "indirect (or reported) speech". For a discussion of the difference between them, see **direct speech**.

orbited For the spelling of this word as a verb, see **t**.

ordain and **ordinance** The spelling difference between these is discussed under **-ain**.

Order of Australia The **Order of Australia** was instituted in 1975, as an Australian society of honor to give recognition to Australian citizens and others for special achievements and meritorious service. A person honored in this way becomes a member of the society, as a Member, Officer or Companion, those being the three levels in ascending order. Strictly speaking one does not "receive" an **Order of Australia**, though that idiom no doubt echoes the earlier system of giving and receiving knighthoods, based on the British practice. From 1976 until 1986 there were the additional orders of Knight and Dame of Australia, introduced by the Fraser government and discontinued by the Hawke government, without prejudice to those who had been awarded them (in all 12 men and 2 women).

The major orders including medals are:

Cross of Valour	*CV*
Knight/Dame of Australia	*KA/DA*
Companion of Australia	*AC*
Officer of Australia	*AO*
Star of Courage	*SC*
Member of Australia	*AM*
Australian Police Medal	*APM*
Bravery Medal	*BM*

The initials corresponding to each order are set immediately after the member's name, with no stops.

ordinance or **ordnance** The first word is much more widely used, in reference to an official regulation or rule which has authority behind it. The second is a collective word for military equipment and supplies, including weapons. The *Ordnance Survey* maps were so called because they were originally commissioned in connection with moving military supplies around on the ground.

For the relationship between **ordinance** and *ordain*, see under **-ain**.

ordinary or **ordinal,** and **cardinal** In ecclesiastical contexts both the **ordinary** and the **ordinal** are reference books. The **ordinary** gives the order for divine service, whereas the **ordinal** is the directory of church services overall, or the forms of service for ordination of members of the clergy. But the term **ordinary** can also be contrasted with **cardinal**: the former refers to any official of the Church (e.g. bishop) in his capacity as an ex officio ecclesiastical authority, and the latter (**cardinal**) to any member of the privileged Sacred College, ranking next after the Pope.

When it comes to numbers, the contrast is between **ordinals** and **cardinals**. The **ordinals** are the numbers which enumerate an order, i.e. *first* (1st), *second* (2nd), *third* (3rd); whereas the **cardinals** are the regular integers used to register how many there are in any set.

organdie, organdy or **organza** The first two are alternative spellings for a type of muslin, a finely woven cotton fabric. The *-ie* spelling is used in Australia, the one with *-y* in the USA. **Organza** is a similar fabric though with more body and stiffness, made out of silk or a synthetic fibre.

orient or **orientate** Fowler thought that **orientate** was "likely to prevail in common figurative use", as it does in the British LOB database. But in the USA and in Australia **orient** is definitely preferred, according to database evidence: in the Australian ACE corpus the verb **orient** outnumbered **orientate** by 18:3. Contrary to Fowler's prediction, **orient** is almost always used figuratively in the Australian data; while **orientate** is only used geographically, as in *orientated towards the north*. In compound adjectives such as in *customer-oriented*, *oriented* again seems to be preferred in Australia.

ortho- In Greek this meant "straight" or "right". In modern English it's built into a handful of semitechnical terms, including *orthodontics*, *orthodox*, *orthogonal*, *orthography* and *orthopedics*. Its major role however has been in the creation of specialised terms in physical chemistry.

orthopedic or **orthopaedic** See under ae/e.

-ose This suffix is found in a number of formal and chemical words. In general use it's found in adjectives, with the meaning "full of" or "given to", as in *bellicose*, *grandiose*, *otiose* and *verbose*. All such words have a pejorative quality, as if it connotes a certain excessiveness. In chemical usage the suffix is perfectly neutral, and used to make nouns which are usually the names of sugars and other carbohydrates. See for example: *glucose* (from which the suffix derives), *fructose* and *lactose*.

The **-ose** suffix sometimes varies with *-ous*, as with *torose/torous*; but in the case of **stratose/stratous** and **viscose/viscous**, there's a contrast in meaning. (See further under those headings.)

o.s.p. See under **decessit sine prole**.

ostensible, ostensive or **ostentatious** All these words have to do with showing something. The most common of the three is **ostentatious**, meaning "putting on a display" as a means to show off one's wealth or importance. **Ostensible** and **ostensive** are rather academic words, both associated with the burden of proof. **Ostensive** means "embodying the very thing it's intended to demonstrate", as printing the word **BLACK** in large black letters shows what "black" means. **Ostensible** means almost the opposite, implying that outward appearances are a false indication of what is underlying. The adverb *ostensibly* enjoys much wider use and currency than the adjective.

other than and **otherwise** *Other* is historically an adjective, yet it has long been used as a pronoun (see next entry), and is on record as an adverb equivalent to **otherwise**. Modern dictionaries recognise it in all three roles, and yet some style commentators object to adverbial uses of **other than**. The following are typical uses of it:

> *They might behave somehow other than arrogantly.*
> *Other than raising an eyebrow, he made no reply.*

Fowler vented a surprising amount of spleen over constructions like those, and purists might still want to substitute **otherwise** in the first sentence and *apart from* in the second. But the *Right Word at the Right Time* affirms that both kinds of sentence are established idiom, and shows that **other than** has indeed developed as an adverb.

The chief point in dispute with **otherwise** is somewhat similar. It arises out of taking the word strictly as an adverb, and the notion that it can only be used in parallel with other adverbs. By that canon, only the first of the following is acceptable:

> *They will finish the operation successfully or otherwise.*
> *They may have succeeded or otherwise.*
> *I'd have her whether she was a trained nurse or otherwise.*

In the second sentence **otherwise** parallels a verb, in the third a noun (phrase), yet such constructions are common enough and communicate satisfactorily. They suggest that *or otherwise* works as a fixed collocation which can be deployed quite freely. The expression is perhaps a little offhanded, but the issue is then one of style rather than grammar.

Note that *or otherwise* may be at least partly redundant when used as a conjunction:

> *We need to get there by midnight, or otherwise we'll be in trouble getting into the hotel.*

In such a sentence, **otherwise**, or just *or*, would be sufficient. The whole phrase may be superfluous in statements like the following:

> *They need to know whether the letter has been approved or otherwise.*

The sentence would be neater without *or otherwise*. If that seems too abrupt, *or not* would do just as well.

other's or **others'** Where to put the apostrophe is the question in each of the following sentences:

> *They took one anothers hand.*
> *The group read each others essays.*
> *They all supported the others emotional problems.*

There is no easy answer in cases such as those, where grammar and logic intersect and the sentences express both mutuality and plurality. Style guides take their cue from the mutual expressions *one another* and *each other* to argue that the singular apostrophe **other's** is the only form possible. But this seems a little awkward when the following noun is plural (as in the second and third sentences), and the wording suggests more than a single exchange. **Others'** seems right for the third, where there's plurality of exchange and a plural noun (and neither *one* nor *each* to call for singular). In the second sentence either **other's** or **others'** is defensible.

For the alleged distinction between *each other* and *one another*, see **each other**.

otherwise See under **other than**.

ought This word is a lone wolf in English grammar. It is actually an estranged relative of the verb *owe*, but its chief function nowadays is as a periphrastic modal which can be used as a substitute for *should* (see further under **auxiliaries** and **modality**).

The use of **ought** is shrinking, because of uncertainties about how to use it in negative statements and questions where many people fall back on *should*. Compare:

You oughtn't to work so late.
    You shouldn't work so late.
Ought she to know about it?
    Should she know about it?

The versions with **ought** may sound a little awkward or old-fashioned, and **ought** is less common in Australian English than in Britain or the USA, according to the evidence of the ACE corpus. Compare 51 instances to 106 and 70.

Other symptoms of uncertainty about the status of **ought** show up in sentences like the following:

He didn't ought to keep it to himself.
He oughtn't keep it to himself.

The first implies that **ought** is no longer an auxiliary in its own right, and therefore needs the support of the auxiliary *do* (*did*) to express the negative. The second would imply exactly the opposite: that **ought** is so well established as an auxiliary, it no longer needs *to* as a link to the following main verb. In other words, it has moved beyond being a periphrastic auxiliary to being a fully fledged auxiliary.

Style guides such as the *Right Word at the Right Time* are inclined to treat both the constructions in the previous paragraph as nonstandard, and to insist that the use of **ought** as a periphrastic auxiliary is as things should be. But elicitation tests in Australia show a preference for **ought** without *to* in negative statements (i.e. as a full auxiliary), as well as a strong tendency to replace it altogether with *should*. The latter is the course of least resistance if you're unsure about **ought** these days.

-ous Many English adjectives end in **-ous**, meaning "full of" or "similar to". The ending came into English with French loanwords such as *courageous*, *dangerous*, *glorious* and *virtuous*, and has since been used to create new adjectives out of English nouns, of which the following are only a few:

> *glamorous hazardous momentous murderous poisonous wondrous*

Many of these adjectives are formed simply by adding **-ous**, or by modifying the last letter, in the case of *y*, to *i*, as in *prodigious*. In a few cases, the adjective in **-ous** parallels a noun ending in *-ion* or *-ity*:

> *cautious   caution*
> *capacious   capacity*

(See further under **-ious**.)

The **-ous** corresponds to the *-ose* in some more latinate adjectives, and occasionally there are parallel formations. (See further under **-ose**.)

Note that **-ous** contrasts with *-us* in pairs of scientific words such as:

> *citrous/citrus*   *mucous/mucus*
> *fungous/fungus*   *oestrous/oestrus*
> *humous/humus*   *phosphorous/phosphorus*

In each case the adjective with **-ous** complements a noun with **-us**, borrowed from Latin (see further under **-us**).

For **callous/callus**, see under that heading.

outward or **outwards** See under -ward.

overawing or **overaweing** See under -e section 1.

overflowed or **overflown** The first is the past form of *overflow*, as in:

> *By 9 pm the river had overflowed the levies.*

The second is the past participle of *overfly*:

> *The accident occurred because the aircraft had overflown the runway.*

overlay or **overlie** These two are sometimes difficult to disentangle. They raise some of the same problems as the simple verbs *lay* and *lie* with their past forms, but *lay* and *lie* also help to distinguish their meanings. The idea of *lying* physically over something is strong in **overlie**, and it may refer either to a covering of snow on the ground:

> *From the air you could see snow overlying the whole countryside.*

Or to geological strata superimposed on each other. A further use is to refer to the accidental smothering of newborn animals by lying on top of them:

> *The hen had overlain two of the chicks.*

Overlay involves the affixing of a layer or special surface to an object, as in printing and other crafts: *The cover was overlaid with gold.* Note how the past form here differs from the last example.

The distinction between the two verbs is less clear-cut in figurative usage, and the choice depends on whether the layer or covering seems to be consciously applied. So it seems more likely that you would speak of the *pessimism overlying a letter*, and *the lawyer's fine words which overlaid her suspicions*.

overlook, oversee and **oversight** The first two words are established verbs, with quite different meanings. **Oversee** means "supervise", as in:
He was commissioned to oversee the building of the factory.
Overlook can mean either "fail to take into account" as in:
They overlooked the need to check the authorship of the letter.
or it can be used in the sense "look over", as in:
Their window overlooked the harbor.
Oversight has a long history as a noun whose meaning corresponds to the first meaning of **overlook**, i.e. "failure to take into account". However it has recently been harnessed as a verb, with a meaning rather like that of **oversee**, "watch with attention, monitor". The usage is current in the public service, and it appeared in both government and religious texts in the Australian ACE corpus. Some find it an ugly use of a noun in the verb role, though that is common enough in the history of English words. (See further under **transfers**.)

overstatement For the rhetorical effects of *overstatement* and *understatement*, see **understatement**.

overtone or **undertone** Their prefixes make these look like a complementary pair, and we might even expect them to contrast. Yet often there's little to choose between them, when applied to the special effect or characteristics of a piece of communication. Should it be *overtones of arrogance* or *undertones of arrogance*?
Various distinctions have been proposed. Fowler argued that *overtones* were the implications of words, on the analogy of musical overtones which are the higher notes produced by a vibrating string above the note actually struck. *Undertones* are explained in terms of an undercurrent, something embedded in an utterance and inferrable from it. This would allow us to draw a distinction between the pervasive quality of a text (its *undertones*), and the more explicit *overtones* of words and phrases in it, and we would then have a distinct use for each of the words. How useful and usable it would be in a given case is another question. Sheer frequency suggests that **overtone(s)** is the more useful of the two, with 6 instances in the Australian ACE corpus, as opposed to one of **undertone**.

ovum For the plural of this Latin word, see **-um**.

owing to or **due to** See under **due to**.

oxymoron In an **oxymoron**, words opposite in meaning are juxtaposed to form a paradoxical figure of speech. Everyday examples are *sweet and sour* (pork), the aphorism *Hasten slowly* and the cliché *thunderous silence*. The American word *sophomore* for a second-year student is explained by *Webster's Dictionary* as an oxymoron in a single word, meaning literally ''wise-foolish''.

Note that the plural of **oxymoron** is usually *oxymora* (see under **-on**). But it was *oxymorons* in Alex Buzo's column on this subject for the *Sydney Morning Herald* (January 1992). There he applies the term to any ad hoc contradiction, for example:

All students must study these optional topics.

It's been a night of near misses as far as direct hits are concerned.

Describing such statements as ''oxymoronic'', and the general phenomenon as ''oxymoronism'', Buzo makes good capital out of the word.

OYO This is an acronym for ''own your own'', used in Melbourne for strata-titled flats. (See further under **home unit**.)

Oz See under **Australia**.

P

-p/-pp- Words ending in **p** generally conform to the common English spelling rules when suffixes are added, witness:
chirruped galloped gossiped hiccuped scalloped walloped
All those verbs have an unstressed syllable before the *p*, and so it's not doubled before the verb suffix is added (see **doubling of final consonant**).

In American English certain other verbs are treated the same way: *worshiped* (usually), and *kidnaped* and *fellowshiped* (by some users); whereas in British and Australian English they are always *fellowshipped, kidnapped, worshipped*. This divergence is exactly like that for words ending in *l*. (See **-l/-ll-**.) Yet *handicapped* is spelled the same way everywhere, and ad hoc creations such as *membershipped* and *workshopped* also run counter to the common rule, perhaps because of the influence of *ship* and *shop* in them. The common meanings of *ship, shop* etc. are irrelevant however, and drawing attention to them with a doubled consonant seems unfortunate. It would be better just to add *-ed*, and have them—and any similar new words—in line with the broadest principles of English spelling.

p. See **pp**.

pace As a one-syllabled word this needs no explanation. But the same four letters can represent a slightly cryptic Latin loanword with two syllables and several pronunciations, including "pacy", "parchay" and "parkay". **Pace** is the ablative form of the more familiar Latin word *pax* "peace", and so it literally means "with peace". More idiomatically it means "with the permission or pardon (of)" or "with apologies (to)" whoever is named immediately after. It offers a respectful apology for going against whatever the person named has said on the subject being discussed. Its proper use is shown in the following:
An Australian alliance with the USA need not **pace** *Harold Holt mean "going all the way".*
As the example shows, **pace** is used with the name of a person (or their title, such as Prime Minister) immediately following. It expresses polite disagreement with some notable statement or opinion expressed by that person. Note that it's not a referencing device like *vide*, or an alternative to *e.g.* for introducing an example. **Pace** may be set in italics as *Webster's English Usage* recommends, although with a name or title always following, it's unlikely to be mistaken or misread.

For a different use of the same word, in *requiescat in pace*, see **RIP**.

paediatrics and **paediatrician** See pediatrician.

paedophile and **paedophilia** See pedophile.

pajamas or **pyjamas** See pyjamas.

Pakistan This remarkable name was coined only half a century ago, to unite the predominantly Muslim provinces of western India. It is close to being an acronym for the five provinces involved:

*P*unjab
*A*fghan province (properly called North West Frontier Province)
*K*ashmir
S*I*nd
Baluchi*STAN*

The name **Pakistan** was taken up after the partition of India in 1947, and applied to the single nation newly created out of Muslim states on both western and eastern sides of India, which were then *West Pakistan* and *East Pakistan* respectively. However the western and eastern states had little in common apart from their religion. Major cultural differences, and sheer geographical separation prevented any real unification between the two, and after years of civil war, the two formally separated in 1971. The eastern provinces renamed themselves *Bangladesh*, and the name **Pakistan** reverted to being that of the western provinces alone. Their official name is the *Islamic Republic of Pakistan*.

palate or **pallet** See under **palette**.

paleo-/palaeo- This Greek prefix meaning "very old, ancient" is probably most familiar in *paleolithic*. The words it forms in English are rarely household words, though scholars in both sciences and humanities know it in one or more of the following:

pal(a)eobotany pal(a)eoecology pal(a)eogeography
pal(a)eography pal(a)eomagnetism pal(a)eontology

Note that when the following word begins with *o* or *a*, **pal(a)eo-** often becomes **pal(a)e-**, as in *pal(a)earctic*.

The spelling with the *ae* digraph has prevailed in Britain, and so also in Australia, while *e* is standard in the USA. The general arguments for simplifying it to *e* are set out at **ae/e**. The particular ones in this case are that the *ae* puts too much weight on an unstressed syllable, and creates monstrous sequences of vowels, especially in examples such as *palaeoecology* and *palaeoethnology*. Though the sequence looks less cumbersome with the *ae* printed as a ligature, the facilities to print ligatures are denied to most of us. Pronunciation is more accurately represented without the *a* in the second syllable, and the word is perfectly recognisable without it. In a 1992 survey of spelling preferences among professional writers in NSW and Victoria, the majority endorsed the spelling with just *e* in *paleolithic*.

palette, pallette, palate or **pallet** All these words are diminutive forms of the Latin word *pala* "spade". That flat shape becomes the **palette** on which artists mix their colors, and as **pallette** it was the name for a particular plate of metal in the armpit of a medieval suit of armor. As **pallet** it was the name for a tool used by the potter to smooth the clay being worked on the wheel. In modern industries the same spelling (**pallet**) is the one used for the wooden platform on which goods are stored before transportation.

Note that the spelling **pallet** is also attached to a quite unrelated word for a mattress of straw, derived from the French word for straw *paille*. And **palate** which is pronounced in exactly the same way as all of the above, is also an unrelated word, from Latin *palatum*.

Apart from their likeness in sound, **palette** and **palate** can almost overlap in meaning when each is figuratively extended. The image of the artist's **palette** is sometimes extended to mean "range of colors", while **palate** is quite often a substitute for "taste", based on the old idea that the taste buds were in the roof of the mouth. So either **palette** or **palate** might be used in an impressionistic comment about the rich tones of a new musical composition. It depends on whether the writer is thinking of the color or the flavor of the music.

palindrome A **palindrome** is a word or string of them which can be read either forwards or backwards with the same meaning. Words which are palindromes include *noon, madam*, and the South Australian placename *Glenelg*. Longer examples include:

don't nod!	(injunction to bored audience)
revolt lover!	(goodbye to romance and all that)
step on no pets!	(warning as you enter premises of an incorrigible cat breeder)
red rum sir is murder	(I'd settle for a red-label beer)

Few *palindromes* get put to a serious purpose. The only well-known exception is: *a man, a plan, a canal, Panama!* used, as it were, to hail the work of Goethals, the US army engineer who completed the canal's construction in 1914, after decades of setbacks.

Those addicted to *palindromes* are also conscious of the next best thing—words or phrases which can be read both ways but with a different meaning each way, such as:

dam/mad devil/lived regal/lager stressed/desserts

There is no standard name for them, though one addict has proposed *semordnilap* for reasons which will be apparent.

pallette, pallet, palette or **palate** See palette.

pan- This Greek element meaning "all" is embedded in words such as:

panacea pandemic pandemonium panegyric
panorama pantechnicon pantheist

The literal meaning of the prefix is not so easy to isolate in such words, however. It's a good deal more noticeable in modern English formations such as *Pan-*

American for a US airline, and in international institutions such as the *Pan-Pacific Congress.*

pandit or **pundit** See pundit.

paneled or **panelled** The choice between these is discussed at **-l/-ll-**.

panic For the spelling of this word when it becomes a verb, see **-c/-ck-**.

papaya, papaw or **pawpaw** See pawpaw.

Papua New Guinea Both culturally and linguistically **Papua** and **New Guinea** are separate entities, and they were managed by different colonial powers until the end of World War I. In the nineteenth century, **Papua** was administered by Britain, and **New Guinea** by Germany. However **Papua** was ceded to Australia in 1905, and **New Guinea** became Australia's mandated territory by resolution of the League of Nations after World War I. Australia has since then administered the two together, and they were forged into a single unit through independence in 1972, with the double-barreled name.

The name is strategic, giving careful recognition and equal status to both **Papua** and **New Guinea**. There is no hyphen between the two names. Citizens refer to themselves in full as *Papua New Guineans*, though those from **Papua** have been known to describe themselves as just *Papuans.* Fortunately the whole nation is united by the use of a common lingua franca: *tok pisin* (also known as *New Guinea pidgin* or *Neo-Melanesian*). In it **Papua New Guinea** is called *Niugini*, a neat and distinctive title. (For more about New Guinea pidgin, see **pidgins.**)

Note that as a geographical term, **New Guinea** refers to the whole island, and therefore includes not only **Papua New Guinea**, but also West Irian, or Irian Jaya—once a Dutch territory, but now part of Indonesia.

papyrus For the plural of this word, see **-us** section 1.

para- These letters represent three different prefixes, one Greek, one derived from Latin and a third which has evolved in modern English. The first, meaning "alongside or beyond" is derived from Greek loanwords such as *paradox, parallel, paraphrase* and *parasite.* Fresh uses of it are mostly found in English scholarly words such as:

paraesthesia paralanguage paramnesia
paraplegic parapsychology parataxis

Note that before a word beginning with *a*, the prefix becomes just *par-*.

The second prefix involving the letters **para-** comes to us through French loanwords such as *parachute* and *parasol.* They embody an Italian prefix meaning "against", a development of the Latin imperative *para* literally "be prepared".

But *parachute* itself is the source of the third meaning for **para-**, found in recent formations such as the following:

parabrake paradrop paraglider paramilitary paratrooper
All such words imply the use of the parachute in their operation.

Note that the word *paramedic* may involve either the first or the third use of *para*. When referring to the medical personnel who provide auxiliary services besides those of doctors and nurses, it belongs with the first set of scholarly words above. But when it's a doctor or medical orderly in the US armed forces, who parachutes in to wherever help is needed, the word is clearly one of the third group.

parable A **parable** uses a simple story to teach a moral truth. The word has strong biblical associations, as the word applied in New Testament Greek to the didactic stories of Jesus Christ. But the definition applies equally to Aesop's fables. A **parable** differs from an *allegory* in that the latter is concerned with more than a single issue, and often involves systematic linking of the characters and events with actual history. (See further under **allegory**.)

paradigm This word is widely used to mean "model", though its older use is in terms of a "model of thinking", an abstract pattern of ideas endorsed by particular societies or groups within them. The term has been applied to the medieval assumption that the sun revolved around the earth, which has now been replaced by the opposite cosmological **paradigm**—that the earth revolves around the sun. Sociologists use the phrase *dominant paradigm* to refer to a system of social values which seems to set the pace for everyone. Rebels try to expose it with the slogan *subvert the dominant paradigm*.

Paradigm is also a synonym for the word "model" in a different sense, that of "exemplar" or just "example". These meanings have always been part of the scope of the word in English, so the following usage is nothing new:

The new guidelines are a paradigm for nonsexist communication in any large organisation.

Some people resist this use of the word, and it fuels their conviction that the phrase *paradigm case* is a tautology. But even that phrase is fully recognised in the *Oxford Dictionary* (1989).

The word **paradigm** has long been used in grammars to refer to the set of different word forms used in the declension or conjugation of a particular word. The often-quoted **paradigm** for the present tense of the Latin verb *amare* "love" is:

amo	"I love"
amas	"you love" (singular)
amat	"he/she/it loves"
amamus	"we love"
amatis	"you love" (plural)
amant	"they love"

For a given context you select the form of the word you need. This idea of selecting one out of a vertical set of options has been extended in modern linguistics to refer to the alternative words or phrases which might be selected at a given point in a sentence. See for example the various *paradigms* in:

Several	*new staff*	*begin*	*on Monday.*
A few	*employees*	*commence*	*next Monday.*
A number of	*assistants*	*start*	*next week.*

The use of **paradigm** in this last sense is the basis on which linguists speak of the *paradigmatic axis* of language, as opposed to the *syntagmatic axis*. For more about the latter, see under **syntax**.

paradise When things are so good it seems like heaven, there are plenty of adjectives to express the feeling. In fact there's a confusion of choice:

paradisiac	*paradisaic*	*paradisic*
paradisiacal	*paradisaical*	
paradisial	*paradisal*	
paradisian	*paradisean*	

Though the major dictionaries give separate entries to several of these, it's clear from their crossreferencing that for almost all of them the preferred spelling/form is *paradisiacal*.

paragraphs For those who cast a casual eye down the page, **paragraphs** are just the visual units that divide up a piece of writing. The *paragraph breaks* promise relief from being continuously bombarded with information. The start of each *paragraph* is still marked by an indent in most kinds of writing and publishing, though in business letters the trend is to set even the first line of each paragraph out at the left hand margin (= "blocked format"). (See further under **indents, letter formats, letter writing** and Appendix VII.)

For the reader, **paragraphs** should correlate with units of thought or action in the writing. They should provide digestible blocks of information or narrative, by which the reader can cumulatively absorb the whole. Ideally (at least in informative and argumentative writing) the **paragraphs** begin with a *topic sentence*, which signals in general terms whatever the *paragraph* is to focus on. The following *paragraph* shows the relationship between topic sentence and the rest:

> *In Sydney it's commonly said—and perhaps believed—that Melbourne is a wetter place. The facts are quite different. Sydney's rainfall in an average year is almost twice that of Melbourne, and in a bad year, a lot more than that. Suburban flooding is a much more frequent problem in Sydney than in Melbourne ...*

The first sentence says what the paragraph is about, the notion that Melbourne is a wetter place (than Sydney). Note that the second brief sentence in fact combines with it to show what the *paragraph* is intended to do, and also works as a kind of topic sentence. Following the statement of the topic, there are specific points to back it up, and so the *paragraph* forms a tightly knit unit around a particular idea.

Readers (especially busy ones) are grateful to writers who provide regular topic sentences. And for writers it's a good habit to get into, because it obliges you to identify the topic of each *paragraph*, and reduces the tendency to shift on to other matters which really deserve a separate *paragraph*. It makes writers much more conscious of the structure of their argument.

1 *How long should a **paragraph** be?* What is considered normal in length varies with the context. Many newspapers use one-sentence **paragraphs** in their ordinary reporting—presumably because they are conscious of the visual effect of longer ones, and are less concerned about giving their readers information in significant units. In scholarly writing and in institutional reports, **paragraphs** are often quite long—as if shorter ones might imply only cursory attention to an issue. For general purposes, **paragraphs** from 3 to 8 sentences long are a suitable size for developing discussion, and some publishers recommend an upper limit of 5/6 sentences. **Paragraphs** which threaten to last the whole page certainly need scrutiny, to see whether the focus has actually shifted and a new *paragraph* is needed.

2 *Continuity of **paragraphs**.* **Paragraphs** need to be in an appropriate order for developing the subject matter. The connections between them can then be made unobtrusively—often embedded in the topic sentence. In the following example, a small but sufficient link with what's gone before is provided by means of the word *different*:

> A *different approach to marketing fiction paperbacks might be to develop automatic vending machines for them, to be installed on railway platforms ...*

The use of *different* is a reminder to the reader that at least one other "approach" has already been discussed, and a sign that a contrasting strategy is coming up. The one word achieves two kinds of *cohesion* with what went before. For a range of other cohesive devices, see under **coherence** or **cohesion**, and **conjunctions**.

Some people advocate including a cohesive or transitional device at the end of each *paragraph*, as well as at the beginning. This can become very tedious if done in every *paragraph*, and is not necessary if there is adequate cohesion at the start of the *paragraph*.

parakeet, parrakeet or **paroquet** These are only some of the spellings for this colorful native bird. Others recorded are *parroket, parroquet, paraquet* and *paraquito*. The origin of the word is much debated; and French, Italian and Spanish ancestors have been found for it, each contributing to the variety of the spellings. In English the spelling **parakeet** is the one preferred in many dictionaries, including *Macquarie, Random House* and the *Oxford Dictionary*. *Webster's* gives preference to **parrakeet**. The spelling with double *r* suggests the influence of *parrot* on it. Both *parrot* and **par(r)akeet** seem to owe their origin to the name *Peter*, in French and Spanish respectively, though the details of their etymologies are still elusive.

parallel This word is well endowed with *l*s, and so the final *l* is not normally doubled when suffixes of any kind are added to it. Hence *paralleled* and *paralleling*; and *parallelism* and *parallelogram*. Yet the spellings *parallelled* and *parallelling* appear as alternatives in some dictionaries, and they make the word conform to the standard British rule for words ending in *l* (see under -l/-ll-). It makes the third syllable rather hefty however, and even Fowler preferred to make an exception of *parallel*, and recommended against using double *l* with it. Citations in the *Oxford Dictionary* show that the spellings with four *l*s have been very little used.

parallel constructions Presenting comparable or contrasting thoughts in a parallel construction is an effective way of drawing attention to their likeness or otherwise. Many ordinary observations become memorable sayings or aphorisms with the help of parallelism:

> *Least said soonest mended.*
> *Run with the hare and hunt with the hounds.*

The use of identical grammatical structures in the two parts of those sayings helps to bind them together into an effective package. In the same way a writer can use a parallel construction to draw attention to ideas which complement or contrast with each other. See for example:

> *The traveller doesn't need to go outside Australasia for sightseeing, or to see the best, get the best or do the best this planet affords ...*
> (G.D. Meudell)

The grammatical structures of the three points in the latter part of the sentence are matched exactly—so exactly that all of them can be read in connection with the final clause.

In the following example, the lack of exact matching makes it difficult to read things in parallel. It shows *faulty parallelism*:

> *The speaker was not able to hold their attention, nor his jokes to amuse them.*

The need for a plural verb in the second statement means that the reader cannot borrow the singular one from the first statement, and the parallelism fails. The benefits of parallelism are easily compromised by noncorrespondence of the two parts, and what results is stylistically worse than if there had been no suggestion of parallelism there at all. A simple change or two is often all that it takes to secure the parallelism:

> *The speaker was unable to hold their attention, or to amuse them with his jokes.*

Parallel constructions can themselves be given extra emphasis through the use of paired conjunctions, such as *neither ... nor, either ... or* (when they express alternative ideas); and with *not only ... but also* or *both ... and* when one idea is added to another. (See further under those headings.)

paralyse or **paralyze** See under **-yse.**

paranoid or **paranoiac** Both serve as adjectives to describe someone suffering from *paranoia*, both in the clinical sense of a severe mental disturbance, or in the ordinary sense of an anxiety that makes someone hypersensitive or suspicious. Psychiatrists prefer to keep **paranoiac** for the clinical meaning, and to allow the general public to use **paranoid** for the ordinary meaning. This distinction is reflected in some dictionaries, but not consistently observed in common usage.

paraphrase A **paraphrase** finds an alternative way of saying something. Dr Samuel Johnson did it impromptu when he first said (of a literary work):
> *It has not wit enough to keep it sweet.*

and immediately afterwards turned it into:
> *It has not vitality enough to preserve it from putrefaction.*

In that famous case, the **paraphrase** has also effected a style change, from plain Anglo-Saxon language to rather formal latinate language. The stylistic change could of course go in the opposite direction—further down the scale of informality:
> *Not enough spark to keep it lively.*

People use *paraphrases* for any of a number of reasons. A style may need adapting to communicate with a different audience from the one originally addressed. So a technical document may need extensive *paraphrasing* for the lay reader. A piece which is written for silent reading may need to be revised for a listening audience. *Paraphrasing* is also a useful way to test your understanding of anything you've read.

Note that the best *paraphrases* work with whole sentences and ideas, and are not produced by finding new words for the slots in an old sentence. (The example quoted from Johnson above is rather limited in this respect.) By totally recasting the sentence you achieve a more consistent style, and more idiomatic English.

parasitic or **parasitical** See under **-ic/-ical.**

parataxis This is an another term for *coordination*. See under **clauses** section 2 *(compound sentences)*.

parcel For the spelling of this word when verb suffixes are added to it, see **-l/-ll-.**

parentheses In the USA this is the standard name for *brackets*, and Australians too are using it increasingly for that purpose. (See under **brackets**.)

parenthesis This is a string of words interpolated into a sentence but grammatically independent of it:
> *The old woman had managed (heaven knows how) to move the cupboard in front of the door.*

The brackets (*parentheses*) show the independence of the *parenthetical* comment, though a pair of dashes would also have served the purpose. Paired commas are sometimes used, but they are not ideal: they imply a closer interrelationship between parenthesis and the host sentence than there actually is. For other punctuation associated with *parentheses*, see under **brackets**.

Because a **parenthesis** interrupts the reading of the host sentence, it should not be too long, nor introduce tangential material which could and should be kept for its own sentence. In examples like the one above, the **parenthesis** is brief and simply adds in an authorial comment on the main point.

parenthetic or **parenthetical** See under -ic/-ical.

parliament The pronunciation of this word confounds its spelling, which has been quite variable even up to a century ago. In earlier times the second syllable was spelled with just *a*, just *e* and just *y* or *i*. The standard spelling comes from Anglo-Latin *parliamentum* (with the Middle English *parli* written into the Latin root *parla-*). The Anglo-Latin spelling began to be recorded in English documents from the fifteenth century, and became the regular spelling in the seventeenth.

parlor or **parlour** See under -or/-our.

parody A **parody** is a humorous or satirical imitation of a literary work (or any work of art). It usually keeps the form and style of the original work, or the genre to which it belongs, and applies them to rather different subject matter. In the example below, Dorothea Mackellar's romantic poem about the Australian landscape is turned into a satire on the more primitive aspects of suburbia. Mackellar's original version appears on the left, and the parody by Oscar Krahnvohl on the right:

I love a sunburnt country	*I love a sunburnt country*
A land of sweeping plains	*A land of open drains*
Of rugged mountain ranges	*Mid-urban sprawl expanded*
Of droughts and flooding rains.	*For cost-accounting gains.*
I love her far horizons	*Broad, busy bulldozed acres*
I love her jewelled sea	*Once wastes of fern and trees*
Her beauty and her terror	*Now rapidly enriching*
The wide brown land for me.	*Investors overseas.*

Those who know the words of the original will find strong satire of its romanticism in the **parody**. Those who only half remember it will still notice the *parodic* effect of using a carefully worked poetic form to express uncompromising social criticism.

paronomasia This is a learned word for *punning*. See further under **puns**.

parrakeet or **parakeet** See parakeet.

parricide or **patricide** While **patricide** is strictly "murder of one's father", **parricide** is "murder of a parent or ancestor, or any person to whom reverence is due". The Latin word *pater* is clearly the formative root behind **patricide**, and is sometimes claimed for **parricide** as well. Another possibility is that **parricide** embodies the same root as the word *parent*. (The modern spelling with two *r*s disguises this, though in Latin the word was often spelled with just a single *r*.) The connection with *parent* is made more likely by the fact that in Roman law *par(r)icidium* was regularly defined in terms of the killing of father *or* mother.

pars pro toto This Latin phrase, literally "part for the whole", is an alternative name for *meronymy* or *synecdoche*. (See further under **synecdoche**.)

participles In traditional grammar terms, English has two **participles**, one called *present* (ending in -*ing*), the other *past* (ending in -*ed* for regular verbs, but with -*en* or -*n* or a change of stem vowel for irregular verbs). The following show the various forms:

| *present*: | rolling | taking | blowing | ringing |
| *past*: | rolled | taken | blown | rung |

The names *present* and *past* are misnomers, since either *participle* can occur in what is technically a present or past tense. In *we were rolling* the *present participle* combines to form the past continuous tense, and in *we have rolled* the *past participle* contributes to the present perfect.

What the **participles** really do in English is create different aspects for the verb, either *imperfect*, also known as *continuous*, or *perfect*, i.e. completed. (See further under **aspect**.) The **participles** also contribute to the active/passive distinction, in that the *present participle* is always **active**, and the past one is normally **passive** (see further under those headings.)

The two kinds of *participle* are frequently used as adjectives in English, as in a *rolling stone* and a *rolled cigarette*. Each type is also capable of introducing a nonfinite clause, witness their role in the following sentences:

Rolling towards them the tyre loomed larger every second.

They found the papers rolled up in a cardboard tube.

(See further under **nonfinite clauses**.)

particles The term *particle* has been used to label various kinds of words which are difficult to classify among the standard grammatical **parts of speech** (see under that heading). It is often applied to the adverb-cum-preposition which is attached to simple English verbs, and becomes integral to their meaning, as with *take up*, *write off* and many more. (See further under **phrasal verbs**.) It also serves to refer to the much censured "preposition" which can occur at the end of a sentence (see **prepositions**, section 2).

partly or **partially** These can certainly serve as synonyms for each other in some contexts. Yet there are also distinctions to be made, if we agree with Fowler that **partly** seems to target the fact that only some part(s) of the whole are concerned, whereas **partially** implies that it's a question of degree over the whole. So a *partly finished report* would be one of which some sections were done and others hardly begun, and a *partially finished report* is one which has been fully drafted, but which needs polishing overall. You might also note that in examples like those, **partly** seems to comment on the noun *report* (only part of the report is done), while **partially** modifies the verbal adjective *finished*, showing the extent to which it is finished.

Those distinctions are fine ones to make, and in many contexts it may not make much difference. Note however that **partially** is stylistically more formal, and grammatically less flexible than **partly**. **Partially** works like a standard adverb, modifying verbs, adjectives and other adverbs; whereas **partly** can be used to modify whole phrases, as in:

> *It's partly because of his unfailing interest*
> > *her fault*
> > *to please my family*
> > *on behalf of my wife*

In all such constructions **partially** is impossible. *Webster's English Usage* notes that this may become the most important distinction between the two words. Be that as it may, the additional uses of **partly** already help to give it much greater currency than **partially**.

parts of speech This is a traditional term for what are now usually called *word classes*. Either way they are the groups into which words may be classified, according to their roles in sentences. The eight such classes which have traditionally been identified for English are:

> *nouns pronouns adjectives verbs*
> *adverbs prepositions conjunctions interjections*

These classes have been the basis of dictionary classifications of words, with the minor addition of *articles*. But for better description of English grammar, recent works such as the *Comprehensive Grammar of English* (1985) diverge more radically. They have created the broader class of *determiner* to include both articles and certain kinds of adjectives (see **determiners**), and separate classes for numerals and for three types of verb (primary, modal and full). (See further under **auxiliary verbs**.) Note also the linguistic distinction between the "closed" and "open" classes of words. The first set includes determiners, pronouns, prepositions, conjunctions and auxiliary verbs—word classes whose members are relatively fixed. The second set includes nouns, adjectives, adverbs and full (main) verbs, whose membership is open-ended.

The English language challenges traditional **parts of speech** in other ways as well. Words can clearly belong to more than one class, e.g. *down* can be either noun, adjective, verb, adverb or preposition, depending on the surrounding words. It proves more useful to think of *word classes* as representing a range of grammatical functions which a word may take on, rather than as a set of pigeon-holes for classifying words. In Latin and Greek, most words had a single function and could be seen as belonging to a particular class; whereas in English their classification must vary with their function. The functions of the English word classes are still discussed under the familiar headings of noun, verb etc.; and it's still conventional to talk of words being *converted* or *transferred* from one class to another when they take on new grammatical roles. In fact this usually means an additional rather than a substitute role. (See further under **transfers**.)

passed or **past** These words are identical in sound and origin (both being derived from the verb *pass*), but only **passed** can now be used for the past tense and past participle of that verb. **Past** was used that way until about a century ago, but it's now reserved for all the other uses of the word, as adjective (*past tense*), adverb (*they marched past*), preposition (*It's past midnight*), and noun (*in the past*).

passim This Latin word, meaning ''in various places'' or ''throughout'', is used in referencing, when you want to indicate that there are relevant details at many points in the work, too many to make it worthwhile noting them all. Some would say that it's not very helpful to do this: if the references are in just one chapter, it looks rather lazy to say ''chapter 6 passim'' instead of giving specific page references. **Passim** is however justifiable when you're referring to a key word which recurs many times on successive pages; or else to an idea whose expression is diffused through the discussion and not in any fixed verbal form.

As a foreign word and/or as a referencing device, **passim** may be set in italics rather than roman. Yet editorial practice is changing on the setting of reference devices (see under **Latin abbreviations**), and the word can scarcely be mistaken for any other if set in roman.

passive verbs People seem to polarise over *passives*; they're either addicted to them or inclined to crusade against them. But **passive verbs** serve more or less legitimate ends, and our use of them should be moderated accordingly.

1 A *passive verb* is one in which the subject undergoes the process or action expressed in the verb, as in:
   The subjects were tested *for HIV antibodies.*
   Several candidates have been included *on the short list.*
As the examples show, **passive verbs** consist of (a) a part of the verb *be* and (b) a past participle. Between them they ensure that the subject is acted upon, and so is a passive rather than an active participant in whatever is going on. Passive constructions like those emphasise the process, rather than who is performing the action, and so are called *agentless passives*. It is possible to express the agent of a *passive verb*, but only as a phrase after it:
   The subjects were tested by the doctor *for HIV antibodies.*

Even in this form, the passive seems to downplay the agent, not allowing it to take up the more prominent position at the start of the sentence (see further under **information focus**).

2 *Style and the passive.* Because **passive verbs** play down the agent (or make it invisible), they are not the stuff of lively narrative, when you want to know who is doing what. Used too often, as in some academic and official styles, they make for dreary reading. But for institutional communication they're all too useful. In their agentless form (i.e. without *by* ...) they avoid saying who is controlling and managing the situation, which is a distinct advantage if you have to break the news that retrenchments are on the horizon:

All staff with less than six months service will be retrenched.

Such wording is less confrontational and perhaps more tactful than:

We, the senior management, will retrench all staff with less than six months service.

The second version with an *active verb* puts a glaring spotlight on the people who have to do the dirty deed. (**Active verbs** must have their agents expressed as the subject: see further under that heading.)

3 *The passive in scientific prose.* Apart from its use in official and corporate documents, the *passive* is a regular component of some kinds of science writing. Its use is occasioned by the fact that science aims to provide objective description of its own procedures, and in terms of processes rather than people. The *agentless passive* allows scientists to report that:

The mixture was heated to 300°C.

without saying who actually did it. Who did it is irrelevant (or should be) as far as the scientific process goes. The *passive* also allows scientists to avoid implying any particular cause and effect in their statements, and to concentrate on what happened until they are ready to look for explanations in physical laws and principles. Not all science writers rely on the passive, and the pressures just discussed are probably stronger in chemistry than in biology. The Council of Biology Editors in the USA has come out in favor of more direct, active reporting of observations, and this should help to counter the ingrained habit of using the *passive*—as if it were a stylistic necessity for professional scientists.

Final note. The *passive* has a place in any writer's stylistic inventory, in spite of the problems associated with it—its dullness, and the fact that it seems to be habit-forming in some institutions and professions. Used occasionally it's a graceful alternative to the active construction, and a useful device for altering the focus or setting up a new topic at the beginning of a sentence. (See further under **topic** and **topicalising**.)

past or **passed** See passed.

past tense Most English verbs show whether the action they refer to happened in the past, rather than the present or some indefinite time in the future. This is the point of difference between:

live/lived send/sent teach/taught write/wrote

The **past tense** is often shown simply by the *-(e)d* suffix, as with *lived* and all regular verbs. Irregular verbs make the **past tense** in other ways, with changes to vowels and/or consonants as illustrated by *sent/taught/wrote*. Just a handful of verbs (old ones ending in *-t* like *hit* and *put*) make no change at all from the present to the past tense (see under **irregular verbs**).

Note that only the *simple past tense* is formed by those means. For compound tenses, auxiliaries are combined with one or other participle, and they in fact mark the tense:

was living (past continuous, progressive)

had been teaching (past perfect continuous)

had written (past perfect)

All such compound tenses express aspect as well as tense (see further under **aspect**).

pasta, paste, pastry, pasty, pâté or **patty** All these words for food go back to the Greek word for "barley porridge". They are, if you like, a tribute to the versatility of European cuisine, and all improve on the shapeless cereal of the original.

In **pasta** the focus on cereal remains, yet this staple Italian food comes in myriads of shapes: *cannelloni, macaroni, ravioli, spirelli, tortellini, vermicelli* etc. The English word **pastry** embodies the same root, and with the *-ry* suffix transforms the cereal substance into the medium out of which shapely pies and pie crusts can be created.

The traditional English **pasty** features both the pastry medium, and its meaty filling, whereas in **paste** and **pâté** the meaning has shifted away from the cereal to the prepared meat. Both **paste** and **pâté** are enjoyed in their own right, though we normally consume them with the help of other cereal items (bread or biscuits).

The English word **patty** sustains both kinds of meaning. What we cook in *patty pans* is again a cereal item, a small pie, tart or cake; whereas the *patties* we cook in a frying pan are a savory item made out of minced meat.

Note that **paté** is often written in English without its circumflex, though the final acute accent lingers to distinguish it from the English word *pate* "head", as in *bald pate*.

pathos In the ancient art of rhetoric, this connoted an appeal to the audience's sense of pity and using it to sway them. **Pathos** contrasted with *ethos*, the attempt to impress the audience through the intrinsic dignity and high moral stance of your presentation.

Neither **pathos** (nor *ethos*) is to be mistaken for **bathos** (see under that heading).

patricide or **parricide** See parricide.

patronymic This is a name which identifies someone in relation to his/her father or ancestor. In Australia *patronymics* are most familiar to us in surnames with the suffixes *-son* or *-sen*, or the prefixes *Fitz-*, *Mac-* or *O'-*. In Russian and some Slavic languages, there are parallel *patronymics* for the surnames of sons (*-ov*) and daughters (*-ova*), as there are in Iceland, with *-sonar* for sons and *-dottir* for daughters.

    Note that the equivalent female term is *metronymic* rather than "matronymic".

patty, pâté or **pasta** See pasta.

pawpaw, papaw or **papaya** The first two spellings are usually used in Australia for the large, soft-bodied tropical fruit with succulent orange-colored flesh. **Pawpaw** is the primary spelling in the *Macquarie Dictionary* (1991), and for the *Sydney Morning Herald.* Yet **papaw** is also current, and preferred by the *Brisbane Courier-Mail* and recommended by News Corporation to its journalists. It is the older spelling by centuries, first recorded in 1624, whereas **pawpaw** was first recorded in 1902.

    Both words seem to be derived from **papaya**, a word which originated in Caribbean Spanish. Yet in Australia **papaya** is often used as the name of one particular variety of the fruit, smaller in size than the **pawpaw** and having bright pink flesh.

    In the USA both **papaya** and what we call **pawpaw** are known by the former name. This is because the word **pawpaw** is put to a different purpose altogether, to name a shrub which is a member of the custard apple family. Its fruit is shaped like a stubby banana and apparently rather tasteless.

peaceable or **peaceful** These are sometimes substituted for each other, but their normal lines of demarcation are that **peaceable** is the one to apply to a person or group of people who are disposed to keep good relations with each other. It can also be applied to human character or intentions. **Peaceful** is applied to nonhuman nouns, such as those referring to situations, periods or general activities which are calm and free of disturbance and conflict.

peccadillo The plural of this word is discussed under **-o**.

peccavi See under **mea culpa**.

pedagogue or **pedagog** See under **-gue/-g**.

pedaled, pedalled or **peddled** See under **pedlar**.

pediatrician or **paediatrician**, and **p(a)ediatrics** See under **ae/e**.

pedlar, peddler or **pedal(l)er** In Australian and British English, the first two are applied to different kinds of trader. **Pedlar** is the older word, applied to an older type of traveling salesman who went from village to village dealing in household commodities, including pots and pans and haberdashery. Their business was quite legal, whereas the word **peddler** was and is reserved for those who deal in illegal drugs or stolen goods. In the USA, **peddler** is applied to both. (See further under **-ar**.)

A **pedaler** or **pedaller** is one who pedals a bicycle or other pedal-powered vehicle. The choice between single and double *l* in that word, and for the verb *pedal* is discussed under **-l/-ll-**.

pedophile or **paedophile,** and **p(a)edophilia** See under ae/e.

peewee or **peewit** These are two of the several names for the Australian *magpie lark* (Grallina cyanoleuca), which looks something like a magpie and sings (a little) like a lark. The name **peewee** suggests its rather plaintive cry. Though sometimes called the **peewit**, it's a quite different bird from the European **peewit** (Vanellus), a kind of plover which makes its nest on the ground. The Australian bird makes its nest high in a tree, using mud as the adhesive, and is in fact called the *mudlark* in Victoria. Yet another name is *Murray magpie*, used in South Australia. Those in NSW and Queensland who are inclined to use **peewee** should certainly prefer it to **peewit**, as do the *Reader's Digest Book of Australian Birds* (1977) and the *Macquarie Dictionary*. The various regional names are all more popular than the straightforward *magpie lark*, according to Bryant's research (1987).

pejorative and **pejoration** This un-English-looking word is used by linguists for several purposes:
1 to refer to affixes which have a derogatory effect on the word they are attached to. This is the effect of prefixes such as **mis-** and **pseudo-**, and occasionally of suffixes such as **-ose** and **-eer**. (See further under individual headings.)
2 to refer to words with disparaging implications, e.g. *shack, wench*.
3 to refer to the process by which some words deteriorate in meaning in the course of time, usually over centuries. So the word *cretin* once meant "Christian", and *silly* once meant "blessed". The word *gay* has undergone **pejoration** in just a few decades this century.

Peking or **Beijing** The capital of China is now known worldwide as **Beijing** (see further under **China**). This reformation of the name is not however likely to affect traditional designations such as *Peking Duck*, the *Pekin(g)ese dog* or the *Peking man*. Restyled with "Beijing" the first two would lose something of their cachet, and the third, its credibility as an ancient human species.

penciled or **pencilled** When *pencil* becomes a verb, it raises spelling questions. See further under **-l/-ll-**.

peninsula or **peninsular** A grammatical distinction lurks in those two spellings: the first makes the word a noun, the second an adjective. Compare:
The Mornington Peninsula is now a commuter region of Melbourne.

But all peninsular traffic has to exit and return by the same route.
See further under **-ar**.

penumbra The plural of this word is discussed under **-a**.

per This Latin preposition, meaning "through, by", has a number of uses in English, mostly as a member of stock Latin phrases which are detailed below. It can also be combined with English words of the writer's own choosing for various meanings. When used in recipes, as in *200 gm cheese per person*, it means "for each", and its meaning is similar in price lists: *$25 per 100*. In the phraseology of commercialese: *to be delivered per courier*, **per** means "by or through the agency of". Some object to such expressions, especially when the simple *by* would do. Yet the meaning embedded in *"per person"* would be hard to express as neatly in other words.

- *per annum* means "by the year", often used after quoting a salary: *$27 450 per annum*, and usually abbreviated in job advertisements as *p.a.*
- *per capita* means "by heads". Its usual context is in economic writing, when statistics are being presented in terms of the individual:
  The per capita consumption of wine has decreased dramatically in Australia over the last two years.
- *per cent*. See **percent**.
- *per diem* means "by the day". In English it's used as a noun to refer to the allowance for daily expenses given by some institutions to traveling employees, apart from the cost of overnight accommodation.
- *per procurationem*. See separate entry.
- *per se* means "by itself" or "for its own sake". In rather formal and theoretical writing it serves to distinguish the intrinsic value of something from its applications. See for example:
  The discovery is of some importance per se, as well as for the directions it suggests for future industries.

per- Only in chemical names is this prefix still productive. There it's applied to inorganic acids and their salts, where it means that they have the maximum amount of the element specified in them. For example: *peroxide*, *perchloride* and *potassium permanganate*. It replaces *hyper-* used in this sense in older chemical nomenclature.

per procurationem This is the full form of a phrase we know better by the abbreviations *per proc.*, *per pro* or just *p.p.* The full Latin phrase means "through the agency (of)", and when followed by capitalised initials it indicates who actually signed the letter, as opposed to the person in whose name it is sent. The usual convention is for *p.p.* and the proxy's initials or signature to appear just above the typed signature of the official sender.

An older convention reported by Fowler and others is for the proxy also to handwrite the official signatory's name, either before the *p.p.* or after their own initials. So a letter going out for James Lombard might be signed in either of the following ways:

Yours sincerely   *Yours sincerely*

J.Lombard pp.RSM   pp.RSM J.Lombard

J. Lombard   J. Lombard
Manager   Manager

More common than either nowadays is the simple use of *p.p.* and the proxy's initials.

Note that the older abbreviation *per pro* (without a stop) was taken by some users to be a combination of two Latin prepositions, and to mean "for and on behalf of". In accordance with this interpretation, they would write it as *per/pro*. With decreasing knowledge of Latin in the community, this variant is disappearing.

For other points of institutional letter writing, see **commercialese, letter writing** and Appendix VII.

percent and **percentage** Percent is an abbreviation for *per centum* "by the hundred". So completely assimilated is it in the shortened form that it's never given a full stop, nor set in italics. It has traditionally been written as two words **per cent**, and in the Australian ACE corpus the two-word form outnumbered **percent** by about 5:1. But the 56 instances of **percent** indicate the likely trend: major American dictionaries such as *Random House* and *Webster's* make it one word, and the *Oxford Dictionary* (1989) confirms that it "frequently" appears that way. In printed texts the numbers accompanying **percent** may be either figures or words, i.e. *10 percent* or *ten percent*, though the ACE corpus showed that the use of words was (1) rare, and (2) confined to very small or round numbers such as *two percent, fifty percent.*

The percent symbol % is freely used in nonfiction in Australia, except in newspapers where it's almost always paraphrased in words. In the Australian ACE corpus overall, the % sign occurs just about as often as the paraphrase. It is always set solid with the preceding number: *10%*. When used in tables, it need not be used with every number in a column of percentage figures, but can simply appear at the top of the column. (Note that the figures in the column may not add up to exactly 100 percent, and the total at the bottom should be left as *99.4%* or *100.2%*, not rounded off.)

When used in continuous text, a percentage figure may take either a singular or a plural verb in agreement with it, depending on whether the entity under discussion is a mass noun or something countable:

In the end 10 percent of the wool was rejected.

Out of the students who came, 10 percent were unprepared.

Percentage is the fully forged abstract noun for **percent**, meaning "proportion calculated in terms of a notional population of 100". However **percentage** is sometimes used loosely to mean "an (unspecified) proportion", as in:

A percentage of the class went to the races.

The statement is so vague as to be useless. Does it mean 95 percent or 10 percent? But it's easily made more useful with the addition of an adjective, such as "large" or "small":

A small percentage of the class went to the races.

Note also the use of **percentage** to mean "advantage", figuratively derived from its use in specifying a profit margin. For example:

There's no percentage in rushing back to the office.

The word is often preceded by *no* (as in that case), or by *any* or *some*. This usage is still regarded as colloquial and casual.

perceptibly or **perceptively** The adverb **perceptively** means "showing fine perception", though it implies the exercise of intelligence and critical judgement, not just powers of observation. **Perceptibly** is more closely related to what is observable. It means "able to be perceived" as in;

He was perceptibly distressed by the things she said.

Just how obvious an effect is, when it's described as "perceptible", can only be assessed in context. Both **perceptibly** and *perceptible* cover a wide range from the conspicuous to the barely noticeable.

perfect aspect See under **aspect**.

perhaps or **maybe** See **maybe**.

peri- This suffix, meaning "around", is embodied in Greek loanwords such as *perimeter, periphery, periscope* and *peristyle*. As those examples show, it's most often used in the dimension of space, and recent medical terms use it to describe a bodily structure in terms of the organ it lies around, as with *pericardium* and *periodontal*. Just occasionally it has formed words in the time dimension, as with *perinatal*, used in relation to the latest stage of pregnancy and the earliest weeks after giving birth.

period In both the USA and Canada, the **period** is the term for the *full stop* used in word and sentence punctuation. (For a discussion of those functions, see **full stop**.) In North America it also serves as the word for the decimal point.

For issues relating to periods of time, see **dating systems**.

periodic or **periodical** As adjectives these are usually interchangeable, like many *-ic/-ical* pairs. Yet in the *periodic table* which classifies the known chemical elements, only the first will do. In *periodical literature* only the second will do, because **periodical** also has an independent life as a noun for a publication issued at regular intervals, e.g. a magazine or journal. For librarians the **periodical** contrasts with the monograph (see under **monogram** or **monograph**). Like many a noun it can qualify other nouns, as it does in *periodical literature.*

perma- This prefix, newly derived from *permanent,* is being put to formative use in the twentieth century, witness *permafrost* from the 1940s, and more recently *permapress* (permanent press) and *permaculture* (that type of agriculture which is self-sustaining and does not require regular plantings).

permanence or **permanency** See under -nce/-ncy.

permissive or **permissible** These adjectives express complementary notions in society's control of its members. **Permissive** is the hands-off approach, tending to permit anything, as in *permissive parents.* **Permissible** implies statutory limits on what is permitted, as in *permissible levels of radiation.*

perpetual calendar This remarkable tool allows us to know exactly what day of the week any date in the past or future might be. Both historians and astrologers are interested in what day of the week people are born on; and those making forward plans for celebrations may be interested in what day of the week Australia Day will be in the year 2000 or 2001.

The calendar was originally developed within the Christian church as an aid to knowing what days of the week the fixed saints days fell on, and how they related to Easter in a given year. The table is based on the date of the first Sunday in the year, and from that a *dominical letter* i.e. a "Sunday letter" is determined for each year. If the first Sunday is actually January 1, the dominical letter for the year is A. If the first Sunday is January 2, the dominical letter is B; if it's January 3, the letter is C, and so on, through to G. Put the other way round, we have a scheme for checking the rotation of days of the week against fixed dates. So:

Dominical letter	A	January 1 =	Sunday
	B		Saturday
	C		Friday
	D		Thursday
	E		Wednesday
	F		Tuesday
	G		Monday

In leap years two dominical letters apply, one for January and February, and the second for March to December. The dominical letters, and their numerical equivalents, are shown on the table in Appendix II, along with a segment of the calendar for the years 1901 to 2001.

For more about the development of the European calendar, see under **dating systems.**

perquisite or **prerequisite** See prerequisite.

persistence or **persistency** See -nce/-ncy.

person For grammarians, the concept of **person** distinguishes between the person speaking (first person), the one spoken to (second person), and the one spoken about (third person). The differences are mostly to be seen among the pronouns:

first person	*I* (me, my, mine) *we* (us, our, ours)
second person	*you* (your, yours)
third person	*he* (him, his) *she* (her, hers) *it* (its) *they* (them, their, theirs)

The only other point in English grammar where **person** makes a difference is in the present tense singular of most verbs. The third person has an *-s* suffix, while the first and second do not. Compare: *I believe* and *you believe* with *s/he believes*. However with the verb *be*, all three *persons* are different: *am, are, is.*

First- or third-person narrative. When writing, the choice of **person** has a significant effect on the style. The choice of *first person*, especially *I*, has the effect of engaging the reader closely in whatever's described and has often been used by narrators for this reason. The use of *first person (plural) we* also tends to involve readers, suggesting a kind of solidarity between writer and reader which is useful for nonfiction writers. The *third person* puts distance between writer and reader, in both fiction and nonfiction. A *third person narrative*, written in terms of *he/she/it/they*, seems to set both writer and reader outside whatever's being described. And continuous use of the *third person* in nonfictional writing can seem very impersonal—which may or may not be the intention. (See further under **I**.)

-person Many have looked to this ending to provide a gender-free way out of some of the problems of sexism in language. So instead of saying *spokesman* or *spokeswoman*, we might use *spokesperson* for both. Unfortunately the word *spokesperson* (or *chairperson* or *salesperson* etc.) is more often used to paraphrase a term ending in *-woman* than one ending in *-man*. This means that people see the word ending in **-person** as a thinly veiled substitute for the one ending in *-woman*, and nothing has been achieved with it.

This is a potential difficulty with any of the substitutes proposed for the endings *-woman* or *-man*. Perhaps invented ones like *-per* (from *person*) or even *-peep* (from *people*) would have a better chance, in that they are more like true suffixes, many of which are gender-free. Yet if "policeper" were only used to replace *policewoman*, it could not become the gender-free alternative.

Better alternatives, for job titles at least, can be found among words which make no reference at all to gender but simply highlight the occupation. (See further under **man**.)

persona non grata In Latin this phrase means "unwelcome person". It has an official use in diplomatic circles, referring to representatives of foreign governments who are unacceptable in the country to which they are accredited.

But it's also used freely in many contexts to refer to someone who has lost their welcome there. The phrase was originally used in English in its positive form *persona grata*, but the negative form is now the one most widely known and used, especially in nondiplomatic contexts.

Because it is a Latin phrase, its plural is *personae non gratae*. (See further under **-a**.)

personal or **personnel** The first word is a common adjective meaning "belonging to the particular person", whose use is illustrated in phrases such as *personal column, personal computer, personal effects* and *personal space*. The word **personnel** is used in companies and government departments as a collective noun for all those employed there. It may take either singular or plural verbs in agreement (see under **collective nouns**).

Like many an English noun **personnel** works occasionally like an adjective, as in the *Personnel Department* of most large institutions and the *Personnel Officer* who heads it. Used in this way, it comes close to the domain of **personal**: see for example *personal development, personnel development*. Both are possible, though the first is about maximising individual potential, and the second represents the management's concern with staff training.

personal pronouns These are the set of pronouns which stand in place of nouns referring to person(s) or thing(s):

Has John brought the letter? Yes, he'*s brought* it.

For the full set of personal pronouns, see **person**. Other kinds of pronoun are presented under **pronoun**.

personification This is a literary device and figure of speech which imputes a personal character to something abstract or inanimate. Poets *personify* the great abstracts of our experience, as did Shakespeare in the simile:

Pity like a naked newborn babe striding the wind ...

In such lofty rhetoric the abstract is given human identity, and demands a human response from us. An atheist might comment that referring to the Christian God as *He* (*His/Him*) in hymns and religious discourse is also a form of **personification**.

Optimism about the future of Australia was *personified* in the voice of the nymph Hope, in verses by Erasmus Darwin (grandfather of Charles Darwin) on his visit to Sydney Cove in 1789:

"There shall tall spires and dome-capped towers ascend,
And piers and quays their massy structures blend;
While with each breeze approaching vessels glide,
And northern treasures dance on every tide!"
    Then ceased the nymph—tumultuous echoes roar,
And Joy's loud voice was heard from shore to shore—
Her graceful steps descending pressed the plain,
And Peace, and Art, and Labour joined her train.

Hope's handmaids are thus *personified* with her in the concluding lines.

Note that the use of *his* (with nonhuman subjects) in literature up to and including the seventeenth century is not necessarily a case of **personification**, because until then *his* served as the possessive for both *he* and *it*. The neuter pronoun *its* first appears at the end of the sixteenth century, and was not in regular use until about 1675. It is absent from the Authorised Version of the Bible, and only begins to appear in Shakespeare texts in the Folio editions of 1623.

Anthropomorphism and personification. Anthropomorphism is a similar device, which gives human form and attributes to the nonhuman, whether a deity, an animal or an object. In ancient art the gods were *anthropomorphised*, and so Athena, goddess of wisdom and justice, was depicted holding balanced scales, and Diana, goddess of the moon, appears as the huntress with bow and arrow in hand. A modern example would be the way a successful yachtsman might describe his boat as "dancing her way to the finishing line".

personnel or **personal** See **personal**.

persuasion The desire to persuade or convince the reader is often a motive for writing, one which calls for special attention to writing technique. Keeping readers with you is all-important, anticipating their attitudes and reactions, and managing the subject matter so that it too brings them inescapably to share your point of view.

We sometimes think of politicians and advertisers as the archetypal persuaders, yet the arts of **persuasion** were highly developed in ancient rhetoric. Then and now, **persuasion** depends on getting the audience on side, by an appeal to emotion or reason. The former was recognised as the more direct method, and meant trying to engage the audience's sympathies with something that touched the heart, or appealed to their better instincts (see further under **pathos**). Nowadays we might feel that the appeal to emotion was sometimes aimed at some instinct lower down the body—gut feeling, or the hip-pocket nerve. Both then and now, the persuader also knew the power of appealing to self-interest, with the *argumentum ad hominem* (see under **ad hominem**).

Persuaders with more respect for the intelligence of their audience are more likely to invoke reason and logic on their side, and to use the force of argument in **persuasion**. Classical rhetoric too recognised the place of *induction* and *deduction* in constructing an argument; and with less formal logic, today's persuaders may compile a convincing list of examples to make a general point, or get us to endorse a premise which leads to an inescapable conclusion. (See further under **induction** and **deduction**.) Either way they are not simply giving us loose information or an extended narrative, but selecting and structuring a telling set of points for maximum effect.

The ultimate key to **persuasion** is in getting the audience or reader to share your value system—to agree that something is worthwhile, or to be condemned. This often comes back to using evaluative words which embed those values in whatever is being talked about. Environmentalists evoke the common concern with preserving natural resources, and so words like "natural", "renewable resource" and "rainforest" are positively charged, while "exploitation" and "pollution" carry negative values. Such values can be shared by many people these days, whether they look to nature for recreation or for raw materials. Advertisers often try to persuade by appealing to the social values latent in their readers, their concern with self-image and social status. So words like "glamor", "luxury" and "sophistication" are used to tap that value system, and help consumers reach for their wallets.

perverse or **perverted** The second adjective makes a much more serious charge than the first. **Perverse** just implies that something defies convention and normal practice, as in:

He took a perverse interest in watching every soap opera ever screened.

The habit described could never be thought of as morally reprehensible, whereas **perverted** does imply an infringement of the common moral code, as in:

He took a perverted interest in child pornography.

Perverted is of course part of a verb, which also refers to a serious moral and/ or legal matter, witness the charge of *perverting the course of justice*.

Note that the abstract noun for **perverse** may be either *perverseness* or *perversity*. *Perversion* however is reserved as the abstract noun for **perverted**.

petaled or **petalled** For the spelling of this word when used as a verb, see -l/-ll-.

petitio principii See **beg the question**.

petrol or **petroleum** These are not strictly synonymous, since they refer to products from different stages of the process of refining oil. **Petroleum** is the natural raw material, also known as "crude oil", "rock oil" and "black gold". Stage by stage in the refining process, **petroleum** yields various fuels, including kerosene (also known as "paraffin"), diesel, liquefied petroleum gas (LPG) and **petrol** itself. Though **petrol** is its standard name in Australia and Britain, the same fuel is *gasoline* or *gas* in the USA.

ph or **f** See **f/ph**.

phalanx This word enjoys some general use, meaning a body of people in close array. Its plural then is *phalanxes*, just as in historical references to the distinctive battle formation used by the Greeks and Macedonians (men packed together under overlapping shields). But for the anatomist who uses the word to mean any of the bones of the fingers or toes, the plural is *phalanges*. For other examples of this type, see **-x** section 3.

The *phalanger* (a zoologist's term for various kinds of possum) takes its name from **phalanx** in the anatomical sense.

pharmacist, chemist or **druggist** The word **pharmacist** is now the standard Australian term for the specialist maker and dispenser of pharmaceutical remedies, who usually doubles as the retailer of other goods associated with health care. In older Australian usage, the **pharmacist** was the

chemist, as older shop signs remind us, and this is still the usual term in Britain. But in Australia those trained in pharmacy moved to identify themselves as *pharmacists*, and the professional *chemist* is nowadays more likely to be a specialist in chemistry who works at a university or research laboratory—a different world from that of the person who runs a suburban pharmacy/chemist's shop. In the USA the word **druggist** is the standard name for the trained pharmacist—not to be confused with the illegal *drug dealer*.

phase or **faze** Though separate in origin and meaning, these raise some confusion and uncertainty because both *ph* and *f*, and *s* and *z* can be interchanged in some other English words.

  Phase serves primarily as a noun, although it has acquired uses as a verb in the last half century, particularly the phrasal verbs *phase in/phase out*, and also as a simple verb meaning (1) "synchronise", and (2) "carry out in stages". Neither of this latter pair is in general use, the first being a technical word, and the second an administrative and institutional expression. Neither is used of people. Given those roles it's perhaps surprising that **phase** could become tangled with the rather informal verb **faze** meaning "disconcert", which is almost always used of people, and typically in a negative construction:

  Contentious meetings never fazed him.

Faze seems to be a variant form of an old dialect word *feeze* meaning "frighten away", recorded in American English from the early nineteenth century. The first evidence of substituting **phase** for **faze** is late in the century, and it has been recorded often enough in the twentieth century to be entered as a variant in *Webster's Dictionary*, but not *Random House* or *Oxford Dictionary* (1989). *Webster's English Usage* (1989) recommends against it, though without great hope that **phase** and **faze** can be confined to their independent roles.

phenomenon and **phenomena** These are the singular and plural form respectively for this Greek loanword, presented in all dictionaries as the standard forms (see further under **-on**). However the *Oxford Dictionary* shows that **phenomena** has been used as the singular since the sixteenth century, and usage notes in both *Collins* and *Random House* dictionaries register it as a current tendency, although one which is infrequent in edited writing. Research by Collins (1979) among young Australian adults showed that between 80 and 90% would think of **phenomena** as a singular.

  An anglicised plural *phenomenons* is registered in larger dictionaries. In *Webster's* and *Random House* it's associated particularly with the use of **phenomenon** to mean "outstanding person".

phil- or **-phile** This Greek root means "loving", and it serves as either first or second element in a number of loanwords and neo-Greek formations including:

  philanthropy philharmonic philologer philosopher

and

  Anglophile audiophile bibliophile zoophile

In modern usage its meaning is quite often "collector (of)", as in *philatelist*, *phillumenist* and *discophile*. Note that the words ending in **-phile** are sometimes spelled without the final *e*, and both *bibliophile* and *bibliophil* are recognised in dictionaries. The abstract noun associated with **-phile** is usually *-philia*, as in *audiophilia*. In a few older cases it can also be *-phily*, as with *bibliophilia* or *bibliophily*, but the *-philia* form is more common.

Philip or **Phillip** Both spellings are widely used, as first names and as surnames **Phil(l)ip(s)**. The original Greek name consisted of *phil-* "loving" and *(h)ippos* "horse". So by rights the name should have one *l* and two *ps* (as it does in *Philippines*).

But as with other borrowed words, it lacks analogies to help fix the number of consonants in the middle, and may gain or lose them (see further under **single for double**). So both spellings are around in the names of people and places. Note that Captain Arthur Phillip used two *ls*, and this dictates the spelling in placenames which commemorate his regime as the first governor of the Australian colony:

> *Phillip (ACT) Phillip Bay (NSW) Phillip Island/Port Phillip Bay (VIC)*
> *Phillip Creek (NT)*

Philippines This nation of many islands (over 7000, of which only about one tenth are inhabited), was named by the Spaniards in 1521 in honor of Philip II of Spain. Until 1898 it was ruled by Spain, but it then came under US control, as part of the treaty which ended the Spanish–American war. After a brief period of Japanese control from 1942 to 1945, it became an independent republic in 1946.

The English spoken in the **Philippines** has a noticeable American coloring, a legacy of the American presence in the first half of this century. But the national language is *Pilipino*, an Austronesian language based mainly on Tagalog. The citizens of the **Philippines** are called *Filipinos*. (See further under **f/ph**.)

Phillip or **Philip** See Philip.

-phobia This word element, meaning "morbid or irrational fear", is well known in formations such as *agoraphobia* and *claustrophobia*; and in ones such as *Anglophobia* and *Judophobia*, where it means "antipathy (to)". The first meaning is the one which has been put to extensive use in modern English to name all kinds of irrational anxieties, such as fear of spiders (*arachnophobia*) and sharks (*galeophobia*), of wet and dry (*hydrophobia/xerophobia*), of death (*necrophobia*), and of the number 13 (*triskaidekaphobia*).

Note that the person suffering from or obsessed with a *phobia* is a *-phobe*, as in *claustrophobe*.

phonesthemes This is the technical name for sounds (usually pairs or sequences of them) which seem to express a particular quality whatever words they appear in. The most noticeable examples are the initial consonant sounds, and those the syllable ends with. The letter *s* is involved in a number of the classic examples. It seems as if "sk" at the start of words such as *scoot*, *skip* and *scuttle* expresses the quick movement implied in all of them, while "sl" suggests either a falling or sliding movement as in *slip*, *slither* or *slouch*, or something slimy or slushy, as in those words and in *sludge*, *slobber* and *sloppy*. "Sp" seems to represent a quick ejective movement in *spit*, *spatter*, *spout* and *spurt*; and "sw" a swaying or swinging movement, as in both of those and in *sweep*, *swirl* and *swagger*.

The closing part of a word also seems to be suggestive of the meaning itself in various cases. Words ending in *-ip* often suggest a brisk, quick movement, as with:

clip flip nip rip skip tip whip

The *le* suffix seems to bring a sense of light movement or sound to most words it's attached to, witness:

crackle crinkle fizzle giggle prattle rustle
scuffle trickle twinkle whistle

(See further under **-le**.)

A further example is in words ending in *-ump*, which are often associated with heaviness and falling weight. See for example:

clump dump hump lump plump slump thump

In some words, the effects of **phonesthemes** at both the beginning and the end of the word are felt, as with *slip* and *slump* from the examples above.

Some of the **phonesthemes** shown above are older than English itself. In other Indo-European languages, words beginning with *sp* also connote senses such as "spit out" or "reject". Yet this kind of sound symbolism also depends on there being a sufficiently large group of such words in a language at any one time. Words embodying **phonesthemes** (like any others) adapt their meanings over the course of time, and may thus dilute the collective effect. And of course there are always other words which coincidentally have the same initial or concluding letters, but whose etymology and current meaning go against the common sound symbolism. Words like *space*, *spade* and *spectrum* could hardly be said to embody any of the sound effects attributed to *sp*, let alone words like *spare*, *special* and *speculation*.

So **phonesthemes** are one of the latent aspects of words, useful to poets for onomatopoeia, and to advertisers in promoting their products, but not a powerful force in ordinary prose. (See further under **onomatopoeia**.)

phonograph or **gramophone** Phonograph is the name given by Edison in 1877 to the cylindrical instrument which was the world's first means of recording and reproducing sound. In 1887 Berliner patented the **gramophone**, a machine which could also record and reproduce sound but did it on a revolving disk.

In the USA, the term **phonograph** was extended to the revolving disk system, and the records used on it were also known as *phonograms*. However the word

phonograph has now been replaced by *record player*. In Britain and Australia, the term **phonograph** went out with the cylinder system of recording, and the revolving disk system has always been known as the **gramophone**. But here too, the dominant term is now *record player*.

phony or **phoney** The first spelling is given preference in American dictionaries, the second in British ones. This balance is matched in Australia, where almost equal numbers of newspaper style guides plump for each, and the *Macquarie Dictionary* (1991) gives equal status to the two spellings.

The origins of the word are uncertain, though most authorities suggest it's linked with the Irish word *fawney*, used to refer to cheap jewellery, and the ring used in confidence tricks. If so the respelling of the word with *ph* is itself **phony**, but we can hardly propose a return to *f* there. We can however give preference to **phony** as the spelling which avoids any spurious connection with the telephone.

phosphorus or **phosphorous** See under **-ous**.

phrasal verbs Many English verbs express their meaning with the aid of a following particle, as in *blow up* ("explode"), *give off* ("emit") and *turn down* ("reject"). Some are followed by two particles, witness:
> *check up on   come up with   face up to*
> *get away with   look down on   walk out on*

These **phrasal verbs** are typically simple and monosyllabic, and the particles are drawn from the commonest and shortest in our preposition/adverb list. *Up* is particularly common in **phrasal verbs**.

In **phrasal verbs**, the particle is closely integrated with the verb, even when an object is interposed between them. So for *turn off* (meaning "extinguish") either *turned off the light* or *turned the light off* will work. This is not possible for similar-looking constructions which are not **phrasal verbs**: *turned off the highway* cannot be rearranged as "turned the highway off". In the second case *off* is a true preposition, which must precede its noun phrase ("the highway"). In the first case *off* is a particle integrated with the verb as a single unit of meaning. The particle of the **phrasal verb** serves to make it transitive (see further under **transitive**).

Phrasal verbs are informal and unpretentious expressions, and often serve as alternatives to a single Latin word, as seen in some of the "translations" shown above. They are very common in conversation, as we string sentences together on the run. In impromptu use they may be overextended, as is sometimes argued, so that *meet up with* is used when just *meet* would do. But subtle differences are perhaps being expressed thereby (see under **meet**).

The presence or absence of prepositions after verbs, and the choice of preposition, is sometimes a matter of dialect difference. (See **prepositions**, section 1.)

phrases A *phrase* is often thought of simply as a multiword unit, contrasting with the single word. So *quick as a flash* is a *phrase* consisting of four words. But for the grammarian a *phrase* is a unit of a clause. It may consist of a single word (such as a name or pronoun) or of several words. In English grammar we distinguish five types of *phrase*:

   noun phrase with a noun as head: *their pet cat/Rex*
   verb phrase with a verb as head: *was lying/lay*
   prepositional phrase with a preposition as first word: *on the bed*
   adjectival phrase with an adjective as head: *most well-bred/pedigree*
   adverbial phrase with an adverb as head: *very endearingly/delightfully*
(See under those headings for more about each.)

pica This word has several meanings in relation to type:
1 For typewriters it is a type size yielding 10 characters to the inch, also known as *ten pitch*.

`This is in the typewriter's pica.`

2 In typesetting the 12 point typesize has been called **pica**.

This is in typesetter's pica.

3 In typesetting, the **pica** is also a unit of linear measurement, equal to just on 4.21 mm or one sixth of an inch, and used to measure the column of print as well as the dimensions of graphics.

Note that the *point* used in measuring the size of a font is one twelfth of a **pica**, i.e. one seventy-second of an inch. In this technical use *point* is often abbreviated as *pt*.

picketed For the spelling of this word when used as a verb, see **t**.

picnic When it becomes a verb, a *k* has to be added. (See **-c/-ck-**.)

pidgins and **creoles** New languages for old. A pidgin is an original system of communication, developed out of existing languages under special circumstances. It usually happens when groups of people who have no language in common try to communicate with each other, using whatever words they hear being used around them. **Pidgins** often develop for the purposes of trade, as did "Bazaar Malay", and the "Bamboo English" used in Korea; but they are also associated with colonial plantations, which employed workers (or slaves) from diverse other places. Both "Black English" in the USA and New Guinea Pidgin originated in this way.

   Pidgins consist of a very basic inventory of words, which work without suffixes and prefixes. Any single word has to do service for a wide range of meanings, witness the use of *arse* in New Guinea pidgin to mean "foundation, basis", and *mary* as the common noun for "woman, wife, girl, maid". Pidgin sentences have the simplest grammatical structure and subordination is rare. Both words and grammatical structures are drawn from the dominant language in the context, typically the language of the colonialist, hence the development of "English-based pidgins", "French-based pidgins" etc.

Pidgins begin life as very restricted languages, sufficient for communication between peoples who have few dealings with each other. But as people resort to *pidgin* more often and the topics of conversation increase, it develops into an *elaborated pidgin* and then becomes the *lingua franca* for people in linguistically diverse regions. This was the way *New Guinea pidgin* grew from its plantation origins to become the lingua franca of the New Guinea region, and now one of the official languages of Papua New Guinea. For many New Guineans it has in fact become their native language, at which point its status is strictly speaking that of a *creole*, no longer a *pidgin*. But the name "New Guinea pidgin" remains with it, and is no doubt still appropriate for those who acquired it as a second language, after their mother tongue.

Some Aboriginal forms of English are really **creoles**, evolved out of the *pidgin* forms of communication which developed between Aborigines and white settlers in remote parts of Australia. Some of the better documented Aboriginal **creoles** are those used across northern Australia from the Kimberleys to the Roper River (NT), known collectively as *Kriol*. Others are to be found in Cape York Peninsula and the Torres Strait islands.

Note that the word *pidgin* is sometimes (rather distractingly) spelled *pigeon*, though the word is more likely to be derived from business than birds. *Pidgin* is probably a reduced form of the word "business", as spoken by those whose language had fewer consonant sounds than English and no "s" sound (rare in Australian and Pacific languages). The connection with "business" is eminently likely, seeing that **pidgins** are often associated with trading. The word *creole* is borrowed from French, though it's ultimately a Spanish and Portuguese word meaning "native to the locality".

pièce de résistance Two of the three words look English, but they shed little light on the meaning of this French phrase. English-speakers use it to mean the "most important item in a collection or program of events", an extension of its original use in reference to the most substantial dish in a meal. The phrase complements **chef d'oeuvre** (see under that heading).

pied à terre This in French is literally "foot on the ground". But in English it refers to a lodging in the city which serves as temporary accommodation for someone whose normal place of residence is out of town, or in another city.

pigmy or **pygmy** These alternative spellings raise a number of issues. The word was spelled with an *i* in earlier English and up to the sixteenth century. The spelling with *y* was then introduced, along with various other respellings which brought older loanwords into line with their classical antecedents. To those who have enough Greek to appreciate it, the spelling **pygmy** is a reminder of the root *pygme* embedded in it, which was the name of an old Greek unit of length, measured from the elbow to the knuckles—rather like the cubit. Fowler preferred the *y* spelling for this reason, and it's the one endorsed by the *Oxford Dictionary*, in spite of the fact that the majority of its citations for the word are spelled with *i*. Etymology seems to have prevailed very strongly over usage in this case, though the major American dictionaries also endorse **pygmy**.

Perhaps there's another issue to reckon with. The spelling **pygmy** does help to prevent the development of any folk etymology that associated the word with ''pig''. That consideration apart, the spelling **pigmy** is more straightforward, not overendowed with *y*s, and allows the word to move with the larger wave of those which vary between *i* and *y*, which are tending towards *i*. (See further under **i/y**.)

Note that when it refers to the *Pygmies*, the dwarf people of equatorial Africa, the word should have a capital letter. (See **capitals**, section 1.)

pimento or **pimiento** These both go back to the Spanish word for pepper, but they are now attached to quite different fruits. **Pimiento** is the sweet and pungently flavored red pepper, the fruit of a shrub (Capsicum annuum) which is also picked and eaten green. Alternative names for it are the *bell pepper*, *sweet pepper* and *capsicum*. **Pimento** is the spice made from the dried berries of a tropical American tree (either *Pimenta droica* or *Pimenta officinalis*), which grows between 6 and 12 m in height. Its alternative name is *allspice*.

In spite of the distinction just described, the names are occasionally substituted for each other. Most often it's the name **pimento** being used for the **pimiento**, but now and then the reverse happens.

Pintupi or **Bindupi** See under **Aboriginal names**.

pis aller See **faute de mieux**.

piscina The plural of this word is discussed under **-a** section 1.

pitiful, pitiable or **piteous** All these revolve around a sense of pity, and the first two are interchangeable in some contexts. In *a pitiful sight* and *pitiable squalor* the adjectives could be exchanged. **Piteous** stands apart. It is the least common of them, and nowadays mostly used to describe vocal sounds, as in *a piteous cry*, where it also implies weakness and faintness.

Note that both **pitiful** and **pitiable** can imply a certain contempt for the condition they describe. A *pitiable effort* or a *pitiful attempt at good relations* carry negative judgements, rather than pity for what is observed. Thus the connotations of **pitiful** and **pitiable** are becoming what they already are for *miserable* and *wretched*. **Pitiful** is probably more widely used than **pitiable**, helped by the fact that its adverb *pitifully* is freely used to express the writer's attitude.

placenames See under **geographical names**.

placenta For the plural of this word, see **-a** section 1.

plagiarism is passing off someone else's writing as if it were your own—
whether it's done on the grand scale by taking over a whole publication, or just
"borrowing" sections, paragraphs or sentences. Any verbatim quotation of a
sentence or more which originates from another writer, and which is not
acknowledged to be theirs, is an act of **plagiarism**. For professional writers, it's
a crime, and for student writers, a dishonest and reprehensible practice, whether
it involves borrowing from fellow students, or from published sources. It shows
a disinclination to engage the mind in writing for oneself, a combination of
intellectual laziness and intellectual theft. Proper quotation and
acknowledgement of sources are a part of good scholarly practice, and a way
of avoiding **plagiarism**.

plain or **plane** These words can have quite similar meanings, and in fact they
derive from the same source, the Latin adjective *planus* "flat or level". The
different spellings became attached to their different uses in the seventeenth
century. The spelling **plane** became the one for mathematical and technical
nouns, including the *vertical plane*, the *(aero)plane*, and the **plane** used to
smooth wood in carpentry. The same word serves as an adjective in *plane
geometry*.

The other spelling **plain** is used as a noun in geographical analysis of
landscapes, as in a *well-watered plain*. It also serves as a general-purpose
adjective meaning "simple, unadorned". *Plain English* aims to be just that, not
complex and convoluted. *Plainsong* (the earliest kind of church music) was sung
in unison without any accompaniment. So spelling distinguishes a *plain surface*,
i.e. one without any decoration, from a *plane surface*, one which may be a
subject for discussion in geometry or mathematics.

Doubts about which spelling to use may arise in figurative expressions, such
as *on the moral plane*. The spelling there confirms that it's a metaphor from
mathematics. But when it's a matter of *one plain one purl* (in knitting), the
image is geographical.

Note that the *plane tree* owes its name to a different source altogether, the
Latin word *platanus*.

Plain English The **Plain English** movement gained momentum in the 1980s
to promote lucid communication between public institutions and people at large.
It aims to reduce the amount of officialese and gobbledygook in government
publications, and also in the fields of law and insurance; and it has enjoyed the
backing of the federal government as well as the Victorian government and the
NSW Law Foundation. The campaign has gathered steam in Britain and in the
USA, and in both places the incomprehensibility of a document has recently
been raised as a defence in law suits.

The **Plain English** campaign emphasises the importance of document design
and especially readable language. Any document needs a clear layout, adequate
white space in the margins and between sections, and effective use of headings
and subheadings to flag their contents. Underlining, color and contrasting

typefaces help to highlight them. Where readability comes in, it's broadly a matter of seeking simple, everyday words whenever possible, and speaking more directly to the reader. Sentences need to be shorter and less intricate, with punctuation that ensures reliable reading. An average of no more than 20 words is recommended. Paragraphs too should be constrained in length, with shorter ones (averaging say 5 lines) for business letters, and longer ones (averaging 10 lines) for larger documents.

1 *What to avoid in* **Plain English**. Part of achieving **Plain English** is being more aware of clichés and other conventional wordiness. Many formulaic phrases such as the following can be paraphrased more simply: *in the event of* often amounts to just plain *if*, and *in respect of* to *about*. High density phrases such as *new employees health and welfare standing committee* are ambiguous and hard to decode, and can be accessed more easily if unpacked as the "standing committee on the health and welfare of new employees". **Plain English** does not necessarily mean restricting the number of words used to express something, especially if it's a complex concept. But if you seem to have enough words for one sentence, it never hurts to stop and begin a new one with the next major concept.

Other structures to avoid in **Plain English** are double or multiple negatives (see under **double negatives**); and double-pronged questions. Most people have to think twice when asked:
Are you over 21 and under 65?
The answers will be more reliable if you ask those two questions separately, or else reword them into a single question:
Are you between 21 and 65 years of age?
The most important principle of **Plain English** is to keep the reader in mind as you write. Think of yourself as communicating to someone, and of how each sentence sounds. Use your ear to test whether they leave the reader gasping for breath.

2 *The importance of* **Plain English**. In the end **Plain English** achieves more than clear communication—though that itself is a substantial benefit. It also reduces reading errors, and complaints and law suits relating to official documents. Apart from saving time and energy and money on all those fronts, it gives citizens a better understanding of government procedures and policies, and of their own rights.

plaintiff or **plaintive** Plaintive is an adjective meaning "sad, mournful", as in the *plaintive cry of the seagull*. **Plaintiff** is a noun referring to the person who raises legal action against another party in a criminal case. (The other party is the defendant.)

Both words derive ultimately from the French adjective *plaintif* meaning "complaining", where the form ending in *f* is masculine and the one with *ve* feminine. In English the gender distinction does not apply, and the woman who raises a law suit is still a *plaintiff*.

plane or **plain**   See **plain**.

plateau   The plural of this word is discussed at **-eau**.

platefuls or **platesful**   See under **-ful**.

platypus   Those who pluralise this word as *platypuses* are taking the most sensible course in a linguistic dilemma. A hybrid word, it was created in the nineteenth century out of Greek elements *platy-* "broad" and *pous* "foot", with the second one latinised as *-pus*. This ending has encouraged the idea that it deserves a Latin plural *platypi*, which is entered as an alternative in some dictionaries.

   Choosing the right plural is the point of a story told by Stephen Murray-Smith about an Australian professor of classics who was asked whether the plural of **platypus** was *platypi* or *platypoi*. "That" he replied "shows an ignorance of three languages". He presumably meant that the Latin *platypi* was wrong because the word is essentially Greek; and the Greek *platypoi* puts it into the wrong declension. (If you're going to go Greek you need *platypodes*. Cf. **octopus**.) Above all it was a mistake to bypass the standard English plural for a word that was coined in English anyway. Among the citations in the *Australian National Dictionary* there is only one for *platypi* from the middle of last century. All the rest are for *platypuses*. Note that conservationists and others may use a zero plural for the word:
   The number of platypus in the river system is declining.
(See further under **zero plural**.)

pleaded or **pled**   The verb *plead* is one of those old irregular verbs which has reverted to being regular, in most parts of the world. **Pleaded** is given as the primary spelling for the past tense in all modern dictionaries, Australian, British and American. **Pled** is given as the second option, but seems to have most currency in American English. The use of *plead* (to rhyme with "led") as the past tense died out in the nineteenth century.

plein air   This French phrase means "open air", although it's not used of anything outdoors like *al fresco*. Instead **plein air** is used in analysing landscape painting that creates the effect and atmosphere of outdoor light, particularly the work of impressionist painters.

   Note that there's no need to hyphenate **plein air** when it serves as a compound adjective: *a plein air depiction of the harbor*.

plenteous or **plentiful**   Both mean "abundant", but the first word now sounds old-fashioned, and is confined to literary and religious diction. **Plentiful** enjoys wide currency, whether it's a matter of the *plentiful supply* of trout in mountain streams, or of good quality bananas at the markets.

pleonasm This means using a combination of words which overlap or duplicate each other in meaning. In some cases it may be viewed negatively, as overwriting or redundancy; in others it seems acceptable either because it's the established idiom, or because it lends intensity to whatever is being said.

1 *The negative side of* **pleonasm** is usually referred to as "redundancy" or "tautology". (Note however that for philosophers the word *tautology* is neutral in meaning. See under **induction**.) Samples of redundancy are all too common in officialese, in the use of unnecessary abstract nouns:

> *the weather conditions for the race*
>
> *problems in the classroom situation*

Redundancy is particularly common in impromptu public speech by politicians and radio announcers, as they try to maintain continuous output with not quite enough ideas for their rate of speaking, as in phrases like:

> *the two twins   new innovations   revert back   paid professional*

More conspicuous examples are the focus of pompous or ponderous statements such as:

> *Traditionally, most of our imports have come from overseas.*
>
> *In New York you can go to a different restaurant every night without going to the same one twice.*

There speakers cover the same ground twice without apparently realising it.

2 *Acceptable* **pleonasms**. Numerous time-honored English phrases are strictly tautologous, witness:

> *free gifts   grateful thanks   past history   usual habit*

Though the adjective adds little to the noun in such expressions, they are sanctioned by usage, and in some cases by the highest authorities in the land. Many *pleonasms* come from law and religion:

> *last will and testament   null and void*
>
> *join together   lift up*

Such expressions do have a function in their original context, in their rhetorical effect and in providing synonyms for less familiar words. Rhetorical emphasis is certainly part of the effect in the very common speech-maker's line:

> *I have one further point to add ...*

The doubling up of *further* and *add* draws attention to the start of a new structural unit in the text, and underscores the final argument. Why should we quibble at that, any more than we do at Shakespeare's dramatic use of tautology in "the most unkindest cut of all"? The double superlative, like the double negative, may be condemned as tautology, or recognised as a resource for intense expression. If you're aiming at hyperbole, **pleonasm** helps to create it in:

> *What wasteful superfluous trivia I had rammed into my head as a kid!*
>
> *As an example of bogus semiotic pseudo-scholarship, this book is priceless.*

See further under **hyperbole** and **figures of speech**.

plink or **plonk** See **vin blanc**.

plough or **plow** See under **gh**.

plummeted For the spelling of this word when used as a verb, see **t**.

pluperfect The past perfect tense is also known as the **pluperfect**. Compare *had arrived* (past perfect) with *have arrived* (present perfect) and see further under **aspect**.

plurals *Plural* forms of words contrast with *singular* ones, to show that more than one item or person is meant. In English the difference is regularly marked on nouns and pronouns, and to a very limited extent on verbs. (For more about the grammar, see further under **number**.) In this entry we concentrate on the plural forms of nouns and noun compounds, as well as proper names, titles and national groups. For the plural forms of numbers and letters, see **letters as words**, and **numbers** and **number style**.

1 *Plurals of nouns.* The letter *s* is the standard English plural suffix, used with many words both ancient and modern. Yet a considerable number of words make their plural in some other way.
a) Several groups take *-es*, including:
  those ending in an "s","z","tch","dg","sh" or "ks" sound such as
    kisses, quizzes, batches, ridges dishes and *boxes.*
  those ending in plain *y* (as opposed to *-ay* etc.) where the *y* changes to *i*
    before adding *-es*, as in *cherries.* (See further under **-y>-i-**.)
  some of those ending in *f* (or *fe*), which changes to *v* before the *-es*, as in
    loaves and *wives.* (See further under **-f>-v-**.)
  some of those ending in *o*, such as *echoes.* (See further under **-o**.)
b) A group of very old words adjust their vowels to show the plural, including
  man>men and *woman>women; foot>feet, goose>geese* and *tooth>teeth; louse>lice* and *mouse>mice.* Note the change of consonant as well in the last pair.
c) Three distinctive words with plurals in *(r)en*: *children, oxen* and *brethren.* The third is an old plural of *brother*, used only in restricted contexts these days. (See **brethren**.)
d) Some words have *zero plural*, i.e. don't change at all from singular to plural, such as *sheep.* (See under **zero plural**.)
e) Loanwords from Latin may have English or Latin plurals. (See under **-a, -is, -us, -um** and **-x**.)
f) Loanwords from Greek may have English or Greek plurals. (See under **-a** and **-on**.)
g) Loanwords from French ending in *eau, ieu* or *iau* may have French plurals in *x*. (See under **eau**.)
h) Loanwords from Italian sometimes have Italian plurals. (See under **Italian plurals**.)
i) Loanwords from Hebrew usually have Hebrew plurals. (See under **-im**.)

2 *Plurals* of compounds. Those that are plain English compounds are pluralised simply by adding *s* at the end, whether they are set solid, spaced or hyphenated:

breakdowns baby-sitters forget-me-nots geography teachers go-betweens
grownups handouts shop assistants wordprocessors tip-offs

The chief exceptions are compounds in which the key noun comes first, as with:

editors-in-chief grants-in-aid ladies-in-waiting
prisoners-of-war passers-by sisters-in-law

The fact that the key noun comes first is also the basis of traditional plurals in:

courts martial governors-general heirs apparent
judges advocate poets laureate sergeants major

However most of those terms can now be pluralised with a *s* at the end, e.g. *court martials*, and we forget that the second word is historically an adjective. Titles of that kind are based on the French word order, which puts the noun first and adjective second. Their traditional plurals in English go back centuries, to when the English language and English law were much more under French influence. For more about **governor-general**, see under that heading.

Uncertainties remain about how to pluralise compounds which are still visibly foreign, especially those from modern French. A few are pluralised in the French way, as with *aides de camp*, *objets d'art* and *pièces de résistance*, no doubt because their structure is clear even in English, and we recognise that the key noun comes first. In cases where this is not transparent, an *s* is simply added to the last word, as in:

cul-de-sacs hors d'oeuvres vol-au-vents

however strange this seems if you know the French words. For the plural of **grand prix**, see under that heading.

The tendency just to add an *s* at the end is even stronger with Latin compounds, witness **postmortem(s)**, **pro forma(s)** and **curriculum vitae(s)**. (See further under those headings.)

3 *Plurals* of proper names and titles. On the somewhat rare occasions when we need to pluralise personal names, we usually add and *s* or *es* in accordance with the general rules for nouns:

The Smiths and the Joneses are on our list.

Note that names ending in *y* never have it changed to *i*:

McNallys are on it too.

When two people share a surname and title, either title or name may bear the plural marker:

Misses Smith   Messrs Smith
Miss Smiths   Mr Smiths

The pluralised title still appears in any formal or corporate address (e.g. on envelopes), whereas the pluralised name is more likely elsewhere. When the surnames are different, the only option is to pluralise the title: *Misses Smith and Jones*; *Messrs Smith and Jones*. Note that there's no plural for the title

Mrs, and we have instead to use *Mesdames*. *Ms* can be pluralised as *Mss* or *Mses*, but neither is much used yet. The plural of *Dr* is simply *Drs*.

4 *Plurals* *of national groups.* The names of national and tribal groups are now usually made in the regular way with *s*: *growing numbers of Khmers* (not *Khmer*). Increasingly people feel that using the zero plural (*Khmer*) is unfortunately like the standard plural for various groups of animals (see further under **zero plurals**). The only national names to keep their zero plurals are ones ending in sibilants, notably *-ese* and *-ish*: *the Japanese, the British*.

plus From its home base in mathematics, this word has been annexed into ordinary usage, as in *total cost plus postage*; and it is now being used for several other purposes, witness the following examples from the ACE corpus:

> *We will give you advice on basic planning, plus quick tips on making your kitchen more efficient.*
> *There are three classes. Upper, middle, and lower. Plus there are some people who live below the lower class ...*

The examples show **plus** working as a preposition/conjunction, and as a conjunct. Its meaning is more than additive: in the first case it is "as well as" and in the second something like "besides which". (See further under **conjunctions**.) These uses of **plus** are recognised in the latest dictionaries, though usually prefaced by the label "informal". *Webster's English Usage* has citations for them from the 1960s, and the *Oxford Dictionary* from the 1970s.

The use of **plus** as a common noun is also established, as in *a big plus*. The preferred plural in all dictionaries is with one *s*, although the Oxford has equal numbers of citations for *pluses* and *plusses*.

Note also the uses of **plus** as an adjective, in *the plus factor* and in *a 20 kg plus tuna* or *a lay trainer plus*, where it has a special role as a post-modifier.

p.m. or **pm** This is the standard abbreviation for times of day which fall between noon and midnight. It stands for Latin *post meridiem* "after midday". Full stops are not essential with it, since it cannot be confused with any other word, and its time function is made clear by the numbers (between 1 and 12) which precede it. However some writers and editors would use stops with it, in accordance with their general policy on lower case abbreviations, and with its counterpart *a.m./am* (see **abbreviations**, section 2). In the Australian ACE corpus there were equal numbers of **p.m.** and **pm**—18 instances of each.

Note that **p.m.** times begin immediately after noon, and so the first minute after 12 noon (= 12 a.m.) is 12.01 p.m. This naturally means that 12 midnight is 12 p.m., and the first minute of the next day is 12.01 a.m.

Note also that by adding **p.m.** you indicate clearly to readers that you're not working with a 24-hour clock. This may be important in making travel arrangements overseas where 24-hour schedules are much more widely used, and ''Arriving at 6.30'' would be unhesitatingly interpreted as a morning arrival. They would expect 18.30 (or *6.30 p.m.*) if you meant the evening.

poetic or **poetical** See under **-ic/-ical**.

point For the use of this word in measuring typefaces, see under **pica**.

pokie, poky or **pokey** This informal word for a poker machine usually appears in the plural, as in *playing the pokies*, which makes the spelling of the singular a real question. Australian authorities all give preference to **pokie**, which helps distinguish it from the adjective **poky** meaning ''cramped''. (See further under **-ie/-y**.) The spelling **pokie** also sets it apart from **pokey**, which is slang for ''jail'' in North America.

polarity Language, like a magnetic field, may be charged either positively or negatively. This **polarity** is rarely an issue in statements about the way things are, because the facts of the situation decide whether it should be positive or negative. Either:
  Schools reopen next Monday. or
  Schools do not reopen next Monday—not until the week after.
But when posing questions we quite often seek to know whether something is or is not:
  Has the boss gone to the conference?
  Would they like a cup of coffee?
In such questions, the polarity has yet to be established, and they are in fact known to many as ''polar questions''. Because they require either ''yes'' or ''no'' for an answer, they are also known as *yes/no questions*. Questions like these differ from *wh-questions*, which require the person answering to offer a piece of information. (See further under **questions**.)
  The **polarity** of a statement has an interesting effect on any tag question that follows it. Compare the following:
  You'd like to come, wouldn't you?
  You wouldn't want to come, would you?
As those sentences show, a positive statement is normally followed by a negative tag question, and vice versa.

political or **politic** These two have diverged, so that **politic** is now confined to the meaning ''judicious, prudent in public affairs'', and **political** covers the broad range of ''belonging to the state or government or a power group and its policies''. **Politic** once covered that ground too, as fossilised in *the body politic*. But the area was taken over by **political** by the mid-eighteenth century.

pollex For the plural of this word, see **-x** section 3.

pollie or **polly** In case there's a need to distinguish between the politician **pollie** and the familiar word for a parrot **polly**, the endings do it. For other words separated by such endings, see **-ie/y**.

For *poly*, see next entry.

poly- This prefix meaning "many" is derived from Greek words such as:

polygamy polygon polyglot polymath polyphonic polysyllabic

In modern English it's mostly used to form new chemical terms, such as:

polyester polymer polypeptide polythene polyunsaturated
polyurethane polyvinyl chloride

A few of the chemical terms have become household words, most notably *polyunsaturated*, and it has helped to generate its own new breed of words, in *polymeat* and *polymilk*—both foods in which there's a relatively high level of polyunsaturated fat. Derivatives from *polyester* are textile blends which incorporate it, such as *polycotton*, *polyviscose* and *polywool*.

Note also that in Britain and the USA, the word *poly* stands in its own right, as an abbreviation for "polytechnic". Its plural according to the *Collins Dictionary* is *polys*.

Polynesia Between them, *Melanesia*, *Micronesia* and **Polynesia** are geographical terms for the various groups of islands in the Pacific, as well as ethnic or anthropological terms for the islands' diverse inhabitants.

Polynesia is the widest of the three, covering the islands from Hawaii in the north to New Zealand in the south, and including Samoa, Tahiti and Tonga. The Melanesian group are west of **Polynesia**, and include Fiji, New Caledonia, Vanuatu and the Solomons. Micronesia embraces a set of small islands east of the Philippines, the best known of which are the Mariana, Caroline and Marshall islands, as well as Kiribati and Nauru.

The three words were coined by the French explorer Dumont D'Urville in the 1820s. All contain the Greek root *-nes-* "island", and so **Polynesia** is the "many-island group", *Micronesia* is the "tiny-island group", and *Melanesia* is the "black-island group". The last group may be so named because of the skin color of their inhabitants, or perhaps because of the dark profile of the islands as seen from sea level.

polysemy Many words have more than one meaning, and **polysemy** "multiple meaning" is the normal state for all our common words. Dictionaries have to enumerate a set of definitions, not just one for each of them. So to talk in terms of the "true meaning" of a word is rather a misconception. Only new words, and especially scientific and technical ones, have a single meaning, and even they tend to gather new meanings around themselves as they gain wider currency. Scientists sometimes lament the fact that "their words" are used differently by others—that expressions like *calorie*, *paranoia* and *quantum leap* have developed nontechnical meanings. But that simply shows **polysemy** working in the usual way.

Some words develop meanings in so many different directions that they might seem to have come from quite independent sources. Thus the *bail* in cricket and in the cowshed make use of one and the same word, though there's no obvious connection, figurative or otherwise, between them. Cases of **polysemy** like that need to be distinguished from *homonymy*, where two or more words from quite separate sources coincide, as with *gibber*, an onomatopoeic word meaning "talk unintelligibly" and *gibber*, the Aboriginal word for "stone or rock". (See further under **homonyms**.)

portico For the plural of this word, see under **-o**.

portmanteau The plural of this word is discussed under **-eau**.

portmanteau words This is Lewis Carroll's term for words which are *blends* of the beginning of one and the end of another. None of the words which he himself coined have gained general currency (*brillig*, *slithy*, *toves* etc.), though the poem "The Jabberwocky" from which they come is quite well known.

The **portmanteau words** which do gain currency are typically nouns referring to something new or newly recognised in our times:
breathalyser brunch electrocute guestimate heliport motel telecast
In examples like those the two components are still recognisable enough to contribute to the meaning of the word. This also seems important in the survival of a blend, and explains the rapid demise of rather obscure ones such as *catalo* (cross between "cattle" and "buffalo") and *incentivation* (a blend of "incentive" and "motivation"). But well-chosen portmanteau words can provide both name and slogan for a new product, witness:
Everlastic Glampoo Soyamaise Sunbrella
Municipal names in Australia occasionally exploit the same principle, with *Ashwood* for Ashburton/Burwood, and *Warranwood* for Warrandyte/Ringwood in the suburbs of Melbourne. *Aldonga* was used for a while to refer to the proposed Albury/Wodonga conglomerate.

possessive adjective Older grammars of English use the term **possessive adjective** for the form of a personal pronoun which precedes and modifies the noun. Examples include: *my*, *you*, *his*, *her*, *its*, *our*, *their*. In more recent grammars of English, the *possessive adjectives* are regarded as one of the groups of **determiners** (see further under that heading and also **possessive pronouns**).

possessive case This is the expression used in some English grammars for what others know as the *genitive case*. The name **possessive** is not however ideal for the English *genitive* since that case expresses other relationships than that of possession or ownership. For the full range of uses, see under **genitive** and **apostrophes**.

possessive pronouns In traditional grammar this term includes both the
possessive adjective/determiner and the "true" pronouns:

> *mine yours hers his its ours theirs*

These words refer to an item already mentioned, and are often the sole item
to express the subject, object or complement of a verb:

> *Mine is the one on the left.*
> *They put yours on the other side.*
> *Which one is theirs?*

Their capacity to stand alone is recognised in modern grammars by the names
"independent possessive" (in the *Contemporary Grammar of English*) and
"absolutes" (in the *Introduction to the Grammar of English*).

Note also *whose*, which is the possessive form of the relative/interrogative
pronoun, as in: *Whose is this?* (See further under **interrogative words**, and
who and **whose**.)

possum or **opossum** Strictly speaking **possum** is not an Australian word,
being a shortened form of the word **opossum** which originated in a North
American Indian language. In the USA **possum** is a colloquial variant of
opossum, but in Australia it has become the standard word. Through the
nineteenth and well into the twentieth century, the word was written here as
'possum to show it was a shortened form, but the apostrophe of omission
has now been dropped.

The word **opossum** was also used in nineteenth century Australia, and it
found its way into various compounds for clothes and other products,
especially the *opossum cloak* worn by Aborigines and some of the early
settlers. The word has disappeared along with the taste for such products.
The only significant survivor is *Opossum Bay* in Tasmania.

post- This prefix, meaning "after", was a preposition in classical Latin. In
Anglo-Latin its life as a prefix began in words like *postponere* and
postmeridianus, which have found their way into English as *postpone* and
postmeridian. In modern English it mostly helps to form adjectives which
designate a period in time, as in:

> *postclassical postdoctoral postglacial postgraduate*
> *posthumous postmedieval postnatal postprandial*

As those examples show, the prefix **post-** normally combines with scholarly,
latinate words. The most notable exceptions are *postdate* and *postwar*. Note
how in those and in other technical terms **post-** works as the antonym of
pre-: *postfix, postlude* and *postposition*.

In expressions such as *postcode* and *postman*, the first element is of course
related to the *post office* and *postal services*, and not a prefix.

post hoc This Latin phrase means literally "after this". It abbreviates the
longer phrase *post hoc ergo propter hoc*, meaning "after this therefore
because of this". It identifies the fallacy of concluding that an event was

caused by whatever preceded it—mistaking sequence in time for a causal relationship. For example, if you pray for a taxi and one comes around the corner immediately after, you might be deluded into thinking that it was prayer-controlled rather than radio-controlled.

postdeterminer See under **determiners**.

postmortem In Latin it means "after death" but in English it's used specifically for the *postmortem examination*, i.e. an autopsy performed on a dead body to establish the cause of death. **Postmortem** often stands instead of the full official phrase; and it has also developed the colloquial meaning "review of a previous event", used when you discuss an event which was less than a resounding success.

Dictionaries often hyphenate the phrase, though this is usually for the adjectival use, and there's no agreement about the noun, whether it should be spaced, hyphenated or set solid. The fact that the term is thoroughly assimilated suggests it should be set solid, as a fully integrated compound. (See further under **hyphens** section 2d.) And if the noun is set solid, so must the adjective be. Some Australian newspapers in Melbourne and Sydney recommend just that—setting the word solid on all occasions—and it seems the most straightforward course to follow.

postscript In anglicised form this is the Latin phrase *post scriptum* or *post scripta*, literally "thing(s) written afterwards". Since the sixteenth century it's been used to preface anything added after the final signature on a letter. These days it applies also to something added to a book after the end of the main text. At the end of letters, it's always abbreviated to *PS*. It appears in capitals, with no full stops nowadays (see further under **abbreviations**). If something further is added after the *PS*, it can be prefaced by *PPS* "post postscript".

potpourri This French phrase means (in reverse order) "rotten pot". However we have to dig deeper into the Spanish phrase *olla podrida* which it imitates, to unearth its meaning. In Spanish it was a culinary term for a miscellany of foods stewed until they were "rotten", i.e. broken down into small pieces, but had developed a wonderful flavor. This at any rate is the Spanish explanation of that otherwise rather puzzling phrase, and shows how the French, and the English could come to use it for something attractive, especially the mixture of dried petals and spices kept as nature's own deodorant.

Both the Spanish *olla podrida* and the **potpourri** can be used in reference to any collection of assorted items, and so to such things as a miscellany of musical or literary pieces. The extension of meaning is like that of *hotchpotch* though the overtones are rather more aesthetic: there's a little *je ne sais quoi* in *potpourri*. (See further under **hotchpot**.)

poule de luxe See under **cocotte**.

pp. or **p.p.** These are really two different abbreviations:

1 The first one **pp.** meaning "pages" as in *pp.1–15* is used in referencing, whenever a series of pages is the focus of a footnote or reference. In bibliographies it serves to show how many pages there are in the journal article or chapter of a book being cited. When referring to a span of pages, **pp.** appears before the numbers, but when it is to the total number of pages in the book, it comes after: *140 pp.* Note that **pp.** is increasingly being omitted before spans of numbers, in running references (see **referencing** section 3).
2 In official letter writing, **p.p.** may be used near the typed signature to indicate that the letter is being signed and sent by proxy. (See further under **per procurationem**.)

practical or **practicable** Is a **practical** suggestion the same as a **practicable** one? It could be, though the two words focus on slightly different things. A **practical** suggestion is one which comes to grips with the situation: while a **practicable** one is a feasible proposition, one that could be put into practice. The tone of the two words is also different, in that **practical** comments and commends in a straightforward way, while **practicable** is more detached and academic in its assessment. With its extra syllable it's a more formal word, so the choice between the two involves style as well as meaning.

The two words have several opposites: for **practicable** the antonyms are *impracticable* and *unpracticable*. Fowler's choice was *impracticable*, which is vindicated in both British and American language databases, though neither word appears in the Australian ACE database. For **practical** there are two kinds of antonym: (1) *theoretical*, and (2) either *impractical* or *unpractical*. Fowler put his weight behind *unpractical* and dismissed *impractical*, perhaps because the *Oxford Dictionary* labeled the latter "rare". But *Oxford* has now removed the label, and offers both American and British citations for it in the last few decades. In the ACE database *impractical* is comfortably represented with 7 instances, while there are none of *unpractical*. Those who know both *unpractical* and *impractical* sometimes use the first one for people: *an unpractical person*, and the second for inanimates: *an impractical scheme*. But this division of labor does not exist for those who use only one of the two terms.

practice or **practise** In Australian and British English **practice** is the standard spelling for the noun, and **practise** for the verb:
Tennis practice was at 10 am. We practised all the new shots.
These complementary spellings are used elsewhere in English to distinguish nouns from verbs (see under **-ce/-se**).

In American English **practice** regularly serves for the verb as well as the noun—a preference which is perhaps in keeping with the avoidance of *-ise* as a verb ending elsewhere. (See **-ise/-ize**.)

pre- This well-worked Latin prefix means "before". In many words including most modern formations, it means "prior in time"; but in older loanwords and a few modern technical words, it can mean "standing in front". We derive it from numerous Latin loanwords such as:

> *preclude predict prefer prefix preliminary prepare prevent*

In modern English it teams up easily with words of both French and Anglo-Saxon origin to make new ones:

> *preadvertise predate predawn predestined preheat prejudge prepaid*
> *preschool preshrunk prestressed preview*

The examples show **pre-** as a formative element in many common nouns, verbs and adjectives, though it also combines with proper names to identify a historical or geological period by the one adjacent to it. For example: *pre-Cambrian, pre-Christian, pre-Shakespearean* and *pre-Raphaelite*. In those cases there's a hyphen between **pre-** and the next word, because of its initial capital.

Note that **pre-** means the same as *ante-*, and they yield a few corresponding pairs:

> *predate/antedate precedent/antecedent prenatal/antenatal*

In each case the word with *ante-* is more restricted in meaning or its context of use. Overall there are many more words with **pre-**, no doubt because of the risk of confusing *ante-* with the very different *anti-*. (See **ante-/anti-**.)

Pre- serves as the contrasting prefix to *post-*, as in *prewar/postwar*. (See further under **post-**.)

precede or **proceed** A mistaken choice between these verbs can easily sabotage your meaning, because **proceed** means "go ahead, advance" while **precede** means "go before", "introduce". Compare:

> *Please proceed to the front of the queue.*
> *A motorcycle escort preceded the parade.*

Grammarians would note that **proceed** is always intransitive, whereas **precede** can be either transitive or intransitive. Since only transitive verbs can work in the passive, **precede** is the only possibility in constructions like:

> *The parade was preceded by a motorcycle escort.*

(See further under **transitive**.)

For the difference in the spelling of the second syllable of each word, see under **-cede/-ceed**.

precedence or **precedent** These differ in meaning and in the grammar of their use. **Precedence** is an abstract noun meaning "priority in rank or importance", most often used in idioms such as *give precedence to*, or *take/have precedence over*. **Precedent** is a countable noun meaning a "model or example from the past", which is used in idioms such as *set a precedent, no precedent for* or *find a precedent for (something) in*. As the phrases show, the words use different prepositions in collocating with what follows. This serves to differentiate them, even when they come close to each other, as in:

The prime minister and his deputy have precedence over the others in speaking.

The office of prime minister has its precedent in the chancellor of Tudor times.

Note that *precedency* is a less common form of **precedence**, given as the second preference in all modern dictionaries. (See further under **-nce/-ncy**.)

precipitate or **precipitous** Both adjectives embody the idea of rushing headlong, though there's an essential difference. **Precipitate** works in the time dimension, and suggests that things are done in a rushed and hurried way, as in a *precipitate decision to go to war*. **Precipitous** is set in the dimension of space, and implies a sharp movement downwards, as in a *precipitous slope*.

Yet **precipitous** is increasingly used in more figurative ways which bring it closer to **precipitate**. When the financial reporter writes of a *precipitous decline in the value of shares*, s/he is no doubt thinking of the way the trend would appear as a line on a graph, a sharp fall which can be reinterpreted as a rapid event. Thus **precipitous** comes to mean "sudden", and is used instead of **precipitate**. Two out of the three instances of **precipitous** in the Australian ACE corpus were of this kind. The trend is perhaps reinforced by the fact that **precipitous** is more common than **precipitate** as an adjective (by 3:1), and **precipitate** is more often used as a verb. Meanwhile the substitution of **precipitous** for **precipitate** is well recognised in modern dictionaries.

précis A précis is a summary version of document (see further under **summary**). The word comes from French with an acute accent which is disappearing in English. In other ways it's only half assimilated. It remains the same when used in the plural (i.e. has a *zero plural*); and though it takes regular English verb suffixes, as in *precising* and *precised*, they are pronounced in the French fashion, without the "s" sound. On the last point compare other French loanwords such as *debut*. (See under **-t**.)

predeterminer See under **determiners**.

predicate This traditional grammar term still has a useful role in identifying the elements of a clause which complement the subject to form a statement. (In transformational grammars the **predicate** is called the *verb phrase*, a usage which conflicts with other important uses of the phrase. See under **verb phrase**.) Together the subject and **predicate** (italicised in the following examples) embody the heart of a clause, as in:

Empty vessels *make the most sound*.

Actions *speak louder than words*.

The pen *is mightier than the sword*.

In statements the subject usually precedes the **predicate**, though some (or all) of the **predicate** comes first in certain questions, negative statements and other inversions (see under **inversions** and **subject**).

1 *Predicates* *always contain a finite verb*, and depending on the nature of that verb, another component. Some grammarians simply call it the "complement", but many others identify three different kinds of complement to the verb namely (a) *object*, (b) *adverb*, (c) *complement* (in a more restricted sense). The three types are illustrated by our three proverbs:

a) *Empty vessels make the most sound.*

   subject/verb/object (SVO)

   Objects are often needed with a verb of action to complete its sense. (See further under **transitive** and **object**.)

b) *Actions speak louder than words.*

   subject/verb/adverb (SVA)

   Some verbs of action take an *adverb* which details it in terms of the manner, place or time in which it takes place. The adverb may be only a single word, or a phrase, as in the example.

c) *The pen is mightier than the sword.*

   subject/verb/complement (SVC)

   Complements in this restricted sense typically come after the verb *be* or another copular or linking verb, and help to detail the subject of the clause. (See further under **copular verbs**.) The use of adjectives in complements is frequent, and sometimes involves special uses of them. A few English adjectives such as *awry* can only appear predicatively (see **adjectives** section 1); and others such as *ill* have different meanings when used predicatively and attributively. Compare *She was ill*, with *an ill omen* and *an ill wind.*

2 *Occasionally a* **predicate** consists of a verb alone, as in:

The telephone rang. (SV)

She had been crying. (SV)

The younger staff used to come. (SV)

As those examples show, the verb component may be a simple verb, or a sequence of auxiliaries and main verb, combining to form a verb phrase. For further extensions of the verb phrase, by infinitives, as in *She begged to come*, and nonfinite clauses, see **catenatives**.

3 For three small groups of verbs, special combinations of the patterns mentioned above, using two components, are required to complete the clause. They are *SVOO*, *SVOA*, and *SVOC*, illustrated in the following:

They gave him fresh clothes. (SVOO)

They put him in an ambulance. (SVOA)

They made him a hero. (SVOC)

The first group requiring *SVOO* (i.e. both indirect and direct objects) are *ditransitive* verbs which involve the transmitting of something to someone. The second group whose pattern is *SVOA* are verbs which express the placing or locating of an object, and the adverb shows where that is. The third type *SVOC* are not very common, just a few verbs which confer a status (notional or actual) on the object, using an extra complement to express it. As in *SVC* clauses, the complement is often an adjective: *They thought/called it miraculous.* Note also the rare *SVCC* pattern, in: *That house is worth a million.*

predominant or **predominate** Both these have served as adjectives in English since the late sixteenth century, though **predominant** was and is the more common of the two. *Webster's English Usage* (1989) notes however that the adverb *predominately* appears rather more often than its adjective **predominate,** and is sometimes thought to be a mistake for *predominantly.* But both adverbs and adjectives are current in the twentieth century.

preface Between the title page of a book and the start of the main text, there may be any or all of the following: *foreword,* **preface,** *introduction.* The boundaries between them, and their location, vary with the publisher and the publication. An *introduction* by the author is these days often as long as a chapter of the book itself; and when it outlines the book's structure and contents it may be treated as the first segment of the main text, and paginated in Arabic numbers with the rest. However when the main text is a reference book, such as a dictionary, even long *introductory essays* are paginated in lower case Roman numbers, and made part of the preliminary matter. (See further under **prelims.**)

The *foreword* and/or **preface** are always paginated in roman. In older bookmaking practice they would both precede the table of contents, and this is still recommended by the *Oxford Dictionary for Writers and Editors* (1981). The reverse is recommended in *Copy-editing* (1991) and the Chicago *Manual of Style*: the table of contents should come first, they suggest, so that a reader can immediately locate all the components of the book, and then begin to read more discursively. The AGPS *Style Manual* (1988) proposes putting the *foreword* before the table of contents and the **preface** after it. This seems a sensible compromise if, as often, the *foreword* is brief (only two or three paragraphs), and is written by someone other than the author—usually a celebrated person whose name lends distinction to the volume. The **preface** is usually written by the author (or editor, if the work is an anthology), and may amount to two or three pages. It typically explains how the book came into being, and acknowledges the contribution of others to it. Sometimes the latter are made on a separate page, with their own heading *acknowledgements.*

In subsequent editions of the book, the *foreword* is likely to remain unchanged, but the **preface** may be modified, or complemented by a separate "Preface to the second edition".

Note that dictionary definitions of *foreword* often make it synonymous with **preface,** and it seems to have originated that way in the nineteenth century, amid moves to replace latinate words with home-grown Anglo-Saxon ones. To some users they are synonyms, though as shown above, those who are involved in the making of books see them as having different functions.

prefixes The meaningful elements we attach to the beginnings of words are **prefixes**. Their distinctiveness can be seen in sets of words like the following:

antiwar/postwar/prewar
inactive/proactive/retroactive

Most of the **prefixes** used in modern English are of classical and especially Latin origin, as are all of those just illustrated. The best known **prefixes** from Old English are *be-* as in *befriend* and *un-* as in *unlikely*.

Prefixes do not usually affect the grammar of the word they are attached to (as suffixes often do). The only **prefixes** which move words from one grammatical class to another are *a-* as in *awash* (verb to adverb), *be-* as in *befriend* (noun to verb), and *en-/em-* as in *enable, empower* (adjective or noun to verb). Very many others modify the meaning, not the grammar of the word.

The kinds of meaning added by **prefixes** can be seen under several headings. There are **prefixes** of time and order (*pre-/post-*), of location (*sub-/super-*), of number (*bi-/tri-*), and of size or degree (*macro-/hyper-*). Others express the reversing of an action (*de-/dis-*), its negation (*un-/in-*), or a pejorative attitude to it (*mal-/mis-*). English words may take **prefixes** from one or two of those groups, but that's the limit, witness: *polyunsaturated, unpremeditated* and *antidisestablishment*.

Note that **prefixes** are generally set solid with the rest of the word. Hyphens appear only when the word attached begins with (1) a capital letter, as with *anti-Stalin*, or (2) the same vowel as the prefix ends in, as with:

anti-inflationary de-escalate micro-organism

Yet in well-established cases, the hyphens become optional, as with *cooperate* and *coordinate*. See further under **co-**, and under **hyphens** section 1.

prelims In publishing this is the colloquial abbreviation for the *preliminary matter*, what is more formally known as the "front matter" of a book. The term **prelims** covers:

• half-title page
• title page
• imprint page
• dedications page and/or epigraph
• table of contents
• table of figures and diagrams
• list of contributors
• foreword, preface and acknowledgements
• list of abbreviations
• maps providing location for text overall

The typical order of appearance is as above, though the location of foreword and preface varies somewhat with the publisher. (See further under **preface**.)

Compare **endmatter**.

premier or **premiere** The word **premier** is an adjective meaning "first in time or rank", both of which were played upon in the numberplate slogan: *NSW* *the premier state*—a rather provocative claim. **Premier** is of course also a noun referring to the chief executive of government in each Australian state, as it does in Canada. (In Britain meanwhile, **premier** is a synonym for *prime minister*.) When referring to the present incumbent, the word is always capitalised: the *Premier of Queensland announced today* ... In the plural and with lower case, *premiers* may refer either to the collective heads of Australian states, or to the winning team in this season's competition: *The Panthers are premiers again.*

The noun **premiere** works in different cultural circles, and is a much more recent borrowing from French. It refers to the first performance of a play or musical composition, or the first showing of a newly made film. Increasingly it's used as a verb too, transitive or intransitive:

The play (was) premiered in Perth before transferring to Melbourne and Sydney.

Its use as a verb dates from 1940 according to the *Oxford Dictionary* and is recognised in all recent dictionaries, though resistance to it is reported in the *Heritage Dictionary*, whose usage panel (86% of them) found it unacceptable. This harnessing of nouns as verbs has a long tradition in English however (see **transfers**). Three instances of verb use are to be found in the Australian ACE corpus.

The grave accent is disappearing fast from the noun **première**, and is certainly not needed when it's used as a verb. That new grammatical role is a sure sign of its being assimilated.

premise, premiss and **premises** In philosophy and logic, the first two spellings are in use to refer to a basic argument or proposition. **Premiss** is the older spelling, dating from the fourteenth century, and the one recommended in the nineteenth century by the American philosopher C.S. Peirce. But contemporary philosophers vary, and ordinary citizens concerned about the assumptions in an argument normally spell the word as **premise**, an alternative form which dates from the sixteenth century.

The plural form **premises**, encountered in reference to real estate and legal rights over it, is from exactly the same source. The very different contexts of use mean there's unlikely to be any confusion, especially when the **premises** of an argument are abstract, and the **premises** which are the subject of a lease are concrete—or at least very tangible. Note that **premises** always has plural verbs and pronouns in agreement, even when referring to a single house:

These modest premises were all I could afford.

prepositional phrases These consist of a preposition followed by a noun, noun phrase or pronoun, witness:

after dinner   after a long evening   after you

They may forge a link with the verb of a clause, with another **prepositional phrase**, or with a noun or adjectival phrase. All four are illustrated and italicised below:

1 The delegation left *for Surfers Paradise.*
2 At the last session *for prospective candidates,* they met her.
3 The search *for meaning* goes on and on.
4 Thankful *for their help,* they forgot their disagreement.

The examples also show the various ways in which prepositional phrases may function in a sentence:

- as adverb (sentence 1) (see further under **predicate**)
- as an extension to the adverb (sentence 2)
- as postmodifier of the noun phrase (sentence 3)
- as postmodifier of the adjectival phrase (sentence 4)

For the term *postmodifier* see under **noun phrases**.

prepositions As their name suggests, **prepositions** go in front (*pre-*), and they often detail the position of something (or its location, direction or relationship to other things). The following list contains the most common of them:

> *about above across after along around as at before below beside*
> *between by down for from in into like near of off on over past*
> *since till than through to under until up with without*

English also has a number of compound prepositions with two or more elements, such as:

> *because of   in front of   instead of   out of   on top of*
> *due to   in regard to   next to   owing to   with reference to*
> *in accordance with*

Within sentences, prepositions typically lead in a noun, noun phrase or pronoun, and with it form a **prepositional phrase**. It may serve one of several functions in a clause. (See previous entry.)

Many English **prepositions** double as adverbs, as a glance at the list above would confirm. The similarity in their roles is clear in the following:

> *They went up the stairs* (preposition) *as the lift was going up* (adverb).

But the very same word *up* can also be a integral part of the meaning of a verb. Compare:

> *He ran up a big bill.*
> *He ran up a big hill.*

In the first sentence *up* is much more intimately involved in the meaning of the verb than in the second. In the second it's an ordinary *preposition,* whereas in the first it becomes a particle in a *phrasal verb.* Its association with the verb is so close that it could not be replaced by any other particle/preposition without drastically altering the verb's meaning. (See further under **phrasal verbs** and **particles**.)

1 *Which **preposition** should you use with...?* Convention dictates that certain verbs and related words are followed by particular prepositions/particles. Words like *compare/comparison* take either *with* or *to,* and *differ/different* may take *from, to* or *than,* depending on the context. The choice sometimes depends on which part of the English-speaking world you belong to. In Australia or Britain, you *fill in* a form, whereas in the USA you would express it as *fill out*. Note also the fact that in American English no *preposition* at all is needed with some verbs which definitely require one in Australian and British English. Compare:

Australian/British	American
agreed on the price	*agreed* the price
cater for a party	*cater* a party
protest against the war	*protest* the war
provide us with a plan	*provide us* a plan
wrote to his MP	*wrote* his MP

2 *Ending sentences with* **prepositions**. The idea that it's incorrect to have a *preposition* at the end of a sentence comes from a limited understanding of what they are and what they do. Many **prepositions** double as adverbs/particles, and can be associated with verbs as much as nouns. As such they can certainly appear at the end of a sentence. Yet a "rule" against ending sentences with **prepositions** was articulated in the eighteenth century, and vigorously taught in the nineteenth and earlier twentieth century. It obliged writers to recast any sentence with a *final preposition* so that the offending item appeared earlier in the sentence. So instead of saying:

They asked which train I was waiting for.

it would be

They asked for which train I was waiting.

As in that case, the result is often rather stiff and sometimes unidiomatic. The awkwardness of observing the rule was unforgettably demonstrated by Churchill, in the comment: "This is a form of pedantry up with which I will no longer put". Thanks to him, the rule is no longer generally respected, though it lives on more vigorously than it should in some computer grammar checkers. (They are always at their most reliable on the most mechanical aspects of language.) We might note that as the last word in a sentence prepositions/particles make a rather limp ending. Still this is a matter of style, not bad grammar.

prerequisite or **perquisite**   A **prerequisite** is a prior condition:

Four years experience is a prerequisite for the course.

A **perquisite** is a benefit or privilege attached to a position, as in the *perquisites of office*. It includes any additional income beyond the fixed wages or salary, and so may refer to anything from tips to the use of a company car. In the latter senses in particular, it's usually abbreviated to *perk*. The word is still slightly informal, though it has been recorded since 1869. Perhaps this is due to the informality of some of the arrangements it connotes.

prescribe or **proscribe**   These both involve the exercise of power and authority. Those who **prescribe** set out rules or a course of action for others to follow, whether it is the judge prescribing the terms of settlement for a case, doctors prescribing medicines, or educators prescribing syllabuses. Those who **proscribe** publicly condemn or prohibit something, as in:

The world can only proscribe what Nazi scientists did.

Smoking is now proscribed in most government buildings.

As those examples show, **proscribe** involves a negative force, while **prescribe** implies a very positive kind of directive. The contrast is perhaps clearest if we compare *prescribed books* (those which a student must read) with *proscribed books* (those banned by the authorities to make it impossible for people to read them).

prescriptive or **descriptive** For the difference between **prescriptive** and **descriptive** approaches to language, see under **descriptive**.

present tense In English the simple forms of verbs, like *smile, walk, discuss,* tend to project events as if they are happening in the here and now—or at least as if there's no time limit on them. Compare the forms *smiled, walked, discussed,* in which the action is set in the past and confined to it. Thus English verbs express either a **present** or a *past* **tense**, the latter being marked by the added *-(e)d* , or some other change to the simple form. (See further under **past tense** and **principal parts**.)

But in certain contexts the **present tense** can express both future and past time. See for example:

My holidays start *tomorrow.*

If it rains, *we'll eat indoors.*

After all that he reappears *with a big grin as if nothing had happened.*

In all such sentences, the tense is expressed through something other than the simple verb. In the first sentence, it's the adverb "tomorrow"; in the second, the verb phrase of the main clause. In the third, the narrator heightens the drama with the use of "reappears", but the other verb makes it clear that the overall context is in the past. This dramatic use of the **present tense** is known as the "historic present" or the "narrative present". Note also that the **present tense** serves to describe ongoing habits and customs, and to make generalisations. For example:

We go to church most Sundays.

The boss likes to have flowers in the office.

The rains come with the change of season.

*Compound **present tenses**.* In ordinary conversation, and in some kinds of writing, the present continuous tense rather than the simple present may be used to project what is happening here and now:

The rains are coming to judge by those big black clouds.

The present continuous creates a span of time in the present, whereas the present perfect marks a moment in it, at which writer and reader can share a retrospective view:

The rains have come.

For more about the continuous and perfect tenses, see **aspect**.

pressure or **pressurise** When used as a verb **pressure** is normally figurative, as in:
They were pressured into taking on more than they could manage.
When it's a case of actually raising atmospheric pressure, the verb to use is **pressurise**:
The cabin was pressurised for takeoff.

presume or **assume** See assume.

presumptuous or **presumptive** In the past, these words were occasionally interchanged, but nowadays they are associated with different aspects of the verb *presume*. **Presumptive** represents its more neutral sense of being based on a *presumption*, as in: *presumptive title* and *heir presumptive*. It occurs much less often than **presumptuous**, a negatively charged word which represents the sense of "presuming too much" or "taking unwarranted liberties".
   Note that **presumptuous** is sometimes pronounced and spelled "presumptious", a spelling which was in use up to the eighteenth century, and which is still fostered by its link with the noun *presumption*. (See further under **-ious**.)

prêt-à-porter This French phrase means "ready to wear", and refers to garments which are mass-produced in standard sizes and sold "off the hook", instead of being made for the individual by a tailor or dressmaker. However inspired their design, clothes bought *prêt-à-porter* are unlikely to qualify as *haute couture* "high fashion". (See further under **haute**.)

pretence, pretense, pretension or **pretentiousness** These overlap considerably, in spite of their different appearances. The first two are simply alternative spellings, **pretence** being used in Britain, and **pretense** in the USA. (See further under **-ce/-se**.) As far as meanings go, we might note that *pretense/pretence* is the abstract noun for the verb *pretend* when it means "feign, put on", as in:
They made a pretense of sympathy.
Pretension picks up the sense of "lay claim to" which is also part of the scope of *pretend*:
He had no pretensions to becoming president.
Pretentiousness embodies the sense of showing off, either socially or intellectually, pretending to sophistication which isn't quite there:
The pretentiousness of his conversation drove his colleagues to despair.
Still the major dictionaries all allow that **pretense/pretence** is sometimes used instead of both **pretension** and **pretentiousness**, and **pretension** for **pretentiousness**. None of them is very flattering.

pretty The idea dies hard that **pretty** is an informal word to use as a qualifier of adjectives or other adverbs. The *Collins Dictionary* has a note to that effect, yet the *Oxford Dictionary* presents it with no restrictive label, and the record shows that it has been in literary use since the sixteenth century, with citations from serious and respected writers in Johnson's dictionary. *Random House* comments that **pretty** is not restricted to informal speech and writing, and is less stilted than other qualifiers such as *relatively*. Among over 90 occurrences of **pretty** in the Australian ACE corpus, more than two thirds were instances of the qualifier; and it appeared in almost all categories of fiction and nonfiction, except government and corporate prose.

preventable or **preventible** The first spelling **preventable** is the older, dating from 1640, and is the one preferred by the *Oxford Dictionary* and all modern dictionaries. The second spelling **preventible** dates only from 1850, and is probably fostered by *preventive* and *prevention*.

preventive or **preventative** The first and shorter spelling is given preference in all dictionaries. **Preventive** is also the older spelling, dating from the seventeenth century. **Preventative** appears to eclipse it in the eighteenth century, but the *Oxford Dictionary* declared its preference for **preventive** because of the better formal relationship with *prevention*. However **preventative** still has some currency as an alternative, especially in phrases like *preventative measures*, and as a noun **preventative** meaning ''prophylactic''.

prima donna In Italian this means ''first lady'', though it's associated with the operatic stage rather than the White House. The term was and is given to the principal female singer in an opera company, though it's now also applied to a temperamental, conceited and autocratic person of either sex. In fact those negative connotations are on record from the mid-nineteenth century, and probably help to explain the arrival in the 1880s of *diva*, another Italian loanword for a great female singer, meaning literally ''goddess'' and still a term which registers admiration.

In English both **prima donna** and *diva* are pluralised in the regular way with *s*, though the Italian plurals *prime donne* and *dive* are sometimes used for their foreign cachet. Perhaps they help to bypass the negative associations of **prima donna** which are now firmly built into the English language in derivative words such as *prima donna-ish* and *prima donna-ism*.

A *prima ballerina* is the matching term in a ballet company identifying the leading female dancer, or one of the highest rank. The only title above that is *prima ballerina assoluta*, a title so rarefied it was only given twice in the history of the Russian Imperial ballet. The expression *prima ballerina* is normally given an English plural, helped by the fact that the word *ballerina* itself is pluralised that way. Yet *prima ballerina* too is developing more general senses. The *Oxford Dictionary* (1989) records both ''important or self-important person'' and ''leading item in its field'', both since 1950. It also recognises the Italian plural *prime ballerine*, which here again may serve to designate outstanding dancers, and distinguish them from leading persons or items in other fields.

prima facie This well-assimilated Latin phrase means literally "by the first face". Less literally it's used to mean "at first sight" or "on the face of it". It has been used in English since the fifteenth century to describe evidence which is sufficient to justify further investigation or judicial proceedings: hence newspaper reporting on the *prima facie case* and *prima facie evidence*. From there it comes to be used occasionally in scholarly argument, of data which looks significant but requires further investigating. Note that there's no need to hyphenate *prima facie* when it serves as a compound adjective. (See **hyphens** section 2c.)

primary auxiliaries See under **auxiliary verbs**.

primus inter pares This Latin phrase means "first among equals". It may be used to identify someone who is the spokesperson for others of equal status; or to suggest that the person who is technically the leader has no special authority over those with whom s/he is associated.

principal or **principle** Most adults cope with one-syllable homophones such as *cede* and *seed*, but three-syllabled ones like **principal/principle** get the better of many. The words do however differ in meaning and function, and we can thus distinguish them.
   Principal is an adjective borrowed from Latin meaning "chief, most important". It has acquired many more meanings as a noun in English, in reference to the head of a school or college, the leader of a section of an orchestra, and those who are the key agents in a law case. In law it also refers to the real assets of an estate (as opposed to the income they earn), and it's used more generally in financial calculations to distinguish the capital sum from any interest or profit associated with it.
   Principle is an abstract word meaning "rule" or "formative characteristic", as in:
   Those groups work on a principle of collaboration.
   The underlying principle of the design is inspired.
Note that because it's an abstract, there are modifiers before and/or after it to specify its meaning. This helps to distinguish it from **principal** as a noun, whose meaning is specific enough in most contexts and needs no elaborating.
   The problem with these words arises from the fact that English preserves the word **principle** and certain others in forms which were peculiar to northern French and Anglo-Norman (see **-le** section 3). The standard French for **principle** is "principe", which does not make a homophone for **principal**.

principal clause See under **clauses**.

principal parts These are the alternative forms of a verb which serve to make the present and past tenses, from which all other forms can be inferred. So for the verb *speak*, the **principal parts** are *speak/spoke/spoken*. The first one of the set provides the necessary stem for *speaks* (3rd singular, present tense) and *speaking* (present participle); and the others provide the past tense and past participle respectively. Although it's customary to give three **principal parts**, this is only essential for irregular verbs. Most regular verbs have just two distinct forms: *laugh* (present) and *laughed* (past), because the past participle is identical with the ordinary past tense. (See further under **irregular verbs**.)

principle or **principal** See principal.

prise or **prize** These spellings represent quite a clutch of different words, both nouns and verbs. In Australian and British English they normally distinguish the verb **prise** "lever off" from the verb **prize** "value greatly". The noun is always **prize**, whether it refers to a special award, or to something captured by strenuous effort. In the USA even the first verb is usually spelled **prize**, which is a straightforward way out of the problem of knowing which spelling to use for which meaning. It coincides also with the standard American use of *-ize* in the choice between *civilize/civilise* etc. (See further under **-ise/-ize**.)

In fact the Australian/British use of **prize** already represents an amalgamation of once separate words. The two noun meanings detailed above are extensions of different roots, with the sense of "special award" coming from the medieval "pris" and Latin *pretium* which also gives us *price*; and the second sense "something captured" is from "prise", part of the French verb meaning "seize" (the source of the English verb **prise**). Meanwhile the verb **prize** "value greatly" is an alternative form of the word *praise*, based on Old French *preisier/prisier*. With all those threads of spelling and meaning intertwined, the American use of **prize** for all of them has something to recommend it.

Note also that in American English *pry* serves as an alternative to *prize* "lever off". (See further under **pry**.)

pro- and **pro** English embraces both older and newer uses of this Latin prefix-cum-preposition. As a prefix it means "forward" or "in front of (in time or space)", as in:

proceed progress project promote propose

In those old loanwords **pro-** is always set solid.

Another older use of **pro-** is to mean "substitute for", which has come down in words such as *proconsul* and *pronoun*, and has generated new formations such as *pro-vice-chancellor*. New words formed this way are hyphenated.

A similar but very recent use of **pro-** is to be found in words like *pro-American*, *pro-communist* and *pro-Israel*, where it means "in favor of". In such words it's always hyphenated, whether the following item bears a capital letter or not. This meaning corresponds quite closely to one associated with *pro* as a preposition in Latin—which perhaps explains both the hyphen and the fact that they can be formed ad hoc with almost any raw material: *pro-daylight saving*.

In addition **pro** has several roles as an independent word in English. In *pros and cons* it refers to arguments in favor of a proposition, a direct use of the

Latin preposition. But **pro** also stands in English as an abbreviation for (1) professional and (2) prostitute.

pro forma This Latin phrase means "as a matter of form". It refers to documents required by law or convention, as in *pro forma letter* and *pro forma invoice*. Nowadays it often serves as an abbreviation for the invoice itself, as in:

A pro forma will be sent with the goods.

No doubt the abbreviation helps to bypass the dirty word *invoice*. To pluralise **pro forma**, use *pro formas*. (The plurals of foreign compounds are discussed under **plurals** section 2.)

pro tem In abbreviated form this is the Latin phrase *pro tempore* "for the time being, temporarily". An informal expression for an interim and often informal arrangement, it can be used in almost any situation. It contrasts thus with the formal *locum tenens*, used of a carefully arranged professional replacement. (See further under **locum tenens.**)

problematic or **problematical** See under -ic/-ical.

proceed or **precede** See precede.

proclaim and **proclamation** See under -aim.

Professor Note that this title is normally written in full in letter salutations or on envelopes. The abbreviation *Prof* is found occasionally in reports although there were only 5 instances of its use in the Australian ACE corpus, compared with more than 40 of the full title used to preface a name. The use/non-use of a stop in the abbreviation is a matter of policy (see **abbreviations** section 2).

profited For the spelling of this word when used as a verb, see **t.**

program or **programme** Program is the standard spelling in the USA, and the one adopted in Australia by the Australian Government *Style Manual* and the *Macquarie Dictionary* (1991) for all uses of the word. In Britain **program** is reserved by many for computer uses, and **programme** applied in all other contexts. This distinction is also made by some Australians, certain influential educational institutions, and parts of the ABC. In the Australian ACE database there are close to 175 instances of *noncomputer* use of **program** compared to 60 of **programme.**

In fact **program** was endorsed by the original *Oxford Dictionary* on two grounds:
1 it was the earlier spelling, used in the word's first recorded appearances in (Scottish) English in the seventeenth century, while the spelling **programme** makes it appearance in the nineteenth century. (We may speculate on whether it was motivated by the desire to "improve" the Scots form or simply an example of "frenchification". See further under **-e.**)

2 it is analogous with *anagram, diagram, histogram, radiogram, telegram* etc., while there are no analogies for *programme*.

Note that when **program** becomes a verb, the final *m* is normally doubled before suffixes, as in *programmed, programming* and *programmer*. In the USA the words are sometimes spelled with a single *m*, but this is not very common, even though it conforms to more general American habits of spelling. The fact that the second syllable is a separable unit may help to explain why. (See further under **doubling of last consonant.**)

prologue or **prolog** See under **-gue/-g**.

pronounce and **pronunciation** The spelling difference between these is a common problem, and inexpert writers sometimes impose the *-oun* of the verb on the second syllable of the noun (''pronounciation''). Until the eighteenth century that was in fact a recognised alternative spelling. But nowadays only **pronunciation** will do, making the word's stem as Latin as the suffix. The spelling of the verb **pronounce** is Anglo-Norman, and a reminder that it was used in English rather earlier than the bookish noun.

Other words related in exactly the same way are **denounce/denunciation** and **renounce/renunciation**.

pronouns A *pronoun* is a small functional word which stands instead of a noun, noun phrase, or name, as *she* may substitute for ''Judith Wright'', or *this* for ''the camera I have in my hand''. There are several kinds of pronouns:

personal	*she, he, you* etc.
possessive	*hers, yours* etc. (see further under **possessive pronouns**)
reflexive	*herself* etc.
demonstrative	*this, that, these, those*
indefinite	*each, any, some, all*
interrogative	*who, which, what, whose, whom*
relative	*who, which, what, whose, whom*

Pronouns usually stand for something which has been mentioned already, though just occasionally a narrative may begin with a pronoun and proceed to explain:

It was the worst interview I've ever had. They sat me in a vast office with the light staring in my face ...

Whether the pronoun anticipates the details (as in that example) or harks back to something detailed earlier, it helps to provide cohesion. (See further under **coherence** or **cohesion**.)

Note that many of the **pronouns** listed above (especially the demonstrative and indefinite groups) also function as **determiners**. (See further under that heading.)

proofreading This is an essential part of checking your own writing, or preparing anyone else's for printing. It involves reading at more than one level—

firstly at the level of ideas and how those ideas are expressed, and secondly at the level of spelling, punctuation and typesetting. This means at least two readings of the MS, since the people who can *reliably* read on both levels at once are as rare as hen's teeth.

The standard *proofreading marks* used to indicate settings and changes to the typesetter are listed in Appendix VI.

propellent or **propellant** *Webster's English Usage* (1989) notes a trend towards using **propellant** for both the noun and adjective, which is confirmed by the *Oxford Dictionary* (1989). It reverses the preference of the original *Oxford Dictionary* for using **propellent** for both of them, though **propellent** still enjoys some currency as the adjective according to *Random House* and *Webster's* dictionaries. (See further under **-ant/-ent**.)

proper names A *proper name* designates a unique person or entity, such as *Percy Grainger*, *Wollongong* or the *University of Melbourne*. Note that in the third case, the proper name consists of common words combined with a proper noun *Melbourne*. **Proper names** can consist entirely of common words, as in *Northern Territory*. As that example shows, it's the uniqueness of the designation which makes it a *proper name*, not the words combined in it.

Proper names—personal, geographical and institutional—are normally distinguished by capital letters on every component except the function words. (So words like *the* and *of* are not capitalised.) However institutional names often shed their capitals when used repeatedly and in abbreviated form in any piece of writing. (See further under **capitals** section 3.)

proper nouns These are single words which serve to identify a unique person or entity, such as *Confucius* or *Tasmania*. They contrast with common nouns such as *man* and *island* which refer to infinite numbers of persons or items of that kind. (See further under **noun**.)

Proper nouns are always capitalised, even when their use in the plural suggests they are no longer unique. Thus we write:

We have three Davids on the staff here.

Although reusable **proper nouns** are not listed with the common nouns in dictionaries, they do have some general kinds of meaning which could be specified. For example, the name *John* is male and Anglo-Saxon, and *Paola* is female and Italian. But for most of us, *Mitsuhiro* and *Masumi* are names of unknown gender, though we may guess that they are Japanese. Some **proper nouns**, or forms of them, have stylistic meaning built into them, and we recognise *Johnno* and *Tassie* as informal proper nouns.

prophecy or **prophesy** Up to about 1700 these were interchangeable, but **prophecy** has since been reserved for the noun, and **prophesy** for the verb. This usage parallels the one observed in Australia and Britain for pairs such as *advice/advise*. (See further under **-ce/-se**.) Note that American authorities are divided on the issue: *Webster's Dictionary* allows either word to stand instead of the other, whereas *Random House* affirms the noun/verb distinction.

proportional or **proportionate** These adjectives both mean "being in proportion", and there's little to choose between them—except that **proportionate** normally appears after the noun, as in *profits proportionate to our investment*, but not before it. **Proportional** is more versatile, and could appear either after or before the noun. The phrase *proportional representation* shows it occurring before the noun. Another small point of difference is that **proportional** seems to express precise numerical ratios, whereas those in **proportionate** are more impressionistic.

This second point also emerges when we compare their opposite forms: *disproportional* points out a disparity in numbers, whereas *disproportionate* suggests a more general lack of proportion.

proposition or **proposal** Either of these could be used when it comes to a proposed plan or business offer. Yet the extra syllable and latinate form of **proposition** makes it the more formal choice, and coincides with the fact that **proposal** is definitely the more common of the two, by a ratio of about 2:1 in the Australian ACE databases. The more formal character of **proposition** is reinforced by its use in scholarly contexts, especially in mathematics and logic.

New idiomatic uses of **proposition** are however increasing its popularity, witness a *commercial proposition*, an *exciting proposition*, a *different proposition altogether*. In phrases like those, applied to anything from the new motel, to a tempting holiday package, to the freshly signed-up football star, **proposition** is far removed from the verb *propose*, and becomes a faintly pretentious synonym for *prospect* or *venture*. **Proposal** retains close links with *propose*.

Another remarkable development is the use of **proposition** as a verb to mean "suggest sexual intercourse with". In this sense it can also work as a noun, and so contrasts dramatically with **proposal** which is always associated with the proposing of marriage.

proprietary or **propriety** The first of these is embedded in certain company titles, such as *BHP* (for *Broken Hill Proprietary Company*), and in the formula *Pty Ltd* as in *Civil and Civic Pty Ltd*. However the word is first and foremost an adjective, as in the phrase *proprietary rights* "rights of ownership". **Propriety** is a noun meaning "concern with conventional manners and the proper code of behavior".

The two words represent two different aspects of the Latin word *proprietas* "property". **Proprietary** relates to what is regarded as the property of an individual, whereas **propriety** grows out of the sense of what is the essential property or character of the social context.

proscribe or **prescribe** See **prescribe**.

prose The ordinary medium of discourse which we write is **prose**. It contrasts with poetry in having no conventional form to dictate the length of lines or the number of lines which form a unit. It contrasts with scripted dialogue or conversation in being continuous monologue.

prospectus For the plural of this word, see under **-us** section 2.

prostrate or **prostate** These two are not to be confused. **Prostate** refers to a gland in the male genital organs, and is often found in the phrase *prostate operation*. **Prostrate** is an adjective meaning "lying collapsed on the ground". In that sense it covers both *prone* "lying face downwards" and *supine* "lying flat on one's back". Yet dictionaries all show that the meaning of **prostrate** is closer to *prone* than *supine*, and that it can be a synonym for the former but not the latter.

Note also the difference between **prostrate** and *supine* when it comes to describing how people respond to another powerful force. **Prostrate** involves total submission and surrender, as in:

Caught red-handed they appeared prostrate before the authorities.

Supine suggests inertness or failure to resist pressure, as in:

The staff are partly to blame in their supine response to this new demand for their time.

Thus **prostrate** implies confrontation with a power that cannot be resisted, whereas *supine* implies that it should have been.

protagonist and **antagonist** In modern English these have been reinterpreted to complement each other, in ways which are sometimes the subject of criticism. Our awareness of *pro-* and *anti-* inclines us to use **protagonist** as "one who fights for something" and **antagonist** as "one who fights against something" (see further under **anti-** and **pro-**).

For those with a knowledge of Greek, including Fowler and the editors of the original *Oxford Dictionary*, this was all very unsatisfactory because the **protagonist** was the leading actor (literally "first actor") in a Greek drama. Fowler therefore claimed that the word could not be made plural (since there was only one **protagonist** in the original context); and he argued that using the adjective "chief" with it (as in *chief protagonist*) was tautologous. They're definitely points for the cognoscenti. The *Oxford Dictionary* (1989) overrules his first point and allows *protagonists* in the plural. Yet it does insist on the word being applied to leaders and prominent people only. It therefore labels as "erroneous" its own set of citations where **protagonist** is used simply to mean "advocate or supporter". Fortunately other modern dictionaries take this usage in their stride, and enter it without any cautionary label.

The fact that people nowadays interpret **protagonist** as embodying *pro-* (the Latin prefix meaning "in support of") is not something to lament or condemn. It confirms that common knowledge of Latin word elements in English is much stronger than the knowledge of Greek—and that people like to make sense of the words they use.

protest against or **protest at** These are used in slightly different ways, since **protest against** often implies an organised protest, whereas **protest at** is more likely to be the voice of an individual. Compare:

> *With their road blockade, the truckies were protesting against the new road tax.*
> *She protested at his disregard for the views of other members of the selection committee.*

Less common alternatives for **protest at** are *protest about* and *protest over*.

Note that in American English, either of the above could be expressed with just *protest*. (See further under **prepositions**.) Yet in Australian and British English too, the verb *protest* stands without a preposition when it means "affirm", as in *protest one's innocence.*

Protestant This term (with a capital *p*) refers to any of the churches which detached themselves from the Catholic Church of Rome at the time of the Reformation. The name was first used of the German princes who spoke out against the counter-Reformation statements of Speyer in 1529. It was then applied to the churches led by Luther and Calvin, and to the Church of England. Further **Protestant** churches were formed in Britain in the next two centuries, detaching themselves from the established Church of England. Dissenting churches, the Methodists, and Presbyterians are therefore also known as *Nonconformist churches*. In the USA the largest **Protestant** churches are the American Baptists, the Mormons and the Jehovah's Witnesses.

Note that the term **Protestant** is not used of the Eastern Orthodox churches, which detached themselves from the Church of Rome about AD 1054.

proto- This Greek prefix means "first in time" or "original". It has developed in English out of words such as *protoplast* and *prototype*, and provided the initial element for many new scientific terms of the nineteenth century, especially in zoology, biology and chemistry. These were followed by a spate of words with **proto-** in the humanities and social sciences. Some are generic terms such as *protoculture, protohistory* and *protosyntax*, while others refer to a specific early language or culture:

> *Proto-Australian Proto-Indo-European Proto-Romance*
> *proto-Baroque proto-Renaissance*

As the examples show, the prefix is capitalised when it forms part of the name of a hypothetical original language, but in lower case when it refers to an early or primitive form of a given culture. Note also the use of a hyphen with **proto-** before a word with a capital, but not in the generic or scientific terms.

proved or **proven** Everywhere in the English-speaking world, **proved** is the dictionaries' primary form for the past participle of the verb *prove*, and **proven** is the second alternative. Database evidence shows that in Australia and Britain

proven is less used than in the USA, where it makes a stronger showing. In the British and Australian databases of one million words (LOB and ACE), **proven** occurs respectively 3 and 4 times (as a verb), as against 11 times in the matching American database (Brown). Even so, the Brown figure is only half that for the use of **proved** for the past participle, so the ratio still runs very much in favor of **proved** for American English. The ratio refutes the claim made in some British style guides that **proven** is the American form.

Note that **proven** is everywhere used for the participial adjective, as in: *proven expertise* and the formula *not proven*, both examples from the ACE corpus.

proverbs See under **aphorism, adage, axiom, maxim** or **proverb.**

provided or **providing** Either of these words can introduce a condition:

> *They'll come provided (that) we guarantee them a bodyguard.*
> *They'll come providing (that) we guarantee them a bodyguard.*

The structures are both equally old, appearing in the fifteenth century with a following *that* and without it, as a quasi-conjunction in the seventeenth. The preference of Fowler and others for **provided (that)** cannot therefore be related to its being older established. In the Australian ACE corpus **provided (that)** is more common by a ratio of 8:1, but whether this is the cause or effect of the style pundits' preference is a moot point. At any rate both expressions are in current use.

Most style commentators agree that these phrases are heavyweight ways of prefacing a condition. If that is the effect you're seeking, they serve your purpose. If not, **provided that** can be reduced to **provided** (as it usually is in ACE), or replaced by *if.* Note that **provided that** seems only to be acceptable when the main clause is positive. Compare:

> *The money is available provided that we spend it before June.*
> *The money is not available provided that we (don't) spend ...(?)*

In the second version **provided that** would have to be replaced by *unless.*

prox. See under **ult.**

proxime accessit See under **cum laude.**

prudent or **prudish** These adjectives recognise very different aspects of human character. **Prudent** implies wisdom and shrewdness, and respect for them in the person or plan credited with them. **Prudish** implies a narrow concern with the conventions of modesty and morality and a tendency to disapprove of others who are more liberal in this regard.

The similarity between the two words suggests a common basis of meaning, but it's deceptive. **Prudent** has a straightforward history going back to an identical Latin adjective meaning "wise". **Prudish** has come to us by a devious route through French. It uses the clipped form (*prude*) of French *prudefemme*, meaning "proud or worthy woman", with the English suffix *-ish* added to make it an adjective. Evidently a certain irony has contributed to its sense development.

pry This is effectively two verbs, one meaning "look inquisitively", and the other "prise". The two are easily distinguished by the following preposition. The first verb only collocates with *into* (*pry into*) and the second with *open* (*pry open*). Neither Australians nor Britons make much use of the second expression, but it is established in American English.

The second verb is believed to be a backformation from *prise*, which was taken as *pries* (as either the third person singular present of a verb, or the plural of the noun) and suggested a base form **pry**. (Compare *fly*.) The same kind of backformation has contributed several nouns to English (see under **false plurals**). The origin of **pry** "look inquisitively" is unknown.

Note the alternative spellings *prier/pryer* for "one who pries" in either of the above senses. The word is far from common, and *prier* is given as the primary spelling in all dictionaries, perhaps following the original *Oxford Dictionary*, which had only a handful of citations, spread over several centuries. As with *drier/flier* we might expect the regular form *pryer* to gain ground, and all the more because of the possibility of confusing *prier* with *prior*.

PS See under **postscript**.

pseudo- Though borrowed from Greek, this prefix meaning "false" first appears in English in medieval religious expressions such as *Pseudo-Christ* and *pseudo-prophet*. There it still functions rather like an adjective, but in the nineteenth century it takes off as a true prefix in countless new formations. At first they are mostly scholarly, and in biological nomenclature **pseudo-** is used in a relatively neutral way to refer to organs which have a function other than the one you might expect (e.g. *pseudocarp*), or a species which resembles another though it's unrelated to it (*pseudoscorpion*).

In other disciplines **pseudo-** has negative connotations, and points to the falseness of appearances, as in *pseudoclassic* and *pseudoscience*. It is freely used in ad hoc pejorative words such as *pseudo-charming*. So common is its use, it has assumed independent status as a noun *pseudo/pseud*, referring to a person deemed to be a sham.

The abbreviation *pseud.* represents *pseudonym*. (See further under **nom de plume**.)

pseudo-cleft sentence See under **cleft sentences**.

psychic or **psychical** See under **-ic/-ical**.

publicly or **publically** The choice between these spellings is discussed under **-ic/-ical**.

punctuation Our *punctuation system* has evolved in tandem with the traditions of writing and printing. Elements of modern **punctuation** made their appearance in England in the seventeenth century, but it was only towards the end of the eighteenth that their use was formalised into a system. The full inventory of *punctuation marks* which appear in modern English are as follows:

(for sentence punctuation)
brackets colon comma dash ellipsis exclamation mark full stop question mark quotation marks semicolon
(for word punctuation)
acute apostrophe cedilla circumflex dieresis grave háček hyphen solidus tilde umlaut

For more about each, see under individual headings.

1 *Developments in* **punctuation**. Not all the punctuation marks listed above are used regularly, and the use of even the most essential ones has varied considerably since the eighteenth century. Any glance at books of prose published more than a century ago will show that *sentence punctuation* was once used much more liberally than nowadays; and even now there are institutions and individuals who prefer heavier rather than lighter punctuation. The British tendency to use more hyphens than Americans when punctuating words is another example of this variability. In business letter writing everywhere there's a growing preference for "open" rather than "closed" punctuation, examples of which are shown in Appendix VII. This trend is motivated partly by the feeling that less **punctuation** means fewer keystrokes for the keyboarder, and less time and effort in the production of the day's letters. Note that the new *punctuation conventions* apply to the more formalised parts of the letter (the address, salutation and signature), and do not affect the main body.

Other factors in the use of **punctuation** are changing ideas about its function. In the past **punctuation** was often placed to coincide with grammatical units, and so almost every phrase in a Victorian novel may be marked off by a comma or semicolon. It served a purpose, given the typically longer sentences of Victorian writing, and reminds us of the fact that **punctuation** should work in partnership with syntax. Less complicated, shorter sentences can be read comfortably with less punctuation. Sentences which function as questions or exclamations need to be finished with the appropriate mark.

2 *Punctuation and speaking*. Some writers and teachers associate **punctuation** with the sound and rhythm of sentences, and see it as a substitute for the stress, pause and intonation of living speech. However the only one of those which it has the means to show regularly is pausing. (Stress can very occasionally be shown by underlining or italics, but ordinary stress and rhythm have to be created by the sequence of words in phrases and sentences.) Early writers on **punctuation** saw the comma, semicolon, colon and full stop as representing increasingly long pauses in sentences. And though we no longer distinguish colon from semicolon in that way, we still regard the comma, (semi)colon and full stop as representing small, medium and large breaks in the structure of sentences. (See further under **colon** and **semicolon**.) Ideally the writer places them at points where readers can safely pause—to coincide with a break or boundary in the structure of information, where they can stop before launching into the next significant unit. Thus **punctuation** serves to highlight information structure, as well as aspects of syntax.

3 *Meaning in punctuation.* **Punctuation** is at bottom a device for separating and/or linking items in the continuous line of writing. Many *punctuation marks* do both at once. Commas often separate one phrase from the next, yet they show that the two belong to the same sentence. Hyphens link the two parts of a compound, but also ensure that the boundary between them is obvious to the reader. Research shows however that **punctuation** works best in supporting distinctions which are already there for the reader in the words, and cannot really "create" ones which are not already felt. The difference between restrictive and nonrestrictive relative clauses cannot be made by commas alone. (See further under **relative clauses**.)

Note finally that **punctuation** is essentially neutral and cannot express the attitudes of the writer without ambiguity. Exclamation marks attached to a particular statement do not clarify whether the writer is shocked or excited by it; and the use of "scare quotes" is similarly ambiguous. (See **quotation marks** section 1.)

pundit or **pandit** This Hindi loanword, originally *pandita*, means "wise man, scholar", and in the form **pandit** it is still a title of honor, witness *Pandit Nehru*. The pronunciation of the word by Indians makes it sound to English ears like "pundit"; and **pundit** is the spelling attached to the extended use of the word in English, when it refers to those who set themselves up as experts, as in *economic pundits with their abstract solutions*. Given this somewhat derogatory use of **pundit**, it's preferable to use the spelling **pandit** whenever the older meaning of the word is intended.

puns A *pun* is a play on words, invoking the meaning of two (or more) at once for humorous effect. Though sometimes called the "lowest form of wit", it all depends on the quality of the *pun*. Shakespeare used **puns** to add allusive dimensions to his dialogue, and contemporary news reporters engage their readers with **puns** in headlines. A nice example to head an article on the aristocratic pursuit of gardening was *HAUGHTY CULTURE*. Advertisers exploit the *pun* in the naming of products, and help them to linger in the mind, witness *ABSCENT* for a deodorant, and *RAINDEERS* for plastic shoe protectors used in the snow belt of North America. As the examples show, a *written pun* commits itself to one meaning by the spelling, and has to rely on the context (verbal/visual/situational) to raise the other.

pupa The plural of this word is discussed under **-a** section 1.

purposely, purposefully or **purposively** The first of these is by far the most common, used to emphasise that something was not just an accident but happened intentionally. Most often it's said in relation to small events:

You purposely took a wrong turning.

Its opposite is *accidentally.*

Purposefully looks beyond the immediate situation, and sees the act as a step towards a preconceived goal:

She walked purposefully across the street to meet him.

Its opposite is *aimlessly.*

Purposively is a more academic word than either of the others, popularised by the theory of ''purposivism'' a century ago. It represents the idea that the behavior of an individual or organism is always directed towards an end, and is not random. Its perspective is detached and behavioristic, whereas both **purposely** and **purposefully** suggest something about what's going on in a person's mind. **Purposively** can be used in connection with nonhuman and inanimate subjects, as in:

A special meeting was arranged purposively two days before.

Neither of the other words would fit properly in that sentence.

pygmy or **pigmy** See **pigmy** or **pygmy**.

pyjamas or **pajamas** The first is the standard spelling in Australia and Britain, the second is the one generally used in the USA, although *Webster's English Usage* notes that **pyjamas** occasionally appears in American fashion catalogues, presumably because of its cachet.

The spelling **pajamas** is slightly closer to the word's origins in Hindi *pajama*, based on a Persian word meaning ''leg garment''. Yet having adapted the word's meaning so that it now refers to a garment for the whole body, we lose part of the argument for keeping the original spelling.

Q

qango or **quango** See **quango**.

QANTAS This name may be written either in full caps, or as **Qantas**, like other well-established **acronyms**. (See further under that heading.)

Outside Australia **QANTAS** could perhaps be mistaken for an Arabic name because it lacks the *u* which goes with *q* in every other English word. Australians know it as an acronym for the *Queensland and Northern Territory Aerial Services*, a name which dates from the founding of the company in 1920 by four men: the chairman, two pilots and a mechanic. During the 1930s and 40s it became *Qantas Empire Airways* (*QEA*) operating the southern hemisphere section of the London–Sydney link in collaboration with British airlines. In 1947 QEA was bought out by the Australian Government, and from then on it operated as a full international airline, once again under the name QANTAS.

QED See under **quod erat demonstrandum**.

Qoran or **Koran** See **Koran**.

qu/k The French *qu* has given us an alternative to *k* in pairs such as **lacquer/lacker**, **lackey/lacquey** and **racket/racquet**. (See further under each of those headings.)

In names such as *Iraq/Irak* and *Qoran/Koran* the *q* represents an Arabic consonant. It tends to be replaced by *k* in the process of anglicisation, though the process itself is uneven. (See further under **Iraq** and **Koran**.)

qua The ordinary English equivalent for this Latin word is "as a ...", but it works in special circumstances. It serves to single out one particular viewpoint or angle from any others which might occur to the audience. See for instance:
Our son's music teacher advised us qua parent that we should not insist too much on daily practice.
I've no complaint about the letter qua letter ... it's just the implications for future contracts.
By convention there's never *a* or *an* between **qua** and the noun following. As the examples show, **qua** may effectively contrast two points of view (those of someone who is both teacher and parent in the first example). It may also draw attention to the distinction between form and meaning or function, as in the second example with the repetition of *letter*.

Qua is useful shorthand for more circuitous phrases such as "in the capacity of". Yet its natural context is academic discourse, and in ordinary kinds of writing it runs the risk of seeming obscure and irritating to those who don't know it, or pretentious to those who do.

quadr- This is the Latin prefix for "four". Its meaning is essential to words such as:

quadrangle quadrella quadrillion quadrophonic quadruped

The examples show that the vowel immediately after the prefix is not to be taken for granted, and dictionaries confirm that quite a few of the **quadr-** words in English have at least two possible spellings. In some cases the vowel of the second syllable is quite clear because of the stress on it, as with the first three above. But those like *quadrophonic* with stress on the first and third syllables leave it unclear as to what the second syllable should be. Is it *quadracycle* or *quadricycle? Quadraplegic, quadriplegic or quadruplegic? Quadrasonic, quadrisonic or quadrosonic?* All those spellings are recognised in modern dictionaries, and any of them would correspond to the standard pronunciation. For *quadraphony* (or is it *quadrophony?*) it depends on whether you stress the first or second syllable. Amid the variety of spellings for those words, the point to note is that the spelling with *a* is acceptable for each of them.

Note however that for mathematical words such as *quadrilateral*, *quadrinomial* and *quadrivalent*, only the spelling with *i* is accepted.

quadriceps For the plural, see under **biceps**.

quadrillion For the value of this number, see **billion**.

qualifiers The adverbs whose role is to affect the force of neighboring words, especially adjectives, are **qualifiers**. They may intensify the adjective, as in *very pleased, extremely annoyed.* Or it may soften their impact, as in *rather excited, somewhat disturbed.*

For more about the first type, see **intensifiers**; for the second, see **hedge words**.

quandary or **quandry** Though this word is often pronounced with two syllables, the only spelling recognised in dictionaries is **quandary**, with three. *Webster's English Usage* (1989) does however have a few citations for **quandry**, and we might expect more if the word appeared more often in print. It remains rather as it was for Samuel Johnson: "a low word".

quandong This is an Aboriginal word, borrowed from the Wiradhuri in central NSW. In the past it was occasionally spelled *quondong* and *quandang*. It refers to two kinds of fruit-bearing native trees:
1 a small tree or shrub (*Santalum acuminatum*) with small bright red fruits, also known as the "native peach". It grows in South Australia.
2 a rainforest tree (*Elaeocarpus angustifolius*) with blue fruits, found in coastal NSW and Queensland and cut for timber. Other names for it are "silver quandong" and "native fig".

The word **quandong** has also been put to colloquial use by urban Australians to refer to someone who takes (or is deemed to take) advantage of another. Citations in the *Australian National Dictionary* since 1960 have it as either a con-man, or a woman who allows herself to be wined and dined but refuses to proceed to a chaser of sex after it. Earlier citations suggest it was associated with stupidity, especially in the phrase *have (the) quandongs.*

quango or **qango** This term originated in Britain in the 1960s as an acronym for *quasi autonomous nongovernment organisation.* The third word in the phrase was however a little mysterious, since *quangos* had government funding and were used to further government policy in specialised areas; and by 1976 the acronym was being explained as *quasi autonomous national government organisation.* But by the 1980s the original explanation was reaffirmed, according to *Oxford Dictionary* citations. The spelling has always included a *u* after the *q* in spite of its being an acronym, making it conform with other common words beginning with *q.*

quarreled or **quarrelled** On the spelling of this verb, see **-l/-ll-**.

quarter This word is differently used in Australia, Britain and the USA when it comes to: (1) telling the time; (2) speaking of fractions.

In reference to times such as *9.15,* Australians and the British say *quarter past nine,* whereas Americans say *quarter after nine.* At 9.45 we say *quarter to ten,* where in different parts of the USA it's *quarter of ten* or *quarter till ten.*

When articulating fractions, Australians speak of *one quarter* and *three quarters.* In the USA it would be *one fourth* and *three fourths.*

quasi- This is quite a recent prefix meaning "apparently", giving new life to a Latin conjunction. It suggests that things are not what they seem, and that the rest of the word is not to be taken at face value. Witness:

quasi-historical quasi-judicial quasi-official quasi-religious

It forms nonce words, especially adjectives and nouns, very freely, e.g. *quasi-expert.* **Quasi-** words are always hyphenated.

quay This spelling seems strange for the pronunciation of the word. In earlier English, it was spelled *key* or sometimes *kay,* and only in the eighteenth century did **quay** become the regular spelling. It represents two spelling principles of the time, that: (1) different spellings should be given to homophones (in this case the homophone was *key*); (2) individual spellings should represent the etymology of the word, as far as possible.

The **quay** spelling satisfied the first principle above, and separated it from *key* as well as *cay* "coral island". But the word owes its *ay* to the second principle, and the fact that it's related to *cay,* ultimately Spanish *cayo* a "shoal or reef sometimes exposed by the tide". The English use of *quay* extends it to mean an artificial causeway or wharf built out to sea above the high-tide level. A dictionary of 1696 shows the first recorded use of the spelling **quay** (alongside *kay*), possibly on the analogy of French *quai*, though *qu* was used to respell *k* in other words during the seventeenth century.

question For **begging the question** and **leading question**, see under their respective headings.

Various subcategories of **questions** are discussed under that heading.

question marks A *question mark* at the end of a string of words confirms that it's a question, or that it should be read as one:

Did you see the advertisement?

He hasn't come yet?

The word order of the first sentence (with subject following the auxiliary verb) sets it up as a question anyway. But the second sentence only becomes a question through the mark at the end. (If spoken, it would of course be marked as a question through rising intonation.)

In the same way, the absence of a *question mark* from an inverted sentence shows that it is not intended as a question, but as a request, invitation or instruction. See for example:

Could I use your phone.

Won't you come in.

Would you close the door.

A *question mark* might perhaps be used in the first of those, if the writer wanted to emphasise the politeness of the request, and the fact that the response was not taken for granted. In the second and third cases, the invitation/instruction assumes compliance and is not up for negotiation.

Note that **question marks** are used only with direct questions, not indirect questions. Compare:

Where were you last night?

I asked where you were last night

Question marks are occasionally used in mid-sentence, beside a date which is uncertain: *Chaucer b. ?1340*, or after a word whose use is questionable. The first is an accepted practice; the second one casts a shadow of doubt on the writer's verbal competence, and should be avoided in a finished MS.

Other punctuation with **question marks**. The *question mark* takes the place of a full stop at the end of a sentence. If there are quotation marks or parentheses it stands inside them, unless it belongs strictly to the carrier sentence. Compare:

She asked "Who are you?"

Did I hear him say "an old friend"?

How can I find out about performances of music (classical)?

It's in that tourist pamphlet (What's On in Brisbane?)

Double **question marks** (*??*), or combinations of question and exclamation marks (*?!* or *!?*), are to be avoided except in informal writing (and in chess). Where they might appear on either side of closing quotation marks (because one belongs to the quote, and the other to the carrier sentence), the sentence should be rearranged to avoid it. Perhaps the **interrobang** will one day solve that problem of needing two punctuation marks at once. (See further under **interrobang**.)

questions A *question* is an interactive means of establishing the facts. Through **questions** we elicit information from others, or ask them to affirm or negate a fact which we ourselves supply. The only **questions** which do not work by interaction like this are *rhetorical questions*. Those who utter them in the course of a monologue mean to provide the answer themselves, and are using the question form only as a way of securing the audience's attention.

1 *Information-seeking* **questions** are also known as *wh-questions* because they're introduced by interrogative words such as *who, when, where, why*:

   Who were you talking to?
   When will the party begin?
   Where should we all meet?
   Why are you waiting?

Note that *how* also counts among the *interrogative words*, and that it too introduces open-ended *wh-questions*.

2 **Questions** *which seek an affirmative or negative as an answer* are known simply as *yes/no questions* or *polar questions*. They are often expressed through inversion of the subject and auxiliary, as in:

   Have you finished?
   Were you thinking of lunch?

Alternatively, a *yes/no question* may take the form of an ordinary statement rounded off with a question mark at the end:

   The show can go on?
   They won't march without us?

In conversation **questions** like those would be accompanied by rising intonation. They might also be followed up by a *tag question*, as in:

   The show can go on, can't it?
   They won't march without us, will they?

3 *Tag* **questions** serve to underscore the subject and verb of the main question, picking up the subject through the appropriate pronoun (*it, they*), and the verb through its auxiliary. (If there's no auxiliary, *do* is recruited for the purpose: *You like the program, don't you?*) Note that the tag question usually has opposite polarity to that of the main question (negative when it's positive and vice versa).

4 *Direct and indirect* **questions**. All the types of **questions** mentioned so far are *direct questions*, i.e. they are expressed as they would be in real interaction with those who supply the answer. At one stage removed are *indirect questions*, ones which report a question through the words of another party:

   They asked when we should all meet.
   They queried why we were waiting.
   They questioned whether the show would go on.

Indirect questions differ from direct ones in that they use regular subject/verb word order. Note that they may adjust the pronouns (turning the second person *you* into first or third person), and modify the tense of the verb. In the examples above a past tense is used following the past tense of the main verb, even though it would have been present tense in the *direct question.* (See further under **sequence of tenses**.) No question mark is used with *indirect questions.*

qui vive   This French tag appears rather curiously in the English phrase *on the qui vive,* meaning "on the alert". In prerevolutionary France, it was the formula by which a sentry accosted anyone approaching, and was intended to elicit the loyal response *Vive le roi* "long live the king". So like *goodbye* it is a remnant of a ritual exchange of greetings. (See further under **adieu**.)

quick   This is first and foremost an adjective, as in *the quick brown fox,* but also works as an adverb, especially in conversational idiom such as *Come quick.* The regular adverb *quickly* is usual in writing. (See further under **zero adverbs**.)
      Note that the comparative form *quicker* is also used as both adjective and as adverb in informal style:
      You'd get there quicker by car.
In writing *more quickly* is usual.

quid pro quo   This Latin phrase means "which in exchange for what". It first appears in the sixteenth century in reference to substituting one medical remedy for another, though Shakespeare used it figuratively, to mean "tit for tat". Nowadays it still serves to refer to whatever is given in retaliation, or where something is expected in return for a favor. The plural is normally *quid pro quos,* not the Latin *quae pro quo.*
      The phrase probably gave rise to the slang word **quid**, a unit of money which varies with the context in which it's used. In the seventeenth century it meant a guinea, and after that a pound. In Australia it now has to be translated into dollars, although it does not pretend to be an exact amount:
      Can you lend me a couple of quid?
As that example shows, the plural is often the same as the singular.

quintillion   For the value of this number, see under **billion**.

quit or **quitted**   The past tense of **quit** is also **quit**, if it's a matter of ceasing to do something:
      She quit smoking a year ago.
But when the word means "leave", the past may be either **quit** or **quitted**, depending on where and who you are. American speakers would say:
      He quit that job after only a few weeks.
Whereas for British speakers it's more likely to be:
      He quitted that job after only a few weeks.
Australians make scant use of **quitted** according to evidence from the ACE corpus: there were five instances of **quit** (meaning "left"), and none of **quitted**.

The form **quitted**, first recorded in the seventeenth century, thus seems to be stalled rather than increasing its grip on the irregular parts of **quit**. (See further under **irregular verbs**.)

quite This is the all-purpose qualifier. It works both as an intensifier to reinforce the following word, as in *quite right*, *quite enough*; and as a hedge word to tone it down, as in *quite amusing*, *quite well*. In some contexts and combinations it's not clear which is intended. If something is *quite original*, is it brilliantly innovative, or just modestly creative? If *quite dangerous*, should you proceed with caution, or evacuate immediately? The word is not the one to choose if you value clear communication. For other less ambiguous qualifiers, see **intensifiers** and **hedge words**.

quiz and **quizzes** See under **-z/-zz-**.

quod erat demonstrandum This weighty Latin phrase **quod erat demonstrandum** means "which was (what had) to be demonstrated". It comes down to us through Euclidean geometry, marking the end of the proof of a theorem. Yet it enjoys wider use as a marker of the conclusion to an argument, when the speaker/writer has pursued the logic of their ideas to the end. It is often abbreviated to *QED*, with each letter pronounced as a separate syllable.

quod vide See q.v.

quorum This enigmatic word is a Latin relative pronoun, a genitive plural meaning "of whom". It has been pressed into service as an abstract noun, and used to refer to the minimum number of people required for a meeting to conduct its business. Its plural in English is *quorums*, since it's not a regular Latin noun. (See further under **-um**.)

English use of **quorum** seems to spring from the wording of commissions which specified the particular number of justices of the peace required to constitute a bench. From there it was applied to all justices, and from the beginning of the seventeenth century it was applied generally to the fixed number needed at a meeting for business to be properly transacted.

quotation marks The common term for the pairs of aerial commas which mark quotations is **quotation marks**, or less formally *quote marks* or *quotes*, the last being freely used among editors (see *Copy-editing* 1992). The older term *inverted commas* which originated in the eighteenth century is losing popularity even in Britain (see further under that heading). **Quotation marks** raise a number of punctuation issues, such as the choice between double and single quotes, and where to locate other punctuation marks in relation to them (see below sections 2 and 3).

1 *Uses of **quotation marks**. Quote marks* identify the words actually uttered or written by someone. They appear at the start and finish of the quoted string of words, except when the quotation runs to several paragraphs. Then the *quote* *marks* appear just at the beginning of each paragraph, until the last one which has them at both beginning and end. Note that no quotation marks at all are needed for block quotations which are indented and set apart typographically (in a smaller or different typeface).

In fact **quotation marks** are often less than essential in separating quoted from nonquoted material. Some famous writers do without them altogether in the articulation of dialogue—including James Joyce, who called them "perverted commas", and preferred to preface segments of dialogue with a dash. (The dash is often used this way in French.) The Authorised Version of the Bible (1611) does without *quote marks*, not as a reaction against them but because their use had not then been systematised. Like many aspects of our punctuation system, **quotation marks** were not in regular use until the later eighteenth century.

A lesser function of **quotation marks** is to draw the reader's attention to a word which is somehow out of the ordinary. It may be technical, or foreign, or a nonce word. It may be a word that the writer feels is an imperfect choice, or one used with ironic implications. *Quote marks* used this way go by various ad hoc names such as "scare quotes", "sneer quotes", "shudder quotes" and "cute quotes". Amid all those effects the *quote marks* may do no more than indicate that the word is not one to take for granted. They draw attention to the word on its first appearance in a text, but after that it appears without them.

Using *quote marks* to highlight words for such a range of different purposes is not ideal. The Chicago *Manual of Style* comments that "mature" writers do not need to rely on *quote marks* to express irony or other attitudes, but can convey the intended emphasis and meaning through the right choice of words, appropriately arranged. If something is still needed for the individual word, you can resort to bold or italic type. Bold and italics are also the answer for technical and foreign terms, or underlining, when special typefaces are not available. This all helps to take the load off **quotation marks** in running text. Most people find they look fussy when used round single words, and alternative fonts help to reduce their overall use. *Quote marks* can then be reserved purely for quoted material, and for translations or glosses of foreign words, as in many entries in this book.

One other conventional use of **quotation marks** is to identify the titles of shorter compositions which form part of an anthology. So *quote marks* are used to embrace the names of lyric poems which are part of a published collection, and songs which make individual tracks on a record or CD. On their use for journal articles, see under **titles**. On the use of **quotation marks** for the names of radio and TV programs, see under **italics**.

2 *Double or single **quotation marks**.* The English-speaking world is rather divided over this. Double quotes are the standard practice in the USA, whereas in Australia and Britain both double and single are in common use. In Australia single quotes are recommended by the Australian Government *Style Manual*,

yet all daily newspapers and many publishers use double quotes. A survey taken
in 1992 among professional writers in Sydney and Melbourne endorsed the use
of double quotes by a majority of more than two thirds. In Britain single quotes
are recommended by Oxford University Press and Cambridge University Press
in their respective style guides, yet once again the British press and other
publishers prefer to differ.

The argument usually raised for single quotes is that they are more elegant
than double quotes—though this suggests it's a matter of taste. Occasionally
arguments of space and efficiency are also raised, though the amount of space
saved is negligible, and there's no difference at all in the number of keystrokes
required of the keyboarder. The chief argument in favor of double quotes is that
they prevent confusion when the typewriter or printer reduces all aerial commas
to a straight vertical or backward-leaning stroke. Compare:

> *(Whose is that?) 'It's John's.'*
>   *"It's John's."*

The use of double quotes ensures that the apostrophe and quote mark are visually
distinct, however limited the type resources.

Note that whether you choose double or single quotes as your normal
practice, you will need the other when it comes to ''quotes within quotes''. The
alternatives are:

> *The announcement was that "The council had decided to disallow the*
> *cutting of 'significant trees', even on private property ..."*

or

> *The announcement was that 'The council had decided to disallow the*
> *cutting of "significant trees", even on private property ...'*

The choice of first level (double or single) entails the other for the second level.
But which level of *quote marks* to choose for the ironically used word is not
discussed in any of the standard style guides. The Australian Government *Style
Manual* uses single quotes for both the first level of quotation and ironic words,
whereas Murray-Smith has double quotes for general purposes and single quotes
for the ironic word. This adds a further dimension of difficulty to using *quote
marks* for ironic and other special purposes. How is the reader to know from
the *quote marks* whether it's an ironic or quoted word, if they appear only
occasionally in the text? The same question can arise within the titles of journal
articles. (See further under **titles**.)

3 *Quotation marks* *with other punctuation.* Which other punctuation marks to
use with *quote marks*, and where to locate them, are vexed and variable issues.
a) *Before the quotation begins.* According to older convention, a quotation is
preceded by a comma:

> *The old woman declared, "I'll let you in on one condition ..."*

This is still quite common practice in novels, though a simple space may
serve the same purpose:

> *The old woman declared "I'll let you in on one condition ..."*

In newspapers and magazines there's a strong tendency to use a colon before quoted material:

> *In his summing up the judge said: "This was a bestial crime which calls for the strongest sentence."*

Note that the quoted material always begins with a capital letter.

b) *Before presentational material.* When a quotation is followed or interrupted by reference to the person who uttered it, any major punctuation mark (exclamation mark, question mark) and the comma which replaces a full stop goes *inside* the closing quote marks:

> *"He's coming!" they exclaimed.*
> *"He's coming?" they asked.*
> *"He's coming," they said.*

That principle is extended to all commas in American editing practice, even those which punctuate the carrier sentence rather than the quotation itself:

> *"Your teacher," they said, "is on that plane."*

The same practice is commonly observed in British printing, according to *Copy-editing* (1992). However it also recognises the alternative British practice represented in *Hart's Rules* (and the *Right Word at the Right Time*), by which the comma would stay outside the closing quote marks when it's not integral to the quotation:

> *"Your teacher", they said, "is on that plane."*

The Australian Government *Style Manual* clearly prefers this practice, although it depends on an awareness of sentence structure not possessed by all those who deal with MS material. Meanwhile the simplicity of the American practice has a lot to recommend it. Note that both British and American editors agree that when a quotation is resumed after the presentational material, the first word is in lower case.

c) *At the end of the sentence.* Where to put the final full stop is again a question on which editorial practices divide. In American English, it always goes inside. In British English the conventions are bewilderingly varied. According to *Hart's Rules* (1983) the position of the full stop depends on whether what's quoted is complete in itself, and completes the carrier sentence at the same time. If it fulfills those conditions, the full stop goes inside; if the quotation is only part of a sentence, the full stop goes outside. Compare:

> *The airline clerk said: "He's on the next plane."*
> *The airline clerk said that he was "on the next plane".*

These conventions are acknowledged in *Copy-editing* (1992), as well as the rather different practice associated with British Standard 5261, by which the full stop only goes inside if the quotation *stands by itself* as a complete sentence. This would mean putting the full stop outside the closing quote marks in both the last two examples. The Australian Government *Style Manual* endorses this latter practice, which has the advantage of making the rules for final punctuation with *quote marks* match up with those for parentheses (see further under **brackets**).

Whether the reader actually notices the position of the final full stop is rather dubious. Editors shed blood, sweat and tears over the issue, wrestling with anomalies not covered by the various rules; and the wastage of editorial time suggests there's a lot to be said for a simple system. The American practice (put it inside) is still the easiest to apply in texts with a lot of dialogue, because it can be applied to quotations of any length, whether in the middle or at the end of a sentence. But for nonfictional writing, the practice of treating final punctuation for quote marks the same way as for parentheses has much to recommend it.

Note that very occasionally a sentence with a quotation needs both question and exclamation marks, or two question marks, or a question mark and a full stop. Once again the authorities disagree. Some authorities (*Right Word at the Right Time*) have it that you should use two of the heavier marks (exclamation marks or question marks) if they are required by the nature of the quotation and the carrier sentence:

Did she really say: "Can I cross your hallowed threshold?"?

However when it's a combination of a full stop with one of the heavier marks, the heavier one subsumes the full stop:

I can't believe she said: "Can I cross your hallowed threshold?"

The Australian Government *Style Manual* (1988) rules that if the marks are the same, you use just one of them, but if they are different you use both. By that rule, the first example above would have only one question mark, and the second would have a full stop after the closing quote marks. Clearly it's a vexed issue when authorities who come to grips with it resolve it in opposite ways. The need for two heavy punctuation marks at the end of a sentence suggests that too much is going on in it, and that ideally it should be recast to disentangle the strands of thought.

quotations For nonfiction writers, **quotations** are essentially a way of bringing someone else's words into your text. A *quotation* may serve to invoke their authority in support of claims or arguments you're making, or as a momentary evocation of their character and style. Journalists and magazine reporters quite regularly resort to quoting statements made by public figures, in order to relieve the straight reportage and introduce a touch of drama. Yet when it happens in every news article, the switch from indirect narrative to directly quoted speech loses its effect, especially when the words quoted are remarkable for their clichés and low level of significance.

In educational and scholarly writing, **quotations** are a means of using the words of another writer to lend weight to your own, without committing plagiarism. Inexperienced writers sometimes use them as a kind of academic showmanship (''Look how many authors I've read''), but it's a mistake to use too many on the same page. As in newspaper reporting, **quotations** seem less significant the more a writer resorts to them. Is the writer capable of expressing things independently, the reader begins to wonder.

*Integrating **quotations***. **Quotations** can only contribute effectively to your prose if they're blended smoothly into the surrounding text. A little effort may be needed to make them dovetail with the carrier sentence, and avoid a rough transition like the following:

Joan Sutherland said that "I'm staying home from now on ..."

Either the carrier sentence, or the quotation itself needs a little adapting:

Joan Sutherland said: "I'm staying home from now on ..."

Joan Sutherland said that she would be "staying home from now on ..."

When the actual wording of the quotation is modified by the writer, the word modified or introduced should be marked with square brackets:

Joan Sutherland said that she would "[stay] home from now on ..."

For more about the use of square brackets, see under **brackets**. The use of ellipsis in quotations is discussed under **ellipsis** section 2.

Quran or **Koran** See Koran.

q.v. This abbreviates the Latin **quod vide**, which translated literally means ''which see'', or more freely ''have a look at that''. It encourages the reader to seek further information under the reference just given, as in *ideas expressed in Psalm 23 (q.v.)*. But like most of the scholarly abbreviations from Latin, it's used less often nowadays.

R

r or **wr** Do you ever *(w)rack your brains* over how to write *(w)rack and ruin*? Dictionaries suggest **rack** for both, though the word comes from different sources for the two phrases. In *racking your brains*, **rack** is easy to justify since it's a figure of speech based on that medieval instrument of torture—as is *nerve-racking*. But in *rack and ruin* the first word is probably related to *wreck*. No doubt the alliteration with *ruin* has helped to promote the spelling of **rack** there, but dictionaries make it quite as acceptable as *wrack and ruin*.

For other homonyms based on **r/wr**, only one or other spelling will do. The curious **wr** spelling seems in fact to persist mostly as a way of distinguishing the following:

rap/wrap reek/wreak rest/wrest retch/wretch right/wright ring wring
rite/write rote/wrote rung/wrung

Note that while *rap* and *wrap* are distinguished for their simple uses, there's some interchange in figurative uses. (See further under **rap up** or **wrap up**, and **rapt, wrapt** or **wrapped**.)

r>z In Australian English personal names with an ''r'' sound in the middle, e.g. *Carolyn*, *Garry* and *Murray* are sometimes refashioned with a ''z'' in the same place, e.g. *Caz*, *Gazza* and *Muzza*. These forms are informal and familiar, used among friends. Thus Barry Humphries projects himself through the character of *Bazza McKenzie* to ingratiate himself with a large Australian audience.

rabies This word takes a singular verb in agreement:

Rabies has not taken hold in Australia fortunately.

In fact **rabies** is a Latin singular (see under **-ies**), though its use with singular verbs in English probably owes more to the fact that it's the name of a disease. (See **agreement** section 3b.)

racist language The problem with **racist language** is that it's not just a means of identifying people as belonging to a particular race or nation. Rather it expresses built-in prejudice against them, a derogatory attitude to their ethnic and cultural differences. In all words like the following, there's a level of contempt:

abo balt boong chink coon dago darkie ding frog gook greasy
gubba Itie Jap kraut nig nigger nip nog polack pommy slant-eye
slope(head) spade spag spic wog Yank yid

At best, such words are offhanded: at worst they are offensive and demeaning. They put people of different races at an instant disadvantage, and encourage others to stereotype them negatively. Though we're all conscious of ethnic and national differences, they are irrelevant in many situations. To draw unnecessary attention to them is as divisive as unnecessary references to gender in sexist language.

When ethnic and cultural differences do need to be acknowledged, it's a matter of choosing the appropriate national term: *Aboriginal, American, Chinese, English, French, Greek, Italian, Korean, Polish, Vietnamese* etc. Terms like those offer a description which is more precise *and* neutral in its connotations.

racket or **racquet** Anyone for tennis? (or squash, or badminton?). Whichever you play, you're free to spell the word either way. The *Macquarie Dictionary* (1991) has the spellings as equals. **Racket** is the original spelling, dating from the sixteenth century along with Henry VIII and royal tennis. Though the alternative *raquet* was also in use, it was not regularly used to distinguish the sporting weapon from *racket* meaning "noise", and only in the nineteenth century was the revised form **racquet** introduced and endorsed in Britain. The French spelling had its special appeal then (see under **frenchification**). But **racquet** never caught on in the USA, and in Britain and Australia, usage of **racket/racquet** has remained quite variable. Both the *Oxford Dictionary* and *Collins* have **racket** as the first choice, though other references such as the *Right Word at the Right Time* argue for **racquet** on grounds of the differentiation it provides. As already noted, in other times and places this has not seemed important.

radio- This prefix has two kinds of use in modern English, to mean:
1 making use of radio waves, as in *radioastronomy, radiofrequency, radiotelephone*
2 associated with radiation, as in *radioactive, radioisotopes, radiotherapy.*

radius The plural of this word is discussed under **-us** section 1.

radix For the the plural of this word, see under **-x** section 3.

railway or **railroad** **Railroad** is the standard American word for what in Australia and Britain is a **railway**, a major transport system which uses heavy rolling stock on a network of parallel rails. Note however that **railway** is used occasionally in the USA to refer to a small streetcar system with light vehicles. And that **railroad** is now used in Australian English as a verb, meaning "rush something through a legal or legislative process".

raise or **rise** Both are essentially verbs, and both by transfer become nouns which can refer to an increase in one's salary. **Raise** is the standard term for this in the USA, and it's quite well known in Australia and Britain. Yet it still sounds either American or casual to our ears. In more formal contexts, i.e. documentary writing and even newspaper reporting, we're likely to use **rise**.

Note that with flour the words are used the other way round. The American term is *self-rising* whereas in Australia and Britain it's *self-raising*.

raison d'être This useful French phrase means "reason for being". It is typically used to justify the existence of abstract entities, such as institutions or policies, not anything which is itself animate.

-rance and **-erance** A few abstract nouns end in **-rance** when you might expect **-erance**. Think of *encumbrance, entrance, hindrance, remembrance* among others which are based on verbs ending in *-er* (*encumber, enter, hinder, remember*). For more about the telescoping of *-er* in other words, see **-er>-r-**.

Unfortunately there are others like *deliverance, sufferance, temperance* and *utterance* in which the *-er* of the verb is not telescoped. Note also that those ending in **-rence**, such as *difference, preference, reference*, never telescope the *-er* in the spelling, even though our normal pronunciation gives them just two syllables.

For the **-ance/-ence** difference, see under that heading.

rang or **rung** See under **ring**.

ranunculus The plural of this word is discussed under **-us** section 1.

rap up or **wrap up** Either spelling will do, if you're aiming for the colloquial Australian idiom which as a verb means "praise highly", or as a noun "high praise". In citations in the *Australian National Dictionary* and in *Australian Colloquialisms* (1990), both spellings are used equally for the noun, although **wrap** seems to be preferred for the verb. That suggests that it would really be more consistent to enter both with the spelling **wrap**, though the *Australian National Dictionary* actually has them at **rap**. The **rap** spelling does however help to distinguish this idiom from another known throughout the English-speaking world: *wrap up*, meaning "bring to a close".

rapt, wrapt or **wrapped** These spellings represent two different words whose meanings coincide in certain idioms. **Rapt** is a rather unusual word meaning "ecstatic", which can be used on its own: *He was rapt*, or with a following phrase: *rapt in thought, rapt in the new secretary*. The last phrase overlaps with a figurative use of the verb *wrap*: *be wrapped (up) in*, meaning "be engrossed with". Thus someone could be *wrapped in the new secretary*, which would amount to much the same as *rapt in her*, except that **wrapped** somehow seems more colloquial and down-to-earth in its style. **Wrapt** is an old past tense of *wrap*, used mostly for the figurative sense "engrossed", but hardly used since the nineteenth century.

For other verbs which have reverted from a *-t* past form to the regular *-ed*, see **-ed**.

rarefy or **rarify** See under **-ify/-efy**.

rather and **rather than** The word **rather** has three roles, as:
1 hedge word: *She writes rather well.*
2 comparative adverb:

a) *The family would rather she played the flute.*
b) *I get the news from radio rather than television.*
c) *He asked for any posting rather than Brazil.*
3 conjunct: *I'm not against strong views. Rather it's a matter of how they're expressed.*

In its second role, **rather** covers a range of meanings, as shown in the set of three sentences above. It may suggest a preference, as in (a), or a very strong determination which allows no alternatives (c). Sentence (b) is somewhere in between and in fact rather ambiguous. Does it express a preference, or a commitment? If the difference is crucial, **rather** needs to be replaced by ''in preference to'' for the first meaning, and ''instead of'' for the second.

Ambiguity can also arise between conjunctive use of **rather** and its use as a hedge word. See for example:
He rather thought she should pay her own way.
Without more context we cannot tell whether **rather** is there to gently modify the verb, or to make a strong contrast equivalent to ''instead''.

*Grammatical options with **rather than***. What form of word to use after **rather than** is sometimes a problem. If two pronouns are being compared with it, the traditional practice is to give the case of the first one to the second:
They're coming to talk to him. Rather him than me.
We rather than they should be doing the program.
However in informal and impromptu speech there's a tendency to use the objective case every time after *than*:
We rather than them should be doing the program.
Neither version sounds ideal, and a better result altogether comes with rephrasing the sentence:
We not they should be doing the program.
Note that when verbs are being compared with **rather**, there are two stylistically equal options:
- To repeat the first form of the verb after **rather**
    He made telephone calls rather than put pen to paper.
- To use the *-ing* form
    He made telephone calls rather than putting pen to paper.

ratio decidendi See under **obiter dictum**.

ravage or **ravish** Both words refer to powerful and usually destructive forces. **Ravage** is used when destruction is spread over a wide area by an impersonal or natural force such as fire or flood. **Ravish** has a specifically human subject and object, and means ''seize, carry off by force'' or ''rape''. Those distinct meanings are there, even when the two words come close, as in: *The landscape was ravaged by napalm, and enemy soldiers ravished the peasant women.*

Surprisingly then, **ravish** can also mean ''overwhelm with delight'', as in *He found her green eyes ravishing.* In fact this meaning has coexisted with the others for centuries, being first recorded in the fourteenth. Yet the word can rarely be taken at face value. Somehow there's an element of hyperbole in **ravish**, keeping the dark and destructive elements of its meaning at bay.

raveled or **ravelled**   For the choice between these, see **-l/-ll-**.

re   This Latin tag is used in official letter writing to identify the subject under discussion. It abbreviates the Latin phrase *in re* "in the matter of", and is not therefore a clipped form of *regarding*, as is sometimes thought. It often prefaces the subject line in a business letter, as in:

> *Dear Editor*
> **re:** *Schedule for production of the annual report*
> *We would propose that ...*

In that position it's often set in lower case, and followed by a colon. However **re** can also appear in upper case and without a colon, as in the following:

> *Dear Editor*
> **Re** *the schedule for the annual report, we would propose that ...*

Re is too well established to need italics, and can even be used informally to replace *concerning* or *regarding*, as in *last night's discussion re the family holiday*. But in general contexts like that, **re** still seems a little awkward with its overtones of business and faintly pretentious Latin character. For more about the conventions of commercial letter writing, see under **commercialese** and Appendix VII.

re-   Drawn originally from Latin, this prefix means "back" or "again". The first meaning is there in words such as: *rebound, recall, recover, repress* and *resound*; the second is in: *rebuild, refill, rejoin, reprint* and *revive*. Yet in many of the French loanwords in which it occurs, its meaning cannot be disentangled from the word itself, witness:

> *receive refuse remember repeat resign reveal*

In modern English words formed with **re-**, the meaning is always "again", a point which is shown up when we compare the new or ad hoc formations with older ones, for example *re-create/recreate, re-mark/remark* and *re-serve/reserve*. The hyphen is vital to identify the meanings of the new words and distinguish them from the old. Further examples are:

> *re-act re-cede re-collect re-count re-cover re-form re-lay*
> *re-lease re-petition re-present re-sort*

Note that in Australian and British English a hyphen is also used when **re-** precedes a word beginning with *e*. See:

> *re-echo re-educate re-election re-emerge re-emphasise re-enter*
> *re-equip re-erect re-establish re-evaluate*

In American English however they are set solid.

-re/-er   The choice between *centre* and *center* is still very much a matter on which American English and Australian/British English divide. The **-er** spelling seems to have been used from the sixteenth to the early eighteenth century; it's found in Shakespeare and in the earliest dictionaries. But *centre* is the headword in both Samuel Johnson and Nathan Bailey's dictionaries of the 1750s, and **-re** spellings became standard in Britain in the decades that followed. Webster however endorsed *center* etc. in his radical dictionary of 1806, and perpetuated the older spellings in the USA. The words affected by this spelling practice are (in their non-American form):

> *calibre fibre goitre litre louvre lustre manoeuvre meagre mitre ochre reconnoitre sabre sepulchre sombre sceptre spectre theatre titre*

Note however that some **-re** words usually keep that spelling even in American English:

> *acre cadre lucre macabre mediocre ogre timbre*

People who use **-re** spellings have the advantage when it comes to forming the derivatives of all those words. The stem of the word remains the same in *centre/central* or *fibre/fibrous*, with just the regular dropping of the final *e* before a suffix beginning with a vowel (see **-e** section 1). Those who use **-er** spellings have to put the stem though a conversion rule before adding suffixes (see under **-er>-r-**). The fact that some of the words above are only spelled **-re** makes **-re** the better choice overall.

For the difference between **metre** or **meter** see further under that heading.

reafforestation, reforestation and **afforestation** The first two words both mean "replanting with trees", and both originated in the 1880s, the first being the British/Australian term and the second the American term. In 1971 the International Forestry Association endorsed **reforestation** as the standard term for silviculturists worldwide: and the decision would appeal to word-watchers as well, given the contradiction or redundancy in **reafforestation**. **Afforestation** itself means "planting with trees", so *re-* does little for the word.

The International Forestry Association in fact uses **afforestation** to mean "planting a species of timber which does not naturally occur in the region", e.g. planting softwood pine trees in Australia. This way it contrasts with **reforestation**, which means "re-establishing the native trees".

This use of **afforestation** may not appeal to those who campaign against the introduction of foreign flora. But at least the word has fewer negative implications than three or four centuries ago, when it implied the planting of trees as a means of increasing the hunting grounds of the rich, and when *afforestation and other oppressions of the poor* made the expansion of forests a desperate political issue.

real or **really** These words can get overused in impromptu conversation, but both have legitimate roles. **Really** is an adverb with dual functions. It can mean "truly, actually", as in *They were really there*. In addition it's often used as an intensifier, as in *They were really great* (see further under **intensifiers**). The two meanings are not always easy to separate however. Both are latent in the second example, and in the ones below where **really** modifies verbs:

> *They really wanted to talk.*

What really worries me is their disinclination to work.

Real has a regular role as an adjective meaning "true, genuine, actual", as in *real friend*, *real pearls*, *real life*. *Real estate* is property in the form of land and the buildings on it, and so tangible rather than paper assets. From meanings like those, **real** comes to be used in phrases like *real facts* and a *real problem*, in which its role is more the intensifier. Some would object to this as a misuse of **real**, though it has already happened with **really**. The problem with such phrases might rather be that they are clichéed.

Another use of **real** which is subject to censure is its informal use as an adverb (once again an intensifier): *They were real smooth.* This is common idiom in the USA, less so in Australia. However everywhere it's considered colloquial, like many of the **zero adverbs** (see further under that heading). In writing it needs to be replaced by some other intensifier.

Note that in *real tennis* the adjective is an old form of *royal*, just as it is in the name *Montreal*.

rebound, redound or **resound** Figurative and idiomatic uses bring these close together, though they have quite separate origins. **Rebound** meaning "bounce back" can be used of a ball springing off the ground, or a noise bouncing off the walls or ceiling. In the second case, it begins to overlap with **resound** "echo", though the imagery is a little different. A noise which *rebounds* seems to set up discrete sound waves, whereas one which *resounds* creates an environment of sound.

Another extension of **rebound** is to refer to an effect resulting from another kind of action, as in:

A cut in import duty will rebound on local industries.

This usage is where it overlaps with the now quite rare verb **redound** "have an effect, contribute to", best known in phrases such as *redounded to their credit*. But apart from its use in idioms like that (which usually refer to honor or disgrace), **redound** is rather a stranger and its use unclear. Where we might once have said: *redound on someone's head*, we're now more likely to say *rebound on someone's head*. Even *redounded to their credit* is these days paraphrased as *resounded to their credit*, whenever the "credit" is a climate of opinion resulting from public discussion. **Redound** has clearly lost out to **rebound** and **resound**.

recalcitrance or **recalcitrancy** See under -nce/-ncy.

reciprocal words Some pairs of words connote actions which complement each other, such as *buy/sell*, *give/take*, *teach/learn*. The common cases like those are no problem to adult users of the language, but less frequent ones such as **lend/loan**, **imply/infer** and **replace/substitute** may be. (See under those headings.)

reclaim and **reclamation** See under -aim.

reconciliation or **reconcilement** Though both can represent the verb *reconcile*, **reconciliation** is the more common of the two. It has developed more specific applications, referring to the coming together of estranged parties, as in the *spirit of reconciliation*, and in the *reconciliation of discrepant evidence*, where it's a matter of seeking consistency and compatibility. **Reconcilement** simply expresses the general meaning of the verb: "act of reconciling".

recourse, resort or **resource** See resource.

recto and **verso** See under verso.

redound, resound or **rebound** See rebound.

reduced forms In the flow of conversation we commonly reduce the sounds and syllables of words, to ease the process of uttering them, and the amount of decoding for the listener. This results in contractions such as *can't* and *would've*, which embody "weak forms" of *not* and *have* respectively. The weak form of *have* is so common that it's sometimes mistakenly spelled "of", in *could of*, *should of*, *would of*, even by adult writers.

　　Reduced forms of syntax are also a common feature of conversation, when we use phrases rather than complete clauses while exchanging ideas:

(have you)　　　　　　*Ever tried parachuting?*
(I wouldn't ever ...)　　*Not on your life.*

The brackets show roughly what's been left out of the utterance, words which would help to make full sentences but contain repetitive material. The exchange is brisker without them.

　　Reduced forms of words and contractions are usually unsuitable for formal writing, and need to be replaced by the full forms. The same applies to elliptical syntax. What can be understood between conversation partners cannot be left out of a monologic written text. **Reduced forms** always suggest informality, and so are counterproductive if dignity and authority are the overtones you're trying to write into your prose.

reductio ad absurdum In Latin this means "reducing (it) to the absurd". It is an argumentative tactic in which an extreme deduction is made from a proposition, one which is obviously contrary to common sense and accepted truth. The technique is used in formal logic to show the falseness of a proposition, but it's also used more informally to discredit someone else's position. For example, those who would insist on a "White Australia" policy sometimes argue that allowing more Asian immigrants in here will result in the *Asianisation of Australia*. The argument thus stretches a proposition (that more Asian immigrants might come to Australia) to an extreme possibility (Australia will be overrun by them), without attempting to consider the issues.

redundancy is a matter of using more words than are needed to express a point. Sometimes it's matter of sheer repetition as in:

They waved a greeting and they went on.

The second *they* seems redundant and clumsy because English grammar allows us to read the subject of the second clause from the first in a coordinated sentence where the two subjects are the same. (See **ellipsis** section 1.) Very occasionally a writer may wish to repeat something which is normally ellipted for the sake of emphasis, but usually it makes for **redundancy**.

Redundancy also arises through the overlap of meaning between different words which are combined in the same phrase or sentence. Compare "the four members of the quartet" with *all members of the quartet*, where the second version avoids **redundancy**. (See further under **pleonasm**.)

Redundant information and strategic repetition. Yet another kind of **redundancy** can occur in communicating information—as when irrelevant details are included, or a detail is reported twice over. To remove irrelevancies you need a clear idea as to the purpose of the whole document, and what its readers need to know. Avoiding unnecessary repetition is a matter of careful organisation, structuring the contents to ensure that things are said at the most productive moment, and not too early so that they have to be repeated. Still a writer may want to foreshadow things at the start of a document, and to summarise them at the end. **Redundancy** is then avoided by ensuring that the foreshadowing section or summary presents things in more general terms than when they are the focus of discussion.

reduplicatives Some English compounds consist of two very similar words, only differing in their first consonants, or their vowels. Examples of the first kind are:

fuddy-duddy hanky-panky heeby-jeebies mumbo-jumbo
razzle-dazzle walkie-talkie

And of the second:

chitchat crisscross dillydally dingdong mishmash
riffraff tittletattle zigzag

One of the two parts of a *reduplicative* (often the second) may be a meaningful word, and the other then plays on its sound. The connotations of **reduplicatives** are usually casual and offhanded, and can be derogatory.

In a small number of cases, English **reduplicatives** involve identical words, as in:

fifty-fifty goody-goody hush-hush never-never
pooh-pooh pretty-pretty tut-tut

As the examples show, they are always the informal word for the concept they refer to. They differ thus from the *reduplicative loanwords* from Aboriginal languages, which are standard vocabulary in Australian English:

bandy-bandy gang-gang mia-mia nulla-nulla willy-willy wonga-wonga

The Aboriginal use of *reduplication* also comes to us in certain placenames, such as *Wagga Wagga* and *Woy Woy*, found in all states and especially Victoria. For all Australians, the hypothetical remote outback place is *Woop Woop*.

reek or **wreak** See wreak.

referencing Writers of reports and scholarly papers often have to refer to other publications to support their own statements and conclusions. There are conventional ways of doing this, so as to provide necessary information for the reader while minimising the interruption. The four main systems are:

- short title
- footnotes or endnotes
- author-date references, also known as the Harvard system, or running references
- number system (including Vancouver style)

The *short title* system is used in general books, while the others are associated with academic publications. The *footnote/endnote* system is mostly used in the humanities, including history and law. *Author-date* references are used in the sciences and social sciences, and the *number* system in science and especially medicine. Some publications use a combination of systems, with author-date references for citing other publications and occasional footnotes for a more substantial comment by the writer or editor. Until recently, footnotes were rather difficult to set or adjust on wordprocessors, and this has probably encouraged wider use of *author-date* references. Other things being equal, *author-date* references are preferable to a *number* system, because they give some immediate information to the reader.

1 *Short title **references*** are cut-down variants of full references, with enough distinctive information to remind readers of the identity of the work being invoked (see **short titles**). They have long been used in footnotes (see below, section 2), but now increasingly within the text itself. With the abbreviated title and (optionally) its date, they provide more immediate information than either author-date references or numbers which take readers away to footnotes or the bibliography. They still depend on full references being given in an accumulated reference list.

2 *Footnotes and endnotes* keep reference material out of the ongoing discussion. Only a superscript number intervenes to guide your eye to the bottom of the page, or to the end of chapter/book when you're ready. The numerals for footnotes can recommence with every page, or run through a whole chapter as is usual for endnotes. Occasionally the enumeration runs through the whole book with all the notes accumulated at the back.

Some writers use footnotes/endnotes to discuss a particular point which might seem to digress from the main argument. These are *substantive* footnotes. But mostly footnotes/endnotes serve to identify source publications, and so must include whatever the reader needs to track them down. In the first reference to any source, it's important to name the author, title, date of publication and the relevant page numbers. Unless there are full details in the bibliography, the footnotes should include the place of publication and also the name of the publisher:

G. *Blainey* Tyranny of Distance *(Melbourne: Sun Books, 1966) pp.23-31*

Note that the author's name or initials come in front of the surname (not inverted as in a bibliography). Questions of punctuating the titles and the order of items are discussed under **bibliographies**: see *Points to note*.

Second and later references to the same work can be cut back, as can endnotes grouped together for the same chapter. The author's name may be sufficient:

Blainey, pp.95-6

However if another work by the same author is cited in the same group of footnotes/endnotes, a short title should be added:

Blainey, Tyranny*, pp.95-6*

The use of Latin abbreviations (**ibid., loc. cit., op. cit.**) is discussed under their respective headings.

3 *Author-date* **references** explain in passing what source publication is being alluded to, but the reference is kept to the bare essentials: just the author's surname, the date of the publication, and the relevant pages indicated by numbers only, with no *pp*. The information is enclosed in brackets, and followed by a comma, full stop etc. as the sentence requires:

Regional usages often stop at state borders in Australia, as did the earliest railway developments (Blainey, 1966:95-6).

Note that final punctuation is never included inside the final bracket of a running reference, even if it would with other kinds of parentheses (see further under **brackets**).

If reference is made to two or more authors with the same surname in the course of an article or book, a distinguishing initial must be added into the basic reference. And if reference is made to more than one publication by the same author in the same year, the two need to be distinguished, as *1966a* and *1966b*, in the running references as well as in the bibliography. The second and subsequent references are identical to the first, except in the case of publications with joint authors. The first reference normally gives the surnames of all authors, unless there are four or more of them, in which case only the first author is named, followed by *et al.* This is the regular practice for second and later references. The author-date system relies very heavily on a full list of references to supply details of the author(s), titles, and the publishing information.

4 *The number system* uses a sequence of superscripts or bracketed numbers on the line of text to refer the reader to publication details in the reference list. More than one number may be used at the same point. Some writers, according to *Webster's Style Manual* (1985), use the brackets to contain both a reference number and a page number, the two being separated by a comma, with the first in italics and the second in roman (e.g. *4*, 216). The reference numbers fix the order of titles in the bibliography, so that they are not alphabetically arranged as for the other referencing systems. (See further under **bibliographies**.)

referendum The plural of this word is discussed under **-um.**

referred or **refereed** On first sight they make a strange pair, but each is regular in its own way. **Referred** is of course the past tense of the verb *refer*, with the final *r* doubled because the syllable it's in is stressed. (See further under **doubling of final consonant**.) **Refereed** is the past tense for a verb made out of the noun *referee*. It loses its final letter (*e*) before the past suffix is added. (See **-ed** section 2.)

reflection or **reflexion** See under **-ction/-xion**.

reflective or **reflexive** The first of these can be used in many contexts, all those where *reflection* itself is used in reference to light, heat or sound, as in *a reflective surface*, or in connection with images and thoughts, as in *an unusually reflective mood for a sportsman*.

    Reflexive is only used in grammar, in reference to such things as *reflexive pronouns* and *reflexive verbs*. (See next entries.)

reflexive pronouns The pronouns ending in *-self* or *-selves* are *reflexive*, and typically refer back to the subject of the sentence. They include:
    myself yourself him/her/itself oneself ourselves yourselves themselves
(For *themself* and *theirselves*, see **themself**.)

    Reflexives are selected to correspond in person and number (and for the third person singular, in gender) with the subject:
    I must see for myself
    He shot himself in the foot.
    They came by themselves.
In cases like those, the *reflexive pronoun* serves as the object of a verb or preposition, and its position in the sentence is fixed.

    Reflexive pronouns can also be used to emphasise any other noun or name in the sentence, standing immediately after it:
    They talked to the premier himself.
    You yourselves might go that way.
Note however that in shorter sentences where the *reflexive* underscores the subject, it can also appear at the other end of the sentence:
    You might go that way yourselves.

reflexive verbs A *reflexive verb* has the same person as its subject and object. In English it can be formed out of an ordinary verb with a reflexive pronoun as object: *The boss cut himself shaving.* But only a handful of English verbs *must* be constructed in that way, like:
    She acquitted herself well at the meeting.
    They didn't behave themselves properly.
In other languages such as French, German and Italian, many common verbs are *reflexive* in their construction. One case is the verb *remember* which is *reflexive* in all three (*se rappeler/ sich erinnern/ricordarsi*), but is certainly not reflexive in English.

reforestation or **reafforestation** See **reafforestation**.

refurbish or **refurnish** Both these words involve you in renovating. But with **refurnish** you're buying new furniture and perhaps soft furnishings. With **refurbish** you're sprucing up and polishing what you already have.

refute According to standard dictionary definitions, this word implies the use of a proof to reject a claim or a charge. Yet the word is often used simply to mean "deny", without any counterevidence or logical disproof being supplied:
> They refuted the suggestion that it was negligence, and changed the subject.

This looser use of the word is confirmed incidentally in larger dictionaries, in the usage notes of the *Heritage* (where it's given as a synonym for "deny"), and in a set of citations given in the *Oxford Dictionary* (1989) which show how *refute ... allegation(s)* has become a regular idiom. Though the *Oxford* labels them "erroneous", the judgement is obviously not felt by others who go into print. *Webster's English Usage* (1989), which also has citation evidence for the usage, notes that the objections to it are stronger in Britain than America.

The message for Australian writers is that **refute** is expanding its territory, and using it to mean "deny" will seem fair enough to many. However it may rankle with those who try to keep words in the state to which they were accustomed, and for them it would be best to replace it with "deny".

regrettably and **regretfully** Both involve regret, but in **regretfully** the feeling is more straightforwardly expressed: *I must regretfully decline*, or else attributed directly to a third party: *He spoke regretfully of his retirement*. In either example the *regret* is expressed openly.

Regrettably is more academic and implies that *regret* is called for: *Regrettably he was not there to speak for himself*. It puts in the writer's evaluation of a situation, and a view which s/he hopes the reader will endorse. **Regrettably** is one of a set of attitudinal adverbs which can be deployed for interpersonal contact in writing. The fact that many of those adverbs end in *-fully* (*delightfully, mercifully, thankfully* etc.) helps to explain why **regretfully** gets mistakenly used for **regrettably**.

regular verbs In English these are the ones which simply add *-ed* to make their past forms, as with *departed* and *rolled*. In the same very large group are all those which add the *-ed* subject to other standard spelling rules, such as:
- dropping the final *e* before the suffix (*arrived, liked*)
- doubling the final consonant before the suffix (*barred, admitted*)

See **-e** section 1, and **doubling of final consonant** for more about those rules.

The **regular verbs** are very numerous because they include not only all newly formed ones, but also most of those we've inherited from Old English. The number of *irregular verbs* has been steadily declining over the centuries, and many which were once irregular have acquired the regular *-ed* past form, at least as an alternative. (See further under **irregular verbs**.)

Note that in Old English, and in discussing other Germanic languages, the **regular verbs** are referred to as "weak" and the irregular ones as "strong".

reindeer The plural of this word is most often just like the singular, i.e. **reindeer**, in keeping with the word *deer* itself. Many other kinds of wild animals have **zero plurals** like this (see under that heading). However the regularised plural *reindeers* is also used occasionally, and is recognised in all major dictionaries.

relaid or **relayed** **Relaid** is the past tense of *re-lay* "lay again":
> *The railway sleepers had to be relaid after the floods.*
Relayed is the past of *relay* "communicate by a radio or electronic network":
> *The program was relayed to country TV stations.*

relation or **relationship** The choice between these becomes an issue when you want to refer to an abstract connection, because there is some stylistic difference. Data from the Australian ACE corpus shows that **relation** in this sense is very much a scholarly word, hardly used outside academic texts, whereas **relationship** is used in this sense equally in general and academic writing. **Relationship** is also used in a wide variety of references to personal, social and political connections e.g. *married relationship, loving relationship,* where **relation** could not appear. By the same token, **relation** reigns supreme in the idiom *in relation to.*

relations or **relatives** Both can refer to your "sisters and your cousins and your aunts". In British English **relations** still has the edge, while in American and Australian English it's **relatives**. In the Australia ACE corpus the instances of **relatives** outnumbered **relations** in this sense by 31:7. One advantage of using *relative* in this way is that it lightens the load borne by *relation*, and leaves it with mostly abstract meanings It also prevents any temporary ambiguity over whether your "political relations" are your cousins in parliament or your contacts with people in power.

relative clauses Otherwise known as *adjectival clauses*, these serve either to define, or to describe and evaluate the noun to which they're attached. They stand right next to it, even if this delays the predicate of the main clause:
> *The old computer that we bought at the markets has never given any trouble.*

1 *Relative clauses* and *pronouns.* **Relative clauses** are usually introduced by one of the relative pronouns (*that, which* etc. See next entry.) But in certain stylistic and grammatical circumstances there may be no pronoun at all. In all but the most formal style, the pronoun can be omitted from relative clauses of which it's the object:
> *The old computer we bought at the markets has never given any trouble.*
But it never happens when the pronoun is the subject, whatever the style:
> *The old computer that came from the markets has never given any trouble.*

Try deleting *that* in that sentence and it undermines the whole structure of the sentence. The reader needs the pronoun to signal the relative clause.

2 *Relative clauses* and *relative adverbs.* Some **relative clauses** are linked to the main clause by adverbs such as *where* and *when*:

> *You remember the place where we met.*
> *I remember the time when we made chocolate-chip damper.*

Both adverbs act as relators of the second clause to a noun in the first one. In fact the relative *when* can be replaced by *that* ("the time that") or even be omitted altogether:

> *I remember the time we made chocolate chip damper.*

The choice between *when/where*, *that* and the complete omission of the relative word makes a scale from formal to informal style.

3 *Sentence relatives.* These are **relative clauses** which relate to the whole preceding clause, not to any one noun in it:

> *They wanted to go home by ferry, which I thought was a good idea.*

Sentence relatives are always prefaced by *which*. Some style guides warn against them, and occasionally it's unclear whether the relative relates to the whole sentence or the last noun in it. Provided there's no such ambiguity *sentence relatives* are no problem, and they serve to add the writer's comment on the main statement or proposition of a sentence.

4 *Restrictive and nonrestrictive relatives.* **Relative clauses** which serve to define or identify something have often been called "restrictive"—which makes "nonrestrictive" all the other kinds which describe or evaluate or add writers' comments. (Alternative names are *defining* and *nondefining* relatives.) Compare the following:

> *People who sign such agreements are crazy.*
> *I met his parents, who signed the agreement.*

In spite of their similarity, the two **relative clauses** differ in that the first one defines the previous noun, whereas the second simply adds descriptive information about what happened.

The distinction between a *relative clause* which defines and one which does something else is not always as clear-cut as in that pair of sentences, and grammarians note ambiguous cases. The tendency to mark restrictive clauses with commas is often overstated (see next entry). Note also that the use of commas with nonrestrictive clauses is more predictable for those which are parenthetic than those which are not. Compare:

> *I met his parents, who signed the agreement, to discuss why he had joined up so young.*
> *To discover why he had joined up so young, I met his parents who signed the agreement.*

The general trend towards lighter punctuation also means that, other things being equal, we're less likely to use a comma with either type of clause.

relative pronouns Most relative clauses are introduced by **relative pronouns**, such as *who, which, whom, whose, that.* *That* can be used as an alternative to any of the *wh-* ones except *whose,* and is not reserved for human antecedents:

> *The doctor who/that came from Sri Lanka ...*
> *The box which/that contained the TV ...*
> *A woman whom/that I'd never seen before ...*
> *The nurse whose face would cure a thousand ills ...*

(For more about **whose**, see under that heading.) The choice between *that* and the *wh-* relatives is sometimes said to depend on whether it prefaces a restrictive or a nonrestrictive relative, with *that* for the restrictive type and *which* for the other (see previous entry). This is an oversimplification of Fowler's original suggestion that they could be used that way, though even he admitted: "It would be idle to pretend it was the practice either of most or of the the best writers." Later style commentators note that while *which* is indeed preferred for nonrestrictive relative clauses, both *that* and *which* can be found with the restrictive type.

Special uses of that. There are contexts in which *that* reigns supreme, or at least predominates:

- after superlatives: *the best wine that I ever drank*
- after ordinal numbers: *the first pub that you come to*
- after indefinites (*some, any, every, much, little, all*):
  > *I'll have any that you can buy ...*
- in a cleft sentence: *It's the label that has a bird on it*
- when the antecedents are both human and nonhuman:
  > *Neither man nor dog that were supposed to be on the tuckerbox were anywhere to be seen.*

That is sometimes said to lend an informal flavor to prose: and when conversing we undoubtedly use it more than *which* in relative constructions. (It saves us some decisions about *who* versus *which* (not to mention *who* versus *whom*)). But *that* has its established place in writing, in all those special contexts just listed, as well as in restrictive relative clauses. So long as *that* gives way occasionally to *which,* it will not mark the style as informal. Sensitive writers notice the need to alternate them in structures such as:

> *He asked which was the one that took my fancy.*
> *That's the one which appeals most.*

Writers can also choose between *which* and *that* according to their relative bulk. *Which* is slightly longer and more conspicuous, and so it's the one to use for a relative clause that needs attention drawn to it. *That* draws less attention to itself, and is useful when you want the clause to merge with the main clause.

relayed or **relaid** See **relaid**.

relevance or **relevancy** See **-nce/-ncy**.

remodeled or **remodelled** For the spelling of this verb, see **-l/-ll-**.

Renaissance or **Renascence** The first spelling is the slightly older one, on record since 1840. It is pure French in its form, whereas the later **Renascence** (first recorded around 1870) is latinate and is more strongly linked with historical scholarship.

Without the initial capital, either can be used of a rebirth or revival. But with capitals both are strongly associated with the flowering of European culture which began in Italy in the fourteenth century and reached Britain in the sixteenth. It marked the end of medieval culture with its emphasis on tradition; yet it was at least partly stimulated by the rediscovery of classical scholarship from Greece and Rome. The reading of classical authors brought many Latin and Greek words into English, and occasioned the respelling of many French loanwords acquired during the previous centuries, according to their classical antecedents. (See further under **spelling**.) The relationship between **Renaissance** and **Renascence** is the same phenomenon, happening in the nineteenth century.

renege or **renegue** Dictionaries and people, spelling and pronunciation are at sixes and sevens over this word. Four centuries after its first appearance it still seeems a misfit. Its nearest relative in English is *renegade*, though **reneg(u)e** itself seems to be a clipped form of the medieval Latin verb *renegare* "deny". In its earliest use in the sixteenth century, *reneg(u)e* had dire overtones of apostasy, and it was only towards the end of the seventeenth century that the word is recorded in association with card-playing. The general meaning "go back on a promise or commitment" appears towards the end of the eighteenth century. However there's little record of it until the twentieth century, perhaps because of the slightly informal flavor that still hangs around it. About 25% of the Heritage usage panel didn't think it was acceptable in writing.

From its links with *renegade* and the Latin *renegare*, we might expect the spelling *reneg*, but it has only been recorded once or twice, according to the *Oxford Dictionary*. Instead the earliest spelling was **renege**, showing the sixteenth century predilection for adding *e* to the ends of words. In this case the final *e* is anomalous, suggesting a soft "j" sound though the word is always pronounced with a hard "g" sound.

The seventeenth century tried to rectify things with the spelling **renegue** which is much more satisfactory as regards the final sound, and it's the spelling endorsed in the *Oxford Dictionary*. However it's not recognised at all in American dictionaries. And because the word seems to have re-entered standard English from the USA, the American spelling **renege** is the best known. Nine out of the ten Oxford citations for it this century are spelled that way, including some from British sources.

The *Macquarie Dictionary* (1991) gives preference to **renege** and acknowledges **renegue** as an alternative. The inflected forms for the first spelling are the rather unsatisfactory *reneged* and *reneging*, and for the second, the hardly used *renegued* and *reneguing*. In spelling terms the latter are to be preferred—unless we derive *renegged* and *renegging* from the fleetingly recorded *reneg*.

renounce and **renunciation** The background to their divergent spellings is discussed at **pronounce**.

rent or **hire** See **hire**.

repairable or **reparable** Both words mean "able to be repaired". But the link with *repair* is stronger as well as more obvious in **repairable**, and it's the one usually applied to material objects which need fixing:
> *Don't throw that clock away—It's still repairable.*
The more latinate **reparable** is more often used of abstract and intangible things needing to be restored or mended, as in:
> *The damage to their self-esteem was reparable.*
Note that the negative of **repairable** is *unrepairable*, and that of **reparable** is *irreparable*.

repellant or **repellent** Modern dictionaries all make **repellent** the primary spelling, for both adjectival and noun uses of this word. **Repellant** is given as an alternative for the noun only in the *Collins Dictionary*, but others including the *Oxford, Webster's* and *Random House* all allow it for either. (See further under **-ant/-ent**.)

repertoire or **repertory** Nowadays these have different domains, though both have links with the stage. A **repertoire** is the range of plays, operas or musical pieces that a company or individual is ready to perform. That usage has now widened to include the stock of abilities or skills possessed by a performer in almost any field. So we speak of a *repertoire of writing styles*, and a *repertoire of tennis strokes*.

    Repertory is simply a latinised form of *repertoire*, most often used now in referring to a *repertory theatre company*, which offers a set of plays for a short season. In the past it could, like **repertoire**, refer to a set of performable items, and also to a repository of some kind of information, but neither is common nowadays.

repetition The **repetition** of any word or phrase in a short space of writing draws attention to it. In a narrative the repeated *he* or *she* is the focus of the action; and in nonfiction a set of key words may be repeated throughout the text because they are essential to the subject. If the writing is technical they *must* be repeated: technical terms cannot be paraphrased without losing the specific point of reference. A certain amount of **repetition** is also important as part of the network of cohesion in any kind of writing. (See further under **coherence** or **cohesion**.)

    Apart from those functional reasons for repeating words and phrases, there may be stylistic or rhetorical ones. This is what gave and still gives great power to Abraham Lincoln's archetypal statement about American democracy, that it was:

"... government of the people, for the people, by the people ..."

The repetition of "people" is made all the more conspicuous by being couched in parallel phrasing. (See further under **parallel constructions**.)

Yet **repetition** is sometimes accidental, or not well motivated. Writers get into a verbal groove when they should be seeking fresh ways of expressing an idea. A thesaurus offers a treasury of alternative words, though many of those grouped together are not synonyms and need to be checked for meaning and stylistic consistency. *Yakka* means "work", but it's suitable only for very informal contexts.

Another way to avoid **repetition** is by varying the grammar of the words you're relying on. Many verbs, nouns and adjectives have partners which can be pressed into service with slight rearrangements of other words around them:

The demonstrators *were protesting about the new road tax.*

Truck drivers demonstrated *yesterday about the new road tax.*

The new road tax was the focus of yesterday's demonstration *outside Parliament House.*

The choice of an alternative word form stimulates a different order and structure for the clause, and creates slots for new information—all of which help to vary your expression.

Alternative function words are discussed at various entries in this book: see especially **conjunctions** and **relative pronouns**.

repetitious or **repetitive** Repetition is usually noticeable, whether or not it serves a purpose. In **repetitious** the effects of repeating are felt to be negative, as in a *repetitious account of their meeting*. In **repetitive**, as in *repetitive strain injury*, the physical fact of repetition is all that's acknowledged, and dictionaries usually present it as the more neutral of the two words. So a *repetitive pattern* in music may not be a focus of criticism, whereas a *repetitious pattern* certainly is. Having said that, we must allow that the two words are sometimes interchanged. So it's best to choose others to make your point about a repeated pattern, if you wish to avoid any possible negative connotations.

replace or **substitute** These are complementary, in that **replace** means "take the place of" and **substitute**, "put in place of". So the following amount to the same thing:

John Tough replaced Ray Rough in Saturday's match.

The manager substituted John Tough for Ray Rough on Saturday.

In the passive they are also complementary:

Ray Rough was replaced by John Tough in Saturday's match.

John Tough was substituted for Ray Rough on Saturday.

With **substitute**, one other construction is possible:

John Tough substituted for Ray Rough on Saturday.

Note that *for* is the particle usually used after **substitute**, whereas *by* or *with* are the ones used in the passive form of **replace**, according to modern dictionaries. Yet *by* was once considered acceptable after **substitute** (judging by the *Oxford Dictionary*'s comment "now regarded as incorrect"), and *substituted with* turns up in technical writing in the Australian ACE corpus. All this suggests the difficulty of separating constructions involving **replace** and **substitute**, as with other reciprocal pairs. (See further under **reciprocal words**.)

reports   In their simplest form **reports** give a retrospective view of an enterprise. Written with the advantage of hindsight, they can offer a perspective on what's more and less important—not a "blow by blow" account of events, but one structured to help readers see the implications.

Apart from reviewing the past, **reports** written in the name of industry and government are expected to develop a strategic plan and recommendations for the future. An environmental impact study for example normally begins with an extended description of the existing environment and its physical, biological and social character. This is followed by discussions of the likely impact of any proposed development on all facets of the site, and then by sets of alternative recommendations.

1 *Structuring reports*. When writing a report it's important to identify the purpose of the investigation, so as to focus the document and define its scope. This prevents it from going in all directions, and from being swollen with irrelevant material. A specific brief may have been supplied for the report (e.g. to examine the causes of frequent lost-time injuries in the machine shop). If not it's a good idea to compile your own brief, and to include it at the front of the report, to show the framework within which the work has been done. If recommendations and a management plan are the expected outcome of a report, these too need to be presented in summary form at the front (often called an *executive summary*), before you go into the details of the inquiry on which they are based.

Any longer report (say more than five pages) needs a table of contents on the first page, to show readers where to go for answers to any particular question. The format for **reports** in government and industry is not standardised (as it is in science), and common sense is your guide in creating a logical structure (e.g. presenting discussion of the status quo before ideas for the future). Within those broad sections, subsections with informative headings need to be devised, ones which can also be used in the table of contents. Tables of statistics are usually housed in an appendix if they occupy full pages, though shorter ones may be included where the discussion refers to them.

2 *Science reports* are written to a conventional format—the so-called *IMRAD* structure which consists of Introduction, Method, Results and Discussion, in that order. Two other details to note are that the Method may be subdivided into subjects, apparatus and procedures; and that the conclusions may be appended

to the end of the Discussion, or else set apart with their own heading: Conclusions. The IMRAD format ensures that scientific experiments and investigations are reported in such a way as to be replicable, and allow the reader to separate the facts of the research (the Method, Results) from their interpretation (Discussion/Conclusion). The science reporting format is also the basic structure for articles in scholarly journals, and for empirical theses and dissertations.

3 *Writing style in* **reports** is necessarily rather formal. Whether written in the name of science or government or industry, they are expected to provide objective and judicious statements on the data examined, and responsible conclusions. They are not a natural vehicle for personal attitudes and values.

Yet the writing style of **reports** need not be dull or overloaded with passives and institutional clichés. (See further under **passive verbs** and **impersonal writing**.) To ensure directness and clarity of style, it always helps to think of the people you're trying to communicate with through the report. Imagine them looking for answers to their questions. Readers are interested in clear, positive analysis—not in hedged statements and tentative conclusions. They respond to vitality in style, and to any attempts to supplement the written word with diagrams and visual aids. (See further under **Plain English**.)

requiescat in pace See **RIP**.

requisite or **requisition** As nouns, these can both mean "item required". But a **requisite** is often just a simple article of food or personal equipment, as in *toilet requisites for going to hospital*. **Requisition** has official overtones. It smacks of supplies for an institution or a national endeavor, as in *army requisitions*. The word **requisition** is often applied to a formal written request or claim for something:
> *Would you put through a requisition for 500 envelopes.*

resin or **rosin** Resin is a broad term, referring to a range of substances obtained from the sap of trees or other plants. It is also applied to similar substances synthesised by chemical processes. **Rosin** refers very specifically to the solid residue of resin from the pine tree which remains when the oil of turpentine has been extracted. A lump of **rosin** to rub on the strings of the violin bow is part of a violinist's equipment.

resister or **resistor** A **resistor** is a component in an electric circuit, whereas a **resister** is a person who puts up a resistance. The two spellings seem to lend support to the idea that *-er* is used for human agents, and *-or* for an instrument or device. Unfortunately there are more *-or* words which defy that "rule" than ones like **resistor** which seem to support it. (See further under **-er/-or**.)

resound, redound or **rebound** See **rebound**.

resource, recourse or **resort** From different sources, these words seem to overlap in their use. However they appear in separate idioms. The least common of them nowadays is **recourse**, a noun which means "someone or something appealed to for help". It appears only in a few phrases such as *with(out) recourse to* and *have recourse to*.

Resort as an abstract noun is also quite uncommon (unlike its more concrete use in *holiday resort*). It survives in the phrase *last resort*, a "course of action adopted under difficult circumstances", and occasionally as a verb meaning "apply to for help". It usually appears in phrases such as *resorted to* and *without resorting to*.

Resource is primarily a noun, used to refer to a means or source of supply in many contexts ranging from *mineral resources* to *resources for teaching*.

The second and third words come close when your *last resource* for amusing the children is perhaps also a *last resort*. However the two phrases are essentially different in meaning. The *last resource* for a farmer battling a bushfire might be his dam water, whereas his *last resort* would be to get in the car and drive to safety.

respectfully or **respectively** Respectfully is a straightforward adverb meaning "full of respect":
They spoke respectfully to the priest.
Respectively has a special role in cuing the reader to match up items in two separate series. They may be in the same sentence, or in adjacent sentences:
Their three sons Tom, Dick and Harry are respectively the butcher, the baker and the garage proprietor of the town.

rest or **wrest** See wrest.

restaurateur or **restauranteur** Strictly speaking, the person who runs a restaurant is a **restaurateur**—at least if we prefer to use the word in the form in which it was borrowed from French in the eighteenth century. Yet the form **restauranteur** has developed among English-speakers (in contexts where the purity of the French connection is neither here nor there) to clarify the link with *restaurant*, its nearest relative in English. It is then a hybrid French/English word, and purists might dub it "folk etymology" although in this instance the spelling adjustment is helpful rather than distracting (see further under **folk etymology**).

Restauranteur is acknowledged as an alternative form in *Webster's Dictionary* and the *Macquarie* (1991), and there are citations for it in the *Oxford Dictionary* from 1949 on, though they're said to be "erroneous". The citations in *Webster's English Usage* go back to 1926, and it's described as a "standard secondary variant", common in speech. The *Oxford Dictionary* also notes the form *restauranter* (without censure), a further reconstruction which makes the word fully English. **Restauranteur** may thus be seen as a transitional form—and perhaps a useful word to refer to a restaurant-owner whose business is not *haute cuisine*. It would not be the first French word to be modified in the process of assimilation into English.

restive or **restless** Surprisingly perhaps, these both imply unsettled or agitated behavior. **Restive** means ''impatient'' or ''chafing at the bit'', and has often been applied to horses, as in:

A pair of restive horses were harnessed to the carriage.

When applied to people, it means they are recalcitrant and inclined to resist control:

By the end of the compulsory conference, the union delegates were restive.

Restless means more simply ''unable to stay still or in one place'', as in:

I had a restless night.

After three years in Queensland he was feeling restless again.

restrictive clauses For the difference between restrictive and nonrestrictive relative clauses, see under **relative clauses** section 4.

résumé This word refers to two kinds of document:

1 a summary overview of events, observations, evidence and such-like, prepared for discussion. (See further under **summary**.)

2 a *curriculum vitae*, as when applicants for a job are requested to *send a copy of their resumé*. This usage originated in North America, but is current and widespread in Australia. (See further under **curriculum vitae**.)

Note that **resumé** often appears without any accent on the first syllable, though the accent on the last syllable is usually in place as a way of distinguishing it from the ordinary verb *resume*. Still the fact that **resumé** is a noun means that there's little chance of confusion.

retain and **retention** Their divergent spellings are discussed under **-ain**.

retch or **wretch** See **wretch**.

retina The plural of this word is discussed at **-a** section 1.

retro- This Latin prefix, meaning ''backwards'' in space or time, is derived from loanwords such as *retroflex, retrograde* and *retrospect*. It appears in some highly specialised scientific words, as well as some from aeronautics and astronautics which make their way into the media, including: *retroengine, retrofire* and *retrorocket*.

revel For the spelling of this word when used as a verb, see **-l/-ll-**.

revenge, avenge and **vengeance** As verbs, the first two are sometimes interchanged. A difference is however to be noted in that the person who *revenges* is usually reacting to an injury or insult which he or she has suffered. **Avenge** is normally used of a third party reacting to another's injury or insult:

He wanted to avenge his son's humiliation.

Note that **revenge** often works as a noun, in which case it means "retaliation or retribution", much the same as **vengeance**. But they differ in the same way as the verbs. **Vengeance** is retribution carried out by a third party, while **revenge** is the retaliatory act of the injured party:

He had his revenge.

The difference between **revenge** and **avenge/vengeance** is also stylistic, in that **revenge** is much more frequent than the others (and not just because it works as both verb and noun). This makes **revenge** less formal and ritual in its overtones than the other two. The ritual element in **vengeance** is no doubt helped by timeless biblical statements such as:

Vengeance is mine; I will repay, saith the Lord. (Romans 12:19)

Reverend The use of the title **Reverend** in combination with other names is discussed under **names** section 2.

reverent or **reverential** Both involve showing *reverence*, and there's little to choose between them, except that **reverent** seems to be applied to people and their ordinary behavior:

Reverent visitors to the chapel spoke in hushed whispers.

Reverential recognises more abstract forms of *reverence*, as in a *reverential rather than critical approach to the classics.*

In terms of frequency **reverent** is more common and at home in everyday contexts. **Reverential** appears less often, and is a more academic word.

reversal or **reversion** These relate to quite different verbs. **Reversal** is the noun associated with *reverse*, as in a *reversal of an earlier decision.* **Reversion** is the noun for *revert*, as in *reversion to a primitive state.*

reverse or **obverse** See under **obverse**.

review or **revue** The spelling **revue** is usually reserved for theatrical shows which offer a mixed program of amusing or satirical songs and skits, often highlighting topical events and themes. **Review** is sometimes applied to such performances, but more often to a serious critical analysis of something such as a book, film, or a government department.

rheme See **topic** section 1.

rhetoric is the ancient and modern art of persuading one's audience. (See further under **persuasion**, and **rhythm**.)

rhetorical questions See under **questions**.

rhyme or **rime** The word **rhyme** was spelled with an *i* for centuries, going back to Old English. In the sixteenth century it was either **rime** or *rhime*, and only in the seventeenth century did **rhyme** appear. Like many respellings of that time, **rhyme** was an attempt to link the word with its classical forebears; in this case it was ultimately the Greek *rhythmos*. However the respelling took some time to catch on, and **rime** was still current in the late eighteenth century, as seen in Coleridge's *The rime of the ancient mariner.*

The spelling **rhyme** helps to distinguish the word from the homonym *rime* "hoar frost", though it makes the word more Greek than it deserves to be. The meaning and spelling which we now give to **rhyme** are a product of its passage through medieval languages.

rhyming slang Informal expressions for many everyday things have been created by **rhyming slang**, and they lend variety to the all-too-familiar. The *rubbidy (dub)* makes a change from "pub", and *egg flip* for a gambling "tip". Some rhyming slang puts on airs, as does *eau de cologne* for "phone" and *aristotle* for "bottle"; while other expressions are perhaps ways of skirting round a problem, such as *Farmer Giles* for "piles" and *AIF* for "deaf". Other obviously Australian examples are *Bass and Flinders* for "windows" and *Barrier Reef* for "teeth".

The examples all show how **rhyming slang** selects a phrase of two or three words to highlight the key word, with the rhyming phrase often an amusing distractor rather than a clue to the key word. Admittedly *to and from* (Australian slang for "Pom") and the offensive *septic tank* (for "Yank") are in the plain-spoken tradition of *trouble and strife* (for "wife"). Yet the amusement of most **rhyming slang** is its seeming irrelevance to what's being referred to, making it hard for the uninitiated to know what is meant. The habit of cutting the rhyming phrase back to a single word, as in *rubbidy* or *elephants* (*elephants trunk* for "drunk") also helps to disguise the reference.

Rhyming slang is certainly for those in the know and works to exclude outsiders. Once such phrases become well known they lose that value and the major motive for their use. Perhaps this helps to explain why few **rhyming slang** terms (as far as we know) ever establish themselves in the standard language.

rhythm This is one of the subtle components of prose. It has a pervasive effect on the reader, yet can only be demonstrated here and there, in particular phrases or sentences. **Rhythm** in prose is certainly no regular **rhythm** as in poetry. It is less like the normal pattern of a sound wave, and much more like the unpredictable patterns of waves on the beach, whose shape and size vary with contextual factors.

We can usefully liken the sentences in a piece of writing to individual waves in their rise and resolution on the shore. Each wave has a clear crest to mark its place in the continuous pattern. In the same way, every sentence needs a clear focus if it's to contribute to the **rhythm** and momentum of the prose. Shapeless sentences with blurred focus are unsatisfactory in terms of **rhythm** as well as meaning. Very long sentences often impair the **rhythm** unless they are carefully constructed. Yet too many short choppy sentences can also disturb the deeper **rhythm** of prose. Continuous variety in sentence length seems in fact to sustain the **rhythm** best, provided each one is focused and balanced in its structure:

In Australia alone is to be found the grotesque, the weird, the strange
scribblings of nature learning how to write. Some see no beauty in our
trees without shade, our flowers without perfume, our birds who
cannot fly, and our beasts who have not yet learned to walk on all
fours. But the dweller in the wilderness acknowledges the subtle
charms of the fantastic land of monstrosities. He becomes familiar with
the beauty of loneliness. Whispered to by the myriad tongues of the
wilderness, he learns the language of the barren and the uncouth, and
can read the hieroglyphs of the haggard gumtrees, blown into odd
shapes, distorted with fierce hot winds, and cramped with cold nights,
when the Southern Cross freezes in a cloudless sky of icy blue.
(Marcus Clarke, 1876)

The passage shows the skilled writer at work, controlling the shape and balance
of sentences. Balance is achieved in the first sentence by inversion of the subject
and predicate. The sentence would lose almost everything if it ran:

In Australia alone the grotesque, the weird, and the strange scribblings of
nature learning how to write are to be found ...

With so much to digest before we reach the verb, it puts a severe strain on
short-term memory. The pile-up of phrases has the effect of smothering the
latent **rhythm**, until the sentence lets us down with an abrupt jolt at the end.
Instead Clarke balanced material on either side of the verb. The passage also
shows how sentence **rhythm** depends on effective use of the phrase and clause.
Note the parallel phrases in the second and fifth sentences which help to create
a satisfying **rhythm** and to control the flow of information.

Rhythm *and rhetoric of the series.* The connection between phrasing and
rhythm can also be seen in the different effects of combining two, three and
four items. When just two are coordinated, the effect is neat, tidy and final,
while the effect of three coordinated items is more expansive, suggesting both
amplitude and adequacy. Both are illustrated in the following:

It is a lamentable fact that young ladies of the present day are not too
clever, too well read, or too accomplished; but it is equally true that the
young men of the same age are no better. (Marcus Clarke, 1868)

Overall the two matching parts of the sentence seem to give the final word on
the younger generation. Yet the three matched phrases within the first part also
suggest a breadth of reference points, in a subject fully considered. Part of the
effect is the careful grading of the three items, each one a little weightier than
the one before, so that it creates a kind of cadence.

Different again is the effect of combining four (or more) items in a series.
A sizable series creates its own local **rhythm**, and temporarily suspends that of
the host sentence—just as the quartet of information seems designed to
overwhelm the reader, and to represent a kind of rhetorical pleading:

Sail up Sydney harbor, ride over a Queensland plain, watch the gathering
of an Adelaide harvest, or mingle with the orderly crowd which throngs to

a Melbourne Cup race, and deny, if you can, that there is here the making
of a great nation. (Marcus Clarke, 1884)

Even from the printed page, the rhythmic effects of well-written prose strike the ear and reinforce the message of the words. The key to writing rhythmical prose is tuning in to the sound of one's own sentences.

rhythmic or **rhythmical** See under **-ic/-ical**.

ricochet Like younger loanwords, **ricochet** has kept a French pronunciation and so rhymes with "say". Yet according to dictionaries, it takes standard English verb endings: *ricocheted, ricocheting*. There is however an alternative English pronunciation to rhyme with "set", and dictionaries note the use of *ricochetted* and *ricochetting* with it. Who really knows, from what's printed, whether the writer would pronounce it one way or the other? What is striking is the fact that 5 out of the 6 *Oxford Dictionary* citations with inflected forms use the double *t*—which seems to tally with the note in the *Random House Dictionary*, that the double *t* form is particularly British. But for all those who maintain the silent *t*, a single *t* is right for the spelling, as with other similar loanwords from French. (See further under **t**.)

rid or **ridded** Dictionaries confirm that overall the past form of *rid* is most likely to be just **rid**. However **ridded** is an alternative for the simple past tense, though not often for the past participle. Idioms such as *be rid of* and *get rid of* help to reinforce the use of **rid** as the past participle. Compare:

He rid(ded) himself of his drug-taking companions.

You are well rid of them.

The regular past **ridded** has actually been on record since the fifteenth century for the past participle, and since the seventeenth for the past tense. But the verb seems to be slow to change from its irregular to regular forms. (See further under **irregular verbs**.)

right or **rightly** **Right** has infinitely more uses than **rightly**. Apart from its adverbial role, it also serves as adjective, noun, verb and interjection. And as an adverb **right** can be either an intensifier, or a counterpart to **rightly**.

Rightly means "properly, justifiably", as in:

You rightly suggest that they should be included.

He was rightly angered by their failure to act.

It also means "correctly", as in:

They guessed rightly that I'd be on the next train.

If I rightly remember, it gets in at 5.30.

In sentences like those, **rightly** often appears before the verb, though it can also appear after it. Note that **right** could also be used for the sense "correctly", but it would have to appear after the verb:

They guessed right that I'd be on the next train.

If I remember right, it gets in at 5.30.

The choice between **right** and **rightly** in those sentences is a matter of style. **Rightly** is definitely the more formal of the two.

But in many contexts there's no choice, and **right** is the only one possible. This is so whenever it means "exactly", as in:

The station is right next to the zoo.
You should apologise right this minute.

This use of **right** as an adverbial pinpointer shades into its use as an intensifier:

The boat was right out to sea.

Right is easily overworked, both as an **intensifier** and as an **interjection** (see under those headings for alternatives). Note also that an alternative is crucial in conversations like the following, where directions are being given:

At the next intersection you turn left. Right?
Right ...

Have you got your bearings now!

Note finally that there's no common ground between **right** and **wright**: see under **wright**.

Right Being on the **Right** in politics, i.e. on the conservative side, puts you in what have traditionally been the government seats in a Westminster-style parliament. Even in opposition, the conservatives remain the **Right** and claim a linguistic advantage never enjoyed by those on the other side of parliament. (See further under **Left**.)

rigor or **rigour** See -or/-our.

rime or **rhyme** See rhyme.

ring or **wring** These two spellings cover three different verbs:
1 **wring** "twist and squeeze"
2 **ring** "encircle" with past form *ringed*
3 **ring** "sound" with past forms *rang* and *rung*

The past form of **wring** is discussed under **wrung**. The second verb is regular and quite stable, whereas the third is irregular and a little unstable in its past forms. In standard English the past tense is *rang* and the past participle *rung*, and the distinction is generally maintained in writing. But in informal Australian speech, *rung* often does service for the simple past tense, and *Collins Dictionary* (1991) acknowledges this in a cautionary usage note. In *Webster's Dictionary* it's presented simply as the less common variant. So for some English-speakers, the verb **ring** ("sound") is aligning itself more with *fling* and *swing*, and less with *sing*. (See further under **irregular verbs**.)

RIP These initials represent the Latin phrase *requiescat in pace* "may s/he rest in peace". The phrase, or the initials, are typically written on tombstones and in death notices, as a solemn farewell from the living to those who have recently died.

rise or **arise** As verbs these have slightly different uses nowadays. **Rise** means "increase, go up or get up"; whereas **arise** has more abstract uses with the meanings "originate or result from". In the past **arise** could be used for some of the more physical senses of **rise**, including "get up", but this is now definitely old-fashioned, and begins to sound archaic.

For the use of **rise** as a noun and alternative to *raise*, see under **raise**.

risky or **risqué** The first is a plain English adjective, used to describe hazardous undertakings of all kinds from climbing sheer cliffs to sinking your capital into prospecting for diamonds in the Australian desert. The second is conspicuously French in its spelling and accent, and draws attention to what the English have always associated with the French, namely a readiness to engage in matters of sexuality. A *risqué story* has sexual implications, and is close to the limits of what is socially acceptable. Of course the word is relative to the context, and what seems **risqué** to some would raise no eyebrows among others.

Note that **risky** has occasionally been substituted for **risqué** for over a century—almost as long as **risqué** itself has been recorded in English. The usage is recognised in major dictionaries, American, British and Australian, and is unmistakable in phrases such as *a risky joke*, *a risky sense of humor*.

rite or **ritual** Rite is much more exclusively associated with religion than **ritual**. Typical uses of **rite** are in *last rites* and in *married according to the rites of the Orthodox Church*, where the word refers to a total religious ceremony. **Ritual** concentrates attention on the particular formal procedure, and is often used in nonreligious contexts nowadays, as when we speak of the *Monday ritual of exchanging football news*, or the *greeting rituals used over the telephone*.

rival On how to spell this word when used as a verb, see **-l/-ll-**.

River or **river** For the use of capitals in referring to the names of *rivers*, see under **geographical names**.

rivet On the spelling of this word when it serves as a verb, see **t**.

road or **street** What's in a name? These words once served to distinguish the connecting routes between towns (= *roads*) from accessways within the town (= *streets*). And in the grids of Australian capital cities, the word **street** predominates. But the distinction has long since been lost in the suburbs, where streets, roads, avenues and crescents are intermingled. The only systematic distinction left is that *lane* designates a minor, narrow way, usually in contradistinction to an adjacent major road, witness *Flinders Lane/Flinders Street* in Melbourne, and *Phillip Lane/Phillip Street* in Sydney.

roman The upright form of type used for all general purposes is known as roman. It contrasts with the sloping *italic* type, used to set off such things as titles and foreign words. (See further under **italics**.) It regularly appears without a capital letter. Compare **Roman numerals**.

roman à clef In French this means literally "novel with a key", but it's used by both French and English to mean a novel in which recent historical events and roles are projected onto fictitious characters. The "key" is the imaginary list which would match the fiction characters with their real-life counterparts. The plural of **roman à clef** should be *romans à clef* according to the French pattern (see **plurals** section 2); but in English it tends to be pluralised as *roman à clefs*. That unfortunately suggests a novel with multiple "keys" rather than several novels.

Roman Catholic On the use of this expression, see under **Catholic** or **catholic.**

Roman numerals Dictionaries show that this expression generally carries a capital letter—except in editorial circles, where references to both *roman* and *arabic* numbers are written without capital letters. For the use of each type of numeral, see under **numbers** and **number style**.

The key symbols in the roman numbering system are:

I (1)   V (5)   X (10)   L (50)   C (100)   D (500)   M (1000)

All intervening numbers can be created by combinations of those letters. The values are essentially created by subtraction from the left and addition on the right of the key symbols. The lower symbol e.g. *I* is subtracted thus in *IV* (4) but added in *VI* (6). Both principles are worked in numbers such as in *XLIX* (= 49), and in *MCMXC* (= 1990).

Romania, Rumania or **Roumania** The Romans gave their name to this easternmost province of their empire, hence the spelling **Romania** which is now the official form in English according to United Nations sources. The spellings **Rumania** and **Roumania** were however used by English writers of the nineteenth century (as far as *Oxford Dictionary* citations go), and they remain the official forms in Spanish and French respectively. The spelling **Rumania** is still preferred by some English-speaking authorities. In American English it's endorsed by the *Random House Dictionary* (where *Webster's* plumps for **Romania**). **Rumania** is used by some Australian newspapers, notably in Victoria, Queensland and Western Australia, whereas **Romania** is used in New South Wales.

roofs or **rooves** The first word is the standard plural for *roof* in all modern dictionaries. **Rooves** is sometimes created by analogy with *hoof/hooves*, but plurals with -*v* are disappearing. (See further under **-f/-v-**.)

root The root of a word is the essential unit of meaning on which various stems and derivative forms may be based. The root underlying *course, current* and *cursive* is the Latin *cur-* meaning "run". Two of the Latin stems from it are *curr-* and *curs-*, while *cours-* has developed in French and English.

rosary or **rosery** The **rosary** or set of beads used to tally personal prayers in the Catholic Church is figuratively a "necklace or garland of roses". It comes from the Latin *rosarium* "rose garden", which was its first meaning in fifteenth century English. By the end of the sixteenth century, its now standard meaning in relation to prayer beads was established.

This left rose-fanciers without a distinctive name for the rose garden, yet it was not until the nineteenth century that the word **rosery** was coined for the purpose. Formed out of the English elements *rose* + *-ery* (along the same lines as *orangery*), it should not be mistaken for a misspelling of **rosary**—however hard it is to separate *-ery* and *-ary* in other words. (See further under **-ary/-ery/ -ory**.)

rosin or **resin** See **resin**.

rotary or **rotatory** Both adjectives mean "turning on or as on an axis", but **rotary** is the everyday word, used in the *rotary engine*, the *rotary clothes hoist* and other appliances. **Rotatory** is the more academic word, applied to things which embody more abstract forms of rotation, such as the *rotatory movement of a satellite* and *rotatory schedules*.

Roumania or **Romania** See **Romania**.

rouse and **arouse** The idea of "awakening" is in both of these, but only **rouse** means this in the direct physical sense:
She roused the sleeping students with a whistle.
With **arouse**, the effect is more internal, and affects emotions and thinking:
His smug words aroused their anger.
Their behavior was so covert as to arouse suspicion.
Note also that **arouse** is the word used of the raising of sexual excitement, which can be psychological, physiological or both.

route or rout In speech these sound quite different, but on paper they look similar, and as verbs they may be identical. The past tense of each is *routed*, and only the context shows whether it's a case of *routed* "drove (the enemy) into retreat" or *routed* "set a course". Compare:
Mounted police routed the angry protesters.
The protest march was routed down George Street.
The same problem can arise with the present participle. *Routing* can be used for either verb, but *routeing* is recommended for *route* by both *Collins* and the *Macquarie* dictionaries, to ensure that it's immediately associated with the right verb. It breaks the normal spelling rule for a final *e* (see **-e** section 1), but it prevents miscommunication.

Royal or **royal** Republicanism is beginning to assert itself in Australia over the use of **Royal**, and we're no longer inclined to give the word a capital on all appearances. In official titles such as the *Royal Melbourne Hospital*, and the *Royal Horticultural Society*, it remains of course, and the Australian Government *Style Manual* demonstrates the capitals in ceremonial contexts such as the *Royal Arms*, *Royal Cipher*, and the *Royal style*. But apart from official titles like those, the word appears without a capital. Australian newspaper style guides agree that a *royal visit* need not be capitalised, nor references to the *royal family*. They also affirm that there's no need to capitalise *royal commission* except when quoting the full title, as in the *Royal Commission into Black Deaths in Custody*. The capitals have lingered on both *royal commission* and *royal assent* (official enactment by the governor-general or state governors of new parliamentary legislation), but this no doubt reflects the heavier use of capitals in legal and legislative writing—rather than any loyalty to royalty. (See further under **capital letters**.)

royal we   See under **we**.

RSI   This abbreviation stands for "repetitive strain injury" (or "repetition strain injury" or "repetitive stress injury")—and the options are a sign of its newness. The first is given priority in both the *Macquarie* and *Collins* dictionaries. It has yet to be entered in the *Oxford Dictionary* and the major American dictionaries. In informal Australian English it's sometimes reduced to "kangaroo paw", while in American English it becomes one of the "cumulative trauma disorders".

RSVP   This French request *répondez s'il vous plaît* (literally "reply if you please") is regularly abbreviated in English as **RSVP**. The abbreviation is used by convention at the bottom of formal written invitations, usually with a date by which to reply, and a contact number or address at which the reply is to be received.

rugby union or **rugby league**   Tradition associates the game of rugby with Rugby School. It supposedly originated in 1823 when a football player picked up the ball and ran with it. By the end of the nineteenth century it had developed its own set of rules and a formal governing body, the *Rugby Union*. The *Rugby League* splintered off from this in 1893.

The **rugby union** game differs from that of **rugby league** in the number of players per side, and in a few rules and points of scoring. They also differ in that **rugby union** is always an amateur sport, whereas **rugby league** is chiefly professional. What used to be called "rugger" is **rugby union**. The word is normally written in lower case.

The pursuit of *rugby* divides NSW and Queensland from the southern and western states of Australia, where *Australian Rules Football* prevails as the weekend spectator sport. (See under **Australian Rules**.)

Rumania or **Romania**   See **Romania**.

rumor or **rumour**   See **-or/-our**.

rung or **wrung**   See **ring** or **wring**, and **wrung**.

running heads   See under **heading, headline** or **header**.

runover lines See **turnover lines**.

rural or **rustic** Both adjectives relate to farming and the countryside, and **rural** is neutral in its connotations, as in *rural incomes* and *rural pastimes*. **Rustic** is rarely neutral, and can be either positively or negatively charged, depending on context. The *rustic gate* in a suburban garden is a feature which lends charm to it, whereas *rustic plumbing* on the same property implies crudeness and backwardness.

Russia It was the largest and most powerful republic in the former USSR (Union of Soviet Socialist Republics), and its name has often been used as a byword for the whole. Such usage was however a double source of dissatisfaction to many within the Soviet Union. For one thing, it was properly the title of the Russian imperial regime which was overthrown in 1917. For another, it designated only one of the seventeen republics, and seemed to overlook the others. And within the various republics there are more than 100 national groupings, including Armenian, Byelorussian, Estonian, Georgian, Latvian, Lithuanian and Uzbek. To refer to the citizens of such nationalities as "Russian" was to extinguish their identity, and point to centralised control from Moscow.

The dissolution of the USSR in 1991 confirms the vigor of nationalist feelings, and it remains to be seen whether any federation will emerge and under what name. The proposed *Union of Soviet Sovereign Republics* has been eclipsed by the *Commonwealth of Independent States*, but what organisation will crystallise out of the present situation is still unclear. In the meantime the Soviet Union's membership at United Nations is being continued in the name of the *Russian Federation*, with the support of eleven members of the Commonwealth of Independent States. Other former members of the Soviet Union are separately represented at United Nations, including Belarus (formerly Byelorussia), Estonia, Latvia, Lithuania and the Ukraine.

rustic or **rural** See **rural**.

℞ or Rx This mysterious symbol appears on doctors' prescriptions prefacing the recipe for a medicament. In fact it represents the Latin word *recipe*, literally "take". As in the scrawled signatures for which doctors are notorious, only the first letter of the word is decipherable.

-ry Strictly speaking this is simply a variant form of the suffix *-ery*. The older spelling of *carpentry* as *carpentery* shows us the process, and it corresponds to the telescoping of *er* to *r* in some other pairs of words (see further under **-er>-r-**). However many of the words with **-ry** are centuries old, and we have no record of them with *-ery*.

One noticeable feature of words ending in **-ry** is that they very often have three syllables, and some scholars believe that the **-ry** helped to maintain this pattern, in words which might otherwise have had four syllables:

artistry bigotry devilry husbandry pedantry
punditry ribaldry rivalry wizardry
Compare:
archery brewery butchery printery robbery smeltery tannery
where three syllables are maintained through the coincidence of *-er* and
-ery. And
eatery finery greenery popery shrubbery thievery
where a single syllable is built up to three with the full *-ery* suffix.

Whatever the historical explanation, either **-ry** or *-ery* is now fixed in the
spelling of such words. Only in the case of *jewelry* and *jewellery* is there a real
choice (see under **jewellery**).

For the choice between *-ery*, *-ary* and *-ory*, see under **-ary/-ery/-ory**.

S

S The letter **s** was the last to acquire a standardised shape in English printing. Even in the late eighteenth century its shape in lower case depended on its position in a word. When it was the last letter it took the shape we know today, but when first or in the middle of a word, printers used a shape rather like an *f*. In roman type it was exactly like f apart from the cross stroke which was only on the left side; in italic, printers used a "long *s*", with a descender below the line of print. The two forms of **s** helped to distinguish any **ss** which were part of the stem of the word from those which were usually the inflection (as with the plural **s**). As it happens, our one and only **s** nowadays is the shape which belonged to the inflection.

-s This is the most important inflection in English, as (1) the plural ending for most nouns and (2) the third person singular present ending for all verbs except auxiliaries.

1 **-s** is the plural inflection for almost all nouns that go back to Old English, and for all assimilated loanwords, including *sticks* and *stones*, *oranges* and *lemons*, and *armadillos* and *aardvarks*. The variant form *-es* is applied to nouns ending in *(s)s*, *sh*, *(t)ch*, *x* or *(z)z*:
   glasses dishes churches patches taxes quizzes
Those which do not take *-(e)s* are usually very recent loans, such as *kibbutzim*, or else ones which preserve their foreign plurals either for scholarly reasons (*phenomena*) or because of the cachet attached to them (*gateaux*). (See further under **plurals**.)

2 **-s** marks verbs in the third person singular present tense, as in *dances*, *rocks*, *rolls*, *sings* and many more. The *-es* variant is reserved for verbs ending in *(s)s*, *sh*, *(t)ch*, *x* or *(z)z*:
   hisses finishes clutches fixes buzzes

Note that the **-s** ending sometimes distinguishes the adverb from the adjective, as with *backwards* and *a backward step*. (See further under **-ward**.) The *-(e)s* ending once marked many more adverbs in English.

's In writing, this inflection is usually the apostrophe **s**, which marks the genitive of English nouns as in the *farmer's son* and the *doctor's answer*. (See further under **apostrophes**.)
   Yet **'s** can also be a contraction of the verb *is* or *has*, as in:
   That's a good idea.
   Where's he put the cat?

These are common contractions in speech and less formal writing. (See further under **contractions** section 2.)

-s/-ss- Whether to write one or two *s*s is a question affecting several kinds of English words when affixes are added.

1 *For nouns ending in a single s*, it's the question of whether to double it before adding the plural suffix *-es*. The answer for nouns of two or more syllables is clear cut: never double the **s**. See for example:

atlases irises proboscises surpluses thermoses

This applies also to Latin loanwords ending in *-us*, such as *cactus(es)* and *syllabus(es)*, whenever they have English plurals (see **-us** section 1). Even with words of one syllable, the pattern is normally the same: *buses, gases, pluses*. Spellings with double **s** are the secondary ones in each case (see further under **bus, gas, plus**).

2 *Verbs ending in s* show rather more variability. The regular rules (see under **doubling of final consonant**) are applied in cases like *chorused, portcullised* and *trellised*. Yet in the cases of *bias* and *focus*, *biassed* and *focussed* are still sometimes seen—in spite of Fowler's preference (and that of the *Oxford Dictionary*) for *biased* and *focused*. With verbs of one syllable (such as *bus* and *gas*), the **s** is usually doubled in Australia and Britain, though less regularly in the USA. (On the spelling of **canvas** and **nonplus** as verbs, see their respective entries.)

3 *Complex words formed with dis-, mis- or trans-* raise the opposite question, when the prefix is before a stem beginning with *s*. Should the two *s* be set side by side, separated by a hyphen, or reduced to one? The answer for words prefixed with *dis-* or *mis-* is to set them solid, as in:

disservice dissimilate dissolve
misshapen misspell misstate

But with *trans-* the "rules" are less clear. Dictionaries record all three forms for some, such as *trans-ship, transship* and *tranship*, but vary in their preferences with *Collins, Webster's* and *Random House* preferring *transship*, and *Macquarie* and *Chambers tranship*. *Transsexual* is given with double *s* in all dictionaries, though the *Oxford Dictionary* (1989) also recognises spellings with a hyphen, and with just one *s*; and it has citations for *trans(s)exual, tran(s)sexualist, trans(s)exualism* and *trans(s)exuality* all showing the variation. Note that *transubstantiation* only ever appears with one *s* because it's a Latin loanword, not an English formation.

sabre or **saber**   See under **-re/-er**.

saccharine or **saccharin**   See under **-ine/-in**.

sack, sac or **sacque**   These spellings show what time and fashion can to do a simple word. The progenitor of them all is Old English *sacc*, an early borrowing from Latin of *saccus* "bag". The spelling **sack** was and is the standard one for a large woven container for heavy products such as potatoes and wheat. The simpler **sac** was introduced in the seventeenth century to refer to a new, loose-fitting style of gown made fashionable by the French. But in the following century **sac** was taken up by biologists in its original sense to refer to a small bag-like structure in the anatomy of a plant or animal, and another spelling had to be found for clothing that went by the same name.

The spelling **sacque** is first recorded in the eighteenth century—a dressed-up form of *sac(k)* with no roots in French, but which no doubt had that je ne sais quoi that is the appeal of other frenchified words. (See further under **frenchification**.) Yet perhaps its French pretensions were too obvious. At any rate it never completely displaced **sack** as the spelling for a loose-fitting gown, and later a coat or jacket of the same style. **Sack** remains the standard spelling for most uses of the word.

said The phrase *the said* is a form of cohesion peculiar to legal documents. In expressions such as *the said Gibson* or *the said premises*, it serves to remind readers that "Gibson" and particular "premises" have been identified earlier on, and that this reference should be connected with that. This is exactly what pronouns do in ordinary English, though not always without ambiguity, and so they're studiously avoided in legal writing. We might also note that the sheer length of legal sentences contributes to the danger of ambiguity, and amid the general wordiness of legal prose, even the cohesive devices need to be bulkier. The phrase *the said* helps to highlight a reference more adequately than a simple pronoun or demonstrative. In any other kind of writing, *the said* looks like overkill.

For other kinds of cohesive devices, see under **coherence** or **cohesion**.

Saint or **St** The conventions for writing saints' names depend on the context: whether it's a reference to the saint himself or herself, or to an institution or place named after them.

The names of saints are only prefaced by **Saint** in books which describe their life and works. Incidental references to them in history books and encyclopedias are usually abbreviated to **St**. In the indexes to religious books, saints' names are entered alphabetically according to their given names, with **Saint** following:

Thomas Aquinas, Saint

In other references **St** is used. Churches are identified this way: *St Mary's Cathedral, St John's Church*, as are other associated institutions: *Brotherhood of St Lawrence, St Vincent de Paul*. Purely secular institutions such as the *St George Building Society* and the *St Kilda Football Club* naturally use the abbreviation. Individuals whose surnames echo a saint's name: *St Clair, St John*, again use the abbreviation, as a glance at the metropolitan phone book will confirm. Likewise geographical names which honor a saint are always written with the abbreviation, whether they're the names of Australian suburbs on the mainland (*St Albans, St Lucia, St Peters*), or of unspoiled places in Tasmania, such as:

Lake St Clair   St Columba Falls   St Helens Isle
St Patricks Head   St Pauls Dome   St Valentines Park

1 *Punctuating saints' names.* Few writers and editors these days put a full stop on **St**, either because (a) it's a contraction rather than an abbreviation, or (b) it carries a capital letter. (For more about these principles, see **abbreviations** section 1.) Note also that there's no apostrophe before the final *s* in placenames containing a saint's name (see **apostrophes**, section 2). However institutions with a saint's name may use an apostrophe, especially ones like *St Vincent's Hospital, St Joseph's College*, which have a religious affiliation. For other institutions, check the telephone directory.

Note that in French, both personal and geographical names may keep the word **saint**(*e*) in full, and connect it to the other word with a hyphen. See for example:

Sainte-Beuve Saint-Quentin Saint-Saens Yves Saint-Laurent
Saint-Germain-des-Pres Saint-Cloud

In compressed lists, maps and timetables, however, placenames like the last two often appear as:

St-Germain-des-Pres St-Cloud

2 *Indexing names with St.* Names prefixed with **St** are indexed as if they were **Saint**, and included after *Sah-* in any list. Other names involving *Saint ...* are integrated with those with **St**, according to their sixth letter. See for example:

St Antony's Home
Saint Honore Cake Shop
St Ignatius College
Saintino Z
St Ives Shopping Village

sake *For his sake ... for my husband's sake ... for God's sake ...* Those phrases show that **sake** normally involves a genitive, and with nouns and names, this means an apostrophe plus *s*. In the past, the same treatment was accorded to all abstract nouns:

for pity's sake   for mercy's sake   for goodness's sake

However Fowler noted that both the final *s* and the apostrophe were beginning to disappear from the last of those. He also noted that there was no need for apostrophe *s* in *for conscience sake*. The *Right Word at the Right Time* creates a compromise rule with the same examples, that the apostrophe alone is to be added if the noun ends in *s*, and if not, then nothing at all is added. Yet the apostrophe in *for goodness' sake* adds no meaning to the idiom, and might as well be omitted.

salination, salinisation and **salinification** Both *desalination* and *desalinisation* are established words for the process of extracting mineral salts from water. The reverse process, by which mineral salts rise from subterranean water to pollute agricultural land, is relatively new. The choice of word for it is not entirely settled although dictionaries give preference to **salinisation**, first recorded in 1928. The first *Oxford Dictionary* citation for **salinification** is from 1979, although it appeared in *Webster's* headword list in 1911 and 1961. **Salination** is recognised by *Webster's* and the *Macquarie Dictionary* (1991) (under **salinisation**), and it expresses the concept more economically than either of the others.

salutary or **salutatory** At the root of both these adjectives is the notion of good health, yet both have moved some distance away from it. **Salutary** now serves to describe something as broadly beneficial or helpful in fostering some positive good, as in *salutary experience* or a *salutary effect on the discussion*.

 Salutatory has strong links with *salutation* "greeting" (which is ultimately a good health wish). So **salutatory** means "offering a welcome", as in a *salutatory letter from my new landlord*.

same This word serves as a shorthand device in business and law, as well as in ordinary English. In commercialese **same** stands instead of the details of an order, to save repeating them all as in:

 Please deliver three cartons of manila folders 297/211 m, and include invoice for same ...

In law also *(the) same* saves tedious repetition:

 The defendant of 31 Low Street Richmond, and his son of the same address ...

These uses are well recognised by the style authorities; yet another common use of *(the) same* gets no mention:

 We arranged a taxi, and the visitors did the same.

Note that there are no overtones of commercialese or legalese in such usage; it is in fact one of the cohesive devices of standard English. (See further under **coherence** or **cohesion**.)

 When **same** is used as an ordinary adjective in comparisons, the following conjunction may be either *as* or *that*:

 It's the same speech as he delivered at yesterday's graduation.

 It's the same speech that he delivered yesterday.

The construction with *as* makes for a more formal style, but the second is commonly used.

sanatorium or **sanitarium** The first is the traditional spelling in Britain for a hospital or residential centre for the chronically ill. The second, according to some, refers to a health resort. But in the USA **sanitarium** is the primary spelling for both, according to *Random House*, while a minority use **sanatorium** for them. People's uncertainty as to which vowel goes where shows up in two other spellings recorded in *Webster's*: *sanitorium* and *sanatarium*

Neither **sanatorium** or **sanitarium** is much used in Australia, though two factors incline us towards the second:

1 the impact of the trademark *Sanitarium*, which comes with the breakfast cereal and other cereal products, and
2 the fact that the spelling **sanitarium** coincides with better known words such as *sanitary*, *sanitise* and *sanitation*; whereas **sanatorium** is supported only by uncommon words such as *sanatory* and *sanative*.

For the plurals, see under -**um**.

sanguine or **sanguinary**   Both these go back to the Latin word for "blood", though only **sanguinary** expresses it now, in phrases such as a *sanguinary encounter with street thugs* which refer to bloodshed or to those with a taste for it. Yet the horrific implications of the word are somehow muted in the latinate word. If its shocking implications are to be communicated, "bloody" or "bloodthirsty" says it more clearly and strongly.

Sanguine came under the influence of medieval ideas about the four bodily humors which affected a person's temperament: blood, phlegm, yellow bile (choler) and black bile (melancholy). Those in whom "blood" was dominant had a cheerful, energetic character, and so **sanguine** now means "confident" and "optimistic".

sanitarium, sanitorium or **sanatorium**   See sanatorium.

sank or **sunk**   See sink.

sans serif   See under serif.

sarcasm   See under irony.

sated, satiated or **saturated**   All three are concerned with the filling of particular needs and capacities, but the first two have much more in common than the third. Both **sated** and **satiated** mean the satisfying of physical and psychological needs to the hilt, even to the point of overindulgence, as in *sated with TV* and *satiated with chocolate*. Some style commentators suggest that **satiated** connotes excess more often than **sated**, though neither is free of pejorative connotations. If a neutral word is needed, some form of the word *satisfy* would be better.

Saturated in ordinary usage means "soaked with a liquid, as much as the medium can absorb":

The carpets were still saturated after the flood.

In military jargon it conveys the idea of an area attacked with so many bombs or fighter aircraft as to render it defenceless.

savanna or **savannah**   The first spelling **savanna** is the primary one in all modern dictionaries. It stays closer to the original loanword from Caribbean Spanish: *zavana* (in modern Spanish *sabana*). The spelling with two *n*s appeared first in the sixteenth century, and the variant with *h* in the seventeenth.

Savannah was the spelling preferred by the *Oxford Dictionary*, and is the one enshrined in *Savannah River* and the town of *Savannah* in Georgia. These geographical names no doubt help to keep *savannah* alive in American English as the alternative spelling for the common word, and it is also registered in *Collins* and *Macquarie* as a secondary form.

savior or **saviour** See -or/-our.

savoir faire and **savoir vivre** The phrase **savoir faire** is French for "knowing what to do"—that almost intuitive knowledge of how to act in any circumstances, which some people possess in larger measure than others. **Savoir vivre** is "knowing how to live". It usually involves experience of good living, and so is more likely to be accessed by those with the means or good fortune to partake of the good life. However **savoir vivre** suggests more refined taste than is associated with *la dolce vita* (see under **dolce vita**).

Note that **savoir faire** is much better established in English, in spite of being the more recently adopted: **savoir vivre** was first recorded in the eighteenth century, **savoir faire** in the nineteenth. There is no need for a hyphen in either.

scale The phrases *large-scale* and *small-scale* carry slightly different meanings, according to whether they refer to the **scale** of a map, drawing or diagram, or to anything else. In ordinary usage, *large-scale* means "extensive", and *small-scale* "small in size", as in a *large-scale/small-scale operation*.

In references to maps etc. things are different. A *small-scale* version covers more ground and offers less detail, whereas the *large-scale* gives you the fine detail of a relatively small area. So a *large-scale* map might be 1:2000, and a *small-scale* map 1:200 000. The differences between *large-scale* and *small-scale* are always relative however.

scallop or **scollop** The first spelling **scallop** is given preference in all dictionaries, and reflects the word's origins in earlier English *scalop* and Old French *escalope* "shell". **Scollop** however reflects the common pronunciation of the word, and is a recognised alternative. Its appearance in the eighteenth century shows how old our present pronunciation is.

Note that when **scallop** becomes a verb the *p* need not be doubled: see under **-p/-pp-**.

scant or **scanty** Scant is now an old-fashioned adjective, hardly used except in stock phrases such as *scant praise*, and *scant regard* (for their safety/health etc.) In such phrases, it only seems to combine with abstract nouns. **Scanty** seems to substitute for it in reference to things concrete and practical, as in *scanty clothes* and a *scanty supply of food*.

scarcely Used on its own this adverb simply judges the extent or likelihood of something:
They scarcely heard the thunder.
The government will scarcely want to go to the polls after that.

Used in tandem with another conjunction, **scarcely** compares the timing of two events:

Scarcely had they finished the roof when it began to rain.
Scarcely had they finished the roof than it began to rain.

The first sentence which uses the temporal *when* is the only correct way of putting it, according to some style commentators. Yet the use of the comparative *than* is quite common, and may indeed sound more idiomatic to some ears. The arguments for it are like those for *hardly than*. (See under **hard** and **hardly**.)

Note the inversion of subject and verb after **scarcely**, and other quasi-negative adverbs. (See further under **negatives**.)

scarfs or **scarves** See under **-f/-v-**.

sceptical or **skeptical** For the choice between these, and between *sceptic/skeptic* and *scepticism/skepticism*, see under **skeptical**.

sceptre or **scepter** See under **-re/-er**.

schema For the plural see **-a** section 1.

schnapper or **snapper** See under **snapper**.

schnorkel or **snorkel** See under **snorkel**.

schwa This vowel sound is less well known to English-speakers than it should be. Apart from being the most common vowel throughout the English speaking world, it's the most common sound altogether in Australian speech. Yet because there's no single letter for it in the alphabet, it goes largely unrecognised. In fact it can correspond to any of the five vowel letters, as italicised in the following:

*a*bout watch*e*s pol*i*tics phot*o*graph nat*u*ral

Schwa is the common vowel sound of unstressed syllables, in individual words, and in strings of them. In *a cup of tea*, the vowels of the first and third words are normally **schwa**.

Being an unstressed vowel, **schwa** has no distinct sound—hence its alternative name "indeterminate vowel". Its indeterminacy means it offers no clues as to the spelling of the syllable it appears in, and many spelling dilemmas, as with *-able/-ible*, *-ant/-ent* and *-er/-or* turn on it.

scientific names Biological classifications have more levels than we're normally aware of. Both botanists and zoologists work with six levels, as shown below:

botany	zoology
Division	*Phylum*
Class	*Class*
Order	*Order*
Family	*Family*
Genus	*Genus*
Species	*Species*

But for ordinary purposes, only the last two levels are used. Most biological names consist of two parts, both of them Latin words, which specify the genus and the species:

Grevillea alpina
Grevillea rosmarinifolia

Occasionally a third word is used to identify the subspecies, as in *Grevillea rosmarinifolia var. divaricata.* Note that the abbreviation *var.* is not used by zoologists before the name of a subspecies. The words designating both species and subspecies may be descriptive, as in the examples above, or may preserve in latinised form the name of the person who identified the species, for example: *Grevillea banksii var. forsteri.* All three words are italicised, but only the first is capitalised, even if the others are disguised proper names. Sometimes an English proper name is printed in roman after the Latin elements, usually in brackets. This is the name of the ''author'', the person who gave the definitive description of the organism in the scientific literature.

Other conventions with scientific names are that when several species of the same genus are mentioned in quick succession, the genus can be abbreviated to an initial (*Grevillea alpina, G. rosmarinifolia*) for the second and subsequent names. Note also that when the Latin word for genus or species is used as the common name for a plant or animal, it's printed with lower case and in roman:

They found grevillea and bottlebrush flowering everywhere.

The naming principles described above apply throughout the natural world, as well as in medicine. They are used in the naming of body organs (*Corpus callosum*, the band of tissue which links the two hemispheres of the brain), and in the names of diseases (*Paralysis agitans* = Parkinson's disease) and microorganisms (*Legionella pneumophila*, the microbe which causes the most familiar form of legionnaire's disease). Note that the initial capital disappears from scientific nomenclature in nonscientific text.

scilicet This Latin tag meaning ''that is to say'' is now found only in scholarly writing belonging to the old school. It was used to introduce a detailed list of things which had only been alluded to in general terms up to that point. The standard abbreviation for **scilicet** is **sc**.

Historically speaking, **scilicet** is a blend of Latin *scire licet*, literally ''*it is permitted to know*''. The authoritarian overtones of that phrase are a reminder of medieval attitudes to knowledge. The word is first recorded in English in 1387, but its history in medieval Latin is much older. Compare *videlicet* under **vide**.

scissors Should the verb accompanying **scissors** be singular or plural? See **agreement** section 3.

scollop or **scallop** See scallop.

Scotch, Scottish or **Scots** Why should it be *Scotch College* in Melbourne, and *Scots College* in Sydney? Part of the answer is that the first was founded in 1851, the second in the 1890s, and during this half century the connotations of the name changed radically.

   Scotch was once the ordinary name for the things of Scotland, traditional fare such as *Scotch broth*, *Scotch egg* and the *Scotch pancake*, as well as natural phenomena such as *Scotch fir*, *Scotch mist* and *Scotch thistle*. The name was endorsed by the **Scots** themselves in the earlier nineteenth century, and enshrined in the writings of Burns and Scott. But the *Oxford Dictionary* noted that the name later became a source of resentment felt to be foisted on them by Southerners. Early twentieth century citations also show that the adjective in colloquial use had acquired the meaning ''parsimonious''—an added reason for replacing it with **Scottish** in the names of products and cultural artifacts associated with Scotland. Hence the modification of *Scotch tartan* to *Scottish tartan* and so on, though the label *Scotch whisky* has remained.

   Broadly speaking, **Scots** is now used in reference to the people, as in *Scotsman* and the *Scots Guards*, while **Scottish** is applied to aspects of the land and its culture, as in *Scottish agriculture* and *Scottish universities*. In some contexts either word is acceptable, as in a *Scots/Scottish accent*.

scrub, brush or **bush** See bush.

seasonal or **seasonable** Seasonal reflects the periodic character of the seasons, the fact that they come and go in a predictable rotation. So *seasonal employment* is work available each year through a particular season. While seasonal is a neutral word, **seasonable** affirms that what's happening is right for the time of year, and to be expected then, as for example in the *seasonable heat of the Sydney summer*. **Seasonable** has in fact been recorded with the meaning ''timely'' since the fifteenth century.

second cousin or **first cousin once removed** See under **cousins**.

second person See under **person**.

Second World War See under **World War**.

self This serves as both prefix and suffix in English, as well as an independent word. As a prefix, it forms new adjective and noun compounds with the greatest ease, using verbs which work reflexively:

   self-addressed self-appointed self-centred self-control

Those examples show that **self-** compounds embody a variety of adverbial relations: for oneself, by oneself, in oneself, of oneself. Note that as a prefix

self- is always hyphenated, but as a suffix, never. As a suffix *-self/-selves* is the key ingredient in English **reflexive pronouns** (see under that heading).

As an independent word, **self** can be a noun, modified by its own adjective as in *your good self* and *his usual self*. Note however that when used on its own and as a substitute for *myself*, it still sounds offhanded. *A holiday for my wife and self* reads like shorthand for *a holiday for my wife and myself*. Some would further argue that to use *myself* (instead of *me*) is unfortunate (see under **me**). However in the sentence above it's natural enough to use *myself* following *my wife*, as Fowler observed. In contexts like that, *myself* seems more elegant than *me* and not an affectation.

self-deprecating, self-deprecatory or **self-depreciatory** See deprecate.

selvage or **selvedge** Selvedge persists as an alternative spelling in most dictionaries, reflecting the origins of the word as "self edge". But **selvage** is the primary spelling in the major British and American dictionaries, and *Oxford Dictionary* citations show that it has been recorded from the fifteenth century on, and is overall the more common spelling. The *-age* spelling links it with others such as *dosage*, *linage* and *shrinkage*, though the internal structure of all such words is more transparent than **selvage**. The *Macquarie Dictionary* (1991) gives equal status to the two spellings.

semantics or **semiotics** These linguistic terms are tossed around in all kinds of contexts these days—so that one hears of the *underlying semantics of a radio interview*, and of the *semiotics of wearing thongs to a dinner party*. Both words have to do with meaning, but **semantics** is still tied to language, to the meanings of individual words or what they add up to in a statement. Misunderstandings are sometimes explained in terms of the *conflicting semantics* of what has been said by the parties involved.

Semiotics is concerned with signs and symbols in the widest sense, the significance of material features of a culture and its codes of behavior. The things we surround ourselves with, and the cut and color of what we wear, all say something about individual identity as well as the different value systems under which we operate.

semi- Derived from scholarly Latin words, this prefix means "half" or "partly". In musical words such as *semibreve* and *semiquaver* it means exactly half of a larger unit; whereas the less precise meaning ("partly") is found in *semiconscious* and *semiarid*.

In spite of its Latin origins, **semi-** is now very much at home in English. It combines with everyday English words, as in:

semidesert semiskilled semisoft semisweet semitrailer

Words prefixed with **semi-** tend to be written without a hyphen, as a glance at recent dictionaries will show. Only in cases where **semi-** is combined with a word beginning with *i* (e.g. *semi-intellectual*) is the hyphen retained.

Compare **demi-**.

semicolon When the average sentence was much longer, **semicolons** were regularly seen as sentence dividers. Nineteenth century novels such as those by Anthony Trollope and Henry James would confirm this. Nowadays the **semicolon** is used much more sparingly, and some writers do without it entirely.

Semicolons now have two very specific functions.

1 The **semicolon** marks the boundary between two independent sentences that are set together as one, usually because the second is strongly related to the first. See for example:

The news of the proposed devaluation got out; there was an immediate run on the stock exchange.

In cases like that, the two sections could equally well have been set as separate sentences, with a full stop between them:

The news of the proposed devaluation got out. There was an immediate run on the stock exchange.

However the version with the **semicolon** emphasises the closeness of the two statements, and draws particular attention to the second. Note that the two could also be linked with a conjunction:

The news of the proposed devaluation got out; and there was …

The news of the proposed devaluation got out, and there was …

Both those are grammatically correct, and there's little to choose between them, except that the **semicolon** makes a more substantial break than the comma.

2 The **semicolon** also serves as a second level of punctuation, in a series of words or phrases which already have commas making some internal divisions. See for example:

The news of the proposed devaluation resulted in an instant drop in the value of shares; a modest fall in interest rates, at least those offered by the larger banks; and a surprising run on property investments, presumably backed by overseas capital.

In a complex list such as that, the demarcation of the three subunits would not be so clear if only commas were used. Here again, the greater ''weight'' of the **semicolon** is put to good use.

semiotics or **semantics** See semantics.

sense, sensibility, sensitivity and **sensitiveness** The first two of these made a title for Jane Austen, and they focus on the common **sense** and good judgement of one character, and the tendency to react emotionally in another. Nowadays we're unlikely to use **sensibility** in that way, and would reserve it for responsiveness to the subtleties of experience and of artistic form. The adjective *sensible* has also moved, from being associated with **sensibility** in its older sense, to being the standard adjective for **sense**.

Both **sensitivity** and **sensitiveness** link up with the adjective *sensitive*, and express the readiness to respond to outside forces. Both words originated in the nineteenth century, and are interchangeable in some general and technical senses. However **sensitivity** is the term usually used for the response of objects to physical forces such as heat and light, not **sensitiveness**; whereas either could be used of human reaction or overreaction to psychological stress. Compare:

The colors don't last because of their sensitivity to sunlight.

Her sensitiveness over being outvoted only seemed to intensify.

sensuous or **sensual** These can be a trap for the unwary, since both mean that the senses are engaged: the question is which senses. **Sensual** often implies the gratifying of physical senses and appetites (including sexual ones) as in *Sensual Massage*, the titillating title of a recent book. **Sensuous** is reserved by some writers for that which appeals to the aesthetic senses, when we refer to the *sensuous words* or imagery of a poet such as Keats. The word **sensuous** was evidently coined by Milton for just this purpose and to prevent confusion with **sensual**.

Yet the distinction between the two is easily blurred when applied to things like food. Is there anything to distinguish a "sensual chocolate cake" from a "sensuous" one? Perhaps the first hints at indulgent excess, while the second simply appreciates the richness. *Random House* suggests that at bottom **sensual** has pejorative connotations which **sensuous** is free of, though that hardly seems to apply in some of the citations in *Webster's English Usage*, including ones from *Gourmet* magazine which use both words in appreciation of rich foods. Modern dictionaries confirm the overlap by giving definitions such as "appealing to the senses" for both words. The interplay between the words makes **sensuous** less aesthetic and innocent than Milton intended. It is also the loser in terms of overall frequency, at least in Australia and the USA, where in equivalent databases the instances of **sensual** outnumbered **sensuous** 7:4 and 6:2 respectively. In the equivalent British corpus, however, the ratio was 1:3, suggesting that the use of **sensual** is constrained by concern about its meaning.

Note that in philosophy the word **sensual** is neutral in meaning and associated with the doctrine of *sensationalism*, which proposes that sensation is the only source of knowledge.

sentences The finite strings of words by which we communicate are **sentences**. A *written sentence* is bounded by a capital letter on its first word, and a full stop after the last. The bounds of *spoken sentences* are often unclear, though in the absence of alternative grammar, they are often analysed in terms of written sentences. For grammarians there are two ways of looking at **sentences**: (1) as utterances which fulfill a particular function; (2) as strings of words with certain common structures.

1 *The functions of **sentences** are usually classified as:*
a) making statements
b) asking questions
c) uttering commands
d) voicing exclamations

Each of those functions is expressed through a standard clause type: (a) declarative (b) interrogative (c) imperative (d) exclamative. Yet there's no one-for-one correspondence between clause type and sentence function. (For examples, see under **commands**.)

2 *The internal structure of a sentence* can be analysed in terms of clause structure: is there one or more of them, and what is the interrelationship between them? The distinctions between simple, complex and compound sentences turn on this. (For a discussion of them, see under **clauses**.) **Cleft sentences** are discussed under their own heading.

Our expectations of **sentences** tend to be modeled on the norms of written syntax, where clauses normally have the full subject and predicate, and any subordinate clause has a main clause to support it. Yet many of the **sentences** exchanged in conversation are not quite like that. Much is understood and left implicit, as in:

Where are you going?
To the movies.
In the city?
Yes, the Hoyts centre in George Street. Can't catch Gallipoli *anywhere else at the moment.*

Apart from the first question, all the **sentences** in that typical piece of dialogue are fragmentary. Grammarians do indeed call them *sentence fragments*. The three in the middle have neither subject nor verb, and consist simply of adverbial phrases. The last is more fully expressed, but still lacks a subject. In terms of scripted dialogue they still count as **sentences**, though they differ from the stuff of nonfictional prose.

3 *Sentences* and style. Whether in fiction or nonfiction, **sentences** are the staple of discourse, and their patterning creates the rhythm of prose. (See under **rhythm**.) Variety in length and structure are both important for their effect on intelligibility as well as rhythm. Too many long *complex sentences* will lose the rhythm and the reader. And too many short ones in quick succession create an awkward, repetitive rhythm which distracts the reader from what's being said. Ideally the occasional short sentence provides relief from longer ones. The target for *average* sentence length in Plain English documents is 20 words. However the average achieved in fiction is around 15 words, and this is the target for mass circulation magazines.

Apart from varying in length, **sentences** need variety in their openings, using topicalising phrases now and then before the grammatical subject, and avoiding anticlimaxes at the end. The sentence is after all an infinitely flexible unit, to be rearranged and stretched and compressed in the interests of an elegant style.

sentiment and **sentimentality** Sentiment has many shades of meaning in reference to thoughts, attitudes and feelings. Its connotations are neutral however, and it relies on modifiers to give it particulars and values, as in a *cheerful sentiment* and a *negative sentiment.*

Sentimentality is somewhat pejorative. It implies an excess of emotion where most people would not indulge it:

> *Her attitude to endangered species showed more sentimentality than scientific sense.*

Note that *sentimental* serves as adjective for both **sentiment** and **sentimentality**: for the first in *sentimental value,* and for the second in *sentimental love-songs.* However the fact that *sentimental* can be linked with **sentimentality** tends to give it a pejorative flavor generally, and so it's better avoided if you wish to make a link with **sentiment.** Calling someone a *sentimental person* is unlikely to sound like a compliment, as *person of sentiment* once did.

sept- This is the Latin prefix for "seven", as in *septet, septuagenarian* and *September* (the seventh month of the Roman year, which has become the ninth month in the modern calendar).

Note that *septic* and *septic(a)emia* embody the Latin form of the Greek word *septikos* "putrid".

sepulchre or **sepulcher**   See under **-re/-er.**

sequence of tenses   The notion of **sequence of tenses** comes from Latin grammar, and is sometimes applied to English. It implies that the tense of the verb in a subordinate clause is influenced by that of the verb in the main clause. For example, when the verb of the main clause is present tense, the subordinate verb is likely to be the same:

> *He says they're coming at noon.*

The use of a past verb in the main clause often results in "backshifting" of the tense in the second clause.

> *He said they were coming at noon.*

In this case the tenses are again matched, though it has traditionally been called "sequencing of tenses".

The *sequencing of tenses* is a significant issue in reported speech (see further under **direct speech**), and in noun clauses which follow verbs of mental process, such as *decide, expect* and *know.* It is also an issue in sentences which express an impossible condition. Compare;

> *If he has any money, he will surely invest it there.*
> *If he had any money, he would surely invest it there.*
> *If he had had any money, he would have invested it there.*

The last sentence shows *sequencing of tenses* in the fullest sense, with the verb in the subordinate clause one tense back from that of the main clause (past perfect/present perfect).

Though the *sequencing/matching of tenses* occurs often enough in certain kinds of subordinate clause, the convention is varied from time to time because of the nature of the material in the clause. If it contains a statement which is believed to be universally true, it will be in the present tense even when the verb of the main clause is past:

They recognised that all life is sacred.

The present is also used when the writer stands between a reported event in the past and one anticipated in the future:

James told us that Monday is a public holiday.

In both cases, the use of the present tense serves to involve readers in the statement and to lend it vividness, as Fowler put it. It would also be possible to put the subordinate clauses into the past and observe the regular sequence of tenses in them—but this would serve to detach the reader from what's being reported.

sergeant or **serjeant** In Australia the two spellings are associated with different institutions. **Sergeant** is the spelling for the army and the police. In parliament it's the *serjeant-at-arms* whose job is to keep order and to evict unruly members. Both spellings have been in use since the fifteenth century, and the major British and American dictionaries allow that **serjeant** is an occasional variant for **sergeant**. However only **sergeant** appears in the Australian ACE corpus, and in the equivalent American database.

serial or **series** In both the audiovisual media and in publishing, material may be divided up and offered in several segments. The **serial** and the **series** are two ways of doing it. A television or radio **serial** continues its story through ongoing episodes as with *A Country Practice*. A **series** presents a set of individually complete stories involving the same set of characters, as in *MASH* or *Dad's Army*. However the two words come together in *miniseries*, which is often a "mini-serial", offering a continuous story in a few larger segments (say two, three or four).

For the librarian **serial** is a general word for the magazine or journal which appears regularly, with a different miscellany of short articles each time from the same general field. A published **series** consists of several independent monographs, each of which finds a major subject in the same field.

The plural of **series** is discussed under **Latin plurals**.

serial comma See under **comma** section 3.

serif *Serifs* are the feet which mark the ends of letters in many typefaces, including the one used for this book. Most people agree that *serif type* is easier to read than its opposite *sans serif* (also written as *sanserif*). However *sans serif letters* may give a "cleaner" and more modern look, and they work well in short messages such as headlines and advertising statements.

The word **serif** is occasionally respelled as *seriph*, either through confusion with the Hebrew word *seraph*, or just through substituting *ph* for *f* in a rather strange word (see **f/ph**). The *f* is more appropriate seeing that the word is believed to be a variant of the Dutch *schreef* meaning a "stroke". It reminds us that the printing industry developed in England with the help of technology and people from the Low Countries.

serjeant or **sergeant** See **sergeant**.

settlor or **settler** See under **-er/-or**.

several or **a few** See under **few**.

sew While the past tense of **sew** is always *sewed*, the past participle can be either *sewn* or *sewed*. The major dictionaries in Australia, Britain and the USA all give priority to *sewn*. Yet there are small differences in the instances found in English databases to suggest that the use of *sewn* for past participle is slightly stronger in Australian and British English than in American English. For some Americans then, **sew** is a regular verb, but for most of the English-speaking world it is a hybrid, with regular past tense (*sewed*) and irregular past participle.

sewage or **sewerage** Strictly speaking **sewerage** is the system of drains which carries waste fluid out of a city. The waste material carried by the system is **sewage**. By those definitions it's tautologous to speak of a *sewerage system* (though not a *sewage system*). Yet the use of the phrase *sewerage system* shows how **sewerage** comes to mean much the same as **sewage**, and it has been on record since 1851. Modern dictionaries often give **sewerage** as a possible synonym for **sewage**, though not vice versa.

sexism in language The identification of gender in English is more pervasive than many would have suspected. Modern English has no masculine and feminine genders like those of French, German, Italian and most other European languages. Yet the grammatical gender built into those languages is mechanical, and probably less harmful than the natural gender which is embedded in some English compounds (*spokesman*, *manpower*), pronouns (generic *he*), and various time-honored idioms (*man in the street*, *man on the land*). See further under **nonsexist language**.

shake The standard principal parts of this verb are *shook* (past tense) and *shaken* (past participle). However in colloquial idioms *shook* also appears as past participle, in *be shook on* "be in love with" and *be shook up* "become agitated".

Shakespearean or **Shakespearian** Since Shakespeare himself varied the spelling of his name (*Shakespere* as well as *Shakspeare*), he would scarcely have bothered about whether the adjective derived from his name should end in *-ean* or *-ian*. Older British dictionaries prefer **Shakespearian**, using the commoner of the two suffixes, while American dictionaries have **Shakespearean**, preserving the final letter of the bard's name. The *Macquarie* (1991) gives equal status to the two spellings.

For other words which vary between *-ian* and *-ean*, see under **-an**.

shall or **will** These are often thought of as alternative ways of expressing the future tense in English. Yet there are few contexts in which they are equally likely, and there are several other ways of expressing futurity, especially in conversation:

I'm going to leave in the morning.

I'm leaving in the morning.

I'll leave in the morning.

In informal English any of those is more likely than **shall** or **will** when it comes to indicating future moves and events. (See also under **present tense**.)

1 *Not simply the future* ... Grammarians have known for centuries that **shall** and **will** could express more than simple futurity, and might indeed express determination or the intention that something should happen. Historically this meaning is associated with **will**, but in modern English it's mostly associated with **shall**, as in legal statements to the effect that:

The Directors shall make a report on the company's financial position available to shareholders twice a year ...

Yet the overlap between intention and futurity can be hazy, and grammarians of the seventeenth and eighteenth centuries devised an odd compromise whereby both **shall** and **will** could express one or the other, depending on the grammatical person involved. Their system was as follows:

I/we shall
you will   expressed simple future
he/she/it/they will

whereas

I/we will
you shall   expressed intention
he/she/it/they
shall

Research by Fries (1925) into the language of English drama showed that this division of labor was artificial; yet the paradigms were enshrined in textbooks of later centuries, and were still being taught a few decades ago. Their relationship with other modal verbs is discussed under **modality**.

2 *Shall and will in statements.* Contemporary English databases show that **will** is commoner by far for expressing the future, and that goes for all persons. **Will** is also the basis of the contraction *'ll* which occurs so often in conversation. (On phonetic grounds *'ll* is unlikely to be a reduced form of **shall**, because the "sh" sound is less likely to merge with surrounding vowels than "w".) The use of **shall** is declining everywhere, though faster in some contexts than others. In Australian and American English **shall** is almost obsolescent in simple statements about the future; and according to the *Right Word at the Right Time*, the same tendency shows in British English.

3 *Shall* and *will* in questions. In questions which seek information about the future, **shall** is often used with first person pronouns, though not with second or third. Compare:

> *When shall we meet again?*
> *Will you come by car?*
> *Will David and Janet come too?*

Questions like these are the one context in which the old rules for **shall** and **will** with particular persons do seem to apply. They also apply in some other kinds of questions, such as those which seek advice or offer instructions or pose a request. Compare:

> *Shall I bring my lunch? Shall we begin?*
> *Will you put it over there please.*

However, it is also possible to frame first-person questions with **will**, especially those which are rhetorical or reflexive in meaning:

> *When will I see them again?*

Overall then **shall** is disappearing, though it lingers in some kinds of questions, and in some stylistic contexts. Its special domains are legal and authoritarian documents where it lays down the law for all parties. Elsewhere **will** is the usual choice.

shammy, chammy or **chamois** See **chamois**.

sharp or **sharply** Most of the time, **sharp** serves as adjective, and **sharply** as an adverb. However **sharp** appears here and there as a zero adverb, in statements about direction, time, and musical pitch:

> *She turned sharp left at the traffic lights.*
> *She arrived at 8 pm sharp.*
> *At first she was singing sharp.*

In sentences like those **sharp** is the only possible choice whether the sentences are spoken or written. Perhaps the clipped form **sharp** seems to embody the punctiliousness and concern with accuracy of the phrases it's embedded in.

> (See further under **zero adverbs**.)

she This pronoun has gender built irrevocably into it, and some would use it assertively, to redress what they see as the prevailing imbalance in the use of *he* and **she**. The use of *he* (*him, his*) has undoubtedly been promoted by its being used for generic purposes, and so there are those who would replace it with **she** and *her*, as in:

> *The doctor must ensure that her paging device is turned on before she goes into the wards.*
> *Before calling the electrician, make sure you can show her where the fuses are.*

Of course it is unfortunate that the use of generic *he* has seemed to reserve many domains for men only; but the attempt to create a generic **she** only creates the same problem. Nor does it help to use male and female pronouns in alternation, as some have suggested, so as to be "evenhanded" and help break down the gender stereotypes:

> *The doctor must ensure that his paging device is turned on before she goes into the ward, and be prepared to respond within one minute to any call made to him by hospital staff. If she is operating, he should hand her device over to one of the theatre nurses ...*

The result of such "evenhandedness" is totally distracting for the reader, since we rely on the continuity of pronouns to provide cohesion in a text. (See further under **coherence** and **cohesion**.) Gender-free continuity cannot be achieved with **she** or *he*, but there are other ways round the problem. (See **he** and/or **she**.)

she- occasionally serves as a prefix. In some words it's a straight gender prefix, as in *she-devil* and *she-goat*, though there are derogatory implications as well in compounds like *she-poetry*. These derogatory implications are believed to be at the heart of a number of Australian tree names, including:

> *she-beech she-bloodwood she-ironbark she-oak she-pine she-teak*

The *she-oak* was said to be so named because its timber was inferior to "real" oak; and the same naming principle could underlie the others. If so, the practice is more developed in Australia than elsewhere in the English-speaking world. The only example in American English is *she-balsam*, a plant for which "inferiority of the timber" is hardly relevant; and in the only British example, *she-holly* appears as the counterpart of the *he-holly*, where *she-/he-* match each other rather than implying the inferiority of one of them.

In the Australian list given above, only *she-oak* is widely known, and increasingly it's being called by the botanical name *casuarina*. It helps to bury a vestige of frontier male chauvinism.

sheafs or **sheaves** See under **-f/-v-**.

shear If Australia still rode on the sheep's back, we might be more certain about the past forms of **shear**. The verb is changing from *shear/shore/shorn* to *shear/sheared* (i.e. from irregular to regular) slowly but surely. A survey taken at the 1992 Style Council showed a majority of Australians (75%) now regularly use *sheared* for the past tense, but 90% preferred *shorn* to *sheared* for the past participle.

The final stage towards complete regularisation has already occurred in situations when the word refers to the cutting or tearing of metal, as in *The bolt had been sheared off*. This too nudges us towards using *sheared* as the all-purpose past form.

sheikh or **sheik** How Arabic do you want to be? **Sheikh** represents the final consonant a little more accurately, which makes it the first preference of the *Oxford Dictionary* and other British and Australian dictionaries. American dictionaries make the less foreign-looking **sheik** their primary spelling, and help the word to assimilate to English spelling—with no obvious loss of meaning. Australian newspapers are divided over whether to endorse the British or

American spelling, with more of them still going for **sheikh**. The choice between the two also surfaces in the variants *sheikhdom/sheikdom*.

sheriff or **sherif** A single letter serves to differentiate the Anglo-Saxon (and American) **sheriff** from the Arab **sherif**. Both are persons of authority, the **sheriff** being a law-enforcement officer, and the **sherif** a prince or ruler. Yet the similarities are pure coincidence. A **sheriff** was originally the "shire reeve", while **sherif** is related to the Arabic word for "noble".

Like many Arabic loanwords **sherif** has alternative spellings in English, and was formerly spelled *shereef* (in accordance with pronunciation which stresses the second syllable). *Webster's Dictionary* makes *sharif* its primary spelling. But all others prefer **sherif**, and the single *f* is all there is to distinguish it in writing from the Anglo-Saxon word. It's little enough with the give and take of double consonants in other loanwords in English. (See **single for double**.)

shew See under **show**.

shibboleth Ancient and modern uses of this word combine to make it an apt label for linguistic fetishes of the twentieth century. The original **shibboleth** was a pronunciation testword used to distinguish those who could pronounce the initial "sh" sound, from others who would make it "s". According to the biblical story (Judges 12:4-6) Jephthah used the word **shibboleth** to distinguish his own Gileadite men from Ephraimites fleeing in disguise.

In modern English the word **shibboleth** has been applied to the catchcry of a distinct party or sect, or a slogan whose impetus is emotional rather than rational, and represents outdated sentiments. The party **shibboleth(s)** still serve to identify members and to exclude those who don't belong.

Many controversial points of English seem to be *shibboleths* for members of a notional party for the protection of pure English. The insistence on *different from*, the avoidance of split infinitives, and the preservation of the subjunctive are planks in the party platform, and endorsed without any critical thought about their basis in contemporary English. More damagingly, they are made the touchstones of "correct" English, to which everyone must adhere or be damned.

This book tries to address issues like those which have tended to become **shibboleths**, to open them up to linguistic analysis, and to discourage their being used as all-powerful criteria for judgements about writing. (See also **fetish**.)

shine The past form of **shine** has traditionally been *shone*, and it's still the standard form when referring to light pure and simple:
The sun had shone all day.
Through the gloom shone the headlights of a large vehicle.
However the alternative *shined* is increasingly used when the word is used metaphorically:
Among all those seasoned performers, she shined brilliantly.
Shined is the form used regularly in references to polishing shoes or other objects:
She shined all the silver for her mother-in-law's visit.

Thus *shined* is gaining ground on *shone* in more than one context, nudging it into line with other regular verbs. (See further under **irregular verbs**.)

-ship Abstract nouns are created with this Old English suffix. They include ones associated with particular skills or pursuits, such as:

courtship friendship horsemanship leadership marksmanship
salesmanship scholarship showmanship workmanship

From these have developed words referring to a distinctive status in a particular field, as in:

apprenticeship championship editorship headship lectureship tutorship

Occasionally the prefix refers not to an individual as in those examples, but to a group or community with a special bond:

fellowship kinship membership township

The association of **-ship**, and especially *-manship* with distinctive skills finds expression in nonce words such as:

brinksmanship gamesmanship oneupmanship

The readiness with which such words are coined and understood is proof of the liveliness of the suffix. They are occasionally turned into verbs e.g. *fellowshipped.* For the spelling of that word, see under **-p/-pp-**.

shishkebab or **shishkabob** See under **kebab**.

shone or **shined** See shine.

shore or **sheared** See shear.

short titles The *short title* reduces the full title of a book or article to its key words, in a phrase of from two to four words:

Full Title	Short Title
Australian Aboriginal Words in English	Australian Aboriginal Words
"New configurations: the balance of British and American English in Canadian and Australian English"	"New configurations"

Titles consisting of fewer than five words are not usually shortened. **Short titles** are now widely used in referencing, as in this book, instead of the traditional Latin abbreviations such as *loc. cit.* and *op. cit.* (See further under **referencing** section 1.)

should or **would** In Australian English there are few points at which you have to stop and think whether to use **should** or **would** for expressing the hypothetical future. The old rules which insisted that **should** (like *shall*) was mandatory with the first person, and **would** (like *will*) with second and third persons (see **shall**

section 1) have gone by the board. Instead **would** is the standard modal for expressing the future-in-past for all three persons:

I said that I would come next week.

You said that you would come next week.

They said that they would come next week.

Only when we're seeking a very formal and respectful effect do we use **should**. Compare:

I would like   *I should like*

I would be honored   *I should be honored*

The choice is generally a matter of style now, not grammar. Yet in just a few contexts either **should** or **would** is required, contexts where something other than future meaning is at stake.

1 *Where* **should** *is still needed.* The major role of **should** nowadays is to express obligation:

A teacher should have a sense of humor.

They should never have been taken on.

Should serves as an alternative to *must* or *ought to* (see further under **ought**). Another use of **should** is to express an assumption about what is likely:

The report should be out by next week.

Should is still the modal used in subordinate clauses that express a wish, a plan, a judgement or a reaction:

They proposed that we should meet on Tuesday.

It's surprising/annoying/right that they should meet us then.

But **should** now appears less and less in conditional statements:

If I should never return, my trophies are to go to the club.

Should they ask any questions, just send them to me in writing.

The use of conditional **should** sounds rather lofty, though the inverted **should** at the start of the clause is still a neat way of prefacing a condition.

2 *When* **would** *is needed.* Apart from being the usual way to express the hypothetical future, **would** expresses willingness and preference, as in *I would like*. It often expresses a moderate degree of probability:

He would have come if he'd known.

Less common uses of **would** are to voice a conjecture, and to formulate a habit:

That would be the first time they admitted it.

She would walk for half an hour every morning.

In some conventional expressions of politeness, **would** is the standard word:

Would the ladies please step this way.

If you would care to look at this screen …

It would be a pleasure.

Note that *'d*, the common contraction of conversation, is a reduced form of **would**. It could hardly be **should**, both for phonetic reasons (the fact that the *w* of **would** often merges with vowels, and the *sh* of **should** is much less likely to), and because **would** itself is much more common (judging from the evidence of English databases).

The relationship of **should** and **would** to other English modals is discussed under **modality**.

should of or **should've**   See under **have** section 3.

shoveled or **shovelled**, **shoveling** or **shovelling**   The choice between these is discussed under **-l/-ll-**.

show   For its past tense **show** always has *showed*, while the past participle can be either *shown* or *showed*. Compare:
> *Never had so many slides been shown in one evening.*
> *Her excitement had showed through all day.*

Yet if you try replacing one participle with the other in those two sentences, they do not work equally well in both. A restriction emerges on *showed*, which as noted in the *Oxford Dictionary* can only be used in active constructions, whereas *shown* can be used in either active or passive. This helps to explain why *shown* is very much more common as past participle than *showed*, by the evidence of English databases: approximately 200 instances of *shown* to 2 or 3 of *showed*.

Note that the use of *shew* (*shewed/shewn*) for **show** etc. is a relic of older usage rather than current style. It makes no showing in the Australian ACE corpus, nor its American counterpart, and there are just 2 instances of *shew* in the British corpus, against more than 300 of **show**.

shred   All dictionaries prefer *shredded* for the past forms (past tense and participle), though **shred** is also recognised. Fowler thought that **shred** was archaic for the past forms, and the most familiar past form of the verb (in phrases like *shredded coconut* and *shredded paper*) serves to reinforce *shredded*. More than 90% of Australians surveyed at the 1992 Style Council used *shredded* for both past forms of **shred**.

shrink   This verb has long had three principal parts: *shrink/shrank/shrunk*. Yet *shrunk* is quite commonly used instead of *shrank* for the past tense, and is certainly not an archaism, as Fowler thought. It is a recognised alternative in comprehensive modern dictionaries in Australia, the USA and Britain, and appears especially with the meaning of reduced physical size, as in the movie title: *HONEY, I SHRUNK THE KIDS.* Note however that *shrank* keeps its place as the past tense for more figurative uses of the verb, as in:
> *They shrank back from the furnace.*

As far as the past participle itself goes, *shrunk* is the regular form:
> *His socks had shrunk in the wash.*
> *The open spaces had all shrunk since the last time I was there.*

The role of *shrunken* is strictly as an adjective, as in *a shrunken physique*, or figuratively *shrunken ideals*.

SI units These are the units of the *Système International* which are the basis of our metric system. (See further under **metrication** and in Appendix IV.)

Sian See under **China**.

sic This Latin word means literally "thus". It's used by scholars when they quote from an earlier source and find themselves wishing to show that the quotation is exactly as it was written, even if the choice of words seems surprising or erroneous.

> *"Sydney Harbor Bridge is one of the most elegant suspension [sic] bridges in the world ..."*
>
> *"To seperate [sic] emotion from pure reason is the ultimate spiritual exercise ..."*

As the examples show, **sic** is placed in brackets immediately after the word in question. It usually appears in italics, and is framed by square brackets rather than parentheses, to show that it's an editorial interpolation. (See further under **brackets**.)

   Sic is essentially a neutral device which says "That's how it was". Yet because it questions the wording of another writer, it introduces a critical element, and done too often it seems rather offensive to the author being quoted (like constant interjections). It can easily trivialise what's being quoted, and distract from the real issues under discussion. The Australian Government *Style Manual* (1988) nevertheless proposed an extension of the use of **sic** to spotlight sexist language in quotations. Once again it would be overdoing it if editors marked every generic use of *he* with **sic**. A general footnote on the matter could draw attention to the problem of sexist language, without intruding on the quotation itself.

sideward or **sidewards** See under **-ward**.

sideways or **sidewise** See under **-wise**.

signaled or **signalled, signaling** or **signalling** The choice between these is discussed under **-l/-ll-**.

signor, signore or **signora** These are Italian titles and forms of address. **Signor** is equivalent to "Mr" and the standard title referring to men, even *Il signor Caruso*. In direct address to men, **Signore** serves as the equivalent of "Sir". **Signora** is used both for "Mrs" in ordinary titles for women, and for "Madam" in direct address.

   Note that the plural of the feminine **signora** is *signore*—identical with the masculine form of address. The plural of the masculine **signore** is *signori*.

silent letters Many English words have **silent letters** in their spelling, i.e. ones which do not correspond to a particular sound in the pronunciation. Quite often they represent sounds which were heard in the word centuries ago, as with *bright*, *knife* and *write*. Other **silent letters** were inserted in early modern

English to connect the English spelling with classical antecedents, as with *debt*, *isle* and *rhyme*; or to distinguish homophones, as with *grille*, *racquet* and *sheriff*. The examples confirm that most letters of the alphabet can be silent in a particular word.

The most *common silent letter* of all in English is *e*. It has developed several roles as a diacritic or marker of the sound values of adjacent letters. Following a *c* or *g*, as in *traceable* or *wage*, the *e* serves to "soften" the sound. (See further under **-ce/-ge**.) In many simple words it serves to show that the vowel before the preceding consonant is either long or a diphthong. Compare:

mate	with	*mat*
mete		*met*
bite		*bit*
rode		*rod*
tube		*tub*

Silent letters have often been the target of spelling reformers, who are inclined to see them as phonetic deadwood. This makes them overlook what **silent letters** do for visual recognition of words, helping us to distinguish homophones at first glance (e.g. *sign/sine*), and forging links between related words whose pronunciation sets them apart (e.g. *sign/signify*). (See further under **spelling**.)

silicon or **silicone**   The ending makes a crucial difference for chemists and for us all. **Silicon** is a hard, nonmetallic element, commonly found in sand. **Silicone** is a plastic compound which includes **silicon**, carbon and oxygen. **Silicon** is the better known of the two, through the *silicon chip* and its uses in electronics, computers and the glass industry. **Silicone** is a synthetic rubber, used for such things as artificial limbs and in cosmetic surgery, and also an ingredient of various lubricants and polishes.

Note that *silica* is an alternative name for another *silicon compound, silicon oxide* (or dioxide).

silvan or **sylvan**   See under **i/y**.

simile   See under **metaphor**.

simple or **simplistic**   Simple is an uncomplicated word which means "straightforward, easy", as in a *simple solution*. A *simplistic solution* is one which is too easy, i.e. it oversimplifies and fails to deal with the complexities of the situation. So **simplistic** is negatively charged, whereas **simple** is neutral or has positive connotations. Because **simplistic** is the longer and more academic-looking word, it's sometimes misguidedly chosen by those who want to make their words more impressive. The result can be disastrous, as in:

This machine represents the latest hi-tech information-retrieval device for the office, and comes with simplistic instructions on how to operate it ...

Heaven help the operator!

simple sentences   See under **clauses** section 1.

since As a conjunction **since** is sometimes ambiguous, because it can express a relationship of either time, or cause and effect:

She hasn't stopped talking since she arrived. (time)

The others just smiled since they were too polite to interrupt. (cause)

The first use is more common than the second, and it coincides with temporal use of **since** as an adverb and preposition. Yet the second (causative) use hangs around as an alternative possibility in sentences such as:

Their children have avoided going out since their father was retrenched.

To settle any ambiguity, it would be better to use a conjunction which is unmistakably temporal or causative. (See further under **conjunctions** section 3.)

sine These letters add up to a one-syllabled word used in mathematics (**sine**); and a two-syllabled word in several borrowed Latin phrases where it means ''without''.

Sine die means ''without (setting) a day''. It is noted when a formal group disbands without deciding on a day for their next meeting. Sometimes it implies indefinite postponement.

For *sine prole*, see under **decessit sine prole**.

Sine qua non means literally ''without which not''. It refers to something indispensable, without which things could not happen or be achieved.

Singapore This is the name of the island at the foot of the Malay peninsula, as well as its capital city. Once part of Malaysia, it has been an independent republic since 1965. Its population comprises a majority of Chinese people, together with some of Malay and Indian origin. The official languages are Malay, Mandarin Chinese, Tamil and English, though English prevails as the language of administration.

Note that the adjective is normally *Singaporean*: only the *Oxford Dictionary* notes the occasional use of *Singaporian*.

single for double In the writing of English words, the use of single or double consonants can be crucial to their identity, witness *latter* and *later*, *supper* and *super*. In some verbs this makes the contrast between present (*write*) and past (*written*), and is once again a fixed and permanent aspect of the spelling. Yet the use of *single and double consonants* is also a variable aspect of some words.

Like many spelling variables its roots go back to the eighteenth century. In Johnson's dictionary of 1755 we notice vacillation over it, in pairs such as *distil* and *instill*, and *downhil* and *uphill*. Discrepancies like those suggest that earlier on in the dictionary he applied a spelling rule which he later abandoned. The ''rule'' is the one which underlies certain distinctive British spellings, such as *appal*, *extol* and *enthral* which contrast with American *appall*, *extoll* and *enthrall*. The principle was also applied in the middle of words such as:

already altogether chilblain dulness fulfil fulness skilful wilful

But the double *l* has returned to **dullness** and **fullness**, and to *fulfill* for many people; and American English has it in **skillful** and **willful**. (See further under individual headings.)

Single for double in loanwords. The tendency to replace double with single consonants can also be seen (though more erratically) in English treatment of loanwords. It creates alternative spellings for some like *cannel(l)oni*, and affects consonants other than *l*, in *cap(p)uc(c)ino*, *gar(r)ot(t)e* and *guer(r)illa*. Sometimes it's seen in the spelling of *diarrhea* as *diarhea* and *hemorrhage* as *hemorhage*. Many loanwords like those are without analogues in English, so there's no clear rationale for keeping the double consonant.

All this helps to explain why the question of single or double consonants vexes many a writer. Unfortunately it does not change the fact that double consonants are fixed into the spelling of many English words. It is still considered a mistake to write *accomodation* for *accommodation*, *exagerate* for *exaggerate* etc.

singular See under **number**.

Sinhalese or **Singhalese** See under **Sri Lanka**.

sink There are two past tenses for this verb: *sank* and *sunk*. *Sank* can be used with both transitive and intransitive constructions, whereas *sunk* is mostly used for the transitive. Compare:

>*The vessel sank without trace.* (intransitive)
>*The dog sank its teeth into the milkman's leg.* (transitive)
>*They sunk a lot of capital into deer farms.* (transitive)

(See further under **transitive**.)

Note also that *sunk* is the regular past participle for the verb whether transitive or not:

>*They have sunk a lot of capital into deer farms.*
>*The vessel had sunk without trace.*

The older past participle *sunken* is rarely found now in the verb phrase, and mostly reserved for use as an adjective, as in *a sunken garden*, *with sunken eyes*. Note however that in technical expressions, *sunk* serves as the adjective: *sunk fence*.

sinus For the plural, see **-us** section 2.

siphon or **syphon** See under **i/y**.

Sir Convention has it that this title of honor cannot be used with a plain surname. This is why the former premier of Queensland was always *Sir Joh Bjelke-Petersen* and a former governor-general *Sir Zelman Cowen*. Note that the same principle applies to *Dame*, as in *Dame Mary Gilmore*.

For the application of the same principle to *Reverend*, see under **names**.

sirup or **syrup** See under **i/y**.

sister-in-law See in-laws.

situ See in situ.

sizable or **sizeable** See under -eable.

skeptic or **sceptic, skeptical** or **sceptical, skepticism** or **scepticism** Skeptical perpetuates the Greek form of the word and was indeed the earlier form in English, which helps to explain its use in American English. It was also the spelling used by Dr Johnson in his dictionary, and the one preferred by Fowler because it works better in terms of English spelling-sound conventions (see **-ce/-ge**).

Sceptical is given preference in Australian and British dictionaries, and though it outnumbers **skeptical** by 11:1 in the Australian ACE corpus, Murray-Smith, author of *Right Words* (1989) thought the **sk** spelling was on the increase. **Skeptical** has the better credentials altogether.

Note that the rationale for choosing between **skeptical** and **sceptical** also carries over to **skeptic/sceptic** and **skepticism/scepticism**.

skilful or **skillful** The older spelling is **skillful**, and it remains standard in the USA. In Britain the spelling was modified to **skilful** in the eighteenth century, and perpetuated through Dr Johnson's dictionary. Australians have inherited the British spelling, though the American one is on the increase here.

slang Broadly speaking **slang** is language which refuses to conform. It sidesteps the vocabulary of standard English, and creates its own, sometimes offhanded and casual (like *sickie* and *rego*), sometimes direct and coarse (like *rip off* and *play silly buggers*). **Slang** has frontiers with colloquial language, as well as with the taboo and obscene.

Unlike standard language **slang** is always somewhat limited in its currency. It's often short-lived, witness words such as *cool, grouse, neat* and *unreal*. Slang words of commendation never seem to last long, and even those for tangible things (*the flicks, black maria*) seem to change with the times. A few **slang** words work their way into the standard: *bus, cheat, dwindle* and *mob* are examples from the eighteenth century. But thousands more live and die in the same century, and even the same decade.

The currency of **slang** is often limited also by being used by a particular group of people, defined by their age, social class, occupation or recreation. A certain use of *rage* has been part of Australian teenage **slang**, just as *googly* is best known among cricketers and their fans. The knowledge of such terms and the natural right to use them goes with belonging to such groups, and the words also serve to exclude those who do not belong. Many **slang** words are limited geographically. Some are just Australianisms, and some only used in a particular state or region, such as the Riverina. (See further under **interstate differences**.)

All these limitations on **slang** help to explain why it's usually avoided in formal prose, and in any writing which has to communicate to a wide audience or withstand the test of time. It is more than a matter of style, if you want to be sure that the meaning gets through. Both Ronald Reagan and Bob Hawke have puzzled the international community with their respective **slang** (Reagan with the American *flaky*, and Hawke with *play funny buggers*). **Slang** is a liability if you forget or don't know the limits of its use.

The vigor and vitality of **slang** still makes it a useful resource now and then for making a point. A phrase like the *golden handshake* expresses a certain indignation about the retirement packages offered to company directors, in a way that the standard phrase never could. The Hansard records of parliament nowadays include the **slang** uttered by members in the course of debate, to ensure that the flavor of the debate comes across along with its substance.

(See further under **colloquialisms**, **flash language**, and **rhyming slang**.)

slash This is an alternative name for the **solidus**, a single oblique stroke (see further under that heading). Slashes used in pairs are *slash brackets*. (See **brackets** section 1.)

Slavic, Slavonic or **Slavonian** In both Australia and America, **Slavic** is the standard form of the adjective referring to the languages and culture of the *Slavs*. In Britain **Slavonic** is the equivalent term. Both **Slavonic** (dating from 1645) and **Slavonian** (from 1598) were based on the geographical name *Slavonia* (a region within Croatia in the former republic of Yugoslavia). But from their earliest use, both **Slavonian** and **Slavonic** could refer more broadly to the language and culture of the *Slavs*, just as **Slavic** (first recorded in 1813) now does.

slay The past forms of this verb depend on whether you're using it in its standard meaning "kill", or the more colloquial "overwhelm with pleasure or amusement". For the first sense the past tense is *slew*, and the past participle *slain*. For the second it becomes a regular verb with *slayed* serving for both past forms.

sled, sledge or **sleigh** Snow transport is remote from most Australians, and our use of all three words is second-hand. All three seem to go back to a Dutch word for a snow vehicle. **Sledge** is the broadest term and the one used in Britain for snow vehicles which either tow loads or people. In North America the **sled** is used for smaller *sledges* which carry goods, and **sleigh** for those which carry people. The **sledge** used for downhill sports is called either a **sled** or *toboggan*. This last word is in fact the one most often heard in Australia, a loanword from Canadian Indians.

slew or **slayed** See under **slay**.

Slovak See under **Czechoslovakia**.

slow or **slowly** Formally speaking **slow** is the adjective, and **slowly** the adverb. But **slow** is often used as the adverb in short utterances and commands, such as *go slow*, and in some compound adjectives such as *slow-release drugs* and *slow-speaking assistant.*

When it comes to comparatives and superlatives, again the adjective forms *slower* and *slowest* often serve as adverbs too, as in:

> *My queue moved slower than yours.*

Compare:

> *My queue moved more slowly than yours.*

The second sentence would be preferable in a formal style, but the first is quite standard, and probably more common. (See further under **zero adverbs**.)

sly The derivatives of this word are usually spelled with *y* rather than *i*: *slyer, slyly, slyness.* (See further under **-y>-i-**.)

small caps This is the common abbreviation for *small capital* letters, ones which have the form of CAPITALS but roughly half their height. (In typographic terms, they are close to the x-height of the regular type.) **Small caps** are used in running text to set words off from those on either side, without making them distractingly LARGE. They are often used for the time abbreviations: AM/PM and AD/BC.

smell The past tense of this verb can be either *smelled* or *smelt* (see further under **-ed**). Note also that it can be followed by either an adjective or an adverb. Compare:

> *It smelled good.*
> *It smelled strongly of coffee.*

In the first sentence, *smelled* acts as a copular verb; in the second it expresses a material event. (See further under **verbs**.)

smoko or **smoke-oh** The spelling **smoko** has established itself as the standard spelling since it first appeared in 1896. **Smoke-oh** was used before then, and occasionally after, most recently by Frank Clune in the 1930s and 1940s. Clune is also the only author recorded in the *Australian National Dictionary* to use *smoke-o.*

The only plural recorded in the *National Dictionary* is *smokos*, as we might expect of a word which is a clipping. (See further under **-o**.)

smoulder or **smolder** The first is the standard spelling in Australia and Britain, the second in the USA. **Smolder** is the older of the two, first recorded as a verb in the fifteenth century. Its origins are rather obscure, and it seems to have gone underground during the seventeenth and eighteenth century—much like the kind of fire it refers to—before being revived by Sir Walter Scott.

snapper or **schnapper** The name **snapper** has been applied to at least three kinds of fish in Australian waters: the *Chrysophrys unicolor* of Western Australia, the *C. auratus* of South Australia, and the *C. guttulatus* of eastern Australia. Elsewhere in the world, the name applies to other species, including a group of food fishes found in the Gulf of Mexico, and the bluefish of the Atlantic coast of North America.

The *Australian National Dictionary* has rather more citations for **snapper** than for **schnapper**, though the germanised spelling seems to persist here. The Fishing Industry Council puts its weight behind *snapper* as the marketing name.

sniveling or **snivelling** The choice between these is discussed under **-l/-ll-**.

snorkel or **schnorkel** The second spelling shows the German origins of this word. It was the name for the ventilation and exhaust tube of a submarine, a figurative name, since as *Schnörchel* it embodies the German verb "snore". In Australian English the word usually refers to the tube which serves as a simple underwater breathing apparatus, and it's usually spelled **snorkel**. **Snorkel** is also a verb nowadays, which can become *snorkeled* or *snorkelled*. The arguments against doubling the final *l* are presented at **-l/-ll-**.

so A chameleon word, **so** takes its color and meaning from the context—either the surrounding words, or the physical context and particular people involved:

Take the flowers and arrange them so. (accompanied by gestures)
They had never been so exhausted. (in comparison with their earlier experience)

As those examples show, **so** is essentially a deictic adverb meaning "in this way" or "to this extent", and the open-endedness of the second meaning makes **so** a general-purpose intensifier: *I was so exhausted/excited/pleased/scared ...* **So** turns up frequently in conversation as an intensifier, and it's useful as an interpersonal cue to involve those with whom we're communicating. Other uses of **so** which invite or leave it to those listening to supply the information are *and so on*, *and so forth*, and *So-and-so said ...*, *you so-and-so*.

In writing **so** takes its meaning from accompanying clauses and sentences, especially when set in a parallel construction:

The doctor has advised her to take a holiday, and you must do so too.

There **so** stands (together with *do*) instead of *take a holiday*. It forges a cohesive link with it (see further under **coherence** or **cohesion**). Note that the clause with **so** matches the first one exactly in its structure. With a mixture of active and passive, the *do so* would not work:

She was advised to take leave and I did so too.

The mismatch of verb structures leaves the reader bemused about how to interpret the second clause.

So as a conjunction. **So** has long been part of compound conjunctions such as *so that* and *and so*. The meaning of *so that* has to be deduced from context, because it can express either purpose or result:

They left early so that they couldn't possibly miss the train.
The train was cancelled so that they waited for hours.

Note that *so that* could be reduced to just **so** in the second sentence, though hardly in the first:

The train was cancelled so they waited for hours.
It could also be expressed as:
The train was cancelled and so they waited ...
The fact that **so** can be interchanged with *and so* suggests that **so** itself is very close to being a coordinating conjunction in modern English. Few grammars yet recognise it as such, probably because it's much more common in speech than writing. In Fries's 1940 data **so** occurred six times more often in his informal written material than the standard prose. With such a solid base of support, its use in writing is likely to increase. (See further under **conjunctions**.)

sobriquet See under **nom de plume**.

social or **sociable** Applied to people, these mean much the same. Compare:
They're very social people.
They're very sociable people.
If there is a difference, it is that **social** embodies the more abstract idea of being inclined to seek the society of others, whereas **sociable** suggests being ready to make friends and be good company.

Beyond that **sociable** has few applications while **social** has very many. It represents the more abstract and impersonal notion of society at large, in phrases such as *social problems* (problems in the structure of society), *social welfare* (services provided for the community), and *social sciences* (the study of human society and human behavior). In all such uses **social** is a neutral and definitive word, which serves to contrast *social sciences* with the *physical/natural sciences*, and *social services* with those provided for such things as health and education. In expressions such as *social events* it often contrasts with events at which matters of business are paramount. A *social club* distinguishes itself from ones set up for more specific purposes, such as a tennis club or a wine club.

The antonym of **sociable** is *unsociable*, which simply means "not disposed to be convivial". *Antisocial* is sometimes used that way as well, as in:
I'm going to be antisocial and watch the TV news.
However *antisocial* can also mean "negatively oriented towards the community at large", as in:
There were antisocial graffiti all over the station walls.
The rare *unsocial* is a little different, and applied to things which are unconducive to social intercourse, as in:
A newspaperman's working hours make for an unsocial way of life.
Once again, the negative forms of **social** have a wider range of meanings than the negative form of **sociable**.

solecism Older usage commentators including Fowler use this word to identify a fault in sentence construction, especially of agreement, as in *you was*. **Solecism** thus contrasted with *barbarism* which was a malformation of a word, for example *brung*. But **solecism** has always had other uses in English, to refer to any error or incongruity, or breach of etiquette, and these are now probably more widely known than its exact linguistic sense.

solidus Editors worldwide use the term **solidus** for the punctuation mark also known in Britain as the *diagonal, slash* or *oblique*. In North America **solidus** (used by the Chicago *Manual of Style*) shares the field with *virgule* (the term preferred by *Webster's Style Manual* as well as *Webster's Dictionary* and *Random House*). In Australia the Government *Style Manual* works with **solidus**, though *slash* is increasingly widely used. Yet another term for it, used by many when dictating or reading punctuation aloud, is *stroke*.

By whatever name, the **solidus** has as its prime function to separate words which are alternatives, and invite the reader to consider each in turn:

They'll arrange road/rail transport for the teams.

Each applicant must bring his/her birth certificate.

For the use of **and/or**, see under that heading.

Sometimes the **solidus** offers alternative readings of the same word:

Everyone can bring their own friend/s.

Style guides are uneasy over using a **solidus** when it means "and" rather than "or", as in:

the June/July recess

the 1990/1 financial year

Most restrict it to cases such as those where there are spans of time or adjacent numbers involved. *Copy-editing* (1992) stands alone in allowing it to have a reciprocal meaning, as in *an oil/water interface*. Others would use an en rule there.

1 *Solidus* with numbers. The **solidus** is conventionally used as a separator in certain kinds of numerical expressions:
* in dates. 21/7/90
* in fractions: 3/4 when the vertical setting is not available
* as a substitute for *per* in expressions of measurement, when the units of measurement are shown as symbols rather than full words, as in *145 km/hr*

In the days before decimal currency, a **solidus** was used to separate the shillings from the pence. So *10/6* meant "ten shillings and sixpence".

2 *Solidus* in poetry and phonetics. When quotations of poetry are integrated with ordinary text, the **solidus** serves to mark the boundary between the lines of the original verse:

The opening lines of the British national anthem: *God save our gracious Queen/Long live our noble Queen* contain two examples of the subjunctive.

In writing phonetics, twin *solidi* (or *slash brackets*) are used to mark the beginning and end of phonemic symbols (see further under **brackets** section 1).

Historical note The word **solidus** is Latin in origin, hence the plural *solidi*. The word referred to the middle denomination of Roman currency, in the series *librae, solidi, denarii*. When abbreviated they were *l.s.d.*, which were then identified with the "pounds, shillings and pence" of British currency. Thus the **solidus** was equated with the shilling. This may explain why the **solidus** is sometimes called the "shilling mark". *Webster's Dictionary* adds that the oblique line which divided the shillings from the pence (in sums like *10/6*) was a straightened form of the "long *s*" used for shillings. (See further under **S**.)

soliloquy See under **monologue**.

sombre or **somber** See under **-re/-er**.

-some This Old English suffix has served to create two kinds of words, though nowadays it seems to produce only nonce formations.
  Firstly, it's the formative element in deriving certain adjectives out of other words, especially verbs:
> *cumbersome fearsome irksome loathsome quarrelsome*
> *troublesome wearisome*
In *wholesome* its base is an adjective (as it was in *handsome*, based on an adjective closely related to *handy*, which meant "convenient" and then "attractive"). In *winsome* the base was *wyn*, an obsolete noun for pleasure.
  A second role of **-some** is to create informal nouns referring to a small group of a specific number, as in *twosome*, *threesome* and *foursome*.

somebody and **someone** For these indefinite pronouns the crucial question is which pronoun to use in agreement with them. The second element (*body/one*) suggests that the following pronoun should be singular, but this involves choosing between *him/his* and *her*, both of which are regrettably specific in terms of gender. Many people therefore prefer to use *them/their*, in spite of their association with the plural. (See further under **agreement** section 2.)

sometimes or **sometime** These indefinite words are definitely fluid in their meanings. Nowadays, **sometimes** is purely an adverb, whereas **sometime** can be either adverb or adjective. Compare:
> *They sometimes arrive unannounced.*
> *Come up and see me sometime.*
> *They flew in sometime last week.*
> *Meet Mr K. resident and sometime Mayor of Richmond.*
The examples show how the time reference in **sometime(s)** varies. **Sometimes** in the first sentence includes both past and future in a statement of a recurrent event. As an adverb **sometime** refers to a particular time, in either the future or the past, depending on the tense of the verb. As an adjective **sometime** means "for a period in the past". However it can also mean "occasional" and even "transient" in the phrase *a sometime thing*. The Gershwin song *A woman is a sometime thing* (1935) may have helped to popularise this meaning and add to it connotations of fickleness. This usage is confirmed by a number of postwar citations in the *Oxford Dictionary*, yet it was rejected by about 70% of the

Heritage Dictionary usage panel, perhaps because of its association with the South and West of the USA.

Note that both words have slightly changed meanings when set as two words:
Some times when I visit he doesn't know me.
We've had some times together.
Can you find some time to meet on Friday?
They'll spend some time in Budapest.
In the first three sentences, *time(s)* means a particular time or occasion; in the fourth, it means a period of time.

son et lumière This is French for "sound and light". For twentieth century tourists it's a way of re-creating history in a time-honored building and its precincts, with the help of floodlighting, pageantry, music and a recorded commentary. The first **son et lumière** was devised in 1952 by French architect Paul Robert-Houdin. The expression has since been applied to other media, including writing which has dramatic and visual qualities, and publications with a wealth of graphic aids, which bring history to life like a **son et lumière** performance.

son-in-law See in-laws.

sophisticated or **sophistical** The first of these is commoner by far, and usually expresses respect for cultivated taste in whatever field it's applied. **Sophistical** describes a kind of argument which is not really respected: though clever and plausible, it is unilluminating, and does not help to resolve issues.

soprano The plural of this is usually *sopranos*. (See under **Italian plurals**.)

sort of For more or less formal uses of this phrase, see under **kind of**.

sotto voce In Italian this is literally "under the voice", i.e. "in an undertone". It refers to something said or sung in a low voice, so that it cannot generally be heard. On stage it's often an aside, used to create dramatic irony.

sound symbolism The sounds of language create patterns and imagery which can contribute to the meaning. (See further under **onomatopoeia** and **phonesthemes**.)

south, southern and **southerly** On early maps the uncharted shape which was eventually to be called *Australia* was sometimes labeled the "Great South Land". But within Australia the terms **south** and **southern** serve to identify the cooler parts of the continent, as in *South Australia* and the *Southern Ocean*. Those from Queensland and the Northern Territory are inclined to speak of those from anywhere south of latitude 28 as "Southerners", a name which is neutral enough. A less-than-neutral use of **south** is to be found in the "Deep South", sometimes used by incorrigible Sydneysiders to refer to Victoria.

As elsewhere in the world, **southerly** is applied to winds and ocean currents which stream from the south. For many Australians the **southerly** has special significance in providing relief from seeringly hot days, with the *southerly buster* in Sydney, and the *southerly doctor* (or *Fremantle doctor*) in Perth.

Southeast Asia or **South-East Asia** For Australians this is a conventional expression for the large geopolitical entity to the north of us, including the southeastern corner of mainland Asia from Malaysia through to Vietnam, and the many offshore islands, from Indonesia to the Philippines. Increasingly the expression is set solid rather than hyphenated.

Southern Hemisphere See under **antipodes**.

southward or **southwards** See under **-ward**.

Soviet Until the breakup of the USSR, **Soviet** was a useful adjective for referring to aspects of the union and its citizens—far preferable to *Russian* for most of the diverse peoples it included. But the word **Soviet** itself is now under a cloud, and *Russian* is returning as the natural candidate, with the *Russian Federation* representing what remains of the USSR at the United Nations. (See further under **Russia**.)

sow The past tense of **sow** is always *sowed*. The past participles can be either *sown* or *sowed*, though *sown* is certainly more common—to judge by the evidence of English databases, and the strong endorsement by 98% of those surveyed at the 1992 Style Council. Dictionaries everywhere register the alternative form *sowed*, which (though it goes back centuries) has yet to dominate and complete the conversion of *sow* to the regular pattern of verbs. (See further under **irregular verbs**.)

SP, **sp.** and **s.p.** In full capitals this abbreviates "starting price" as in *SP bookmaker*. In lower case with a final stop only (**sp.**) it stands for one of several words, including *specimen, species* and *spelling*. With two stops (**s.p.**) it represents the Latin *sine prole*: see **decessit sine prole**.

-speak George Orwell bequeathed us this suffix via the term *newspeak*, which he coined in the novel *1984* for a type of language that people had reason to be uneasy about. It has helped to generate words for various new styles of communicating, such as *adspeak, computer speak* and *science speak*. Such compounds are faintly pejorative, though more because of the jargon in them than because they threaten society as we know it. The use of the suffix in *Hawkespeak, Jospeak* and *Thatcherspeak* highlights their idiosyncrasies of speech, but is not particularly sinister. Compare **-ese**.

special pleading This phrase originated in the courts where it refers to a lawyer's statement of the particular issues affecting the case about to be heard. It also points out new matter which will be presented to refute the arguments of the opposing counsel. From these strictly legal applications, the phrase has been reinterpreted to mean an unprofessional style of argumentation found in many ordinary contexts—a one-sided style of argument, which concentrates on what is favorable to the case being argued, and avoids counterissues.

speciality or **specialty** See **specialty**.

specially or **especially** Though *special* has supplanted *especial* in contemporary English, **especially** is much more common now than **specially**— according to the evidence of English databases. **Especially** dominates by 10:1 in the Australian ACE corpus, and by 18:1 in the equivalent British corpus. This large difference in frequency is because **especially** works as a general-purpose subjunct and modifier of adjectives and whole phrases, as in:
> *There was nothing especially difficult in the plan.*
> *He wanted it especially for his children.*

The meaning of **especially** ranges from "very" (an intensifier) in the first example, to "above all" (a particulariser) in the second. In conversation **specially** could be used in such sentences, but in writing it would look somewhat informal.

Specially does however have its own uses in prose, where it means "for a specific purpose", as in:
> *a chair which is specially designed for people with short legs* or
> *These cards were made specially for the Governor-General.*

As in those examples, it typically modifies the past participle of a verb, and is technically an adjunct rather than a subjunct. (See further under **adverbs**.) **Especially** could not be used in such sentences without blurring the meaning.

specialty or **speciality** These words can apply either to a special product, or to a special pursuit, and dictionaries confirm that they are interchangeable. English databases show that Americans prefer **specialty** for both meanings, while the British prefer **speciality** with its extra syllable. Australian English is heir to both, and they are about equally represented in the ACE corpus.

species For the plural of this word, see under **Latin plurals**.

spectre or **specter** See under **-re/-er**.

speed The past forms of this can be either *sped* or *speeded*, though they carry slightly different meanings. *Sped* is used for the ordinary sense of quick motion by a train, tram, bus, car or even skis or a skateboard. *Speeded* is used in two special contexts. One is when it's a matter of excessive speed, as in:
> *The truck had speeded all the way to Albury.*

The second is the more abstract use of **speed**, as in:
> *The work must be speeded up to meet the deadline.*

spell When it means "give the letters of a word", the past form may be either *spelled* or *spelt*. (See further under **-ed**.) Either form may be used in related figurative expressions such as:
> *He spelled/spelt out all the duties of the secretary.*

The news spelled/spelt doom for them all.
When *spell* means "give a spell (or rest) to", the only possible past is *spelled.*

spelling, rules and **reform** English spelling is the product of a long period
of evolution. It embodies the changing culture of centuries of history. It
preserves mutants and fossils along with the mainstream of more or less
regularly spelled words. Some claim that about 85% of English words conform
to spelling rules, though the irregular ones are the focus of most comment and
criticism. See for example sets such as:
   cough dough plough rough through thorough
   (words with the same spelling but different sounds)
   eat meet key quay chief receive people police ski amoeba faeces
   (multiple spellings for the same sound)
In cases like those you have to know the whole word to get the spelling right.

1 *Spelling adjustments of the past.* Attempts to reconnect the **spelling** of
English words with their sounds are to be found in almost every century. Anglo-
Norman scribes revised the **spelling** of various consonants and vowels in the
wake of the Norman Conquest; and in the thirteenth century an English monk
demonstrated an experimental *spelling system* in a poem called *Ormulum,*
attempting to use single and double consonants more consistently. The
introduction of printing to England in the fifteenth century created many
alternative spellings as printers grappled with new technology. They reduced
the blank spaces in a line by adding an extra *e* to words here and there, or
swapping an *i* for a *y.*
   All these arbitrary changes to words (as well as changes in pronunciation
which complicated the relationship between sounds and letters) left sixteenth
century scholars skeptical about basing a word's **spelling** on its sound, and more
inclined to look for a firm basis in its historical form. Renaissance scholarship
brought to light the classical antecedents of many English words, showing how
the **spelling** had diverged over the centuries, and confirming some of the
respellings which had already begun to filter through from French sources. And
while the movement towards classical respelling petered out in France, it
continued in England, linking words with their ultimate etymology. This
principle accounts for the bracketed letters in all of the following, which were
earlier spelled without them:
   a(d)venture   dou(b)t   fau(l)t   recei(p)t   t(h)rone
Some of the medieval and Renaissance respellings were misguided. Words with
no classical ancestry were touched up according to classical spelling analogies:
   a(d)miral   from Arabic (made like *admire*)
   i(s)land   from Old English (made like *isle*)
   s(c)ythe   from Old English (made like *scissors*)
Debate continued as to whether it was more useful to base **spelling** on the
etymology or the sounds of a word. But the **spelling** of most common words
was standardised during the seventeenth century, and only fine-tuning took place

in the eighteenth century, such as removing ''superfluous letters'' (as in *logic(k)* and *music(k))*, and the respelling of *k* with the French *qu*, as in *quay* and *cheque*.

2 *Standardisation.* In comparison with pronunciation, **spelling** is very highly standardised, yet not all English words have the same **spelling** everywhere. The biggest divide in **spelling** is between *British standard spelling* and the American standard, both of which are known in Australia. *American spelling* sometimes differs from British when it preserves the older forms (as with *check* and *skeptic*), which were taken across the Atlantic in the seventeenth and eighteenth century, before the words had been subjected to fine-tuning and frenchification. Later British spelling often differentiates words (such as *ensure/insure* and *kerb/ curb*) which have the same **spelling** in American English. In general *British spellings* follow those of Dr Johnson's dictionary of 1755, while *American spellings* are in line with those of Noah Webster's later dictionaries of 1828 and 1838. *American spelling* applies the rules to more of the susceptible words in any set, and is less inclined to create exceptions on grounds of etymology. In Britain the reverse is true. So American English uses *-ize* everywhere possible, allowing it in words like *advertize* and *comprize* where etymology argues for *-ise*. It even extends the rule to words like *analyze* (rather than *analyse*). The following entries deal with the major points on which *American* and *British spelling* differ:
   ae   i/y   -ise/-ize   -l/-ll-   oe   -or/-our   -re/-er
Overall *American spelling* is more standardised than that of British or Australian English, though it is not without its own anomalies.

3 *Spelling rules.* All varieties of English make use of certain conventional practices in **spelling**, which are detailed at the following entries, together with examples:
   -e   -c/-ck   -ce/-ge   doubling of final consonant   -f/-v-
   i>y   i before e   -o   -y>-i-

4 *Spelling reform.* Because *English spelling* is neither perfect nor fully standardised, there is scope for streamlining it. Yet most reformers recognise that it would take an enormous effort to overhaul the present system, even in one English-speaking country like Australia, let alone through the whole English-speaking world. There is no constitutional authority to enforce **spelling** changes, and even if there were, it seems doubtful whether people would be willing to follow it to the letter. Dr Johnson doubted whether British citizens of the eighteenth century would have been willing to obey the dictates of a language academy, and his arguments still ring true today:
   The edicts of an English academy would probably be read by many only that they might be sure to disobey them ... The present manners of our nation deride authority ...
Yet we can perhaps achieve something by modest adjustments, preferring more regular **spellings** wherever they are already used by a group of significant size,

or familiar even as minority variants in Australia. The argument applies to **spellings** such as *archeology, artifact, color, defense, fulfill, spoiled, traveler,* and many others. None of those **spellings** is revolutionary. They simply represent further applications of rules which are applied in many other words.

A more controversial step, though still not revolutionary, would be to extend a *standardised spelling* to all words in large sets such as the following:

-able/-ible   -ant/-ent   -ary/-ery/-ory   -er/-or

The rationale for using one rather than the other is buried in individual word history, and one or two pairs in each set are already interchangeable, for example: *collapsable/collapsible, dependant/dependent, accessary/accessory, convener/convenor.* Because there's no distinction in meaning or sound for those suffixes, it seems perverse that differences in **spelling** should be maintained for so many of them, differences which may get the better of otherwise excellent writers. It would be a kindness to all to allow alternatives, or else to suggest that the most common suffix in each set (*-able, -ent, -ary, -er*) be used for all words formed with it. Those who wished could continue to use the *traditional spelling* for each word in the set, but others could use a *standardised spelling* for the suffix, without fear of being ridiculed for bad spelling. It seems unfortunate when adults with a full secondary education still have to reach for the dictionary, and it reflects on the arbitrary details of the *spelling system* as much as on their education and competence. A few systematic reforms like those mentioned would tidy up the system, and lighten the load for everyone, without allowing that "anything goes".

spill The past forms of *spill* can be either *spilled* or *spilt*. Only when the word serves as an adjective, as in *spilt milk*, is the spelling fixed. (See further under the heading **-ed**.)

spin From having three principal parts *spin/span/spun*, this verb is now reduced to two, with *spun* used for both past tense and participle. *Span* and *spun* were equally matched in the nineteenth century, according to *Oxford Dictionary* citations, but *spun* has prevailed in the twentieth century for both literal and figurative uses of the word.

spiraled or **spiralled**, **spiraling** or **spiralling** See under **-l/-ll-**.

spiritual or **spirituous** **Spiritual** has everything to do with the spirit and the human soul, and strong religious overtones. **Spirituous** is totally secular. It relates only to spirits in the sense of distilled alcoholic beverages. The word is little used, though it's often seen above the doorway of the public bar, identifying the publican as a *licensed vendor of fermented and spirituous liquors*.

spit Modern dictionaries all allow either *spat* or **spit** for the past form of this verb. *Macquarie* and *Collins* give preference to *spat*, and this was greatly preferred by those surveyed at the 1992 Style Council, with a 100% vote for *spat* as the past tense, and 91% for the past participle (the rest being *spitted* and *spitten*). In the USA however **spit** is preferred, according to both *Webster's* and *Random House*, which makes it one of the verbs with **zero past tense**. (See further under that heading.)

splendor or **splendour** See under -**or/-our**.

split infinitive The "problem" of the **split infinitive** is the fruit of a misconception about English infinitives, the assumption they consist of two parts (*to* + the verb itself: *to read*), and that the two parts can never be split. In fact English infinitives do not necessarily come with the preceding *to* (see **infinitives**); and **split infinitives** were used for centuries before they became the bête noire of nineteenth century grammarians. Their censure has cast long shadows into the twentieth century, extended now by the computer style checker which can so easily be programmed to pick them up.

Reactions to the **split infinitive** still beg the question as to what is wrong with it. The answers to that question vary from "It's ungrammatical" to "It's inelegant". The first comment has no basis, as we've seen. The second is often subjective, though individual cases do need to be examined in their own terms. Having an adverbial phrase between the *to* and the verb can make awkward reading, as in:

I wanted to above all be near her.

It reads more smoothly as:

I wanted above all to be near her.

Yet there's no alternative place for the adverbial phrase in:

He wanted to more than match that offer.

A single-word adverb runs in smoothly enough, especially an intensifier:

He wanted to really talk to her.

If we made a point of not splitting the infinitive in that case, the result is less elegant and more ambiguous:

He wanted really to talk to her.

In some cases, the effort to avoid splitting the infinitive alters the meaning of the sentence. Compare:

He failed completely to follow the instructions.

He failed to completely follow the instructions.

There's little virtue in a sentence which avoids the **split infinitive** so clumsily as to make obvious what the writer was trying not to do:

The failure adequately to brief the pictorial editor was inexcusable.

Most style guides including Fowler recommend a judicious approach to splitting infinitives, and do not endorse the knee-jerk reaction of nineteenth century pedagogues or the twentieth century computer style checker. The consensus is *Don't* split an infinitive if the result is an inelegant sentence. *Do* split infinitives to avoid awkward wording, to preserve a natural rhythm, and especially to achieve the intended emphasis and meaning.

spoil The past form of this can be either *spoiled* or *spoilt*. (See further under -**ed**.) However in phrases such as a *spoilt child* where the word is an adjective, it's most often *spoilt*.

spoonfuls or **spoonsful** See under -**ful**.

spouse equivalent This term (or the extended *designated spouse equivalent*) is occasionally heard in administrative contexts as a way of referring to people involved in a domestic arrangement other than that of man and wife. Its value is that it is gender-free, and it can therefore be applied to either partner in a heterosexual relationship, as well as in homosexual ones.

But however useful the term is in legal and official documents, it leaves unsolved the problem of how to introduce or refer to one's *de facto* in ordinary conversation. (See further under **de facto**.)

spring The past tense of this verb may be either *sprang* or *sprung*, according to the major dictionaries everywhere. However all make *sprang* the primary spelling.

square brackets For the uses of square brackets, see under **brackets**.

square metres or **metres square** The order of the words makes a large difference to the size of the area being described. A room whose area is *6 square metres* may be 2 metres long and 3 metres wide (the two dimensions multiplied together make the square metrage). But if the room is *6 metres square*, its walls are all 6 metres long (its dimensions 6 m x 6 m), and the room is definitely square in shape. The first would be about the size of a ship's cabin: the second large enough for table tennis.

Note that the *square* in *a house of 17 squares* was equivalent to 100 square feet (or 10 feet square). In pre-metric days it served as a unit of floor space when advertising real estate.

squirreling or **squirrelling** For the choice between these, see under -**l/-ll-**.

Sri Lanka Since 1972 this has been the official name of the large Indian Ocean island which was formerly *Ceylon*. The largest single group within the Sri Lankan community (75%) are *Sinhalese*, who originated from Northern India. The Tamils from South India are the next largest group (20%). Since 1956 Sinhala has been the official language, though Tamil serves some official purposes in some areas.

Note that *Sinhalese* has replaced the older spelling of the same word (*Singhalese*). Earlier still it was *Cinghalese*.

-ssie or **-zzie** These are alternative spellings for the ending of a number of Australian colloquialisms such as:

cossie/cozzie (swimming costume)   mossie/mozzie (mosquito)
possie/pozzie (position)   pressie/prezzie (present)

The spellings with *zz* identify better the sound of the abbreviated word, whereas those with *ss* keep a visual link with the word they represent. In the case of *mozzie* and *prezzie*, the spelling with *zz* also prevents any spurious connections with *moss* and *press* respectively, and this would help to account for their strong showing in *Australian National Dictionary* citations. Yet *cossie* and *possie* are definitely preferred to their counterparts with *zz*, as are *Aussie* and *Tassy*. Those proper names are indeed the first words of this type to be recorded, beginning with *Tassy* in the last decade of the nineteenth century.

Note that *-y* is sometimes used instead of *-ie* for the final syllable, as in *possy* etc. This tends to make the words look more established than they feel. The *-ie* ending is more in keeping with their informal style. (See further under **ie/y**.)

St or **Saint** See **Saint**.

-st This ending is fixed in *against*, but the tide of usage has turned against it in *amidst*, *amongst* and *whilst*. (See **amid(st)** and **among(st)**, **while** or **whilst**.) In all of them the final *t* is something acquired over the centuries, like verdigris on a copper roof. The suffix was originally just *(e)s* as with some other adverbs (see further under **-s**); but from the sixteenth century the *t* seems to have been added on by analogy with the superlative ending.

stadium For the plural of this word, see under **-um**.

staff Like many old words ending in *f*, **staff** has a plural in which *ff* is replaced by *v* to create *staves*. Yet *staves* is no longer the regular plural for most applications of the word: only in historical and ceremonial contexts, and when it refers to the set of five lines on which music is scored is *staves* still used. For other uses, as when it refers to "sticks or rods", either *staves* or *staffs* may be used. When referring to the bodies of people who carry out the work of a company or institution, *staffs* is the only plural.

> *The staffs of all metropolitan state schools were on strike.*

Note that when used in this last sense, **staff** is a collective noun. The verb in agreement with it could therefore be either singular or plural:

> *They told me the staff was on strike.*
> *They told me the staff were on strike.*

(See further under **agreement** section 4.)

stalactite or **stalagmite** Most people need a mnemonic to remind them which of these grows downwards and which grows upwards—as well as which has *c* and which has *g* in it. Both questions are answered if you remember that **stalactites** descend from the ceiling or top of the cave (which gives you the *c* and *t* of the spelling); whereas **stalagmites** grow from the ground or mud on the cave floor (the *g* and *m* are there).

Both words are neoclassical, dating from the seventeenth century but formed with Greek stems: the first embodies a verbal adjective meaning "dripping or trickling", and the second a noun meaning a "drop".

stamen The plural of this botanical word for the pollen-bearing organ of a flower is usually *stamens*. Very rarely it appears as *stamina*, which is its correct Latin plural. This is one and the same word as *stamina* meaning "physical resilience". In Latin *stamen/stamina* meant "thread(s)", and as Roman myth had it, the threads of life were spun by the Fates until a person's dying day. So the idea that *stamina* related to longevity is very old, though our use of it to refer to someone's staying power on the tennis court (and elsewhere) is relatively new.

stanch or **staunch** See **staunch**.

standard English People sometimes speak of **standard English** as if it were a simple reference norm, like a standard gauge on the railway. How do expressions like *eccentric, off-beat, way-out* and *flaky* measure up to the standard? There is no easy answer, because words are not physical objects with linear dimensions. A standard in language is more abstract and more value-laden. The notion of **standard English** is often invoked by those who want to claim that a certain expression is correct and that another is effectively substandard.

   A less value-ridden approach to standard is to recognise that many expressions have a particular stylistic, regional or social character, which limits their usefulness in other contexts. Words with strong colloquial associations (such as *way-out*) are unsuitable for formal prose. *Eccentric* meanwhile is on the more formal side of the style range. This suggests that we could well define **standard English** as the kind of language which has no strong stylistic connotations, or—put the other way round—language which is neutral in style. An enormous body of words can in fact be used in any kind of context, forming a broad band between colloquial and slang on the one hand, and formal and technical language on the other.

FORMAL		TECHNICAL
	S T A N D A R D E N G L I S H	
COLLOQUIAL		SLANG

Apart from being stylistically neutral, **standard English** is neutral as to region. It avoids words with a strong local flavor, or ones which might not be understood outside the region of the world in which they are current idiom. An American colloquialism such as *flaky* is unsuitable for international communication. **Standard English** is free of regionalisms, so that by its use of words it could have originated anywhere in the English-speaking world. In this sense it's close to the notion of **international English** (see further under that heading.)

   The most contentious aspect of **standard English** is how far it is or can be neutral in social terms. Many would associate **standard English** with "educated

English'', and this seems to make it the prerogative of those who have enjoyed access to a full formal education. Yet **standard English** should not be equated with written English or bookish modes of expression. Again we would assert its neutrality in the social-educational spectrum of usage, so that **standard English** occupies the middle ground between illiterate expression and pedantic usage. It prefers *you* to *youse*, and would not go out of its way to use *whom*. (See further under **whom** and **youse**.)

Standard English is not the exclusive property of any social or regional group, but a resource to which English-speakers at large have access.

standard units See under **SI units**, **metrication** and Appendix IV.

stank or **stunk** See under **stink**.

state To capitalise or not to capitalise, that is the question. A capital letter serves to distinguish the *State of Victoria* from a *state of mind*, though the phrases themselves show perfectly clearly that **state** in the first is an administrative unit, and in the second a general condition. In *State of Victoria* the capital letter is part of a legal title, but in nonlegal contexts it's less essential than some authorities would have you believe. In plural references to the *Australian states* it's scarcely necessary (not being part of an official title), though the Australian Government *Style Manual* (1988) claims that *State* is "nearly always capitalised ... in any context".

Yet data from the ACE corpus shows a gradation in the use of a capital letter, even with the singular form of the word. In government documents *State* is almost always found with upper case; in newspapers it usually is, as in the many references to *State Government*; in magazines and journals the lower case is common, as in references to *state schools*. The gradation seems to correspond with the level of control on style. In government documents the *Style Manual's* recommendations are strictly observed; for many newspapers, the use of a capital for *State* is also prescribed by their style guide, though this does not prevent occasional appearances of *state coffers*, *state selectors* and *state development fund*, among others. But articles in magazines and journals are edited by a wide variety of people according to their own lights, and the references to **state** (= an Australian **state**) are often uncapitalised.

All this suggests that lower case is the natural state for an Australian **state** in contexts where it is generic rather than titular. In phrases like "any state of Australia" or "state legislation" the word speaks for itself, and there's no need or justification for upper case. (For the general principles of reducing capitalised words to lower case when their use is generic or plural, see under **capitals** section 1b.)

Compare **federal**.

statements In terms of sentence functions, **statements** contrast with questions and exclamations. A statement simply offers a piece of information and is not primarily intended to stimulate a reaction from the reader or listener. Contrast the ways in which questions, commands and exclamations work: they are indeed designed to elicit a response, either linguistic, behavioral or emotional, from the other party.

Sentences which are **statements** are phrased with the verb in the indicative, and always end with a full stop. (See further under **indicative** and **mood**.)

stationary or **stationery** The choice of spelling is in line with the grammar of the two words. Given the choice between -*ary* and -*ery*, the second spelling is only applied to nouns, whereas the first can be for either nouns or adjectives (see further under **-ary/-ery/-ory**). **Stationery** is therefore the only possible spelling for the noun referring to paper goods, and this leaves **stationary** for the adjective meaning ''not moving''. But the mistaken use of the latter in an advertisement for *a stationary cabinet* suggests the need to look for furniture which doesn't get up and walk away.

statistics For the choice between a singular or plural verb with this, see **-ic/-ics**. For the treatment of numbers in written documents, see **numbers** and **number style**.

status The plural of this word is discussed under **-us** section 2.

status quo This elliptical Latin phrase means the ''state in which ...''. It refers to an existing state of affairs, in contrast with proposed changes and alternatives. Sometimes it seems to imply a state which has been discontinued, as in *things have returned to the status quo*. Strictly speaking the phrase should then be *status quo ante*, the ''state in which (things were) before''—though that phrase is much less well known.

staunch or **stanch** **Staunch** is the more common spelling in Australia for the verb meaning ''stop the flow of or from'', yet either spelling is acceptable:
> *The ambulance officer staunched/stanched the blood from the damaged artery.*

In American usage as well as British, *stanched* seems to be the primary spelling, at least by its treatment as the primary headword in dictionaries. British style guides are more variable on the matter. While Fowler preferred **stanch**, the *Right Word at the Right Time* makes **staunch** its equal, and the *Bloomsbury Good Word Guide* hints that **stanch** is now slightly old-fashioned. Perhaps things are a-changing.

For the adjective meaning ''loyal'', **staunch** is very much the usual spelling everywhere, and **stanch** very rare. It derives ultimately from the same source as the verb, as is clear from its original meaning ''watertight''.

staves or **staffs** See staff.

stem This is the part of a word to which affixes are attached, the common element in sets of words like:
> *escalate escalator escalating de-escalated*

The **stem** can appear in more than one form in different words. In the case of *escalat(e)* it appears with and without a final *e*. In others like *refer(r)*, the final consonant may be doubled in some words but not others, witness:

refers   reference   referred   referring

In other languages such as French and Italian, individual *stems* vary a good deal more than in those English examples. See for example the set of *stems* for the French verb *venir* "come":

viens   venons   viennent   viendrai

Compare **root**.

stencil   Should it be *stenciled* or *stencilled* etc.? See under **-l/-ll-**.

step or **steppe**   These are now quite different words: **step** being the spelling for the English word meaning "level support for the foot when ascending or descending" (among other things), and **steppe** the spelling for the vast treeless plain of Russia. However the Russian word was simply spelled **step** in English up till the nineteenth century, which is in keeping with the original spelling. The spelling **steppe** is borrowed from French, though it might otherwise seem to owe something to the "olde Englysshe" mode of archaising familiar words.

-ster   There's life in this very old suffix, judging by the various nonce words which are still being created with it, including *bopster*, *jivester* and *popster*, to refer to the devotees of new twentieth century musical forms. Better known examples are the words for writers and composers of various kinds: *pulpster*, *punster*, *rhymster*, *songster* and *wordster*; as well as those for "con-artists" in other fields: *gangster*, *huckster*, *shyster*, *tipster* and *trickster*. Almost all recent formations are deprecating in some way, except *youngster*, and words such as *dragster*, *roadster*, *speedster*, *teamster*, which refer to a means of transport or those who use them.

According to the *Oxford Dictionary* **-ster** has an intricate history. It was originally a female agentive which paralleled *-er* for males. Yet scattered evidence in the following centuries suggests that it gradually became associated with the professional conduct of a trade by either men or women, whereas the *-er* suffix was used for the occasional practitioner. Thus the *brewer*, *spinner* and *weaver* turned their hand to the trade from time to time, while those whose livelihood depended on it were named *brewster*, *spinster* and *webster* respectively. (The modern word *pollster* represents the same kind of formation.) The evidence on this use of **-ster** varies in different parts of Britain, but the suffix evidently continued to be applied to women in the south until 1500, even though by 1300 it could be applied to men, with the professional meaning, in the north. However the gender and professional/part-time distinctions were complicated by the pejorative overtones of the suffix, which begin to be registered by 1400 and continue with many formations. The word *spinster* now seems to suffer from them all.

stigma This Greek loanword has both Greek and English plurals: *stigmata* and *stigmas*. *Stigmata* is very strongly associated with religious tradition in the Catholic Church (the mystical marks which symbolise the piercing of nails on the crucified body of Christ). *Stigmas* is the usual plural in secular use (when it means a mark of disgrace), and in its various scientific uses.

stimulus and **stimulant** Both these are used to refer to a physiological mechanism that stimulates the function of a body organ. The **stimulus** is normally that which initiates a process, while the **stimulant** increases it. Elsewhere their roles are quite different. **Stimulant** means a food (such as chocolate) or drink (such as coffee) or medication (such as pep pills) that stimulates the body. **Stimulus** is a more abstract word for anything which motivates and mobilises us to action.

Note that the plural of **stimulus** is still usually *stimuli*, in keeping with its Latin origin, though *stimuluses* is common enough in informal contexts. (See **-us** section 1.)

stink The past tense of this is either *stank* or *stunk*, with all dictionaries giving preference to *stank*. Yet as with some other verbs ending in *-ink* (*shrink*, *sink*), the past participle form with *-unk* is being used increasingly for the past tense itself. (The changeover is already complete for *slink*.) The use of *stunk* for the past tense has in fact been recorded since the sixteenth century.

stoa The plural of this word is discussed under **-a** section 1.

stops The word *stop* is sometimes used as:
1 a term for any punctuation mark
2 a shortened form of *full stop*, especially when it's a question of how to punctuate abbreviations.
For further information about particular punctuation marks, see under individual headings.

storey or **story** In Australian and British English, these spellings differentiate the word for the floor or level of a building, from the word for a tale or account of something. This distinction is however less than a century old. The *Oxford Dictionary* had both spelled **story**, and the same happens in American English. The plural for the first spelling is *storeys*, while for the second it's *stories*.

Whether the two words come from one and the same source is a matter for scholars to debate. Some trace both words back to the Latin *storia*, with the picturesque notion that the levels of older buildings were differentiated by the different tales told in their windows. Others suggest that **storey** "level of a building" developed, like the noun *store*, from an Old French verb *estorer* "build".

The Australian/British use of **storey** entails *multistorey* where Americans use *multistory*. For other derivatives like *two-storey* there are even more variants:

either *two-storey* or *two-storeyed* for Australians and the British, and *two-story* or *two-storied* for Americans.

For the question as to whether the second stor(e)y is the first or second floor, see **floor** and **storey**.

straight or **strait** As single words, these need to be carefully distinguished. **Strait** is a noun referring to a narrow stretch of water which opens out at either end, as in the *Torres Strait*. **Straight** is an adjective describing a line or edge with no curves or kinks in it. It can also be an adverb meaning "directly" or "immediately":

Head straight for the post office.
Go straight to bed.

From **strait** and **straight** are derived *straitened* and *straightened* respectively. *Straitened* means "restricted" as in *straitened circumstances*, and *straightened* means "made straight" as in a *straightened street*.

Note that both *straitjacket* and *straitlaced* are strictly speaking compounds of **strait**, though both are occasionally spelled with *straight*. *Straightjacket* has been recorded frequently since the sixteenth century, and is recognised in dictionaries as an alternative. No doubt people think of the garment as one which keeps your arms and legs straight (not just one which restricts your movements). Likewise it's tempting to reinterpret *straitlaced* as *straightlaced*, i.e. "keeping to the straight and narrow", though dictionaries are less inclined to recognise it as an alternative.

strata By origin this is the plural of the Latin word *stratum* (see further under **-um**). In English however **strata** has been used as a singular word from time to time since the eighteenth century. Nowadays **strata** occurs as a singular, especially in reference to a level in society, and it has developed its own English plural: *stratas*. This trend is frowned on by usage commentators, but it is no stranger than our use of *candelabra* and *agenda* as singular words. (See also **media**.)

Note that **strata** also exists in its own right in law in the expression *strata title*, referring to system which gives people ownership rights to a particular floor in a multistorey building. (See under **home unit**.)

strategy or **stratagem** A **strategy** is an overall plan or method for tackling a problem or managing a campaign. A **stratagem** is a specific trick or ruse, used to deceive. They differ thus in scale, as well as their implications: a **stratagem** involves deviousness, whereas a **strategy** means legitimate planning.

Both words go back ultimately to Greek *strategos* "a general". But **stratagem** entered English in the fifteenth century with a French modification to the spelling of the second syllable. **Strategy** arrived in the seventeenth century, amid the English Renaissance when the classical forms of words were better known.

stratose or **stratous** Both adjectives are related to the word *strata*, but they belong in different fields. **Stratose** is a botanical term meaning "arranged in layers", first recorded in 1881. **Stratous** is older, used since 1816 in meteorology to refer to a layered cloud formation. It corresponds to the noun *stratus*. (See further under **-ous**.)

stratum In technical writing the plural of this word is *strata*, as for similar Latin loanwords (see **-um**). In less formal contexts it becomes *stratums*, partly because of the tendency to reinterpret **strata** as singular. See under that heading.

street For the differences between **street** and *road*, see under **road**.
Note that in Australian and British English we usually say:
I live in Market Street.
In American English the idiom is:
I live on Market Street.
Americans can indeed omit the word *Street* altogether, as in:
My place is on the corner of Smith and Market.
But that idiom is still uncommon in Australia.

streptococcus The plural of this word is discussed under **-us** section 1.

stride The past tense of this verb is definitely *strode*, but a good deal of doubt hangs over its past participle. Dictionaries all give it as *stridden*, just like the verb *ride*. But the *Comprehensive Grammar of English* (1985) allows that it may be also be *strode*; and some of those surveyed at Style Council 1992 (15%) supplied the regular form *strided*. Just under half (47%) endorsed *stridden*, and 38% were for *strode*. But many expressed discomfort about the choice, and an uncertainty which would incline them to paraphrase the word.

strike *Struck* now serves for both past tense and past participle of this verb:
The clock struck one.
The phantom raspberry-blower had struck again.
Note however that the old past participle *stricken* survives as an adjective in metaphorical uses of the word, as in *stricken with age* and *poverty-stricken*.

string, stringed and **strung** In *string instrument*, the word **string** is essentially a noun, and the phrase refers to instruments with *strings* such as the violin and cello, which produce sound through their vibrations (just as the phrase "wind instruments" identifies the sound-producing medium of the flute, oboe etc.). **String** also works as a verb meaning "fit with strings", witness the phrase *stringed instrument* found in musicological descriptions:
The Japanese koto is a stringed instrument like a long zither.
Stringed was once the regular past form of the verb **string**, but it's now confined to the role of definitive adjective, as in that example. In expressions freely formed **strung** has taken its place:
The zither was strung with fresh wire for her visit.
I had to play with a badly strung instrument.

Beyond the world of music **strung** is also the regular past form of **string**, both as an independent word, and as part of a compound:

They strung the discussion out for the whole morning.

They were hamstrung by the lack of funds for the project.

strived or **strove** The past tense of *strive* can be **strove** or **strived**, and the past participle either *striven* or again *strived*. The major American dictionaries register the alternatives, which help to regularise this old irregular verb. **Strived** is heard occasionally in Australian English too, though not yet registered in dictionaries here. A survey taken at Style Council 1992 showed that 20% would use it for the past tense, and 12% for the past participle.

structure in writing See under **headings and subheadings.**

stub See under **tables**.

stucco For the plural see **-o**.

stunk or **stank** See stink.

stupefy See under **-ify/-efy**

sty or **stye** These are alternative spellings for the small swelling which comes up like a boil on an eyelid. Dictionaries regularly cite **sty** first but all recognise **stye** as well. For some (*Collins, Webster's*) the longer form is made equal rather than a lesser option.

But when referring to the enclosure for pigs, **sty** is the only option in most dictionaries.

Note that the plural for **sty** is *sties*, whereas that for **stye** is of course *styes*.

style Some do it with style—and others presumably without it. But writing always has a **style** or *styles* built into it and generated by the very language used. Whether the **style** is formal or informal depends on the words and the idiom used. (See further under **formal words** and **colloquialisms**.) A lively **style** makes use of active verbs and concrete imagery, and avoids too many abstractions and nominalisations. (See further under **abstract nouns** and **nominal**.) A clear **style** is helped by effective use of sentences, so that their length and structure correspond with the units of meaning being expressed.

Certain writing *styles* have strong links with particular institutions. Documents written in the name of government often embody *officialese*, just as those associated with business often contain *commercialese*. Legal writing and scientific writing have recurrent features, such as long sentences, and passive and impersonal constructions. Many academic writers have a **style** which is abstract and impersonal, in keeping with the theoretical emphasis of university work. Thus the writing **style** of many people employed by those institutions is at least somewhat institutionalised. It may indeed be seen as part of their professional competence. Yet no-one would deny the negative aspects of institutional *styles*, and the need to consciously combat them with **Plain English** (see further under that heading).

Institutional and professional writing often involves **style** in that other sense of *house style*, the conventions of spelling, word form, punctuation and usage to be used by everyone who works for that company or department or publisher. The *style guide* which describes the house style is intended to standardise the documents or publications produced, and so is normative or prescriptive.

Individual writers are free to cultivate their own **style** in both senses of the word: to create their own flexible "house" style according to the various contexts in which they write; and to create their own distinctive *writing style*, making it clear and lively, and attractive and readable.

stylus For the plural of this word, see under **-us** section 1.

stymie, stymy or **stimy** Golfers coined this word for the frustrating situation when an opponent's ball lies directly between yours and the hole. For them the uncertainty of the spelling is of no consequence, but it becomes a question for others when the word is used in the general sense of "thwart". Dictionaries all prefer **stymie** to the others, and propose *stymieing* for the present participle. However research into actual usage in Britain shows that the instances of *stymying* considerably outnumber those of *stymieing*, as if writers prefer to treat it in the same way as *die*, *lie* and *tie*. (See under **i>y**.)

sub- This Latin prefix meaning "below", is found in all kinds of verbs, adjectives and nouns of which the following are just a token:

submarine submerge submit subordinate subterranean

Sub- often means "below" in physical terms, as in *subcutaneous*, *subsoil* and *subway*. From this it has developed metaphorical meanings, such as "inferior to", in *subhuman, subnormal* and *substandard*. It can also mean "below" in terms of structure or organisation:

subcommittee subcontract subdivide sublet subplot
subroutine subsection subtitle

In a handful of words, this meaning is further extended to designate a rank or position by reference to the one immediately above it, as in:

subdean subeditor sublieutenant

sub poena See under **habeas corpus**.

sub rosa This Latin phrase means "under the rose", but in English (and other languages such as Dutch and German) it's used to mean "confidentially" or "privately". The phrase has a long history. Some trace it back to the ancient Egyptian god Horus, whose symbol was the rose. Horus was identified by the Greeks with Harpocrates, their god of silence, who was represented as a naked boy sucking his finger. In Roman myth, Harpocrates was given a rose by Cupid, to bribe him not to disclose the amorous affairs of Venus. Thus the rose became the symbol of silence in western civilisation. In more recent times it was sculptured on the ceilings of banquet rooms, as a reminder to the diners that what was said in their cups was not to be repeated outside. A rose was also set above the door of some sixteenth century confessionals. At this point however the secular symbolism of the rose begins to overlap with its symbolism in the Christian tradition, where it was associated with the Virgin Mary and other female saints. (See also **rosary** or **rosery**.)

subconscious or **unconscious** The prefixes make some difference to the meaning of these words. **Subconscious** as an adjective means "just below the level of consciousness", as in:

The smile revealed his subconscious relief at the decision to discontinue the project.

Unconscious as an ordinary adjective means "having lost consciousness":

The victim lay unconscious on the footpath.

Note however that in psychology **unconscious** is used both as noun and adjective in the *unconscious (mind)* to refer to mental processes and psychic material which a person cannot bring into consciousness. The word **subconscious** is sometimes used nontechnically in the same way:

My subconscious is telling me I need a drink.

subject The grammatical **subject** of a clause is the person or thing which operates the verb:

On Thursday I leave for the markets at 5 am.
Wholesale business begins much earlier.
The stalls are opened for shoppers at 5.30.

The easiest way to locate the **subject** of a clause is to identify the verb and make it the focus of a question:

Who or what leaves? ("I")
Who or what begins? ("wholesale business")
Who or what are opened? ("the stalls")

In statements, a **subject** almost always comes befor the verb, though in questions it's usually delayed until after the auxiliary part of the verb phrase. (See under **inversion**.)

The **subject** is often the first item in a sentence, hence the standard pattern of SVO (subject verb object) etc., discussed under **predicate**. However the **subject** can be preceded by a conjunction, and adverb or adverbial phrase, as in the first example sentence above. Any kind of phrase which precedes the **subject** draws attention to itself, and can be used to alter the focus of discussion. (See further under **topic**.)

subjective case This is a name used by some English grammarians for the case of the subject of a clause. Traditionally it has been called the **nominative case**. (See further under that heading.)

subjunctive The **subjunctive** is an obsolescent concept in English grammar. In older English, the *subjunctive forms* of verbs diverged from those in the indicative, and were used for special purposes such as expressing a wish or a hypothesis. Compare:

God save the Queen (subjunctive, for a wish)

God saves the Queen (indicative, for a plain statement)

English once had both present and past forms of the **subjunctive**, but for most verbs the only residue of all that is the *third person singular present subjunctive*. As shown in the example above, it differs from the indicative in having no *-s* suffix. Only for the verb *be* is there a set of alternative forms for the *present subjunctive*, all of which are different from the indicative. Compare:

I am   you are   he/she/it is   we are   they are (indicative)

(if) *I be   you be   he/she/it be   we be   they be* (subjunctive)

The verb *be* also retains some distinct forms for its *past subjunctive*, at least in the singular. Compare:

I was   you were   he/she/it was   we were   they were
(indicative)

(if) *I were   you were   he/she/it were   we were   they were*
(subjunctive)

1 *Survivals of the **subjunctive***. In twentieth century English, we still use the **subjunctive** in conventionalised wishes and other formulaic phrases. For example:

Be that as it may.   Come what may.   Far be it from me.

If I were you.   If need be.   As it were.   God bless you.

Heaven forbid.   Come Sunday.   Convention be damned.

It is also used more flexibly in subordinate clauses expressing a condition or determination:

If he were the world's best manager I wouldn't mind.

I move that he be given a second chance.

Note the use of the *were* **subjunctive** to express an "unreal" condition especially after *as though* and *as if*. But after plain *if* there's a growing tendency to replace the **subjunctive** with indicative, whether the condition is strictly real or unreal:

If he was the world's best manager I wouldn't mind.

In discussing this and other constructions with the **subjunctive**, the *Comprehensive Grammar of English* (1985) stresses its association with formal style.

2 *Regional difference*. The use of the **subjunctive** is sometimes said to be stronger in American English than elsewhere, and research shows that this is because of American preference for the **subjunctive** in many kinds of mandative statements. They are the ones prefaced by verbs like *move* and others including:

advise ask beg demand desire direct insist move order propose
recommend request require stipulate suggest urge

Adjectives such as *essential, important, necessary* and *vital*, and conjunctions such as *in order that* and *on condition that*, also introduce mandative clauses which in American English take the **subjunctive**. They sometimes preface a *negative subjunctive*: *(that) they not be allowed/overlooked/ expected* etc. In British and Australian English, the **subjunctive** in mandative statements and negative ones is often replaced by *should*:

> *I demand that he should be allowed a second chance.*

The decline of the **subjunctive** in British and Australian English means it strikes the ear as grammatically unusual, and literary or formal in tone. Fowler himself noted that it could sound pretentious, and that there was no point in straining to use it. The *Right Word at the Right Time* also warns against using it when it sounds "awkward". The roles of the **subjunctive** are more than covered by other forms of the verb, especially modal verbs (see further under **modality**). We need not lament its passing.

subjuncts See under **adverbs**.

subordination and **the subordinate clause** For the grammatical issues, see under **clauses** sections 3 and 4.

For the role of *subordinate clauses* in controlling the delivery of information, see **information focus**.

substantial or **substantive** Both words are related to the noun *substance*, and though both could appear in the same context, they differ in focus. **Substantial** is the commoner of the two by a factor of about 14:1, on the evidence of the ACE corpus. It has the more physical meaning of "large in size or proportion", as in *a substantial distance* or *a substantial contribution*. The meaning of **substantive** is more abstract, and implies that there are real issues in whatever's being described that way, such as *a substantive argument*. The same discussion paper could be both **substantial** and **substantive**—if it was long and large as well as significant in terms of the issues it raised. However a weary reader would no doubt prefer it to be **substantive** rather than **substantial**.

substitute or **replace** See under **replace**.

such and **such as** Like other words with expanding grammatical roles, **such** has been the target of a good deal of censure. For many dictionaries it's just a pronoun and adjective, as in the following:

> *Such is the fate of many of us.* (pronoun)
> *Such people are hard to talk to.* (adjective)

For grammarians however, the **such** of the second sentence is a *determiner* rather than an adjective (see further under **determiner**). The familiar construction *such a* as in *such a change* has also challenged analysis, with the *Comprehensive Grammar of English* (1985) inclined to treat **such** there as a *predeterminer*.

The dictionaries which call attention to *such a* as in *such a rude comment* tend to call it an intensifying adverb, comparable to its use in *such rude replies*. This adverbial use of **such** is sometimes dubbed "colloquial" and it undoubtedly gets extensive use in conversation. But it appears often enough in print for *Webster's English Usage* to conclude that it qualifies as standard usage. The Australian ACE corpus has nearly 70 examples spread over all categories of writing, though there are undoubtedly more of them in the fiction genres.

1 *Combinations with* **such.** **Such** has come under fire when used with relative conjunctions (*that, who, which*):

> *The document was phrased in such a way that made it thoroughly incomprehensible.*
> *The increase applies only to such members of staff who have more than ten years of service.*

The usage commentators would replace the relative pronoun in each of those sentences with *as*. Yet Fowler noted that the use of the relative pronoun was quite common, and that it was very like a perfectly acceptable construction expressing a result:

> *The document was phrased in such a way that we could make no sense of it.*

This slightly varied version of the first sentence above makes it an adverbial rather than a relative clause, and suggests another way out of trouble. In fact **such** is something of an overkill in the two original sentences: if it's simply omitted, the sentences make their respective points more effectively.

2 *Such as* to introduce examples. **Such as** has traditionally been preferred to *like* as a way of introducing examples:

> *His preference was for tropical fruits such as pineapple and pawpaw.*

Nowadays the use of **such as** in such contexts helps to make the style more formal, whereas using *like* would make it more informal.

Note that when pronouns follow **such as**, it's normal to have them in the accusative case:

> *Do you want an extra driver such as me?*

It was once argued that the nominative form (*I*) ought to be used in such cases, on the basis that **such as** introduces the remnant of an elliptical clause *(such as I could be)*. Modern grammarians are less inclined to argue from what is not there, and to allow that **such as** is effectively a preposition rather than a (compound) conjunction—which means that the accusative *me* is the natural case to use.

3 *Such* as a cohesive device. **Such** is a powerful cohesive device, which is no doubt why it's used in legal documents:

> *Any person found borrowing test instruments for use at home, or using such for private purposes while on government premises will be prosecuted under Section 513 of the* Government Property Act.

The intricate language of law makes it necessary perhaps to have special cohesive devices like **such**, instead of ordinary and unobtrusive ones like the pronoun *it*. Whatever the necessity in legal writing, using **such** elsewhere as a pronoun creates an official and rather pompous style.

suffixes These are the add-on units at the ends of words which modify their grammar and/or meaning, witness:

hyphen hyphens hyphenate hyphenated hyphenation

In that set of words there are two essential types of **suffixes**:
• inflectional
• derivational (or lexical).

1 *Inflectional suffixes* are ones like the plural *-s* and the past tense *-ed*, which simply adapt the basic word *within* its own grammatical class (noun or verb in those cases). A plural noun is still a noun, just as a past tense verb is still a verb. The range of *inflectional suffixes* in English is quite small in comparison with those of other European languages. (See further under **inflections**.)

2 *Derivational suffixes* have a much more radical effect on the word they're attached to, often moving it from one grammatical class to another. In the set above, *-ate* converts the noun *hyphen* into a verb, while *-ion* turns the verb into an abstract noun. Note that **suffixes** which convert concrete nouns to abstract ones (*cork* > *corkage*), or to agentive nouns (*wharf* > *wharfie*) and vice versa, are also considered to be derivational. The range of derivational suffixes in English is very large, comprising both those maintained from Old English (e.g. *-dom, -ship*), as well as many acquired via French and Latin loanwords (e.g. *-ery, -ment*), and even some from Greek (e.g. *-archy, -ology*). Others are the fruit of internal development in English itself, over the course of centuries (e.g. *-ful, -man*).

Suffixes can be grouped in terms of their effect on the grammar of words, those which convert:
• verbs into nouns, either agentive (*-er, -ant, -or* etc.) or abstract (*-al, -ation, -ment* etc.)
• adjectives/nouns into verbs (*-en, -ify, -ise*)
• adjectives into adverbs (*-ly*)
• nouns/adjectives into nouns/adjectives (*-an, -ese, -ite* etc.)
• concrete nouns into other types of noun (*-eer, -hood, -y*)

English words often carry more than one *suffix*, though four derivational ones seem to be the limit. The noun *editorialising* (*edit/or/ial/is/ing*) is a useful mnemonic for this. All *derivational suffixes* precede *inflectional* ones. The last *derivational suffix* decides the grammatical role of the word. Note that words with three or four *derivational suffixes*, each of which in turn modifies the word's role, put some strain on the reader; and writing which uses too many multi-suffixed words is heavy-going. The details of many common **suffixes** are discussed under individual headings.

sui generis In Latin this means literally "of its own kind". It is used of something which (or someone who) stands apart as the only one of their kind.

Strictly speaking it's an adverbial phrase, not a noun, a usage which the *Oxford Dictionary* dubbed "illiterate". The reason for such heavy censure is not however obvious to those without Latin, and the grammar of the phrase is ambiguous in English sentences such as *This publication is **sui generis***.

sulfur or **sulphur** The spelling **sulfur** is often thought of as the American choice where Australian and British English would use **sulphur**. But for some years **sulfur** has been the standard spelling for scientists everywhere in the world, recommended by the International Union of Pure and Applied Chemistry. The recommendation flows on to the names of *sulfur compounds* such as *sulfuric acid*, *copper sulfate* and *hydrogen sulfide*, and the spelling of the word *sulfurous* when used in technical contexts.

Outside the context of chemistry, Australians still typically use **sulphur**, and it's the only spelling in the ACE corpus. Fauna such as the *sulphur-crested cockatoo* and the *sulphur-bottom* (= blue whale) retain the traditional spelling, and it persists in nontechnical uses of the word, as when describing the *sulphurous smell from the hotsprings*.

In fact **sulfur** is the sounder spelling altogether. The word originated in Latin (not Greek), and its earliest spellings were **sulfur** and *sulpur*. The introduction of *ph* into the spelling is thus a scholarly mistake. (See further under **spelling** section 1.)

summa cum laude See under **cum laude**.

summary How different are the following:
abridgement abstract precis résumé summary synopsis
All refer to a shortened or summary version of a text, and are sometimes used loosely as substitutes for each other. Yet they do differ in the way they summarise the original text.

An *abridgement* gives you a shortened version of the text of a book. The less important parts are cut out, and the rest remains in the author's own words.

An *abstract* is a very brief statement (usually one or two paragraphs) about the work reported at large in a document. The abstract pinpoints the issues addressed and the results of the inquiry, as well as the conclusions drawn from it. The term is much used in reporting the essence of academic research.

A *precis* restates the contents of a piece of writing in a much more limited number of words (usually specified). Compression is achieved by repackaging the ideas in alternative wording.

A *résumé* is an overview of action so far taken or of something proposed. (For other uses of the word, see the individual entry for **résumé**.)

A *synopsis* give you a bird's eye view of the various topics discussed in a work, without detailing what is said about each.

The word **summary** itself may be reserved for a brief recapitulation of the points argued in a piece of writing. However it's often used to cover reporting of the main substance of a document, and thus in much the same way as *synopsis*. For *executive summary*, see **reports** section 1.

super- This is a Latin prefix meaning "above", derived from words such as:
   superficial superlative superordinate supersede supervisor
In modern English formations, it often means "above and beyond", as in:
   superhuman supernatural superpower supersonic superstructure
This meaning has been extended in popular formations to mean "outstanding, very special", as in *superman* and *supermarket*, and this extension has proved useful to advertisers, with their generic *superproduct*, as well as *superwash*, *supercleaner* etc.

Note that the agricultural *superphosphate* is not a trade name but an older chemical use of **super-**, equivalent now to *per-*. (See under **per-**.)

As an independent word *super* for a while meant "great", and was used very freely in conversation to express approval: a *super holiday, It was just super!* Fowler rails at overuse of the word, but it has succumbed to the oblivion which overtakes all heavily indulged words. Its chief uses nowadays as an independent word are semitechnical: in reference to the highest grade of petrol, and as an abbreviation for *superannuation* (allowance).

supercede or **supersede** See **supersede**.

supercilious and **superciliary** Both these words focus on the eyelid (in Latin *supercilium*). The literal meaning is there in **superciliary**, a recent scientific word used in anatomy and zoology to refer to a ridge or mark above the eye. **Supercilious** is the common adjective for "haughty", an attitude which even the Romans associated with raising one's eyebrows.

superlative In common usage this word means "excellent" and lends itself to hyperbole, as on a menu card which describes a dish as:
   A superlative combinative of fresh seafood, lightly cooked in batter and
   served with a garnish of roasted pinenuts ...
For grammarians the word refers to the highest degree of comparison for an adjective. (See **adjectives** section 2.)

For the question of double superlatives, see **pleonasm** section 2.

superordinate In logic and language this refers to a concept or word which is at a higher level of generality or abstraction, as *residence* is in relation to *house, home unit, hut, mansion* and *weekender*. The **superordinate** stands as a cover term for a whole class of more specific words, and includes them within its ambit. Between the **superordinate** and the specific terms (*hyponyms*), there's a strong bond of meaning which can be exploited to provide cohesion. (See further under **coherence** or **cohesion**, and **hyponyms**.)

supersede or **supercede** The spelling **supersede** is the standard one, reflecting the etymology of the word. (The first element is the prefix *super-*, the second the Latin root *sed-* meaning "sit".) But because it's the only word in

English which uses the root that way, and because there are several words with the root *ced-* meaning "yield", it's tempting to use it in spelling the word. **Supercede** appears often enough in American English for *Webster's* and *Random House* to register it as a variant, and *Webster's English Usage* has several recent citations for it from edited prose. Other modern dictionaries do not recognise it, although the *Oxford Dictionary* notes it as a "variant, now erroneous" of **supersede**, recorded from the fifteenth to the nineteenth century.

For other words ending in *-cede*, see **-cede/-ceed**.

supper or **dinner** See under **dinner**.

suppose or **supposing** Either of these can be used when you wish to voice a suggestion or a hypothetical ("what if") idea:

Suppose/supposing you ask whether ...
Suppose/supposing it is now found that ...

Some stylists prefer **suppose** for a more formal effect, and it's easier to justify in terms of grammar. There were in fact more instances of this use of **suppose** than of **supposing** in the Australian ACE corpus (7:3). All instances of **suppose** were from scholarly writing, whereas one of the 3 of **supposing** was from a magazine article.

Supposing is the only possibility when the word means "assuming":

We'll go to the gallery, always supposing it's open today.

In such sentences **supposing** works as a kind of conjunction for a subordinate clause.

sur- This prefix comes to us in French loanwords such as:

surface surpass surplus surprise survey survive

As the French form of *super*, it essentially means "above", although that meaning is submerged in most of the words just listed. The pronunciation of some of them (especially *surprise*) seems to erode the suffix away, hence the spelling *suprise* found in children's writing. However **sur-** appears in full force in a few English formations such as:

surcharge surclip surprint surtax surtitle

And of course in *surname*.

surprised by or **surprised at** The particle following **surprised** holds the key to two different meanings. When the phrase means "caught unawares", it's **surprised by**: whereas **surprised at** means "struck with amazement". Compare:

They were surprised by the night watchman.
She was surprised at how quickly it had grown.

In some contexts either meaning might apply, and so it would be possible to use **surprised by** in the second sentence. However **surprised at** could not be used in the first without changing its meaning.

surveil or **surveille** The first spelling is the one recognised in all major dictionaries for this new verb, backformed from *surveillance*. The *Oxford Dictionary* allows **surveille** as an alternative, in spite of its being poorly supported by citations. **Surveil** is stressed on the second syllable, which helps to explain the double *l* in *surveilled* and *surveilling* even in American English. Even so it's slightly at variance with the common conventions for doubling *l* because its vowel is a digraph. (See further under **doubling of final consonant**.)

susceptible to or **susceptible of** In common use **susceptible** is followed by **to**:
> *The plant was susceptible to frost and to many kinds of bugs.*
> *They're susceptible to pressure from other colleagues.*
In such cases it means "easily affected or influenced by". In its more abstract use, where it means "capable of", **susceptible** is followed by **of**:
> *The paper was susceptible of several interpretations.*
This usage sounds very formal nowadays.

suspect or **suspicious** These adjectives differ in that **suspect** applies to the object of suspicion, while **suspicious** describes the attitude of the person holding the suspicion. Compare:
> *Their commitment to the project was very suspect.*
> *I was suspicious about their reasons for joining the group.*
Suspicious is however also used to mean "giving rise to suspicion", especially in police reporting on *suspicious circumstances*.
The adverb *suspiciously* has to do service for both adjectives, as in:
> *The children were suspiciously quiet.*
> (their behavior was suspect)
> *The teacher looked suspiciously round the room.*
> (he had reason to be suspicious)
Note that the colloquial adjective *suss* covers both **suspicious** and **suspect**. The adjective *suss* and the verb *suss (out)* are normally spelled with two *ss*, whereas the noun *sus* meaning a "suspect" has only one.

suspense or **suspension** Both have you suspended, but they work in different worlds. **Suspense** hangs you up emotionally, as in:
> *I'm still in suspense over the scholarship application.*
> *The play kept us in suspense until the last act.*
Suspension is usually a physical state of being suspended. It may be in the air as on a *suspension bridge*, or close to the ground when it's the *suspension of a car*. In chemistry the word refers to being suspended in a liquid, as when particles of chalk form a *suspension in water*. One other use of **suspension** is more an administrative matter: the *suspension of one's driving licence* (or anything else) means that certain rights have been temporarily withdrawn, or that a regular system of some kind has been discontinued.

Note also that for editors in North America **suspension** is the technical term for one kind of *contraction*. (See **contractions** section 1.)

suspicious or **suspect** See suspect.

swam or **swum** See swim.

swap or **swop** The first spelling **swap** is the primary one in all major dictionaries, and the one which expresses the presumed etymology of the word. It seems to come from an old onomatopoeic verb *swappen*, meaning "strike or slap hands (in a bargain)". The alternative spelling **swop** expresses the modern pronunciation, and has been on record for centuries. According to Gowers in the 1965 edition of *Fowler*, **swop** was the more common of the two in Britain, and Murray-Smith echoes his comment in Australia in 1988. Yet the most recent dictionaries (*Collins* and *Macquarie* 1991) still give priority to **swap**.

swat or **swot** These two spellings can be interchanged, though dictionaries link them with two different words. **Swat** is the preferred spelling for "strike (a fly)" or "instrument for striking flies". **Swot** is the primary spelling for the colloquial verb "stuff oneself with information for exams", and for the related nouns meaning "hard study" or "person who studies (too) hard".

swear words This phrase covers the wide variety of coarse, blasphemous and obscene language used in swearing, and in angry or excited exclamations. Their effect is to shock or offend, though the degree of offense depends on how inured those listening are to them. Intensifiers such as *bloody* and *fucking* are used so often in some quarters (such as a football crowd or building site) that they cease to be shocking or to offend those around. However **swear words** which are deliberately used to insult are likely to create shock waves even when the person targeted is thoroughly used to them. This is the reason why people can be charged with "swearing and offensive language"—not that the police are unaccustomed to such words.

See further under **four-letter words** and **taboo words**.

swell The normal past forms of this verb are *swelled* (past tense) and *swollen* (past participle), as in:

Her ankle swelled immediately after the accident.

Her ankle was badly swollen.

Note however that *swelled* can also serve as past participle for things which increase in number:

By noon the crowds had swelled to 12 000.

The use of *swelled* rather than *swollen* in that sentence makes it an observation of fact, since *swollen* has acquired rather negative connotations and tends to suggest that something has gone wrong, or is developing in an undesirable way. The negative associations of *swollen* carry over to its use as an adjective, as in *eyes swollen with crying*, and the more idiomatic *swollen head*. The negative associations are also there in *swelled head*, known in Australian and American English but not in Britain.

swim The standard past tense of this verb is *swam* and the past participle *swum*. However the past tense is not entirely stable, and *swum* is quite often heard in casual conversation. Dictionaries which acknowledge it label it as "old-fashioned or dialectal", and its use in the poetry of Tennyson could be explained one way or the other. In Australia it's certainly not an archaism, and its currency suggests the label "colloquial" rather than any other.

swiveled or **swivelled, swiveling** or **swivelling** For the choice between these, see under **-l/-ll-**.

swollen or **swelled** See under **swell**.

swop or **swap** See **swap**.

swot or **swat** See **swat**.

swum or **swam** See **swim**.

syllabify, syllabicate or **syllabise** These were coined in the nineteenth, eighteenth and seventeenth century respectively. Modern dictionaries show by their crossreferencing that the first **syllabify** has eclipsed the other two, at least in Australia and the USA. British dictionaries give equal status to the first two.

syllables and **syllabification** The boundaries of **syllables** in both speech and writing are far from clear-cut. Linguists debate them, and typesetters and others who divide words at the end of a line often vary in where they make the break, for practical reasons. Dictionaries differ over them partly because of the question as to whether to go by the sounds or the structure of the word. The principles are discussed under **wordbreaks**.

syllabus The plural of this word is discussed under **-us** section 1.

syllogism A **syllogism** is one of the classical forms of deductive argument. See further under **deduction**.

sylvan or **silvan** See under **i/y**.

symbols and **symbolism** A *symbol* stands for something beyond itself. In specialised fields such as chemistry, mathematics and logic, there are conventional **symbols**; in others, writers create their own. The first group are often like abbreviations, witness the chemical **symbols** C for carbon and N for nitrogen. They also serve as symbols for SI units, C for the coulomb, and N for the newton. These conventional **symbols** are never given stops like other abbreviations. For the **symbols** used in the SI set, see Appendix IV.

The **symbols** created by writers are different altogether. They are focal images which carry significance beyond themselves by being developed steadily through the language and substance of a literary work. **Symbols** often begin unobtrusively in a poem or the narrative of a novel, grounded in its physical world. But they reappear in successively different contexts, and take on a complexity of values which help to give the original physical image its greater power. The albatross of Coleridge's *Ancient Mariner* begins as part of the oceanic ambience, yet becomes a *symbol* of an evil system of values. In Carey's *Oscar and Lucinda*, the **symbolism** of glass is developed slowly but surely from its first introduction as the mysterious object in Lucinda's hand. It is both the plain object of manufacture, and the metaphysical medium of the church which is the apex of aspirations in the novel. Through the work the *symbol* becomes a force much more important than it originally seemed, and a unifying element in a long and complex narrative.

Symbols differ from metaphors in being much less closely tied to the specifics of language for their effect. For the difference between **symbolism** and allegory, see **allegory**.

sympathy with or **sympathy for**   The particle after it makes a difference to the meaning of *sympathy*. **Sympathy with** is an intellectual identification with someone's values and point of view—endorsing their ideas. **Sympathy for** is an emotional identification with the problems of others—feeling compassion for them.

symposium   For the plural of this word, see under **-um.**

synagogue or **synagog**   See under **-gue/-g.**

sync or **synch**   Both these are clipped forms of *synchronise*, used in discussing the operation of computers and film-making. But the word appears increasingly in general usage, especially in the phrase *out of sync(h)*, and so it raises spelling questions that impinge on us all.

Sync is the primary spelling in the dictionaries, and it works neatly until you want to use it as a verb and attach the standard verb suffixes to it. Dictionaries which address the problem show that the forms used are *synced* and *syncing*, which are less than ideal in terms of the general spelling rule by which a *c* is normally softened to "s" by a following *e* or *i*. To avoid this a *k* could be introduced, as in *trafficking*. (See further under **-c/-ck-.**) But *syncked* and *syncking* are not among the forms in the citations of the *Oxford Dictionary* (1989); and the evidence of similar words like *arc* is that the forms with *k* are not popular.

The alternative spelling **synch** avoids the problem of what to do before the verb suffixes, but it suffers from others: it appears to rhyme with "winch", and could even be a misspelling of "cinch".

If we settle the question by frequency of usage, **sync** remains the spelling to use. *Oxford Dictionary* citations show that it outnumbers the cases of **synch** by 17:7, and is preferred overwhelmingly in technical contexts.

synecdoche   This is the classical name for a figure of speech in which either:

- a part of a familiar object is used to refer to the whole, or
- the name of the whole stands for the part.

An example of the first is *put a prawn on the barbie* (where the prawn is just part of the barbecue feast). The second can be illustrated by the use of *Canberra* to refer to the national government which is instituted there.

Either type of **synecdoche** works allusively, inviting the reader to translate the expression offered into something broader, or more specific. Note that the first type of **synecdoche** is also known as *metonymy*.

synonyms "Words with the same meaning" is a common definition of **synonyms**. But when you ask whether *chair* and *seat*, or *tap* and *faucet*, or *buy* and *purchase* are **synonyms**, clearly there's more to be said. Words embody many kinds of meaning: denotative, connotative and stylistic; and relatively few words match up on all those dimensions. The denotation of *chair* is more specific than *seat*. (A *chair* has legs and can be moved around independently, whereas a *seat* at the opera is different on both counts.) The connotations of *faucet* make it American, whereas *tap* is at home in Australia. The stylistic overtones of *purchase* are much more formal than those of *buy*. Few pairs of words like those are perfect **synonyms**.

Yet words which diverge more than any of those can function as **synonyms** for each other. So *high* can stand for *secondary* when referring to schooling, even though it could never do so in *secondary symptom*. The fact that you can interchange them in one particular phrase without changing the meaning makes them **synonyms** there, for the purposes of the argument.

Writers often search for **synonyms** as a way of varying their expression, and the ultimate collection of **synonyms** is a thesaurus. However the thesaurus groups together words which differ in style, in connotation and even denotation. Any possible substitute word needs to be checked with the dictionary for its suitability.

synopsis See under **summary**.

syntax This term is often used in alternation with *grammar* in talking about the structure of English. But when we get down to details it's important to distinguish them. *Grammar* is the broader term, embracing:

1 **syntax** (= the grammatical relations between words as they're strung together in phrases, clauses and sentences)
2 *morphology* (= the grammar of words as shown by their suffixes and inflections)

Because there are relatively few inflections in modern English, **syntax** is much more important in our grammar.

Syntax embodies the principles that underlie the *syntagmatic axis* of any language. This is the so-called "horizontal" dimension of meaning, vested in the order of words, and the way that adjacent words set up expectations about

each other's roles. We become most conscious of this axis of meaning when it's unclear, as in the following headline:
CLEANER TRAINS IN TEN YEARS
If we take the first word as a noun, it becomes the subject of the verb we anticipate in *trains*—and we get a vision of the most thoroughly trained cleaner in the universe. Yet if we read the first word as a comparative adjective, we anticipate that the second word is the noun it describes—and it paints a gloomy picture of railway car maintenance.

Compare the *paradigmatic axis*, under **paradigm**.

synthetic Apart from its everyday uses, this word has two technical meanings in relation to the use of language. A *synthetic language* is one which has many kinds of inflections to express the grammatical relations between words. So *synthetic languages* like Latin contrast with those like English or Chinese, in which grammatical meaning is vested much more in the syntactic arrangements of words. (See further under **syntax**.)

A *synthetic statement* is one whose validity is tested by empirical evidence. (See further under **induction**.)

syphon or **siphon** See under **i/y**.

syrup or **sirup** The first spelling is given preference in all dictionaries, Australian, British and American, and **sirup** is very much the secondary spelling, even in the USA. The word seems thus to resist the general trend to replace *y* with *i* (see under **i/y**).

systematic or **systemic** The first of these has many more uses, to describe something that embodies a system, e.g. a *systematic methodology for research*, and by extension, anything or anyone that's well organised (a *systematic secretary*). The latter use has positive overtones.

Systemic is still an academic word, used in medicine to refer to diseases or drugs which affect the whole body; and in other fields to designate theoretical approaches which analyse the parts of something in relation to the whole. *Systemic grammar* shows how sentences and parts of them relate systematically to the larger functions of language.

T

t Two-syllable words ending in *-t* raise various spelling issues when they become verbs. For some like *budget* and all those in the list below, it's the question as to whether the **t** should be doubled before the verb suffixes (especially *-ed* and *-ing* are added):

ballot banquet billet blanket bracket buffet bullet docket facet ferret fidget fillet jacket junket limit market orbit picket plummet profit rivet rocket target ticket trumpet

The answer is clear: provided the syllable ending in *-t* is unstressed, the *t* remains single, so they become *budgeting*, *marketed*, *targeting* etc. The same principle applies to similar three-syllabled verbs such as *benefiting* and *deposited*. (See further under **doubling of final consonant**.)

For the spellings associated with *bayonet* and *combat*, see **bayonet** and **combated** or **combatted**.

*New French loanwords which end in a silent **t** raise other questions. What happens when they serve as verbs?

ballet beret bouquet buffet cabaret chalet crochet debut depot parquet sachet valet

The final **t** remains silent even when the standard English verb suffixes are added, as in *balleting*, *debuted*, *valeting*. Their spelling is thus very straightforward, though the relationship between spelling and sound is quite unconventional for English.

The verb *ricochet* is a special case, with two pronunciations and two sets of spellings. (See **ricochet**.)

Note that *-t* itself is a verb suffix on a number of English verbs, as in: *crept, dealt, kept, left, meant, slept* etc. For the choice between *-t* and *-ed* on the following:

burn dream kneel lean leap learn smell spell spill spoil

see under **-ed**.

tabbouleh, tabooli or **tabouli** See tabouli.

table d'hôte See à la carte.

tableau For the plural of this word in English, see **-eau**.

tables A *table* is an effective and efficient way of communicating a lot of numerical information in a small space. **Tables** allow the reader to make instant comparisons horizontally and vertically, and to see overall trends. They are (or should be) designed to be read independently of the surrounding text, and must contain all the information necessary for that reading.

Every *table* needs an explanatory title, highlighting its topic or the general trends which it shows. The wording must be specific enough to allow browsing readers to make sense of the figures, and may therefore run to two or three lines. Beneath the title comes the *box* containing the column headings for the *table*, showing what kind of entries are entered in the *field* or *body* of the *table*, and what unit of measurement they're calibrated in. (Abbreviations can be freely used in column headings.) The unit should be chosen to minimise excess zeros or nonsignificant ones in the figures cited. (So *59 kg* is preferable to *59 000 gm.*) The set of figures must be expressed in terms of the same unit for easy comparison. If percentages are used, readers also need to know the actual size of the population analysed, and the raw number (n = whatever) should be given in the footnotes to the *table*.

The relationship between age of respondents and their support for a set of spelling changes

	Age groups		
	10-25	26-45	46+
Spelling changes	% support	% support	% support
1 Change *-our* words to *-or* (colour>color)	38	41	55
2 Use *-er* for all agent words (investor>invester)	22	32	42
3 Use *-able* for all words with *-ible* (digestible>digestable)	61	56	63
4 Use *-l* for *-ll-* before suffixes (traveller>traveler)	50	56	59
5 Drop final *e* from root before *-able* (likeable>likable)	61	63	68
6 Reduce *ae* to *e* (paediatrics>pediatrics)	38	73	75
7 Reduce *oe* to *e* (homoeopath>homeopath)	38	67	73
	n = 18	n = 158	n = 232

Note that **tables** these days have a minimum of horizontal rules drawn in, and no vertical lines, to allow the eye to move freely across and down.

The side headings in a *table*, known collectively as the *stub*, are set flush with the margin, as the numbering is in the table example. Turnover lines may be indented if there's sufficient space (as in the example) or else set flush left with a line space between each heading. The headings begin with a capital letter, but have no final full stops. The wording of all headings needs to be made consistent. In the example, all headings begin with an imperative form of the verb. (See further under **lists**.)

taboo words Words which many people avoid because of the offense they may give are **taboo words**. In twentieth century English they typically involve private subjects such as defecation (*shit*), urination (piss) and copulation (fuck): (see further under **four-letter words**).

Earlier on in English, and still in other languages, **taboo words** link up with religion. Religion is often a focus of taboos, and religious words uttered without reverence are naturally an offense to those who take religion seriously. Some of our common expletives are disguised religious references: *by Crikey* is a veiled form of "by Christ"; and *bloody* is believed to be a disguised form of "by our Lady". In those forms they are less directly blasphemous, and do not seem to violate religious taboos—though *bloody* can still be offensive to some as a **swear word** (see further under that heading).

All this shows that **taboo words** are the ones which evoke the taboo subject in a blatant or blasphemous way. Disguised expletives and latinate words like *copulation* do not violate taboos as *by Christ* and *fuck* do. In writing, as in speaking, even taboo subjects can be handled provided taboo language is avoided.

Note that *taboo* can also be spelled *tabu*, which is as the Tongan word was originally written down. However all modern dictionaries prefer *taboo*.

tabouli, tabouleh, tabbouleh or **tabooli** These spellings, and other permutations and combinations like them, are used to refer to a Lebanese salad made of cracked wheat, parsley and tomato. The word is a recent borrowing (1955) from Arabic, where it appears as *tabbula*, and is apparently a derivative of *tabil* "spice". Both the *Oxford Dictionary* and *Random House* prefer the spelling **tabbouleh**, but the spelling with one *b* and a final *i* is given priority by the *Macquarie Dictionary*.

tabula rasa In Latin this means "a tablet scraped clean"—a clean slate. But in English this phrase is used where someone knows nothing about a subject and is ready to receive any information about it. Psychologists use it to refer to the human mind at birth.

tag questions See under **questions**.

tant pis See under **faute de mieux**.

target For the spelling of this word when used as a verb, see **t**.

tasseled or **tasselled** See under **-l/-ll-**.

Tassie or **Tassy** The informal name for Tasmania and Tasmanians was first recorded in the 1890s. Its spelling has varied, being originally *Tassy* but with **Tassie** and *Tazzie* appearing around World War I. As with other *-ssie/-zzie* words, the spelling with *-ssie* has most currency, probably because it leaves intact the first syllable of the name. (See further under **-ssie/-zzie**.)

Other informal names for a Tasmanian are the rather pejorative *Tasmaniac* (dating from 1867) and *Taswegian* (a recent name first recorded in 1961). (See further under **-mania** and **-wegian**.)

tautology This is a matter of saying the same thing twice over, as in: *A capacity crowd completely filled the stadium.* A **tautology** involves redundancy, though there are times when it serves a purpose. (See **pleonasm** section 2.)

For philosophers **tautology** is another name for an analytic statement, i.e. one which is self-defining or self-validating. (See further under **induction**.)

Tazzie See under **Tassie**.

tea or **dinner** See **dinner**.

tea-tree or **ti-tree** The name **tea-tree** has been loosely applied to a number of aromatic trees and shrubs in the melaleuca and leptospermum families. The name evidently records the fact that Captain Cook's surgeon and naturalist mistook a species of leptospermum for a North American plant which was used as a substitute for tea. Later settlers in Australia did not find that **tea-tree** provided a very palatable drink, and it has since been used more for its pliable bark, and for its oil.

Yet the spelling **tea-tree** has prevailed over **ti-tree**. The latter was in vogue in the 1890s, but appears only as the lesser alternative before and after that. The spelling **ti-tree** suggests some confusion with the New Zealand *ti-tree* which is a palm-like cabbage tree.

technical or **technological** The first is a good deal older than the second. **Technical**, in use since the seventeenth century, was and is applied to all kinds of *techniques*, in many different fields from art to arithmetic and from angling to leatherwork. **Technological** as the adjective associated with *technology* is a twentieth century word, and refers more exclusively to the applications of science to industry. Both *technology* and **technological** have a learned ring to them, and *institutes of technology* give university-style degrees, while *technical colleges* do not.

Differences like those are matched in the words *technologist* and *technician*. When used as a job title, *technologist* presupposes skills equivalent to those of a four-year degree plus some postgraduate study or training. The *technician* meanwhile has skills equivalent to those of two-year associate diploma. In the Australian Standard Classification of Occupations (1990), there are about forty job titles which involve *technician* for every one involving *technologist*.

technologese This word takes its place alongside *commercialese, journalese* and *legalese* in designating the writing style which goes with a particular institution or profession. The suffix *-ese* has negative overtones, and so **technologese** suggests writing loaded with technical conventions and clichés which make it an unattractive style for many. Yet the word **technologese** (or *technobabble* as Murray-Smith called it) does represent the "technophobe's" point of view—that of people who feel excluded by technical language.

Technical writing in science, computers, or any other specialised field is somewhat dependent on jargon, which allows specialists to communicate precisely and efficiently with each other. The use of technical terms is perfectly legitimate in documents intended for a limited readership. It is however unfortunate if technical expressions are spread thickly in documents meant for the general reader, and the specialist author seems oblivious of the obstacles they raise. Technical writers certainly need to be able to adjust their style for a nontechnical audience—if they have any ambitions to communicate with the public, let alone win them over. The typically impersonal style of technical and scientific writing needs to be avoided, and consciously replaced with lively and direct expression. (See further under **impersonal writing** and **passive verbs**.)

technological or **technical** See **technical**.

tele- These letters represent two Greek prefixes, one in common usage, the other mostly confined to philosophy.

1 The very familiar prefix **tele-** means "distant" or "over a distance". It derives from *telescope*, first recorded in English in the seventeenth century along with new developments in optics. Other **tele-** words are monuments to technological developments, including *telegraph* (1794), *telephone* (1835), *telemeter* (1860) and *television* (1909). In both *television* and *telecommunication*, the Greek prefix forms a linguistic hybrid with a Latin word; and it now combines with very ordinary English words in *telemotor, teleprinter, teletext* and *teletype*.

Note that some other simple formations with **tele-** are really blends of *telephone* or *television* and other words:
   telecast teledex telemovie teleplay teleprompter televiewer

2 The much less common prefix is **tele-** or *teleo-* meaning "end or goal". Best known in the philosophical term *teleology*, it refers to the theoretical approach which looks for evidence of design in nature, and for the ultimate purpose in any phenomenon.

tempera or **tempura** These similar words are very different in origin, though by coincidence eggs are involved in both. **Tempera** is an Italian word for a method of mixing paint, combining the pigments with egg yolk. It was once known as *distemper*, but that word has been annexed by home decorators to refer to paints which are made with sizing materials less expensive than eggs.

A new word had to be found for the original egg-based technique of fine art, and **tempera** has been used in English for this since 1832.

Tempura is a Japanese word meaning "fried food". It refers to a dish in which seafood or vegetables are deep-fried in a very light batter, again making good use of egg yolk.

template or **templet** Templet is the original spelling of this word for a pattern or mould used to reproduce a design on another surface or in another medium. The word comes from Latin *templum* "timber, beam" via French (where a diminutive ending *-et(te)* was added on), and so **templet** meant "small timber". But this background was obscure to English users, and the spelling **template** attempts to make sense of the second syllable. (For other examples, see **folk etymology**.) The revised spelling has largely displaced the earlier one, and all modern dictionaries give **template** as the primary spelling.

temporary or **temporal** The time in **temporary** is always limited, and sometimes very brief: a *temporary appointment*, a *temporary shelter from the storm*. The pressure of time seems to be felt in the word itself, which is commonly pronounced with only three syllables (sometimes only two). Children occasionally write it as "tempory" (or "tempary") for the same reason.

Temporal relates to time at large. In grammar and linguistics it means "expressing a time factor", as in *temporal conjunction*. In religion however it expresses finite human time, in contrast with eternal, spiritual time. So the *Lords Temporal* (in the English House of Lords) have a lesser brief than the *Lords Spiritual*.

tempura or **tempera** See tempera.

tend or **attend** See attend.

tensed verb See under **finite verbs**.

tenses Any language has its ways of indicating whether an event is in the past, present or future; and many do it through the forms of their verbs and especially through different inflections. The sets of inflections (or other formal changes) which represent time differences are the **tenses** of a language.

English has only two **tenses** in this sense: present and past. They are the time differences represented in the forms *rest/rested* and *write/wrote*. (See further under **present tense** and **past tense**.) The future is expressed in English through compound verbs, i.e. ones involving auxiliaries:

will rest/write
shall rest/write
am/is/are going to rest/write
am/is/are about to rest/write

(See further under **future tense**.) The English future has much in common with compound verbs which express such things as obligation, inclination and possibility:

must rest/write
might rest/write
could rest/write
(See further under **modality**.)
    See also **sequence of tenses**.

terminology Technical terms go with any specialised activity, whether it is the craft of knitting (one purl one plain) or computing (booting the DOS) or any other. Nonspecialists are effectively excluded by such terminology, and the word *jargon* is often used to express their sense of frustration and alienation. When writing for a general reader, it's important to use words in common use wherever possible, and to provide an explanation beside any technical terms which cannot be avoided (or else a glossary at the back of the document). Above all, technical **terminology** should not be applied in fields other than the one it belongs to. It may be tempting to say of someone who's just got up and is acting like a zombie that "he hasn't yet booted the DOS". But neither the point nor the joke will get through to those who know nothing of computers. (See further under **jargon**.)

terminus or **terminal** As nouns, these are both associated with public transport, and can both mean a "station at the end". **Terminus** is the older word for the final station on a train, tram or local bus line, where the passengers get on and off. **Terminal** has always been the point of arrival and departure for aircraft, including helicopters, for shipping, and more recently for long-distance buses.
    In computing, a **terminal** (never a **terminus**) is the word for the workstation which accesses a computer network.
    Note that **terminus**, like other Latin words ending in *-us*, has two plurals: *termini* and *terminuses*. In everyday English the latter is more common. (See further under **-us** section 1.)

terminus ante quem and **terminus ad quem** In historical writing these Latin phrases are both used to refer to the final point of a period in which something must be dated. The first means literally "endpoint before which (something happened)". The second, "endpoint towards which (something was heading or tending)", implies less certainty about the continuity of events up to the terminal date. The contrasting phrase for the beginning of the dating period is *terminus a quo*, the "point from which (a certain period began)".

terra In both Latin and Italian, this is the word for "earth" or "land". English has it in several borrowed phrases:
• *terra cotta* from Italian is literally "cooked earth". This is the clay out of which reddish, unglazed pottery is made, and a name for the pottery itself.
• *terra firma* from Latin is "solid land", nowadays used to distinguish solid, dry land from sea. Originally it seems to have been used in reference to the

mainland, as contrasted with offshore islands, though this use became obsolete in the eighteenth century.

- *terra incognita* from Latin is "unknown (or unexplored) land". It frequently appears on early maps of Australia.
- *terra nullius* from Latin means "land of no-one". It embodies the nineteenth century legal notion that when European settlers arrived in Australia there were no title-holders to the land. The concept has now been discredited in the *Native Title Act* (1993).

terrible or **terrific** Colloquial use has reduced the element of terror in both of these. We still confront it in formal usage such as in *Ivan the Terrible* and *terrible destruction*. But in many of its appearances, **terrible** is a general-purpose negative, witness: a *terrible performance*. The associated adverb is often just an intensifier: *It's terribly kind of you*, with no negative value at all.

Terrific has become a general word of commendation, as in: a *terrific film*, though to most ears it sounds rather exaggerated. Its adverb also serves as an intensifier: *It's terrifically exciting*.

Compare **horrible, horrid, horrendous, horrific** or **horrifying**.

tertium quid This is the Latin equivalent of a Greek phrase which means the "third something". In English it has several uses. In scholarly argument it refers to a notional elusive something which is related to but distinct from two other known entities. A more specific use of the word is to refer to that which is a medium between two others, or an intermediate between opposites.

Another, less academic use of the phrase is to refer to the third party in an "eternal triangle", a use which is immortalised in a Kipling story which begins: "Once upon a time there was a man and his wife and a tertium quid".

tête à tête This French phrase means literally "head to head". Most often it's used of a private conversation between two people, though it has also been applied to an S-shaped piece of furniture for seating two people face to face. The phrase is usually given hyphens, though they are unnecessary when it's printed in italics, or even when it serves as a compound adjective. (See **hyphens** section 2c iii.)

Compare the Italian phrase *a quattr'occhi*, discussed under **au pair**.

-th This Old English suffix is found on numerical adjectives (*fourth, fifth* etc.), and in a number of common abstract nouns, such as:

> *breadth depth filth growth health length stealth strength truth warmth wealth width*

It has formed hardly any words since the seventeenth century, only *illth* (1860), which was coined by Ruskin as an opposite to *wealth* (in its older sense of "well-being"), but never caught on.

Note that *drought* and *height* were once "droughth" and "heighth". The spellings with just *-t* began to be used in the thirteenth century, and have long since prevailed.

than Questions about the grammar of this word were energetically debated in the eighteenth century, and are still asked in the twentieth. By origin it is a conjunction, used to introduce a subordinate clause of comparison, as in:

He knows more than I do about their history.

The use of the subject pronoun *I* anticipates the verb *(do)*, and confirms that a clause is to follow. For grammarians, this is proof that **than** is a conjunction. And for some of them: "once a conjunction, always a conjunction"—in spite of common constructions like the following:

He knows more than me about their history.

In that version of the sentence, the object pronoun *me* shows that **than** is operating as a preposition, which normally takes an object. Prepositional use of **than** with an object pronoun has been recorded since the sixteenth century, yet prescriptive grammarians still argue that the subject pronoun is the proper one to use; and they would adapt the second sentence to:

He knows more than I about their history.

To many people this sounds less natural, but the grammarians argue that it is an elliptical version of the first sentence above, i.e. that a whole clause is understood after it, and so *I* is still the correct form of the pronoun. Yet there's no need for this elaborate argument if we allow that **than** can work as a preposition as well. There are ample examples in *Webster's English Usage* of **than** with object pronouns—and even the *Oxford Dictionary* recognised the use of the phrase *than whom*. To insist that **than** is always a conjunction flies in the face of evidence, and to replace object pronouns after **than** with subject pronouns sounds rather lofty these days.

Note that in practice this issue only arises when **than** precedes one of the first or third person pronouns, the ones that have distinct forms for the subject and object (*I, we, he, she, they*). For the second person pronoun *you*, the third person *it*, and for nouns and proper names, the forms are just the same.

He knows more than his teacher about their history.

Grammarians may still debate whether **than** introduces a phrase or an elliptical clause, but there's generally no problem for the writer. The only thing to watch for is the occasional ambiguity, as in:

She's kinder to her dog than the children.

To settle the ambiguity in sentences like that, you need to spell the point out more fully. (See further under **ellipsis**.)

Other issues with **than**:

1 *Than and what.* The most extended use of **than** as a preposition is to be seen in sentences such as:

He wanted it more than what I did.

Constructions like that, which give **than** an object in *what*, are generally considered nonstandard. The *what* is unnecessary because the sentence could perfectly well be:

He wanted it more than I did.

However the construction *than what* is occasionally heard in impromptu talk, and is one of the various redundancies that occur when we construct sentences on the run. It should be edited out of written documents.

2 *Following* **than**—it's possible to use either an infinitive or an *-ing* form of the verb. Compare:

She rushed on rather than let me catch up.

She was rushing on rather than letting me catch up.

As those examples show, the *-ing* form usually follows a continuous/progressive form of the main verb, and the infinitive goes with other aspects and tenses.

3 *Than with quasi-comparatives.* A number of adjectives and adverbs imply comparisons without having the standard comparative suffixes such as *-er*. Thus collocations like *different than* and *superior than* are quite often heard, as alternatives to *different to/from* or *superior to*; and sequences such as *hardly ... than* and *scarcely ... than* as alternatives to *hardly ... when* and *scarcely ... when*. Purists are inclined to argue that **than** has no place in such phrases, and the comparison is definitely implicit rather than explicit in the form of words. Yet common idiom endorses such structures. (See further under **different, hardly** and **scarcely**.)

thank you and **thanks** These expressions differ a little in style. **Thank you** is the standard and neutral way of expressing one's gratitude:

Thank you for your attention.

Thanks is more informal, and works either as a friendly acknowledgement or a brisk refusal:

Thanks for being with us.

No thanks. I've had enough.

The expression *many thanks* gets the best of both worlds. It embodies warmer feeling than **thank you**, while avoiding the informality of **thanks**.

Note that when **thank you** becomes a compound noun or adjective, it is either set solid or hyphenated, as in *said their thankyous* and *wrote a thank(-)you note*.

that The workhorse of the English language, **that** has uses as a demonstrative pronoun and adjective, as three kinds of conjunction, and occasionally as an adverb.

1 *As a demonstrative* **that** complements *this*. **That** represents something further away than whatever we might apply *this* to: *This goes with that* as they say in a certain fashion store. **That** draws attention to something at a remove from the reader and writer, whereas *this* draws them together over it. In conversation **that** often refers to something in the physical context, whereas in writing **that** must have an antecedent in the text itself:

To go to Japan—that was her number one ambition.

As in that example, **that** is as useful a cohesive device as any of the personal pronouns. (See further under **coherence** and **cohesion**.)

2 *That* as a conjunction. **That** serves to introduce any of three kinds of clause: relative (adjectival), noun and adverbial. It also appears in several compound conjunctions: *in order that, provided that* and *so that*.

a) When **that** introduces a relative clause it can be and often is omitted, depending on both grammatical and stylistic factors. As the object of the relative clause it often disappears, as in:

The program (that) we heard yesterday had a powerful impact.

Compare:

A program that had a powerful impact was broadcast yesterday.

In the second sentence **that** is the subject of the relative clause and must remain. Yet the deletion of **that** as objective pronoun is normal in conversation, and quite common in writing these days.

(For the choice between **that** and *which*, see **relative pronouns**.)

b) When **that** introduces a noun clause, after a verb which expresses a mental or verbal process, it's often omitted:

We knew (that) the idea was yours.

He said (that) it was his.

Here again **that** is likely to be omitted in speech as well as informal writing.

c) In adverbial clauses **that** can again be omitted. See for example:

We were so exhausted (that) we didn't care.

The construction without **that** smacks of lively speech with its strong emphasis—far removed from the decorum of formal writing.

Note finally the newish construction which combines **that** with *enough* rather than *so*:

We were exhausted enough that we didn't care

In the construction with *enough*, **that** cannot be omitted.

3 *That* as an adverb. Adverbial uses of **that** are now accepted when they modify other adverbs, as in:

Is it that far to Kalgoorlie?

But the use of **that** to modify adjectives is still quite colloquial:

They were that excited about the trip to Kakadu.

The more formal word for modifying adjectives is *so*.

the This common and humble word is surprisingly significant in conveying ideas. In the grammar of English it signals that a noun is to follow, and it very often implies that the noun is one with which the reader is already acquainted, as in:

The result was not declared immediately.

Effectively **the** says: "You know which one I mean", and reminds us of an earlier reference to the same thing in the text. Thus it's an important cohesive device (see further under **coherence** or **cohesion**.) **The** often links up with a phrase introduced by an indefinite article (*a* or *an*). Yet **the** makes connections with all kinds of noun phrases, and can forge a link with a whole clause or sentence, as in:

He said he would come. The answer was not what they'd expected ...

1 *Other uses of the.* Instead of working cohesively with earlier information, **the** sometimes appeals to common knowledge, as when we speak of *the government, the radio, the sun* or *the world.* The first two invoke social and cultural experience; the third and fourth appeal to knowledge of the universe. Common knowledge is also invoked in the so-called "generic" use of **the** with a singular noun:

The platypus may soon become a threatened species.
In the one-teacher school, older students act as mentors to younger ones.

2 *The in titles and designations.* The titles of many publications include an article, witness Thea Astley's novel *The Acolyte* or a reference book such as *The Gentle Art of Flavoring.* In such cases, *The* needs a capital, as an intrinsic part of the title, even when it's cited in mid-sentence:

Thea Astley won the Miles Franklin Award in 1972 for The Acolyte.

However style guides agree that if retaining the *The* makes an awkward sentence, it can be dropped:

Have you read his Gentle Art of Flavoring?

Likewise it's accepted that when referring to titles prefaced by *A* or *An* (e.g. *A New English Dictionary*), the indefinite article may have to be replaced by **the**. It would not be capitalised as part of the title:

Information on many a cultural question can be found among the words in the New English Dictionary.

The no longer needs to be cited in the mastheads of newspapers and magazines such as the *Age*, the *Bulletin*, according to the Australian Government *Style Manual* (1988). Earlier style guides used to enjoin including it, perhaps because *The Times* was known to insist on it. But the preferences of less well-known publications could be hard to ascertain, and so the simple practice of leaving *The* out makes a reliable rule for all. Anticipating this, some publications such as *New Scientist* have deliberately shed *The* from their mastheads. The practice also simplifies adjectival use of such titles, as in:

They have a collection of one hundred Age *editorials.*

The use of italics for newspaper titles is discussed at **italics** section 5.

One other place where **the** is dropped is in definitive designations for people, when they appear immediately after the proper name as in:

Peter Carey, (the) author of Oscar and Lucinda *and ex-advertising man, has a gift for graphic description.*

The practice of dropping **the** in such designations is common in newspaper reporting, even before personal names:

Author and ex-advertising man Peter Carey has ...

As a broad introductory phrase, this is a feature of journalese, but little used elsewhere. (See further under **journalism**.) Note however that **the** can be omitted from an introductory phrase in any style when it refers to a unique office:

He was voted co-president in his second year.

In his role as coach, he was a tireless motivator.

theatre or **theater** See under -re/-er.

theirself and **theirselves** See under **themself**.

theme For the **theme** and *rheme* of a sentence, see under **topic**.

themself This word is more often heard than seen, and the few modern dictionaries that register it label it as "colloquial" and "nonstandard". Yet if we allow the use of *they/them/their* for referring to the singular (see **they**), **themself** seems more consistent than *themselves* after an indefinite pronoun:

Anyone who arrives late must let themself in by the back door.

Themself has the double advantage of being singular and gender-free— preferable to *himself*, or *himself/herself*.

Themself was in fact standard English until the mid-sixteenth century, when it was replaced by *themselves*. The *Oxford Dictionary* labels it obsolete, yet *Webster's English Usage* (1989) has fresh citations for it from the twentieth century. It serves a purpose, just as *yourself* does alongside *yourselves*.

Note also the alternatives *theirselves* and *theirself*, registered in the *Oxford Dictionary* (1989) and the major American dictionaries, though as nonstandard items. They are of course consistent in their makeup with *myself, ourselves, yourself, yourselves* in using a possessive adjective for the first element. However both *themself* and the regular *themselves* match up with *himself* and *itself* in using the object pronoun. The two sets provide conflicting analogies, but with the second set at least the third person reflexives are consistent with each other.

thence See under **hence**.

there This is primarily a demonstrative adverb meaning "in/on/at/towards that place". In writing it's often used to refer to a place already mentioned, whether physical, geographical or abstract:

Turn to the diagram on p.10 and look at the details there.

We went there by bus.

The discussion moved to government policy on the environment, and there he got thoroughly confused.

There also combines with other adverbs/prepositions of place to form compound adverbs:

down there   over there   up there

Note that *from there* is now used instead of *thence* (see further under **hence**); and that **there** itself has taken over from *thither*.

The other most important use of **there** is as the introductory slot-filler in a sentence which explains how things are:

There's no place like home.

There are seventeen pubs and no bookshops in the town.

Grammarians often refer to this as *existential there*, the counterpart of "ambient *it*" in *It's raining*. This similarity between them explains why some dictionaries label *existential there* a pronoun, though it's not a substitute for a previously mentioned word like a normal pronoun. Both words do however function as "dummy subjects" in the examples above, and so are called "dummy elements" in the *Introduction to the Grammar of English* and some others.

Existential there can be used with either singular or plural verbs, as shown in the examples above. The verb agreement is decided strictly by the following noun phrase, as least in formal writing. In speech however, *there is* (or *there's*) is increasingly used as a fixed phrase even before plural nouns. In fiction samples in the Australian ACE corpus there were 10 instances (5% of all instances of *there's*) representing casual talk. Examples included:

There's tears in her eyes.

There's no misters in this country.

Before a series of singular nouns, *there is/was* is widely acceptable in writing as well as speech:

In that village there is a post office, a garage and a tiny church.

Note that *existential there* is sometimes used with other verbs:

After all that there remained the small matter of money.

There comes a time for all of us to retire from politics.

On the bed there lay a small figure.

However constructions like these may sound a little contrived nowadays.

thereafter, thereby, therefor, therein, thereon, thereunder etc.

All these, and others like them, are at home in legal documents where they serve to avoid the standard pronouns. **Thereafter** only means "after it/that", but it's more conspicuous than the plain phrase in a long sentence and may perhaps reduce ambiguity. (Compare **the said**.)

In other kinds of writing, these words sound very formal and slightly archaic. The only one which enjoys some general use is **thereby**:

He was unexpectedly moved to a new section, and thereby avoided the problem for a while.

On **therefore**, see the next entry.

therefore
This is a connecting word meaning "consequently" or "for that reason". It forges a logical link between one statement and what follows, as in:

The weather deteriorated and they therefore thought that the game was cancelled.

In sentences like that, **therefore** works as a conjunct, not as a full *conjunction* (the grammatical connection depends on *and*). Traditional grammarians and dictionaries are still disinclined to recognise **therefore** as a full conjunction (in spite of the famous *I think therefore I am*), and would correct the following sentence:

The weather deteriorated, therefore they thought the game was cancelled.
The sentence would only be correct, in their view, if punctuated with a
semicolon:

The weather deteriorated; therefore they thought the game was cancelled.
The semicolon makes the difference because its function is to mark the boundary
between two independent statements in the same sentence (see further under
semicolon). The difference between the two sentences is of course purely visual.
Although **therefore** has yet to be generally recognised as a *conjunction*, it is
accorded the special status of "sentence connector" in the *Collins Dictionary*
(1991). See further under **conjunctions**.

therein, thereon, thereunder See under **thereafter**.

thesaurus The plural of this word is discussed under **-us** section 1.

they, them, their When we need pronouns in the third person plural, **they**
(and **them** and **their**) are there to serve our purpose. Yet being gender-free,
they're increasingly used instead of *he/she* in singular applications as well:

*Each member of the group must be prepared to bring in samples of their
work to discuss.*

Their avoids the need for the sexist *his*, or the clumsy *his/her*.

After indefinite pronouns **their** helps to give the statement the broadest
possible reference:

Everyone has to consider their future.

Purists might still say that to use "plural" **their** after *everyone* is incorrect, but
many people nowadays use *they/them/their* in agreement with indefinite
pronouns and adjectives such as *any(one), every(one), no-(one)* and *some(one)*,
without noticing that it's happening. Australian research finds the singular *they/
them/their* in a range of documents from advertising to legislation. *Webster's
English Usage* has numerous citations from fiction and nonfiction sources,
stretching back to the sixteenth century. Language historians would note that
the trend towards using **they** for both plural and singular is exactly what
happened with *you* some centuries ago. (See further under **ye** and **you**.)

third person The **third person** is a grammarian's phrase for the person(s) or
thing(s) being talked about in a sentence. The difference between **third person**
and the *first* or *second* is clearest in the perspectives involved in our English
pronouns, as in:

I am firm. *(first)*

You are stubborn. *(second)*

He is pig-headed. *(third)*

In conversations we use all three persons, whereas in most writing the **third
person** is used disproportionately in conveying information. Some formal and
institutional styles oblige writers to keep entirely to the **third person** and avoid
the first and second persons entirely, which makes for detached and impersonal
prose. See further under **person** (first or third-person narrative).

Third World Coined in French (as "tiers monde"), this term was used after World War II to refer to the least developed countries of Asia, Africa, Latin America and the Pacific. It had both political and cultural implications: that the countries concerned were not politically linked with either western alliances such as NATO or the Soviet bloc; and that they had neither an industrial infrastructure nor a high standard of living.

The term can be explained either by assuming that the **Third World** is the newest international frontier after the "Old World" (Europe) and the "New World" (North America)—or by the idea that the "First World" and the "Second World" are, respectively the West and former Soviet bloc, and then the **Third World** includes all those not aligned to the first two. In the Chinese view, however, they are the **Third World**. This then requires a further expression "Fourth World", for referring to the poorest and most dependent nations of the world.

this has a number of idiomatic uses. For the choice between **this** and *next*, as in *this Saturday* and *next Saturday*, see **next.**

For the uses of **this** and *that*, see under **that.**

tho See **though.**

-thon See under **-athon.**

thorax The plural of this word is discussed at **-x** section 2.

thou and **thee** These were once the ordinary English pronouns by which English-speakers addressed each other. They were used for the individual, while *ye/you* were for more than one person. This division of labor was maintained in the King James Bible, and it underlies the difference between two otherwise similar comments:

O thou of little faith.

O ye of little faith.

The first was said by Jesus to Peter, when the disciple seemed to be thinking twice about his ability to walk on water. The second was addressed to the crowd assembled to hear the sermon on the mount.

In fact this biblical grammar was somewhat old-fashioned in its own day. Shakespeare's plays suggest that by about 1600, the singular/plural distinction between **thou** and *ye* had already been replaced by a style distinction in which *thou/thee* was used for friendly and intimate address to an individual, while *ye/you* was for neutral, public and more distant address, to either an individual or a group. This is comparable to the distinction still made in French, German and other modern European languages. But for some reason the distinction was short-lived in English, and by the end of the seventeenth century **thou/thee** had been replaced by *you* for almost all second person uses, both singular and plural. Only in religious language did **thou/thee** live on, in the special form of address

to the divinity; and their lofty overtones could then be harnessed in literary
rhetoric:

O wild west wind, thou breath of autumn's being ...

though or **although** In spite of appearances, **though** is not to be thought of
as simply a cut-down, informal version of **although**. Admittedly there are
sentences like the following, in which either one could be used to mean "despite
the fact that":

Though the door is still intact, the lock needs attention.
Although the door is still intact, the lock needs attention.

The choice of **although** entails greater formality and emphasis.

Although most often occurs at the start of the sentence, and draws attention
to itself there. **Though** is more flexible, appearing at the start and at the end of
sentences, as well as in between. It carries more variety of meanings than
although. In mid-sentence it becomes a synonym for *but*:

I wouldn't stake my hopes on it though I'd consider it a hopeful sign.

At the end of a sentence **though** is a synonym for "however":

I wouldn't stake my hopes on it though.

In that position it often serves to qualify the thrust of the previous statement.

These uses of **though** have developed in informal talk, but they're common
enough now in print, as the *Right Word at the Right Time* shows. In databases
of written English, the use of **though** to mean "however" runs at about 8% of
all instances of the word.

Other roles of **though** (but not **although**) are to combine with *as* and *even*
in compound conjunctions:

As though it had been commissioned, the sun began to shine.
*Even though we were indoors, the sunshine seemed to brighten the
conversation.*

Note that *even though* seems more emphatic than either **although** or **though**,
and can draw extra attention to a concessive statement when it's needed.

Both **though** and **although** have alternative spellings in *tho'/tho* and *altho'/
altho*. Unlike many abbreviations, they have no effect on the pronunciation of
the word, and they do tidy up the surplus letters. In spite of this, neither
abbreviation has caught on generally. (There was just one instance of *tho* in the
Australian ACE corpus.) The forms with apostrophe declare their informality,
and those without it are perhaps too different from the regular spelling. Whatever
the reasons, these eminently sensible forms are mostly confined to advertising
and technical writing, according to *Webster's English Usage* (1989)—i.e. to
styles of writing which are more independent of the standard conventions of
English.

thrash and **thresh** In Australian English these are two separate words, **thrash**
meaning "beat" and **thresh** meaning "separate the grains of wheat from the
ears that contain them". Originally they were one and the same word
"thresshe", the variant spelling with an *a* making its appearance in the sixteenth

century. The different spellings were subsequently linked with the different strands of meaning. But there are signs of a return to the original situation, except that it's **thrash** which is gaining ground. It sometimes replaces **thresh** when referring to harvesting, and it's also the one used for new figurative meanings, in:

The dog was thrashing about in the water and

Let's thrash out this problem over lunch.

through With the meaning "from one end to another", this word can be used in the dimensions of either space or time. Compare:

They walked through the park.

They worked through the night.

In such cases, **through** governs a noun which is a unit of space or time. Those uses of **through** are established worldwide.

A rather different use of **through** has developed in American English, in which it links two words which specify the beginning and the end of a time period:

The gallery will be open Monday through Thursday.

Here **through** means "from Monday up to and including Thursday"—though it's a neater way of saying it, and it has the advantage of making it clear that the period runs until the end of Thursday. In Australian English when we say *Monday to Thursday* it's not certain whether the period includes the whole of Thursday. The use of **through** to clarify the period is now widely recognised and understood outside North America, and it's beginning to catch on in Australia.

Note that the spelling *thru* is not generally used in documentary writing, even though it quite often appears on street signs (*NO THRU ROAD*), and in catalogues and advertisements. It renders the word simply and directly, and has everything to recommend it. It was one of the set of words which major American institutions such as the National Education Association and the *Chicago Tribune* tried to establish, during nearly a century of spelling reform. (See further under **gh**.) The word *thruway* is a monument to the endeavor, but represented only by references to the *New York Thruway* in the Australian ACE database. There are no instances of *thru* itself.

throwaway terms Because languages reflect the culture of the people who use them, they also show something of their values and attitudes to others— those they admire and those for whom they have no respect. Every language has expressions like the English *Chinese burn, Dutch courage, French leave* and *Mexican carwash*, which enshrine stereotyped criticism of the peoples concerned.

Throwaway expressions have no factual basis, though they sometimes emerge in a century when relations with another country are particularly vexed. The *Oxford Dictionary* notes that rivalry between the English and the Dutch in the seventeenth century seems to have been the matrix for various phrases critical of the Dutch, including *Dutch auction, Dutch bargain, Dutch gold, Dutch treat* and *Dutch uncle*. The phrases imply stereotypes of the Dutch as stingy and moralising. **Throwaway terms** for the French tend to project them as licentious, witness *French kiss, French letter* and *doing french*. Speakers of languages other than English return the compliment. To express what the English call *French leave*, there are expressions in Italian, French and Norwegian which translate as "leave like an Englishman".

The prejudices and stereotypes embodied in **throwaway terms** are very persistent, and it would be better for neighborly relations if they passed into oblivion. Dictionaries too can do their bit by removing the capital letter from **throwaway terms**, so that there's no subconscious stimulus to read them as national or geographical terms. The fact that *French Guiana* comes just before *French leave* in the headword list is no reason to insist on keeping the capital letter on the second.

thru or **through** See through.

thus This has two roles, as:
1 a demonstrative adverb meaning "in this way"
2 a conjunct meaning "consequently".

Both uses of **thus** contribute to the cohesion of a piece of writing (see **coherence** and **cohesion**). The second is particularly useful in argument, suggesting logical connections between one statement and another. Note that it is a *conjunct* rather than a *conjunction* (see further under **conjunctions** section 3).

tic or **tick** These spellings serve to differentiate a medical word from several others. **Tic** is reserved for a convulsive motion by the muscles of the face, while **tick** covers all of the following:
- the small bloodsucking insect
- the small sound made by a clock
- the small mark ($\checkmark$) used to check items off
- the cover of a mattress or pillow

Apart from those standard uses, **tick** is also found in informal idioms such as *just a tick* (= moment) and *on tick* (= credit).

The words spelled **tick** make a remarkable set of homonyms, and the fact that several imply something small also suggests that there's some sound symbolism at work in the word. (See further under **phonesthemes**.)

ticketed For the spelling of this verb, see t.

tidbit or **titbit** See titbit.

tight or **tightly** The first of these can be either an adjective as in a *tight fist*, or an adverb, especially in informal idioms such as *hold tight* and *sit tight*. It usually follows the verb it modifies.

Tightly is the regular adverb which expresses the firmness of a grip, as in *clamped tightly between the teeth*, or the closeness of an arrangement, as in *tightly packed congregation*. It can appear either before or after the verb, as in those examples. (See further under **zero adverbs**.)

tilde This accent is most familiar in Spanish and Portuguese, though it has different functions in each. In Spanish it only occurs with *n*, as in *señor*, to show that it's pronounced to rhyme with "tenure" rather than "tenor". In Portuguese it appears with *a* and *o* to show that they are nasal vowels, whether as single sounds or as the first vowel in a diphthong as in *curação*.

till or **until** In most contexts these are equally good, witness:
We'll delay the discussion till you come.
We'll delay the discussion until you come.
Until seems a little more formal, yet **till** is certainly not an abbreviated form of it. **Till** was established centuries before **until**. Both words can be used as prepositions and conjunctions, in the dimensions of time and space.
Two cautions to note with **till/until**:
1 to combine *up* with either of them (*up till/up until*) is strictly redundant, though it's occasionally used for special emphasis
2 there is no need or justification for *'til*, when **till** stands in its own right and not as a contraction of *until*.

timber or **timbre** These words mean quite different things and are not merely different spellings for the same word like *center/centre*. **Timber** is of course the collective word for wood which has been harvested and sawn up for use in buildings etc. It originated in Old English as the word for "wood" or "wooden construction".
Timbre is the quality of sound made by a musical instrument, or the singing or speaking voice. It depends on the relative intensities of the overtones accompanying the fundamental. It derives from the French word for a small bell. A rare alternative spelling for **timbre** is *tamber*, coined by British linguists in the 1920s to render the sound of the French word.

time In the Anglo-Saxon tradition, **time** of day was reckoned in terms of two equal parts, with twelve hours before noon (*a.m.*) and twelve before midnight (*p.m.*). Questions about which of the threshold hours belong to which are discussed at the entry for **p.m.** With the twenty-four hour clock, neither *a.m.* nor *p.m.* are needed, and the problem disappears altogether.
For matters of *historical time*, see **dating systems**. For *geological time*, see **geological eras** and Appendix III.
For the use of the apostrophe in expressions such as *six months time* or *one year's time*, see under **apostrophes** section 2.

time zones Australia stretches 4000 kilometres from east to west, and is divided into three **time zones**. The eastern states (Queensland, New South

Wales, Victoria and Tasmania) work by Australian Eastern Standard Time; South Australia and Northern Territory by Central Standard Time (half an hour behind Eastern Standard); and Western Australia by Western Standard Time (two hours behind Eastern Standard).

Daylight saving adjustments are applied independently by each state to standard time, and their sovereign right to decide when summertime begins and ends can result, temporarily, in further **time zones**. In March 1992 there were five **time zones**, when South Australia and Tasmania maintained daylight saving longer than the rest.

tingeing or **tinging** See -e section 1d.

-tion Many abstract nouns in English end this way, though strictly speaking the *-t* belongs to the stem, and the suffix is *-ion*. (See further under the headings **-ation** and **-ion**.)

tipstaff The plural of this word is *tipstaves* according to the *Macquarie* and the major American dictionaries. For the *Collins Dictionary* it's *tipstaffs*. Compare the two plural forms of **staff**, discussed under that heading.

tire or **tyre** See under **tyre**.

tiro or **tyro** Dictionaries diverge on which spelling to use for this Latin loanword meaning a "novice". In classical Latin it was **tiro**, and this is the spelling preferred in the *Oxford Dictionary* and other British authorities. However the immediate source of the word for English was medieval Latin where it was **tyro**, and this is the preferred spelling in *Webster's* and *Macquarie* dictionaries. Because of its rarity there's no pressure to settle the spelling one way or the other. For other classical words spelled with both *i* and *y*, see under **i/y**.

The plural of the word has also varied, though modern dictionaries recommend the English plural *tiros* or *tyros*. The Latin plural *tyrones* was last recorded in 1824.

titbit or **tidbit** The first spelling is preferred in Australian and British English, the second in American English. The word is something of a mystery, but both Bailey and Johnson record that *tid* could mean such things as "nice, delicate, tender, soft", which seem to come closer to the meaning than *tit*, a "small animal or object". This suggests that the American **tidbit** is closer to the origin of the word. Yet the British spelling **titbit** also dates from the eighteenth century.

titer or **titre** See -re/-er.

titles The **titles** of publications and creative works demand special treatment to set them apart from ordinary strings of words. This entry deals in turn with books, journal articles, newspapers and magazines and audiovisual media. For the **titles** used by people, see under **forms of address**.

1 *Book titles* are distinguished in print by italics, and in handwriting or typing by underlining. On the question of which words in the title to capitalise, all agree that the first word must carry a capital letter, but after that there's considerable divergence. Opinions range from minimal use of capitals to something like maximal:

a) capitalise nothing apart from any proper names:

   For the term of his natural life

b) capitalise all nouns:

   For the Term of his natural Life

c) capitalise all nouns and adjectives:

   For the Term of his Natural Life

d) capitalise all nouns, adjectives, pronouns, verbs and adverbs (i.e. everything except function words):

   For the Term of His Natural Life

Librarians and bibliographers work with minimal capitals (option (a)), yet options (b) to (d) are well established in literary tradition. For many people there's virtue in using option (a) in lists and bibliographies (see further under **bibliographies**), but using one of the other options for titles quoted in the course of a written discussion. Option (b) is quite sufficient whenever an italic typeface or underlining is used to set the title apart from the text in which it's embedded.

Note also that these options allow us to contrast the title and subtitle of a book with heavier and lighter capitalisation. Thus any of the options (b) to (d) can be used for the main title, and option (a) for the subtitle, as in:

   The Life and Times of the English Language: the marvellous history of the English tongue

The use of option (a) for the subtitle also settles a minor bone of contention over whether to capitalise the first word of the subtitle or not. The principle of minimal capitals means lower case for everything (except proper names) in the subtitle, as shown above.

2 *The use of short titles* (an abbreviated form of the book's title) is on the increase. They replace the Latin *ibid.* etc. in footnotes, and also appear in the main text in second and subsequent allusions to a publication. In both places, it's helpful to have more than minimal capitalisation. (See further under **short titles**.)

3 *Titles of journal articles.* The setting of the **titles** of scholarly articles varies from journal to journal, reflecting the decisions and preferences of individual editors. An established style is to enclose the *title* of the article in quotation marks, and to use italics (or underlining) for the name of the journal. The more recent style does away with quotation marks, and simply uses typography to contrast the title of the article (in roman) with the name of the journal (in italics). Abbreviations for the stock items in journal references (such as *J* for *Journal*) are increasingly used, especially in the Vancouver style. (See **bibliographies** section C.)

4 *Titles of newspapers and magazines.* The mastheads of newspapers and magazines are set in italics, without *The* (see further under **the**). The date of issue and the edition, where necessary, are given as well as the section number or name, if the paper is produced in separate units. Page references are optional according to both the Chicago *Manual of Style* and *Copy-editing* (1992)

5 *Titles of radio and TV programs, feature films, sound recordings etc.* The **titles** of these are capitalised, as for books. Again it's desirable to have more than minimal capitalisation when the titles are cited amid running text, and options (b), (c) or (d) serve the purpose. Quotation marks are sometimes used to distinguish the subunits of a TV or radio series (as with individual poems in an anthology). Otherwise the **titles** of audiovisual items are distinguished chiefly by the use of italics (see further under **italics**). For more details about citing **audiovisual media**, see under that heading.

titre or **titer** See -re/-er.

ti-tree or **tea-tree** See tea-tree.

to This small word is the focus of several usage questions about how it relates to verbs and to particular adjectives.

1 *To with verbs.* **To** is commonly thought of as an essential part of the infinitive of English verbs, but it's not necessarily so (see **infinitives**). For a discussion of the so-called "split infinitive", as in *to really understand*, see **split infinitive**.

   To often serves as the link between quasi-auxiliaries or catenatives and the main verb, as with:
   dare to   had to   going to   need to   ought to   try to   want to
Note that the **to** is sometimes omitted with **dare**, **need** and **ought**, especially in negative statements (see under those individual headings).

2 *To after certain adjectives.* **To** has always been used after adjectives (and adverbs), especially those which suggest likeness or closeness, for example:
   adjacent to   close to   similar to   near to
It also works with many kinds of words to suggest a particular orientation or relative position, as with:
   amenable to   averse to   comparable to   conducive to   different to
   oblivious to   susceptible to
For some of those, the collocation with **to** is an alternative, but for others it's the only one used. Those with a related verb (*compare, differ*) often have alternatives. (See further under **compare**, **different** and **oblivious**.)

toboggan or **sled** See sled.

toilet or **toilette** When first borrowed into English in seventeenth century (as *toilette*), this French loanword referred to a cloth associated with dressing and grooming. Within the context of getting dressed it developed a number of other meanings, almost all of which have been disabled since about 1900, because as **toilet** it then became the standard word for a lavatory.

The older and wider associations with dressing and grooming live on in derivatives such as *toilet bag*, *toilet set* and *toiletries*, and in the occasional use of **toilette** (with French pronunciation) to refer to personal ablutions. In writing, the French spelling helps to distance the word from the WC. No longer is it possible to say: *She appeared in a blue toilet*, as was said a century ago; and the thought of a **toilet** being a "reception held while dressing" (an eighteenth century usage) is unthinkable. The word's history is a living example of the operation of language taboos. (See further under **taboo words**.)

tolerance or **toleration**   These abstract nouns both embody the verb *tolerate*, but the first is the broader and more sympathetic word. It implies a characteristic willingness to give place to attitudes and practices other than one's own. **Tolerance** also has some more technical meanings:
- in medicine and pharmaceutics "capacity to endure", as in *low tolerance for alcohol*;
- in engineering "acceptable deviation from the specified dimensions", as in *the measurements have tolerances of only 1 mm.*

Toleration is mostly used of a specific instance of **tolerance**, as in:
Don't count on her toleration of his throwaway lines about Queenslanders.
It implies more strongly than **tolerance** that there are limits to what one would put up with. This is still so when it comes to *religious toleration*, which often suggests the need to accept other religions because of their presence in the community, not through any desire to endorse them.

Note that the negative form for both **tolerance** and **toleration** is *intolerance*.

ton, tonne or **tun**   The word **ton** belongs to the imperial system of weights and measures, and is the equivalent of 2240 lb. The extended names *gross ton* or *long ton* help to distinguish it from the *short ton* of 2000 lb, which is used in the USA. (The latter is therefore sometimes called the "American ton" by outsiders.) The **tonne** is a metric unit of mass equal to 1000 kg. See further under **imperial system** and Appendix V.

Ton derives from **tun**, a word for a large cask of wine or beer, which has also served as a unit of measurement for liquids. The spelling **ton** was simply a variant of **tun** that became the word for a standard of weight during the seventeenth century. **Tonne** was borrowed from French in the nineteenth century, though it too is ultimately the same word.

The word *tonnage* relates to *tons* and the imperial system, and there's not yet an equivalent for *tonnes* in the metric system. One could suggest *tonneage*, though that goes against standard rules of English spelling (see **-e** section 1). Perhaps there's no need to worry about finding a term, because *tonnage* will simply become the standard term relating to the metric **tonne** as the change to metrication completes itself.

topic The beginning of a sentence is its most important part. Whatever is there is foregrounded for the reader as the ongoing focus of interest, whether it's something talked about in the preceding sentence(s), or a new focus of attention. Compare:

A) *James Rand had always wanted to go to Africa. He had met Moroccans in Spain who seemed to exude the mystery of the dark continent. He also knew there was business to be cultivated in Nigeria, and he could amuse himself with a little big game hunting as recreation.*

B) *James Rand had always wanted to go to Africa. But until things had settled down in Nigeria, it wasn't the place to look for business. It wasn't far from the big game hunting grounds however ...*

Notice how version (A) seems to focus on JR the man himself, whereas version (B) is concerned with the location. These different perspectives develop from the different openings to the second and third sentences. Both versions begin with a statement about the man and the place, but (A) turns the spotlight on *he*, and (B) on *it*. Thus the focus of the passage, and what it foregrounds, is controlled by what appears at the beginnings of sentences.

1 *Sentence positions.* The all-important first "slot" in the sentence is often referred to as the **topic**. The rest of the sentence is then known as the *comment*. In these terms the first sentence above is structured thus:

> TOPIC   COMMENT
> *James Rand   had always wanted to go to Africa.*

Note that the **topic** position can be occupied by different grammatical items. It's often a name, pronoun or noun phrase which is the grammatical subject of the sentence. But it can also be an opening adverbial phrase or clause, as in sentence two of version (B):

But until things had settled down in Nigeria ...

Note also that the **topic** may be preceded by a conjunction/conjunct (in that case *but*), which gives no substance but helps to show that the focus is changing. In closely argued writing the **topic** is quite often preceded by a conjunct and/ or an interpersonal cue such as *perhaps, regrettably*, which again helps to frame the **topic** item for the reader.

What happens in the *comment* slot (the latter part of the sentence) is less important for information focus. It does however serve to introduce information which can be developed in the following sentence. The reference to *Africa* in the *comment* of the first sentence gives the writer a basis from which to develop the subject and to refer to ''Moroccans'' in the second sentence (version A) and ''Nigeria'' (version B), and then to ''big game'' in the third sentence.

Note that some linguists replace the terms **topic** and *comment* with *theme* and *rheme* respectively.

2 *Topicalising phrases.* Because the **topic** position is so important, what goes there should not be dictated by the routine grammar of the clause. Ordinarily a clause begins with its subject, as noted above; yet something else can be put ahead of it to highlight the point at issue. The phrase or clause which does that is known as a *topicalising phrase/clause*. In documentary writing there are stock topicalising phrases which serve to alter the focus:

In a similar/later/larger study, JB found that …

From a historical/theoretical point of view, the problem …

For other examples, see under **dangling participle**.

Other ways of getting something into **topic** position are:

- using the passive. It puts the spotlight on the object of the verb instead of the subject. Compare:

The Moroccans embodied all the mystery of the dark continent.

All the mystery of the dark continent was embodied in the Moroccans he met.

- using **cleft sentences** (see under that heading).

topic sentences These are the sentences that signal what a paragraph is to be about. (See under **paragraphs**.)

tormentor or **tormenter** Dictionaries always give first preference to **tormentor**, but the major ones also present **tormenter** as an acceptable alternative.

tornado, hurricane or **cyclone** See **cyclone**.

torpedo For the plural, see under **-o**.

torturous or **tortuous** The first word has *torture* in it, and **torturous** means "causing pain and distress", as in:

He suffered a torturous death from lung cancer.

The second word **tortuous** means "twisting, winding", and so is often found in the phrase *a tortuous path*. In fact both words could be applied to a grueling bushwalk on a narrow and difficult track.

In figurative use, especially in relation to an argument, **tortuous** is more likely and more common as a way of saying that what's said was complicated and hard to follow. (That is, unless the words uttered were very distressing to the hearer, in which case it would be **torturous**.) The two words are often confused, and if there's any risk of misunderstanding, they should be replaced: **tortuous** with "convoluted" and **torturous** with "excruciating".

total of Which should it be:

A total of 34 soldiers was recruited.

A total of 34 soldiers were recruited.

Traditional grammar would insist on the first, arguing that the verb has to agree with *total*. The alternative view is that the second sentence is also possible, either (1) because *total* works as a collective noun, or (2) because **total of** works as a numerical phrase like *a lot of* or *a number of*, which normally take plural verbs. (See further under **agreement** section 4.)

totaled or totalled Whether to double or not to double the *l* is discussed at **-l/-ll-**.

toto See **in toto**.

tour de force This French phrase means literally "feat of strength". In English it usually refers to a feat of technical skill, as in:

The soprano's high trills were a tour de force.

The phrase can be used admiringly, but it often implies that what was done was spectacular rather than having particular artistic or intellectual value.

tout de suite In English this is usually taken to mean "at once, immediately", while in French it means "following straight on". Thus it's open to the same kind of ambiguity as *momentarily* as to how soon the intended action will actually take place. (See **momentous** or **momentary**.)

The phrase is sometimes pronounced in English as "toot sweet", but is not to be mistaken for the Italian *tutti frutti* "all fruits", a confection or icecream made with a variety of fruits.

toward or **towards** The choice between these is simply a matter of where you live. In Australia and Britain people generally plump for **towards**, whereas in North America it's **toward**. The difference is most marked in Britain however, where according to corpus evidence **towards** outnumbers **toward** by more than 20:1. In Australia the ratio is more like 7:1, while in the USA it's the reverse: 1:7 in favor of **toward**.

Note that the word is a preposition, and therefore a different case from the adjectives/adverbs ending in *-ward(s)*. (See further under **-ward** or **-wards**.)

toweling or **towelling** For the choice between these, see **-l/-ll-**.

town names Australia's towns and suburbs are often named after places and people elsewhere, but with some inconsistencies in the spelling. You might wonder for instance why it's *Moonie* in Queenland, *Mooney Mooney* in New South Wales, and *Moonee (Ponds)* in Victoria. Unless you look closely at the *Postcode Book*, you may not notice the numerous interstate differences, including the following:

Armadale VIC	*Armidale NSW*
Balaclava VIC	*Balaklava SA*
Berri SA	*Berry NSW*
Berridale NSW	*Berriedale TAS*
Boolaroo NSW	*Booleroo SA*
Boya WA	*Boyer TAS*
Branxholm TAS	*Branxholme VIC*
Carina QLD	*Carine WA*
Cradoc TAS	*Cradock SA*
Currajong QLD	*Kurrajong NSW*
Dimboola VIC	*Dimbulah QLD*

Forest TAS	*Forrest VIC, WA*
Forestdale QLD	*Forrestdale WA*
Girraween NSW	*Girrawheen WA*
Leichardt VIC	*Leichhardt NSW*
Montagu TAS	*Montague VIC*
Nerrena VIC	*Nerrina VIC*
Paringa SA	*Paringi VIC*
Paterson NSW	*Patterson VIC*
Peron WA	*Peronne VIC*
Ranelagh TAS	*Raneleigh VIC*
Rocklea QLD	*Rockley NSW*
Surry Hills NSW	*Surrey Hills VIC*
Stewart VIC	*Stuart QLD*
Teatree TAS	*Ti Tree NT*
Woodforde SA	*Woodford NSW, QLD, VIC*
York Town TAS	*Yorketown SA*

Note also the divergent treatment of names involving *Mac*. (See **Mac** or **Mc**.)

toxemia or **toxaemia** See under **ae/e**.

trachea The plural is discussed under **-a** section 1.

trademarks When first created, **trademarks** and *tradenames* are jealously guarded commercial property, which can only be used by the company that owns them. Yet the company no doubt rejoices to hear their product name become a household word. If your fortunes depend on HOOVER it is reassuring to hear people using the word *hoover* as a noun or verb to refer to any vacuum cleaner or to vacuum cleaning—as if it's the only product of its kind on the market. It is also a linguistic event, showing that the word is becoming generic and that it merits a place in dictionary headword lists.

The point at which a word moves from being a *tradename* to being a generic word is in one sense a matter of law. Unpleasant lawsuits have been fought over what was considered by one party to be a protected *tradename*, and by the other to be common lexical property. Dictionaries are sometimes invoked to show whether or not the word is generic, and can find themselves in the gun for including words which began life as *tradenames*. Their defense is to say that such words would not be in the list if they were not already generic, and to note at the same time that the word originated as a *trademark*. A surprising number of household words began life as **trademarks**, including:

biro crimplene daks doona fibro kleenex laundromat levis masonite
plasticine polaroid primus technicolor thermos

There are many more.

Newspapers and mass-circulating magazines are more often challenged over the use of a *tradename* than dictionaries. They are vulnerable because they also contain advertising, and editorial use of *tradenames* may be seen as promoting one product at the expense of others. Most newspapers take no risks therefore, and urge their journalists to avoid **trademarks** altogether by means of a paraphrase, e.g. "sticking plaster" instead of *bandaid*. Their other strategy when the word cannot be avoided (as in verbatim quotes) is to capitalise it, which helps to show that it's a unique, proper name and not being used carelessly. Yet the effect can be quite unfortunate, witness: *It was just a Bandaid solution to the agricultural problem, according to the minister.* The use of the capital letter invites a literal rather than figurative interpretation of *bandaid*. A way out in this case would be to put quote marks round "bandaid solution".

traffic For the spelling of this word when it serves as a verb, see **-c/-ck-**.

tranquilliser, tranquillizer or **tranquilizer** Either the first or second spelling may be found in Britain, and the second or third in the USA. In Australia the most common spelling is the first, reflecting the general preference for *-ise(r)* over *-ize(r)*, and the tendency to follow British practice in doubling a final *l* before adding endings. The use of double *l* seems particularly misguided in this case, since it's not usually indulged before *-ise*. (Compare **equalise**, **totalisator**, and see further under **-l/-ll-**.) The British spelling is probably influenced by *tranquillity*, where the difference in stress justifies the double *l*. The ideal spelling for Australians would be *tranquiliser*, though it has yet to be listed in dictionaries.

trans- This Latin prefix meaning "across, through" comes to us in a large number of loanwords, especially verbs, but also adjectives and related nouns:
>   *transfer transfigure transform translate translucent transmigrate*
>   *transmit transcribe transparent transpose*
In modern English the prefix has mostly helped to create geographical adjectives. Following *trans-Atlantic* (1779) came:
>   *transalpine trans-Andean trans-Canadian transcontinental*
>   *trans-Pacific transpolar trans-Siberian*
An exceptional example where **trans-** is used more figuratively is *transsexual*. For the spelling of *tran(s)sexual* and *tran(s)ship*, see **-s/-ss-**.

transcendent and **transcendental** In common usage either of these may be used to mean "surpassing ordinary standards or limits", though they have few applications in everyday life. **Transcendental** is most familiar in the phrase *transcendental meditation*, a profound yet fully conscious state of relaxation deeper than sleep, which is reached by a technique derived from Hinduism. In western philosophy **transcendental** is used in reference to a particular style of argumentation, whereas **transcendent** refers to that which is beyond experience. In Christian theology **transcendent** is the term used to express the idea of a divinity existing beyond the created world. Still in the realms of the abstract, **transcendental** is used in mathematics to describe a number which cannot be produced or expressed by algebraic operations.

transexual or **transsexual** See under -s/-ss-.

transferable, transferrable or **transferrible** The first spelling is preferred in all dictionaries, though the pronunciation it implies (with stress on the first syllable) is not the most common. The second spelling with two *rs* (suggesting stress on the second syllable) is also registered in the larger dictionaries as an alternative. Only the largest dictionaries record the third, rather latinate spelling, but by their evidence it is archaic.

Compare **inferable**.

transferer or **transferor** The spelling with *-er* is the one to use for general purposes, whereas the one with *-or* is for legal uses. *Webster's Dictionary* registers yet other spellings with two *rs*: *transferrer/transferror*, which accord well with common pronunciation (with stress on the second syllable) but are rarely seen.

transfers Words and compounds often acquire new roles and meanings by being *transferred* from one grammatical class to another. Shakespeare made it happen in the much quoted *It outherods herod*; and a striking modern example can be seen in: *The concept has been Laura Ashleyed*. The grammatical process is no stranger than the one we accept in sentences like the following:

They were short-changed at the restaurant.

He buttonholed me in the corridor.

The conversion of nouns and noun compounds to verbs has fostered innumerable new usages since the Middle English period, when the number of distinctive inflections for all classes of words was reduced to the small number we know today. Many of those produced by Shakespeare are now unremarkable elements of the English language. Even recent examples are quickly assimilated, such as the following, all from the first half of the twentieth century:

audition contact date debate feature package

page pressure process service

The reverse process, by which verbs are converted into nouns, is also common enough. The following are all very old **transfers** of this kind:

aim contest fall hunt laugh lift look move push

reject ride scan shudder sneeze split

Adjectives also lend themselves to conversion, and have generated new verbs all through the history of English. Examples from the thirteenth, fourteenth and fifteenth century include:

black blind blunt brown calm crisp dim dirty

empty equal humble secure treble

Even comparative adjectives can become verbs, witness *better* and *lower*.

All those examples show that English permits and even encourages such **transfers**. Some English-users nevertheless react to new **transfers**, especially cases where nouns work as verbs, as with *action, impact, interface* and *profile* for example. Those four are by now widely used, and are not examples of the most objectionable kind, where the writer hasn't taken the trouble to find the right form of word for the job:

The architecture document was vocabularied so as to obstacle-course the project for the would-be understander.

A concentrated collection of ad hoc **transfers** like that is enough to make anyone shudder, and we might note that examples involving words of more than two syllables seem extra awkward. But the shift of one and two-syllabled words from one class to another goes on unnoticed all the time, without people turning a hair.

Note that the linguistic name for **transfers** or conversions of words from one grammatical class to another is *zero derivation* (because the word changes class without any derivational suffix. See further under **suffix**.)

tranship or **transship** See under -s/-ss-.

transient or **transitory** These both mean that something will not linger. In their connotations however they differ, since **transitory** can have a certain elegiac melancholy about it, as in *the transitory freshness of youth*. **Transient** is more matter of fact about the brevity of things, and *transient visitors* are simply ''short-term'' ones.

transitive and **intransitive** In traditional grammar these words identify an aspect of the way verbs work. A *transitive verb* is one with a direct object as the focus of the action it expresses, as with *pick (a team)* or *send (a letter)*. *Intransitive verbs* are ones without an object, such as *appear* and *vanish*. But many verbs can be used either transitively or intransitively, witness:

Transitive	Intransitive
They flew me to Darwin.	*The bird flew away.*
She boiled the kettle.	*The kettle boiled.*

Note that verbs in the passive are automatically regarded as **transitive**, because they involve using the object of a verb as the subject. Compare:

A messenger was dispatched to Rome. (passive/transitive)
They dispatched a messenger to Rome. (active/transitive)

Reflexive verbs are also regarded as **transitive**, because of the reflexive pronouns which function as their objects:

She drove herself to the airport.

Note that in all the examples so far the verb has one object and is therefore *monotransitive*. Compare *ditransitive* verbs, which have both indirect and direct objects in that order (see **object** section 2).

1 *Transitivity extended.* Certain other kinds of verbs are **transitive** by virtue of the noun clause which is their normal object. Typically they are verbs which express a mental or verbal process, such as *say*, *think* etc. See for example;

I know he'll do well.

The idea of transitivity is also extended by some grammarians to verbs which take an infinitive, because they regard the infinitive as a noun, and as the object of the verb. (See further under **verbal nouns**.) This makes *like* a **transitive** verb in the following construction:

They liked to swim after work.

The alternative analysis is to regard *to swim* as a complement of the catenative verb *like*, and the verb phrase is then **intransitive**.

2 *Phrasal and prepositional verbs* can be difficult to categorise in terms of transitivity. Compare:

He can't live down his past.
He lives down the road.

Recent grammars such as the *Comprehensive Grammar of English*, as well as the *Collins Dictionary* (1991) would take *live down* in the first sentence as a **transitive** verb—*down* being a particle closely linked with the verb, rather than prefacing the following noun, as in the second sentence, where it's a preposition.

3 *Copular verbs* also challenge the **transitive/intransitive** distinction, as in *I feel uneasy*. They are usually felt to have more in common with **intransitive** verbs, because the item after the verb is not its object but a complement for the subject. (See further under **copular verbs**.)

Note also that in spite of the problems in applying traditional notions of transitivity, the terms **transitive** and **intransitive** persist in dictionaries. Recent grammars and especially the *Introduction to Functional Grammar* (1985) take seriously the need to reanalyse the concept of transitivity for English.

transitory or **transient** See transient.

transparence or **transparency** When referring to a photographic image, only **transparency** will do. Either word can be used for the abstract noun that describes the quality of being transparent, though even there **transparency** is more common.

transsexual or **transexual** See under -s/-ss-.

transship or **tranship** See under -s/-ss-.

traveled or **travelled**, **traveler** or **traveller**, **traveling** or **travelling** The choice between these is discussed under -l/-ll-.

travelogue or **travelog** See under -gue/-g.

tread The regular past forms of this verb are *trod* (past tense) and *trodden* (past participle). The form *trod* is sometimes used instead of *trodden*:

He's trod his muddy shoes on the new carpet.

Examples of this usage have been on record since the sixteenth century, and it's an accepted variant in Australia.

treasonable or **treasonous** These are equivalent, though **treasonable** is the one for most purposes. It serves in law, as in *treasonable offence*, as well as in ordinary usage, as a general synonym for "traitorous". The use of

treasonous has steadily declined, and even to Fowler it was largely a poetic word. Dictionaries confirm the trend by crossreferencing the less common **treasonous** to **treasonable**.

treble or **triple** See triple.

tri- This Latin prefix for "three" is found in common words such as:
triangle tricycle trident trifecta triplet tripod
Yet it also plays a vital part in scientific words, in chemistry:
trichloride trioxide tritium trinitrotoluene (TNT)
and in medicine:
triceps tricuspid trinodal trivalve
Tri- appears in time words like *trimonthly* and *triweekly*, where it means "happening every three months/weeks". In the same way *triennial* means "every three years". Note however that *tricentennial* is actually less common than *tercentenary* as the word for "three hundredth anniversary", even though it matches up better with *bicentennial/bicentenary*.
   The prefix **tri-** appears with a shortened vowel in words such as *trilogy*, *trinity* and *trivial*. Note that the last word is probably connected with *trivium*, the three-part curriculum that was the foundation level of medieval schooling.

trialed or **trialled**, **trialing** or **trialling** Working as a verb is still relatively new for *trial*, and the spelling is unstable. The *Macquarie Dictionary* (1991) recommends the spellings with two *l*s, in keeping with British practice on verbs ending in *l*. Yet at least one Australian education department has recommended the forms with one *l*, which are more regular. (See further under **-l/-ll-**.)

triceps For the plural see under **biceps**.

trillion For the value of this number, see under **billion**.

triple or **treble** Both these are modern forms of the Latin *triplus*, which comes to us direct in **triple**, and as **treble** via Old French and Middle English. Both words can now work as adjectives, nouns or verbs, though from the evidence of English databases there are some differences in the use of each. Overall British English prefers **treble**, using it as noun, verb and adjective, while **triple** works the same way in American English. Australian usage has something each way: in the ACE corpus both words are found as verbs, though there are three instances of **treble** to one of **triple**, and **triple** alone appears as adjective and noun. The tendency here is to give more roles to *triple* and fewer to *treble*.
   Writers who use both words sometimes maintain a distinction made by Fowler, that **treble** means something has become three times as great as a known reference point, e.g. *Costs have trebled since 1980*; whereas **triple** means "consisting of three parts or difference entities" as in *triple alliance* or *triple jump*. Yet the *Macquarie* and *Collins* dictionaries both allow that **triple** can mean "(become) three times as great".

For musicians, however, the two words still stand far apart. **Treble** refers to the highest voice part in a musical score, and to instruments whose range corresponds to it, such as the *treble recorder*. **Triple** refers to musical rhythm in which there are three beats to a bar (as in a waltz), which contrasts with duple and quadruple time signatures (as in a march).

triumphant or **triumphal** The first of these expresses a personal feeling of triumph, as in *She was triumphant after winning the contract*. **Triumphal** has ceremonial overtones, as in a *triumphal arch* or *triumphal march*.

trivia This Latin loanword is the plural of *trivium*, a word used in medieval schooling for the lower or elementary curriculum. In modern English **trivia** means "petty details", though the largest dictionaries allow that it may be construed as either plural or singular: *all these trivia/all this trivia*. *Webster's English Usage* (1989) finds the two patterns about equally common. The use of **trivia** with singular agreement seems not to have raised as much angst as **data** and **media** (see under those headings).

-trix This is sometimes thought of as a feminine suffix, because it identifies the feminine gender in pairs like *aviatrix/aviator*. Strictly speaking however, the operative ending is *-ix*, since the *t* and *r* belong to the stem. Either way it appears in very few other words in English, only *executrix* and *testatrix*, which are confined to law and do not undermine women's opportunities more generally. Compare **-ess**.

Note the case of loanwords like *matrix* and *cicatrix*, where the ending is a reminder of the fact that they have both Latin and English plural forms. (See further under **-x**.)

trolley or **trolly** These spellings once served to distinguish a type of lace (**trolly**) from a four-wheeled vehicle (**trolley**). But the former is now hardly known, and so **trolly** is beginning to be reused as a simple variant for **trolley** in reference to supermarket vehicles etc., according to *Oxford Dictionary* citations.

trompe l'oeil This French phrase means literally "deceive the eye". It refers to a type of painting which creates the illusion of three dimensional space as hyperreal art does; or to interior decor which suggests spatial features which are not there, such as painted panels which make a passage seem longer or a room look larger.

troop or **troupe**, **trooper** or **trouper** Both words are derived from French *troupe* an "organised group of people", but usually associated with different activities. A **troupe** is a group of actors or entertainers, as in a *troupe of street theatre artists*, though just occasionally this is written as **troop**. The spelling **troop** is usually reserved for an organised unit of boy scouts, or to a subdivision of a cavalry regiment. In military usage, the plural *troops* refers to the whole body of soldiers, not particular units within it.

The distinction between **troupe** and **troop** carries over to **trouper** and **trooper**. **Trouper** refers to a member of an entertainment group, and **trooper** to either a cavalryman or a mounted policeman. The first is proverbially a committed and experienced performer, the second the archetypal champion at swearing. Compare:

He carried on like a trouper.

He swore like a trooper.

However the *Oxford Dictionary* (1989) shows that the more familiar spelling **trooper** is sometimes used where we might expect the other, as in "a fine trooper".

truism This is a word to be wary of. In technical usage, a **truism** is a tautology, i.e. a self-validating statement, like: *A triangle has three sides.* But the word is also commonly used to refer to a self-evident truth, one which requires no proof. As such it may be either an axiom, or worse, a platitude—so obvious that it does not bear uttering. This last possibility makes **truism** an unreliable word, and one to avoid if you want to stress the fundamental truth or factuality of something, as in:

It's a truism that homosexual behavior exposes people to AIDS.

With **truism** embedded in it, the statement runs the risk of either being thought pretentious, or to mean that you think the observation is superfluous. Either way you need to express the thought in other words.

trumpet For the spelling of this word when used as a verb, see under **t.**

try to or **try and** **Try to** is standard English and acceptable anywhere. **Try and** often replaces it in informal promises and instructions, as in:

I'll try and keep in touch with her.

Try and come soon.

Though **try and** is often criticised as illogical, it seems to express a supportive attitude, as Fowler noticed. It therefore has a particular interpersonal role to play, which may be as important in certain kinds of writing as in speech. It probably has no place in institutional writing, hence the censure often applied to it.

Note that the use of **try and** is always associated with *try* itself, and no other parts of the verb. We cannot use *and* after *tries, trying* or *tried*. (*And* cannot replace *to* in *He tries to make the best of it.*)

Some style guides warn against using **try and** in negative statements, perhaps because Fowler did. Yet a negative instruction like *Don't try and crack hardy over it* sounds natural enough, and with its supportive implications it may be more appropriate than *Don't try to* in some contexts.

tsar or **czar** See under **czar.**

tumor or **tumour** See under **-or/-our.**

tun or **ton** See ton.

tunneled or **tunnelling** See -l/-ll-.

turbid or **turgid** Writing which fails to communicate may be **turbid** (muddy, unclear, confused) or **turgid** (inflated, pompous), or both. When trying to identify the problem, you need to know which, although generalised criticism of a style often conflates the two. Our ability to separate them is hampered by the fact that neither is much used now in its essential physical sense: **turbid** in reference to a liquid with particles stirred up in it, and **turgid** as "swollen". Either way, plain English is needed as an antidote to **turbid** and **turgid** writing.

turfs or **turves** The choice of plurals is discussed under **-f/-v-**.

turnover lines *Turnover(s)* is the editorial term used in Australia and Britain for line(s) which run on to the next one. In the USA they are known as *runover lines*.

    After a paragraph indent *turnovers* are of course set flush left. But in an index or the stub of a table, *turnovers* go the other way and are normally indented 1 em from the left alignment in an index, or the left margin in a table. (See **indexing** and **tables**.) In captions to pictures, the *turnovers* may be aligned on the left, indented, or even centred.

twingeing or **twinging** The choice between these is discussed under **-e** section 1d.

-ty This masquerades as an English suffix in abstract nouns such as:
    casualty certainty cruelty frailty loyalty safety
All of those have closely related adjectives from which they might seem to be derived. In fact the nouns were borrowed ready-made from French, and none have been formed independently in English. Compare **-ity**.

type of For questions of agreement relating to this phrase, see under **kind of**.

typhoid or **typhus** **Typhoid** means "typhus-like" and is a reminder that these two different diseases have similar symptoms, and that **typhus** was the one first identified.

    Typhus was the name given in 1759 by de Sauvages to a severe and often fatal infection, characterised by (among other things) great lassitude and the eruption of reddish spots. It was associated with crowded human habitations, such as camps, hospitals, jails and ships, hence some of the earlier names for it: *camp fever*, *jail fever*. Only recently has it become known that the disease is an infection from micro-organisms transmitted by fleas and lice in crowded places.

    Typhoid fever has similar febrile symptoms, and was not distinguished from **typhus** until the mid-nineteenth century. Its source is a dangerous bacillus in contaminated food or drink, which causes severe intestinal inflammation and ulceration—again often fatal.

typhoon, tornado or **cyclone** See **cyclone**.

tyre or **tire** In Australian and British English, these two spellings are used to distinguish the rubber shock-absorber round the rim of a wheel (**tyre**) from the verb meaning "exhaust" (**tire**). In American English **tire** serves for both meanings.

The words are quite separate in origin. **Tire** meaning "exhaust" goes back to Old English, whereas **tyre** is a contracted form of *attire*, a loanword from French. At first this word referred to any kind of wheel covering, and could mean the metal rim on a cart wheel. Later they were made of wood or cork. The use of rubber was a byproduct of nineteenth century colonialism, and the first inflatable rubber **tyre** was patented in 1890. All through this time, the word could be spelled either **tire** or **tyre**, and the spelling **tire** was endorsed by the *Oxford Dictionary*, and by Fowler in the 1920s. However the spelling **tyre** was the one used in the patent, and subsequently taken up in Britain as the twentieth century evolved. It has no etymological justification, but appeals to those who prefer that homophones should not be homographs as well. The grammar of the two words serves to keep them apart however, and Americans do without **tyre**, at no obvious cost to their industrial development.

tyro or **tiro** See tiro.

U

U and **non-U** No other letter of the alphabet has the touch of class that now goes with **U**. In the late 1950s it acquired unforgettable social and linguistic significance as the letter/symbol for "upper class", and especially for the speech habits of the British aristocracy. Class differences in speech had certainly been recognised before in Shaw's *Pygmalion* which dramatised the contrast between the language of the upper crust and the working class. **U** and **non-U** are a little different in that they focus on the differences between upper and middle class: differences in pronunciation and the choice of words, as well as greetings and modes of address. The following are some of the different word choices made by the two groups:

U	non-U
drawing room	*lounge*
jam	*preserve*
lavatory	*toilet*
napkin	*serviette*
rich	*wealthy*
scent	*perfume*
vegetables	*greens*
writing paper	*notepaper*

The **U** list comprises traditional expressions, whereas those in the **non-U** list are often more recent French loans. In comparison with the older words they perhaps have a certain air to them—that slight pretension that goes with French words and spellings elsewhere. (See further under **frenchification**.)

The terms **U** and **non-U** were coined by Alan Ross in an academic article published in 1954. They might never have caught on but for the reprinting of the article two years later in a small anthology of essays titled *Noblesse Oblige*, edited by Nancy Mitford. Since then the language has of course moved on, and some of Ross's **non-U** words have eclipsed their **U** equivalents. The terms **U** and **non-U** have been extended to refer to social conventions, not just linguistic behavior, and to ones which may not be linked with class. Thus **non-U** can mean something like "unfashionable", as in *Skivvies are definitely non-U for our children*, especially in Australia where it's unclear who might constitute the upper class.

The idea that people's use of words reveals something of their identity is as old as the word **shibboleth** (see under that heading). Since the 1950s the connections between language and society have been the subject of systematic research, and *social dialects* are now considered as important in the total picture of language variation as geographical dialects. (See further under **dialect**.)

U-ey or **U-ie** The colloquial abbreviation for *U-turn* is very much an Australian invention, though the term itself is known in other parts of the English-speaking world. Like many a colloquialism, it has only recently made its appearance in print, and the spelling is not yet standardised. Citations in the *Australian National Dictionary* are mostly for **U-ey** (apart from odd ones for *Uy* and *youee*). The *Macquarie Dictionary* (1991) also lists **U-ie**, which is the usual spelling for informal abbreviated words of this type. (See further under **-ie/-y**.)

UK These days **UK** stands for the United Kingdom of Great Britain and Northern Ireland. The "United Kingdom" wasn't built in a day, but over centuries by strategic treaties. England and Wales were united by treaty in 1536, and Scotland joined in 1707 to form *Great Britain.* The so-called "Act of Union" brought the whole of Ireland into the "United Kingdom" in 1801, but in 1921 the south of Ireland (Eire) regained its independence, and now only Northern Ireland remains.

The abbreviation **UK** is useful shorthand on envelopes and wherever space is at a premium. In phrases like *UK government* the abbreviation is more accurate than "British government" would be in the same place, though the latter is preferred in official documents. The abbreviation needs no stops because it's in upper case (see further under **abbreviations**).

ukulele or **ukelele** The first spelling represents exactly the two Hawaiian words for a popular musical instrument. Surprisingly they are *uku* "flea" and *lele* "jumping". The second spelling is a variant which shows how our common pronunciation of the word turns the second vowel into a **schwa** (see under that heading). Dictionaries all give preference to **ukulele**, yet **ukelele** is to be found in some well respected musical references.

ulna For the plural of this word, see **-a** section 1.

Ulster See under **Irish**.

ult. This Latin abbreviation was once used regularly in business letters:
Thank you for your letter of 23 ult.
It stood for *ultimo mense* "last month"; and it contrasted with *inst.* (*instante mense* "this month") and *prox.* (*proximo mense* "next month"). All three smack of older styles of correspondence. Modern letter writers give the name of the month, as in:
Thank you for your letter of 23 August.
(See further under **commercialese**.)

ultimatum For the plural of this word, see under **-um**.

ultra In Latin **ultra** was an adverb and preposition meaning "beyond". In modern English it works as a prefix for various adjectives, with the meaning "beyond the range of", as in *ultrasonic* and *ultraviolet.* Some scientific formations of this kind have become household words, witness *UHT milk* ("ultra-heat-treated"), and the *UHF wave band* which means "ultra-high frequency". But in common words **ultra** often means "extremely or very", as in *ultrafashionable* and *ultramodern.*

Ultra can also be used as an independent adjective, as in:

They were voting with the ultra conservatives.

Its use as a noun for "one who goes to extremes" can be seen in:

Punks are the ultras of counterfashion.

In both these uses, and some of the compound adjectives, **ultra** carries the value judgement "excessive". This meaning seems to have originated in the French loan *ultrarevolutionary,* first recorded in 1793, and is latent in many nonscientific words which have been coined with *ultra-* since then.

ultra vires This Latin phrase means "beyond the powers (of)". It represents the judgement that a particular issue is beyond the legal power and authority of a person, committee or institution to deal with.

Compare it with *intra vires* meaning "within the powers (of)", which affirms that the issue in hand is within the jurisdiction of the authority concerned.

-um This ending on a word of two or more syllables is usually a sign that it's a Latin loanword, as for:

aquarium atrium colloquium compendium condominium consortium crematorium curriculum emporium encomium equilibrium forum fulcrum gymnasium honorarium mausoleum maximum medium memorandum millennium minimum moratorium ovum podium referendum rostrum sanatorium sanctum serum solarium spectrum stadium stratum symposium ultimatum vacuum

The key question is their plurals, whether they should be Latin ones with *-a* or English ones with *-ums,* or perhaps either. Overall, the more the word appears in everyday use, the more likely it is to take the English plural, as with *aquariums, compendiums, condominiums, emporiums, forums, gymnasiums, referendums, ultimatums* and *vacuums.* Those which most often appear in scholarly or institutional contexts make more use of their Latin plurals, e.g. *colloquia, curricula, memoranda* and *millennia.* These tendencies were the general preferences of professional writers surveyed in Melbourne and Sydney in 1992, though between 20 and 30% preferred English plurals even for words in the latter group. A few scholarly words ending in **-um** are always found with Latin plurals, namely *addenda, corrigenda, desiderata, errata* and *ova.*

Some words ending in **-um** always have English plurals, notably flowers and plants such as:

capsicum chrysanthemum delphinium geranium nasturtium

as well as a miscellany of other everyday words:

album asylum conundrum harmonium museum nostrum pendulum premium quorum vademecum vellum

The reasons why these make their plurals only in the English way are intertwined with their individual histories; but in general terms it's because they do not have straightforward connections with Classical Latin nouns.

Note finally that for some words the Latin and English plurals mean different things:

- *mediums*—the means or material for doing something; spiritualist links with the supernatural

   media—channels of communication, especially mass communication: particular materials or techniques of art

- *stadiums*—sports grounds

   stadia—stages of a disease.

umlaut This accent consists of two strokes which in German and Swedish are placed above a back vowel to show that it is pronounced further forward in the mouth than the same vowel without **umlaut**. So the first syllable of the German *Hütte* "hut" and *Hut* "hat" sound a little different, rather like the difference between "Hugh" and "who".

Umlauts also appear in some other languages such as Hungarian, but loanwords from there are so few that their use of the **umlaut** is unfamiliar. German loanwords such as *Fräulein* and *Führer* are however seen occasionally in English with their umlauts. When the **umlaut** is unavailable in English typing and printing fonts, an *e* is sometimes inserted after the umlauted vowel as a substitute. Our normal spelling of *muesli* embodies this practice, whereas in (Swiss) German it's *müsli*.

Like other accents, the **umlaut** marks a word or name as being not English—which is no doubt why *umlauts* are sometimes sprinkled freely on names which are worth more if they look foreign. Australian wine labels such as *Rhinë Kellër* (with *umlauts* on the wrong vowels) probably hope to price themselves up with imported wines.

Compare **dieresis**.

un- Negative words are created very freely in English with this prefix. Most simply it means "not", as in adjectives such as:

   unable uncertain uncommon unfit unjust untidy unusual unwilling

When attached to a verb, **un-** reverses the action expressed in it, as in:

   uncover undo undress unleash unload unlock untie unwind

Note however that in both *unfurl* (= "furl") and *unloosen* (= "loosen"), **un-** has zero value.

In longer adjectives, especially those ending in *-able*, **un-** is tending to replace the Latin negative prefix *in-*. So *unescapable* is more and more used instead of *inescapable* etc. (See further under **in-/un-**.)

unattached participle See **dangling participle**.

unaware or **unawares** Unaware is usually an adjective, though occasionally it appears as an adverb. Compare:

Unaware of what was going on behind, the speaker carried on.
They were caught unaware by the strike.

Unawares is only ever an adverb, used without modification:

They came upon the snake unawares.

The use of **unawares** seems however to be declining, and only survives with a handful of verbs, including *catch, come upon* and *take.*

unconscious or **subconscious** See under **subconscious**.

under- This English prefix has both physical and figurative functions. It means:

1 "below or underneath", as in *undercarriage, underground, undermine, underpants, undertow*
2 "less than normal", as in *underestimate, undernourished, underprivileged, underweight*
3 "lower in status or rank", as in *underdog, undergraduate, underofficer, undersecretary, understudy.*

Under- combines freely with both English and Latin/French words, and with nouns, verbs and adjectives.

underhand or **underhanded** The first is the usual form of the word meaning "crafty, deceptive":

The company used underhand methods to save money at their employees' expense.

Just occasionally **underhanded** is used with that same meaning, though the extra syllable is unnecessary and adds nothing.

Note also the use of **underhand** in ball games such as tennis and squash, to refer to a stroke which begins below the shoulder. And that **underhanded** is used in American English to mean "short of staff". It thus becomes a synonym for *shorthanded.*

underlay or **underlie** Underlay is most commonly a noun, which **underlie** never is. But as verbs they can be confused. One way to distinguish them is to note that **underlay** involves putting a layer under something, whereas **underlie** means being that layer or foundation for something else. Compare:

Before finishing the collar she underlaid it with stiffening.
A layer of sand underlies the topsoil.

Note that the past participle of **underlay** is *underlaid*, while that of **underlie** is *underlain.*

understatements Provided your readers know what you're referring to, *understatement* can be as effective as overstatement in drawing attention to it. For example, if you have been severely reprimanded by someone, you could say that X had "come down like a ton of bricks on you". But if others know X's style, it may be just as effective—and more amusing—to say that "X told you how to improve yourself". *Understatement* suggests restrained judgement, whereas overstatement implies a willingness to dramatise or exaggerate things. (See further under **figures of speech**.)

undertone or **overtone** See **overtone**.

undiscriminating See under **discriminating** or **discriminatory**.

undistributed middle Using the **undistributed middle** term in a syllogism is a logical fallacy. (See **fallacies** section 2.)

undoubtedly, indubitably and **doubtless** All these are adverbs which aim to banish the reader's doubts, and therefore have an interpersonal role to play in writing (see **interpersonal**).

Of the three, **undoubtedly** is the most forceful and widely used. **Indubitably** is also a strong word, but it can only be used in very formal styles. **Doubtless** is less strong, and perhaps a little old-fashioned now. Compare:

He will doubtless appear in a few minutes.
He will no doubt appear in a few minutes.

Note that because **doubtless** is established as an adverb, there's strictly no need for *doubtlessly*. Dictionaries do however recognise it, and its existence suggests the discomfort people feel with zero adverbs. *Doubtlessly* can never be misread as an adjective, whereas **doubtless** could.

unexceptional or **unexceptionable** See under **exceptional**.

uni- The Latin prefix for "one" is found in everyday English words such as *uniform, unilateral* and *unisex*. It appears in scientific words such as *unidirectional, unipolar* and *univalve*. The same prefix is the first component in *unanimous* and *unanimity*, and it's integrated into loanwords such as: *unify, union, unit* and *unity* whose meanings focus on "oneness".

Compare **mono-**.

uninterested See under **disinterested**.

Union Jack In Australia this is usually taken as the name of the British national flag of red, white and blue, which represents the union of England, Wales, Scotland and Northern Ireland. The pattern combines the cross of St George (for England), of St Andrew (for Scotland), and of St Patrick (for Ireland). Its official name is the "Union flag", but it acquired the name "jack" long ago from being flown on the jack staff at the bows of British sailing ships.

unique This word has received an extraordinary amount of critical attention, with various rights and wrongs made to hang on its use. In its primary and historical sense, the word singles something out as the only one of its kind:

Sydney's Opera House is a unique building.

In this absolute sense, the word cannot be qualified by words such as *more, most* or *very*. By implication, there are no degrees of uniqueness. Yet Fowler and others argued that some modifiers such as *almost, really, truly* and *absolutely* could be used with it, because they focused on whether the state of uniqueness had actually been achieved. Fowler also allowed that *quite unique* was possible, provided you were using *quite* as an intensifier rather than as a hedge word. (See further under **quite**.)

All this debate turns on the idea that **unique** has an absolute meaning, yet this very point is also not to be taken for granted. For one thing it may be impossible to know whether something is the only example of its kind; for another the word is often uttered amid a certain amount of hype which tends to devalue it. Modern dictionaries and style guides all recognise that **unique** is these days used to mean such things as "outstanding", "remarkable" and "unusual"—some reporting it without comment, others saying that it's a "loose" application of the word, or one objected to by some people.

Now if we allow that words change and expand their range of meaning in the course of time, we see that this is what's happening with **unique**. With its extended meaning, it can reasonably be qualified by words such as *more*, *most* and *very*, and they in fact show that it's not being used in an absolute sense. Those who regret that **unique** is changing in this way should take comfort from the fact that they can still express the absolute meaning by other words such as *sole*.

units of measurement The SI system is discussed at **metrication**, and set out in full in Appendix IV. For **imperial weights** and **measures**, see under that heading. Note that the symbols representing units of measurement in either system do not take stops (see further under **abbreviations**).

unless This word helps to introduce clauses that express a negative condition. Thus it's often equivalent to *if … not*, as in:

Unless it snows, we'll move house tomorrow.

The positive equivalents to **unless** are the compound conjunctions *in case* and *provided that*.

unlike For the problems posed by this word in negative sentences, see the final note on **like** or **as**.

unloose or **unloosen** See under **loose**.

unpractical or **impractical** See under **practical**.

unsanitary or **insanitary** Both are perfectly acceptable, though some modern dictionaries seem to lend weight to the second by giving a separate entry to **insanitary**, and simply treating **unsanitary** in a block entry on words prefixed with *un-*.

unsatisfied or **dissatisfied** See **dissatisfied**.

unshakable or **unshakeable** See under **-eable**.

until or **till** See **till**.

upper case For the origins of the name, see under **lower case**. For the use of upper case/capital letters, see **capital letters**.

upward or **upwards** See under -ward.

urban or **urbane** The first of these adjectives means simply "associated with the city", as in *urban transport* or *urban development*. The second word **urbane** implies a social style which is smooth and sophisticated, a sense which embodies the stereotyped contrast between the manners of city dwellers and those of less polished country people.

In the sixteenth century, the two words were simply spelling variants for the same meaning. But the meaning "sophisticated" developed in the seventeenth century, and the spelling **urbane** has since been attached to it.

urethra The plural is discussed under -a section 1.

-us This ending is very often found on Latin loanwords, and often means that their plurals need special attention. They come from several Latin declensions, and their Latin plurals are still used extensively in writing, though often replaced by English plurals in speech.

1 *Many -us words are from the Latin second declension* or modeled after it. Examples include:

> *abacus agapanthus antechinus bacillus cactus crocus focus fungus gladiolus hibiscus incubus narcissus nucleus papyrus radius ranunculus stimulus streptococcus stylus syllabus terminus uterus*

In Latin the regular pattern was for the **-us** ending to become *-i* in the plural (*stimulus* > *stimuli*), and this often happens in English too. The Latin plural is occasionally replaced by the regular English one (*stimuluses*), especially for the names of flowers and plants e.g. *cactuses.* But the English plural involves a concentration of sibilants at the end of the word, and this may explain why English plurals have been slower to catch on with this group of Latin loans than with others, such as those ending in *-um.* In a survey of professional writers conducted in Melbourne and Sydney in 1992 only *focus* and *syllabus* were voted English plurals by more than 70% in both groups, though *stylus* and *terminus* were also anglicised by the Sydney group. The English plural is however the only one for **-us** words whose grammar or contemporary meaning is independent of classical Latin, such as *bonus, chorus, campus, circus* and *virus.*

Note that the plural for *genius* depends on the intended meaning (see **genius**).

2 *A small number of -us words come from the fourth Latin declension,* where the plural was spelled the same way as the singular (it was a *zero plural*). English loanwords from this group include:

> *apparatus census f(o)etus hiatus impetus nexus prospectus sinus status*

All these words are given regular *-s* plurals in English, and only *apparatus* is occasionally found with its Latin zero plural. They should never be given plurals in *-i*, as if they were members of the second declension.

3 *An even smaller group of -us words are from the Latin third declension.* Their plurals have a characteristic inflection with *-ra*, and a preceding change of vowel. The three commonest loanwords involved are *corpus*, *genus* and *opus* which become *corpora*, *genera* and *opera* respectively. All three are informally given English plurals: *corpuses*, *genuses* and *opuses*.

4 *Some -us words are not Latin nouns at all*, and so are not heirs to any Latin plural suffix. They include *ignoramus*, *minus*, *omnibus* and *rebus*, which can only be given English plurals: *ignoramuses*, *minuses*, *omnibuses* and *rebuses*. Most scholars prefer to give English plurals also to words whose source material is Greek rather than Latin, as with *thesaurus*, as well as **hippotamus, octopus** and **platypus** (see under those headings).

USA This is the standard abbreviation for the United States of America, often reduced to *US*. The reduced abbreviation is actually more common than the fuller one, and occurs more than twice as often in the Australian ACE corpus, occurring very commonly as an adjective in phrases such as *US government* and *US president*. This use of *US* is strictly speaking more accurate than using "American" in the same phrases, because *American* refers rather loosely to the whole continent, not the **USA** in particular (see further under **America**).

The abbreviation *US* is often used informally for the noun as well, as in *going to the US next year*. The usage may be seen in newspapers and less formal writing, though in formal documents it's replaced by "the United States".

No stops are needed in either **USA** or *US*, because they are in upper case (see further under **abbreviations**).

usable or **useable** With these two there's no question that **usable** is to be preferred. It appears as the first spelling in all modern dictionaries; and it was preferred by the *Oxford Dictionary* both because of the larger number of citations for it, and the fact that it embodied one of the standard spelling rules of English, the dropping of *e* before a suffix beginning with a vowel (see **-e** section 1). **Usable** also corresponds better with *usage*.

usage or **use** The first of these is sometimes no more than an inflated substitute for the second, as in:
The usage of public transport has declined in the last two decades.
In such cases the verbal noun **use** would be preferable to the more abstract **usage**.

Usage comes into its own as a reference to a prevailing linguistic or social habit. Compare the roles of the two words in:
Common usage now sanctions the use of different than.
As that example shows, **use** needs postmodification, to specify what is being used, whereas **usage** has enough intrinsic meaning to stand on its own.

useable or **usable** See **usable**.

used to This verb phrase is a curious remnant of an older idiom. It refers to a custom or habit, as in:

We used to sleep in every morning.

The expression is fixed in the past tense, and as with other fringe auxiliaries there's some uncertainty as to how its negative works. Should it be:

We used not to get up early (This makes it an auxiliary, which takes the negative itself.)

We did not use to get up early (This makes it a lexical verb, which needs an auxiliary to precede the negative.)

The second construction is preferred by the majority of Australians, according to Collins's research (1979). Yet *did not use* seems rather strange since there's no longer an infinitive "use" pronounced to rhyme with "loose". Some writers therefore make it *didn't used to*, though that too seems unsatisfactory because it doubles the past tense marking. According to *Webster's English Usage* (1989), *didn't use to* is usual and correct in American English; and it's also preferred in Britain, according to the *Comprehensive Grammar of English*. Both regard the status of *didn't used to* as dubious.

When it comes to phrasing questions with **used to**, there are the same alternatives:

Used you to get up early?

Did you use(d) to get up early?

The second construction: *did you use* is overwhelmingly preferred to *used you to* in British and American English, and in Australian English as well. Yet Collins's research also showed Australians' discomfort in using the dubious *use to*, and an inclination to avoid it by means of paraphrase. The following are some of the alternatives for construing the question above:

Did you get up early when you were younger?

Did you make a habit of getting up early?

Were you used to getting up early?

USSR See **Russia**.

utilise or **use** Most of the time **utilise** seems to appear as a heavyweight substitute for **use**, as in:

If the fax machine fails, would you utilise the telephone.

There's little justification for **utilise** when it only serves to make the statement sound more important.

Yet for some writers **utilise** still connotes something more than **use**, i.e. the implication that a resource has been turned to good account, and used in a profitable, effective or ingenious way:

They utilised the water of the nearby creek to cool the engine.

This subtle extra dimension of **utilise** is unfortunately jeopardised by pretentious use of it elsewhere.

V

-v-/-f- The letters **v** and **f** are alternatives in some verbs which derive from older English nouns ending in *-f* or *-fe*, e.g. *knifed/knived*. The words are all ones which as nouns have **v** in their plural forms (see further under **-f/-v-**). The use of **v** or **f** sometimes affects the meaning, as shown in the table below.

noun	verb	inflected verbs
hoof	*hoof*	*hoofed/hooved*
knife	*knife/knive*	*knifed/knived*
leaf	*leaf* "have leaves"	*leafed/leaved*
	leaf "turn pages"	*leafed*
loaf	*loaf* "be idle"	*loafed*
	loaf "shape like loaf"	*loaved/loafed*
roof	*roof/roove* "put roof on"	*roofed/rooved*
	roove "secure with a washer"	*rooved*
sheaf	*sheaf/sheave*	*sheafed/sheaved*

The **v/f** option once applied also to adjectives such as *elvish/elfish* and *wolvish/wolfish*. But in contemporary English the spellings with **f** are more common, and those with **v** are regarded in all dictionaries as secondary alternatives.

vacation This word has yet to become the standard word for "holiday" in Australia, as it is in USA. We still speak in terms of "holiday pay", and "going on holiday". Yet tourist pamphlets increasingly try to tempt us with "a dream vacation on Hayman Island", or with the line "Why not a vacation in the Maldives?" This still tends to link **vacation** with expensive and fashionable long-distance holidays, rather than the annual break from work.

In some Australian institutions however, **vacation** certainly refers to a significant break in the working year. In law it refers to the intermission in the legal year, and the *long vacation* is part of the regular calendar in universities and colleges. No doubt this institutional use of **vacation** will combine with fashionable use to spread the word.

vaccinate See under **inoculate**.

vacuity or **vacuousness** The first of these is the established abstract noun, on record since the sixteenth century, with a range of meanings from physical emptiness to absence of mind or purpose. **Vacuousness** is the ad hoc noun from *vacuous*, recorded only sporadically since seventeenth century. The *Oxford*

Dictionary citations show it being more often used figuratively, to refer to lack of mental engagement or sense of direction.

vacuum The plural of this word is discussed under **-um.**

vademecum This Latin phrase means literally ''go with me''. It has been used since the seventeenth century to refer to portable reference manuals on subjects as diverse as theology and theatre, opera and archeology etc. etc.

vagary Until about a century ago, this could mean a physical ''wandering or rambling''. But for centuries it has also been used more figuratively to mean a digression in a discourse, and to capricious conduct. This last meaning is often enshrined in plural use of the word, as in the *vagaries of the money market.*
   Note that when *vagaries* refers to erratic patterns of thought or speech, its meaning overlaps with ''vagueness'', as in:
   We couldn't follow the vagaries of that senile mind.
The temptation to find ''vague'' in *vagaries* is all the stronger because common pronunciation now puts the stress on the first syllable. The older pronunciation with stress on the second syllable did not lend itself to this coincidence of ideas.

vagina For the plural, see **-a** section 1.

valency or **valence** The first has been the usual Australian spelling of this scientific word. The second is on the increase here because of the use of textbooks from North America, where it is the standard spelling. Some interchange between them also results from the common vacillation between *-ncy* and *-nce* in such pairs. (See further under **-nce/-ncy.**)
   Note also *valance*, a quite independent word now mostly known in the context of soft furnishings. It refers to a hanging piece of drapery which covers the upper part of a window, or the lower part of a piece of furniture. In earlier motoring *valance* was also the name for a cover over the wheel of a car, which reduced drag and prevented mud splashing up.

valiant or **valorous** Both mean ''brave or courageous'' but there's a stylistic difference. **Valorous** is the more formal word, and the one used in official recognitions of bravery, as in military and police *awards for valorous conduct.* **Valiant** comes up in everyday references, and can be used of moral and political courage, as in:
   He was a valiant campaigner for conservation issues.

valor or **valour** For the choice between these, see **-or/-our.**

valuable and **invaluable** Note that these are not antonyms. **Invaluable** is not the reverse of **valuable** (i.e. ''having no value'') but rather ''extremely valuable''—so much so that you can't put a price on it. Put another way, something which is **invaluable** is more than just **valuable**. The word which works as an antonym for both **valuable** and **invaluable** is *valueless*. If there's any doubt about them, *priceless* is a safe synonym for **invaluable**, and *worthless* (or *valueless*) for the opposite.

van and **von** In Dutch and German these are unremarkable particles meaning "from". They quite often appear as the first element in proper names, as in *Van Gogh* and *Von Trapp*, and in English the question arises as to whether they should bear capital letters or not. The style for famous historical personages can be settled by reference to a dictionary of biography, whereas that for someone with whom we're corresponding should be checked against previous letters or the telephone directory. The general trend is for such names to acquire a capital on the Van/Von in English (see under **capital letters**, section 1).

The names raise further questions when it comes to indexing. In principle, their place depends on whether the particle is capitalised or not, so that *van Dam* would be alphabetised with the *D*s and *Van Dam* with the *V*s. Yet this is rather unpredictable and mysterious for English speakers who are unaware that **van** and **von** are merely particles. There's therefore good reason to group such names all together under *V*, as happens in Australian telephone directories. At *V* itself, the individual's preference for a capital letter or not is shown. (This is comparable to the usual practice for names beginning with **Mac** or **Mc**. See further under that heading.) A crossreference at the other point in the index where the **van/von** name might otherwise appear would help also.

Van Diemen's Land The name **Van Diemen's Land** was given to Tasmania in 1642 by Abel Tasman, in honor of the then governor of the Dutch East Indies. The governor's name is less flatteringly built into *Vandemonia* (with the play on "pandemonia"), as an unofficial designation for Tasmania as a penal colony. Records in the *Australian National Dictionary* show that *Vandemonia* was never greatly used, though the closely related *Vandemonian* had some currency as the adjective for things Tasmanian, and its non-Aboriginal inhabitants. Tasmania became the official name in 1855.

Vancouver style This is a type of number referencing system developed in the late 1970s and used especially in biomedical journals (see **referencing** section 4). The numbers may be italicised (in parentheses, square brackets or superscripted) to set them apart from the line of text. Clusters of references are permitted e.g. ...*[1,4]*. The **Vancouver style** entails a number of conventions to compress the details of a reference (see further under **bibliographies** section C).

vapor or **vapour** The choice between them is discussed under **-or/-our**.

variety in writing Variety is vital for writing to keep the reader with you. Even a shortish piece of writing is a relatively long monologue to direct at a reader, and if the style is pedestrian and repetitious, readers are likely to switch off. Writers need therefore to consciously vary their style, by such things as:
- varying the form of their sentences, both in length and structure (see **sentences**)

- varying their choice of words by looking for synonyms (see **synonyms**)
- varying the word forms they choose (see under **-ation** and **nominal**). This incidentally helps to vary both the vocabulary and the shape of sentences.

vegetarian or **vegan** Both *vegetarians* and *vegans* maintain a meat- and fish-free diet, but the **vegan** takes vegetarian principles much further and avoids eating any animal produce, including eggs, milk, butter and cheese. Vegetarian diets have of course been obligatory at various times and seasons in earlier centuries, and in other cultures. But the idea of voluntary *vegetarianism* contrasting with the omnivorous eating habits of others seems to arise with the first record of **vegetarian** in 1839. **Vegan** first appears in 1944.

veld or **veldt** Modern dictionaries almost all prefer the shorter spelling, in line with usage in South Africa itself. **Veldt** is still used outside South Africa, and it represents the original Dutch word as well as common pronunciation.

venal or **venial** See venial.

vendor or **vender** These spellings both date from the last decade of the sixteenth century. **Vendor** originated in law and still represents the role of anyone who disposes of property by sale. **Vender** is the ordinary spelling for one who sells things, often in the street. But it runs second to **vendor** in all modern dictionaries and databases, perhaps because the verb *vend* on which it's based is so rare. The adjective found in *vending machine* is the most familiar member of the verbal set.

vengeance or **revenge** See revenge.

venial or **venal** The spelling marks the crucial difference between that which is pardonable (**venial**) and that which involves bribery (**venal**). Compare:
She had the disarming but venial habit of plying him with questions.
A venal police force is the first symptom of the breakdown of law and order.
Both adjectives have their own abstract nouns: *veniality* and *venality*, where once again the *i* in the second syllable makes a big difference in meaning.
   Note that because a *venial sin* is forgivable, it can be atoned by prayer and other good works. In theological terms it's the opposite of a "mortal sin", i.e. one which means spiritual death and condemns the soul to hell.

venturous or **venturesome**, **adventurous** or **adventuresome** All these are recognised in modern dictionaries as words meaning "daring, or ready to take risks". **Venturous** has been put to good use in many of the classics of English literature, yet dictionary crossreferencing suggests that **venturesome** and **adventurous** are now the primary members of each pair. Database evidence in Australia and elsewhere shows that **adventurous** is rather more common than **venturesome**: the ratio was 5:1 in the ACE corpus.

veranda or **verandah** Both spellings are recognised yet the first and shorter one is given priority in all dictionaries. It was preferred by the *Oxford Dictionary*, probably because it was closer to the word's etymology in the Portuguese and Hindi word *varanda*. But *Oxford* citations show that **verandah** was popular in the nineteenth century (perhaps because the final *h* linked it with *maharajah* and Anglo-India); and this preference is continued in contemporary Australia, judging by evidence from the ACE database, where instances of **verandah** outnumber those of **veranda** by almost 4:1.

verb phrase This means different things in different grammars.

1 *In traditional grammar* **verb phrase** meant the finite verb of a clause when it consisted of more than one word:
was playing
was being played
will have been played
would have been being played
The **verb phrase** has a *main verb* (*playing/played*) as its head, and the first of the accompanying auxiliaries marks the verb's tense. (See **auxiliary verbs**.)

2 *In modern grammars* the term **verb phrase** is given extended applications. It refers to simple finite verbs as well as compound ones like the examples in section 1; and it's also applied to the nonfinite **verb phrase**. Nonfinite *verb phrases* may also be simple or compound, and constructed with either infinitives or participles (i.e with *be/being* or *have/having*), as in the following:
You saw her buy it.   *I wanted to buy it.*
I'd like to have bought it.   *It had stopped ticking.*
He'll get it repaired.   *I saw it being worked on.*

Thus, many English clauses contain nonfinite verbs to complement the finite ones, and the syntactic implications are still being weighed up in the most recent grammars (e.g. the *Comprehensive Grammar of English* and the *Introduction to the Grammar of English*).

3 *In transformational-generative grammars* the term **verb phrase** comes close to meaning the "predicate" of a clause. A sentence is said to consist of an NP + VP, i.e. a noun phrase which is the subject, and a **verb phrase** which includes not only the verb but also its object (also a noun phrase), and/or any adverbial phrases attached:

NP	VP		
The assistant	put the clock	on the counter.	
(S)	(V)	(O)	(A)
subject	verb	object	adverbial

Because the idea of the **verb phrase** has developed so considerably in recent decades, it's vital to know which analysis is being used before entering into discussions about its role.

verbal The more you deal with language, the more ambiguous this word seems. It can mean:

1 "spoken" (as opposed to "written") as in a *verbal agreement*

2 "in words" (as opposed to pictures) as in *communicate by verbal rather than visual means*

3 "using verbs" (rather than nouns) as in *verbal style* (see further under **nominal**).

   Much of the time **verbal** is used in the first of those senses, and this is the one enshrined in its use as a verb in Australian English. It refers to a police procedure in which comments offered by a prisoner are recorded and presented in court, often as evidence against him. The inflected forms of the verb are often printed as *verballed/verballing*, though there's strictly no need to double the *l*. (See under **doubling of final consonant**.)

   In ordinary contexts the ambiguity of **verbal** presents no problems, especially in standard idioms such as *verbal agreement*. But in discussing language itself, precision is important, and linguists prefer to paraphrase the word: with "spoken/oral" for the first sense above; "using words" for the second sense; and "using verbs" for the third.

verbal nouns These are nouns which embody the action or process of a verb. They take various forms including:

● the suffix *-ing* (see further under **gerunds**)

● abstract suffixes such as *-ation*, *-ity* and *-ment*

● no suffix at all (see further under **transfers**)

Note that using too many abstract **verbal nouns** creates a *nominal style* which may be undesirable (see under **nominal**).

   Note also that some grammarians regard infinitives as **verbal nouns**, because they seem to function in the same way as *-ing* forms. Compare:

   They were famished but declined to eat uncooked meat.
   They were famished but declined eating uncooked meat.

Alternatively the infinitive may be analysed as part of the **verb phrase** or clause complement (see **verb phrase** section 2).

verbiage and **verbosity** Both mean an excess of words, but while **verbiage** applies to the text itself and the expression used in it, **verbosity** can also be applied to the writer or speaker. Compare:

   With its verbiage removed, the letter would be only half as long.
   I'd send them to a course on Plain English, to cure their verbosity.

verbs The *verb* is the prime mover of the clause, and the item that makes something happen. **Verbs** may be classified in three ways, in terms of their meaning, their grammatical roles and their grammatical form.

Many **verbs** are dynamic and express events. They may be physical events such as *push*, *pull*, *rise* and *fall*, which can be observed by anyone; or the verbal (speech) events referred to in **verbs** of communicating such as *call*, *exclaim*, *speak* or *shout*. Other **verbs** express internal, mental events, such as *decide*, *hope*, *remember* and *think*. Yet another group embody states of being, as do *involve*, *mean* and *seem*. The last ones are **copular verbs** (see under that heading).

In terms of their grammatical role in the verb phrase, **verbs** may be either auxiliaries or main verbs—or catenatives which have some properties of both (see further under **auxiliary verbs** and **catenatives**). They may be finite or nonfinite (see **finite verbs**). **Verbs** may be transitive or intransitive, according to whether they take an object or not (see further under **transitive**). They may be active or passive, according to whether their subject is the operator of the verb phrase or not (see further under **voice**). Some **verbs** have strong links with a following particle (see further under **phrasal verbs**).

In form **verbs** may be *simple* or *compound*, depending on whether there's one or more of them in the verb phrase (see **verb phrase** section 2). They may vary in form according to *tense* and/or *aspect*, with the addition of particular inflections, especially *-ed*. Those which change in this way are *regular verbs*. Those which change in other ways to show tense and aspect are discussed under **irregular verbs**. (See also **principal parts**.)

verso This word is short for the Latin phrase *verso folio*, which is used in book production to refer to the left-hand page of an open book. The right-hand page is **recto** i.e. *recto folio*.

versus This Latin word, meaning "against", is at home in everyday English, witness its use in sporting contests: *Tonight's cricket: Australia versus West Indies*. In law it's conventionally used to refer to the opposing parties in a law suit: *Kramer versus Kramer*.

Note that while **versus** is regularly abbreviated to *v.* in the titles of law suits, in other contexts either *v.* or *vs.* can be used. In the names of law suits it's put into italics, along with the names on either side of it. (See further under **italics**.) But elsewhere the abbreviation is left in roman, like others borrowed from Latin which have become commonplace.

vertebrae This is the regular Latin plural of *vertebra*, a word for the individual bone of the spinal column. Compare:
She has cracked a vertebra.
He damaged three vertebrae in the fall.

However like many a well-used loanword, this one also has an English plural
vertebras, which is at home in informal contexts. For other examples, see **-a**
section 1.

vertex or **vortex** The first word **vertex** means "apex". It mostly appears in
mathematical and scientific writing, in reference to the apex of a cone or triangle,
or to the crown of the head (in anatomy and zoology). The related adjective is
vertical.

    Vortex means a "whirlpool (of water, air or fire) around an axis". It can
also be used figuratively, of whirling forces which threaten to engulf people.

    Both words have Latin plurals *vertices/vortices* as well as English ones
vertexes/vortexes, for use in specialised and everyday contexts respectively (see
further under **-x** section 2).

veterinary or **veterinarian** The first of these is usually an adjective as in
veterinary surgeon, though it occasionally stands alone as a noun. The second
veterinarian is always a noun.

veto The plural of this is discussed under **-o**.

via This Latin loanword means "by way of". Its essential use is to spotlight the
route by which you go from A to B, as in *flying to London via Kuala Lumpur*.
During the twentieth century its use has been extended to refer to the channel
by which something is transferred, as in:
    We receive the signal via satellite.
    I'll return the tapes to you via your brother.
The first of those extensions is accommodated in modern dictionaries by the
gloss "by means of", and the *Oxford Dictionary* (1989) has citations for it. It
could also cover the second example, though some style commentators draw a
line between the two, allowing that *via* can be used of an impersonal channel
of communication but not yet with people. In either case it's arguable that a
simple English preposition would do just as well: *by* in the first sentence, and
through in the second.

vice or **vise** In Australia and Britain **vice** serves as the spelling for three
different words:
1 the Latin loanword/prefix discussed in the next entry
2 the word meaning "bad habit"
3 the word for a mechanical device which grips an object while it's being
    worked on.
    In American English, the first two are spelled **vice** while the third is **vise**.
Both **vice** and **vise** were used for the mechanical device in medieval times, but
only in the USA has **vise** been maintained to distinguish it from its homonyms.

vice, vice- and **vice versa** The Latin word **vice** has two syllables when it
means "in place of", as in:
    The secretary attended the meeting vice the society's president.

Vice is used particularly when someone is deputed to take on the role or duties of another person in a given context. From this usage, **vice-** comes to be used as a prefix in words like: *vice-captain*, *vice-president* and *viceroy*, to refer to the person who is the regular deputy for a senior executive.

The same word appears in **vice versa**, literally "with the place turned around" or more approximately "with things the other way round". It can be used when either the order of items, or people's roles, are being reversed. Compare:

They will visit the publisher and then have lunch, or vice versa.
Then you must contact me or vice versa.

The expression has been thoroughly assimilated into English since the seventeenth century, and is sometimes abbreviated to *v.v.*

Victoria and **Victorian** In Australia the adjective **Victorian** carries a geographical and political value in relation to the state of **Victoria**, as well as a historical/cultural one in relation to Queen Victoria (1837–1901). At this end of the twentieth century, historical use of **Victorian** sometimes makes it a byword for "old-fashioned"—which is why some institutions in **Victoria** prefer to avoid it, as do the *Victoria Police*.

Until 1851 **Victoria** was officially the *Port Phillip District of New South Wales*. Its good farming land led explorer Thomas Mitchell to dub it "Australia Felix", where the Latin adjective means "happy, fertile, productive".

vide, videlicet and **viz.** These instructions are all based on the Latin verb "see". **Vide** is the imperative, sometimes found on its own but more often in the crossreferencing instruction *quod vide*. It is usually abbreviated to **q.v.** (see under that heading).

Videlicet is a telescoping of *videre licet*, literally "it is permitted to see". It introduces a more precise explanation of something already stated in general terms. (Compare *scilicet*, used to introduce examples.) **Videlicet** is rarely seen in full nowadays, and is much better known in the abbreviated form **viz.** The *z* is the printer's equivalent of the scribal ʒ, which was the standard abbreviation for *-et*. Thus **viz.** is strictly speaking a **contraction** (see further under that heading).

Vietnam For most of three decades following World War II, **Vietnam** was divided into a northern communist zone with Hanoi as its capital, and a southern zone whose capital was Saigon. The country was reunified in 1976, as the Socialist Republic of Vietnam, and Saigon renamed as Ho Chi Minh City.

Note that the name is normally written as a single word, even though it is two words *Viet Nam* for United Nations and other official purposes. Of the dictionaries which register the name, both *Macquarie* (1991) and *Random House* mention *Viet Nam* as an alternative; and the *Oxford Dictionary* (1989) has it in just one citation but uses **Vietnam** in its definitions. There are no instances of *Viet Nam* in the Australian ACE corpus, as against 46 of **Vietnam**.

vigor or **vigour** For the choice between these, see under **-or/-our**.

villain or **villein** Historically speaking, these are simply alternative spellings for the medieval word for a farm laborer. The word was however used with derogatory connotations as early as the fourteenth century, and they are strong enough to do disservice to honest farmhands. Yet only since the nineteenth century have the two spellings been regularly used to differentiate the scoundrel **villain** from the medieval farm worker **villein**. Modern dictionaries still allow that **villain** may be used for **villein**, but not vice versa.

vin blanc This French phrase for "white wine" appears on some respectable Australian wine labels. It has however been more fully naturalised as the Australian word *plonk*, which is believed to represent *blanc*. The process of assimilation began during World War I, in expressions such as *vin blank*, *von blink* and even *point blank*, all of which are associated with wine of poor quality. Both *plonk* and *plink* seem to have originated this way. Yet the existence of the two words seems in fact to have raised the idea that they were different, and citations in the *Australian National Dictionary* show that *plonk* is now (since World War II) felt to be a cut above *plink*. Or, put the other way round, *plink* is cheap *plonk*.

virgule See **solidus**.

virtuosos or **virtuosi** The choice between these is discussed under **Italian plurals**.

virus The plural of this word is discussed at **-us** section 1.

vis à vis In French this means literally "face to face". From this it comes to mean "opposite", and in earlier times it could mean a carriage or piece of furniture which one shared with another person sitting opposite.
　　Nowadays it's most commonly used in the abstract sense of "in relation to" or "with regard to", as in:
　　We discussed the arrangements vis à vis their costs.
Note that the phrase is often written without an accent in English, especially when printed in roman. Most dictionaries give it hyphens, though being a foreign phrase there's little risk of its components being misconstrued without them (see further under **hyphens** section 2c).

viscous or **viscose** From the fifteenth century on, these were interchangeable as adjectives meaning "sticky, glutinous". **Viscose** disappeared from the record in the eighteenth century, but was signed up for service again in the late nineteenth century as the name of an artificial fibre or sheet made from cellulose. For similar pairs, see under **-ose**.

visible or **visual** The essential difference between these is that **visible** emphasises the fact of being seen, as in *visible signs of emotion*. **Visual** points to the fact that sight rather than any other form of perception is involved, as in:

Drivers need aural cues as well as visual ones for maximum safety.
Yet **visual** is used in some scientific contexts where we might expect **visible**, as in *visual symptoms* (of a disease), and *visual rays of the sun*. Note also that **visible** is developing along more metaphorical lines with the meaning "in the public eye". See for example:
Ministers of Education are more visible than they used to be.

visit or **visitation** Anyone can pay a **visit**, but a **visitation** implies extra formality at the least, and often has official or ominous connotations as well. Thus it's used for the formal visits of clergymen to those in hospital, or of government inspectors. It used to be used of the appearance of supernatural or quasi-supernatural forces, against which mankind seemed powerless, as in the *visitation of God's wrath* and *visitations of the plague*, though phrases like those sound archaic now.

visual or **visible** See **visible**.

viva voce This Latin phrase meaning literally "with living voice" is occasionally used to mean "by word of mouth". In British and Australian universities it refers to an oral examination at which students are quizzed by one or more examiners. Colloquially such an exam is a *viva*.

viz. See under **vide** and **Latin abbreviations**.

vocabulary This is a collective term for words when we think of them as items with particular meanings, not as components in the grammar of a phrase, clause or sentence. The choice of words is a crucial factor in any style. (See further under **colloquialisms**, **formal words** and **nominal**.)
For suggestions on how to vary your vocabulary, see **variety in writing**. The internal structure of words is discussed at **words**.

vocal chords or **vocal cords** See **chord**.

vocative This is one of the six grammatical cases recognised in Latin and other languages. It is associated with direct address, and so the personal name in the following sentence is in the **vocative** case:
John, would you bring the coffee?
In English the **vocative** case has no special inflection, whereas in Latin it did, at least in some declensions. It appears in the Latin quotation given by Shakespeare to the dying Julius Caesar: *Et tu Brute*, where *Brute* is the **vocative** of *Brutus*.

vogue words Fowler created this term for trendy expressions used by people to show they are swimming with the cultural tide. Earlier this century the vogue words included ones like "modern" and "progressive", which have been replaced at this end of the century by ones like *alternative* and *sustainable*. As those examples show, **vogue words** often embody current values, and reflect changes in them.

Some **vogue words** are drawn from the technology of the times, so current ones like *global village* can be invoked to show how advanced we are when talking about satellite links, and our *intelligent building* may be the one in which the fibre-optic cable is about to reach the computers on the fourth floor. As those examples show, there's often an element of hyperbole in the use of **vogue words** and expressions.

Yet many **vogue words** are less obviously connected with cultural developments—simply expressions which have somehow become very popular, such as:

crisis   dialogue   facelift   front runner   grassroots   marathon

Such words are grist for reports on almost anything in the mass media, and quickly become clichés. Today's **vogue words** are likely to be old hat before 2001, just because they're worked so hard. Those used as intensifiers, such as *cosmic*, *fantastic*, *mega* and *unreal* wear out even faster.

Apart from the **vogue words** in general usage, there are those which get overworked in academic and bureaucratic or corporate discourse. They include words like:

factor framework image interface parameter profile
situation syndrome target

Whatever weight they bring with them is undermined by their being overused and often redundant in phrases like the *classroom situation*. When not redundant they are still rather abstract words, and should not be used as makeshift expressions where something more precise is needed.

All the **vogue words** mentioned above achieve less than the users might hope by way of communicating. Yes, they are the buzz words of the moment, but by being trendy they draw attention to themselves, rather than the point or information you might want to get across.

voice In traditional grammar **voice** is the term used to cover the *active* and *passive* forms of the verb phrase, which show different relationships between the verb and its subject. In languages such as Latin there were separate sets of inflections for active and passive verbs. In modern European languages, including English, the passive is usually expressed through a compound verb. (See further under **active verbs** and **passive verbs**.)

volcano The plural of this word is discussed under **-o**.

Von The alphabetisation of names beginning with **Von** is discussed under **van** and **von**.

vortex or **vertex** See vertex.

vowels A *vowel* is at the heart of any syllable we pronounce. *Consonants* are the sounds that accompany the *vowel*, coming before and/or after it. In Australian English there are about twenty different **vowels** (including diphthongs) by the standard analysis based on the International Phonetic

Alphabet. A complete inventory of the Australian vowels and consonants is to be found in Appendix I.

The Roman alphabet has only five vowel letters (a,e,i,o,u) which naturally means that they correspond to more than one sound in English. Even vowel digraphs generally represent more than one vowel, witness the different sounds for *ea* in *beat, great, hear* and *heart,* or for *oo* in *flood, good, goose* and *poor.*

One consequence of this is that readers make more use of consonants than **vowels** in identifying written words. If every *vowel* in a sentence is blanked out we have a fair chance of reconstructing the words from the consonants and the inherent grammar, better than with only the **vowels**. So while **vowels** are indispensable to spoken language, the consonants are more fundamental to the written word, at least in English.

vox populi This Latin phrase is an abbreviated version of *vox populi vox Dei* "the voice of the people is the voice of God". From the fifteenth century on it was often cited to affirm the importance of common opinion.

In the twentieth century the phrase has been further curtailed to *vox pop,* but given new life in the title of radio and TV programs where brief statements extracted from street interviews are compiled to give a spectrum of opinion on a current issue.

vs. or v. See under **versus**.

vulgar When Fowler or the *Oxford Dictionary* called an expression **vulgar** it did not mean "rude" or "obscene". Rather it implied that the word belonged to popular usage, and was therefore not valued by anyone who took writing style seriously. Yet it also served to discredit more informal styles of writing, and underlies some of the shibboleths of twentieth century usage, which make formal English the only correct form. (See further under **shibboleth** and **barbarism**.)

vulva For the plural, see **-a** section 1.

W

waddy, waddie, wady or **wadi** The word **waddy** (also sometimes **waddie**) was borrowed from the Dharuk Aborigines of Port Jackson. We usually associate it with an Aboriginal war club, though last century it was also a byword for a tree, or any piece of wood. It also served then as a verb meaning "beat up or kill with a club". The spelling stabilised as **waddy** about the middle of the nineteenth century, and this helps to distinguish it from the Arabic loanword **wadi** or **wady** "dry water course", which is also used in Australia. The plural of **waddy** is of course *waddies*, whereas that of **wadi** is either *wadis* or *wadies*.

wagon or **waggon** The first spelling is preferred in all modern dictionaries. The spelling with two *g*s was popular in eighteenth century Britain, and appears in many dictionaries of the time, and in the citations in Dr Johnson's dictionary, though he himself chose *wagon* for the headword. The *Oxford Dictionary* shows that the point was much disputed in the first half of the nineteenth century, and though it also prefers **wagon** it notes the persistence in Britain of **waggon** late in the century. In the USA the preferred spelling has always been **wagon**, in keeping with the word's longer history and its etymology in the Dutch word *wagen*.

wait or **await** In twentieth century English **wait** is usually an intransitive verb, and **await** is transitive. Compare:
We're waiting for them to arrive.
We're awaiting their arrival.
As in those sentences, **await** usually has an abstract noun as its object. The use of a human or concrete object now sounds strangely formal: *We await her (plane).* In contrast *wait for* takes human or concrete items as objects.
    Note that there are special idiomatic uses of **wait** in which it works transitively:
You'll have to wait your turn.
The cook will have to wait table as well.
Shall we wait lunch for them?
Apart from these, **wait** is usually intransitive and has a preposition immediately following it. (See also next entry.)

wait on or **wait for** In conversation **wait on** serves as an alternative to **wait for**, as in:
We're still waiting on Philippa.

Yet its right to appear in print has been challenged for nearly two centuries. Doubts about its status may well relate to the fact that the *Oxford Dictionary* declared it obsolete in the nineteenth century. Perhaps the fact that **wait on** has other uses helped to strengthen the feeling that it ought not to do the job of **wait for** as well. At any rate, its recognised meanings included "serve ", as in:

Her mother had also waited on the Queen.

and "serve at table":

Able seamen were recruited to wait on the officers in the dining room.

It also appears in the more abstract sense of "be dependent or consequent on", as in:

The project now waits on confirmation from the Canberra office.

These several meanings—and the one in the first sentence above—are clear from the context. There is thus no problem if **wait on** appears in print in the sense "wait for". *Webster's English Usage* (1989) has ample citations from round the world to show that many writers have no inhibitions about using it that way.

waiter or **waitress** The push towards nonsexist language means that **waiter** is preferred by many, whether the person attending your table is male or female. The same service is performed by either, and it's unnecessary to draw attention to the gender of the person concerned, except when their dress (or lack of it) makes it something you cannot overlook. Most dictionaries now define **waiter** in gender-free terms: and the Australian Government *Style Manual* (1988) recommends **waiter** to replace **waitress**. (See further under **-ess**.)

The verb **waiter** is backformed from *waitering* "working as a waiter", and it fills a necessary gap if you want to explain what you do for a part- or full-time income. However it still has an informal ring to it. (See further under **backformation**.)

waive or **wave**, **waiver** or **waver** The word **waive** originated in Anglo-French law, and even in nonlegal use it still has official overtones:

The committee must agree to waive that prerequisite.

You'll need an official waiver.

Wave is a very old English word, whose roles as noun and verb are usually quite distinct from **waive**. They only come close in idioms such as *wave aside* meaning "dismiss". For example:

He waved aside my offer of payment.

Still *wave aside* differs from **waive** in being a personal dispensation rather than an institutional one.

Note also the verb **waver** borrowed from Old Norse. Its only chance of being confused with **waiver** is on the rare occasions when it's used as a noun:

There wasn't a waver in the grim line of protesters.

The two words are distinct in meaning, since **waver** suggests indecision whereas **waiver** always connotes some form of decision-making.

wake, waken, awake or **awaken** There's confusion of choice here: all four have or have had both transitive and intransitive uses, i.e. as meaning "emerge from sleep" as well as "rouse (someone)". (See further under **transitive.**)

Nowadays the verbs **awaken** and **awake** are both a little old-fasioned except in figurative use, as in *awaken their suspicions* and *awake to the alarming prospect of war.* In such expressions, **awaken** is a transitive verb, and **awake** intransitive. A further point to note is that the adjective **awake** can be used freely in both figurative and nonfigurative senses, as in: *stay awake* and *be awake to the problem.*

In Australian English **wake** and especially *wake up* is the most common of all four, from evidence in the ACE corpus. It serves for the intransitive verb "emerge from sleep":

Without daylight saving I wake too early.

I woke up at dawn.

Meanwhile **wake** shares with **waken** the transitive meaning "rouse":

Don't wake(n) the baby.

You've woken/wakened the baby.

Wake is usually an irregular verb in Australian and British English (with **wake**, *woke, woken* as its principal parts). In American English however the regular forms **wake**, *waked* are the primary ones. These differences are a reminder that there were two Old English verbs meaning "wake", one strong, one weak, which seem to have coalesced in Middle English, leaving us not altogether sure which of their various forms to use.

wallaby This word was borrowed from the Dharuk Aborigines in the Port Jackson area. The word's spelling varied considerably till the mid-nineteenth century, with *wullubee, wallable, wallabi* and *wallaba* among the variants recorded. The last spelling comes closest to the Aboriginal essence of the word *walaba.*

The plural is usually *wallabies*, though **wallaby** is used collectively by zoologists and sportsmen. (See further under **zero plurals.**)

wallop For the spelling of this word when it serves as a verb, see **-p/-pp-**.

-ward or **-wards** These endings on adjectives and adverbs imply movement in a particular direction: *backward(s), forward(s)* etc. In Australia and Britain, the common practice is to use **-ward** for the adjective, and **-wards** for the adverb. Compare:

That seems a backward step.

I don't believe in going backwards.

The same distinction can be applied to all the following as well:

downward(s) eastward(s) heavenward(s) homeward(s) inward(s)
landward(s) northward(s) onward(s) outward(s) seaward(s) sideward(s)
southward(s) upward(s) westward(s)

In American English meanwhile, the form with **-ward** is mostly used for adverb as well as adjective, as in:

They headed westward across the Mississippi.

Yet the tendency to use the same form for both adverb and adjective can be observed in Australian English with *forward*. Compare:

She stepped forward from the group.

The plan shows forward thinking.

The ratio of 95:7 for *forward/forwards* in the ACE corpus shows a definite decline in the differentiation between the two forms. It is echoed by the variable ratios for the adverb of several others, not always weighted towards the **-wards** form.

The preposition **toward(s)** shows a similar trend: see **toward** or **towards**.

warden or **warder** In Australia and Britain **warden** is the name for officials of several kinds ranging from *traffic wardens* to the *Warden of Trinity College* (University of Melbourne). In nineteenth century Australia, *wardens* were responsible for managing goldmining sites.

In the USA, the **warden** is the superintendent of a prison—at which point there could be confusion with **warder**, an older term for a prison guard. In fact the US prison guard is called a *jailer* (see **jailer** or **jailor**), while in both Australia and Britain the **warder** is now a "prison officer".

warrantor or **warranter** See under -er/-or.

warranty or **warrantee** This word originated as **warranty** in fourteenth century feudal law, but two centuries later began to be used in its commercial sense of a "pledge as to the reliability of goods sold". The second spelling **warrantee** is labeled as erroneous by the *Oxford Dictionary*, though citations for it go back to the seventeenth century. The vacillation over its spelling is exactly like that for *guaranty/guarantee*, and all four come from the same French source word.

The domain of **warranty/warrantee** has been encroached on by *guaranty/ guarantee*, though some distinguish them in terms of the commitment to repair or replace offered by the latter, and the pledge that the goods have been fully tested and checked before being marketed, offered by the former.

warrigal This is another name for the dingo, Australia's wild dog. Both *dingo* and **warrigal** were early loanwords from the Dharuk Aborigines of Port Jackson. While *dingo* has remained the standard term for the dog, **warrigal** has a number of other meanings, including "stranger" or "wild Aborigine", i.e. one not accustomed to European ways. The word also appears in Australian English as an adjective meaning "wild, untamed", usually in reference to animals. In the late nineteenth and early twentieth century **warrigal** is also recorded meaning "wild horse".

Apart from its range of meanings, **warrigal** has also had a range of spellings, including *warragal, warragul, warregal* and *warrigul*, mostly in the nineteenth century. The Gippsland town of *Warragul* preserves one of them.

waste or **wastage** Style guides remind us that **wastage** should be kept for loss by wear and tear, decay and other natural processes, so that its use is distinct from that of **waste**, which involves careless use of resources. Compare:

We hope to reduce the work force by natural wastage.

The lecture was a waste of time.

The comparison helps to show that **waste** has negative connotations, whereas **wastage** is neutral.

Yet both the *Oxford Dictionary* and more recent dictionary definitions suggest that the distinction just illustrated is not watertight, and that **wastage** can now include human *wastefulness*. The pressure to inflate language means that **wastage** appears as a synonym for the shorter **waste**, and then it takes on negative connotations. So if you want a neutral word to refer to natural attrition of a resource, it's safer to seek an alternative to **wastage**.

wave or **waive**, **waver** or **waiver** See **waive** or **wave**.

way This simple noun has a number of additional roles which are common in conversation, and increasingly seen in print. It serves as an adverb in:

He was way down the corridor.

Her answers were way out.

There **way** means "a long distance", though its use shades into that of an intensifier as the second example shows. The usage is well established, and has been recorded since 1849.

Way also has a conjunctive role to play in sentences such as:

They don't sing the way they used to.

In traditional grammar, this use of *the* **way** was regarded as elliptical for *in the way that*, and many writers would spell it out like that in formal contexts. But in everyday communication, spoken and written, *the* **way** works as a compound conjunction, and as an informal alternative to both *as* and *how*:

She mustn't suffer the way her mother did.

That's the way the cookie crumbles.

English databases show that *the* **way** is used relatively more freely as a conjunction in fiction than in nonfiction, though the stylistic divide is sharper in Britain than in the USA. Research by Mittins in 1970 showed Britons reacting strongly to its appearance in formal speech and writing, whereas American research reported in *Webster's English Usage* (1989) found it was unexceptionable.

-ways or **-wise** See **-wise** section 1.

we Questions of grammar and style are raised by this pronoun. Its use is often slightly self-conscious, and some people are in two minds about when it should be **we** and when *us*. Thus **we** is occasionally used as a substitute for *us* as in:
This is a familiar experience for we blind people.
In speech this could pass unnoticed (masked by the appositional structure), and *Webster's English Usage* (1989) cites a number of examples from print. But in formal writing *us* would still be expected in such a context following a preposition.

We also raises some stylistic issues. The use of **we** by a single writer can be seen as presumptuous: it's often called "using the royal *we*", though not usually regarded as treasonable. Newspaper editors do it, speaking on behalf of the nation—or just their newspaper; and it's done increasingly by scientists or other academic writers as they seek to involve the whole academic community in their argument. It is unlikely to raise eyebrows unless the opinion attributed to *we/us* is contrary to that of the reader. Persuaders and narrators of all kinds use **we** to establish solidarity with their audience, and create a feeling of common identity. It thus serves a rhetorical purpose in many contexts. (See further under **person**, first and third person narrative.)

weak forms See under **reduced forms**.

weasel For the spelling of this word when it's used as a verb, see under **-l/-ll-**.

weave The usual past forms of this verb are *wove* (past tense) and *woven* (past participle). For example:
She wove tapestries as a hobby.
There was a fine thread of gold woven into the border.
But when **weave** is used figuratively in describing the movement of a person or a vehicle, the past form is *weaved:*
The cyclist weaved his way through the traffic.

wed This old English verb has gained new currency through newspaper headlines, where *marry* would be too bulky a word. The regular past form is *wedded*, but this too is reduced to **wed**, especially for the past participle, when space is limited.

-wegian This suffix owes its origins to *Norwegian*, which was first recorded in the seventeenth century and paralleled in the eighteenth by *Galwegian* (from either Galloway in Scotland or Galway in Ireland). Walter Scott extended the pattern by extending it to *Glaswegian*, and it has remained popular, in spite of the comment that "Glasgovian" would be easier to justify. *Taswegian*, first recorded in 1961, has even less justification, except as an alternative to *Tasmaniac*.

welch or **welsh** See welsh.

well or **good** See good.

well and **well-** The adverb **well** is used to modify parts of verbs, as in:

They were well dressed.

Their children were well behaved.

In sentences like those, **well** and the word following are independent parts of the verb phrase, and are not to be hyphenated.

But when the same combinations form compound adjectives and become part of a noun phrase, then they need hyphens, as in:

We saw well-dressed adults and well-behaved children.

The use of a hyphen with **well** depends thus on how it works in relation to the grammar of the phrase or sentence—not whether it's part of an established compound.

Note that compound adjectives with **well-** may be made comparative and superlative in one of two ways:

- with *better/best*
- with *more/most*

Compare:

They wanted a better known architect for the job.

They wanted a more well-known architect for the job.

and

He was the best loved author of his generation.

He was the most well-loved author of his generation.

Some authorities such as the *Oxford Guide to English Usage* indicate their preference for the forms with *better* and *best*, and they are certainly neater. Yet they lose a shade of meaning which is there in *well-known* and *well-loved*—an indication of celebrity.

In practice, the forms with *better/best* are not suitable for all the adjectives compounded with **well-**, and only *more/most* seem to work. See for example:

He chose the most well-done steak on the barbecue.

A more well-rounded person you couldn't imagine.

In such cases the idiomatic meaning of the compound is lost if **well-** is converted into *better/best*. The problem is deepened by the fact that *better/best* are related to *good* as well as **well**, which also lends ambiguity to many **well-** compounds.

welsh or **welch** All dictionaries make **welsh** the primary spelling for this colloquial word meaning "duck one's responsibilities" (financial or otherwise). **Welch** is the secondary alternative, but it's the one to prefer if you wish to play down any possible disparagement of the people of Wales. The word may have originated as a "throwaway term", expressing English prejudice against the Welsh, though some dictionaries simply say its origins are obscure. (See further under **throwaway terms**.)

were The usual role of **were** is as the plural past tense of *be*. For its use to express wishes, suppositions and conditions, see under **subjunctive**.

west, western or **westerly**   These all appear in lower case when they stand
as geographical words, referring to a point, area or direction which is 90° left
of the north/south axis for a given place. The meaning is always relative:
compare *west of the Dividing Range* with *the western suburbs of Melbourne*.
Note that both **west** and **western** normally mean "to(wards) or in the west".
But when **west** or **westerly** are applied to winds or ocean currents, they mean
"from the west".

Both *West* and *Western* also appear with capital letters as the first element
in geographical names, such as *West Indies*, *West Pakistan*, *Western Australia*
and *Western Samoa*. In the USA *West* appears as the second element in *Midwest*
(the central and northern farming lands), and in *Far West* (the states west of the
Rocky Mountains). The "Wild West" was never strictly a geographical term,
but rather a notional frontier region where stable government and law and order
had yet to be established.

For the world at large, the *West* has become a political designation for the
capitalist countries of Europe and North America, as opposed to the communist
or socialist states of eastern Europe and the former Soviet Union. The adjective
western also contrasts with *eastern* in broad cultural terms, as in *western
medicine*. Here the implied contrast is between European culture and traditions,
and those of Asia. Note that the verb *westernise* "adapt to the culture and
customs of the West" is usually written without a capital letter.

Note also that in suburban Sydney, the term *westie* or *Westie* is a colloquial
and sometimes derogatory reference to someone who lives in the further western
region, and whose culture and life style are thought to be rather rough.

Western Australia   Australia's largest state has many syllables to its name,
though there's one less for the individual resident and the general adjective:
West Australian. Compare:

  the premier of Western Australia
  The average West Australian supports daylight saving.
  the West Australian vote in the Senate

A telescoped form of the word *Westralia(n)* was coined by the *Bulletin* in the
1890s; but it has no official status, and has never caught on.

westward or **westwards**   See under -**ward**.

wet   The past forms of the verb **wet** are often just the same:

  The rain wet the dust on the window frames.
  The child has wet the cushion.

Wetted is used for the past tense when some deliberate action is involved, as
in:

  She wetted her lips with a quick pass of the tongue.

In passive sentences, the choice between *wetted* and **wet** again helps to show
whether or not the event described happens by accident:

  The wall had been wet by a broken pipe for years.

To prevent the roof catching fire, the gutters should be wetted.
(See also **whet**.)

wharfie or **wharfy** See under **-ie/-y**.

wharfs or **wharves** The choice between these is discussed under **-f/-v-**.

what The use of **what** is straightforward in questions such as the direct *What's the matter?* and the indirect *You asked what I thought*. As an interrogative pronoun it's the only possible option. But as an interrogative adjective, it is a matter of choice. Compare:
What train did you catch?
Which train did you catch?
In a question like that, either **what** or *which* would do, though the first implies that the questioner knows nothing about the times of the trains, whereas the second suggests that s/he knows something about them.

What also has a special use as a relative pronoun, equivalent to *that which* or *those which*:
I did what I thought was right.
They looked for provisions and brought what there were.
As those examples show, the verb following **what** may be singular or plural, depending on its agreement with singular or plural nouns in the sentence. Note also that **what** is not a simple relative, and so it should not appear in sentences like: ''The man what came to the door looked upset.'' Instead it should be *who* or *that* came. Never use **what** where a relative pronoun (*that, who, whom* or *which*) would fit in.

Note finally how **what** sometimes appears unnecessarily in comparative clauses:
She remembered the meeting more closely than (what) I did.
I'd like the same choice as (what) I had before.
In such sentences the conjunctions *than* and *as* are quite enough to join the two clauses.

For the use of **what** in topicalising clauses such as *What the world needs now ...*, see under **cleft sentences** and **information focus**.

whatever or **what ever** See under **-ever**.

whence Like *hence* and *thence*, this word now draws attention to itself as being either formal or slightly old-fashioned. (See under **hence**.)

where- In earlier English there was a large set of conjunctions compounded with **where-**:
whereat wherefore wherefrom wherein whereof whereon
wheresoever whereto whereunder wherewith
None of these is current in ordinary usage, and if used they bring a slightly stuffy or old-fashioned flavor to the style. They are easily paraphrased with *which*, so that *whereat* becomes ''at which'', and so on.

The only **where-** conjunctions which remain in general use are *whereas* and *wherever. Whereby* is restricted to some formal constructions such as *a means whereby* ...; and *whereupon* survives in certain traditional styles of narrative. Other remnants of the set are used as nouns: *whereabouts, wherewithal* and *wherefores* (as in *whys and wherefores*).

whereabouts Should it be:

> *Their whereabouts remain a secret* or
> *Their whereabouts remains a secret.*

According to *Webster's English Usage* the first is rather more likely than the second, though both are established. The issues are discussed further under **agreement** section 3.

whet The past form of this verb is always *whetted*, whether it means literally "sharpen", or more figuratively "incite, excite". Compare the past of *wet*, which can be either *wet* or *wetted.* (See under **wet**.) The two verbs come rather close together in figurative uses such as:

> *The walk had whetted their appetites.*
> *They had already wetted their whistle.*

(The idiom *wet one's whistle* goes back to the fourteenth century, to Chaucer in the *Reeve's Tale*.)

whether In indirect questions **whether** is equivalent to *if*, though it's slightly more formal in style:

> *The student asked whether/if she would record the lecture.*

In some cases **whether** is preferable to *if* to prevent ambiguity. (See under **if**.) But in other contexts **whether** is the only possible conjunction:

- when there's a preposition: *His appointment depends on whether we have enough money in reserve.*
- when there are alternatives to introduce: *You must make a decision whether to go or not.*
- when the meaning is "regardless of X or Y": *Whether they want him or not, he'll arrive.*

Note that when *whether or not* sets up the alternatives, they do not need to be underscored by antonyms, as in *Whether or not we succeed or fail* ... The point comes through more clearly as either:

> *Whether or not we succeed* ... or
> *Whether we succeed or fail* ...

whetted or **wetted** See whet.

which This word has several roles, in introducing direct and indirect questions, as well as relative clauses, all of **which** raise different questions of style.

1 *In direct (and indirect) questions*, **which** can be an interrogative pronoun or an adjective:

> *Which is your car?*

Which bus do we take to the station?
In either case **which** implies a set of known alternatives. Compare the use of *what* as an interrogative (see **what**).

2 *In relative clauses,* **which** often serves as an alternative to *that* in reference to things:
I bought tickets at the kiosk which/that was opposite the bank.
The choice between **which** and *that* may be purely stylistic, or influenced by the grammar of the clause it introduces. (See further under **relative pronouns**.)

3 Which is sometimes used to introduce a relative clause that refers back to a whole preceding clause, not just something within it. The difference can be seen in:
James is bringing his new wife, which is great.
James is bringing his new wife who is great.
In the first of those sentences, **which** effectively summarises the whole of the preceding statement and is a "sentential relative". The construction used to be frowned on, but the *Comprehensive Grammar of English* (1985) treats it as a regular part of English syntax.

4 Another use of **which** that has only recently become acceptable is when it stands at the start of a sentence, when it makes a cohesive link with the previous one. For example:
He finished up by saying that we should all work together on the project.
Which is exactly what we'd hoped for.
Traditional grammarians might urge that **which** be replaced by one of the demonstratives (*this/that*); or that a dash should replace the full stop after "project" and **which** be printed without a capital letter, to link the two sentences in the conventional way. The *Right Word at the Right Time* argues that a sentence starting with **which** is an effective summary device at the end of an article—but its effectiveness depends on its being used only rarely.

while or **whilst** With its several meanings **while** is potentially ambiguous. Its essential and oldest use is as a temporal conjunction:
The Titanic *was sinking while the band played on.*
Note that this temporal use of **while** usually goes with use of a continuous (*-ing*) verb in the main clause.
  While has also been used since the sixteenth century to introduce a clause which expresses some sort of contrast or opposition to the main clause:
While it's not my favorite place, it'll do for tonight.
The adults wanted a quiet evening while the children pressed for a video.
The degree of contrast is weaker in that second example, and is even further reduced in sentences such as the following:
The barbecue is planned for Friday, while Sunday is our sailing day.
In such sentences **while** has neither temporal nor contrastive value, and some would deprecate this "modern colourless use", as the *Oxford Dictionary* calls

it. There are always alternative words to clarify the meanings of **while**, including *when*, *(al)though*, *whereas* and even *and*. In fact the meaning is rarely ambiguous because the temporal use of **while** usually goes with a continuous verb, and the contrastive use usually puts **while** at the start of the sentence.

The choice between **while** and **whilst** is a matter of both regional dialect and style. **Whilst** is rare in American English (it did not appear in the Brown corpus), whereas in comparable databases in Britain and Australia there were 66 and 34 instances respectively. Even so **whilst** is conspicuous by its absence from the daily press in Australia and Britain, and is most frequently represented in formal and literary nonfiction. Two thirds of the instances in the ACE corpus were in bureaucratic, academic or crafted prose (belles lettres). This suggests that **whilst** is on the wane here too. (Compare **amid(st)**.)

whingeing or **whinging** See -**e** section 1d.

whisky or **whiskey** Within the trade, these two spellings distinguish the grain-based spirits of Scotland, Australia and Canada (**whisky**) from those of Ireland and the USA (**whiskey**). However **whisky** is also the common spelling for such spirits of whatever source in Australian and British English (whatever type); and **whiskey** works the same way in American English.

whiz or **whizz** Both spellings are recognised in modern dictionaries, though there are differences in their application. Australian and American dictionaries prefer **whiz**, whether it's:
- the colloquial word for an expert or something remarkable or
- an onomatopoeic word for the sound of a rapidly moving object (noun or verb).

Whizz is given as a secondary spelling for both.

The *Oxford Dictionary* prefers **whizz** for both words, with **whiz** or *wiz* as alternatives for the first word (it seems diffident about the idea that it owes its origins to *wizard*), and only **whiz** as alternative for the second.

Those who use **whiz** as the verb still double the *z* before adding suffixes such as *-ed*, *-ing* and *-er* (see further under **z/zz**), which makes it identical with **whizz**.

The preference for *whizbang* or *whizzbang* correlates simply with the use of **whiz/whizz**. The first spelling is preferred by the major American dictionaries, and the second by the Oxford. Note also the distinction between the American *whizkid* "exceptional person", and the British slang *whizzboy* "pickpocket".

who and **whose** Who works as a pronoun both interrogative and relative for referring to people:
Who goes there?
The stranger who greeted me in the foyer is a visiting writer.
Note however that either **who** or *which* may be used after words which refer to collectives of people, such as *committee, team* etc.:
It was a committee which operated quite autocratically.

It was the committee who agreed to those terms.
The use of *which* in such cases projects the committee as a single administrative unit, whereas **who** makes them individual people.

*The domain of **whose*** is a little different. It serves as the possessive form for both **who** and *which* (for both people and things) in relative clauses:
The soldier whose arm was raised in salute had disappeared.
We were sideswiped by a car whose brakes had failed.
Yet the idea that **whose** can only be applied to people dies hard, and many a sentence has been made awkward by the use of *of which* rather than **whose**. Compare this version of the second sentence above:
We were sideswiped by a car the brakes of which had failed.
Fowler had to argue strenuously for the use of **whose** in reference to inanimates, and the controversy even then was 150 years old. Note however that when **whose** serves as an interrogative word at the start of a sentence, it is effectively limited to people. Compare:
Which of the cars does this street directory belong to?
Whose car does this street directory belong to?
The use of **whose** in the second sentence concentrates attention on the car's owner, and cannot relate to the car itself.

whom As the object form of *who*, **whom** is a remnant of the once much more extensive case system in English (see further under **cases**). Its use overall has declined, and while it survives in writing it's quite rare in speech. Its decline is more marked in Australia and the USA than in Britain. In comparable databases of one million words, **whom** appeared 219 times in British English, as opposed to 146 in American English, and 117 in Australian English

1 Whom is an interrogative/relative pronoun which according to traditional grammar should appear whenever *who* is the object of a verb or a preposition. Yet usage on this point was already changing at the end of the eighteenth century, when Noah Webster argued that it should be:
Who did she marry? rather than
Whom did she marry?
Webster noted that *who* rather than **whom** was the idiom people used, and he would not endorse the efforts of his contemporaries who rewrote passages of Shakespeare and other classical authors, to ensure that **whom** appeared according to the rules. Then as now it seems that when it's the *first word* in a question, *who* is preferred to **whom**. **Whom** is preferred when it comes second i.e. after a preposition:
To whom were you speaking?
Compare what happens when the preposition moves to the other end of the sentence:
Who were you speaking to?

The two constructions show the contrast between formal and standard/informal styles, with the second now commonly used in writing as well as speech. In both direct and indirect questions, **whom** makes for a high style:

They asked to whom I was speaking.

Compare:

They asked who I was speaking to.

2 In relative clauses **whom** can be replaced by *that* or a zero relative. Compare:

She needs someone in whom she can confide.
She needs someone that she can confide in.
She needs someone she can confide in.

Once again relative **whom** continues in writing after any preposition, and especially in phrases such as *all of whom/both of whom/ten of whom*. For example:

They chose the first three applicants, none of whom had a car.

In partitive constructions like those there is no alternative to **whom**, and it seems to be a stronghold for it. More than two thirds of the instances of **whom** in the Australian ACE corpus were following a preposition. Elsewhere **whom** represents a formal stylistic choice because there are less formal options; and it correlates more strongly with nonfiction than fiction in the ACE data.

3 *Inappropriate use of **whom***. Style guides these days have as much to say about using **whom** in the wrong place as failing to use it where formal style might require it. Examples of the problem go back to Shakespeare and the King James Bible, as in *Whom do men say that I am?* If we agree that the first word is the complement of *I am*, then *who* is the word to agree with it.

Yet grammarians differ on the issue, and with a different analysis Jespersen found this use of **whom** unexceptionable. In questions and statements involving a kind of parenthesis, it's common enough for writers to use **whom** instead of *who*:

They asked me whom I thought was most suitable for the job.

Within the Australian ACE corpus there are several examples. The *New Yorker* found enough to run a column titled "The Omnipotent Whom", but discontinued it when the editor found that "almost nobody knew what was wrong with them".

This extra use of **whom** is unlikely to turn the tide in its favor. Rather, the doubts about where **whom** should or should not be used confirm that its place in modern English grammar is insecure. Given the risks involved in using it, it's not surprising if writers avoid it.

Whorfian principle One of the tantalising questions of language is whether it influences the society and culture we live in, or whether they determine it. Are we predestined to see the world as we do because we speak English, or any other language, or does our language simply reflect what happens in our culture?

The relationship between language and culture was one of the profound questions raised by Benjamin Lee Whorf, an American linguist of the 1930s. Whorf was an engineer by profession, but he spent any leave he had investigating the unwritten language of American Indians, and eventually became a full-time field worker.

While working with the Hopi Indians, Whorf ascertained that they made no use of tense with their verbs, and it occurred to him that this went hand in hand with their stable, very traditional lifestyle, which recognised no landmarks of history and anticipated no change of state in the future. It seemed to Whorf that the absence of tenses in language worked against any possible perception of historical change, and that language could perhaps condition the outlook of a people. The latter hypothesis is now generally referred to as the **Whorfian principle**.

Yet linguistic evidence often allows either the Whorfian or a counter-Whorfian interpretation. Many Aboriginal languages have highly developed case systems and demonstratives to express the location and direction of objects. You could argue that these linguistic resources have supported a nomadic way of life, *or* that they have developed in response to the necessities of that lifestyle. Many people would prefer a compromise interpretation: that such language resources develop hand in hand with a nomadic lifestyle, and are not simply a cause or effect of it. Language has a dynamic relationship with culture.

This dynamic reinterpretation of the *Whorfian hypothesis* lends strength to attempts to rid Australian English of sexist and racist elements. While they are there, they may sustain and foster sexist and racist attitudes in the community. By consciously replacing them with nonsexist and nonracist words, we have some hope of consolidating equal opportunity attitudes and practices.

whose See under **who**.

wh-words See **interrogative words**.

widow or **widower** The *-er* ending on **widower** now marks it as the male counterpart of **widow**, and gives us a clear gender distinction between the two words. Several centuries ago **widow** served to refer to either women or men who had lost their spouse, showing how fluid the gender in a word can be. The gender distinction which we now make between **widow** and **widower** confers no obvious advantage on the latter, and has not attracted attention in the debate about sexist language.

wilful or **willful** The first spelling is standard in Australia and Britain, the second in the USA. **Wilful** is the older spelling, originating in the fourteenth century, while **willful** makes its first appearance in the seventeenth—early enough to cross the Atlantic and establish itself in American English.

will For the choice between **will** and *shall*, see under **shall**.

willy-willy For the difference between **willy-willy** and *cyclone*, see **cyclone**.

For the origin and structure of the term, see further under **Aboriginal words** and **Australian English**.

winey or **winy** See under **-y/-ey.**

wiry or **wirey** See under **-y/-ey.**

-wise or **-ways** In certain words **-wise** and **-ways** are alternatives, as in *lengthwise/lengthways*. Other examples are:

> *cornerwise/cornerways crosswise/crossways edgewise/edgeways*
> *endwise/endways leastwise/leastways longwise/longways*
> *sidewise/sideways*

Your preference for one or the other may be influenced by the fact that the forms with **-wise** are more common in American English, and those with **-ways** in British English.

Other uses of **-wise**:

1 **-Wise** is the only possible ending in long-established words such as *clockwise*, *likewise* and *otherwise*. In those it means "in the manner (of)", just as in newer adverbs created with nouns, such as *crabwise*.

2 A very different use of **-wise** is to mean "clever, smart", in compound adjectives such as *streetwise*. No quibbles seem to be raised about words formed in this way, though they can be quite ad hoc:

> *He's as computerwise as anyone in this department.*

Being adjectives, these **-wise** words are built into the core of the sentence either predicatively (as in the example) or attributively (see further under **adjectives**).

3 Yet another more disputed use of **-wise** is in creating ad hoc adverbs which mean "where X is concerned", as in:

> *Computerwise it's the only possible solution.*

These **-wise** words often occur at the beginning of a sentence. They announce a new focus of attention, and are in fact a topicalising device. (See further under **topic** and **information focus**.) They also serve as convenient shorthand for a longer phrase. But being rather conspicuous at the start of a sentence, they are a ready target for those who react negatively to innovations in language. Words formed this way are probably more often spoken than written, though that's no reason to ban them from writing. The grammar of the sentence distinguishes them from the matching adjectives, as the examples above show. They need not arouse any objection if used skilfully and sparingly.

wisteria or **wistaria** The glorious climbing plant with pendant clusters of blue flowers is usually said to be named after Caspar Wistar 1761–1818, an American anatomist, scientist or doctor, depending on which dictionary you consult. The spelling **wistaria** renders the surname more closely, and it's the first one in the *Oxford Dictionary* and British dictionaries, but **wisteria** gets first preference in American ones, and in the *Macquarie Dictionary*. This is because **wisteria** was the spelling used by Thomas Nuttall, curator of the Harvard botanical gardens 1822–34, and the man who gave the flower its name. Other forces, such as the parallel between **wisteria** and a variety of other words *hysteria, diphtheria, cafeteria* etc. have probably helped to reinforce that spelling.

Apart from the spelling, we may wonder whether the plant was actually named after *Caspar Wistar* the anatomist etc., or whether it might not reflect some appreciation of the work of another Caspar Wistar, actually the grandfather of the anatomist, who was founder of the American glass industry in New Jersey. The products of Wistar the elder's foundry (known as Wistarberg glass) were beautiful green vessels decorated with swirls and threads of applied glass—rather reminiscent of the tendrils of the **wisteria** plant.

witch's hat, witches' hat or **witches hat**   This compound is hexed with logical problems when you try to write it down in its contemporary sense of "road marker". All is well when you simply want it as an item of millinery:

She went in Elizabethan dress, topped off with a witch's hat.

But not when it comes to saying that:

The traffic lanes had been changed with witch's hats ...

There the singularity of the witch and the plurality of hats are at odds. If however we go for **witches' hats** we seem to imply a coven of witches that has left behind tokens of their visit. For the moment **witches hats** seems the best solution, for a generic expression so often used in the plural—taking advantage of the fact that the apostrophe is receding from various kinds of attributive expressions (see **apostrophes** section 2). In the longer run *witch hats* would banish the hex for good.

without   This was once the opposite of *within*, and a synonym for "outside". So in Shakespeare's *Macbeth*, a servant could say of visitors: *They are, my lord, without the palace gate.* This meaning of **without** goes back to Old English. The modern meaning "lacking" began to appear in Middle English, but has completely taken over: and the old meaning can only be revived in a contrived way by combining it with *within*, as in *a house clean within and without*.

Note that in Australian English, **without** is only used to introduce nonfinite clauses. For example:

We'll have trouble getting there without stopping for petrol.

In some British and American dialects, **without** is used as a conjunction to introduce a finite clause, as in:

We'll have trouble getting there without we stop for petrol.

wolfish or **wolvish**   See under **-v-/-f-**.

woman   See under **lady**.

womera or **woomera**   See **woomera**.

wonga   Whether as **wonga** or *wonga-wonga*, this Aboriginal loanword has diverse sources and applications. It can mean:

1 A corroboree. This use, recorded only since 1946, invokes a word from Aboriginal languages spoken in northwestern Northern Territory.

2 An Australian bulrush (also known by the Aboriginal name *cumbungi*), whose root was eaten by the Aborigines in western Victoria and along the Lachlan River in New South Wales. It was first recorded in 1865, but not often since then.

3 The ground-feeding pigeon *Leucosarcia melanoleuca*, found on the east coast from Victoria to Mackay. The name, first recorded in 1821, was probably borrowed from the Dharuk people of the Sydney area. The bird has since been referred to variously as *wonga-wonga (pigeon)*, *wonga pigeon*, and just **wonga**.

4 The climbing plant *Pandorea pandarana*, with its clusters of showy cream or pale brown flowers. It grows naturally in eastern and southeastern Australia, but was already being cultivated in the 1890s, according to Morris's *Austral English*. First recorded as *wonga-wonga vine*, it's nowadays often reduced to *wonga vine*.

There may be a connection between the third and fourth items above (listed under the same headword in the *Australian National Dictionary*) but it is unexplained.

woollen or **woolen** The spelling **woollen** is unusual, in that consonants are not normally doubled after a vowel which is a digraph (i.e. consists of two letters). Compare *leaden*, *wooden* etc. In American English this convention is observed with the spelling **woolen**. But in British and Australian English, **woollen** is the primary spelling. It matches the use of double *l* in other derived words such as *traveller*, though they normally have at least two syllables (see **-l/-ll-**). Perhaps *woolly*, the regular adjective from *wool* is also an influence.

woomera or **womera** Two different Aboriginal words for different weapons underlie these two spellings, though the relationship between words and weapons is a challenge to Aboriginal scholarship. Both words come from the Dharuk Aborigines, and were first recorded in the 1790s.

The more distinctive word of the two **woomera** is the name for the throwing stick Aborigines used to propel a dart or spear. According to *Australian Aboriginal Words*, it corresponds to the Dharuk word "wamara". In English the spelling is most often **woomera**, though **womera**, *wommara*, *wommera* and *womra* are among the others recorded.

The less well-known word, given in the *Australian National Dictionary* as **womera**, refers to an Aboriginal weapon like a club or boomerang. It renders a Dharuk word which sounded like "wumerang", and may simply have been a variant of *boomerang* as *Australian Aboriginal Words* has it. In some of the *National Dictionary* citations it's evidently thrown like a boomerang, yet in others it's a hand-held weapon used to club victims. Spelling variants for the word include those associated with **woomera**, among others, which complicates the identification of the object.

word classes See **parts of speech**.

word order In English, **word order** is a significant factor in grammar (syntax). The normal **word order** for statements has the subject preceding the verb, and the verb before its object or complement. This basic order is modified for questions and occasionally for other grammatical reasons. (See under **inversion**.)

Beyond the essential grammar of **word order**, we can and do vary the position of elements of the sentence for reasons of style and emphasis. Knowing that the beginning of a sentence is its most conspicuous part, we may well want to move a significant phrase into that position (see further under **topic**). Adverbs and adverbial phrases can often be moved around; and a sentence with a lot of them reads better when they are not all clustered together at the end. Compare:

The speaker drew attention again at the end of his·speech to the number of members absent from the meeting.

At the end of his speech, the speaker again drew attention to the number of members absent from the meeting.

The second version is clearer and more effective.

wordbreaks In printed texts, especially those with narrow colunms, it's necessary from time to time to divide the last word in the line, and put some of it on the line below. Readers are notified that the word has been divided by the hyphen placed after the first part. Longer words can often be divided in more than one place, as with *re + spect + ive + ly*. Thus the *wordbreak* can be made so as to optimise the use of space at the end of the line.

Some dictionaries indicate the points at which words can be divided, but those that do are far from unanimous about it. Some go by the pronunciation of the word and how the sounds combine in the syllables; others go by the word's structure. Compare:

tran + scend   with   *trans + cend*
des + pite   *de + spite*

American dictionaries are often said to go by the pronunciation, and British ones by the structure; yet both compromise between the two principles on particular words. Because English words are so diverse in structure and spelling, the best general practice is to ask what the reader would make of the string of letters on the upper line. Will they provide a helpful lead on the rest of the word—or prove distracting? Clearly it's not ideal to break *mother* into *moth + er*, nor *therapist* into *the + rapist*.

Apart from that basic principle, the following points are worth noting:

1 words of less than six letters should not be divided

2 words of one syllable should not be divided

3 other things being equal, there should be at least three letters of the word on each line—unless for example the word begins with a two-letter prefix e.g. *indebted, recaptured*

4 letters which are part of the same digraph should stay together, thus *budg + et*, and *feath + er* or *fea + ther*

5 it helps to have a consonant to begin the second part of the word, thus *boome + rang*—except where word structure overrules this as with *draw + ing, system + atic* etc

6 a *wordbreak* between two or more consonants (so long as they are not a digraph) is usually acceptable, as in *democ + racy, dif + ferent* and *ser + vice*

7 breaking a compound at the junction of its two parts is always acceptable, as in *Anglo + Saxon, awe + inspiring* and *heavy + duty*

8 proper names of any length should not be broken.

words We take them for granted, yet it's quite difficult to define what they are. Loosely speaking they are the strings of letters which are separated by space from their neighbors in the line of print. So *foot, foothold* and *UFO* all qualify, as would *foot-and-mouth* (in *foot-and-mouth disease*).

Compounds test our definition of *word*, because the hyphens in *foot-and-mouth* seem to make it a *word*, even though they would be three separate words in other contexts. Compare: *The disease affects both foot and mouth.* In that sentence the same **words** make up a phrase, whereas in *foot-and-mouth* they form a compound adjective. (See further under **hyphens**, section 2.) Yet many recognised compounds such as *cash register* do not have hyphens and are set with space between their components. Does that disqualify them as **words**? The answer depends on whether you want to include all compounds in the definition, or only those which are visually unified by means of hyphens or being set solid.

Other issues affecting the definition of *word* come up when we ask whether *armor* and *armour* are different **words**, or *adaption* and *adaptation*, or *orange* and *oranges*, *child* and *children*. Linguists handle these differences with special terminology, saying that in each pair we have the same *lexeme* but variant spelling or morphology. The reverse problem also arises—the need to recognise that *bear* "large furry animal" and *bear* "carry" are different lexemes/words.

In the examples of the previous paragraph we used *word meanings* to help decide on their status as individuals or members of the same lexeme. The grammar of words is also part of their identity, and we have to recognise the functionary types that simply string a sentence together, such as *a, to, my,* as well as those which embody the distinctive semantic content: *snake, came, waterhole.* Note that the former (*function words*) can be just one or two letters, whereas the latter (*content words*) are almost always a minimum of three.

In fact we seem to need several definitions of *word* for different purposes, depending on whether we're thinking of **words** as printed items on the page, or in terms of their linguistic form, function and meaning.

World War The two world wars of this century may be written as either:

World War I   or   *First World War*
World War II   *Second World War*

All style guides agree that the words should be capitalised. They vary only in that the Chicago *Manual of Style* and other American sources seem to prefer *World War I/II*, while Murray-Smith plumped for *First/Second World War,* without giving his reasons. The *Australian Writers' and Editors' Guide* (1991) treats the two forms as equal alternatives.

worshipped or **worshiped** The choice between these spellings is discussed under **-p/-pp-**.

would or **should** See **should**.

would of or **would've** See **have** section 3.

woven or **weaved** See under **weave**.

wr or **r** For most words there's no choice between these. See under **r or wr**.

wrang or **wrung** See **wrung**.

wrap up or **rap up** See **rap up**.

wrapped or **wrapt** See under **rapt**.

wrath or **wroth** The first word is old-fashioned, and the second definitely archaic. Since neither is in current use, people make little of the dictionary distinction between **wrath** as the noun, and **wroth** the adjective. Fowler reported the use of **wrath** as both adjective and noun; and more recently the *Right Word at the Right Time* noted that some people use **wroth** as a noun. The state of confusion suggests that the words should be laid to rest. Requiescant in pace.

wreak or **reek** While the first word is contracting to a few savage idioms such as *wreak havoc, wreak vengeance*, the second is expanding its domain. Writers are therefore more likely to need **reek**, in either its physical sense of "smell" or the figurative extension in which it implies being suffused with a particular quality. Compare its use in:
> *The house reeked of popcorn.*
> *His comments reek of other ambitions.*

wrest or **rest** Rest as a verb meaning "take it easy" is almost the opposite of **wrest**, which means "take by force or struggle". It is often used figuratively, as in:
> *The home team wrested victory from their opponents in the last five minutes of play.*
Note that *wrestle* (where the emphasis is on struggle, either physical or metaphorical) is derived from **wrest**. (See **-le**.)

wretch or **retch** Neither word has pleasant associations. **Retch** is an involuntary spasm which precedes vomiting, while **wretch** is an emotionally charged word to describe someone pitiable or despicable, occasionally used as a term of abuse.

wright or **write** Writers sometimes pause over the spelling of *playwright*, with the thought that it could perhaps be "playwrite"—though it would be an akward use of the verb **write**. The noun **wright** is the only possibility, a rare word which in Old English was the ordinary term for "worker" but now survives only in compounds such as *playwright, shipwright, wheelwright*. Note that the *wr* in **wright** and **write** distinguishes both from the homophones *right* and *rite*. For other examples see **r** or **wr**.

wring or **ring** See under **wrung**.

wrong or **wrongly** Wrong can be an adjective or noun, as well as an adverb:

> *He gave the wrong answer.*
> *A grave wrong was committed there.*
> *The plan went wrong after a few days.*

In the last sentence **wrong** is a **zero adverb** (see further under that heading).

Wrongly only works as an adverb, though it cannot be freely interchanged with **wrong** in that role. It could not replace **wrong** in the third example, or in the many ordinary idioms with *do, get, go* and *have*, such as *Don't get me wrong*. On the other hand, only **wrongly** can be used with more formal expressions such as *was wrongly accused/attributed/decided/judged* etc. Note that although **wrongly** comes before the past participle in those examples, it can also come after the verb:

> *He had applied the concept quite wrongly.*

Compare **right** or **rightly**.

wrung, wrang or **wringed** What is the past form for the verb *wring*? Dictionaries register only the first as current, though the *Oxford Dictionary* confirms that the second and third and various others made their mark in earlier centuries. In modern standard use, **wrung** serves for both past tense and past participle:

> *The lawyer wrung his hands nervously.*
> *She had wrung his heart.*

With **wrung** as its only past form, *wring* works like *fling* and *sling*, rather than *ring* which has two past forms (*rang/rung*). (See further under **irregular verbs**.)

wurlie or **wurley** This word for an Aboriginal shelter (or any temporary shelter) is believed to be a loan from the Gaurna people in the vicinity of what is now Adelaide. Its spelling has been very variable, often with *wh*, and with *ir* rather than *ur* in the middle. In the twentieth century **wurlie** has been more common than **wurley**, by a ratio of 4:1 in the *Australian National Dictionary* citations. The plural *wurlies* (from either **wurlie** or *wurly*) has also been more numerous than *wurleys*.

X

-x The letter **-x** often marks a spot needing special attention—especially at the ends of nouns in English. For some groups the plurals are as you might expect, for others not.

1 Those which have regular English plurals with *-es*:

a) everyday words of one syllable such as *box, fax, flax, flux, fox, hex, jinx, lynx, tax, wax*; plus a few commercial names such as *durex, kleenex, pyrex, telex, wettex*;

b) common Latin loanwords of two or more syllables such as *annex, crucifix, equinox, paradox, reflex, spinifex*;

c) words appearing in general humanistic and linguistic study such as *affix, circumflex, prefix, suffix, syntax*.

2 Latin loanwords which have both English plurals in *-es* and Latin ones where *-ces* replaces the *-x*. They include:

apex, appendix, helix, ibex, index, latex, matrix, phalanx, thorax, vertex, vortex

In writing for the general public, they have English plurals, but in scholarly and scientific writing they use Latin ones. Note that for some of those the Latin plural also involves a change of the stem vowel. More details are given at individual entries on **apex**, **appendix**, **index**, **matrix**, and **vertex** or **vortex**. The plural forms of **phalanx** are discussed under that heading.

3 Latin loanwords which are only seen with Latin plurals. They remain the specialised terminology of science, medicine, mathematics, paleography and theology; and they maintain regular Latin plurals with:

a) *-ces*: *anthrax, calix, calyx, caudex, cicatrix, codex, cortex, fornix, pollex, radix*; or

b) *-ges*: *coccyx, larynx* and *pharynx*.

Note finally that **-x** itself appears as a plural suffix for a number of French loanwords, such as *adieux, fabliaux, gateaux* etc. Such words also have *-s* plurals. (See further under **-eau**.)

xanthorrh(o)ea See under **yakka**.

Xian See under **China**.

-xic or **-ctic** See under **-ctic/-xic**.

-xion or **-ction** See under **-ction/-xion**.

Xmas This abbreviation for Christmas is over a thousand years old. The *X* represents the Greek letter *chi*, which is the first letter in the Greek form of the name *Christ*. In the first centuries of Christianity the letter *chi* was often used as a symbol of the faith, and there are citations for its use in abbreviations for *Christian* in the fifteenth and sixteenth centuries. But in modern English **Xmas** is considered informal, and only to be used in greeting cards or headlines, where space has to be conserved.

X-ray or **x-ray** To capitalise or not to capitalise, that is the question. The trend is certainly to write this with a lower case letter. Its use as both adjective and verb confirm that it is well assimilated, and English databases in Australia, Britain and USA show that the word appears as often without a capital letter as with it. The major American dictionaries have lower case as their preferred spelling, and in Australia Murray-Smith recommended the lower case form, as do half the newspaper style guides which comment on the issue. The other half still recommend a capital letter, as does the *Macquarie Dictionary* (1991). *Collins Dictionary* notes that either form is acceptable.

Y

y/i For words whose spelling varies between *y* and *i* (e.g. *gypsy/gipsy*), see **i/y**.

-y Both nouns and adjectives in English have this ending:

1 *Adjectives* formed with it have simply added **-y** to a single-syllabled noun, as in *cloudy, dirty, risky, woody, wordy* and countless others. With *crazy, edgy, icy, shady* and others, the final *-e* of the noun (*craze, edge* etc.) has disappeared before the addition of **-y**, in accordance with the standard rule (see **-e** section 1, as well as **-y/-ey**). Note that when the basic word itself ends in **-y**, the adjective ending is *-ey*, as with *clayey* and *flyey*. Plural nouns can also provide the base for such adjectives, as in *newsy* and *rootsy*. Many adjectives of this kind are formed ad hoc and do not appear in dictionaries.

2 *Nouns* ending in **-y** fall into two major groups:
a) abstract and often rather formal words like *capacity, novelty, revelry, tracery,* many of them borrowed ready-made from French or Latin. (See further under **-ity** and **-ry**.)
b) informal words which are always English formations. Some are associated with talking to children, such as *doggy, nanny, piggy*; but many are used freely by adults: *brolly, footy, hippy, telly*. Note that most words of this kind can also be spelled with *-ie*, as with *footie, hippie*. (See further under **-ie/-y**.)

-y/-ey Some well-established English words ending in *y* have variant spellings in *ey*. They include *nouns* such as:
> *bog(e)y curts(e)y doil(e)y fog(e)y stor(e)y troll(e)y whisk(e)y*

In some cases different meanings are attached to the different spellings (see under individual headings for each).

Adjectives whose spelling can be either **-y** or **-ey** are typically informal words of the twentieth century, or ones which are only beginning to be used in writing. The nouns on which they are based are much more familiar in print, and some writers and editors prefer to preserve the whole noun within the spelling of the adjective. Others allow them to lose the final *-e*, in keeping with the general rule of English spelling (see **-e** section 1). For example:
> *bon(e)y cag(e)y chanc(e)y cliqu(e)y dic(e)y dop(e)y gam(e)y hom(e)y*
> *lin(e)y mous(e)y nos(e)y phon(e)y pric(e)y ston(e)y win(e)y wir(e)y*

The spellings without *e* are the more regular ones, bringing the word into line with other adjectives with the suffix **-y** (see under **-y**).

If there is any problem in recognising the regular spellings, it would be with examples like *gamy*, where dropping the *-e* leaves only three letters to indicate the root word. Yet even two letters are enough for *icy*. Overall there's little reason to delay spelling these words in the regular way. For *phon(e)y* it only helps to perpetuate a spurious etymology (see **phony**).

-y>-i- When *y* occurs at the end of a word after a consonant, it often changes to *i* before inflections beginning with *-e*. It happens with:

- verbs ending in **-y**. These change to *i* before *-ed*, as in *apply>applied*, *copy>copied*, *try>tried*. The same change is seen before *-er*, in agent words such as *copier*.
- nouns ending in **-y**. These change before the plural suffix *-es*, as with *city>cities*, *estuary>estuaries*, *spy>spies*. Note however that proper nouns ending in **-y** do not change for the plural: *three Hail Marys, four Gregorys*. Compounds also resist the change, witness *laybys, standbys*.
- adjectives with two syllables change *y* to *i* before *-er/-est*: *gloomier/gloomiest*. Note however that this is not necessarily done with one-syllabled words, as seen in common examples such as **drier/dryer** (see further under that heading).

The change of a final *y* to *i* also affects many other words formed with suffixes. The following are just a token:

alliance beautify bounciness denial gloomily marriage
merriment pitiless plentiful reliable

Only when the suffix begins with **-i** does the final *y* remain, for example in *allying* and *copyist*.

The major exceptions to y/i change are words in which a vowel precedes the final *y* before the suffix. Note the unchanged *y* before regular inflexions in:

verbs	e.g. *delayed, employed, surveyed*
nouns	e.g. *alloys, days, donkeys, guys*
adjective	e.g. *coyer/coyest, greyer/greyest*

The change to *i* does however take place in three very common verbs, where the suffix is fused with the root:

lay>laid pay>paid say>said

and in two rather uncommon nouns:

obsequy>obsequies soliloquy>soliloquies

But otherwise the presence of a vowel before the final *y* seems to inhibit the change, in numerous formations such as:

betrayal conveyance employment joyless playful repayable

yabby or **yabbie** This Aboriginal word for a small freshwater crayfish is borrowed from the Wemba people of Central and Western Victoria. The spelling with *y* for the second syllable is by far the more common in *Australian National Dictionary* citations, perhaps because it's not an informal abbreviation of an English word (see further under **-ie/-y**).

yacca, yacka or **yakka** See yakka.

yack, yak and **yackety-yak** This slang word meaning "talk incessantly" is used worldwide. The major American dictionaries make **yak** their primary spelling, whereas the *Oxford Dictionary* (1989) has it as **yack**—even though **yak** prevails in the citations given. Perhaps **yack** is preferred as a way of distinguishing the word from the **yak** which is a bovine animal. The extended forms *yacket*, *yackety* and **yackety-yak** also give the word an unmistakable identity.

Beyond these the *Oxford Dictionary* records the use of the agent noun *yacker*, "a person who ya(c)ks on", derived in the normal way from the verb *ya(c)k*. Here again *yakker* is the spelling actually endorsed in the *Oxford's* citations. For Australians this word overlaps with two others: the not-so-common verbal noun *yacker* (or *yakker*) which itself means "talk", and the very familiar word meaning "work". (See next entry.)

yakka, yakker, yacker, yacka or **yacca** These various spellings represent two different Aboriginal words, meaning (1) "work" and (2) "grasstree".

The first word came from the Jagara people around Moreton Bay in the mid-nineteenth century, and was spelled **yakker** or **yacker** until World War II. The *Australian National Dictionary* has no postwar citations for the verb, and it keeps the spelling **yakker** for it, while making **yakka** (for which there are ample postwar citations) the spelling for the still very active noun. The spelling **yakka** helps to distinguish it from *yacker/yakker* meaning "talk" (see previous entry).

On rare occasions the spellings **yacca** and **yacka** have also been used for "work", though they are normally associated with the second word, the Australian "grasstree". This Aboriginal loanword probably comes from a South Australian language, though the etymology is obscure. The **yacca** is often called a *blackboy*, even though this was originally used for the West Australian *kingia*, a separate but similar genus. (It produces a spherical flower head on a lofty stalk, which is the analogue of the spear that protrudes from grasstrees native to other states.) The name *xanthorrh(o)ea* is given to grasstrees at large because of the yellow gum which exudes from them, used as an adhesive by Aborigines, and the basis of a small export industry for European settlers around the turn of the century.

Yankee Outside the USA this term is used rather casually and sometimes disparagingly to refer to Americans and things American (see further under **racist language**). To Americans themselves it has historical overtones: it originally referred to the inhabitants of New England, and subsequently to northerners at large, especially those who fought for the Union in the Civil War. The abbreviated form *Yank* was applied in World War II to American soldiers overseas, and since then to any American.

The origin of **Yankee** is debated. Most dictionaries trace it back to *Jan Kees*, a derisive nickname meaning ''John Cheese'', which was supposedly applied by early Dutch settlers in New York to the English colonists in Connecticut. It was then interpreted as a plural by English-speakers, and the singular **Yankee** derived from it. (For other words derived this way, see **false plurals**.) Other scholars believe the word comes from one used by American Indians in reference to the English, which rendered them as *Yenggees*.

ye and **you**   Until about 1600 **ye** and **you** shared the role of the second person plural pronoun, with **ye** used when the word was the subject of a clause, and **you** when it was the object. (See further under **case**.) The King James Bible still observes this in:

Ye have not chosen me; I have chosen you.

But this case distinction was already breaking down in Shakespeare's and Ben Jonson's plays, and early seventeenth century grammarians made the two words interchangeable. **You** was in fact taking over, and by the eighteenth century **ye** had been ousted from the standard language and survived only in literary and lofty use. The takeover went still further, for **you** also subsumed the singular roles of *thou/thee* (see further under **thou**).

The lack of case distinction between **you/ye** was no great loss, since English syntax helps to show subject and object. But the merging of plural and singular second persons leaves English without a simple way of showing whether someone's remarks are meant solely for the person addressed, or for others whom s/he represents as well. Many an invitation has been complicated by this fact. Expressions such as *you both* and *you all* help to clarify the situation, and in informal contexts *you guys* and *you lot*, as well as *youse/yous* (see further under **youse**). Still there's no regular way of expressing the singular/plural distinction in the English second person.

1 *Other roles of you* go beyond the second person. **You** has long served as an indefinite pronoun, as in:

After all that, you'd think he would compromise.

In such sentences, **you** is an informal substitute for *one*, a pronoun which is somewhere between second and first person (see further under **one**). A more formal but still ultimately indefinite use of **you** is often recommended in the name of Plain English, to paraphrase of the impersonal style which besets government documents. Writers are urged to translate:

All tax returns must be filed by October 31 into
You must file your tax return by October 31.

For the moment this style is so new that it has all the directness of the normal second person address. But the effect is likely to wear off as the style becomes institutionalised, and reduce its force to a generalised and indefinite **you**.

2 *Old-fashioned Ye*. The **Ye** found in quasi-old shop signs such as *Ye Olde Tea Shoppe* is unrelated to the second person pronoun. The *Y* is an attempt to match the Old English character þ "thorn" (borrowed from the runic alphabet) which represented "th". So **Ye** is simply *The*. In Tudor handwriting and printing, *y* was used instead of *th* in *the* and a number of other words: *that, they, this* (and sometimes *them, their, this*) to save space. It ceased to be common practice by the eighteenth century, but it lingers in the **Ye** of pub and shop signs, wherever the whiff of antiquity seems to be a commercial asset.

yet This can serve as a conjunction, conjunct or adverb, as shown in the following sentences:
> *He offered no help, yet assumed his right to sell our project.*
> *They stayed home. Yet they must have thought about coming ...*
> *It hasn't come yet.*

In the first sentence, **yet** serves as a synonym for "but", and in the second for "however", though it seems to make the contrast more gently than either of them (see further under **conjunctions**). In the third sentence **yet** serves as a gentler alternative to "still". Compare *It still hasn't come.* The choice of **yet** rather than one of its synonyms is a matter of style and emphasis.

yodel The question of whether to double the *l* when verb suffixes are added is discussed under **-l/-ll-**.

yoghurt, yogurt and **yoghourt** The first two spellings are equally acceptable in Australia, and in the Australian ACE database there were 5 instances of **yoghurt** to 2 of **yogurt**. **Yogurt** is preferred in the USA, and was the primary spelling for the *Oxford Dictionary*, though its evidence is curious and contradictory. The word appeared in many different forms from the seventeenth century on (the *Oxford* lists no fewer than eleven different spellings), yet the preference given to **yogurt** is surprising in that it's absent from the citations, and does not render the original Turkish word so closely. The spelling which does is **yoghurt**, and under such circumstances the Oxford usually gives preference to the etymological spelling. Given that **yogurt** appears both as a variant spelling and in the headword as well—while **yoghurt** is left out—we may suspect that **yoghurt** was intended as the headword spelling.

Be that as it may, **yogurt** remains the primary spelling in the *Oxford Dictionary* (1989), with **yoghurt** now as the secondary alternative. This still seems curious in the light of the fact that each occurs only once in the five citations from the twentieth century, while **yoghourt** is in three of them. Perhaps the editors are using product labels or other evidence for their spelling preference, but it would be good to know what that evidence is.

Yogyakarta See under **Jakarta**.

Yolngu See under **Aboriginal** or **Aborigine**.

you See under **ye** and **you**.

yours faithfully and **yours sincerely** The use of **yours faithfully** at the close of a formal letter is declining. It was once used widely in official and commercial correspondence in which the relationship was strictly one of business. **Yours sincerely** was then reserved for letters to friends. Nowadays, businesses seek friendly relationships with their customers; and within corporations and bureaucracies, the tone of communication is generally collaborative rather than distant and authoritarian. Either way **yours sincerely** is more in keeping with the prevailing style, whether or not the correspondents are acquainted. **Yours faithfully** is increasingly reserved for correspondence addressed to the unknown reader (*Dear Sir/Madam*) at a government institution, and in legal correspondence.

   For more about the changing style of business letters, see **commercialese**.
   For the layout of letters, see Appendix VII.

youse or **yous** This is a slang form of *you*, often addressed to a group of people. The spelling **yous** suggests that it's plural, on the analogy of regular nouns. The analogy is imperfect, however, seeing that the word is a pronoun; and dictionaries allow either spelling, with the *Oxford Dictionary* (1989) putting **yous** first, and *Random House*, *Webster's* and the *Macquarie Dictionary* making it **youse**. The three instances in the Australian ACE corpus are all **youse**.

   Its status and meaning are unsettled. Although it seems to fill a gap in the English pronoun system (see further under **ye** and **you**), it's not invariably used in plural situations, as the major dictionaries show. *Webster's* notes its occasional use to address one person as representing "another or others". Its number value is therefore somewhat indeterminate, and its use may have more to do with informality of style than with exactness over the number of people being addressed. Yet its informality is such that it's unacceptable as a general-purpose form of address, and dictionaries enter it with restrictive labels or cautionary notes. The *Oxford Dictionary* dubs it "dialectal", while the *Random House Dictionary* associates it with urban speech in northern USA, in New York, Boston and Chicago. In Australia it's heard in casual exchanges in both metropolitan and country speech, but still associated with a shortage of education.

-yse/-yze These are alternative spellings for words like:
   analyse catalyse dialyse electrolyse hydrolyse paralyse
In Australian and British English, the **-yse** spellings are the usual ones, but in American English those with **-yze** are standard. Spellings such as *analyse* and *paralyse* are backed by etymology, and match better with the related nouns *analysis* and *paralysis*. However for most people the endings **-yse/-yze** are not meaningfully different from *-ize/-ise*, especially when *y* and *i* change places in many English words. The American use of *analyze*, *paralyze* etc. makes those words conform to the much larger set of verbs with *-ize* (see **-ise/-ize**).

yucky or **yukky**, **yuck** or **yuk** Dictionaries prefer **yucky** as the spelling for this not-so-charming adjective, though they do allow **yukky** as an alternative.

The exclamation of distaste on which it's based is similarly listed as **yuck** rather than **yuk**, although citations in the *Oxford Dictionary* show that the latter is probably more common. The preference for *-ck* spellings may reflect the inclination to anglicise the form of curious new elements in the vocabulary (see further under **k/c**). In American English there's the added motive of distinguishing it from another recent slang word: **yuk** meaning "loud laugh".

Yugoslavia This name means a state for "Southern Slavs", though it covered a diverse group of people inhabiting the western side of the Balkan peninsula, amalgamated in 1918 out of Serbia, Montenegro and parts of the Austro-Hungarian empire. Until 1990 **Yugoslavia** consisted of six socialist republics: Bosnia-Herzegovina, Croatia, Macedonia, Montenegro, Serbia and Slovenia. There were three official languages: Serbo-Croatian, Slovenian and Macedonian, with Serbs and Macedonians using the Cyrillic alphabet, and Croats and Slovenians the Roman. In religion too the population of **Yugoslavia** has been divided, with a majority adhering to the Eastern Orthodox Church, and others to Roman Catholicism and to Islam. Such diversity became the basis of division and civil war, and by May 1992 three states (Bosnia-Herzegovina, Croatia and Slovenia) had declared their independence and been recognised as separate members of the United Nations. Macedonia's attempt to assert its independence has been complicated by controversy over the use of that name with Greece. Serbia and Montenegro are still closely allied and retain the name **Yugoslavia**.

Dictionaries still recognise *Jugoslavia* as an alternative spelling for **Yugoslavia**, but it has never been much used, and the *Oxford Dictionary*'s citations for it are confined to the first half of the twentieth century.

yuk and **yukky** See under **yucky**.

yuppie This is the primary spelling in almost all dictionaries for this faintly derogatory word of the 1980s. The *-ie* ending makes the word more informal (see further under **-ie/y**), though the capital letter (*Yuppie*) sometimes given to it reminds us of its formal origins as an acronym (other spellings: *Yuppy* and *yuppy* are also registered in dictionaries). In fact it's an amalgam of two acronyms: *young urban professional*, and *young upwardly mobile person*. As originally coined, **yuppie** and *yumpie* identified two social types both preoccupied with the acquisition of status symbols, but distinguishable by the superior education of the first, and the conspicuous social pretensions of the second. By now the word **yuppie** has outperformed *yumpie*, incorporated its image as part of its own, and left it ambiguous whether the *u* stands for "urban" or "upwardly mobile", and whether the *p* is "professional" or just "person".

In Australia Murray-Smith identified three such types of *nouveaux riches*, with the comment that various older suburbs were being repopulated by *yuppies*, *yumpies* and *yummies* ("young upwardly mobile Marxists").

-yze/-yse See -yse.

Z

z/zz Very few words allow you to choose between one or two *z*s at the end—only **friz(z)** and **whiz(z)** (see further under those headings). Beyond those there are a few which always have a single **z**, and a lot which always have double **z**.

Those with single **z** are mostly colloquial words, such as *biz, squiz* and *swiz*. They're often abbreviations, as *biz* is for "business" and *swiz* for "swizzle". The word *quiz* may likewise have originated as a clipped form of "inquisitive" or "inquisition", though it's now a standard English word. Note that all such words double the **z** before suffixes are added to them. The plural of *quiz* is *quizzes*, and *quizzed* is the past tense. Derivatives such as *quizzical* also show the trend towards doubling.

The majority of words ending in **z** have two, and double **z** is the regular spelling with:

> *buzz chizz fizz fuzz jazz mozz razz tizz zizz*

Such words need no special treatment, whatever inflections are added.

zero adverbs The fact that many English adverbs are formed with suffix *-ly* leads some people to assume that all adverbs have it. Thus the adverb for *slow* is expected to be *slowly*, and the adverb *doubtless* is quite often tidied up as *doubtlessly*. A moment's thought shows that many kinds of adverbs never end in *-ly*:

- adverbs that double as prepositions: *above, after, before*
- negative adverbs: *not, never, no*
- adverbs of time: *often, soon, then*
- focusing adverbs: *also, even, only*
- modifying adverbs: *rather, quite, very*

Other adverbs can appear both with and without *-ly*, according to context and idiom. They include:

> *bad cheap clean clear close deep direct easy fair flat high loud*
> *quick right sharp short slow tight wide wrong*

Research shows that for some of these, the form without *-ly* is actually more common. This is so for *cheap, close, flat, high, right, wrong*, all of which are caught up in idioms which require the zero form. See for example:

> *going cheap   come close   fall flat   fly high*

Where there is a choice, the zero form is usually more colloquial. Compare *come quick* with *come quickly*. Occasionally the zero and *-ly* forms differ in meaning. (See **direct, just** and **low**.)

Overall the use of *-ly* is slightly more common in American English than British English, according to the evidence of language databases. This is in keeping with the general tendency for American speakers to prefer rule-governed forms where they are available.

zero conjunction Not all subordinate clauses are introduced by a subordinating conjunction. English allows the conjunction *that* to be omitted before a noun clause, as in:

   I thought (that) you were in the office.

And it allows any relative pronoun to be omitted when it's the object of the relative clause:

   I'm the person that/whom *you heard on the radio.*

These omissions are no longer confined to speech and informal writing. (See further under **that.**)

zero derivation This is a linguist's term for words which take on a new grammatical role without any derivational suffix. (See further under **suffixes,** and for examples, see **transfers.**)

zero past tense A number of common English verbs of one syllable ending in *t* or *d* have no special form for the past tense (or the past participle). Compare:

   You just cut out the order form and send it off. (present)
   I cut my finger as I was doing the vegetables. (past)

Other verbs with zero past forms are:

   bid burst hit hurt let put set shed shut split spread thrust

(See further under **irregular verbs.**)

zero plurals Several kinds of English nouns are the same whether they're singular or plural. They include:

- collective words for animals, e.g. *deer, fish, pheasant, sheep,* especially when they're the quarry for hunting
- a few Latin loanwords whose plurals were the same as the singular in Latin, including *series, species, status* (see further under **Latin plurals** and **-us** section 2)
- a few French loanwords, such as *chassis, chamois*

For all such words, the plural is shown by the use of a plural verb.

   Note also the various English words that already end in a plural *s* and whose form is invariant:

   binoculars clothes dregs gallows linguistics means news pyjamas

For them there is no singular nor can they be further pluralised. Most take plural verbs (see **agreement** section 3).

zinc See under **-c/-ck-.**

Zionist See under **Israel.**

zombie or **zombi** When you reach this end of the alphabet you may not care how this word is spelled. But if you wish to express that detached mental state in the approved spelling, most dictionaries give preference to **zombie,** while listing **zombi** as an alternative. The second spelling is slightly more foreign, and as close as anyone can get to the original African word, now current only in the Kongo word *nzambi*. The word referred to the python god worshipped in voodoo ceremonies, who was believed to have the power to bring a dead person back to life. The word then became associated with the corpse thus revived, and so to the person who behaves like the living dead.

-zzie/-ssie See -ssie.

Appendix I

INTERNATIONAL PHONETIC ALPHABET SYMBOLS FOR AUSTRALIAN ENGLISH SOUNDS

Vowels

/i/	as in	"s*ea*t", "sw*ee*t"
/ɪ/	as in	"s*i*t"
/e/	as in	"s*e*t"
/eɪ/	as in	"s*a*te", "s*ay*", "sl*eigh*"
/æ/	as in	"s*a*t"
/aɪ/	as in	"s*igh*t", "s*i*te"
/ʌ/	as in	"sh*u*t"
/ɪə/	as in	"sh*ear*", "s*eer*"
/eə/	as in	"sh*are*"
/ə/	as in	"*a*side", "cid*er*"
/ɜ/	as in	"s*er*ve"
/a/	as in	"sh*ar*d"
/aʊ/	as in	"sh*ou*t"
/ɒ/	as in	"sh*o*t"
/ɔɪ/	as in	"s*oi*l"
/ɔ/	as in	"sh*or*t", "s*ough*t", "s*aw*", "s*ore*"
/oʊ/	as in	"sh*ow*"
/ʊ/	as in	"s*u*gar"
/u/	as in	"sh*oo*t", "sh*oe*", "s*ou*venir"
/ʊə/	as in	"s*ewer*"

Consonants

/b/	as in	"*b*et"
/d/	as in	"*d*ebt"
/f/	as in	"*f*ed", "*ph*oto"
/g/	as in	"*g*et"
/dʒ/	as in	"*j*et", "e*dge*"
/h/	as in	"*h*ead"
/tʃ/	as in	"*ch*eddar", "ha*tch*"
/k/	as in	"*k*ettle", "*c*at", "*q*uit", "e*x*cite"
/l/	as in	"*l*et"
/m/	as in	"*m*et"
/n/	as in	"*n*et"
/ŋ/	as in	"si*ng*", "a*n*chor"
/p/	as in	"*p*et"
/r/	as in	"*r*ed"
/s/	as in	"*s*aid", "*c*edar"
/ʃ/	as in	"*sh*ed", "*ch*evron"
/t/	as in	"*t*etanus"
/ð/	as in	"*th*en"
/θ/	as in	"*th*read"
/v/	as in	"*v*et"
/w/	as in	"*w*et", "s*u*ede"
/j/	as in	"*y*et"
/z/	as in	"*z*ed", "*x*erox"
/ʒ/	as in	"*ge*nre", "bei*ge*"

Appendix II

PERPETUAL CALENDAR 1901–2001

Years 1901–2001				Months											
				J	**F**	**M**	**A**	**M**	**J**	**J**	**A**	**S**	**O**	**N**	**D**
	25	53	81	4	0	0	3	5	1	3	6	2	4	0	2
	26	54	82	5	1	1	4	6	2	4	0	3	5	1	3
	27	55	83	6	2	2	5	0	3	5	1	4	6	2	4
	28	56	84	0	3	4	0	2	5	0	3	6	1	4	6
01	29	57	85	2	5	5	1	3	6	1	4	0	2	5	0
02	30	58	86	3	6	6	2	4	0	2	5	1	3	6	1
03	31	59	87	4	0	0	3	5	1	3	6	2	4	0	2
04	32	60	88	5	1	2	5	0	3	5	1	4	6	2	4
05	33	61	89	0	3	3	6	1	4	6	2	5	0	3	5
06	34	62	90	1	4	4	0	2	5	0	3	6	1	4	6
07	35	63	91	2	5	5	1	3	6	1	4	0	2	5	0
08	36	64	92	3	6	0	3	5	1	3	6	2	4	0	2
09	37	65	93	5	1	1	4	6	2	4	0	3	5	1	3
10	38	66	94	6	2	2	5	0	3	5	1	4	6	2	4
11	39	67	95	0	3	3	6	1	4	6	2	5	0	3	5
12	40	68	96	1	4	5	1	3	6	1	4	0	2	5	0
13	41	69	97	3	6	6	2	4	0	2	5	1	3	6	1
14	42	70	98	4	0	0	3	5	1	3	6	2	4	0	2
15	43	71	99	5	1	1	4	6	2	4	0	3	5	1	3
16	44	72	00	6	2	3	6	1	4	6	2	5	0	3	5
17	45	73		1	4	4	0	2	5	0	3	6	1	4	6
18	46	74		2	5	5	1	3	6	1	4	0	2	5	0
19	47	75		3	6	6	2	4	0	2	5	1	3	6	1
20	48	76		4	0	1	4	6	2	4	0	3	5	1	3
21	49	77		6	2	2	5	0	3	5	1	4	6	2	4
22	50	78		0	3	3	6	1	4	6	2	5	0	3	5
23	51	79		1	4	4	0	2	5	0	3	6	1	4	6
24	52	80		2	5	6	2	4	0	2	5	1	3	6	1

Days of the week

S	1	8	15	22	29	36
M	2	9	16	23	30	37
T	3	10	17	24	31	
W	4	11	18	25	32	
T	5	12	19	26	33	
F	6	13	20	27	34	
S	7	14	21	28	35	

The three tables allow you to discover what day of the week any date this century fell on, e.g. the date of Australia's Bicentennial celebrations on 26 January 1988.
- Read across from the relevant year (*1988*) to the **Months** table and extract the number for January (in this case *5*).
- Add that number to the actual day of the month (*26*) = *31*.
- Check that composite number on the **Days of the week** table above to find the actual day ... *Tuesday*.

Appendix III

GEOLOGICAL ERAS

Era	Years BP	Period	Epoch	Evolutionary events
Precambrian	4550 m.	Archean		hardening of earth's crust
	2500 m.	Early Proterozoic		spores; bacteria; marine algae
	1600 m.	Riphean		
	650 m.	Vendian		
Paleozoic	570 m.	Cambrian		marine invertebrates
	500 m.	Ordovician		primitive fish
	430 m.	Silurian		shellfish; fungi
	395 m.	Devonian		age of fishes; first amphibians
	345 m.	Carboniferous		age of amphibians; first insects
	280 m.	Permian		development of reptiles
Mesozoic	225 m.	Triassic		first dinosaurs
	190 m.	Jurassic		age of dinosaurs; flying reptiles
	136 m.	Cretaceous		last dinosaurs; modern insects
Cenozoic	65 m.	Tertiary	Paleocene	development of mammals
	53 m.		Eocene	modern mammals; modern birds
	37 m.		Oligocene	browsing mammals
	26 m.		Miocene	grazing mammals
	5 m.		Pliocene	formation of Alps, Andes, Himalayas
	1.8 m.	Quaternary	Pleistocene	widespread glacial ice; early man
	.1m		Holocene (Recent)	modern man

Adapted from the *Cambridge Encyclopedia of Earth Sciences* (1981)

Appendix IV

INTERNATIONAL SYSTEM OF UNITS (SI UNITS)

Physical quantity

Base SI units	SI unit	Symbol
length	metre	m
mass	kilogram	kg
time	second	s
electric current	ampere	A
thermodynamic temperature	kelvin	K
amount of substance	mole	mol
luminous intensity	candela	cd

Supplementary units		
plane angle	radian	rad
solid angle	steradian	sr

Derived SI units		
energy	joule	J
force	newton	N
pressure	pascal	Pa
frequency	hertz	Hz
power	watt	W
electric charge	coulomb	C
potential difference	volt	V
resistance	ohm	Ω
capacitance	farad	F
conductance	siemens	S
inductance	henry	H
magnetic flux	weber	Wb
magnetic flux density	tesla	T
luminous flux	lumen	lm
illumination	lux	lx

Prefixes for SI units

exa-	E	10^{18}	deci-	d	10^{-1}
peta-	P	10^{15}	centi-	c	10^{-2}
tera-	T	10^{12}	milli-	m	10^{-3}
giga-	G	10^{9}	micro-	μ	10^{-6}
mega-	M	10^{6}	nano-	n	10^{-9}
kilo-	k	10^{3}	pico-	p	10^{-12}
hecto-	h	10^{2}	femto-	f	10^{-15}
deka- (deca-)	da	10^{1}	atto-	a	10^{-18}

Appendix V

INTERCONVERSION TABLES FOR METRIC AND IMPERIAL MEASURES

Metric unit		Symbol	Conversion factor to imperial unit	
Length	centimetre	cm	1 cm	= 0.394 inches
	metre	m	1 m	= 3.28 feet or 1.09 yards
	kilometre	km	1 km	= 0.621 mile
area	square centimetre	cm²	1 cm²	= 0.155 sq. inches
	square metre	m²	1 m²	= 10.8 sq. feet or 1.20 sq. yds
	hectare	ha	1 ha	= 2.47 acres
	square kilometre	km²	1 km²	= 0.386 sq. mile
volume	cubic centimetre	cm³	1 cm³	= 0.0610 cubic inches
	cubic metre	m³	1 m³	= 35.3 cubic feet or 1.31 cubic yards or 27.5 bushels
volume *(fluid)*	millilitre	mL	1 mL	= 0.0352 fluid ounces
	litre	L	1 L	= 1.76 pints
	cubic metre	m³	1 m³	= 220 gallons
mass	gram	g	1 g	= 0.0353 ounces
	kilogram	kg	1 kg	= 2.20 pounds
	tonne	t	1 t	= 0.984 ton
velocity	kilometre per hour	km/h	1 km/h	= 0.621 miles per hour
angular velocity	radians per second	rad/s	1 rad/s	= 9.55 revolutions per minute
energy	kilojoule	kJ	1 kJ	= 0.948 British thermal units
	megajoule	mJ	1 mJ	= 9.48×10^{-3} therms
force	newton	N	1 N	= 0.225 pound-force
pressure	kilopascal	kPa	1 kPa	= 0.145 pounds per square inch
(meteorology)	millibar	mb	1 mb	= 0.0295 inch of mercury
power	kilowatt	kW	1 kW	= 1.34 horsepower
temperature	degree Celsius	°C	$(°C \times \frac{9}{5}) + 32 = °F$	

Imperial unit		Symbol	Conversion factor to metric unit
length	inch	in	1 in = 25.4 millimetres
	foot	ft	1 ft = 30.5 centimetres
	yard	yd	1 yd = 0.914 metres
	mile		1 mile = 1.61 kilometres
area	square inch	in^2	1 in^2 = 6.45 sq. centimetres
	square foot	ft^2	1 ft^2 = 929 sq centimetres
	square yard	yd^2	1 yd^2 = 0.836 sq. metres
	acre	ac	1 ac = 0.405 hectares
	square mile	sq.mile	1 sq.mile = 2.59 sq. kilometres
volume	cubic inch	in^3	1 in^3 = 16.4 cubic centimetres
	cubic foot	ft^3	1 ft^3 = 28.3 cubic decimetres
	cubic yard	yd^3	1 yd^3 = 0.765 cubic metres
	bushel	bus	1 bus = 0.0364 cubic metres
volume *(fluid)*	fluid ounce	fl oz	1 fl oz = 28.4 millilitres
	pint	pt	1 pt = 568 millilitres
	gallon	gal	1 gal = 4.55 litres
mass	ounce	oz	1 oz = 28.3 grams
	pound	lb	1 lb = 454 grams
	ton		1 ton = 1.02 tonnes
velocity	mile per hour	mph	1 mph = 1.61 kilometres per hour
angular velocity	revolution per minute	rpm	1 rpm = 0.105 radians per second
energy	British thermal unit	Btu	1 Btu = 1.06 kilojoules
			1 therm = 106 megajoules
force	pound-force	lbf	1 lbf = 4.45 newtons
pressure	pound per square inch	psi	1 psi = 6.89 kilopascals
(meteorology)	square inch of mercury	inHg	1 inHg = 33.9 millibars
power	horse power	hp	1 hp = 0.746 kilowatts
temperature	degree Fahrenheit	°F	$(°F - 32) \times \dfrac{5}{9} = °C$

Appendix VI

SELECTED PROOFREADING MARKS

Action	Marking on text of MS	Marginal indicator
Leave as printed	words to be retained	(stet)
Delete character	words to be retained	
Delete and close up	words to be retained	
Delete string of characters	words not to be retained	
Insert in text	words be retained	to / [each new item to be followed by a /]
Substitute in text	words to be regained	t/
Insert as superior or superscript	"words to be retained	[for quote marks, apostrophes and superscript letters or figures]
Insert hyphen	words to be remarked	/–/
Insert or substitute	words retained remarked	,/ [for comma, semicolon, question mark, exclamation mark]
Insert or substitute	words retained Remarking	⊙/ [for colon, full stop]
Insert or substitute	words retained remarked	Ø/ [for solidus]
Change to capital letter	words to be retained	(caps)
Change to lower case	wORDS to be retained	(l.c.)
Change to italic	words to be retained	(ital)
Change to roman	words (to) be retained	(rom)

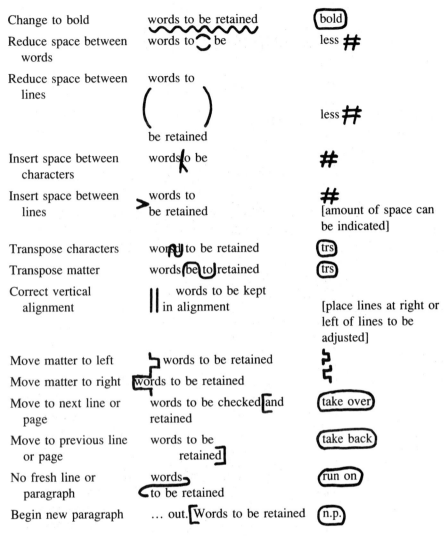

Change to bold	words to be retained	bold
Reduce space between words	words to ⌒ be	less #
Reduce space between lines	words to ( ) be retained	less #
Insert space between characters	words⋏o be	#
Insert space between lines	> words to be retained	# [amount of space can be indicated]
Transpose characters	word~~ to be retained	trs
Transpose matter	words ⌐be⌐to⌐ retained	trs
Correct vertical alignment	‖ words to be kept in alignment	[place lines at right or left of lines to be adjusted]
Move matter to left	⌐words to be retained	
Move matter to right	words to be retained	
Move to next line or page	words to be checked⌐and retained	take over
Move to previous line or page	words to be retained⌐	take back
No fresh line or paragraph	words⌐ to be retained	run on
Begin new paragraph	… out.⌐Words to be retained	n.p.

Notes

- Words used as marginal indicators are ringed to show that they are instructions and not to be set as part of the text.
- If there are several corrections for the same line, divide them between the left and right margins, and present in left-to-right order on each side.
- Editorial corrections to the MS are conventionally made on the text itself between the lines, assuming that the MS is double-spaced. Marginal marks are designed for easy reference by the proofreader/typesetter.

For a comprehensive listing of proofreading marks, consult the Australian Government *Style Manual* (1988).

Appendix VII

FORMATS FOR LETTERS

1 An official letter, with fully blocked format and open punctuation

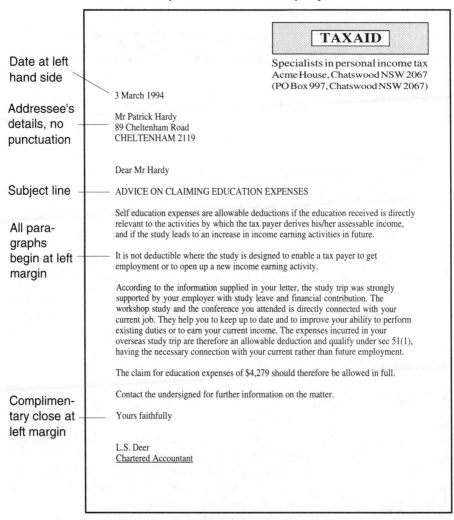

Date at left hand side

Addressee's details, no punctuation

Subject line

All para- graphs begin at left margin

Complimen- tary close at left margin

3 March 1994

Mr Patrick Hardy
89 Cheltenham Road
CHELTENHAM 2119

Dear Mr Hardy

ADVICE ON CLAIMING EDUCATION EXPENSES

Self education expenses are allowable deductions if the education received is directly relevant to the activities by which the tax payer derives his/her assessable income, and if the study leads to an increase in income earning activities in future.

It is not deductible where the study is designed to enable a tax payer to get employment or to open up a new income earning activity.

According to the information supplied in your letter, the study trip was strongly supported by your employer with study leave and financial contribution. The workshop study and the conference you attended is directly connected with your current job. They help you to keep up to date and to improve your ability to perform existing duties or to earn your current income. The expenses incurred in your overseas study trip are therefore an allowable deduction and qualify under sec 51(1), having the necessary connection with your current rather than future employment.

The claim for education expenses of $4,279 should therefore be allowed in full.

Contact the undersigned for further information on the matter.

Yours faithfully

L.S. Deer
Chartered Accountant

TAXAID

Specialists in personal income tax
Acme House, Chatswood NSW 2067
(PO Box 997, Chatswood NSW 2067)

Letter style
- formal explanation
- language is neutral, logical
- mostly third person, some use of *you*

2 A more personal letter, with semiblocked format and closed punctuation

<table>
<tr>
<td>

RED SHIELD APPEAL

APPEAL OFFICE,
P.O. BOX 1264,
PARRAMATTA 2124.

April, 1994

Dear Mrs Peters,

As the Volunteer Chairman of the Annual Red Shield Appeal of The Salvation
Army, I am often asked why, in these difficult economic times, both my
company and I give generously to the campaign. I thought you might be
interested in some of my reasons:

- These "hard financial times" mean that The Salvation Army must help more
  people, more often, and thus they need far more help from us, their friends.

- I feel a responsibility to others in the community. My firm and I have
  prospered over the years so we have a responsibility for the well-being of
  those who need help. The Salvos offer the best vehicle for turning
  intentions into actual assistance.

- Our gifts to The Salvation Army allow us to provide care for the people
  who most need it, anonymously, with no strings attached. Through The
  Salvos we can reach the poor, the aged, the young, the lost and the
  helpless.

- The Salvation Army Red Shield Appeal is an ideal opportunity to help our
  fellow people in the most effective way.

I hope that you will follow my example and give generously to The Salvation
Army 1993 Red Shield Appeal.

Yours sincerely

Bill McNamara,
Parramatta & Sydney West
Appeal Chairman

</td>
<td>

Sender's
address at right
hand side,
punctuated

Date at right
hand side

Paragraphs
or sections
of letter are
indented to
enhance com-
munication

Complimentary
close set
centre-page,
and here
punctuated

</td>
</tr>
</table>

Letter style   • courteous but with human emphasis
                    • has emotive and evaluative elements
                    • interactive stance: *I, you, our*

Appendix VIII

LAYOUT FOR ENVELOPES (AS RECOMMENDED BY AUSTRALIA POST)

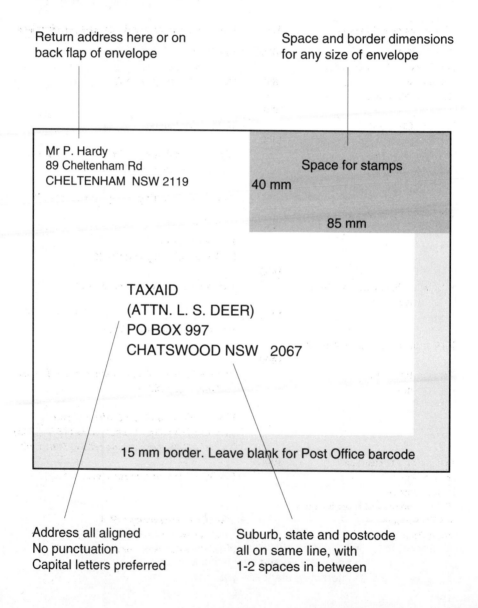

Return address here or on back flap of envelope

Space and border dimensions for any size of envelope

Mr P. Hardy
89 Cheltenham Rd
CHELTENHAM NSW 2119

Space for stamps

40 mm

85 mm

TAXAID
(ATTN. L. S. DEER)
PO BOX 997
CHATSWOOD NSW   2067

15 mm border. Leave blank for Post Office barcode

Address all aligned
No punctuation
Capital letters preferred

Suburb, state and postcode all on same line, with 1-2 spaces in between

Appendix IX

TIME LINE FOR THE ENGLISH LANGUAGE AND AUSTRALIAN ENGLISH

Major historical events	AD	Language periods and seminal publications
Arrival of Angles, Saxons and Jutes in England	**400**	*Old English*
Viking invasions begin	**800**	"Beowulf" ms (late 900s)
Reign of King Alfred		
	1000	
Norman Conquest		*Middle English*
	1300	
		Wyclif's translation of the Bible (c.1380)
		Chaucer's *Canterbury Tales* (1390)
	1400	
		First printing in English by Caxton (1477)
Discovery of America		
	1500	
		Modern English
		Shakespeare's plays (1591–1612)
	1600	
Pilgrim Fathers leave for North America		Authorised Version of Bible (1611)
	1700	
		Johnson's dictionary (1755)
European settlement of Australia		
	1800	
Transportation ends		Webster's *American Dictionary of the English Language* (1828)
Gold rushes		
		First publication of the *Bulletin* (1880)
		New English (Oxford) Dictionary (1884–1933)
		Morris's *Dictionary of Austral English* (1892)
Federation of Australia	**1900**	
World War I		Fowler's *Modern English Usage* (1926)
World War II		
British withdrawal from Singapore		
ANZUS treaty		*Macquarie Dictionary* (1981)
Australia's Bicentennial		*Comprehensive Grammar of English* (1985)
		Australian National Dictionary (1988)
	2000	

Appendix X

LIST OF REFERENCES

—*American Heritage dictionary of the English language* (Houghton Mifflin 1969)

—Appleton, R and Appleton, B *Cambridge dictionary of Australian places* (Cambridge University Press 1992)

—*Australian Aboriginal words in English* (Oxford University Press 1990)

—*Australian colloquialisms* → Wilkes

—Australian Government Publishing Service *Style manual for authors, editors and printers* 4th ed. (Australian Government Publishing Service 1988)

—*Australian national dictionary* (Oxford University Press 1988)

—*Australian standard classification of occupations* (Australian Bureau of Statistics 1990)

—*Australian writers' and editors' guide* (Oxford University Press 1991)

—Ayto, J A minuscule question: orthography and authority in dictionaries *Euralex 92 proceedings.*

—Baker, SJ *The Australian language* 2nd ed (1966; repr. Currawong 1978)

—Baron, D *Grammar and gender* (Yale University Press 1986)

—Benson, M et al. *Lexicographic description of English* (John Benjamins 1986)

—Bliss, AJ *A dictionary of foreign words and phrases in English* (Routledge Kegan Paul 1966)

—*Bloomsbury good word guide* (Bloomsbury Publishing 1988)

—Bryant, P South East lexical usage region of Australian English *Australian Journal of Linguistics* 9 (1989)

—Butcher, J *Copy-editing* (Cambridge University Press 3rd ed. 1975; 1992)

—*Cambridge encyclopedia of earth sciences* → Smith

—*Chambers English dictionary* 7th ed. (Chambers/Cambridge University Press 1988)

—Chicago *Manual of style* 13th ed. (University of Chicago Press 1981)

—*Collins English dictionary* 3rd (Aust) ed.(HarperCollins 1991)

—Collins, PC *Dare* and *need* in Australian English *English Studies* 59 (1978)

—Collins, PC Elicitation experiments on acceptability in Australian English *Working Papers of the Speech and Language Research Centre, Macquarie University* (1979)

—Collins, PC Semantics of some modals in Australian English *Australian Journal of Linguistics* 8 (1988)

—*Comprehensive grammar of English* Quirk R, Greenbaum S, Leech G, and Svartvik J (Longman 1985)

—*Copy-editing* → Butcher

—Creswell, TJ *Usage in dictionaries and dictionaries of usage* (University of Alabama Press 1975)

—Crystal, D *Who cares about English usage?* (Penguin 1984)

—Dabke, R *Morphology of Australian English* (Wilhelm Fink 1976)

—*Editing Canadian English* (Douglas and McIntyre 1987)

—*Field guide to Australian birds* 2 vols (Rigby 1974)

—*Fowler's modern English usage* (Oxford University Press 1926; ed. E Gowers 1965, repr. 1968)

—Francis, WN and Kucera, H *Frequency analysis of English: usage and lexicon* (Houghton Mifflin 1982)

—Fries, CC The periphrastic future with *shall* and *will* in modern English *Publications of the Modern Language Association of America* 40 (1925)

—Fries, CC *American English grammar* (Appleton Century Crofts 1940)

—Gowers, E *Complete plain words* 2nd ed. (Penguin 1973)

—*Grammar and gender* → Baron

—Halliday, MAK *Introduction to functional grammar* (Edward Arnold 1985)

—*Hart's rules for compositors and readers* 39th ed. (Oxford University Press 1983; repr. 1989)

—Howard, P *Dictionary of diseased English* (Routledge Kegan Paul 1977)

—Huddleston, R *Introduction to the grammar of English* (Cambridge University Press 1984)

—*Introduction to the grammar of English* → Huddleston

—*Introduction to functional grammar* → Halliday

—*Indexing, the art of* → Knight

—Jesperson, O *Growth and structure of the English language* 9th ed. (Macmillan 1948)

—Johansson, S and Hofland, K *Frequency analysis of English vocabulary and grammar* 2 vols. (Oxford University Press 1989)

—Johnson, S *A dictionary of the English language* (1755: facsimile Longman 1989)

—Kirkman, J *Good style for scientific and engineering writing* (Pitman 1980)

—Kjellmer, G On the spelling of English *millennium. Studia Neophilologica* 58 (1986)

—Knight, GN *Indexing, the art of* (Allen and Unwin 1979)

—Leech, G *An A-Z of English grammar and usage* (Edward Arnold 1989)

—Levin, B *In these times* (Sceptre 1988)

—*Macquarie dictionary* 2nd ed. (Macquarie Library 1991)

—*Macquarie dictionary of new words* (Macquarie Library 1990)

—*MLA Style manual* (Modern Language Association of America 1985)

—Mittins, W et al. *Attitudes to English usage* (Oxford University Press 1970)

—Morris, EE *A dictionary of Austral English* (1892; repr. Sydney University Press 1972)

—Murray-Smith, S *Right words* 2nd ed. (Viking 1989)

—*Naming systems of ethnic groups* (Australian Government Publishing Service 1990)

—*Oxford dictionary* = *New English dictionary* 13 vols (Oxford University Press 1884–1933)

—*Oxford English dictionary* 2nd ed. 20 vols (Oxford University Press 1989)

—*Oxford dictionary for writers and editors* (Oxford University Press 1981)

—*Oxford guide to the English language* (Oxford University Press 1984)

—Peters, PH ed. *Style in Australia: proceedings of Style Council 86* (Dictionary Research Centre 1987)

—Peters, PH ed. *Frontiers of style: proceedings of Style Councils 87 and 88* (Dictionary Research Centre 1990)

—Peters, PH ed. *Australian style into the nineties: proceedings of Style Councils 90 and 91* (Dictionary Research Centre 1992)

—Peters, PH ed. *Style on the move: proceedings of Style Council 92* (Dictionary Research Centre 1993)

—*Random House dictionary* 2nd ed. (Random House 1987)

—*Reader's Digest complete book of Australian birds* (Reader's Digest 1976/7)

—Reed, AW *Placenames of Australia* (Reed 1973)

—*Right word at the right time* (Reader's Digest, 1985)

—Schonnell, F *A study of the oral vocabulary of Australian adults* (University of Queensland Press 1955)

—*SBS world guide* (Text Publications 1992)

—Smith, DG *Cambridge encyclopedia of earth sciences* (Cambridge University Press 1981)

—Style Council → Peters

—*Terminology Bulletin No. 342: country names* (United Nations Secretariat 1990, plus corrigenda 1991/2)

—*Watch your language* 2nd ed. (Australian Broadcasting Corporation 1992)

—*Webster's third new international dictionary* (Merriam-Webster 1961: repr. 1986)

—*Webster's dictionary of English usage* (Merriam-Webster 1989)

—*Webster's standard American style manual* (Merriam-Webster 1985)

—Wilkes, G *Dictionary of Australian colloquialisms* (1978; 2nd ed. reset Oxford University Press 1990)